6/99

WILDLIFE WATCHER'S HANDBOOK

The National Wildlife Federation's

WILDLIFE WATCHER'S HANDBOOK

*A Guide to Observing Animals
in the Wild*

JOE LA TOURRETTE

Illustrations by Cheryl Ziebart

AN OWL BOOK
HENRY HOLT AND COMPANY
NEW YORK

Henry Holt and Company, Inc.
Publishers since 1866
115 West 18th Street
New York, New York 10011

Henry Holt® is a registered trademark
of Henry Holt and Company, Inc.

Published in Canada by Fitzhenry & Whiteside Ltd.,
195 Allstate Parkway, Markham, Ontario L3R 4T8.

Library of Congress Cataloging-in-Publication Data
La Tourrette, Joe.
The National Wildlife Federation's wildlife watcher's handbook: a guide to
observing animals in the wild / Joe La Tourrette and the National Wildlife
Federation.—1st ed.
p. cm.
"An Owl book."
Includes index.
1. Wildlife watching—North America—Guidebooks. 2. Wildlife viewing
sites—North America—Guidebooks. 3. North America—Guidebooks.
I. National Wildlife Federation. II. Title.
QL151.L37 1997
591.973—dc20
96-44345

ISBN 0-8050-4685-2

Henry Holt books are available for special promotions
and premiums. For details contact: Director, Special Markets.

First Edition 1997
Illustration on page 81 by Brenda Guiberson; illustration on page 136 by Jackie
Aher. Photo credits: page 7, Steve Terrill; pages 11 and 15, Chuck Place; pages
13 and 27, Thomas Kitchin (Tom Stack & Associates); page 18, John Gerlach;
page 21, Jack W. Dykinga; page 24, Dominique Braud (Tom Stack & Associates).

Printed in the United States of America
All first editions are printed on acid-free paper. ∞

1   3   5   7   9   10   8   6   4   2

Contents

Foreword

Aldo Leopold, one of the founders and leading thinkers of the conservation movement, said in 1947 that "the practice of conservation must spring from a conviction of what is ethically and esthetically right."

Firsthand experience with the wilderness is the surest way to develop that conviction, and this book is your passport. It will tell you where to find wildlife, how best to view it, how to equip yourself for hours, days, or weeks in the field, and how to find wildlife close to home. Most important, the book will teach you how to ensure that your interest in wildlife and your desire to be near it does not harm the habitat upon which animals and plants depend for their existence.

Protecting the wild creatures and places that bring wonder to so many of us has been the primary goal of the National Wildlife Federation since its inception in 1936. Across the decades, the federation has been instrumental in the protection of animals ranging from bald eagles, waterfowl, and songbirds to gray wolves, grizzlies, and sea otters. The federation has also worked to protect the places that all of Earth's creatures depend upon for life, from wetlands to forests, from prairies to streams. The federation has helped build the key bastions of wildlife and environmental protection: the Endangered Species Act, the Clean Air Act, the Marine Mammal Protection Act, the Wilderness Act, and many other critical laws through which the country expresses its ethics and esthetics.

Yet these protections are only as potent as the citizenry wants them to be. Without strong, well-informed public support, these laws are only so much ink on paper. That support grows out of the joy that so many people find in the wild; out of their concern for the conservation of the wild places they love; and out of the desire to get outdoors and meet nature firsthand.

The National Wildlife Federation's *Wildlife Watcher's Handbook* will help enhance your experience of the wilderness. For the novice, it will create passages to new worlds. For the seasoned outdoor enthusiast, it will sharpen skills already developed. For all readers, it will contribute to that "conviction of what is ethically and esthetically right."

—Mark Van Putten, president,
National Wildlife Federation

I want to thank the following friends for their support and help in reviewing my manuscript: Wendy Hudson, Defenders of Wildlife; Charles Gibilisco, Washington Department of Fish and Wildlife; Margot Boyer; and my wife, Kathy La Tourrette.

WILDLIFE WATCHER'S HANDBOOK

Introduction

If you are not an active wildlife watcher, but you are buying this book as a first step toward becoming one, you are about to join the ranks of those who enjoy one of North America's most popular and fastest-growing outdoor activities.

If observing or photographing wildlife is already a part of your life, the National Wildlife Federation's *Wildlife Watcher's Handbook* will provide you with a lot of valuable information about the location and habits of North American wildlife as well as pointers for successful wildlife viewing and photography.

The National Wildlife Federation (NWF), North America's largest wildlife conservation organization, has for more than sixty years stood in the vanguard of national and international efforts to conserve wildlife resources and increase public knowledge, understanding, and enjoyment of wildlife through educational programs such as Nature Quest and NatureLink and through publications such as *Ranger Rick* and *National Wildlife* magazines. *Wildlife Watcher's Handbook* is the first of a series of books designed to help members and the general public get maximum enjoyment from their outdoor experiences.

Most Americans and Canadians value wildlife as an important

part of their national culture. In 1991, the U.S. Fish and Wildlife Service published the results of a national survey showing that more than half of all U.S. residents engage in some type of wildlife-related recreation every year. Some of these people are hunters, some are sport anglers, and many enjoy simply watching and photographing wildlife. More than half of the respondents in the survey engaged in all three types of wildlife recreation. Over 57 percent of hunters, for instance, also listed themselves as wildlife watchers or photographers.

Watching wildlife is not only one of our most enjoyable and fastest-growing outdoor recreation pursuits, it has also become an important part of our economy. The U.S. Fish and Wildlife Service estimated that wildlife viewers and photographers spent more than $18 billion in 1991 in the pursuit of watchable wildlife—compared with expenditures of $5.8 billion for movie tickets and $5.9 billion on sporting events—and that bird watching alone supports about 200,000 jobs in the United States.

As the population of the United States and Canada expands, and as important wildlife habitat is altered or lost to various types of development, the cost of protecting habitat and providing outdoor recreational opportunities is escalating. For many years, hunters and sport anglers paid for most U.S. wildlife-conservation programs through license fees and excise taxes collected on firearms, outboard motors, and fishing tackle. But these revenues are no longer adequate to meet the overall needs of wildlife or to address growing public demand for wildlife-recreation opportunities. Efforts currently are under way at national and state levels to find new ways both to meet public demand and to pay for wildlife conservation and wildlife recreation programs.

The National Wildlife Federation and its affiliates are involved in a number of these important efforts, including the National Watchable Wildlife Program and Teaming with Wildlife, a national effort to create a trust fund for state-level conservation efforts, funded by user fees paid on certain outdoor equipment. The National Watchable Wildlife Program was initiated in 1990 by the International Association of Fish and Wildlife Agencies; four national conserva-

tion groups, including the National Wildlife Federation and Defenders of Wildlife; and eight federal land-management agencies, including the U.S. Forest Service and the U.S. Fish and Wildlife Service. The program is designed to help meet growing public demand for wildlife recreation, to increase public awareness of the habitat needs of wildlife, and to build a new base of public support for wildlife conservation.

The most immediate and visible result of the national program has been the establishment of a network of thousands of designated Watchable Wildlife sites around the United States and the publication, by Defenders of Wildlife and Falcon Press, of wildlife viewing guides for twenty-two states so far. Many designated Watchable Wildlife sites are described in the viewing guides, and all are identified along roadways by standardized brown-and-white signs that feature the distinctive Watchable Wildlife binoculars logo.

Canada has established a comparable Watchable Wildlife program with similar binoculars-logo signs and publication of provincial viewing guides.

Publication of *Wildlife Watcher's Handbook* is a valuable addition
to the recreational and educational objectives of the National
Watchable Wildlife Program. In the following pages, you will find
valuable information on where wildlife lives in North America,
when it is most visible, where to go and view it, how to observe it,
and how to prepare yourself for the outings that will put you in
visual contact with our most interesting and colorful wildlife species.

Examples used throughout this book come from my own personal experiences, from those of friends and acquaintances, and from many excellent written sources, including the series of wildlife viewing guides mentioned above.

The NWF staff and I hope that this handbook helps to increase your understanding and appreciation of wildlife and enhances your ability to get out in nature and safely enjoy the magnificent and diverse wildlife resources of North America.

1

Where Wildlife Lives—
Habitat Regions of the United
States and Canada

The United States and Canada can be divided into at least eight broad habitat regions, each with its own diversity of plant communities and wildlife (biodiversity). The boundaries of these habitat regions are not formal, official, or fixed by nature. In fact, I see them as more of a continuum, with broad transitional areas between habitat regions and large islands of other habitat types within each region. Wildlife species living within these habitat regions are usually not fixed either, but a definite relationship does exist between the plant communities and the wildlife found within each habitat region.

Eastern Deciduous Forest

The Eastern Deciduous Forest Habitat Region extends from the Atlantic Ocean to eastern Texas and from the Great Lakes to the Gulf of Mexico, covering roughly the eastern third of the United States and Canada. The Eastern Deciduous Forest is composed of many different forest communities, but most of them are dominated by specific groupings of broad-leaved or deciduous trees that gradually blend into each other with changes in topography and climate.

When the first European settlers came ashore in this habitat region in the 1600s, they stood at the edge of an almost solid forest that extended west to the Mississippi River and slightly beyond. Although about 95 percent of this original forest was cleared for farms, cities, and transportation corridors, it is now reestablishing itself where farmland has been abandoned. In southern Canada, New England, and the Great Lakes area, the Eastern Deciduous Forest Habitat Region is characterized by hardy deciduous trees, such as sugar maple, beech, and basswood, intermingled with coniferous pine and hemlock. As the forest extends south along the Atlantic Coast and the Appalachian Mountains, other tree species gradually become dominant, including shagbark hickory and many varieties of oak. The American chestnut was the most common tree in this region until about a hundred years ago, when an imported disease began killing the trees. Today, the American chestnut hovers near extinction.

As the Eastern Deciduous Forest spreads south into the Mississippi Valley and northern Florida, it gradually becomes dominated by deciduous trees typical of the Deep South, including magnolia, southern red oak, and live oak. The southern pine forests that dominate the coastal plains of the Atlantic and Gulf states are within the greater deciduous forest region, but ecologists classify them as subclimax forests, meaning that if these are left undisturbed, they eventually will be replaced by broad-leaved trees.

The Eastern Deciduous Forest region also includes many thousands of square miles of beaches, coastal marshes, and rich estuaries along the Atlantic and Gulf Coasts. These wetlands provide habitat for many species of resident and migratory birds, mammals, and other wildlife. Brown pelicans are common summer inhabitants of the Atlantic Coast, as are laughing gulls and Atlantic bottle-nosed dolphins. The Gulf Coast, from Florida to Texas, is world famous for populations of rails, sandpipers, and other migratory shorebirds. The sole surviving natural population of whooping cranes winters on an island along the Texas Gulf Coast.

The Eastern Deciduous Forest is home to a large number and diversity of wildlife species, both resident and migratory. White-tailed deer, black bears, wild turkeys, raccoons, and opossums live in the densely forested habitats of the Eastern Deciduous Forest, as do many species of small mammals, turtles, woodpeckers, and owls—as well as warblers and other neotropical songbirds, species that winter in the tropical habitats of the New World. The Appalachian Mountains and Atlantic Coast serve as major migration corridors for many thousands of hawks, vultures, and other birds of prey each fall and spring. The coastal estuaries and marshes of the Atlantic and Gulf Coasts provide nesting, resting, and wintering habitat for literally millions of shorebirds, waterfowl, and other migratory birds. The southern forested part of the Eastern Deciduous Forest—including coastal pine forests and cypress swamps—harbors many resident species of birds, small mammals, and reptiles, such as alligators, not found farther north.

Some wildlife-viewing highlights of this habitat region are:

Carter Caves State Resort Park, accessible from Interstate 64 in eastern Kentucky near the border with Ohio and West Virginia, is an excellent place to explore natural limestone caves and see the oak-hickory and mixed pine and hardwood forests described by E. Lucy Braun in her classic book *Deciduous Forests of Eastern North America*. Here you may see white-tailed deer, red and gray foxes, beavers, and other wetland-dependent wildlife. In the winter thousands of endangered Indiana bats hibernate in Bat Cave.

Hanging Rock State Park, about 25 miles north of Winston-Salem, North Carolina, offers more than 18 miles of hiking trails and a breathtaking panorama of the mixed deciduous and hardwood forest of the Piedmont region of North Carolina. A diverse wildlife population includes white-tailed deer, bobcats, and gray foxes, which are sometimes observed at night by campers. The park hosts a variety of neotropical songbirds, whippoorwills, and migratory raptors, including turkey vultures, black vultures, and broad-winged hawks, which can be observed from Hanging Rock in autumn and spring.

Shenandoah National Park, in Virginia's Blue Ridge Mountains, a short drive west of Washington, D.C., gives motorists an excellent opportunity to observe white-tailed deer and other wildlife typical of the Eastern Deciduous Forest. The park is bisected by the 105-mile-long Skyline Drive and by the Appalachian Trail. The national park boasts more than 1,100 species of flowering plants, including 18 varieties of orchids. The park is also home to almost 6,000 white-tailed deer, more than 300 black bears, and a host of small mammals. About 200 bird species have been observed in the park.

Gus A. Engling Wildlife Management Area, about 100 miles northeast of Waco, Texas, is one of the most scenic and diverse places in East Texas to view wildlife of the Eastern Deciduous Forest. Rolling hills of oak, hickory, sweet gum, elm, and dogwood surround Catfish Creek, a tributary of the Trinity River. Beaver Pond and Dogwood Nature Trails provide visitors with good opportunities to view beavers and other wetland wildlife species, even alligators, as well as many native mammals and birds. The management area has active bird rookeries, a sphagnum moss bog, and many sloughs and marshes that attract wintering waterfowl and other waterbirds.

Northern Coniferous Forest

North of the Canadian border, the Eastern Deciduous Forest yields to a broad belt of coniferous, or evergreen, trees that extend west from New England and Quebec to the Canadian Rockies, north to the arctic tundra, and south into the Sierra Nevada, Cascade, and Rocky Mountain ranges of the western United States. The Northern Coniferous Forest Habitat Region, or boreal forest region, of Canada is characterized by short summers, long winters, and heavy snowfall. The dominant trees, all across the boreal forest, are white spruce, black spruce, and balsam fir. The cold climatic conditions that characterize the boreal forests also exist in western mountain ranges, but in the mountains the dominant tree species change to a mixture of western hemlock, tamarack, and various pines and firs. Aspens grow in moister canyons and draws.

Many of the wildlife species common in the Eastern Deciduous Forest continue to be found in the Northern Coniferous Forest region, including white-tailed deer and black bear, but as trees become more widely dispersed and humans less intrusive, species such as moose, wolverines, lynx, timber wolves, snowshoe hares, and northern flying squirrels become more common. Boreal forests are home to a smaller number and diversity of bird species than are other habitat regions, but some residents, such as the boreal owl and boreal chickadee, are rarely found outside the boreal forest. Other wildlife found in the Northern Coniferous Forest region includes porcupines, red squirrels, fishers, great gray owls, gray jays, and spruce grouse.

In the Western Rockies, Cascades, and Sierra Nevada mountains, the diversity of wildlife species increases along with the diversity of trees and plant communities, resulting in greater biodiversity than the boreal forest can exhibit. White-tailed deer have expanded

their range into many wooded areas of the West, but the dominant large animals of the western mountains remain mule deer and Rocky Mountain elk plus many typically mountain species, such as bighorn sheep, mountain goats, mountain quail, cougar, blue grouse, mountain chickadees, pine grosbeaks, and northern goshawks. Wolves and grizzly bears were systematically eliminated from most areas south of the Canadian border but, under protection of the federal Endangered Species Act, are being reintroduced to or are reestablishing themselves naturally in areas such as Yellowstone National Park and the North Cascades of Washington.

Some wildlife-viewing highlights of this habitat region are:

Brule River State Forest, about 35 miles east and south of Duluth, Minnesota, is one of the best locations in Wisconsin to observe wildlife of the northern coniferous or boreal forest. The forest includes a mix of coniferous black spruce, white cedar, and balsam fir bogs as well as northern hardwood trees found in eastern deciduous forests. The Brule River is excellent for canoeing and kayaking, with a variety of both flat-water and white-water experiences. Bald eagles and ospreys roost along the river, which hosts runs of spawning coho and chinook salmon, as well as steelhead and anadromous brown trout, which spend most of their lives in Lake Superior. The white cedar swamps associated with the upper Bois-Brule bog contain more than 38 bird species, and the managed forest harbors bobcats, snowshoe hares, great gray owls, and other species associated with the boreal forest.

Rocky Mountain National Park, conveniently located near Estes Park, Boulder, and Fort Collins, Colorado, protects 400 square miles of Rocky Mountain coniferous forest and its wildlife. On mountainsides and in meadows you can observe herds of Rocky Mountain elk, bighorn sheep, and mule deer. Moose can sometimes be seen in willow thickets of the Kawuneeche Valley. The tundra-topped peaks within the park—some of the mountains are more than 14,000 feet tall—provide ideal habitat for alpine wildlife such as brown-capped rosy finches, white-tailed ptarmigan, bighorn sheep, and pikas (short-eared relatives of rabbits).

Mount Nebo Scenic Loop, south of Provo, Utah, offers a scenic mountain drive through many of the forest communities of the Wasatch Mountain Range. Road turnouts present many opportunities to view mule deer, Rocky Mountain elk, migrating hawks, and sometimes moose. The Uinta National Forest maintains over 100 miles of hiking and horseback trails, including the Nebo Basin Trail, which winds through fields of wildflowers to the 11,877-foot summit of Nebo's north peak. Trails are also open in the winter for cross-country skiing.

Sequoia and Kings Canyon National Parks, east of Fresno, California, are the best places on earth to see giant sequoias, the world's largest trees. These trees are among the oldest in the world too—the General Sherman tree is between 2,300 and 2,700 years old. The two parks, totaling almost a million acres, protect some of the most pristine forests in the Sierra Nevada Range, from oak and chaparral foothills through thick coniferous forests to the crest of 14,495-foot Mount Whitney, the highest mountain in the lower forty-eight states. Black bear, mule deer, cougars, yellow-bellied

marmots, California bighorn sheep, and more than 200 bird species range through the combined national parks.

Tundra Habitat Region

North of Canada's coniferous forest lies the tundra, an almost treeless belt of frozen land that encircles the top of the globe. Tundra vegetation begins where the tree line ends. It is composed of low-growing shrubs, grasses, sedges, and lichens that are able to withstand the constant wind and to grow in the shallow soils that overlie a perennially frozen stratum called permafrost. During the tundra's short summer season, surface ice melts, creating a huge system of shallow lakes and bogs useful to many wildlife species.

Tundra also occurs as a habitat type at elevations above tree line on western mountains, where ecologists call it alpine, rather than arctic, tundra.

Wildlife of the arctic tundra must be adapted to long, cold winters and very short summers. Year-round residents include musk oxen, barren-ground caribou, tundra wolves, and polar bears, as well as smaller wildlife such as arctic fox, snowy owls, rock ptarmigan, snow buntings, and Lapland larkspurs. Many arctic tundra species hibernate during the coldest winter months. Some, such as the arctic fox and the ptarmigan, grow white fur or plumage as camouflage against snow. Hundreds of thousands of ducks, geese, and other migratory birds spend summers nesting in potholes and other open water created by melting permafrost.

Wildlife of the alpine tundra, in the Rockies and other western mountain ranges, includes Dall's bighorn sheep, hoary marmots, and mountain goats (which aren't really goats at all but are closely related to antelope).

The arctic tundra is so remote, difficult to get to, and potentially hazardous that most outdoor enthusiasts are best advised to visit there with a professional guide or as part of an organized tour. The tundra is vast and improved road access is limited. The summer season is very short, and travel to the arctic wilderness at any other time of the year is difficult, if not foolhardy. If you want to observe arctic tundra wildlife, two places in particular are definitely worth the effort of getting to them:

The Arctic National Wildlife Refuge, in the far north of Alaska, offers a unique opportunity to observe thousands of barren-ground caribou in May and June, when the animals congregate on the coastal plain to give birth and to fatten up for the long winter. The short, three-month warm season also offers 24-hour daylight viewing of other wildlife, including snowy owls, arctic foxes, and thousands of nesting waterfowl and migratory shorebirds. In August and September, lesser snow geese stop here on their long southward migration to wintering habitat.

Wood Buffalo National Park, just south of Great Slave Lake, straddles the Canadian provinces of Alberta and the Northwest Territories. This is Canada's largest national park, and includes elements of both the tundra and the boreal forest habitat regions. The park protects one of North America's two remaining herds of wild bison (the other is in Yellowstone National Park) and is the only nesting

site in the world for whooping cranes. In addition to bison, wolves, and other tundra wildlife, the park's Athabasca–Peace River delta provides nesting habitat for many thousands of waterfowl and other migratory birds.

Pacific Coast Forest

The Pacific Coast Forest Habitat Region extends along the Pacific Coast from southeast Alaska to just north of San Francisco Bay in California. Rainfall is abundant in this region, ranging from about 40 inches in Eureka, California, to 130 inches in Kodiak, Alaska. This high rainfall, coupled with moderate temperatures, has created an extensive forest and wildlife community quite different from that of the Northern Coniferous Forest, even though many of the same tree species are found in the Rockies and on the drier slopes of the Cascades and Sierra Nevada.

In coastal Alaska, the Pacific Coast Forest region is dominated by western hemlock, western red cedar, and Sitka spruce. As you travel south through the region, other tree species, such as grand fir, Pacific silver fir, and Douglas fir become more dominant. Coastal redwood trees were once dominant in the Coast Range of northern California, but most of the large stands of redwood forest were commercially logged many years ago.

The range of wildlife species that occurs in the Pacific Coast Forest region differs from that of the Northern Coniferous Forest region, although, as in the case of trees, many of the same species are found in both. The Pacific Coast is protected from extremes of hot and cold by offshore currents, and such a climate attracts wildlife adapted to wet, generally moderate weather.

Coastal forest wildlife species include Roosevelt elk, black-tailed deer (a subspecies of mule deer), black bear, cougars, Douglas squirrels, northern flying squirrels, blue grouse, and the most famous denizen of Pacific Northwest mature forests, the northern spotted owl. Other common birds include the Steller's jay, the red-breasted nuthatch, the brown creeper, the rufous-sided towhee, the Oregon junco, and the ubiquitous common crow.

Timber wolves and grizzly bears were once common along the Pacific Coast but have been all but eliminated south of the Canadian border. The greater Pacific Coast Forest region includes the Pacific Coast itself, with its associated shoreline, coastal estuaries, and large inland extensions of the sea, such as the Georgia Straits and Puget Sound, which are home to an abundance and great diversity of wildlife, from bald eagles and Pacific salmon to millions of wintering waterfowl and migrating shorebirds. This region also includes California's Central Valley, a huge, arid expanse of grasslands and agricultural land punctuated by wetlands, where you can observe many wildlife species, including the native tule elk and a vast array of waterfowl.

Some wildlife-viewing highlights of this habitat region are:

Coquihalla Canyon Provincial Park, about 90 miles east of Vancouver, British Columbia, provides hiking access to a mixed cedar, hemlock, and Douglas fir forest and wildlife typical of the

Pacific Coast Forest Habitat Region. The Coquihalla River provides spawning habitat for salmon and steelhead trout, which can be observed from a viewpoint struggling upstream against the rapids. The forest offers habitat for black-tailed deer, varied thrushes, black-throated gray warblers, and other songbirds. Water ouzels (dippers) and belted kingfishers can be seen feeding in the shallow riffles and pools of the river.

Mount Rainier National Park, about 60 air miles southeast of Seattle, Washington, contains a wide diversity of plant communities and wildlife habitats, from subalpine meadows to streamside corridors and low-elevation, old-growth forests. This is one of the best places in the Pacific Northwest to see the huge old-growth Douglas fir trees that once covered the Cascade Range before the forests were logged for timber. The park has more than 300 miles of trails and four visitor centers. Black-tailed deer are common throughout the park. Roosevelt elk are best observed in the fall and spring, when they migrate between high meadows and wintering habitat along forested river bottoms. Many other wildlife species associated with mature Pacific Coast forests live in the park, including the northern spotted owl, the Douglas squirrel, the goshawk, and a variety of songbirds.

Strawberry Hill, in Neptune State Park, is one of the best places on the Oregon coast to observe harbor seals hauled out on rocks near the shore. At any time of year you can see a hundred or more seals, although calm days, low tides, and summer are best for viewing.

Prairie Creek Redwoods State Park and nearby **Redwood National Park,** both on the northern California coast, are the two best places left in California to drive or walk among giant coastal redwood trees and observe Roosevelt elk, black bear, and other wildlife associated with the greater Pacific Coast Forest region. Elk can often be seen from the Drury Scenic Parkway, at Elk Prairie campground and Gold Bluffs Beach, and along Highway 101 south

of the national park. Black bear are also resident here, and over 260 species of birds have been sighted within the combined park boundaries. The Smith River, which flows through the national park, is California's last major free-flowing river, and is famous for its runs of steelhead trout and chinook salmon.

Shrub-steppe Desert

Deserts are defined as places where evaporation exceeds rainfall. The deserts of western North America originated millions of years ago, when the uplift of two tiers of mountain ranges that parallel the Pacific Ocean from southern British Columbia into Mexico began blocking oceanic precipitation.

The Shrub-steppe Desert Habitat Region of the western United States incorporates a huge expanse of landlocked desert that extends from central Nevada north to the Columbia Basin of eastern Washington and from the eastern slopes of the Sierra Nevada to eastern Utah and southwest Wyoming. Much of the Shrub-steppe Desert, including the Great Basin of Nevada and Utah, is 4,000 feet or more above sea level, giving rise to bitterly cold winter temperatures. Annual precipitation hovers between 6 and 18 inches, so the region is mostly treeless except for intermittent stands of juniper and pinyon pine in the foothills; willows, aspen, and cottonwoods in moister canyons and draws; and larger trees such as ponderosa and lodgepole pine at the higher elevations of internal mountain ranges. Shrub-steppe Desert vegetation is dominated by sagebrush, deerbrush, rabbitbrush, shadscale, and other high-desert shrubs and bunchgrasses.

In many ways, the Shrub-steppe Desert is a transitional zone between the Northern Coniferous Forest; the grasslands of eastern New Mexico, Colorado, and Wyoming; and the warmer Southwest Desert. Wildlife diversity in the desert is similarly transitional. Mule deer live throughout the Shrub-steppe Desert, as do black-tailed hares (jackrabbits), badgers, coyotes, golden eagles, prairie falcons, sage grouse, and ferruginous hawks. Pronghorn antelope and white-tailed deer also occur in parts of the Shrub-steppe Desert. Some desert areas, including the Klamath Basin of Oregon and Bear River, Utah, provide critical nesting and wintering habitat for hundreds of thousands of ducks, geese, and other birds that migrate north and south in the Pacific Flyway (see the map on page 37).

Some wildlife-viewing highlights of this habitat region are:

Sheldon National Wildlife Refuge, about 140 air miles north of Reno, Nevada, provides vast unbroken expanses of sagebrush, steep rock outcroppings, and scattered springs (cold and hot), lakes, creeks, and associated wetlands. This is an isolated desert area but an excellent location to see pronghorn antelope, which migrate from Oregon in the summer; golden eagles; mule deer; sage grouse; bighorn sheep, which were recently reintroduced to the area; and many species of waterfowl, which nest here and use the area during spring and fall migration. A number of wild horses and burros also roam the refuge, descendants of animals turned loose around the turn of the century. Many reptiles and amphibians are associated with the Shrub-steppe Desert Habitat Region.

Golden Spike National Historic Site, just north of the Great Salt Lake in Utah, celebrates the spot where the cross-country railroad was completed in 1869. The area also provides excellent shrub-steppe desert habitat and viewing opportunities for a wide variety of wildlife species. Both sharp-tailed and sage grouse can be observed on their strutting grounds, or leks, in the early spring. Other species seen here are mule deer, badgers, burrowing owls, and golden eagles.

Malheur National Wildlife Refuge, southeast of Burns, Oregon, is one of the most productive and popular wildlife viewing areas in the Northwest, especially during the spring and fall. Malheur is a major desert stopover area during spring migration for northern pintail ducks, snow geese, white-fronted geese, tundra swans, Canada geese, and lesser sandhill cranes. Greater sandhill cranes, joined by thousands of mallards, canvasbacks, and other waterfowl, stop here again during their fall migration to California's Central Valley and other wintering areas. The extensive marshes of Malheur also attract nesting waterfowl in the summer and populations of bald eagles and rough-legged hawks in the winter, when they feed on small rodents and ducks.

Tex Creek Wildlife Management Area, about 30 miles east of Idaho Falls, Idaho, is a 27,000-acre refuge made up of large expanses of sagebrush, bitterbrush, and other shrubs as well as aspen, willow, and other streamside vegetation. In the winter months, this is an excellent place to view up to 3,000 mule deer, 2,000 Rocky Mountain elk, and a smaller number of moose. The desert shrubs and grass also provide excellent habitat for sage grouse, sharp-tailed grouse, and chukar partridge, introduced from India many years ago. During the warmer months, the management area is a good place to view a wide variety of songbirds.

Southwest Desert Habitat Region

The Southwest Desert Habitat Region includes the Mohave Desert of southern California and Nevada, the Sonoran Desert of Arizona, and the Chihuahuan Desert, which extends from southern New Mexico into Mexico. Like the Shrub-steppe Desert to the north, the Southwest Desert has relatively low rainfall (3 to 13 inches). But the average air temperature is considerably higher, resulting in plant communities and wildlife that differ from those of the Shrub-steppe Desert. Plants of the Southwest Desert are adapted either to resist or to evade drought. Drought resisters such as cacti generally store water in their tissue, reducing the loss of moisture to the atmosphere. Drought evaders include thousands of annual flowers whose seeds sprout only when soil is moist enough to allow them to flower and produce a new crop of seeds.

Dominant plants in much of the Southwest Desert are the creosote bush, which is distributed widely; mesquite; and a variety of other shrubs, cacti, yucca plants, and native bunchgrasses. Willows and cottonwood trees often grow in canyons and draws where there is greater soil moisture.

Wildlife of the Southwest Desert is surprisingly rich, diverse, and well adapted to hot summer temperatures and a general scarcity of water. Like the plants, desert wildlife is adapted either to resist or evade drought conditions by avoiding direct sunlight, by being nocturnal, or, like many insects and some amphibians, by staying underground until enough rain falls to allow them to complete their life cycles. Some Southwest Desert wildlife species also live farther north in the Shrub-steppe Desert, including coyotes, black-tailed hares, prairie falcons, burrowing owls, and badgers. But many other species are uniquely adapted to this hot desert environment, including the kit fox, cactus wren, Gila monster, sidewinder, roadrunner, desert bighorn sheep, and a number of kangaroo rat species, which can live their whole lives without actually drinking any water. White-tailed deer also are common in parts of the Southwest Desert region.

Some wildlife-viewing highlights of this habitat region are:

Death Valley National Park, in southern California, receives the least annual rainfall of any place in the Northern Hemisphere, 1.84 inches, yet it is one of the largest, most interesting, and most biologically diverse places in the United States to observe the flora and fauna of the Southwest Desert Habitat Region. The park, formerly a national monument, covers more than 2 million acres and ranges from 282 feet below sea level to mountain peaks more than 11,000 feet high. Death Valley contains more than 1,000 species of plants, including hundreds of annual wildflowers that bloom only after enough rain has fallen, and 400 wildlife species, including desert bighorn sheep, kit foxes, roadrunners, sidewinders, and 14 species of bats, which emerge at sunset to feed on insects. Death Valley is one of the most reliable places in California to observe desert tortoises, which have been classified as an endangered species.

Organ Pipe Cactus National Monument, southwest of Phoenix, Arizona, exhibits an extraordinary showcase of the plants and animals of the Sonoran Desert. There are 26 species of cactus in the park, plus many dozens of desert wildflowers, including the organ pipe, the largest cactus in the United States. Most of the wildflowers bloom in the early spring; cacti usually bloom later in the spring or summer. Organ Pipe is an excellent place to observe wildlife of the Southwest Desert, including bighorn sheep, roadrunners, coyotes, and javelinas, although many of these species are primarily nocturnal. Quitobaquito Spring, within the national monument, is a true oasis, which attracts many species of birds, including vermilion flycatchers and phainopepla. The spring and small pond, both near the Mexican border, harbor an endangered species of desert pupfish, which can tolerate salinity levels up to three times saltier than the ocean.

Valley of Fire State Park, about 40 miles northeast of Las Vegas, Nevada, near the shore of Lake Mead, is a valley of ancient sandstone formations, including giant caves and arches. The desert landscape is dominated by creosote bush, burro bush, and several cactus species, including beavertail and cholla, plus a spectacular array of blooming wildflowers in the spring. Desert ravens, golden eagles, roadrunners, sage sparrows, antelope ground squirrels, and a variety of desert lizards and snakes are visible during the day, as well as turkey vultures and red-tailed hawks, which soar overhead. At night, the desert comes alive with kangaroo rats, pocket mice, and the predators that stalk them, including coyotes and kit foxes. Desert tortoises are rarely seen here and totally protected by state and federal law.

Big Bend National Park, on the border between Texas and Mexico, is one of the finest wildlife viewing areas in all of North America. Here, the Rio Grande cuts through the Chisos Mountains, described in the *Texas Wildlife Viewing Guide* as a "green island in a desert sea"—meaning the Chihuahuan Desert. Float trips down the river, plus more than 150 miles of hiking trails, provide opportunities to observe many wildlife species found in the Southwest Desert, including almost 80 species of mammals, over 400 species of

birds, and 56 species of reptiles. Some wildlife seen at Big Bend, including the Carmen Mountains white-tailed deer, are found nowhere else in the United States.

Greater Grassland Habitat Region

The Greater Grassland Habitat Region is the largest and most diverse in North America, covering the interior of the continent from eastern Montana and Colorado to western Indiana, and from Alberta into Mexico. At least seven basic types of grassland community occur in North America, from the tallgrass prairies bordering the Eastern Deciduous Forest to the desert grasslands of southern Texas. During the past two hundred years, most of the original grassland communities were eliminated or altered by livestock grazing and farming practices. Less than 2 percent of virgin tallgrass prairies survive today.

Prior to European settlement, prairies (French for grasslands) and other grassland communities supported one of the largest concentrations of herbivorous (plant-eating) wildlife in the world, exceeded only by the great herds of East Africa. In 1600, North American grasslands supported an estimated 45 million bison and an equal number of pronghorn antelope, along with the gray wolves and other predators that preyed upon and traveled with the herds. The teeming numbers of bison and pronghorn are gone forever, although a few small herds do remain.

Many of the wildlife species living in the Greater Grassland region today also are found in surrounding desert and forest regions. These animals include mule deer, white-tailed deer, sharp-tailed grouse, badgers, Swainson's and rough-legged hawks, and coyotes (which now fill the ecological niche once occupied by wolves). Other grassland wildlife species include greater prairie chickens, horned larks, prairie dogs, and the main predator of prairie dogs, the endangered black-footed ferret. The prairie pothole portion of the Greater Grassland region is a major breeding area for ducks, geese, swans, and thousands of other migratory birds that traverse the Central Flyway.

Some wildlife-viewing highlights of this habitat region are:

Hoosier Prairie Nature Preserve, about 15 miles southeast of Chicago, near Griffith, Indiana, is a large (439 acres) remnant of the prairie landscape that once covered much of the Midwest. This area, made up of tallgrass prairie, freshwater marsh, and dry, oak-savanna uplands has a great diversity of flora and fauna unique to the prairie ecosystem. The area is known for its summer and fall wildflowers, as well as songbirds, which are most visible in the spring and summer. The site, including a one-mile walking trail, is managed by the Indiana Division of Nature Preserves.

Parkhill Prairie Preserve is a 436-acre preserve located in Collin County, Texas, about 35 miles north of Dallas. The park features one of the last surviving examples of native blackland tallgrass prairie, which once covered 12 million acres of Texas. This preserve provides a large array of year-round viewing opportunities, including wildflowers in the spring, and many species of birds and other wildlife, including coyotes, armadillos, and red-tailed hawks. Park-hill Prairie also harbors a unique species of crayfish that was unknown anywhere until it was discovered here in 1990. Collin County maintains a system of nature trails, boardwalks, and overlooks, which are open to the public.

Kalsow Prairie State Preserve is a 160-acre preserve located about 20 miles due west of Fort Dodge, Iowa. This is one of Iowa's finest remaining tallgrass prairies, dominated by big bluestem, Indian grass, and northern dropseed in dry areas and Indian grass, Canada wild rye, and slough grass in wetter places. Bison, elk, marbled godwits, and other historical prairie wildlife are gone, but these remnant prairies still support a diversity of wildlife, including upland sandpipers, sedge wrens, bobolinks, western meadowlarks, red foxes, and an occasional badger. Kalsow Prairie contains a number of large earth mounds, called mima mounds, which are of unknown origin and found in only one other place, south of Olympia, Washington. Kalsow Prairie is managed by the Iowa Department of Natural Resources.

Little Missouri National Grassland, more than a million acres of diverse prairie and badlands habitat in southwestern North Dakota, provides opportunities to see several hundred wildlife species associated with the Greater Grassland Habitat Region. The northern part of the national grassland, the McKenzie District, includes rolling prairie, badlands, woody draws, and high buttes that are home to bighorn sheep, elk, pronghorn antelope, white-tailed deer, and mule deer. The southern half, called the Medora District, contains the only stands of limber pine and natural ponderosa pine in North Dakota. A 58-mile self-guided auto tour of the Medora District begins and ends in the town of Medora, North Dakota. The auto tour offers additional opportunities to view wild turkeys, white-tailed deer, pronghorn antelope, golden eagles, prairie dogs, and black-footed ferrets. From March through mid-May sharp-tailed grouse can sometimes be observed on their dancing grounds, or leks.

Tropical Hardwood Habitat Region

The Tropical Hardwood Habitat Region of North America is relatively small, occurring only in southern Florida, including the Florida Keys. This is the only place in North America, outside Mexico, where naturally occurring tropical plant communities are found—including mangrove swamps, palmetto prairies, and such hardwood trees as gumbo-limbos and West Indies mahoganies.

Wildlife of the Tropical Hardwood Forest includes many species found farther north in the Eastern Deciduous Forest region, including black bear, white-tailed deer, brown pelicans, bobcats, and cougars (called panthers in Florida, where the animal is federally listed as an endangered species). Other resident wildlife that occurs in relative abundance includes American alligators, eastern diamondback rattlesnakes, and a list of long-legged wading birds, such as wood storks, roseate spoonbills, great egrets, and glossy ibises. Southern Florida, along with certain Caribbean islands, provides wintering habitat for many species of neotropical songbirds and other migratory birds. The region's offshore coral reefs harbor species of tropical fish and other wildlife found nowhere else in North America.

Some wildlife-viewing highlights of this habitat region are:

Gumbo-Limbo Environmental Complex, in Red Reef Park, is owned and managed by the City of Boca Raton, Florida. The complex, which includes a nature center, canoe trails, a boardwalk through the mangrove swamp, and a 40-foot-high observation tower, provides opportunities to experience at least three native vegetation communities: the coastal dunes, a sabal palm hammock, and a mangrove swamp. Wildlife observed from the visitor center and trails includes brown pelicans, ospreys, manatees, giant orb spiders, and land crabs. In May, the nature center sells tickets to watch the annual return of sea turtles, which nest on the beaches.

Lignumvitae Key State Botanical Site, a 280-acre island in the Florida Keys, is managed by the Florida Division of Recreation and Parks to preserve a remnant tropical forest of 65 trees and shrubs, including gumbo-limbo, strangler fig, mahogany, and the small, flowering lignumvitae. The island is small but important because it preserves a unique, virgin plant community that has been virtually eliminated on the rest of the Florida Keys. White-crowned pigeons, black-whiskered vireos, mangrove cuckoos, and neotropical warblers are among the unusual wildlife species you may encounter here. The key can be reached only by a three-hour boat ride from Indian Key. One-hour guided tours of the island are given by park rangers.

2

Timing—The Secret to Finding
and Observing Wildlife

U nlike trips to a museum, theme park, or zoo, successful observation of animals in the wild usually requires some advance planning to make sure you are at the right place at the right time to find the species you want to observe, photograph, or study. If you understand a few fundamentals about how animals make use of the hours of the day and the seasons of the year, you can readily improve your chances of locating wildlife. Many North American wildlife species, such as elk, eagles, and waterfowl, migrate or otherwise make adjustments in their biological rhythms to cope with temperature extremes, weather changes, predation, and the availability of food and water. As wildlife watchers, if we do not learn something about wildlife activities and movements, and if we don't plan our hikes and excursions to accommodate these habits, we might miss out on some of the most exciting observations that nature has to offer.

Some species are easy to find, because as individual animals they stay in one general area their whole lives and are active and visible year-round. Deer, for example, are known to be territorial. Some individual deer spend their entire lives within a single square mile of forest.

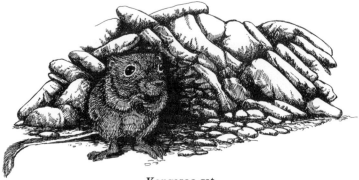

Kangaroo rat

In some parts of the globe, wildlife observation is relatively easy to do. In subtropical and warm-desert climates, for example, animals are not normally stressed by weather or food shortages. Consequently, they do not migrate widely or hide away for long periods of time. In the tropics, you can also observe a variety of species year-round. Even in northern climates, you can usually count on seeing squirrels and many other small mammals at any time of year, along with blue jays, chickadees, juncos, tufted titmice, and other resident birds.

Animals engage in two fundamental types of behavioral modifications that can affect when to see them: daily, or circadian, cycles and seasonal cycles. Let's look at each separately.

Daily (Circadian) Activity Cycle

Animals make adjustments in their daily schedules to optimize access to food and water, to avoid temperature extremes, and to minimize the chances of falling victim to predators. Generally speaking, in warmer months, midday is not the best time to view active wildlife. Early morning and very late afternoon or evening are better. Some exceptions to this rule are daytime insect eaters such as woodpeckers, and hawks and vultures, which ride midday thermal air currents over river valleys and large bodies of water.

Because they are unable to regulate body temperature, reptiles and amphibians are active only when air and ground temperatures are suitable. This may be during the night in summer, when direct sunlight can quickly overheat them, and at midday in winter, when these animals have a greater need for extra warmth.

Many wildlife species, from bats and owls to deer and desert kangaroo rats, are active only at night or during early-morning or late-afternoon hours. Unless you are willing to get up before the sun or stay up late, you might not even know that these species are around. White-tailed deer, for example, live in the wooded areas of many eastern cities, but rarely show themselves during the day.

Time of day is not the only factor that governs wildlife behavior. The feeding activity of coastal shorebirds and some sea ducks, for example, is governed not by time of day but by ocean tides, which alternately cover and expose small invertebrates and other food items that the birds seek in the intertidal area. For you as a wildlife watcher, it is not enough to know where wildlife lives. You also need to know when animals are "working" and when they are at home.

Biologists use one of three terms to describe animals according to the time of day when they are active. Diurnal animals, such as songbirds, are out during the day. Crepuscular species, such as deer, are active around dusk and dawn. Nocturnal species, such as most owls, are active at night.

Seasonal Cycles

Hibernation and Estivation

Hibernation is a form of deep sleep during which animals remain inactive or dormant during cold-weather months. The flip side is estivation, in which some, mostly desert, species become inactive in summer to escape heat and conserve moisture. Most reptiles and amphibians—from snakes and turtles to salamanders and frogs—hibernate, particularly in northern climates. Cold weather even triggers hibernation

Black bear

in alligators, which dig hibernation burrows. Among estivating creatures are the spadefoot toads of the Southwest Desert region, which bury themselves underground, becoming active and surfacing only during the brief period when rains visit the desert.

Many small mammals fatten up in autumn, then hibernate all winter—including bats, jumping mice, and, of course, groundhogs (woodchucks), which supposedly emerge on February 2 to signal the end or continuation of winter. Grizzly bears and black bears hibernate in dens during cold weather, but they do not sleep as deeply as rodents do and sometimes come out of their dens during warm winter days.

Migration

The overwhelming majority of birds, as well as other wildlife species sought by wildlife watchers in North America, are migratory, traveling in spring and fall between summer and winter habitats. Most birds follow established migration routes, and some of these routes are used so heavily by waterfowl and other birds that they are called flyways—sort of aerial freeways for birds. The four recognized routes in North America (see the maps on pages 34–37) are the Atlantic, Mississippi, Central, and Pacific Flyways.

Many waterfowl and other birds use these flyways to migrate thousands of miles between northern breeding grounds and southern winter habitats. Lesser snow geese in the Pacific Flyway breed on Wrangel Island in Siberia and winter along the Pacific Flyway, all the way from British Columbia's Fraser River Valley to the Central Valley of California. White pelicans nest in the prairie states and Canadian provinces, then migrate south to winter in the Gulf states and Florida. Swainson's hawks nest in the Midwest but in autumn fly to wintering habitat in Argentina, Bolivia, and Uruguay—more than 4,000 miles south.

Over half the birds that nest in the United States winter in South America, Central America, or Mexico. These neotropical migrants include hummingbirds, shorebirds, waterbirds, birds of prey, and many species of warblers and other songbirds. Wildlife enthusiasts who visit Central American rain forests during our winter will find many familiar North American bird species among the tropical foliage.

Migrating birds do not always take the shortest route between winter and summer grounds. Many hawks, storks, and other birds that migrate from the United States to Latin America fly hundreds of miles out of their way to avoid traveling over the open waters of the Gulf of Mexico. During their travels, migratory birds stop at traditional resting places to feed and gain energy for the rest of their voyage. Check with your state or provincial wildlife agency for information on migratory-bird stopover sites in your area. Among the most heavily used by migrating birds are Delaware Bay, on the

Atlantic Flyway

Mississippi Flyway

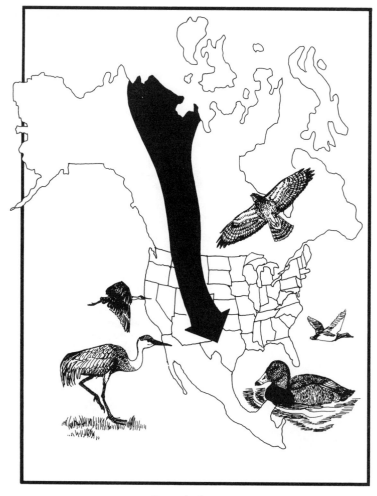

Central Flyway

Pacific Flyway

East Coast; the Cheyenne Bottoms wetlands of Kansas; the Platte River in central Nebraska; the prairie pothole region of the northern Midwest; the Gulf Coast; San Francisco Bay; and Mono Lake, in south-central California. Many federal, state, and provincial wildlife refuges also attract migratory waterfowl, particularly when wetlands on private property are drained away, forcing more and more birds to retreat to refuges and parks. Sites such as these can offer true wildlife spectacles—hundreds of thousands of shorebirds or waterfowl on the wing or feeding together on shore and in shallow water.

Not all birds migrate in a north–south direction, and not all migratory wildlife are birds. Many redhead ducks and evening grosbeaks breed in midwestern wetlands and then, instead of flying south in the fall, wing their way in an easterly direction to winter on the Atlantic Coast as far north as New Jersey. California gray whales, taken off the federal Endangered Species List in 1994, breed in the warm waters of Baja California, Mexico, then migrate as much as 7,000 miles north each spring to feed and raise young in rich arctic waters. The spring migration of barren-ground caribou on the Arctic National Wildlife Refuge in Alaska, mentioned in Chapter 1, is an extraordinary annual event. Even "resident" elk and deer in the West migrate vertically in the mountains each fall and spring to pursue favored food sources and to escape severe weather.

Knowing which species migrate, which migration routes they take, and when you can expect to see them in your neighborhood or nearby wildlife refuge will give you a distinct advantage in finding and observing wildlife.

3

Tips for Observing
Important Groups of
Watchable Wildlife

W e all get lucky sometimes and see a remarkable wildlife event in our backyard or neighborhood. My wife and I did one Saturday morning when we looked out from our deck and watched a Cooper's hawk nail a backyard crow. And last winter I heard a scratching on my front porch and opened the door to find a huge porcupine. But the most remarkable wildlife viewing experiences are likely to occur at times and places that we select to take advantage of known wildlife habitat preferences. So the more we know about the habits and behavior of wildlife, the better our chances will be to successfully time our outings and position ourselves to observe the species we want to see.

Some wildlife species can be seen only in certain habitat regions or along specific migration routes, while other species are virtually continental in distribution. No matter where these animals are found, however, they will exhibit fairly predictable habits and behavior. The same can be said for certain groups of animals—bears and native cats, for instance—whose nocturnal habits and secretive behavior are similar enough that it is possible to make general statements about how to locate and observe them.

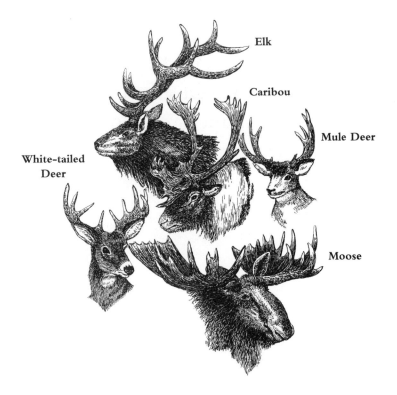

Here is some basic information about the location and habits of certain wildlife; this information is intended to help you locate, observe, and appreciate wildlife anywhere in North America. Rather than trying to review all watchable wildlife species in North America here, I have focused on species and groups that I think are especially valued and sought after in North America.

Deer, Elk, Moose, and Caribou

These magnificent animals are all members of the deer family, or Cervidae. All habitat regions in North America have at least one member of the deer family.

The white-tailed deer is the most common and wide-ranging

species of the deer family in North America, native to every eastern and midwestern state and Canadian province as well as parts of the Pacific Northwest and the Southwest. Whitetails are the only deer species found in the Eastern Deciduous Forest Habitat Region, and they are closely associated with deciduous forests throughout the rest of their range. White-tailed deer, which can weigh more than 200 pounds, take their name from their distinctive white tail, which they wag frequently when moving or alarmed.

Mule deer are found throughout the West and in the more westerly grasslands of the Midwest. They are closely associated with the mountain ranges of the Northern Coniferous Forest and Shrub-steppe Desert Habitat Regions and with the western Grassland Habitat Region. Male mule deer (bucks) are generally larger than white-tailed deer bucks—extremely large individuals can weigh up to 400 pounds. Mule deer populations overlap white-tailed deer ranges in many midwestern and western states and provinces. Black-tailed deer, a variety of mule deer, inhabit the Pacific Coast Forest Habitat Region from Alaska to southern California. Mule deer and black-tailed deer have black tips on their tails. White-tailed deer occur in growing numbers throughout much of their range. In the East they have been helped particularly by the recovery of their woodland habitat. Mule deer show signs of decline in some parts of the West because of increasing land development for commercial use, as well as for housing development.

The Rocky Mountain elk, a large number of the deer family that may stand 5 feet tall at the shoulder and weigh up to 800 pounds, inhabits the coniferous mountain ranges of western Canada and the western United States. Roosevelt elk are darker than Rocky Mountain elk and inhabit the coastal areas of British Columbia and the Pacific Coast states. The tule elk, a slightly smaller animal considered a separate species by some biologists, occurs now in only a few locations in California's Central Valley. Elk once ranged throughout most of the lower forty-eight states and were numerous during the colonial era as far east as Pennsylvania. Uncontrolled hunting and habitat loss wiped the animals out in many areas. Attempts to reintroduce elk from the West into parts of the East and even into such western states as Oklahoma, which lost its native subspecies, have met with mixed success because subspecies from one region do not generally do well ecologically in other regions. Introduced individuals of this large-hoofed species also run into conflicts with people who have a commercial interest in the land, notably farmers on whose crops the elk sometimes feed.

The moose, the largest member of the deer family, ranges from Alaska across forested regions of Canada and parts of Minnesota to Maine, and also across the Rocky Mountain states from Utah to Washington. Moose stand 7 to 9 feet tall at the shoulder and weigh up to 1,400 pounds. With their dark brown bodies, long, gangly legs, huge size, and massive antlers, moose are seldom mistaken for any other animal.

Two species of caribou are found in North America. Woodland caribou live in small herds, ranging over much of the boreal forest region of Canada; their range extends into the United States in only two specific areas of Alaska, Idaho, and Washington. Barren-ground caribou, or wild reindeer, are found in large migratory herds in the arctic tundra region of Alaska and far northern Canada. Caribou are larger than deer, about the size of elk. Woodland caribou live in dense stands of forest and are not easily observed. Lighter-colored barren-ground caribou are visible in large herds on the tundra, when they are gathered after their annual spring migration.

Deer, elk, and moose usually feed on grasses, herbaceous plants, and the leaves of deciduous trees during warmer months and on woody vegetation and the needles of coniferous trees during winter. Moose feed in shallow lakes and wetlands during spring and summer; in winter, they eat the foliage and bark from trees that grow out of the snow. In the winter, caribou seek the shelter of the forest and browse on shrubs and small trees. In the summer, after their migration to more open, lower elevations, barren-ground caribou feed on grass, moss, and especially lichens; caribou can often be seen "eating on the run" during their migration.

Deer and elk are mostly nocturnal but may feed during the early morning hours and at dusk. Moose and caribou may be active day or night. Deer and elk normally bed down during the day, although mule deer and elk are sometimes active on winter days. Historically, white-tailed deer were active during the day, but increasing human interaction has made them more nocturnal. Adult male deer, elk, and moose are usually solitary except during the mating season, when they congregate with females. Exceptions are white-tailed bucks, which travel in small groups much of the year, and moose, which band together in winter. Female white-tailed deer (does) and elk (cows) can be seen in groups at any time of the year. Mule deer does usually travel alone with their young. Caribou tend to stay in large herds year-round, although male woodland caribou often keep to themselves during summer months.

Young deer (fawns) and young elk and moose (calves) are born in spring and raised by their mothers. Males play no part in raising their young and are never seen alone with fawns or calves. During most of the year, male deer, elk, and moose can be distinguished easily from females because the males bear antlers; females do not. The caribou is the only North American member of the deer family in which both males and females produce antlers. Antlers begin growing in spring and reach their full size and beauty in time for fights among males during the fall mating season (or rut). Deer and moose shed their antlers in winter, but elk shed them in early spring.

Antlers differ from horns in several ways. During growth, antlers are nourished by blood that reaches them from a network of veins that grows in the velvet-like tissue that covers the antlers. When the antlers are fully grown, the velvet dries up and falls off, usually helped by the animal as it rubs its antlers on shrubs and other objects. Antlers are solid calcium. Horns are nourished by a blood supply in a porous, bony core that is covered with the smooth, hard outer substance we call horn. Antlers are shed each year and regrown. Horns are permanent, except in the case of the pronghorn antelope, which sheds the outer cover of the horns yearly.

Rocky Mountain elk and mule deer usually migrate to lower elevations in autumn to escape winter weather. During migration, they are often easy to observe. Both these species can also be seen during winter, even by day, when they feed in large groups in river valleys and other lower-elevation areas. Many traditional wintering areas in the West have been converted to orchards, farms, or home sites, forcing migratory animals to bunch up in the limited areas still available to them, often on public wildlife lands.

In places like Jackson Hole, Wyoming; Stonewall, Colorado; and Yakima, Washington, elk are fed hay by wildlife agencies to tide them over the worst winter-weather conditions. Feeding stations are good places to observe these magnificent animals up close, although you may see mostly cows at the feeders, since bulls tend to stay on the edges of the herd.

Mule deer can also be seen in winter habitat all over the intermontane West, including wildlife management areas near Silver Lake, Oregon; Winthrop, Washington; Huntsville, Utah; and Carson City, Nevada. Roosevelt elk and coastal black-tailed deer also congregate in winter but usually in thick coniferous forests, where they are hard to see.

White-tailed deer and moose do not generally migrate, but their feeding habits nevertheless change in winter. When deciduous trees drop their leaves, white-tailed deer lose their protective cover, so they often concentrate in coniferous forests, where they still have something to hide behind. Big Meadows, on Virginia's Skyline Drive in Shenandoah National Park, is a reliable place to see white-tailed deer up close any time of year.

Moose also congregate into herds during winter and may be visible when they travel and feed in groups, sometimes in deep snow.

Woodland caribou are secretive and difficult to observe throughout their range in the Northern Coniferous Forest region. Barren-ground caribou can be seen in groups of 10,000 or more during and after their spring migration, but one must travel to the arctic tundra of Alaska or northern Canada to experience this last great spectacle of large animal migration in North America.

Deer, elk, moose, and caribou always should be observed from a safe distance, not only as protection for people (all four can be dangerous to humans during the fall rut and when raising their young) but also for the sake of the animal. Getting too close can frighten the animals, interrupting their feeding behavior or causing them to use energy to flee. This can be harmful, especially for females with young or for all individuals during winter, when they are physically stressed by cold weather and forced to live off fat reserves.

Deer, elk, and moose are legally hunted from October through December throughout much of North America. Wearing blaze orange or red caps and vests as a warning to hunters is recommended when you are observing wildlife in the fall, even if it reduces your viewing success.

Birds of Prey

Wildlife watchers the world over have a strong affinity for birds of prey, or raptors, and the United States and Canada offer many opportunities to observe them. Most hawks, eagles, falcons, and vultures are migratory and so are best seen when they are moving between summer breeding habitat and winter feeding areas, which for many species are separated by thousands of miles.

Raptors have been persecuted for many years by people who believe that these birds prey heavily on livestock or compete with humans for game animals. Though they do take an occasional chicken or other free meal, hawks, eagles, and other raptors do minimal damage to livestock or game populations. In fact, birds of prey help to reduce the inroads of crop-eating rodents and rabbits.

Bald eagles, ospreys, peregrine falcons, and certain other birds of prey were almost eliminated in North America by the use of DDT and other persistent pesticides, but populations have rebounded since the banning of DDT in the United States in 1972. Raptor populations generally are healthy and can be observed fairly consistently throughout North America during all or part of the year.

All birds of prey are fully protected by the federal Migratory Bird Treaty Act. The bald eagle and peregrine falcon are also listed under the Endangered Species Act; the bald eagle was upgraded from endangered to threatened in 1994 because of continued signs of its recovery.

The bald eagle is the only large North American bird of prey with a solid white head, neck, and tail. However, this characteristic pattern occurs only on adult birds at least five years old. Young are uniformly dark brown or mottled brown and white.

Bald eagles nest in many areas of the United States and Canada, though they are scarce in the Midwest and in the Great Basin region of the West. They are particularly numerous in Alaska, where dozens of the birds can sometimes be seen in a single roost. Their winter range is roughly the same as their summer range, though some eagles shift southward in cold winter.

Bald eagles are primarily fish eaters and are seldom seen far from water. In the Pacific Northwest, eagle migration coincides with salmon migration, so the best time to observe them there is during late fall and winter, when the eagles gather in large groups along salmon-bearing streams.

Golden eagles live in mountains and high-desert areas of the western United States and Canada. They are slightly larger than bald eagles and have dark plumage. Because they lack the adult bald eagle's white head and trim, observers often confuse golden eagles with immature bald eagles. Golden eagles generally do not migrate, although some birds in northern Canada do move south in winter. Golden eagles feed mostly on rabbits and small rodents. They do not gather in large groups as bald eagles do, so they are most often observed in mountainous areas as single birds or pairs. Golden eagles are not common anywhere, but you are most likely to find them perched on power poles, in trees, or on rock ledges. Golden eagle nests, like those of bald eagles, are usually platforms of sticks on cliffs or in tall trees.

Hawks with thickset bodies and broad, relatively short tails are called buteos. Included here are red-tailed hawks, red-shouldered hawks, broad-winged hawks, Swainson's hawks, ferruginous hawks, and rough-legged hawks. Most North American buteos breed in northern areas and migrate south for winter. Red-tailed hawks and other buteos often can be observed soaring in wide circles over open land, bodies of water, and river valleys, but are also seen from the road perched in trees or on telephone poles. They prey mostly on small mammals.

Hawks with long tails and short, rounded wings are called accipiters. Included here are goshawks, sharp-shinned hawks, and Cooper's hawks. Accipiters live in wooded areas, where they feed on birds and some small mammals. They do not soar like buteos but often move from tree to tree with an almost bouncing motion.

Ospreys are large brown-and-white fish-eating hawks with heads that are mostly white but with broad, black eye stripes.

Observers sometimes mistake ospreys for bald eagles, but they are much smaller and have distinctive, boomerang-shaped wings. Ospreys feed exclusively on fish, which they catch by swooping talons-first into the water. They are common all over North America, from high mountain lakes to the seacoast, and are especially plentiful along the Atlantic Coast, where they perch and nest on pilings. The aerial feeding of ospreys is easy to observe, since they almost always hunt over open water.

Falcons are birds of prey with long, accipiter-like tails and pointed wings. Famous for their beauty and supurb flying skills, falcons are sought after by wildlife watchers and photographers as well as falconers, who train the birds for sport hunting.

Peregrines are the best-known falcons in North America. Many peregrines, as well as the larger gyrfalcons and the smaller merlins, nest in the far north and migrate south to winter along the Pacific Coast. Other peregrine falcons nest in the lower forty-eight states—even on the ledges of inner-city buildings—then winter in the southwestern states and Mexico. Prairie falcons live in the arid West, from the Canadian prairies to the southwestern desert.

The most common falcon in North America is the small American kestrel, or sparrow hawk, which is commonly seen in open grasslands or farmlands, but sometimes can be seen even in cities.

Peregrine falcons and gyrfalcons eat small birds, which they catch in midair, using power dives of up to 200 miles per hour. Prairie falcons and kestrels eat a variety of small mammals, ground birds, and even grasshoppers. Except for the relatively common kestrel, the chances of seeing a falcon in most of the United States and Canada are slim. Their numbers were never large and are even lower now, due to past DDT poisoning. The best place to see a peregrine falcon might be in a city such as Seattle, Washington; Baltimore, Maryland; or Salt Lake City, Utah, where falcon pairs released under a federal recovery plan have built nests and fledged young on the ledges of office buildings.

Biologists have classified vultures as birds of prey for many years, but recent evidence suggests that vultures actually belong in the stork family. I include them here with the raptors out of respect for the old tradition.

Vultures feed exclusively on dead animals (carrion). Two species soar over North America. The turkey vulture is large and black, with a red, featherless head and a wingspan of up to 32 inches. It occurs across most of North America. The black vulture, with a black, featherless head, is slightly smaller. It ranges primarily in the southeastern states. Vultures, also called buzzards, are like large hawks but can usually be distinguished when in flight by the V, or dihedral, shape of their outstretched wings. In spring and fall, turkey vultures can often be seen migrating with other raptors along the Atlantic coast and the Appalachian Mountains.

Most raptors migrate to warmer climates before winter. Many species retreat to South America when winter comes. For example, virtually all of North America's 450,000 Swainson's hawks migrate to Argentina when winter comes. Some species—and even individuals of widely migrating species—may winter in North America. Routes and times of migration are fairly consistent for each species, so you can plan raptor-watching trips with virtual assurance of seeing the birds. During autumn and spring, large numbers of hawks and vultures pass over well-known hawk lookout points in Pennsylvania, New York, New Jersey, and the Great Lakes states and provinces. In autumn, many hawks also migrate south along the Atlantic Coast, where they can be seen at dozens of well-known lookout points from Nova Scotia to New Jersey. At these hawk lookout points, observers commonly see hundreds of hawks spiraling on warm air currents, or thermals, in groups that raptor aficionados call kettles.

Eagles, hawks, and other raptors also migrate along the Pacific Coast and inland valleys of the West and Midwest, but the topography and climate do not provide as many consistent or well-known hawk-watching opportunities as are found in the East. Manzano, New Mexico; Hawk Hill, in San Francisco; and the eastern slope of the Rockies near Lincoln, Montana, are three of the best hawk lookout points in the western United States.

The best time of year to see large numbers of raptors in the West is from November to March, when the birds gather in their wintering habitat. The Skagit and Nooksack Rivers in Washington are famous for their wintering concentrations of bald eagles that have migrated south from Alaska and Canada to meet the upstream migration of Pacific salmon. So is Haines, Alaska, where up to 3,000 eagles can be seen together during salmon migration. Red-tailed and rough-legged hawks often winter in open farm country, along with snowy owls, an arctic species that sometimes comes south when northern winters are particularly severe.

North America's raptors include 18 species of owl. The largest is the great gray owl of the boreal forests of Alaska and Canada, which measures up to 33 inches from head to tail. The smallest is the elf owl of the Southwest Desert region, which is only about 6 inches long. The most widely distributed owl in North America is probably the great horned owl, which ranges across all Canadian provinces and the continental United States. Other owls common in North America are barn owls, screech owls, and barred owls. All owls are carnivorous, and most are nocturnal, feeding on mice, rats, flying squirrels, other small mammals, and even other birds, including other owls. Some owls, including pygmy owls, burrowing owls, and snowy owls, hunt during the day for rodents and other small animals.

Because they are nocturnal, finding and observing owls requires a willingness to venture into the woods or the desert at night—or to prowl around old farm buildings where some owls, including barn owls, often nest and roost. You need to use your ears more than your eyes in locating owls. Owls are noisy birds, so you sometimes can locate their roosts and nests by simply sitting quietly on a log and listening for their calls. You can also initiate calling by briefly playing recordings or imitating owl calls. Owls—particularly screech owls, great horned owls, and tiny saw-whet owls—respond readily to recordings or imitations of their calls or the calls of prey. You should always limit use of calls and recordings, however, because they confuse and fatigue the birds.

Once you have located an owl by its call, move quietly in the direction of the call until you are so close that the bird senses your presence and stops calling. At that point, it is sometimes possible to

Barn owl

approach an owl quietly and illuminate it with a flashlight. The bird usually will sit still just long enough for you to confirm its identification before it flies off into the darkness.

You can locate owl roosts during the day by looking for owl pellets or telltale whitewash droppings under trees, on shaded rock ledges, or around old farm buildings. If you do come across a sleeping owl during the day, you should observe it for only a few minutes, then leave as quietly as you arrived.

All you really need for observing owls at night is a flashlight, a field guide, a warm jacket, and maybe a tape recorder to play back or record calls. Cassette tapes of bird calls can be purchased from outdoor stores and catalogues, including the National Wildlife Federation catalogue.

Waterfowl

At least 39 species of ducks, 7 species of geese, and 2 wild swan species occur in North America. Most of these waterfowl migrate between northern nesting grounds and southern wintering areas. Migrating waterfowl move north and south in great numbers along the Pacific, Central, Mississippi, and Atlantic Flyways. The United States, Canada, and Mexico are working together, through the North American Waterfowl Management Plan, to restore waterfowl populations to the levels of the early 1970s.

Dabbling ducks (dabblers) are associated with shallow ponds, creeks, and freshwater marshes. This group includes mallards, black ducks, pintails, gadwalls, shovelers, teal, and wigeon. Dabblers eat on land or upend their bodies to feed on shallow aquatic vegetation. When surprised, dabbling ducks spring into the air and fly almost straight up. Male dabblers (drakes) have brighter colors than do the females (hens), including an iridescent patch of feathers, called a speculum, on the trailing edges of their wings.

Diving ducks (divers) are associated with saltwater and estuaries, although they migrate inland in the spring to breed and raise young on lakes, rivers, and freshwater marshes. This group of ducks includes canvasbacks, redheads, goldeneyes, buffleheads, scaup, and harlequin ducks. Divers submerge fully to feed on underwater vegetation, fish, crustaceans, and other small organisms. Divers do not take off straight up; instead, they fly across the surface of the water, gathering speed like an airplane.

Wild geese are found all across North America during the breeding, wintering, and migration seasons. Species include the Canada goose, American and black brant, emperor goose, Ross's goose, snow goose, blue goose, and white-fronted goose. The Canada goose is by far the most abundant and widely distributed goose species. Canada geese also show the greatest variation in size, ranging from the Atlantic Canada goose, which grows to three feet or longer, to the mallard-sized cackling goose of the Pacific Flyway.

Two species of wild swan live in North America, the trumpeter swan and the tundra (or whistling) swan. Domesticated mute swans, originally from Europe, are often planted in parks and private lakes. All swans are white and much larger than geese, with necks longer than their bodies.

Waterfowl can be observed almost any time of year, but the best time to observe large groups of the birds is during the fall and spring migrations and when waterfowl are concentrated in wintering habitat. In fall, at the onset of cold weather, the birds begin to move south along well-established routes within each flyway. They usually travel in large groups, often at high altitudes, and stop only to rest and feed. Canada geese fly in large V formations; snow geese fly in wavy lines. Sometimes waterfowl feed in coastal estuaries, sometimes in cornfields or on row crops, depending on their preferences and the availability of food. Some saltwater diving ducks, including scaup, goldeneyes, and harlequin ducks, migrate south for the winter, then migrate again in the spring, when they fly inland to nest and raise their young on freshwater lakes and rivers.

Wintering waterfowl seek areas with open (unfrozen) water and available food and will go as far south as they need to go to find them. Many waterfowl are not particular about where they winter, as long as they have sufficient food and water. If the weather turns cold, wintering birds will pick up and move farther south. If it warms up, they might stay in one spot for most of the winter. In mild winters, some Canada geese and mallard ducks do not migrate at all.

Many important feeding and wintering areas in all four waterfowl flyways are in public ownership and are managed as federal or state wildlife refuges. Most public lands are open year-round for wildlife watching—with reasonable rules to keep the public from disturbing or stressing the birds—and some refuges are also open for fall hunting. Thousands of private farm ponds and midwestern potholes also accommodate millions of ducks, geese, and swans each winter.

Because different flyways provide different habitat conditions, they also attract different mixes of waterfowl species. Black ducks, for instance, are normally seen only in the Atlantic Flyway. Techniques and materials used by waterfowl hunters to attract birds, such as blinds, camouflage, and duck and goose calls, can be used effectively at other times of year to attract and observe waterfowl and other flyway travelers. As you would with other migrating and wintering wildlife, however, keep your presence unknown or keep your distance. Use binoculars and spotting scopes. If you want to observe waterfowl and other wildlife on private land, be sure to ask permission from the landowner.

Shorebirds

Perhaps no group of wildlife species is more interesting to observe and study than those sandpipers, knots, snipe, avocets, oystercatchers, plovers, and other migratory birds known collectively as shorebirds. These birds are beautiful in flight. They are also fascinating to study because they spend so much of their lives migrating and cover so many thousands of miles between their breeding and wintering habitats. Many sandpipers nest in Siberia or Alaska, then winter in southern California and on south as far as Chile. One incredible example of shorebird migration is the bristle-thighed curlew, which nests in the vicinity of the Yukon River Delta in Alaska, then flies across the Pacific Ocean to winter on Tahiti and other South Pacific islands. Shorebirds, like waterfowl, migrate south and north along predictable routes, or flyways, but they are even more inflexible than waterfowl in the timing and stopover pattern of their migration flights. Shorebirds use a tremendous amount of energy in flight and, without the right habitat and adequate food at each stopover, will not put on enough weight to negotiate the next leg of their flight. For example, most of the world's population of western sandpipers stops and feeds in Grays Harbor, Washington,

Sandpipers

each spring on their northward migration to nest in the Arctic. If this particular estuary were no longer available or suitable for shorebirds, the whole Pacific Coast population of this species could be jeopardized.

Unless you happen to live in or visit the remote tundra and boreal forests of Alaska and Canada in the late spring or early summer, you are unlikely to see most shorebirds in their breeding habitat. The best times to view them are usually during their long spring and fall migrations, when thousands of birds gather to rest and feed in coastal estuaries, wetlands, and exposed freshwater mudflats. In such places as Humboldt Bay National Wildlife Refuge, California; Padre Island National Seashore, Texas; and Brigantine National Wildlife Refuge, New Jersey, thousands of sandpipers and other shorebirds can be observed at one time. They fly in perfectly coordinated formations, then land together on shallow beaches and mudflats to feed on small crustaceans left exposed by outgoing tides. Peregrine falcons, merlins, and other birds of prey also gather at these stopovers to feed on shorebirds.

Finding and observing shorebirds is not especially difficult, since many coastal beaches and inland mudflats are visited by shorebirds during the spring, fall, or winter. Identifying shorebirds to the species level can be a challenging experience, especially for beginning wildlife watchers. First of all, migrating shorebirds are very skittish, making it difficult to get close enough to make a positive identification. Also, many shorebirds look alike, even when you do get close enough to observe them. Some lack any obvious field marks, and even those change from season to season as the birds molt. Often, all you can do is get the best look you can, then carefully list or sketch all the characteristics you see, including size, shape, color of legs and plumage, and shape of bill. Later, when you are able to consult and compare field guides, you can figure out what you saw. If you have a good description, and you know which species should or should not be seen in a particular area, you can usually winnow down the list of possible species by the process of elimination.

Grays Harbor, Washington, was recently recognized as one of the most important shorebird sites in the Western Hemisphere; other critical shorebird sites recognized by the Western Hemisphere Shorebird Reserve Network include San Francisco Bay; Great Salt Lake, Utah; Delaware Bay; Stillwater, Nevada; Copper River Delta, Alaska; and the Bay of Fundy on the east coast of Canada.

Sandhill Cranes

Sandhill cranes are not waterfowl and certainly not shorebirds, but they are one of the most beautiful, interesting, and sought-after migratory bird species in North America, at least by midwestern wildlife watchers. Sandhill cranes are about four feet tall and gray in color, with black-tipped wings and a distinctive red patch on their foreheads. They have long legs and necks and are sometimes confused with herons or other wading birds, although cranes occupy their own family, Gruidae, in the scheme of bird classification. Sandhill cranes are known for their beautiful plumage and their distinctive, frenzied dance, performed by both males and females.

Considered on the brink of extinction in the 1930s, sandhill populations have grown steadily to the point where there are almost 600,000 birds in North America. The sandhill crane's larger, white cousin, the endangered whooping crane, has not fared so well. Less than 200 whooping cranes remain in North America, breeding in

Canada each year and wintering at the Aransas National Wildlife Refuge on the Gulf Coast of Texas.

Sandhill cranes nest in northwestern Canada, Alaska, and parts of Siberia. They winter in Mexico, New Mexico, and, along with whooping cranes, along the Gulf Coast of Texas. They migrate up to 6,000 miles each spring and fall and spend up to two months on the wing during each migration.

The best time to observe sandhill cranes is during their northward migration in the early spring—from mid-February to the end of March—and the best place to see them in large numbers is along Nebraska's central Platte River Valley. Here, the public can see up to half a million birds—80 percent of the North American population—at one time. Some birders congregate at places such as the National Audubon Society's Lillian Annette Rowe Sanctuary. Other visitors observe the cranes from secondary roads along the Platte River between Kearney and Grand Island, Nebraska. Sandhill cranes can also be observed in other places in the Grassland and Shrub-steppe Desert Habitat Regions, including the Columbia National Wildlife Refuge in eastern Washington and Malheur National Wildlife Refuge in eastern Oregon.

Bats

Bats are the most abundant mammals on Earth, except for rodents, and are found in every state, province, and habitat type in North America. Bats are the only mammals that truly fly. Their wings are formed by a skin membrane stretching between the hand and finger bones. All bats found in North America are insect eaters, except for a few tropical fruit and nectar-eating bats that occasionally wander north from Mexico. All North American bats are largely nocturnal, and except for some species that migrate to warmer climates in winter, most hibernate during cold seasons. The eyes of bats are almost useless, but the bat's poor eyesight is compensated by its use of sonar (echolocation), which allows bats to fly and to feed on insects in almost total darkness. Bats also have large ears and incredibly acute hearing.

Bats sleep during the day and through the winter in dark, quiet places, including caves, hollow trees, and buildings. Some species are solitary sleepers, but many others spend the daylight hours in large colonies. All hang upside down when they sleep. North American bats do not attack or bite humans but should never be handled, since they are sometimes rabid. One species, the vampire bat, feeds on the blood of mammals, biting animals while they sleep and lapping up their blood. Vampire bats usually do not live in the United States; they are denizens of tropical areas in Mexico and Central and South America. Bat observation records include only one lone vampire reported in southern Texas.

Bats are fascinating to observe, especially at dusk as they leave their roosts in large numbers. They begin emerging from daytime roosts about an hour before dark, then usually fly to a stream, lake, or pond to drink before spending the night catching and eating insects. Bats are the only major predators of night-flying insects. One bat may eat up to 3,000 or more insects in one night, including many mosquitoes that might otherwise be out biting humans.

The best way to observe bats is with a spotting scope or binoculars as the sun goes down. Try to be as quiet as possible, since bats are easily startled by loud noises. One of the most famous bat-watching places in North America is in downtown Austin, Texas, where from April to October you can see as many as 750,000 Mexican free-tailed bats at a time leaving their roost under the Congress Avenue Bridge at dusk. Many natural caves, including Carlsbad Caverns National Park in New Mexico, Nickajack Caves in Tennessee, Lewis and Clark Caverns in Montana, Florida Caverns State Park in Florida, and Maquoketa Caves State Park in Iowa are also famous for their bat-watching opportunities.

Bears and Native Cats

Three species of bears and six species of native cats occur in North America. All are relatively uncommon and secretive in their habits. Cats are basically meat eaters. Biologists classify bears as carnivores, but in fact the animals eat mostly fruit, berries, and other vegetable material. The exception to this is the polar bear, which feeds almost exclusively on meat in its nearly vegetation-free habitat. Grizzly bears and black bears hibernate during cold weather, disappearing into winter dens. Unlike hibernating rodents, hibernating bears maintain a relatively high body temperature and metabolic rate. During warm periods in winter, hibernating bears may even awaken and wander outside their dens before returning to sleep. Male and nonpregnant polar bears do not hibernate, but pregnant females do, giving birth in their dens.

Black bears are the most common and most widely distributed bears in North America, ranging across Alaska and Canada, down western mountain ranges, and through most of the Eastern Deciduous Forest Habitat Region, including Florida. Black bears are relatively small, weighing between 200 and 400 pounds. Their color ranges from the almost white Kermode bear of British Columbia to the bluish glacier phase found in parts of Alaska and the Yukon to the much more common light brown and black varieties. An estimated 50 percent of black bears in the Rocky Mountains are black, the rest brown. Most of the black bears in the East are in fact black.

Grizzly bears once roamed over much of the western United States and Canada. Although viable populations are still found in Canada, Alaska, and the northern Rocky Mountains, including Yellowstone and Glacier National Parks, they are listed as threatened in the lower forty-eight states. Grizzly bears are much larger than black bears. The Alaska or Kodiak brown bear, a subspecies of grizzly, may weigh 1,500 pounds or more. Grizzlies have a distinctive hump above their shoulders, which often can be used to distinguish them from black bears. Grizzlies also have a more dished face, and their claws tend to be longer and straighter than those of the black bear.

Polar bears are found only in the extreme north of Alaska and Canada, in tundra above the Arctic Circle. Their fur is white or yellowish white, and they rival the grizzly in size. Polar bears eat mostly seals and other marine mammals, plus birds and fish when they can capture them.

Cougar

Cougars are the largest native cats in North America (except for jaguars, which once occurred in Texas and parts of the Southwest but are now largely missing from North America), weighing up to 200 pounds. They are widely distributed in western Canada and the United States. A handful—fewer than fifty animals—remain in southern Florida, a tiny remnant of the once-large eastern cougar population. Cougars, also called pumas, mountain lions, and panthers, prefer mountains and forested habitat away from human disturbance, where they prey mostly on deer. Cougars have unspotted tawny to gray coats.

Bobcats and lynx are much smaller than cougars, weighing about 30 pounds, with pointed ears (tufted, in the case of the lynx) and short tails. Bobcats have spotted coats and are widely distributed across the United States and southern Canada. Lynx are slightly larger than bobcats, are not spotted, and occur across the Northern

Coniferous Forest region of Canada and the northern United States. Bobcats eat rabbits and other small mammals; lynx eat mostly snow-shoe hares.

Jaguars and ocelots live in mountainous areas of Mexico and are occasionally reported in the southernmost parts of Arizona, New Mexico, and Texas. Jaguars are larger than cougars, while ocelots are much smaller, weighing about 40 pounds. Both jaguars and ocelots are spotted.

Bears and native cats have many habits in common, and many of the same considerations should be taken into account when trying to observe them. All bears and native cats are secretive, and most are nocturnal. Most people go their whole outdoor lives without ever seeing a bear or cat in the wild. When they do see one, it is usually only a fleeting glimpse—unless the animal is sick, injured, or, as in the case of some park bears, habituated to humans. Most national parks have taken steps to reduce dangerous encounters between humans and bears, but these parks are probably still the best places in the lower forty-eight states to observe bears safely in the wild. Grizzly bears can be seen in Glacier and Yellowstone National Parks or fishing in groups along coastal salmon streams in Alaska and Canada. Black bears can sometimes be seen in parks and refuges in the Eastern Deciduous Forest Habitat Region, including Blueberry Hill, near Goshen, Vermont; and Great Smoky Mountains National Park, which straddles the North Carolina–Tennessee border. Polar bears occur only in the Arctic Tundra Habitat Region.

Native cats are strict predators and usually stalk or travel the trails used by deer, rabbits, and other favored prey animals. Cougars and bobcats often watch wildlife trails from trees or rock ledges and will almost always see you before you see them. Bears are sometimes encountered on trails by hikers. All bears and native cats are potentially dangerous, especially if they are surprised or have their young with them. Grizzlies and polar bears are especially dangerous.

If you do encounter a bear or cat in the wild, you should try to stay calm, talk softly, leave the animal plenty of room to escape, and slowly back away. Never turn your back on or run from a bear or large cat.

Fish

Observing fish can be as enjoyable as any other wildlife-viewing experience, but of course there are different ground rules for getting in touch with these animals. In order to view fish in their natural habitat, you must either wait for them in a place where they are known to pass by or congregate near the surface of the water, or you must insert yourself into their environment by looking or going underwater. Below is a short discussion of each way to view fish.

Surface Viewing

Fish can sometimes be seen with the naked eye in streams, lakes, and spring-fed pools where the water is exceptionally clear or where the fish come near the surface to feed or spawn. In other places, visitor centers offer underwater rooms where fish can be seen as they swim by. In Wisconsin, large lake sturgeon can be viewed as they gather to spawn on the shore of Lake Winnebago. At Cass County France Park in Indiana, 6-foot-long paddlefish can be seen swimming in an old quarry lake, and at Lake Tahoe, on the California-Nevada border, kokanee salmon can be observed from a large underwater viewing room at the headwaters of the Truckee River. Many dams on the Columbia and Snake Rivers in the Pacific Northwest also have viewing rooms where adult salmon can be seen negotiating fish ladders to spawn in upstream tributaries. Big Bend Manatee Viewing Center, in Florida's Tampa Bay, offers a close-up view of many freshwater fish species, as well as manatees. State, provincial, and federal fish hatcheries, when open to the public, are almost always good places to view trout and other game fish, even though the fish are not yet in the wild.

Observing fish from the surface can be enhanced by wearing sunglasses with polarizing lenses, which will reduce the surface glare of the water. Fish have very good eyes and hearing, so you should stand or sit very quietly and keep your own shadow away from the fish. Fish also have a well-developed sense of smell—salmon find

their way back to their spawning grounds by the unique smell of each tributary stream—something to keep in mind if you put your hands or feet in the water.

Snorkeling and Scuba Diving

If you really want to see fish up close, you should try immersing yourself into their environment by using snorkels and shallow dives or by learning how to dive deeper and stay underwater longer with the use of scuba equipment (*scuba* stands for self-contained underwater breathing apparatus). Coral reefs off the southern Atlantic coast of Florida—including Biscayne National Park and John Pennekamp Coral Reef State Park—are also excellent places to observe fish with the use of snorkels or scuba gear. If you decide to do this, be sure you read the regulations carefully. Collecting coral reef is illegal; in fact touching the reef is even discouraged, since corals are fragile, living organisms. Touching or feeding fish is also not a good idea, for all the reasons I mention in the next chapter. Snorkeling and diving are discussed in more detail in Chapter 8, along with some great places to view fish.

Whales and Other Marine Mammals

Whales, dolphins, porpoises, sea otters, seals, and other marine mammals are found in all oceans of the world and occasionally in rivers.

All whales and porpoises belong to the order Cetacea. Scientists divide whales as a group into two types. Baleen whales, such as gray and humpback whales, lack teeth. Instead, their mouths are lined with horny baleen plates, which they use to strain out their food, composed of small marine organisms, from the huge quantities of water that they take in as they swim with their mouths open. The second group is the toothed whales, including dolphins, porpoises, beaked whales, and sperm whales. They feed on fish, squid, seals, and other marine mammals. Seals and sea lions are classified as pinnipeds, from the Latin for fin foot. Sea lions differ from seals in being able to rotate their hind flippers forward for use on land and in having small external ears.

Sea otters and river otters are classified as mustelids, a group that includes mink, weasels, and badgers.

Sea otters and many whale and pinniped species were hunted almost to extinction during the nineteenth and early twentieth centuries. With the passage of the Marine Mammal Protection Act in 1972 and the initiation of international treaties that restrict or ban the commercial killing of whales, we have seen a comeback of marine mammal populations in recent years, including the right whale, blue whale, and California gray whale, all of which were once on the brink of extinction. The gray whale has rebounded so well, in fact, that the species was removed from the Endangered Species list in 1994. With this recent increase in marine mammal populations has come a growing public demand to see these magnificent creatures, giving rise to a new tourism industry that puts the public in contact with whales and other marine mammals.

Large whales, such as blue, fin, and sperm whales, are most likely to be seen in the open ocean, although some migratory whales, including humpback, right, and gray whales, often swim near shore

or come into bays and estuaries. In the fall of 1985, a humpback whale, dubbed Humphrey by the media, spent weeks swimming around in the Sacramento River in California, to the delight of the public and TV camera crews. Migrating gray whales often stop to rest and feed in Grays Harbor or Puget Sound in Washington State. To view whales in open water, travel in a boat at least the size of a commercial fishing vessel, and go with people who know where and when whales should be visible. In most cases, professional outfitters or charter-boat operators are your best bet and are generally available for hire anywhere there are whales to be seen. Check with your local fisheries agency or chamber of commerce for reputable outfitters.

Seeing porpoises and orcas (killer whales) is not as difficult as finding larger whales. Small whales, dolphins, and porpoises can often be seen just offshore along the Atlantic or Gulf coasts or in protected waters like Chesapeake Bay, Florida's Tampa Bay, or the Inland Passage of Alaska and Canada. There are places in the San Juan Islands of Washington's Puget Sound, as well as in the Gulf Islands of British Columbia, where you have a pretty good chance of seeing orcas from shore during the summer months, or you can hire an outfitter to take you out in a small boat, which will get you closer to the whales. Off the Outer Banks of North Carolina, pods of Atlantic bottle-nosed dolphins swim so close to the beach every afternoon that they almost join human swimmers and surfers. With porpoises, dolphins, and orcas, the first thing you usually will see is a dorsal fin slicing through the water. If you go out in a boat to observe whales, remember it is against the law to approach any marine mammal closer than 100 yards. If you plan to watch from shore, remember to bring binoculars or a spotting scope.

Seals and sea lions are generally easier to see than whales because they haul themselves out of the water at regular intervals and at habitual resting places. Since passage of the Marine Mammal Protection Act, harbor seals and California sea lion populations have increased dramatically, so these animals can be seen at hundreds of places along the Pacific Coast. One of the best places to view sea lions up close is the small boat marina at San Francisco's Fishermen's Wharf. Pacific sea otters pop up sometimes in offshore kelp beds all along the Pacific Coast, although the best place to see them might be the Monterey Bay Aquarium in California. River otters are basically freshwater animals but can sometimes also be viewed in estuaries and shallow saltwater bays, where they feed on fish.

Never approach seals or sea lions, especially on land. Seals are very afraid of humans; sea lions are large and bad-tempered.

Amphibians and Reptiles

North America is home to 142 species of amphibians and 236 species of reptiles. Together, these groups occupy almost every habitat region on the continent, from the open ocean (sea turtles) to the eastern deciduous forests to the Southwest desert.

All amphibians and reptiles are ectothermic, or cold-blooded, which means that their body temperatures are dependent on the temperature of the air or water surrounding them.

North American amphibians include frogs, toads, salamanders,

and newts. Frogs and toads are the most numerous and widespread amphibians in North America. They are also the most visible. The main difference between frogs and toads is their appearance. Frogs have smooth skin and long legs and live in or near water. Toads have shorter legs and rough or warty skin and live in moist places away from water. Salamanders also have smooth skin and four legs, but their bodies are lizard-shaped, with long tails. Some salamander species live in water, some on land, and some divide their time between the water and the land. Newts are salamanders that live on land but spend a few weeks in water each spring to breed.

Amphibians are carnivorous, capturing and eating insects, worms, snails, and slugs. Large bullfrogs occasionally even eat small rodents and ducklings. Most adult amphibians are nocturnal and secretive. Many are naturally camouflaged to blend in with background colors. Most also hibernate or estivate to escape temperature extremes.

North American reptiles include snakes, lizards, turtles, alligators, and the rare American crocodile. Snakes, lizards, and turtles are found in the lower forty-eight states and southern Canada. Alligators are found in coastal areas from North Carolina to Texas. The American crocodile, an endangered species, lives in only a few locations in Florida. The abundance and diversity of reptiles is greatest in tropical and warm desert climates.

All reptiles have dry, scaly skin that holds moisture, so they are generally better adapted to life on land than are amphibians. Reptile eggs also have hard shells, like those of birds, which protect the young from drying out on land.

Most reptiles are carnivorous, including snakes, alligators, most lizards, and some turtles, which eat slow-moving prey like insect larvae, shellfish, and worms. Other turtle species and some lizards are vegetarians or omnivores, including some sea turtles, desert tortoises, and the chuckwalla lizard of the Southwest Desert.

Most reptiles are active during the day. In fact, alligators, turtles, and many lizards can often be observed sunning themselves during the middle of the day. Some snakes are nocturnal. As with amphibians, many reptiles hibernate or estivate during part of the year to escape temperature extremes. Generally speaking, most reptiles are active only when the air temperature is above 60 degrees Fahrenheit. They also avoid hot, direct sunlight, as they can quickly overheat and die.

Most amphibians and reptiles are largely overlooked by wildlife watchers and the educational media, even though, as a group, these creatures are among the most beautiful and interesting wild animals in North America. The following tips should be considered in finding and observing amphibians and reptiles:

⇥ The best time to look for amphibians is during cool, damp weather in the spring, summer, and fall, particularly during early morning and evening hours. Look for salamanders in forested areas, where they are likely to be under rocks, logs, or damp leaves on the ground. Look for tree frogs on or near—no surprise—trees. Look for larger frogs at the edges of open water. Amphibians are harmless to humans, but should be handled only briefly and carefully.

⇥ The best time to look for reptiles is on warm days in the spring and fall. Most are inactive in the winter and on hot summer days. Although some turtles and small snakes are shy and harmless, most reptiles are aggressive and should be observed only from a safe distance. Rattlesnakes, copperheads, coral snakes, and water moccasins are very poisonous, as are Gila monsters in the Southwest

Desert. Even many nonpoisonous snakes have sharp teeth and will bite if provoked. Snapping turtles are especially bad-tempered, and alligators are potentially fatal, especially to small children and pets. If you are bitten by a reptile, even a nonpoisonous snake, you should get medical attention as soon as possible to avoid infection.

4

Field Awareness—Making the Most of Your Senses and Knowledge

Observing wildlife in the field is a rewarding but often challenging experience. Birds, mammals, and other wildlife spend most of their time and energy searching for food and trying to avoid danger. Accordingly, evolution has equipped most species with finely tuned senses of smell, hearing, and eyesight, all the better to monitor their environment for danger or food. Their often superior senses give them a distinct advantage over us when we are looking for them and they are trying to avoid us. In the following pages I offer some basic information and tools that are intended to help you offset your natural disadvantage in the field and help increase your chances of observing, understanding, and enjoying a whole range of wildlife in various natural habitats.

Frame of Mind

As is true in any other pursuit, your attitude and mind-set will have a great deal to do with your success in finding and observing wildlife. If you are like me, you will try to squeeze a day or two of hiking and wildlife watching into a schedule already packed with business and family obligations. But if you approach your wildlife excursion as just another scheduled activity, chances are you will never make the mental transition between simply getting something done and having a focused, relaxing, and rewarding wildlife-viewing experience.

Before you strap on your pack, grab your binoculars, and move down the trail, you should try to shift your mind and body into a lower gear than you normally use in your day-to-day life. If you don't slow down, you are likely to find yourself taking an aerobic walk rather than a nature hike. You might experience good cardio-vascular training, but wildlife will detect your approach, and you will see very few animals.

Try to purge your mind of the hectic thoughts that characterize the rest of your life—the frustrating situation you had at the office yesterday, the repair job you need to do on your roof. If you can force yourself to sit down for a few minutes, try to conjure up in your mind that nagging to-do list, then either set it aside or write it down to deal with later.

I always carry a small notebook and a pen or pencil with me when I go out in the field. Then as I invariably start to mentally download the phone calls I forgot to make last week and the business contacts I need to make next week, I quickly jot them down, then stuff the notebook into my pocket or pack. It doesn't take long before I've cleaned most of the routine clutter out of my mind, and I become better able to focus on the environment around me.

The timing of a nature hike or trip can also be important. Personally, I find that my mind is less cluttered and more focused after a good night's sleep—and not surprisingly, I usually see more wildlife and enjoy my outings more in the early morning hours.

Moving Slowly and Quietly

When you actually head down the trail, or get to wherever you plan to observe wildlife, try to keep your speed in first or second gear. You are likely to see more wildlife in a slow two-mile walk than in a five-mile aerobic march. Try to vary your pace. Walk slowly for a while. Pick up your pace if the habitat lacks promise for the type of wildlife you are seeking. Then when you get to a likely spot, stop altogether and either stand still, crouch down, or take a seat. Try to blend into the background by positioning yourself against a back-drop, such as a tree or a pile of rocks, and keep your profile as low as possible. Look and listen for signs of wildlife. If you detect wildlife and want to get closer, try stalking, which is discussed later in this chapter.

Try always to walk as quietly as possible and to keep conversa-tion to a bare minimum. If you do talk with companions, keep your voices as low as possible. Remember, most animals have the advan-tage when it comes to detecting intruders, including humans. Some mammals, for instance, can hear up to 60,000 cycles (the measure-ment of sound rate and vibration), at least 12 times the range of human ears. Remember, also, that for most wildlife the human voice is a danger signal—except of course for jays, gulls, squirrels, and other animals habituated to people and looking for a handout.

If you hike or travel with children, do more than just nag them to be quiet. Instead, make a special effort to have them understand that loud noises, even small voices, will frighten away wildlife. Try to make "being sneaky" part of the positive experience of watching wildlife. If you bring pets along—which I do not recommend—keep them leashed and quiet, if possible.

Sitting Still

It's pretty amazing what you can see if you just sit still, even out in the open. The eyes of most wild animals require some slight move-ment to separate an object from general background shapes and colors, and any object that is not moving will usually not elicit any alarm. This is especially true with mammals, since most mammal species see only in shades of black, white, and gray. Birds see in color, but they also respond to movement more than they do to other alarm signals.

As you sit or stand still, focus your senses on your surroundings and try to detect individual birdcalls and other wildlife sounds. Even though the human ear is not as sensitive as that of other mammals and birds, we can hear a lot of sounds if we sit still, remain quiet, and condition ourselves to focus attention on the environment around us.

If you want to see creatures you might easily overlook, then don't be reluctant to get "down and dirty." Sometimes, the most interesting species are animals you can see only by getting down on hands and knees. On college field trips to Death Valley, one of my botany professors, Frits Went, encouraged students to see beyond the obvious cacti and desert shrubs and look for interesting "belly plants"—small annual desert flowers that could be seen only by literally getting down on your belly. The same idea applies to woods and wetlands and to finding many small critters likely to remain invisible to the permanently bipedal. When you stop to rest and listen for wildlife, look for small plants and animals that live in or under dead logs, under rocks, and in other such microhabitats. This is especially important if you are traveling with children. Kids want to do more than just watch wildlife from a distance; they want to touch and handle things. So when you stop to rest, let your children explore the immediate vicinity. Encourage them to look for plants and animals under rocks and logs; then be prepared to answer their questions.

Stalking

Much has been written about the art of stalking, or sneaking up on, wildlife. And stalking can really work if you know the location of an animal—by a pattern of tracks, for instance—and try carefully to approach it undetected.

One of the secrets of stalking is to move slowly enough to avoid making unexpected or abnormal sounds. Even the snap of a twig or a scrape on a rock can be enough to send wildlife on its way.

Here are a few pointers that will help you become a stealthy wildlife viewer:

➣ *Wait for rain.* Going on a woodland outing after a rainstorm allows you to take advantage of footpaths silenced by moisture—no brittle leaves or snapping twigs.

➣ *Try to keep downwind of quarry likely to perceive your scent.* This may mean going out of your way to approach an animal from a new direction. Wet your finger and hold it in the air. The side that cools is the side from which air is moving. You want to get downwind of the animal so that air is moving from it to you.

➣ *Be wary.* As you approach wildlife, avoid staring at it directly, as some animals take this as a sign of aggression. Keep your target in sight by looking off to one side, so that you can watch for any behavior that might indicate alarm. A deer will often raise its head, flick its tail, or begin to move slowly toward cover when alarmed. Blue jays and squirrels sound an alarm that alerts not only other jays and squirrels but every creature around. If an animal seems to detect you, freeze in place and momentarily look away. If the animal goes back to eating or other normal behavior, try moving a little closer. If the alarm signals go up again, you are probably as close as you are going to get to that particular animal or group of animals. This is the best time to get a closer look with a pair of binoculars or to get your best shot with a camera.

❧ *Be careful.* It is dangerous to approach large animals such as bears or moose or to approach any animal that is with its young. If you decide to try stalking wildlife in the field, be certain that your approach is not so threatening that you put yourself in danger.

Getting Off the Beaten Path

Many parks and refuges have well-defined and marked trails that managers want the public to use in order to protect habitat, prevent accidents, and keep people from getting lost. I fully appreciate the need for these rules in parks and other developed areas, and I never advise wildlife watchers to break the rules. However, I encourage you to stray off the beaten path whenever you can do so without breaking rules or trampling fragile vegetation. Animals tend to avoid places and routes where people gather, unless they are habituated to people and looking for a handout. The tendency of wildlife to avoid people significantly diminishes your chances of seeing wildlife on heavily used trails. Try taking side paths off the main trail, or even an animal trail, and walk as far as your comfort level allows. Make note of some landmarks back to the main trail, then stand or sit quietly. In a few quiet minutes you are likely to see more wildlife than will the whole stampede of people moving back and forth on the main trail.

Looking in All the Right Places

As you search for wildlife, you should get into the habit of looking at a variety of habitats and inspecting the same habitat at various eye levels. If you look only in one direction or at only one level, you are likely to miss a lot of wildlife. My wife takes fifth-grade students on nature hikes in the forest every spring. She tells them to stop and listen, then to look away from the trail, from side to side, and especially up in the trees. Many birds and mammals nest or roost in trees or position themselves on rock ledges from which they can see enemies and prey without being seen.

A good place to look for wildlife is in the transition area or margin between two different kinds of habitat. These areas, which biologists call edge habitat, or ecotones, often provide two or more of an animal's basic needs in close proximity to each other. One example of edge habitat would be a meadow next to a wooded area, where a deer or rabbit can feed in the open but dash to cover and safety when frightened. Another would be a cattail marsh on the edge of a pond, where ducks, muskrats, and other wildlife can swim or feed in open water without getting too far from the cover offered by the cattails. Riparian zones—trees and shrubs that parallel a river or stream—are also good places to see wildlife.

Looking for Signs of Life

All wildlife species leave signs of their activities and travels. Some signs are fairly obvious, such as fresh tracks and active bird nests. Others, such as deer scrapes, deer bedding areas, or tree damage done by bears, are more subtle, and detection might require some assistance from field guides or more experienced wildlife watchers. As you go out on nature hikes to observe wildlife, begin to learn and look for those signs that will add to your knowledge of wildlife habits and your total enjoyment of wildlife observation. Here are some of the more obvious signs to look for in the field:

SENTINEL OF THE FOREST

A twig cracks, there is a low grunt, something moves quietly through the trees.

If you are very quiet, you might see the lone bull elk as he raises his head and sniffs the air, cued to your presence in his domain.

Hidden so that you may never see him, the elk bull lies closely but rest assured, nature is near.

Trails

Deer, elk, and other wildlife are creatures of habit. They tend to use the same routes over and over as they move between feeding, watering, and resting areas. Look for trails where vegetation has been trampled or where soil has been gouged and rutted from repeated use. Wooded areas are often crisscrossed by myriad animal trails or by runs that go left and right off the main trail. If you spot an animal trail and you feel safe, try following it. If by bending over slightly you are able to navigate the trail without being snagged by branches, you are using the trail of a deer or larger animal—maybe even an elk or moose, depending on where you are. If you have to get down on your hands and knees to see into a trail, it was probably made by a rabbit or other small mammal.

In desert areas, look for telltale ruts and tracks that mark the habitual trails of kangaroo rats, pocket mice, and other nocturnal mammals. In grasslands, look for permanent and temporary trails where the grass has been pushed down and bent.

Dens, Beds, and Burrows

Many small animals and their natural predators are nocturnal, sleeping during the day in dark, protected places such as hollowed-out logs, woodpiles, caves—even under the low branches of a shrub. Other animals are active during the day and sleep in open beds or lays, often no more than depressions in the ground, sometimes lined with grass. Included here are elk, deer, and Canada geese. You are unlikely to surprise a deer in its bed, unless it is a very young fawn, but you can usually find a deer bed by looking for other deer signs, including droppings (scat) or stiff hair on nearby trees and shrubs.

Sometimes animals aren't even very particular about where they bed down. My in-laws lived in a Seattle suburb where a raccoon took up residence in their backyard for almost two years. The raccoon slept under a shrub and, amazingly, coexisted with their dog the whole time.

The dens or burrows of other animals, including marmots, foxes, and raccoons, can be identified in the field by noting certain signs around the entrance—including hair, tracks, bones, feathers, and of course, scats. Some birds, notably burrowing owls, nest in the subterranean burrows of other animals, such as prairie dogs.

Never stick your hand into a suspected animal den, even if you think it is unoccupied. Many people have been surprised and bitten by animals ranging from ground squirrels to badgers to black widow spiders. Be especially cautious near any den or burrow if you think it contains young animals.

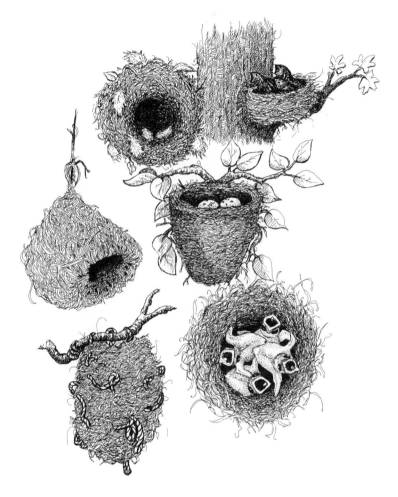

Nests

Identification of nests and eggs is one sure way to know which species of birds are found in an area, at least during spring and summer. Nest watching is rewarding in itself, especially if the nests are in or near your backyard. You can watch the birds go through the whole process of breeding, egg incubation, and raising their young.

More than 500 bird species breed regularly or occasionally in just the twenty-two states west of the Mississippi River, and every species has its own unique way of protecting its eggs from temperature extremes and predators. Many shorebirds, such as oystercatchers and killdeer, do nothing more than scrape a depression in the ground. Others, including robins, grackles, and many warblers, build elaborate nests in trees, using grass, straw, mud, and other available materials. Woodpeckers and many owl species build nests in the cavities of trees, both dead and alive. The ladder-backed woodpecker, found in southwestern deserts, locates its nest in holes made in cactus and yucca plants—a daunting barrier for most potential predators.

Nest sizes also vary greatly, from hummingbird nests only an inch across to the bulky, stick-bristling nests of large hawks and other birds of prey. Bald eagle nests, used and added to year after year by the same birds, may measure up to 10 feet in diameter and weigh several hundred pounds. If you find an active bird nest, keep your distance, especially if it contains eggs or young birds.

Moving in too close could disrupt adult birds as they go about the business of raising young and perpetuating their species. Observe the nest with binoculars or a spotting scope. Many good field guides for birds include illustrations or descriptions of nests. A number of field guides for nests have also been published, including the Peterson field guides to western (and eastern) birds' nests. Remember, it is a federal offense to collect the nests, eggs, or feathers of migratory birds.

Scats

Scats—animal droppings—are among the best ways to identify which animals are living within a given area. In fact, research biologists often depend on scat analysis to determine the eating habits of wildlife. Some scats, particularly those of mammals, are distinctive in color and shape, and many field guides include illustrations of common animal scats along with tracks and other identifying features.

Depending on where you find scats—outside dens or burrows, for instance—you may be able to tell not only which species left the droppings but how long ago the animal was there (that is, if you want to look that closely).

The scats of small carnivores such as coyotes, foxes, and bobcats are hard to tell apart in the field, as are whitewash bird droppings, which serve to signal the presence of birds but fail to help in the identification of species. Look for animal scats along the trail; near dens, burrows, and animal beds; and under trees, rock ledges, and other places where animals roost.

Owl Pellets

Owl pellets are not scats. Owls generally eat their prey whole, and as they digest the food, undigestible hair, feathers, and bones are coughed up as pellets, usually held together with small-mammal hair. Hawks and other birds of prey also cough up pellets, but most hawks are able to digest the bones they swallow, so their pellets usually do not include bones.

The size and shape of owl pellets usually will tell you the species and size of the owl. The pellets of great horned owls are the largest you are likely to find, usually an inch or more in diameter and up to about 3 inches long. Long-eared and barn owl pellets can be almost as large. Since most owls are nocturnal, the discovery of owl pellets might be the only way you will know that owls are around.

Owl pellets make terrific teaching aids. Last summer, I participated in NatureLink, a program conducted annually by the National Wildlife Federation and its state affiliates to give an outdoor experience to inner-city kids and their families. One Saturday, I brought along a bag of owl pellets in case of rain. It did rain, but the owl pellets kept the children occupied all afternoon. I had the kids tear the pellets apart and try to identify the various bones and tiny skulls. Teachers often microwave owl pellets to help ensure that no diseases are passed on to children. Look for owl pellets under trees, in places where you see whitewash droppings, and in barns and other farm buildings.

Tracks

The surest and perhaps most enjoyable way to identify wildlife without actually seeing the animals is by identifying their footprints or tracks. In the winter, when there is snow on the ground, it is fun to follow along a farm road or trail and look for the tracks of birds, rodents, and larger animals, including deer, elk, and predators such as coyotes and foxes. It is particularly interesting to see the tracks of both predators and prey heading down the same trail. I recently followed the tracks of a snowshoe hare on a wildlife refuge near Spokane, Washington, when I came across the equally distinct and fresh tracks of a coyote in the snow—moving right behind the hare. I followed the combined tracks until they disappeared. I never saw the hare or the coyote, but I am sure there was a story of winter survival at the end of those tracks. Snow is not the only medium that preserves wildlife tracks well. Beaches and desert sands, particularly if damp and slightly compacted, preserve tracks beautifully, as does mud of almost any color and consistency.

Often a tail mark is an important clue in following tracks—with lizards and alligators, for instance. With snakes, the body and tail track is usually the only sign you will see. The sidewinder rattle-

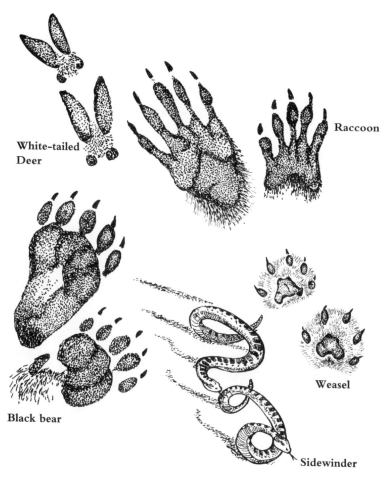

White-tailed Deer

Raccoon

Black bear

Weasel

Sidewinder

snake leaves a very distinctive track in the sand dunes (see the illustration above).

Track identification, like nest identification, is an interesting and rewarding spin-off of wildlife watching. Most mammal field guides and some bird guides as well include drawings of common tracks. If you want to know even more about tracks, look for specific field guides in bookstores.

Tracking wildlife, like stalking it, is an art that can be developed with a certain amount of practice. Human cultures that still practice subsistence hunting use tracking to pursue and capture wildlife for food. Tracking a snowshoe hare in fresh snow is relatively easy. Tracking animals in wooded or grassy habitats is a more difficult undertaking, especially when the tracks are hours or days old. If you are interested in knowing more about the art of tracking, a number of excellent books are available. My favorite is *Tom Brown's Field Guide to Nature Observation and Tracking*.

Keeping a Low Profile

I mentioned earlier that one of the most successful things you can do to observe wildlife is to just sit still and let animals come to you. Your success can be enhanced even more by the use of certain deceptive practices that mask the senses of wildlife and allow or persuade them to come closer than they ordinarily would. Many of these techniques and devices were developed and marketed for hunting, but they work just as well for people who want only to watch or photograph wildlife.

Camouflage

Your success in seeing and identifying wildlife species will depend on how well you blend in with the natural background and how successful you are at not alarming the animals. Imagine how much you might see and experience if you could make yourself totally invisible to wildlife. Use of camouflage can make you almost invisible, especially to mammals and other wildlife that cannot see color. I talk in Chapter 5 about the need to wear clothing that is comfortable and weather resistant, as well as subdued in color and capable of blending in with natural surroundings. Camouflage is not generally a necessity; you can do quite well with earth-tone fabrics. On the other hand, if you want to give yourself the best possible visual advantage, you might look into some of the camouflage clothing and equipment used by hunters, who have essentially the same objectives as wildlife watchers—to get as close as possible to wildlife in the field.

Inexpensive camouflage clothing, including gloves and caps, can be found in many sporting-goods stores and may be ordered from outdoor catalogue companies. One caution: If you plan to spend time in the woods during hunting season, you should seriously consider wearing a vest and cap of hunter-orange material. Such garments could keep you from being shot accidentally. Sporting-goods manufacturers offer hunter-orange camouflage patterns that warn hunters but also break up your outline, helping to conceal you from deer and other mammals that do not see in color.

Blinds

As I mentioned before, many animals' alarm signals are set off by movement, making it important to either move slowly or sit quietly if you want to see animals up close. But even sitting quietly in camouflage clothing might not be enough to observe some wildlife species up close. If you plan to spend time in one location, such as a watering hole or a marsh frequented by waterfowl, you should think about making some sort of blind, either from natural materials or camouflage fabric. The more concealing the blind, the better, but almost any concealing object can function as a blind, as long as it has been in one spot long enough for wildlife to get used to it. Once habituated to the blind, the animals will ignore it. Even sitting in an automobile is preferable to standing out in the open, since the shape of a motor vehicle is more benign to most wildlife than the human shape.

Make every attempt to enter your blind unnoticed, preferably in the dark. Once inside, sit or stand as quietly as possible. Take a camera. This might be the closest you ever get to some wildlife species in their natural habitat, a perfect photo opportunity.

Calling, Baiting, and Decoys

Sometimes wildlife can be enticed to venture close through a combination of concealment techniques and natural-like sounds or visual stimuli. Many wildlife species are social and respond readily to imitations of their calls and to dummy animals that lead them to believe they are joining others of their kind to feed or rest. Birds in particular are attracted to groups of other birds.

The most commonly used dummies are duck and goose decoys. These are consistently effective in bringing birds in close from hundreds of yards away, especially when the decoys are used with duck calls and a blind or camouflage clothing. Waterfowl are often not choosy about whom they feed and socialize with, as long as the birds on the water look natural. Mallards, for instance, will fly into a group of pintail or teal decoys almost as readily as mallard decoys—as long as nothing else, like a fidgeting human or restless dog, frightens them away.

Waterfowl are not the only gullible animals, and socializing is not the only stimulus that will draw animals close. Decoys also work with wild turkeys, crows, and many predators, including hawks and owls looking for a quick meal or trying to chase an apparent interloper from their territory.

Decoys do not fool most predators for long, but they can work long enough to give you a quick look at something—a hawk, for instance—that you would never see otherwise. Decoys are also effective with many mammals. Squirrels, for example, are normally quite territorial, and the literature is full of stories about squirrels ferociously attacking stuffed animals placed in their territories.

Many species can be lured close by imitating their natural sounds. Some bird-watchers make all kinds of squeaking or pishing sounds to bring songbirds in close.

For those of us not proficient at imitating birdcalls unaided, a little handheld metal and wood device called the Audubon Bird Call works quite effectively. Interestingly, this little birdcall was developed in Italy, where songbirds are legally hunted. If you want to get serious about calling wildlife in close, you might also try some of the predator or varmint calls on the market. Imitations of rabbits or rodents in distress can lure in predators such as coyotes, foxes, and even owls. Or you can take a battery-powered tape recorder along and play the pre-recorded calls of birds and small mammals. If you decide to use a varmint call or tape recorder, please don't do it often or for long durations—these false alarms can waste the time and energy that a predator needs to find food.

Recording What You See

Details of an animal's appearance (size, shape, color), its behavior, and its habitat are important for positive identification. Many animals can be positively identified in the field only by noticing details. Some warblers and other songbirds, for instance, look so much alike that the only way to tell them apart is by noting very minor differences in plumage. In many bird species, males and females do not even resemble each other (biologists call such differences sexual dimorphism).

Appearance

Male birds usually have bright plumage; most females are drab. As you observe wildlife, notice the following characteristics:

⇢ *Size.* Size is usually the most obvious characteristic for telling two animal species apart. A swimming muskrat or nutria—both are aquatic rodents—might look like a beaver from a distance, but a beaver is much larger than a muskrat or nutria. Downy and hairy woodpeckers have almost identical plumage, but the hairy is a larger bird. Size is not always easy to estimate from a distance. Try to use nearby objects as reference points. If need be, you can measure reference objects after the animals have departed.

⇢ *Shape.* The shape of an animal or its body parts can also be an important characteristic for identifying wildlife. The quickest way to tell canvasback ducks from redhead ducks is the shape of the head:

canvasbacks have a longer, more sculpted shape to their heads. Virtually the only way to tell some shorebirds apart is by the shape of their bills. For example, long-billed curlews have a bill that curves sharply down, and marble godwits, which resemble curlews in the field, have bills that most definitely curve up.

᛫᛫ *Color.* Color can be the most distinctive characteristic for some species or for telling apart males and females of the same species. Color can change with the season. Many animals living in cold climates acquire white plumage or fur during winter. A good example is the snowshoe hare. It is dark brown in summer, but as the days grow shorter in autumn, its dark pelt is gradually replaced with white fur. Another example is the ptarmigan, a grouse-like bird, which acquires white plumage to help it survive the long winters of the arctic tundra.

᛫᛫ *Sound.* Most birds and mammals make very distinctive sounds. Being able to hear and recognize these calls will add tremendously to your enjoyment of watching wildlife. With owls, coyotes, and other mainly nocturnal animals, a call might be the only sign you will ever get that they are nearby.

As you move along the trail or sit quietly around a campfire at night, listen for the calls of wildlife. If you recognize a call, try to get closer for a look. If you do not recognize the call, try to describe it in your field notebook or better yet, record it with a tape recorder for future identification. If you want to increase your proficiency before going into the field, listen to tapes or CDs of birdcalls at home or in your car. Commercial recordings can sometimes be checked out of libraries.

Animal Behavior

You should pay attention to and record what an animal or group of animals is doing while you are watching. For most wildlife watchers, simply identifying wildlife is not enough. We want to know why an animal is where it is and what it is doing there.

Some behavior is obvious; other behavior is not, especially if you are observing species new to you. The longer you observe particular animals or groups of animals, and the closer you get to wildlife, the easier it will be to define and understand their exact behavior. Most wildlife behavior can easily be grouped into the following categories:

❧ *Feeding.* Many group feeding activities are obvious. The grazing activity of a herd of bison or deer can hardly be mistaken for anything else. The same goes for ducks or shorebirds feeding in an intertidal area. But other feeding behavior is not so obvious. Woodpeckers may appear to be randomly knocking holes in a tree when they actually are searching for wood-boring insects in a very systematic way. Some animals hunt by actively searching for prey or plant material; an example would be a bat weaving and darting through the air pursuing tiny insects. Some predators hunt by waiting for prey to come to them. On many occasions, I have watched great blue herons standing perfectly still in a pool of water for so long that they seemed to be sleeping. But a sudden flash of blue-gray color and a fish in the heron's bill usually proves otherwise.

Alligators, like herons, are deceptively still when hunting, which has meant an untimely end for many stray dogs and other small animals in Florida. Alligators, incidentally, can easily outrun a dog from a standing (or sleeping) start.

❧ *Mating and Courtship.* Reproduction is the strongest impulse driving animal behavior, and wildlife will go to extraordinary lengths to attract a mate. Birds, mammals, and other wildlife engage in what seems like excessive, even bizarre, behavior when their hormones are raging—not too unlike teenaged humans. The most remarkable behavior for male elk and deer is the aggressive way they defend their territory during the fall mating season or rut. The spring courtship rituals of many wading birds and ducks resemble frenzied dances performed across the surface of the water. Many of these courtship rituals look comical to us, but they serve an important reproductive function for the wildlife.

❧ *Maintenance.* Maintenance behavior is that related to normal body care and comfort. Even normal maintenance activities might look strange at first if you are observing a new animal. Once, when my family vacationed in the Everglades, we noticed large cormorant-like birds called anhingas standing immobile on tree limbs with their wings held straight out. At first my children could not figure out what the birds were doing, since they did not seem to be feeding, sleeping, or interacting with other wildlife. It turns out that the feathers of an anhinga's wings are not waterproof like those of most waterbirds. The anhingas were simply drying their wings so they could fly and hunt fish again.

Habitat

Last but definitely not least, you should carefully note the location and habitat conditions of the wildlife you are observing. Good field guides are organized by both appearance and habitat. The location and type of habitat a particular bird or small mammal is occupying can be very important in making a positive identification, as well as in understanding the habits and needs of that animal.

5

Going Prepared—Maximizing Your Comfort, Safety, and Enjoyment of Wildlife

About a year ago, I read a news story about a family outing to gather mushrooms that resulted in the death of one person and hospitalization of another. These losses were caused not by eating poisonous mushrooms, but by getting lost and spending the night in the forest without adequate clothing, food, shelter, or even a flashlight. This was a tragic end to what started out to be a family day hike close to home. Gathering mushrooms or watching wildlife can be enjoyable and rewarding experiences if you are prepared for them and know what you are doing. They can also be frustrating, uncomfortable, even risky ordeals if you do not do some basic planning.

The following pages provide a discussion of preparations, clothing, and equipment you should consider before planning an outing to observe wildlife—whether the outing is a one-day car trip or day hike or an extended trip into the backcountry. Included in this discussion are equipment and precautions you should take to ensure your comfort and safety, as well as things you can do to maximize your understanding and enjoyment of watchable wildlife.

Weather Reports

Regardless of the frustrations we all have felt when meteorologists fail to forecast the weather correctly, the truth is that weather satellites and computer technology have made weather forecasting quite accurate in recent years. Daily newspaper weather reports are remarkably accurate, and those of radio and TV even more so, since they are updated hourly. On-line services, such as America Online and Prodigy, also have up-to-date weather forecasts. As weather science and communication technology advance, weather reports will become increasingly more accurate and available to the general public. Regardless of the type of outing you are planning, a detailed weather report will help you make wiser choices in packing your gear and selecting that all-important accoutrement, clothing.

Clothing

After you have a pretty good idea of the weather to expect on your wildlife-viewing trip, select clothing that is comfortable and that will protect you from the elements. Wearing the proper garments is particularly important for serious hiking, bicycling, or canoeing.

Proper outdoor clothing provides three basic functions: it transports, or wicks, perspiration away from your skin; it keeps you warm; and it protects you from the elements—mostly wind, rain, and intense sunlight. In the case of wildlife observation, clothing should also make you as inconspicuous to wildlife as possible.

Whether you are viewing bighorn sheep in the Arizona desert or getting a glimpse of wintering bald eagles in Minnesota, many of the same general rules for clothing apply. First, select garments loose enough to give you a full range of movement but not so baggy that they will snag on underbrush. There is no outdoor experience quite as miserable as hiking in tight shorts or pants—unless, of course, your tight pants happen to be wet.

Second, wear clothes that are relatively light in weight, even in the winter. A heavy wool coat or down jacket might be comfortable if you are sitting on a log looking at winter songbirds, but it could make you sweat up a storm once you start hiking—and sweating is the last thing you want to do in cold weather because of the threat of hypothermia as sweat evaporates and cools you. Hypothermia is a very dangerous condition during which you begin to lose heat faster than you can produce it, so your body temperature begins to drop. The first sign of hypothermia is uncontrollable shivering. The best way to stay comfortable while hiking or exercising in cold weather is by layering your clothes (a lesson we can learn from ducks and geese, which nature has decked out in an outer layer of waterproof feathers and an inner layer of insulating down). Choose your field clothing so you can add or remove garments as the air temperature and your body temperature change.

The best clothing selection for outdoor activities requires three layers. Begin with an inner layer next to your skin, one that absorbs moisture and keeps your skin dry by transporting water to the middle layer. In warm weather, a cotton T-shirt might be ideal as the inner (or only) layer. Net underwear is highly recommended by some hikers, especially in hot weather, since the air pockets in the net provide good insulation while allowing maximum contact between the skin and the air, which carries off excess perspiration and keeps you cool. In very cold weather, wool underwear is more appropriate. Wool provides better insulation than cotton and absorbs up to a third of its weight in water before it begins to feel wet. Polypropylene is a synthetic fabric that wicks perspiration away from the body better than almost any other natural or synthetic material.

The second layer of clothing should give added insulation, absorb perspiration, and provide some protection against the elements. Cotton shirts or sweaters are comfortable in mild weather, even cool spring and fall weather, but are not recommended when it is raining or very cold. The main problem with cotton, even cotton flannel, is that it loses its insulative quality when it gets wet. A better fabric for the middle layer is light wool or wool blends.

These lighter-weight wool fabrics have good insulative value, even when wet.

The third, outer layer of clothing is intended to give you a first line of protection against wind and rain and sometimes additional insulation from cold weather. The commercial market offers a dizzying array of outerwear fabrics, ranging from plastic rain gear (which nobody recommends) to rubber ponchos (which hardly anyone recommends) to simple nylon shells to jackets and parkas made from Gore-Tex, a synthetic fabric that is not only waterproof but breathable, allowing moisture to move in one direction only—away from the body. Plastic or rubber outerwear is discouraged because they will not let moisture escape from the inner and middle layers of fabric. When you select outerwear for watching wildlife, pick fabrics that minimize glare—unless you decide to wear hunter orange—since shiny surfaces might give you away to wildlife. Also, avoid nylon outerwear that rustles when you move.

Most people you see hiking or watching wildlife wear blue jeans, which are sturdy and comfortable in most weather conditions, as long as they are not too tight. The main disadvantage with denim is that, like any other cotton fabric, it soaks up water easily and is absolutely miserable to wear when wet. In cold and wet weather, I prefer the green wool pants I was issued when I was commissioned a state game warden. These pants have the added advantage over denim of blending in better with surrounding vegetation. You can usually find similar green or gray wool pants in military surplus stores. In summer, I like to wear cotton shorts, even though they are not a good option if you expect to encounter heavy underbrush or teeming insect populations.

When you start out on a nature hike in warm weather, consider packing enough extra clothing to create a layered effect if the weather unexpectedly turns colder or wet, or if you start out in a warm area but know you will end up in a cooler place, such as higher elevations, dense forest, or a cave. Also, on all nature hikes, wear or take along a hat or cap. In warm weather, a light cotton or mesh cap will help protect you from the sun. In my case, this is critical, since the natural protection disappeared from my head a few years ago. If you plan to spend much time in direct sunlight, buy a wide-brimmed cotton or straw hat. In cold or wet weather, a waterproof hat or wool cap will conserve a lot of body heat. Up to half your body heat is lost from your neck and head, where blood flows closest to the surface.

Regardless of whether you are seeking protection from heat, rain, or cold, try to select outerwear with big, easily accessible pockets so that you don't have to get into your backpack or day pack every time you want to reach your binoculars, field guide, or handkerchief. The best birding jacket I ever owned was a Carter's denim farm coat with big pockets in the front.

Footwear

Selecting socks and shoes or boots is probably the most important decision you will make in outfitting yourself for nature hikes. But even more than other clothing, footwear is a matter of personal choice about which I hesitate to make any firm recommendations.

Comfort is, of course, the primary consideration in selecting shoes or boots that you plan to use for hiking or extended walking, and I include under comfort here both protection from pain and protection from moisture and cold. Another consideration, when picking footwear for stalking and observing wildlife, is stealth—that is, how quietly you can move through the woods.

Running shoes, designed for comfort and speed, are ideal for some wildlife-watching trips, especially if the terrain is not too rough. The biggest disadvantage of running shoes is that they are not even slightly waterproof—although with the right kind of socks, even wet running shoes are not a major problem, at least in warm weather. A good pair of leather walking shoes will also work for most wildlife-watching expeditions, as long as the terrain is not too rough and the weather not too wet.

But if you plan to get serious about wildlife watching and hiking, I recommend that you buy a good pair of high-top boots that will give you ankle support and protect your feet and lower legs from sharp rocks and underbrush. The choices are many when you start looking at boots. For example, a product information guide for hiking boots published by Recreational Equipment, Inc. (REI), lists thirty different boot styles in five different categories, ranging from lightweight hiking boots with rubber soles and mixed leather and Cordura nylon uppers to all-leather extended backpacking and mountaineering boots that are probably suitable for scaling Mount Everest. It is not uncommon for a good pair of mountaineering boots to cost more than $300.

When buying shoes, pay special attention to comfort. Even if your new footwear feels comfortable in the shoe store, you should always break it in before taking off on any extended walk or hike. One author I consulted recommended standing in a bucket of water with your new boots on, then walking around until they are dry. Most other hiking and footwear guides simply recommend that you break in boots by starting with short hikes, gradually increasing the distance until they are really comfortable.

Another consideration is the weight of the shoes or boots you are planning to buy. The U.S. Army Research Institute of Environmental Medicine reportedly found that it takes six times as much energy to carry a pound on your feet as on your back. If you plan to engage in serious mountain climbing and happen to look at some wildlife on the way up and down, consider a heavy-duty pair of hiking boots. Otherwise, opt for a pair of boots or shoes that are as light as possible, while combining comfort and durability.

Personally, when I go on wildlife hikes, I wear a pair of high-topped leather boots with Gore-Tex on the upper part. The Gore-Tex makes them waterproof and lighter in weight than 100 percent leather boots. If I have room in my day pack, I also carry a pair of running shoes in case I want to give my feet a break, especially in warm weather. Moccasins, with their soft soles, are also recommended by some naturalists for stalking wildlife in wooded habitats (see Chapter 4).

Any discussion of footwear should also mention socks . . . and wool. Socks insulate your feet in cold weather, help keep them dry and cool in warm weather, and provide padding to prevent soreness and blisters. And wool or wool-blend materials are almost universally recommended for use with hiking boots, even in warm weather, where they keep your feet dry better than cotton or any synthetic fabric can. Cotton socks are fine for short day hikes in walking or running shoes, but wool can be worn with these same shoes and will give you the added advantage of keeping your feet warm and dry, even when your shoes are wet. The layering effect can also be used effectively for socks, as long as the outer layer is wool or a wool blend and the inner layer is polypropylene or some other fabric designed to wick water away from the skin.

Whatever sock you wear, be sure it fits properly. Socks that are too tight will impede blood circulation and make your feet cold. Loose, baggy socks will wrinkle up, give you blisters, and generally drive you crazy.

Packs

By the time you pull together everything you need (or that I suggest you need) for serious wildlife watching, you could have a pile in your living room the size of a Volkswagen. You can stuff a lot of equipment in your pockets, but you are going to feel pretty awkward trying to walk very far. Besides, what will you do when the weather warms up, and you want to take off your outer layer of clothing?

This need for baggage space leads to the recommendation that you should have some kind of backpack or day pack if you plan to get very far from your car in pursuit of watchable wildlife. What kind of pack is best? As with hiking boots, unless you know what you are looking for, you can easily end up buying more than you really need.

If your primary interest is backpacking and you plan to check out some wildlife on the way, you should look at serious backpacking equipment, including a good pack with an aluminum frame. This could cost you as much as $300, but it is something you really need if you plan to hike into an area and spend the night. However, if you plan to go only on day hikes, a frame pack is a waste of money. All you usually need for a day hike—or a one-day canoe or kayak trip—is a day pack. Nylon day packs cost as little as $20. Military surplus stores sell perfectly functional canvas packs for about the same price. For years I got by with an old canvas Boy Scout pack, until it got too small for all my junk. If your nature hike is fairly short, you might even want to skip the day pack and opt for a belt pack that will allow you easy access to your binoculars, field guides, and camera.

Maps

One of the first things you should fold up and put into your day pack is a functional map of the area you plan to visit. Personally, I cannot really enjoy any outdoor trip unless I have with me some kind of map that shows topographic features. Fortunately, maps are inexpensive and fairly easy to find. Most outdoor equipment stores and even many stationery stores sell a wide variety of road maps and topographic maps, suitable for finding and observing wildlife. State and county road maps work well for making sure you do not get lost while driving on public roads. But road maps alone do not provide the kind of topographic or natural-history information you will probably want on a nature outing. Instead, I recommend maps that give both up-to-date road information and information on such things as trails, streams, lakes, and other natural landmarks.

U.S. Geological Survey (USGS) topographic, or topo, maps are the most consistently accurate and detailed maps you can buy for any kind of outdoor recreation, including wildlife viewing. These maps, published by the federal government, cover the entire United States and are updated periodically. The 7.5-minute-series maps have a scale of 1:24,000, which means that each square mile (numbered section) is almost 3 inches square on the map. If you are planning a trip or outing to a specific area, and you want a lot of topographic detail, USGS maps could be your best choice. Otherwise, they might not be worth the money—not to mention the space to store them—since each $3 map covers an area of only about seven by nine miles. USGS maps can be purchased in many outdoor recreation and map stores, as well as directly from the USGS. Write to USGS Map Sales, P.O. Box 25286, Building 810, Denver Federal Center, Denver, Colorado 80225-0286, or phone USGS at 303-236-4200. The Canadian equivalent of USGS maps can be ordered from the Canada Map Office, Department of Energy, Mines, and Resources, 615 Booth Street, Ottawa, Ontario K1A 0E9, Canada. The phone number for Canadian maps is 613-952-7000.

Approximately 200 million acres of public land in the United States are managed by the U.S. Forest Service (USFS) through a system of 156 national forests. The Forest Service publishes maps for each national forest, which include good road and trail coverage, some topographic and natural-history information, and the precise location of USFS campgrounds and other recreation sites. USFS maps are color-coded for land ownership—which can be helpful in keeping you from straying onto private land—and published at a scale of 1:126,000 (2 square miles per inch). They are also printed on both sides, which gives you a lot more map coverage per dollar than a USGS map, with only a modest loss in detail. USFS maps cost about $3 apiece at USFS offices and, like USGS maps, are available at many map and outdoor-recreation stores.

The DeLorme Map Company of Freeport, Maine, began publishing a series of state-map atlases or gazetteers in 1976. The company has completed atlases for twenty-nine states and hopes eventually to offer coverage of the entire United States. In my opinion, these gazetteers are the best things to come along in many years for wildlife watchers and other outdoor recreationists. First of all, you get map coverage for an entire state in one 15.5-inch-by-11-inch book that is reasonably priced. This is especially nice if you do a lot of traveling and cannot afford to rent a U-Haul for your maps. At a scale of 1:250,000, the gazetteers provide enough detail on roads, topography, and natural landmarks to keep most travelers on the right track. They also are designed with outdoor recreation in mind, with precise locations and descriptions of outdoor-recreation areas, historical sites, trails, wildlife areas, and fishing streams. I never start an automobile trip without at least my state gazetteer in the car. If you plan to go on wildlife watching trips outside of a specific area or national forest, consult the gazetteer for your state. DeLorme gazetteers are sold in many outdoor-recreation and book stores or can be ordered directly.

Other Map Products

Some state and provincial land agencies publish their own topographic maps, often at a scale of 1:100,000, which can be very useful for outdoor trips and outings. A number of private companies also publish maps oriented to certain sectors of the outdoor-recreation market, such as hiking, bicycling, or cross-country skiing. Many of these companies use USGS maps as their base maps, then add highlighted detail for trails and other features. One map company, Trails Illustrated of Evergreen, Colorado, publishes good, enhanced USGS maps on waterproof material. However, before buying any private outdoor-recreation maps, make sure they meet your particular needs. Some privately published, so-called outdoor-recreation maps are nothing more than road maps with some basic recreation information superimposed on them.

Compass

When used alone, a compass will give you the approximate direction in which you are heading. Combined with a good map, a compass is a surefire way to make sure you never get lost, regardless of weather or other factors. Remember, your compass will always point to the magnetic North Pole, which will usually vary from the direction of true north shown on most topographic maps. Every USGS map has a diagram in the bottom margin that shows the variation between true north and magnetic north. Orienting yourself to any particular USGS map requires only that you put the map and

your compass on a flat surface and let the compass needle point to magnetic north. At that point, you can orient your map, and your hike, to true north, south, east, and west. DeLorme gazetteer maps are similarly aligned with true north and south. The variation between magnetic and true, along with orientation directions, is provided on the inside cover of each state gazetteer volume.

Before you try orienteering with a compass and map in the wilderness, practice with a map of your own city or neighborhood.

If you buy a compass, get a real one, preferably an orienteering compass made of clear plastic and designed especially for use with topographic maps. Don't buy one of those little round compasses (without degrees marked on them) that you see in toy departments. They don't hold up in wet weather and are not accurate enough for anything other than giving you a general sense of direction. A good compass can be purchased for as little as $15 from an outdoor recreation store or catalogue.

Recently, stores and catalogues have started marketing a high-tech alternative to the compass. Called Global Positioning Systems (GPS), these devices, developed for the Department of Defense for navigation and targeting, work by locking onto high-frequency radio signals emitted from GPS satellites orbiting the Earth. These units triangulate signals from three or more satellites and give you your exact position in latitude and longitude. Once you program in the coordinates of your destination, the GPS unit will not only tell you where you are but will keep you on track, regardless of weather or time of day.

GPS units are serious navigational devices that can keep you from getting lost. They could even save your life in an emergency. The prices of GPS units currently start at about $200, but like most electronic equipment, these prices are likely to drop as more units are manufactured and sold. As wonderful as these high-tech units are, I would still want to pack on any long hike a good set of topographic maps for orienting myself to road and other land features. I would also pack my old compass in case of GPS-unit battery failure.

One piece of high-tech equipment now becoming so commonplace that it seems virtually low tech is the cellular phone. I never go on a long outing without taking along my cellular phone. Just having it in my pack gives me a more secure feeling in case some emergency should arise, whether it is a medical emergency or the more likely realization that I left the coffeepot turned on at home and need to call a neighbor to turn it off. Cell phones do not work everywhere, however. The geographic range may be restricted by the type of service you have. Or in mountainous areas, your phone signal may be blocked or too weak to reach the nearest relay station. I would advise you to check with your cellular phone carrier before heading for the mountains with your cell phone.

Water and Food

The romantic notion that hikers can quench their thirst from pure, clean mountain streams is hopelessly out of date. The fact is, in many areas of the country, water coming out of seemingly pristine streams or mountain lakes might be contaminated with organisms such as *Giardia lamblia*, a protozoan that can cause severe intestinal disorders. The simple solution to this potential problem is to carry drinking water with you, even on a short hike.

I cannot stress too much how important it is to drink a lot of liquids when hiking or climbing. Most people can go a few days without food, but we all need constantly to replenish our bodies with water, especially in dry climates and warm weather.

Carrying water should not be a major problem on many day hikes, but you should avoid packing more water than you need for the day. A simple quart-sized canteen or plastic water bottle is usually all most people need for a few hours. Remember, a quart of water weighs two and a half pounds. For longer hikes, or even as a precaution, I would recommend including a small bottle of water purification tablets in your first-aid kit. If your canteen runs dry, and you do not have any purification tablets, somehow boil available water, which will kill any waterborne organisms, including *Giardia*.

Conserve water by taking small sips during the day. If you find yourself developing a headache, especially during warm weather, rest in the shade and have a few sips of water. A headache can be the first sign of dehydration.

Personally, I would never consider going on a wildlife outing without taking something to eat. First, because I am an unrepentant snacker with a sweet tooth. Second, because there is always the chance that I will be delayed long enough to miss a meal. Even if the delay is my idea—for example, I can't tear myself away from watching a flock of swans—it is a lot more comfortable and enjoyable without the hunger pangs. Candy bars will work, although most survival guides recommend fruits, nuts, and other high-energy snacks.

Sunblock and Sunglasses

If you read or listen to the news, you know that severe sunburn and skin cancer are on the rise around the world owing to an increase in the amount of ultraviolet rays reaching the Earth's surface from space. Ozone, a layer of modified oxygen located about 15 miles up in the atmosphere, absorbs most of the dangerous ultraviolet radiation entering the Earth's atmosphere. But because of recent increases in human-generated pollutants, this protective ozone layer is being depleted, allowing more ultraviolet rays to reach the Earth's surface.

The only good thing you can say about the increase in ultraviolet rays is that it has spurred the development of excellent sunblocking lotions that effectively protect against most ultraviolet rays for hours after application. Most pharmacies, supermarkets, and department stores have a good selection of sunblock formulas, ranging from 8 to about 50 SPF. The SPF number indicates how well a particular lotion will block ultraviolet rays, compared with having no protection at all. For instance, an SPF number of 30 means the lotion will give you 30 times the amount of ultraviolet protection you would have without applying any sunblock lotion. Many of the early sunblock lotions used para-aminobenzoic acid (PABA) as their active ingredient. Some people are allergic to PABA, but effective alternatives have been found. Most modern sunblock lotions are also labeled as waterproof, which is a real advantage against intermittent rain or perspiration.

I strongly recommend carrying a tube of sunblock lotion on any nature hike during which your skin might be exposed directly to sunlight. Obviously, sunny days are the worst for sunburn, but ultraviolet rays also penetrate clouds. Sunblock should be applied to your face, especially under your eyes and on your ears and nose. Read the directions on the sunblock tube for recommended frequency of application.

I also suggest that you wear sunglasses, especially if you are going to be traveling over water or snow. Buy sunglasses that block both the ultraviolet and the infrared rays of the sun. Cheap sunglasses that do not block these rays can actually result in damage to your eyes.

Insect Repellent

When observing wildlife, carry a can or bottle of insect repellent for use against mosquitoes, gnats, and biting flies. These insects are particularly prevalent and obnoxious around still water and wetlands. I've tried a lot of insect repellents, and I prefer those with a high percentage of the active ingredient N,N-diethyl-toluamide, or DEET. Some people are more susceptible to insect bites than others. But there are places, such as Alaska in the summer, where if you have a heartbeat and a body temperature above 90 degrees, you will be eaten alive by mosquitoes—that is, if you do not avail yourself of a repellent. Most pharmacies and supermarkets carry a good selection of insect repellents in various forms, including small bottles and aerosol cans.

First-aid Kit

Encounters with wildlife can occasionally be dangerous—for example, if you get too close to a snapping turtle's jaws or accidently come across a poisonous snake. But the injuries most likely to happen in the field result in nothing more life-threatening than a blister, scrape, or small cut. However, even minor injuries can turn into major problems if untreated, so you should carry a basic first-aid kit in your pack if you plan to do any serious hiking or canoeing. Many stores sell excellent pre-packed first-aid kits that will get you through most minor medical emergencies.

Outfitting Children

This is probably a good time to talk about some of the special needs of children on nature hikes and other outings. Although hiking or canoeing with kids is a great way to introduce them to the wonders of nature and to instill them with a conservation ethic, you should not assume that all their preferences and physical needs are going to match yours. First of all, most small children have high energy levels and must be fed on a regular basis, or they will get cranky. Make sure you or the kids pack enough snacks and water for the whole outing. Children also have low tolerances for pain and discomfort, especially if they are doing something that was organized by adults, like a nature hike or canoe trip. They also get cold faster than adults, so you must make sure that their shoes and clothes are appropriate for the weather and terrain.

If children become wet and cold—or if one of them gets a heel blister from the wrong kind of shoes or socks—they will be miserable, and so will you. Most kids like to run, but they can wear out faster than adults. Recreational Equipment Inc. (REI) recommends that children between two and four years old be allowed to hike $1/2$ mile to 2 miles on their own, but that they should stop and rest every 10 to 15 minutes. Children five to seven can hike for 1 to 3 hours each day, covering 3 to 4 miles over easy terrain, with a rest every 30 to 45 minutes. Children eight to nine years old can hike all day long and cover 6 to 7 miles in a day. REI also recommends that a child's pack not exceed 20 percent of his or her body weight.

Make sure that children not only learn about wildlife but are comfortable and safe. If you plan for the special needs of children, you will have a more enjoyable and productive wildlife watching trip. If you do not, you and the kids might have a miserable outing.

Flashlight and Extra Batteries

A battery-powered flashlight is important, whether you plan to be out after dark (some of the best wildlife experiences occur at night) or whether you just pack it for emergencies. If you use good maps and a compass (or a GPS), you will probably never get lost on a nature hike. But you really never know when you might be delayed, and it is a good idea to have a flashlight along to illuminate the trail and, if necessary, to signal your location to others.

If you are actually planning to be out after dark and will be using a flashlight to illuminate your way, your batteries will last longer if you get in the habit of switching the light on for only brief periods of time—enough, for instance, to make sure you are staying on the trail. Your eyes also will adjust to the darkness better if you turn your light on for only brief periods.

Take along a spare flashlight bulb and extra batteries. To keep your flashlight from accidentally turning itself on during storage in your pack, take the batteries out or reverse them when the light is not in use.

Knife

Last year, some campers were attacked by a rabid cougar while backpacking in California's Sierra Nevada Mountains. They did not have a firearm in their camp, but they were somehow able to wrestle the cat to the ground and kill it with a knife. If I were to ask those people the most important piece of equipment they had packed on that trip, I guess they would say their knife.

I have never seen a cougar in the wild and probably never will, but I always pack a folding knife on my belt when I am hiking or canoeing somewhere looking for wildlife. A sharp knife has many purposes on a nature hike—from cutting brush to allow a better view of a bird, to cutting adhesive tape for a bandage, to spreading cheese on a cracker. Either invest in a good folding knife like a Buck or a Shrader or buy a knife with a fixed blade and a leather case. Never hike with an unsheathed knife, or you may have greater need for your first-aid kit than you ever wanted.

Matches

In the old days, when most adults puffed away on tobacco, almost everyone carried matches in pocket or purse. Now, because most Americans and Canadians are nonsmokers, we have to make a conscious effort to remember to pack matches. You are unlikely ever to need to make a fire while out pursuing watchable wildlife, but you should have the ability to make one if you really need to, whether to boil drinking water or to build a warming fire should you be delayed after dark.

Pack some wooden matches in a waterproof container—a small

plastic bottle or film can will do—or carry metal matches, which start a fire by being scraped with a knife blade. Metal matches can be purchased in most outdoor-equipment stores. Avoid packing butane cigarette lighters on nature hikes, since they often leak.

If you do build a fire, make sure it is completely out before moving down the trail. Either drown the fire with water or make sure it is completely buried with soil and no longer smoldering.

Opticals

Binoculars

A pair of binoculars is probably the single most important tool you will need for watching birds and other wildlife. You don't have to spend a lot of money for binoculars, but if you plan to spend much time in the field observing wildlife, you should buy the best pair you can afford. Improved technology and increased competition have brought the price of good binoculars down to what most amateur wildlife watchers can afford.

In addition to price, you should consider magnification, brightness, and field of view before pulling out your checkbook to pay for a pair of binoculars. All binoculars are marked with two numbers, separated by an x. The first is the magnification number, usually between 6x and 10x, which means that an object will appear 6 to 10 times larger than normal. The second number is the diameter in millimeters of the front lens, which determines how much light is gathered and how bright your images will be. The higher the second number, the brighter the image, especially when the amount of natural light is limited, as in deep woods. To optimize light availability, the second number should be at least five times the magnification number. A third set of numbers—for example, 375 feet at 1,000 yards—indicates the field of view or width of the image.

Magnification, and to lesser degrees brightness and field of view, are a matter of personal preference for wildlife watchers. Ten-power binoculars are great for bringing small animals up close, but may not let in as much light as 7x or 8x instruments; that might be a real disadvantage when observing wildlife on overcast days, in deep woods, or in the evening. For some people, 10x binoculars also are difficult to hold steady. Many wildlife watchers prefer 7x or 8x binoculars, figuring that what they lose in magnification is made up for in greater light-gathering capability and field of vision.

Field of vision is important when you are scanning the horizon for birds and other movement. Magnification is more important if you are watching relatively still wildlife, especially from a distance, or animals up close, such as in your backyard. If you think you might do some very close-up watching, buy close-focusing binoculars, which give you a clear image at less than 10 feet from the subject.

The size and weight of the binoculars you select could be important, especially when you think about all the other stuff you will want to carry on an outing, such as field guides. Luckily, there are some good, lightweight binoculars on the market that are also inexpensive. I recently purchased a shirt-pocket-size pair for under $100, and carry them in the glove compartment of my pickup at all times.

If you plan to spend a lot of time in the field in less-than-ideal weather, you should pay a little bit more and get a pair of binoculars that is both sturdy and waterproof. Buy a pair that feels good in your hands. If you wear eyeglasses, get binocular eyepieces, large, soft eye cups that allow you to compensate for the extra distance your eyes must be from the lens.

The most important recommendation I can make for purchasing a pair of binoculars is that you try out a number of different styles, sizes, and magnifications before making a final selection. Find a shop or department store that offers a good selection; then try out as many pairs in your price range as you can. If store personnel object to your trying out the binoculars, go to another dealer.

If you are making your selection in a large department store, focus the binoculars on a variety of close-up, mid-range, and distant objects. If you are in a small shop, get permission to step outside and focus on distant objects. A good pair of binoculars is an important consideration if you plan to do any serious wildlife observation, so take your time in making a choice. You will not regret the time you spent shopping when you are in the field.

Spotting Scopes

Binoculars are almost always better than the naked eye when watching anything but large animals up close. But there are occasions when even binoculars are inadequate, such as when observing small birds and distant wildlife. Consequently, many nature watchers eventually invest in a spotting scope.

The magnifying power of scopes generally ranges from 20x to 60x. Older models used interchangeable lenses to achieve a range of magnification, but most modern spotting scopes are equipped with zoom lenses that very quickly allow you to shift from an initial observation at 20x to a very close inspection of a bird or other animal at up to 60x magnification.

As with binoculars, there is more than just magnification to consider when shopping for a spotting scope. The light-gathering capability, like that of binoculars, is a function of the size of the outer, or objective, lens, which is generally in the range of 50mm to 60mm in traditional scopes. Newer scopes, with objective lenses as high as 85mm, can double the amount of light gathered with a 60mm lens.

A spotting scope can really be used effectively only if stabilized on something like a photographic tripod or modified rifle mount. Without some sort of support, even an individual with the steadiest of hands will find it almost impossible to see anything but light and blurred images, even at the lowest setting of 20x power.

Compared with binoculars, spotting scopes are heavy and cumbersome to carry on hikes or canoe trips. However, great improvements have been made in recent years in both optics and materials, so it is now possible to buy a reasonably priced compact scope that weighs a pound or less. Despite their size, scopes are worth the effort in many situations: use by groups (where everyone can share one scope), in backyards, or in opportunities to observe something like a hawk or eagle nest, which is fairly stationary but requires keeping your distance. I probably would not recommend a spotting

scope to someone just learning how to identify and observe wildlife. But for any wildlife watcher advanced enough to consider purchasing a scope, I offer much the same advice as for binoculars: take your time; try out a number of models and styles; then buy the best scope you can get within your budget.

Cameras

Photography is very important for some wildlife watchers. In fact, for many people, photography is the main reason they get into wildlife observation. And that is fine, since most wildlife photographers have a genuine respect and appreciation for the animals they photograph. For me and many others, packing a camera is a way to ensure good recorded memories and maybe—just maybe—to capture a rare but memorable photographic moment.

For what it's worth, my greatest photographic opportunities have come along when I was not in possession of a camera. Most particularly, I remember the duck-hunting trip on a frozen tributary of the Columbia River when a group of us, all cameraless, sat and watched in fascination as seven bald eagles and four playful river otters tried to share half a dozen duck carcasses.

Many books have been written about wildlife photography, and I will not try to offer a short course here. (I do, however, recommend a photography course for anyone interested in any kind of serious photography.) Instead, I will offer a few general pointers on selecting cameras for use in the field.

First, do not go overboard in buying a new camera and accessories if you plan to take only snapshots of your canoe trips or hiking companions. There are many inexpensive and very lightweight 35mm cameras on the market, even some with small zoom lenses, all of which are more than adequate for recording great memories and will use either slide or print film.

On the other hand, if you really want to be prepared for serious wildlife photography, you should take along a 35mm single-lens reflex (SLR) camera and enough lenses, film options, and other accessories to photograph from a variety of distances and during various weather and lighting conditions. Most SLR cameras come equipped with a standard 50mm to 55mm lens, which basically gives you the same-size image as your unaided eye. For close-up or distance photography—and most wildlife photography is distance photography—you should have a selection of telephoto lenses as well as a zoom lens. Zoom lenses commonly range from 70mm to 200mm. A single macro-zoom lens will allow you to focus on everything from the distant horizon to subjects as close as a few inches away. Anything larger than a 300mm lens is very difficult to use without a tripod.

Before I leave the subject of wildlife photography, I want to offer a few additional thoughts based on my own experience and that of a number of authors. First of all, the faster the shutter speed, the more motion a camera will arrest in a photo, and the less light will reach the film. For these reasons, fast shutter speeds are good for moving birds and bright, sunny days. Also, the smaller the lens opening (aperture) of your camera, the greater the depth of field and overall sharpness of the image. So ideally you should try to shoot wildlife at a smaller aperture (F16 end of the dial) and, unless the animals are moving, at a slower shutter speed.

The larger the ASA number on your film, the faster the film is in capturing the image. For landscape shots with slide film, slower films such as Kodachrome 25 work well. For general wildlife photography, medium-speed films, such as Ektachrome 64 or Fujichrome 100, are recommended by some authors. For fast-moving wildlife, faster ASA films can work well, along with faster shutter speeds of 1/500 second or more. Early morning hours are generally the best time of the day for photographing wildlife. The animals are more active, and the morning light yields brighter colors and sharper contrasts between colors.

The final piece of advice is that unless you are using a telephoto lens, the animal you photograph will almost always look farther away in your photo than it did when you were focusing on it with your camera. The first time I ever photographed a bald eagle roosting in a tree, I was sure I was close enough to get a great shot. Then I got the film developed and found that I had actually gotten a picture of a small white-capped bird about half a mile away in a tree. In this case, I took care of the problem by enlarging the photo to the approximate size of a roadside billboard, then cropping out an 8-by-11-inch piece with the eagle intact. This enlargement hangs on my wall, along with a similarly grainy photo of a peregrine falcon.

Field Guides and Viewing Guides

Learning to identify birds and other wildlife in the field is the first step toward fully enjoying the experience of wildlife observation. The identity of some species will be obvious. For instance, you will probably not need a field guide to identify a mature bald eagle roosting in a tree. But if the eagle is an immature bird (without the distinctive white head) or if the bird is soaring overhead, chances are you will not be able to conclusively identify it as an eagle unless you consult a bird book or field guide for data on such things as size, coloration, and range. Most of your field observations will be of birds and mammals that are less easy to identify than a mature bald eagle. So when going out on the trail, take along field guides or other materials that will help you to identify and understand the animals you are watching.

Field guides, as opposed to textbooks and large-format coffee-table books, are intended for use in the field. They should be rugged enough to sustain a lot of unintentional abuse, yet small enough to carry in a small pack or large pocket. They also should include enough information, including illustrations, to allow you to identify animals by systematically eliminating similar species on the basis of appearance, behavior, and habitat.

When you first walk into a bookstore to look at wildlife field guides, you will be taken aback by not only the number but also the variety and specialization of the books. Since the late Roger Tory Peterson published his first edition of the classic *Field Guide to the Birds* in 1934, interest has grown steadily not just in bird watching but in wildlife viewing in general. This growing interest has spawned a huge inventory of good, popular field guides for a vast array of animals—birds, mammals, butterflies, amphibians and reptiles, fish, whales, even birds' nests and animal tracks. There are so many good field guides on the market now that I find it impossible to recommend a single book or set of books that will serve the needs of all nature watchers. Each publisher organizes its guides in a different way, and each emphasizes different information. As a minimum, a good field guide should include color photographs, range maps, and brief natural-history and habitat information about species and groups of species. Beyond that, it is really a matter of what strikes you as attractive and usable. Most serious wildlife watchers end up with a whole collection of different field guides anyway, for cross-reference, if nothing else. Thayer Birding Software even sells interactive CD-ROM programs that combine field-guide information and imagery with authentic songs of North American birds.

In the introduction, I mentioned the National Watchable Wildlife Program, which includes the Wildlife Viewing Guide series published by Falcon Press in cooperation with Defenders of Wildlife, the National Wildlife Federation, and many state and federal wildlife agencies. This excellent series, published for twenty-four states so far, gives wildlife watchers a choice of 65 to 199 hand-picked wildlife viewing sites in each state. Similar viewing guides have been published for some Canadian provinces, including Alberta, British Columbia, and Yukon Territory.

Other Equipment

I have covered the basic items required for most backpacking and hiking trips, but a few miscellaneous items remain, including toilet tissue and an extra pair of eyeglasses, if you use glasses. You may want to sketch wildlife and take detailed field notes about where and when you see interesting critters, so a notebook and a pen or pencil are also good additions.

6

Where to Observe Wildlife— Public and Private Lands

Both the U.S. and Canadian governments have long histories of setting aside and managing land for the public, offering these lands for timber production, wildlife protection, and outdoor recreation, among other uses. Approximately a third of the land area of the United States is in public ownership—740 million acres—and except for military bases, most of this land is open for public recreation. The same situation holds in Canada, where a large percentage of the country is in public ownership, mainly as federal or provincial parks, wildlife areas, and timber reserves. Although some parks and wildlife refuges are required to charge admission fees to cover their administrative and land-stewardship costs, most public land, in particular federal land, is free for public use.

The secret to getting full enjoyment from your public lands is knowing where they are, when they are open, and what to expect when you get there—especially what types of wildlife-viewing opportunities are available. Whenever I plan a vacation or extended business trip to another part of the country, I send postcards to chambers of commerce and visitor bureaus in the area, asking for information about parks, refuges, and opportunities for nature hikes. At the same time, I locate nearby wildlife refuges on a state road map and drop postcards to them asking for similar information.

I always get a good response to my postcard inquiries, and by doing some advance planning, I do not waste valuable vacation time trying to decide where I want to go to observe wildlife. In 1995, my family vacationed with friends on the Outer Banks of North Carolina. Before we departed, I had lined up free guided birding walks at Pea Island National Wildlife Refuge and two day-long guided kayaking trips, one through the recently established Alligator River National Wildlife Refuge.

Check the reference desk at your public library for a book called *The World Chamber of Commerce Directory*, which will provide you with current addresses for chambers of commerce and state tourist bureaus all over North America. You also can get current information about parks, refuges, and other public wildlife lands in both Canada and the United States by calling or writing to the agencies listed in Appendix 1.

Public land is set aside and managed for a variety of different purposes, and each category of land has different rules and conditions for public use. Below, I briefly discuss some of the major categories of public and private lands available to the general public for wildlife viewing and other outdoor pursuits.

National Parks

The United States has one of the largest and finest systems of national parks in the world, consisting of 369 protected units totaling more than 83 million acres in forty-nine states, the District of Columbia, Puerto Rico, the Virgin Islands, and Guam. These sites include sixty-four national parks and seventy-three national monuments as well as many smaller historical sites. The National Park Service is administered by the Department of Interior.

Most national parks were established primarily to provide the public with fine scenery. By protecting scenery, the parks also incidentally protected wildlife and other natural resources.

Today, national parks put a much greater emphasis on wildlife protection. Gone are the days when federal agents attempted to wipe out the wolves and mountain lions of Yellowstone National Park. National parks feature managed trail systems, interpretive centers, and even lodges and restaurants to enhance the public's enjoyment. Most of the educational programs and facilities in the parks are geared toward creating a better understanding of wildlife. Even historical sites and battlefields managed by the National Park Service usually provide interpretive programs on the natural history of the area and excellent opportunities to observe on-site wildlife.

Our national parks are the crown jewels of our public land system, in that they protect some of the very best examples of our biological and cultural heritage—from the large parks such as Yellowstone, Yosemite, and Grand Canyon to many small historical sites all around the country. The only problem with national parks, for those of us who want to view wildlife, is that visitation is so high, especially in the summer, that you sometimes have to work hard to get away from the crowds and see wildlife that is not habituated to people. For example, during summer, you are more likely to see traffic jams than bears in Yellowstone National Park, which takes in 3 million visitors a year—with the great bulk of them coming in summer. The Great Smoky Mountains National Park, on the border of Tennessee and North Carolina, has an even bigger annual tourist load, tallying nearly 9 million recreational visits in 1994.

Many of us grew up seeing black bears in the national parks. Although they were usually hanging around garbage dumps and roadsides, where they could always find a steady supply of tourist handouts, the bears were very visible to park visitors. I would not suggest a return to the old days, but now that most parks manage trash, automobile traffic, and bears better than they did twenty years ago, the only way many people will see bears—or most other wildlife, for that matter—is by hiking away or otherwise distancing themselves from campgrounds and other crowded settings in the park. Even the hiking and canoeing trails in our most popular national parks grow so crowded during peak seasons that the chance of seeing wildlife is sometimes pretty slim.

If you plan to visit a popular park in hope of observing wildlife, I suggest you get out on the trail very early in the morning—or better yet, visit the park before or after the peak tourist season. In spring, autumn, and winter, even Yellowstone's roads are relatively empty. Also, try to hike off the main roads and trails. Surveys show that most park visitors do not get more than a quarter mile off paved roads, so if you hike even a relatively short distance, you might significantly improve your chances of finding wildlife.

Most national parks and many other sites managed by the National Park Service charge an entrance fee. If camping is available, park personnel also collect a fee for each campsite. For information about individual national parks or about parks within a particular region of the United States, contact the appropriate National Park Service regional office listed in Appendix 1.

National Wildlife Refuges

The U.S. Fish and Wildlife Service (FWS), another agency of the Department of the Interior, protects 92.3 million acres of habitat in more than 450 wildlife refuges scattered across the United States, from Florida to Alaska and Hawaii. Congress has also designated federal wildlife refuges in U.S. territories, including Puerto Rico and the Virgin Islands, as well as many uninhabited offshore islands.

Although most federal refuges were established to conserve, protect, and enhance waterfowl and other migratory wildlife (a primary FWS management responsibility), most provide excellent habitat and opportunities for viewing both migratory and resident wildlife. One good example is Ding Darling National Wildlife Refuge, on Florida's Sanibel Island, which winters many thousands of migratory birds, including white pelicans, blue-winged teal, and red-breasted mergansers. The refuge is also a great place to observe alligators, river otters, brown pelicans, wood storks, and other year-round Florida residents.

National Wildlife Refuges are open for public enjoyment—some even for hunting—but public use is always secondary to wildlife protection. For example, Nisqually National Wildlife Refuge, near my home in Washington State, was a popular local jogging area until refuge managers determined that runners were disturbing nesting and breeding waterfowl. Closing the Nisqually refuge dikes to runners was not a completely popular decision with local runners, but the refuge managers, under federal law, had to do what was best for wildlife.

FWS also operates a system of federal fish hatcheries in coastal areas around the country. These hatcheries are often overlooked as great places to see not only salmon and other migrating fish but also eagles, herons, otters, and other fish-eating wildlife attracted to these areas. Entrance to many national wildlife refuges and hatcheries is free; others charge a small daily admission fee. Possession of a federal migratory waterfowl stamp will get you into any national wildlife refuge for free. Information on refuges and hatcheries is available from the FWS regional offices listed in Appendix 1.

National Forests

The U.S. Forest Service (USFS), within the federal Department of Agriculture, administers a vast system of 156 national forests that stretches from Alaska to Puerto Rico and covers 191 million acres, an area the size of California, Oregon, and Washington combined.

National forests are open to the public and are required by law to be managed under a multiple-use concept that allows for timber harvest, mineral development, grazing, and other commercial uses as well as protection of fish, wildlife, and other natural resources. Logging activities have sometimes gotten out of balance with the protection of wildlife. This has resulted in predicaments like that of the national forests of the Pacific Northwest, where accelerated harvest of old-growth timber jeopardized sensitive species such as the northern spotted owl, which requires large stands of mature Douglas fir.

In any case, our national forests are almost always great places to get away from crowded conditions and observe wildlife in its native habitat. USFS boasts of more than 100,000 miles of trails and 100,000 recreational sites nationwide; the current emphasis on recreation and wildlife habitat will probably be expanded as commercial logging is slowed in many national forests, particularly in the West. The U.S. Forest Service also has its own watchable-wildlife program, called Eyes on Wildlife, which provides good opportunities and interpretive material for people seeking to observe wildlife in national forests.

National forests tend to be much larger than national wildlife refuges, and more open in terms of access and management than either refuges or national parks. In most cases, national forest roads and recreational facilities are more primitive than those found in refuges or parks. This makes it easier to get away from the crowds, but also makes it imperative that you be prepared with proper maps and equipment before heading out to explore your national forests. Admission to national forests is free, although some USFS districts charge nominal fees for overnight camping. Recently, the Forest Service has begun contracting the summer management of some campgrounds and other attractions to private companies, which also charge nominal fees. USFS maps were mentioned in Chapter 5. To get these maps and other information in advance of a nature trip, contact one of the regional Forest Service offices listed in Appendix 1.

Bureau of Land Management

The Bureau of Land Management (BLM), also part of the Department of the Interior, manages more public land than any other single government agency: 270 million acres, mostly in the Western states. Like national forests, BLM lands are managed under the multiple-use concept, which allows for timber harvest, grazing, mining, and other revenue-producing activities as well as fish and wildlife protection and outdoor recreation. BLM lands are also wide open for most public recreation, including hiking and wildlife watching, with appropriate rules and regulations to protect natural and cultural resources. In recent years, BLM has increased its emphasis on the protection and restoration of wetlands and other wildlife habitat and has expanded Watchable Wildlife opportunities for the public.

If you live in or are visiting the West, check out wildlife-viewing opportunities on BLM lands. While in college, I spent my summers doing BLM wildlife-habitat surveys, and I had many excellent wildlife-viewing experiences in the field. The most memorable was a quiet, almost spiritual encounter with a full-curl desert bighorn ram on a rocky cliff north of Las Vegas, Nevada. The experience sent me back to college that fall to change my major from accounting to wildlife biology.

BLM lands are similar to national forests in that they are usually less crowded, developed, and controlled than are most parks and refuges. The roads and facilities are sometimes primitive at best, so you should be well prepared with good maps, proper attire, and essential equipment. BLM offices are fewer and farther apart than those of the Forest Service and the National Park Service. For information on BLM lands and wildlife-viewing opportunities, contact one of the state offices listed in Appendix 1.

State Parks and Wildlife Management Areas

Like the federal government, state legislatures have responded to public demand for outdoor recreation by funding the purchase and management of millions of acres of land for wildlife protection and public recreation. State-administered lands, like federal public lands, are generally open for public access and enjoyment, with some rules and regulations to protect the environment and ensure public safety.

State parks often protect some of the best wildlife habitat in the country. But my experience has been that, like national parks, state parks are well known and attract large numbers of campers, boaters, and other recreationists. State parks are especially crowded during summer months, so wildlife-viewing opportunities might be best pursued in the off-season, before or after the summer crowds.

State wildlife-management areas and state forest lands, on the other hand, are often overlooked by the public, except for hunters during the fall hunting season. State wildlife-management areas are generally more primitive than parks, but they attract a wide variety of resident and migratory wildlife. State parks that charge entrance fees during the summer season often suspend the fees (and seasonal fee collectors) in the fall, winter, and spring. State wildlife-management areas and forests are free in most states. Some, including Texas, require a special pass for public use. A list of contact addresses and phone numbers for state parks and wildlife areas is provided in Appendix 1.

Canadian Parks, Wildlife Areas, and Migratory Bird Sanctuaries

Canada manages a very large network of national and provincial parks, forests, and wildlife refuges. The official terminology for Canadian public lands differs a little from that used in the United States, but like U.S. parks and refuges, those in Canada usually are open to outdoor recreationists. Appendix 1 provides a list of contact addresses and phone numbers for Canadian federal and provincial parks and wildlife lands.

Canada's federal park agency, Parks Canada, administers a system of 36 national parks, 4 national marine conservation areas, and 800 national historic sites. Parks Canada seeks to protect lands that represent all of Canada's 39 natural regions. With this goal in mind, the federal government plans to add 16 new parks to the system in the future.

The Canadian Wildlife Service, a division of Environment Canada, manages almost 5 million acres of wildlife habitat across Canada, for purposes of conservation, research, and public education. Included within this land base are 98 migratory bird sanctuaries and 49 national wildlife areas. Migratory bird sanctuaries emphasize protection of waterfowl and other migratory birds. National wildlife areas are established to protect critical habitat both for migratory wildlife and for endangered or threatened species. A marine national wildlife area, for example, is being established in Isabella Bay, Baffin Island, Northwest Territories, for the endangered bowhead whale. Most sanctuaries and wildlife areas are open to the public, although they are sometimes closed during critical nesting and molting seasons. Many wildlife areas have trails and interpretive exhibits, but most are unstaffed and lack on-site visitor services.

Canada's federal park and refuge system is augmented by many provincial parks and wildlife management areas. Each province, from Nova Scotia and New Brunswick in the east to the Yukon Territory in the far northwest, has its own way of classifying and managing provincial land. Contact each province individually for information on location and visitation rules (see Appendix 1).

Private Lands Open to the Public

A number of conservation organizations, including The Nature Conservancy, National Audubon Society, and local land trusts, purchase important wildlife-habitat areas either to turn over to governmental wildlife agencies or to keep and manage for conservation. These lands often are open to the public for guided tours or for hiking, canoeing, and other recreation, though the organizations usually charge an admission fee and/or ask for donations to help cover the cost of managing and protecting the land. Look in your phone book for Audubon Society and Nature Conservancy offices near you or call one of the offices listed in Appendix 2. DeLorme gazetteers and other recreation maps also show the location of many of these private wildlife preserves.

Don't overlook or discount other private lands when you are searching for places to hike and observe wildlife. Often you can find wonderful wildlife-viewing opportunities on farms, ranches, forests, beaches, and other private lands not specifically managed for conservation. Always ask permission before entering private lands, but don't be totally discouraged by no-trespassing signs. In some cases, a sign means just that—keep off this land or you will be prosecuted—

but often the landowner is willing to allow access, especially for nonconsumptive recreation such as hiking and wildlife viewing, provided that you get permission in advance. Landowners are justifiably concerned about fire, vandalism, and accident liability on their property, and by posting their land they can screen the people who enter and can talk to them about appropriate conduct and possible hazards.

Landowners might want to write down your name and address before allowing access to their land. They might even charge you a nominal user fee. But it hardly ever hurts to approach a farmer, rancher, or private timber company and ask permission to view wildlife. The worst they can say is no.

7

Opportunities Close to Home

So far, this book has focused on techniques and opportunities for observing and studying wildlife away from home—on vacations, camping trips, and planned wildlife excursions. The fact is, for many Americans and Canadians, some of the most accessible and rewarding wildlife-viewing opportunities might be in places much closer to home: in regional and municipal parks, greenbelts and trail systems; in zoos and wild animal parks; even in their own neighborhoods or backyards. Below is a summary of some of the wildlife-viewing opportunities available locally to city dwellers and suburbanites.

Urban Parks and Natural Areas

As was mentioned in Chapter 4, many birds and other wildlife species seek out a diversity of habitat types, including riparian zones and edge habitat on the margins of open space and forested areas, which offer both food and nearby cover. Many urban parks by design emphasize the kind of habitat diversity sought by resident and migratory wildlife—large trees, open grassy areas, native plants, water, and protection from most predators. In addition to traditional urban parks, which attract a lot of songbirds, waterfowl, and small mammals, many progressive cities, counties, and regional park districts have acquired land and developed large natural parks and forests specifically managed as open space and habitat for native wildlife, from neotropical songbirds to big animals like deer, elk, and bighorn sheep.

In addition to their value as wildlife habitat, many local and regional parks are located where they offer good points of view for seeing wildlife in other, adjacent habitats. An example is Discovery Park in Seattle, which not only provides great habitat for black-tailed deer, bald eagles, and a host of other wildlife species but also, as a former military gun battery, gives the public an unmatched vantage of Puget Sound and its wildlife—including seabirds, birds of prey, and the occasional whale that wanders into Elliott Bay from the ocean. As with any other wildlife-watching experience, successful wildlife observation in urban and regional parks requires that you be aware of the times of day and seasons when wildlife is visible and when human activities do not interfere with wildlife or your enjoyment of it.

Below are some examples of urban parks and locally managed wildlife preserves that provide excellent wildlife viewing opportunities.

Denver, Colorado: Denver Mountain Park System, City and County of Denver, 2300 Fifteenth Street, Denver, CO 80202. Phone: 303-964-2580.

The Denver Park System includes several large mountain areas outside the city. The 2,340-acre Genesee Park includes fenced pastures that support small herds of bison and elk, as well as picnic areas, hiking trails, and the peak of Genesee Mountain. Genesee Park is home to mule deer and many small mammals, such as snowshoe hares, coyotes, and porcupines. Bird inhabitants include blue grouse, red-tailed hawks, owls, woodpeckers, and an occasional wild turkey. Other features of the Denver park system are Stapleton Park, with its self-guided nature trail marked with signs in English and Braille, and the spectacular high-mountain view from Summit Lake Park and Mount Evans.

Fort Worth, Texas: Fort Worth Nature Center and Refuge, City of Fort Worth Parks Department, 9601 Fossil Ridge Road, Fort Worth, TX 76135. Phone: 817-237-1111.

Only a few miles from downtown Fort Worth, this 3,500-acre sanctuary offers nature programs, maps, and exhibits, in addition to 25 miles of walking trails. Several habitats are represented, including wetland ecosystems, river-bottom forest along the Trinity River, prairie, canyons, and live-oak groves. Wildlife inhabitants include white-tailed deer, coyotes, skunks, raccoons, armadillos, and a small herd of bison. Prairie wildflowers attract a variety of butterflies.

New York, New York: Central Park, c/o Central Park Conservancy, The Arsenal, Central Park, New York, NY 10021. Phone: 212-315-0385.

In the midst of Manhattan's urban buzz, New York residents and visitors can seek out a quieter experience in 843-acre Central Park, home to small mammals including squirrels, raccoons, chipmunks, moles, and opossums; and to turtles, lizards, and skunks. But the widest variety is found in the bird population. Common resident and migrant birds include the double-crested cormorant, green heron, American black duck, mallard, and red-tailed hawk. More than 150 bird species have been spotted here in recent years. Contact the Central Park Conservancy for a full listing.

Philadelphia, Pennsylvania: Fairmount Park, Fairmount Park Commission, P.O. Box 21601, Philadelphia, PA 19131. Phone: 215-685-0044.

Lying along the Schuylkill River in midtown Philadelphia, 8,700-acre Fairmount Park offers a variety of natural settings, including wooded hills, lakes, ponds, and springs. At least 20 species of mammals, including bats, opossums, deer, raccoons, and skunks, dwell in the park, along with snakes, salamanders, and fish. More than 50 bird species breed here, and another 100 stop while migrating or over-wintering. The varied bird population includes northern cardinals, mockingbirds, ring-necked pheasants, great horned owls, and various woodpeckers, warblers, and other songbirds.

Phoenix, Arizona: Phoenix Mountain Preserves, City of Phoenix Outdoor Programs, 17642 North Fortieth Street, Phoenix, AZ 95032. Phone: 602-262-6861.

The City of Phoenix maintains an impressive system of seven mountain preserves, including Dreamy Draw Recreation Area, Echo Canyon Recreation Area, and Papago Park. South Mountain Park, at 16,500 acres the world's largest municipal park, includes 58 miles of trails for horseback riding, hiking, and mountain biking. South Mountain Park includes remarkable geological features, ancient petroglyphs, and a variety of desert flora and fauna. Several species of snakes and lizards are found here, including Gila monsters, horned lizards, geckos, and chuckwallas. Look for hardy desert mammals such as black-tailed hares, ringtail cats, coyotes, javelinas, and kit foxes. Bird populations come and go with seasonal water supplies, but desert arthropods like sun spiders, scorpions, and centipedes are found year-round.

Portland, Oregon: Forest Park Hoyt Arboretum, 4000 Southwest Fairview Boulevard, Portland, OR 97221. Phone: 503-228-8733 or 503-797-1850.

Forest Park, overlooking the confluence of the Columbia and Willamette Rivers, is the United States' largest park contained within the boundaries of a city. The nearly 5,000-acre park includes abundant natural forest and extensive recreational trails. While most city parks are island habitats, Forest Park's 8-mile length connects directly to open spaces to the north and west, serving wildlife as both a home base and a travel corridor to areas outside the city. More than 60 mammal species are found here, including northern flying squirrels, black-tailed deer, raccoons, pocket gophers, mountain beavers, coyotes, and even black bears and cougars.

Seattle, Washington: Discovery Park, City of Seattle Parks Department, 3801 West Government Way, Seattle, WA 98199. Phone: 206-386-4236.

At 534 acres, Discovery Park is the largest of Seattle's parks. A former military base, it includes walking trails, historic sites, the Daybreak Star Center for Indian culture, and the 115-year-old West Point Lighthouse. Douglas fir and cedar forest, tallgrass meadows, brushy wetland, and Puget Sound beachfront provide a variety of habitats for small mammals and deer. More than 230 resident and migrant birds are reported to use the park, including owls, hawks, bald eagles, and shorebirds. Bird tours are offered spring and fall. Marine shoreline species range from mussels and barnacles to harbor seals and the occasional orca whale seen offshore.

Zoos and Wildlife Parks

Urban zoos are not what they used to be in most North American cities. The concrete bunkers with metal bars have been replaced in many cases with natural-looking exhibits that attempt to re-create the natural habitats of featured wildlife. These modern exhibits play at least two important functions: They educate the public about the natural habitat needs and relationships of wildlife, and they give zoo animals a more interesting and stimulating environment in which to live—which yields more alert, active, and natural-acting animals and a more positive visiting experience for the public.

In addition to upgrading urban zoos, some zoological societies, regional park districts, and private foundations have developed, on the outskirts of cities, wild-animal parks in which animals roam in massive fenced enclosures. In these parks, the public can observe animals in more natural and relaxed conditions than a traditional urban zoo can offer. Some of these animal parks allow the public to drive through in cars, while others provide trams driven by tour guides Disneyland-style. Some parks feature native animals in native or almost-native habitats. Others have a mixture of native and exotic animals.

While visiting zoos and wildlife parks is certainly not the same as observing wildlife in its natural habitat, it can be enjoyable and educational. If you plan your trips around crowded days and times, modern zoos and animal parks can be good places to observe animals up close and to practice using binoculars, spotting scopes, and cameras.

Below are some examples of wild animal parks that provide excellent viewing opportunities to see native wildlife. Before visiting, I recommend calling these parks to get current information on fees and operating hours.

Eatonville, Washington: Northwest Trek Wildlife Park, Eatonville, WA 98323. Phone: 206-832-6117.

Operated by the Metropolitan Park District of Tacoma, Northwest Trek is a large, open-air zoological park located in the foothills of the Cascade Mountains, near Mount Rainier National Park. A 435-acre enclosure allows Roosevelt elk, woodland caribou, blacktailed deer, and other native wildlife to roam around. The park recently added a grizzly bear exhibit. A tour tram takes visitors through the enclosed area.

Nashville, Tennessee: Grassmere Wildlife Park, 3777 Nolensville Road, Nashville, TN 37211. Phone: 615-833-1534.

Once a farm, the Grassmere site is now managed and operated by the nonprofit Friends of Grassmere. This beautiful park features the historic Croft Family Farmstead, an aviary, and a Cumberland River exhibit. Wildlife includes cougar, black bear, bison, elk, wolves, and otters. Free parking, wheelchair access, no pets.

Peoria, Illinois: Wildlife Prairie Park, R.R. #2, Peoria, IL 61615. Phone: 309-676-0998.

Wildlife Prairie Park's extensive facilities include a restored prairie, a pioneer homestead, a large playground area, a railroad, cross-country ski trails, nature walks, interpretive programs, picnic sites, and limited overnight lodging. Wildlife includes woodchucks, badgers, coyotes, foxes, wolves, raccoons, cougars, deer, elk, and many resident and migratory birds.

Waycross, Georgia: Okefenokee Swamp Park, Waycross, GA 31501. Phone: 912-283-0583.

Located at the headwaters of the Suwannee and St. Marys Rivers, Okefenokee Swamp Park features wildlife exhibits, wilderness walks, an observation tower, Pioneer Island, a short tour of Indian waterways, and native animals in their own habitat. Canoe rentals and boat tours are available for an additional fee. Wildlife includes black bears, river otters, flamingos, and alligators.

Backyard Wildlife Watching

Some of the most enjoyable wildlife watching in North America can be experienced from the comfort of your own home by observing the birds, small mammals, and other wildlife that reside in your yard or that stop by for a snack or drink.

Like wildlife watching anywhere, backyard observation can be approached either actively or passively. You can go about your normal business and hope something interesting will come by, or you can try to attract wildlife to your property.

The numbers and diversity of the wildlife you see in your backyard will depend on how many basic habitat needs your yard can fulfill and how the habitat components of your property fit with the rest of your neighborhood "ecosystem." Property lines mean nothing to wildlife. Indeed, fences, depending on their design, can make great perches for birds and terrific aerial pathways for squirrels, opossums, and other four-legged wildlife.

Wild animals are constantly searching for the various components of their required habitat—food, water, and cover. If your yard has some important habitat component not found on your neighbor's property—a pond, for instance, or a large tree—you might well attract wildlife that would not appear in your neighbor's yard.

There are many simple things you can do to attract wildlife and just about as many excellent books and magazine articles available to tell you how to do it. The National Wildlife Federation, through its Backyard Wildlife Habitat Program, provides a wealth of information about designing your backyard to attract wildlife, as well as an opportunity to register your own property as a Backyard Wildlife

Habitat. For information about how to get involved in the Backyard Wildlife Habitat Program, you may call the National Wildlife Federation at (800)477-5560. Ask for the information packet that includes a program application, a booklet on planning and planting a habitat, and *The Backyard Naturalist*, a book about one person's experiences and efforts to attract wildlife to his yard. Another of my favorite sources is the backyard-birding series offered by *Wild Bird* magazine.

Your objective in embarking on any serious backyard wildlife projects should be twofold: to attract a variety of interesting wildlife and to be able to see the wildlife you attract. Here are three categories of steps you can take to attract and accommodate wildlife:

Landscaping

Plants are probably the most important component of backyard wildlife habitat, and your selection of trees, shrubs, and grass will have a lot to do with the species and diversity of wildlife attracted to your yard. So will the spacing and arrangement of plants, water, and other habitat features. Some bird species, such as chickadees and blue jays, seek dense trees or thick brush. Others, such as bluebirds and mockingbirds, prefer open areas. Most birds and small mammals, however, prefer a mixture of deep-foliage and open areas that meet a variety of their habitat needs.

In the East, where deciduous forests are abundant, wildlife is often attracted to open spaces or the edge habitat at the margin of open areas and thick deciduous forest. In the open deserts and plains west of the Mississippi River, even a single tree in your yard might provide important habitat for some animal. Trees and shrubs, such as hackberry and cherry trees, provide abundant fruit and flowers for wildlife. Other trees, including many coniferous or evergreen species, are favored as nesting or roosting habitats.

Many excellent books and other references are available to help landowners select plants favored by wildlife. Most good plant nurseries can also advise home owners about which trees and plants work best to attract wildlife.

Structures

Birdhouses and nest boxes are simple to build and, if placed properly, usually quite effective in attracting cavity-nesting birds such as woodpeckers, bluebirds, and purple martins. Many outdoor stores and plant nurseries sell inexpensive birdhouses and bird feeders. Birds that are not cavity nesters will not be attracted to birdhouses. In fact, robins and some owls are often content to nest on a simple shelf, or even on an unused shelf in your toolshed, as long as they have twenty-four-hour access to the nest.

You can add to the attractiveness of your property for nesting birds by placing some nesting materials in your yard. String, yarn, even an old straw broom will work well for nest builders.

In winter, wildlife that does not hibernate or migrate south can often use a little help from human friends. In addition to providing winter species with food, carefully placed bird feeders and feeding trays also provide a lot of viewing opportunities for backyard wildlife watchers. As with nest boxes, the design and location of your feeders, as well as the type of food you offer, will influence which wildlife species are attracted to your yard. Design and location will also determine how well birds are protected from their most common and effective predators—domestic cats. Check your reference materials for cat-proof designs. If you begin feeding birds in the fall or early winter, you should stick with the feeding until spring. Feeding will encourage even migratory birds to stick around through the cold months. If you cut off the food supply in mid-winter, birds dependent on you will die.

Hanging feeders work well for most finches and grosbeaks, including cardinals, whereas ground-feeding birds like juncos and mourning doves will be more attracted to flat feeding trays placed close to the ground. Suet can be offered to wildlife in many ways, including mesh bags and screened boxes attached to trees or buildings.

Locating and putting up a feeding structure is the easy part of feeding wildlife. If you go to the trouble to do that, you should make sure you stock the feeding station with the right groceries. Seeds are a sure bet for many birds year-round. Most commercially prepared seed mixes contain sunflower seeds, millet, and other desirable seed species. You can also buy individual seeds and mix your own.

Water

A dependable source of fresh water could be the single most important and attractive habitat feature in your yard. Even wildlife that is

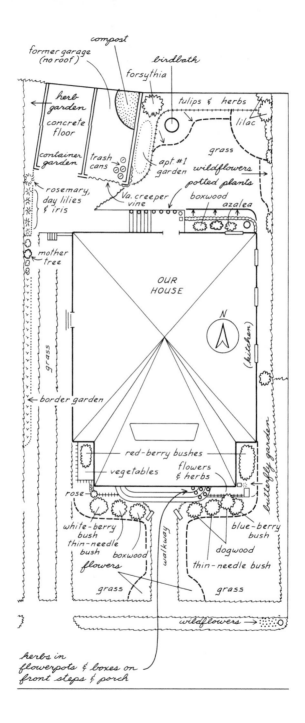

compost

former garage
(no roof)

forsythia

birdbath

herb
garden

concrete
floor

container
garden

trash
cans

tulips & herbs

lilac

grass

wildflowers

apt. #1
garden

potted plants

boxwood

azalea

rosemary,
day lilies
& iris

Va. creeper
vine

mother
tree

OUR
HOUSE

N

(kitchen)

grass

border garden

red-berry bushes

vegetables

flowers
& herbs

rose

white-berry
bush

thin-needle
bush

boxwood

walkway

blue-berry
bush

dogwood

thin-needle bush

flowers

grass

grass

butterfly garden

wildflowers

herbs in
flowerpots & boxes on
front steps & porch

not attracted by nest boxes and feeding stations might drop by for a drink or a bath. Water is a scarce commodity in the summer almost anywhere, and in the Southwest Desert Habitat Region year-round, so a small pond, a concrete birdbath, or better yet, a fountain or small stream will attract birds and a whole host of small mammals, reptiles, amphibians, and other wildlife—many of them nocturnal.

Ponds and birdbaths should be designed with wildlife in mind. For instance, to avoid drowning small birds, a birdbath should be no more than 3 inches deep, and ponds should have rocks in the center to offer a safe resting spot. Instructional materials that offer help with all types of backyard-habitat design are available from the National Wildlife Federation.

One key to attracting a lot of interesting and visible backyard wildlife is the placement and overall relationship of the various habitat components, including trees, shrubs, garden plants, water, and artificial structures. The diagram on page 136 shows a good habitat design for your yard, if you happen to live in a neighborhood with mature trees—the ideal design depends of course on your location. Notice the variety of shrubs and herbs, as well as their arrangement, which leaves plenty of open space and edge habitat. Notice also that the birdbath is located near edge habitat among lawn, garden, and, in this case, a single forsythia bush. This arrangement allows a margin of safety from predators but keeps animals visible from the house. The birdbath is also at least 3 feet tall, which will discourage cats and other predators—although not aerial predators such as a sharp-shinned hawk.

I want to stress how important it is to maintain the habitat you create for wildlife. For example, a yard landscaped with wildlife in mind can quickly lose its habitat value if the trees are pruned so severely that they lose their ability to conceal or if the margin of the lawn and garden gets so overgrown that it no longer functions as an edge habitat. Also, nest boxes, feeders, birdbaths, and other structures should be cleaned out annually to prevent the transmission of parasites and disease-carrying organisms to the next generation of birds.

8

Getting There:
Travel and Viewing Alternatives

Americans and Canadians are hooked on automobile travel, whether for good (convenience, individual planning) or for bad (pollution, heavy traffic). For the wildlife watcher, our society's emphasis on automobile travel has created a boon: most of our recreational opportunities, including some of the best wildlife viewing, are in places easily accessible by car. Our major parks, refuges, and public trailheads are almost all served by good roads, and most campgrounds are designed for car camping. Also, automobiles sometimes make adequate blinds—animals are less likely to flee a parked or slowly moving motor vehicle than they are to avoid people on foot. The National Watchable Wildlife Program, discussed earlier, was designed with motorists in mind in order to make wildlife watching as easy and convenient as possible. The standard brown-and-white-binoculars logo shown in the Introduction is specifically intended to help motorists find designated Watchable Wildlife sites.

For those of you who do not own automobiles or who are willing to leave your cars at home, there are workable alternative modes of travel that will take you to places where you can view wildlife in its natural habitat. The alternatives will probably not be as quick or convenient as automobile travel and might be more expensive up front (unless you factor in car payments, insurance, fuel, and repairs), but you can get to a lot of good wildlife-viewing locations in North America without a car. In fact, in Alaska's Denali National Park, cars are forbidden; visitors have to travel by foot, on bicycles, or in buses provided for them.

Alternatives to Automobiles

Both Amtrak in the United States and VIA Passenger Train Network in Canada travel to, or at least very near, many of our finest national parks, state parks, and wilderness areas. Areas not served by train are usually served by bus companies. Many great wildlife areas can also be visited by flying into nearby cities and either renting a car or taking a tour bus, if available.

Some good books and guides on non-auto travel are available, including Lee Cooper's *How to Get to the Wilderness Without a Car*, which give information about parks and wilderness areas served by train, bus, and scheduled airline. Should you decide to take a wildlife-oriented vacation without an automobile, consult books like this to get a general idea of available transportation alternatives.

Once you decide on the region or location you want to visit, then find a good travel agent to help you with up-to-date travel schedules and accommodations. Airline, train, and bus routes and schedules frequently change. If you have enough planning time, you should also remember to write or call for information from local chambers of commerce or the appropriate state and provincial tourism bureaus listed in Appendix 1.

Wildlife Tours

Perhaps the most exciting alternative to individual or family automobile travel is the growing ecotourism industry: tour companies that specialize in packaged, wildlife-oriented travel and vacations.

The kinds of treks and photo safaris we traditionally associate with Africa and other exotic locations are now available to wildlife habitats all over North America, from the Florida Everglades to the Canadian tundra. Some ecotours are scheduled by area—the Grand Canyon, for instance, or the Rio Grande between Texas and Mexico. Other tours or tour companies specialize in certain groups of wildlife, such as birds of prey or wintering neotropical birds. There are many advantages to joining a tour, especially for travel in an area with which you are not familiar. First, all your basic food and shelter needs are taken care of by the tour operators, leaving you free to focus on the landscape and wildlife around you. Second, most experienced tour guides know where and when to look for wildlife and what you are seeing when you do spot an interesting animal. Many summer-tour guides are professional wildlife biologists, teachers, or biology students during the rest of the year. Outfitters and guides can also get you into remote places you would not venture to alone, even if you did have permission—for instance, some of the coastal rivers in Alaska where grizzly bears can be observed in the fall feeding on salmon. Some tours through groups such as Earthwatch or the National Wildlife Federation even offer travelers a chance to assist with ongoing wildlife research projects.

The main disadvantages to joining a tour group are price and schedule. All that special attention and access to out-of-the-way places does not come without a price tag, and as with any other tour, the guide's schedule becomes your schedule. If you enjoy totally unstructured vacations, you might be frustrated by any tour, no matter how much you get to see and do.

To find out more about ecotours in North America, contact the National Wildlife Federation or one of the tour companies listed in Appendix 3.

Horseback Riding

All through this book, the main emphasis has been on walking and hiking, because most people on nature outings travel by foot. But there are a number of other great ways of leaving the crowds behind and viewing wildlife, including horseback riding in the backcountry. Travel by horse enables you to explore easily the interior of many large parks, national forests, and, especially, designated wilderness areas, which are closed to motorized vehicles. Horses are quiet and they keep an eye on the trail, allowing you to spend your time watching for wildlife. You can also cover a lot more miles in a day on a horse than on foot.

Many national parks, national forests, and state parks have developed equestrian trails for people who bring their own horses as well as for licensed outfitters and guides. Day rides are fun, especially for novice riders, but to really see the interior of most parks and wilderness areas by horseback you should contact a licensed outfitter and arrange for a pack trip that includes some overnight stays. On guided pack trips, you normally spend four to six hours in the saddle each day, which allows plenty of personal time for off-trail exploration by foot, as well as wildlife watching in the evening and early morning. Like other tour operators, pack outfitters normally take care of all meals and other chores, so you can relax and enjoy the wilderness.

Backcountry outfitters tend to be concentrated in the southwestern desert and the Rocky Mountains, but guided trips are available in almost every habitat region of North America, including the eastern states and eastern Canadian provinces. There is no national organization of backcountry horse outfitters, but many states and provinces do have organizations. Check with a local riding association or tack shop to find backcountry outfitters.

Mountain Bikes

Mountain bikes can propel you away from crowds and into the backcountry almost as quietly as hiking, and bikes, like horses, will get you there a lot faster than your feet. Like horses, mountain bikes are legal in many areas that are closed to trail bikes and other motorized vehicles—a major exception being in Forest Service–designated wilderness areas, where trail bikes are prohibited. Unlike horseback riding, mountain biking usually requires that you keep your eye on the trail, not on the trees and rocks around you. You may not see as much on the trail as hikers do, but if your time is limited, you can get farther away from civilization and see a lot of wildlife once you get to your destination.

Mountain bikes have been around for only a few years, but the sport is one of the fastest growing in North America. Mountain-bike technology is a spin-off from ten-speed road bikes with light alloy frames and multiple gears, but mountain bicycles are designed specifically with trails and primitive roads in mind. With their flat handlebars, strong suspension systems, and fat, knobby tires, they not only are sturdy but offer a relatively comfortable ride.

Many of the horse trails in national parks, national forests, and state and provincial parks are also open to mountain biking, and a number of mountain-biking tour companies have opened up around North America, especially in the southwestern and Rocky Mountain states.

Rafting, Canoeing, and Kayaking

Some of the finest wildlife viewing opportunities in North America occur on major lake systems and river corridors, many of which are inaccessible by foot, mountain bike, or even horseback.

Canoes and sometimes kayaks are widely available to rent for day trips and short overnight excursions in such waters. My family rented canoes in the Everglades National Park a few years ago and had a wonderful day observing alligators, waterbirds, and giant orb spiders along the canals. The spiders were a real hit with my daughters!

For longer trips or for trips over white water, it is almost mandatory that you be an experienced canoeist or that you sign up with a licensed outfitter. In the eastern United States, including West Virginia, many guided trips are one-day excursions. In the West, where rivers generally are longer and access points farther apart, guided trips may last a week or more. Although every outfitter is different, and every trip has its own pace, most trips allow for four to six hours on the water each day, with the rest of your time ashore and available for hiking or simply scanning the horizon with binoculars for birds of prey and other wildlife.

Regardless of the type of float trip you take, you should be in a good position to see wildlife. In flat-water areas, such as the Everglades or the Boundary Waters Canoe Area in northern Minnesota and Ontario, your canoe or kayak will allow you to approach wildlife fairly closely. Even on white-water rafting or kayaking trips, long stretches of flat water between rapids usually offer a chance to catch birds and other wildlife by surprise. Depending on the region you are in and the river you float, you can see a wide variety of animals near water, including moose, bald eagles, golden eagles, bighorn sheep, cougar, black bear, salmon, river otters, beaver, and many songbirds.

Guided river-rafting trips are not cheap—generally costing $100 to $150 per person per day—but they are both exciting and very relaxing. And on such trips, like backcountry horseback riding and other guided trips, most of the work is done by the outfitters, leaving you plenty of time to explore the hillsides and canyons for wildlife.

The Boundary Waters Canoe Area, the Saint Croix International Waterway in Maine and Quebec, and the Okefenokee Swamp in Georgia are three great flat-water areas where you can view wildlife by canoe or kayak. Okefenokee supports a dense alligator population, and the big reptiles will cruise right under your canoe. The Rio Grande, separating Texas and Mexico, is one of the best rivers in North America for floating and wildlife observation, as is the Skagit River in Washington State, where hundreds of bald eagles gather in autumn and winter to feed on spawned-out salmon.

Sea Kayaking

I have not spent much time in sea kayaks, but I have just enough experience that I can recommend sea kayaking as one of the best methods for approaching and observing aquatic birds and other wildlife. I hope to do more sea kayaking in the future.

Sea kayaks are larger, heavier, more stable, and more comfortable than either the canoes or the kayaks used for white-water trips. They are maneuverable enough to navigate large bays—even the open ocean at times—as well as the smallest side channels and shallow estuaries. And because sea kayaks ride low on the water and are virtually soundless, they allow you to get very close to wildlife, both on the water and near the shoreline. I have watched sea kayakers in Puget Sound glide right through a raft of scoters—large sea ducks—while hardly disturbing a single duck. You can enjoy sea kayaking in small groups on day excursions, or you can arrange for longer guided tours. In either case, you can expect to get a lot of exercise, maybe get wet, and see some unexpectedly interesting wildlife. Last summer, on a guided day trip in Currituck Sound, behind the Outer Banks of North Carolina, I missed most of the large wading birds I wanted to see, but I did see my first water moccasin, which swam within 2 feet of my kayak—I got a good look but kept my hands in the boat!

Guided sea kayaking trips are available all over North America, depending on the season, from the Outer Banks to Pukaskwa National Park in Ontario and the inland waters of Puget Sound and Georgia Straits in Washington and British Columbia.

Snorkeling and Scuba Diving

Snorkeling and scuba diving are the only ways—other than maybe glass-bottomed boats—that you can observe fish and other underwater organisms up close. And there are hundreds of places in North America where you can successfully use snorkels and face masks or scuba gear to observe fish in both freshwater and saltwater habitats.

The advantages of snorkeling are that the equipment is inexpensive to buy or rent, the technique is easy to learn, and you may float for hours without having even to lift your head out of the water. The disadvantage is that you are restricted to the surface or as deep as you can dive while holding your breath. For shallow water in streams or for many coral reefs, snorkeling is a great way to explore the underwater environment. In most cases, you won't even need to be a strong swimmer, since the water will float you. As long as you wear fins, you should be able to move around and make shallow dives easily. However, you should get some instruction before you venture into the water wearing a snorkel and mask; you will need to know how to clear your snorkel for breathing when you surface from a dive. Also, remember to apply a lot of waterproof sunblock to your back and the backs of your legs, or risk getting burned to a crisp.

To observe fish in deeper water, you should learn to use scuba equipment. The equipment is relatively expensive, but once you have purchased or rented it, your main expense, other than travel and money paid to charter-boat operators, is the air you must put into the tanks before each dive. Basic diving instruction is widely available in North America and offered year-round—in swimming pools if necessary.

Also, many tour operators and even resorts specialize in snorkeling and scuba trips. Some of the best places in North America to snorkel and dive are off Florida's Atlantic Coast, including the Florida Keys; Los Angeles and San Diego, California; Alaska (in wet suits or dry suits); and British Columbia, where you can observe octopuses among the rocks in waters off Vancouver Island.

Ferries and Excursion Boats

While not as exciting or personal as sea kayaking or canoeing, the hundreds of ferries and excursion boats that ply the lakes, large

Gray whale

rivers, and coastal waters of North America present some excellent opportunities for observing wildlife.

My first sighting of an orca whale was from the deck of a ferry-boat in Washington's Puget Sound, and during the past twenty years that I have lived in the Pacific Northwest, I have made many other memorable wildlife sightings from ferries, including harlequin ducks, and even Dall's porpoises swimming in the bow wave of the boat that goes between Port Angeles, Washington, and Victoria, British Columbia. Last summer, on a short ferry ride in the Back Bay area of Virginia, we came so close to nesting ospreys we could almost reach out and touch them.

I have not had the occasion to ride the Alaska ferry between Bellingham, Washington, and Juneau, Alaska, but I understand the wildlife viewing can be spectacular.

Whenever you have occasion to ride a ferry, take an excursion boat, or engage in some of the other activities mentioned in this chapter, carry a pair of binoculars and a couple of field guides. You never know what you might see.

9

Safety and Ethics of
Wildlife Viewing

Viewing wildlife in its natural habitat carries responsibilities to wildlife, yourself, other recreationists, and the landowners and land managers who are responsible for wildlife habitat. Below, I have summarized some basic things you should remember and heed while you are out looking for and watching wildlife. Some of these things were already covered earlier, but they are important enough to bear repeating:

⇥ *Come prepared.* Wear or pack clothing appropriate for the conditions you anticipate, and pack extra clothing for unexpected contingencies. Weather might change while you are in the field, or you might get lost and have to spend the night outdoors. Always pack water, some food, a flashlight, maps, and a compass, especially if you are entering a new area.

If you are canoeing or kayaking, make sure you have proper flotation devices in the boat. Take care of yourself in the field. Don't get chilled or overheated by the sun. Use insect repellent and sunblock when appropriate. Check yourself for ticks periodically if you are hiking in woods. If you are driving into remote areas, make sure your automobile has enough fuel. Take precautions so your health and safety don't become someone else's problem.

❧ *Leave your pets at home.* Pets and wildlife do not mix. If you must take your dog, keep it leashed at all times and clean up its droppings—remember, you might be the next one to come down the trail. Most unleashed dogs cannot resist chasing or otherwise harassing wildlife. Even leashed pets will make unnecessary noises and reduce your ability to blend into the environment and see interesting wildlife.

❧ *Keep your distance from wildlife.* It is all right to move quietly in the direction of wildlife or even to stalk wildlife for a short while. But when the animals begin to show signs of alarm or stress, stop or move away. Try not to get so close that you make wildlife run or fly away. Animals that are startled and forced to flee may use up critical energy reserves, abandon their young, or dart into traffic. They also become more vulnerable to predators when frightened and distracted.

Signs of distress in animals include aggressive behavior, alarm calls, skittish movements, or in the case of birds, circling repeatedly or diving. Never approach animals during breeding season or when they are with young. Even normally shy animals like opossums might be aggressive if they feel threatened or cornered. Some wildlife species are always dangerous for humans and should be given wide berth, including venomous snakes, alligators, cougars, bears, bison, and moose.

The chances of meeting a bear or cougar on the trail are slim, but if you should run into one, try to stay calm, talk softly, and slowly back away from the animal until you are safely out of its space. Give any large animal plenty of room to escape from you. Never turn your back and never run—you cannot outrun a bear or cougar, and running might stimulate the animal to chase and attack you. If you are with small children, pick them up so they won't panic and run. If you know you are in bear country, check with the local land-managing agency to get more detailed information on basic bear safety precautions.

❧ *Don't feed or touch wildlife.* It is never a good idea to feed wild animals, unless you are using acceptable backyard feeders (see

Chapter 7). Animals that are fed by hand lose their natural fear of humans. This can lead to many unpleasant results, usually at the expense of the wildlife. For example, in the late 1970s and early 1980s, Yellowstone National Park officials, in an effort to prevent confrontations between humans and bears, were forced to kill many grizzlies that had grown accustomed to eating garbage and handouts.

Most snack foods are not good for wildlife, and giving animals handouts can keep them from eating nutritious foods that are part of their natural diet. Habituated animals might even begin to eat paper and other litter, which can damage their digestive tracts. Deer at Lassen Volcanic National Park in California were hand-fed cigarettes and became addicted to tobacco. Dolphins and other marine animals fed by people may become less wary around humans, resulting in injuries from boat propellers or snagging by fishing hooks.

Touching wildlife is also a bad idea. Many small animals, such as squirrels, chipmunks, and raccoons, may bite when startled, and they sometimes carry diseases such as plague and rabies. Even road-killed animals can harbor parasites and disease and should never be handled without gloves.

✒ *Never pick up or move baby animals.* You should never pick up or move young birds or other wildlife, even if they appear abandoned or orphaned. The parents are probably close by, gathering food or watching from the shadows. If you are concerned about the welfare of a young animal—a fawn by the road or a seal pup on the beach, for instance—you should report the location to the site manager or your local wildlife agency.

✒ *Respect the rights of other people to enjoy their recreation.* If you come across other wildlife watchers, sport fishers, or hunters in the field, try not to do anything that would ruin or diminish their experience. Keep conversation quiet and try not to make unnecessary noise. If you are passing near wildlife being watched, move slowly so you do not frighten it away. If a particular blind or wildlife-viewing site is being used, wait your turn or come back later. Remember, your roles might be reversed next time.

Elk

❧ *Respect the rights of private landowners.* It is almost always illegal to enter private property without permission. Always obey posted signs. When you ask permission from a landowner or manager, inquire about any special rules you should obey. Stay clear of livestock, and leave fences and gates the way you found them, unless the landowner tells you otherwise.

❧ *Leave wildlife habitat in better shape than you found it.* Respect private and public land as you would your own. Pick up litter, even if it was left by someone else. Bury or carry out your own waste. Repair or report acts of vandalism. Teach others, especially children, how to respect the outdoors.

10

Getting Involved in Wildlife Conservation

North America's wildlife resources are among the richest in the world, and in many cases they are available for our prudent use and enjoyment. But these resources will not continue to be available for future generations unless active steps are taken now to ensure their survival. Wildlife exists only where there is adequate and suitable habitat, and many of our most productive habitats are being steadily altered or eliminated by development activities, ranging from the filling and paving of wetlands for roads and industrial parks to the systematic clear-cut logging of mature coniferous forests on our public lands.

We do not have to choose between economic growth and wildlife protection. We can have both. We can protect critical wildlife habitat and still develop suitable land for homes, businesses, and transportation systems. As a society, we can make intelligent choices about where and how development will be accommodated to cause the least amount of adverse impact on wildlife and other environmental resources. As individuals, we can also get directly involved by supporting public and private efforts to conserve wildlife and wildlife habitat for future generations. Below are some ways you can get involved in wildlife conservation.

Join a Wildlife Conservation Organization

There are a number of organizations in the United States and Canada that do an excellent job of educating the public and decision-makers about wildlife conservation. By collecting donations and membership dues, these groups get the funding they need to stay involved in efforts to identify and conserve our most critical wildlife and wildlife habitat. The following organizations are some of the most effective and worthy of public support. Donations to these groups, other wildlife organizations, or federal, state, and provincial wildlife agencies are usually tax-deductible.

National Wildlife Federation

The National Wildlife Federation (NWF) is the largest wildlife conservation and advocacy group in North America. The National Wildlife Federation, working with the Canadian Wildlife Federation (CWF) and state and provincial local affiliate organizations, accomplishes its conservation and educational goals in many ways, including sponsorship of this book, publication of *National Wildlife, International Wildlife, Ranger Rick,* and *Your Big Backyard* magazines, as well as development of new television programming.

The NWF and its affiliates also contribute directly to many important wildlife research, conservation, and educational efforts all over North America. Nature Quest is an outdoor education program aimed at educators, naturalists, and youth leaders. NatureLink, one of NWF's newest programs, works with affiliate organizations to sponsor three-day educational weekends in the outdoors for inner-city children and their families.

The goals of the affiliate groups mirror those of the national organization but focus more on local and regional issues. The Washington Wildlife Federation, for instance, works to protect habitat for wild populations of Pacific salmon. In a similar way, the Minnesota Conservation Federation puts a strong emphasis on reducing pollution in Lake Superior and its tributary rivers. Appendix 2 includes addresses and phone numbers for the NWF and the CWF. NWF regional offices and the Canadian Wildlife Federation can also put you in touch with their affiliate state and provincial organizations.

National Audubon Society

The National Audubon Society (NAS) works to conserve wildlife and educate the public about the needs of wildlife through its publications, travel programs, and system of nature sanctuaries. In my opinion, the National Audubon Society's greatest strength is its network of 515 local chapters, all over the United States, which not only work on local conservation issues but also sponsor field trips, fund-raising birdathons, winter bird counts, and other functions that get their members out in the field to observe and monitor birds and other wildlife. The NAS is closely affiliated with the Canadian Nature Federation, which has 145 affiliated groups across Canada. Addresses and phone numbers for the National Audubon Society and its nine regional offices, as well as the Canadian Nature Federation, are listed in Appendix 2.

Defenders of Wildlife

Defenders of Wildlife is a relatively small but effective wildlife advocacy group that focuses on protecting and restoring native wildlife species, habitats, and biological diversity. Defenders is also a lead sponsoring organization of the National Watchable Wildlife Program and the Watchable Wildlife Series of state-by-state viewing guides, published by Falcon Press. The address and phone number for Defenders of Wildlife's national office are included in Appendix 2.

Donate Land or Money
for Wildlife Habitat Protection

The surest way to permanently protect important wildlife habitat is by acquiring it outright or acquiring a conservation easement, a legal document which guarantees protection of the wildlife habitat, while allowing the landowner to use his/her land in ways that are compatible with habitat protection. Federal, state, and provincial agencies own and manage millions of acres of important habitat in North America, but they cannot do the job of habitat protection alone. In the United States and Canada, three organizations—actually two organizations and a system of local land trusts—do a superb job, in my opinion, of identifying habitat that is threatened or critical for wildlife and then acquiring the land or some interest in the land, such as a conservation easement.

These organizations—the Nature Conservancy, Ducks Unlimited, Inc., and local land trusts—all accept donations of land that fit their definition of critical habitat. They also use cash donations to purchase other critical lands. The National Wildlife Federation also accepts land donations for conservation through its Land Gifts Program (800-332-4949).

The Nature Conservancy

The Nature Conservancy and the Nature Conservancy of Canada are nonprofit organizations committed to the protection of biological diversity through the acquisition and protection of ecologically significant lands throughout North America. The Nature Conservancy works closely with educational institutions, industry, wildlife agencies, and other conservation groups to identify and protect ecologically significant areas. The conservancy also owns and manages a large system of nature sanctuaries, many of which are open to the public.

Addresses and phone numbers for the Nature Conservancy and the Nature Conservancy of Canada are listed in Appendix 2.

Ducks Unlimited, Inc.

Ducks Unlimited and Ducks Unlimited, Canada, put their primary emphasis on the direct protection, restoration, and enhancement of wetlands and adjacent upland habitat, primarily for waterfowl and associated wildlife. Working through regional offices and local chapters, Ducks Unlimited sponsors and participates in projects that show direct habitat results on the ground, not just for ducks and geese but for other wetland-dependent wildlife, including shore-birds, many neotropical migrant songbirds, even juvenile fish. Ducks Unlimited participates in many habitat acquisition projects. The organization also restores and enhances wetland wildlife habitat all across North America. Addresses and phone numbers for Ducks Unlimited are provided in Appendix 2.

Local Land Trusts

The local land-trust movement is one of the most exciting and fastest-growing efforts in North America for protecting and man-aging important wildlife habitat and other critical lands. Land trusts are nonprofit organizations set up within a local community—or sometimes within a state or regional area—to protect lands that are particularly important to that local community. Most land trusts are operated by volunteer board members, although some of the larger trusts have professional staff. Most land trusts acquire conservation lands, either in fee-title or as permanent conservation easements, from local residents who want to make sure their land will always be kept as open space. Some land trusts also use donated funds to pur-chase land or easements that they think are important. You might have a local land trust in your community. If not, you might want to organize one. The primary national organization that assists with the organization of local land trusts is the Land Trust Alliance. Their address and phone number in Washington, D.C., is listed in Appendix 2.

Support Federal, State, and
Provincial Wildlife Programs

Federal, state, and provincial wildlife agencies protect and manage millions of acres of important wildlife habitat in North America. These agencies are supported by the public through taxes and through collection of hunting and fishing license fees, but they often need additional help, especially for habitat protection and nongame programs aimed at protecting wildlife species that are neither hunted nor fished. There are a number of ways the public can directly help support these wildlife programs:

Donate your time. Most wildlife agencies have active volunteer programs and are always looking for people to help out with projects ranging from staffing informational booths at a fair to planting trees or mending fences at a wildlife-management area. If you have time to volunteer, contact one of the wildlife agencies listed in Appendix 2.

Buy a hunting license and/or a waterfowl conservation stamp. Even if you do not hunt, your dollars will be used to protect, enhance, and manage habitat for all wildlife species. Some states and provinces also have special programs to generate revenue for nongame wildlife programs. In Washington State, the nongame, or wildlife diversity, program is funded by the sale of personalized license plates. Other states allow you to allocate a portion of your state income-tax refund for nongame wildlife.

Leave an endowment of land or money in your will. Most wildlife agencies—as well as all of the conservation groups listed above—eagerly accept tax-exempt donations from individuals, businesses, and estates.

Appendix 1

Public Land Management Agencies

Federal Public Lands

National Parks

Alaska Region National Park
Service
2525 Gambell Street
Anchorage, AK 99503-2892
(907) 271-2737

Mid-Atlantic Region National
Park Service
143 South Third Street
Philadelphia, PA 19106-2818
(215) 597-7018

Midwest Region National Park
Service
1709 Jackson Street
Omaha, NE 68102-2571
(402) 221-3471

North Atlantic Region National
Park Service
15 State Street
Boston, MA 02109-3572
(617) 223-5199

Pacific Northwest Region
National Park Service
915 Second Avenue
Seattle, WA 98104
(206) 220-7450

Rocky Mountain Region
National Park Service
P.O. Box 25287
Denver, CO 80225-0287
(303) 969-2000

Southeast Region National Park
Service
75 Spring Street SW
Atlanta, GA 30303-3378
(404) 331-5187

Southwest Region National Park
Service
P.O. Box 728
Santa Fe, NM 87504-0728
(505) 988-6012

Western Region National Park
Service
600 Harrison Street, Suite 600
San Francisco, CA 94107-1372
(415) 556-0560

National Wildlife Refuges

U.S. Fish and Wildlife Service

Alaska Regional Office
1011 East Tudor Road
Anchorage, AK 99503
(907) 786-3545

Great Lakes–Big Rivers Regional
Office (IA, IL, IN, MI, MN,
MO, OH, WI)
Federal Building
1 Federal Drive
Fort Snelling, MN 55111
(612) 725-3507

Mountain-Prairie Regional
Office (CO, KS, MT, ND,
NE, SD, UT, WY)
Denver Federal Center
134 Union Boulevard
P.O. Box 25486
Denver, CO 80225
(303) 236-8145

Northeast Regional Office (CT,
DC, DE, MA, MD, ME, NH,
NJ, NY, PA, RI, VA, VT,
WV)
300 Westgate Center Drive
Hadley, MA 01035
(413) 253-8200

Pacific Regional Office (CA, HI,
and Pacific Islands, ID, NV,
OR, WA)
Eastside Federal Complex
911 NE Eleventh Avenue
Portland, OR 97232-4181
(503) 231-6214

Southeast Regional Office (AL,
AR, FL, GA, KY, LA, MS,
NC, PR, SC, TN, VI)
1875 Century Boulevard
Atlanta, GA 30345
(404) 679-7152

Southwest Regional Office (AZ,
NM, OK, TX)
500 Gold Avenue SW, Room
3018
Albuquerque, NM 87102
(505) 766-1829

Bureau of Land Management

Alaska State Office
222 West Seventh Avenue, #13
Anchorage, AK 99513-7599
(907) 271-5076

Arizona State Office
3707 North Seventh Street
P.O. Box 16563
Phoenix, AZ 85011
(602) 417-9503

California State Office
2135 Butano Drive
Sacramento, CA 95825
(916) 979-2800

Colorado State Office
2850 Youngfield Street
Lakewood, CO 80215
(303) 239-3701

Eastern States Regional Office
7450 Boston Boulevard
Springfield, VA 22153
(703) 440-1700

Idaho State Office
3380 Americana Terrace
Boise, ID 83706
(208) 384-3001

Montana State Office
222 North Thirty-second Street
P.O. Box 36800
Billings, MT 59107
(406) 255-2904

Nevada State Office
850 Harvard Way
P.O. Box 12000
Reno, NV 89520
(702) 785-6590

New Mexico State Office
1474 Rodeo Drive
P.O. Box 27115
Santa Fe, NM 87502-0115
(505) 438-7501

Oregon State Office
1515 SW Fifth Avenue
P.O. Box 2965
Portland, OR 97208
(503) 952-6001

Utah State Office
324 South State Street
P.O. Box 45155
Salt Lake City, UT 84145-0155
(801) 539-4010

Wyoming State Office
2515 Warren Avenue
P.O. Box 1828
Cheyenne, WY 82003
(307) 775-6001

National Forests

Alaska Region
Federal Building
709 West Ninth Street
P.O. Box 21628
Juneau, AK 99802
(907) 586-8863

Eastern Region
310 West Wisconsin Avenue,
  Room 500
Milwaukee, WI 53203
(414) 297-3693

Intermountain Region
Federal Building
324 Twenty-fifth Street
Ogden, UT 84401
(801) 625-5354

Northern Region
Federal Building
200 East Broadway
P.O. Box 7669
Missoula, MT 59807
(406) 329-3511

Pacific Northwest Region
333 SW First Street
P.O. Box 3623
Portland, OR 97208
(503) 326-2971

Pacific Southwest Region
630 Sansome Street
San Francisco, CA 94111
(415) 705-2870

Appendix 1

Rocky Mountain Region
11177 West Eighth Avenue
P.O. Box 25127
Lakewood, CO 80225
(303) 236-9431

Southern Region
1720 Peachtree Road NW
Atlanta, GA 30367
(404) 347-4191

Southwestern Region
Federal Building
517 Gold Avenue SW
Albuquerque, NM 87102
(505) 842-3292

Parks Canada

Alberta Region
220 Fourth Avenue SE,
   Room 552
Calgary, AB T2P 3H8, Canada
(403) 292-4401

Atlantic Region Historic
   Properties
1869 Upper Water Street
Halifax, NS B3J 1S9, Canada
(902) 426-3436

National Capital Region
Publications Unit,
Communications Branch
25 Eddy Street, Room 10H2
Hull, PQ K1A 0M5, Canada
(819) 994-6625

Ontario Region
500–516 Yonge Street
North York, ON M2N 6L9,
   Canada
(416) 954-9243; (800) 839-8221

Pacific and Yukon Region
300 West Georgia Street
Vancouver, BC V6B 6C6,
   Canada
(604) 666-0176

Prairies and Northwest
   Territories Region
45 Forks Market Road
Winnipeg, Man. R3C 4T6,
   Canada
(204) 983-2290

Quebec Region
3 Buade Street
Haute-Ville
P.O. Box 6060
Quebec, PQ G1R 4V7, Canada
(418) 648-4177; (800) 463-6769
and
Guy-Favreau Complex
200 René-Lévesque Boulevard
   West
West Tower, Sixth Floor
Montreal, PQ H2Z 1X4, Canada
(514) 283-2332; (800) 463-6769

Canadian Wildlife Service

British Columbia and the Yukon:

Canadian Wildlife Service,
  Environment Canada
P.O. Box 340
Delta, BC V4K 3Y3, Canada
(604) 940-4700

*Manitoba, Saskatchewan, Alberta,
and the Northwest Territories:*

Canadian Wildlife Service,
  Environment Canada
4999 Ninety-eighth Avenue,
  Second Floor
Edmonton, AB T6B 2X3,
  Canada
(403) 468-8919

*Nova Scotia, New Brunswick,
Newfoundland, and
Prince Edward Island:*

Canadian Wildlife Service,
  Environment Canada
P.O. Box 1590
Sackville, NB E0A 3C0, Canada
(506) 364-5044

Ontario:

Canadian Wildlife Service,
  Environment Canada
49 Camelot Drive
Nepean, ON K1A 0H3, Canada
(613) 952-2403

Quebec:

Canadian Wildlife Service,
  Environment Canada
1141 Route de l'Eglise C.P.
  10 100
Sainte-Foy, PQ G1V 4H5,
  Canada
(418) 648-7225

State and Provincial Lands

Alabama

Department of Conservation and
  Natural Resources
Division of State Parks &
  Division of Game and Fish
64 North Union Street
Montgomery, AL 36130
(205) 242-3486

Alaska

Department of Fish and Game
P.O. Box 25526
Juneau, AK 99802
(907) 465-4100

Division of Parks and Outdoor
  Recreation
P.O. Box 107001
Anchorage, AK 99510-7001
(907) 762-2600

Arizona

Game and Fish Department,
    Wildlife Management Division
2221 West Greenway Road
Phoenix, AZ 85023-4312
(602) 942-3000

Arizona State Parks Board
1300 West Washington Avenue
Phoenix, AZ 85007
(602) 542-4172

Arkansas

Department of Parks and
    Tourism
One Capitol Mall
Little Rock, AR 72201
(501) 682-7777

Game and Fish Commission
2 Natural Resources Drive
Little Rock, AR 72205
(501) 223-6300

California

Department of Fish and Game
1416 Ninth Street
Sacramento, CA 95814
(916) 653-7664

Department of Parks and
    Recreation
1416 Ninth Street
P.O. Box 942896
Sacramento, CA 94296-0001
(916) 653-8380

Colorado

Department of Natural Resources
Division of Parks and Outdoor
    Recreation
1313 Sherman Street, Room 618
Denver, CO 80203
(303) 866-3437

Department of Natural Resources
Division of Wildlife
6060 Broadway
Denver, CO 80216
(303) 297-1192

Connecticut

Department of Environmental
    Protection
79 Elm Street
Hartford, CT 06106-5127
Wildlife Division (860) 424-3011
State Parks Division
(860) 424-3200

Delaware

Department of Natural Resources
    and Environmental Control
89 Kings Highway
P.O. Box 1401
Dover, DE 19903
Division of Fish and Wildlife
(302) 739-5295
Division of Parks and Recreation
(302) 739-4401

Florida

Department of Environmental
  Protection
Recreation and Parks
3900 Commonwealth Boulevard
Tallahassee, FL 32399-3000
(904) 488-6131

Game and Fresh Water Fish
  Commission
Division of Wildlife
620 South Meridian Street
Tallahassee, FL 32399-1600
(904) 488-1960

Georgia

Department of Natural Resources
Wildlife Resources Division
2070 U.S. Highway 278, SE
Social Circle, GA 30279
(404) 918-6401
Parks, Recreation, and Historic
  Sites Division (404) 656-2770

Hawaii

Department of Land and Natural
  Resources
Division of Forestry and Wildlife
1151 Punchbowl Street
Honolulu, HI 96813
(808) 587-0166

Department of Land and Natural
  Resources
Division of State Parks
P.O. Box 621
Honolulu, HI 96809
(808) 587-0300

Idaho

Fish and Game Department
600 South Walnut
P.O. Box 25
Boise, ID 83707
(208) 334-3700

State Parks and Recreation
P.O. Box 83720
Boise, ID 83720-0065
(208) 334-4199

Indiana

Indiana Department of Natural
  Resources
Division of Fish and Wildlife &
  Division of State Parks
402 West Washington Street,
  Room W255B
Indianapolis, IN 46204-2748
(317) 232-4200

Iowa

Department of Natural Resources
Fish and Wildlife Division &
  Parks, Recreation, and
  Preserves Division
Wallace Building, East Ninth and
  Grand Avenue
Des Moines, IA 50319-0034
(515) 281-5145

Kansas

Department of Wildlife and Parks
900 SW Jackson Street, Suite 502
Topeka, KS 66612-1233
(913) 296-2281

Kentucky

Department of Fish and Wildlife
   Resources
One Game Farm Road
Frankfort, KY 40601
(502) 564-3400

Department of Parks
Capitol Plaza Tower,
   Tenth Floor
Frankfort, KY 40601
(502) 564-2172

Louisiana

Department of Wildlife and
   Fisheries
P.O. Box 98000
Baton Rouge, LA 70898-9000
(504) 765-2800

Office of State Parks
Department of Culture,
   Recreation, and Tourism
P.O. Box 44426
Baton Rouge, LA 70804
(504) 342-8111

Maine

Department of Conservation
Bureau of Parks and Recreation
State House Station 22
Augusta, ME 04333
(207) 287-3821

Department of Inland Fisheries
   and Wildlife
284 State Street, Station 41
Augusta, ME 04333
(207) 287-2766

Maryland

Department of Natural Resources
State Forest and Park Service &
   Fish, Heritage, and Wildlife
   Administration
Tawes State Office Building
580 Taylor Avenue
Annapolis, MD 21401
(410) 974-3987

Massachusetts

Department of Environmental
   Management
Division of Forests and Parks
100 Cambridge Street, Room
   1905
Boston, MA 02202
(617) 727-3163

Division of Fisheries and Wildlife
100 Cambridge Street, Room
   1901
Boston, MA 02202
(617) 727-3155

Michigan

Department of Natural Resources
Wildlife and Parks and
   Recreation
P.O. Box 30028
Lansing, MI 48909
(517) 335-4623

Minnesota

Department of Natural Resources
Division of Parks and Recreation
    & Division of Fish and
    Wildlife
500 Lafayette Road
St. Paul, MN 55155-4001
(612) 296-6157

Mississippi

Department of Wildlife, Fisheries,
    and Parks
2906 North State Street
P.O. Box 451
Jackson, MS 39205
(601) 362-9212

Missouri

Department of Conservation
Wildlife Division
P.O. Box 180
Jefferson City, MO 65102-0180
(314) 751-4115

Department of Natural Resources
Division of Parks and Recreation
P.O. Box 176
Jefferson City, MO 65102
(314) 751-3443

Montana

Department of Fish, Wildlife, and
    Parks
1420 East Sixth
P.O. Box 20071
Helena, MT 59620
(406) 444-2535

Nebraska

Game and Parks Commission
Wildlife and State Parks
2200 North Thirty-third Street
P.O. Box 30370
Lincoln, NE 68503-0370
(402) 471-0641

Nevada

Department of Conservation and
    Natural Resources
Division of State Parks &
    Division of Wildlife
Capitol Complex
123 West Nye Lane
Carson City, NV 89710
(702) 687-4360

New Hampshire

Department of Resources and
    Economic Development
Division of Parks
172 Pembroke Road
P.O. Box 1856
Concord, NH 03302-1856
(603) 271-3254

Fish and Game Department
Wildlife Division
2 Hazen Drive
Concord, NH 03301
(603) 271-3422

New Jersey

Department of Environmental
    Protection
Division of Fish, Game, and
    Wildlife
401 East State Street, CN 400
Trenton, NJ 08625-0400
(609) 292-2965

Department of Environmental
    Protection
Division of Parks and Forestry
401 East State Street, CN 404
Trenton, NJ 08625-0404
(609) 292-2733

New Mexico

State Parks and Recreation
    Division
P.O. Box 1147
Santa Fe, NM 87504-1147
(505) 827-7173

Department of Game and Fish
Division of Wildlife
P.O. Box 25112
Santa Fe, NM 87504
(505) 827-7911

New York

Department of Environmental
    Conservation
Division of Fish and Wildlife
50 Wolf Road
Albany, NY 12233
(518) 457-5690

New York State Office of Parks,
    Recreation, and Historic
    Preservation
The Governor Nelson A.
    Rockefeller Empire State Plaza
    Agency, Building 1
Albany, NY 12238
(518) 474-0456

North Carolina

Department of Natural Resources
State Parks and Recreation &
    Wildlife Resources
    Commission
P.O. Box 27687
Raleigh, NC 27611
(919) 733-4984

North Dakota

Parks and Recreation
    Department
1835 Bismarck Expressway
Bismarck, ND 58504
(701) 221-5357

State Game and Fish Department
100 North Bismarck Expressway
Bismarck, ND 58501
(701) 221-6300

Ohio

Department of Natural Resources
Division of Parks and Recreation
    & Division of Wildlife
Fountain Square
Columbus, OH 43224
(614) 265-6565

Oklahoma

Department of Wildlife
   Conservation
1801 North Lincoln
P.O. Box 53465
Oklahoma City, OK 73152
(405) 521-3851

Tourism and Recreation
   Department
2401 North Lincoln, Suite 500
Oklahoma City, OK 73105-4492
(405) 521-2409

Oregon

Department of Fish and Wildlife
2501 SW First Avenue
Portland, OR 97201
(503) 229-5410

Parks and Recreation
   Department
1115 Commercial Street NE
Salem, OR 97310-1001
(503) 378-6305

Pennsylvania

Department of Environmental
   Resources
Bureau of State Parks
Public Liaison Office, Sixteenth
   Floor, MSSOB
P.O. Box 2063
Harrisburg, PA 17105-2063
(717) 783-2300

Game Commission, Bureau of
   Wildlife Management
2001 Elmerton Avenue
Harrisburg, PA 17110-9797
(717) 787-4250

Puerto Rico

Comite Despertar Cidreno
   Wildlife
P.O. Box 123
Cidra, PR 00739
(809) 739-5492

Department of Natural and
   Environmental Resources
P.O. Box 5887
Puerta de Tierra Station
San Juan, PR 00906
(809) 724-8774

Rhode Island

Department of Environmental
   Management
Fish, Wildlife, and Estuarine
   Resources
Stedman Government Center
Wakefield, RI 02879
(401) 227-2774

Department of Environmental
   Management
Parks and Recreation
2321 Hartford Avenue
Johnston, RI 02919
(401) 227-2774

South Carolina

Department of Natural Resources
Division of Wildlife
Rembert C. Dennis Building
P.O. Box 167
Columbia, SC 29202
(803) 734-3888

Department of Parks, Recreation,
    and Tourism
Edgar A. Brown Building
1205 Pendleton Street
Columbia, SC 29201
(803) 734-0122

South Dakota

Game, Fish, and Parks
    Department
Division of Parks and Recreation
    & Division of Wildlife
523 East Capitol
Pierre, SD 57501-3182
(605) 773-3387

Tennessee

Department of Environment and
    Conservation, State Parks
401 Church Street
Nashville, TN 37243
(615) 532-0109

Wildlife Resources Agency
Wildlife Management Division
Ellington Agricultural Center
P.O. Box 40747
Nashville, TN 37204
(615) 781-6500

Texas

Parks and Wildlife Department
4200 Smith School Road
Austin, TX 78744
(512) 389-4800

Utah

Department of Natural Resources
Division of Wildlife Resources
1594W North Temple
Salt Lake City, UT 84114
(801) 538-4700

Division of Parks and Recreation
1594W North Temple,
    Suite 116
Salt Lake City, UT 84114
(801) 538-7220

Vermont

Agency of Natural Resources
Department of Forests, Parks, and
    Recreation
Waterbury Complex
103 South Main, Bldg. 10 South
Waterbury, VT 05671
(802) 241-3670

Department of Fish and Wildlife
103 South Main, Bldg. 10 South
Waterbury, VT 05671
(802) 241-3700

Virgin Islands

Department of Planning and
 Natural Resources
Division of Fish and Wildlife
Suite 231, Nisky Center
St. Thomas, VI 00803
(809) 774-3320

Virginia

Department of Conservation and
 Recreation
Division of State Parks
203 Governor Street, Suite 306
Richmond, VA 23219
(804) 786-2132

Department of Game and Inland
 Fisheries
Fish and Wildlife Management
4010 West Broad Street
P.O. Box 11104
Richmond, VA 23230
(804) 367-1000

Washington

Department of Fish and Wildlife
Wildlife Management Program
600 Capitol Way North
Olympia, WA 98501
(360) 902-2200

State Parks and Recreation
 Commission
7150 Cleanwater Lane, KY-11
Olympia, WA 98504-5711
(360) 753-5757

West Virginia

Division of Natural Resources
Wildlife Resources
1900 Kanawha Boulevard
East Charleston, WV 25305
(304) 558-2754

Tourism Department,
 Division of Parks
Capitol Complex, Building 6,
 Room 451-B
Charleston, WV 35305-0662
(800) 225-5982

Wisconsin

Department of Natural Resources
Bureau of Wildlife Management
 & Bureau of Parks and
 Recreation
P.O. Box 7921
Madison, WI 53707
(608) 266-2621

Wyoming

Game and Fish Department
Wildlife Division
5400 Bishop Boulevard
Cheyenne, WY 82006
(307) 777-4600

State Parks and Historic Sites
2301 Central Avenue, Barrett
 Building
Cheyenne, WY 82002
(307) 777-6323

Alberta

Department of Environmental
  Protection
Natural Resources Services
Main Floor, North Tower,
  Petroleum Plaza
9945 108th Street
Edmonton, AB T5K 2G6,
  Canada
(403) 427-6749
Park Services (403) 427-2924

British Columbia

Ministry of Environment
Parks Department
810 Blanshard Street, Fourth
  Floor
Victoria, BC V8V 1X4, Canada
(604) 387-5002

Wildlife Branch
780 Blanshard Street
Victoria, BC V8V 1X4, Canada
(604) 387-9731

Manitoba

Natural Resources Services
Box 24
1495 Saint James Street
Winnipeg, Man. R3H 0W9,
  Canada
(204) 945-7761

Parks and Natural Areas
Box 50
1495 Saint James Street
Winnipeg, Man. R3H 0W9,
  Canada
(204) 945-4362

New Brunswick

Department of Natural Resources
  and Energy
Fish and Wildlife Branch
P.O. Box 6000
Fredericton, NB E3B 5H1,
  Canada
(506) 453-2440

Newfoundland

Wildlife Division
Building 810, Pleasantville
P.O. Box 8700
St. John's, NF A1B 4J6, Canada
(709) 729-2542

Northwest Territories

Department of Economic
  Development and Tourism
Government of the Northwest
  Territories
Parks and Visitor Services
Box 1320
Yellowknife, NT X1A 2L9,
  Canada
(403) 873-7902

Department of Renewable
  Resources
Government of the Northwest
  Territories
Wildlife Management
Scotia Centre Box 21 600
5102 Fiftieth Avenue
Yellowknife, NT X1A 3S8,
  Canada
(403) 873-7411

Nova Scotia

Natural Resources Services
136 Exhibition Street
Kentville, NS B4N 4E5, Canada
(902) 679-6091

Department of Natural
    Resources: Parks and
    Recreation
R.R. #1, Belmont
Colchester County, NS
    B0M 1C0, Canada
(902) 662-3030

Ontario

Ministry of Natural Resources
Room M-1-73, MacDonald
    Block
900 Bay Street
Toronto, ON M7A 2C1,
    Canada
(416) 314-2000

Prince Edward Island

Department of Environmental
    Resources
Fish and Wildlife Division
P.O. Box 2000
Charlottetown, PEI C1A 7N8,
    Canada
(902) 368-4684

Quebec

Department of Recreation,
    Fish, and Game
Place de la Capitale 150, Boul.
    René-Lévesque Est
Quebec, PQ G1R 4Y1, Canada
(418) 644-282
Recreation and Parks
(418) 644-9393

Saskatchewan

Environment and Resource
    Management
Parks and Facilities
3211 Albert Street
Regina, SK S4S 5W6, Canada
(306) 787-2846
Wildlife Branch (306) 787-2309

Yukon Territory

Department of Renewable
    Resources
Parks and Outdoor Recreation
P.O. Box 2703
Whitehorse, YT Y1A 2C6,
    Canada
(403) 667-5261
Fish and Wildlife (403) 667-5715

Appendix 2

Wildlife Conservation Organizations

National Wildlife Federation

National Headquarters

National Wildlife Federation
1400 Sixteenth Street NW
Washington, DC 20036-2266
(202) 797-6800

NWF Natural Resource Centers

Alaska Natural Resource
Center
750 West Second Avenue,
Suite 200
Anchorage, AK 99501
(907) 258-4800

Canadian Wildlife Federation
2740 Queensview Drive
Ottawa, ON K2B 1A2,
Canada
(613) 721-2286

Great Lakes Natural Resource
Center
506 East Liberty
Ann Arbor, MI 48104-2210
(313) 769-3351

Mid-Atlantic Office
1400 Sixteenth Street NW
Washington, DC 20036
(202) 797-6693

Northeast Natural Resource
Center
18 Baldwin Street
Montpelier, VT 05602
(802) 229-0650

Northern Rockies Natural
Resource Center
240 North Higgins
Missoula, MT 59802
(406) 721-6705

Prairie Wetlands Resource
  Center
1605 East Capitol Avenue
Bismarck, ND 58501
(701) 222-2442

Rocky Mountain Natural
  Resource Center
2260 Baseline Road, Suite 100
Boulder, CO 80302
(303) 786-8001

South Central Office
4505 Spicewood Springs,
  Suite 300
Austin, TX 78759
(512) 346-3934

Southeastern Natural Resource
  Center
1401 Peachtree Street NE,
  Suite 240
Atlanta, GA 30309
(404) 876-8733

Western Natural Resource
  Center
921 SW Morrison, Suite 512
Portland, OR 97205
(503) 222-1429

National Audubon Society

National Headquarters

National Audubon Society
700 Broadway
New York, NY 10003
(212) 979-3000

Regional Offices

Alaska-Hawaii Office
308 G Street, Suite 217
Anchorage, AK 99501
(907) 276-7034

Great Lakes Office
692 North High Street,
  Suite 208
Columbus, OH 43215
(614) 224-3303

Mid-Atlantic Office
1104 Fernwood Avenue,
  Suite 300
Camp Hill, PA 17011
(717) 763-4985

Northeast Office
1789 Western Avenue
Albany, NY 12203
(518) 869-9731

Rocky Mountain Office
4150 Darley, Suite 5
Boulder, CO 80303
(303) 499-0219

Southeast Office
102 East Fourth Avenue
Tallahassee, FL 32303
(904) 222-2473

Southwest Office
2525 Wallingwood, Suite 301
Austin, TX 78746
(512) 327-1943

West Central Office
200 Southwind Place,
    Suite 205
Manhattan, KS 66502
(913) 537-4385

Western Office
555 Audubon Place
Sacramento, CA 95825
(916) 481-5332

Defenders of Wildlife

National Headquarters

Defenders of Wildlife
1101 Fourteenth Street NW,
    Suite 1400
Washington, DC 20005
(202) 682-9400

West Coast Office

Defenders of Wildlife
1637 Laurel Street
Lake Oswego, OR 97201
(503) 697-3222

The Nature Conservancy

National Headquarters

The Nature Conservancy
1815 North Lynn Street
Arlington, VA 22209
(703) 841-5300

Regional Offices

California Region
201 Mission Street, Fourth
    Floor
San Francisco, CA 94105
(415) 777-0487

Eastern Region
201 Devonshire Street, Fifth
    Floor
Boston, MA 02110
(617) 542-1908

Florida Region
222 South Westmonte Drive,
    Suite 300
Altamonte Springs, FL 32714
(407) 682-3664

Midwest Region
1313 Fifth Street SE, Room
    314
Minneapolis, MN 55414
(612) 331-0700

The Nature Conservancy of
Canada
110 Eglinton Avenue West,
Suite 400
Toronto, ON M4R 2G5,
Canada
(416) 932-3202

New York Region
91 Broadway
Albany, NY 12204
(518) 463-6133

Pacific/Hawaii Region
1116 Smith Street, Suite 201
Honolulu, HI 96817
(808) 537-4508

Southeast Region
P.O. Box 2267
Chapel Hill, NC 27515-2267
(919) 967-5493

Western Region
2060 Broadway, Suite 230
Boulder, CO 80302
(303) 444-1060

Ducks Unlimited, Inc.

National Headquarters

Ducks Unlimited, Inc.
One Waterfowl Way
Memphis, TN 38120-2351
(901) 758-3825

Regional Offices

Ducks Unlimited, Canada
P.O. Box 1160
Stonewall, Man. R0C 2Z0,
Canada
(204) 467-3000

Great Plains Region
3502 Franklin Avenue
Bismarck, ND 58501
(701) 258-5599

Southern Region
193 Business Park Drive,
Suite E
Jackson, MS 39213
(601) 956-1936

Western Region
3074 Gold Canal Drive
Rancho Cordova, CA
95670-6116
(916) 852-2000

The Land Trust Alliance

The Land Trust Alliance
1319 F Street NW, Suite 501
Washington, DC 20004
(202) 638-4725

Appendix 3

Ecotours

Abercrombie and Kent and
  Society Expeditions
1520 Kensington Road,
  Suite 212
Oak Brook, IL 60521
(800) 323-7308

American Museum of Natural
  History
Discovery Tours
Central Park West at Seventy-
  ninth Street
New York, NY 10024
(800) 462-8687

Cornell Adult University
626 Thurston Avenue
Ithaca, NY 14850
(607) 255-6260

Cross Cultural Adventures
P.O. Box 3285
Arlington, VA 22203
(703) 204-2717

Earthwatch
60 Mt. Auburn Street
P.O. Box 403-N
Watertown, MA 02272
(617) 926-8200

Ecotour Expeditions
39 Mt. Pleasant Street, Suite 2
P.O. Box 1066
Cambridge, MA 02238
(800) 688-1822

Foundation for Field Research
P.O. Box 2010
Alpine, CA 91903
(619) 445-9264

International Expeditions
One Environs Park
Helena, AL 35080
(800) 633-4734

International Fund for Animal
  Welfare
Natural Habitat Wildlife
  Adventures
One Sussex Station
Sussex, NJ 07461
(800) 543-8917

Journeys International
4011 Jackson Road
Ann Arbor, MI 48103
(800) 255-8735

Mountain Travel-Sobek
6420 Fairmount Avenue
El Cerrito, CA 94530
(800) 227-2384

National Audubon Society
700 Broadway
New York, NY 10003
(212) 979-3000

National Wildlife Federation
NWF Expeditions
1400 Sixteenth Street NW
Washington, DC 20036
(800) 606-9563

Nature Expeditions
    International
474 Willamette
P.O. Box 11496
Eugene, OR 97440
(800) 869-0639

Oceanic Society Expeditions
Ft. Mason Center, Building E
San Francisco, CA 94123
(800) 326-7491

Questers Tours and Travel
257 Park Avenue South
New York, NY 10010
(800) 468-8668

Salen Linbald Cruising
333 Ludlow Street
P.O. Box 120076
Stamford, CT 06912
(800) 223-5688

Sierra Club
Outings Department
85 Second Street
San Francisco, CA 94105
(415) 977-5522

Smithsonian Institution
National Associate Program
Study Tours and Seminars
1100 Jefferson Drive SW
Washington, DC 20560
(202) 357-4700

Victor Emanuel Nature Tours
P.O. Box 33008
Austin, TX 78764
(800) 328-8368

Wildland Journeys
3516 NE 155th Street
Seattle, WA 98155
(800) 345-4453

Wildlife Conservation
    International
217 East Eighty-fifth Street,
    Suite 200
New York, NY 10028
(212) 879-2588

Bibliography

Arnosky, Jim. 1991. *Secrets of a Wildlife Watcher*. New York: Beechtree Books. 80 pages.

Blount, Steve, and Herb Taylor. 1984. *The Joy of Snorkeling; An Illustrated Guide*. New York: Macmillan. 112 pages.

Braun, Lucy. 1964. *Deciduous Forests of Eastern North America*. Hafner Publishing Co. 596 pages.

Brown, Cindy Kilgore. 1994. *Vermont Wildlife Viewing Guide*. Helena, Mont.: Falcon Press. 63 pages.

Brown, Tom. 1983. *Tom Brown's Field Guide to Nature Observation and Tracking*. New York: Berkley Books. 282 pages.

Burt, William H., and Richard P. Grossenheider. 1980. *A Field Guide to the Mammals of North America*. The Peterson Field Guide Series. New York: Houghton Mifflin. 289 pages.

Carpenter, Leslie Benjamin. 1990. *Idaho Wildlife Viewing Guide*. Helena, Mont.: Falcon Press. 104 pages.

Carr, John N. 1992. *Arizona Wildlife Viewing Guide*. Helena, Mont.: Falcon Press. 95 pages.

Cerulean, Susan, and Ann Morrow. 1993. *Florida Wildlife Viewing Guide*. Helena, Mont.: Falcon Press. 136 pages.

Clark, Jeanne L. 1992. *California Wildlife Viewing Guide*. Helena, Mont.: Falcon Press. 159 pages.

———. 1993. *Nevada Wildlife Viewing Guide*. Helena, Mont.: Falcon Press. 87 pages.

Cole, Jim. 1990. *Utah Wildlife Viewing Guide.* Helena, Mont.: Falcon Press. 88 pages.

Cooper, Lee W. 1985. *How to Get to the Wilderness Without a Car.* Fairbanks, Alaska: Frosty Peak Books. 213 pages.

Detweiler, Esme. 1983. *Bradford Angier's Backcountry Basics.* Mechanicsburg, Pa.: Stackpole Books. 358 pages.

Doan, Marlyn. 1982. *Hiking Light.* Seattle: Mountaineers Press. 194 pages.

Duda, Mark Damian. 1994. *Virginia Wildlife Viewing Guide.* Helena, Mont.: Falcon Press. 95 pages.

Fischer, Carol, and Hank Fischer. 1990. *Montana Wildlife Viewing Guide.* Helena, Mont.: Falcon Press. 104 pages.

Fodor's Great American Sports and Adventure Vacations. 1994. New York: Fodor's Travel Publications. 346 pages.

Graham, Gary L. 1992. *Texas Wildlife Viewing Guide.* Helena, Mont.: Falcon Press. 160 pages.

Gray, Mary Taylor. 1992. *Colorado Wildlife Viewing Guide.* Helena, Mont.: Falcon Press. 128 pages.

Hamel, Paul. 1993. *Tennessee Wildlife Viewing Guide.* Helena, Mont.: Falcon Press. 96 pages.

Harrison, Hal. 1979. *Field Guide to Nests.* Western ed. Boston: Houghton Mifflin. 279 pages.

Heintzelman, Donald S. 1979. *A Manual for Bird Watching in the Americas.* New York: Universe Books. 255 pages.

Jackson, Laura Spess. 1995. *Iowa Wildlife Viewing Guide.* Helena, Mont.: Falcon Press. 95 pages.

Judd, Mary K. 1995. *Wisconsin Wildlife Viewing Guide.* Helena, Mont.: Falcon Press. 95 pages.

Knue, Joseph. 1992. *North Dakota Wildlife Viewing Guide.* Helena, Mont.: Falcon Press. 95 pages.

Kruse, Barclay, and The REI Staff. 1983. *How to Select and Use Outdoor Equipment.* Tucson, Ariz.: HP Books. 160 pages.

La Tourrette, Joe. 1992. *Washington Wildlife Viewing Guide.* Helena, Mont.: Falcon Press. 96 pages.

Lynn, Carolyn Hughes. 1994. *Kentucky Wildlife Viewing Guide.* Helena, Mont.: Falcon Press. 79 pages.

MacCarter, Jane S., and Cindy Kilgore Brown. 1994. *New Mexico Wildlife Viewing Guide.* Helena, Mont.: Falcon Press. 96 pages.

Marchington, John, and Anthony Clay. 1974. *An Introduction to Bird and Wildlife Photography.* London: Faber and Faber. 149 pages.

McKinley, Michael D. 1983. *How to Attract Birds*. San Francisco: Ortho Books. 96 pages.

O'Keefe, M. Timothy. 1992. *Diving to Adventure! How to Get the Most from Your Diving and Snorkeling*. Lakeland, Fla.: Larsen's Outdoor Publications. 160 pages.

Osborne, Richard, John Calambokidis, and Eleanor M. Dorsey. 1988. *A Guide to Marine Mammals of Greater Puget Sound*. Anacortes, Wash.: Island Publishers. 191 pages.

Pasquier, Roger. 1977. *Watching Birds; an Introduction to Ornithology*. Boston: Houghton Mifflin. 301 pages.

Peterson, Roger Tory. 1980. *A Field Guide to the Birds*. Boston: Houghton Mifflin. 384 pages.

————. 1990. *A Field Guide to Western Birds*. Boston: Houghton Mifflin. 432 pages.

Roe, Charles E. 1992. *North Carolina Wildlife Viewing Guide*. Helena, Mont.: Falcon Press. 95 pages.

Roth, Charles E. 1982. *The Wildlife Observer's Guidebook*. Englewood Cliffs, N.J.: Prentice-Hall. 239 pages.

Seng, Phil T., and David J. Case. 1992. *Indiana Wildlife Viewing Guide*. Helena, Mont.: Falcon Press. 104 pages.

Shelford, Victor E. 1963. *The Ecology of North America*. Urbana: University of Illinois Press. 610 pages.

Smith, Robert L. 1966. *Ecology and Field Biology*. New York: Harper and Row. 686 pages.

Stidworthy, John. 1989. *Reptiles and Amphibians*. New York: Facts on File. 96 pages.

Stokes, Donald, and Lillian Stokes. 1986. *Guide to Animal Tracking and Behavior*. Boston: Little, Brown. 418 pages.

Udvardy, Miklos D. F. 1977. *The Audubon Society Field Guide to North American Birds*. New York: Alfred A. Knopf. 854 pages.

Wareham, Bill. 1991. *British Columbia Wildlife Viewing Guide*. Edmonton, Alberta: Lone Pine Publishing. 96 pages.

Whitaker, John O. 1980. *The Audubon Society Field Guide to North American Mammals*. New York: Alfred A. Knopf. 745 pages.

Yuskavitch, James A. 1994. *Oregon Wildlife Viewing Guide*. Helena, Mont.: Falcon Press. 95 pages.

Zakreski, L. A. 1977. *The Budget Backpacker*. New York: Winchester Press. 274 pages.

Index

Turkey

Thrace &
Marmara
p142

İstanbul
p58

İzmir & the
North Aegean
p174

Western
Anatolia
p280

Ephesus, Bodrum
& the South Aegean
p218

Antalya & the
Turquoise Coast
p322

Ankara &
Central Anatolia
p415

Cappadocia
p463

Eastern
Mediterranean
p384

Black Sea Coast
p509

Northeastern
Anatolia
p537

Southeastern
Anatolia
p570

THIS EDITION WRITTEN AND RESEARCHED BY

James Bainbridge,
Brett Atkinson, Stuart Butler, Steve Fallon, Will Gourlay,
Jessica Lee, Virginia Maxwell

AYA SOFYA (P65),
İSTANBUL

LIBRARY OF CELSUS (P227),
EPHESUS

SIEGFRIED LAYDA / GETTY IMAGES ©

MIGUEL CARMINATI / GETTY IMAGES ©

ON THE ROAD

Contents

HORSE RIDING,
NEVŞEHIR (P483)

ON THE ROAD

BALLOONING, ORTAHISAR (P487)

AYHAN ALTUN / GETTY IMAGES ©

Contents

Welcome to Turkey

A richly historical land with some of the best cuisine you will ever taste, a variety of scenery from beaches to mountains, and the great city of İstanbul.

An Epic History

When you set foot in Turkey, you are following in the wake of some remarkable historical figures. Turkey has hosted A-list history-book figures including Julius Caesar, who famously 'came, saw and conquered' near Amasya, and St Paul, who criss-crossed the country. Byzantine Christians cut cave churches into Cappadocia's fairy chimneys, and Ottoman sultans luxuriated in İstanbul's Topkapı Palace, ruling an empire that stretched from Budapest to Baghdad. At other points in history, Romans coursed down the Curetes Way at Ephesus (Efes), medieval Armenians built Ani's churches, whirling dervishes gyrated with Sufi mysticism, and the Lycians left ruins on Mediterranean beaches.

Cultural Depth

Of course, Turkey's current inhabitants are just as memorable. The gregarious Turks are understandably proud of their heritage, and full of information (of variable accuracy) about subjects from kilims (flat-weave rugs) to the Aya Sofya's floating dome. Turkey's long history, coupled with its unique position at the meeting of Europe and Asia, has given it a profound depth of culture. Immersing yourself in that culture is as simple as soaking in an ancient hamam, eating a kebap and tasting influences brought along the Silk Road, or visiting the ruins scattering the fields, bays and hills.

Culinary Exploration

The best thing about sampling Turkey's delicious specialities – from meze on a Mediterranean harbour to a pension breakfast featuring products from the kitchen garden – is they take you to the heart of Turkish culture. For the sociable and family-oriented Turks, getting together and eating well is a time-honoured ritual. So get stuck into olive oil-lathered Aegean vegetables, spicy Anatolian kebaps and dishes from Turkey's many other corners – and as you drink a tulip-shaped glass of çay and contemplate some baklava for dessert, remember that eating is deepening your understanding of Turkey.

Landscapes & Activities

The greatest surprise for first-time visitors to Turkey is the sheer diversity found between its Aegean beaches and eastern mountains. In İstanbul, you can cruise – on the Bosphorus as well as through markets and nightclubs – in a Westernised metropolis offering equal parts romance and overcrowded insanity. In Cappadocia and the southwestern coasts, mix trekking, horse riding and water sports with meze-savouring on a panoramic terrace. Then there are the less-frequented eastern quarters, where weather-beaten relics add lashings of lyricism to mountain ranges. It's hardly surprising Turkey has attracted so many folk over the centuries. Come and discover their legacy for yourself.

Why I Love Turkey

By James Bainbridge, Author

Turkey's charm lies somewhere between its stunning landscapes such as Cappadocia; the constant surprises provided by its storied history; and the hearty locals, who are always ready to chat over a çay or Efes beer. As the old Turkish saying goes: 'A cup of coffee commits one to 40 years of friendship.' This proverb nails the addictive qualities of the Turkish lifestyle, enjoyed by people who are blessed with a land of ancient bazaars and sandy beaches, magnificent ruins and soaring mountains – and who are keen to make sure visitors love it as much as they do.

For more about our authors, see page 704

Above: Galata Bridge (p92) and Aya Sofya (p65), İstanbul

Turkey

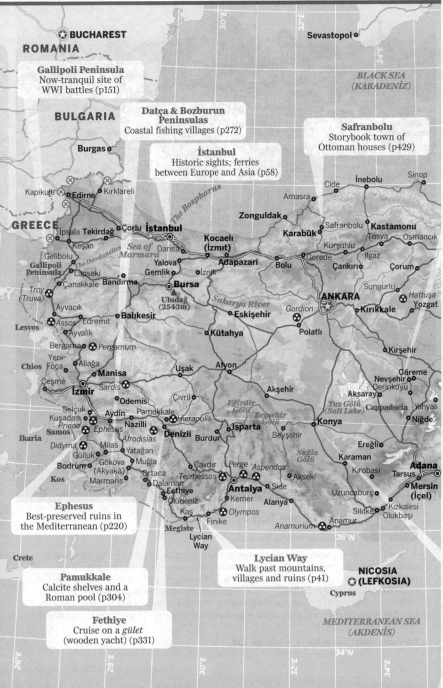

Gallipoli Peninsula
Now-tranquil site of
WWI battles (p151)

Datça & Bozburun Peninsulas
Coastal fishing villages (p272)

İstanbul
Historic sights; ferries
between Europe and Asia (p58)

Safranbolu
Storybook town of
Ottoman houses (p429)

Ephesus
Best-preserved ruins in
the Mediterranean (p220)

Lycian Way
Walk past mountains,
villages and ruins (p41)

Pamukkale
Calcite shelves and a
Roman pool (p304)

Fethiye
Cruise on a *gület*
(wooden yacht) (p331)

ROMANIA
BUCHAREST
Sevastopol

BLACK SEA
(KARADENİZ)

BULGARIA

Burgas

GREECE
Kapıkule
Edirne
Kırklareli
İpsala
Tekirdağ
Çorlu
Keşan
Gelibolu
Gallipoli Peninsula
Lapseki
Çanakkale
Bandırma
Troy (Truva)
Ayvacık
Assos
Edremit
Ayvalık
Lesvos
Bergama
Pergamum
Yeni
Foça
Aliağa
Chios
Çeşme
İzmir
Sardis
Manisa
Odemiş
Selçuk
Aydın
Pamukkale
Kuşadası
Priene
Nazilli
Samos
Ephesus
Afrodisias
Ikaria
Didyma
Milas
Yatağan
Güllük
Bodrum
Gökova (Akyaka)
Muğla
Kos
Marmaris
Ortaca
Dalaman
Çavdır
Fethiye
Ölüdeniz
Kaş
Finike
Megiste
Lycian Way
Crete

İstanbul
Kocaeli (İzmıt)
Darıca
Yalova
Gemlik
İznik
Adapazarı
Bolu
Bursa
Uludağ (2543m)
Eskişehir
Sakarya River
Gordion
ANKARA
Kütahya
Polatlı
Uşak
Afyon
Akşehir
Çivril
Hierapolis
Isparta
Beyşehir
Denizli
Burdur
Perge
Aspendos
Termessos
Antalya
Side
Kemer
Alanya
Olympos

Amasra
Cide
İnebolu
Sinop
Zonguldak
Karabük
Safranbolu
Kastamonu
Kurşunlu
Tosya
Osmancık
Gerede
Çankırı
Çorum
Sungurlu
Hattuşa
Kırıkkale
Yozgat
Kırşehir
Nevşehir
Göreme
Derinkuyu
Aksaray
Cappadocia
Yahyalı
Tuz Gölü (Salt Lake)
Niğde
Konya
Ereğli
Karaman
Kirobası
Adana
Tarsus
Mersin (İçel)
Uzuncaburç
Kızkalesi
Silifke
Olukbaşı
Anamur
Anamurium

Eğirdir Gölü
Beyşehir Gölü
Suğla Gölü
Akseki

The Bosphorus
Sea of Marmara
The Dardanelles

NICOSIA (LEFKOSIA)
Cyprus
MEDITERRANEAN SEA
(AKDENİZ)

N 0 ⎯⎯ 200 km
0 ⎯⎯ 100 miles

RUSSIA

Grozny

Ani
Eerie ruins of a former
Armenian capital (p561)

Cappadocia
Surreal fairy chimneys
and cave dwellings (p463)

Kaçkar Mountains
Hike through high-
altitude pastures (p542)

Sukhumi

Kutaisi

GEORGIA

Sumela Monastery
Cliff-face monastery
surveys valleys (p531)

TBILISI

Batumi
Sarp
Hopa

Vanadzor

Bafra

Samsun

Giresun

Ünye
Ordu

Trabzon Rize

Sumela
Monastery

Mt Kaçkar
(Kaçkar Dağı)
(3937m)

Artvin

Göle

Yusufeli

Gyumri

ARMENIA

YEREVAN

Kars

Ani

Sarıkamış

Kağızman

Lake
Sevan

Amasya

Niksar

Reşadiye

Gümüşhane

Bayburt

Kelkit River

Tortum

Horasan

İğdır

Tuzluca

Mt Ararat
(Ağrı Dağı)
(5137m)

Turhal

Tokat
Koyulhisar
Suşehri

Refahiye

Erzincan

Pasinler

Erzurum

Ağrı

Doğubayazıt

Gürbulak/
Bazargan

Sivas

Zara

Tercan

Patnos

Şarkışla

Divriği

Tunceli

Bingöl

Mt Nemrut
(Nemrut Dağı)
(3050m)

Muradiye

Özalp

IRAN

Keban
Dam

Muş

Lake Van
(Van Gölü)

Van

Kayseri

Gürün

Elazığ

Karakaya Dam

Murat River

Malatya

Mt Nemrut
(Nemrut Dağı)
(2150m)

Tatvan

Bitlis

Gevaş

Gürpınar

Başkale

Sero

Göksun

Elbistan

Doğanşehir

Gölbaşı
Kahta
Atatürk
Dam

Batman

Baykan

Siirt

Çatak

Esendere

Yüksekova

Kahramanmaraş

Adıyaman

Siverek

Diyarbakır

Kurtalan

Hakkari

Mt Cilo
(Cilo Dağı)
(4168m)

Kozan

Gaziantep
(Antep)

Karatepe

Araban

Hilvan

Viranşehir

Mardin

Şırnak

Tigris River

Osmaniye

Ceyhan

Kilis

Birecik

Barak

Şanlıurfa
(Urfa)

Harran

Qamishle

Nussaybin

Mosul

Arbil

İskenderun

Elbeyli

Akçakale

Ceylanpınar

Antakya
(Hatay)

Reyhanlı
Bab al-
Hawa

Aleppo
(Halab)

Lake
al-Assad

Mt Nemrut (Nemrut Dağı)
Giant stone heads litter
a mountain (p587)

Kirkük

Yayladağı

Lattakia

Konya
Dervishes whirl at the
Mevlâna Festival (p454)

Deir ez-Zur

IRAQ

Tripoli

Palmyra

Euphrates River

SYRIA

ELEVATION

3000m
2500m
2000m
1500m
1000m
700m
500m
200m
100m
0

LEBANON

BEIRUT

Turkey's
Top 19

1

Crossing Between Continents

1 In İstanbul (p58), you can board a commuter ferry and flit between Europe and Asia in under an hour. Every day, a flotilla takes locals up the Bosphorus and over the Sea of Marmara, sounding sonorous horns as it goes. Morning services share the waterways with diminutive fishing boats and massive container ships, all accompanied by flocks of shrieking seagulls. At sunset, the tapering minarets and Byzantine domes of the Old City are thrown into relief against a dusky pink sky – it's the city's most magical sight.

Cappadocia

2 Cappadocia's hard-set honeycomb landscape looks sculpted by a swarm of genius bees. The truth – the effects of erosion on rock formed of ash from megalithic volcanic eruptions – is only slightly less cool. Humans have also left their mark here, in the Byzantine frescoes in rock-cut churches and in the bowels of complex underground cities. These days, Cappadocia (p463) is all about good times: fine wine, local dishes and five-star caves; horse riding, valley hikes and hot-air ballooning. There's enough to keep you buzzing for days. Görkündere Vadısı (Love Valley; p472)

IZZET KERIBAR / GETTY IMAGES ©

IZZET KERIBAR / GETTY IMAGES ©

Ephesus

3 Undoubtedly the most famous of Turkey's ancient sites and considered the best preserved ruins in the Mediterranean, Ephesus (p223) is a powerful tribute to Greek artistry and Roman architectural prowess. A stroll down the marble-coated Curetes Way provides myriad photo opportunities – not least the Library of Celsus with its two storeys of columns, and the Terraced Houses, their vivid frescoes and sophisticated mosaics giving insight into the daily lives of the city's elite. Much of the city is yet to be unearthed. Library of Celsus (p227)

Hamams

4 At many hamams in Turkey, plenty of extras are on offer: bath treatments, facials, pedicures etc. We recommend you stick with the tried and true hamam experience – a soak and a scrub, followed by a good (and optional) pummelling. After this cleansing ritual and cultural experience, the world (and your body) will never feel quite the same again; do leave time to relax with a çay afterwards. For a memorable hamam, seek out Antalya's atmospheric old quarter (p369) or historic Sultanahmet (p106), İstanbul. Cağaloğlu Hamamı (p107), İstanbul

WIBOWO RUSLI / GETTY IMAGES ©

IZZET KERIBAR / GETTY IMAGES ©

Aya Sofya

5 Even in mighty İstanbul, nothing beats the Aya Sofya, or Church of the Divine Wisdom (p65), which was for centuries the greatest church in Christendom. Emperor Justinian had it built in the 6th century, as part of his mission to restore the greatness of the Roman Empire. Gazing up at the floating dome, it's hard to believe this fresco-covered marvel didn't single-handedly revive Rome's fortunes.

Meyhanes

6 Say *şerefe* (cheers) to Efes-drinking Turks in a *meyhane* (tavern). A raucous night mixing meze with rakı (anise spirit) and live music is an honoured Turkish activity. Melon, white cheese and fish go particularly well with the *aslan sütü* (lion's milk; the clear rakı turns white when added to water) and the soundtrack ranges from romantic ballads to *fasıl,* lively local gypsy music. A great place to sample Turkish nightlife is Beyoğlu (p123), İstanbul, where the *meyhane* precincts around İstiklal Caddesi heave with people on Friday and Saturday nights.

THOMAS ROCHE / GETTY IMAGES ©

IZZET KERIBAR / GETTY IMAGES ©

Lycian Way

7 Acclaimed as one of the world's top 10 long-distance walks, the Lycian Way (p41) follows signposted paths for 500km between Fethiye and Antalya. This is the Teke Peninsula, once the stamping ground of the ancient and mysterious Lycian civilisation. The route leads through pine and cedar forests in the shadow of mountains rising almost 3000m, and past villages, stunning coastal views and an embarrassment of ruins at ancient cities such as Pınara, Xanthos, Letoön and Olympos. Walk it in sections (unless you have plenty of time and stamina). Kale (p360)

Sumela Monastery

8 The improbable cliff-face location of Sumela Monastery (p531) is more than matched by the surrounding verdant scenery. The gently winding road to the Byzantine monastery twists past rustic riverside fish restaurants, and your journey from nearby Trabzon may be pleasantly hindered by a herd of fat-tailed sheep en route to fresh pastures. The last few kilometres afford tantalising glimpses across pine-covered valleys of Sumela's honey-coloured walls, and the final approach on foot leads up a forest path to the rock-cut retreat.

Beaches

9 Turkey's beaches are world-famous, offering a reliable summer mix of sun, sand and azure waters. Heading the bucket list are Mediterranean and Aegean beauties such as Kaputaş (p348), a tiny cove with dazzling shallows near Kalkan, and Patara, Turkey's longest beach. Many of the finest Mediterranean *plajlar* (beaches) dot the Lycian Way footpath, while other stretches of Turkish sand offer activities, such as windsurfing in Alaçatı and Akyaka, or locations far from the holiday crowds, for example beaches on the Aegean islands of Gökçeada and Bozcaada. Kaputaş (p348)

AYHAN ALTUN / GETTY IMAGES ©

IZZET KERIBAR / GETTY IMAGES ©

Ani

10 Ani (p561) is a truly exceptional site. Historically intriguing, culturally compelling and scenically magical, this ghost city floating in a sea of grass looks like a movie set. Lying in blissful isolation right at the Armenian border, the site exudes an eerie ambience. Before it was deserted in 1239 after a Mongol invasion, Ani was a thriving city and a capital of both the Urartian and Armenian kingdoms. The ruins include several notable churches, as well as a cathedral built between 987 and 1010.

Nemrut Dağı

11 One man's megalomania echoes across the centuries atop Nemrut Dağı's (p587) exposed and rugged summit. A gently emerging sunrise coaxes stark shadows from the mountain's giant sculpted heads, and as dawn breaks, the finer details of the immense landscape below are gradually added. While huddling against the chill of a new morning, a warming glass of çay could not be more welcome. And when your time on the summit is complete, don't miss the graceful Roman bridge crossing the nearby Cendere River.

Pamukkale

12 Famed for its intricate series of travertines (calcite shelves), and crowned by the ruined Roman and Byzantine spa city of Hieropolis, the 'Cotton Castle' (p305) is one of Turkey's most unusual treasures. Explore ruins such as the Roman theatre and soak your feet in the thermal water filling the crystal travertines before tiptoeing down to Pamukkale village past a line of the saucer-shaped formations. An optional extra is a dunk in Hieropolis' Antique Pool amid toppled marble columns.

OKAN METIN / GETTY IMAGES ©

WIBOWO RUSLI / GETTY IMAGES ©

WALTER BIBIKOW / GETTY IMAGES ©

JEAN-BERNARD CARILLET / GETTY IMAGES ©

KEN WELSH / GETTY IMAGES ©

Gallipoli Peninsula

13 The narrow stretch of land guarding the entrance to the much-contested Dardanelles (p151) is a beautiful area, where pine trees roll across hills above Eceabat's backpacker hang-outs and Kilitbahir's castle. Touring the peaceful countryside is a poignant experience for many: memorials and cemeteries mark the spots where young men from far away fought and died in gruelling conditions. The passionate guides do a good job of evoking the futility and tragedy of the Gallipoli campaign, one of WWI's worst episodes.
Anzac Cove (p155)

Kaçkar Mountains (Kaçkar Dağları)

14 Rippling between the Black Sea coast and the Çoruh River, the Kaçkars (p542) rise to almost 4000m, affording superb hiking in summer. Spending a few days crossing the *yaylalar* (mountain pastures) between hamlets like Olgunlar and Ayder is one of Turkey's top trekking experiences, and the lower slopes offer cultural encounters. The local Hemşin people serve their beloved, fondue-like *muhlama* (cornmeal cooked in butter) in villages with Ottoman bridges and Georgian churches.

Whirling Dervishes

15 The *sema* (whirling dervish ceremony) crackles with spiritual energy as the robe-clad dervishes spin, a constellation of dancers performing this trancelike ritual. The ceremony begins and ends with chanted passages from the Koran and is rich with symbolism; the dervishes' conical felt hats represent their tombstones, and the dance signifies relinquishing earthly life to be reborn in mystical union with God. You can see a *sema* in locations including İstanbul, Cappadocia, Bursa and Konya; the latter's Mevlâna Museum (p454) is a Turkish icon.

IZZET KERIBAR / GETTY IMAGES ©

NEIL OVERY / GETTY IMAGES ©

Safranbolu

16 Listed for eternal preservation by Unesco in 1994, Safranbolu (p429) is Turkey's prime example of an Ottoman town brought back to life. Domestic tourists descend here full of nostalgia to stay in half-timbered houses that seem torn from the pages of a children's storybook. And the magic doesn't end there. Sweets and saffron vendors line the cobblestone alleyways, and artisans and cobblers ply their centuries-old trades beneath medieval mosques. When the summer storms light up the night sky, the fantasy is complete.

Gület Cruising

17 Known locally as a 'blue voyage' (*mavi yolculuk*), a cruise lasting four days and three nights on a *gület* (traditional wooden sailing boat) along the western Mediterranean's Turquoise Coast is the highlight of many a trip to Turkey. The cruises (p366) offer opportunities to explore isolated beaches, watch sunsets and, above all, get away from it all, offshore and offline – a rare treat nowadays. The usual route is Fethiye–Olympos, stopping at Mediterranean highlights such as Butterfly Valley, while aficionados say the Fethiye–Marmaris route is even prettier.

Bazaar Shopping

18 Turkey has a market for every mood – from İstanbul's famously clamorous Grand Bazaar (p88) to the donkeys winding through Mardin's hillside bazaar (p603), and from the traditional shadow puppets in Bursa's *kapalı çarşı* (covered market) to the silk scarves in Şanlıurfa's ancient caravanserai. To take home the finest Turkish carpets you need a sultan's fortune, but don't be discouraged. Find something you like, drink some çay with the shopkeeper and accept that you might not bag the world's best deal but you'll hone your haggling skills. Grand Bazaar (p88)

GARY YEOWELL / GETTY IMAGES ©

18

Datça & Bozburun Peninsulas

19 These mountainous peninsulas, stretching from Marmaris towards the Greek island of Symi, form a scenic dividing line between the Aegean and Mediterranean. From *gület*-building Bozburun village to the ruins of Knidos at the tip of the Datça Peninsula (p272), the adjoining fingers of land mix holiday charm with rustic tranquility. Eski Datça has cobbled lanes, while Selimiye is an up-and-coming village with some good restaurants. In summer, ferries cross daily between the Datça Peninsula and Bodrum. Bozburun Peninsula (p272)

CHRIS WINSOR / GETTY IMAGES ©

19

Need to Know

For more information, see Survival Guide (p653)

Currency
Türk Lirası (Turkish lira; ₺)

Language
Turkish and Kurdish

Visas
To stay for up to 90 days, most Western nationalities either don't require visas or should purchase one in advance from www.evisa.gov.tr (typically €20 to €60).

Money
ATMs are widely available. Credit and debit cards are accepted by most businesses in cities and tourist areas.

Mobile Phones
SIM cards are cheap and widely available, but the networks block unregistered foreign phones. Registration costs ₺100; secondhand Turkish phones cost from ₺50.

Time
Eastern European Time (GMT/UTC plus two hours); from late March until late October, Eastern European Summer Time (GMT/UTC plus three hours).

When to Go

İstanbul
GO Apr–May, Sep

Eastern Anatolia
GO May–Jun, Sep

Cappadocia
GO May, Sep–Oct

Aegean
GO May–Jun, Sep

Mediterranean
GO Apr, Sep–Oct

- Desert, dry climate
- Warm to hot summers, mild winters
- Mild to hot summers, cold winters

High Season
(Jun–Aug)

➡ Prices and temperatures highest

➡ Expect crowds, book ahead

➡ Turkish school holidays mid-June to mid-September

➡ İstanbul's high season April–May and September–October

➡ Christmas and Easter also busy

Shoulder Season
(May & Sep)

➡ Fewer crowds, apart from around Kurban Bayramı holiday (currently in September)

➡ Warm weather in spring and autumn, especially in the southwest

➡ İstanbul's shoulder season is June–August

Low Season
(Oct–Apr)

➡ October is autumn; spring starts in April

➡ Accommodation in tourist areas close or offer discounts

➡ High season in ski resorts

➡ İstanbul's low season is November to March

Useful Websites

Lonely Planet (www.lonelyplanet.com/turkey) Info, bookings and forum.

Turkey Travel Planner (www.turkeytravelplanner.com) Useful travel info.

Turkish Cultural Foundation (www.turkishculture.org) Culture and heritage.

Go Turkey (www.goturkey.com) Official tourism portal.

Good Morning Turkey (www.goodmorningturkey.com) Turkish news in English, German and Russian.

All About Turkey (www.allaboutturkey.com) Multilingual introduction.

Important Numbers

Local codes are listed under the names of locations.

Turkey country code	☏90
International access code from Turkey	☏00
Ambulance	☏112
Fire	☏110
Police	☏155

Exchange Rates

Australia	A$1	₺1.88
Canada	C$1	₺1.97
Europe	€1	₺2.78
Japan	¥100	₺1.87
New Zealand	NZ$1	₺1.74
UK	£1	₺3.51
USA	US$1	₺2.24

For current exchange rates see www.xe.com.

Daily Costs

Budget: Less than ₺135

➡ Dorm bed: €6-24

➡ İstanbul–Gallipoli Peninsula bus ticket: ₺30

➡ *Balık ekmek* (fish sandwich): ₺5-10

➡ Beer: ₺7-10

Midrange: ₺135-350

➡ Double room ₺90-180

➡ Double room in İstanbul and Bodrum: €90-200

➡ İstanbul–Cappadocia flight: from ₺85

➡ Fish and meze meal: ₺25

➡ Boat day trip: ₺35

Top end: More than ₺350

➡ Double room: more than ₺180

➡ Double room in İstanbul and Bodrum: more than €200

➡ Four-day *gület* cruise: €165-275

➡ Hot-air balloon flight: €175

➡ Car hire per day: €20

Opening Hours

Hours are listed in this book when businesses deviate from the following standard opening hours.

Information 8.30am-noon & 1.30-5pm Mon-Fri

Restaurants and cafes Breakfast 7.30-10am, lunch noon-2.30pm, dinner 6.30-10pm

Bars 4pm-late

Nightclubs 11pm-late

Shops 9am-6pm Mon-Fri (longer in tourist areas and big cities – including weekend opening)

Government offices & banks 8.30am-noon & 1.30-5pm Mon-Fri

Arriving in Turkey

Atatürk International Airport (İstanbul) Havataş (Havaş) airport buses run to Taksim Meydanı every 30 minutes (₺10, one hour); the metro runs every 10 minutes to Zeytinburnu (₺4), from where trams run to the centre (₺4), taking one/1½ hours total from the airport to Sultanahmet/Taksim Meydanı; a taxi to Sultanahmet/Taksim Meydanı costs ₺45/55; hotels offer a free pick-up for stays of longer than three days.

Sabiha Gökçen International Airport (İstanbul) Havataş (Havaş) airport buses run to Taksim Meydanı (₺13, 1½ hours); a taxi to Taksim Meydanı/Sultanahmet costs ₺100/130.

Büyük İstanbul Otogarı (Big İstanbul Bus Station) The metro runs to Zeytinburnu (₺4), from where trams runs to the centre (₺4); a taxi to Sultanahmet or Taksim Meydanı costs ₺35; some bus companies provide a *servis* (free shuttle) to the centre.

Getting Around

Bus Generally efficient and good value, frequent services between the major cities and tourist spots. Often fewer services in winter.

Air Domestic flights are an affordable way of reducing travel time. More choices from İstanbul.

Train The growing network of high-speed services offers rapid routes across Anatolia. The bus is often quicker than normal trains.

Car A great way to explore rural areas, with rental operators in cities and airports. Drive on the right. Petrol is expensive.

Ferry Regular services cross the Sea of Marmara and link parts of the Aegean coast.

For much more on **getting around**, see p668

First Time Turkey

For more information, see Survival Guide (p653)

Checklist

➡ Check your passport will be valid for at least six months after entering Turkey.

➡ Check if you need a visa and purchase it at www.evisa.gov.tr.

➡ Inform your credit card provider of your travel plans.

➡ Purchase travel insurance and record provider's details.

➡ Check travel vaccinations are up to date.

➡ Organise airport transfer or onward connection.

➡ Book flights and hire car online.

➡ Book accommodation for popular areas.

What to Pack

➡ Passport

➡ Paper copy of e-visa

➡ Credit and debit cards

➡ Bank's contact details

➡ Back-up euros/dollars

➡ Oral rehydration salts

➡ Conservative clothing for mosque visits

➡ Toilet roll

➡ Soap or handwash

➡ Chargers and adaptor

Top Tips for Your Trip

➡ Turkey is like a few countries rolled into one: the east is sparsely populated and devoutly Muslim, whereas much of the Aegean, Mediterranean and İstanbul are more Westernised.

➡ Turkey is predominantly Muslim, but certainly tolerant and welcoming to non-Muslims.

➡ Turkey is a nationalistic country: Turkish flags and portraits of founding father Atatürk are ubiquitous; be respectful, as Turks are extremely proud.

➡ Make an effort to get off the beaten track – the hospitality and home cooking in little villages are a memorable experience.

What to Wear

İstanbul and the Aegean and Mediterranean resort towns are used to Western dress, including bikinis on the beach and short skirts in nightclubs. In eastern and central Anatolia, people are conservative; even men should stick to long trousers. In staunchly Islamic cities, even T-shirts and sandals are inadvisable. Women do not need to cover their head unless they enter a mosque. To decrease the likelihood of receiving unwanted attention, dress on the conservative side.

Sleeping

It's generally not necessary to book accommodation in advance. But if you are visiting a popular place such as İstanbul or Bodrum in high season, it is worth reserving well ahead.

➡ **Boutique hotels** Small and intimate; normally a historic building.

➡ **Pensions** Family-run guesthouses offer an authentic experience.

➡ **Luxury hotels** World-class service and myriad facilities.

➡ **Self-catering** Villas and apartments are popular in coastal areas.

➡ **Resorts** Family-friendly options on the coast, with package deals.

➡ **Hostels** Backpacker options with dorms.

➡ **Campsites** Mostly on the coast, and have ablutions and facilities.

➡ **Budget hotels** Cheap options often lacking the charm and cleanliness of pensions.

Islam & Ramazan

Turkey is predominantly Islamic, but tolerant of other religions and lifestyles – especially western Turkey, where there are as many bars as mosques and it is sometimes easy to forget you are in an Islamic country. Do bear in mind, however, that Ramazan, the holy month when Muslims fast between dawn and dusk, currently falls in the summer. Cut the locals some slack; they might be grumpy if they are fasting in hot weather. Don't eat, drink or smoke in public during the day, and if you aren't a fasting Muslim, don't go to an *iftar* (evening meal to break fast) tent for cheap food.

Blue Mosque (p68), İstanbul

Bargaining

Haggling is common in bazaars, as well as for out-of-season accommodation and long taxi journeys. In other instances, you're expected to pay the stated price.

Tipping

Turkey is fairly European in its approach to tipping and you won't be pestered for baksheesh. Tipping is customary in restaurants, hotels and taxis; optional elsewhere.

➡ **Restaurants** A few coins in budget eateries; 10% to 15% of the bill in midrange and top-end establishments.

➡ **Hotel porter** Give 3% of the room price in midrange and top-end hotels only.

➡ **Taxis** Round up metered fares to the nearest 50 kuruş.

Language

English is widely spoken in İstanbul and touristy parts of western Turkey; less so in eastern and central Anatolia, where knowing a few Turkish phrases, covering relevant topics such as accommodation, is invaluable. Turkish is fun to learn as pronunciation is easy. Learning Turkish is more useful than Kurdish, as most Kurds speak Turkish (but not vice versa). Many Turks speak German.

Etiquette

➡ **Religion** Dress modestly and be quiet and respectful around mosques.

➡ **Hospitality** Generous Turks take it seriously; you may receive a few invitations to dine or drink çay together.

➡ **Restaurants** Generally, whoever extended the invitation to eat together picks up the bill.

➡ **Alcohol** Bars are common, but public drinking and inebriation are less acceptable away from tourist towns.

➡ **Greetings** Turks value respect; greet or acknowledge people.

➡ **Language** Learn a few Turkish phrases; immeasurably helpful and appreciated by Turks.

➡ **Relationships** Do not be overly tactile with your partner in public; beware miscommunications with locals.

➡ **Politics** Be tactful; criticising Turkish nationalism can land you in prison.

➡ **Shopping** Visiting the bazaar, be prepared to haggle and drink tea with shopkeepers.

➡ **Queues** Turks can be pushy in public situations; be assertive.

What's New

Transport Links

New metro lines make it easier to navigate İstanbul, with the Marmaray running under the Sea of Marmara and another line crossing the Golden Horn. The latest addition to Anatolia's high-speed train network, the İstanbul–Ankara service cuts the journey to 3½ hours. The world's longest gondola links Bursa with Uludağ and hourly dolmuşes (minibuses) between Ürgüp and Avanos make it easier to explore Cappadocia.

Karaköy

The neighbourhood on İstanbul's Bosphorus shore has taken off as the ever-changing city's hip new area, complete with a new jazz venue, Nublu İstanbul. (p126)

Gallipoli Simulation Centre

The high-tech museum's 11 rooms of 3D simulation equipment bring the naval and land battles at Gallipoli to life. (p154)

Troy Museum

A state-of-the-art new museum at the archaeological site is set to contain the 'Troy Gold', 24 gold jewellery pieces dating to c 2400 BC. (p169)

Şanlıurfa Archeopark

The park comprises the Şanlıurfa Archeology Museum (p579), which sheds light on the Stonehenge-like Göbekli Tepe nearby, and the Edessa Mosaic Museum, with mosaics from Roman villas. (p579)

Carpet Museum

One of a few new museums in İstanbul, the Carpet Museum fills an 18th-century *imaret* (soup kitchen) with 14th- to 20th-century carpets from mosques nationwide. (p83)

Museum of Seljuk Civilisation

Multimedia displays cover the empire's artistry, culture and history in the appropriate surrounds of Kayseri's Çifte Medrese, a Seljuk seminary and hospital. (p505)

Bosphorus Tour

Dentur Avrasya's new cruises allow you to hop on and off en route up İstanbul's famous strait between Europe and Asia. (p105)

Surp Giragos Kilisesi

Diyrabakır's wooden-ceilinged Armenian church (p597) is fully restored. Kick off a visit with breakfast in the leafy courtyard of the new Diyarbakır Kahvaltı Evi. (p599)

Kılıç Ali Paşa Hamamı

Joining the ranks of İstanbul's beautiful Ottoman hamams, this 16th-century beauty, designed by the great architect Mimar Sinan, has reopened after a seven-year restoration. (p107)

Moving Museums

Van Museum (p613) and Antakya's Hatay Archaeology Museum (p410), respectively famous for their collections of Urartian artefacts and Roman and Byzantine mosaics, have moved to purpose-built new premises.

For more recommendations and reviews, see lonelyplanet.com/Turkey

If You Like...

Bazaars

Centuries ago, Seljuk and Ottoman traders travelled the Silk Road, stopping at caravanserais to do business – the tradition is still alive and so is haggling in Turkey's labyrinthine bazaars.

Grand Bazaar Hone your bargaining skills in İstanbul's original and best shopping mall. (p88)

Şanlıurfa Bazaar Narrow alleyways, shady courtyards and proximity to Syria give Şanlıurfa's bazaar a Middle Eastern flavour. (p580)

Eski Aynalı Çarşı Bursa's 14th-century Old Mirrored Market houses shadow-puppet shops. (p287)

Spice Bazaar Jewel-like *lokum* (Turkish delight) and pyramids of spices provide eye candy at İstanbul's fragrant bazaar. (p92)

Hamams

Hamams are also known as Turkish baths, a name coined by Europeans introduced to their steamy pleasures by the Ottomans. Have a massage or just soak in the calming atmosphere.

Sefa Hamamı This restored 13th-century gem in Kaleiçi (Old Antalya) retains many of its Seljuk features. (p369)

Ayasofya Hürrem Sultan Hamamı Süleyman the Magnificent's luxurious hamam has been serving İstanbul since 1557. (p106)

Yeni Kaplıca 'New thermal bath' is actually Bursa's oldest, founded by the 6th-century Byzantine emperor Justinian I. (p290)

Kelebek Turkish Bath Spa Cappadocia's most luxurious hamam experience, with a full range of spa-style added extras. (p470)

Beaches

Turkey is surrounded by the Mediterranean, the Aegean, the Black Sea and the Sea of Marmara, offering numerous beaches for reclining by the 'wine-dark sea' (as Homer called the Aegean).

Kaputaş The pale sandy cove and brilliant azure waters near Kalkan look brochure-perfect. (p348)

Kabak Take a steep ride down to the Mediterranean beach community. (p341)

Patara One of the Mediterranean's longest beaches, with 18km of white sand, ruins and sea turtles. (p346)

Aegean islands A ruined monastery overlooks Bozcaada's Ayazma Beach (p176), and you might have Gökçeada's beaches (p170) to yourself.

Museums

In a country marked by great dynasties, from Hittite hill men to Ottoman sultans, every self-respecting town has a museum to preserve its local history.

İstanbul Options range from classics like the İstanbul Archaeology Museums to contemporary galleries. (p82)

Göreme Open-Air Museum Only in surreal Cappadocia could a valley of rock-cut Byzantine churches be called a museum. (p466)

Museum of Anatolian Civilisations Ankara's star attraction examines the ancient civilisations that warred and waned on the surrounding steppe. (p417)

Museum of Underwater Archaeology Housed in Bodrum's 15th-century Castle of St Peter, it displays bounty from ancient shipwrecks. (p253)

Gaziantep Zeugma Mosaic Museum Showcases virtually complete Roman floor mosaics, rescued from a dam site. (p571)

Cities

Turks are a regionalist bunch; they will invariably tell you their town is *en çok güzel* (the most beautiful) – but these are the best places to experience urban Turkey.

İstanbul The world's only city on two continents, the megacity was once the capital of empires. (p58)

Antalya The classically beautiful and stylishly modern gateway to the Turkish Riviera. (p365)

İzmir Turkey's third-largest city is right on the Aegean; its *kordon* (seafront promenade) is a joy. (p200)

Antakya (Hatay) The site of the biblical Antioch has a distinctively Arabic feel. (p409)

Van Near mountain-ringed Lake Van, the Anatolian city begins its day with its famous local *kahvaltı* (breakfast). (p611)

Diyarbakır Compelling heartland of Kurdish culture, with fascinating mosques and churches concealed within massive city walls. (p595)

Boutique Hotels

From half-timbered Ottoman mansions to Greek stone houses, Turkey's architectural gems are increasingly being converted into small, one-off hotels. These distinctive properties offer a local experience with a stylish twist.

Cappadocia Take up residence in a fairy chimney (rock formation) and experience troglodyte life in luxury. (p463)

Alaçatı Scores of the Aegean village's stone Greek houses have been converted into boutique digs. (p214)

Top: İstiklal Caddesi (p94), İstanbul
Bottom: Harbour, Behramkale (Assos; p179)

Ottoman Anatolia Among rocky bluffs, Safranbolu and Amasya are idyllic settings for hotels in Ottoman piles. (p415)

Kaleiçi A smattering of boutique hotels adds further charm to Antalya's Roman-Ottoman old quarter. (p370)

Mehmet Ali Ağa Konağı This 19th-century pile's Mansion Suite includes the original *selamlik* (public quarters) and *haremlik* (family quarters). (p274)

History

Turks are proud of their long, eventful history, and it's easy to share their enthusiasm at the country's mosques and palaces, ruins and museums.

İstanbul The city's historic significance can be felt everywhere, but particularly among Sultanahmet's ancient monuments. (p58)

Gallipoli Peninsula Poignant memorials and cemeteries recall the battles fought here in WWI. (p151)

Greek villages Places like Ayvalık **old town** recall Greeks displaced by the population exchange of the 1920s. (p185)

Christianity Christian sites include Cappadocia's rock-cut Byzantine monasteries, and the northeastern valleys' medieval Georgian churches. (p480)

Hattuşa Explore off the beaten track to the remote capitals of less-renowned Anatolian civilisations, including the Hittite HQ. (p438)

Ruins

Whether in a city centre or atop a craggy cliff, the country's ruins bring out the historical romantic in you. Excavations continue at many, giving new glimpses of ancient history.

Ephesus The best-preserved classical city in the eastern Mediterranean evokes daily life in Roman times. (p223)

Nemrut Dağı Atop Mt Nemrut are the toppled heads of statues built by a megalomaniac pre-Roman king. (p655)

Pergamum The Hellenistic theatre is a vertigo-inducing marvel and the Asclepion was Rome's pre-eminent medical centre. (p189)

Göbekli Tepe Predating Stonehenge by 6500 years, Şanlıurfa's Neolithic site may be history's first place of worship. (p579)

Armenian Eastern Anatolia's Armenian ruins include Ani (p561), the former capital, and Akdamar Island's 10th-century church. (p610)

Activities

Turkey's many outdoor activities make the most of its beautiful and diverse terrain, ranging from mountain ranges to beaches – and çay and baklava, or Efes beer and meze, await afterwards.

Walking Opportunities range from half-day wanders through Cappadocia's valleys to 500km Mediterranean trails. (p39)

Canyoning The 18km-long Saklıkent Gorge near Fethiye is the top spot for canyoning. (p42)

Water sports On the Aegean and Mediterranean, diving, windsurfing, kiteboarding, canoeing and waterskiing are on offer. (p41)

Adventure Eastern Anatolia offers adrenaline-pumping activities such as white-water rafting and mountain walking. (p43)

Kekova Island Sea kayak over walls, shattered amphorae and other remains of the Lycian 'sunken city'. (p359)

Skiing Ski resorts across the country include Bursa's Uludağ (p295) and Cappadocia's Erciyes Dağı. (p505)

Landscape

Apart from a toe sticking into Europe, Turkey is part of Asia, so it should come as no surprise that its landscapes are varied and stunning.

Cappadocia The fairy chimneys and smooth valleys are best explored on foot or horseback. (p463)

Northeastern Anatolia Mountains and rugged scenery including Turkey's highest peak, Mt Ararat (Ağrı Dağı; p537).

Amasra to Sinop A great drive takes you past Black Sea beaches and green hills. (p513)

Behramkale The hillside village has dreamy views of the Aegean coast. (p179)

Lakes The mountain-ringed lakes of Eğirdir, Bafa, Van and İznik are among Turkey's unsung glories.

Datça and Bozburun Peninsulas Raw landscape dividing the Aegean and Mediterranean, riddled with coves and pine forests. (p272)

Nemrut Dağı Mountain-top stone heads gaze at the Anti-Taurus Range. (p655)

Ala Dağlar National Park Waterfalls crash down limestone cliffs in the Taurus Mountains. (p135)

Food & Drink

Turkey has epicurean indulgence nailed, from

TIM GERARD BARKER / GETTY IMAGES ©

Kabak coast (p341)

street snacks to gourmet restaurants. Not only does every region offer local dishes, you can sample them in individualistic eateries and on panoramic terraces.

Cappadocia Home Cooking Sample true home-style Cappadocian cooking, surrounded by the family's organic garden in a valley village. (p496)

Limon Aile Lokantası On the Bodrum Peninsula, Limon offers an original take on the much-loved Aegean meze-and-seafood experience. (p264)

Beyoğlu rooftop bars Toast İstanbul from above with breathtaking views across the Bosphorus and Golden Horn. (p123)

İmam Çağdaş Discover Gaziantep baklava, reputedly the planet's best, amid the epicurean city's storied streets. (p576)

Kahvaltı Sokak The restaurants on Van's 'breakfast street' are the ultimate place to eat a Turkish breakfast. (p614)

Hatay Sultan Sofrası Syrian and Arab culinary influences abound in Antakya, for example in the mezes and spicy kebaps here. (p413)

Architecture

Turkey's legacy of mighty empires has left a bounty of imposing buildings: palaces, mosques, churches, monas-

teries and caravanseries are a few of the ancient structures evoking bygone eras.

İstanbul Glorious edifices include the greatest surviving Byzantine building, the Aya Sofya (p65), and the Topkapı Palace. (p75)

İshak Paşa Palace Perched above the steppe, this 18th-century pile mixes Seljuk, Ottoman, Georgian, Persian and Armenian styles. (p565)

Ulu Cami & Darüşşifa Stone portal carvings so intricate that locals say they prove the existence of God. (p452)

Boutique hotels Restored historic properties range from Safranbolu's Ottoman mansions to the Aegean's old Greek villages. (p431)

Month by Month

January

The dead of winter. Even İstanbul's streets are empty of crowds, local and foreign, and snow closes eastern Anatolia's mountain passes and delays buses. Accommodation in tourist areas is mostly closed.

✴ New Year's Day

A surrogate Christmas takes place across the Islamic country, with decorations, and exchanges of gifts and greeting cards. Celebrations begin on New Year's Eve and continue through this public holiday. Over Christmas and New Year, accommodation fills up and prices rise.

March

As in the preceding months, you might have sights to yourself outside the country's top destinations, and you can get discounts at accommodation options that are open.

✴ Çanakkale Deniz Zaferi

Turks descend on the Gallipoli (Gelibolu) Peninsula and Çanakkale to celebrate what they call the Çanakkale Naval Victory – and commemorate the WWI campaign's 130,000 fatalities. The area, particularly the Turkish memorials in the southern peninsula, is thronged with visitors. 18 March. (p163)

✴ Nevruz

Kurds and Alevis celebrate the ancient Middle Eastern spring festival with much jumping over bonfires and general jollity. Banned until recently, Nevruz is now an official holiday with huge parties, particularly in Diyarbakır, although political tensions can lead to muted celebrations. 21 March.

✴ Mesir Macunu Festivalı

An altogether different way of marking the spring equinox, Manisa's Unesco-protected festival celebrates *Mesir macunu* (Mesir paste), a scrumptious treat made from dozens of spices that once cured Süleyman the Magnificent's mother of illness. 21 to 24 March. (p211)

April

Spring. April and May are high season in İstanbul and shoulder season elsewhere. Not a great month to get a tan in northern Turkey, but you can enjoy balmy, breezy weather in the southwest.

✴ İstanbul Tulip Festival

İstanbul's parks and gardens are resplendent with tulips, which originated in Turkey before being exported to the Netherlands during the Ottoman era. Multicoloured tulips are often planted to resemble the Turks' cherished 'evil eye'. Flowers bloom from late March or early April. (p108)

☆ İstanbul Film Festival

For a filmic fortnight, cinemas around town host a packed program of Turkish and international films and events (http://film.iksv.org/en). An excellent crash course in Turkish cinema, but book ahead.

🎖 Anzac Day, Gallipoli Peninsula

The WWI battles for the Dardanelles are commemorated again, this time with more emphasis on the Allied soldiers. Antipodean pilgrims sleep at Anzac Cove before the dawn services; another busy time on the peninsula. 25 April.

May

Another good month to visit. Shoulder season continues outside İstanbul, with attendant savings, but spring is going strong and Aegean and Mediterranean beaches are heating up.

🏃 Windsurfing

In Turkey's windsurfing centre, Alaçatı (www.alacati.info), the season begins in mid-May. The protected Aegean bay hosts the Windsurf World Cup in August and the season winds down in early November, when many of the eight resident schools close.

☉ Ruins, Mosques, Palaces & Museums

This is your last chance until September to see the main attractions at famous Aegean and Mediterranean sights such as Ephesus

Top: Diving, Kaş (p353)
Bottom: Erciyes Dağı Ski Resort (p505)

without major crowds, which can become almost unbearable at the height of summer. (p223)

🏃 Dedegöl Dağcılık Şenliği

Dedegöl Mountaineering Festival sees Eğirdir's mountaineering club scramble up Mt Dedegöl (2998m) – simply because they can, now spring is thawing the Taurus Mountains. Register to join the free two-day event, which includes a night at the base camp. 19 May. (p317)

June

Summer. Shoulder season in İstanbul and high season elsewhere until the end of August. Expect sizzling temperatures, inflexible hotel prices and crowds at sights – avoided by visiting early, late or at lunchtime.

🍴 Cherry Season

June is the best month to gobble Turkey's delicious cherries, which Giresun introduced to the rest of the world. On the Sea of Marmara, Tekirdağ's Kiraz Festivalı (Cherry Festival) in mid-June celebrates the juicy wonders.

🎆 Kafkasör Kültür ve Sanat Festivalı, Artvin

Join the crush at the *boğa güreşleri* (bloodless bull-wrestling matches) at Artvin's Caucasus Culture and Arts Festival, held in the Kafkasör Yaylası pasture, 7km southwest of the northeastern Anatolian mountain town. Late June or early July. (p555)

🎆 Historic Kırkpınar Oil-Wrestling Festival, Edirne

In a sport dating back over 650 years, brawny *pehlivan* (wrestlers) from across Turkey rub themselves from head to toe with olive oil, and grapple. Late June or early July.

July

This month and August turn the Aegean and Mediterranean tourist heartlands into sun-and-fun machines, and temperatures peak across the country. The blue skies bring out the best in the hot-blooded Turkish personality.

🎆 Kültür Sanat ve Turizm Festivalı, Doğubayazıt

The Kurdish town between Mt Ararat and the romantic İshak Paşa Palace hosts its Culture and Arts Festival, allowing you to immerse yourself in Kurdish heritage through music, dance and theatre performances. June or July. (p565)

🏃 Mountain Walking

Out in the northeastern Anatolian steppe, the snow clears from atop the Kaçkar Mountains (Kaçkar Dağları) and Mt Ararat (Ağrı Dağı, 5137m), Turkey's highest peak, allowing multiday treks and sublime *yaylalar* (highland pasture) views in July and August. www.culture-routesinturkey.com.

🎆 Music Festivals

Turkey enjoys a string of summer music jamborees,

including İstanbul, İzmir and Bursa's highbrow festivals (http://muzik.iksv.org/en). The cities host multiple pop, rock, jazz and dance music events, while summer playgrounds such as Alaçatı and the Bodrum Peninsula turn into mini-Ibizas. June to August.

August

Even at night, the weather is hot and humid; pack sun cream and anti-mosquito spray. Walking and activities are best tackled early in the morning or at sunset.

🎆 Cappadocian Festivals

Two festivals take place in the land of fairy chimneys (rock formations). A summer series of chamber music concerts are held in the valleys and, from 16 to 18 August, sleepy Hacıbektaş comes alive with the annual pilgrimage of Bektaşi dervishes. (p471)

🎆 Cultural Festivals

Aspendos Opera & Ballet Festival takes place in this awesome Roman theatre near Antalya (June or August to September), and Bodrum's atmospheric 15th-century Castle of St Peter hosts the International Bodrum Ballet Festival (July to August; www.bodrumballetfestival.gov.tr). (p379)

September

İstanbul's second high season begins; elsewhere, it's shoulder season – temperatures, crowds and prices lessen. Accommodation and activities, such as boat trips, begin winding down for the winter.

🏃 Diving

The water is warmest from May to October and you can expect water temperatures of 25°C in September. Turkey's scuba diving centre is Kaş on the Mediterranean, with operators also found in Marmaris, Bodrum, Kuşadası and Ayvalık on the Aegean.

🎊 İstanbul Biennial

The city's major visual-arts shindig, considered to be one of the world's most prestigious biennials (http://bienal.iksv.org/en), takes place from early September to early November in odd-numbered years. Venues around town host the internationally curated event.

October

Autumn is truly here; outside İstanbul, many accommodation options have shut for the winter. Good weather is unlikely up north, but the Mediterranean and Aegean experience fresh, sunny days.

🏃 Walking

The weather in eastern Anatolia has already become challenging by this time of year, but in the southwest, autumn and spring are the best seasons to enjoy the scenery without too much sweat on your brow (www.trekkinginturkey.com and www.cariantrail.com).

November

Even on the coastlines, summer is a distant memory. Rain falls on İstanbul and the Black Sea, southern resort towns are deserted and eastern Anatolia is ensnarled in snow.

🎊 Akbank Jazz Festival

From late October to early November, İstanbul celebrates its love of jazz with this eclectic line-up of local and international performers (www.akbanksanat.com). Going for 25 years, it's the older sibling of July's İstanbul Jazz Festival.

🎊 Karagöz Festival, Bursa

A week of performances celebrate the city's Karagöz shadow-puppetry heritage, with local and international puppeteers and marionette performers. Originally a Central Asian Turkic tradition, the camel-hide puppet theatre developed in Bursa and spread through the Ottoman Empire. November of odd years.

December

Turks fortify themselves against the cold with hot çay and kebap-induced layers. Most of the country is chilly and wet or icy, although the western Mediterranean is milder and day walks there are viable.

🏃 Ski Season

Hit the slopes: the Turkish ski season begins at half a dozen resorts across the country, including Cappadocia's Erciyes Dağı (Mt Erciyes), Uludağ (near Bursa), Palandöken (near Erzurum) and Sarıkamış, near Kars. Late November to early April.

🏃 Snow in Anatolia

If you're really lucky, after skiing on Erciyes Dağı, you could head west and see central Cappadocia's fairy chimneys looking even more magical under a layer of snow. Eastern Anatolia is also covered in a white blanket, but temperatures get brutally low.

Itineraries

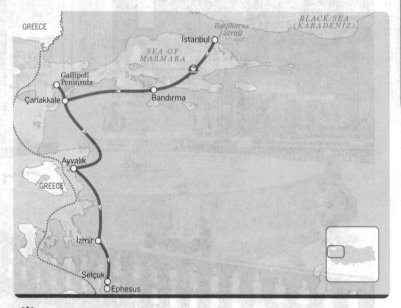

 **Classic Turkey**

Most first-time visitors to Turkey arrive with two ancient names on their lips: İstanbul and Ephesus. This journey across the Sea of Marmara and down the Aegean coast covers both.

You'll need at least three days in **İstanbul** to even scratch the surface of its millennia of history. The top three sights are the Aya Sofya, Topkapı Palace and the Blue Mosque, but there's a sultan's treasury of other sights and activities, including a cruise up the Bosphorus, nightlife around İstiklal Caddesi, and the Grand Bazaar.

From İstanbul, instead of schlepping out to the city's main otogar (bus station), hop on a ferry to Bandırma. From there, you can take the train straight down to Selçuk (for Ephesus) via İzmir, but it's more interesting to catch a bus to **Çanakkale**, a lively student town on the Dardanelles. A tour of the nearby **Gallipoli Peninsula's** poignant WWI battlefields is a memorable experience. From Çanakkale, it's a 3¼-hour bus ride to **Ayvalık**, with its tumbledown old Greek quarter and fish restaurants. Finally, another bus ride (via İzmir) reaches **Selçuk**, a pleasantly rustic town and the base for visiting glorious **Ephesus**, the best-preserved classical city in the eastern Mediterranean.

Top: Ulu Camii (p286), Bursa

Bottom: Anıt Kabir (p419), Ankara

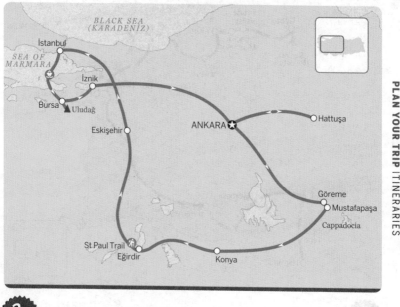

3 WEEKS

Cappadocia Meander

Travellers are often confronted with a tough choice when deciding where to go in Turkey after İstanbul: Cappadocia or the southwestern coast. If you feel drawn to the former's fairy-tale landscape, there are a few worthwhile stops en route across Anatolia.

After following the **İstanbul** leg of the Classic Turkey itinerary, hop on a ferry across the Sea of Marmara to **Bursa**. The city, recently proclaimed a World Heritage Site, does a good line in Ottoman mosques and mausoleums, İskender kebaps and Karagöz shadow puppets; and nearby, the world's longest gondola climbs to **Uludağ's** ski resort. Head north to lakeside **İznik**, its Ottoman tile-making heritage on display between Roman-Byzantine walls.

Next, bus it to **Ankara**, the Turkish capital. The city is no match for that show-stealer on the Bosphorus, but two key sights here give an insight into Turkish history, ancient and modern: the Anıt Kabir, Atatürk's hilltop mausoleum, and the Museum of Anatolian Civilisations, a restored 15th-century *bedesten* (covered market) packed with finds from the surrounding steppe. Tying in with the latter, a detour east takes in the isolated, evocative ruins of **Hattuşa**, which was the Hittite capital in the late Bronze age.

Leave three days to explore Cappadocia – base yourself in a cave hotel in **Göreme**, the travellers' hang-out surrounded by valleys of fairy chimneys. The famous rock formations line the roads to sights including Göreme Open-Air Museum's rock-cut frescoed churches and the Byzantine underground cities at Kaymaklı and Derinkuyu. Among the hot-air balloon trips, valley walks and horse riding, schedule some time to just sit and appreciate the fantastical landscape in çay-drinking villages such as **Mustafapaşa**.

Fly straight back to İstanbul or, if you have enough time and a penchant for Anatolia's mountains and steppe, continue by bus. Stop in **Konya** for lunch and tour the turquoisedomed Mevlâna Museum, containing the tomb of the Mevlâna (whirling dervish) order's 13th-century founder, en route to **Eğirdir**. Lakeside Eğirdir, with its road-connected island and crumbling old Greek quarter ringed by beaches and the Taurus Mountains, is a serene base for walking sections of the **St Paul Trail**. Again, you can fly back to İstanbul from here, but vibrant **Eskişehir** is a worthwhile stop-off, with its studentdriven nightlife, river gondola rides and picturesque old town.

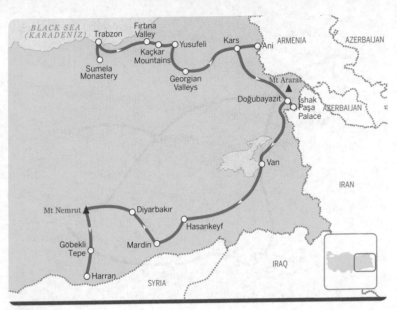

4 WEEKS Eastern Delights

From the Black Sea shore to the borders of the Middle East, Turkey's little-visited eastern reaches are sweeter than *bal* (honey) for adventurous travellers.

Start with a couple of days in buzzing **Trabzon**, where sights include the 13th-century Aya Sofya, then move south to visit **Sumela Monastery**, peering down on a forested valley from its rock face. Head along the coast and drive up the **Fırtına Valley**, with its Ottoman humpback bridges and Hemşin culture. Circle the **Kaçkar Mountains**, or tackle a multiday trek over the top, to **Yusufeli**, where the Çoruh River white-water rafting is worth sampling before a dam floods the area. The onward journey to Kars through the **Georgian Valleys** is one of Turkey's most scenic, heading over mountains, through gorges and past crumbling castles to medieval churches in hill villages.

Russian-influenced **Kars** is an intriguing city surrounded by the vast Anatolian steppe. The star attraction here is nearby **Ani**, once a thriving Armenian capital, and now a field strewn with magnificent ruins. Spend a couple of days in the area, where weather-beaten Armenian and Georgian churches hide in corners of the steppe. Next, head south past **Mt Ararat** (Ağrı Dağı, 5137m), Turkey's highest mountain, to **Doğubayazıt**. Perched above the predominantly Kurdish border town, **İshak Paşa Palace** surveys the plains, resembling a romantic scene from *One Thousand and One Nights*.

Continue south to **Van**, on the shore of the vast, mountain-ringed lake of the same name. Take a couple of days to see the 10th-century church on Akdamar Island in the lake, and 17th-century Hoşap Castle. Heading southwest, **Hasankeyf** is a sort of Cappadocia in miniature, set to be submerged by a dam; and honey-coloured **Mardin**, with its minarets, churches and castle, overlooks the roasting Mesopotamian plains.

Next, enter the Byzantine city walls at **Diyarbakır**, the heartland of Kurdish culture, before climbing **Mt Nemrut** (Nemrut Dağı) to see the gigantic stone heads left by a megalomaniac pre-Roman king – one of eastern Turkey's most famous sights. Head south to finish with a final hit of history at Şanlıurfa's Neolithic **Göbekli Tepe**, perhaps the world's first place of worship, and **Harran**, which hosted Abraham in 1900 BC and is one of the planet's oldest continuously inhabited spots.

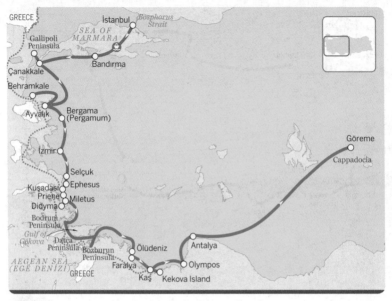

Palm Trees & Fairy Chimneys

4 WEEKS

If you have a kind boss, you don't have to choose between Cappadocia's wavy valleys and the coast's white-sand beaches – prepare to spend many hours on buses and check out both areas.

Follow the Classic Turkey itinerary, and add an extra stop in **Behramkale**, where you can survey the Aegean from an old Greek village scattered around a hilltop temple; or **Bergama**, overlooked by the vertigo-inducing theatre in Pergamum's Greco-Roman acropolis.

From Ephesus, hit the southern Aegean coast in cruise port **Kuşadası**, which offers 'PMD' day trips to the ruins of **Priene**, **Miletus** and **Didyma**. These sites, respectively two ancient port cities and a temple to Apollo, are interesting additions to an Ephesus visit. Spend a day or two eating calamari and drinking cocktails on the chichi **Bodrum Peninsula** and cross the Gulf of Gökova by ferry to the **Datça Peninsula**. With their fishing villages and rugged hinterland of forest-covered mountains, Datça and the adjoining **Bozburun Peninsula** are excellent for revving up a scooter or just putting your feet up.

Continuing along the Mediterranean coast, beautiful **Ölüdeniz** is the spot to paraglide from atop Baba Dağ (Mt Baba; 1960m) or lie low on a beach towel. You're now within kicking distance of the 509km-long Lycian Way. Hike for a day through superb countryside to overnight in heavenly **Faralya**, overlooking Butterfly Valley; further inroads into the trail will definitely top your 'next time' list.

Also on the Lycian Way, laid-back **Kaş'** pretty harbourside square buzzes nightly with friendly folk enjoying the sea breeze, views, fresh meze, and a beer or two. One of Turkey's most beguiling boat trips departs from here, taking in the sunken Lycian city at **Kekova Island**. From Kaş, it's a couple of hours to **Olympos**, famous for the naturally occurring Chimaera flames and beach tree houses.

A 1½-hour bus journey reaches the city of **Antalya**. Its Roman-Ottoman quarter, Kaleiçi, is worth a wander, against the backdrop of a jaw-dropping mountain range. Finally, drag yourself away from the beach and catch the bus north to claim your cave in **Göreme**, beatific base for a few days in Cappadocia's surreal moonscape.

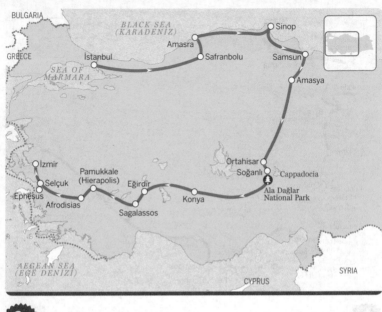

Anatolian Circle
3 WEEKS

This trip leaves out only eastern Anatolia, which is a mission in itself, and takes in both obscure gems and prime sights.

Begin with a few days among mosques, palaces and some 14 million folk in **İstanbul**, former capital of the Ottoman and Byzantine empires. Next, head east to **Safranbolu**, with its winding streets of Ottoman mansions, before turning north to **Amasra**, where Turkish holidaymakers wander the Byzantine castle and eat fresh fish on the two harbours. Amasra is the beginning of the drive through rugged hills to **Sinop**, another pretty Black Sea port town and the birthplace of Greek philosopher Diogenes the Cynic.

Next, it's a 6½-hour bus journey via **Samsun** to **Amasya**, with its Ottoman houses, Pontic tombs and castle. Take it all in from a terrace by the Yeşilırmak River, and drink several tulip-shaped glasses of çay, before another long bus ride across the Anatolian steppe to **Cappadocia**. This enchanting land of fairy chimneys and cave churches is wholeheartedly back on the beaten track, but you can escape the tour buses by exploring the valleys on foot or horseback. Likewise, Göreme and Ürgüp are the usual bases, but you could stay in a less-touristy village such as **Ortahisar**, with its craggy castle. South of central Cappadocia, see rock-cut churches without the crowds in **Soğanlı**, where Byzantine monastic settlements occupy two valleys; and head into the **Ala Dağlar National Park** for some of Turkey's most breathtaking scenery in the Taurus Mountains (Toros Dağları).

Konya, its magnificent mosques recalling its stint as capital of the Seljuk sultanate of Rum, makes a convenient lunch stop en route to Eğirdir. Lakeside **Eğirdir** has views of the Taurus Mountains and little-visited local sights such as **Sagalassos**, a ruined Greco-Roman city at an altitude of 1500m. There are more impressive classical ruins at **Hierapolis**, an ancient spa city overlooking the village of **Pamukkale** from atop the travertines, a mountain of calcite shelves. Nearby **Afrodisias**, once a Roman provincial capital, is equally incredible; you might have the 30,000-seat stadium to yourself.

From Denizli (near Pamukkale), it's just a few hours' journey by bus or train to **Selçuk**, base for visiting **Ephesus**. From Selçuk, you can fly back to İstanbul from nearby **İzmir**, or continue overland via our Classic Turkey itinerary.

Plan Your Trip
Turkey's Outdoors

Whether you want to shoot downstream in a raft, sail over archaeological remains, tackle challenging summits or explore the countryside on horseback, Turkey offers superb playgrounds for active travellers from aspiring kayakers to dedicated skiers. Safety standards are good too, provided you stick to reputable operators with qualified, English-speaking staff.

Walking & Trekking

Walking in Turkey is increasingly popular among both Turks and travellers, and a growing number of local and foreign firms offer walking holidays here. The country is blessed with numerous mountains, from the Taurus ranges in the southwest to the Kaçkars in the northeast, which all provide fabulous hiking opportunities. Hiking is also the best way to visit villages and sights rarely seen by holidaymakers, and it will give you a taste of life in rural Turkey.

Hiking options range from challenging multiday hikes, including Mt Ararat (Ağrı Dağı), Turkey's highest summit and a possible location of Noah's Ark, to gentle afternoon strolls, such as in Cappadocia.

For more information on hiking in Turkey, visit **Trekking in Turkey** (www.trekkinginturkey.com) and **Culture Routes in Turkey** (www.cultureroutesinturkey.com).

Safety Advice

Bar a few well-known and well-maintained trails, most are not signposted and it's recommended to hire a guide, or at least seek local advice before setting off.

Weather conditions can fluctuate quickly between extremes, so come prepared and check the local conditions.

Top Regions

Antalya & the Turquoise Coast

The western Mediterranean offers the widest array of activities, including sea kayaking, boat trips, diving, two waymarked walking trails, canyoning, rafting and paragliding.

Cappadocia

Excellent for a half- or full-day hike, with a surreal landscape of curvy valleys and fairy chimneys (rock formations). There are also mountain-walking opportunities, horse riding, and skiing on Erciyes Dağı (Mt Erciyes).

Eastern Anatolia

Head to the eastern wilds, especially the northern part, for serious adrenaline fixes – mountain walking, white-water rafting, horse riding, skiing, snowboarding and cross-country skiing.

South Aegean

Bring your swimming trunks to the more-popular stretch of the Aegean, where operators in spots such as Bodrum, Marmaris and Akyaka offer boat trips galore, and water sports including diving, waterskiing, windsurfing and kiteboarding.

ANDERS BLOMQVIST / GETTY IMAGES ©

DANITA DELIMONT / GETTY IMAGES ©

Top: Rafting (p43),
Çoruh River
Bottom: Paragliding
Ölüdeniz (p43)

Day Walks

For half- and full-day walks, Cappadocia is unbeatable, with a dozen valleys that are easily negotiated on foot, around Göreme and the Ihlara Valley. These walks, one to several hours in length with minor gradients, are perfectly suited to casual walkers and even families. The fairy chimneys are unforgettable, and walking is the best way to do the landscapes and sights justice – and discover areas that travellers usually don't reach. After all, there aren't many places in the world where you can walk between a string of ancient, rock-cut churches in a lunar landscape.

Long-Distance Trails

Culture Routes in Turkey has developed two iconic waymarked trails, the Lycian Way and St Paul Trail, plus several new long-distance routes, which range from the Carian Trail in the south Aegean to Abraham's Path around Şanlıurfa. The routes are best tackled in spring or autumn and you don't have to walk them in their entirety; it's easy to bite off a small chunk. Consult the websites on p39 for information, guidebooks and maps covering the trails.

Lycian Way

Chosen by British Newspaper *The Sunday Times* as one of the world's 10 best walks, the Lycian Way covers 509km between Fethiye and Antalya, partly inland, partly along the coast of ancient Lycia, via Patara, Kalkan, Kaş, Finike, Olympos and Tekirova. Highlights include stunning coastal views, pine and cedar forests, laid-back villages, ruins of ancient cities, Mt Olympos and Baba Dağ. Kate Clow, who established the trail, describes it in detail in walking guide *The Lycian Way*.

St Paul Trail

The St Paul Trail extends 500km north, from Perge, 10km east of Antalya, to Yalvaç, northeast of Eğirdir Gölü (Lake Eğirdir). Partly following the route walked by St Paul on his first missionary journey in Asia Minor, it's more challenging than the Lycian Way, with more ascents. Along the way you'll pass canyons, waterfalls, forests, a medieval paved road, Roman baths and an aqueduct, and numerous quaint villages.

HIKER'S DILEMMA: ARARAT OR KAÇKARS

Zafer Onay (p569), a trekking guide based in Doğubayazıt, guides hikers on Mt Ararat and in the Kaçkars. 'Mt Ararat is a great climb, but landscapes in the Kaçkars are more scenic; they form a range, which means you can expect more diversity. It's more colourful, you can see wildflowers and, if you're lucky, you can spot bears and ibex. Birdwatching is also an option in the Kaçkars.'

St Paul Trail, by Kate Clow and Terry Richardson, describes the trail in detail. Eğirdir is a good place to base yourself, with an activities centre geared towards walking the trail.

Mountain Walks

Turkey is home to some seriously good mountain walking.

Mt Ararat (p568) Turkey's highest mountain, the majestic and challenging 5137m Mt Ararat, near the Armenian border, is one of the region's top climbs and can be tackled in five days (including acclimatisation) from nearby Doğubayazıt. You'll need to be cashed up and patient with all the bureaucracy – a permit is mandatory.

Kaçkar Mountains (p542) In northeastern Anatolia, the Kaçkars are increasingly popular with Europeans. They offer lakes, forests and varied flora, at altitudes from about 2000m to 3937m. There are numerous possible routes, ranging from a few hours to several days, notably the multiday Trans-Kaçkar Trek.

Cappadocia (p463) Southern Cappadocia has good mountain walks, including 3268m Mt Hasan and the Taurus Mountains in Ala Dağlar National Park.

Water Sports

Lounging on a white-sand beach is certainly tempting, but there are many opportunities to dip your toes in the sea.

Scuba Diving

OK, the Red Sea it ain't, but where else in the world can you swim over amphorae and broken pottery from ancient

DO YOU WANNA GÜLET?

For a boat trip along the Aegean or Mediterranean coast, there are endless possibilities, ranging from day trips – out of pretty much everywhere with a harbour, from Ayvalık in the north Aegean all the way around the coast to Alanya in the eastern Mediterranean – to chartering a graceful *gület* (traditional wooden yacht) for a few days of cruising around beaches and bays. The most popular *gület* route is between Demre (Kale; near Olympos) and Fethiye, although aficionados say the route between Marmaris and Fethiye is prettier.

shipwrecks? Turkey also offers a wide choice of reefs, drop-offs and caves. The waters are generally calm, with no tides or currents, and visibility averages 20m (not too bad by Mediterranean standards). Pelagics are rare, but small reef species are prolific. Here you can mingle with groupers, dentex, moray eels, sea bream, octopus and parrotfish, as well as the occasional amberjack, barracuda and ray. You don't need to be a strong diver; there are sites for all levels of proficiency. For experienced divers, there are superb expanses of red coral to explore (usually under 30m of water).

The standard of diving facilities is high, and you'll find professional dive centres staffed with qualified, English-speaking instructors. Most centres are affiliated with internationally recognised dive organisations. Compared with other countries, diving in Turkey is pretty cheap, and it's also a great place to learn. Most dive companies offer introductory dives for beginners and reasonably priced open-water certification courses.

While it is possible to dive all year, the best time is May to October, when the water is warmest (you can expect up to 25°C in September).

Top Dive Spots

Kaş is Turkey's scuba-diving hub, with excellent Mediterranean dive sites and numerous operators. On the Aegean coast, Marmaris, Bodrum, Kuşadası and Ayvalık also have a reputation for good diving.

Sea Kayaking & Canoeing

Maps clearly show the tortuous coastline in the western Mediterranean area, with its secluded coves, deep blue bays, pine-clad mountains, islands shimmering in the distance, and laid-back villages. Paddling is the best way to comfortably access pristine terrain – some inaccessible by road – and experience the breathtaking scenery of the aptly named Turquoise Coast. Adding excitement to the journey, you might see flying fish and turtles, and if you're really lucky, frolicking dolphins.

Day trips are the norm, but longer tours can be organised with overnight camping under the stars on deserted beaches. They should include transfers, guides, gear and meals. There are also paddling spots on the Aegean coast, including Akyaka.

Top Paddling Spots

Kekova Sunken City (p359) This magical spot, with Lycian ruins partly submerged 6m below the sea, perfectly lends itself to a sea-kayaking tour from Kaş. This superb day excursion, suitable for all fitness levels, allows you to glide over underwater walls, foundations and staircases submerged by 2nd-century earthquakes, clearly visible through crystal-clear waters.

Patara (p346) Canoeing trips on the Xanthos River offer a unique opportunity to glide past jungle-like riverbanks and discover a rich ecosystem, with birds, crabs and turtles. Ending your journey on Patara beach, Turkey's longest, adds to the appeal.

Canyoning

Canyoning is a mix of climbing, hiking, abseiling, swimming and some serious jumping or plunging – down waterfalls, river gorges, and water-polished chutes in natural pools. Experience is not usually

SADDLE UP!

Cappadocia is Turkey's top spot for horse riding, with numerous good riding tracks criss-crossing the marvellous landscapes. Outfits including Cappadocia's own horse whisperer are ready to take you on guided rides, ranging from one-hour jaunts to fully catered treks. The best thing about riding here is that you can access terrain you can't otherwise get to.

necessary, but water confidence and reasonable fitness are advantageous. Expect adventure centres offering canyoning to provide wetsuits, helmets and harnesses, and outings to be led by a qualified instructor. The 18km-long Saklıkent Gorge (p344), southeast of Fethiye, features leaping into natural pools, swimming through narrow passages, scrambling over rocks and abseiling down waterfalls.

White-Water Rafting

Stick to the more reputable operators, as it's important to choose one with the experience, skills and equipment to run a safe and exciting expedition. Your guide should give you a comprehensive safety talk and paddle training before you launch off downstream. Top rafting spots:

Çoruh River (p544) Come to Yusufeli from June to August for fantastic white-water rafting; and come before 2018, when the area is set to be flooded by a dam. Thanks to rugged topography and an abundance of snowmelt, the iconic Çoruh River and its tributaries offer world-class runs with powerful grade 2 to 5 rapids. An added thrill is the breathtaking scenery along the sheer walls of the Çoruh Gorge. Trips generally last three hours.

İspir and Barhal Rivers (p551) Also near Yusufeli, the fainter of heart can take a mellower but equally scenic trip on these tributaries of the Çoruh.

Çamlıhemşin (p545) On the other side of the Kaçkars, offering gentler rapids and impressive scenery.

Köprülü Kanyon (p379) In the western Mediterranean region, near Antalya.

Saklıkent Gorge (p344) An 18km-long gorge near Fethiye.

Zamantı River (p499) In Cappadocia's Ala Dağlar National Park.

Windsurfing & Kitesurfing

The PWA (Professional Windsurfers Association) World Cup takes place in Alaçatı, on the Çeşme Peninsula. With constant, strong breezes (up to 25 knots) and a 2km-long beach with shallows and calm water conditions from mid-May to early November, Alaçatı is a world-class windsurfing destination and a prime kitesurfing spot. It's also an ideal place to learn, with English-speaking instructors and an array of classes available. Alternatively, Akyaka (near Marmaris) is increasingly popular for windsurfing and kite boarding.

PARAGLIDING

Picture yourself gracefully drifting over the velvety indigo of the sea, feeling the caress of the breeze. Paragliding from the slopes of Baba Dağ (1960m) in Ölüdeniz, which has consistently excellent uplifting thermals from late April to early November, is top notch. For beginners, local operators offer tandem flights, for which no training or experience is required. You just have to run a few steps and the rest is entirely controlled by the pilot, to whom you're attached with a harness. Parasailing is also available in Ölüdeniz, while Kaş and Pamukkale are also popular for paragliding.

Winter Sports

Don't expect the Alps, but powder junkies will be genuinely surprised at the quality of Turkey's infrastructure and the great snow conditions from December to April. Whether you're a seasoned or novice *kayakcı* (skier), there are options galore. Most ski resorts have been upgraded in recent years and feature good facilities, including well-equipped hotels – and at lower prices than many Western European resorts.

Most hotels offer daily and weekly packages including lift passes and full board. Equipment rental and tuition are available, though English-speaking instructors are hard to find. Most resorts cater to snowboarders, and some offer cross-country skiing and snowshoeing.

Ski Resorts

Uludağ (p295) Near Bursa, this major resort has chain hotels and a gondola from the city's outskirts. It's popular on winter weekends.

Palandöken (p542) A major resort on the outskirts of Erzurum.

Sarıkamış (p565) Surrounded by pines, this low-key resort near Kars has deep, dry powder.

Davraz Dağı (p319) Mt Davraz rises between three lakes near Eğirdir, offering Nordic and downhill skiing and snowboarding.

Erciyes Dağı (p505) Above Kayseri in the Cappadocia region, Mt Erciyes offers empty pistes and a developing resort.

Spinach and cheese *gözleme*

Plan Your Trip

Eat & Drink Like a Local

Turks love to eat and are ferociously proud of their national cuisine, treating it as reverently as any of the country's museum collections or archaeological sites. This is for good reason – food here is packed with flavour, prepared with great expertise and enjoyed with gusto.

The Year in Food

Turkish cuisine is resolutely and deliciously seasonal.

Spring (Mar–May)

Kalkan (turbot), *levrek* (sea bass), *mezgit* (whiting) and *karides* (shrimp) are in plentiful supply, often enjoyed with new-season lemon. Salads feature artichoke, broad bean, radish and cucumber; strawberries and green plums are plentiful.

Summer (Jun–Aug)

Sardalya (sardines) and *ıstakoz* (lobster) are summer treats. Meze spreads draw on freshly harvested artichoke, broad bean and walnut. Salads feature cucumber, corn and tomato; watermelon and fig start four-month seasons.

Autumn (Sep–Nov)

Locals celebrate the start of the four-month *hamsi* (anchovy), *palamut* (bonito) and *lüfer* (bluefish) seasons, as well as the short *çupra* (gilthead sea bream) season. Pomegranates appear in October.

Winter (Dec–Feb)

The best season for fish; December is known for its *hamsi* and January for *istavrit* (horse mackerel), *lüfer* and *palamut*. Chestnuts are harvested and roasted on street corners.

Food Experiences

Keen on the idea of a gastronomic odyssey? You've come to the right country.

Meals of a Lifetime

Asitane (p117) & **Matbah** (p115) İstanbul restaurants that research and recreate Ottoman dishes devised for the palace kitchens at Topkapı and Dolmabahçe.

Levissi Garden (p343) Marvellous Mediterranean meals served in a 400-year-old building in an atmosphere-laden former Greek village.

Cappadocia Home Cooking (p496) Rustic treats enjoyed in a family home surrounded by an organic garden on the edge of the Ayvalı Gorge.

Okyanus Balık Evi (p517) The best seafood restaurant on the Black Sea coast, with a strict 'only in season' policy and an unusual meze selection.

Diyarbakır Kahvaltı Evi (p599) Lavish and delectable village-style breakfasts served in the courtyard of a heritage mansion.

Cheap Treats

Balık ekmek Grilled fish fillets stuffed into bread with salad and a squeeze of lemon; sold at stands next to ferry docks around the country.

Simit Bread ring studded with sesame seeds; sold in bakeries and by street vendors.

Midye dolma Mussels stuffed with spiced rice and sold by street vendors.

Döner kebap Lamb cooked on a revolving upright skewer then thinly sliced and served in bread with salad and a sprinkling of sumac.

Gözleme Thin savoury crepes filled with cheese, spinach, mushroom or potato; particularly popular in central Anatolia.

Dare to Try

Kokoreç Seasoned lamb/mutton intestines stuffed with offal, grilled over coals and served in bread; sold at *kokoreçis* (*kokoreç* stands).

Boza Viscous tonic made from water, sugar and fermented barley that has a reputation for building up strength and virility. Best sampled at historic Vefa Bozacısı (p123) in İstanbul.

İşkembe or kelle paça çorba Tripe or sheep's trotter soup; the former is reputed to be a hangover cure.

Şalgam suyu Sour, crimson-coloured juice made by boiling turnips and adding vinegar; particularly popular in the eastern Mediterranean city of Mersin.

Ayvalık tost Toasted sandwich crammed with cheese, spicy sausage, pickles, tomatoes, ketchup, mayonnaise and anything else its creator can think of; named after the north Aegean town where it was invented.

Local Specialities

İstanbul

It's the national capital in all but name and Turks relocate here from every corner of the country, meaning that regional cuisines are well represented within the local restaurant scene. The Syrian-influenced dishes of Turkey's southeast are particularly fashionable at the moment, but the number one choice when it comes to dining out is almost inevitably a Black Sea–style fish restaurant or *meyhane* (tavern). The only dishes that can be said to be unique to the city are those served at Ottoman restaurants where the rich concoctions enjoyed by the sultans and their courtiers are recreated.

Thrace & Marmara

In Marmara – and especially in its capital, Edirne – liver reigns supreme and is usually served deep-fried with crispy fried chillies and a dollop of yoghurt. Dishes in Thrace are dominated by fish rather than offal, and the locals are fond of sweet treats such as Gökçeada island's *efi badem* (sugar-dusted biscuits made with almond, butter and flour). In recent years, local wineries here have been producing some of the country's most impressive vintages and can be visited by following the newly created Thracian Vineyard Route.

Döner kebap

The Aegean

Mezes made with seafood, freshly picked vegetables, wild herbs and locally produced olive oil are the backbone of Turkish Aegean cuisine, providing a delicious inducement for visitors. Fish dominates menus on the coast, but inland villagers love their lamb, serving it in unusual forms such as *keşkek* (lamb mince and coarse, pounded wheat). The island of Bozcaada is dotted with picturesque vineyards supplying its three well-regarded local wineries with grapes.

Western & Central Anatolia

Turkey's heartland has a cuisine dominated by kebaps. Regional specialities that have become national treasures include the rich and addictive İskender, or Bursa, kebap (döner lamb on a bed of crumbled pide, topped with yoghurt, hot tomato sauce and browned butter) and the Tokat kebap (skewers of lamb and sliced eggplant hung vertically, grilled, then baked in a wood-fired oven and served with roasted garlic). Both take their names from the cities where they originated. Popular

---

TURKISH COFFEE

A thick and powerful brew, *Türk kahve* (Turkish coffee) is usually drunk in a couple of short sips. If you order a cup, you will be asked how sweet you like it – *çok şekerli* means 'very sweet', *orta şekerli* 'middling', *az şekerli* 'slightly sweet' and *şekersiz* or *sade* 'not at all'. Though you shouldn't drink the grounds in the bottom of your cup, you may want to read your fortune in them – check the Turkish Coffee/Fortune Telling section of the website of İstabul's longest-established purveyor of coffee, **Kurukahveci Mehmet Efendi** (www.mehmetefendi.com) for a guide.

Simit (sesame-encrusted bread rings; p45)

sweets include *kestane şekeri* (candied chestnuts).

The Mediterranean

The eastern Mediterranean is home to three towns with serious foodie credentials: Silifke, Adana and Antakya. Silifke is known for its yoghurt, Adana for its eponymously titled kebap (minced beef or lamb mixed with powdered red pepper then grilled on a skewer and dusted with slightly sour sumac) and Antakya for its wealth of Syrian-influenced dips, salads, croquettes and desserts. The best-loved of these desserts is *künefe,* layers of vermicelli-like noodles cemented together with sweet cheese, doused in sugar syrup and served hot with a sprinkling of pistachio. Both gooey and crispy, it's dangerously addictive – consider yourself warned.

Black Sea

Hamsi (anchovies) are loved with a passion along the Black Sea (Karadeniz) coast. Generations of cooks have used this slim silver fish in breads, soups and pilafs,

thrown them on the grill or dusted them with flour before snap-frying them. It's not the only culinary reason to head here, though. *Muhlama* (cornmeal cooked with butter and cheese), *karalahana çorbası* (collard soup) and the decadently rich *Laz böreği* (flaky pastry layered with custard and hazelnuts) are other dishes that demand gastronomic investigation.

Southeastern Anatolia

Top of this region's foodie hit parade is Gaziantep (Antep), destination of choice for lovers of pistachio. The local examples are plump and flavoursome, showcased in the city's famous baklava and *katmer* (thin pastry sheets layered with clotted cream and nuts, topped with pistachio, baked and served straight from the oven). Also notable is Şanlıurfa (Urfa), home to Urfa kebap (skewered lamb with tomatoes, sliced onion and hot peppers) and the country's best examples of the Arabic-influenced wafer-thin pizza known as *lahmacun.* Other regional treats include sweet apricots from Malatya.

FROE MEL KAPITZA / GETTY IMAGES ©

Turkish coffee (p46)

Northeastern Anatolia

Fruits of the forest and field are on show in this far-flung corner of the country. Flowery honey from small producers is slathered on bread and topped with ultra-creamy *kaymak* (clotted cream) in a breakfast ritual that is now being emulated across the country, and *kaz* (duck) and lamb are roasted or stewed in dishes reminiscent of those served in neighbouring Iran, Georgia and Armenia. Unusual drinks include *reyhane,* made from purple basil.

How to Eat & Drink

Like all countries with great national cuisines, Turkey has rules and rituals around where and when to eat. Here's a quick guide, but see the menu decoder on p640 for more information.

When to Eat

Kahvaltı (breakfast) Usually eaten at home, although *böreks* (sweet or savoury filled pastries) and *simit*s are popular eat-on-the-run alternatives.

Ögle yemeği (lunch) Usually eaten at a cafe, *lokanta* (eatery serving ready-made dishes) or fast-food stand around noon.

Akşam yemeği (dinner) The main meal of the day, eaten with family and/or friends around 6pm (rural areas) and 7.30pm to 8pm (cities).

Where to Eat

Balık restoran Fish restaurant.

Hazır yemek lokanta (often abbreviated to *lokanta*) Eatery serving ready-made meals.

Kebapçı Kebap restaurant.

Köfteçi Köfte (meatball) restaurant.

Meyhane Tavern where mezes, grilled meats and fish are enjoyed and where live music is sometimes performed.

Ocakbaşı Kebap restaurant where customers watch meat being grilled over coals.

Pideci Pide maker or seller.

Menu Decoder

Ana yemekler Main courses; usually meat or fish dishes.

Bira Beer; the most popular local tipple is Efes Pilsen.

Dolma Something stuffed with rice and/or meat.

İçmeklar Drinks

Meze Small tapas-like hot or cold dish eaten at the start of a meal.

Porsiyon Portion, helping. *Yarım porsiyon* is a half-portion.

(Kırmızı/Beyaz) Şarap (Red/White) Wine

Servis ücreti Service charge

Su Water; *maden suyu* is mineral water.

Tatlı(lar) Sweets; often baklava, stewed fruit or a milk-based pudding.

Zeytinyağlı Food cooked in olive oil.

Plan Your Trip

Travel with Children

Çocuklar (children) are the beloved centrepiece of family life in Turkey, and your children will be welcomed wherever they go. Your journey will peppered with exclamations of Maşallah (glory be to God) and your children will be clutched into the adoring arms of strangers.

Turkey for Kids

Travelling in family-focused Turkey is a blessing with kids big and small – waiters play with babies, strangers entertain and indulge at every turn, free or discounted entry to sights is common. Do bear in mind, however, that facilities are often lacking and safety consciousness rarely meets Western norms.

Children's Highlights

Accommodation

➡ Cappadocian cave hotels, Olympos tree houses and Kabak's beach retreats offer novel accommodation.

Activities

➡ In the western Mediterranean region, mix beach-based fun and water sports with activities such as tandem paragliding.

➡ The Aegean is good for a relaxed seaside holiday, with beaches, Kuşadası and Marmaris' water parks and the Bodrum area's resorts.

➡ Cappadocia offers activities including horse riding and hot-air ballooning.

Best Regions for Kids

Ephesus, Bodrum & the South Aegean

Ruins such as Ephesus for older children, plus beaches for kids of all ages. Holiday spots like Kuşadası, Bodrum, Marmaris and Akyaka offer plenty of sights, facilities, resorts, water parks and sports, with less touristy coastline nearby.

Antalya & the Turquoise Coast

Water sports and activities from tandem paragliding to sea kayaking over submerged ruins. With younger children, holiday towns like Kaş offer picturesque lanes and sandy beaches.

Cappadocia

The fantastical landscape of fairy chimneys (rock formations) and underground cities will thrill older children, as will cave accommodation. A safe, relaxing rural area with activities including horse riding, hot-air ballooning and walking.

İzmir & the North Aegean

More Aegean beaches. İzmir's kordon (seafront) is a child-friendly promenade – spacious, flat, pretty and offering numerous eating options. Bozcaada island is easy to negotiate and enjoy, with safe swimming beaches and good cycling.

➡ Teenagers will enjoy walking in Cappadocia or the Kaçkar Mountains.

➡ Cooking courses are available in locations such as İstanbul.

Historic Sites

➡ For older children and teenagers, Turkey offers numerous major sights, from Ephesus to Ani, Pergamum to Mt Nemrut (Nemrut Dağı).

➡ Ruins such as İstanbul's Hippodrome (p69) offer plenty of space for toddlers to expend energy.

➡ Children will love the creepy atmosphere of İstanbul's subterranean Basilica Cistern, with walkways suspended over the water.

➡ Exploring Cappadocia's fairy chimneys, caves and underground cities will prove memorable for older kids.

➡ At Mediterranean spots such as Patara and Kekova, you can mix ruins with beach, boat trips and sea kayaking.

Museums

➡ The Rahmi M Koç museums in İstanbul (p106) and Ankara (p421) are interactive museums with planes, trains and automobiles on display.

➡ İstanbul Modern (p94) gallery has multimedia exhibits to amuse and engage.

➡ Children under 12 receive free or discounted entry to many museums and monuments.

Transport

➡ Ferries in İstanbul and İzmir are popular.

➡ İstanbul's funiculars and antique tram are novelties.

➡ The world's longest gondola climbs Uludağ (2543m) from Bursa.

➡ *Fayton* (horse-drawn carriage) rides and bikes are offered on İstanbul's Princes' Islands.

Treats

➡ Turkey does sweet treats as well as it does kebaps – including baklava, *dondurma* (ice cream) and *lokum* (Turkish delight).

Planning

Accommodation

➡ Many hotels in all price ranges have family suites.

➡ Self-catering apartments and villas are common in tourist areas such as Bodrum.

➡ Cots are increasingly common; many hotels will organise one with advance notice.

➡ Resorts offer kids' clubs and hotels in tourist areas may be able to arrange babysitting.

Eating

➡ Children's menus are uncommon outside tourist areas, but restaurants will often prepare special dishes for children.

➡ High chairs are by no means common, but increasingly widespread in tourist areas (apart from İstanbul).

Facilities

➡ Public baby-changing facilities are rare, but found in some chain restaurants.

➡ Breastfeeding in public is uncommon; best to do so in a private or discreet place.

➡ Seaside towns and cities often have playgrounds, but check the equipment for safety.

Getting Around

➡ Buses often lack functioning toilets, but they normally stop every few hours.

➡ Free travel on public transport within cities, and discounts on longer journeys, are common.

➡ Most car-rental companies can provide baby seats for a small extra charge.

➡ Dangerous drivers and uneven surfaces make using strollers an extreme sport.

➡ A 'baby backpack' is useful for walking around sights.

Health

➡ Consider giving children the BCG tuberculosis vaccine if they haven't had it.

➡ In hot, moist climates, any wound or break in the skin may lead to infection. The area should be cleaned and then kept dry and clean.

➡ Encourage your child to avoid dogs and other mammals because of the risk of rabies and other diseases.

➡ For children and pregnant or breastfeeding women, double-check drugs and dosages prescribed for travel by doctors and pharmacists, as they may be unsuitable. The same applies to practitioners in Turkey.

➡ Some information on the suitability of drugs and recommended dosage can be found on travel-health websites.

Products

➡ Pasteurised UHT milk is sold in cartons everywhere, but fresh milk is harder to find.

➡ Consider bringing a supply of baby food – what little you find here, your baby will likely find inedible – or it will just be mashed banana.

➡ Migros supermarkets have the best range of baby food.

➡ Most supermarkets stock formula (although it is very expensive) and vitamin-fortified rice cereal.

➡ Disposable *bebek bezi* (nappies or diapers) are readily available.

➡ The best nappies are Prima and Huggies, sold in pharmacies and supermarkets; don't bother with cheaper local brands.

Resources

➡ Lonely Planet's *Travel with Children* has practical information and advice.

➡ This book's chapters including İstanbul have boxed texts on seeing the respective destinations with children.

Safety

➡ In hotels and other buildings, look out for open power points.

➡ Many taps are unmarked and reversed (cold on the left, hot on the right).

On the street, watch for:

➡ Turkey's notorious drivers, particularly those on pavement-mounting mopeds.

➡ Crudely covered electric mains.

➡ Open stairwells.

➡ Serious potholes.

➡ Open drains.

➡ Carelessly secured building sites.

Regions at a Glance

Given Turkey's vast scale, it makes sense to focus your travels on one or two regions. This need not confine you to one part of the country – domestic flights are an affordable way to cross the Anatolian steppe in a few hours. A visit to mighty İstanbul can easily be paired with a bus or train to western Turkey's many highlights, or a flight east for off-the-beaten-track adventures. While there are many constants throughout Turkey and the food is certainly excellent everywhere, this is an incredibly diverse country offering varied experiences. Each region has its own charms, so choose wisely and you could find yourself white-water rafting in wild northeastern Anatolia, sauntering through cosmopolitan İstanbul or sun bathing on a Mediterranean beach.

İstanbul

History
Nightlife
Shopping

History

The megacity formerly known as Constantinople and Byzantium was the capital of a series of empires. The Aya Sofya, a church-turned-mosque-turned-museum, is the grandest remnant of the Byzantine Empire; Ottoman landmarks include the Blue Mosque and Topkapı Palace.

Nightlife

Beyoğlu is an exhilarating melting pot between the dusk and dawn calls to prayer, when up-for-it crowds swirl through its rooftop bars, pedestrian precincts and bohemian nightclubs.

Shopping

The city's famous bazaars include the sprawling Grand Bazaar, the Spice Bazaar, and the Arasta Bazaar with its carpet and ceramics stores. There are markets and malls galore, including Kadıköy's food market on the Asian side, while worthwhile neighbourhoods range from Çukurcuma, with its antiques and collectables, to Galata for avant-garde fashion.

p58

Thrace & Marmara

History
Battlefields
Architecture

History

Turkey's northwest corner is famous for the Gallipoli Peninsula, the site of WWI battles, and Troy. A ferry ride from Gallipoli and Çanakkale is Gökçeada island, with its Greek heritage and slow-paced Aegean lifestyle, and further north is Edirne, once capital of the Ottoman Empire.

Battlefields

Over 100,000 soldiers died on the now-tranquil Gallipoli Peninsula, a pilgrimage site for Australians, New Zealanders and Turks. Touring the memorials, battlefields and trenches is simply heart-wrenching.

Architecture

Edirne's Ottoman gems include Selimiye Camii, one of the finest works of the great architect Mimar Sinan. Gökçeada's hilltop villages of tumbledown Greek houses are time capsules, while Çanakkale's Ottoman old town has mosques, hamams and a 19th-century clock tower.

p142

İzmir & the North Aegean

History
Village Life
Food

History

The hilltop ruins of Pergamum are renowned as some of Turkey's finest. There are also numerous, less-visited sites along the Biga Peninsula and echoes of the population exchange with Greece in Ayvalık and Bozcaada town's old Greek quarters. Look out, too, for İzmir's unique Sephardic synagogues and the Ayvacık area's descendents of Turkmen nomads.

Village Life

In laid-back spots such as Bozcaada island, the Biga Peninsula, Behramkale, Ayvalık and Bergama, life has an alluringly slow rural pace. Changing seasons and weekly markets are still the main events.

Food

This is the place to try Aegean *balık* (fish) and rakı (anise spirit) on a seafront terrace. There's even a saying about one town's pescatarian excellence: 'rakı, *balık,* Ayvalık'.

p174

Ephesus, Bodrum & the South Aegean

History
Nightlife
Sun & Surf

History

Romans once bustled along the Curetes Ways at Ephesus, Turkey's most visited ruins. Less-frequented sites include eerie Priene, a hilltop Ionian city; Miletus, an ancient port; Didyma's Temple of Apollo, once the world's second-largest temple; and Knidos, a Dorian port on the Datça Peninsula.

Nightlife

Bodrum's tourist machine has created a mean nightlife, with waterfront bar-clubs on its twin bays. Another sexy Bodrum Peninsula sundowner spot is Türkbükü, summer playground of İstanbul's jet set.

Sun & Surf

The Bodrum Peninsula's beaches are excellent for sunning, swimming and water sports; and the Datça and Bozburun peninsulas hide secluded coves and azure waters. *Gület* (traditional Turkish wooden yacht) cruises take in the coastline between Marmaris and Fethiye.

p218

Western Anatolia

History
Ruins
Fresh Air

History

Bursa was the Ottoman capital before Constantinople, İznik's gateways and Aya Sofya recall its Byzantine greatness, and the Phrygian Valley's rock-hewn monuments survive from the distant Phrygian era. Meanwhile, Eskişehir mixes its pastel-painted Ottoman quarter with today's lively cultural scene and nightlife.

Ruins

Hierapolis, a ruined ancient spa city, famously stands atop Pamukkale's glistening white travertines. Quieter sites include Afrodisias, a grand provincial Roman capital, and Sagalassos, a Pisidian-Hellenistic-Roman city in the Taurus Mountains.

Fresh Air

Two long-distance hiking paths, the Phrygian Way and St Paul Trail, respectively wind through the Phrygian Valley, and over the Taurus Mountains from the Mediterranean to western Anatolia's serene Lake District. Above Bursa, Uludağ ('Great Mountain'; 2543m) is one of Turkey's best ski resorts.

p280

Antalya & the Turquoise Coast

History
Beaches
Ruins

History

The western Mediterranean region's coves and valleys are layered with history. Even its two waymarked paths, the Lycian Way and St Paul Trail, name check historical folk who passed through. The former trail crosses the Teke Peninsula, littered with sepulchres and sarcophagi left millennia ago by the Lycians.

Beaches

Patara, Turkey's longest beach, and İztuzu Beach near Dalyan both shelter Lycian ruins and nesting sea turtles. Olympos is famed for its 'tree house' accommodation and the naturally occurring flames of Chimaera. For solitude, take a high-suspension vehicle down to Kabak's cliff-flanked beach.

Ruins

The trademark funerary monuments of the Lycian civilisation still nestle in spectacular spots such as Xanthos, Pınara and Kaleköy, while other gems include Antalya's Roman-Ottoman antique quarter.

p322

Eastern Mediterranean

History
Food
Christian Sites

History

History has a fairy-tale quality here: Kızkalesi Castle (Maiden's Castle) seemingly floats offshore, and Zeus is said to have imprisoned hydra-headed Typhon in the Gorge of Hell. Karatepe-Aslantaş Open-Air Museum preserves the ruins of an important town for the late-Hittite kings of Cilicia.

Food

Seafront fish restaurants abound on this stretch of coast, and Antakya is a Turkish and Arab culinary melting pot. The city's influences from nearby Syria include lemon wedges and mint, which accompany kebaps and local specialities.

Christian Sites

The early Christian and Old Testament sites in Tarsus include St Paul's ruined house, where pilgrims drink from the well. Paul and Peter both preached in Antakya (the biblical Antioch), and Silifke's Church of St Thekla recalls Paul's early follower.

p384

Ankara & Central Anatolia

History
Architecture
Ruins

History

This is where the whirling dervishes first whirled, Atatürk began his revolution, Alexander the Great cut the Gordion knot, King Midas turned everything to gold, and Julius Caesar uttered his famous line: *'Veni, vidi, vici'* ('I came, I saw, I conquered').

Architecture

Safranbolu and Amasya are Ottoman heritage towns, with boutique hotels occupying their half-timbered, black-and-white houses. Konya's turquoise-domed Mevlâna Museum is a Turkish icon and Sultanhanı is Anatolia's largest remaining Seljuk *han* (caravanserai).

Ruins

Hattuşa was the Hittite capital over 3000 years ago, and stone stars explode above the doors of Divriği's 780-year-old mosque complex. There are Pontic tombs in the cliffs above Amasya, and Gordion's Phrygian tomb (c 700 BC) might be the world's oldest wooden structure.

p415

Cappadocia

History
Hiking
Caves

History

Cappadocia was a refuge for Byzantine Christians, who carved monastic settlements into the rock, left frescoes on the cave walls and hid from Islamic armies in underground cities. You can see all these relics and relive the area's history on horseback.

Hiking

This is one of Turkey's best regions for going walkabout, with options ranging from gentle saunters through the dreamy valleys to serious missions. South of leafy Ihlara Valley, 3268m Mt Hasan and the Ala Dağlar National Park are both challenging.

Caves

Cappadocia's tuff cliff faces and surreal fairy chimneys (rock formations) are riddled with caves. Some are occupied by centuries-old churches, others by full-time cave-dwellers. Many are now hotels, offering an experience of the troglodyte lifestyle in comfort and style.

p463

Black Sea Coast

History
Local Secrets
Scenery

History

Anatolia's north coast was once the Kingdom of Pontus, and Ottoman Greeks tried to create a post-WWI Pontic state here. Impressive ruins include Sumela, the Byzantine monastery clinging to a cliff face, and Trabzon's 13th-century church-turned-mosque Aya Sofya.

Local Secrets

The Black Sea (Karadeniz) offers experiences unknown to non-Turkish holidaymakers, such as sipping çay in tea-producing Rize, wandering Amasra and Sinop's ancient fortifications, and staying in Ordu and Ünye's old Greek and Armenian quarters.

Scenery

The *yaylalar* (mountain pastures) above towns like Giresun and Ordu offer rugged scenery, as does the coastline west of Sinop. The winding road from Amasra to Sinop is Turkey's answer to California's Hwy 1, and there are more coastal vistas around Yason Burnu.

p509

Northeastern Anatolia

History
Outdoor Activities
Slow Travel

History

Medieval Armenian and Georgian churches and castles dot the steppe, and isolated Ani was a Silk Road trading centre. Near the Iranian border, mountainside İshak Paşa Palace is one of the most impressive examples of 18th-century Ottoman architecture.

Outdoor Activities

Yusufeli is a white-water rafting and trekking centre; hikers can head to the Kaçkar Mountains and Mt Ararat; and snow bunnies to Palandöken and Sarıkamış.

Slow Travel

To enjoy mountainous countryside at a mellow pace, head up to the *yaylalar* in the Kaçkar Mountains or northeast of Artvin near Georgia. Nestled in the landscape are villages, ruins, traditional wooden houses and the beginnings of the Caucasus region, which stretches east to the Caspian Sea and north to Russia.

p537

Southeastern Anatolia

History
Food
Architecture

History

The many remains of past civilisations in southeastern Anatolia include Lake Van's island church, built by an Armenian king, the statues atop Mt Nemrut, and Şanlıurfa's Neolithic Göbekli Tepe. A dam will soon submerge the historic village of Hasankeyf; on the bright side, Gaziantep Zeugma Mosaic Museum showcases Roman mosaics rescued from a dam site.

Food

With Kurdish and Arabic influences, the area's cuisine is a knockout. Top places to try local dishes are Gaziantep, with the planet's tastiest pistachio baklava, and Şanlıurfa, home of Urfa kebaps.

Architecture

History has left stunning buildings throughout the region – including mystery-shrouded Şanlıurfa, Mardin's gold-coloured labyrinth of lanes, basalt-walled Diyarbakır, and the Morgabriel and Deyrul Zafaran monasteries.

p570

On the
Road

İstanbul

POP 14 MILLION

Why Go?

Some ancient cities are the sum of their monuments. But others, such as İstanbul, factor a lot more into the equation. Here, you can visit Byzantine churches and Ottoman mosques in the morning, shop in chic boutiques during the afternoon and party at bars and clubs throughout the night. In the space of a few minutes you can hear the evocative strains of the call to prayer issuing from the Old City's tapering minarets, the sonorous horn of a crowded commuter ferry crossing between Europe and Asia, and the strident cries of a street hawker selling fresh seasonal produce. Put simply, this marvellous metropolis is an exercise in sensory seduction like no other.

Ask locals to describe what they love about İstanbul and they'll shrug, give a small smile and say merely that there is no other place like it. Spend a few days here, and you'll know exactly what they mean.

Best Places to Eat

➡ Klemuri (p118)

➡ Antiochia (p118)

➡ Zübeyir Ocakbaşı (p118)

➡ Meze by Lemon Tree (p121)

➡ Develi Baklava (p115)

Best Places to Stay

➡ Hotel Ibrahim Pasha (p111)

➡ Sirkeci Mansion (p111)

➡ Hotel Empress Zoe (p111)

➡ Marmara Guesthouse (p109)

➡ Marmara Pera (p113)

When to Go
İstanbul

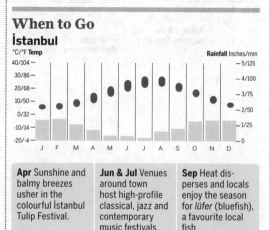

Apr Sunshine and balmy breezes usher in the colourful İstanbul Tulip Festival.

Jun & Jul Venues around town host high-profile classical, jazz and contemporary music festivals.

Sep Heat disperses and locals enjoy the season for *lüfer* (bluefish), a favourite local fish.

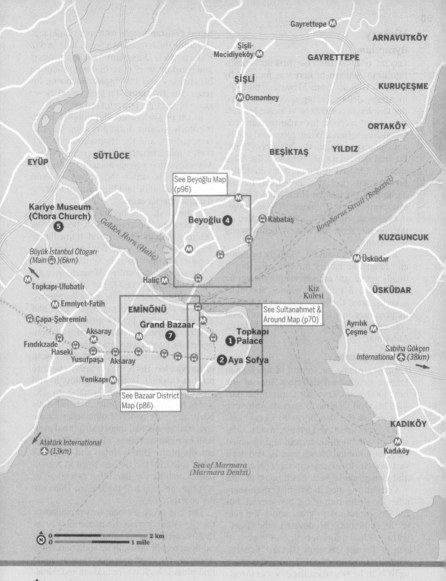

İstanbul Highlights

❶ Uncover the secrets of the seraglio in opulent **Topkapı Palace** (p75).

❷ Marvel at the interior of **Aya Sofya** (p65), one of the world's truly great buildings.

❸ Surrender to the steam in an Ottoman-era **hamam** (p106).

❹ Head to **Beyoğlu** (p123) for drinks at a rooftop bar

followed by dinner at one of the many restaurants.

❺ Admire the extraordinary Byzantine mosaics at the **Kariye Museum** (Chora Church; p93).

❻ Take a **ferry trip** (p102) along the mighty Bosphorus, up the Golden Horn or to the Princes' Islands.

❼ Lose yourself in the hidden caravanserais and labyrinthine lanes of the **Grand Bazaar** (p88).

❽ Contemplate the cutting edge at a **contemporary art gallery** (p94).

❾ Kick back with the locals at a traditional **çay bahçesi** (tea garden; p122).

History

Byzantium

Legend tells us that the first historically significant settlement here was founded by Byzas, a colonist from Megara, a port city in Attica. Before leaving Greece, he asked the Delphic oracle where to locate his new colony and received the enigmatic answer: 'Opposite the blind.' When Byzas and his fellow colonists sailed up the Bosphorus in 657 BC, they noticed a small colony on the Asian shore at Chalcedon (modern-day Kadıköy). Looking left, they saw the superb natural harbour of the Golden Horn (Haliç) on the European shore. Thinking, 'Those people in Chalcedon must be blind', they settled on the opposite shore and named their new city Byzantium.

Byzantium submitted willingly to Rome and fought its battles for centuries. But it finally got caught out supporting the wrong side in a civil war. The winner, Septimius Severus, razed the city walls and took away its privileges in AD 196. When he relented and rebuilt the city, he named it Augusta Antonina.

Constantinople

Another struggle for control of the Roman Empire determined the city's fate for the next 1000 years. Emperor Constantine pursued his rival Licinius to Augusta Antonina, then across the Bosphorus to Chrysopolis (Üsküdar). Defeating Licinius in 324, Constantine solidified his control and renamed Augusta Antonina 'New Rome'. He laid out a vast new city to serve as capital of his empire and inaugurated it with much pomp in 330.

Constantine died in 337, just seven years after the dedication of his new capital, but the city continued to grow under the rule of the emperors. Theodosius I ('the Great'; r 379–95) had a forum built on the present site of Beyazıt Meydanı (Beyazıt Square), while his son Theodosius II ordered massive walls built in 413, when the city was threatened by the marauding armies of Attila the Hun. Flattened by an earthquake in 447 and hastily rebuilt within two months, the Theodosian Walls still surround the Old City today.

Theodosius II died in 450 and was succeeded by a string of emperors, including the ambitious Justinian (r 527–65). Three years before taking the throne, Justinian had married Theodora, a strong-willed former courtesan. Together they further embellished Constantinople with great buildings, including the famous Aya Sofya, built in 537. Unfortunately, Justinian's building projects and constant wars of reconquest exhausted his treasury and his empire. Following his reign, the Byzantine Empire would never again be as large, powerful or rich.

Much of ancient Constantinople's building stock remains, including churches, palaces, cisterns and the Hippodrome. In fact, there's more left than most people realise. Any excavation reveals ancient streets, mosaics, tunnels, water and sewage systems, houses and public buildings buried beneath the modern city centre.

Mehmet II, who became known as Fatih (meaning 'the Conqueror'), became the Ottoman sultan in 1451 and immediately departed his capital in Edirne, aiming to conquer the once-great Byzantine city.

In four short months, Mehmet oversaw the building of Rumeli Hisarı (the great fortress on the European side of the Bosphorus) and also repaired Anadolu Hisarı, built half a century earlier by his great-grandfather Beyazıt I. Together these fortresses controlled the strait's narrowest point.

The Byzantines had closed the mouth of the Golden Horn with a heavy chain to prevent Ottoman boats from sailing in and attacking the city walls on the northern side. Not to be thwarted, Mehmet marshalled his boats at a cove (where Dolmabahçe Palace now stands) and had them transported overland by night on rollers, up the valley (present site of the Hilton Hotel) and down the other side into the Golden Horn at Kasımpaşa. Catching the Byzantine defenders by surprise, he soon had the Golden Horn under control.

The last great obstacle was provided by the city's mighty walls. No matter how heavily Mehmet's cannons battered them, the Byzantines rebuilt the walls by night and, come daybreak, the imperious young sultan would find himself back where he'd started. Finally, he received a proposal from a Hungarian cannon founder called Urban, who had come to help the Byzantine emperor defend Christendom against the infidels. Finding that the Byzantine emperor had no money, Urban was quick to discard his religious convictions and instead offered to make Mehmet the most enormous cannon ever seen if appropriately recompensed. Mehmet gladly accepted and the mighty cannon breached the walls, allowing the Ottomans into the city.

On 28 May 1453 the final attack began, and by the evening of the 29th the Turks were in complete control of the city. The last Byzantine emperor, Constantine XI Palaiologos, died fighting on the walls.

İstanbul

Seeing himself as the successor to great emperors such as Constantine and Justinian, Mehmet at once began to rebuild and repopulate the city. He chose the conspicuous promontory of Seraglio Point as the location for his ostentatious palace, Topkapı, and he also repaired and fortified Theodosius II's walls. İstanbul was soon the administrative, commercial and cultural heart of his growing empire.

The building boom Mehmet kicked off was continued by his successors, with Süleyman the Magnificent and his architect Mimar Sinan being responsible for an enormous amount of construction. The city was endowed with buildings commissioned by the sultan and his family, court and grand viziers; these include the city's largest and grandest mosque, the Süleymaniye (1550). Later sultans also added mosques, and in the 19th century numerous palaces were built along the Bosphorus, among them Dolmabahçe.

As the Ottoman Empire grew to encompass the Middle East and North Africa as well as half of Eastern Europe, İstanbul became a fabulous melting pot of nationalities. On its streets people spoke Turkish, Greek, Armenian, Ladino, Russian, Arabic, Bulgarian, Romanian, Albanian, Italian, French, German, English and Maltese.

However, what had been the most civilised city on earth in the time of Süleyman eventually declined along with the Ottoman Empire, and by the 19th century İstanbul had lost much of its former glory. Nevertheless, it continued to be known as the 'Paris of the East' and, to affirm this, the first great international luxury express train, the famous *Orient Express,* connected İstanbul and the French capital in 1883.

After founding the Turkish Republic, Mustafa Kemal Atatürk decided to leave behind the imperial memories of İstanbul and set up his new government in Ankara, a city that could not be threatened by gunboats. Robbed of its status as the capital of a vast empire, İstanbul lost much of its wealth and atmosphere. The city's streets and neighbourhoods decayed, its infrastructure was neither maintained nor improved and virtually no economic development occurred.

The city stayed this way until the 1990s, when a renaissance took place. Since this time, public transport has been massively upgraded and continues to be improved, suburbs have been reinvigorated and parklands now line the waterways. When İstanbul won the right to become the European Capital of Culture in 2010, other ambitious projects were undertaken and many major

İSTANBUL HISTORY

İSTANBUL IN...

Two Days

With only two days, you'll need to get cracking! On day one, visit the **Blue Mosque** (p68), **Aya Sofya** (p65) and the **Basilica Cistern** (p75) in the morning, grab a quick lunch in **Hocapaşa Sokak** in Sirkeci and then follow our walking tour of the **Grand Bazaar** (p88) in the afternoon. Head to **Beyoğlu** in the evening.

Day two should be devoted to **Topkapı Palace** (p75) and the **Bosphorus**. Spend the morning at the palace, then board one of the private excursion boats at Eminönü or the hop-on/hop-off service at Kabataş for a **Bosphorus cruise**. Afterwards, walk up through Galata to **İstiklal Caddesi** and have a drink at a **rooftop bar** before dinner nearby.

Four Days

Follow the two-day itinerary, and on your third day visit the **İstanbul Archaeology Museums** (p82) or **Museum of Turkish & Islamic Arts** (p73) in the morning, have lunch in or around the Grand Bazaar and then visit the **Süleymaniye Mosque** (p88) in the afternoon. For dinner, head back across Galata Bridge to **Beyoğlu**. Day four could be devoted to contemporary **art galleries** and Orhan Pamuk's **Museum of Innocence** (p95) in Beyoğlu, or to a ferry trip up the Golden Horn to **Eyüp**. At night, the bar, restaurant and club scenes on the other side of **Galata Bridge** once again await.

İstanbul

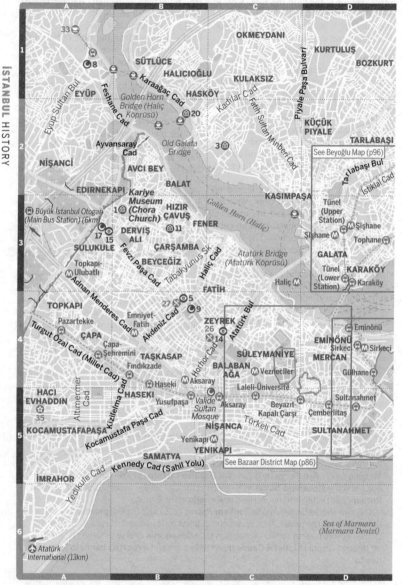

OKMEYDANI

KURTULUŞ

BOZKURT

SÜTLÜCE

HALICIOĞLU

KULAKSIZ

33

8

Feshane Cad

Karaağaç Cad

EYÜP

Eyüp Sultan Bul

HASKÖY

Kadlar Cad

Fatih Sultan Minberi Cad

Piyale Paşa Bulvarı

KÜÇÜK PIYALE

TARLABAŞI

Golden Horn Bridge (Haliç Köprüsü)

20

Ayvansaray Cad

Old Galata Bridge

3

See Beyoğlu Map (p96)

Tarlabaşı Bul

İstiklal Cad

NİŞANCI

AVCI BEY

BALAT

EDIRNEKAPI

Kariye Museum (Chora Church)

HIZIR ÇAVUŞ

KASIMPAŞA

Golden Horn (Haliç)

Tünel (Upper Station)

Şişhane

Şişhane

Tophane

Büyük İstanbul Otogarı (Main Bus Station) (6km)

1

DERVIŞ ALI

FENER

11

ŞULUKULE

17

15

Topkapı-Ulubatlı

ÇARŞAMBA

BEYCEĞIZ

Fevzi Paşa Cad

Tabakyunus Sk

Haliç Cad

Atatürk Bridge (Atatürk Köprüsü)

GALATA

KARAKÖY

Tünel (Lower Station)

Haliç

Karaköy

Adnan Menderes Cad

FATİH

27

5

9

TOPKAPI

Pazartekke

Emniyet-Fatih

Akdeniz Cad

ZEYREK

26

14

Atatürk Bul

SÜLEYMANIYE

EMİNÖNÜ

Eminönü

Sirkeci

Sirkeci

ÇAPA

Turgut Özal Cad (Millet Cad)

Çapa Şehremini

TAŞKASAP

Fındıkzade

BALABAN AĞA

Vezn|ciler

MERCAN

Gülhane

Altımermer Cad

Haseki

Aksaray

Laleli-Üniversite

Beyazıt-Kapalı Çarşı

Sultanahmet

HACI EVHADDIN

35

HASEKI

Yusufpaşa

Valide Sultan Mosque

Aksaray

Çemberlitaş

Horhor Cad

Kızıtelma Cad

Kocamustafa Paşa Cad

NİŞANCA

Türkeli Cad

SULTANAHMET

KOCAMUSTAFAPAŞA

Yenikapı

İMRAHOR

Yedikule Cad

Kennedy Cad (Sahil Yolu)

SAMATYA

YENİKAPI

See Bazaar District Map (p86)

Sea of Marmara (Marmara Denizi)

Atatürk International (13km)

---

buildings have benefited from painstaking restoration.

İstanbul's cultural transformation is just as marked. The seedy dives of Beyoğlu have been replaced by arty cafes, bars and boutiques, transforming the neighbourhood into a bohemian hub. Galleries such as İstanbul Modern, ARTER and SALT have opened here, showcasing Turkey's contemporary art to the world. The live-music scene in the city has also exploded, making İstanbul a buzzword for creative, energetic music

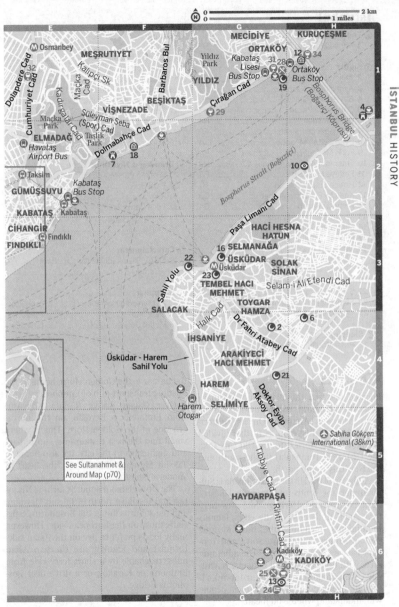

with a unique East–West twist. And a new generation of artisans is refining and repositioning the city's traditional crafts industries – making for exciting and unexpected shopping experiences.

In short, İstanbul is a cosmopolitan and sophisticated megalopolis that has well and truly reclaimed its status as one of the world's great cities.

İstanbul

◉ Sights

Located between the Black and Marmara Seas, the Bosphorus strait divides Europe from Asia and Anatolia. On its western shore, European İstanbul is further divided by the Golden Horn into the Old City (aka the Historical Peninsula) in the south and the New City in the north.

At the tip of the Historical Peninsula is Sultanahmet, the centre of İstanbul's Unesco-designated World Heritage Site. It's here that you'll find most of the city's famous monuments, including the Blue Mosque (Sultan Ahmet Camii), Aya Sofya and Topkapı Palace (Topkapı Sarayı). The adjoining area, with hotels to suit all budgets, is actually called Cankurtaran (*jan*-kur-tar-an), although if you say 'Sultanahmet' most people will understand where you mean.

Up the famous Divan Yolu boulevard from Sultanahmet you'll find the Grand Bazaar (Kapalı Çarşı). To its north is the Süleymaniye Mosque, which graces the top of one of the Old City's seven hills, and further on are the Western Districts. Downhill from

the bazaar is the Golden Horn, home to the bustling transport hub of Eminönü.

Over Galata Bridge (Galata Köprüsü) from Eminönü is Beyoğlu, on the northern side of the Golden Horn. This is where you'll find the best restaurants, shops, bars and nightclubs in the city. It's also home to Taksim Meydanı (Taksim Sq), the heart of 'modern' İstanbul.

The city's glamour suburbs include Nişantaşı and Teşvikiye, north of Taksim Meydanı, and the suburbs lining the Bosphorus, especially those on the European side. However, many locals prefer to live on the Asian side. Üsküdar and Kadıköy are the two Asian hubs, reachable by a short ferry ride from Eminönü or Karaköy, or a drive over Bosphorus Bridge.

◉ Sultanahmet & Around

It's not surprising that many visitors to İstanbul never make it out of Sultanahmet – after all, few cities have such a concentration of sights, shops, hotels and eateries within easy walking distance.

★ **Aya Sofya**   MUSEUM

(Hagia Sophia; Map p70; ☏ 212-522 1750; www.
ayasofyamuzesi.gov.tr; Aya Sofya Meydanı 1; adult/
child under 12yr ₺30/free; ☺9am-6pm Tue-Sun
mid-Apr–Sep, to 4pm Oct–mid-Apr; 🚇Sultanah-
met) There are many important monuments
in İstanbul, but this venerable structure –
commissioned by the great Byzantine emperor Justinian, consecrated as a church in
537, converted to a mosque by Mehmet the
Conqueror in 1453 and declared a museum
by Atatürk in 1935 – surpasses the rest due
to its innovative architectural form, rich history, religious importance and extraordinary
beauty.

➡ **Ground Floor**

As you enter the building and walk into the
inner narthex, look up to see a brilliant mosaic of *Christ as Pantocrator* (Ruler of All)
above the third and largest door (the Imperial Door). Through this is the building's main
space, famous for its dome, huge nave and
gold mosaics.

The focal point at this level is the apse,
with its magnificent 9th-century mosaic of
the *Virgin and Christ Child*. The mosaics
above the apse once depicted the archangels
Gabriel and Michael; today only fragments
remain.

The Byzantine emperors were crowned
while seated in a throne placed within the
omphalion, the section of inlaid marble in
the main floor.

Ottoman additions to the building include a *mimber* (pulpit) and *mihrab* (prayer
niche indicating the direction of Mecca);
large 19th-century medallions inscribed
with gilt Arabic letters; a curious elevated
kiosk known as the *hünkar mahfili*; and an
ornate library behind the omphalion.

Looking up towards the northeast (to
your left if you are facing the apse), you will
see three mosaics at the base of the northern tympanum (semicircle) beneath the
dome. These are 9th-century portraits of St
Ignatius the Younger, St John Chrysostom
and St Ignatius Theodorus of Antioch. To
their right on one of the pendentives is a
14th-century mosaic of the face of a seraph
(six-winged angel charged with the care-
taking of God's throne).

In the side aisle to the northeast of the
Imperial Door is a column with a worn copper facing pierced by a hole, known as the
Weeping Column. Legend has it that the
pillar was blessed by St Gregory the Miracle
Worker and that putting one's finger into the
hole can lead to ailments being healed if the
finger emerges moist.

Aya Sofya

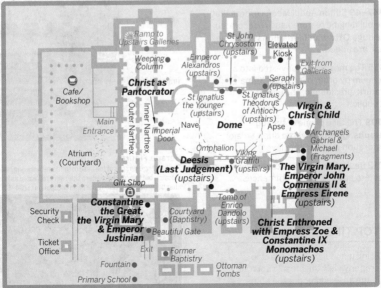

Aya Sofya

TIMELINE

537 Emperor Justinian, depicted in one of the church's famous **mosaics ❶**, presides over the consecration of Byzantium's new basilica, Hagia Sophia (Church of the Holy Wisdom).

557 The huge **dome ❷**, damaged during an earthquake, collapses and is rebuilt.

843 The second Byzantine Iconoclastic period ends and figurative **mosaics ❸** begin to be added to the interior. These include a depiction of the Empress Zoe and her third husband, Emperor Constantine IX Monomachos.

1204 Soldiers of the Fourth Crusade led by the Doge of Venice, Enrico Dandolo, conquer and ransack Constantinople. Dandolo's **tomb ❹** is eventually erected in the church whose desecration he presided over.

1453 The city falls to the Ottomans; Mehmet II orders that Hagia Sophia be converted to a mosque and renamed Aya Sofya.

1577 Sultan Selim II is buried in a specially designed tomb, which sits alongside the **tombs ❺** of four other Ottoman Sultans in Aya Sofya's grounds.

1847–49 Sultan Abdül Mecit I orders that the building be restored and redecorated; the huge **Ottoman Medallions ❻** in the nave are added.

1935 The mosque is converted into a museum by order of Mustafa Kemal Atatürk, president of the new Turkish Republic.

2009 The face of one of the four **seraphs ❼** is uncovered during major restoration works in the nave.

2012 Restoration of the exterior walls and western upper gallery commences.

TOP TIPS

Bring binoculars if you want to properly view the mosaic portraits in the apse and under the dome.

Ottoman Medallions
These huge medallions are inscribed with gilt Arabic letters giving the names of God (Allah), Mohammed and the early caliphs Ali and Abu Bakr.

⑦

Imperial Loge

Omphalion

Imperial Door

Seraph Figures
The four huge seraphs at the base of the dome were originally mosaics, but two (on the western side) were recreated as frescoes after being damaged during the Latin occupation (1204–61).

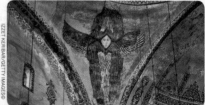

Dome
Soaring 56m from ground level, the dome was originally covered in gold mosaics but was decorated with calligraphy during the 1847–49 restoration works overseen by Swiss-born architects Gaspard and Giuseppe Fossati.

Christ Enthroned with Empress Zoe and Constantine IX Monomachos
This mosaic portrait in the upper gallery depicts Zoe, one of only three Byzantine women to rule as empress in their own right.

Ottoman Tombs
The tombs of five Ottoman sultans and their families are located in Aya Sofya's southern corner and can be accessed via Kabasakal Caddesi. One of these occupies the church's original Baptistry.

②

⑥

③

④

Aya Sofya Tombs

⑤

Former Baptistry

Astronomer's House & Workshop

①

Exit

Ablutions Fountain

Primary School

Main Entrance

Constantine the Great, the Virgin Mary and the Emperor Justinian
This 11th-century mosaic shows Constantine (right) offering the Virgin Mary the city of Constantinople. Justinian (left) is offering her Hagia Sophia.

Grave of Enrico Dandolo
The Venetian doge died in 1205, only one year after he and his Crusaders had stormed the city. A 19th-century marker in the upper gallery indicates the probable location of his grave.

HENRICUS DANDOLO

DON'T MISS

AYA SOFYA TOMBS

Part of the Aya Sofya complex but entered via Kabasakal Caddesi and thus often overlooked by tourists, these tombs (Aya Sofya Müzesi Padişah Türbeleri; Map p70; Kabasakal Caddesi; ⊙9am-5pm; 🚇 Sultanahmet) FREE are the final resting places of five sultans – Mehmed III, Selim II, Murad III, İbrahim I and Mustafa I – most of whom are buried with members of their families. The ornate interior decoration in the tombs features the very best Ottoman tilework, calligraphy and decorative paintwork.

Mehmed's tomb dates from 1608 and Murad's tomb from 1599; both are adorned with particularly beautiful İznik tiles. Next to Murad's tomb is that of his five children; this was designed by Sinan and has simple but beautiful painted decoration.

Selim's tomb, which was designed by Sinan and built in 1577, is particularly poignant as it houses the graves of five of his sons, murdered on the same night in December 1574 to ensure the peaceful succession of the eldest, Murad III. It also houses the graves of 19 of Murad's sons, murdered in January 1595 to ensure Mehmet III's succession. They were the last of the royal princes to be murdered by their siblings – after this, the younger brothers of succeeding sultans were confined to the kafes (cage) in Topkapı Palace instead.

The fifth tomb is Aya Sofya's original Baptistry, converted to a mausoleum for sultans İbrahim I and Mustafa I during the 17th century.

➡ Upstairs Galleries

To access the galleries, walk up the switchback ramp at the northern end of the inner narthex. When you reach the top, you'll find a large circle of green marble marking the spot where the throne of the empress once stood.

In the south gallery (straight ahead and then left) are the remnants of a magnificent *Deesis* (Last Judgement). This 13th-century mosaic depicts Christ with the Virgin Mary on his left and John the Baptist on his right.

Further on, at the eastern (apse) end of the gallery, is a 11th-century mosaic depicting *Christ Enthroned with Empress Zoe and Constantine IX Monomachos*.

To the right of Zoe and Constantine is a 12th-century mosaic depicting *The Virgin Mary, Emperor John Comnenus II and Empress Eirene*. The emperor, who was known as 'John the Good', is on the Virgin's left and the empress, who was known for her charitable works, is to her right. Their son Alexius, who died soon after the portrait was made, is depicted next to Eirene.

In the north gallery, look for the 10th-century mosaic portrait of the Emperor Alexandros.

➡ Exiting the Building

As you leave the outer narthex, be sure to look back to admire the 10th-century mosaic of *Constantine the Great, the Virgin Mary and the Emperor Justinian* on the lunette of the inner doorway. Constantine (right) is offering the Virgin, who holds the Christ Child, the city of İstanbul; Justinian (left) is offering her Hagia Sophia.

Just after you exit the building through the Beautiful Gate, a magnificent bronze gate dating from the 2nd century BC, there is a doorway on the left. This leads into a small courtyard that was once part of a 6th-century Baptistry. In the 17th century the Baptistry was converted into a tomb for sultans Mustafa I and İbrahim I. The huge stone basin displayed in the courtyard is the original font.

On the opposite side of Aya Sofya Meydanı are the Baths of Lady Hürrem (Ayasofya Hürrem Sultan Hamamı), built between 1556 and 1557. Designed by Sinan, the hamam was commissioned by Süleyman the Magnificent in the name of his wife Haseki Hürrem Sultan, known to history as Roxelana.

Blue Mosque   MOSQUE

(Sultanahmet Camii; Map p70; Hippodrome; ⊙ closed to tourists during the 5 daily prayer times & Fri sermon; 🚇 Sultanahmet) İstanbul's most photogenic building was the grand project of Sultan Ahmet I (r 1603–17), whose tomb is located on the north side of the site facing Sultanahmet Park. The mosque's wonderfully curvaceous exterior features a cascade of domes and six slender minarets. Blue İznik tiles adorn the interior and give the building its unofficial but commonly used name.

The mosque's architect, Sedefhar Mehmet Ağa, managed to orchestrate the sort of visual wham-bam effect with the mosque's exterior that Aya Sofya achieved with its interior. Its curves are voluptuous, it has six minarets (more than any other mosque at the time it was built) and its courtyard is the biggest of all the Ottoman mosques. The interior has a similarly grand scale: the İznik tiles number in the tens of thousands, there are 260 windows and the central prayer space is huge.

To best appreciate the mosque's design, enter the complex via the Hippodrome rather than from Sultanahmet Park. Once inside the courtyard, which is the same size as the mosque's interior, you'll appreciate the building's perfect proportions.

The mosque is such a popular attraction that admission is controlled so as to preserve its sacred atmosphere. Only worshippers are admitted through the main door; tourists must use the south door (follow the signs).

Great Palace Mosaic Museum   MUSEUM
(Map p74; ☎ 212-518 1205; Torun Sokak; admission ₺10; ⊙ 9am-5.30pm Tue-Sun mid-Apr–Sep, to 3.30pm Oct–mid-Apr; ⊖ Sultanahmet) When archaeologists from the University of Ankara and the University of St Andrews (Scotland) excavated around the Arasta Bazaar at the rear of the Blue Mosque in the 1930s and 1950s, they uncovered a stunning mosaic pavement featuring hunting and mythological scenes. Dating from early Byzantine

times, it was restored from 1983 to 1997 and is now preserved in this museum.

Thought to have been added by Justinian to the Great Palace of Byzantium, the pavement is estimated to have measured from 3500 to 4000 sq metres in its original form. The 250 sq metres that is preserved here is the largest discovered remnant – the rest has been destroyed or remains buried underneath the Blue Mosque and surrounding shops and hotels.

The pavement is filled with bucolic imagery and has a gorgeous ribbon border with heart-shaped leaves. In the westernmost room is the most colourful and dramatic picture, that of two men in leggings carrying spears and holding off a raging tiger.

The museum has informative panels documenting the floor's history, rescue and renovation.

Hippodrome   PARK
(Atmeydanı; Map p70; ⊖ Sultanahmet) The Byzantine emperors loved nothing more than an afternoon at the chariot races, and this rectangular arena was their venue of choice. In its heyday, it was decorated by obelisks and statues, some of which remain in place today. Recently re-landscaped, it is one of the city's most popular meeting places and promenades.

Originally, the arena consisted of two levels of galleries, a central spine, starting boxes and the semicircular southern end known as the Sphendone (Map p70; Hippodrome; ⊖ Sultanahmet), parts of which still

---

ℹ MUSEUM PASS İSTANBUL

Most visitors spend at least three days in İstanbul and cram as many museum visits as possible into their stay, so the recent introduction of this discount pass (www.muze.gov.tr/museum_pass) is most welcome. Valid for 72 hours from your first museum entrance, it costs ₺85 and allows entrance to Topkapı Palace and Harem (p75), Aya Sofya (p65), the İstanbul Archaeology Museums (p82), the Museum of Turkish & Islamic Arts (p73), the Great Palace Mosaic Museum and the İstanbul Museum of the History of Science & Technology in Islam (p83). Purchased individually, admission fees to these sights will cost ₺125, so the pass represents a saving of ₺40. Its biggest benefit is that it allows you to bypass ticket queues and make your way straight into the museums – something that is particularly useful when visiting ever-crowded Aya Sofya.

As well as giving entry to these government-operated museums, the pass also gives discounts on entry to privately run museums including the Museum of Innocence (p95), the Pera Museum (p98) and the Rahmi M Koç Museum (p106); on ticket prices for the Bosphorus ferry tours operated by İstanbul Şehir Hatları (p136); and on guided walking tours operated by İstanbul Walks (p108).

The pass can be purchased from some hotels and also from the ticket offices at Aya Sofya, Topkapı Palace, the Great Palace Mosaic Museum and the İstanbul Archaeology Museums.

Sultanahmet & Around

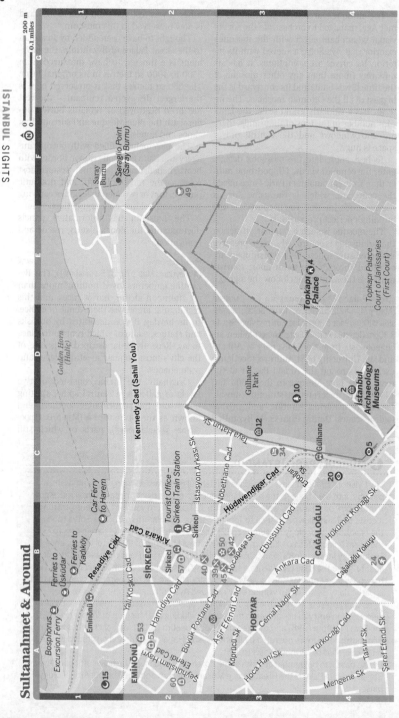

N
0   200 m
0   0.1 miles

Golden Horn
(Haliç)

Bosphorus
Excursion Ferry

Ferries to
Üsküdar

Ferries to
Kadıköy

Eminönü

Car Ferry
to Harem

Saray
Burnu

Seraglio Point
(Saray Burnu)

Kennedy Cad (Sahil Yolu)

Gülhane
Park

Topkapı Palace

Topkapı Palace
Court of Janissaries
(First Court)

İstanbul
Archaeology
Museums

Gülhane

Tourist Office –
Sirkeci Train Station

Sirkeci

Sirkeci

İstasyon Arkası Sk

Nöbethane Cad

Taya Hatun Sk

Hüdavendigar Cad

Erdoğan Sk

ÇAĞALOĞLU

Hükümet Konağı Sk

Çağaloğlu Yokuşu

Ankara Cad

Ebussuud Cad

Cemal Nadir Sk

HOBYAR

Aşir Efendi Cad

Köprülü Sk

Hoca Hanı Sk

Mengene Sk

Türkocağı Cad

Tasvir Sk

Şeref Efendi Sk

Hocapaşa Sk

Ekşeoğlu Sk

Büyük Postane Cad

Şeyhülislam Hayri
Efendi Cad

Hamidiye Cad

Yalı Köşkü Cad

Reşadiye Cad

Ankara Cad

EMİNÖNÜ

SİRKECİ

Eminönü

15

53

51

60

57

40

39

45

42

50

12

34

10

2

4

49

5

20

24

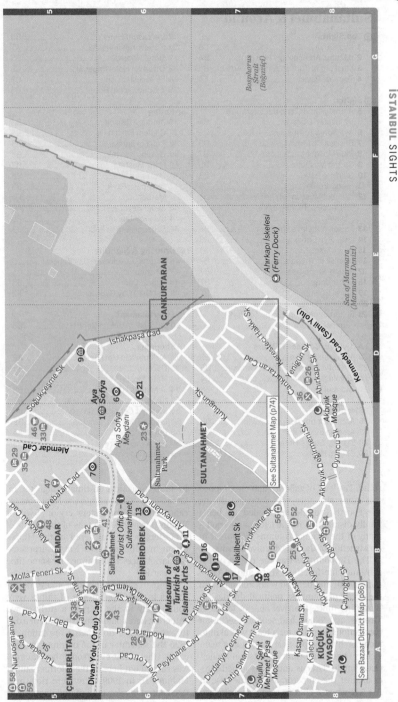

Bosphorus Strait (Boğaziçi)

Sea of Marmara (Marmara Denizi)

Ahırkapı İskelesi (Ferry Dock)

CANKURTARAN

Kennedy Cad (Sahil Yolu)

İshakpaşa Cad

Soğukçeşme Sk

9

Aya Sofya

Aya Sofya Meydanı

6

21

23

SULTANAHMET

Kutluğun Sk

Cankurtaran Cad

Terbıyık Hakkı Sk

Akbıyık Sk

Keresteci Hakkı Sk

36

26

Akbıyık Mosque

Ak bıyık Değirmeni Sk

Oyuncu Sk

See Sultanahmet Map (p74)

Alemdar Cad

46

33

29

35

47

Yerebatan Cad

7

Alayköşkü Cad

ALEMDAR

48

22 32

41

Sultanahmet

Tourist Office – Sultanahmet

1

13

Tavukhane Sk

56

52

30 54

55

25

8

Nakilbent Sk

BİNBİRDİREK

Armdani Cad

11

16

19

17

18

Oğul Sk

Küçük Ayasofya Cad

Molla Feneri Sk

Museum of Turkish & Islamic Arts

3

Amdani Cad

Tezgahçılar Cad

Üçler Sk

Tezgahçılar Sk

Nuruosmaniye Cad

Türbedar Sk

58

59

ÇEMBERLİTAŞ

Çatal Çeşme Sk

44

37

38

43

27

28

Bab-ı Ali Cad

Divan Yolu (Ordu) Cad

Işık Sk

İmran Öktem Cad

Klodfarer Cad

Piyer Loti Cad

Peykhane Cad

Dizdariye Çeşmesi Sk

Katip Sinan Camii Sk

Sokullu Şehit Mehmet Paşa Mosque

Kasap Osman Sk

Kaleci Sk

KÜÇÜK AYASOFYA

14

Çayıroğlu Sk

Kadırga Limanı Cad

See Bazaar District Map (p86)

Sultanahmet & Around

stand. The level of galleries that once topped this stone structure was damaged during the Fourth Crusade and ended up being totally dismantled in the Ottoman period – many of the original columns were used in construction of the Süleymaniye Mosque.

The Hippodrome was the centre of Byzantium's life for 1000 years and of Ottoman life for another 400 years and has been the scene of countless political dramas. In Byzantine times, the rival chariot teams of 'Greens' and 'Blues' had separate sectarian connections. Support for a team was akin to membership of a political party and a team victory had important effects on policy. Occasionally, Greens and Blues joined forces against the emperor, as was the case in AD 532 when a chariot race was disturbed by protests against Justinian's high tax regime – this escalated into the Nika riots (so called after the protesters' cry of Nika!, or Victory!), which led to tens of thousands of protesters being massacred in the Hippodrome by imperial forces. Not unsurprisingly, chariot races were banned for some time afterwards.

Ottoman sultans also kept an eye on activities in the Hippodrome. If things were going badly in the empire, a surly crowd gathering here could signal the start of a disturbance, then a riot, then a revolution. In 1826 the slaughter of the corrupt janissary corps (the sultan's personal bodyguards) was carried out here by the reformer Sultan Mahmut II. In 1909 there were riots here that caused the downfall of Abdülhamit II.

Despite the ever-present threat of the Hippodrome being the scene of their downfall, emperors and sultans sought to outdo one another in beautifying it, adorning the centre with statues from the far reaches of their empire. Unfortunately, many priceless statues carved by ancient masters have disappeared from their original homes here. Chief among the villains responsible for such thefts were the soldiers of the Fourth Crusade, who invaded Constantinople, a Christian ally city, in 1204. After sacking Aya Sofya, they tore all the plates from the Rough-Stone Obelisk (Map p70) at the Hippodrome's southern end in the mistaken belief that they were solid gold (in fact, they were gold-covered bronze). The crusaders also stole the famous quadriga (team of four horses cast in bronze), a copy of which now sits atop the main door of the Basilica di San Marco in Venice (the original is inside the basilica).

Near the northern end of the Hippodrome, the little gazebo with beautiful stonework is known as Kaiser Wilhelm's Fountain (Map p70). The German emperor paid a state visit to Sultan Abdülhamit II in 1898 and presented this fountain to the sultan and his people as a token of friendship in 1901. The motifs on the dome's interior feature Abdülhamit's *tuğra* (monogram) and the first letter of Wilhelm's name, representing their political union.

The immaculately preserved pink granite Obelisk of Theodosius (Map p70) in the centre was carved in Egypt during the reign of Thutmose III (r 1549–1503 BC) and erected in the Amon-Re temple at Karnak. Theodosius the Great (r 379–95) had it brought from Egypt to Constantinople in AD 390. On the marble billboards below the obelisk, look for the carvings of Theodosius, his wife, sons, state officials and bodyguards watching the chariot-race action from the *kathisma* (imperial box).

South of the obelisk is a strange column coming up out of a hole in the ground. Known as the Spiral Column (Map p70), it was once much taller and was topped by three serpents' heads. Originally cast to commemorate a victory of the Hellenic confederation over the Persians in the battle of Plataea, it stood in front of the temple of Apollo at Delphi from 478 BC until Constantine the Great had it brought to his new capital city around AD 330. Though badly damaged in Byzantine times, the serpents' heads survived until the early 18th century. Now all that remains of them is one upper jaw, housed in the İstanbul Archaeology Museums (p82).

★ Museum of Turkish & Islamic Arts   MUSEUM
(Türk ve İslam Eserleri Müzesi; Map p70; www.tiem.gov.tr; Atmeydanı Caddesi 46; adult/child under 12yr ₺20/free; ⊙ refer to website; Sultanahmet) This Ottoman palace on the western edge of the Hippodrome was built in 1524 for İbrahim Paşa, childhood friend, brother-in-law and grand vizier of Süleyman the Magnificent. Undergoing a major renovation at

GREAT PALACE OF BYZANTIUM

Constantine the Great built the Great Palace soon after he declared Constantinople to be the capital of the Roman Empire in AD 330. Successive Byzantine leaders left their mark by adding to it, and the complex eventually consisted of hundreds of buildings over six levels. These included throne rooms, audience chambers, churches, chapels, stadiums and thermal baths, all enclosed by walls and set in terraced parklands stretching from the Hippodrome over to Aya Sofya (Hagia Sophia) and down the slope, ending at the sea walls on the Sea of Marmara. The palace was finally abandoned after the Fourth Crusade sacked the city in 1204, and its ruins were pillaged and filled in after the Conquest, becoming mere foundations of much of Sultanahmet and Cankurtaran.

Various pieces of the Great Palace have been uncovered – many by budding hotelier 'archaeologists'. The mosaics in the Great Palace Mosaic Museum (p69) once graced the floor of the complex, and excavations at the Sultanahmet Archaeological Park (Map p70; Kabasakal Caddesi) in Kabasakal Caddesi, near Aya Sofya, have uncovered other parts of the palace. Controversially, some of these excavations were subsumed into a new extension of the neighbouring luxury Four Seasons Hotel before public outcry stalled the project.

For more information, check out www.byzantium1200.com, which has computer-generated images that bring ancient Byzantium to life.

Sultanahmet

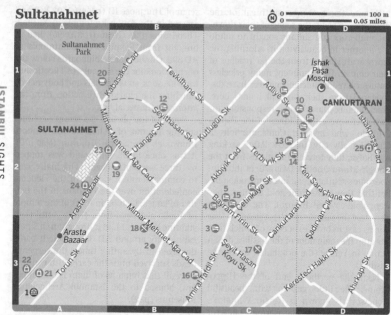

N 0 _____ 100 m
0 _____ 0.05 miles

Sultanahmet

the time of research, it has a magnificent collection of artefacts, including exquisite examples of calligraphy and one of the world's most impressive collections of antique carpets.

Born in Greece, İbrahim Paşa was captured in that country as a child and sold as a slave into the imperial household in İstanbul. He worked as a page in Topkapı, where he became friendly with Süleyman, who was the same age. When his friend became sultan, İbrahim was made in turn chief falconer, chief of the royal bedchamber and grand vizier. This palace was bestowed on him by Süleyman the year before he was given the hand of Süleyman's sister, Hadice, in marriage. Alas, the fairy tale was not to last for poor İbrahim. His wealth, power and influence on the monarch became so great that others wishing to influence the sultan became envious, chief among them Süleyman's powerful wife, Haseki Hürrem Sultan (Roxelana). After a rival accused İbrahim of disloyalty, Roxelana convinced her husband that İbrahim was a threat and Süleyman had him strangled in 1536.

Artefacts in the museum's collection date from the 8th and 9th centuries up to the 19th century. They include *müknames* (scrolls outlining an imperial decree) featuring the sultan's *tuğra* (monogram); Iranian book binding from the Safavid period (1501–1786); and Holbein, Lotto, Konya, Uşhak, Iran and Caucasia carpets.

Basilica Cistern   CISTERN

(Yerebatan Sarnıçı; Map p70; ☑ 212-512 1570; www. yerebatan.com; Yerebatan Caddesi 13; admission officially ₺20 for foreigners but in reality ₺10; ⊙ 9am-6.30pm mid-Apr–Sep, till 5.30pm Nov–mid-Apr; ⓐ Sultanahmet) This subterranean structure was commissioned by Emperor Justinian and built in 532. The largest surviving Byzantine cistern in İstanbul, it was constructed using 336 columns, many of which were salvaged from ruined temples and feature fine carved capitals. Its symmetry and sheer grandeur of conception are quite breathtaking, and its cavernous depths make a great retreat on summer days.

Like most sites in İstanbul, the cistern has an unusual history. It was originally known as the Basilica Cistern because it lay underneath the Stoa Basilica, one of the great squares on the first hill. Designed to service the Great Palace and surrounding buildings, it was able to store up to 80,000 cu metres of water delivered via 20km of aqueducts from a reservoir near the Black Sea, but was closed when the Byzantine emperors relocated from the Great Palace. Forgotten by the city authorities some time before the Conquest, it wasn't rediscovered until 1545, when scholar Petrus Gyllius was researching Byzantine antiquities in the city and was told by local residents that they were able to miraculously obtain water by lowering buckets into a dark space below their basement floors. Some were even catching fish this way. Intrigued, Gyllius explored the neighbourhood and finally accessed the cistern through one of the basements. Even after his discovery, the Ottomans (who referred to the cistern as Yerebatan Saray) didn't treat the so-called Underground Palace with the respect it deserved – it became a dumping ground for all sorts of junk, as well as corpses.

The cistern was cleaned and renovated in 1985 by the İstanbul Metropolitan Municipality and opened to the public in 1987. It's now one of the city's most popular tourist attractions. Walking along its raised wooden platforms, you'll feel the water dripping from the vaulted ceiling and see schools of ghostly carp patrolling the water – it certainly has bucketloads (forgive the pun) of atmosphere.

★ Topkapı Palace   PALACE

(Topkapı Sarayı; Map p70; ☑ 212-512 0480; www. topkapisarayi.gov.tr; Babıhümayun Caddesi; palace adult/child under 12yr ₺30/free, Harem adult/child under 6yr ₺15/free; ⊙ 9am-6pm Wed-Mon mid-Apr–Oct, to 4pm Nov–mid-Apr; ⓐ Sultanahmet) Topkapı is the subject of more colourful stories than most of the world's museums put together. Libidinous sultans, ambitious courtiers, beautiful concubines and scheming eunuchs lived and worked here between the 15th and 19th centuries when it was the court of the Ottoman Empire. Visiting the palace's opulent pavilions, jewel-filled Treasury and sprawling Harem gives a fascinating glimpse into their lives.

Mehmet the Conqueror built the first stage of the palace shortly after the Conquest in 1453, and lived here until his death in 1481. Subsequent sultans lived in this rarefied environment until the 19th century, when they moved to the ostentatious European-style palaces they built on the shores of the Bosphorus.

Before you enter the palace's Imperial Gate (Bab-ı Hümayun), take a look at the ornate structure in the cobbled square just outside. This is the rococo-style Fountain of Sultan Ahmet III, built in 1728 by the sultan who so favoured tulips.

The main ticket office is in the First Court, just before the gate to the Second Court.

➡ **First Court**

Pass through the Imperial Gate into the First Court, which is known as the Court of the Janissaries or the Parade Court. On your left is the Byzantine church of Hagia Eirene, more commonly known as Aya İrini.

➡ **Second Court**

The Middle Gate (Ortakapı or Bab-üs Selâm) led to the palace's Second Court, used for the business of running the empire. In Ottoman times, only the sultan and the *valide sultan* (mother of the sultan) were allowed through

Topkapı Palace (Topkapı Sarayı)

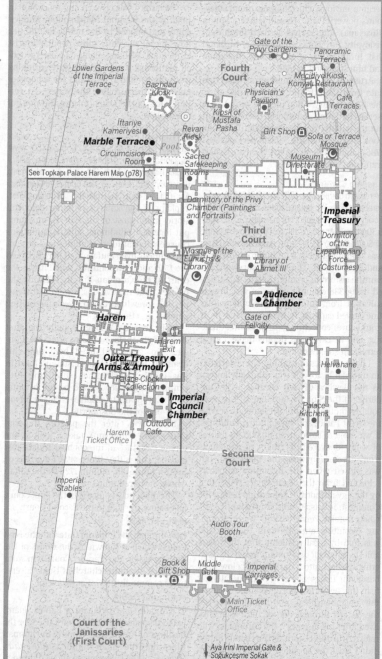

İSTANBUL SIGHTS

Gate of the Privy Gardens

Panoramic Terrace

Lower Gardens of the Imperial Terrace

Fourth Court

Baghdad Kiosk

Head Physician's Pavilion

Mecidiye Kiosk; Konyalı Restaurant

Café Terraces

İftariye Kameriyesi

Kiosk of Mustafa Pasha

Gift Shop

Sofa or Terrace Mosque

Marble Terrace

Revan Kiosk

Pool

Museum Directorate

Circumcision Room

Sacred Safekeeping Rooms

See Topkapı Palace Harem Map (p78)

Dormitory of the Privy Chamber (Paintings and Portraits)

Imperial Treasury

Dormitory of the Expeditionary Force (Costumes)

Third Court

Mosque of the Eunuchs & Library

Library of Ahmet III

Audience Chamber

Gate of Felicity

Harem

Harem Exit

Helvahane

Outer Treasury (Arms & Armour)

Palace Clock Collection

Imperial Council Chamber

Palace Kitchens

Outdoor Cafe

Harem Ticket Office

Second Court

Imperial Stables

Audio Tour Booth

Book & Gift Shop

Middle Gate

Imperial Carriages

Main Ticket Office

Court of the Janissaries (First Court)

Aya İrini Imperial Gate & Soğukçeşme Sokak

the Middle Gate on horseback. Everyone else, including the grand vizier, had to dismount.

The Second Court has a beautiful parklike setting. Unlike typical European palaces, which feature one large building with outlying gardens, Topkapı is a series of pavilions, kitchens, barracks, audience chambers, kiosks and sleeping quarters built around a central enclosure.

The great Palace Kitchens on the right (east) as you enter have been closed to the public for a number of years while awaiting restoration. When they reopen they may hold a small portion of Topkapı's vast collection of Chinese celadon porcelain, valued by the sultans for its beauty but also because it was reputed to change colour if touched by poisoned food.

On the left (west) side of the Second Court is the ornate Imperial Council Chamber (Dîvân-ı Hümâyûn). The council met here to discuss matters of state, and the sultan sometimes eavesdropped through the gold grille high in the wall. The room to the right showcases clocks from the palace collection.

North of the Imperial Council Chamber is the Outer Treasury, where an impressive collection of Ottoman and European arms and armour is displayed.

➡ Harem

The entrance to the Harem is beneath the Tower of Justice on the western side of the Second Court. If you decide to visit – and we highly recommend that you do – you'll need to buy a dedicated ticket.

As popular belief would have it, the Harem was a place where the sultan could engage in debauchery at will. In more prosaic reality, these were the imperial family quarters, and every detail of Harem life was governed by tradition, obligation and ceremony. The word 'harem' literally means 'forbidden' or 'private'.

The sultans supported as many as 300 concubines in the Harem, although numbers were usually lower than this. Upon entering the Harem, the girls would be schooled in Islam and in Turkish culture and language, as well as the arts of make-up, dress, comportment, music, reading, writing, embroidery and dancing. They then entered a meritocracy, first as ladies-in-waiting to the sultan's concubines and children, then to the *valide sultan* (mother of the sultan) and finally – if they were particularly attractive and talented – to the sultan himself.

The sultan was allowed by Islamic law to have four legitimate wives, who received the title of *kadın* (wife). If a wife bore him a son she was called *haseki sultan*; *haseki kadın* if it was a daughter.

Ruling the Harem was the *valide sultan*, who often owned large landed estates in her own name and controlled them through black eunuch servants. Able to give orders directly to the grand vizier, her influence on the sultan, on the selection of his wives and concubines, and on matters of state was often profound.

The earliest of the 300-odd rooms in the Harem were constructed during the reign of Murat III (r 1574–95); the harems of previous sultans were at the now-demolished Eski Saray (Old Palace), near current-day Beyazıt Meydanı.

The Harem complex has six floors, but only one of these can be visited. This is approached via the Carriage Gate. Inside the gate is the Dome with Cupboards. Beyond it is a room where the Harem's eunuch guards were stationed. This is decorated with fine Kütahya tiles from the 17th century.

Beyond this room is the narrow Courtyard of the Black Eunuchs, also decorated with Kütahya tiles. Behind the marble colonnade on the left are the Black Eunuchs' Dormitories. In the early days white eunuchs were used, but black eunuchs sent as presents by the Ottoman governor of Egypt later took control. As many as 200 lived here, guarding the doors and waiting on the women of the Harem.

At the far end of the courtyard is the Main Gate into the Harem, as well as a guard room featuring two gigantic gilded mirrors. From this, a corridor on the left leads to the Courtyard of the Concubines and Sultan's Consorts. This is surrounded by baths, a laundry fountain, a laundry, dormitories and private apartments.

Further on is Sultan Ahmet's Kiosk, decorated with a tiled chimney, followed by the Apartments of the Valide Sultan, the centre of power in the Harem. From these ornate rooms the *valide sultan* oversaw and controlled her huge 'family'. Of particular note is the Salon of the Valide with its lovely 19th-century murals featuring bucolic views of İstanbul.

Past the adjoining Courtyard of the Valide Sultan is a splendid reception room with a large fireplace that leads to a vestibule covered in Kütahya and İznik tiles dating from the 17th century. This is where the princes, *valide sultan* and senior concubines waited

Topkapı Palace Harem

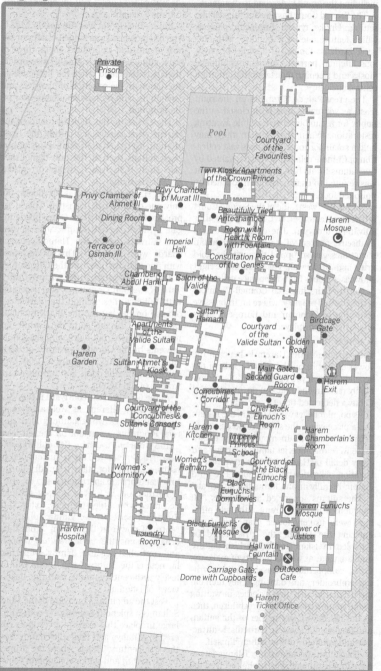

Private Prison

Pool

Courtyard of the Favourites

Twin Kiosk Apartments of the Crown Prince

Privy Chamber of Murat III

Privy Chamber of Ahmet III

Dining Room

Beautifully Tiled Antechamber

Harem Mosque

Room with Hearth; Room with Fountain

Imperial Hall

Terrace of Osman III

Consultation Place of the Genies

Chamber of Abdül Hamit I

Salon of the Valide

Sultan's Hamam

Apartments of the Valide Sultan

Courtyard of the Valide Sultan

Birdcage Gate

Golden Road

Harem Garden

Sultan Ahmet's Kiosk

Main Gate; Second Guard Room

Harem Exit

Concubines' Corridor

Courtyard of the Concubines & Sultan's Consorts

Chief Black Eunuch's Room

Harem Kitchen

Imperial Princes School

Harem Chamberlain's Room

Women's Hamam

Courtyard of the Black Eunuchs

Women's Dormitory

Black Eunuchs Dormitories

Harem Eunuchs' Mosque

Harem Hospital

Laundry Room

Black Eunuchs' Mosque

Tower of Justice

Hall with Fountain

Carriage Gate; Dome with Cupboards

Outdoor Cafe

Harem Ticket Office

before entering the handsome Imperial Hall for an audience with the sultan. Built during the reign of Murat III, the hall was redecorated in baroque style by order of Osman III (r 1754–57).

Nearby is the Privy Chamber of Murat III, one of the most sumptuous rooms in the palace. Dating from 1578, virtually all of its decoration is original and is thought to be the work of Sinan. The recently restored three-tiered marble fountain was designed to give the sound of cascading water and to make it difficult to eavesdrop on the sultan's conversations. The gilded canopied seating areas are later 18th-century additions.

Continue to the Privy Chamber of Ahmed III and peek into the adjoining dining room built in 1705. The latter is lined with wooden panels decorated with images of flowers and fruits painted in lacquer.

Northeast (through the door to the right) of the Privy Chamber of Murat III are two of the most beautiful rooms in the Harem – the Twin Kiosk/Apartments of the Crown Prince. These two rooms date from around 1600; note the painted canvas dome in the first room and the fine İznik tile panels above the fireplace in the second. The stained glass is also noteworthy.

To the east of the Twin Kiosk is the Courtyard of the Favourites. Over the edge of the courtyard (really a terrace) you'll see a large pool. Just past the courtyard (but on the floor above) are the many small dark rooms that comprised the *kafes* where brothers or sons of the sultan were imprisoned.

From here, a corridor leads east to a passage known as the Golden Road and then out into the palace's Third Court.

Note that the visitor route through the Harem changes when rooms are closed for restoration or stabilisation, so some of the areas mentioned here may not be open during your visit.

➡ **Third Court**

The Third Court is entered through the Gate of Felicity. The sultan's private domain, it was staffed and guarded by white eunuchs. Inside is the Audience Chamber, constructed in the 16th century but refurbished in the 18th century. Important officials and foreign ambassadors were brought to this little kiosk to conduct the high business of state. The sultan, seated on a huge divan, inspected the ambassadors' gifts and offerings as they were passed through the doorway on the left.

Right behind the Audience Chamber is the pretty Library of Ahmet III, built in 1719.

On the eastern edge of the Third Court is the Dormitory of the Expeditionary Force, which now houses a rich collection of imperial robes, kaftans and uniforms worked in silver and gold thread. Also here is a fascinating collection of talismanic shirts, which were believed to protect the wearer from enemies and misfortunes of all kinds.

On the other side of the Third Court are the Sacred Safekeeping Rooms. These rooms, sumptuously decorated with İznik tiles, house many relics of the Prophet. When the sultans lived here, the rooms were opened only once a year so that the imperial family could pay homage to the memory of the Prophet on the 15th day of the holy month of Ramazan.

Next to the sacred Safekeeping Rooms is the Dormitory of the Privy Chamber, which houses an exhibit of portraits of 36 sultans. The highlight is a wonderful painting of the *Enthronement Ceremony of Sultan Selim III* (1789) by Konstantin Kapidagli.

➡ **Treasury**

Located on the eastern edge of the Third Court, Topkapı's Treasury features an incredible collection of objects made from or decorated with gold, silver, rubies, emeralds, jade, pearls and diamonds. The building itself was constructed during Mehmet the Conqueror's reign in 1460 and was used originally as reception rooms.

In the first room, look for the jewel-encrusted Sword of Süleyman the Magnificent and the Throne of Ahmed I (aka Arife Throne), which is inlaid with mother-of-pearl and was designed by Sedefhar Mehmet Ağa, architect of the Blue Mosque. It's one of four imperial thrones on display here. The Treasury's most famous exhibit, the Topkapı Dagger, is in the fourth room. The object of the criminal heist in Jules Dassin's 1963 film *Topkapi*, the dagger features three enormous emeralds on the hilt and a watch set into the pommel. Near it is the Kasıkçı (Spoonmaker's) Diamond, a teardrop-shaped 86-carat rock surrounded by dozens of smaller stones. First worn by Mehmet IV at his accession to the throne in 1648, it's the world's fifth-largest diamond.

➡ **Fourth Court**

Pleasure pavilions occupy the palace's Fourth Court. These include the Mecidiye Köşkü, which was built by Abdül Mecit (r 1839–61) according to 19th-century European models.

Topkapı Palace

DAILY LIFE IN THE IMPERIAL COURT

A visit to this opulent palace compound, with its courtyards, harem and pavilions, offers a fascinating glimpse into the lives of the Ottoman sultans. During its heyday, royal wives and children, concubines, eunuchs and servants were among the 4000 people living within Topkapı's walls.

The sultans and their families rarely left the palace grounds, relying on courtiers and diplomats to bring them news of the outside world. Most visitors would go straight to the magnificent **Imperial Council Chamber** ❶, where the sultan's grand vizier and Dîvân (Council) regularly met to discuss affairs of state and receive foreign dignitaries. Many of these visitors brought lavish gifts and tributes to embellish the **Imperial Treasury** ❷.

After receiving any guests and meeting with the Dîvân, the grand vizier would make his way through the ornate **Gate of Felicity** ❸ into the Third Court, the palace's residential quarter. Here, he would brief the sultan on the deliberations and decisions of the Dîvân in the ornate **Audience Chamber** ❹.

Meanwhile, day-to-day domestic chores and intrigues would be underway in the **Harem** ❺ and servants would be preparing feasts in the massive **Palace Kitchens** ❻. Amid all this activity, the **Marble Terrace** ❼ was a tranquil retreat where the sultan would come to relax, look out over the city and perhaps regret his sequestered lifestyle.

DON'T MISS

There are spectacular views from the terrace above the Konyalı Restaurant and also from the Marble Terrace in the Fourth Court.

Harem
The sultan, his mother and the crown prince had sumptuously decorated private apartments in the Harem. The most beautiful of these are the Twin Kiosks (pictured), which were used by the crown prince.

Harem Ticket Office

Middle Gate

Aya İrini

Imperial Gate

Imperial Council Chamber
This is where the Dîvân (Council) made laws, citizens presented petitions and foreign dignitaries were presented to the court. The sultan sometimes eavesdropped on proceedings through the window with the golden grille.

TONY SOUTER/GETTY IMAGES©

Audience Chamber
Surrounded by a colonnade of 22 columns, this recently restored pavilion was where the sultan sat on a canopied throne to receive his grand viziers and foreign dignitaries.

Marble Terrace
This gorgeous terrace is home to the Baghdad and Revan Kiosks, the tiled imperial circumcision room and the İftariye Kameriyesi, a viewing platform with a gilded canopy. During Ramazan, the sultan would enjoy his *iftar* (breaking of the fast) here.

Circumcision Room

Baghdad Kiosk

Revan Kiosk

Kiosk of Mustafa Pasha

Library of Ahmet III

Head Physician's Pavilion

Dormitory of the Privy Chamber
Arms & Armour

Sacred Safekeeping Rooms

⑦

Mecidiye Kiosk

⑤

Outer Treasury

③

①

④

②

Terrace

⑥

Dormitory of the Expeditionary Force (Costume Collection)

Ticket Office

Gate of Felicity
This rococo-style gate was used for state ceremonies, including the sultan's accession and funeral. A 1789 work by court painter Kostantin Kapidagli records the enthronement ceremony of Sultan Selim III.

REINHARD DIRSCHERL/ROBERT HARDING©

Palace Kitchens
Keeping the palace's 4000 residents fed was a huge task. Topkapı's kitchens occupied 10 domed buildings with 20 huge chimneys, and were workplace and home for 800 members of staff.

Imperial Treasury
One of the highlights here is the famous Topkapı Dagger, which was commissioned in 1747 by Sultan Mahmud I as a lavish gift for Nadir Shah of Persia. The shah was assassinated before it could be given to him.

ART DIRECTIONS & TRIP/ALAMY©

İSTANBUL FOR CHILDREN

Children of all ages will enjoy the **Rahmi M Koç Museum** (p106) in Hasköy, which offers loads of activities and gadgets. The spooky **Basilica Cistern** (p75), with its upside-down heads on columns, is also usually a hit. Older children will enjoy the **ferry trip** down the Bosphorus, particularly if it's combined with a visit to the fortress of **Rumeli Hisarı** (p103) – but beware of the steep stairs here, which have no barriers. On **Büyükada** and **Heybeliada**, two of the Princes' Islands, you can hire bikes or circle the island in a *fayton* (horse-drawn carriage), which is lots of fun.

If you're staying in Sultanahmet, there are **playgrounds** in Kadırga Park, near Little Aya Sofya, and in **Gülhane Park** (p83). If you're staying in Beyoğlu, there's one right at the water's edge next to the Fındıklı tram stop – very scenic, but be sure to watch your toddlers carefully!

If you need to resort to bribery to ensure good behaviour, look for the **Mado** (227 3876; İskele Meydanı, Ortaköy; 7am-2am; Ortaköy) chain of ice-cream shops – there are additional branches on Divan Yolu in Sultanahmet and on İstiklal Caddesi in Beyoğlu.

Beneath this is the Konyalı restaurant, which offers wonderful views from its terrace but is let down by the quality of its food. West of the Mecidiye Köşkü is the Head Physician's Pavilion. Interestingly, the head physician was always one of the sultan's Jewish subjects. Nearby, you'll see the Kiosk of Mustafa Pasha, sometimes called the Sofa Köşkü. During the reign of Ahmet III, the Tulip Garden outside the kiosk was filled with the latest varieties of the flower.

Up the stairs at the end of the Tulip Garden is the Marble Terrace, a platform with a decorative pool, three pavilions and the whimsical İftariye Kameriyesi, a small structure commissioned by İbrahim I ('the Crazy') in 1640 as a picturesque place to break the fast of Ramazan.

Murat IV built the Revan Kiosk in 1636 after reclaiming the city of Yerevan (now in Armenia) from Persia. In 1639 he constructed the Baghdad Kiosk, one of the last examples of classical palace architecture, to commemorate his victory over that city. Notice its superb İznik tiles, painted ceiling and mother-of-pearl and tortoiseshell inlay. The small Circumcision Room (Sünnet Odası) was used for the ritual that admits Muslim boys to manhood. Built by İbrahim I in 1640, the outer walls of the chamber are graced by particularly beautiful tile panels.

⭐ **İstanbul Archaeology Museums** MUSEUM (İstanbul Arkeoloji Müzeleri; Map p70; 212-520 7740; www.istanbularkeologi.gov.tr; Osman Hamdi Bey Yokuşu, Gülhane; adult/child under 12yr ₺15/ free; 9am-6pm Tue-Sun mid-Apr–Sep, to 4pm Oct–mid-Apr; Gülhane) This superb museum showcases archaeological and artistic treasures from the Topkapı collections. Housed in three buildings, its exhibits include ancient artefacts, classical statuary and an exhibition tracing İstanbul's history. There are many highlights, but the sarcophagi from the Royal Necropolis of Sidon are particularly striking.

The complex has three main parts: the Archaeology Museum (Arkeoloji Müzesi), the Museum of the Ancient Orient (Eski Şark Eserler Müzesi) and the Tiled Pavilion (Çinili Köşk). These museums house the palace collections formed during the late 19th century by museum director, artist and archaeologist Osman Hamdi Bey. The complex can be easily reached by walking down the slope from Topkapı's First Court, or by walking up the hill from the main gate of Gülhane Park.

➡ **Museum of the Ancient Orient**

Located immediately on the left after you enter the complex, this 1883 building has a collection of pre-Islamic items collected from the expanse of the Ottoman Empire. Highlights include a series of large blue-and-yellow glazed-brick panels that once lined the processional street and the Ishtar Gate of ancient Babylon. These depict real and mythical animals such as lions, dragons and bulls.

➡ **Archaeology Museum**

On the opposite side of the courtyard is this imposing neoclassical building housing an extensive collection of classical statuary and sarcophagi plus a sprawling exhibit documenting İstanbul's history.

The main draws are two dimly lit rooms where the museum's major treasures –

sarcophagi from the Royal Necropolis of Sidon and surrounding area – are displayed. These sarcophagi were unearthed in 1887 by Osman Hamdi Bey in Sidon (Side in modern-day Lebanon). The *Alexander Sarcophagus* and *Mourning Women Sarcophagus* are truly extraordinary works of art.

In the next room is an impressive collection of ancient grave-cult sarcophagi from Syria, Lebanon, Thessalonica and Ephesus. Beyond that is a room called The Columned Sarcophagi of Anatolia, filled with amazingly detailed sarcophagi dating from between 140 and 270 AD. Many of these look like tiny temples or residential buildings; don't miss the *Sidamara Sarcophagus* from Konya.

Further rooms contain Lycian monuments and examples of Anatolian architecture from antiquity.

The museum's 'Anatolia and Troy Through the Ages' and 'Neighbouring Cultures of Anatolia, Cyprus, Syria and Palestine' exhibitions are upstairs, as is a fascinating albeit dusty exhibition called İstanbul Through the Ages that traces the city's history through its neighbourhoods during different periods: Archaic, Hellenistic, Roman, Byzantine and Ottoman. It is likely that these exhibitions will be overhauled in the near future.

The museum's famed Statuary Galleries had been closed for renovation for a number of years when this book went to print and a completion date was not available. A downstairs gallery showcasing Byzantine artefacts was also closed.

➡ Tiled Pavilion

The last of the complex's museum buildings is this handsome pavilion, constructed in 1472 by order of Mehmet the Conqueror. The portico, with its 14 marble columns, was constructed during the reign of Sultan Abdülhamid I (1774–89) after the original one burned down in 1737.

On display here are Seljuk, Anatolian and Ottoman tiles and ceramics dating from the end of the 12th century to the beginning of the 20th century. The collection includes İznik tiles from the period between the mid-14th and 17th centuries when that city produced the finest coloured tiles in the world. When you enter the central room you can't miss the stunning *mihrab* from the İbrahim Bey İmâret in Karaman, built in 1432.

Carpet Museum   MUSEUM
(Halı Müzesi; Map p70; ✆ 212-512 6993; www.hali muzesi.com; Soğukçeşme Sokak; ⊙ 9am-4pm Tue-Sun; 🚇 Sultanahmet or Gülhane) FREE Housed in an 18th-century *imaret* (soup kitchen) built behind the Aya Sofya complex, this recently opened museum is entered through a spectacular baroque gate and gives the visitor an excellent overview of the history of Anatolian carpet-making. The carpets, which have been sourced from mosques throughout the country, date from the 14th to 20th centuries.

There are three galleries, each entered through Tardis-like humidity-controlled entrances. The first, in the *me'kel* (dining hall) features early Anatolian-era carpets with geometric and abstract designs; these are sometimes called Holbein carpets in honour of Dutch artist Hans Holbein the Younger, who often depicted them in his paintings. Also here are examples of the best-known type of Turkish carpets: Uşak (Ushak) carpets of the 16th and 17th centuries.

The second gallery, in the *aşhane* (kitchen), displays rugs with central and eastern Anatolian motifs including star-shaped medallions and keyholes; the latter is said to have been inspired by the mosque *mihrab*. Don't miss the particularly fine 19th-century Hereke rug that came from the Mustafa Mosque in Sirkeci.

The third gallery, in the *fodlahane* (bakery), is the most impressive, with a huge 17th-century Uşak carpet from the Süleymaniye Mosque and another 19th-century example from the Blue Mosque.

The museum was free at the time of research, but an entry fee may apply in the future.

Gülhane Park   PARK
(Gülhane Parkı; Map p70; 🚇 Gülhane) Gülhane Park was once the outer garden of Topkapı Palace, accessed only by the royal court. These days crowds of locals come here to picnic under the many trees, promenade past the formally planted flowerbeds, and enjoy wonderful views over the Golden Horn and Sea of Marmara from the Set Üstü Çay Bahçesi teahouse (p122) on the park's northeastern edge.

Recent beautification works have seen improvements to walkways and amenities, and have included the opening of a new museum, the İstanbul Museum of the History of Science & Technology in Islam (İstanbul İslam Bilim ve Teknoloji Tarihi Müzesi; Map p70;

📋 212-528 8065; www.ibttm.org; Has Ahırlar Binaları, Gülhane Parkı; admission ₺10; ⊙ 9am-4.30pm Wed-Mon; 🚇 Gülhane).

Next to the southern entrance is the Alay Köşkü (Parade Kiosk), now open to the public as the Ahmet Hamdi Tanpınar Literature Museum Library (Ahmet Hamdi Tanpınar Edebiyat Müze Kütüphanesi; Map p70; 📋 212-520 2081; Gülhane Parkı; ⊙ 10am-7pm Mon-Sat; 🚇 Gülhane) FREE.

Across the street and 100m northwest of the park's main gate is an outrageously curvaceous rococo gate leading into the precincts of what was once the grand vizierate, or Ottoman prime ministry, known in the West as the Sublime Porte (Map p70; 🚇 Gülhane). Today the buildings beyond the gate hold various offices of the İstanbul provincial government (the Vilayeti).

Little Aya Sofya   MOSQUE
(Küçük Aya Sofya Camii, SS Sergius & Bacchus Church; Map p70; Küçük Ayasofya Caddesi; 🚇 Sultanahmet or Çemberlitaş) FREE Justinian and his wife Theodora built this little church sometime between 527 and 536, just before Justinian built Aya Sofya. You can still see their monogram worked into some of the frilly white capitals. The building is one of the most beautiful Byzantine structures in the city despite being thoroughly 'mosque-ified' during a recent restoration.

Named after Sergius and Bacchus, the two patron saints of Christians in the Roman army, the building has been known as Little (Küçük in Turkish) Aya Sofya for much of its existence. Its dome is architecturally noteworthy and its plan – an irregular octagon – is quite unusual. Like Aya Sofya, its interior was originally decorated with gold mosaics and featured columns made from fine green and red marble. The mosaics are long gone, but the impressive columns remain. The church was converted into a mosque by the chief white eunuch Hüseyin Ağa around 1500; his tomb is to the north of the building. The minaret and *medrese* (seminary) date from this time.

The *medrese* cells, arranged around the mosque's forecourt, are now used by second-hand booksellers and bookbinders. In the leafy forecourt there is a tranquil *çay bahçesi* where you can relax over a glass of tea.

◉ **Bazaar District**

Crowned by the city's first and most evocative shopping mall – the famous Grand

🏃 **Grand Bazaar**
Grand Bazaar

START ÇEMBERLITAŞ TRAM STOP
END SAHAFLAR ÇARŞISI
LENGTH 1KM; THREE HOURS

Visitors are often overwhelmed by the bazaar's labyrinthine layout and vociferous touts, but if you follow this walking tour, you should enjoy your visit.

Start at the tram stop next to the tall column known as ❶ **Çemberlitaş**, which was erected by order of Emperor Constantine to celebrate the dedication of Constantinople as capital of the Roman Empire in 330. From here, walk down Vezir Han Caddesi and you will soon come to the entrance to the ❷ **Vezir Han**, a *han* (caravanserai) built between 1659 and 1660 by the Köprülüs, one of the Ottoman Empire's most distinguished families.

Continue walking down Vezir Han Caddesi until you come to a cobbled pedestrianised street on your left. Walk along this until you come to the ❸ **Nuruosmaniye Mosque**, commissioned by Mahmut I in 1748. In front of you is one of the major entrances to the Grand Bazaar, the Nuruosmaniye Kapısı (Nuruosmaniye Gate, Gate 1), adorned by another sultan's seal.

The brightly lit street now in front of you is Kalpakçılarbası Caddesi, the busiest street in the bazaar. Originally named after the *kalpakçılars* (makers of fur hats) who had their stores here, it's now full of jewellers, who pay huge amounts per year in rent for this high-profile location. Start walking down the street and then turn right and take the marble stairs down to the ❹ **Sandal Bedestenı**, a 17th-century stone warehouse featuring 20 small domes. This warehouse has always been used for the storage and sale of fabric (*sandal* means fabric woven with silk).

Exit the Sandal Bedestenı on its west side, turning right into Sandal Bedestenı Sokak and then left into Ağa Sokak, which takes you into the oldest part of the bazaar, the ❺ **İç (Inner) Bedesten**, also known as the Eski (Old) Bedesten. This has always been an area where precious items are stored and sold, and today it's where most of the bazaar's antique stores are located.

Exiting the *bedesten* from its south door, walk down to the first cross-street,

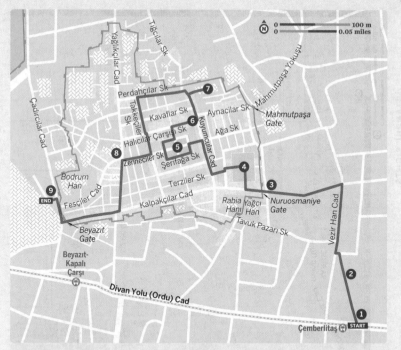

Halıcılar Çarşışı Sokak, where popular shops including Abdulla Natural Products and Derviş are located.

Walking east (right) you will come to a major cross-street, Kuyumcular Caddesi (Street of the Jewellers). Turn left and walk past the little kiosk in the middle of the street. Built in the 17th century and known as the ❻ **Oriental Kiosk**, it now houses a jewellery store but was once home to the most famous *muhallebici* (milk pudding shop) in the district. A little way further down, on the right-hand side of the street, is the entrance to the pretty Zincirli (Chain) Han, home to one of the bazaar's best-known carpet merchants. Returning to Kuyumcular Caddesi, turn sharp left into Perdahçılar Sokak (Street of the Polishers). Walk until you reach Takkeçiler Sokak, where you should turn left. This charming street is known for its marble *sebils* (public drinking fountains) and shops selling kilims (pileless woven rugs). Turn right into Zenneciler Sokak (Street of the Clothing Sellers) and you will soon come to a junction with another of the bazaar's major thoroughfares, Sipahi Sokak (Avenue of the Cavalry Soldiers). ❼ **Şark Kahvesi**, a traditional coffeehouse, is right on the corner.

Turn left into Sipahi Sokak and walk straight until you return to Kalpakçılarbası Caddesi. Turn right and exit the bazaar from the Beyazıt Kapısı (Beyazıt Gate, Gate 7). Turn right again and walk past the market stalls to the first passage on the left, and you will find yourself in the ❽ **Sahaflar Çarşısı** (Old Book Bazaar), which has operated as a book and paper market since Byzantine times. From here, you can exit to Beyazıt Meydanı and make your way down Divan Yolu Caddesi to Sultahnamet or continue walking north along the walls of İstanbul University to the Süleymaniye Mosque.

Many visitors choose to combine a visit to the Grand Bazaar with one to the Spice Bazaar at Eminönü. To do this, backtrack through the bazaar to the Mahmutpaşa Kapısı (Mahmutpaşa Gate, Gate 18) and follow busy Mahmutpaşa Yokuşu all the way down the hill to the Spice Bazaar.

This street and the streets to the west of the Spice Bazaar (collectively known as Tahtakale) are the busiest mercantile precincts in the Old City. This is where locals come to buy everything from coffee cups to circumcision outfits – a wander around here will give you a glimpse into the real, rather than touristy, İstanbul.

ISTANBUL SIGHTS

Bazaar District

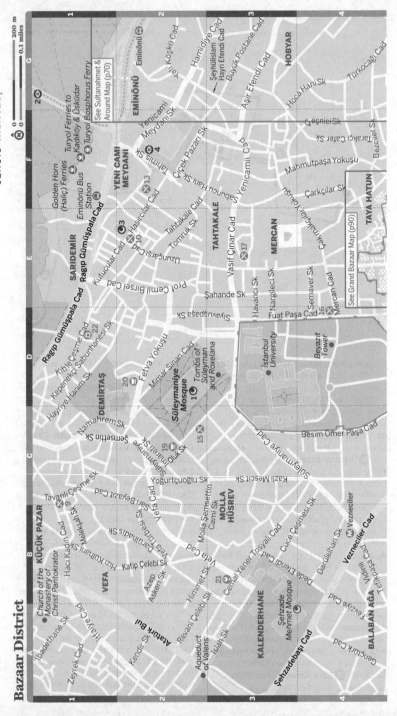

G1 — Turyol Ferries to Kadıköy & Üsküdar
G1 — Turyol Bosphorus Ferry

See Sultanahmet & Around Map (p70)

Eminönü

EMINÖNÜ

HOBYAR

Golden Horn (Haliç) Ferries
Eminönü Bus Station

YENI CAMI MEYDANI

SARIDEMIR

Ragıp Gümüşpala Cad

TAHTAKALE

MERCAN

See Grand Bazaar Map (p90)

TAYA HATUN

Ragıp Gümüşpala Cad

DEMIRTAŞ

Süleymaniye Mosque

Tombs of Süleyman and Roxelana

Istanbul University

Beyazıt Tower

Beşim Ömer Paşa Cad

Church of the Monastery of Christ Pantokrator

KÜÇÜK PAZAR

VEFA

MOLLA HÜSREV

Vezneciler

BALABAN AĞA

Aqueduct of Valens

Şehzade Mehmet Mosque

KALENDERHANE

Şehzadebaşı Cad

200 m
0.1 miles

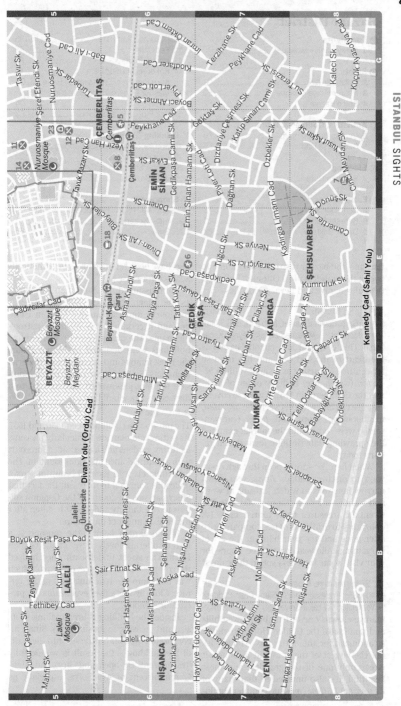

Bazaar District

Bazaar – the bazaar district is also home to two of the grandest of all Ottoman buildings the Süleymaniye and Beyazıt Mosques.

★ **Grand Bazaar**   MARKET
(Kapalı Çarşı, Covered Market; Map p90; ⊙ 8.30am–7pm Mon-Sat; Ⓜ Vezneciler, Ⓡ Beyazıt-Kapalı Çarşı) This colourful and chaotic bazaar is the heart of the Old City and has been so for centuries. Starting as a small vaulted *bedesten* (warehouse) built by order of Mehmet the Conqueror in 1461, it grew to cover a vast area as laneways between the *bedesten*, neighbouring shops and *hans* (caravanserais) were roofed and the market assumed the sprawling, labyrinthine form that it retains today.

When here, be sure to peep through doorways to discover hidden *hans*, veer down narrow laneways to watch artisans at work and wander the main thoroughfares to differentiate treasures from tourist tack. It's obligatory to drink lots of tea, compare price after price and try your hand at the art of bargaining. Allow at least three hours for your visit; some travellers spend three days!

★ **Süleymaniye Mosque**   MOSQUE
(Map p86; Professor Sıddık Sami Onar Caddesi; Ⓜ Vezneciler, Ⓡ Laleli-Üniversite) The Süleymaniye crowns one of İstanbul's seven hills and dominates the Golden Horn, providing a landmark for the entire city. Though it's not the largest of the Ottoman mosques, it is certainly one of the grandest and most beautiful. It's also unusual in that many of its original *külliye* (mosque complex) buildings have been retained and sympathetically adapted for reuse.

Commissioned by Süleyman I, known as 'the Magnificent', the Süleymaniye was the fourth imperial mosque built in İstanbul and it certainly lives up to its patron's nickname. The mosque and its surrounding buildings were designed by Mimar Sinan, the most famous and talented of all imperial architects. Sinan's *türbe* (tomb) is just outside the mosque's walled garden, next to a disused *medrese* building.

➡ **Mosque**

The mosque was built between 1550 and 1557. Its setting and plan are particularly pleasing, featuring gardens and a three-sided forecourt with a central domed ablutions fountain. The four minarets with their 10 beautiful *şerefes* (balconies) are said to represent the fact that Süleyman was the fourth of the Osmanlı sultans to rule the city and the 10th sultan after the establishment of the empire.

In the garden behind the mosque is a terrace offering lovely views of the Golden Horn. The street underneath once housed the complex's *arasta* (street of shops), which was built into the retaining wall of the terrace. Close by was a five-level *mülazim* (preparatory school).

Inside, the building is breathtaking in its size and pleasing in its simplicity. Sinan incorporated the four buttresses into the walls of the building – the result is wonderfully 'transparent' (ie open and airy) and highly reminiscent of Aya Sofya, especially as the dome is nearly as large as the one that crowns the Byzantine basilica.

The *mihrab* is covered in fine İznik tiles, and other interior decoration includes window shutters inlaid with mother-of-pearl, gorgeous stained-glass windows, painted *muqarnas* (corbels with honeycomb detail), a new and quite spectacular persimmon-coloured floor carpet, painted pendentives and medallions featuring fine calligraphy.

➡ Külliye

Süleyman specified that his mosque should have the full complement of public services: *imaret* (soup kitchen), *medreses*, hamam, *tabhane* (inn for travelling dervishes), *darüşşifa* (hospital) etc. Today the *imaret*, with its charming garden courtyard, houses the Dârüzziyafe Restaurant and is a lovely place to enjoy a çay. On its right-hand side (north) is a *tabhane* that was being restored at the time of research and on its left-hand side (south) is Lale Bahçesi (p123), a popular tea garden set in a sunken courtyard.

The main entrance to the mosque is accessed via Professor Sıddık Sami Onar Caddesi, formerly known as Tiryaki Çarşışı (Market of the Addicts). The buildings here once housed three *medreses* and a primary school; they're now home to the Süleymaniye Library and a raft of popular streetside *fasulye* (bean) restaurants that used to be tea houses selling opium (hence the street's former name). On the corner of Professor Sıddık Sami Onar Caddesi and Şifahane Sokak is the *darüşşifa*, under restoration.

The still-functioning Süleymaniye Hamamı is on the eastern side of the mosque.

➡ Tombs

To the right (southeast) of the main entrance is the cemetery, home to the tombs of Süleyman and his wife Haseki Hürrem Sultan (Roxelana). The tilework in both is superb. Peek through the windows of Süleyman's tomb to see jewel-like lights in the dome. In Roxelana's tomb, the many tile panels of flowers and the delicate stained glass produce a serene effect.

➡ Surrounding Area

The streets surrounding the mosque are home to what may well be the most extensive concentration of Ottoman timber houses on

THE GREATEST OTTOMAN ARCHITECT

Sultan Süleyman the Magnificent's reign is known as the golden age of the Ottoman Empire, in part due to his penchant for embellishing İstanbul with architectural wonders. Most of these monuments were designed by architect Mimar Sinan, who managed to perfect the design of the classic Ottoman mosque.

Born in 1497, Sinan was a recruit to the *devşirme,* the annual intake of Christian youths into the Janissaries (Ottoman army). He became a Muslim (as all such recruits did) and eventually took up a post as a military engineer in the corps. Süleyman appointed him the chief of the imperial architects in 1538 and he went on to design a total of 321 buildings, 85 of which are still standing in İstanbul.

Most Sinan-designed mosques have a large forecourt with a central *şadırvan* (ablutions fountain) and domed arcades on three sides. On the fourth side stands the mosque, with a two-storey porch. The main prayer hall is covered by a large central dome rising much higher than the two-storey facade, and surrounded by smaller domes and semidomes.

İstanbul's superb Süleymaniye Mosque is the grandest and most visited of his mosques, so if you only have time to visit one of his masterpieces, make it this one. The Atik Valide Mosque (p100) in Üsküdar is similar to the Süleymaniye in many ways, most notably in the extent of its *külliye* (mosque complex, often including hamam, *medrese*, hospital, cemetery and soup kitchen). The much smaller, tile-encrusted Rüstem Paşa Mosque (p91) is exquisite, well rewarding anyone who makes the effort to see it.

Sinan didn't only design and construct mosques. The Çemberlitaş Hamamı (p107), Ayasofya Hürrem Sultan Hamamı (p106) and Kılıç Ali Paşa Hamamı (p107) are also his work, giving you a perfect excuse to blend your architectural studies with a pampering hamam session.

Sınan's works survive in other towns of the Ottoman heartland, particularly Edirne, the one-time capital of the empire.

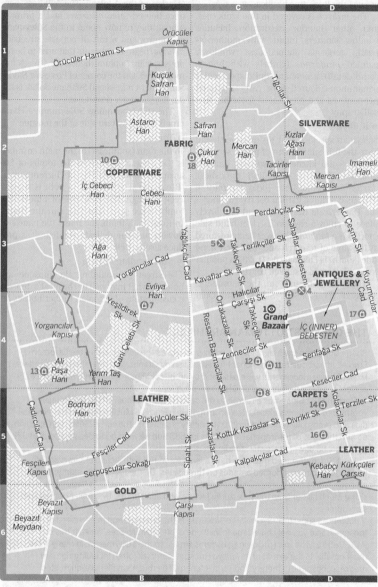

the historical peninsula, many of which are currently being restored as part of an urban regeneration project. To see some of these, head down Felva Yokuşu (between the *tabhane* and Sinan's tomb) and then veer right into Namahrem Sokak and into Ayrancı

Sokak. One of the many Ottoman-era houses here was once occupied by Mimar Sinan; it now houses a cafe.

Alternatively, from Professor Siddık Sami Onar Caddesi head southwest into narrow Ayşekadin Hamamı Sokak (look for the 'Sü-

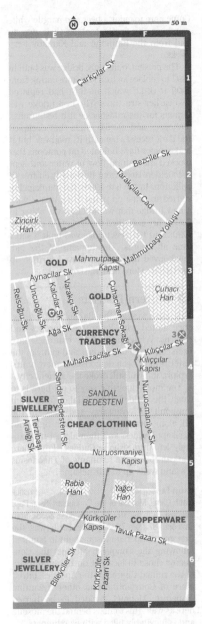

home to a number of pretty timber houses built in the late 19th and early 20th centuries.

Rüstem Paşa Mosque MOSQUE
(Rüstem Paşa Camii; Map p86; Hasırcılar Caddesi, Rüstem Paşa; MHaliç, ☒Eminönü) Nestled in the middle of the busy Tahtakale shopping district, this diminutive mosque is a gem. Dating from 1560, it was designed by Sinan for Rüstem Paşa, son-in-law and grand vizier of Süleyman the Magnificent. A showpiece of the best Ottoman architecture and tilework, it is thought to have been the prototype for Sinan's greatest work, the Selimiye in Edirne.

At the top of the two sets of entry steps there is a terrace and the mosque's colonnaded porch. You'll immediately notice the panels of İznik tiles set into the mosque's facade. The interior is covered in more tiles and features a lovely dome, supported by four tiled pillars.

The preponderance of tiles was Rüstem Paşa's way of signalling his wealth and influence – İznik tiles being particularly expensive and desirable. It may not have assisted his passage into the higher realm, though, because by all accounts he was a loathsome character. His contemporaries dubbed him Kehle-i-Ikbal (the Louse of Fortune) because he was found to be infected with lice on the eve of his marriage to Mihrimah, Süleyman's favourite daughter. He is best remembered

leymaniye Kütüphanesi' sign in the middle of the souvenir stands) and follow it and Kayserili Ahmetpaşa Sokak down through the Molla Hüsrev district, which is slowly being restored as part of the Süleymaniye Urban Regeneration Project. Kayserili Ahmetpaşa Sokak is for plotting with Roxelana to turn Süleyman against his favourite son, Mustafa. They were successful and Mustafa was strangled in 1553 on his father's orders.

The mosque is easy to miss because it's not at street level. There's a set of access stairs on Hasırcılar Caddesi and another on the small street that runs right (north) off Hasırcılar Caddesi towards the Golden Horn.

Spice Bazaar
MARKET

(Mısır Çarşısı, Egyptian Market; Map p86; ⊘8am-6pm Mon-Sat, 8am-7pm Sun; 🚊 Eminönü) Vividly coloured spices are displayed alongside jewel-like *lokum* (Turkish delight) at this Ottoman-era marketplace, providing eye candy for the thousands of tourists and locals who make their way here every day. As well as spices, stalls sell caviar, dried herbs, nuts and dried fruits. The number of stalls selling tourist trinkets increases annually, yet this remains a great place to stock up on edible souvenirs, share a few jokes with the vendors and marvel at the well-preserved building.

New Mosque
MOSQUE

(Yeni Camii; Map p70; Yenicamii Meydanı Sokak, Eminönü; 🚊 Eminönü) Only in İstanbul would a 400-year-old mosque be called 'New'. Dating from 1597, its design references both the Blue Mosque and the Süleymaniye Mosque, with a large forecourt and a square sanctuary surmounted by a series of semidomes crowned by a grand dome. The interior is richly decorated with gold leaf, coloured İznik tiles and carved marble.

Galata Bridge
BRIDGE

(Galata Köprüsü; Map p86; 🚊 Eminönü or Karaköy) To experience İstanbul at its most magical, walk across the Galata Bridge at sunset. At this time, the historic Galata Tower is surrounded by shrieking seagulls, the mosques atop the seven hills of the city are silhouetted against a soft red-pink sky, and the evocative scent of apple tobacco wafts out of the nargile (water-pipe) cafes under the bridge.

During the day, the bridge carries a constant flow of İstanbullus crossing to and from Beyoğlu and Eminönü, a handful or two of hopeful anglers trailing their lines into the waters below, and a constantly changing procession of street vendors hawking everything from fresh-baked *simits* (sesame-encrusted bread rings) to Rolex rip-offs. Underneath, restaurants and cafes serve drinks and food all day and night.

Come here to enjoy a beer and nargile while watching the ferries making their way to and from the Eminönü and Karaköy ferry docks.

The present, quite ugly, bridge was built in 1992 to replace an iron structure dating from 1909 to 1912, which in turn had replaced two earlier structures. The iron bridge was famous for the ramshackle fish restaurants, teahouses and nargile joints that occupied the dark recesses beneath its roadway, but it had a major flaw: it floated on pontoons that blocked the natural flow of water and kept the Golden Horn from flushing itself free of pollution. In the late 1980s the municipality started to draw up plans to replace it with a new bridge that would allow the water to flow. A fire expedited these plans in the early 1990s and the new bridge was built a short time afterwards. The remains of the old, much-loved bridge were moved further up the Golden Horn near Hasköy.

⊙ Western Districts

This area west of the Bazaar District was once dotted with Byzantine churches and cisterns. While most of the churches have been converted to mosques and many of the cisterns have been demolished, a few hours' exploration will still evoke the ancient city.

The most enjoyable way to get here is to catch the Golden Horn (Haliç) ferry from Eminönü to Ayvansaray and walk up the hill along Dervişzade Sokak, turn right into Eğrikapı Caddesi and then almost immediately left into Şişhane Caddesi. From here you can follow the remnants of Theodosius II's land walls up to Edirnekapı.

Fatih Mosque
MOSQUE

(Fatih Camii, Mosque of the Conqueror; Fevzi Paşa Caddesi, Fatih; 🚊 31E, 32, 336E, 36KE & 38E from Eminönü, 87 from Taksim) The Fatih was the first great imperial mosque built in İstanbul following the Conquest. Mehmet the Conqueror chose to locate it on the hilltop site of the ruined Church of the Apostles, burial place of Constantine and other Byzantine emperors. Mehmet decided to be buried here as well – his tomb is behind the mosque and is inevitably filled with worshippers.

The original *külliye*, finished in 1470, was enormous. Set in extensive grounds, it included 15 charitable establishments such as *medreses*, a hospice for travellers and a caravanserai. Many of these still stand – the most interesting is the multidomed *tabhane* to the southeast of the mosque. Its columns are said to have been originally used in the Church of the Apostles.

Unfortunately, the mosque you see today is not the one Mehmet built. The original stood for nearly 300 years before toppling in an earthquake in 1766. The current baroque-style mosque was constructed between 1767 and 1771.

The front courtyard of the mosque is a favourite place for locals to congregate. On Wednesday the streets behind and to the north of the mosque host the **Çarşamba Pazarı** (Fatih Pazarı, Wednesday Market), a busy weekly market selling food, clothing and household goods.

Fethiye Museum   MUSEUM

(Fethiye Müzesi, Church of Pammakaristos; http://ayasofyamuzesi.gov.tr; Fethiye Caddesi, Çarşamba; admission ₺5; ◉9am-6pm Thu-Tue mid-Apr–Sep, to 5pm Oct–mid-Apr; 🚌33ES, 44B, 36C, 90, 399B&C from Eminönü, 55T from Taksim) Not long after the Conquest, Mehmet the Conqueror visited this 13th-century church to discuss theological questions with the Patriarch of the Orthodox Church. They talked in the southern side chapel known as the **parecclesion**, which is decorated with gold mosaics and is now open as a small museum.

Mihrimah Sultan Mosque   MOSQUE

(Mihrimah Sultan Camii; Ali Kuşçu Sokak, Edirnekapı; 🚌31E, 32, 36K & 38E from Eminönü, 87 from Taksim) The great Sinan put his stamp on the entire city, and this mosque, constructed in the 1560s next to the Edirnekapı section of the historic land walls, is one of his best works. Commissioned by Süleyman the Magnificent's favourite daughter, Mihrimah, it features a wonderfully light and airy interior with delicate stained-glass windows and an unusual 'bird cage' chandelier.

Occupying the highest point in the city, the mosque's dome and one slender minaret are major adornments to the city skyline; they are particularly prominent on the road from Edirne. Remnants of the *külliye* include a still-functioning **hamam** (Ali Kuşçu Sokak, Edirnekapı) on the corner of Ali Kuşçu and Eroğlu Sokaks.

⭐ Kariye Museum (Chora Church) MUSEUM

(Kariye Müzesi; 📞212-631 9241; http://ayasofyamuzesi.gov.tr; Kariye Camii Sokak, Edirnekapı; admission ₺15; ◉9am-6pm Thu-Tue mid-Apr–Sep, to 5pm Oct–mid-Apr; 🚌31E, 32, 36K & 38E from Eminönü, 87 from Taksim, 🚋Ayvansaray) İstanbul has more than its fair share of Byzantine monuments, but few are as drop-dead gorgeous as this mosaic- and fresco-laden church. Nestled in the shadow of Theodosius II's monumental land walls and now a museum overseen by the Aya Sofya curators, it receives a fraction of the visitor numbers that its big sister attracts but offers an equally fascinating insight into Byzantine art.

The building was originally known as the Church of the Holy Saviour Outside the Walls (Chora literally means 'country'), reflecting the fact that when it was first built it was located outside the original city walls built by Constantine the Great.

What you see today isn't the original church. Instead, it was reconstructed at least five times, most significantly in the 11th, 12th and 14th centuries. Virtually all of the interior decoration – the famous mosaics and the less renowned but equally striking frescoes – dates from 1312 and was funded by Theodore Metochites, a poet and man of letters who was *logothetes*, the official responsible for the Byzantine treasury, under Emperor Andronikos II (r 1282–1328). One of the museum's most wonderful mosaics, found above the door to the nave in the inner narthex, depicts Theodore offering the church to Christ.

Today the Chora consists of five main architectural units: the nave, the two-storied structure (annexe) added to the north, the inner and the outer narthexes and the chapel for tombs (parecclesion) to the south. In 2013 a major restoration of the church commenced. This will be undertaken in stages, involves closure of parts of the museum and is likely to take a number of years (the estimated date of completion is August 2015). At the time of research the nave and the two-storey annexes on the northern side of the building were closed for stage one of the restoration. Stage two will see the inner narthex closed and stage three the outer narthex and parecclesion. It may not be worth visiting during stage three.

➡ Mosaics

Most of the interior is covered with mosaics depicting the lives of Christ and the Virgin Mary. Look out for the *Khalke Jesus*, which shows Christ and Mary with two donors – Prince Isaac Comnenos and Melane, daughter of Mikhael Palaiologos VIII. This is under the right dome in the inner narthex. On the dome itself is a stunning depiction of Jesus and his ancestors (*The Genealogy of Christ)*. On the narthex's left dome is a serenely beautiful mosaic of *Mary and the Baby Jesus Surrounded by Ancestors*.

In the nave are three mosaics: *Christ*; *Mary and the Baby Jesus*; and the *Dormition of the Blessed Virgin (Assumption)* – turn around to see the latter, as it's over the main door you just entered. The 'infant' being held by Jesus is actually Mary's soul.

➡ Frescoes

To the right of the nave is the **parecclesion**, a side chapel built to hold the tombs of the church's founder and his relatives, close friends and associates. This is decorated with frescoes that deal with the themes of death and resurrection, depicting scenes taken from the Old Testament. The striking painting in the apse known as the *Anastasis* shows a powerful Christ raising Adam and Eve out of their sarcophagi, with saints and kings in attendance. The gates of hell are shown under Christ's feet. Less majestic but no less beautiful are the frescoes adorning the dome, which show Mary and 12 attendant angels.

◉ Beyoğlu & Around

The suburb of Beyoğlu (*bay*-oh-loo) rises from the shoreline north of Galata Bridge and incorporates both Taksim Meydanı (Taksim Sq) and the city's grandest boulevard, İstiklal Caddesi. In the mid-19th century it was known as Pera and acknowledged as the 'European' quarter of town. Diplomats and international traders lived and worked here, and the streets were showcases for the latest European fashions and fads.

All this changed in the decades after the republic was formed. Embassies moved to Ankara, the glamorous shops and restaurants closed, the grand buildings crumbled and Beyoğlu took on a decidedly sleazy air. Fortunately the '90s brought about a rebirth and Beyoğlu is once again the heart of modern İstanbul, full of galleries, cafes and boutiques. Here, hip new restaurants and bars open almost nightly, and the streets showcase cosmopolitan Turkey at its best. Put simply, if you miss Beyoğlu, you haven't seen İstanbul.

The best way to get a feel for this side of town is to spend an afternoon or day exploring by foot. If you're based in Sultanahmet, catch the tram to Kabataş and the connecting funicular up to Taksim Meydanı. Then work your way down İstiklal Caddesi, exploring its many side streets along the way. At the foot of the boulevard is Tünel Meydanı (Tünel Square); follow Galipdede Caddesi downhill and you will be able to explore the historic neighbourhood of Galata before walking across Galata Bridge to Eminönü, from where you can catch a tram or walk back up to Sultanahmet. All up it's a walk of at least two hours from Taksim Meydanı – but dedicating a full day will be more rewarding.

★ İstanbul Modern   ART GALLERY
(İstanbul Modern Sanat Müzesi; Map p96; www. istanbulmodern.org; Meclis-i Mebusan Caddesi, Tophane; adult/student/under 12yr ₺17/9/free; ⊙10am-6pm Tue, Wed & Fri-Sun, to 8pm Thu; ⏸Tophane) The big daddy of a slew of newish, privately funded art galleries in the city, this impressive institution has a stunning location on the shores of the Bosphorus, an extensive collection of Turkish 20th-century paintings on the ground floor, and a constantly changing and uniformly excellent program of mixed-media exhibitions by local and international artists in the basement galleries. There's also a well-stocked gift shop, a cinema that shows art-house films and a stylish cafe-restaurant with superb views of the Bosphorus.

★ İstiklal Caddesi   STREET
(Independence Ave; Map p96) Once called the Grand Rue de Pera but renamed İstiklal (Independence) in the early years of the republic, Beyoğlu's premier boulevard is a perfect metaphor for 21st-century Turkey, being an exciting mix of modernity and tradition. Contemporary boutiques and cutting-edge cultural centres are housed in its grand 19th-century buildings, and an antique tram traverses its length alongside crowds of pedestrians making their way to the bustling cafes, bistros and bars that Beyoğlu is known for.

At the boulevard's northern end is frantically busy Taksim Meydanı, the symbolic heart of the modern city and the scene of often-violent protests in recent years. Another square, Galatasaray Meydanı, is at the boulevard's midpoint, close to Beyoğlu's much-loved Balık Pazarı (Fish Market) and Çiçek Pasajı (Flower Passage). At its southern end is Tünel Meydanı and the relatively tranquil district of Galata, home to atmospheric cobblestone lanes and traces of a fortified settlement built by Genoese merchants in the 13th century.

SALT Galata
CULTURAL CENTRE

(Map p96; ☑ 212-334 2200; www.saltonline.org/en; Bankalar Caddesi 11, Karaköy; ☺ noon-8pm Tue-Sat, to 6pm Sun; ☒ Karaköy) **FREE** The descriptor 'cultural centre' is used a lot in İstanbul, but is often a misnomer. Here at SALT Galata it really does apply. Housed in a magnificent 1892 bank building designed by Alexandre Vallaury and cleverly adapted by local architectural firm Mimarlar Tasarım, this cutting-edge institution offers an exhibition space, auditorium, arts research library, cafe and glamorous rooftop restaurant.

Galata Tower
TOWER

(Galata Kulesi; Map p96; Galata Meydanı, Galata; admission ₺19; ☺ 9am-8pm; ☒ Karaköy) The cylindrical Galata Tower stands sentry over the approach to 'new' İstanbul. Constructed in 1348, it was the tallest structure in the city for centuries, and it still dominates the skyline north of the Golden Horn. Its vertiginous upper balcony offers 360-degree views of the city, but we're not convinced that the view (though spectacular) justifies the steep admission cost.

Galata Mevlevi Museum
MUSEUM

(Galata Mevlevihanesi Müzesi; Map p96; www.mekder.org; Galipdede Caddesi 15, Tünel; admission ₺5; ☺ 9am-4pm Tue-Sun; Ⓜ Şişhane, ☒ Karaköy, then funicular to Tünel) The *semahane* (whirling-dervish hall) at the centre of this *tekke* (dervish lodge) was erected in 1491 and renovated in 1608 and 2009. It's part of a complex including a *meydan-ı şerif* (courtyard), *çeşme* (drinking fountain), *türbesi* (tomb) and *hamuşan* (cemetery). The oldest of six historic Mevlevihaneleri (Mevlevi *tekkes*) remaining in İstanbul, the complex was converted into a museum in 1946.

The Mevlevi *tarika* (order), founded in the central Anatolian city of Konya during the 13th century, flourished throughout the Ottoman Empire. Like several other orders, the Mevlevis stressed the unity of humankind before God regardless of creed.

Taking their name from the great Sufi mystic and poet, Celaleddin Rumi (1207–73), called Mevlana (Our Leader) by his disciples, Mevlevis seek to achieve mystical communion with God through a *sema* (ceremony) involving chants, prayers, music and a whirling dance. This *tekke*'s first *şeyh* (sheikh) was Şemaî Mehmed Çelebi, a grandson of the great Mevlana.

Dervish orders were banned in the early days of the Turkish Republic because of their ultraconservative religious politics. Although the ban has been lifted, only a handful of functioning *tekkes* remain in İstanbul, including this one and the İstanbul Bilim Sanat Kültür ve Eğitim Derneği in Fatih. Konya remains the heart of the Mevlevi order.

Beneath the *semahane* is an interesting exhibit that includes displays of Mevlevi clothing, turbans and accessories. The *mahfiller* (upstairs floor) houses the *tekke*'s collection of traditional musical instruments, calligraphy and *ebru* (paper marbling).

The *hamuşan* is full of stones with graceful Ottoman inscriptions, including the tomb of Galip Dede, the 17th-century Sufi poet whom the street is named after. The shapes atop the stones reflect the headgear of the deceased, each hat denoting a different religious rank. To see the dervises whirl, see the boxed text on p101.

★ Museum of Innocence
MUSEUM

(Masumiyet Müzesi; Map p96; ☑ 212-252 9748; www.masumiyetmuzesi.org; Çukurcuma Caddesi, Dalgıç Çıkmazı, 2; adult/student ₺25/10; ☺ 10am-6pm Tue-Sun, till 9pm Thu; Ⓜ Taksim, ☒ Tophane) The painstaking attention to detail in this fascinating museum/piece of conceptual art will certainly provide every amateur psychologist with a theory or two about its creator, Nobel Prize–winning novelist Orhan Pamuk. Vitrines display a quirky collection of objects that evoke the minutiae of İstanbullu life in the mid-to-late 20th century, when Pamuk's novel, *The Museum of Innocence,* is set.

Occupying a modest 19th-century timber house, the museum relies on its vitrines, which are reminiscent of the work of American artist Joseph Cornell, to retell the story of the love affair of Kemal and Füsun, the novel's protagonists. These displays are both beautiful and moving; some, such as the installation using 4213 cigarette butts, are as strange as they are powerful.

Pamuk's 'Modest Manifesto for Museums' is reproduced on a panel on the ground floor. In it, he asserts 'The resources that are channeled into monumental, symbolic museums should be diverted to smaller museums that tell the stories of individuals.' The individuals in this case are fictional, of course, and their story is evoked in a highly nostalgic fashion, but in creating this museum Pamuk has put his money where his mouth is and come out triumphant.

Beyoğlu

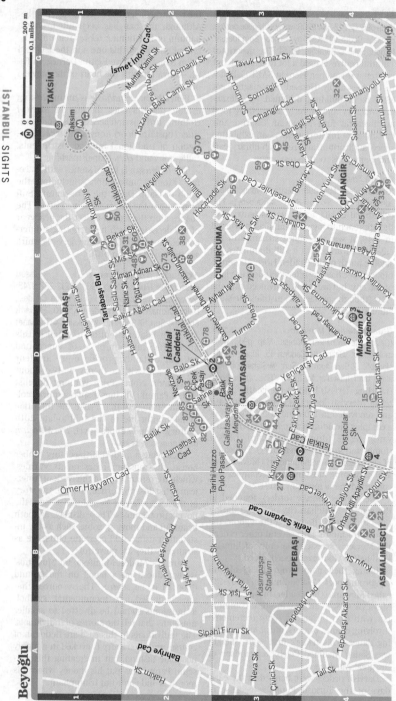

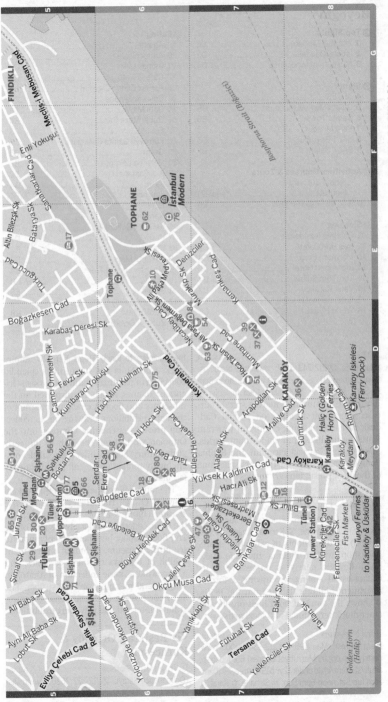

Beyoğlu

ARTER
GALLERY

(Map p96; ☑212-243 3767; www.arter.org.tr; İstiklal Caddesi 211; ⊙11am-7pm Tue-Thu, noon-8pm Fri-Sun; Ⓜ Şişhane, Ⓕ Karaköy, then funicular to Tünel) FREE A stunning marble spiral staircase, prominent location on İstiklal Caddesi, and international exhibition program featuring the likes of Mona Hatoum, Sarkis, Marc Quinn, Patricia Piccinini and Sophia Pompéry make this four-floor art space one of the most prestigious art venues in town.

SALT Beyoğlu
CULTURAL CENTRE

(Map p96; ☑212-377 4200; www.saltonline.org/en; İstiklal Caddesi 136; ⊙noon-8pm Tue-Sat, to 6pm Sun; Ⓜ Şişhane, Ⓕ Karaköy, then funicular to Tünel) Its three floors of exhibition space, bookshop, walk-in cinema and cafe make SALT Beyoğlu nearly as impressive as its Galata-based sibling. Occupying a former apartment building dating from the 1850s, it shows the work of both high-profile and emerging international and local artists.

Pera Museum
MUSEUM

(Pera Müzesi; Map p96; ☑212-334 9900; www.peramuzesi.org.tr; Meşrutiyet Caddesi 65, Tepebaşı; adult/student/child under 12yr ₺15/8/free; ⊙10am-7pm Tue-Sat, noon-6pm Sun; Ⓜ Şişhane, Ⓕ Karaköy,

then funicular to Tünel) Head here to admire works from Suna and İnan Kıraç's splendid collection of paintings featuring Turkish Orientalist themes, which are displayed on the museum's 2nd floor. A changing program of thematic exhibitions drawing on the collection provides fascinating glimpses into the Ottoman world from the 17th to the early 20th century. Some works are realistic, others highly romanticised – all are historically fascinating.

The most beloved painting in the Turkish canon – Osman Hamdı Bey's *The Tortoise Trainer* (1906) – is the stand-out work in the Kıraç collection and is always part of the 2nd-floor display, but there's plenty more to see in the museum, including a permanent exhibit of Kütahya tiles and ceramics, and a somewhat esoteric collection of Anatolian weights and measures on the 1st floor. The 5th floor hosts a constantly changing program of international travelling exhibitions.

◎ Beşiktaş, Ortaköy & Kuruçeşme

Dolmabahçe Palace
PALACE

(Dolmabahçe Sarayı; ☑212-327 2626; www.millisaraylar.gov.tr; Dolmabahçe Caddesi, Beşiktaş; adult

Selâmlık ₺30, Harem ₺20, joint ticket ₺40, student/child under 7yr ₺5/free; ☯9am-3.30pm Tue-Wed & Fri-Sun Apr-Oct, to 2.30pm Nov-Mar; 🚇Akaretler, 🚇Kabataş then walk) These days it's fashionable for architects and critics influenced by the less-is-more aesthetic of the Bauhaus masters to sneer at buildings such as Dolmabahçe. The crowds that throng to this imperial pleasure palace with its neoclassical exterior and over-the-top interior fit-out clearly don't share their disdain, though, flocking here to visit its Selâmlık (Ceremonial Suites), Harem and Veliaht Dairesi (Apartments of the Crown Prince). The latter is home to the recently opened National Palaces Painting Museum (Milli Saraylar Resim Müzesi; ☎212-236 9000; Dolmabahçe Caddesi, Beşiktaş; ☯9am-4pm Tue, Wed & Fri-Sun; 🚇Akaretler, 🚇Kabataş then walk).

More rather than less was certainly the philosophy of Sultan Abdül Mecit I (r 1839–61), who decided to move his imperial court from Topkapı to a lavish new palace on the shores of the Bosphorus. For a site he chose the *dolma bahçe* (filled-in garden) where his predecessors Sultans Ahmet I and Osman II had filled in a little cove in order to create a royal park complete with wooden pleasure kiosks and pavilions.

Abdül Mecit commissioned imperial architects Nikoğos and Garabed Balyan to construct an Ottoman-European palace that would impress everyone who set eyes on it. Traditional Ottoman palace architecture was eschewed – there are no pavilions here, and the palace turns its back to the splendid view rather than celebrating it. The designer of the Paris Opera was brought in to do the interiors, which perhaps explains their exaggerated theatricality. Construction was finally completed in 1854 and the sultan and his family moved in two years later. Though it had the wow factor in spades, Abdül Mecit's extravagant project precipitated the empire's bankruptcy and signalled the beginning of the end for the Osmanlı dynasty. During the early years of the republic, Atatürk used the palace as his İstanbul base and died here on 10 November 1938.

The tourist entrance to the palace is near the ornate clock tower, designed by Sarkis Balyan between 1890 and 1895 for Sultan Abdül Hamid II (r 1876–1909). There is an outdoor cafe near here with premium Bosphorus views and extremely reasonable prices (yes, really).

The palace is set in well-tended gardens and is entered via its ornate imperial gate. It is divided into three sections: the Selâmlık, Harem and Veliaht Dairesi. Entry is via a compulsory and dreadfully rushed guided tour (up to 50 people per group), which focuses on the Selâmlık but visits parts of the Harem as well; you can visit the National Palaces Paintings Museum by yourself. In busy periods, English-language tours leave every 10 minutes or so; during quiet times every 25 minutes is more likely.

Note that visitor numbers in the palace are limited to 3000 per day and this ceiling is often reached on weekends and holidays – come midweek if possible, and even then be prepared to queue (often for a long period and in full sun). If you arrive before 3pm (summer) or 2pm (winter), you must buy a combined ticket to tour both the Selâmlık and Harem; after those times you can take only one tour (we recommend opting for the Selâmlık). Admission here is not covered by the Museum Pass İstanbul.

The nearby Dolmabahçe Mosque (Dolmabahçe Camii) on Muallim Naci Caddesi was designed by Nikoğos Balyan and completed in 1853.

◉ Asian Shore

Although most of İstanbul's noteworthy sights, shops, bars and eateries are on the European side of town, many locals prefer to live on the Asian (aka Anatolian) shore, citing cheaper rents and a better standard of living. For others, the best thing about living in or visiting this side of town is the scenic ferry ride between the continents.

ÜSKÜDAR

Üsküdar (oo-skoo-dar) was founded about two decades before Byzantium, and was originally called Chrysopolis. The Ottomans called it Scutari. Unwalled and therefore vulnerable, it became part of the Ottoman Empire at least 100 years before the Conquest.

Today Üsküdar is a bustling working-class suburb with a handful of important Ottoman mosques that attract visitors. If coming to Üsküdar, take the İstanbul Şehir Hatları ferry from Eminönu, a Dentur Avrasya ferry from Kabataş or Beşiktaş, or a Turyol ferry from Eminönu or Karaköy. Alternatively, take the Marmaray metro from Vezneciler or Sirkeci.

Judging that Scutari was the closest point in İstanbul to Mecca, many powerful Ottoman figures built mosques here to assist their passage to Paradise. Every year a big caravan set out from here, en route to Mecca and Medina for the Haj, further emphasising the suburb's reputation for piety.

As you leave Üsküdar dock, the main square, Demokrasi Meydanı (currently being redeveloped as part of the massive Marmaray transport project), is right in front of you. Its northeastern corner is dominated by the Mihrimah Sultan Mosque (Mihrimah Sultan Camii; Paşa Limanı Caddesi; ☮Üsküdar), sometimes referred to as the İskele (ferry dock) Camii. This mosque was designed by Sinan for Süleyman the Magnificent's daughter and built between 1547 and 1548.

South of the square is the Yeni Valide Mosque (Yeni Valide Camii, New Queen Mother's Mosque; Demokrasi Meydanı; ☮Üsküdar). Featuring a wrought-iron 'birdcage' tomb in its overgrown garden, it was built by Sultan Ahmet III from 1708 to 1710 for his mother, Gülnuş Emetullah.

West of the square, overlooking the harbour, is the charming Şemsi Ahmed Paşa Mosque (Şemsi Paşa Camii, Kuskonmaz Camii; Paşa Limanı Caddesi; ☮Üsküdar). Designed by Sinan and built in 1580 for grand vizier Şemsi Paşa, its modest size and decoration reflect the fact that its benefactor occupied the position of grand vizier for only a couple of months under Süleyman the Magnificent. Its *medrese* has been converted into a library and there's a popular *çay bahçesi* on its southern side.

The Atik Valide Mosque (Atik Valide Camii; Valide İmaret Sokak; ☮Üsküdar) is another of Sinan's works, and is considered by many experts to be among his best designs. It was built for Valide Sultan Nurbanu, wife of Selim II (The Sot) and mother of Murat III, in 1583. Nurbanu was captured by Turks on the Aegean island of Paros when she was 12 years old, and went on to be a successful player in the Ottoman court. Murat adored his mother and on her death commissioned Sinan to build this monument to her on Üsküdar's highest hill.

The nearby Çinili Mosque (Çinili Camii, Tiled Mosque; Çinili Hamam Sokak; ☮Üsküdar) is unprepossessing from the outside, but has an interior made brilliant with İznik tiles, the bequest of Mahpeyker Kösem (1640), wife of Sultan Ahmet I and mother of sultans Murat IV and İbrahim (r 1640–48).

To find the Atik Valide and Çinili Mosques, walk up Hakimiyet-i Milliye Caddesi until you get to the traffic circle. Continue up Dr Fahri Atabey Caddesi for about 1km until you get to little Sarı Mehmet Sokak, on your left. From here you'll spot the minarets of Atik Valide Mosque. To get to the Çinili Mosque from the Atik Valide Mosque, walk east along Çinili Camii Sokak for about 300m, after which it turns north and runs uphill. The Çinili Mosque is about 200m further on. All up it's about a 25-minute walk to the Çinili Mosque from the main square.

Further up the hill is the recently constructed Şakirin Mosque (cnr Huhkuyusu Caddesi & Dr Burhanettin Üstünel Sokak; ▯6, 9A, 11P, 11V, 12A, 12C), one of the city's most impressive examples of contemporary architecture. It's located opposite the Zeynep Kamil Hospital, a 10-minute walk from the Atik Valide Mosque.

KADIKÖY

Although this is the site of the city's first colony (originally called Chalcedon), Kadıköy has nothing to show of its historic beginnings. Instead, locals and visitors come here to visit the suburb's fabulous fresh produce market (Kadıköy Pazarı; the streets around Güneşlibahçe Sokak; ☺Mon-Sat; ▯Kadıköy). To get here, take the İstanbul Şehir Hatları ferry from Eminönü, Karaköy or Beşiktaş, or a Turyol ferry from Eminönü or Karaköy.

Kadıköy and the affluent suburbs stretching southeast to Bostancı are also the Asian side's entertainment hubs. For alternative culture, head to Kadife Sokak to check out its independent cinema, grunge boutiques, tattoo studios and hugely popular bars. And to see the wealthy at play, cruise down Bağdat Caddesi in neighbouring Moda, which is full of shops, restaurants and cafes.

To the north of Kadıköy is the neoclassical Haydarpaşa Train Station, resembling a German castle. In the early 20th century when Kaiser Wilhelm of Germany was trying to charm the sultan into economic and military cooperation, he presented the station as a small token of his respect. Now decommissioned, it recently suffered damage in a fire and its future is uncertain.

Buses 12 and 12A link Kadıköy and Üsküdar, as do frequent dolmuşes (minibuses).

🏃 Activities

Ferry Cruises

During the 18th and 19th centuries the Bosphorus, Golden Horn and Sea of Marmara were alive with caiques (long, thin rowboats), their oars dipping rhythmically

---

SEEING THE DERVISHES WHIRL

If you thought the Hare Krishnas or the Harlem congregations were the only religious orders to celebrate their faith through music and movement, think again. Those sultans of spiritual spin known as the 'whirling dervishes' have been twirling their way to a higher plane ever since the 13th century and show no sign of slowing down.

There are a number of opportunities to see dervishes whirling in İstanbul. The best-known of these is the weekly ceremony in the *semahane* (whirling dervish hall) in the Galata Mevlevi Museum (Galata Mevlevihanesi Müzesi; Map p96; Galipdede Caddesi 15, Tünel; performances ₺40; ☺performances 5pm Sat & Sun; ▯Karaköy, then funicular to Tünel) in Tünel. This one-hour ceremony is held on Saturdays and Sundays at 5pm and costs ₺40 per person. Come early (preferably days ahead) to buy your ticket.

Another, much longer and more authentic, ceremony is held at the EMAV Silivrikapı Mevlana Cultural Center (EMAV Silivrikapı Mevlana Kültür Merkezi; www.emav.org; Yeni Tavanlı Çeşme Sokum 8, Silivrikapı; ▯Çapa-Şehremini) on Thursday evenings between 7.30pm and 11pm. This includes a Q&A session (in Turkish), prayers and a *sema*. You'll need to sit on the ground for a long period. Admission is by donation.

For a more touristy experience, the Hocapaşa Culture Centre (Hodjapasha Culture Centre; Map p70; ☏212-511 4626; www.hodjapasha.com; Hocapaşa Hamamı Sokak 3b, Sirkeci; performances adult ₺60-80, child under 12yr ₺40-50; ▯Sirkeci), housed in a beautifully converted 15th-century *hamam* near Eminönü, presents whirling dervish performances five evenings per week throughout the year.

Remember that the ceremony is a religious one – by whirling, the adherents believe that they are attaining a higher union with God – so don't talk, leave your seat or take flash photographs while the dervishes are spinning or chanting.

into the currents as they carried the sultan and his courtiers from palace to pavilion and from Europe to Asia. The caiques are long gone, but in their place are the sleek speedboats of the moneyed elite and the much-loved public ferries used by the rest of İstanbul's population. A trip on one of these ferries – whether it be the short return trip to Kadıköy or Üsküdar, on which you cross from Europe to Asia and back again, or one of the longer trips detailed below – is an essential activity while you are in İstanbul.

Bosphorus Ferry

The major thoroughfare in İstanbul is the mighty Bosphorus strait, which runs from the Sea of Marmara (Marmara Denizi) to the Black Sea (Karadeniz), located 32km north of the city centre. In modern Turkish, the strait is known as the Boğaziçi or İstanbul Boğazı (from *boğaz*, meaning throat or strait). On one side is Asia; on the other, Europe. If you have a Museum Pass İstanbul you will receive a 25% discount.

Departure Point: Eminönü

Hop onto a boat on the Eminönü quay. The tour that we have outlined here follows the route of the *Uzun Boğaz Turu* (Long Bosphorus Tour) operated by Istanbul Şehir Hatları; for details of this and other options see the Getting There & Around section (p104).

It's always a good idea to arrive 30 minutes or so before the scheduled departure time and manoeuvre your way to the front of the queue that builds in front of the doors leading to the dock. When these open and the boat can be boarded, you'll need to move fast to score a good seat. The best spots are on the sides of the upper deck near the bow. The Asian shore is to the right side of the ferries as they make their way up the Bosphorus, Europe is to the left.

As you start your trip, you'll see the small island and tower of Kız Kulesi on the Asian side near Üsküdar. This squat tower is one of the city's most distinctive landmarks. In ancient times, a predecessor of the current 18th-century structure functioned as a toll-booth and defence point; the Bosphorus could be closed off by means of a chain stretching from here to Seraglio Point. More recently, the tower featured in the 1999 Bond film *The World is Not Enough*.

On the European shore, you'll pass grandiose Dolmabahçe Palace (p98). In his travelogue *Constantinople in 1890*, French writer Pierre Loti described this and the neighbouring Çırağan Palace as 'a line of palaces white as snow, placed at the edge of the sea on marble docks', a description that remains as accurate as it is evocative.

Beşiktaş to Kanlıca

After a brief stop at Beşiktaş, Çırağan Palace (☎212-326 4646; www.ciragan-palace. com; Çırağan Caddesi 32, Ortaköy; ◻Çırağan) looms up on the left. Next to it is the long yellow building occupied by the prestigious Galatasaray University. On the Asian shore is the Fethi Ahmed Paşa Yalı, a wide white building with a red-tiled roof that was built in the pretty suburb of Kuzguncuk in the late 18th century. The word *yalı* comes from the Greek word for 'coast', and describes the waterside wooden summer residences along the Bosphorus built by Ottoman aristocracy and foreign ambassadors in the 17th, 18th and 19th centuries, now all protected by the country's heritage laws. To your left a little further on is the pretty Ortaköy Mosque (Ortaköy Camii, Büyük Mecidiye Camii; İskele Meydanı, Ortaköy; ◻Ortaköy), its dome and two minarets dwarfed by the adjacent Bosphorus Bridge, opened in 1973 on the 50th anniversary of the founding of the Turkish Republic.

Under the bridge on the European shore is the Hatice Sultan Yalı, once the home of Sultan Murad V's daughter, Hatice. On the Asian side is Beylerbeyi Palace (Beylerbeyi Sarayı; www.millisaraylar.gov.tr; Abdullah Ağa Caddesi, Beylerbeyi; adult/student/child under 7yr ₺20/5/free; ◷9am-4.30pm Tue, Wed & Fri-Sun Apr-Oct, till 3.30pm Nov-Mar; ◻Beylerbeyi Sarayı), a baroque-style building that was built for Sultan Abdül Aziz I (r 1861–76). Look for its whimsical marble bathing pavilions on the shore; one was for men, the other for the women of the harem.

Past the suburb of Çengelköy on the Asian side is the imposing Kuleli Military School (Çengelköy; ⛴Eminönü-Kavaklar tourist ferry), built in 1860 and immortalised in Irfan Orga's wonderful memoir, *Portrait of a Turkish Family*. Look for its two 'witch-hat' towers.

Almost opposite Kuleli on the European shore is Arnavutköy ('Albanian Village'), which boasts a number of gabled Ottoman-era wooden houses. On the hill above it are buildings formerly occupied by the American College for Girls. Its most famous alumni was Halide Edib Adıvar, who wrote about the years she spent here in her

1926 autobiographical work, *The Memoir of Halide Edib*.

Arnavutköy runs straight into the glamorous suburb of Bebek, famous for upmarket shopping and chic cafes. As the ferry passes, look out for the mansard roof of the Egyptian consulate (Bebek; ☑ Eminönü-Kavaklar tourist ferry), an art nouveau minipalace built for Emine Hanım, mother of the last khedive (viceroy) of Egypt, Abbas Hilmi II. It's just south of the waterside park. In the park itself is the Ottoman Revivalist–style Bebek Mosque.

Opposite Bebek is Kandilli, the 'Place of Lamps', named after the lamps that were lit here to warn ships of the particularly treacherous currents at the headland. Among the many *yalıs* here is the huge red Kont Ostorog Yalı, built in the 19th century by Count Leon Ostorog, a Polish adviser to the Ottoman court; Pierre Loti came here when he visited İstanbul in the 1890s. A bit further on, past Kandilli, is the long, white Kıbrıslı ('Cypriot') Mustafa Emin Paşa Yalı, which dates from 1760.

Next to the Kıbrıslı Yalı are the Büyük Göksu Deresi (Great Heavenly Stream) and Küçük Göksu Deresi (Small Heavenly Stream), two brooks that descend from the Asian hills into the Bosphorus. Between them is a grassy, shady delta, which the Ottoman elite thought just perfect for picnics. Foreign residents, who referred to the place as 'the sweet waters of Asia', would often join them. If the weather was good, the sultan joined the party – and did so in style. Sultan Abdül Mecit's version of a picnic blanket was the rococo pavilion Küçüksu Kasrı (☑ 216-332 3303; Küçüksu Caddesi, Beykoz; adult/student/child under 7yr ₺5/1/free; ☺ 9am-4.30pm Tue, Wed & Fri-Sun Apr-Oct, till 3.30pm Nov-Mar; ☒ Küçüksu), constructed from 1856 to 1857. You'll see its ornate cast-iron fence, boat dock and wedding-cake exterior from the ferry.

Just before the Fatih Bridge, the majestic structure of Rumeli Hisarı (Fortress of Europe; ☑ 212-263 5305; Yahya Kemal Caddesi 42; admission ₺10; ☺ 9am-noon & 12.30-4.30pm Thu-Tue; ☒ Rumeli Hisarı) looms over a pretty village of the same name on the European shore. Mehmet the Conqueror had Rumeli Hisarı built in a mere four months during 1452 in preparation for his planned siege of Constantinople. For its location he chose the narrowest point of the Bosphorus, opposite Anadolu Hisarı (Fortress of Asia), which had been built by Sultan Beyazıt I in 1391. In doing so, Mehmet was able to control all traffic on the strait, thereby cutting off the city from resupply by sea. Just next to the fortress is a clutch of popular cafes and restaurants.

There are many architecturally and historically important *yalıs* in and around Anadolu Hisarı. These include the Köprülü Amcazade Hüseyin Paşa Yalı, built for one of Mustafa II's grand viziers in 1698 and the oldest *yalı* on the Bosphorus. Next door, the Zarif Mustafa Paşa Yalı was built in the early 19th century by the official coffeemaker to Sultan Mahmud II. Look for its upstairs salon, which juts out over the water and is supported by unusual curved timber struts.

Almost directly under the Fatih Bridge on the European shore is the huge stone Tophane Müşiri Zeki Paşa Yalı, a mansion built in the early 20th century for a field marshal in the Ottoman army. Later, it was sold to Sabiha Sultan, daughter of Mehmet VI, the last of the Ottoman sultans, and her husband İmer Faruk Efendi, grandson of Sultan Abdül Aziz. When the sultanate was abolished in 1922, Mehmet walked from this palace onto a British warship, never to return to Turkey.

Past the bridge, still on the Asian side, is the charming suburb of Kanlıca, famous for its rich and delicious yoghurt, which can be sampled at the two cafes in front of the ferry stop or on the boat itself. This is the ferry's second stop and, if you so choose, you can stop and explore before reboarding the boat on its return trip or heading back to Üsku-dar by bus. From here you can also catch a ferry across to Emirgan or Bebek on the European side and return to town by bus.

High on a promontory above Kanlıca is Hıdiv Kasrı (Khedive's Villa; www.beltur.com.tr; Çubuklu Yolu 32, Çubuklu; ☺ 9am-10pm; ☒ Kanlıca) FREE, an art nouveau villa built by the last khedive of Egypt as a summer residence. Restored after decades of neglect, it now functions as a restaurant (mains ₺10-20.50) and garden cafe (tosts ₺4-4.50, cake ₺6). The villa is an architectural gem, and the extensive garden is superb, particularly during the İstanbul Tulip Festival in April. To get here from the ferry stop, turn left into Halide Edip Adivar Caddesi and then turn right into the second street (Kafadar Sokak). Turn left into Haci Muhittin Sokağı and walk up the hill until you come to a fork in the road. Take the left fork and follow the

'Hıdiv Kasrı' signs to the villa's car park and garden.

Kanlıca to Sarıyer

Opposite Kanlıca on the European shore is the wealthy suburb of Emirgan. It's well worth coming here to visit the impressive Sakıp Sabancı Museum (Sakıp Sabancı Müsezi; ☑ 212-277 2200; http://muze.sabanciuniv.edu; Sakıp Sabancı Caddesi 42, Emirgan; adult/student/child under 8yr ₺15/8/free; ☉10am-5.30pm Tue, Thu & Fri-Sun, to 7.30pm Wed ; 🚊Emirgan), which hosts world-class travelling exhibitions. The museum is also home to MüzedeChanga (p122), a restaurant with a terrace that has sweeping Bosphorus views. If you're after a simpler snack, there's a branch of the popular chain eatery Sütiş (p122) opposite the ferry dock. It has outdoor seating and an all-day breakfast menu.

On the hill above the museum is Emirgan Woods, a huge public reserve that is particularly beautiful in April, when it is carpeted with thousands of tulips.

North of Emirgan, there's a ferry dock near the small yacht-lined cove of İstinye. Nearby, on a point jutting out from the European shore, is the suburb of Yeniköy. This was a favourite summer resort for the Ottomans, as indicated by the cluster of lavish 18th- and 19th-century *yalıs* around the ferry dock. The most notable of these is the frilly white Ahmed Afif Paşa Yalı, designed by Alexandre Vallaury, architect of the Pera Palas Hotel in Beyoğlu, and built in the late 19th century. On the opposite shore is the suburb of Paşabahçe, famous for its glassware factory.

Originally called Therapeia for its healthy climate, the little cove of Tarabya to the north of Yeniköy on the European shore has been a favourite summer watering place for İstanbul's well-to-do for centuries, although modern development has sullied some of its charm. For an account of Therapeia in its heyday, read Harold Nicholson's 1921 novel, *Sweet Waters*.

North of Tarabya are some of the old summer embassies of foreign powers. When the heat and fear of disease increased in the warm months, foreign ambassadors and their staff would retire to these palatial residences, complete with lush gardens. Such residences extended north to the village of Büyükdere, which is also notable for its churches and for the Sadberk Hanım Museum (☑212-242 3813; www.sadberkhanimmuzesi.org.tr; Piyasa Caddesi 27-29; adult/student ₺7/2;

☉10am-4.30pm Thu-Tue; 🚊Sarıyer), named after the wife of the late Vehbi Koç, founder of Turkey's foremost commercial empire. There's an eclectic collection here, including beautiful İznik and Kütahya ceramics, Ottoman silk textiles, and Roman coins and jewellery. The museum is a 10-minute walk from the next ferry stop, at Sarıyer.

Sarıyer to Anadolu Kavağı

After stopping at Sarıyer, the ferry sails on to Rumeli Kavağı, known for its fish restaurants. After a short stop here it then crosses the strait to finish the journey at Anadolu Kavağı. Once a fishing village, its local economy now relies on the tourism trade and its main square is full of mediocre fish restaurants and their touts.

Perched above the village are the ruins of Anadolu Kavağı Kalesi (Yoros Kalesi; Anadolu Kavağı; 🚊Eminönü-Kavaklar tourist ferry), a medieval castle that originally had eight massive towers in its walls. First built by the Byzantines, it was restored and reinforced by the Genoese in 1350, and later by the Ottomans. Unfortunately, the castle is in such a serious state of disrepair that it has been fenced so that no one can enter and enjoy its spectacular Black Sea views. As a result, we suggest giving the steep 25-minute walk up here a miss.

ℹ Getting There & Around

Most day-trippers take the Long Bosphorus Tour (*Uzun Boğaz Turu*) operated by **İstanbul Şehir Hatları** (İstanbul City Routes; www.sehirhatlari.com.tr). The ferry travels the entire length of the strait in a 90-minute one-way trip and departs from the *iskele* (ferry dock) at Eminönü daily at 10.35am. From April to October, there is an extra service at 1.35pm. A ticket costs ₺25 return (*çift*), ₺15 one way (*tek yön*). The ferry stops at Beşiktaş, Kanlıca, Sarıyer, Rumeli Kavağı and Anadolu Kavağı (the turnaround point). It is not possible to get on and off the ferry at stops along the way using the same ticket. The ferry returns from Anadolu Kavağı at 3pm (plus 4.15pm from April to October).

From March to October, İstanbul Şehir Hatları also operates a two-hour Short Bosphorus Tour (*Kısa Boğaz Turu*) that leaves Eminönü daily at 2.30pm, picking up passengers in Ortaköy 20 minutes later. It travels as far as the Fatih Bridge before returning to Eminönü. Tickets cost ₺12. From November to February, the service is limited to Saturdays, Sundays and holidays.

On Saturday evenings between early June and mid-September there is a special Moonlit Night Cruise (*Mehtaplı Geceler Turu*) leaving from

Bostancı and picking up passengers in Eminönü at 6.25pm. After further pick-ups in Üsküdar and Beşiktaş, the ferry makes its way up the strait to Anadolu Kavağı, stops there for two hours and then returns at 10.30pm, arriving at Eminönü just past midnight. On board, Turkish musicians entertain passengers. Tickets cost ₺20.

Note that if you have a Museum Pass İstanbul you will receive a 25% discount on the ticket prices of these tours. Check www.sehirhatlari. com.tr for timetable and fare updates for all ferry services, as these often change.

A newly introduced and attractive alternative to the Long Bosphorus Tour is to take the hop-on/hop-off service operated by **Dentur Avrasya** (☑ 444 6336; www.denturavrasya. com) from the *iskele* behind the petrol station at Kabataş. This costs ₺15, leaves six times daily at 12.45pm, 1.45pm, 2.45pm, 3.45pm, 4.45pm and 5.45pm, and allows passengers to alight at Emirgan, Küçüksu Kasrı and Beylerbeyi Sarayı and then re-board the ferry on the same ticket. It would be very rushed to try to make three stops within one afternoon (you would need to take the first service), but two stops is achievable. Just be aware that Küçüksu Kasrı and Beylerbeyi Sarayı close at 3.30pm (winter) and 4.30pm (summer).

Another option is to buy a ticket for a cruise on a private excursion boat. Although these only take you as far as Anadolu Hisarı and back (without stopping), the fact that the boats are smaller means that you travel closer to the shoreline and so are able to see a lot more. The entire trip takes about 90 minutes and tickets cost ₺12. A number of companies offer these tours from Eminönü; of these **Turyol** (☑ 0212-512 1287; www. turyol.com) is probably the most reputable. Its boats leave from the dock on the western side of the Galata Bridge every hour from 11am to 6pm on weekdays and every 45 minutes or so from 11am to 7.15pm on weekends. Boats operated by other companies leave from near the Boğaz İskelesi, from near the Haliç İskelesi and from the Ahirkapı İskelesi near Sultanahmet.

There's also a full 5½-hour tour operated by Dentur Avrasya leaving daily at 11.15am from behind the petrol station at Kabataş (₺20). It stops for three hours in Anadolu Kavağı.

If you wish to return from Sarıyer by bus rather than ferry, lines 25E and 40 head south to Emirgan. From Emirgan, 22, 22RE and 25E head to Kabataş and 40, 40T and 42T go to Taksim. All travel via Rumeli Hisarı, Bebek, Ortaköy, Yıldız and Beşiktaş.

If you decide to catch the ferry to Anadolu Kavağı and make your way back to town by bus, catch bus 15A, which leaves from a square straight ahead from the ferry terminal en route to Kavacık. Get off at Kanlıca to visit Hıdiv Kasrı or to transfer at Beykoz to bus 15, which will take

you south to Üsküdar via Çengelköy, the Küçüksu stop (for Küçüksu Kasrı) and the Beylerbeyi Sarayı stop (for Beylerbeyi). Buses 15F or 15BK take the same route but continue to Kadıköy.

All bus tickets cost ₺4 (₺2.15 with an İstanbulkart travel card).

Golden Horn Ferry

Most visitors to İstanbul know about the Bosphorus cruise, but not too many have heard about the *Haliç* (Golden Horn) trip. Until recently, this stretch of water to the north of Galata Bridge was heavily polluted and its suburbs offered little to tempt the traveller. All that's changing these days, though. The waters have been cleaned up, beautification works are under way along the shores, and the Haliç suburbs are being gentrified. Spending a day hopping on and off the ferry and exploring will give you an insight into a very different – and far less touristy – İstanbul.

Departure Point: Eminönü

The ferry starts in Üsküdar on the Asian side and stops in Karaköy before taking on most passengers at the Haliç İskelesi (Golden Horn Ferry Dock) on the western side of the Galata Bridge at Eminönü. The dock is behind a car park next to the Zindanhan Jewellery building.

After passing underneath the Atatürk Bridge, it stops at Kasımpaşa on the opposite side of the Golden Horn. This area is where the Ottoman imperial naval yards were located between the 16th and early 20th centuries, and some of the original building stock remains. The palace-like building to the left of the *iskele* is the 19th-century Bahriye Nezareti, where the Ministry for the Navy was once based. It is currently undergoing a major restoration. On the hill above is an 18th-century building that was originally the Naval Academy but was converted to a hospital in the 1850s; French soldiers were treated here during the Crimean War. There are plans to redevelop the shipyards here into a huge complex including shops, hotels and restaurants, although locals seem sceptical that this will go ahead in the near future.

Kasımpaşa to Hasköy

As the ferry makes its way to the next stop, Hasköy, you can see the fascinating Western District suburbs of Fener and Balat on the western (left) shore.

Fener is the traditional home of the city's Greek population and, although few Greeks

 İSTANBUL ACTIVITIES

are resident these days, a number of important Greek Orthodox sites remain. The prominent red-brick building on the hill is the Phanar Greek Orthodox College (Megali School or Great School), the oldest house of learning in İstanbul. The school has been housed in Fener since before the Conquest – the present building dates from 1881. Sadly, it currently has a total enrolment of under 100 students.

The church building you can see in the waterside park is the Gothic revival Church of St Stephen of the Bulgars.

The next suburb, Balat, was once home to a large proportion of İstanbul's Jewish population but is now crowded with migrants from the east of the country.

Passing the derelict remains of the original Galata Bridge on its way, the ferry then docks at Hasköy. In the Ottoman period, this part of the city was home to a naval shipyard and a sultan's hunting ground. Today, it has two sights of interest to visitors: the splendid Rahmi M Koç Museum (Rahmi M Koç Müzesi; ☑212-369 6600; www.rmk-museum.org.tr; Hasköy Caddesi 5, Hasköy; museum adult/student & child ₺12.50/6, submarine ₺7/5; ☉10am-5pm Tue-Fri, to 6pm/8pm Sat & Sun winter/summer; ☒47, 47E, 47Ç, 47N from Eminönü & 36T, 54HT, 54HŞ from Taksim, ⛴Hasköy), dedicated to the history of transport, industry and communications in Turkey; and Aynalıkavak Kasrı (Aynalıkavak Pavilion; ☑212-256 9750; www.millisaraylar.gov.tr; Aynalıkavak Caddesi, Hasköy; adult/student & child ₺5/1; ☉9am-4.30pm Tue, Wed & Fri-Sun Apr-Oct, to 3.30pm Nov-Mar), an ornate 18th-century imperial hunting pavilion set in extensive grounds. The museum is located directly to the left of the ferry stop. To get there, walk southeast (right) along Hasköy Caddesi, veer left into Okmeydanı Caddesi and then right into Sempt Konağı Sokak, which runs into Kasimpaşa-Hasköy Caddesi.

Hasköy to Sütlüce

The ferry's next stop is at Ayvansaray on the opposite shore. From here, you can walk up the hill alongside Theodosius II's monumental land walls to visit the Kariye Museum (Chora Church; p93).

From Ayvansaray, the ferry crosses to Sütlüce and then returns to the western shore to terminate at Eyüp. This conservative suburb is built around the Eyüp Sultan Mosque (Eyüp Sultan Camii, Mosque of the Great Eyüp; Camii Kebir Sokak, Eyüp; ☉tomb 9.30am-4.30pm; ☒36CE, 44B or 99 from Eminönü, ⛴Eyüp), one of the most important religious sites in Turkey. After visiting the complex, many visitors head north up the hill to enjoy a glass of tea and the wonderful views on offer at the Pierre Loti Café (p123).

ℹ️ Getting There & Around

Haliç ferries leave Üsküdar every hour from 7.30am to 8.45pm and travel up the Golden Horn to Eyüp, picking up most of their passengers at Eminönü; the last ferry returns from Eyüp at 8.45pm. Note that services are reduced on Sundays and holidays. The ferry trip takes 55 minutes (35 minutes from Eminönü) and costs ₺4 per leg (₺2.15 if you use an İstanbulkart). Check www.sehirhatlari.com.tr for timetable and fare updates.

If you wish to return from Eyüp by bus rather than ferry, buses 36CE, 44B and 99 travel from outside the ferry stop at Eyüp via Balat, Fener and Karaköy to Eminönü. Bus 39 travels to Aksaray via Edirnekapı, allowing you to stop and visit the Kariye Museum.

To return to Taksim from Hasköy or Sütluce by bus, take bus 36T, 54HT or 54HŞ. For Eminönü, take bus 47, 47E, 47Ç or 47N. All bus tickets cost ₺4 (₺2.15 if you use an İstanbulkart travel card).

🚶 Hamams

A visit to a hamam is a quintessential Turkish experience. We've listed six here – four tourist hamams in historic buildings on the historical peninsula, one historic hamam in Beyoğlu and one modern hamam that is known for its fantastic massages. The tourist hamams are pricey and their massages generally are short and not particularly good, but you'll be in gorgeous historic surrounds – weighing up these facts and deciding whether or not to go is up to the individual. For a total pampering experience, head to one of the luxe five-star hotel spas in the city – the Ritz Carlton, Çırağan Palace Kempinski and Four Seasons İstanbul at the Bosphorus all have excellent spas offering indulgent hamam treatments.

Ayasofya Hürrem Sultan Hamamı   HAMAM (Map p70; ☑212-517 3535; www.ayasofyahamami. com; Aya Sofya Meydanı 2; bath treatments €85-170, massages €40-75; ☉8am-10pm; ☒Sultanahmet) Reopened in 2011 after a meticulous restoration, this twin hamam is now offering the most luxurious traditional bath experience in the Old City. Designed by Sinan between 1556 and 1557, it was built just across the road from Aya Sofya by order of Süleyman the Magnificent and named in honour of his wife Hürrem Sultan, commonly known as Roxelana.

The building's three-year, US$13 million restoration was closely monitored by heritage authorities and the end result is wonderful, retaining Sinan's austere design but endowing it with an understated modern luxury. There are separate baths for males and females, both with a handsome *soğukluk* (entrance vestibule) surrounded by wooden change cubicles. Though relatively expensive, treatments are expert and the surrounds are exceptionally clean. The basic 35-minute treatment costs €85 and includes a scrub and soap massage, olive-oil soap and your personal *kese* (coarse cloth mitten used for exfoliation). In warm weather, a cafe and restaurant operate on the outdoor terrace.

Kılıç Ali Paşa Hamamı   HAMAM
(Map p96; ☑ 212-393 8010; http://kilicalipasahamami.com; Hamam Sokak 1, off Kemeraltı Caddesi, Tophane; self-service ₺100, bath service ₺130; ⊙ women 8am-4pm, men 4.30pm-midnight; ⬛ Tophane) It took seven years to develop a conservation plan for this 1580 Sinan-designed building and complete the meticulous restoration and boy oh boy, it was worth the wait. The hamam's interior is simply stunning and the place is run with total professionalism, ensuring a clean and enjoyable Turkish bath experience.

Commissioned by Admiral Kılıç Ali Paşa, who also endowed the nearby mosque and *medrese*, the hamam was originally used by the *levends* (marine forces in the Ottoman navy) but fell into disrepair last century. It reopened in late 2012.

Cağaloğlu Hamamı   HAMAM
(Map p70; ☑ 212-522 2424; www.cagaloglu-hamami.com.tr; Yerebatan Caddesi 34; bath, scrub & massage packages €50-110; ⊙ 8am-10pm; ⬛ Sultanahmet) Built in 1741 by order of Sultan Mahmut I, this gorgeous hamam offers separate baths for men and women and a range of bath services that are – alas – radically overpriced considering how quick and rudimentary the wash, scrub and massage treatments are. Consider signing up for the self-service treatment (€30) only.

Çemberlitaş Hamamı   HAMAM
(Map p86; ☑ 212-522 7974; www.cemberlitashamami.com; Vezir Han Caddesi 8; self-service ₺60, bath, scrub & soap massage ₺90; ⊙ 6am-midnight; ⬛ Çemberlitaş) There won't be too many times in your life when you'll get the opportunity to have a Turkish bath in a building dating back to 1584, so now might

well be the time to do it – particularly as this twin hamam was designed by the great architect Sinan and is among the most beautiful in the city.

The building was commissioned by Nurbanu Sultan, wife of Selim II and mother of Murat III. Both of its bath chambers have a huge marble *sıcaklık* (circular marble heat platform) and a gorgeous dome with glass apertures. The *camekan* (entrance hall) for men is original, but the women's version is new.

It costs around ₺60 to add an oil massage to the standard bath package, but all massages and treatments here are perfunctory so we'd suggest giving this a miss and opting for the cheaper self-serve option. Tips are meant to be covered in the treatment price and there's a 20% discount for ISIC student-card holders.

Ambassador Spa   HAMAM
(Map p70; ☑ 212-512 0002; www.istanbulambassadorhotel.com; Ticarethane Sokak 19; Turkish bath treatments €40-60, remedial & aromatherapy massage €25-80; ⊙ 9am-10pm; ⬛ Sultanahmet) There's no Ottoman ambience on offer at the shabby spa centre of this hotel just off Divan Yolu, but all treatments are private, meaning that you get the small hamam all to yourself. Best of all is the fact that the signature 60- or 75-minute 'Oriental Massage' package includes a facial massage, hamam treatment and expert 30-minute oil massage.

Gedikpaşa Hamamı   HAMAM
(Map p86; ☑ 212-517 8956; www.gedikpasahamami.com; Emin Sinan Hamamı Sokak 65-67, Gedikpaşa; bath, scrub & soap massage ₺70; ⊙ men 6am-midnight, women 9am-11pm; ⬛ Çemberlitaş) This Ottoman-era hamam has been operating since 1475. Its shabby interior isn't as beautiful as those at Çemberlitaş and Cağaloğlu, but services are cheaper and there are separate hamams, small dipping pools and saunas for both sexes. Best of all is the fact that the masseuses in the women's section occasionally break into song while working.

The operators will sometimes transport guests to and from Sultanahmet hotels at no charge – ask your hotel to investigate this option.

🦜 Courses

Note that prices for courses are often set in euros or US dollars rather than Turkish lira.

Cooking Alaturka   COOKING
(Map p74; ☑ 0536 338 0896; www.cookingalatur-
ka.com; Akbıyık Caddesi 72a, Cankurtaran; cooking
class per person €65; ⓢ Sultanahmet) Dutch-
born Eveline Zoutendijk opened the first
English-language Turkish cooking school
in İstanbul in 2003 and since then has built
a solid reputation for her convivial classes,
which offer a great introduction to Turkish
cuisine and are suitable for both novices
and experienced cooks. The delicious results
are enjoyed over a five-course meal in the
school's restaurant (p115).

☞ Tours

Note that most tour companies in İstanbul
set their charges in euros or US dollars rather than in Turkish lira.

★ İstanbul Walks   WALKING TOUR
(Map p70; ☑ 212-516 6300; www.istanbulwalks.
com; 2nd fl, Şifa Hamamı Sokak 1; walking tours
€30-80, child under 6yr free; ⓢ Sultanahmet) Specialising in cultural tourism, this company
is run by history buffs and offers a large
range of guided walking tours conducted
by knowledgeable English-speaking guides.
Tours concentrate on İstanbul's various
neighbourhoods, but there are also tours of
major monuments, a Turkish Coffee Trail,
and a tour of the Bosphorus and Golden
Horn by private boat. Student discounts are
available.

★ İstanbul Eats   WALKING TOUR
(http://istanbuleats.com; most walks per person
US$125) Full-day culinary walks around the
Old City, Bazaar District, Beyoğlu, Kadıköy
and the Bosphorus suburbs, as well as an
evening spent sampling kebaps in Aksray's
'Little Urfa' district. All are conducated by
the dedicated foodies who produce the excellent blog of the same name, and involve
lots of eating.

Turkish Flavours   WALKING TOUR
(☑ 0532 218 0653; www.turkishflavours.com; tour
per person US$145) A well-regarded outfit of-
fering foodie walks, Turkish Flavours runs
a five-hour 'Market Tour' that starts at Eminönü's Spice Bazaar and then takes a ferry
to Kadıköy, where it tours the Karaköy produce market and finishes with a lavish lunch
at Çiya Sofrası (p121).

Urban Adventures   WALKING, CULTURAL TOURS
(☑ 0532 641 2822; www.urbanadventures.com;
tours adult €25-39, child €20-30) The international tour company Intrepid offers a

program of city tours including a popular
four-hour guided walk around Sultanahmet and the Bazaar District. Also on offer
is the 'Home Cooked İstanbul' tour, which
includes a no-frills dinner with a local family in their home plus a visit to a neighbourhood teahouse for tea, a nargile and a game
of backgammon.

İstanbulodos   PHOTOGRAPHY TOUR
(☑ 0535 675 6491; www.istanbulodosviaggio.com;
tour per group €110) Having lived in İstanbul
for many years, New York–born photographer Monica Fritz recently made the decision to share some of the secrets she has
learned about the city with fellow shutter-
bugs. Her five-hour tours of the Grand Bazaar introduce participants to hidden *hans*
and passageways as well as taking to the
roof à la James Bond in *Skyfall*.

Monica also offers tours of Galata, Balat
and the Asian suburbs. The cost covers
groups of up to 10 participants and includes
lunch in a local eatery.

✷ Festivals & Events

During the warmer months İstanbul is buzzing with arts and music events, giving plenty
of options when it comes to entertainment.
The big-name arts festivals are organised by
the İstanbul Foundation for Culture & Arts
(İKSV; ☑ 0212-334 0700; www.iksv.org/english; Sadi
Konuralp Caddesi 5, Şişhane; Ⓜ Şişhane). Tickets to
most events are available from Biletix (☑ 216-
556 9800; www.biletix.com).

April

İstanbul Tulip Festival   FLOWERS
The tulip (*lale* in Turkish) is one of İstanbul's
traditional symbols, and the local government
celebrates this fact by planting more than
three million of them annually. These bloom
in late March and early April, endowing almost every street and park with vivid spring
colours and wonderful photo opportunities.

İstanbul Film Festival   FILM
(http://film.iksv.org/en) If you're keen to view
the best in Turkish film and bump into a
few local film stars while doing so, this is the
event to attend. Held early in the month in
cinemas around town, it's hugely popular.
The program includes retrospectives and recent releases from Turkey and abroad.

June

★ İstanbul Music Festival   MUSIC
(http://muzik.iksv.org/en) The city's premier
arts festival includes performances of opera,

dance, orchestral concerts and chamber recitals. Acts are often internationally renowned and the action takes place in atmosphere-laden venues including Aya İrini in Sultanahmet.

July

Efes Pilsen One Love MUSIC
(www.oneloveistanbul.com) This two-day music festival is organised by the major promoter of rock and pop concerts in Turkey, Pozitif. International headline acts play everything from punk to pop, electronica to disco.

İstanbul Jazz Festival MUSIC
(http://caz.iksv.org/en) An exhilarating hybrid of conventional jazz, electronica, drum 'n' bass, world music and rock. Venues include Salon in Şişhane, and parks around the city.

September

⭐**İstanbul Biennial** ARTS
(http://bienal.iksv.org/en) The city's major visual-arts shindig takes place from early September to early November in odd-numbered years. An international curator or panel of curators nominates a theme and puts together a cutting-edge program that is then exhibited in a variety of venues around town.

October

Akbank Jazz Festival MUSIC
(www.akbanksanat.com) This older sister to the İstanbul Jazz Festival is a boutique event, with a program featuring traditional and avant-garde jazz, as well as Middle Eastern fusions and a special program of young jazz. Venues are scattered around town.

November

İstanbul Design Biennial DESIGN
(http://istanbuldesignbiennial.iksv.org/) A new addition to the İKSV's stellar calendar of festivals, this event sees the city's design community celebrating their profession and critically discussing its future. It's held in even-numbered years.

🛏 Sleeping

Every accommodation style is available in İstanbul. You can live like a sultan in a world-class luxury hotel, doss in a hostel dorm, or relax in a well-priced boutique establishment.

Hotels reviewed here have rooms with private bathroom and include breakfast in the room price. Exceptions are noted in the reviews. All prices given are for high season and include the KDV (*katma değer vergi-si;* value-added tax). During low season (November to mid-March, but not around Christmas or Easter) you should be able to negotiate a discount of at least 20% on the price. Before you confirm any booking, ask if the hotel will give you a discount for cash payment (usually 5% or 10%), whether a pick-up from the airport is included (it often is if you stay more than three nights) and whether there are discounts for extended stays. Book as far ahead as possible if you will be visiting during the high season.

Note that almost all hotels in İstanbul set their prices in euros, and we have listed them as such here.

🛏 Sultanahmet & Around

The Blue Mosque (Sultan Ahmet Camii) gives its name to the quarter surrounding it. This is the heart of Old İstanbul and is the city's premier sightseeing area, so the hotels here and in the adjoining neighbourhoods to the east (Cankurtaran), south (Küçük Aya Sofya) and northwest (Binbirdirek, Çemberlitaş, Alemdar and Cağaloğlu) are supremely convenient. The area's only drawbacks are the number of carpet touts and the lack of decent bars and restaurants. Note, too, that some of the hotels in Cankurtaran can be noisy – late at night the culprits are the hostels and bars on Akbıyık Caddesi, which play loud music; early in the morning your sleep may be disturbed by the sound of the call to prayer issuing from the İşak Paşa Mosque behind Adliye Sokak.

⭐**Marmara Guesthouse** PENSION €
(Map p74; ☎212-638 3638; www.marmaraguesthouse.com; Terbıyık Sokak 15, Cankurtaran; s €30-70, d €40-85, f €60-100; ❄@🛱; 🚇Sultanahmet) There are plenty of family-run pensions in Sultanahmet, but few can claim the Marmara's levels of cleanliness and comfort. Manager Elif Aytekin and her family go out of their way to make guests feel welcome, offering plenty of advice and serving a delicious breakfast on the vine-covered, sea-facing roof terrace. Rooms have comfortable beds, good bathrooms and double-glazed windows.

Members of the same family operate the similarly impressive **Saruhan Hotel** (Map p86; ☎212-458 7608; www.saruhanhotel.com; Cinci Meydanı Sokak 34, Kadırga; s €30-65, d €35-75, f €52-105; ❄@🛱; 🚇Çemberlitaş) in the predominantly residential pocket of Kadırga.

APARTMENT LIVING

We all daydream about packing our bags and escaping to live in another country at some stage in our lives. In İstanbul, it's easy to hire an apartment and do just that for a week or two.

There's a rapidly proliferating number of short-term apartment rentals on offer here, all of which are furnished and most of which come with amenities such as wi-fi, washing machines and weekly maid service. Many are located in historic apartment blocks and offer spectacular views – just remember that the usual trade-off for this is a steep flight of stairs.

The following companies are worth investigating; most have three- or four-day minimum rental periods:

1001 Nites (www.1001nites.com; apt €100-135) Run by an American expat. Locations in Sultanahmet, Çukurcuma and Cihangir.

Galateia Residence (Map p96; ☎ 212-245 3032; www.galateiaresidence.com; Şahkulu Bostan Sokak 9, Galata; apt from €140; ✲ ☎; Ⓜ Şişhane, Ⓕ Karaköy, then funicular to Tünel) Serviced apartments in a wonderful location close to the Galata Tower. Perfect for business travellers, but a 30-day minimum stay applies.

İstanbul Apartments (☎ 0212-249 5065; www.istanbulapt.com; apt from €50; ✲ @) Run by an urbane Turkish couple, with properties in Cihangir, Tarlabası and off İstiklal.

istanbul!place Apartments (http://istanbulplace.com/; apt 1-bed €80-121, 2-bed €109-230, 3-bed €115-270) Stylish and well-set-up apartments in the Galata district managed by an English-Turkish couple.

Manzara Istanbul (☎ 212-252 4660; www.manzara-istanbul.com; apt from €70; ✲ ☎) Long-term operation run by a Turkish-German architect. Locations are mainly in Galata, Cihangir and Kabataş.

Hotel Alp Guesthouse
HOTEL €

(Map p74; ☎ 212-517 7067; www.alpguesthouse.com; Adliye Sokak 4, Cankurtaran; s €35-60, d €55-80, f €80-110; ✲ @ ☎; Ⓕ Sultanahmet) The Alp lives up to its location in Sultanahmet's premier small-hotel enclave, offering a range of attractive, well-priced rooms. Bathrooms are small but very clean, and there are plenty of amenities. The roof terrace is one of the best in this area, with great sea views, comfortable indoor and outdoor seating, and free tea and coffee.

Hotel Peninsula
HOTEL €

(Map p74; ☎ 212-458 6850; www.hotelpeninsula.com; Adliye Sokak 6, Cankurtaran; s €30-55, d €35-70, f €80-130; ✲ @ ☎; Ⓕ Sultanahmet) Hallmarks here are friendly staff, comfortable rooms and bargain prices. There's a terrace with sea views and hammocks, and a breakfast room with outdoor tables. Basement rooms (d €30-55, f €65-90) are dark, but have reduced prices. The same owners operate the slightly more expensive and comfortable Grand Peninsula (Map p74; ☎ 212-458 7710; www.grandpeninsulahotel.com; Cetinkaya Sokak 3, Cankurtaran; s €35-50, d €45-80, f €85-100; ✲ @ ☎), a few streets away.

Hanedan Hotel
HOTEL €

(Map p74; ☎ 212-516 4869; www.hanedanhotel.com; Adliye Sokak 3, Cankurtaran; s €30-55, d €45-70, f €70-110; ✲ @ ☎; Ⓕ Sultanahmet) The 11 rooms at this cheap, clean and comfortable choice feature double-glazed windows, satellite TV and small white marble bathrooms. One large and two interconnected rooms are perfect for families, and the pleasant roof terrace overlooks the sea and Aya Sofya.

Cheers Hostel
HOSTEL €

(Map p70; ☎ 212-526 0200; www.cheershostel.com; Zeynep Sultan Camii Sokak 21, Cankurtaran; dm €16-22, d €60-80, tr €90-120; ✲ @ ☎; Ⓕ Gülhane) The dorms here are worlds away from the impersonal barracks-like spaces in bigger hostels. Bright and airy, they feature wooden floorboards, rugs, lockers and comfortable beds; most have air-con. Bathrooms are clean and plentiful. It's a great choice in winter because the cosy rooftop bar has an open fire and a great view. Private rooms aren't as nice.

Bahaus Hostel
HOSTEL €

(Map p74; ☎ 212-638 6534; www.bahausistanbul.com; Bayram Fırını Sokak 11, Cankurtaran; dm

€11-24, d €60-70, without bathroom €50-60; ⊕ ⓢ; 🅷 Sultanahmet) A small, clean and secure operation, Bahaus stands in stark and welcome contrast to the huge institutional-style hostels found on nearby Akbıyık Caddesi. Dorms (some female-only with bathroom) have curtained bunks with good mattresses, reading lights and lockers; they can be hot in summer. Top marks go to the plentiful bathrooms, entertainment program and rooftop terrace bar.

Metropolis Hostel   HOSTEL €

(Map p74; ☑ 212-518 1822; www.metropolishostel. com; Terbıyık Sokak 24, Cankurtaran; dm €11-18, d €88-140, without bathroom €64-88; ⊕ @ ⓢ; 🅷 Sultanahmet) Located in a quiet street where a good night's sleep is assured, this friendly place offers a mix of dorms – at least one female-only and all with comfortable beds, reading lamps and private lockers. Showers and toilets are clean but in limited supply. Guests love the rooftop terrace with its sea views and enjoy the busy entertainment program.

Zeynep Sultan Hotel   HOTEL €

(Map p70; ☑ 212-514 5001; www.zeynepsultanhotel.com; Zeynep Sultan Camii Sokak 25, Alamdar; s €39-69, d €49-79; ⊕ @ ⓢ; 🅷 Sultanahmet or Gülhane) There aren't many hotels in the world that can boast a Byzantine chapel in the basement, but this one can. Room decor doesn't date back in time quite as far, but it's certainly faded. Front rooms are nice and light, with clean but basic bathrooms and satellite TV. Breakfast is served on the rear terrace with an Aya Sofya view.

Ahmet Efendi Evi   PENSION €

(Map p70; ☑ 212-518 8465; www.ahmetefendievi. com; Keresteci Hakkı Sokak 23, Cankurtaran; s €35-65, d €45-80, f €65-140; ⊕ @ ⓢ; 🅷 Sultanahmet) Mr Ahmet's House has a true home-away-from-home feel and is a particularly good choice for families. In a predominantly residential area (a rarity in Sultanahmet), it offers nine rooms that vary in size; the family rooms have kettles and DVD players.

Big Apple Hostel   HOSTEL €

(Map p74; ☑ 212-517 7931; www.hostelbigapple. com; Bayram Fırını Sokak 12, Cankurtaran; dm €15-21, s €50-75, d €55-85; ⊕ @ ⓢ; 🅷 Sultanahmet) It may be lacking a traveller vibe, but the compensations at this recently renovated hostel include six- and 14-bed air-conditioned dorms with comfortable beds, as well as hotel-style private rooms with private bath-

room and satellite TV. Added to this is a rooftop bar-breakfast room with sea views.

Agora Guesthouse & Hostel   HOSTEL €€

(Map p74; ☑ 212-458 5547; www.agoraguesthouse. com; Amiral Tafdil Sokak 6, Cankurtaran; dm €12-20, s €45-65, d €55-90; ⊕ @ ⓢ) Worth considering for its comfortable bunk beds (all with lockers underneath) and clean, modern bathrooms. Drawbacks: an inadequate number of showers and toilets and a lack of natural light in the basement dorms.

★Hotel Ibrahim Pasha   BOUTIQUE HOTEL €€

(Map p70; ☑ 212-518 0394; www.ibrahimpasha. com; Terzihane Sokak 7; r standard €100-195, deluxe €145-285; ⊕ @ ⓢ; 🅷 Sultanahmet) This exemplary designer hotel has a great location just off the Hippodrome, a comfortable lounge with open fire, and a terrace bar with knockout views of the Blue Mosque. All of the rooms are gorgeous but some are small – opt for a deluxe one if possible. Urbane owner Mehmet Umur is a mine of information about the city.

★Sirkeci Mansion   HOTEL €€

(Map p70; ☑ 212-528 4344; www.sirkecimansion. com; Taya Hatun Sokak 5, Sirkeci; standard r €120-215, superior & deluxe r €220-325, f €220-295; ⊕ @ ⓢ ⌕; 🅷 Gülhane) The owners of this terrific hotel overlooking Gülhane Park know what keeps guests happy – rooms are impeccably clean, well sized and loaded with amenities. It has a restaurant where a lavish breakfast is served, an indoor pool and a hamam. Top marks go to the incredibly helpful staff and the complimentary entertainment program, which includes walking tours and afternoon teas.

★Hotel Empress Zoe   BOUTIQUE HOTEL €€

(Map p74; ☑ 212-518 2504; www.emzoe.com; Akbıyık Caddesi 10, Cankurtaran; s €65-90, d €110-140, ste €160-275; ⊕ ⓢ; 🅷 Sultanahmet) Named after the feisty Byzantine empress, this is one of the most impressive boutique hotels in the city. There's a range of room types but the garden suites are particularly enticing as they overlook a gorgeous flower-filled courtyard where breakfast is served in warm weather. You can enjoy an early-evening drink there, or while admiring the sea view from the terrace bar.

Sarı Konak Hotel   BOUTIQUE HOTEL €€

(Map p74; ☑ 212-638 6258; www.istanbulhotel-sarikonak.com; Mimar Mehmet Ağa Caddesi 26, Cankurtaran; s/d €59-179, tr €79-199, ste €119-299;

✳ @ ☎; 🏠 Sultanahmet) Guests here enjoy relaxing on the roof terrace with its Sea of Marmara and Blue Mosque views, but also take advantage of the comfortable lounge and courtyard downstairs. Rooms are similarly impressive – the deluxe rooms are spacious and elegantly decorated, the superior rooms are nearly as nice, and standard rooms, though small, are very attractive. Suites have kitchenettes.

Burckin Suites Hotel HOTEL €€
(Map p70; ☏ 212-638 5521; www.burckinhotel. com; Klodfarer Caddesi 18, Binbirdirek; s €50-109, d €60-119; ✳ @ ☎; 🏠 Sultanahmet) An offer of four-star amenities at three-star prices is always enticing, and such is the case here. Rooms are small but the decor is attractive and there are plenty of amenities. The main draw is the rooftop terrace restaurant-bar, which has a wonderful view of Aya Sofya and the Sea of Marmara.

Ottoman Hotel Imperial HOTEL €€
(Map p70; ☏ 212-513 6150; www.ottomanhotelimperial.com; Caferiye Sokak 6; s from €110, d from €130, ste from €215; ✳ @ ☎; 🏠 Sultanahmet) This four-star hotel is in a wonderfully quiet location just outside the Topkapı Palace walls. Its large and comfortable rooms have plenty of amenities and are decorated with Ottoman-style objets d'art – opt for one with an Aya Sofya view or one in the rear annexe. No roof terrace, but the excellent Matbah (p115) restaurant is based here.

Hotel Uyan HOTEL €€
(Map p74; ☏ 212-518 9255; www.uyanhotel.com; Utangaç Sokak 25, Cankurtaran; s €50-60, d standard €75-99, deluxe €95-200; ✳ @ ☎; 🏠 Sultanahmet) The Uyan's quietly elegant decor nods towards the Ottoman style, but never goes over the top – everyone will feel at home here. Rooms are comfortable and most are of a decent size; the exceptions are the budget singles, which are tiny but serviceable. Breakfast is enjoyed in the top-floor space or on the terrace.

Hotel Şebnem HOTEL €€
(Map p74; ☏ 212-517 6623; www.sebnemhotel.net; Adliye Sokak 1, Cankurtaran; s €50-80, d €60-120, f €80-140; ✳ @ ☎; 🏠 Sultanahmet) Simplicity is the rule here, and it works a treat. Rooms have wooden floors, recently renovated bathrooms and comfortable beds; two have a private courtyard garden. The large terrace upstairs functions as a bar and nargile cafe and has views over the Sea of Marmara.

Hotel Nomade BOUTIQUE HOTEL €€
(Map p70; ☏ 212-513 8172; www.hotelnomade. com; Ticarethane Sokak 15, Alemdar; s €60-100, d €70-110; ✳ ☎; 🏠 Sultanahmet) Designer style and budget pricing don't often go together, but the Nomade bucks the trend. Just a few steps off busy Divan Yolu, it offers simple rooms that some guests find too small – request the largest possible. Everyone loves the roof-terrace bar (smack-bang in front of Aya Sofya).

Osman Han Hotel HOTEL €€
(Map p74; ☏ 212-458 7702; www.osmanhanhotel. com; Çetinkaya Sokak 1, Cankurtaran; d & tw €80-140, t €130-169; ✳ @ ☎; 🏠 Sultanahmet) Amenity levels at this small hotel are high – rooms have comfortable beds, free minibars, tea/coffee facilities and satellite TV; opt for a slightly larger deluxe room if possible, as the bathrooms in the standard rooms are cramped (request 41 or 42). The breakfast room and terrace have sea views, and guests are free to use the kitchen.

Dersaadet Hotel HOTEL €€
(Map p70; ☏ 212-458 0760; www.hoteldersaadet. com; Kapıağası Sokak 5, Küçük Aya Sofya; s €70-105, d standard €70-130, d & t deluxe €110-160; ✳ @ ☎; 🏠 Sultanahmet) 'Dersaadet' means 'Place of Happiness' in Turkish – and guests are inevitably happy at this well-run place. A restored Ottoman house, it offers extremely comfortable rooms; three have charming hamam-style bathrooms and half have sea views. The terrace restaurant has Sea of Marmara and Blue Mosque views.

Arcadia Blue Hotel HOTEL €€€
(Map p70; ☏ 212-516 9696; www.hotelarcadiablue. com; İmran Öktem Caddesi 1, Bindirbirek; s €125-255, d €135-255, sea view r €165-355; ✳ @ ☎; 🏠 Sultanahmet) Views of Aya Sofya, the Blue Mosque, the Bosphorus and the Sea of Marmara certainly make breakfast (or the complimentary afternoon aperitivo) memorable at the terrace restaurant-bar of this recently renovated hotel. Rooms are extremely comfortable; all are a good size but the sea-view versions are worth their higher price tag. There's a hamam (charged) and a gym (free).

🛏 Beyoğlu & Around

Most visitors to İstanbul stay in Sultanahmet, but Beyoğlu is becoming a popular alternative. Stay here to avoid the touts in the Old City, and because buzzing, bohemian Beyoğlu has the best wining, dining and shopping in the city. It's also where most of the designer hotels and apartment rentals are located.

Getting to/from the historical sights of Old İstanbul from Beyoğlu is easy: you can either walk across Galata Bridge (approximately 45 minutes), or use the Taksim Meydanı–Kabataş or Tünel Meydanı–Karaköy funicular connections to the tram.

World House Hostel HOSTEL €
(Map p96; ☑212-293 5520; www.worldhouseistanbul.com; Galipdede Caddesi 85, Galata; dm €14-18, d €68, tr €78; @🛜; Ⓜ Şişhane, 🔁 Karaköy, then funicular to Tünel) Hostels in İstanbul are usually impersonal hulks with jungle-like atmospheres, but World House is reasonably small and very friendly. Best of all is its location close to Beyoğlu's entertainment strips but not too far from the sights in Sultanahmet. There are large and small dorms (one shower for every six beds), but none are female-only.

★Marmara Pera HOTEL €€
(Map p96; ☑212-251 4646; www.themarmarahotels.com; Meşrutiyet Caddesi 1, Tepebaşı; s €109-160, d €135-199; ❄@🛜⛱; Ⓜ Şişhane, 🔁 Karaköy, then funicular to Tünel) A great location in the midst of Beyoğlu's major entertainment enclave makes this high-rise modern hotel an excellent choice. Added extras include a health club, a tiny outdoor pool, and a truly fabulous buffet breakfast spread, and the Mikla (p123) rooftop bar and restaurant. Rooms with a sea view are approximately 30% more expensive.

Has Han Galata BOUTIQUE HOTEL €€
(Map p96; ☑212-251 4218; www.hahsan.com.tr; Bankalar Caddesi 7, Galata; r €150-180, ste €180-215; ❄🛜; Ⓜ Şişhane, 🔁 Karaköy) Located on the cosmopolitan side of the Galata Bridge, this recently opened establishment has nine well-appointed and beautifully decorated rooms and an in-house cafe. The happening neighbourhood of Karaköy is close by, and the Old City is a relatively short walk away.

Richmond Hotel HOTEL €€
(Map p96; ☑212-252 5460; www.richmondhotels.com.tr; İstiklal Caddesi 227; d €120-210, tr €180-260, ste €280-320; ❄@🛜; Ⓜ Şişhane, 🔁 Karaköy, then funicular to Tünel) Behind its 19th-century facade, the Richmond is modern, comfortable and well run. Rooms have been renovated in recent years and are a good size; light sleepers should request one at the rear as the hotel's location on ever-busy İstiklal

Caddesi means that those at the front can be noisy. The Leb-i Derya bar on the 6th floor is a definite draw.

★Witt Istanbul Hotel BOUTIQUE HOTEL €€€
(Map p96; ☑212-293 1500; www.wittistanbul.com; Defterdar Yokuşu 26, Cihangir; d ste €195-385, penthouse & superior king €385-450; ❄@🛜; Ⓜ Taksim, 🔁 Tophane) Showcasing nearly as many designer features as an issue of *Wallpaper* magazine, this stylish apartment hotel in the trendy suburb of Cihangir has 18 suites with kitchenette, seating area, CD/DVD player, iPod dock, espresso machine, king-sized bed and huge bathroom. Penthouse and superior king suites have fabulous views. It's a short but steep climb from the Tophane tram stop.

TomTom Suites BOUTIQUE HOTEL €€€
(Map p96; ☑212-292 4949; www.tomtomsuites.com; Tomtom Kaptan Sokak 18; ste €169-649; ❄@🛜; Ⓜ Şişhane, 🔁 Karaköy, then funicular to Tünel) We're more than happy to beat the drum about this suite hotel occupying a former Franciscan nunnery off İstiklal Caddesi. Its contemporary decor is understated but elegant, with particularly impressive bathrooms, and each suite is beautifully appointed. There's also a rooftop bar-restaurant with fantastic views

Vault Karaköy BOUTIQUE HOTEL €€€
(Map p96; ☑212-244 6434; www.thehousehotel.com; Bankalar Caddesi 5, Karaköy; r €125-320, ste €210-800; ❄@🛜; Ⓜ Şişhane, 🔁 Karaköy) Han Tümertekin's US$40 million fit-out of this new hotel epitomises the modern city, being an exciting and evocative meld of old and new. It occupies a grand bank building complete with vaults (hence the name); the hotel's public areas are full of art and include a lobby restaurant and bar. There's also a summer roof terrace, a gym and a spa complete with sauna, steam room and hamam.

🛏 Kadıköy

Hush Moda HOSTEL €
(☑216-330 1122; www.hushhostels.com; Güneşlibahçe Sokak 50b; dm ₺35-45, d ₺120-145, without bathroom ₺90-120; ❄@🛜; 🚢 Kadıköy, Ⓜ Kadıköy) The new metro link between the Old City and Asian suburbs has made Kadıköy a viable accommodation location at last, and the Hush flashpacker operation has responded by opening two hostels here. This is the best of the two. Most private rooms have air-con (dorms don't), there's a terrace

bar and guests can use the kitchen (the produce market is nearby).

✖ Eating

İstanbul is a food-lover's paradise, with visitors being spoiled for choice when it comes to choosing a cafe, *meyhane* (Turkish tavern), *lokanta* (eatery serving ready-made food), *ocakbaşı* (grill house) or restaurant. Unfortunately, Sultanahmet has the least impressive range of eating options in the city. Rather than eating here at night, we recommend crossing Galata Bridge and joining the locals in Beyoğlu. At lunchtime, head to Hocapaşa Sokak in Sirkeci, where there are plenty of good cheap eateries, or to the Grand Bazaar area.

For a good local foodie website, check İstanbul Eats (http://istanbuleats.com).

✖ Sultanahmet & Around

Sefa Restaurant TURKISH €
(Map p70; ☑ 212-520 0670; www.sefarestaurant.com.tr; Nuruosmaniye Caddesi 17, Cağaloğlu; portions ₺8-14, kebaps ₺13-20; ⊙ 7am-5pm; ☑; ⓕ Sultanahmet) This popular place near the Grand Bazaar describes its cuisine as Ottoman, but what's really on offer are *hazır yemek* (ready-made dishes) and kebaps at extremely reasonable prices. You can order from an English menu or choose daily specials from the bain-marie. Try to arrive early-ish for lunch because many of the dishes run out by 1.30pm. No alcohol.

Erol Lokantası TURKISH €
(Map p70; ☑ 212-511 0322; Çatal Çeşme Sokak 3, Cağaloğlu; portions ₺6-14; ⊙ 11am-9pm Mon-Sat; ☑; ⓕ Sultanahmet) One of the last *lokantas* in Sultanahmet, Erol wouldn't win any awards for its interior design but might for its food – the dishes in the bain-marie are made fresh each day using seasonal ingredients and are really very good. Opt for a meat or vegetable stew served with buttery pilaf.

Şehzade Cağ Kebabı KEBAP €
(Map p70; ☑ 212-520 3361; Hocapaşa Sokak 3a, Sirkeci; kebap ₺15; ⊙ 11.30am-7.30pm Mon-Sat; ⓕ Sirkeci) Cooked on a horizontal rather than vertical spit, the Erzurum-style lamb kebap that this humble joint is known for is tender, very slightly charred and oh-so-delicious. Served on warm *lavaş* bread with a side-serve of tangy lemon, it's fast food of the highest order. Get here early at lunchtime to score one of the streetside tables.

Güvenç Konyalı TURKISH €
(Map p70; ☑ 212-527 5220; Hocapaşa Hamam Sokak 4, Sirkeci; soups ₺8, mains & pides ₺12-25; ⊙ 7am-9pm Mon-Sat; ⓕ Sirkeci) Specialities from Konya in central Anatolia are the draw at this bustling place just off the much-loved Hocapaşa Sokak food strip. Regulars come for the spicy *bamya çorbası* (sour soup with lamb and chickpeas), *etli ekmek* (flatbread with meat) and meltingly soft slow-cooked meats from the oven. No alcohol.

Hocapaşa Pidecisi PIDE €
(Map p70; ☑ 212-512 0990; www.hocapasa.com.tr; Hocapaşa Sokak 19, Sirkeci; pides ₺8-15; ⊙ 11am-8pm; ⓕ Sirkeci) This much-loved place has been serving piping hot pides straight from its oven since 1964. Accompanied by pickles, they can be eaten at one of the outdoor tables or ordered *paket* (to go).

Sofa Cafe Restaurant RESTAURANT, BAR €
(Map p74; ☑ 212-458 3630; Mimar Mehmet Ağa Caddesi 32, Cankurtaran; burgers ₺14, pastas ₺15-20, Turkish mains ₺17-35; ⊙ 11am-11pm; ⓕ Sultanahmet) Ten candlelit tables beckon patrons into this friendly cafe-bar just off Akbıyık Caddesi. There's a happy hour (in fact three) between 3.30pm and 6.30pm each day and a decidedly laid-back feel. The food is cheap but tasty, the glasses of wine are generous and the Efes is cold, meaning that there's plenty to like.

Sedef Beyaz KEBAP €
(Map p70; Divan Yolu Caddesi 21b; döner from ₺6; ⊙ 11am-8.30pm; ⓕ Sultanahmet) Locals swear that this is the best döner kebap in Sultanahmet, and keep the chef busy shaving thin slices of meat or chicken with his enormous knife every lunchtime. A portion stuffed into fresh bread *(yarım ekmek)* costs ₺6 to ₺10 to take away, depending on the size and meat. Prices are higher in the next-door cafeteria.

Çiğdem Pastanesi CAFE €
(Map p70; Divan Yolu Caddesi 62a; cappuccino ₺7, glass of tea ₺2.50, pastries ₺1-4, cakes ₺2.50-7.50; ⊙ 8am-11pm; ⓕ Sultanahmet) Strategically located on the main drag between Aya Sofya Meydanı and the Grand Bazaar, Çiğdem has been serving locals since 1961 and is still going strong. Pop in for a quick cup of tea or coffee accompanied by a cake, *börek* (filled pastry) or *açma* (Turkish-style bagel).

Hafız Mustafa SWEETS €
(Map p70; www.hafizmustafa.com; Muradiye Caddesi 51, Sirkeci; börek ₺5, baklava ₺6-7.50, puddings

₺6; ⊘7am-2am; 🚇Sirkeci) Making locals happy since 1864, this *şekerlemeleri* (sweets shop) sells *lokum* (turkish delight), baklava, milk puddings, pastries and *börek*. Put your sweet tooth to good use in the upstairs cafe, or choose a selection of indulgences to take home (avoid the baklava, which isn't very good).

There's a second branch on **Divan Yolu Caddesi** (Map p70; ☎212-514 9068; Divan Yolu Caddesi 14, Sultanahmet; ⊘9am-midnight; 🚇Sultanahmet) – look for the 'Edebiyat Kıraathanesi' sign – and a third on **Hamidiye Caddesi** (Map p70; ☎212-513 3610; www.hafizmustafa.com; Hamidiye Caddesi 84; ⊘8am-8pm Mon-Sat, 9am-8pm Sun; 🚇Eminönü) close to the Spice Bazaar.

Ahırkapı Balıkçısı
SEAFOOD ₺₺

(Map p70; ☎212-518 4988; Keresteci Hakkı Sokak 46, Cankurtaran; meze ₺5-30, fish ₺30-50; ⊘5.30-10pm; 🚇Sultanahmet) For years we promised locals that we wouldn't review this neighbourhood fish restaurant. We sympathised with their desire to retain the place's low profile, particularly as it's tiny and authentically Turkish. However, other decent options are so scarce on the ground that we've finally decided to share the secret. Get here early to score a table.

Cooking Alaturka
TURKISH ₺₺

(Map p74; ☎212-458 5919; www.cookingalaturka.com; Akbıyık Caddesi 72a, Cankurtaran; set lunch or dinner ₺55; ⊘lunch Mon-Sat & dinner by reservation Mon-Sat; ☝; 🚇Sultanahmet) Dutch-born owner-chef Eveline Zoutendijk and her Turkish colleague Fehzi Yıldırım serve a set four-course menu of simple Anatolian dishes at this hybrid cooking school–restaurant near the Blue Mosque. The menu makes the most of fresh seasonal produce, and can be tailored to suit vegetarians or those with food allergies (call ahead). No children under six years at dinner and no credit cards.

★Balıkçı Sabahattin
FISH ₺₺₺

(Map p74; ☎212-458 1824; www.balikcisabahattin.com; Şeyit Hasan Koyu Sokak 1, Cankurtaran; mezes ₺10-30, fish ₺30-65; ⊘noon-midnight; 🚇Sultanahmet) The limos outside Balıkçı Sabahattin pay testament to its enduring popularity with the city's establishment, who join cashed-up tourists in enjoying its limited menu of meze and fish. The food here is the best in Sultanahmet, though the service is often harried. You'll dine under a leafy canopy in the garden (one section smoking, the other nonsmoking).

Be sure to choose your fish from the display near the restaurant entrance – cold mezes are chosen from trays brought to your table. If you're lucky, waiters will bring free desserts at the end of the meal (both the figs and the quince are delicious). This and water are included in a ₺5 cover charge.

★Matbah
OTTOMAN ₺₺₺

(Map p70; ☎212-514 6151; www.matbahrestaurant.com; Ottoman Imperial Hotel, Caferiye Sokak 6/1; mezes ₺10-19, mains ₺28-60; ⊘noon-11pm; ☝; 🚇Sultanahmet) One of a growing number of İstanbul restaurants specialising in so-called 'Ottoman Palace Cuisine', Matbah offers dishes that were first devised in the palace kitchens between the 13th and 19th centuries. The menu changes with the season and features unusual ingredients such as goose. Surrounds are attractive, the staff are attentive and there's live oud music on Friday and Saturday nights.

🍴 Bazaar District

★Develi Baklava
SWEETS ₺

(Map p86; ☎212-512 1261; Hasırcılar Caddesi 89, Eminönü; portion ₺8-9; ⊘6.30am-7pm Mon-Sat; Ⓜ Haliç, 🚇Eminönü) As with many things Turkish, there's a ritual associated with eating baklava. Afficionados don't use a knife and fork. Instead, they turn their baklava upside down with the help of an index finger and thumb, and pop it into the mouth. To emulate them, head to this famous shop close to the Spice Bazaar, one of the city's best *baklavacıs*.

★Bereket Döner
KEBAP ₺

(Map p86; Hacı Kadın Caddesi, cnr Tavanlı Çeşme Sokak, Küçük Pazar; döner ekmek ₺3; ⊘11am-8pm Mon-Sat; Ⓜ Halıc or Vezneciler) The best döner in the district (maybe even the city) can be found at this local eatery in the run-down Küçük Pazar shopping strip between Eminönü and Atatürk Bulvarı. Definitely worth the trek.

★Fatih Damak Pide
PIDE ₺

(☎212-521 5057; www.fatihdamakpide.com; Büyük Karaman Caddesi 48, Zeyrek; pide ₺12-16; ⊘11am-11pm; Ⓜ Vezneciler) It's worth making the trek to this *pidecisi* (pide restaurant) overlooking the Fatih İtfaiye Park near the Aqueduct of Valens, as its reputation for making the best Karadeniz (Black Sea)–style pide on the

CHEAP EATS AROUND THE GRAND BAZAAR

Lunch is an important part of the day for the shopkeepers, artisans and porters who work in and around the Grand Bazaar. As well as providing an excuse for a welcome break, it's also a chance to chat with fellow workers and catch up with the local gossip. Of the hundreds of food stands in the streets and laneways in and around the Grand Bazaar, the following are our favourites. Most have a few stools for customers, a few are take-away only.

Note that when ordering döner (sliced lamb from revolving upright skewer) or *koko-reç* (seasoned, girlled lamb.mutton intestines in *ekmek* (bread), you will usually have to choose from three sizes: *çeyrek* (a quarter of a loaf), *yarım* (half a loaf) or *bütün* (a whole loaf). The term *dürüm* applies when meat is served in thin *lavaş* bread ('*dürüm*' means 'wrapped').

Gazientep Burç Ocakbaşı (Map p90; Parçacılar Sokak 12, off Yağlıkçılar Caddesi, Grand Bazaar; kebaps ₺13-22; noon-4pm Mon-Sat; Vezneciler, Beyazıt-Kapalı Çarşı) The *usta* (master chef) at this simple place presides over a charcoal grill where choice cuts of meats are cooked to perfection. We particularly recommend the spicy Adana kebap and the delectable *dolması* (eggplant and red peppers stuffed with rice and herbs).

Dönerci Şahin Usta (Map p90; 212-526 5297; www.donercisahinusta.com; Kılıççlar Sokak 7-9, Nuruosmaniye; döner kebap from ₺7; 11am-3pm Mon-Sat; Çemberlitaş) Ask any shop-keeper in the Grand Bazaar about who makes the best döner in the immediate area, and he is likely to give the same answer: 'Şahin Usta, of course!'.

Pak Pide & Pizza Salonu (Map p86; 212-513 7664; Paşa Camii Sokak 16, Mercan; pides ₺7-10; 11am-3pm Mon-Sat; Eminönü or Beyazıt Kapalı Çarşı) Finding this worker's *pideci-si* (pide restaurant) is an adventure in itself (it's hidden in the steep narrow lanes behind the Büyük Valide Han) but your quest will pay off when you try the fabulous pides, which are served straight from the oven.

Aynen Dürüm (Map p90; Muhafazacılar Sokak 29; dürüm kebap ₺8; 7am-6pm Mon-Sat; Çemberlitaş) You'll find this perennially busy place just inside the Grand Bazaar's Kılıççılar Kapısı (Kılıççılar Gate), near where the currency dealers ply their noisy trade. Patrons are free to doctor their choice of grilled meat (we like the chicken) with pickled cucumber, grilled and pickled green chillies, parsley, sumac and other accompaniments that are laid out on the communal bench.

Dürümcü Raif Usta (Map p86; 212-528 5997; Küçük Yıldız Han Sokak 6, Mahmutpaşa; dürüm kebap ₺9; 11.30am-6pm Mon-Sat; Çemberlitaş) The assembly line of staff assist-ing the *usta* at this place attests to the excellence and popularity of its speciality, Adana or Urfa kebap served with raw onion and parsley and wrapped in *lavaş* bread. Note that the Adana is spicy, Urfa isn't.

Kokoreçci Erdinç Usta (Map p86; 0212-514 6029; Kılıççlar Sokak 33, Nuruosmaniye; kokoreç from ₺4; 9am-6pm Mon-Sat; Çemberlitaş) Devotees of offal flock here for the *kokoreç*: seasoned lamb intestines stuffed with sweetbreads or other offal, seasoned with red pepper and oregano, wrapped around a skewer and grilled over charcoal.

Meşhur Dönerci Hacı Osman'ın Yeri (Map p86; Fuat Paşa Caddesi 16, Mercan; döner from ₺3.50; 11am-5pm Mon-Sat; Vezneciler, Beyazıt-kapalı Çarşı) This döner stand oc-cupying an elegant Ottoman *sebil* (fountain) outside the Ali Paşa Camii is hugely popular with students from nearby İstanbul University.

Bena Dondurmaları (Map p86; 212-520 5440; Gazı Atik Ali Paşa Camii 12b; ice cream per scoop ₺0.75, desserts ₺2.50-5; 10am-6pm Mon-Sat; Çemberlitaş) There's inevitably an afternoon queue in front of this tiny *dondurma* (Turkish ice-cream) shop in the courtyard of the Atik Ali Paşa Camii near the Çemberlitaş tram stop. Though the *dondurma* is an undeniable draw, we tend to opt for the *fırın sütlaç* (rice pudding) or decadent *trileçe* (cream-soaked sponge cake with a caramel topping).

Historic Peninsula is well deserved and the free pots of tea served with meals are a nice touch.

Siirt Şeref Büryan Kebap
ANATOLIAN €

(☑212-635 8085; www.serefburyan.com; İtfaye Caddesi 4, Kadın Pazarı; büryan ₺12, perde pilavi ₺12; ⊘9.30am-10pm Sep-May, till midnight Jun-Aug; ⓜVezneciler) Those who enjoy investigating regional cuisines should head to this four-storey eatery in the Kadın Pazarı (Women's Market) near the Aqueduct of Valens. It specialises in two dishes that are a speciality of the southeastern city of Siirt: *büryan* (lamb slow-cooked in a pit) and *perde pilavi* (chicken and rice cooked in pastry). Both are totally delicious.

Kuru Fasulyeci Erzincanlı Ali Baba
TURKISH €

(Map p86; www.kurufasulyeci.com; Professor Sıddık Sami Onar Caddesi 11, Süleymaniye; beans with pilaf & pickles ₺12; ⊘7am-7pm; ☑; ⓜVezneciler, 🚇Laleli-Üniversite) Join the crowds of hungry locals at this long-time favourite opposite the Süleymaniye Mosque. It's been dishing up its signature *kuru fasulye* (white beans cooked in a spicy tomato sauce) accompanied by pilaf (rice) and pickles since 1924. The next-door *fasulyeci* (restaurant specialising in beans) is nearly as old and serves up more of the same. No alcohol.

Hamdi Restaurant
KEBAP €€

(Map p86; ☑212-528 8011; www.hamdirestorant.com.tr; Kalçın Sokak 17, Eminönü; mezes ₺9-14, kebaps ₺25-32; ⓜHaliç, 🚇Eminönü) Hamdi Arpacı arrived in İstanbul in the 1960s and almost immediately established a street stand near the Spice Bazaar where he grilled and sold tasty kebaps made according to recipes from his hometown Urfa, in Turkey's southeast. His kebaps became so popular with locals that he soon acquired this nearby building, which has phenomenal views from its top-floor terrace.

Sur Ocakbaşı
KEBAP €€

(☑212-533 8088; www.surocakbasi.com; İtfaiye Caddesi 27; kebaps ₺13-25; ⓜVezneciler) Indulge in some peerless people-watching while enjoying the grilled meats at this popular place in the Kadınlar Pazarı. The square is always full of locals shopping or enjoying a gossip, and tourists were a rare sight before Anthony Bourdain filmed a segment of *No Reservations* here and blew Sur's cover.

Fes Cafe
CAFE €€

(Map p86; Ali Baba Türbe Sokak 25, Nuruosmaniye; sandwiches ₺14-22, salads ₺16-20, pasta ₺18-20; ⊘closed Sun; ☑; 🚇Çemberlitaş) After a morning spent trading repartee with the touts in the Grand Bazaar, you'll be in need of a respite. Those who want a cafe with a Western-style ambience and menu are sure to be happy with this stylish cafe just outside the Nuruosmaniye Gate. Sandwiches, salads and pastas feature on the menu. There's a second branch inside the **Grand Bazaar** (Map p90; ☑212-527 3684; Halicilar Caddesi 62, Grand Bazaar; ⊘9.30am-6.30pm Mon-Sat; 🚇Beyazıt-Kapalı Çarşı).

✖ Western Districts

Kömür Turk Mutfağı
TURKISH €

(☑212-521 9999; www.komurturkmutfagi.com; Fevzi Paşa Caddesi 18, Fatih; veg portion ₺7-8, meat portion ₺10-15, grills ₺13-32; ⊘5am-11pm; ☑; 🚌31E, 32, 336E, 36KE & 38E from Eminönü, 87 from Taksim) Located amid the wedding-dress shops on Fatih's main drag is this five-floor *Türk mutfağı* (Turkish kitchen) where brides-to-be join businessmen and worshippers from the nearby Fatih Mosque for lunch. The gleaming ground-floor space has a huge counter where ready-made dishes are displayed and where fresh meat and fish can be cooked to order.

★ Asitane
OTTOMAN €€€

(☑212-635 7997; www.asitanerestaurant.com; Kariye Oteli, Kariye Camii Sokak 6, Edirnekapı; starters ₺16-26, mains ₺32-50; ⊘11am-midnight; ☑; 🚌31E, 32, 36K & 38E from Eminönü, 87 from Taksim, 🚢Ayvansaray) This elegant restaurant next to the Kariye Museum serves Ottoman dishes devised for the palace kitchens at Topkapı, Edirne and Dolmabahçe. Its chefs have been tracking down historic recipes for years, and the menu is full of versions that will tempt most modern palates, including vegetarians. Dine inside or in the pretty outdoor courtyard during summer.

✖ Beyoğlu & Around

★ Karaköy Güllüoğlu
SWEETS, BÖREK €

(Map p96; www.karakoygulluoglu.com; Kemankeş Caddesi, Karaköy; portion baklava ₺5-10, portion börek ₺6-7; ⊘8am-11pm; 🚇Karaköy) This Karaköy institution has been making customers deliriously happy and dentists obscenely rich since 1947. Head to the register and order a *porsiyon* (portion) of whatever baklava takes your fancy (*fıstıklı* is pistachio, *cevizli* walnut and *sade* plain), preferably with a glass of tea. Then hand your ticket over to the servers. The *börek* here is good, too.

Asmalı Canım Ciğerim
ANATOLIAN €
(Map p96; Minare Sokak 1, Asmalımescit; portion ₺22, half portion ₺14; ⊠ Karaköy, then funicular to Tünel) The name means 'my soul, my liver', and this small place behind the Ali Hoca Türbesi specialises in grilled liver served with herbs, *ezme* (spicy tomato sauce) and grilled vegetables. If you can't bring yourself to eat offal, fear not – you can substitute the liver with lamb if you so choose. No alcohol, but *ayran* (yoghurt drink) is the perfect accompaniment.

Datlı Maya
BAKERY €
(Map p96; www.datlimaya.com; Türkgücü Caddesi 59, Cihangir; cakes & pastries ₺2-5; ⊙ 8am-10pm; Ⓜ Taksim, ⊠ Kabataş, then funicular to Taksim) A tiny cafe-bakery located behind the Firuz Ağa Mosque in Cihangir, Datlı Maya is as popular as it is fashionable. The old wood-fired oven produces cakes, *lahmacun*s (Arabic pizzas), pides (Turkish-style pizza), *börek*s and breads, all of which can be taken away or enjoyed in the tiny upstairs dining area.

İnci Pastanesi
DESSERTS €
(Map p96; Mis Sokak 18; tea & dessert ₺10; ⊙ 7am-midnight; ⊠ Karaköy, then funicular to Tünel) A Beyoğlu institution, İnci was forced out of its historic İstiklal Caddesi premises in 2012 but has reopened here and continues to delight devotees with its profiteroles covered in chocolate sauce. We're also particularly partial to the moist chocolate cake filled with candied fruit, but usually ask the staff to hold the chocolate topping.

Helvetia Lokanta
TURKISH €
(Map p96; General Yazgan Sokak 8-12, Asmalımescit; soup ₺6, portions ₺5-13; ⊙ 8am-10pm Mon-Sat; ⊉; Ⓜ Şişhane, ⊠ Kabataş, then funicular to Tünel) This tiny *lokanta* is popular with locals (particularly of the vegetarian and vegan variety), who pop in here for inexpensive soups, salads and stews that are cooked fresh each day. No alcohol, and cash only.

★Klemuri
ANATOLIAN €€
(Map p96; ☑212-292 3272; www.klemuri.com; Büyük Parmakkapi Sokak 2; starters ₺8-12, mains ₺12-23; ⊙ noon-11pm Mon-Sat; ⊉; Ⓜ Taksim, ⊠ Kabataş, then funicular to Taksim) The Laz people hail from the Black Sea region, and their cuisine relies heavily on fish, kale and dairy products. One of only a few Laz restaurants in the city, Klemuri serves delicious home-style cooking in bohemian surrounds. There's a well-priced wine list, a dessert (*Laz böreği*, a flaky pastry layered with custard and hazelnuts) that has attained a cult following and interesting choices for vegetarians and vegans.

★Antiochia
ANATOLIAN €€
(Map p96; ☑212-292 1100; www.antiochiaconcept. com; General Yazgan Sokak 3c, Asmalımescit; mezes ₺10-12, mains ₺18-28; ⊙ lunch Mon-Fri, dinner Mon-Sat; ⊠ Karaköy, then funicular to Tünel) Dishes from the southeastern city of Antakya (Hatay) are the speciality at this foodie destination. Mezes are dominated by wild thyme, pomegranate syrup, olives, walnuts and tangy home made yoghurt, and the kebaps are equally flavoursome – try the succulent *şiş et* (grilled lamb) or *dürüm* (wrap filled with minced meat, onions and tomatoes). There's a discount at lunch.

★Zübeyir Ocakbaşı
KEBAPS €€
(Map p96; ☑212-293 3951; Bekar Sokak 28; meze ₺7-9, kebaps ₺22-45; ⊙ noon-1am; ⊠ Kabataş, then funicular to Taksim) Every morning, the chefs at this popular *ocakbaşı* (grill house) prepare the fresh, top-quality meats to be grilled over their handsome copper-hooded barbecues that night: spicy chicken wings and Adana kebaps, flavoursome ribs, pungent liver kebaps and well-marinated lamb *şiş* kebaps. Their offerings are famous throughout the city, so booking a table is essential.

Çukur Meyhane
TURKISH €€
(Map p96; ☑212-244 5575; Kartal Sokak 1; mezes ₺7-16, mains ₺12-17; ⊙ noon-1am Mon-Sat; ⊉; Ⓜ Taksim, ⊠ Kabataş, then funicular to Taksim) Despite their long and much-vaunted tradition in the city, it is becoming increasingly difficult to find *meyhanes* serving good food. Standards have dropped in many of our old favourites (sob!), and we are constantly on the search for replacements. Fortunately, Çukur fits the bill. On offer is a convivial atmosphere, great food and relatively cheap prices. Book ahead on weekends.

Gram
MODERN TURKISH €€
(Map p96; ☑212-243 1048; www.grampera.com; Meşrutiyet Caddesi 107, Asmalımescit; small/large salad plate ₺16/25, soup ₺11, mains ₺22-33; ⊙ 10.30am-6.30pm Mon-Fri, 10.30am-6.30pm Sat; Ⓜ Şişhane, ⊠ Karaköy, then funicular to Tünel)

London has Ottolenghi, İstanbul has Gram. This pocket-sized place in fashionable Asmalımescit embraces the open kitchen concept and serves its daily changing menu of fresh and healthy dishes to a coterie of ultra-loyal regulars. Arrive early at lunchtime to claim a place on the shared tables in the rear kitchen/dining room. We love the self-service salad spread.

Aheste
CAFE €€

(Map p96; ☑ 212-245 4345; www.ahestegalata. com; Serdar-ı Ekrem Caddesi 30, Galata; breakfast ₺9-21, soups ₺12-15, sandwiches ₺18-22; ⊙9am-midnight; Ⓜ Şişhane, ⓕ Karaköy) A perfect example of the casual, design-driven cafe model that has been trending in İstanbul over the past few years, Aheste is a small place that's equally alluring for breakfast, morning tea, lunch or dinner. The home-baked cakes and pastries are European-style and delicious, the perfect accompaniment to good Italian-style coffee. Meals are light and packed with flavour.

Karaköy Lokantası
TURKISH €€

(Map p96; ☑ 212-292 4455; www.karakoylokan-tasi.com; Kemankeş Caddesi 37a, Karaköy; mezes ₺8-18, portions ₺8-14, mains ₺19-25; ⊙noon-4pm & 6pm-midnight Mon-Sat, 6pm-midnight Sun; ☑; ⓕ Karaköy) Known for its gorgeous tiled interior, genial owner and bustling vibe, Karaköy Lokantası serves tasty and well-priced food to its loyal local clientele. It functions as a *lokanta* during the day, but at night it morphs into a *meyhane* , with slightly higher prices. Bookings are essential for dinner.

Jash
ANATOLIAN €€

(Map p96; ☑ 212-244 3042; www.jashistanbul.com; Cihangir Caddesi 9, Cihangir; mezes ₺9-22, mains ₺22-45; ⊙noon-11pm; Ⓜ Taksim, ⓕ Kabataş, then funicular to Taksim) Armenian specialities such as *topik* (a cold meze made with chickpeas,

pistachios, onion, flour, currants, cumin and salt) make an appearance on the menu of this bijou *meyhane* in trendy Cihangir. Come on the weekend, when an accordion player entertains diners and unusual dishes including *harisa* (chicken with a hand-forged wheat and butter sauce) are on offer.

Journey
INTERNATIONAL, CAFE €€

(Map p96; ☑ 212-244 8989; www.journeycihangir. com; Akarsu Yokuşu 21, Cihangir; breakfast ₺14-25, sandwiches ₺16-19, mains ₺16-39; ⊙9am-2am; ☑; Ⓜ Taksim, ⓕ Kabataş, then funicular to Taksim) This classy lounge cafe located in the expat enclave of Cihangir serves a great range of Mediterranean comfort foods, including sandwiches, soups, pizzas and pastas. Most of the dishes use organic produce, there's a thoughtful wine list, and vegetarian and vegan options are on offer. The crowd is 30-something and the ambience is laid-back. Great stuff.

Social
RESTAURANT, BAR €€

(Map p96; ☑ 212-293 3040; Sıraselviler Caddesi 72, Cihangir; salads ₺18-25, pasta ₺17-32, burgers ₺21-24; ⊙8am-3.30am; ☎☑; Ⓜ Taksim, ⓕ Kabataş, then tram to Taksim) The spacious courtyard at the rear of this hipster hang-out is the main draw, but the food provides strong backup. A huge menu features fresh and delicious salads, authentic burgers, and an array of sandwiches, pastas and pizzas. Patrons drink everything from coffee to cocktails, and particularly enjoy the party vibe on Friday and Saturday nights.

Asmalı Cavit
TURKISH €€

(Asmalı Meyhane; Map p96; ☑ 212-292 4950; Asmalımescit Sokak 16, Asmalımescit; mezes ₺6-20, mains ₺18-24; ☑; Ⓜ Şişhane, ⓕ Karaköy, then funicular to Tünel) Cavit Saatcı's place is an old-style *meyhane* that, like other old-timers on this street, has stood the test of time and

FISH SANDWICHES

The city's favourite fast-food treat is undoubtedly the *balık ekmek* (fish sandwich), and the most atmospheric place to try one of these is at the Eminönü end of the Galata Bridge. Here, in front of fishing boats tied to the quay, are a number of stands where mackerel fillets are grilled, crammed into fresh bread and served with salad; a generous squeeze of bottled lemon is optional but recommended. A sandwich will set you back a mere ₺6 or so, and is delicious accompanied by a glass of the *şalgam* (sour turnip juice) sold by nearby pickle vendors.

There are plenty of other places around town to try a *balık ekmek* – head to any *iskele* (ferry dock) and there's bound to be a stand nearby. Alternatively, Fürreyya Galata Balıkçısı (Map p96; www.furreyyagalata.com), a tiny place opposite the Galata Tower, serves an excellent versions for ₺8.

 İSTANBUL EATING

retained a local following. The menu offers all the usual dishes (mezes, fried calamari, *börek* stuffed with meat, fried liver, kebaps). Bookings essential.

Enstitü CAFE, RESTAURANT €€
(Map p96; www.istanbulculinary.com; Meşrutiyet Caddesi 59, Tepebaşı; starters ₺10-20, mains ₺15-30; ⊙7.30am-10pm Mon-Fri, 10am-10pm Sat; ✐; Ⓜ Şişhane, ⓖ Karaköy, then funicular to Tünel) This chic but casual venue would be equally at home in Soho, Seattle or Sydney. A training venue for the İstanbul Culinary Institute (Enstitü; Map p96; ✆212-251 2214; www.istanbulculinary.com; Meşrutiyet Caddesi 59, Tepebaşı), it offers freshly baked cakes and pastries, a limited lunch menu that changes daily and a more-sophisticated dinner menu that makes full use of seasonal products. Prices are a steal considering the quality of the food.

Tarihi Karaköy Balık Lokantası FISH €€
(Map p96; ✆212-243 4080; Kardeşim Sokak 30, Karaköy; fish soup ₺8, mains ₺20-38; ⊙noon-4pm Mon-Sat; ⓖKaraköy) Seafood is expensive in most of İstanbul's restaurants, so it's always a pleasure to sample the fresh and perfectly prepared fish dishes at this old-style fish restaurant in the run-down quarter behind the Karaköy Balıkcılar Çarşısı (Karaköy Fish Market). No frills, no alcohol, no dinner service. Don't get it mixed it up with its far-more-expensive sibling, Tarihi Karaköy Balıkçısı Grifin.

Cafe Privato CAFE €€
(Map p96; ✆212-293 2055; http://privatocafe.com; Tımarcı Sokak 3b; breakfast ₺30; ⊙9am-midnight; Ⓜ Şişhane, ⓖ Karaköy, then funicular to Tünel) This enclave off Galipdede Caddesi in Galata has been reinvented over the past couple of years, trading in its rough-and-ready heritage for up-to-the-minute casual-chic credentials. Privato is the best-loved of the new cafe arrivals and is well worth visiting for its *köy kahvaltısı* (village breakfast) or for a drink (espresso and Turkish coffee, range of herbal teas, house-made *limonata*).

Kahve 6 CAFE €€
(Map p96; ✆212-293 0849; Anahtar Sokak 13, Cihangir; breakfast ₺11-19, sandwiches ₺10-19, pastas ₺15-19; ⊙9am-10pm; ▣✐; Ⓜ Taksim, ⓖ Kabataş, then funicular to Taksim) An expat haven in Cihangir, Kahve Altı (Coffee 6) has a pretty interior salon where patrons take advantage of free wi-fi, and a popular rear courtyard where groups of friends rendezvouz. The menu is simple but deserves kudos for its emphasis on local, natural and seasonal produce (often organic). No alcohol.

Kafe Ara CAFE €€
(Map p96; Tosbağ Sokak 8a, Galatasaray; sandwiches ₺16-22, salads ₺16-25; ⊙7.30am-midnight Mon-Thu, to 1am Fri & Sat, to 10pm Sun; ✐; Ⓜ Şişhane, ⓖ Kabataş, then funicular to Taksim) This casual cafe is named after its owner, legendary local photographer Ara Güler. It occupies a converted garage with tables and chairs spilling out into a wide laneway opposite

DON'T MISS

BALIK PAZARI

Accessed off İstiklal Caddesi, Galatasaray's Balık Pazarı (fish market; ⓖ Kabataş, then funicular to Taksim) is full of small stands selling *midye tava* (skewered mussels fried in hot oil), *kokoreç* (grilled sheep's intestines stuffed with peppers, tomatoes, herbs and spices) and other snacks. You'll also find shops selling fish, caviar, fruit, vegetables and other produce; most of these are in Duduodaları Sokak on the left (southern) side of the market.

Many of the shops have been here for close to a century and have extremely loyal clienteles – check out the following places:

Sütte Şarküteri (Map p96; ✆212-293 9292; Balık Pazarı, Duduodaları Sokak 13; ⊙8am-10pm) Delicious charcuterie, *kaymak* (clotted cream) and take-away sandwiches

Tarihi Beyoğlu Ekmek Fırını (Map p96; Balık Pazarı, Duduodaları Sokak 5) Fresh bread

Üç Yıldız Şekerleme (Map p96; ✆212-293 8170; www.ucyildizsekerleme.com; Balık Pazarı, Duduodaları Sokak 7; ⊙7am-8.30pm Mon-Sat, 9am-6pm Sun) Jams, *lokum* (Turkish delight) and sweets

Petek Turşuları (Map p96; Balık Pazarı, Duduodaları Sokak 6) Pickles

Reşat Balık Market (Map p96; ✆212-293 6091; Balık Pazarı, Sahne Sokak 30) for caviar and the city's best *lakerda* (strongly flavoured salted kingfish).

the Galatasaray Lycée and serves an array of well-priced salads, sandwiches and Turkish staples such as *köfte* (meatballs) and *sigara böreği* (pastries filled with cheese and potato). No alcohol.

★ **Meze by Lemon Tree**   MODERN TURKISH €€€
(Map p96; ☑212-252 8302; www.mezze.com.tr; Meşrutiyet Caddesi 83b, Tepebaşı; mezes ₺10-30, 4-course degustation menu for 2 persons ₺160; ☺7-11pm; ☑; Ⓜ Şişhane, Ⓕ Karaköy, then funicular to Tünel) Chef Gençay Üçok creates some of the most interesting – and delicious – modern Turkish food seen in the city, and serves it in an intimate restaurant opposite the Pera Palace Hotel. We suggest opting for the degustation menu or sticking to the wonderful mezes here rather than ordering mains. Bookings essential.

Duble Meze Bar   MODERN TURKISH €€€
(Map p96; ☑212-244 0188; www.dublemezebar. com; 7th fl, Meşrutiyet Caddesi 85; cold mezes ₺10-18, hotel mezes ₺16-40; ☺6pm-2am; ☑; Ⓜ Şişhane, Ⓕ Karaköy, then funicular to Taksim) Commanding expansive Golden Horn views from its location atop the Palazzo Donizetti Hotel, Duble is an exciting modern take on the traditional *meyhane* experience. On sultry nights, local glamour pusses love nothing better than claiming a designer chair in the glass-sheathed dining space, ordering a cocktail and grazing the menu of 35 different mezes.

Lokanta Maya   MODERN TURKISH €€€
(Map p96; ☑212-252 6884; www.lokantamaya. com; Kemankeş Caddesi 35a, Karaköy; starters ₺16-28, mains ₺34-52; ☺noon-5pm & 7-11pm Mon-Sat; ☑; Ⓕ Karaköy) Critics and chowhounds alike adore the dishes created by chef Didem Şenol at her stylish restaurant near the Karaköy docks. Didem is the author of a successful cookbook focusing on Aegean cuisine; her food is light, flavoursome, occasionally quirky and always assured. You'll need to book for dinner; lunch is cheaper and more casual.

Mikla   MODERN TURKISH €€€
(Map p96; ☑212-293 5656; www.miklarestaurant. com; Marmara Pera Hotel, Meşrutiyet Caddesi 15, Tepebaşı; prix fixe à la carte dinner menu ₺160; ☺6-11.30pm Mon-Sat; Ⓜ Şişhane, Ⓕ Karaköy, then funicular to Tünel) Local celebrity chef Mehmet Gürs is a master of Mod Med, and the Turkish accents on the menu here make his food memorable. Extraordinary views, luxe surrounds and professional service complete

the experience. In summer be sure to have a drink at the rooftop bar beforehand.

✖ Ortaköy & Kuruçeşme

Eateries on and around the Golden Mile (along Muallim Naci and Kuruçeşme Caddesis in Ortaköy and Kuruçeşme) can get pricey, and if you're on a tight budget you should probably limit yourself to brunch – as most young locals do. On weekends, the stands behind the Ortaköy Mosque do brisk business selling *gözlemes* (savoury pancakes) and *kumpir* (baked potatoes filled with your choice of sour cream, olive paste, cheese, chilli or bulgur).

✖ Kadiköy

Etabal   HONEY €
(☑216-414 9977; www.etabal.com.tr; Güneşli Bahçe Sokak 28; yoghurt & honey tub ₺4; Ⓔ Kadıköy) To sample one of the market's greatest treats, stop at this honey shop and ask for a serve of yoghurt with a generous swirl of honey from the comb on top. Simply sensational.

Baylan Pastanesi   SWEETS €
(☑216-336 2881; www.baylanpastanesi.com.tr; Muvakkithane Caddesi 9; ☺7am-10pm; Ⓔ Kadıköy) Its front window and interior have stood the test of time (the cafe opened in 1961 and its appearance has hardly changed since then), and so too has the popularity of this Kadıköy institution. Regulars tend to order a decadent ice-cream sundae or an espresso coffee and house-made macaroon.

Çiya Sofrası   ANATOLIAN €€
(www.ciya.com.tr; Güneşlibahçe Sokak 43; mezes ₺7-8, portions ₺16-22; ☺11am-11pm; Ⓔ Kadıköy) Known throughout the culinary world, Musa Dağdeviren's *lokanta* showcases dishes from the region surrounding the chef-owner's home city of Gaziantep and is a wonderful place to try Turkish regional specialities. Its next-door *kebapçı* (kebaps ₺18 to ₺40) sells a huge variety of tasty meat dishes. Neither sells alcohol.

Kadı Nimet Balıkçılık   FISH €€
(☑216-348 7389; Serasker Caddesi 10a; mezes ₺7-16, fish mains ₺15-35; ☺noon-midnight; Ⓔ Kadıköy) Tucked in behind the market's best fish stall, which has the same owners, is this much-loved restaurant. Make your choice from the cold mezes on display, choose your fish and let the waiters do the rest. Cold beer or rakı (aniseed brandy) are the usual accompaniments.

✗ Bosphorus Suburbs

Sütiş
CAFE €

(☎ 212-323 5030; www.sutis.com.tr; Sakıp Sabancı Caddesi 1, Emirgan; ⊙ 6am-1am; ☒ 22, 22RE & 25E from Kabataş, 40, 40T & 42T from Taksim) The Bosphorus branch of this popular chain has an expansive and extremely comfortable terrace overlooking the water. It's known for serving all-day breakfasts and milk-based puddings – we recommend the *simit* (sesame-encrusted bread rings) with honey and *kaymak* (clotted cream). Watching the valet-parking ritual on weekends is hilarious.

Tapasuma
MODERN TURKISH €€€

(☎ 216-401 1333; www.tapasuma.com; Kuleli Caddesi 43, Çengelköy; ⊙ 11.30am-midnight; ☒ 15) Set in a restored 19th-century rakı distillery (*suma* is a Turkish word meaning unadulterated spirit), this recently opened, super-stylish restaurant associated with the luxury Sumahan on the Water hotel has a waterside location and a jet-setter vibe. The menu focuses on Turkish mezes with a modern twist, which are artfully displayed on an 8m-long marble bar.

MüzedeChanga
MODERN TURKISH €€€

(☎ 212-323 0901; www.changa-istanbul.com; Sakıp Sabancı Müzesi, Sakıp Sabancı Caddesi 42, Emirgan; starters ₺20-34, mains ₺40-55; ⊙ 10.30am-1am Tue-Sun; ☒ 22, 22RE & 25E from Kabataş, 40, 40T & 42T from Taksim) A glamorous terrace with Bosphorus views is the main draw of this design-driven restaurant at the Sakıp Sabancı Museum. The food is good, if overpriced, and is best enjoyed at a weekend brunch. If you don't feel like visiting the museum, door staff will waive the entry fee and point you towards the restaurant.

🍺 Drinking & Nightlife

It may be the biggest city in a predominantly Islamic country, but let us assure you that İstanbul's population likes nothing more than a drink or three. If the rakı-soaked atmosphere in the city's *meyhanes* isn't a clear enough indicator, a foray into the thriving bar scene will confirm it.

The city's bohemian and student set tends to gravitate to the bars in Beyoğlu's Cihangir, Asmalımescit, Karaköy and Nevizade enclaves or head over the water to grungy Kadife Sokak in Kadıköy on the city's Asian side, which is known to everyone as Barlar Sokak (Bar Street).

Alternatively, you can check out the alcohol-free, atmosphere-rich *çay bahçesis* (tea gardens) or *kahvehanı* (coffeehouses) dotted around the Old City. These places are where the locals go to sample that great Turkish institution, the nargile (water pipe), accompanied by a cup of *Türk kahve* (Turkish coffee) or çay.

The city's most famous nightclubs are on the 'Golden Mile' between Ortaköy and Kuruçeşme on the Bosphorus. To visit any of the venues on this sybaritic strip you'll need to dress to kill and be prepared to outlay loads of lira – drinks start at ₺30 for a beer and climb into the stratosphere for wine, imported spirits or cocktails. Booking the restaurants at these venues is a good idea, because it's usually the only way to get past the door staff – otherwise you'll be looking at a lucky break or a tip of at least ₺100 to get the nod.

The Beyoğlu clubs are cheaper, more avant-garde and relatively attitude-free. All venues are busiest on Friday and (especially) Saturday nights, and the action doesn't really kick off until 1am or 2am.

🍺 Sultanahmet & Around

Set Üstü Çay Bahçesi
TEAHOUSE

(Map p70; Gülhane Parkı, Sultanahmet; ⊙ 9am-10.30pm; ☒ Gülhane) Come to this terraced tea garden to watch the ferries plying the route from Europe to Asia while at the same time enjoying an excellent pot of tea (for one/two people ₺8/14) accompanied by hot water (such a relief after the usual fiendishly strong Turkish brew). Add a cheap *tost* (toasted cheese sandwich; ₺3) to make a lunch of it.

Cihannüma
BAR, RESTAURANT

(Map p70; ☎ 212-520 7676; www.cihannumaistanbul.com; And Hotel, Yerebatan Caddesi 18; ⊙ noon-midnight; ☒ Sultanahmet) We don't recommend eating at this restaurant on the top-floor of the And Hotel near Aya Sofya, but the view from its narrow balcony and glass-sheathed dining room is one of the best in the Old City (Aya Sofya, Blue Mosque, Topkapı Palace, Galata Tower and Bosphorus Bridge), so it's a great choice for a late-afternoon coffee or sunset drink.

Cafe Meşale
NARGILE CAFE

(Map p74; Arasta Bazaar, Utangaç Sokak, Cankurtaran; ⊙ 24hr; ☒ Sultanahmet) Located in a sunken courtyard behind the Blue Mosque,

Meşale is a tourist trap par excellence, but still has loads of charm. Generations of backpackers have joined locals in claiming one of its cushioned benches and enjoying a tea and nargile. It has sporadic live Turkish music and a bustling vibe in the evening.

Derviş Aile Çay Bahçesi
TEA GARDEN

(Map p74; Mimar Mehmet Ağa Caddesi; ⊙7am-midnight Apr-Oct; 🚇Sultanahmet) Superbly located directly opposite the Blue Mosque, the Derviş beckons patrons with its comfortable cane chairs and shady trees. Efficient service, reasonable prices and peerless people-watching opportunities make it a great place for a leisurely tea, nargile and game of backgammon.

Caferağa Medresesi Çay Bahçesi
TEA GARDEN

(Map p70; Soğukkuyu Çıkmazı 5, off Caferiye Sokak; ⊙8.30am-4pm; 🚇Sultanahmet) On a fine day, sipping a çay in the in the gorgeous courtyard of this Sinan-designed *medrese* near Topkapı Palace is a delight. Located close to both Aya Sofya and Topkapı Palace, it's a perfect pit stop between sights. There's simple food available at lunchtime.

Kybele Cafe
BAR

(Map p70; www.kybelehotel.com; Yerebatan Caddesi 35; ⊙7.30am-11.30pm; 🚇Sultanahmet) The lounge bar-cafe at this hotel close to the Basilica Cistern is chock-full of antique furniture, richly coloured rugs and old etchings and prints, but its signature style comes courtesy of the hundreds of colourful glass lights hanging from the ceiling.

🍸 Bazaar District

★Erenler Nargile ve Çay Bahçesi
TEA GARDEN

(Map p86; Yeniçeriler Caddesi 35, Beyazıt; ⊙7am-midnight; 🚇Beyazıt-Kapalı Çarşı) Set in the vine-covered courtyard of the Çorlulu Ali Paşa Medrese, this nargile cafe near the Grand Bazaar is the most atmospheric in the Old City.

★Mimar Sinan Teras Cafe
NARGILE CAFE

(Map p86; 📞212-514 4414; www.mimarsinanterascafe.com; Mimar Sinan Han, Fetva Yokuşu 34-35, Süleymaniye; ⊙8am-1am; 🚇Vezneciler or Haliç, 🚇Laleli-Üniversite) A magnificent panorama of the city can be enjoyed from the spacious outdoor terrace of this popular student cafe in a ramshackle building in the shadow of the Süleymaniye Mosque. Head here during the day or in the evening to admire the view

over a coffee, unwind with a nargile or enjoy a glass of çay and a game of backgammon.

Lale Bahçesi
TEA GARDEN

(Map p86; Şifahane Caddesi, Süleymaniye; ⊙9am-11pm; 🚇Vezneciler, 🚇Laleli-Üniversite) Make your way down the stairs into the sunken courtyard opposite the Süleymaniye Mosque to discover this charming outdoor teahouse, which is popular with students from the nearby theological college and İstanbul University.

Vefa Bozacısı
BOZA BAR

(Map p86; www.vefa.com.tr; cnr Vefa & Katip Çelebi Caddesis, Molla Hüsrev; boza ₺3; ⊙8am-midnight; 🚇Vezneciler, 🚇Laleli-Üniversite) This famous *boza* bar was established in 1876 and locals still flock here to drink the viscous tonic (ie, *boza*), which is made from water, sugar and fermented barley and has a slight lemony tang. Topped with dried chickpeas and a sprinkle of cinnamon, it has a reputation for building up strength and virility, and tends to be an acquired taste.

🍸 Western Districts

★Pierre Loti Café
CAFE

(Gümüşsuyu Balmumcu Sokak 1, Eyüp; ⊙8am-midnight; 🚉Eyüp) Many visitors head to this hilltop cafe after visiting the Eyüp Sultan Mosque (p106). Named for the famous French novelist who is said to have come here for inspiration, it offers lovely views across the Golden Horn and is a popular weekend destination for locals, who relax over tea, coffee, ice cream and nargile.

🍸 Beyoğlu & Around

★Mikla
BAR

(Map p96; www.miklarestaurant.com; Marmara Pera Hotel, Meşrutiyet Caddesi 15, Tepebaşı; ⊙from 6pm Mon-Sat summer only; 🚇Şişhane, 🚇Karaköy, then funicular to Tünel) It's worth overlooking the occasional uppity service at this stylish rooftop bar to enjoy what could well be the best view in İstanbul. After a few drinks, consider moving downstairs to eat in the classy restaurant.

★MiniMüzikHol
CLUB

(MMH; Map p96; 📞212-245 1718; www.minimuzikhol.com; Soğancı Sokak 7, Cihangir; ⊙10pm-late Wed-Sat; 🚇Taksim, 🚇Kabataş, then funicular to Taksim) The mothership for innercity hipsters, MMH is a small, slightly grungy venue near Taksim that hosts the best dance party in town on weekends, and live sets by local and international musicians midweek. It's best after 1am.

★360 BAR
(Map p96; www.360istanbul.com; 8th fl, İstiklal Caddesi 163; ⊙noon-2am Sun-Thu, to 4am Fri & Sat; Ⓜ Şişhane, 🚋 Karaköy, then funicular to Tünel) İstanbul's most famous bar, and deservedly so. If you can score one of the bar stools on the terrace you'll be happy indeed – the view is truly extraordinary. It morphs into a club after midnight on Friday and Saturday, when a cover charge of around ₺40 applies.

★Tophane Nargile Cafes CAFE
(Map p96; off Necatibey Caddesi, Tophane; ⊙24hr; 🚋 Tophane) This atmospheric row of nargile cafes behind the Nusretiye Mosque is always packed with locals enjoying tea, nargile and snacks. Follow your nose to find it – the smell of apple tobacco is incredibly enticing. It costs around ₺50 for a 'VIP package' (tea, one nargile and some snacks to share) or around ₺25 for tea and nargile only.

★Karabatak CAFE
(Map p96; ☑ 212-243 6993; www.karabatak.com; Kara Ali Kaptan Sokak 7, Karaköy; ⊙8.30am-10pm Mon-Fri, 9.30am-10pm Sat & Sun; 🚋 Tophane) Hipster central for caffeine fans, Karabatak imports Julius Meinl coffee from Vienna and uses it to conjure up some of the city's best coffee. The outside seating is hotly contested, but the quiet tables inside can be just as alluring. Take your choice from filter, espresso or Turkish brews and order a panino (filled bread roll) or sandwich if you're hungry.

★Dem TEAHOUSE
(Map p96; ☑ 212-293 9792; www.demkarakoy.com; Hoca Tahsin Sokak 17, Karaköy; ⊙10am-10pm; 🚋 Tophane) We have witnessed long-term expat residents of İstanbul fight back tears as they read the menu at Dem. Their reaction had nothing to do with the price list (which is very reasonable) and everything to do with the joy of choosing from 60 types of freshly brewed tea, all served in fine china cups and with milk on request.

★Unter BAR
(Map p96; ☑ 212 244-5151; http://unter.com.tr; Kara Ali Kaptan Sokak 4, Karaköy; ⊙9am-midnight Tue-Thu & Sun, till 2am Fri & Sat; 🚋 Tophane) This scenester-free zone epitomises the new Karaköy style: it's glam without trying too hard, and has a vaguely arty vibe. The

ground-floor windows open to the street in fine weather, allowing the action to spill outside during busy periods. Good cocktails and a wine list strong in boutique Thracian drops are major draws, as is the varied food menu.

Cihangir 21 BAR
(Map p96; ☑ 212-251 1626; Coşkun Sokak 21, Cihangir; ⊙9am-2.30am; Ⓜ Taksim, 🚋 Kabataş, then funicular to Taksim) The great thing about this neighbourhood place is its inclusiveness – the regulars include black-clad boho types, besuited professionals, expat loafers and quite a few characters who defy categorisation. There's beer on tap (Efes and Miller), a smoker's section and a bustling feel after work hours; it's quite laid-back during the day.

Indigo CLUB
(Map p96; http://indigo-istanbul.com; 1st-5th fl, Mısır Apt, 309 Akarsu Sokak, Galatasaray; ⊙10pm-5am Fri & Sat, closed summer; Ⓜ Taksim, 🚋 Kabataş, then funicular to Taksim) This is Beyoğlu's electronic-music temple and dance-music enthusiasts congregate here on weekends for their energetic kicks. The program spotlights top-notch local and visiting DJs or live acts.

Urban BAR
(Map p96; www.urbanbeyoglu.com; Kartal Sokak 6a, Galatasaray; ⊙11am-1am; Ⓜ Taksim, 🚋 Kabataş, then funicular to Taksim) A tranquil bolthole in the midst of İstiklal's mayhem, Urban is where the preclub crowd congregates at night and where many of them can be found kicking back over a coffee during the day. The vaguely Parisian interior is a clever balance of grunge and glamour.

5 Kat BAR, RESTAURANT
(Map p96; www.5kat.com; 5th fl, Soğancı Sokak 7, Cihangir; ⊙5pm-1am Mon-Fri, 11am-1am Sat & Sun; Ⓜ Taksim, 🚋 Kabataş) This İstanbul institution has been around for over two decades and is a great alternative for those who can't stomach the style overload at many of the high-profile Beyoğlu bars. In winter drinks are served in the boudoir-style bar on the 5th floor; in summer action moves to the outdoor roof terrace. Both have great Bosphorus views.

Mavra CAFE, BAR
(Map p96; ☑ 212-252 7488; Serdar-ı Ekrem Caddesi 31a, Galata; breakfast ₺9-27, sandwiches & burgers ₺9-22, pastas ₺15-20; ⊙9.30am-2am

Mon-Sat, till midnight Sun; M Şişhane, 🚡 Karaköy, then funicular to Tünel) Serdar-ı Ekrem Caddesi is one of the most interesting streets in Galata, full of ornate 19th-century apartment blocks, avant-garde boutiques and mellow cafes. Mavra was the first of the cafes to open on the strip, and remains one of the best, offering simple food and drinks (caffè latte ₺6, beer ₺9) amid decor that is thrift-shop chic.

Manda Batmaz COFFEEHOUSE
(Map p96; Olivia Geçidi 1a, off İstiklal Caddesi; ⏰ 9.30am-midnight; M Şişhane, 🚡 Karaköy, then funicular to Tünel) He's been working at this tiny coffeehouse for two decades, so Cemil Pilik really knows his stuff when it comes to making Turkish coffee. The name translates as 'so thick that even a water buffalo won't sink in it', and Cemil's brew is indeed as viscous as it is smooth.

Araf CLUB
(Map p96; www.araf.com.tr; 5th fl, Balo Sokak 32; ⏰ 5pm-4am Tue-Sun; M Taksim, 🚡 Kabataş, then funicular to Taksim) Grungy English teachers, Erasmus exchange students and Turkish-language students have long claimed this as their favoured destination, listening to world music and swilling some of the cheapest club beer in the city. Wednesday night is comedy night.

Club 17 GAY
(Map p96; Zambak Sokak 17; ⏰ 11pm-5am; M Taksim, 🚡 Kabataş, then funicular to Taksim) Rent boys outnumber regulars at this narrow bar. At closing time the crowd spills out into the street to make final hook-up attempts possible. It's quiet during the week but jam-packed late on Friday and Saturday.

Hazzo Pulo Çay Bahçesi TEA GARDEN
(Map p96; Tarihi Hazzo Pulo Pasaji, off İstiklal Caddesi; ⏰ 9am-midnight; M Şişhane, 🚡 Karaköy, then funicular to Tünel) There aren't as many traditional teahouses in Beyoğlu as there are on the Historic Peninsula, so this picturesque cobbled courtyard full of makeshift stools and tables is beloved of local 20-somethings. Order from the waiter and then pay at the small cafe near the narrow arcade entrance.

Bigudi LESBIAN
(Map p96; Terrace fl, Mis Sokak 5; ⏰ 10.30pm-5am Sat; M Taksim, 🚡 Kabataş, then funicular to Taksim) The city's only lesbian club is open for one night only and is resolutely off-limits to non-females. To find it, look for the Dizzel Bar on the ground floor and then head upstairs. The Şarlo Cafe Pub (Map p96; 5th fl, Mis Sokak 5; ⏰ 4pm-1am; M Taksim, 🚡 Kabataş, then funicular to Taksim) on the 5th floor is open to women, men and the transgendered, and offers special events including a queer tango night every second Wednesday.

Leb-i Derya BAR, RESTAURANT
(Map p96; www.lebiderya.com; 6th fl, Kumbaracı Yokuşu 57, Galata; ⏰ 4pm-2am Mon-Thu, to 3am Fri, 10am-3am Sat, to 2am Sun; M Şişhane, 🚡 Karaköy, then funicular to Tünel) On the top floor of a dishevelled building off İstiklal, Leb-i Derya has wonderful views across to the Old City and down the Bosphorus, meaning that seats on the small outdoor terrace or at the bar are highly prized. Note that the venue can close early on quiet winter nights.

Atölye Kuledıbı BAR
(Map p96; Galata Kulesi Sokak 4, Galata; ⏰ noon-midnight Mon-Thu, to 2am Fri & Sat; M Şişhane, 🚡 Karaköy, then funicular to Tünel) Good music (sometimes live jazz) and a welcoming atmosphere characterise this bohemian place near the Galata Tower.

Kiki BAR, CLUB
(Map p96; ☎ 212-243 5306; www.kiki.com.tr; Sıraselviler Caddesi 42, Cihangir; ⏰ 6pm-2am Mon-Wed, to 4am Thu-Sat; M Taksim, 🚡 Kabataş, then funicular to Taksim) Kiki has a loyal clientele who enjoys its burgers and drinks, but mainly comes for the music (DJs and live sets). Regulars tend to head to the rear courtyard. There's a second branch in Ortaköy (☎ 212-258 5524; http://kiki.com.tr; Osmanzade Sok 8, Ortaköy; ⏰ 5pm-1am Tue-Fri, to 5am Fri & Sat, to midnight Sun).

Love Dance Point GAY
(www.lovedp.net; Cumhuriyet Caddesi 349, Harbiye; ⏰ 11.30pm-5am Fri & Sat; 🚡 Kabataş, then funicular to Taksim, then walk) Going into its second decade, Love DP is easily the most Europhile of the local gay venues, hosting gay musical icons and international circuit parties. Hard-cutting techno is thrown in with gay anthems and Turkish pop. This place attracts the well-travelled and the unimpressionable, as well as some straight hipsters from nearby Nişantaşı.

Tek Yön GAY
(Map p96; 1st fl, Siraselviler Caddesi 63, Taksim; ⏰ 10pm-4am; M Taksim, 🚡 Kabataş, then funicular to Taksim) This sleek premises features

İSTANBUL ENTERTAINMENT

the city's largest gay dance floor as well as a garden popular with smokers and cruisers. The core clientele is hirsute and fashion-challenged (and that includes the drag queens). Cuddly bears abound.

Ortaköy & Kuruçeşme

Reina CLUB

(☎ 212-259 5919; www.reina.com.tr; Muallim Naci Caddesi 44, Ortaköy; ☑ Ortaköy) According to its website, Reina is where 'foreign heads of state discuss world affairs, business people sign agreements of hundred billions of dollars and world stars visit'. In reality, it's where Turkey's C-list celebrities congregate, the city's nouveau riche flock and an occasional tourist gets past the doorman to ogle the spectacle. The Bosphorus location is truly extraordinary.

Sortie CLUB

(☎ 212-327 8585; www.sortie.com.tr; Muallim Naci Caddesi 54, Kuruçeşme; ☑ Şifa Yurdu) Sortie has long vied with Reina for the title of reigning queen of the Golden Mile, nipping at the heels of its rival dowager. It pulls in the city's glamour pusses and poseurs, all of whom are on the lookout for the odd celebrity guest.

Kadıköy

★ Fazıl Bey COFFEEHOUSE

(www.fazilbey.com; Serasker Caddesi 3; ☑ daily; ☑ Kadıköy) Making the call as to who makes the best Turkish coffee in İstanbul is no easy task, but our vote goes to Fazıl Bey, the best-loved *kahvehan* (coffeehouse) on Serasker Caddesi. Enjoying a cup while watching the passing parade of shoppers has been a popular local pastime since 1923.

Karga Bar BAR

(☎ 216-449 1725; www.kargabar.org; Kadife Sokak 16; ☑ 11am-2am; ☑ Kadıköy) Karga is one of the most famous bars in the city, offering cheap drinks, loud music and avant-garde art on its walls. There's a small courtyard downstairs to enjoy a late-afternoon beer.

☆ Entertainment

It's rare to have a week go by when there's not a special event, festival or performance somewhere in town.

For an overview of what's on, make sure you pick up a copy of *Time Out İstanbul* magazine when you hit town, and also check its website and that of Yabangee (http://ya-

bangee.com/), a website geared towards expat residents. Tickets for major events are available through the Biletix (☎ 216-556 9800; www.biletix.com) website.

☆ Beyoğlu & Around

★ Babylon LIVE MUSIC, CLUB

(Map p96; www.babylon.com.tr; Şehbender Sokak 3, Asmalımescit; ☑ lounge from 5pm, club from 8.30pm Tue-Thu, from 10.30pm Fri & Sat, closed summer; ☑ Şişhane, ☑ Karaköy, then funicular to Tünel) İstanbul's pre-eminent live-music venue has been packing the crowds in since 1999 and shows no sign of losing its mojo. The eclectic program often features big-name international music acts, particularly during the festival season. Most of the action occurs in the club, but there's also a lounge with DJ; access this from Jurnal Sokak.

Munzur Cafe & Bar LIVE MUSIC

(Map p96; ☎ 212-245 4669; www.munzurcafebar.com; Hasnun Galip Sokak 17, Galatasaray; ☑ 1pm-4am, music from 9pm; ☑ Taksim, ☑ Kabataş, then funicular to Taksim) Hasnun Galip Sokak in Galatasaray is home to a number of *Türkü evleri,* Kurdish-owned bars where musicians perform live, emotion-charged *halk meziği* (folk music). This simple place, which is two decades old, has stood the test of time and is well worth a visit. It has a great line-up of singers and expert *bağlama* (lute) players.

Nardis Jazz Club JAZZ

(Map p96; ☎ 212-244 6327; www.nardisjazz.com; Kuledibi Sokak 14, Galata; ☑ 9.30pm-12.30am Mon-Thu, 10.30pm-1.30am Fri & Sat, closed Aug; ☑ Şişhane, ☑ Karaköy) Named after a Miles Davis track, this intimate venue near the Galata Tower is run by jazz guitarist Önder Focan and his wife Zuhal. Performers include gifted amateurs, local jazz luminaries and visiting international artists. It's small, so you'll need to book if you want a decent table.

Nublu İstanbul JAZZ

(Map p96; ☎ 212-249 7712; www.nubluistanbul.net; Sıraselviler Caddesi 55, Taksim; ☑ 10pm-3am Wed-Sun Oct-May; ☑ Taksim, ☑ Kabataş, then funicular to Taksim) This ultra-cool venue is run by – or at least in association with – New York–based saxophonist and composer, İlhan Ersahin. Note that the club closes during summer and has a tendency to move location; check its website or Facebook page for venue updates and the program.

Garajistanbul
CULTURAL CENTRE

(Map p96; ☑212-244 4499; www.garajistanbul. org; Kaymekem Reşet Bey Sokak 11a, Galatasaray; Ⓜ Şişhane, ☒ Kabataş, then funicular to Tünel) This performance space occupies a former parking garage in a narrow street behind İstiklal Caddesi and is about as edgy as the city's performance scene gets. It hosts contemporary dance performances, poetry readings, theatrical performances and live jazz.

Salon
LIVE MUSIC

(Map p96; ☑212-334 0752; www.saloniksv.com; Ground fl, İstanbul Foundation for Culture & Arts, Sadi Konuralp Caddesi 5, Şişhane; ⊙ Oct-May; Ⓜ Şişhane, ☒ Karaköy, then funicular to Tünel) This intimate performance space in the İstanbul Foundation for Culture & Arts (İKSV) building hosts live contemporary music (classical, jazz, rock, alternative and world music) as well as theatrical and dance performances; check the website for program and booking details. Before or after the show, consider having a drink at X Bar (⊙ noon-midnight Mon-Sat), on the seventh floor of the same building.

Sport

There's only one spectator sport that really matters to Turks: football (soccer). Eighteen teams from all over Turkey compete from August to May, and four of these – Fenerbahçe (nickname: the Golden Canaries), Galatasaray (the Lions), Beşiktaş (the Black Eagles) and Kasımpaşa SK (the Apaches) – are based in İstanbul. The top team of the first division plays in the European Cup.

Matches are usually held on weekends, normally on a Saturday night. Almost any Turkish male will be able to tell you which is the best match to see. Tickets are sold at the clubhouses at the *stadyum* (stadium) or through Biletix (☑216-556 9800; www. biletix.com), and usually go on sale between Tuesday and Thursday for a weekend game. Open seating is reasonably priced; covered seating – which has the best views – can be expensive. If you miss out on tickets you can get them at the door of the stadium, but they are usually outrageously overpriced.

To join local supporters watching a broadcast of the match, head to the Tophane Nargile Cafes (p124).

🛍 Shopping

If you love shopping, you've come to the right place. Despite İstanbul's big-ticket historic sights, many travellers are surprised to find that the highlight of their visit was shopping, particularly searching and bartering for treasures in the city's atmospheric bazaars. The best of these are the Grand Bazaar and Arasta Bazaar, which specialise in carpets, jewellery, textiles and ceramics.

For Turkish musical instruments, check out the shops along Galipdede Caddesi, which runs between Tünel Meydanı and the Galata Tower in Beyoğlu. For designer fashions, head to the upmarket shopping area of Nişantaşı, and for avant-garde fashion go to Serdar-ı Ekrem Caddesi in Galata or to Cihangır. Antique hunters should wander through the streets of Çukurcuma in Beyoğlu.

Come energised, come with maximum overdraft and – most importantly – come with room in your suitcase.

🛍 Sultanahmet

★ Cocoon
CARPETS, TEXTILES

(Map p70; ☑212-638 6271; www.cocoontr.com; Küçük Ayasofya Caddesi 15 & 19; ⊙ 9am-6pm; ☒ Sultanahmet) There are so many rug and textile shops in İstanbul that choosing individual businesses to recommend is incredibly difficult. We had no problem whatsoever in singling this one out, though. Felt hats, felt-and-silk scarves and textiles from central Asia are artfully displayed in one store, while rugs from Persia, Central Asia, the Caucasus and Anatolia adorn the other.

There's a third branch selling hamam items at Shop 93 in the Arasta Bazaar (Map p74; Arasta Bazaar 43 (old door No 93); ⊙ 9am-7pm; ☒ Sultanahmet).

★ Özlem Tuna
JEWELLERY, HOMEWARES

(Map p70; ☑212-513 1361; www.ozlemtuna.com; 5th fl, Nemlizade Han, Ankara Caddesi 65, Eminönü; ⊙ 10am-5pm Mon-Fri, by arrangement Sat; ☒ Sirkeci) A leader in Turkey's contemporary design movement, Özlem Tuna produces super-stylish jewellery and homewares that she sells from her atelier overlooking Sirkeci Train Station. Her pieces use form and colours that reference the city (tulips, seagulls, gold, Bosphorus blue) and include hamam bowls, coffee and tea sets, serving bowls, trays, rings, earrings, cufflinks and necklaces.

★ Jennifer's Hamam
BATHWARE

(Map p74; ☑212-518 0648; www.jennifershamam. com; 135 Arasta Bazaar; ⊙ 9am-9pm Apr-Oct, 9am-7pm Nov-Mar; ☒ Sultanahmet) Owned by Canadian Jennifer Gaudet, this shop stocks

1. Balık Pazarı (p120) 2. Grand Bazaar (p88)
3. Spice Bazaar (p92) 4. Arasta Bazaar (p127)

İstanbul's Bazaars

Turks have honed the ancient arts of shopping and bargaining over centuries. In İstanbul, the city's Ottoman-era bazaars are as much monuments as marketplaces, spaces showcasing architecture and atmosphere that are nearly as impressive as the artisan wares offered for sale.

The Grand Bazaar

One of the world's oldest and best-loved shopping malls, the Grand Bazaar, has been luring shoppers into its labyrinthine lanes and hidden *hans* (caravanseries) ever since Mehmet the Conqueror ordered its construction in 1461. Come here to purchase carpets and kilims, bathwares, jewellery and textiles. Be sure to investigate its fabulous fast-food opportunities too.

The Spice Bazaar

Seductively scented and inevitably crammed with shoppers, this building opposite the Eminönü ferry docks has been selling goods to stock household pantries since the 17th century, when it was the last stop for the camel caravans that travelled the legendary Spice Routes from China, Persia and India. These days it's a great place to source dried fruit and spices.

The Arasta Bazaar

Nestling in the shadow of the Blue Mosque, this elongated open arcade of shops has a quiet, laid-back atmosphere that stands in stark contrast to the crowded and noisy Grand and Spice Bazaars. Come here for carpets and kilims, bathwares, ceramics and textiles.

Produce Markets

İstanbul is blessed with fabulous fresh produce markets. Consider visiting the following markets:

➜ Kadıköy Produce Market (p101)
➜ Balık Pazarı, Beyoğlu (p120)
➜ Kadınlar Pazarı, Zeyrek (İtfaiye Caddesi, Fatih; 🚇Aksaray)
➜ Çarşamba Pazarı, Fatih (p93)

top-quality hamam items including towels, robes and *peştemals* (bath wraps) produced using certified organic cotton on old-style shuttled looms. It also sells natural soaps and *keses* (coarse cloth mittens used for exfoliation). Prices are set, with no bargaining.

There's another branch within the Arasta Bazaar (Map p74; Arasta Bazaar 125; ◷ 9am-9pm Apr-oct, 9am-7pm Nov-Mar; ⊠ Sultanahmet) and also nearby Öğül Sokak (Map p70; Öğül Sokak 20; ◷ 9am-6pm; ⊠ Sultanahmet).

Yilmaz Ipekçilik TEXTILES
(Map p74; ☑ 212-638 4579; www.yilmazipekcilik.com/en; İshakpaşa Caddesi 36; ◷ 9am-9pm Mon-Sat, to 7pm winter; ⊠ Sultanahmet) Well-priced hand-loomed silk textiles made in Antakya are on sale in this slightly out-of-the-way shop. Family-run, the business has been operating since 1950 and specialises in producing good-quality scarves, shawls and *peştemals*.

Mehmet Çetinkaya Gallery CARPETS, TEXTILES
(Map p70; ☑ 212-517 6808; www.cetinkayagallery.com; Tavukhane Sokak 7; ◷ 9.30am-7.30pm; ⊠ Sultanahmet) Mehmet Çetinkaya is known as one of the country's foremost experts on antique oriental carpets and kilims. His flagship store-cum-gallery stocks items that have artistic and ethnographic significance, and is full of treasures. There's a second shop selling rugs, textiles and objects in the Arasta Bazaar (Map p74; Arasta Bazaar 58; ⊠ Sultanahmet).

Khaftan ART, ANTIQUES
(Map p70; Nakilbent Sokak 33; ◷ 9am-6.30pm; ⊠ Sultanahmet) Gleaming Russian icons, delicate calligraphy (old and new), ceramics, Karagöz puppets and contemporary paintings are all on show in this attractive shop on the hill beneath the Hippodrome.

🏛 Bazaar District

★ Abdulla Natural Products TEXTILES, BATHWARE
(Map p90; www.abdulla.com; Halıcılar Çarşışı Sokak 62, Grand Bazaar; ◷ 8.30am-7pm Mon-Sat; Ⓜ Vezneciler, ⊠ Beyazıt-Kapalı Çarşı) The first of the Western-style designer stores to appear in this ancient marketplace, Abdulla sells top-quality cotton bed linen and towels, handspun woollen throws from eastern Turkey, cotton *peştemals* and pure olive-oil soap. There's another branch in the Fes

Cafe (Map p86; Ali Baba Türbe Sokak 25, Nuruosmaniye; ⊠ Çemberlitaş) in Nuruosmaniye.

★ Ümit Berksoy JEWELLERY
(Map p90; ☑ 212-522 3391; İnciler Sokak 2-6, Grand Bazaar; ◷ 8.30am-7pm Mon-Sat; Ⓜ Vezneciler, ⊠ Beyazıt-Kapalı Çarşı) Jeweller Ümit Berksoy handcrafts gorgeous Byzantine-style rings, earrings and necklaces using gold and old coins, as well as more contemporary pieces at his tiny atelier just outside the İç Bedesten.

★ Derviş TEXTILES, BATHWARE
(Map p90; www.dervis.com; Keseciler Caddesi 33-35, Grand Bazaar; ◷ 8.30am-7pm Mon-Sat; Ⓜ Vezneciler, ⊠ Beyazıt-Kapalı Çarşı) 🌿 Gorgeous raw cotton and silk *peştemals* share shelf space here with traditional Turkish dowry vests and engagement dresses. If these don't take your fancy, the pure olive-oil soaps and old hamam bowls are sure to step into the breach. There are other branches in Halıcılar Çarşısı Sokak (Map p90; Halıcılar Çarşışı Sokak 51, Grand Bazaar) and in the Cebeci Han (Map p90; ☑ 0532 256 0107; Cebeci Han 10, Grand Bazaar), also in the bazaar.

Muhlis Günbattı TEXTILES
(Map p90; www.muhlisgunbatti.net; Perdahçılar Sokak 48, Grand Bazaar; ◷ 8.30am-7pm Mon-Sat; Ⓜ Vezneciler, ⊠ Beyazıt-Kapalı Çarşı) One of the most famous stores in the Grand Bazaar, Muhlis Günbattı specialises in *suzani* fabrics from Uzbekistan. These beautiful bedspreads, tablecloths and wall hangings are made from fine cotton embroidered with silk. As well as the textiles, it stocks top-quality carpets, brightly coloured kilims and a small range of antique Ottoman fabrics richly embroidered with gold.

Yazmacı Necdet Danış TEXTILES
(Map p90; Yağlıkçılar Caddesi 57, Grand Bazaar; ◷ 8.30am-7pm Mon-Sat; Ⓜ Vezneciler, ⊠ Beyazıt-Kapalı Çarşı) Fashion designers and buyers from every corner of the globe know that when in İstanbul, this is where to come to source top-quality textiles. It's crammed with bolts of fabric of every description – shiny, simple, sheer and sophisticated – as well as *peştemals,* scarves and clothes. Murat Danış next door is part of the same operation.

Mekhann TEXTILES
(Map p90; ☑ 212-519 9444; Divrikli Sokak 49, Grand Bazaar; ◷ 8.30am-7pm Mon-Sat; Ⓜ Vezneciler,

Beyazıt-Kapalı Çarşı) Bolts of richly coloured hand-woven silk from Uzbekistan and a range of finely woven shawls join finely embroidered bedspreads and pillow slips on the crowded shelves of this Grand Bazaar store, which sets the bar high when it comes to quality.

Ak Gümüş
HANDICRAFTS

(Map p90; Gani Çelebi Sokak 8, Grand Bazaar; 9am-7pm Mon-Sat; Beyazıt-Kapalı Çarşı, Vezneciler) Specialising in Central Asian tribal arts, this delightful store stocks an array of felt toys and hats, as well as jewellery and other objects made using coins and beads.

Haşimi Ticaret
ANTIQUES

(Map p90; Ali Paşa Han, Grand Bazaar; 8.30am-7pm Mon-Sat; Vezneciler, Beyazıt-Kapalı Çarşı) Head towards the Sahaflar Çarşışı from the Yorgancilar Kapısı (Gate 11) to find this veritable Aladdin's Cave of a shop, which is crammed with old wooden boxes and other artefacts sourced from Turkey, Afghanistan and Pakistan. Bargain hard.

Silk & Cashmere
CLOTHING

(Map p70; www.silkcashmere.com; Nuruosmaniye Caddesi 69, Nuruosmaniye; 9.30am-7pm Mon-Sat; Çemberlitaş) The Nuruosmaniye branch of this popular chain sells cashmere and silk-cashmere-blend cardigans, sweaters, tops and shawls. All are remarkably well priced considering their quality. There's another, smaller, store inside the Grand Bazaar (Map p90; Kalpakçılar Caddesi 74; Vezneciler, Beyazıt-Kapalı Çarşı).

Dhoku
CARPETS

(Map p90; www.dhoku.com; Takkeçiler Sokak 58-60, Grand Bazaar; 8.30am-7pm Mon-Sat; Vezneciler, Beyazıt-Kapalı Çarşı) One of the new generation of rug stores opening in the bazaar, Dhoku (meaning 'texture') sells artfully designed wool kilims in resolutely modernist designs. Its sister store, Ethnicon (Map p90; www.ethnicon.com; Takkeçiler Sokak, Grand Bazaar), opposite Dhoku, sells similarly stylish rugs in vivid colours and can be said to have started the current craze in contemporary kilims.

Altan Şekerleme
FOOD & DRINK

(Map p86; 212-522 5909; www.altansekerleme.com; Kıble Çeşme Caddesi 68, Eminönü; 8am-7pm Mon-Sat, 9am-6pm Sun; Haliç, Eminönü) It's not just kids who like candy stores. İstanbullus of every age have been coming to this shop in the Küçük Pazar (Little Bazaar) precinct below the Süleymaniye Mosque since 1865, lured by its cheap and delectable *lokum* (Turkish delight), *helva* (sweet made from sesame seeds) and *akide* (hard candy).

Ali Muhiddin Hacı Bekir
FOOD

(Map p70; www.hacibekir.com.tr/eng; Hamidiye Caddesi 31 & 33, Eminönü; 8am-8pm Mon-Sat; Eminönü) Many people think that this historic shop, which has been operated by members of the same family for over 200 years, is the best place in the city to buy *lokum*. Choose from *sade* (plain), *cevizli* (walnut), *fıstıklı* (pistachio), *badem* (almond) or *roze* (rose water). There are other branches in Beyoğlu (Map p96; 212-244 2804; www.hacibekir.com.tr; İstiklal Caddesi 83; Taksim, Kabataş, then funicular to Taksim Meydanı) and Kadıköy (216-336 1519; Muvakkithane Caddesi 61; kadıköy).

Sofa
ART, JEWELLERY

(Map p86; 212-520 2850; www.kashifsofa.com; Nuruosmaniye Caddesi 53, Nuruosmaniye; 9.30am-6.30pm Mon-Sat; Çemberlitaş) Investigation of Sofa's three floors of artfully arranged clutter reveals an eclectic range of pricey jewellery, prints, textiles, calligraphy, Ottoman miniatures and contemporary Turkish art.

Vakko İndirim
CLOTHING, ACCESSORIES

(Vakko Sale Store; Map p70; Sultan Hamamı Caddesi 8a, Eminönü; 9.30am-6pm Mon-Sat; Eminönü) This remainder outlet of İstanbul's famous fashion store should be on the itinerary of all bargain hunters. Top-quality men's and women's clothing – often stuff that's been designed and made in Italy – is sold here for a fraction of its original price.

Beyoğlu & Around

Hiç
HOMEWARES, HANDICRAFTS

(Map p96; 212-251 9973; www.hiccrafts.com; Lüleci Hendek Caddesi 35, Tophane; 10.30am-7pm Mon-Sat; Şişhane, Tophane) Interior designer Emel Güntaş is one of İstanbul's style icons, and this recently-opened contemporary crafts shop in Tophane is a favourite destination for the city's design mavens. The stock includes cushions, carpets, kilims, silk scarves, lamps, furniture, glassware, porcelain and felt crafts. Everything here is artisan-made and absolutely gorgeous.

★**Nahıl** HANDICRAFTS, BATHWARE
(Map p96; ☎212-251 9085; www.nahil.com.tr; Bekar Sokak 17; ☻10am-7pm Mon-Sat; Ⓜ Taksim, 🚡 Kabataş, then funicular to Taksim) The felting, lacework, embroidery, all-natural soaps and soft toys in this lovely shop are made by economically disadvantaged women in Turkey's rural areas and all profits are returned to them, ensuring that they and their families have better lives.

Beyoğlu Olgunlaşma Enstıtüsü HANDICRAFTS
(Map p96; www.beyogluolgunlasma.k12.tr; İstiklal Caddesi 28; ☻9am-5pm Mon-Fri; Ⓜ Taksim, 🚡 Kabataş, then funicular to Taksim) This is the ground-floor retail-outlet-gallery of the Beyoğlu Olgunlaşma Enstıtüsü, a textile school where students in their final year of secondary school learn crafts such as felting, embroidery, knitting and lacemaking. It sells well-priced examples of their work, giving them a taste of its commercial possibilities.

Old Sandal SHOES
(Map p96; ☎212-292 8647; www.oldsandal.com.tr; Serdar-ı Ekrem Sokak 10a, Galata; ☻11am-7.30pm; Ⓜ Şişhane, 🚡 Karaköy, then funicular to Tünel) Owning a pair of Hülya Samancı's handmade shoes, boots or sandals is high on many local wishlists. Pop into this tiny store in the shadow of the Galata Tower to admire these 100% leather creations for men and women.

Lale Plak MUSIC
(Map p96; ☎212-293 7739; Galipdede Caddesi 1, Tünel; ☻noon-7pm; Ⓜ Şişhane, 🚡 Karaköy, then funicular to Tünel) This small shop is crammed with CDs, including a fine selection of Turkish classical, jazz and folk music. It's a popular hang-out for local musicians.

Mephisto MUSIC
(Map p96; ☎212-249 0696; www.mephisto.com.tr; İstiklal Caddesi 125; ☻9am-midnight; 🚡 Kabataş, then funicular to Taksim) If you manage to develop a taste for local music while you're in town, this popular store is the place to indulge it. As well as a huge CD collection of Turkish popular music, there's a select range of Turkish folk, jazz and classical music. It also stocks DVDs and has an upstairs cafe. There's another branch in Kadıköy (☎216-414 3519; www.mephisto.com.tr; Muvakkithane Caddesi 5; 🚢 Kadıköy).

Selda Okutan JEWELLERY
(Map p96; ☎212-514 1164; www.seldaokutan.com; Ali Paşa Değirmeni Sokak 10a, Tophane; ☻closed

Sun; 🚡 Tophane) Selda Okutan's sculptural pieces featuring tiny naked figures have the local fashion industry all aflutter. Come to her design studio in Tophane to see what all the fuss is about.

İstanbul Modern Gift Shop GIFTS
(Map p96; www.istanbulmodern.org; Meclis-i Mebusan Caddesi, Tophane; ☻10am-6pm Tue, Wed & Fri-Sun, 10am-8pm Thu; 🚡 Tophane) It's often difficult to source well-priced souvenirs and gifts to take home, but this stylish shop in the İstanbul Modern gallery boasts plenty of options. It stocks T-shirts, CDs, stationery, coffee mugs, homewares, jewellery and cute gifts for kids.

İKSV Tasarım Mağazası JEWELLERY, HOMEWARES
(İKSV Gift Shop; Map p96; ☎212-334 0830; www.iksvtasarim.com; İstanbul Foundation for Culture & Arts, Sadi Konuralp Caddesi 5, Şişhane; ☻10am-7pm Mon-Sat; Ⓜ Şişhane, 🚡 Karaköy, then funicular to Tünel) A secret to sourcing a great souvenir of your trip to İstanbul? Ignore the mass-produced junk sold in many shops around the city and instead head to a museum or gallery store like this one. Run by the İstanbul Foundation for Culture & Arts (İKSV), it sells jewellery, ceramics and glassware designed and made by local artisans.

A La Turca CARPETS, ANTIQUES
(Map p96; ☎212-245 2933; www.alaturcahouse.com; Faikpaşa Sokak 4, Çukurcuma; ☻10.30am-7.30pm Mon-Sat; Ⓜ Taksim, 🚡 Kabataş, then funicular to Taksim) Antique Anatolian kilims and textiles are stacked alongside top-drawer Ottoman antiques in this fabulous shop in Çukurcuma. This is the best area in the city to browse for antiques and curios, and A La Turca is probably the most interesting of its retail outlets. Ring the doorbell to gain entrance.

Paşabahçe GLASS
(Map p96; ☎212-244 0544; www.pasabahce.com; İstiklal Caddesi 314; ☻10am-8pm; Ⓜ Taksim, 🚡 Karaköy, then funicular to Tünel) Established in 1934, this local firm manufactures excellent glassware from its factory on the Bosphorus. Three floors of glassware, vases and decanters feature, and prices are very reasonable. Styles are both traditional and contemporary. There are other stores at the Zorlu, İstinye Park and Kanyon shopping malls, as well as near the Grand Bazaar (Map p70; ☎212-522 1622; www.pasabahce.com; Nuruosmaniye Caddesi 66, Nuruosmaniye; 🚡 Çemberlitaş).

🏠 Beşiktaş, Ortaköy & Kuruçeşme

Lokum
FOOD

(🖉 212-287 1528; www.lokumistanbul.com; Arnavutköy-Bebek Caddesi 15, Arnavutköy; ⊙9am-7pm Mon-Sat; 🚇 Arnavutköy) *Lokum* (Turkish delight) is elevated to the status of artwork at this boutique on the border of Kuruçeşme and Arnavutköy. Owner-creator Zeynep Keyman aims to bring back the delights, flavours, knowledge and beauty of Ottoman-Turkish products such as *lokum, akide* candies (traditional boiled lollies), cologne water and scented candles. The gorgeous packaging makes these treats perfect gifts.

🏠 Kadıköy

Soy
HOMEWARES

(🖉 216-330 0030; www.soy.com.tr; Leylek Sokak 20b; ⊙call for appointment; 🚇 Kadıköy) A few years ago, entrepreneur and committed foodie Emir Ali Enç identified a market opportunity for quality copper cookware made in Turkey. The resulting range of handmade serving bowls, coffee pots and saucepans has quickly developed a loyal fan base both here and overseas, and can be seen at his showroom on the edge of Kadıköy and Moda.

If you are keen to purchase a pot or two, you'll need to give Emir a lead time of seven to 10 days. Orders can be shipped overseas.

Mesut Güneş
TEXTILES

(🖉 216-337 6215; www.mesutgunes.com.tr; Yasa Caddesi 46; ⊙8.30am-6pm Mon-Sat; 🚇 Kadıköy) It may not look like much from the front, but this shop often sells top-quality towels and sheets manufactured in Turkey for major international brands (eg Frette) for a fraction of their usual price.

ℹ️ Information

DANGERS & ANNOYANCES

İstanbul is no more nor less safe a city than any large metropolis, but there are a few dangers worth highlighting:

➡ Bag-snatchings and muggings occasionally occur on Beyoğlu's side streets.

➡ There are semi-regular police crackdowns on gay venues in the city, especially hamams and saunas. Many have closed but those that remain open are in constant danger of being raided by police for 'morality' reasons.

➡ Males travelling alone or in pairs should be wary of being adopted by a friendly local who is keen to take them to a club for a few drinks – many such encounters end up at *pavyons*, sleazy nightclubs run by the mafia where a drink or two with a female hostess will end up costing hundreds – sometimes thousands – of euros. If you don't pay up, the consequences can be violent.

➡ In 2013 an American woman was murdered while exploring a stretch of the historic city walls. Though an isolated incident, it was a reminder that travellers (especially those who are solo) should be careful when exploring derelict buildings/areas.

➡ If a shoeshine guy drops his brush in front of you, ignore it – it's a time-tested scam to con you into paying for his services.

EMERGENCY

Ambulance (🖉 112)

Fire (🖉 110)

Police (🖉 155)

Tourist Police (🖉 212-527 4503; Yerebatan Caddesi 6) Across the street from the Basilica Cistern.

MEDIA

Time Out İstanbul Published monthly, the printed English edition of this magazine is the best source for details about upcoming events – you can pick it up at the airport, at newspaper booths in Sultanahmet and at some bookshops. There's also a website.

The Guide İstanbul Listings-heavy bimonthly guide to the city published in printed and online editions.

MEDICAL SERVICES

Although they are expensive, it's probably best to visit one of the private hospitals listed here if you need medical care when in İstanbul. Both accept credit-card payments and charge ₺200 to ₺250 for a standard consultation.

American Hospital (Amerikan Hastenesi; 🖉 212-311 2000, 212-444 3777; www.americanhospitalistanbul.org/ENG; Güzelbahçe Sokak 20, Nişantaşı; ⊙24hr emergency department; 🚇 Osmanbey)

Memorial Hospital (🖉 212-314 6666, 444 7888; www.memorial.com.tr/en; Piyalepaşa Bulvarı, Okmeydanı; 🚇 Şişli) Pediatric, general medicine and dentistry clinics.

MONEY

ATMs are everywhere in İstanbul and include those conveniently located near Aya Sofya Meydanı in Sultanahmet, in the Grand Bazaar and all along İstiklal Caddesi in Beyoğlu.

The 24-hour *döviz bürosus* (exchange bureaux) in the arrivals hall at Atatürk International Airport offer rates comparable to those offered by city bureaux. Other exchange bureaux can be found on Divan Yolu in Sultanahmet, near the Grand Bazaar and around Sirkeci station in Eminönü.

POST

İstanbul's central PTT (post office) is in a convenient location between Sirkeci Train Station and the Spice Bazaar.

TELEPHONE

If you are in European İstanbul and wish to call a number in Asian İstanbul, you must dial 216, then the number. If you are in Asian İstanbul and wish to call a number in European İstanbul dial 212, then the number. Don't use the area codes if you are calling a number on the same shore.

TOURIST INFORMATION

When this book was being researched, the Ministry of Culture & Tourism was operating four tourist information offices around town; a fifth was scheduled to open in the Atatürk Cultural Centre on Taksim Meydanı when renovations there were complete. The Sultanahmet office is the least helpful.

Tourist Office – Atatürk International Airport (☑ 212-465 3547; International Arrivals Hall, Atatürk International Airport; ⊙9am-9pm)

Tourist Office – Karaköy (Map p96; Karaköy International Maritime Passenger Terminal, Kemankeş Caddesi, Karaköy; ⊙9.30am-5pm Mon-Sat; ⓘ Karaköy)

Tourist Office – Sirkeci Train Station (Map p70; ☑ 212-511 5888; Sirkeci Gar, Ankara Caddesi, Sirkeci; ⊙9am-6pm mid-Apr–Sep, 9am-5.30pm Oct–mid-Apr; ⓘ Sirkeci)

Tourist Office – Sultanahmet (Map p70; ☑ 212-518 8754; Hippodrome, Sultanahmet; ⊙9.30am-6pm mid-Apr–Sep, 9am-5.30pm Oct–mid-Apr; ⓘ Sultanahmet)

ⓘ Getting There & Away

İstanbul is the country's foremost transport hub.

AIR

Atatürk International Airport (IST, Atatürk Havalimanı; ☑ 212-463 3000; www.ataturkairport. com) Located 23km west of Sultanahmet. The international terminal *(Dış Hatlar)* and domestic terminal *(İç Hatlar)* operate at or close to capacity, which has prompted the Turkish government to announce construction of a new, much larger, airport 50km north of the city centre. The first stage of the new airport's construction is due to be completed by 2018 but the facility won't be fully operational until 2025.

There are car-hire desks, money-exchange offices, stands of mobile-phone companies, a tourist information desk, a pharmacy, ATMs and a PTT in the international arrivals hall and a 24-hour supermarket on the walkway to the metro. The left-luggage service (₺18 to ₺25 per suitcase per 24 hours) is to your right as you exit customs.

Sabiha Gökçen International Airport (SAW, Sabiha Gökçen Havalimanı; ☑ 216-588 8888; www.sgairport.com) Located 50km east of Sultanahmet, at Pendik/Kurtköy on the Asian side of the city, this airport is used by cut-price European carriers. There are car-hire desks, exchange offices, stands of mobile-phone companies, a minimarket and a PTT here.

BUS

The **Büyük İstanbul Otogarı** (Big İstanbul Bus Station; ☑ 212-658 0505; www.otogaristanbul. com) is the city's main bus station for both inter-city and international routes. Often called simply 'the Otogar' (Bus Station), it's located at Esenler in the municipality of Bayrampaşa, about 10km west of Sultanahmet. The metro service from Aksaray stops here (₺4; Otogar stop) on its way to the airport; you can catch this to Zeytinburnu and then easily connect with a tram (₺4) to Sultanahmet or Beyoğlu. A taxi will cost approximately ₺35 to both Sultanahmet and Taksim.

There's a second, much smaller, otogar at **Alibeyköy** where buses from central Anatolia (including Ankara and Cappadocia) stop en route to Esenler. From here, passengers can take a *servis* (service bus) to Taksim; the transfer is included in the ticket cost. The only problem with this option is that *servis* drivers rarely speak English and passengers sometimes have to wait for a *servis* – it's probably easier to go to Esenler.

The city's third otogar is on the Asian shore of the Bosphorus at **Harem**, south of Üsküdar and north of Haydarpaşa Train Station, but this will probably be decommissioned in the near future. Some bus companies have already relocated to an otogar at **Ataşehir**, on the Asian side at the junction of the O-2 and O-4 motorways. From Ataşehir, *servises* transfer passengers to Asian suburbs including Kadıköy and Üsküdar.

TRAIN

At the time of research, only one international service – the daily *Bosfor Ekspresi* between İstanbul and Bucharest via Sofia – was operating in and out of İstanbul, departing at 10pm daily (€39 to €59 plus couchette surcharge). The service included a bus link between Sirkeci Gar (Sirkeci Train Station) and Çerkezköy, a two-hour drive northwest of İstanbul. Check **Turkish State Railways** (TCDD; www.tcdd.gov.tr) for details.

A new fast train service between Ankara and Pendik, 20km southeast of Kadıköy on the Asian side of town, commenced in July 2014. The journey takes approximately 3½ hours and ticket prices start at ₺70. Unfortunately, Pendik is difficult to access. You'll need to take a ferry to Kadıköy then the M4 metro to the end of the line at Kartal. From Kartal, bus 251 and taxis travel the last 6km to Pendik Gar. There are future plans to link Pendik with the M4 metro but a timetable for this has yet to be announced.

❶ Getting Around

TO/FROM THE AIRPORT

Atatürk International Airport

Bus If you are staying near Taksim Meydanı, the Havataş (Havaş) airport bus departs from outside the arrivals hall. Buses leave every 30 minutes between 4am and 1am; the trip takes between 40 minutes and one hour, depending on traffic. Tickets cost ₺10 and the bus stops in front of the Point Hotel on Cumhuriyet Caddesi, close to Taksim Meydanı.

Hotel Shuttles Many hotels will provide a free pick-up service from Atatürk airport if you stay with them for three nights or more. There are also a number of cheap (one way €5) but very slow shuttle-bus services from hotels to the airport for your return trip.

Metro There's an efficient metro service from the airport to Zeytinburnu, from where it's easy to connect with the tram to Sultanahmet, Eminönü, Karaköy and Kabataş. There are funiculars from Karaköy to Tünel Meydanı and from Kabataş to Taksim Meydanı.

The metro station is on the lower ground floor beneath the international departures hall – follow the 'Metro/Subway' signs down the escalators and through the underground walkway. You'll need to purchase a *jeton* (ticket token; ₺4) or purchase and recharge an İstanbulkart (travel card; ₺10) from the machines at the metro entrance. Services depart every six to 10 minutes from 6am until midnight. When you get off the metro, the tram platform is right in front

of you. You'll need to buy another token (₺4) to pass through the turnstiles. The entire trip from the airport takes around 50 to 60 minutes to Sultanahmet, 60 to 70 minutes to Eminönü and 85 to 95 minutes to Taksim.

Taxi Around ₺45 to Sultanahmet, ₺55 to Taksim Meydanı and ₺75 to Kadıköy.

Sabiha Gökçen International Airport

Bus Havataş airport buses travel from the airport to Taksim Meydanı between 4am and 1am. There are also services to Kadıköy between 4.15am and 12.45am. Tickets cost ₺13 to Taksim (90 minutes) and ₺8 to Kadıköy (60 minutes). If you're heading towards the Old City from Taksim, you can take the funicular from Taksim to Kabataş (₺4) followed by the tram from Kabataş to Sultanahmet (₺4). From Kadıköy, ferries travel to Eminönü (₺4).

Hotel Shuttles Hotels rarely provide free pick-up services from Sabiha Gökçen. Shuttle-bus services from hotels to the airport for return trips cost €12 but are infrequent – check details with your hotel.

Taxi Around ₺100 to Taksim and ₺130 to Sultanahmet.

BUS

The city bus system operated by **İstanbul Elektrik Tramvay ve Tünel** (İETT, Istanbul Electricity, Tramway and Tunnel General Management; www.iett.gov.tr) is extremely efficient, though traffic congestion in the city means that bus trips can be very long. The major bus stands are underneath Taksim Meydanı and at Beşiktaş,

SERVICES FROM İSTANBUL'S OTOGAR

DESTINATION	FARE (₺)	DURATION (HR)	DISTANCE (KM)
Alanya	80	12	860
Ankara	50–55	6	450
Antalya	70–75	12	740
Bodrum	70–75	12½	860
Bursa	30	4	230
Çanakkale	45	6	340
Denizli (for Pamukkale)	70	11	665
Edirne	30	2½	235
Fethiye	70	12	820
Göreme	60	12	725
İzmir	60	9	750
Kaş	90	14	1090
Konya	75	10	660
Kuşadası	65	12	555
Marmaris	75	12½	805
Selçuk	65	11	1107
Trabzon	75	17	1110

Kabataş, Eminönü, Kadıköy and Üsküdar; most services run between 6am and 11pm. You must have an İstanbulkart before boarding

The most useful bus lines for travellers are those running along both sides of the Bosphorus and the Golden Horn, those in the Western Districts and those between Üsküdar and Kadıköy. Note that İstanbulkart transfer charges are slightly lower on buses than they are on trams and ferries.

FERRY

The most enjoyable way to get around town is by ferry. Crossing between the Asian and European shores, up and down the Golden Horn and Bosphorus, and over to the Princes' Islands, these vessels are as efficient as they are popular with locals. Some are operated by the government-owned **İstanbul Şehir Hatları** (İstanbul City Routes; www.sehirhatlari.com.tr); others by private companies including **Turyol** (☑ 0212-512 1287; www.turyol.com) and Dentur Avrasya (☑ 444 6336; www.denturavrasya.com). Timetables are posted at *iskelesis* (ferry docks).

On the European side, the major ferry docks are at the mouth of the Golden Horn (Eminönü and Karaköy), at Beşiktaş and next to the tram stop at Kabataş, 2km past the Galata Bridge.

The ferries run to two annual timetables: winter (mid-September to May) and summer (June to mid-September). Tickets are cheap (usually ₺4) and it's possible to use an İstanbulkart on most routes.

Ferries ply the following useful two-way routes:

➡ Beşiktaş–Kadıköy
➡ Beşiktaş–Üsküdar
➡ Eminönü–Anadolu Kavağı (Bosphorus Cruise)
➡ Eminönü–Kadıköy
➡ Eminönü–Üsküdar

➡ Emirgan–Kanlıca–Anadolu Hisarı–Bebek (weekends only)
➡ İstinye–Emirgan–Kanlıca–Anadolu Hisarı–Kandilli–Bebek–Arnavutköy–Çengelköy
➡ Kabataş–Kadıköy
➡ Kabataş–Kadıköy–Kınalıada–Burgazada–Heybeliada–Büyükada (Princes' Islands ferry)
➡ Kabataş–Üsküdar
➡ Karaköy–Kadıköy (some stop at Haydarpaşa)
➡ Karaköy–Üsküdar
➡ Sarıyer–Rumeli Kavağı–Anadolu Kavağı
➡ Üsküdar–Karaköy–Eminönü–Kasımpaşa–Hasköy–Ayvansaray–Sütlüce–Eyüp (Golden Horn Ferry)

FUNICULAR

There are two heavily used funiculars (*funiküleri*) in the city.

A funicular called the Tünel carries passengers between Karaköy, at the base of the Galata Bridge (Galata Köprüsü), to Tünel Meydanı. The service operates between 7am and 10.45pm and a *jeton* costs ₺4.

The second funicular carries passengers from Kabataş – at the end of the tramline – to Taksim Meydanı, where it connects to the metro. The service operates from 6am and midnight and a *jeton* costs ₺4.

METRO

Metro service are operated by **İstanbul Ulaşım** (www.istanbul-ulasim.com.tr) and run every two to 10 minutes between 6am and midnight. *Jetons* cost ₺4 and İstanbulkarts can be used.

The **M1A** connects Aksaray with the airport, stopping at 15 stations including the otogar along the way. There are plans to add a link between Aksaray and Yenikapı, southwest of Sultanahmet.

The **M2** connects Yenikapı with Taksim, stopping at three stations along the way: Vezneciler, near the Grand Bazaar; on the new bridge across

---

ⓘ İSTANBULKARTS

İstanbul's public transport system is excellent, and one of its major strengths is the İstanbulkart, a rechargeable travel card.

İstanbulkarts are simple to operate: as you enter a bus or pass through the turnstile at a ferry dock or metro station, swipe your card for entry and the fare will automatically be deducted from your balance. The cards offer a considerable discount on fares (₺2.15 as opposed to the usual ₺4, with additional transfers within a two-hour journey window; ₺1.60 for the first transfer, ₺1.50 for the second and ₺1.30 for the third). They can also be used to pay for fares for more than one traveller (one swipe per person per ride).

The cards can be purchased from machines at metro and funicular stations for a non-refundable charge of ₺10, which includes ₺4 in credit. If you buy yours from a street kiosk near a tram or bus stop (look for an 'Akbil', 'Dolum Noktası' or 'İstanbulkart' sign), you will pay ₺8 including a plastic cover or ₺7 without. These won't include any credit.

Cards can be recharged with amounts between ₺5 and ₺150 at kiosks or at machines at ferry docks, metro and bus stations. Machines will only accept ₺5, ₺10 or ₺20 notes.

İstanbul Public Transport

Funicular
Tram
Train
Metro & LRT

Haciosman
Darüşşafaka
Atatürk Oto Sanayi
İTÜ Ayazağa
Sanayi
4. Levent
Levent
Gayrettepe
Şişli Mecidiyeköy
Osmanbey
Taksim

Bağcılar
Güneştepe
Yavuzselim
Soğanlı
Akıncılar
Güngören
Merter Tekstil Merkezi
Mehmet Akif

Üçyüzlü
Seyrantepe
Menderes
Esenler

Şişhane
Galatasaray
Tünel
Odakule
Kabataş
Fındıklı Mimar Sinan Üni
Tophane
Karaköy

SEA OF MARMARA
(MARMARA DENİZİ)

the Golden Horn (Haliç); and at Şişhane, near Tünel Meydanı in Beyoğlu. From Taksim, another service travels northeast to Hacıosman via nine stations.

The **Marmaray line** connects Kazlıçeşme, west of the Old City, with Ayrılak Çeşmesi, on the Asian side. This travels via a tunnel under the Sea of Marmara, stopping at Yenikapı, Sirkeci and Üsküdar en route.

The **M4** connects Kadıköy and Ayrılak Çeşmesi with Kartal.

TAXI

All taxis have digital meters, but some drivers ask for a flat fare, or pretend the meter doesn't work so they can gouge you at the end of the trip. The best way to counter this is to tell them no meter, no ride. Avoid the taxis waiting for fares near Aya Sofya Meydanı – these guys are almost inevitably rip-off merchants.

Taxi fares are very reasonable, and rates are the same during day and night. It costs around ₺15 to travel between Beyoğlu and Sultanahmet.

Few taxis have seat belts. If you catch a taxi over either of the Bosphorus bridges, it is your responsibility to cover the toll (₺3.40). The driver will add this to your fare.

TRAM

An excellent *tramvay* (tramway) service operated by İstanbul Ulaşım runs from Bağcılar, in the city's west, to Zeytinburnu (where it connects

with the metro from the airport) and on to Sultanahmet and Eminönü. It then crosses the Galata Bridge to Karaköy (to connect with the Tünel) and Kabataş (to connect with the funicular to Taksim Meydanı). A second service runs from Cevizlibağ, closer to Sultanahmet on the same line, through to Kabataş. Services run every five minutes from 6am to midnight. The fare is ₺4; *jetons* are available from machines at every tram stop and İstanbulkarts can be used.

A small antique tram travels the length of İstiklal Caddesi in Beyoğlu from a stop near Tünel Meydanı to Taksim Meydanı. Electronic tickets (₺4) can be purchased from the ticket office at the Tünel funicular, and İstanbulkarts can be used.

AROUND İSTANBUL

Princes' Islands

Most İstanbullus refer to the Princes' Islands as 'The Islands' (Adalar). The group lies about 20km southeast of the city in the Sea of Marmara and makes a great destination for a day's escape, particularly as the ferry ride here is so enjoyable.

In Byzantine times, refractory princes, deposed monarchs and others who had

Around İstanbul

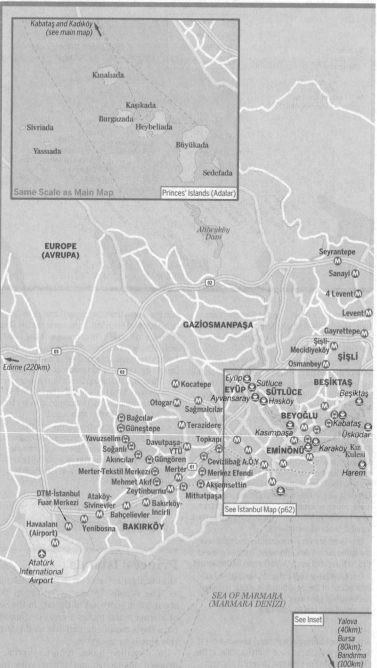

Kabataş and Kadıköy
(see main map)

Kınalıada

Kaşıkada

Burgazada
Sivriada
Heybeliada

Yassıada

Büyükada

Sedefada

Same Scale as Main Map

Princes' Islands (Adalar)

Alibeyköy
Dam

**EUROPE
(AVRUPA)**

Seyrantepe

Sanayi Ⓜ

02

4 Levent Ⓜ

Levent Ⓜ

GAZİOSMANPAŞA

Gayrettepe Ⓜ

Şişli-
Mecidiyeköy Ⓜ

ŞİŞLİ

03

Osmanbey Ⓜ

Eyüp

Edirne (220km)

03

Sütluce

EYÜP

SÜTLÜCE

BEŞİKTAŞ

Ⓜ Kocatepe

Ayvansaray

Hasköy

Beşiktaş

Otogar Ⓜ

Ⓜ
Sağmalcılar

BEYOĞLU

Terazidere

Kabataş

Ⓔ Bağcılar

Ⓜ

Kasımpaşa

Ⓔ Güneştepe

Üsküdar

Yavuzselim

Davutpaşa-

Topkapı

EMİNÖNÜ

YTÜ

Karaköy Kız

Soğanlı

Kulesi

Akıncılar

Güngören

Cevizlibağ A.Ö.Y

Harem

Merter-Tekstil Merkezi

Merter

01

Merkez Efendi

Mehmet Akıf

Akşemsettin

Zeytinburnu

DTM-İstanbul

Mithatpaşa

Fuar Merkezi

Ataköy-

Sivinevler

See İstanbul Map (p62)

Bakırköy-

Bahçelievler

İncirli

Havaalanı

Yenibosna

BAKIRKÖY

(Airport)

Atatürk
International
Airport

*SEA OF MARMARA
(MARMARA DENİZİ)*

See Inset

Yalova
(40km);
Bursa
(80km);
Bandırma
(100km)

outlived their roles were interned on the islands. A ferry service from İstanbul was started in the mid-19th century and the islands became popular summer resorts with Pera's Greek, Jewish and Armenian business communities. Many of the fine Victorian villas built by these wealthy merchants survive today.

You'll realise after landing that there are no cars on the islands, something that comes as a welcome relief after the traffic mayhem of the city. Except for the necessary police, fire and sanitation vehicles, transport is by bicycle, *fayton* (horse-drawn carriage) and foot, as in centuries past.

The islands are busiest on holidays and in summer, and ferries can be unpleasantly crowded on weekends at this time; consider visiting mid week instead. In winter, many hotels, restaurants and shops close for the season.

◉ Sights & Activities

There are nine islands in the group; the conventional ferry stops at four of these and the Dentur Avraysa/Mavi Marmara ferries stop at the two largest (Heybeliada and Büyükada) – we describe the conventional ferry trip here. Year-round there are 16,000 permanent residents scattered across the six islands that are populated, but numbers swell to 100,000 or so during the summer months when İstanbullus – many of whom have holiday homes here – come to escape the city heat.

After boarding a ferry at Kabataş, try to find a seat on the right side of the boat so that you can view the various islands as the ferry approaches them.

Heading towards the Sea of Marmara, passengers are treated to fine views of Topkapı Palace, Aya Sofya and the Blue Mosque on the right and Kız Kulesi, Haydarpaşa Train Station and the distinctive minaret-style clock towers of Marmara University on the left.

After a quick stop at Kadıköy, the ferry makes its way to the first island in the group, Kınalıada. This leg takes 30 minutes. After this, it's another 15 minutes to the island of Burgazada and another 15 minutes again to Heybeliada, the second-largest of the islands. Büyükada is another 15 minutes from here.

◉ Heybeliada

Heybeliada (Heybeli for short and Halki in Greek) is popular with day-trippers, who

İSTANBUL PRINCES' ISLANDS

come here on weekends to walk in the pine groves and swim from the tiny (but crowded) beaches. The island's major landmark is the hilltop Haghia Triada Monastery, which is perched above a picturesque line of poplar trees in a spot that has been occupied by a Greek monastery since Byzantine times. The current monastery complex dates from 1844 and housed a Greek Orthodox theological school until 1971, when it was closed on the government's orders. The Ecumenical Patriarchate of Constantinople is waging an ongoing campaign to have it reopened. The complex includes a small church with an ornate altar as well as an internationally renowned library, which is home to many old and rare manuscripts. To visit the library, you'll need to gain special permission from the abbot, Metropolitan Elpidophoros. A *fayton* will charge ₺30 to bring you here from the centre of town.

The delightful walk from the *iskele* up to the Merit Halki Palace (☏ 216-351 0025; www.halkipalacehotel.com; Refah Şehitleri Caddesi 94; s/d €110/160; @ 🛜 🛋) hotel at the top of Refah Şehitleri Caddesi passes a host of large wooden villas set in lovingly tended gardens. Many laneways and streets leading to picnic spots and lookout points are located off the upper reaches of this street. To find the hotel, turn right as you leave the ferry and head past the waterfront restaurants and cafes to the plaza with the Atatürk statue. From here walk up İşgüzar Sokak, veering right until you hit Refah Şehitleri Caddesi. If you don't feel like walking up to the hotel (it's uphill but not too steep), you can hire a bicycle (₺10 per hour, ₺25 per day) from one of the shops in the main street or a *fayton* to take you around the island. A 25-minute tour (*küçük tur*) costs ₺45 and a one-hour tour (*büyük tur*) costs ₺58; the *fayton* stand is behind the Atatürk statue. Some visitors spend the day by the pool at the Merit Halki Palace, which is a good idea, as the waters around the island aren't very clean and many of the beaches are privatised. Towels and chaise longues are supplied, and there's a pleasant terrace restaurant for meals or drinks. There is a charge for nonguests using the pool (weekdays/weekends ₺40/60).

👁 Büyükada

The largest island in the group, Büyükada (Great Island) is impressive viewed from the ferry, with gingerbread villas climbing up the slopes of the hill and the bulbous twin cupolas of the Splendid Otel providing an unmistakable landmark.

The ferry terminal is an attractive building in the Ottoman Revival style; it dates from 1899.

The island's main drawcard is the Greek Orthodox Monastery of St George, located in the 'saddle' between Büyükada's two highest hills. To walk here, head from the ferry to the clock tower in İskele Meydanı (Dock Sq). The shopping district (with cheap eateries) is left along Recep Koç Sokak. Bear right onto 23 Nisan Caddesi, then head along Çankaya Caddesi up the hill to the monastery; when you come to a fork in the road, veer right. The walk, which takes at least one hour, takes you past a long progression of impressive wooden villas set in gardens. After 40 minutes or so you will reach a reserve called 'Luna Park' by the locals. The monastery is a 25-minute walk up an extremely steep hill from here. As you ascend, you'll sometimes see pieces of cloth tied to the branches of trees along the path – each represents a prayer, most made by female supplicants visiting the monastery to pray for a child.

There's not a lot to see at the monastery. A small and gaudy church is the only building of note, but there are fabulous panoramic views from the terrace, as well as the pleasant Yücetepe Kır Gazinosu restaurant. From its tables you will be able to see all the way to İstanbul and the nearby islands of Yassıada and Sivriada.

The Museum of the Princes' Islands (Adalar Müzesi Hangar Müze Alanı; ☏ 216-382 6430; www.adalarmuzesi.org; Aya Nikola Mevkii; adult/child under 12yr ₺5/free, free Wed; ☉ 9am-7pm Tue-Sun Mar-Nov, to 6pm Dec-Feb) is also worth a visit, with exhibits covering local lifestyle, famous residents and local food. It's hard to locate, so we recommend taking a *fayton* (₺26).

Bicycles are available for rent in several of the town's shops (₺10 per hour, ₺40 per day), and shops on the market street can provide picnic supplies. The *fayton* stand is to the left of the clock tower. Hire one for a long tour of the town, hills and shore (one hour, ₺80) or a shorter tour of the town (₺70). It costs ₺30 to be taken to Luna Park.

🍴 Eating

Unfortunately, most of the restaurants on the islands are unremarkable and pricey.

Yücetepe Kır Gazinosu
Restaurant   TURKISH €

(☑216-382 1333; www.yucetepe.com; Monastery of St George, Büyükada; mezes ₺6-8, mains ₺12-16; ⊙daily Apr-Oct, Sat & Sun only Nov-Mar; 🚍Büyükada) At the very top of the hill where the Monastery of St George is located, this simple place has benches and chairs on a terrace overlooking the sea and İstanbul. Dishes are simple but good – the *köfte* (meatballs) are particularly tasty. You can also enjoy a beer or glass of tea here.

Heyamola Ada Lokantası   TURKISH €€

(☑216-351 1111; www.heyamolaadalokantasi. com; Mavi Marmara Yalı Caddesi 30b, Heybeliada; mezes ₺9-12, fish ₺18-20, set brunch ₺25; ⊙9am-midnight, closed Mon Nov-Apr; 🚍Heybeliada) Opposite the İDO dock. this busy place wows customers with a huge array of mezes (try the baked saganaki cheese), delicious fish mains (order *mezgit*, whiting, if it's on offer), and an interesting and affordable wine list featuring plenty of boutique labels.

Pelikan Balıkçısı   SEAFOOD €€

(☑216-382 1282; www.pelikanbalik.com; Şehit Recep Koç Caddesi 20, Büyükada; fish soup ₺7, fish mains ₺15-30 or by kg; ⊙11am-9.30pm, to midnight Jun-Aug; 🚍Büyükada) The cheery slogan (Hello Fish!) on the sign outside this simple place one street back from the waterfront promenade says it all. Fresh fish is available daily, with yesterday's leftovers used in the tasty fish soup. The friendly waiters probably won't care if you opt for a fish sandwich or a plate of fried *hamsi* (anchovy) instead of the more-expensive grills on offer.

ℹ Getting There & Away

At least eight **İstanbul Şehir Hatları** (İstanbul City Routes; www.sehirhatlari.com.tr) ferries run to the islands each day between 6.50am and 7.40pm (to 9pm June to mid-September), departing from the Adalar İskelesi (ferry dock) at Kabataş. The most useful departure times for day-trippers are 8.40am, 10.40am and noon (8.30am, 9.30am, 10.30am and 11.30am June to mid-September). On summer weekends, board the vessel and grab a seat at least half an hour before departure time unless you want to stand the whole way. The trip costs ₺6 (₺3.85 with an İstanbulkart) to the islands and the same for each leg between the islands and for the return trip. To be safe, check the timetable at www.se-hirhatlari.com.tr, as the schedule often changes.

Ferries return to İstanbul every two hours or so. The last ferry of the day leaves Büyükada at 8.15pm and Heybeliada at 8.30pm (10.40pm and 10.55pm June to mid-September).

There are also regular Mavi Marmara ferries operated by **Dentur Avraysa** (☑444 6336; www.denturavrasya.com). These are on smaller boats and leave from the *iskele* behind the petrol station at Kabataş. As there are only two stops (Heybeliada and Büyükada), the trip is faster. Ferries depart Kabataş every 30 minutes from 9.30am to 11.30am, at 1pm and then every hour from 2.30pm to 7.30pm. The last return service is at 7.30pm. Tickets cost ₺6; İstanbulkarts are not valid.

Thrace & Marmara

Why Go?

Grand narratives have unfolded in this corner of Turkey for millennia, leaving an extraordinary archaeological site (Troy), a city full of Ottoman buildings (Edirne), historically significant battlefields (Gallipoli) and a culturally fascinating and physically beautiful island outpost (Gökçeada) for visitors to explore. It was here that Alexander the Great crossed the Hellespont on his conquering march to Persia, and where the Achaeans (Greeks) and Trojans fought the war immortalised by Homer in the *Iliad*. Mehmet II launched his campaign to conquer Constantinople from the Ottoman capital of Edirne, and nearly 500 years later Allied forces landed on the Gallipoli (Gelibolu) Peninsula, triggering a bloody stand-off with Turkish troops that would drag on for nine long months and help to define the modern nations of Turkey, Australia and New Zealand.

Best Places to Eat

➡ Barba Yorgo Taverna (p173)

➡ Kilye Suvla Lokanta (p162)

➡ Mustafanın Kayfesi (p172)

➡ Yalova (p166)

Best Places to Stay

➡ Anemos Hotel (p172)

➡ Anzac Hotel (p165)

➡ Gallipoli Houses (p159)

➡ Hotel Edirne Palace (p148)

➡ Pansyon Agridia (p172)

When to Go

Edirne

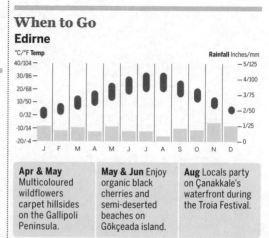

| Apr & May Multicoloured wildflowers carpet hillsides on the Gallipoli Peninsula. | May & Jun Enjoy organic black cherries and semi-deserted beaches on Gökçeada island. | Aug Locals party on Çanakkale's waterfront during the Troia Festival. |

Edirne

📞 0284 / POP 150,260

Capital of the Ottoman Empire before Mehmet II conquered Constantinople and moved his court there, Edirne is blessed with imperial building stock, a notable culinary heritage and a lingering and much-cherished sense of civic grandeur. Close to the Greek and Bulgarian borders, the city has a European flavour that is best appreciated in summer, when locals party on the banks of the Tunca and Meriç Rivers and cheer on the contestants at the world-famous Kırkpınar oil-wrestling festival.

Thrace & Marmara Highlights

❶ Visit the World Heritage–listed Selimiye Mosque (p145) in the former Ottoman capital of **Edirne**.

❷ Sample local wine and food while following the newly established **Thracian Vineyard Route** (p149).

❸ Investigate the fascinating Greek heritage and windswept landscape on the Aegean island of **Gökçeada** (p162).

❹ Walk in the footsteps of WWI soldiers and contemplate the horrors of war on the **Gallipoli Peninsula** (p151).

❺ Laze away an afternoon admiring the view over the Dardanelles at a waterfront çay bahçesi (tea garden) in **Çanakkale** (p163).

❻ Admire Trojan gold and other ancient artefacts in the newly opened museum at the **Troy** archaeological site (p169).

Edirne

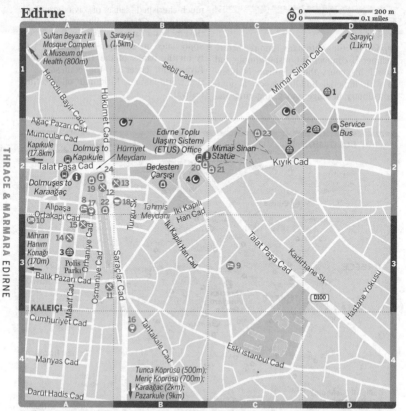

Sultan Beyazıt II Mosque Complex & Museum of Health (800m)
Sarayiçi (1.5km)
Sebil Cad
Mimar Sinan Cad
Sarayiçi (1.1km)
Horozlu Bayır Cad
Hükümet Cad
Ağaç Pazarı Cad
Mumcular Cad
Kapıkule (17.8km)
Dolmuş to Kapıkule
Talat Paşa Cad
Hürriyet Meydanı
Edirne Toplu Ulaşım Sistemi (ETUS) Office
Mimar Sinan Statue
Kıyık Cad
Service Bus
Dolmuşes to Karaağaç
Bedesten Çarşısı
Alipaşa Ortakapı Cad
Tahmis Meydanı
İki Kapılı Han Cad
İki Kapılı Han Cad
Talat Paşa Cad
Kadirhane Sk
Mihran Hanım Konağı (170m)
Polis Parkı
Osmaniye Cad
Orhaniye Cad
Turgu Sk
Saraçlar Cad
Balık Pazarı Cad
Maarif Cad
KALEİÇİ
Cumhuriyet Cad
Tahtakale Cad
Manyas Cad
Tunca Köprüsü (500m); Meriç Köprüsü (700m); Karaağaç (2km); Pazarkule (9km)
Darül Hadis Cad
Eski İstanbul Cad
Hastane Yokuşu
D100

Edirne

⊙ Sights
1 Edirne Archaeology & Ethnography Museum D1
2 Edirne Turkish and Islamic Art Museum D2
3 Kırkpınar Evi A3
4 Old Mosque B2
5 Selimiye Foundation Museum C2
6 Selimiye Mosque C1
7 Üç Şerefeli Mosque B2

⊜ Sleeping
8 Efe Hotel A2
9 Hotel Edirne Palace C3
10 Sarı Pansiyon A3

⊗ Eating
11 Balıkçım Yasem A3

12 Balkan Piliç A2
13 Köfteci Osman B2
14 Melek Anne A3
15 Niyazi Usta A3

⊜ Drinking & Nightlife
16 Çalgılı Meyhane B4
17 Kahverengi A2
18 Mado B2

⊜ Shopping
19 Ali Paşa Covered Bazaar A2
20 Arslanzade B2
21 Keçecizade C2
22 Keçecizade A2
23 Selimiye Arastası C2
24 Turkuaz A2

History

Emperor Hadrian made Hadrianopolis (later Adrianople) the main centre of Roman Thrace in the early 2nd century AD. In the mid-14th century the nascent Ottoman state began to grow in size and power, and in 1363 its army crossed the Dardanelles, skirted Constantinople and captured Adrianople, renaming it Edirne and making it the third capital of the Ottoman Empire.

The city functioned in this role until 1453, when Constantinople was conquered and became the new capital. Subsequent sultans continued to acknowledge Edirne's historical importance by maintaining its industries and preserving its buildings. It was briefly occupied by imperial Russian troops in 1829, during the Greek War of Independence, and in 1878, during the Russo-Turkish War of 1877–78, but remained relatively unscathed by these events. Its role as a fortress defending Ottoman Constantinople and Eastern Thrace during the Balkan Wars of 1912–13 was more significant, and it suffered heavy losses of life and property at this time.

When the Ottoman Empire collapsed after WWI, the Allies handed Thrace to the Greeks and declared İstanbul an international city. In the summer of 1920 Greek armies occupied Edirne, only to be driven back by forces under the command of Atatürk. The Treaty of Lausanne (1923) ceded Edirne and eastern Thrace to the Turks.

◉ Sights & Activities

Selimiye Mosque MOSQUE
(Selimiye Camii) Modern-day architects such as Zaha Hadid and Frank Gehry may be superstars of their profession, but neither is as prolific and revered as was the great Ottoman architect Mimar Koca Sinan (1497–1588). Sinan's best-known buildings adorn the İstanbul skyline and include the magnificent Süleymaniye Mosque, but many believe that his greatest achievement was this exquisite mosque, which is Edirne's major landmark.

Built between 1569 and 1575 by order of Sultan Selim II at the city's highest point, the mosque features four striking 71m-high minarets and was positioned in the centre of an extensive *külliye* (mosque complex) including a *medrese* (Islamic school of higher studies), *darül Hadis* (Hadith school) and *arasta* (arcade of shops). The main entrance is through the western courtyard, home to a lovely marble *şadırvan* (ablutions fountain).

Inside, the broad, lofty dome – at 31.3m, marginally wider than that of İstanbul's Aya Sofya – is supported by eight unobtrusive pillars, arches and external buttresses, creating a surprisingly spacious interior. As they only bear a portion of the dome's weight, the walls are sound enough to hold dozens of windows, the light from which brings out the interior's colourful calligraphic decorations.

Unesco added the mosque and its *külliye* to its World Heritage list in 2011.

Edirne Turkish and Islamic Art Museum MUSEUM
(Edirne Türk-İslam Eserleri Müzesi; ☑225 5748; admission ₺5; ⊘9am-6.30pm Tue-Sun) The small rooms of the elegant *darül Hadis* (Hadith school) in the northeastern corner of the Selimiye's courtyard house an eclectic collection of Ottoman-era artefacts including calligraphy, weaponry, glass, woodwork, ceramics, costumes and jewellery. Some of the rooms feature mannequins in ethnographic-style displays; our favourite is the Circumcision Room (check out the look on the young boy's face!). The handsome 'Tekke Works Room' displays dervish-related Korans, prayer rugs and musical instruments.

Selimiye Foundation Museum MUSEUM
(Selimiye Vakıf Müzesi; ☑212 1133; ⊘9am-5pm Tue-Sun) **FREE** Similar to the Edirne Turkish and Islamic Art Museum, this museum is housed in an equally handsome building in the Selimiye's *külliye* (mosque complex; this time in a *medrese* in the southeastern corner of the courtyard) and showcases a collection of art and artefacts drawn from mosques and religious buildings in and around Edirne.

Edirne Archaeology & Ethnography Museum MUSEUM
(Edirne Arkeoloji ve Etnografya Müzesi; ☑225 1120; Kadır Paşa Mektep Sokak 7; admission ₺5; ⊘9am-6.30pm Tue-Sun) Behind the Selimiye Mosque is this museum with two sections: one archaeological and the other ethnographic. Highlights of the archaeological section include Thracian funerary steles featuring horsemen. The ethnographic section showcases carpets, embroidery, textiles, calligraphy and jewellery; don't miss the wooden objects decorated in the Edirnekâri style, a lacquering technique developed locally during the Ottoman era.

Üç Şerefeli Mosque MOSQUE
(Üç Şerefeli Cami; Hükümet Caddesi) Edirne's *merkez* (town centre) is visually dominated by this mosque, which was built by order of Sultan Murat II between 1437 and 1447 and has four strikingly different minarets. Its

name refers to the *üç şerefeli* (three balconies) on the tallest minaret; the second tallest has two balconies and the remaining two have one balcony each.

The mosque has a wide and beautifully decorated interior dome mounted on a hexagonal drum and supported by two walls and two massive hexagonal pillars. In a style emulated by later Ottoman architects, the partly covered courtyard features a portico with small, beautifully decorated domes.

Old Mosque   MOSQUE
(Eski Camii; Muaffıklarhane Sokak) Though not as prominent on Edirne's skyline as the Selimiye and Üç Şerefeli mosques, the Eski (Old) Mosque is an important landmark in the city and has a large and loyal local congregation. Built between 1403 and 1414, it is the oldest of the city's imperial mosques and features a square, fortress-like form and an arcaded portico topped with a series of small domes. Inside, there are huge calligraphic inscriptions on the walls.

The mosque originally had an extensive *külliye*, but today only its handsome *bedesten* (covered bazaar) remains. This comprises 36 strongrooms covered by 14 domes in two rows of seven. The *bedesten* was the centre of commercial activity in Edirne in the 15th century and the strongrooms were needed to secure valuable goods including jewellery, armour and carpets. Sadly, its stores today sell merchandise that is considerably less impressive.

Kaleiçi   HISTORIC AREA
Roughly translated, *kaleiçi* means 'inside the castle'. In Edirne it is used to describe the old streets to the south of Talat Paşa Caddesi and west of Saraçlar Caddesi. Dating from the medieval period, this is the heart of the old city and it retains a number of ornately decorated timber houses dating from the 18th, 19th and early 20th centuries, as well as a couple of handsome stone civic buildings.

When exploring, look out for the **Kırkpınar Evi** (Kırkpınar House; 212 8622; www.kirkpinar.com; Maarif Caddesi; 10am-noon & 2-6pm) opposite Polis Parkı (Police Park). Its collection of memorabilia associated with oil wrestling is drab, but the building itself is a good example of Edirne's traditional houses. Some of these have undergone recent restoration (the Mihran Hanım Konağı in Gazipaşa Caddesi is a good example), but many are in a sad state of disrepair. Other interesting buildings include the police sta-

tion in Maarif Caddesi and the recently restored Great Synagogue in Manyas Caddesi, which was built in 1906; unfortunately, the synagogue is closed to the public.

◉ North of the Centre

Sultan Beyazıt II Mosque Complex MOSQUE
(Beyazıt II Camii ve Külliyesi; Beyazıt Caddesi, Yıldırım Beyazıt Mahallesi) Standing in splendid isolation on the banks of the Tunca River, this complex was commissioned by Sultan Beyazıt II and built between 1484 and 1488. The mosque's design lies midway between the Üç Şerefeli and Selimiye models: its prayer hall has one large dome, similar to the Selimiye, but it also has a courtyard and fountain like the Üç Şerefeli. The *külliye* includes a *tabhane* (travellers hostel), *tımarhane* (asylum), *tıp medresesi* (medical school) and *darüşşifa* (hospital).

The complex is a 10-minute taxi (₺10) ride from the centre or a longish but pleasant walk down Horozlu Bayır Sokak and across the Yalnıgöz and Sultan Beyazıt II bridges. The Yalnıgöz (Lonely Arch, or Lone Eye) dates from 1570 and was designed by Mimar Sinan; the Beyazıt II dates from 1488. Alternatively, dolmuşes (shared taxis) to Yenimaret ('Y.Maret') from opposite the tourist office pass the complex; you'll need a *dolmuşkart* to ride (see p150).

Museum of Health   MUSEUM
(Sağlık Müzesi; 224 0922; http://saglikmuzesi.trakya.edu.tr; adult/child under 15yr ₺10/free; 9am-5.30pm) The extremely beautiful *darüşşifa* (hospital) and *tıp medresesi* (medical school) in the Sultan Beyazıt II mosque complex now house this museum tracing the history of Islamic medicine. Overseen by Trakya Üniversitesi, the museum highlights innovative treatments developed and utilised in the hospital and medical school here from 1488 to 1909. Mannequins dressed as Ottoman-era doctors, patients and medical students are used in scenes illustrating various medical procedures, and interpretative panels explain the connection between the hospital's physical design and treatments.

Sarayiçi   HISTORIC AREA
It was here, in the 15th century, that Sultan Murat II built the Eski Sarayı (Old Palace). Little remains of this grand structure, which was blown up just before the Russo-Turkish War of 1877–78 to prevent the Russians cap-

KIRKPINAR OIL-WRESTLING FESTIVAL

Officially known as the Tarihi Kırkpınar Yağlı Güreş Festivali (Historic Kırkpınar Oil-Wrestling Festival; http://kirkpinar.org), this testosterone-charged sporting event is famous throughout Turkey and attracts enormous crowds to Edirne for one week in late June or early July every year. The crowds come to cheer on muscular men skimpily clad in a pair of *kispet* (tight leather shorts) and lathered in olive oil, who attempt to wrestle their opponents to the ground or lift them above their shoulders. And no, this is not a headline event on the international gay festival circuit – it's serious, ultra-macho sport, Turkish style.

According to local legend, the festival's origins go back to 1363, when the Ottoman Sultan Orhan Gazi sent his brother Süleyman Paşa with 40 men to conquer the Byzantine fortress at Domuz. The soldiers were all keen wrestlers, and after their victory challenged each other to bouts. Two of them were so evenly matched that they fought for days without any clear result, until both of them finally dropped dead. When the bodies were buried under a nearby fig tree, a spring mysteriously appeared. The site was given the name Kırkpınar ('40 Springs'), in the wrestlers' honour.

The annual three-day contest has been held in Sarayiçi on the outskirts of Edirne since the birth of the republic, and is now preceded by four days of wrestling-themed festivities. Wrestlers, who are classed not by weight but by height, age and experience, compete in 13 categories – from *minik* (toddler) to *baş* (first class) – and dozens of matches take place simultaneously in the Sarayiçi stadium. Bouts are now capped at 30 or 40 minutes, after which they enter 'sudden death' one-fall-wins overtime. When all the fights are decided, prizes are awarded for gentlemanly conduct and technique, as well as the coveted and hotly contested *başpehlivan* (head wrestler) title.

Entry to the first day of the wrestling is free, but tickets are required for the next two. There's a ticket box at the venue, or you can purchase tickets from Biletix (www.biletix.com). Note that accommodation in and around the city over this week fills up fast.

---

turing weapons stored inside. Fortunately, the kitchens where Ottoman palace cuisine was developed have been rebuilt. Today, an area that was once the sultans' private hunting reserve is home to a modern stadium where the famous Kırkpınar oil-wrestling festival is held.

Near the stadium, which is flanked by bronze sculptures of wrestling *başpehlivan* (champions), stands the Adalet Kasrı (Justice Hall; 1561), a stone tower with a conical roof that dates from the time of Süleyman the Magnificent. In front of it are two square columns: on the Seng-i Hürmet (Stone of Respect) to the right, people would place petitions to the sultan, while the Seng-i İbret (Stone of Warning) on the left displayed the heads of high-court officers who had managed to anger the sultan.

Behind the Justice Hall is the small Fatih Köprüsü (Conqueror Bridge; 1452). Across it and on the right is a sombre Balkan Wars memorial; straight ahead and to the left are the scattered ruins of the Eski Sarayı.

To get here, walk north along Hükümet Caddesi and cross the Tunca River on Saraçhane Köprüsü (Saddler's Bridge; 1451); or head north on Mimar Sinan Caddesi and Saray Yolu, and cross the river on Kanumi/

Saray Köprüsü (Kanumi/Palace Bridge), which was designed by Mimar Sinan in 1560. Alternatively, it's a scenic 1km walk along the road to the north of the river from the Sultan Beyazıt II mosque complex.

◉ South of the Centre

In fine weather, the social scene in Edirne moves to the banks of the Tunca and Meriç Rivers, a 20- to 25-minute walk from the tourist office on Hürriyet Meydanı. To join the party, follow Saraçlar Caddesi past the stadium and cross the Tunca Köprüsü, an Ottoman stone humpback bridge dating back to 1615, and then the longer and extremely graceful Meriç Köprüsü, built in 1847. The area around the bridges is packed with restaurants, tea gardens and bars, all great places to come for a drink or a meal in warm weather. The best ones are those on the southern side of the Meriç River, which offer perfect sunset river vistas.

⊨ Sleeping

Sarı Pansiyon PENSION €
(☑ 212 4080; www.saripansiyon.com; Mehmet Karagöz Sokak 17; s/d without bathroom ₺40/80; ☎) Named for its daffodil-yellow exterior,

this unassuming place offers simple rooms with single beds and satellite TV. Shared bathrooms are clean, with 24-hour hot water. The location is convenient but is opposite a school, so it can be noisy in the morning. Though the elderly owner doesn't speak English, he will happily use his computer's translation program to communicate.

Efe Hotel HOTEL €€
(☑213 6080; www.efehotel.com; Maarif Caddesi 13; s/d ₺95/140; ❋@🖲) A time-warp feel dominates at this old-timer on busy (read: noisy) Maarif Caddesi. Rooms have nana-esque decor with worn furniture and fittings, and the basement bar-restaurant where breakfast is served has tartan carpet that must have been ultra-fashionable in the 1970s. It's clean, though, and the English-speaking manager goes out of his way to be helpful.

★ Hotel Edirne Palace HOTEL €€€
(☑214 7474; www.hoteledirnepalace.com; Vavlı Cami Sokak 4; s €45-80, d €60-90; ❋@🖲) Tucked into the backstreets below the Old Mosque, this modern business hotel offers comfortable, bright and impeccably clean rooms with a good range of amenities. Staff are extremely helpful and breakfast is slightly better than average. It's definitely the best sleeping option in the city centre.

Mihran Hanım Konağı HOTEL €€€
(☑225 6409; www.mihranhanim.com; Gazipaşa Caddesi 30; s/d €100/150; ❋🖲) The closest Edirne has to a boutique hotel, this 1905 wooden mansion in the heart of the Kaleiçi area has been fully restored and opened its doors to guests in 2013. Highlights include the winding staircase and the magnificent upstairs foyer. Its nine rooms are comfortable but have disappointingly dowdy decor; each is equipped with tea- and coffee-making facilities.

✖ Eating

The city centre is full of *ciğercisi* (liver restaurants) serving the city's signature dish, *ciğer tava* (thinly sliced calf's liver deepfried and eaten with crispy fried red chillies). It's usually enjoyed with a chaser of *ayran* (yoghurt drink). Other local specialities include *badem ezmesi* (marzipan) and *gaziler helva* (veteran's helva), a rich concoction of butter, flour, milk, sugar and almond.

There's a wide assortment of eateries along Saraçlar and Maarif Caddesis. Note that most of the riverside restaurants south of the centre are open only in summer and are often booked solid at weekends.

Balıkçım Yasem FISH €
(☑225 4247; Balıkpazarı Caddesi 9; fish sandwich ₺4, cooked fish ₺8-12) Appropriately located near the fish fountain just off Saraçlar Caddesi, this tiny eatery next to the city's busiest fishmonger cooks up fresh catch of the day and serves it to a constant stream of takeaway customers or at its five tables on the street.

Niyazi Usta KEBAP €€
(☑213 3372; www.cigerciniyaziusta.com.tr; Alipaşa Ortakapı Caddesi 5/2; porsyon ₺12, half porsyon ₺6; ⊙9am-9pm) This bright, modern and very friendly joint is perhaps the best place in town to try a *porsyon* (portion) of *ciğer tava*. Wash it down with a glass of *ayran* (yoghurt drink) or *şalgam* (sour turnip juice).

Balkan Piliç TURKISH €€
(☑225 2155; Saraçlar Caddesi 14; porsyon ₺4.50-12; ⊙11am-4pm Mon-Sat) The *piliç* (chicken) roasting in the window signals the house speciality at this extremely popular *lokanta* (eatery serving ready-made food). Order a *porsyon* (portion) with a side order of *pilav* (plain rice or rice cooked with bulgur or lentils). Alternatively, choose from the daily-changing array of meat and vegetable stews in the bain-marie.

Köfteci Osman TURKISH €€
(☑214 1717; http://edirnelikofteciosman.com; Saraçlar Caddesi 3; ciğer or köfte ₺12; ⊙11am-10pm) Widely recommended by locals for its tasty *ciğer tava* and *köfte* (meatballs), Osman has a prime location at the top of the city's main pedestrian drag so is easy to locate. Efficient waiters ensure that the indoor and outdoor tables turn over quickly.

Melek Anne CAFE €€€
(☑213 3263; www.melekanne.com; Maarif Caddesi 18; mains ₺23; ⊙8am-10pm; 🖉) In this liver-obsessed city, 'Angel Anne' is one of the few places catering to vegetarians. Occupying a 120-year-old house with a shady attached garden, it serves a daily-changing menu of home-style, ready-made dishes, including *mantı* (Turkish ravioli), *yaprak sarma* (stuffed vine leaves), hearty vegetable stews and *köfte*.

♥ Drinking & Nightlife

There are *cay bahçesis* (tea gardens) all over town. The most popular are near the Tunca and Meriç bridges south of the centre, in the Polis Parkı on Maarif Caddesi, and around the Mimar Sinan statue in the city centre. Most of the bar action is in the northern side streets between Saraçlar and Maarif Caddesis or along the street joining the two bridges.

Çalgılı Meyhane   PUB, RESTAURANT
(☑213 8945; Saraçlar Caddesi; ⊘9pm-late) A boozy atmosphere, friendly staff and live *halk meziği* (folk music) five days per week are the attractions at this traditional Turkish tavern. Basic *meyhane* (pub) food is available, but it's fine to stick with drinks only; a huge tankard of ice-cold Efes costs a mere ₺12. Make sure that you tip the musicians before you leave.

Kahverengi   BAR
(☑214 4210; www.kahverengibistro.com; Orhaniye Caddesi 14; ⊘10am-3am) Its laid-back ambience, pleasant outdoor deck and bargain snack-and-beer combo deals make Kahverengi popular with a youthful local clientele. Efes is the tipple of choice, but there are also imported beers and luridly coloured cocktails on offer.

Mado   CAFE
(☑225 6236; Saraçlar Caddesi; ☎) Local residents are as enamoured of the Mado chain of *dondurma* (Turkish ice cream) cafes as the rest of their compatriots, and flock to this huge branch near Hürriyet Meydanı to have coffee with friends, watch the football or play a game of *tavla* (backgammon) in upstairs Cafe M.

🛍 Shopping

Traditional Edirne souvenirs include *meyve sabunu* (fruit-shaped soaps) and *badem ezmesi* (marzipan).

Keçecizade   FOOD & DRINK
(☑212 1261; www.kececizade.com; Saraçlar Caddesi 50) The residents of Edirne are particularly partial to sweet treats, as is evident by the huge number of *şekerlemes* (sweet shops) scattered through the city. Keçecizade is one of two popular local chains specialising in *lokum* (Turkish delight) and *badem ezmesi*, and is a good place to sample both. There's another branch (☑225 2681; www.kececizade.com; Belediye Dükkanları (Eski Camii Karşısı) 4) opposite the Old Mosque.

Arslanzade   FOOD & DRINK
(www.arslanzade.com.tr; Belediye Dükkanları (Eski Camii Karşısı) 2) Keçecizade's main competitor,

---

THRACIAN VINEYARD ROUTE

Vines have been cultivated in Thrace (Trakya) since ancient times. Homer wrote about the honey-sweet black wine produced here in his *Iliad*, and generations of local farmers have capitalised on the rich soil, flat geography and benign climate of this region to grow grapes to be used for wine and spirit production.

In late 2013 the Turkish government introduced new regulations on alcoholic drinks that made it illegal to advertise, publicise or sell alcohol over the internet. The wine industry initially went into shock, but it quickly realised that to stay viable it would need to look at alternative methods of marketing its products. One of the most innovative solutions was developed by a group of 12 boutique wine producers in this region, who banded together to devise the Trakya Bağ Rotası (Thracian Vineyard Route; www.trakyabagrotasi.com). Inspired by Italy's hugely successful Strade del Vino (Wine Roads) network, this local equivalent aims to entice visitors to visit Thracian vineyards, enjoy local gastronomy, investigate regional heritage and admire the area's stunning scenery. Guided tours of the vineyards are offered from the first 'bud breaks' in late April to the harvest in October.

The route passes through mountains, forests and a variety of micro-climates surrounded by three seas (the Sea of Marmara, the Aegean Sea and the Black Sea). Eight of the vineyards have restaurants and cafes where local wine and food are matched, and three offer accommodation. One of these, the highly regarded Arcadia Vineyards (☑0533 514 1490; www.arcadiavineyards.com), is an hour's drive southeast of Edirne and is most definitely worth a detour en route to/from İstanbul or the Gallipoli Peninsula. Another, Barbare (☑212-257 0700; www.barbarewines.com), is just outside Tekirdağ on the road to the Gallipoli Peninsula.

Arslanzade produces *badem ezmesi* and *lokum* but also offers delicious *devâ-i misk helvası* (sweet made with sugar, egg white and 41 different spices) and *kallavi kurabiye* (biscuit made with pistachio, saffron and honey).

Ali Paşa Covered Bazaar   MARKET
(☺7am-sunset) Mimar Sinan designed this long and highly atmospheric bazaar in 1569. Inside, Turkuaz (☑ 214 1171; Ali Paşa Çarşısı 125) is one of the best spots in the city to buy *meyve sabunu*.

Selimiye Arastası   MARKET
(Selimiye Arcade; ☺sunrise-sunset) Also known as the Kavaflar Arastası (Cobblers' Arcade), this historic market below the Selimiye Mosque was part of the original *külliye* (mosque complex). Shops include branches of Arslanzade (p149) and Keçecizade (p149).

❶ Information

Banks and money exchanges are clustered around the Ali Paşa Covered Bazaar on Talat Paşa Caddesi.

Tourist Office (☑ 213 9208; edirnetourisminformation@gmail.com; Hürriyet Meydanı 17; ☺8.30am-5.30pm daily 15 Apr–30 Sep, closed Sat & Sun 1 Oct–14 Apr) Very helpful, with English-language brochures and a city map.

❶ Getting There & Around

BUS & DOLMUŞ

Edirne's otogar (bus station) is 9km southeast of the centre on the access road to the E80. *Servises* (shuttle buses) provided by the bus companies provide free transfers between the otogar and the city centre for ticketed passengers. From Edirne, the **servises** depart from outside the ramshackle *çay bahçesi* on the outer southwest corner of the Selimiye Mosque complex approximately 45 minutes before ticketed departure times. A taxi between the otogar and the city centre costs ₺28.

Dolmuşes service the city and also travel to the Bulgarian and Greek borders. Tickets are not available on board, so you will need to purchase a pre-paid *dolmuşkart* from the **Edirne Toplu Ulaşım Sistemi** (ETUS) office in the Belediye Dükkânları (Eski Camii Karşısı) on Talat Paşa Caddesi opposite the Old Mosque.

Çanakkale (₺35, four hours) At least four buses daily on **Truva** (www.truvaturizm.com) and **Metro** (www.metroturizm.com.tr).

İstanbul Frequent buses to the Büyük Otogar in Esenler (₺30, 2¾ hours) on Metro, Ulusoy and Nilüfer. Demand is high, so book ahead.

Kapıkule (₺7, 25 minutes) Dolmuşes run to this Bulgarian border crossing, 18km northwest,

from a stop near the Şekerbank branch opposite the tourist office on Talat Paşa Caddesi.

Pazarkule The nearest Greek border post is 9km southwest of Edirne. Catch a dolmuş to Karaağaç (₺3, 15 minutes) from the stop on the southern side of Talat Paşa Caddesi near the tourist office and tell the driver that you want to go to Pazarkule.

Sofia (Bulgaria) (₺65, 5½ to 6½ hours) Five services daily on Metro Turizm.

Tekirdağ
☑ 0282 / POP 150.920

Overlooking an attractive bay on the northern shore of the Sea of Marmara, Tekirdağ features a bustling waterfront area complete with parks, playgrounds and *çay bahçesis*. Though definitely not worth a trip in itself, the waterfront and a scattering of timber houses dating from the 18th century make the town a reasonable pit stop en route to/from Greece or the Gallipoli Peninsula.

The small **tourist office** (☑261 1698; www.tekirdagkulturturizm.gov.tr; ☺8.30am-5.30pm) is located near the main *iskele* (jetty) on Atatürk Bulvarı.

◉ Sights

Tekirdağ Archaeological & Ethnographic Museum   MUSEUM
(Tekirdağ Arkeoloji ve Etnografya Müzesi; ☑261 2082; Rakoczi Caddesi 1; ☺9am-5pm Tue-Sun) **FREE** Housed in the Tekirdağ Vali Konağı (Governor's Mansion), a fine Ottoman Revival–style building dating from 1927, this modest museum gives a fascinating glimpse into the history of Thrace. The most striking exhibit is the setting of marble furniture and silver plates from the Naip tumulus (burial mound) dating back to the late 4th century BC; this would have formed a celebratory setting for the serving of wine.

To get here from the tourist office, walk west along the waterfront for about 1km, cross Atatürk Bulvarı and walk up the steep flight of stairs to Vali Konağı Caddesi. The museum is to the right.

Rákóczi Museum   MUSEUM
(Rakoczi Müzesi; ☑263 8577; Hikmet Çevik Sokak 21; admission ₺3; ☺9am-noon & 1-5pm Tue-Sun) This house museum is a shrine to Prince Ferenc (Francis) II Rákóczi (1676–1735), who led the first Hungarian uprising against the Habsburgs between 1703 and 1711. Forced into exile, the Transylvanian was given asylum by Sultan Ahmet III in 1720 and lived in this

pretty 18th-century timber *konak* (mansion) for a number of years. The *konak*'s interior fittings are good-quality reproductions, as the originals were returned to Kassa in Hungary (now Košice in Slovakia). Displays include portraits, weapons and letters.

The museum is west of the Tekirdağ Archaeological & Ethnographic Museum, on the opposite side of the road.

Namık Kemal House
MUSEUM

(Namık Kemal Evi; ☑ 262 9128; Namık Kemal Caddesi 7; ⊙ 8.30am-noon & 1-5pm Mon-Fri) **FREE** Another house museum celebrating a great man, this time Tekirdağ's most famous son, Namık Kemal (1840–88). A nationalist poet, journalist and social reformer, Kemal had a strong influence on Atatürk, who called him 'the father of my ideas'. Exhibits in the 19th-century timber and stone house include photographs of Kemal, Atatürk and old Tekirdağ. You'll find it close to the Tekirdağ Valiliği (Governor's Office).

🛏 Sleeping

Golden Yat Hotel
HOTEL €€

(☑ 261 1054; www.goldenyat.com; Yalı Caddesi 21; s ₺90-110, d ₺130-150; ❋ 🞉) The pick of a limited bunch of sleeping options in town, this 1970s-era hotel opposite the waterfront claims three-star status but is looking increasingly worn each time we visit. Front rooms can be noisy, but the quieter and slightly cheaper options at the rear are smaller and darker.

🍴 Eating

Tour buses often pause for lunch in Tekirdağ, pulling up opposite the waterfront at the row of restaurants serving the city's famous *Tekirdağ köftesi (*bullet-shaped *köfte* served with a spicy red sauce).

Özcanlar
KÖFTE €€

(☑ 263 4088; www.ozcanlarkofte.com; Liman Karşısı 68, Atatürk Bulvarı; köfte ₺10-25) The most popular of the *köfte* restaurants overlooking the waterfront, Özcanlar has been serving up a limited range of soups, meat dishes and local desserts since 1953. Tables on the outdoor terrace fill fast, as the cafeteria-style dining room can be noisy.

❶ Getting There & Away

The otogar is located 1km northeast of the main waterfront promenade. Arriving by bus from İstanbul (₺17, 2½ hours) or Edirne (₺17, two hours), it's an easy walk down Çiftlikönü

Caddesi. Buses to/from Eceabat (₺37, three hours) and Çanakkale (₺37, 3½ hours) travel via both the otogar and the waterfront and can be flagged down along Atatürk Caddesi.

Dolmuşes travel throughout the town and its outlying suburbs. Tickets cost ₺1.75 and can be purchased from the driver.

Gallipoli (Gelibolu) Peninsula
☑ 0286

Today, the Gallipoli battlefields are protected landscapes covered in pine forests and fringed by idyllic beaches and coves. However, the bloody battles fought here in 1915 are still alive in Turkish and foreign memories and hold important places in the Turkish, Australian and New Zealand national narratives. Australians and New Zealanders view the peninsula, which is now protected as the Gallipoli Historical National Park (Gelibolu Yarımadası Tarihi Milli Parkı; Map p152; http://gytmp.milliparklar.gov.tr), as a place of pilgrimage and visit here in their tens of thousands each year, but they are outnumbered by Turks, who, drawn by the legend of the courageous 57th regiment and its commander, Mustafa Kemal (the future Atatürk), are travelling here in ever-increasing numbers to pay their respects.

Two dates attract the largest crowds each year: the Turkish naval victory in the Dardanelles is commemorated in Çanakkale on 18 March, and the Allied landings are commemorated on 25 April. Politicians' speeches and plenty of flag-waving are the main features of the Turkish commemoration (they did win, after all), but a more sombre mood prevails at the dawn service marking the anniversary of the landing of the Australian and New Zealand Army Corps (Anzacs), which attracts up to 10,000 travellers from Down Under each year.

The most convenient base for visiting the battlefields is Eceabat, on the western shore of the Dardanelles, but it is an ugly and noisy town – Çanakkale, on the eastern shore, is accessed via car ferry (25 minutes) from Eceabat and is a much better option. Also worth considering as a base is the unspoiled island of Gökçeada, a 75-minute car-ferry ride from Kabatepe. Very few options exist in the battlefield area itself.

Having your own transport will maximise your opportunities for exploration and is highly recommended. The alternative is

THRACE & MARMARA GALLIPOLI (GELIBOLU) PENINSULA

Gallipoli Peninsula

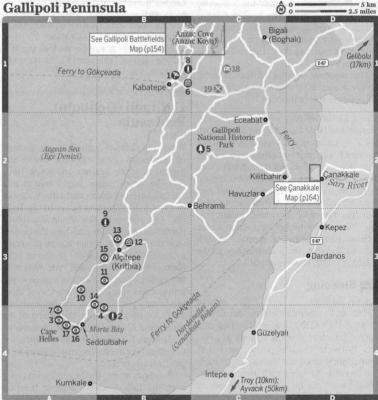

Gallipoli Peninsula

⊙ Sights
1 Brighton Beach	B1
2 Çanakkale Şehitleri Anıtı	B4
3 Cape Helles British Memorial	A4
4 French War Memorial & Cemetery	B4
5 Gallipoli Historical National Park	C2
6 Gallipoli Simulation Centre	B1
7 Lancashire Landing Cemetery	A4
8 Mehmetçiğe Derin Saygı Anıtı	B1
9 Nuri Yamut Monument	B3
10 Pink Farm Cemetery	A3
11 Redoubt Cemetery	B3
12 Salim Mutlu War Museum	B3
13 Sargı Yeri Cemetery	B3
14 Skew Bridge Cemetery	A3
15 Twelve Tree Copse Cemetery	B3
16 'V' Beach Cemetery	A4
17 Yahya Çavuş Şehitliği	A4

⊜ Sleeping
18 Gallipoli Houses	C1

⊗ Eating
19 Doyuranlar Aile Çay ve Gözleme	C1

to base yourself in Çanakkale or Eceabat, where eating, drinking and sleeping options are close at hand and where you will be able to hire a private guide with transport or join an organised bus tour of the battlefields.

Many tour companies offer one-day tours from İstanbul that involve 10 to 12 hours'

travel time in a minibus. We do not recommend these as they are exhausting and we have received reports of drivers exceeding speed limits and driving dangerously so as to minimise time on the road.

The website Visit Gallipoli (www.anzac-site.gov.au) is full of useful information.

History

Not even 1500m wide at its narrowest point, the Strait of Çanakkale (Çanakkale Boğazı), better known as the Dardanelles or the Hellespont in English, has always offered the best opportunity for travellers – and armies – to cross between Europe and Asia Minor.

King Xerxes I of Persia forded the strait with a bridge of boats in 481 BC, as did Alexander the Great a century and a half later. In Byzantine times it was the first line of defence for Constantinople, but by 1402 the strait was under the control of the Ottoman Sultan Beyazit I (r 1390–1402), which allowed his armies to conquer the Balkans. Beyazit's great-grandson Mehmet the Conqueror fortified the strait as part of his grand plan to conquer Constantinople (1453), building eight separate fortresses. The strait remained fortified after he defeated the Byzantines, signalling to foreign powers that this strategic sea passage was firmly in Ottoman hands.

The Ottomans remained neutral at the outbreak of WWI, but in October 1914 they joined the Central Powers and closed the Dardanelles, blocking the Allies' major supply route between Britain, France and their ally Russia. In response, the First Lord of the British Admiralty, Winston Churchill, decided that it was vitally important that the Allies take control of both the strait and the Bosphorus, which meant capturing İstanbul. His Allied partners agreed, and in March 1915 a strong Franco-British fleet attempted to force the Dardanelles. It was defeated on 18 March in what the Turks commemorate as the Çanakkale Naval Victory (Çanakkale Deniz Zaferi).

Undaunted, the Allies devised another strategy to capture the strait. On 25 April, British, Australian, New Zealand and Indian troops landed on the Gallipoli Peninsula; in a diversionary manoeuvre, French troops landed at Kum Kale near Çanakkale. The landings on the peninsula were a disaster for the Allies, with the British 29th Division suffering horrendous losses at Cape Hellas and the Anzac troops landing at a relatively inaccessible beach north of their planned landing point near Gaba Tepe (Kabatepe). Rather than overcoming the Turkish defences and swiftly making their way across the peninsula to the strait (the planned objective), the Allies were hemmed in by their enemy, forced to dig trenches for protection and stage bloody assaults to try to improve their position. After nine months of ferocious combat but little headway, the Allied forces withdrew in December 1915 and January 1916.

The outcome at Gallipoli was partly due to bad luck and leadership on the Allied side, and partly due to reinforcements to the Turkish side brought in by General Liman von Sanders. But a crucial element in the defeat was that the Allied troops landed in a sector where they faced Lieutenant Colonel Mustafa Kemal. A relatively minor officer, the future Atatürk had managed to guess the Allied battle plan correctly when his commanders did not, and he stalled the invasion in spite of bitter fighting that wiped out his regiment. Kemal commanded in full view of his troops throughout the campaign, miraculously escaping death several times. Legend has it that at one point a piece of shrapnel hit him in the chest but was stopped by his pocket watch. His brilliant performance made him a folk hero and paved the way for his promotion to *paşa* (general).

The Gallipoli campaign – in Turkish the Çanakkale Savaşı (Battle of Çanakkale) – resulted in a total of more than half a million casualties, of which 130,000 were deaths. The British Empire saw the loss of some 36,000 lives, including 8700 Australians and 2700 New Zealanders. French casualties numbered 47,000 (making up over half the entire French contingent); 8800 Frenchmen died. Half the 500,000 Ottoman troops were casualties, with almost 86,700 killed.

⊙ Sights

Gallipoli Historical National Park encompasses 33,500 hectares of the peninsula. There are several different signage systems in use: normal Turkish highway signs; national-park administration signs; and wooden signs posted by the Commonwealth War Graves Commission. This can lead to confusion because the foreign and Turkish troops used different names for the battlefields, and the park signs don't necessarily agree with those erected by the highway department. We've used both English and Turkish names.

There are currently 40 Allied war cemeteries at Gallipoli, and at least 20 Turkish ones. The principal battles took place on the peninsula's western shore, around Anzac Cove (Anzac Koyu), 12km northwest of

Gallipoli Battlefields

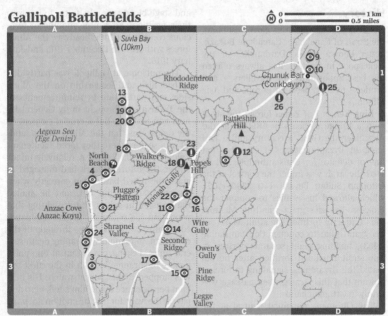

0 ——— 1 km
0 ——— 0.5 miles

Gallipoli Battlefields

◎ Sights

1 57 Alay Cemetery	B2
2 Anzac Commemorative Site	B2
3 Anzac Cove (Anzac Koyu)	A3
4 Arıburnu Cemetery	A2
5 Arıburnu Sahil Anıtı	A2
6 Baby 700 Cemetery	C2
7 Beach (Hell Spit) Cemetery	A3
8 Canterbury Cemetery	B2
9 Chunuk Bair New Zealand Cemetery & Memorial	D1
10 Conkbayırı Atatürk Anıtı	D1
11 Courtney's & Steele's Post Cemetery	B2
12 Düztepe Monument	C2
13 Embarkation Pier Cemetery	B1
14 Johnston's Jolly	B3
15 Kanlısırt Kitabesi	B3
16 Kesikdere Cemetery	B2
17 Lone Pine Cemetery	B3
Mesudiye Topu	(see 6)
18 Nek	B2
19 New Zealand No 2 Outpost Cemetery	B1
20 No 2 Outpost Cemetery	B1
21 Plugge's Plateau Cemetery	B2
22 Quinn's Post Cemetery	B2
23 Sergeant Mehmet Monument	B2
24 Shrapnel Valley Cemetery	A3
25 Suyatağı Anıtı	D1
26 Talat Göktepe Monument	C1

Eceabat, and in the hills east of the cove. If you wish to identify a particular grave when you are here, the Commonwealth War Graves Commission website (www.cwgc.org) will be a useful resource.

◉ Northern Peninsula

About 3km north of Eceabat, the road to Kabatepe heads west into the park. We describe the sites in the order most motorists are likely to visit them.

Gallipoli Simulation Centre

If you are travelling independently, be sure to start your tour at this extremely impressive and informative museum (Çannakale Destanı Tanıtım Merkezi; Map p152; ☑ 810 0050; http://canakkaledestani.milliparklar.gov.tr; Kabatepe; admission ₺13; ⊙ 9.30-11am & 1.30-5pm) roughly 1km east of the village of Kabatepe. Opened with great fanfare in 2012, it comprises 11 gallery rooms in which high-tech 3D simulation equipment takes the viewer on a historical journey through the Gallipoli naval and land campaigns, taking both the Turkish and Allied points of view. The technology allows visitors to choose their presentation language and interact with the display. There's a small cafe in which you can recover if it all gets a bit too realistic.

Kabatepe Village

The small harbour here was probably the object of the Allied landing on 25 April 1915. In the predawn dark it is possible that uncharted currents swept the Allies' landing craft northwards to the steep cliffs of Arıburnu – a bit of bad luck that may have sealed the campaign's fate from the start. Today there's little in Kabatepe except for a campground, cafe and dock for ferries to Gökçeada island. Just north of the promontory is the stretch of sand known as Brighton Beach (Map p152), a favourite swimming spot for Anzac troops during the campaign. Today, this is the only officially sanctioned swimming spot on the peninsula. A small Gelibolu Milli Parkı (Gallipoli National Park) office here sells maps, souvenirs and snacks.

Anzac Cove

Heading north along the coastal road from Brighton Beach, it's a short drive to Beach (Hell Spit) Cemetery (Map p154). Before it, a rough track cuts inland to Lone Pine (1.5km) and, across the road from the car park at the cemetery, another track heads inland to Shrapnel Valley Cemetery (Map p154) and Plugge's Plateau Cemetery (Map p154).

Following the road for another 400m from the turn-off, or taking the footpath from Beach Cemetery past the WWII bunker, brings you to Anzac Cove (Map p154). This now extremely narrow stretch of sand beneath and just south of the Arıburnu cliffs was where the ill-fated Allied landing began on 25 April 1915. Ordered to advance inland, the Allied forces at first gained some ground but later in the day met with fierce resistance from the Ottoman forces under the leadership of Mustafa Kemal, who had foreseen where they would land and disobeyed an order to send his troops further south to Cape Helles.

In August of the same year a major offensive was staged in an attempt to advance beyond the beach up to the ridges of Chunuk Bair and Sarı Bair (Yellow Slope). It resulted in the battles at Lone Pine and the Nek, the bloodiest of the campaign, but little progress was made.

Another 300m along is the Arıburnu Sahil Anıtı (Arıburnu Coastal Memorial; Map p154), a moving Turkish monument with Atatürk's famous words of peace and reconciliation, spoken in 1934:

'To us there is no difference between the Johnnies and the Mehmets...You, the mothers, who sent your sons from faraway countries, wipe away your tears; your sons are now lying in our bosom...After having lost their lives in this land, they have become our sons as well.'

Just beyond the memorial is Arıburnu Cemetery (Map p154) and, 750m further north, Canterbury Cemetery (Map p154). Between them is the Anzac Commemorative Site (Anzac Tören Alanı; Map p154) at North Beach, where dawn services are held on Anzac Day. This is where the much-photographed Anzac monument is located. From it, look up towards the cliffs and you can easily make out the image in the sandy cliff face nicknamed 'the Sphinx' by young diggers (Aussie infantrymen) who had arrived from Australia via Egypt.

Less than 1km further along the seaside road on the right-hand side are the cemeteries at No 2 Outpost (Map p154), set back inland from the road, and New Zealand No 2 Outpost (Map p154). The Embarkation Pier Cemetery (Map p154) is 200m beyond the New Zealand No 2 Outpost on the left.

Towards Lone Pine

Returning to the Gallipoli Simulation Centre, you should then follow the signs to Lone Pine, just under 3km uphill.

En route, the first monument you'll come to, Mehmetçiğe Derin Saygı Anıtı (Map p152), on the right-hand side of the road about 1km from the junction, is dedicated to 'Mehmetçik' (Little Mehmet, the Turkish 'tommy' or 'digger'), who carried a Kiwi soldier to safety.

Another 1200m brings you to the Kanlısırt Kitabesi (Bloody Ridge Inscription; Map p154), which describes the battle of Lone Pine from the Turkish viewpoint.

Lone Pine

Lone Pine (Kanlısırt; Map p154), 400m uphill from Kanlısırt Kitabesi, is perhaps the most moving of all the Anzac cemeteries. Australian forces captured the Turkish positions here on the afternoon of 6 August 1915. During the battle, which was staged in an area the size of a soccer field, over 4000 men died and thousands more were injured. The trees that shaded the cemetery were swept away by a forest fire in 1994, leaving only one: a lone pine planted from the seed of the original solitary tree, which stood here at the beginning of the battle and gave the battlefield its name.

The tombstones carry touching epitaphs and the cemetery includes the grave of the youngest soldier to die here, a boy of just 14. The remains of trenches can be seen just behind the parking area.

From here, it's another 3km up the one-way road to the New Zealand Memorial at Chunuk Bair.

Johnston's Jolly to Quinn's Post

Progressing up the hill from Lone Pine, the ferocity of the battles becomes more apparent; at some points the trenches are only a few metres apart. The order to attack meant certain death to those who followed it, and virtually all did as they were ordered on both sides.

The road marks what was the thin strip of no-man's land between the two sides' trenches, as it continues to the cemeteries Johnston's Jolly (Kırmızı Sırt; Map p154), 200m on the right beyond Lone Pine, Courtney's & Steele's Post (Map p154), roughly the same distance again, and Quinn's Post (Map p154), 100m uphill.

57 Alay & Kesikdere Cemeteries

About 1km uphill from Lone Pine, across the road from the Little Mehmet statue, is the cemetery (57 Alay Şehitliği; Map p154) and monument for the Ottoman 57th Regiment, which was led by Mustafa Kemal and was almost completely wiped out on 25 April while halting the Anzac attempt to advance to the high ground of Chunuk Bair.

The statue of an old man showing his granddaughter the battle sites represents Hüseyin Kaçmaz, who fought in the Balkan Wars, the Gallipoli campaign and at the fateful Battle of Dumlupınar during the War of Independence. He died in 1994 aged 111, the last surviving Turkish Gallipoli veteran.

Down some steps from here, the Kesikdere Cemetery (Map p154) contains the remains of another 1115 Turkish soldiers from the 57th and other regiments.

Sergeant Mehmet Monument & the Nek

About 100m uphill past the 57th Regiment Cemetery, a road goes west to the Sergeant Mehmet Monument (Map p154), dedicated to the Turkish sergeant who fought with rocks and his fists after he ran out of ammunition, and the Nek (Map p154). It was at the Nek on the morning of 7 August 1915 that the 8th (Victorian) and 10th (Western Australian) Regiments of the third Light Horse Brigade vaulted out of their trenches into withering fire and were cut down before they reached the enemy line, an episode immortalised in Peter Weir's 1981 film *Gallipoli*.

Baby 700 Cemetery & Mesudiye Topu

About 200m uphill on the right from the access road to the Nek is the Baby 700 Cemetery (Map p154) and the Ottoman cannon called the Mesudiye Topu (Map p154). Named after its height above sea level in feet, Baby 700 was the limit of the initial attack, and the graves here are mostly dated 25 April.

Düztepe & Talat Göktepe Monuments

The Düztepe Monument (Map p154), uphill from the Baby 700 Cemetery, marks the spot where the Ottoman 10th Regiment held the line. Views of the strait and the surrounding countryside are superb. About 1km further on is a monument (Map p154) to a more recent casualty of Gallipoli: Talat Göktepe, chief director of the Çanakkale Forestry District, who died fighting the devastating forest fire of 1994.

Chunuk Bair

At the top of the hill, some 500m past the Talat Göktepe Monument, turning right at the T-junction takes you east to the Suyatağı Anıtı (Watercourse Monument; Map p154). Having stayed awake for four days and nights, Mustafa Kemal spent the night of 9 August here, directing part of the counterattack to the Allied offensive.

Back at the T-junction, turn left for Chunuk Bair (known as Conk Bayiri in Turkish), the first objective of the Allied landing in April 1915, and now the site of the Chunuk Bair New Zealand Cemetery and Memorial (Conkbayırı Yeni Zelanda Mezarlığı ve Anıtı; Map p154) and the Conkbayırı Atatürk Anıtı (Conkbayırı Atatürk Memorial; Map p154), a huge statue of the Turkish hero.

As the Anzac troops made their way up the scrub-covered slopes on 25 April, Mustafa Kemal brought up the 57th Infantry Regiment and gave them his famous order: 'I am not ordering you to attack, I am ordering you to die. In the time it takes us to die, other troops and commanders will arrive to take our places.'

Chunuk Bair was also at the heart of the struggle for the peninsula from 6 to 10 August 1915, when some 16,000 men died on this ridge. The Allied attack from 6 to 7 August, which included the New Zealand Mounted Rifle Brigade and a Maori contingent, was deadly, but the attack on the following day was of a ferocity which, according to Mustafa Kemal, 'could scarcely be described'.

◉ Southern Peninsula

From Kabatepe it's about 12km to the village of Alçıtepe, formerly known as Krithia. A few metres north of the village's main intersection is the Salim Mutlu War Museum (Salim Mutlu Müsezi; Map p152; admission ₺1; ⊙8am-8pm), a hodgepodge of rusty finds from the battlefields, giving a sense of just how much artillery was fired. At the main intersection, a sign points right to the Turkish Sargı Yeri Cemetery (Map p152), approximately 1.5km away, with its enormous statue of 'Mehmet' and solid Nuri Yamut Monument (Map p152). Take the first left for the Twelve Tree Copse Cemetery (Map p152), 2km away, and the Pink Farm Cemetery (Map p152), 3km away.

From Pink Farm, the road passes the Lancashire Landing Cemetery (Map p152). Turn right 1km before Seddülbahir village for the Cape Helles British Memorial (Map p152), a commanding stone obelisk honouring the 20,000-plus Britons and Australians who perished in this area and have no known graves. The initial Allied attack was two-pronged, landing on 'V' Beach at the tip of the peninsula as well as Anzac Cove. Yahya Çavuş Şehitliği (Sergeant Yahya Cemetery; Map p152) remembers the Turkish officer who led the resistance to the Allied landing here, causing heavy casualties. 'V' Beach Cemetery (Map p152) is visible 500m downhill.

North of Seddülbahir, the road divides; the left fork leads to the Skew Bridge Cemetery (Map p152), followed by the Redoubt Cemetery (Map p152). Turn right and head east, following signs for Abide or Çanakkale Şehitleri Anıtı at Morto Bay, and you'll pass the French War Memorial & Cemetery (Map p152). French troops, including a regiment of Africans, attacked Kumkale on the Asian shore in March 1915 with complete success, then re-embarked and landed in support of their British comrades-in-arms at Cape Helles, where they were virtually

---

GALLIPOLI UNDER THREAT

It seems a world away from the early 1980s, when Australian film director Peter Weir spent two days scampering over the hills of the Gallipoli Peninsula and saw not a living soul. The numbers of visitors have grown by leaps and bounds since then and most of these are Turks. *Belediyes* (town and city councils) from Edirne to Van send their citizens here by the busload, and tens of thousands of Turkish students come here between March and September each year as a result of the government stipulation that every Turkish school student must make an organised excursion to the Gallipoli battlefield at least once.

This increased popularity has made conservation of the national park particularly challenging, and many people feel that the local government and park administration don't always handle the situation effectively. In recent years the flow of bus and coach traffic has become extremely heavy, and supposed 'improvements' such as car parks and road-widening schemes have caused considerable damage to some areas, most shockingly at Anzac Cove. Other changes are having an effect on the visitor experience, notably at the major Turkish monuments (Chunuk Bair, 57 Alay Cemetery, Çanakkale Şehitleri Anıtı), where snack and souvenir stands promote an atmosphere that is carnival-like rather than contemplative.

Crowds of travellers also turn up for the dawn Anzac Day memorial service on 25 April, one of the most popular events in Turkey for foreign visitors, and almost a rite of passage for young Australians in particular. In fact, the service has become so popular that the Turkish and Commonwealth governments were forced to devise a ballot scheme for tickets in 2015, the centenary of the landings.

All of this means that travellers are best to time their visits for dates other than Anzac Day (25 April) and Çanakkale Naval Victory Day (18 March). It's also sensible to avoid weekends between mid-March and mid-June and again in September, when most Turks visit.

wiped out. The rarely-visited French cemetery is extremely moving, with rows of metal crosses and five white-concrete ossuaries each containing the bones of 3000 soldiers.

The Çanakkale Şehitleri Anıtı (Çanakkale Martyrs' Memorial; Map p152), also known as the Abide (Monument), is a gigantic stone structure that commemorates all the Turkish soldiers who fought and died at Gallipoli.

☞ Tours

Guided tours are popular ways to explore the battlefields. The recommended tour providers listed below generally offer three-hour morning tours and five- or six-hour afternoon tours, including transport by minibus and guide. Most also include lunch.

Think carefully about what tour company you book with. While researching, we tested one high-profile outfit that was operating a dodgy cash-only policy and whose guide provided historically dubious information and hassled for tips. Needless to say, it's not listed here. We have heard similar stories about this and other companies from many readers.

★ Crowded House Tours   TOUR
(☑ 814 1565; www.crowdedhousegallipoli.com; Huseyin Avni Sokak 4, Eceabat) Based at the Eceabat hotel of the same name, this is the most professional of the tour companies operating on the peninsula and is heartily recommended, especially if you can join a tour led

by the affable and extremely knowledgeable Bülent 'Bill' Yılmaz Korkmaz. Its core offering is an afternoon tour of the main Anzac battlefields and cemeteries (€20).

Other options include a morning tour of Cape Helles (€25), a morning snorkelling around a WWI shipwreck at Anzac Cove (€15), an afternoon tour by boat of the Anzac landing sites (€50) and two-day Gallipoli and Troy packages from İstanbul (prices on application).

Bülent Korkmaz also leads walking tours of the battlefields.

Hassle Free Travel Agency   TOUR
(☑ 213 5969; www.anzachouse.com; Cumhuriyet Meydanı 59, Çanakkale) Operating from its base in Çanakkale, this long-standing company offers a half-day tour of the Anzac battlefields and cemeteries (€40) and a package including a boat trip to the Anzac landing beaches, a snorkel at Anzac Cove and a visit to the Kabatepe Simulation Centre (€50). It also offers Gallipoli and Troy tours with onward transportation to İstanbul or Selçuk/ Ephesus.

Kenan Çelik   TOUR
(☑ 217 7468; www.kcelik.com; half-/full-day tours for small groups €120/150) One of Turkey's foremost experts on the Gallipoli campaign, Kenan Çelik has retired from his position as lecturer in English language and literature at Çanakkale Onsekiz Mart University and

WALKING THE BATTLEFIELDS

The best way to explore the battlefields is undoubtedly in the footsteps of the original combatants. Walking the hills and around the gullies of this landscape offers a glimpse into the physical challenges that troops faced in 1915. It also allows walkers to enjoy the wonderful views and landscape of the national park.

The Australian Government's Department of Veterans Affairs website (www.anzacsite. gov.au) includes details of a one-day walk exploring the main area held by Anzac troops during the campaign. This starts in North Beach, includes sites such as Anzac Cove and Lone Pine, and ends on the high ground near the Nek and Walker's Ridge. Walk instructions, downloadable audio commentary and plenty of historical information is available on the website.

Crowded House Tours offers several walking tours. Expert guides lead a number of trails including a one-day tour of the batlefields of the Anzac sector; a half-day 'New Zealand Trail' following the advance of NZ troops to Chunuk Bair; and a full-day walk around the Helles sector following the paths of British troops. Guides will try to accommodate special interests, including visiting particular graves. Tours cost between €47 and €255 per person depending on how many people are in the group. The cost includes lunch and transport to/from the start and finish points from Eceabat or Çanakkale.

Walkers should be sure to bring sturdy shoes, as the terrain can be steep and difficult in parts. Hats and sunblock are essential in the warmer months; a rain jacket is useful at other times of the year. Don't forget water and food.

now concentrates on conducting private tours of the battlefields. He offers full-day tours concentrating on significant Anzac or Turkish sites, and can also cover Suvla Bay and Cape Helles.

The prices cited assume that the client has transportation. If not, an extra charge of €50/100 applies.

🛏 Sleeping & Eating

There are a number of accommodation options around Seddülbahir in the southern part of the peninsula, but none are worthy of recommendation.

★ **Gallipoli Houses** BOUTIQUE HOTEL €€€
(Map p152; ☑ 814 2650; www.thegallipolihouses. com; Kocadere; s €45-60, standard d €55-70, superior & deluxe d €65-95; ⊗ closed mid-Nov–mid-Mar; ❈) Located in a farming village within the national park, this is the intelligent accommodation choice when visiting the peninsula. The 10 rooms are split between the original stone house and a purpose-built section with countryside views. Note that there is usually a minimum stay of two nights and that children under the age of 10 are not accommodated.

Rooms are spacious and comfortable, and there is a pleasant bar area where guests can enjoy a drink and chat before dinner (€15). A lunch box costs €7. Eric, the Belgian co-host, and his Turkish wife Ozlem are equally at ease preparing home-cooked Turkish cuisine as tailoring a battlefields itinerary.

Doyuranlar Aile Çay ve Gözleme TURKISH €
(Map p152; ☑ 814 1652; mains ₺6-10; ⊗ from 7.30am; ☎) The village women in charge of this roadside eatery and *çay bahçesi* (tea garden) midway between Eceabat and Kabatepe serve up huge breakfast platters, *köfte* (meatballs) and *menemen* (eggs scrambled with white cheese, tomatoes and peppers), but regulars opt for the house speciality: crisp and delicious *gözleme* (savoury pancakes) washed down with a glass of *ayran* (yoghurt drink).

❶ Information

BACKGROUND RESEARCH

Peter Weir's 1981 film *Gallipoli* is a classic of Australian cinema and is well worth viewing before your visit. In 2014, Australian–New Zealand actor Russell Crowe released his directorial debut, *The Water Diviner*. The film tells the story of an Australian father who makes his way to Turkey to ascertain the fate of his three sons, all missing in action after the Battle of Gallipoli.

Reading at least one of following books before your visit will allow you to make the most of your time here:

Gallipoli Award-winning Australian historian and journalist Les Carlyon's 2001 book is highly regarded by military historians and is a gripping, magnificently written account of the campaign.

Gallipoli Battlefield Guide (Çanakkale Muharebe Alanları Gezi Rehberi) The English-language version of this reference book by Gürsel Göncü and Şahin Doğan was published in 2006 and is still available at some bookshops in Çanakkale and Eceabat.

Exploring Gallipoli: Australian Army's Battlefield Guide to Gallipoli This ebook was written by Lieutenant Colonel Glenn Wahlert, a historian with the Australian Army History Unit, and released in 2012.

Gallipoli Military historian Peter Hart, an oral historian at the Imperial War Museum's sound archive, focuses on the contribution of British troops to the campaign in his 2011 book.

Gallipoli This 1956 classic by the Australian-born foreign correspondent Alan Moorehead was re-released in a Perennial Classics edition in 2002.

❶ Getting There & Around

With your own transport you can easily tour the northern battlefields in a day. Trying to do both the northern and southern parts of the peninsula is possible within one day, provided you get a very early start.

DOLMUŞ

The only regular public-transport options on the peninsula are the dolmuş between Eceabat and Kilitbahir (₺1.50, every 45 minutes) and the dolmuş between Eceabat and Kabatepe (₺3.50, 15 minutes). The latter meets ferries from Gökçeada year-round and makes more frequent runs in the summer months. There are usually a couple of dolmuşes each day from Kilitbahir to Seddülbahir and Alçıtepe, but the timetable changes frequently.

FERRY

Gestaş (☑ 444 0752; www.gestasdenizulasim. com.tr) operates ferries across the Dardanelles between Çanakkale and Eceabat and Çanakkale and Kilitbahir. It also crosses the Aegean between Kabatepe and Gökçeada.

TAXI

A taxi between Kabatepe and Eceabat will cost approximately ₺40.

1. Lone Pine cemetery (p155) **2.** Anzac Cove (p155)
3. Cape Helles British Memorial (p157)

Gallipoli Battlefields

Pilgrimage is the oldest – and often the most rewarding – form of travel. In Turkey there are a number of ancient pilgrimage destinations, but only one dates from modern times and draws both local and international visitors: the pine-scented peninsula where the bloody Gallipoli campaign of WWI unfolded.

Cemeteries

There were almost 130,000 Turkish and Allied deaths at Gallipoli and the battlefields are home to more than 60 meticulously maintained cemeteries. Places for contemplation and commemoration include the Allied cemeteries at Beach (Hell Spit), Arıburnu (Anzac Cove), Lone Pine, Chunuk Bair and V Beach; and the Turkish 57 Alay (57th Regiment) and Kesikdere cemeteries.

Memorials

Gallipoli is a place where bravery and sacrifice are honoured and where the narratives of modern nations have been forged. The most famous memorial on the peninsula is the Arıburnu Sahil Anıtı (Arıburnu Coastal Memorial), which records Atatürk's famous words of peace and reconciliation between the 'Johnnies' and the 'Mehmets'. Other memorials include the stone obelisk at Cape Helles that commemorates the 20,000-plus Britons and Australians who perished on the southern peninsula and have no known graves.

Landing Beaches

Few places are so closely associated with national identity as Anzac Cove, where Australian and New Zealand troops landed on 25 April 1915. Today, the annual Anzac Day dawn service is held at nearby North Beach. Casualties at Anzac Cove were relatively minor, as opposed to those incurred on the five beaches at Cape Helles – most notably V and W Beaches – where thousands of deaths occurred.

Eceabat

☑ 0286 / POP 5541

Eceabat (ancient Maydos) is an unremarkable waterfront town on the southern shore of the Dardanelles. It is notable only for its proximity to the main Gallipoli battlefields and for its ferry link to Çanakkale. Ferries dock by the main square (Cumhuriyet Meydanı), which is ringed by hotels, restaurants, ATMs, a post office, bus-company offices, and dolmuş and taxi stands.

🛏 Sleeping

Hotel Crowded House   HOSTEL €

(☑ 814 1565; www.crowdedhousegallipoli.com; Hüseyin Avni Sokak 4; s/d/tr €23/30/39; ❇@🛜) The one decent budget hotel close to the battlefields, Crowded House has basic rooms with comfortable beds and clean bathrooms. The hotel's biggest draw is its association with the tour company of the same name – these guys can organise everything you will need when visiting Gallipoli, and do so in a friendly and professional fashion.

A simple breakfast is included in the room charge, and there's a courtyard restaurant at the rear where other meals (including summer barbecues) are on offer.

🍴 Eating

Liman Balık Restaurant   FISH €€

(Liman Fish Restaurant; ☑ 814 2755; www.limanrestaurant.net; İstiklal Caddesi 67; meze ₺6-16, mains ₺10-25; ⊗noon-10pm; 🛜) Next to the water (Liman means 'Harbour'), this laid-back place is particularly pleasant on summer nights, when seats on the outdoor terrace are highly prized (book ahead). The food, service and wine list are unexpectedly impressive. Choose meze from the refrigerated cabinet and make sure that you inspect the catch of the day before ordering your fish.

★ Kilye Suvla Lokanta   MODERN TURKISH €€€

(☑ 814 1000; www.suvla.com; Suvla Winery, Çınarlıdere 11; pizza ₺15-28, salads ₺12-18, mains ₺25; ⊗lokanta noon-3pm, tasting room & concept store 8.30am-5.30pm) Since launching its first vintages in 2012, local outfit Suvla has taken Turkey's wine scene by storm. Its 60 hectares of certified organic vineyards are located near Kabatepe, but its winery, complete with restaurant, tasting room and produce store, is on Eceabat's outskirts. The food here is as impressive as the industrial-chic setting, and is worth a dedicated visit.

Suvla produces wines in five categories, ranging from its base tipples, the Kabatepe Kırmızı (Red), Beyaz (White) and Blush, to the mightily impressive Grand Reserve Cabernet Sauvignon and Roussane Marsanne. All can be sampled in the winery's tasting room (tastings ₺7 to ₺30) or in the restaurant, which features a huge glass wall looking into an ageing room full of oak barrels. The menu ranges from modern twists on Turkish classics such as *köfte* to fresh salads and Turkish-style pizzas.

The winery is at the end of a road off Atatürk Caddesi, in the southwestern corner of town.

🍷 Drinking & Nightlife

Boomerang Bar   BAR

(Cumhuriyet Caddesi 102) Run by Mersut, a rakı (aniseed brandy)–loving local who revels in his role as host, the Boomerang is a kitschy beach shack that somehow makes the perfect place for a beer after touring the battlefields. It's at the town's northern entrance. Free camping is unofficially available on a nearby stretch of rocky beach.

ℹ Information

Free maps of the town are available from the information booth at the ferry port.

ℹ Getting There & Away

Çanakkale Ferries cross the Dardanelles in both directions (per person/car ₺2.50/29, 25 minutes) every hour on the hour between 7am and midnight, and roughly every two hours after that. Contact **Gestaş** (☑ 444 0752; www.gestasdenizulasim.com.tr). The ticket box is right next to where passengers enter the ferries.

Bus tickets can be purchased from the Truva and Metro offices on the ground floor of the Grand Eceabat Hotel building opposite the port.

Kabatepe In summer there are regular dolmuşes to Kabatepe ferry dock (₺3.50, 15 minutes); in winter they only meet the ferries. If asked, the dolmuş will drop you at the Gallipoli Simulation Centre, 750m southeast of the bottom of the road up to Lone Pine and Chunuk Bair.

Kilitbahir Dolmuşes every 45 minutes (₺1.50, 10 minutes).

İstanbul Buses to the Büyük Otogar in Esenler leave regularly (₺45, five hours); those to Ataşehir Otogar near Kadıköy on the Asian side are less frequent. **Truva Turizm** (☑ 212 2222; www.truvaturizm.com) offers the best service.

Kilitbahir

Just across the Narrows from Çanakkale, Kilitbahir (Lock of the Sea) is a tiny fishing harbour dominated by a massive fortress that was closed for restoration at the time of research. Built by Mehmet the Conqueror in 1452 and given a grand seven-storey interior tower a century later by Süleyman the Magnificent, it and Çimenlik Kalesi in Çanakkale ensured that the Ottomans retained control of the Dardenelles.

The text next to the huge image of the soldier on the hill to the right of Kilitbahir reads 'Traveller halt! The soil you tread once witnessed the end of an era'.

Gestaş (✆ 444 0752; www.gestasdenizulasim.com.tr) operates a ferry service to/from Çanakkale (per person/car ₺1.50/24, 20 minutes) every 30 to 60 minutes between 7am and 11.15pm.

Çanakkale

✆ 0286 / POP 116,078

If you thought that Çanakkale was only worth visiting as a launching point for the battlefields, think again. The presence of the highly regarded Çanakkale Onsekiz Mart University endows this small city with a sizeable student population that loves nothing more than eating, drinking and partying in the atmospheric cobbled lanes around the *saat kulesi* (clock tower, built 1897) and along the sweeping *kordon* (waterfront promenade). Joining their revelries is a highlight of any visit.

The undisputed hub of the region, Çanakkale is replete with mythological associations. It was from the ancient town of Abydos immediately north that Leander swam across the Hellespont every night to see his love Hero; and it was in the Dardanelles that Helle, the daughter of Athamas, was drowned here in the legend of the Golden Fleece, giving the waterway its ancient name. Close by and still existing are the remnants of ancient Troy, which Homer wrote about in his epic poem the *Iliad*.

◎ Sights & Activities

Dardanelles Straits Naval Command Museum MUSEUM
(Çanakkale Boğaz Komutanliği Deniz Müzesi; ✆ 213 1730; Çimenlik Sokak; park entrance free,

museum admission ₺6; ⊙ 9am-noon & 1.30-5pm Tue, Wed & Fri-Sun) At the southern end of the *kordon* is a park dotted with guns, cannons and military artefacts. Behind the park is **Çimenlik Kalesi** (Meadow Castle), built by order of Mehmet the Conqueror in 1452, and near the park entrance is a small military museum containing exhibits on the Gallipoli battles and some war relics. Museum ticket-holders can also board the replica of the *Nusrat* minelayer, which played a significant role in the Çanakkale Naval Victory.

Trojan Horse MONUMENT
Wolfgang Petersen's 2004 movie *Troy* has had a big impact on the Çanakkale region, including boosting visitor numbers to the archaeological site and endowing the northern stretch of the *kordon* with this wooden horse, which was used in the film shoot. There's a model of the ancient city and information displays underneath.

Kent Müzesi MUSEUM
(City Museum; ✆ 214 3417; www.canakkalekentmuzesi.com; Fetvane Sokak 31; ⊙ 10am-7pm Tue-Sun Apr-Aug, to 5pm Sep-May) FREE The lives of Çanakkale's residents since Ottoman times are the focus of this small museum, which has drawn on oral histories for the content of many of its display panels. There are also photographs, newspaper articles and a few artefacts on show.

Yalı Hamam HAMAM
(Çarşı Caddesi 5; full treatment ₺45; ⊙ 8am-11pm) Women may not feel comfortable in this 17th-century hamam, as it is a mixed facility and the attendants are all male. That said, it's clean, the *göbektaşı* (raised platform used for massage) is piping hot, and the massage will please those who like a bit of a pummel.

⭐ Festivals & Events

Çanakkale is almost unbearably overcrowded around the following events.

Çanakkale Naval Victory COMMEMORATION
(Çanakkale Deniz Zaferi) Turks celebrate this day on 18 March.

Anzac Day COMMEMORATION
Australians and New Zealanders descend on the Gallipoli Peninsula on and around 25 April.

Çanakkale

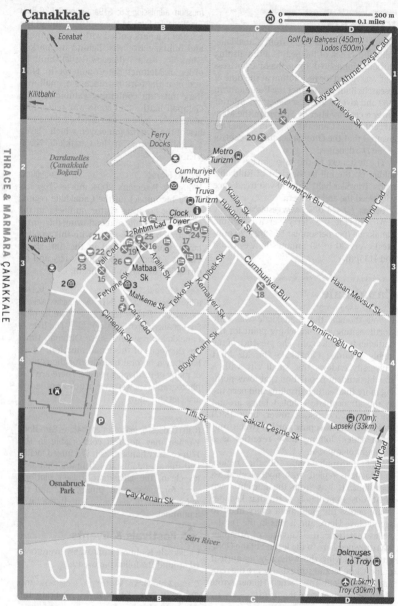

Troia Festival

CULTURAL

(Troia Festivali) Parades, concerts and exhibitions take over the *kordon* (waterfront promenade) and big-name Turkish music acts perform at free concerts in Cumhuriyet Meydanı for five days in mid-August.

Hellespont & Dardanelles Swim

SPORT

On 30 August (Turkey's Victory Day), the Dardanelles Strait is closed to maritime traffic for 1½ hours when swimmers race the 4.5km from Eceabat to Çanakkale (www.swimhellespont.com).

Çanakkale

THRACE & MARMARA ÇANAKKALE

🛏 Sleeping

If you intend to be in town on 18 March or 25 April, book well in advance and be prepared to pay a premium.

Anzac House Hostel   HOSTEL €
(☑213 5969; www.anzachouse.com; Cumhuriyet Meydanı 59; dm/s/d without bathroom & excluding breakfast ₺25/45/70; ☎) Recent years haven't been kind to Çanakkale's only backpacker hostel, with comfort and cleanliness levels plunging since the days when it was run by the Hassle Free tours outfit. Fortunately, that crew is still based on the ground floor and was due to reclaim the lease in late 2014, promising a full renovation and improvement in services.

★ Anzac Hotel   HOTEL €€
(☑217 7777; www.anzachotels.com; Saat Kulesi Meydanı 8; s €30-40, d €40-55; ❄@) An extremely professional management team ensures that this recently renovated and keenly priced hotel opposite the clock tower is well maintained and has high levels of service. Rooms are a good size, with tea- and coffee-making facilities and double-glazed windows. The convivial bar on the mezzanine shows the *Gallipoli* and *Troy* movies every night. Parking costs €2.50.

The same team operates the nearby **Grand Anzac** (☑216 0016; www.anzachotels.com; Kemalyeri Sokak 11; s €35-45, d €45-60; ❄@☎) and **Comfort Anzac** (☑217 2018; www.anzachotels.com; Kemalyeri Sokak 44; s €35-45, d €45-60) hotels, which offer slightly larger rooms at a marginally higher price. The Grand Anzac also has a restaurant.

Hotel Limani   HOTEL €€€
(☑217 2908; www.hotellimani.com; Yalı Caddesi 12; s ₺90-160, d ₺140-240; ❄@☎) Overlooking the harbour, the Limani deserves its reputation as Çanakkale's best top-end hotel. Rooms are on the small side, but are comfortable and have pretty, very feminine decor. It's worth paying extra for a land or sea view, as the budget alternatives are windowless. The downstairs restaurant-bar serves decent meals and a mighty fine buffet breakfast.

Hotel des Etrangers   BOUTIQUE HOTEL €€€
(☑214 2424; http://hoteldesetrangers.com.tr; Yalı Caddesi 25-27; r €90-100; ❄☎) This historic hotel (Troy archaeologist Schliemann himself once stayed here) is an atmospheric sleeping choice offering eight rooms with whitewashed wooden floors, inlaid timber ceilings and tasteful country-style furniture. The four rooms at the front are larger and have small balconies overlooking the harbour and bustling Yalı Caddesi. Note that windows aren't double glazed and the location can be noisy.

Artur Hotel   HOTEL €€€
(☑213 2000; www.hotelartur.com; Cumhuriyet Bulvarı 28; s ₺150, d ₺200; ❄@☎) A bland but safe choice, this modern business hotel close to the ferry port offers large rooms with comfortable beds and clean but frill-free bathrooms. It is slated for a renovation in 2015, so prices may rise.

🍴 Eating

The *kordon* is lined with licensed restaurants and cafes.

Çonk Coffee
CAFE €

(Kemalyeri Sokak 3; snacks from ₺3; ☺8am-10pm) A display of old radios, cameras and photographs adorns the walls of this small and extremely friendly cafe, which serves Turkish and espresso coffee, hot dogs, sandwiches and the city's best *tost*s (toasted sandwiches).

Hüsmanoğlu Babalığın Torunları
SWEETS €

(☑217 7733; www.peynirhelvasi.net; Yalı Caddesi 29; per kilogram ₺18) Locals love *peynir helvası* (a dessert of flour or semolina, butter and sugar) and often head to this store or nearby Babalık Peynir Helvası (☑217 3610; Yalı Caddesi 47) to buy a tray full of this rich treat to take home.

Cevahir Ev Yemekleri
TURKISH €

(☑213 1600; Fetvane Sokak 15; meals from ₺8; ☺11am-9pm) Cheap and cheerful is the motto at this popular *ev yemekleri* (eatery serving home-cooked food) close to the clock tower. Choose from bean, vegetable and meat dishes in the bain-marie. Set meals including a bowl of soup, salad and main dish with rice are available for less than ₺10. No alcohol.

Assos Cafe
CAFE €€

(☑0532 784 6484; Kayserili Ahmet Paşa Caddesi 27; meals ₺10-20; ☺8am-2am; 🛜) Head to this hipster hang-out near the Trojan Horse for a hamburger, fajita or pizza washed down with cold Efes. Getting louder as the night gets older, the music is indie rather than Turkish pop (Nick Cave was on the turntable when we last visited). Regulars like to meet up with friends, use the free wi-fi and play *tavla* (backgammon).

Gülen Pide
KEBAP, PIDE €€

(☑212 8800; Cumhuriyet Bulvarı 27; pides ₺7.50-11.50, kebaps ₺11.50-25; ☺11am-10pm) The open kitchen here produces pides, *lahmacun*s (Arabic-style pizzas) and kebaps that are enjoyed in a cafeteria-style space with white-tiled floors and high ceilings. Quality is so-so, but the waiters are friendly and prices are reasonable.

★Yalova
SEAFOOD €€€

(☑217 1045; www.yalovarestaurant.com; Gümrük Sokak 7; mezes ₺6-22, mains ₺20-40) Locals have been coming here for slap-up meals since 1940. A two-storey place on the *kordon*, it serves seafood that often comes straight off the fishing boats moored out front. Head upstairs to choose from the meze and fish displays, and be sure to quaff some locally produced Suvla wine with your meal.

Kavala
FISH €€€

(Kavala Balık Lokantası; ☑214 3519; Kayserili Ahmetpaşa Caddesi 5; meze ₺6-22, mains ₺15-40; ☺noon-midnight) The outdoor terrace of this extremely friendly place on the northern stretch of the *kordon* is always packed with locals, so you should book ahead to secure a table or be prepared to sit inside. The decor is Greek island style, but the food is traditional Turkish, with all the usual meze and fish standards on offer.

🍷 Drinking & Nightlife

Çanakkale is full of students, so it has a healthy cafe, bar and club scene. Fetvane Sokak near the clock tower has so many bars and clubs that locals call it Barlar Sokağı (Bar Street). The city is unusual in that many of the *çay bahçesi* (tea gardens) and cafes along the *kordon* serve alcohol as well as tea.

★Yalı Hanı
TEA GARDEN, BAR

(Fetvane Sokak 26; ☺closed winter months) Hidden in the wisteria-covered courtyard of a late-19th-century caravanserai is this atmospheric hybrid *çay bahçesi* and bar that doubles as a performance and film-festival venue. It's a favourite haunt of boho types, who linger over glasses of wine and earnest conversation after checking out the art exhibitions that are often held in the upstairs space.

★Golf Çay Bahçesi
TEA GARDEN

(Tea Garden; Gazi Bulvarı; ☺8am-10pm) One of the best spots to be when the sun sets over the Dardanelles, Golf has a huge outdoor terrace where you can enjoy a beer or glass of tea while admiring the view. It's just past the northern end of the *kordon*, near the Necip Paşa Mosque.

Şakir'in Yeri
CAFE, BAR

(☑217 3877; Gümrük Sokak 1; ☺7am-midnight) Dominating the cafe action at the southern end of the *kordon*, Şakir'in Yeri is as popular for breakfast (the pastries are delicious) as it is for afternoon games of *tavla* (backgammon) and sunset drinks. The people-watching opportunities both here and at the similarly popular Donanma Aile Çay Bahçesi, opposite, are stellar.

Öküz Kültür Cafe Bar
BAR

(☑ 214 1655; http://okuzkultur.com/tr/canakkale/; Fetvane Sokak 17; ⊙ from noon) A busy program of live music (everything from electronica to Turkish folk) and regular happy hours makes this a mainstay of the student party scene.

Lodos
CLUB

(☑ 0531 424 2500; https://tr-tr.facebook.com/LodosBar17; Nara Sokak 1; ⊙ 5pm-1.30am) This thumping club at the northern end of the *kordon* (waterfront promenade) spins Turkish pop for its party-focused patrons and offers drink deals for early birds. Check its Facebook page for the program.

Hayal Kahvesi
CLUB

(☑ 217 0470; www.hayalkahvesicanakkale.com; Saat Kulesi Yanı; ⊙ 5pm-1.30am) Live rock bands take the stage every night at this old-timer near the clock tower.

ⓘ Information

Çanakkale is centred on its harbour, with a PTT booth, ATMs and public phones right by the docks, and hotels, restaurants, banks and bus offices all close by.

Tourist Office (☑ 217 1187; İskele Meydanı 67; ⊙ 8.30am-5.30pm Mon & Fri, 10am-12.30pm & 1.30-4pm Sat & Sun) Strategically located between the ferry pier and the clock tower, this office can supply a city map, information about the battlefields and dolmuş timetables.

ⓘ Getting There & Away

AIR

Anadolu Jet (www.anadolujet.com), operated by Turkish Airlines, flies to/from Ankara three times per week (₺260, 90 minutes). A municipal minibus meets flights and travels into the city centre (₺2); by taxi it's ₺20.

FERRY

Bozcaada (₺15) Passenger ferry only. Departs Wednesday, Saturday and Sunday at 9am, returning at 7pm.

Eceabat (₺2.50/29 per person/car, 25 minutes) Departs every hour on the hour between 5am and midnight, and every one to two hours after that.

Gökçeada (₺2.50/29 per person/car, 2½ hours, Sunday at 8.30pm)

Kilitbahir (₺1.50/24 per person/car, 20 minutes) Departs every 30 to 60 minutes between 7.30am and 12.30am from either the main pier or the smaller pier to the south.

BUS

The easiest way to get to/from Çanakkale on public transport is by bus. The otogar is 1km inland of the ferry docks, beside a large Carrefour supermarket, but many buses pick up and drop off at the ferry dock. We have noted services offered by **Metro Turizm** (☑ 213 1260; www.metroturizm.com.tr) and **Truva Turizm** (☑ 212 2222; www.truvaturizm.com) as they offer the most frequent service schedules, but other companies also service the city.

Ankara (₺57, 10 hours) One daily on Truva and two on Metro.

Bursa (₺35, 4½ hours) At least four daily on both Truva and Metro.

Edirne (₺35, 4½ hours) At least two daily on both Truva and Metro.

İstanbul (₺45, six hours) Services to the Büyük Otogar in Esenler on the European side (Metro and Truva) and to the Ataşehir Otogar near Kadıköy on the Asian side (Truva).

İzmir (₺40, 5¾ hours) Via Ayvalık (₺30, 3¼ hours) Frequent services on Truva and Metro.

Troy (Truva)
☑ 0286

History

This area was first inhabited during the early Bronze Age (late 4th millennium BC). The walled cities called Troy I to Troy V (3000–1700 BC) had cultures similar to that of the Bronze Age, but Troy VI (1700–1250 BC) took on a different Mycenae-influenced character, doubling in size and trading prosperously with the region's Greek colonies. By the time of Troy VI, the city probably covered the entire plateau, making it one of the largest towns in the Aegean region. An earthquake brought down the city walls in 1350 BC, but these were rebuilt. There is evidence of widespread fire and slaughter around 1250 BC (Troy VII), which leads many historians to believe that this is when the Trojan War occurred. What is known of the economic and political history of the Aegean region in this period suggests that the real cause of the war was intense commercial rivalry between Troy and the mercantile Mycenaean kingdom, the prize being control of the Dardanelles and the lucrative trade with the Black Sea.

The city was abandoned by the end of the 2nd millennium BC but was reoccupied by Greek settlers from Lemnos in the 8th century BC (Troy VIII, 700–85 BC). In 188 BC it was identified by the Romans

Troy (Truva)

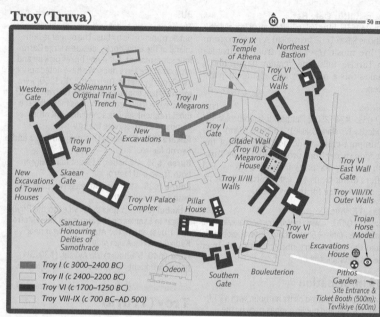

Troy IX Temple of Athena
Northeast Bastion
Troy VI City Walls
Western Gate
Schliemann's Original Trial Trench
Troy II Megarons
Troy I Gate
Citadel Wall (Troy II) & Megaron House
Troy VI East Wall Gate
New Excavations
Troy II Ramp
Troy II/III Walls
Troy VIII/IX Outer Walls
New Excavations of Town Houses
Skaean Gate
Troy VI Palace Complex
Pillar House
Troy VI Tower
Trojan Horse Model
Sanctuary Honouring Deities of Samothrace
Excavations House
Pithos Garden
Troy I (c 3000–2400 BC)
Troy II (c 2400–2200 BC)
Troy VI (c 1700–1250 BC)
Troy VIII-IX (c 700 BC–AD 500)
Odeon
Southern Gate
Bouleuterion
Site Entrance & Ticket Booth (500m); Tevfikiye (600m)

as the Ilion of Homer and recognised as the mother city of Rome (Ilium Novum), being granted exemption from taxes. The city prospered under Roman rule and survived a severe earthquake in the early 6th century. Abandoned once again in the 9th century, it was reoccupied in the later Byzantine period and not finally deserted until well into the Ottoman period.

The archaeological site was added to Unesco's World Heritage list in 1998. In the Unesco citation, the ruins are described as the most significant demonstration of the first contact between the civilisations of Anatolia and the Mediterranean world.

Discovering Troy

Up until the 19th century, many historians doubted whether ancient Troy had ever existed. One man who was convinced of its existence – to an almost obsessive level – was the German businessman Heinrich Schliemann (1822–90), who in 1870 received permission from the Ottoman government to excavate a hill near the village of Hisarlık, which archaeologists had previously identified as a possible site for the city.

Schliemann was more of an eager treasure hunter than a methodical archaeologist

and he quickly tore open the site, uncovering the remains of a ruined city, which he confidently identified as the Troy of Homeric legend. He also found a great cache of gold artefacts that he named 'Priam's Treasure'.

In his haste, Schliemann had failed to appreciate that Troy was not a single city but rather a series of settlements built one on top of the other over the course of about 2500 years. Subsequent archaeologists have identified the remains of nine separate Troys, large sections of which were damaged during Schliemann's hot-headed pursuit of glory. Furthermore, it was soon established that his precious treasures were not from the time of Homer's Troy, but from the much earlier Troy II.

Schliemann's dubious antics continued after the excavation, when he smuggled part of Priam's Treasure out of the Ottoman Empire. Much of it was displayed in Berlin, where it was seized by invading Soviet troops at the end of WWII. Following decades of denials about their whereabouts, the treasures were eventually found hidden away in the Pushkin Museum in Moscow, where they remain today.

⊙ Sights

Ruins of Troy   ARCHAEOLOGICAL SITE
(☑283 0536; adult/child under 12yr ₺20/free;
☺8am-7pm Apr-Oct, to 4.30pm Nov-Mar) If you
come to Troy expecting a rebuilt ancient city
along the lines of Ephesus, you'll be disappointed. The site resembles an overgrown
archaeological dig and it's very difficult to
imagine what the ancient city would have
looked like. Fortunately, an informative
audioguide (₺10) helps to evoke the ancient
city for those who are visiting without a tour
guide.

As you approach the ruins, take the stone
steps up on the right. These bring you out on
top of what was the outer wall of Troy VIII/
IX, from where you can gaze on the fortifications of the east wall gate and tower of
Troy VI.

Go back down the steps and follow the
boardwalk to the right, between thick stone
walls and up a knoll, from where you can
look at some original (as well as some reconstructed) red-brick walls of Troy II/III.
The curved protective roof above them is
the same shape and height as the Hisarlık
mound before excavations began in 1874.

Continue following the path, past the
northeast bastion of the heavily fortified city
of Troy VI, the site of a Graeco-Roman Troy
IX Temple of Athena and, later, the walls of
Troy II/III. You can make out the stone foundations of a megaron (building with porch)
from the same era.

Next, beyond traces of the wall of Early/
Middle Troy (Troy I south gate) are more remains of megarons of Troy II, inhabited by

a literal 'upper class' while the poor huddled
on the plains.

The path then sweeps past Schliemann's
original trial trench, which cut straight
through all the layers of the city. Signs
point out the nine city strata in the trench's
15m-high sides.

Just round the corner is a stretch of wall
from what is believed to have been the
two-storey-high Troy VI Palace Complex,
followed by traces from Troy VIII/IX of a
sanctuary to unknown deities. Later, a new
sanctuary was built on the same site, apparently honouring the deities of Samothrace.
Eventually, the path passes in front of the
Roman Odeon, where concerts were held,
and, to the right, the Bouleuterion (Council
Chamber), bringing you back to where you
started.

⟲ Tours

Two Gallipoli Peninsula tour companies
(p158) offer half-day guided tours of Troy (€
25 to €32). Both will also organise a full-day
program including a morning at Troy, lunch
in Eceabat and an afternoon on the battlefields (around €75). Local guide Uran Savaş
is based in the village of Tevfikiye, next to
the ruins. He runs Trpoa Pension, speaks excellent English and conducts private tours of
the archaeological site (₺150).

🛏 Sleeping & Eating

The vast majority of visitors stay in Çanakkale and visit Troy on a day trip. However,
those camping or in a campervan may wish
to stay nearby.

THRACE & MARMARA TROY (TRUVA)

DON'T MISS

TROY'S NEW MUSEUM

The number of visitors to Troy has been steadily growing since the release of the *Troy*
movie in 2004 (take a bow, Brad Pitt) and as a result Turkey's Ministry of Culture and
Tourism is building a state-of-the-art museum for the archaeological site. A national
architectural competition was launched in 2011 and the winner, İstanbul-based firm
Yalın Mimarlık, was announced in 2012. Its winning design features a cubic building that
is inspired by the form of an excavated artefact. Clad in rusty metal panels, the cube is
accessed via a ramp leading underground and will include conservation laboratories
and storage areas for the Troy collection, as well as a cafe and exhibition spaces where
artefacts excavated from the site will be displayed. These will include the 'Troy Gold', a
collection of 24 gold jewellery pieces that were found at or near Troy and that date to
c 2400 BC. Loaned to Turkey by the Penn Museum in Pennsylvania, USA, they are sure
to be a highlight and also send a message to the Pushkin Museum in Russia that if
Priam's Treasure were to be loaned or gifted to the museum it would be given a fitting
home. The new museum is due to open in mid-2015.

Troia Pension PENSION €

(☎283 0571; www.troiapension.com; Truva Mola Noktası, Tevfikiye; camp/campervan sites without breakfast €15, s/d €20/50; ✴☎) A short walk from the ruins is this simple place behind a cafe and souvenir store. Run by tour guide Uran Savaş, it offers four twin rooms and powered sites for visitors with tent or campervan; these include squeaky-clean showers and toilets as well as a facility for changing toilet water in vans. Meals are available in the cafe.

❶ Getting There & Away

Dolmuşes to Troy (₺5, 35 minutes, hourly) leave on the half-hour between 9.30am and 4.30pm (7pm April to mid-October) from a station at the northern end of the bridge over the Sarı River in **Çanakkale** and drop passengers at the archaeological site's car park. Returning, dolmuşes leave on the hour between 7am and 5pm (8pm in summer).

Gökçeada

☑0286 / POP 8830

'Heavenly Island' is a spectacular Aegean outpost 11 nautical miles from the Gallipoli Peninsula. On weekends and holidays during the summer months it is popular with residents of İstanbul and İzmir, who are drawn by its unspoiled landscape, sandy beaches and Greek-influenced culture. At other times of the year it is a tranquil, windswept place where visitors are rare and the surroundings are truly bucolic.

It's a mystery to us why Gökçeada isn't more popular as a base for those visiting the battlefields. A ferry links the island with Kabatepe at the heart of the Gallipoli Peninsula, carries both cars and passengers, and takes only 75 minutes. There is a small but alluring range of accommodation options on offer and plenty of opportunities for swimming, windsurfing, trekking and cultural tourism.

Gökçeada was once a predominantly Greek (Rum) island known as Imbros or İmroz. During WWI it was an important base for the Gallipoli campaign; indeed, Allied commander General Ian Hamilton stationed himself at the village of Aydıncık (then Kefalos) on the island's southeastern coast. Along with its smaller island neighbour to the south, Bozcaada, Gökçeada was ceded to the new Turkish Republic in 1923 as part of the Treaty of Lausanne but was exempted from the population exchange, retaining a predominantly Greek population. However, in 1946 the Turkish authorities installed the first wave of Turkish settlers from the Black Sea region, starting a clear but unstated process of 'Turkification' that reached its height in the 1960s and 1970s when up to 6000 ethnic Turks from the mainland – many from the east – were relocated here. Greek schools were forceably closed, many Greek churches were desecrated and 90% of the island's cultivatable land was appropriated from Greek residents, most of whom had had no choice but to leave. In 1970, the island was renamed Gökçeada by the Turkish government. These days, there are approximately 250 Greek residents, most of whom are elderly.

The island's inhabitants earn their living through fishing, sheep- and cattle-rearing, farming and tourism. There are three small-scale wine producers and a larger olive-oil

Gökçeada

industry that uses fruit from Ladolia trees that are claimed to be unique to the island.

◉ Sights

Inland Greek Villages

Heading west from Gökçeada Town, better known as Merkez (Centre), you'll pass Zeytinli (Aya Theodoros) after 3km, Tepeköy (Agridia) another 7km on, and Dereköy (Shinudy) another 5km west. All were built on hillsides overlooking the island's central valley to avoid pirate raids. Many of the stone houses in these villages are deserted and falling into disrepair, particularly at Dereköy, which is reminiscent of the ghost town of Kayaköy, near Fethiye. However, thanks to a few enthusiastic and entrepreneurial residents of Greek heritage in Zeytinli and Tepeköy, the villages are discovering the benefits of small-scale tourism and some former residents and their families are returning. In 2013, the Aya Todori Greek Primary School in Zeytinli reopened after a 50-year closure, and in 2014 the first baby in 40 years was born to a resident of Tepeköy, a joyous event celebrated both on the island and as far away as Athens and İstanbul.

Zeytinli and Tepeköy are surrounded by green-grey scree-covered hills, with spectacular views over the countryside. If you have your own transport, they make idyllic bases for an island stay. If day-tripping, be sure to sample a cup of the island's famous dibek coffee (Turkish-style coffee that is ground on a dibek stone) in one of Zeytinli's traditional Greek cafes.

Yukarı Kaleköy

Perched on the hillside above the harbour at Kaleköy is 'High Kaleköy' (formerly Kastro), a pretty village built around a ruined Genoese fortress. Overlooking the Aegean island of Samothrace (Samothraki), most of its buildings date from the time when its residents were Greek; sadly all were forced out in the 1960s and 1970s. There's a disused church, a charming coffee shop, a couple of restaurants, a number of pensions and two boutique hotels, making the village an excellent base for the visitor. A dolmuş links both it and the harbour with Merkez.

Down on the harbour, the beach and nearby fish restaurants are popular with touring Turks. The coastline between Kaleköy and Kuzulimanı forms a *sualtı milli parkı* (national marine park).

Eski Bademli

Another hilltop Greek village, Eski Bademli (Old Bademli) looks down on ugly Yeni Bademli (New Bademli) and over the valley to the Aegean. The village has cobbled lanes, old stone houses and plenty of almond trees (*bademli* is the Turkish word for almond).

Beaches

The sand beach at Aydıncık is the best on the island. It is adjacent to Tuz Gölü (Salt Lake), a favourite shelter for pink flamingos between November and March. Both are popular for windsurfing and kitesurfing, and the lake is rich in sulphur and reputed to be good for the skin. Further west there are good beaches at Kapıkaya and Uğurlu.

✨ Festivals & Events

Greek Easter   RELIGIOUS
Many former residents return to the island for the celebrations.

Festival of the Virgin Mary   RELIGIOUS
(Panayia) Church services and feasts on 15 August.

🛏 Sleeping & Eating

In summer, it's not unusual for locals to approach and offer you a spare room in their house (*ev pansiyonu*) for considerably less than the prices charged by pensions and hotels. Many establishments close during the low season.

🛏 Merkez

Taylan Hotel   HOTEL €
(☑887 2451; omertaylanada@hotmail.com; Atatürk Caddesi; s/d ₺50/80; ⊙year-round; ❋🛜) On the main street in Merkez, this place has seen better days, but it's clean, the management is friendly (though not bilingual) and there's a bustling downstairs restaurant. The Ada Hotel (☑887 2400; http://gokceadaaotel.com; Atatürk Caddesi; ❋🛜), two doors down, offers similar rooms and prices and is operated by members of the same extended family.

Meydanı Pastanesi   PATISSERIE €
(☑887 4420; www.efibadem.com.tr/meydani; Atatürk Caddesi 31; tea & efi badem ₺1.75; ⊙6am-11pm) Every visitor to Gökçeada makes their way to the island's most popular cafe at some stage, lured by its most famous creation, the *efi badem*. A sugar-dusted biscuit made with almonds, butter and flour, it is

the perfect accompaniment to a glass of tea. Pastries, other biscuits and slices of pizza are also available.

Avlu Şarap Evi TURKISH €€

(☑ 0533 662 8224; Kadri Üçok Caddesi 13; fish at market prices; ⊙ 2pm-midnight summer only) On sultry summer nights, local tend to gravitate towards the front courtyard of this small wine house; when live musicians perform, the action moves into the stone-walled interior. *Meyhane*-style fish, seafood and grilled meats are on the menu.

🛏 Yukarı Kaleköy

★ Anemos Hotel BOUTIQUE HOTEL €€€

(☑ 887 3729; www.anemos.com.tr; Yukarı Kaleköy 98; bargain/standard/superior r ₺250/320/400; ⊙ year-round; ❉ 🛜 ⛱) *Anemos* means 'wind' in Turkish, and this gorgeous hotel certainly brought the winds of change to Gökçeada, introducing the concept of the boutique hotel and attracting clients from the mainland who would previously have headed to style-setting Bodrum for their vacations. Ground-floor bargain rooms are smallish; standard are spacious; and superior are large (some have private terraces). All are well appointed.

Views from the expansive pool terrace are utterly gorgeous, service is excellent and meals made with locally grown organic produce are available. The breakfast buffet, which is included in the room cost, is lavish and delicious.

Castle BOUTIQUE HOTEL €€€

(☑ 0554 676 5155; http://hotelthecastle.com; Yukarı Kaleköy 29-30; standard r ₺225, ste ₺300; ⊙ Apr-Nov; ❉ 🛜) Most of the old houses on the island were built using the golden-hued stone you'll see scattered across the landscape. High in Yukarı Kaleköy, with wonderful views, is this charming hotel that incorporates two old Greek houses that were built this way. There are five good-size standard rooms sleeping three, and four larger suites sleeping four. All have kitchenettes.

Yakamoz RESTAURANT €

(☑ 887 2057; www.gokceadayakamoz.com; Yukarı Kaleköy; mains ₺25-35; ⊙ lunch & dinner) For a sundowner with million-dollar views over the water, head to the terrace restaurant at the Yakamoz Motel.

★ Mustafanın Kayfesi BREAKFAST, CAFE €€

(☑ 887 2063; www.mustafaninkayfesi.com; village breakfast plate ₺12.50; ⊙ 9am-9pm) Look for the freestanding belltower of the Ayia Marina church to find this welcoming cafe, which is tucked into the adjacent garden. The village-style breakfast is delicious, and the Turkish coffee is the best on the island. In the late afternoon, a nargile (water pipe) and coffee combo (₺13) really hits the spot.

🛏 Aydıncık

Şen Camping CAMPING GROUND €

(☑ 898 1020; camping per person ₺10; ⊙ May-Sep) 🅿 The water almost laps the tent sites at this Aydıncık campsite. Though it's looking a bit run-down, the place is neat and all sites include bathroom use. The restaurant and cafe-bar are popular in the high season. If you're keen to windsurf, there's equipment hire and an in-house instructor.

Gökçeada Sörf Eğitim Merkezi Oteli RESORT €€€

(Gökçeada Surf Training Centre Hotel; ☑ 898 1022; www.surfgokceada.com; s/d ₺180/280; ⊙ May-Sep; ❉ 🛜) They take windsurfing seriously at this resort, offering guests six-lesson packages over three to four days (₺380). Surrounded by gardens that lead straight to the sandy beach, it offers 46 rooms with tiled floors and sand-coloured walls. The beach cafe-bar and restaurant are definite draws.

🛏 Zeytinli

Zeytindali Hotel BOUTIQUE HOTEL €€€

(☑ 887 3707; www.zeytindalihotel.com; Zeytinliköy 168; s/d ₺180/220; ⊙ May-Oct; ❉ 🛜) Two rebuilt Greek stone houses at the top of the old village showcase island style and comfort. The 16 rooms – each named after a Greek god – have satellite TVs and views of the village or the sea; wi-fi is only available in the lobby and on the terrace. The ground-floor restaurant is popular with day-trippers.

🛏 Tepeköy

★ Pansyon Agridia PENSION €

(☑ 887 2138; info@pansyonagridia.com; per person ₺50; ⊙ year-round) Owner Dimitris Assanakis is extremely proud of his whitewashed pension perched on the village's highest point. There are three simply decorated rooms with good beds; a double and twin share a bathroom and the second twin has an en suite. All can be hot in summer, but the balcony with its magnificent view over the valley well and truly compensates.

Kudos goes to Dimitris' mother, who makes the delicious, largely organic breakfasts using eggs, fruit, vegetables and spring water from the village.

Barba Yorgo Pansyon   PENSION €

(☑ 887 3592; www.barbayorgo.com; r per person ₺45; ☻ May–mid-Sep) 'Papa George' is the big-spirited owner of Tepeköy's much-loved taverna and he also oversees nine pension rooms spread across three houses in the village; two have private bathrooms and seven have shared facilities. All have stone walls, wooden floorboards and mountain views.

★ Barba Yorgo Taverna   AEGEAN €€€

(☑ 887 4247; www.barbayorgo.com; mains ₺20-25; ☻ May-Sep) A good time is assured at this atmospheric village restaurant overlooking vineyards and the 1780 Ayios Yioryios church. The menu includes goat stew, wonderfully tender octopus and platefuls of meze, all washed down with carafes of the house-made wine (Baba Yorgo produces a knock-your-socks-off retsina, an eminently quaffable red blend and a more sophisticated organic cabernet sauvignon).

🛍 Shopping

Gökçeada is one of only nine Turkish cittaslow cities (http://cittaslowturkiye.org) and is committed to producing organic foodstuffs. At the forefront of this endeavour is Elta-Ada (☑ 887 3287; www.elta-ada.com.tr), a farm that produces organic olive oil, dairy products (soft white cheeses, yoghurt and butter) and assorted fruits and vegetables. Shops around the main square in Merkez sell locally produced products including artisan-made soap, olive oil, jams, honey and dibek coffee. These include Elta-Ada's kiosk (Cumhuriyet Meydanı; ☻ 8am-9pm summer), opposite the Pegasus Otel; Ada Rüzgarı (☑ 887 2496; www.adaruzgari.com; Suluoğlu İş Merkezi 24b); and Ekozey (Atatürk Caddesi).

İmroza Sabun Atölyesi ve Mağazası (İmroz Soap Factory and Shop; ☑ 887 2388; www.imroza.com), on the road to the ruined fortress in Yukarı Kaleköy, produces and sells a range of all-natural soap.

ℹ Information

Facilities such as a bank, ATMs and a post office are found 6km inland at Merkez, where most of the island's population lives.

Tourist Office (☑ 887 3005; Cumhuriyet Meydanı; ☻ 9am-2pm & 3-7pm) In a timber kiosk next to the main dolmuş stop in Merkez.

ℹ Getting There & Away

AIR

In summer, **Seabird Airlines** (☑ 0850 811 0732; www.flyseabird.com) operates seaplane services between İstanbul and Gökçeada.

FERRY

Check the **Gestaş** (☑ 444 0752; www.gestasdenizulasim.com.tr) website and with your hotel for departure times, because these change according to the season.

Gallipoli Peninsula Ferries cross the Aegean between Kabatepe and Gökçeada (per person/car ₺2.50/29, 75 minutes) three times daily each way from September to May, five times daily in June and July and even more regularly in August.

Çanakkale Ferries leave Çanakkale on Sunday at 8.30am (per person/car ₺2.50/29, 2½ hours) and return from Gökçeada on Monday at 8.30am.

ℹ Getting Around

CAR

Note that the only petrol station is 2km from Merkez on the Kuzulimanı road. There are three car-hire companies on the island, including **Gökçeada-Rent-A-Car** (☑ 887 2417; www.gokceadarentacar.net; Atatürk Caddesi 84), in Merkez, which charges ₺100 per day for a small car.

DOLMUŞ

Ferries dock at Kuzulimanı, from where you can take a dolmuş to Merkez (₺2, 15 minutes, eight per day). Change at Merkez to continue to Kaleköy, 5km further north (₺1.50, 25 minutes). Some of the Kaleköy dolmuşes stop in Yeni Bademli and Yukarı Kaleköy en route.

TAXI

It costs ₺250 to hire a taxi for half a day and tour the island. Otherwise, short trips cost:

- Kuzulimanı–Merkez (₺15, 10 minutes)
- Kuzulimanı–Kaleköy (₺25, 20 minutes)
- Kuzulimanı–Yukarı Kaleköy (₺30, 25 minutes)
- Merkez–Kaleköy (₺10, five minutes)
- Merkez–Zeytinli (₺15, 10 minutes)
- Merkez–Tepeköy (₺20, 20 minutes)
- Merkez–Aydıncık (₺25, 15 minutes)

İzmir & the North Aegean

Includes ➡

Best Places to Eat

- ➡ Asma Yapraği (p216)
- ➡ Sakız (p206)
- ➡ Cabalımeyhane (p178)
- ➡ Lal Girit Mutfağı (p188)
- ➡ Fokai Restaurant (p197)

Best Places to Stay

- ➡ Assos Alarga (p180)
- ➡ Alaçatı Taş Otel (p214)
- ➡ Rengigül Konukevi (p177)
- ➡ Macaron Konağı (p185)
- ➡ Lola 38 Hotel (p197)

Why Go?

This relatively short stretch of coast is first and foremost a magnet for holidaymakers. Beaches along the Ege Deniz (Aegean Sea), including the Biga Peninsula, are superb (and often empty), while on the Çeşme Peninsula, Alaçatı offers world-class windsurfing. At the same time, this region is a colossus for history buffs. The hilltop ruins of Pergamum and Assos are breathtaking sites of antiquity, while others lie hidden along peninsulas inhabited by descendants of the Turkmen nomads. İzmir, Turkey's third-largest city, is a buzzing, Euro-centric metropolis with an attractive bazaar and seafront *kordon* (promenade) and a fair few ancient sites of its own.

No matter where you go in this region, the Greek influence is inescapable. Many towns experienced the great population exchange of the early 20th century and today, in places like Ayvalık and on the island of Bozcaada, the architecture, music and food seem like bittersweet echoes from across the sea.

When to Go

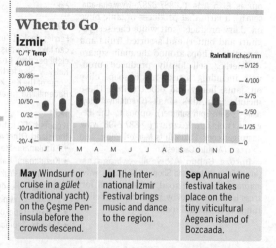

İzmir

May Windsurf or cruise in a *gület* (traditional yacht) on the Çeşme Peninsula before the crowds descend.

Jul The International İzmir Festival brings music and dance to the region.

Sep Annual wine festival takes place on the tiny viticultural Aegean island of Bozcaada.

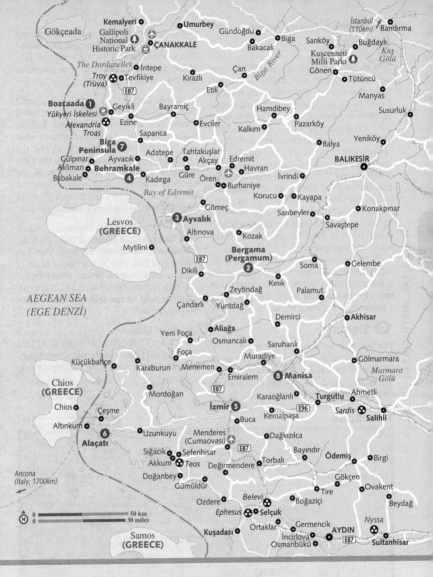

İzmir & the North Aegean Highlights

1 Ferry over to idyllic **Bozcaada** (p176) to lounge on the beach and indulge in fine local wine and dining.

2 Take a cable car to the Acropolis at **Bergama** (Pergamum; p189), one of the country's finest ancient sites.

3 Wander the crumbling,

atmospheric back streets of the old town in **Ayvalık** (p183).

4 Climb the cobbled streets of **Behramkale** (Assos; p179) to the Temple of Athena and its glorious sea views.

5 Enjoy the seafront *kordon* (promenade) restaurants and the nightlife of **İzmir's Alsancak district** (p201).

6 Windsurf by day and party by night in **Alaçatı** (p214), the glamour town of the Çeşme Peninsula.

7 Motor around the **Biga Peninsula** (p181), with its ruins, villages and beaches.

8 Journey to **Manisa** (p210) for its mosques, museums and 'power paste'.

Bozcaada

📞 0286 / POP 2650

This stylish Aegean island is still relatively unknown outside the well-heeled urban Turkish travel set. Every summer it seems a new batch of expatriate İstanbullus open up another pension, wine bar or restaurant but even at capacity it's still all charm, with a warren of picturesque, vine-draped old houses and cobbled streets huddling beneath a huge medieval fortress.

Windswept Bozcaada (Tenedos in Greek) has always been known to wine connoisseurs, and vineyards still blanket its sunny slopes. The island is small – just under 40 sq km – and easy to explore. Lovely unspoilt sandy beaches line the coast road to the south and southwest.

Many businesses shut down outside the high season (mid-June to mid-September); some restaurants and bars open their doors only at weekends and on Wednesdays, when a market fills the main square.

◎ Sights

The best beaches lie on the south and southwest coasts and include Akvaryum, Ayazma, Sulubahçe and Habbele. Tuzburnu Beach below the lighthouse to the southeast is also passable but rocky. Ayazma is by far the most popular and best equipped, boasting several cafes as well as the small, abandoned Greek Orthodox Aya Paraşkevi Monastery uphill. In summer you can rent umbrellas and deckchairs at Ayazma.

Bozcaada Castle CASTLE
(Bozcaada Kalesi; admission ₺5; ⊙10am-1pm & 2-6pm) Bozcaada town's colossal fortress dates to Byzantine times, but most of what you see are later additions made by the Venetians, Genoese and Ottomans. Over the dry moat and within the double walls are traces of a mosque, ammunition dumps, a barracks, an infirmary and Roman pillars. It sits right next to the ferry terminal.

Local History Research Museum MUSEUM
(Yerel Tarih Arastırma Müzesi; ☑0532 215 6033; Lale Sokak 7; adult/child ₺5/3; ⊙10am-8pm mid-Jun–mid-Sep) This is a treasure trove of island curios – maps, prints, photographs, seashells and day-to-day artefacts. It is located 100m west of the ferry terminal and is well signposted.

Church of St Mary CHURCH
(Meryem Ana Kilisesi; 20 Eylül Caddesi 42/A) This beautiful old church in the old Greek neighbourhood to the west of the fortress is rarely open.

Bozcaada

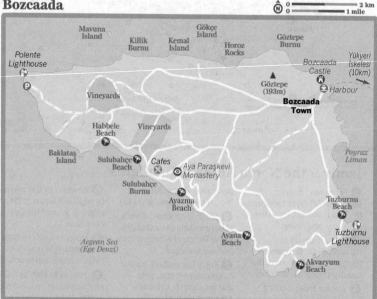

🛏 Sleeping

Headscarf-wrapped ladies may greet you at the *iskele* (pier) and offer you their spare room; if not, wander through the old Greek quarter west of the castle and Çınar Çarşı Caddesi. The traditional Turkish neighbourhood lies to the south of the castle.

Aki Hotel
PENSION €€

(📋697 0307; www.akihotelbozcaada.com; Hamam Sokak 1; s ₺90-150, d ₺120-180; ❉🖥) Above a gift shop in the Turkish quarter, Aki's seven rooms won't win any beauty pageants, but they are clean, well equipped and very central. Excellent bathrooms; room 2 faces a quiet square.

Kale Pansiyon
PENSION €€

(Castle Pension; 📋697 8617; www.kalepansiyon.net; İnönü Caddesi 69; s/d ₺60/120; ❉🖥) Reached via a steep climb from the old Greek quarter, and with commanding views from the top of town, the family-run 'Castle' has 14 simple but fastidiously clean rooms and a garden for breakfast. Of its two houses, the one on the right has better bathrooms; light wooden floors and kilims (pileless woven rugs) are found throughout.

Ergin Pansiyon
PENSION €€

(📋0542 404 5413, 697 0038; www.erginpansiyon.com; Çınar Çarşı Caddesi 24; s/d ₺50/100; ❉🖥) With 16 rooms in four separate buildings, the Ergin has something for everyone. The cheapest of the rooms are at this address opposite the ferry pier. The decorative disasters include mixing green walls and orange blankets, but the delicious Turkish breakfast served in the courtyard and the rooftop terrace with its castle view make up for those shortcomings.

★ Rengigül Konukevi
BOUTIQUE HOTEL €€€

(Colourful Rose Guesthouse; 📋697 8171; www.rengigul.net; Atatürk Caddesi 31; s/d ₺160/180; 🖥) This flower-bedecked Greek townhouse from 1876 has seven tastefully decorated, antique-strewn rooms (Özcan, the owner, also owns an art gallery), a cosy lounge and library area, and a large, peaceful walled garden. The breakfast table here is the most attractive and lavish in Bozcaada. Some rooms share a bathroom.

Latife Hanım Konağı
BOUTIQUE HOTEL €€€

(Madam Latife Mansion; 📋690 0030; www.latifehanimkonagi.com; Atatürk Caddesi 23; s/d ₺100/200; ❉@🖥) One of the more afford-

---

---

able boutique hotels in the Greek quarter, this newcomer with a dozen rooms leaves history at the renovated doorstep and welcomes you into a stark-white, ultra-cool interior. Rooms are large, and the views from the 2nd-floor roof terrace are commanding.

9 Oda
BOUTIQUE HOTEL €€€

(Dokuz Oda; 📋0532 427 0648; www.dokuzoda.com; 20 Eylül Caddesi 43; s/d ₺119/250; ❉🖥) Greek-owned 'Nine Rooms' is essentially two renovated buildings with a total of 17 rooms on either side of a pretty cobblestone street. Kosta, a Bozcaada native, has conceived a clean-lined island retreat. Polished floorboards, earthy colours and the odd *objet d'art* help keep the calm. Room 301 is a gem.

Kaikias Otel
BOUTIQUE HOTEL €€€

(📋697 0250; www.kaikias.com; Eskici Sokak 1; r ₺165-300; ❉🖥) Overlooking a tiny square near the castle, this artful 22-room hotel in two buildings is an attraction in itself – from the reception's planted ceiling to the antiques and artefacts, such as a bookcase of flaking tomes behind protective glass. We love step-down room 3 and the wine cellar visible through the glass floor.

🍴 Eating

Local specialities include *kurabiye* (biscuits) made with *bademli* almonds and *sakızlı* (mastic). Buy them at **Bozcaadalı Veli Dede** (📋697 0436; www.velidede.com.tr; Cuhuriyet Meydanı 9; ⊙6am-9pm) next to the Corvus wine shop.

★ **Cabalımeyhane** AEGEAN €€

(☑697 0118; www.cabalimeyhane.com; Kazanlar Sokak 12; mains ₺14-30, meze ₺8) This new Greek-style seafood restaurant and meze bar perches right on the water in the shadow of Bozcaada Castle. Try the pumpkin with walnuts (*cevizli kabak*), the scrumptious melted goat's cheese (*keçi peyniri eritme*) and the paper-wrapped squid (*kağıtta kalamar*).

Ada Café CAFE €€

(☑697 8795; www.bozcaada.info; Çınar Çeşme Caddesi 35/A; mains ₺8-17.50, wine per glass from ₺10; ◷8.30am-1.30am Apr-Oct) Melih and Semra have presided over this popular cafe and gourmet larder since 1994. Ada serves wholesome, simple food like fresh thyme salad and a crispy house *börek* (filled pastry). In summer try *gelincik şerbeti*, a frothy sherbet drink made from poppy flowers.

Café at Lisa's CAFE €€

(☑697 0182; Kurtulus Caddesi 1; mains ₺18; ◷9am-midnight; ☎) Lisa is an Australian expat who runs the cutest cafe on the island, a sure thing for good coffee, chocolate cake, pasta and pizza. Grab an outside table beneath the big tree.

Boruzan SEAFOOD €€€

(☑697 8414; www.boruzanrestoran.com; Yalı Caddesi 10; mains ₺20-25, meze ₺8-10; ◷9am-midnight) A buzzing harbourside place, blue-and-white Boruzan is particularly good for meze, which feature produce from the restaurant's own vegetable patch, and simple seafood dishes, such as *kalamar tava* (grilled squid) and octopus balls. A branch opens in summer at Ayazma Beach.

Yakamoz SEAFOOD €€€

(☑697 0398; Yalı Caddesi 14; mains ₺20, meze ₺8-20; ◷8am-midnight) Another seafood restaurant facing the harbour, 'Phosphorescence' lights the way with its massive meze trays groaning under the weight of things fishy, olive oily and yoghurty. Excellent wine list and helpful staff.

🍷 Drinking & Nightlife

Polente BAR

(☑697 8605; İskele Caddesi 41; ◷9am-3am; ☎) The welcoming, Greek-blue Polente, fronting the main square, plays an eclectic mix of music, including Latin and jazz, and attracts an equally eclectic mix of locals and visitors. Its cocktails, made with anything in season (cherries, mulberries, grapes), are inspired.

BOZCAADA'S FINE WINE

Bozcaada has been one of Turkey's great wine-growing regions since ancient times, when enormous quantities of wine were used to fuel the debauchery at festivals for the wine god Dionysus. Nobody is quite sure why, but some magical alchemy of the island's climate, topography and soil make-up perfectly suits the growing of grapes. Among the island's main winemakers are Corvus, Talay, Ataol, Yunatçılar and newcomer Amadeus (www.amadeuswine.com).

Unfortunately, due to new government regulations it is all but impossible to taste wine in Bozcaada before you buy it. Two indigenous grape varietals are Vasilaki for the production of white wine and Kuntra (or Karasakız) for red.

Corvus (www.corvus.com.tr; Çınar Çarşı Caddesi 53; ◷10am-6pm, to 9.30pm mid-Jun–mid-Sep), which has a shop on the main street, belongs to Turkish architect Reşit Soley. Its wines, such as red Karga (Crow) and white Zeleia Vasilaki, have impressed wine critics internationally.

Talay (www.talay.com.tr; Lale Sokak 3; ◷8am-6pm) has a shop behind the ATMs on the main square. You can also visit the winemaker's fermentation tanks behind the Ziraat Bankası.

Yunatçılar, which markets its wine under the Çamlıbağ (www.camlibag.com.tr) label, was the first Turkish-owned winery (1925) to be founded on the island. It makes a delightful Merlot-Kuntra blend and a decent rosé.

If travelling in September, try to coincide with the annual Bozcaada Wine Festival, with tours of the wine houses and lectures on the processes of viticulture. It takes place over the first weekend of the month.

Bakkal   BAR
(☑ 0543 210 9410; www.bozcaadabakkal.com; Lale Sokak 22) This super-cool cafe called 'Grocery' serves local Corvus wine (glass ₺10), smoothies, espressos and sandwiches (around ₺20). Seating is at little tables on the lane or inside among corner-store products for sale.

ℹ Information

At the wooden **information booth** (İskele Caddesi; ⊘ 9am-6pm daily Jun–mid-Sep, when boats arrive Fri-Sun rest of the year) near the ferry pier, you can pick up a map from some of the hotels and cafes.

There's a row of ATMs on the main square in Bozcaada town near the PTT.

ℹ Getting There & Away

BOAT

Gestaş (☑ 444 0752; www.gestasdenizulasim.com.tr) ferries run daily to Bozcaada from Yükyeri İskelesi (Yükyeri Pier; 30 minutes, return per person/car ₺6/58), 4km west of Geyikli, south of Troy. They leave the mainland at 9am, 11am, 1pm, 5pm and 7pm and depart the island at 7.30am, 10am, noon, 4pm and 6pm. Departures increase to 14 a day in high season.

Hydrofoils sail from Çanakkale (55 minutes, one-way ₺15) on Wednesday, Saturday and Sunday (depart 9am, return 7pm). Make sure you double-check departure times, as they do change.

BUS

Hourly dolmuşes (minibuses that stop anywhere along a prescribed route) link the Çanakkale otogar (bus station) with Geyikli (₺10) via Ezine, with connections to Yükyeri İskelesi (₺3). Dolmuşes meet the ferry from Bozcaada and run to Geyikli and to Ezine (₺6), from where there are services to Çanakkale and destinations to the south such as Behramkale (Assos) and Gülpınar.

ℹ Getting Around

Located around the corner from the main square, **Akuz** (☑ 0545 541 9514) hires out mountain bikes (₺20/35 per half/full day), motorbikes motorbikes (₺50/100 per half/full day) and cars (₺100 per day).

DOLMUŞ

Hourly dolmuşes leave from near the *iskele* in Bozcaada town and travel to Ayazma Beach (₺3). In summer, more-frequent dolmuşes also serve Ayazma via Sulubahçe Beach, and there's a service to Polente Feneri (Polente Lighthouse) on the westernmost point for watching sunsets.

TAXI

A taxi from Bozcaada town to Ayazma costs about ₺30.

Behramkale (Assos)

☑ 0286 / POP 1200

The hilltop village of Behramkale contains the ancient Greek settlement of Assos. This spreads out around the Temple of Athena and, at the bottom of a steep hill, there's a former working harbour with a small pebble beach. Here the old stone buildings and warehouses have been transformed into hotels and fish restaurants.

Try to avoid visiting on weekends and public holidays from the beginning of April to the end of August, when tourists pour in by the coach load. Locals often refer to the two areas as *liman* (harbour) and *köyü* (village). There are few facilities other than an ATM and pharmacy in the village.

History

The Mysian city of Assos was founded in the 8th century BC by colonists from Lesvos, who built its great temple to Athena in 530 BC. The city enjoyed considerable prosperity under the rule of Hermeias, a former student of Plato who encouraged philosophers to live in Assos. Aristotle himself lived here from 348 to 345 BC and ended up marrying Hermeias' niece, Pythia. Assos' glory days came to an abrupt end with the arrival of the Persians, who crucified Hermeias and forced Plato to flee.

Alexander the Great drove the Persians out, but Assos' importance was challenged by the ascendancy of Alexandria Troas to the north. From 241 to 133 BC the city was ruled by the kings of Pergamum.

St Paul visited Assos briefly during his third missionary journey, walking here from Alexandria Troas to meet St Luke before boarding a boat for Lesvos. In late Byzantine times the city dwindled to a village.

◉ Sights & Activities

Temple of Athena   RUIN
(admission ₺8; ⊘ 8am-5pm, to 7pm Apr-Sep) On top of the 238m-high hill above the village is this impressive temple built in 530 BC in a mixture of Doric and Ionic styles. The short tapered columns with plain capitals are hardly elegant, and the concrete reconstruction hurts more than helps, but the site and

the view out to Lesvos are spectacular and well worth the admission fee.

Other Ruins   RUIN

Scramble down the path from the Temple of Athena or walk along the road to the harbour to find the necropolis. Assos' sarcophagi (from the Greek, 'flesh-eaters') were famous. According to Pliny the Elder, the stone was caustic and 'ate' the flesh off the deceased in 40 days. To the south and southeast you'll see the ruins of a 2nd-century BC gymnasium and south of the agora a heavily restored theatre and basilica.

Ringing the hill are stretches of the city walls of medieval Assos, which are among the most impressive medieval fortifications in Turkey.

Hüdavendigar Camii   MOSQUE

Next to the entrance to the Temple of Athena, this 14th-century mosque is a simple structure – a dome on squinches set on top of a square room – built before the Turks had conquered Constantinople and assimilated the lessons of Aya Sophia. It was constructed with materials from a 6th-century church and is one of just two remaining Ottoman mosques of its kind in Turkey (the other is in Bursa). Hüdavendigar is, in fact, a poetic name for that city.

🛏 Sleeping

The most atmospheric accommodation is found in the peaceful hilltop village, though the harbour has a bit more going on. In high season, virtually all the hotels around the harbour insist on *yarım pansiyon* (half board).

🛏 Village

Dolunay Pansiyon   PENSION €€

(☑721 7172; www.dolunaypansiyon.com; s/d ₺60/120; 🕸🛜) In the centre of the village on the main square, this basic family-run place has five spotless rooms. There's also a small terrace with sea views where you can enjoy a scenic breakfast, as well as a lovely courtyard.

Tekin Pansiyon   PENSION €€

(☑721 7099; http://tekinpansiyon.tripod.com; s/d ₺45/90; 🕸🛜) This simple place fulfills the basic pension requirements, and even though the eight rooms face away from Behramkale's panoramic views, the little tables in the open gallery overlook village goings-on.

★ Assos Alarga   BOUTIQUE HOTEL €€€

(☑0537 663 1338, 721 7260; www.assosalarga. com; Behramkale 88; r ₺260-350; 🕸@🛜🏊) Located in the quiet end of the village just below the Temple of Athena, this stunner of a place has just three rooms (another two are on the way), guaranteeing stellar service from Ece, the affable owner. The room called Orsa has the floorboards, beautiful bookshelves and desk, while Viya and Bakla have kilims and stylishly rustic furnishings.

All rooms have amazing views over the mountains and very cool bathrooms. There's a deluxe outdoor pool, garden, ping-pong tables and even a piano.

Assosyal Otel   BOUTIQUE HOTEL €€€

(☑721 7046; www.assosyalotel.com; Alan Meydanı 8; s/d ₺200/310; 🕸🛜) Opposite Assos Alarga, this 16-room hotel has helped pull Behramkale into the 21st century. Contemporary lines arc across old stone, vine-clad walls. Tea in the courtyard (with fireplace) feels timeless. The light brown and beige rooms are minimally furnished, with deluxe, raised beds and stunning mountain-facing terraces. The glass and metal garden sculptures set the playful mood.

There are no TVs in the guestrooms, but you're more than welcome to watch the stars with the telescope in the common room.

🛏 Harbour

Dr No Antik Pansiyon   PENSION €

(☑721 7397; www.assosdrnoantikpansiyon.com; Antik Liman; s ₺50-70, d ₺100-140; 🕸) No sign of an evil conspiracy at this simple, friendly pension with seven cramped rooms and a pleasant outdoor area. It's the best budget option down at the harbour.

Yıldız Otel   PENSION €€

(☑721 7025; http://bert-genzink1.magix.net/website; Antik Liman; s ₺60-100, d ₺120-200; 🕸) The Star is drifting into post-retro territory with its tired decor, but it's friendly, the upstairs terrace is sublime and the seven rooms are adequately sized. Breakfast is served on the pier. The owners operate another hotel just east along the coast at Kadırga.

Assos Kervansaray Hotel   HOTEL €€€

(Map p164; ☑721 7093; www.assoskervansaray. com; Antik Liman; with sea view s ₺140-210, d ₺190-280; 🕸🛜🏊) The most reliable place to stay down by the ancient harbour, but something of an oddity all the same, the Kervansaray is housed in a 19th-century acorn warehouse. The hotel's 70 smart rooms have small bathrooms and plasma-screen TVs concealed in wooden cases; four of the rooms (including No 305) have sea-facing balconies. The outdoor pool almost laps into the sea.

Assos Nazlıhan Hotel RESORT €€€
(✆721 7385; www.assosnazlihanspahotel.com; Antik Liman; s ₺155-180, d ₺250-310; ❈🅟) Partly remodelled as a spa resort (where a decent treatment is available), the Nazlıhan's older section has two floors with 36 rooms mostly facing an internal courtyard. The newer section is actually pretty flash, with stone-faced walls, wood-panelled bath-tubs at the foot of the beds, and very small, tiled bathrooms. Room 103 has you practically in the sea.

🍴 Eating & Drinking

Proximity to the sea accounts for the higher prices on the harbour. Be sure to check the cost of fish and bottles of wine before ordering.

🍴 Village

Ehl-i Keyf TURKISH €
(✆721 7106; gözleme ₺7-10, meze ₺6; ❂8am-midnight; 🅟) The multilevel 'Tame Fun' is just that, combining excellent, fresh food with attentive service and a very pleasant outlook. Choose from a long menu of *ızgara* (grills) and *gözleme* (stuffed savoury crêpes) amid flowering plants, old carriages and even a beached barque. Also good for coffee; watch the mechanical bear do the grinding outside.

WORTH A TRIP

BIGA PENINSULA

The isolated Biga Peninsula, with its assorted ruins, makes a good day trip – provided you travelling are under your own steam. The peninsula also boasts some relatively isolated beaches, which, while not entirely off the beaten track, are seldom as crowded as others further south.

Ten kilometres southeast of Geyikli lie the ruins of **Alexandria Troas**, scattered around the village of Dalyan. After the death of Alexander the Great in 323 BC, one of his generals, Antigonus, took control of this land, founding the city of Antigoneia in 310 BC. This site feels secret, with visitors exploring among its great grass-strewn ruins. Recent excavations have revealed a bathing complex and a temple; there are some new explanatory signboards. The stone arches and crystal-clear inscriptions are impressive.

Some 34km south is **Gülpınar**, a one-street farming village once the ancient city of **Chryse** (Krysa), famous for its 2nd-century BC Ionic temple to Apollo – and for its mice. Apparently an oracle had told Cretan colonists to settle where 'the sons of the earth' attacked them. Awakening to find mice chewing their equipment, they took it as an omen and built a temple to Apollo Smintheus (Apollo Lord of the Mice). The 5m-tall cult statue of the god, of which only a fragment remains, had marble mice carved at its feet.

The ruins of the **Apollon Smintheion** (www.smintheion.com; admission incl museum ₺5; ❂8am-5pm, to 7.30pm mid-Jun–mid-Sep) are signposted 300m down a side road as you enter the village. It's a large site with a small museum and includes a partially reconstructed temple, a Roman baths complex from the 1st to 3rd centuries AD, and a large gymnasium. Also found here, and now covered for protection, are the wonderful reliefs and column drums with illustrated scenes from the Iliad, which recounts the Apollo Smintheion priest Chryse's feud with Agamemnon.

From Gülpınar, a road heads 9km west past an enormous and unsightly residential development to **Babakale** (ancient Lekton), the westernmost point of mainland Turkey. It's a sleepy place that seems almost overawed by its 18th-century **fortress**, the last Ottoman castle built in present-day Turkey.

Above the harbour, the **Uran Hotel** (✆0286-747 0218; Babakale Köyü; s/d ₺40/70; ❈) has seven simple but sea-breeze-fresh rooms with tiny bathrooms; two have small balconies overlooking the castle and sea. The hotel also has also a delightful terrace and a good and reasonably priced **fish restaurant** (mains ₺15).

There are buses from Gülpınar (₺2, 15 minutes) and daily services from Ezine (₺8, 1½ hours). They arrive in the village centre.

Assos Köyüm Restaurant   TURKISH €€
(☑ 721 7424; mains ₺15-20; ☺ 7am-3am) Serving *mantı* (Turkish ravioli), *avcı boreği* ('hunter's *börek*'; pastry filled with meat or cheese) and a good range of meze, this restaurant has a lovely terrace overlooking the main square and great views to the sea from the rooftop. It's one of the only eateries in the village with beer available.

Aile Çay Bahçesi   TEA GARDEN
(Family Tea Garden; tea ₺1, soft drinks ₺3; ☎) For a coffee or Coke on the main square, this place has a pleasant shaded terrace offering attractive views and good company.

✕ Harbour

Uzunev   SEAFOOD €€
(☑ 721 7007; Antik Liman; mains ₺15-25, meze ₺15; ☺ 8am-3am) The 'Long House' is the pick of the seafront restaurants and garners the liveliest crowd, especially on weekends in high season. Blue wooden chairs line the terrace, while inside it feels like a warm Turkish pub. Try the succulent speciality, sea bass à l'Aristotle (steamed in a special stock) or the varied seafood meze.

Çakır Restaurant   SEAFOOD €€
(☑ 721 7048; mains ₺15-20; ☺ noon to midnight) About as chilled out as dining can get, this restaurant at the Çakır brothers' pension overlooks a pebble beach and rickety wooden platforms above the water. You can choose meze and mains such as *kalamar* (squid) and *köfte* (meatballs) from the fridge.

❶ Getting There & Away

BAY OF EDREMIT
In the summer, dolmuşes connect Behramkale with Küçükkuyu (₺8, one hour); otherwise a taxi costs ₺40 to ₺45.

BİGA PENINSULA
Dolmuşes run to Behramkale from Gülpınar (₺3, one hour).

ÇANAKKALE
Regular buses run from Çanakkale (₺18, 1½ hours); alternatively take a more frequent one to Ayvacık (₺15, one hour), where you can pick up a dolmuş to Behramkale (₺5, 30 minutes). Try to get to Ayvacık as early in the day as you can to catch a dolmuş to Behramkale. If you miss the last one, Ayvacık has a couple of hotels, or a taxi to Behramkale will cost around ₺30.

❶ Getting Around

In summer, there's a shuttle service throughout the day between the village and the harbour (₺2.50, every 30 minutes), or it's about a half-hour walk. Dolmuşes also head south to the beach at Kadırga (₺2.50).

Ayvacık

☑ 0286 / POP 7760

Heading to or from Behramkale you may have to transfer in Ayvacık, which has a big Friday market where villagers go to sell fruit, vegetables and baskets. Those in long satiny overcoats or brightly coloured head scarves are the descendants of Turkmen nomads who settled in this area.

Ayvacık is famous for its diminutive carpets; some 20 villages and Turkmen communities in the region still produce them. Two kilometres out of Ayvacık, opposite the Total garage on the main road to Çanakkale, is the headquarters of the Dobag Project (Dobag Projesi; ☑ 712 1274; www.dobag-teppiche.de; ☺ 9am-6pm), which was set up in 1981 to encourage villagers to return to weaving carpets from naturally dyed wool. The prices charged by the village women are cheaper than those found in big-city bazaars. The great majority of carpets are exported, and the prices are not extravagant considering what goes into the process: every stage – shearing, carding, spinning, weaving, knotting and dyeing – is done by hand. The upstairs exhibition hall may be empty out of season; phone ahead to organise a village tour.

Bay of Edremit

☑ 0286

Some 23km from Behramkale, the coastal road meets the 550 Hwy, which then runs east along the north shore of the Bay of Edremit.

Turn left here, towards Ayvacık, and head 4km northwest into the hills to reach the village of Yeşilyurt, set among pine forests and olive groves. The yellow stone walls of many restored houses have been beautifully enhanced by red brick and wood, and the picturesque village offers plenty of boutique hotels including the lovely Öngen Country Hotel (☑ 752 2434; www.ongencountry.com; half board s/d ₺190/380; ✳ ☎) with 30 rooms perched high above Yeşilyurt at the end of a steep, cobbled road.

Back on the coastal highway, pause in Küçükkuyu to inspect the excellent **Adatepe Zeytinyağı Museum** (✆0286-752 1303; www.adatepedukkan.com; ⏰9am-6.30pm) **FREE**, housed in an old olive-oil factory and explaining the process of making olive oil. The neighbouring shop is excellent and very comprehensive, selling olive oil and every olive-oil product imaginable.

From Küçükkuyu, head 4km northeast into the forested hills to visit the pretty village of **Adatepe**, a cluster of restored stone houses below a lizard-like rock formation said to be Zeus' ancient altar. The area is great for walking, with waterfalls, plunge pools for swimming and, near the falls at Başdeğirmen, a Roman bridge. At the top of Adatepe you'll find the blissfully tranquil **Hünnap Han** (✆752 6581; www.hunnaphan. com; s/d ₺175/250), a restored country house with nine traditionally decorated rooms, a lovely garden and a stone courtyard.

Buses stop in Küçükkuyu every hour en route to Çanakkale (₺20) and İzmir (₺23). A taxi from Küçükkuyu to Adatepe or Yeşilyurt costs ₺20. In summer, dolmuşes run to Behramkale (₺8, one hour); a taxi costs ₺50.

The road continues east, past hillside after hillside of holiday villages, hotels and second-home developments. From Güre, follow the brown signpost and head 2.5km north into the hills to find **Alibey Kudar Etnografya Galerisi** (Alibey Kudar Ethnographic Gallery; www.etnografya-galerisi.com; admission ₺2; ⏰8am-7pm) in Tahtakuşlar village. Jum-bled exhibits such as a domed tent frame and ancient wagon provide an insight into the local villages inhabited by descendants of Turkmen people who moved here in the 15th century. The world's largest leatherback sea turtle – 1.97m long and weighing in at 360kg – is under glass here.

In Akçay, 10km west of Edremit, **Demre Tour** (✆384 8586; www.demretour.com.tr; Cumhuriyet Bulvarı 27; tour incl lunch ₺70) runs daily 4WD safaris to Mt Ida National Park (Kazdağı Milli Parkı), departing at 10.30am and returning at 7pm.

There is a good lunch stop near the seafront in Akçay. Turn right off the main street on to Turgut Reis Caddesi to find the multicoloured **Zeyyat Lokanta** (✆384 9998; mains ₺10; ⏰8am-10pm), which has outside seating and dishes up good home cooking and sumptuous breakfasts.

Ayvalık

✆0266 / POP 37,300

Ayvalık is an attractive, work a day port with a secret. Distinctively free of the tourist hustle, the palm-tree-lined waterfront and smattering of fish restaurants are much like elsewhere on the Aegean, but wander a few streets back to find an old Greek village in spirited abandon. Cars are squeezed out of the narrow, cobblestone lanes by horse-drawn carts and locals headed for the market. Colourful, shuttered

---

GHOSTS FROM THE PAST

The early 1920s hold mixed memories for Ayvalık. Pride over its role in the Turkish War of Independence – it was here that the first shots were fired – is tempered by what happened afterwards. The Ottoman Greeks, who made up the majority of the population in Ayvalık, were forced to abandon the land of their ancestors and relocate to the Greek island of Lesvos, while some Turks from that island were, in turn, forced to start new lives in Ayvalık. Despite the enormous distress this must have caused, the Ayvalık–Lesvos exchange is nonetheless regarded as one of the least damaging episodes of the period because of the proximity of the two communities, which enabled people from both sides to continue visiting their former homes – mixed though their emotions must have been during those trips. Furthermore, both communities were involved in the production of olive oil, and so would have found much that was familiar in the other.

Today, whispers from the past are everywhere here. Some elderly locals can speak Greek and many of the town's former Greek Orthodox churches remain standing, though converted into mosques. In 1923 the former Ayios Yannis (St John's) church became the **Saatlı Camii** ('Clock Mosque', so named for its clock tower and now minaret). The former Ayios Yioryios (St George's) is today the **Çınarlı Camii**, named after the *çınar* (plane trees) that grew here. The grand Greek cathedral was never converted but has now been turned into the Taksiyarhis Memorial Museum (p185).

Ayvalık

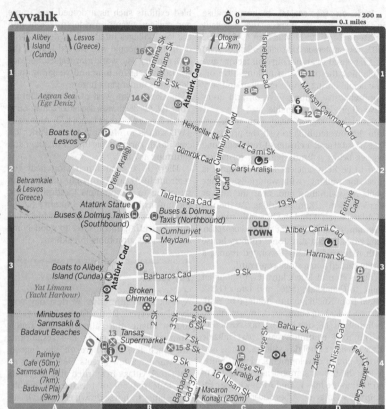

IZMIR & THE NORTH AEGEAN AYVALIK

Ayvalık

doors conceal all-day cafes and craft stores, time lapses in the afternoon sun.

Aegean olive-oil production is centred in Ayvalık, and there are lots of shops selling the end product. The broken chimney in the town centre belonged to a now-abandoned olive-oil factory; there are ongoing plans to turn it into a local museum. Ayvalık is also the springboard to the island of Lesvos in Greece.

◉ Sights & Activities

There are a number of good sandy beaches a few kilometres south of the city. The oddly named **Sarımsaklı Plaj** (Garlic Beach) is the most popular and will inevitably be the most crowded, as this is package-holiday territory. Stay on the bus a bit longer until you reach **Badavut Plaj** (Badavut Beach) to the west and you'll find some quieter stretches.

Taksiyarhis Memorial Museum CHURCH
(Taksiyarhis Anıt Müzesi; Mareşal Çakmak Caddesi; admission ₺3; ⊙8am-5pm Mon-Sat) This erstwhile Greek Orthodox cathedral, parts of which date back to the 15th century, was completely renovated in 2013 and positively shimmers in the noonday sun. Note the *catedra* (bishop's seat) decorated with pelicans and a crown, the wonderful pulpit and the 18th-century icons in the apse. The cathedral is huge, with three naves and a free-standing belfry.

Old Town HISTORIC AREA
Other than the Taksiyarhis church there are few specific sights here, but Ayvalık's old town is a joy to wander around, with its maze of cobbled streets lined with wonderfully worn-looking Greek houses. You can pick up a map called *A Walking Tour of Ayvalık* with information about sights, including the former Greek Orthodox churches, at selected cafes and hotels.

Markets MARKET
Thursday sees one of the region's largest and most vibrant markets, and stalls seem to fill the whole town. Seek out the **köy pazarı** (village market), which takes place next to the main **pazar yeri** (Marketplace). A small daily **fish market** (Balık Pazarı) takes place on the seafront next to the terminal for the ferry to Alibey Island (Cunda)

🛏 Sleeping

Kelebek Pension PENSION €€
(☑312 3908; www.kelebek-pension.com; Mareşal Çakmak Caddesi 108; s/d ₺60/100; ❄🛜) Yet another change in management has not detracted from this colourful seven-room pension where you can see the sea from your bedroom (eg rooms 4 or 5). The white-and-blue building has a terrace for having breakfast in the fresh air. Room 7 at the top is the choicest.

Bonjour Pansiyon PENSION €€
(☑312 8085; www.bonjourpansiyon.com; Çeşme Sokak 5; s/d without bathroom ₺50/100; ❄) In a fine-looking old mansion that once belonged to an ambassador to the sultan, this place has a faded grandeur feel, with aged furniture and antique knick-knacks filling every corner. The 11 rooms are immaculately presented, and you receive a terrific welcome from the owners, Yalçin and Hatice.

An excellent buffet breakfast is served in the courtyard and there's a laundry room.

Istanbul Pansiyon PENSION €€
(☑312 4001; www.istanbulpansiyonayvalik.com; Neşe Sokak Aralığı 4; s/d ₺60/110; ❄🛜) This lovely pension on the edge of the bazaar opens onto a quiet public square. The pretty blue and pink exterior gives way to six spacious rooms, four facing the inner courtyard. Breakfast is a delight under a green canopy in the lush garden.

Taksiyarhis Pension HOSTEL €€
(☑312 1494; www.taksiyarhispension.com; Mareşal Çakmak Caddesi 71; dm ₺30, s/d without bathroom ₺50/100; ❄🛜) This 120-year-old Greek house, behind the eponymous former cathedral, is one of the more stylish in Ayvalık. There's a vine-shaded terrace with sweeping views across the city, a communal kitchen and a decent book exchange. Rooms are rustic chic with exposed wooden beams; room 3 has a loft and 11 is a small dormitory. Breakfast costs ₺15 extra.

⭐ **Macaron Konağı** BOUTIQUE HOTEL €€€
(☑312 7741; www.macaronotel.com; 18 Sokak 54; s ₺85-115, d ₺175-260; ❄@🛜) The 'Marjoram Guesthouse' is a fragrant hostelry, with 13 rooms in an ancient Greek priest's dwelling (1880) known as 'Papa's House'. Everything – from the stone staircase and old Victrola to the lovely inner courtyard garden and room with a working fireplace (No 6) – combines to create what is arguably the nicest place to stay in the old town.

Hotel Ayvalık Palas HOTEL €€€
(☑312 1064; www.ayvalikpalashotel.com; Gümrük Meydanı Oteler Aralığı 1; s ₺60-100, d ₺120-200; ❄🛜) Not the prettiest seafront hotel, but the location is spot-on and it's anonymous and serviceable, plus there's a huge car park (₺10), a luxury in Ayvalık. Many of the 33 rooms face the sea.

🍴 Eating

Palmiye Cafe CAFE **€**
(☑ 312 1188; Atatürk Caddesi 78; börek ₺5; ⏰ 9am-9pm) A very friendly cafe along the seafront serves delicious baked goods, both sweet and savoury. The back section is popular with courting young bloods.

Hatipoğlu Pastaneleri SWEETS, ICE CREAM **€**
(Atatürk Caddesi 12; tea/Turkish coffee ₺1.50/3.50; ⏰ 7am-1am, to 3am in summer) With a great selection of traditional Turkish pastries and cakes, this friendly patisserie makes a terrific breakfast or tea stop. Try *lok* (sponge cake oozing honey; ₺5), the Ayvalık speciality, and add a scoop of *sakızlı dondurma* (mastic ice cream).

Deniz Kestanesi SEAFOOD **€€**
(☑ 312 3262; www.denizkestanesi.com; Karantina Sokak 9; mains ₺15-25, meze ₺6-25; ⏰ 10am-midnight) The 'Sea Urchin' is a stylish indoor/outdoor affair, right on the waterfront, with wooden floors, high ceilings, leather chairs and great views of Alibey Island's twinkling lights. Meat dishes are available in addition to meze and *balık* (fish), including bass, bream and mullet.

Balıkçı SEAFOOD **€€€**
(☑ 312 9099; Balıkhane Sokak 7; mains ₺17-25; ⏰ 8am-midnight) Run by a local association of fishermen and marine environmentalists, this is a fine place to sample local seafood and settle into the tiled terrace. Or sit inside for a better view of the Turkish troubadours, who get a singalong going from 8.30pm onwards daily in summer and on Wednesday, Friday and Sunday the rest of the year.

Cafe Caramel CAFE
(☑ 312 8520; Barbaros Caddesi 8 Sokak; ⏰ 8am-10pm Mon-Sat) Lovely Yasemin fronts this nostalgic cafe in the old town. Jazz soundtracks, an extensive cake and dessert menu, home-made soda and simple meals like *mantı* and *menemem* (scrambled eggs with peppers and tomatoes) done well. Caramel hits the sweetest spot and has a loyal following.

🍷 Drinking & Entertainment

Muhabbet Sokağı, the evocatively named 'Fondness St', which runs parallel to the seafront one block in from Atatürk Caddesi, is lined with bars and clubs that resound until the wee hours.

White Knight Café PUB
(☑ 312 3682; Cumhuriyet Meydanı 13; beer ₺8; ⏰ 10am-2am; 🛜) This pub-cafe behind the Atatürk statue is a mellow place for a libation, except when major football matches are shown. Very popular with Ayvalık's small expat community.

Sanat Fabrikası Tiyatrosu THEATRE
(Arts Factory Theatre; ☑ 312 3045; www.sanat-fabrikasi.com.tr; Barbaros Caddesi 4 Sokak 1-3; ⏰ 9am-1am) Ayvalık's hub for live performance attracts an appreciative, youthful crowd to its cosy theatre. The attached bar is ideal for a drop-in drink before, after or during a show and can get, well, lively at weekends.

🛍️ Shopping

Çöp Madam HANDICRAFTS
(☑ 312 6095; Alibey Cami Caddesi 2; ⏰ 9am-5pm) A cooperative for unemployed women who make colourful bags, jewellery and other bits and pieces out of recycled materials. It's next to a popular tea house, about 250m east of the ferry terminal.

Antikacılar Çarşısı ANTIQUES
(Otelier Araliği; ⏰ 9am-6pm) Buy old coins, jewellery and bric-a-brac, plus retro magazines and posters, in this quaint covered market in the same building as the Hotel Ayvalık Palas.

AYVALIK-STYLE FAST FOOD

Ayvalık may have made its name as an olive-oil producer, but these days it's better known throughout Turkey for a rather less-refined culinary offering – *Ayvalık tost* (Ayvalık toast). The town's take on fast food is essentially a toasted sandwich, crammed with all manner of ingredients, including cheese, *sucuk* (spicy veal or beef sausage), salami, pickles and tomatoes. These fillings are then lathered in ketchup and mayonnaise (unless you specifically request otherwise).

It's available at cafes and stalls throughout town, but **Avşar Büfe** (Atatürk Caddesi; Ayvalik toast ₺5, with just cheese ₺4; ⏰ 24hr May-Sep, 7am-3am Oct-Apr) and the surrounding eateries with communal tables and benches are good places to try it.

DIVING & CRUISING AROUND AYVALIK

The waters around Ayvalık are famed among divers for their rare deep-sea red coral at sites like Deli Mehmet and Kerbela. Another boon for the industry was the discovery of a wrecked jet in 2009. Dive companies in Ayvalık can organise trips to see these places and their attendant marine life, including moray eels, grouper, octopus and sea horses. One of the better options is **Korfez Diving Center** (☎ 0532 266 3589, 312 4996; www.korfezdiving.com; Atatürk Bulvari Özaral Pasaji 147; ☺ Mar-Nov), which moors its boat by the fish market. A day's diving costs ₺175 and dive courses start at ₺875.

In addition to the dive sites and summer ferries to Lesvos, cruising boats head around the bay's islands, including Alibey (Cunda), and stop here and there for swimming, sunbathing and walking. They generally depart at 11am and return by 6.30pm and cost around ₺70 per person, including lunch.

ℹ Information

Find internet cafes in the maze of streets around Gümrük Caddesi, northwest of the Atatürk statue, including **Ares Internet Cafe** (Talatpaşa Caddesi, Eski Matbaa Sokak 3; per hour ₺1.5; ☺ 8am-1am).

Post Office (Atatürk Caddesi 127) At the northern end of town on the main street.

Tourist Office (☎ 312 2122; Yat Limanı Karşısı; ☺ 8am-noon & 1-5pm Mon-Fri) You can get information from this kiosk on the waterfront south of the main square (if/when open).

ℹ Getting There & Away

BOAT

From May to September, boats sail daily to Mytilini (Midilli in Turkish) in Lesvos, Greece, at 9am (one-way passenger/car ₺85/175, 1½ hours) and return to Ayvalık (€30/60) on the same day at 6pm. From October to May, boats sail to Lesvos at 9am on Tuesday, Thursday and Saturday, and return to Ayvalık the same days.

Note that times do change and you must make a reservation (in person or by telephone) 24 hours before departure. When you pick up your tickets, bring your passport.

For information and tickets, contact **Jale Tour** (☎ 331 3170; www.jaletour.com; Yeni Liman Karşısı) or **Turyol** (☎ 331 6700; www.turyolonline.com; Yeni Liman Karşıı).

BUS

Bergama

Hourly Bergama (₺8, 1½ hours, 45km) buses leave Ayvalık otogar between 9am and 7pm and travel south through town, so you can jump on at the main square.

Çanakkale

If coming from Çanakkale (₺30, 3¼ hours, 200km, three daily), smaller companies may drop you on the main highway (Hwy 550), from where you'll have to catch a dolmuş to the centre. Larger companies, such as Ulusoy, provide a *servis* (shuttle bus) to their offices in the centre.

Edremit

Regular dolmuşes go from Ayvalık otogar (₺8, one hour) to Edremit between 7am and 8.45pm each day.

İzmir

There are hourly buses to/from İzmir (₺22, 2½ hours, 150km) departing from Ayvalık otogar.

CAR

The inland route to Bergama, via Kozak, is much more scenic and only marginally slower than the coast road, winding through idyllic pine-clad hills. Backtrack north for 10km towards Edremit, then turn east.

ℹ Getting Around

BUS & DOLMUŞ

Town Centre

Dolmuş taxis (white with red stripes running around them) serve the town centre, stopping to put down and pick up passengers along a series of short set routes. You can catch them at the main square. Fares are typically ₺2.

Otogar

Ayvalık city buses (₺2) run through town between the otogar and the main square.

South

City buses continue from the main square to the tourist office and the beaches around Sarımsaklı. Minibuses (₺2.50) also depart for the beaches from beside the Tansaş supermarket south of the main square.

CAR

Navigating Ayvalık old town's fiendishly narrow lanes can be an extremely stressful experience. You'd be better off parking at one of the car parks along the waterfront. They generally cost ₺10 to ₺12 per day.

TAXI

From the otogar to the town centre costs ₺25.

Alibey Island (Cunda)

📞 0266 / POP 3500

Named after a hero of the Turkish War of Independence, Alibey Island (Alibey Adası), known to the locals as Cunda Island (Cunda Adası), lies just offshore, facing Ayvalık across the water to the west. It can be reached by ferry or by dolmuş taxi – it's linked to the mainland by a causeway – and is generally regarded as a quieter extension of Ayvalık itself, with residents of both communities regularly shuttling back and forth between the two.

The ferry docks at a small quay lined with fish restaurants. Behind these sits a small, distinguished-looking town made up of old (and in parts rather dilapidated) Greek stone houses. As with Ayvalık, the people here were compelled into a population exchange in the early 1920s, in this instance with Muslims from Crete.

Just to the east of the ferry pier is the town's main square. There are a half-dozen ATMs on the seafront and an information board with maps in the car park at the eastern end of the esplanade. Behind the square is a small tourist market with stalls selling jewellery and other trinkets.

One of the most famous relics of the town's Greek past, the Taksiyarhis church (1873) – not to be confused with the older church of the same name in Ayvalık – perches on a small hill, just inland from the tourist market. Though it avoided being turned into a mosque, the church suffered severe damage during an earthquake in 1944, and today stands in picturesque decrepitude. Inside are some faded and rather forlorn-looking frescoes. You'll also see a few Greek-style windmills that vaguely recall Mykonos but went into retirement decades ago.

The prettiest parts of the island are to the west, where there are good beaches for sunbathing and swimming, and north, much of which is taken up by the Pateriça Nature Reserve. This has good walking routes and, on the north shore, the ruins of the Greek Ayışığı Manastır ı (Moonlight Monastery).

🛏 Sleeping

Tutku Pansiyon PENSION €€
(📞 327 1965; www.tutkupansiyon.com; Sahil Restorantları ve Taş Kahve Arkası; s/d ₺75/150; ❄🛜) Alibey's best budget pension, 'Passion' is centrally located, beside a cool wine house and a few streets back from the water. It

has five small, simple rooms with red tiled floors, small TVs and fridges. Owners Şevket and Abidin are relaxed and hospitable.

Ada Kamping CAMPING GROUND €€
(📞 327 1211; www.adacamping.com; campsite per person ₺30 plus tent/caravan ₺10/20, caravan/bungalow per person ₺80/120; ☺ Apr-Nov) This large, well-equipped camping ground lies 3km west of town. The air-conditioned bungalows are simple but spotless, although the caravans and grounds are a little worn-looking. The site boasts its own beach and waterside restaurant (mains ₺15), plus a kitchen for guest use.

Taş Bahçe BOUTIQUE HOTEL €€€
(📞 327 2290; www.tasbahcebutikotel.com; 15 Eylül Caddesi 33; r ₺200-275) The lovely 'Stone Garden' is a boutique hotel in two newly built townhouses that look centuries old. It's on the main road into town about 100m from the seafront, but the windows in the 10 rooms have double-glazing, ensuring island tranquillity. We love the canopy beds, the views of the church and town, and the lovely garden where breakfast is served.

🍴 Eating & Drinking

⭐ **Lal Girit Mutfağı** CRETAN €€
(Ruby Cretan Cuisine; 📞 327 2834; Altay Pansiyon Yanı 20; mains ₺12-20, meze ₺8; ☺ 10am-midnight) At this charming restaurant serving home cooking (for real) and local hang-out, Emine serves delicious Girit (Cretan) dishes learned from her grandmother, including *peynirli kabak* (zucchini with feta cheese) and *briam* (mixed baked vegetables in tomato sauce). You can even BYO fish (₺10) and they'll cook it for you.

Cunda Lezzet Diyarı SEAFOOD €€
(📞 327 1016; Sahil Yolu 16; meze ₺6-12; ☺ 11am-midnight) Even by Turkish standards, the fridge in this small blue-and-white restaurant is heaving with meze. Hot dishes include Aegean staples such as octopus casserole.

Papalina SEAFOOD €€€
(📞 327 1041; Sahil Boyu 7; mains ₺15-25, meze ₺7; ☺ 8am-1am) Named after the *papalina balığı*, a popular local sprat (one portion ₺10), this place has a lovely position right next to the fishing boats at the western end of the pier and a cheery, bustling atmosphere.

Taş Kahve BAR
(www.taskahve.com.tr; Sahil Boyu 20; tea ₺1.50, beer ₺8; ☺ 7am-midnight) It's worth the trip to

the island just to sip tea and talk fishing in this cavernous venue adorned with coloured glass windows, period black-and-white photos and artwork on its cracked concrete walls.

❶ Getting There & Away

BOAT
Boats to Alibey Island (₺5, 20 minutes) run to/from Ayvalık pier every 15 minutes from June to early Sepetember and hourly between 10am and midnight the rest of the year.

CAR & DOLMUŞ
From the centre of Ayvalık, taxis head for the island (₺2.50, 20 minutes) via the causeway. They run from 6am to midnight and drop off at the eastern end of the island's esplanade.

TAXI
It typically costs ₺30 between the island and central Ayvalık.

Bergama (Pergamum)

📞 0232 / POP 62,400

Bergama, a laid-back market town, is the modern successor to the once-powerful ancient city of Pergamum. Unlike Ephesus, which heaves with tourists year-round, Pergamum is for the most part a site of quiet, classical splendour. Those who do make it here are invariably enamoured with the uncrowded access to the Asclepion, ancient Rome's pre-eminent medical centre, and the staggering mountainside Acropolis, easily reached by cable car.

There has been a town here since Trojan times, but Pergamum's heyday was during the period between Alexander the Great and the Roman domination of all Asia Minor, when it was one of the Middle East's richest and most powerful small kingdoms. Pergamum was inscribed on Unesco's World Heritage list in June 2014, the 999th site in the world (and the 14th in Turkey) to be so honoured.

History

Pergamum owed its prosperity to Lysimachus, one of Alexander the Great's generals, who took control of much of the Aegean region when Alexander's far-flung empire fell apart after his death in 323 BC. In the battles over the spoils, Lysimachus captured a great treasure, estimated at over 9000 gold talents, which he entrusted to his commander in Pergamum, Philetaerus, before going off to fight Seleucus for control of Asia Minor.

But Lysimachus lost the battle and was killed in 281 BC. Philetaerus then set himself up as governor.

Philetaerus, a eunuch, was succeeded by his nephew and heir Eumenes I (263–241 BC), who was in turn followed by his adopted son, Attalus I (241–197 BC). Attalus declared himself king, expanding his power and forging an alliance with Rome.

During the reign of Attalus' son, Eumenes II (197–159 BC), Pergamum reached its golden age. He founded a library that would in time rival that of Alexandria, Egypt, then the world's greatest repository of knowledge. This was partly due to the large-scale production here of *pergamena* (parchment), the writing material made from stretched animal skin and more durable than papyrus.

Eumenes also added the Altar of Zeus to the buildings already crowning the Acropolis, built the 'middle city' on terraces halfway down the hill, and expanded and beautified the Asclepion. Much of what he and the other kings built hasn't survived the ravages of the centuries (or the acquisitive enthusiasm of Western museums, notably the Pergamon Museum in Berlin), but what remains is impressive, dramatically sited and well worth visiting.

Eumenes' brother Attalus II (160–138 BC) kept up the good work, but under the short rule of his son, Attalus III (138–133 BC), the kingdom began to fall apart. With no heir, Attalus III bequeathed his kingdom to Rome, and Pergamum became the Roman province of Asia in 129 BC.

Along with İzmir, Sardis and Ephesus, Pergamum is one of the Seven Churches of the Revelation (or Apocalypse), the major churches of early Christianity mentioned by St John the Divine in the New Testament's last chapter. The phrase 'where Satan has his throne' (Rev 2:13) may refer to the Red Hall.

◉ Sights & Activities

Bergama Acropolis   RUIN
(Bergama Akropol; www.muze.gov.tr/akropol; Akropol Caddesi 2; admission ₺25, audioguide ₺10; ⊙ 8am-7pm Apr-Sep, to 5pm Oct-Mar) The road leading up to the Acropolis, Bergama's richest archaeological site, wends 5km from the Red Hall to a car park at the top, with some souvenir and refreshment stands nearby. A much easier way to go is to follow the signposts along Akropol Caddesi to the lower station of the Bergama Acropolis Cable Car (Bergama Akropolis Teleferik;

Acropolis

At the northern end of the theatre terrace is the ruined Temple of Dionysus, while to the south is the Altar of Zeus (also known as the Great Altar), which was originally covered with magnificent friezes depicting the battle between the Olympian gods and their subterranean foes. However, 19th-century German excavators were allowed to remove most of this famous building to Berlin, leaving only the base behind.

Piles of rubble on top of the Acropolis are marked as five separate palaces, including that of Eumenes II, and you can also see fragments of the once-magnificent defensive walls as well as barracks.

To escape the crowds and get a good view of the theatre and Temple of Trajan, walk downhill behind the Altar of Zeus, or turn left at the bottom of the theatre steps, and follow the sign to the antik yol (ancient street) past the Upper Agora and the bath-gymnasium. Within what was once a sprawling residential area of the Middle City is modern Building Z (2004) protecting part of a peristyle court and some fantastic floor mosaics. Look for the grotesque masks with wild animals, the child Dionysus with Silenus supping from a cup and the remnants of tinted stucco on the walls. More baths, gymnasia and the sumptuous Palace of Attalus I before reaching the Lower Agora. From here you can exit, follow the road left for 700m and, before reaching the cable car lower station, turn right down the steep road to Akropol Caddesi leading into town.

www.facebook.com/akropolisteleferik; Akropol Caddesi; return ₺6; ☺8am-7pm Apr-Sep, to 5pm Oct-Mar). The ride up takes five minutes and is worth it for the views alone. You can easily explore as you make your way down.

From the Upper City at the top, a line of rather faded blue dots marks a suggested route around the main structures – you might instead consider hiring the audioguide for ₺10. These structures include the library that helped put Pergamum on the map and the colossal marble-columned Temple of Trajan (Trajaneum), built during the reigns of the emperors Trajan and Hadrian and used to worship them as well as Zeus. It's the only Roman structure surviving on the Acropolis, and its foundations were used as cisterns during the Middle Ages.

Immediately downhill from the temple, descend through the tunnel to the impressive and unusual vertigo-inducing, 10,000-seat Hellenistic theatre. Its builders decided to take advantage of the spectacular view (and conserve precious space on top of the hill) by building the theatre into the hillside. In general, Hellenistic theatres are wider and rounder than this, but at Pergamum the hillside location made rounding impossible and so it was increased in height instead.

Asclepion RUIN

(Asklepion; www.muze.gov.tr/asklepion; Prof Dr Frieldhelm Korte Caddesi 1; admission/parking ₺20/5; ☺8am-7pm Apr-Sep, to 5pm Oct-Mar) An ancient medical centre, the Asclepion was founded by Archias, a local who had been cured at the Asclepion of Epidaurus (Greece). Treatments included mud baths, the use of herbs and ointments, enemas and sunbathing. Diagnosis was often by dream analysis. The Asclepion may not be as dramatic as the Acopolis, but in many ways it is complete and evocative of the times and how ancient people lived.

The Asclepion is 2km uphill from the town centre as the crow flies (but it's a winding road), signposted from the Lead Mosque (Kurşunlu Cami) on Cumhuriyet Caddesi opposite the PTT. A second road (Asklepion Caddesi and Prof Dr Frieldhelm Korte Caddesi) runs from the southern end of Cumhuriyet Caddesi, southwest of town.

It's closed to motorists and we don't recommend walking it, as it passes through a large military base; if you do, be off it by dusk and don't take photos.

Pergamum's Asclepion came to the fore under Galen (AD 129–216), who was born here and studied in Alexandria, Greece and Asia Minor before setting up shop as physician to Pergamum's gladiators. Recognised as perhaps the greatest early physician, Galen added considerably to the knowledge of the circulatory and nervous systems, and also systematised medical theory. Under his influence, the medical school at Pergamum became renowned throughout the ancient world. His work was the basis for Western medicine well into the 16th century.

The Roman Via Tecta, a colonnaded sacred way, leads from the entrance to the sanctuary, where you'll see the base of a column carved with snakes, the symbol of Asclepios, the god of medicine. Just as the snake sheds its skin and gains a 'new life', so the patients at the Asclepion were supposed to 'shed' their illnesses. Signs mark a circular Temple of Asclepios, a library and, beyond it, a heavily restored Roman theatre.

There are latrines over a channel in the southwest corner of the main courtyard and you can take a drink from the sacred well in the centre. From here pass along the vaulted tunnel to the treatment centre, a temple to another god of medicine called Asclepius. Patients slept in the round temple hoping that Telesphorus would send a cure or diagnosis in a dream. The names of Asclepius' two daughters, Hygieia and Panacea, have passed into medical terminology.

Soft drinks, snacks and souvenirs (including parchment) are available from the stalls by the car park.

Red Hall
RUIN

(Kızıl Avlu; Kınık Caddesi; admission ₺5; ☉ 8am-7pm Apr-Sep, to 5pm Oct-Mar) The cathedral-sized Red Hall, sometimes called the Red Basilica, was originally built as a giant temple to the Egyptian gods Serapis and Isis in the 2nd century AD. It's still an imposing-looking place, though rather scattered and battered. At the time of research, the structure was closed for renovation, which will see some of the hall's severely damaged high walls repaired.

During its pagan pomp, this must have been an awe-inspiring place. In his Book of Revelation, St John the Divine wrote that this was one of the Seven Churches of the Apocalypse, singling it out as the 'throne of the devil'. Look for a hole in the podium in the centre which allowed a priest to hide and appear to speak through the 10m-high cult statue. The building is so big that the early Christians didn't convert it into a church but built a basilica inside it dedicated to St John, of course. The most intact section, the southern rotunda, was used for religious and cult rituals; once covered in marble panels, it is now red brick.

Along with the glass-sided lantern at the northern (main) entrance, the curious red flat-brick walls of this large, roofless structure are visible from midway down the roads to the Acropolis and town centre. You can easily walk to the Red Hall, or stop your taxi here on your way to/from the Acropolis.

İZMIR & THE NORTH AEGEAN BERGAMA (PERGAMUM)

Asclepion

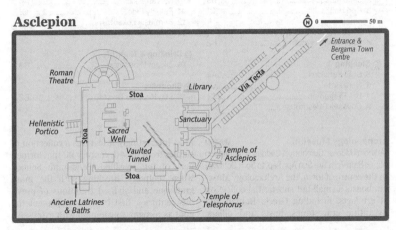

Roman Theatre

Library

Via Tecta

Entrance & Bergama Town Centre

Stoa

Hellenistic Portico

Sanctuary

Stoa

Sacred Well

Vaulted Tunnel

Temple of Asclepios

Stoa

Ancient Latrines & Baths

Temple of Telesphorus

Ⓝ 0 ▬▬▬▬ 50 m

Bergama

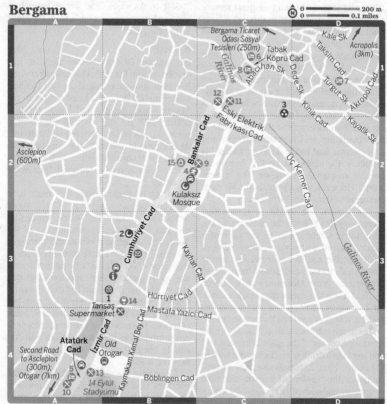

N
0 ——————— 200 m
0 ——————— 0.1 miles

Asclepion (600m)

Bergama Ticaret Odası Sosyal Tesisleri (250m)

Kale Sk

Acropolis (3km)

Acropolis (3km)

Kulaksız Mosque

Eski Elektrik Fabrikası Cad

Tansaş Supermarket

Second Road to Asclepion (300m); Otogar (7km)

Old Otogar

14 Eylül Stadyumu

Bergama

⊙ Sights
1 Archaeology Museum B3
2 Lead Mosque B3
3 Red Hall C1

⊙ Activities, Courses & Tours
4 Hacı Hekim Hamamı B2

⊙ Sleeping
5 Gobi Pension A4
6 Hera Hotel C1
7 Les Pergamon D1
8 Odyssey Guesthouse C1

⊗ Eating
9 Bergama Sofrası C2
10 Kervan A4
11 Paksoy Pide C1
12 Sarmaşık Lokantası C1
13 Simge Pastanesi A4

⊙ Drinking & Nightlife
14 Zıkkım Birahanesi B3

⊙ Shopping
15 Şen Naoe Ev Tekstil B2

Archaeology Museum   MUSEUM
(Arkeoloji Müzesi; Cumhuriyet Caddesi 6; admission
₺5; ⊙8am-7pm Tue-Sun Apr-Sep, to 5pm Oct-Mar)
In the centre of town, the Archaeology Museum boasts a small but substantial collection
of artefacts, including Greek, Roman and
Byzantine gravestones, busts and pillars.

Most interestingly, it features a collection of
statues from the 4th century BC that formed
part of the so-called 'Pergamum School'
when sculptors, breaking with the more
grotesque and stylised traditions of previous centuries, first began to represent the
gods as recognisably human with expressive

features. Other finds from the surrounding sites include a smashed Roman tablet listing city laws, discovered at the Lower Agora on the Acropolis.

Look out, too, for the scale replica of the Altar of Zeus (the original is in the Pergamon Museum in Berlin) and, in the main hall, finds from the nearby, and now underwater, site of Allianoi. The ethnography gallery focuses on the crafts and customs of the Ottoman period, with dioramas representing folk dancing and carpet weaving.

Hacı Hekim Hamamı   HAMAM
(☑ 631 0102; www.hacihekimhamami.com.tr; Bankalar Caddesi 42; hamam ₺25, scrub & massage ₺40; ☺ men 6am-11pm, women 8.30am-7pm) This 16th-century hamam just north of the Kulaksız Mosque has separate entrances for men and women and charges ₺40 for the full works. It's one of the nicer hamams you'll find in provincial Turkey.

🛏 Sleeping

The northern end of Cumhuriyet Caddesi, in the old part of town, is the best area to stay.

Odyssey Guesthouse   PENSION €
(☑ 631 3501; www.odysseyguesthouse.com; Abacıhan Sokak 13; dm ₺25, s/d from ₺50/85, s/d without bathroom ₺40/70; ❇ @ ☎) The pension in this grand old house is excellent, with superb views of all three archaeological sites from the upstairs terrace lounge. The main building has six basic doubles, with excellent showers; the other building has three rooms. Self-caterers enjoy the small kitchenette and separate sleeping area. There's a book exchange and a copy of Homer's *Odyssey* in every room.

Gobi Pension   PENSION €
(☑ 633 2518; www.gobipension.com; İzmir Caddesi 18; s/d ₺55/85, s/d without bathroom ₺35/65; ❇ @) This very popular family-run place has 12 bright rooms. Those at the front have double glazing to keep the traffic noise out and those at the back overlook a garden; some have balconies. It's well set up for travellers, with a kitchen, laundry service and help on hand from terrifically friendly Gobi and his son Mustafa.

Hera Hotel   BOUTIQUE HOTEL €€€
(☑ 631 0634; www.hotelhera.com; Tabak Köprü Caddesi 38; s/d €60/80; ❇ ☎) A pair of 200-year-old Greek houses have been cobbled into the most sophisticated accommodation. Each of the 10 rooms, named after

mythological Greek deities, feature timber ceilings, parquet floors, kilims and curios hand-picked by the erudite couple in charge. Zeus (€120) is a beautiful suite with two balconies, while Nike, in the second building, just does it.

The breakfast on the rooftop with views of the Acropolis comes highly recommended.

Les Pergamon   BOUTIQUE HOTEL €€€
(☑ 632 3935; www.lespergamon.com; Taksim Caddesi 35; s/d €70/95; ❇ ☎) Now in the same stable as the Hera Hotel, this gorgeous but somewhat chaotically run stone property once served as a Greek school. The six rooms have their own names as well as high ceilings, wooden floors, grey, black or violet bedspreads and rugs. Some bathrooms are in the original stone. Zeus (€130) is a touch more regal; Serapis is a single.

Even if you don't stay, splurge on a meal in the Kybele restaurant, with garden seating in the warmer months.

🍴 Eating & Drinking

There's a row of tree-shaded pubs around Zıkkım Birahanesi.

Bergama Sofrası   TURKISH €
(☑ 631 5131; Bankalar Caddesi 44; mains ₺8-12; ☺ 10am-5am) Sit outside next to the hamam or inside the diner-like interior, with its clean surfaces and open kitchen under bright lights. The spicy *köfte* (₺8) is the speciality. It's best to eat here at lunch when the food is still fresh.

Simge Pastanesi   BAKERY €
(☑ 631 1034; Atatürk Caddesi 1; baklava & ice cream ₺4; ☺ 24hr) The family-run Simge Pastanesi is considered the best patisserie in town.

Paksoy Pide   PIDE €
(☑ 633 1722; İstiklal Meydanı 39; pide ₺5-8.50; ☺ 6am-11pm) Pint-sized Paksoy is clean and patronised by locals. Watch the chef rolling and flipping the pide classics in front of the oven.

Sarmaşık Lokantası   TURKISH €
(☑ 632 2741; İstiklal Meydanı 6; mains ₺8; ☺ 8am-11pm) One of the more dependable local restaurants on the main street, the 'Ivy' has a heavy rotation of ready-made stews, soups and rice dishes.

Kervan   PIDE, KEBAP €€
(☑ 633 2632; Atatürk Caddesi 16; mains ₺6-10; ☺ 8am-11pm) Kervan is popular among locals

for its large outdoor terrace and good dishes. The menu features a range of kebaps, pide, çorba (soup) and, for dessert, künefe (syrup-soaked dough and sweet cheese sprinkled with pistachios).

Bergama Ticaret Odası Sosyal Tesisleri
TURKISH €€

(📋 632 9641; Ittihati Terakki Caddesi; mains ₺18-24; 🕙 9am-midnight) Run by the local chamber of commerce, this wonderfully restored restaurant has an outdoor terrace with panoramic views, reasonable food and a license. It's located in a park 300m up the hill behind the main street.

Market
MARKET

(🕙 8am-6pm Mon) Bergama has a bustling Monday market, which stretches from the old otogar to past the Red Hall. It's great for fresh fruit and veg. Böblingen Caddesi and the area around the old bus station are good for picnic supplies. Cheese, olives, fresh bread and dried fruit are all sold.

Zıkkım Birahanesi
PUB

(Cumhuriyet Caddesi; mains ₺6-10, beer ₺7; 🕙 10.30am-1am) With shady garden seating just off the main road, this cool beer garden makes a welcome midtown pit stop, offering ice-cold Tuborg, köfte and piyaz (whitebean salad).

🛍 Shopping

Şen Naoe Ev Tekstil
HANDICRAFTS

(📋 633 4488; Kapalı Çarşı 9; 🕙 8am-9pm Jun-Sep, 10am-5pm low season) This lovely Japanese-run shop in the old Bedesten (Covered Bazaar) sells exquisite handwoven hamam towels, shawls, tablecloths and the like.

ℹ Information

Modern Bergama lies spread out on either side of one long main street, which changes names, and along which almost everything you'll need can be found, including hotels, restaurants, banks, the PTT and the museum.

Tourist Office (📋 631 2852; İzmir Caddesi 11, Hükümet Konağı; 🕙 8.30am-noon & 1-5.30pm) Just north of the museum in the main provincial office; supplies a useful map.

ℹ Getting There & Away

BUS

Bergama's *yeni* (new) otogar lies 7km from the centre, at the junction of the İzmir–Çanakkale highway and the main road into town. From 6am to 7pm, a free *servis* (shuttle bus) runs between there and the *eski* (old) otogar in the town centre. Outside these hours you will have to take a taxi (₺25). Some buses from Çanakkale drop you at the junction near the otogar, from where you can walk to the bus station and pick up the *servis*.

Ankara ₺65, 8½ hours, 480km, nightly
Ayvalık ₺10, 1¼ hours, 60km, hourly
İstanbul (via Bursa) ₺55, 11 hours, 250km, two daily, with additional services in high season
İzmir ₺12, two hours, 110km, every 45 minutes

DOLMUŞ

In the early morning and evening, half-hourly dolmuşes to Ayvalık and Çandarlı leave from the old otogar; at other times, they leave from the new otogar.

WORTH A TRIP

KALEM ISLAND

Should you discover that you've woken up in paradise, no doubt you've spent the night at **Kalem Island Oliviera Resort** (📋 0232-677 8023; www.olivieraresort.com; Kalem Adası, Bademli Köyü; r with half board low/high season from €240/360; 🕙 mid-May–Sep), one of the most beautiful places on (errr, make that off) the Turkish Aegean coast. The resort sits on its own private island, Kalem Adası (Reed Island), just 450m from the shore near Bademli village, which is 18km northwest of Çandarlı. The resort now counts 44 rooms in four different categories that range from five ultra-comfortable Palm rooms in a lovely stone cottage to seven luxurious Chateau suites, with polished wooden floors and Jacuzzis. Facilities abound – there's a spa with treatments and a host of water sports (sailing, diving, windsurfing) as well as a pool and a small but perfectly groomed Blue Flag beach. For sustenance, choose from among four bars and restaurants.

But it's Kalem's great natural beauty that is its major draw card. Gentle hills covered with olive groves lead down to lovely hidden coves and the turquoise waters off the west coast have earned it the nickname 'the Maldives of Turkey'. The endless gardens are a delight and are complemented by scores of ancient columns, busts and urns – all on loan from the Archaeology Museum in İzmir. Seriously worth a detour.

ℹ Getting Around

Bergama's sights are so spread out that it's hard to walk round them all in one day. The Red Hall is about a kilometre from the tourist office, the Asclepion is 2km away and the Acropolis is over 5km away.

BUS

Between 6am and 7pm, half-hourly buses run through town between the old otogar and the market area (₺1.75), 200m past the Red Hall at the foot of the road up to the Acropolis.

TAXI

A convenient option is to book a 'city tour'. From the centre to the Asclepion, Red Hall and Acropolis, with 30 minutes at the first two sights and an hour at the latter, should cost around ₺70. Taxis wait around some of the mosques and the two otogars. Individual fares from the taxi rank near Hacı Hekim Hamamı are about ₺10 to the Asclepion, and ₺15 to the Acropolis.

Çandarlı

📞 0232 / POP 5300

The small, tranquil resort town of Çandarlı (ancient Pitane) sits on a peninsula jutting into the Aegean, 33km southwest of Bergama. It's dominated by the small but stately restored 15th-century Venetian **Çandarlı Castle** (Çandarlı Kilesi; ⊙ 24hr) FREE and has a sandier beach than some of its neighbours.

Local tourism fills most of the pensions in high summer. Out of season, Çandarlı is pretty much a ghost town.

Shops, internet cafes and the PTT are in the centre, 200m behind the seafront. The castle, pensions and restaurants line the seashore. Market day is Friday.

🛏 Sleeping

Most of the hotels and pensions lie west of the castle, facing a thin strip of coarse sand.

Otel Samyeli   HOTEL €€
(📞 673 3428; www.otelsamyeli.com; Sahil Plaj Caddesi; s/d/tr ₺60/120/180; ❄) Facing the beach, the Samyeli has 20 simple, spotless and cheerful rooms (double room 20 and triple 21 have great sea views). The halls are decorated with old sewing machines and typewriters and there's a seafront fish restaurant (mains ₺15 to ₺25).

Kaffe Pansiyon   PENSION €€
(📞 673 3122, 0545 689 8789; Sahil Plaj Caddesi; s/d ₺50/100; 📶) This pretty basic pension above quite a lovely cafe has 15 small rooms and

wi-fi is in the lounge only. But the price is right, and some rooms face the sea.

🍴 Eating & Drinking

For fresh fruit, the daily *çarşı* (market) in the shadow of the town mosque is a good place to replenish. There's also a Tanşaş supermarket, and ice cream stalls on the seafront east of the castle.

Deniz Restaurant   SEAFOOD €€
(📞 673 3124; Sahil Plaj Caddesi; mains ₺15, meze ₺5; ⊙ 11am-midnight) With tables right on the seafront, the 'Sea' is friendly and good value, serving all the usual meze and fish dishes as well as meat options.

Altıhan   SEAFOOD €€€
(📞 673 1056; Sahil Plaj Caddesi; mains ₺20-25; ⊙ 11am-midnight) Probably the most upmarket restaurant on the Çandarlı seafront, the Altıhan has a clean, modern look and feel to it and great views.

ℹ Getting There & Away

Frequent buses run between Çandarlı and İzmir (₺12, 1½ hours) via Dikili (₺3, 20 minutes). At least six dolmuşes run daily to/from Bergama (₺5, 30 minutes).

Foça

📞 0232 / POP 28,500

Sometimes called Eski Foça (Old Foça) to distinguish it from its newer (and rather dull) neighbour, Yeni Foça, over the hill, this happy-go-lucky holiday town straddles both the Büyük Deniz (Big Sea) and the picturesque Küçük Deniz (Small Sea). Its Ottoman-Greek houses are among the finest on the Aegean coast and open onto a storybook esplanade where children fish and couples stroll from pension to restaurant in the shadows of Beşkapılar castle.

Foça was the site of ancient Phocaea, which takes its name from the seals (*phoce* in Greek) basking offshore at Siren Rocks, and was founded in the 8th century BC. During their golden age (5th century BC), the Phocaeans were great mariners, sending swift vessels, powered by up to 50 oars, into the Aegean, Mediterranean and Black Seas; see a replica opposite Beşkapılar. They also founded Samsun on the Black Sea, as well as towns in Italy, Corsica, France and Spain.

More recently, this was an Ottoman-Greek fishing and trading port. It's now a prosperous middle-class resort, with holiday villas gathered on the outskirts and a thin, dusty beach with some swimming platforms. There are some more secluded beaches to the north heading towards Yeni Foça.

The otogar is just inland from the Büyük Deniz. Heading north from here, with the Büyük Deniz and its accompanying tour boats on your left, takes you through the centre of town to the Küçük Deniz. You'll pass the tourist office, the PTT, the *belediye* (town hall) and banks, before reaching the harbour after around 350m. Continue north along the Küçük Deniz' shore for most of the pensions.

⊙ Sights

Ancient Phocaea RUIN
FREE Little is left of the ancient Ionian settlement in Foça: a ruined theatre, the remains of an aqueduct near the otogar and and traces of two shrines to the goddess Cybele. Some 7km east of town on the way to the İzmir highway and on the left side of the road lies an *anıt mezarı* (monumental tomb) from the 4th century BC.

Temple of Athena RUIN
This site above the outdoor sanctuary of Cybele, with two shrines to that goddess, has yielded a beautiful griffin and a horse's head believed to date to the 5th century BC. Excavations continue in the summer and the site is still not open to the public.

Beşkapılar FORTRESS
(Five Gates) If you continue west past the outdoor sanctuary of Cybele, you'll come to the city walls and the partially rebuilt Beşkapılar, effectively the docking area of a castle, built by the Byzantines, repaired by the Genoese and the Ottomans in 1539, and clearly much restored since.

Dış Kale FORTRESS
Guarding the town's southwestern approaches, the late 17th-century 'Outer Castle' is best seen from the water (on a boat trip) as it's inside a military zone.

🏃 Activities

Between late April and early October, boats leave daily at about 11am from both the Küçük Deniz and Büyük Deniz for day trips around the outlying islands. Trips include various swim stops en route and return about 5pm. Most drop anchor at Siren Rocks, and typically cost ₺35, including lunch and tea.

Valinor: the Lord of the Boats BOAT TOUR
(☑ 798 6317; www.valinortour.com; Büyük Deniz) One of the better boat trip operators is Valinor: The Lord of the Boats, based in front of the *jandarma* (police) station on the Büyük Deniz.

Belediye Hamamı HAMAM
(☑ 812 1959; 115 Sokak 22; hamam ₺15, scrub & massage ₺40; ⊙ 8am-midnight) The full works cost ₺40 at this tourist-friendly hamam above the Büyük Deniz.

🛏 Sleeping

There's some very good accommodation here at all budget levels and camping grounds on the coast north of Foça.

FOÇA'S SEALS

Foça's offshore islands provide refuge to some of the last remaining Mediterranean monk seals, an endangered species once common throughout the region. There are thought to be about 600 left in the world, so you shouldn't bank on seeing one. Thankfully, much of Foça's offshore area is now a protected zone, the extent of which was increased in 2007.

The seals' habit of basking on rocks and their wailing plaintive cries are believed to have been the inspiration for the legend of the Sirens, as featured in Homer's *Odyssey*.

According to legend, the sirens were strange creatures, half-bird, half-woman, who lived on rocky islands. They used their beautiful, irresistible singing voices to lure sailors towards their perilous perches, where the ships would be dashed against the rocks, and the sailors killed. Odysseus, so the story goes, only managed to resist their entreaties by having himself lashed to his ship's mast.

Appropriately enough, one of the seals' favourite modern basking spots is Siren Kayalıkları (Siren Rocks) on Sickle Island (Orak Adası), just off Foça's northern shore.

For more information on the Mediterranean monk seal, contact the Ankara-based SAD-AFAG (Underwater Research Society-Mediterranean Seal Research Group; ☑ 0312-230 3520; www.sadafag.org; Akıncılar Sokak 10), which oversees protection programs on the coast.

Siren Pansiyon
PENSION **€€**

(☑ 0532 287 6127, 812 2660; www.sirenpansiyon.com; 161 Sokak 13; s ₺50-70, d ₺70-110; 🛜) This excellent 13-room pension is very popular with budget travellers. The location is superb, in a quiet spot just off the seafront promenade, and return guests continually rave about Remzi's hospitality, the excellent kitchen and the rooftop terrace.

İyon Pansiyon
PENSION **€€**

(☑ 812 1415; www.iyonpansion.com; 198 Sokak 8; s ₺60-70, d ₺110-130; ❄🛜) İyon is a great choice for independent travellers. The mood on the two terraces is unobtrusive yet communal. The 10 rooms are simple but up to date, and the five downstairs open onto a lovely shared courtyard. There are sea views from an upstairs room and the reception/breakfast area. The welcoming Tutar family can arrange boat trips with lunch (₺45).

Villa Dedem Hotel
HOTEL **€€**

(☑ 812 1215; www.villadedemhotel.com; Sahil Caddesi 66; s ₺60-90, d ₺100-150; ❄🛜) This 18-room hotel enjoys a central quayside location, but you might struggle to bag a room in summer, as it tends to welcome the same families back year after year. Still, if you get lucky, try to get one of the eight rooms with sea view and balcony.

★ Lola 38 Hotel
BOUTIQUE HOTEL **€€€**

(☑ 812 3826; www.lola38hotel.com; Reha Midilli Caddesi 140; r ₺250-400; ❄🛜) Not unlike sleeping inside a wedding cake, this eight-room symphony in pink and turquoise is a novelty. It's a converted Greek stone house on the quiet end of the Küçük Deniz and is lots of fun, quite posh and supremely comfortable. Those tired of the humdrum hotel room will revel in this place. Choose one of the four garden rooms.

Bülbül Yuvası Hotel
BOUTIQUE HOTEL **€€€**

(Nightingale's Nest; ☑ 812 5152; www.bulbulyuvasi.com.tr; 121 Sokak 20; r ₺225-450; ❄🛜) The 'Nightingale's Nest' is a designer refuge, with 11 beautifully appointed rooms featuring heavy drapery and wooden floors. Caria and Veria are a little pokey for the price, while the sea views (and spa) from the Alalia I and Larissa II rooms lift them up a category. It's down a dead-end lane, so silence predominates.

✖ Eating & Drinking

Foça's dining scene is mostly Turkish pescatarian. There is a decent Tuesday market, which is a good place to stock up for a picnic, as well as various grocery stores. The market spreads through the back streets of the old town.

Harika Köfte Evi
KÖFTE **€**

(☑ 812 5409; Belediye Karşısı; mains ₺10; ☺ 8am-midnight) In addition to four types of *köfte* – reputedly the best in town – the 'Wonderful Köfte House' serves various types of *çorba* (soup) and *tavuk şiş* (roast skewered chicken kebap).

Çarşı Lokantası
TURKISH **€€**

(☑ 812 2377; Küçük Deniz Caddesi 18; mains ₺8-18; ☺ 8am-midnight) This *lokanta* is excellent for lunch. A mixed plate (with meat) typically includes *köfte*, stew, *kalamar* and half a dozen vegetables and starches, sprinkled with herbs and spices by the friendly Mesut and Fatoş. Treat yourself to a Turkish pastry with ice cream.

Letafet
TURKISH **€€**

(☑ 812 1191; 197 Sokak 3; mains ₺15-35; ☺ 9am-2am) This swish place is hidden behind a white wall in the old town, but the giveaway is the loud music and the din of ambient noise and clinking cutlery. Happy diners enjoy classic Turkish cuisine at reasonable prices here.

Foça Restaurant
SEAFOOD **€€**

(☑ 812 2446; Sahil Caddesi 56; mains ₺15-25, meze ₺6; ☺ 9am-midnight) Highly recommended by locals, this seafood restaurant enjoys a prominent position on the quay just opposite the sanctuary of Cybele. The meze here are particularly good.

★ Fokai Restaurant
TURKISH **€€€**

(☑ 812 2186; 121 Sokak 8; mains ₺20; ☺ noon-midnight) Overlooking the Büyük Deniz, Fokai is the best restaurant in town. The atmosphere is understated and the service is sincere. In summer, the terrace fills with Turks and foreign tourists chowing down yummy and unusual meze like *pancar* (beetroot) preparations, superb seafood grills and casseroles. There's pretty good pizza, too.

Keyif
BAR

(Sahil Caddesi 42a; beer ₺8-10) Funky for Foça (it's got a glitter ball) 'Pleasure' offers both Western music and live Turkish performers. Dancing has been known to take place inside.

1. Northern shore, Bozcaada (p176) **2.** Temple of Trajan (p190), Bergama **3.** Konak Meydanı (p201), İzmir **4.** Harvesting grapes (p178), Bozcaada

İzmir & the North Aegean Highlights

Travellers are spoiled for choice in this region and, at the risk of sounding cliché, there really is something for everyone here. Its ancient cities bring history alive, the beaches are seldom as frenetic as elsewhere, the food and wine are among the country's best and the ghosts of times past are ever present.

Ruins

The ancient city of Pergamum (now Bergama) is at the top of everyone's list of places to visit, and Assos in Behramkale is as dramatically situated as you'll find anywhere. But don't miss the wealth of ruins at lesser-known sites like Apollon Smintheion on the Biga Peninsula or Sardis east of İzmir.

Beaches

The beaches at Bozcaada are rightfully celebrated and easily accessible. But go the extra kilometre to take the plunge at Çeşme's Diamond Beach or the one at Çandarlı. And if you prefer to be on rather than in the water, head for Alaçatı Surf Paradise, the centre for windsurfing in Turkey.

Memories

The north Aegean has been colonised for millennia and is one of the most ethnically diverse regions in Turkey. Reminders of the region's multilayered past are seen, felt and sometimes even heard especially in places like Ayvalık, where many Greeks made their home before independence, and İzmir with its community of Sephardic Jews.

Food & Drink

Those rich, multi-ethnic influences are especially palpable in the region's cuisine, which has taken much from the Greek, Cretan and Jewish styles of cooking. Some of the finest vineyards in Turkey are found at Bozcaada, where you'll find descendants of vines planted by the Greeks.

ⓘ Information

Look for internet cafe just off the main square (eg on 194 Sokak).

Tourist Office (☑ 812 1222; Cumhuriyet Meydanı; ☺ 8.30am-noon & 1-5.30pm Mon-Fri, 10am-7pm Sat Jun-Sep) Very helpful, with lots of brochures and a decent map in several languages.

ⓘ Getting There & Around

BICYCLE

Rent bicycles from **Göçmen** (☑ 812 3743; 119 Sokak 2; per hourr/day ₺5/20; ☺ 9am-8pm) near the hamam.

BUS

Bergama

Take the bus to Menemen/İzmir, jump off on the highway (Hwy 550) and flag down any bus heading north.

İzmir & Menemen

Between 6.30am and 9.15pm (11pm in summer), half-hourly buses run to İzmir (₺5, 1½ hours, 86km), passing through Menemen, where there are connections to Manisa.

Yeni Foça

Three to five city buses run daily to/from Yeni Foça (₺4, 30 minutes, 22km). They pass pretty little coves, beaches and camping grounds along the way.

CAR

If you're staying in the area for a few days, you might want to hire a car from **MNB Oto Kirala-ma** (☑ 812 1987; www.mnbrentacar.com; 123 Sokak 6; per day ₺85), behind the police station on the Büyük Deniz.

İzmir

☑ 0232 / POP 2.8 MILLION

The grand port city of İzmir, the third-largest in Turkey, is a proudly liberal, long-time centre of commerce that has emerged as a smart alternative base for travel in the west of the country. Formerly the Greek city of Smyrna, İzmir lives by its seafront *kordon* (promenade), which, especially around leafy Alsancak, is as fetching and lively as any in the world.

With its Levantine, Greek, Armenian and Jewish heritage, İzmir is quite distinct from the rest of Turkey. Indeed, its fellow countrymen sometimes still regard İzmiris with a degree of suspicion and that's nothing new: the Ottomans referred to the city as Gavur İzmir (Infidel Smyrna). Even today

İzmir retains its liberal, laid-back feel. During Ramazan, when some bars in İstanbul and elsewhere close, it's business as usual in the countless watering holes on the balmy *kordon*.

İzmir is also developing a reputation for its cultural and civic foresight. The International İzmir Festival in June and July is adventurous and vast, while a number of decrepit industrial buildings have found new life as communal and creative spaces.

History

İzmir was once Smyrna, a city founded by colonists from Greece sometime in the early part of the 1st millennium BC. Over the next 1000 years it would grow in importance as it came under the influence of successive regional powers: first Lydia, then Greece, and finally Rome. By the 2nd century AD it was, along with Ephesus and Pergamum, one of the three most important cities in the Roman province of Asia. Under Byzantine rule, however, its fortunes declined as the focus of government turned north to Constantinople. Things only began to look up again when the Ottomans took control in 1415, after which Smyrna rapidly became Turkey's most sophisticated and successful commercial city.

After the collapse of the Ottoman Empire at the end of WWI, the Greeks invaded, but were eventually expelled following fierce fighting which, along with a subsequent fire, destroyed most of the old city. The day that Atatürk recaptured Smyrna (9 September 1922) marked the moment of victory in the Turkish War of Independence. The events of 1922 are commemorated in the rather top-heavy monument gracing the waterfront.

◉ Sights & Activities

İzmir is best seen on foot. Between the early 17th and early 20th centuries, İzmir had one of the Ottoman Empire's largest populations of Levantines. The international expat community was drawn here when İzmir was one of the empire's principal trading hubs, and its influence can still be seen. Areas such as Bornova, northeast of the centre, have whole streets of Levantine houses, which reveal the various nationalities' different temperaments. French- and British-built houses have open balconies, as their owners didn't mind being glimpsed from the street, whereas the more-conservative Italians had closed balconies and the Greeks had no balconies.

The best way to see İzmir's different houses and other sights is by foot.

Kordon
WATERFRONT

It's difficult to imagine life in İzmir without its iconic seafront promenade. A triumph of urban renewal, the pedestrianised confines of the west-facing *kordon* are home to a great selection of bars and restaurants that attract droves of people at the end of the day to watch the picture-perfect sunsets. Inland to the east, the Alsancak district is now the focus of the city's nightlife and fashion.

At the southern end of the *kordon* is the new Arkas Art Centre (Arkas Sanat Merkezi; ☑464 6600; www.arkassanatmerkezi.com; 1380 Soka 1; ☉10am-6pm Tue, Wed, Fri-Sun, to 8pm Thu) FREE, housed in the former French consulate. As worthwhile as the rotating exhibits here are, the centre demands a visit just to see the interior of the sumptuous edifice built in 1906.

A 15-minute spin in a horse-drawn carriage along the *kordon* costs ₺20 for four people.

Konak Meydanı
SQUARE

On a pedestrianised stretch of Cumhuriyet Bulvarı, this wide plaza, named after the prominent Ottoman-era Government House (Hkümet Konağı; 1872) to the east, marks the heart of the city. It's the site of the late Ottoman Konak Clock Tower (Konak Saat Kulesi) designed by the Levantine French architect Raymond Charles Père in 1901 to mark the 25th anniversary of Sultan Abdül Hamit II's coronation. Beside it is the lovely Yalı Camii (Shore Mosque; Konak Meydanı; 1755) covered in Kütahya tiles.

Jutting into the sea to the north is the 1890 Konak Pier (Konak Iskelesi; Atatürk Caddesi). It is the work of Gustave Eiffel, who designed Paris' famous tower. The former Customs House was converted into an upmarket shopping mall in 2004.

Zübeyde Hanım Museum Ship
MUSEUM

(Zübeyde Hanım Müze Gemisi; Pasaport Pier; ☉10am-noon & 2-6pm) The M/V *Zübeyde Hanım*, named after Atatürk's beloved mother, is a 50m-long, 307-tonne ferry built in 1987 and used in İstanbul until early 2014, when it opened as a museum devoted to rescue operations at sea. It's worth a visit to see some of the old medical equipment and ship's furnishings.

Agora
RUIN

(Agora Caddesi; admission ₺5; ☉8.30am-7pm Apr-Sep, to 5.30pm Oct-Mar) The ancient Agora, built for Alexander the Great, was ruined in an earthquake in AD 178, but rebuilt soon after by the Roman emperor Marcus Aurelius. Reconstructed Corinthian colonnades, vaulted chambers and arches give you a good idea of what a Roman bazaar looked like. A Muslim cemetery was later built on the site and many of the old tombstones can be seen around the perimeter. The site is entered on the south side, just off Gazi Osmanpaşa Bulvarı.

Archaeology Museum
MUSEUM

(Arkeoloji Müzesi; ☑489 0796; www.izmirmuzesi.gov.tr; Halil Rifat Paşa Caddesi 4, Bahri Baba Parkı; admission ₺10; ☉8.30am-7pm Tue-Sun Apr-Sep, to 5pm Oct-Mar) İzmir's Archaeology Museum is a little dry, but look out for the beautifully decorated sarcophagi, the head of a gigantic statue of Domitian that once stood at Ephesus, and the impressive frieze from the mausoleum at Belevi (250 BC). It's a short walk up the hill from Konak Meydanı.

Ethnography Museum
MUSEUM

(Etnografya Müzesi; ☑483 7254; Halil Rifat Paşa Caddesi 3, Bahri Baba Parkı; ☉8.30am-5.30pm Tue-Sun) FREE The Ethnography Museum occupies the former St Roche Hospital just beside the Archaeology Museum. The lovely, old four-storey stone building houses colourful displays (including dioramas, photos and information panels) of local arts, crafts and customs. You'll learn about everything from camel wrestling, pottery and tin-plating to felt-making, embroidery and weaponry.

Kemeraltı Market
MARKET

(Kemeraltı Çarşısı; ☉8am-8pm) Kemeraltı Market is İzmir's heart and soul, and a great place to get lost for a few hours. There are bargains galore, especially in leather goods, clothing and jewellery. Seek out the flower and bead markets, then stop for a reviving shot of Turkish coffee and baklava in one of the delightful cafes at its core. Anafartalar Caddesi rings the main bazaar area and is its principal thoroughfare.

Within the main bazaar, the glorious Kızlarağası Han (Kızlarağası Inn; Kemeraltı Market; ☉8am-5pm) caravanserai (1744) is a much smaller, calmer version of İstanbul's famous Covered Bazaar. It's touristy, with many items from the far end of the Silk Road (China), but good for a wander. There's a cafe in the courtyard, where merchants once tethered their camels.

The bazaar also contains Hisar Camii (Fortress Mosque; Kemeraltı Market), the city's

İZMİR & THE NORTH AEGEAN İZMİR

İzmir

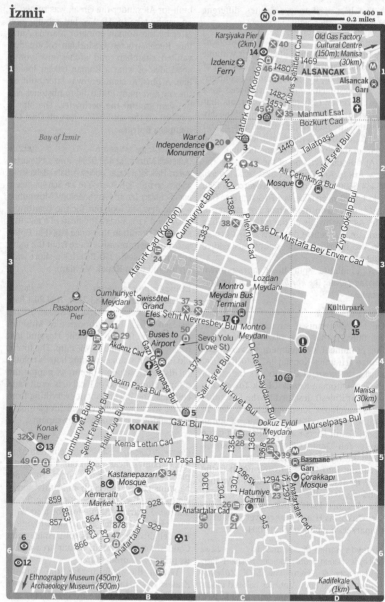

N 0 ———— 400 m
0 ———— 0.2 miles

Karşiyaka Pier
(2km)

İzdeniz
Ferry

Old Gas Factory
Cultural Centre
(150m); Manisa
(30km)

ALSANCAK

Alsancak
Garı

Bay of İzmir

Mahmut Esat
Bozkurt Cad

War of
Independence
Monument

Ali Çetinkaya Bul

Mosque

Dr Mustafa Bey Enver Cad

Lozdan
Meydanı

Kültürpark

Montrö
Meydanı Bus
Terminal

Cumhuriyet
Meydanı

Swissôtel
Grand
Efes Şehit Nevresbey

Pasaport
Pier

Şehit Nevresbey

Montrö
Meydanı

Buses to
Airport

Sevgi Yolu
(Love St)

Akdeniz Cad

Gazi Osmanpaşa Bul

Kazim Paşa Bul

Manisa
(30km)

Konak
Pier

KONAK

Gazi Bul

Dokuz Eylül
Meydanı

Mürselpaşa Bul

Kema Lettin Cad

Fevzi Paşa Bul

Basmane
Garı

Kastanepazarı

Çorakkapı
Mosque

Mosque

Kemeraltı
Market

Hatuniye
Camii

Anafartalar Cad

Ethnography Museum (450m);
Archaeology Museum (500m)

Kadifekale
(1km)

---

largest mosque. The interior is quintessentially İzmiri: the blue-and-gold motifs on the domed ceiling are simpler and less Oriental than classic Ottoman designs. Also look out for the roses and grapes carved along the bottom of the women's gallery and the designs on the stone staircase.

City Museum & Archive MUSEUM
(Ahmet Piristina Kent Arsivi ve Muzesi, Apikam);
293 3900; www.apikam.org.tr; Şair Eşref

İzmir

Bulvarı 1; ⊙8.30am-5.30pm Mon-Sat May-Sep, 8am-5pm Oct-Apr) FREE Housed in a fire station built by the British in 1923, this small but perfectly formed museum has displays on İzmir's history and a courtyard cafe.

Kültürpark PARK
Much of İzmir's town centre between Alsancak and Basmane was destroyed in the 1922 fire as this had been a Greek neighbourhood for centuries. Today it contains Kültürpark, which helps inject a little greenery into the city and attracts strolling couples and joggers. Specific attractions include a 50m parachute tower, a gorgeous Ferris wheel, some contemporary sculptures on the west side of the pond, and exhibition halls for events including the International İzmir Festival (p205).

İzmir Museum of History & Art MUSEUM
(İzmir Tarih ve Sanat Müzesi; ☑445 6818; www.izmirmuzesi.gov.tr/izmir-muze-mudurlugu-izmir-tarih-ve-sanat-muzesi.aspx; Kültürpark; admission ₺3;

⊙8.30am-5.30pm Tue-Sun) Containing three separate departments (Sculpture, Ceramics and Precious Artefacts), this museum, renovated in 2014, gives a good overview of the region's artistic heritage. Look out for the 2nd-century-AD high relief of Poseidon and Demeter from the Agora, the late Neolithic anthropomorphic vase, and the seated Aphrodite from the Roman period.

Atatürk Museum MUSEUM
(Atatürk Müzesi; www.izmirmuzesi.gov.tr/izmir-muze-mudurlugu-ataturk-muzesi.aspx; Atatürk Caddesi 248; ⊙8.30am-5.30pm Tue-Sun) FREE During İzmir's 19th-century heyday, the *kordon* was lined with stately offices and fine houses. Built by a carpet merchant, this is one of the city's best preserved residences, which traces the life and times of one Mustafa Kemal Atatürk. Atatürk stayed here intermittently between 1930 and 1934; in 2014 it was turned into a museum in his honour.

Kadifekale

FORTRESS

(Velvet Castle; Rakım Elkutlu Caddesi) In the 4th century, Alexander the Great chose a secure site for Smyrna's acropolis on Mt Pagos, southeast of the modern city centre, erecting the fortifications that still crown the hill. The view from 'Velvet Fortress' is magnificent, especially just before sunset. Bus 33 from Konak will carry you up the hill.

İzmir's Churches

CHURCH

İzmir retains a number of churches that are still used by the Christian faithful, including the oldest Christian house of worship in the city, the Church of St Polycarp (Sen Polikarp Kilisesi; Vali Kazım Dirik Caddesi; ☺9am-noon & 3-6pm Mon-Sat), built in 1625 with the permission of Sultan Süleyman the Magnificent.

It honours the city's patron saint who was martyred by the Romans at Kadifekale in 155 AD. Note the charming frescoes in which the 19th-century restorer, French architect Raymond Charles Père, included his own likeness.

St John's Cathedral (Şehit Nevresbey Bulvarı), consecrated in 1874, was partly financed by Sultan Abdülaziz and the main altar was a gift from Pope Pius IX.

The more austere Anglican St John's Church (Ziya Gökalp Bulvarı) in Alsancak was consecrated in 1902.

İzmir Mask Museum

MUSEUM

(İzmir Mask Müzesi; ☑465 3107; www.izmirmask-muzesi.com; Cumbalı Sokak 22; admission ₺4; ☺10am-7pm) Tucked away in an old house on a street filled with bars, this little museum spread over three floors has an interesting collection of ceremonial and decorative masks from around the world as well as death masks of the great and the not so good (Mao, Trotsky etc).

Şifalı Lüks Hamamı

HAMAM

(Şifalı Luxury Hamam; ☑484 8430; Anafartalar Caddesi 660; bath & massage ₺40; ☺8am-11pm men, 9am-5pm women) This super-clean hamam dating from the 16th century has a lovely domed and marble interior.

THE JEWS OF İZMİR & THEIR SYNAGOGUES

When the Jews were expelled from Spain and Portugal by King Ferdinand and Queen Isabella in 1492, many settled in cities of the Ottoman Empire, in particular Constantinople (İstanbul), Salonika (now Thessaloniki in Greece) and Smyrna (today's İzmir). For several centuries they were the predominant power in commerce and trade; indeed, the sultan is said to have commented: 'Ye call Ferdinand a wise king, he who makes his land poor and ours rich.' Jews, who followed the Sephardic tradition and spoke a medieval Spanish language called Ladino, enjoyed a tolerance under the Muslim Ottomans unknown in Christian Europe and, unlike in the West, there were no restrictions on the professions Jews could practice.

In Ottoman times, Jews were concentrated in the Mezarlıkbaşı quarter or around Havra Sokağı (Synagogue St), both of which are located in or around Kemeraltı Market (p201). Here they built some three dozen synagogues in traditional Spanish style, eight of which remain in varying conditions. The İzmir Project (☑421 5195; www.izmirjewishheritage.com; admission €7, full-day group tour €125) is an international initiative trying to save these synagogues and create a living cultural monument to the city's rich Sephardic Jewish heritage; two of them – Etz Hayim and Bet Hillel – are in the process of being restored. Contact staff at the İzmir Project to gain access to some of the synagogues; a full-day guided tour will take you to all synagogues still standing as well as the four remaining cortijos (yahudhane in Turkish), distinctive Sephardic Jewish family compounds with a courtyard and fountain.

Also worth visiting is Karataş, an area about 3km south of the centre of town, where most members of the city's 2500-strong Jewish community live. Here you'll find Bet Israel (☑421 4709; Mihat Paşa Caddesi 265), the city's largest synagogue built in 1907, and the Asansör, a lift (elevator) built in the same year by a Jewish banker to facilitate trade between Karataş and the coastline – the alternative is 155 steps. At the foot of the lift a plaque marks the typical old İzmir house where Darío Moreno (1921–68), the late Jewish singer of 'Canım İzmir' (My Dear İzmir), lived. The street – Dario Moreno Sokağı – is named after him. You'll hear a recording of this erstwhile heartthrob singing in the lift.

✦ Festivals & Events

International İzmir Festival FESTIVAL
(Uluslararası İzmir Festivalı; www.iksev.org/tr/iz-mir-festivali) From mid-June to mid-July the annual International İzmir Festival offers performances of music and dance at İzmir's Kültürpark as well as in Çeşme and Ephesus.

🛏 Sleeping

İzmir's waterfront is dominated by large high-end business hotels, while inland there are more budget and midrange options, particularly in Kemeraltı and near Basmane train station.

🛏 Kemeraltı & Basmane

Just southwest of Basmane train station, 1294 Sokak and 1296 Sokak offer many options in restored Ottoman houses. West of the station 1368 Sokak is also a happy hunting ground.

Güzel İzmir Oteli HOTEL €
(☑483 5069; www.guzelizmirhotel.com; 1368 Sokak 8; s/d from ₺65/80; ✸@🖧) It's all change at the 'Pretty', making this budget option in Basmane even more attractive. The 30 rooms, though small, have been given a thorough facelift, there are lovely old photos of Smyrna, a sunny, sunny breakfast room and even a small fitness centre. Room 307 is larger than most and 501 gives on to the terrace.

Hotel Baylan Basmane HOTEL €€
(☑483 0152; www.hotelbaylan.com; 1299 Sokak 8; s/d ₺75/120; ✸@🖧) The 30-room Baylan is among Basmane's best options. The entrance via the huge car park is a little disconcerting, but inside is a spacious and attractive hotel with a welcoming terrace-cum-garden in back. All rooms have polished floorboards and large bathrooms.

Konak Saray Hotel BOUTIQUE HOTEL €€
(☑483 7755; www.konaksarayhotel.com; Anafartalar Caddesi 635; s/d ₺100/135; ✸@🖧) The 27 rooms in this restored old Ottoman house (1855) in a less touristy part of the bazaar have been given an update, with minibar and desk. The rooms facing the atrium are smaller but modern and well priced for what they offer. There's also a great top-floor restaurant.

Otel Antik Han HOTEL €€
(☑489 2750; www.otelantikhan.com; Anafartalar Caddesi 600; s/d/tr ₺75/110/140; ✸@) Said to have once belonged to Atatürk's father, this restored Ottoman building (1857) has 30 pleasant, if somewhat threadbare, rooms with plasma-screen TVs and minibars. The tranquil central courtyard is a world away from the hustle and bustle of the market outside. The hotel also has six charming little loft 'suites' that cost the same price as rooms.

Konak Saray Agora Hotel HOTEL €€
(☑484 1424; www.agorakonaksaray.com; Kestelli Caddesi 113; s/d ₺120/150; ✸🖧) This branch of the Konak Saray is in a renovated Ottoman home above the Agora. The 30 small rooms are modern and certainly lack any design pretensions in the drab brown and white colour schemes; the best views are from rooms 504 or 602. There's a lobby restaurant.

Met Boutique Hotel BOUTIQUE HOTEL €€€
(☑483 0111; www.metotel.com; Gazi Bulvari 124; d ₺180-400; ✸🖧) A boutique hotel really in name only, this flash hotel in the business district has 38 sleek rooms with strong colour schemes of red and black and white and streamlined furniture. It could, however, do with stand-alone desks or some extra space. But the lobby cafe area is genuinely funky and the service is worthy of the world's great cities.

🛏 Alsancak & Kordon

North of Gazi Bulvarı is more pleasant, though the hotels here are firmly in midrange or even top-end territory.

★ Otel Kilim HOTEL €€€
(☑484 5340; www.kilimotel.com.tr; Atatürk Caddesi; s ₺145, d ₺210-260; ✸🖧) This extremely well-run hotel in the Pasaport section of the *kordon* attracts a swathe of return visitors – including us. The 70 rooms are generous (both in dimensions and minibar contents) with lovely showers and vintage photos of İzmir. Some seven rooms face the sea – room 703 is the choicest – though the others have good side views.

Kordon Otel Pasaport HOTEL €€€
(☑484 8181; www.kordonotel.com.tr; Akdeniz Caddesi 2; s/d €90/120; ✸🖧) Fabulous new addition to the seafront stable of hotels, the aptly named Kordon has 60 rooms, all of which have sea views (though only a dozen have balconies). It's a sleekly designed place, with boldly patterned carpets, up-to-date

bathrooms and enormous suites. The rooftop bar, open for cocktails till 2am, is to die for.

İzmir Palas Oteli
HOTEL €€€

(☑ 465 0030; www.izmirpalas.com.tr; Atatürk Caddesi; s/d from ₺150/200; ❄@🛜) Established in 1927, the 138-room Palas is a 10-storied beast, but it's popular, quite comfortable (protracted renovations are now complete), and the location is tremendous overlooking the bay. The fine Deniz seafood restaurant is on the doorstep. The phone chargers in the lobby are a nice touch.

Myhotel
BOUTIQUE HOTEL €€€

(☑ 445 3838; www.myhotel.com.tr; Cumhuriyet Bulvarı 132; s/d ₺160/190; ❄🛜) In a brilliant location just a street back from the sea, the chaotically run but still charming Myhotel is a low-key alternative to the fancier chain hotels nearby. The lobby bar and restaurant are super-cool and the 30 spacious rooms have had a refit (though 360-degrees of chocolate brown might get old after a couple of days).

✖ Eating

The mostly seafood *kordon* restaurants have outside tables with views of the bay but some are quite pricey. On and around Kıbrıs Şehitleri Caddesi in Alsancak, you'll lose the sunset views but gain on atmosphere.

Reyhan
CAFE €

(☑ 444 7946; Dr Mustafa Bey Enver Caddesi 24; cheesecake ₺9.75; ⊙7am-midnight) This institution is serious about sweet stuff, with a professional taster and headset-wearing waitstaff. Decadent delights like strawberry (or raspberry or cherry) cheesecake and almond-cream cake with pineapple and almonds sit alongside favourites like carrot cake.

Sir Winston Tea House
CAFE €

(☑ 421 8861; www.sirwinstonteahouse.com.tr; Dr Mustafa Bey Enver Caddesi 20a; sandwiches ₺15-19, tea ₺4.50-8; ⊙8.30am-midnight Mon-Fri, to 1am Sat & Sun) On a street known for its cafes, this is one of the best, serving dozens of teas, hot and cold coffees, good salads and pastas. There's shady seating outside.

Atıştır Cafe
CAFE €

(☑ 465 2919; 1379 Sokak; filled jacket potatoes ₺7.50-10, set menus ₺6-16; ⊙9am-11pm) 'Snacking', located on a lane running north of Şehit Nevresbey Bulvarı, and half a dozen neighbouring eateries offers enormous jacket (baked) potatoes (*kumpir*) with a choice of

fillings that would sink a battleship. Great place for a filling lunch.

Karagöz
DESSERTS €

(☑ 445 6597; 902 Sokak 25; baklava & ice cream ₺2; ⊙8am-8pm) This little hole-in-the-wall in the Kemeraltı Market is known for its excellent homemade ice cream and baklava.

Yengeç Restaurant
SEAFOOD €€

(☑ 464 5757; Atatürk Caddesi 314a; mains ₺12-25, meze ₺6; ⊙10am-midnight) Our favourite seafood restaurant on the *kordon*, the 'Crab' serves some of the best fish dishes in coastal Turkey. Even better, the price is always right and the staff are both welcoming and very helpful.

Topkapı Restaurant
TURKISH €€

(☑ 484 4141; Anafartlar Caddesi 783; mains ₺12-18, meze ₺5-6; ⊙24hr) This very pleasant modern place that never sleeps serves up some of the best *ızgara* (grills) in the city. Excellent soups (₺6 to ₺10) as well. Located just opposite the Basmane train station.

Kırçiçeği
KEBAP, PIDE €€

(☑ 464 3090; Kıbrıs Şehitleri Caddesi 83; pide ₺10, kebaps ₺17; ⊙24hr) İzmir's poshest soup kitchen also serves great pide, including the cheese and spinach varieties, kebaps and *lahmacun* (Arabic-style 'pizza'). A blowout Turkish breakfast is ₺19.

★ Sakız
MODERN TURKISH €€€

(☑ 464 1103; www.sakizalsancak.com; Şehit Nevresbey Bulvarı 9a; mains ₺18-38, meze ₺6-16; ⊙11am-11pm Mon-Sat) Sakız, specialising in Aegean and Cretan cuisine, is the most inventive restaurant in İzmir. Its fresh meze include shrimps wrapped in filo pasty and *köz patlıcan* (smoked aubergine with tomatoes and peppers), while some of the unusual mains are sea bass with milk thistle and haddock with Aegean herbs.

Sit on the lovely informal terrace and order à la carte or from the endless set menu for two (€60), which includes wine. Live traditional guitar music sets the scene on Wednesday, Friday and Saturday.

Deniz Restaurant
SEAFOOD €€€

(☑ 464 4499; Atatürk Caddesi 188b; mains ₺30-35; ⊙11am-11pm) This old favourite on the *kordon* is attached to the İzmir Palas hotel and trades a little on its reputation – and it's far from good value – but the meze like octopus in oregano and baked sardines are worth the added expense.

The house speciality is *tuzda balık* (fish baked in a block of salt that's broken at your table). It's suitable for three or four people.

Asansör Restoran   RESTAURANT €€€
(☑ 261 2662; Şehit Nihat Bey Caddesi 76a; mains ₺20-35; ⊙ 8am-midnight) Asansör is a 'destination' restaurant rising high above the Jewish quarter and accessed via a charming historic elevator. Inside is a formal, white-tablecloth venue with decent food; most people come for the views in any case. Perhaps more charming though is a light meal and a beer at the terrace cafe, especially in summer. It's about 3km from the town centre.

%100   RESTAURANT, CAFE €€€
(☑ 441 5593; Atatürk Caddesi 19, Konak Pier; mains ₺30-35) At the end of Konak Pier, %100 has a lengthy menu, with steak, sushi and pizza highly recommended by our table. It's a great place for a lazy cocktail (₺25) or a coffee break by the water's edge. Service is excellent.

🍸 Drinking & Entertainment

Alsancak plays host to the city's hottest nightlife, particularly in the clubs and bars on side streets such as 1452, 1453 and 1482 Sokak.

Sunset Cafe   BAR
(☑ 463 6549; Ali Çetinkaya Bulvarı 2a; beer ₺6; ⊙ 7am-2am) On the edge of the boulevard, the Sunset makes a great end-of-day watering hole, with tables on the pavement and a relaxed, youthful crowd. The cheap beer flows freely.

Tyna   BAR
(☑ 422 5151; Ali Çetinkaya Bulvarı 5, Cumhuriyet Bulvarı 98a; beer ₺8; ⊙ 8am-1am) The outside tables are hot property at this pizzeria on a small square. Most just come for a beer though there's pizza (from ₺14) and a good set menu for ₺27.

Pasaport Mado   CAFE
(☑ 489 5489; www.mado.com.tr; Atatürk Caddesi 142; ⊙ 8am-midnight) Pasaport Mado is one of the more modern of the many seafront cafes running south from the police station.

Miko   LIVE MUSIC
(☑ 463 2657; www.miko.com.tr; 1452 Sokak 11) This very chilled pub and bar with a vaguely nautical theme in Alsancak features everything from Latino and classical guitar to contra-bass. Decent pizzas (₺12.50 to ₺16), too.

Jackson's   CLUB
(☑ 422 6045; 1453 Sokak 17; ⊙ 6pm-3am) Probably the most popular club in Alsancak, with both live music and DJs, Jackson's is housed in what was once the British consul's residence; the rack behind the bar was used for displaying china.

1888   CLUB
(☑ 421 6690; www.1888.com.tr; Cumhuriyet Bulvarı 248; ⊙ 6pm-3am) This dance club set around an Ottoman-era courtyard hosts everything from film and cultural festivals to parties.

Old Gas Factory Cultural Centre   CULTURAL CENTRE
(Tarihi Havagazı Fabrikası Kültür Merkezi; ☑ 293 1091; Liman Caddesi) The mid-19th-century Ottoman Gas Company is İzmir's latest cultural precinct, with two brick warehouses now containing art exhibitions and workshops. It's located 500m east of Alsancak's 19th-century train station, complete with colourful stained-glass windows and a steam train outside.

🛍 Shopping

Konak Pier Shopping Centre   MALL
(Atatürk Caddesi, Konak Pier; ⊙ 10am-10pm) On the jetty built by Gustave Eiffel, this modern mall is spacious and stylish. There's a cinema, good local fashion stores, two smart waterside cafes and a couple of restaurants. A branch of Remzi Kitabevi (☑ 489 5325; www.remzi.com.tr; ⊙ 10am-10pm) has a large selection of English-language books for both adults and children.

Atı Souvenir   SOUVENIRS, GIFTS
(☑ 0553 321 3348; www.atisouvenir.com; 869 Sokak 7; ⊙ 8am-9pm) For traditional Turkish souvenirs, try this place in the market with *tavla* (backgammon sets), waterpipes and lovely beaded jewellery.

Arma Kitap & Cafe   BOOKS
(☑ 465 0771; Atatürk Caddesi 312a; ⊙ 8am-midnight) Not the widest selection of English-language titles at this very popular bookshop and cafe by the sea, but plenty of good international magazines. Sevgi Yolu (Love St) is lined with stalls selling used books.

ℹ Information

Banks, ATMS and internet cafes are found all over the centre.

Post Office (Cumhuriyet Meydanı) The main post office is south of Cumhuriyet Meydanı facing Pasaport Pier.

Tourist Office (☑ 483 5117; 1344 Sokak 2; ☺ 8.30am-7.30pm May-Sep, 8am-5pm Oct-Apr) Inside the ornately stuccoed İl Kültür ve Turizm Müdürlüğü building just off Atatürk Caddesi, this office is unhelpful to the point of being hostile.

ⓘ Getting There & Away

AIR

There are many flights to İzmir's **Adnan Menderes Airport** (☑ 455 0000; www.adnanmenderesairport.com) from European destinations.

Turkish Airlines (☑ 484 1220; www.thy.com; Halit Ziya Bulvarı 65) offers direct flights from İstanbul (both airports), Adana, Ankara, Antalya, Diyarbakır, Erzurum, Gaziantep, Kayseri, Kars, Malatya, Samsun, Sivas, Trabzon and many European destinations, including London. Other airlines serving İzmir include:

Atlasjet (www.atlasjet.com)
İzair (www.izair.com.tr)
Onur Air (www.onurair.com.tr)
Pegasus Airlines (www.flypgs.com)
Sun Express (www.sunexpress.com.tr)

BUS

İzmir's mammoth otogar lies 6.5km northeast of the city centre. For travel on Friday or Saturday to coastal towns located north of İzmir, buy your ticket a day in advance; in high season, two days in advance. Tickets can also be purchased from the bus companies' offices in the city centre, mostly found at Dokuz Eylül Meydanı in Basmane.

Long-distance buses and their ticket offices are found on the lower level of the otogar; regional buses (to Selçuk, Bergama, Manisa, Sardis etc) and their ticket offices are on the upper level. City buses and dolmuşes leave from a courtyard in front of the lower level.

Short-distance buses (eg to the Çeşme Peninsula) leave from a smaller local bus terminal in Üçkuyular, 6.5km southwest of Konak. But they pick up and drop off at the otogar as well.

Details of daily bus services to important destinations are listed in the table.

TRAIN

Most intercity services, including Ankara, Bandırma and Manisa, now arrive at and depart from **Alsancak Garı** with some pulling into **Basmane Garı**. For northern or eastern Turkey, change at Ankara.

Ankara

There are daily trains to Ankara (₺37, 14 hours), leaving at 6.30pm and travelling via Eskişehir (₺32, 12 hours).

Bandırma

There are daily trains to/from Bandırma (₺23, six hours) at 8.20am/2pm. Trains usually coordinate with the ferry to/from İstanbul.

SERVICES FROM İZMİR'S OTOGAR

DESTINATION	FARE (₺)	DURATION (HR)	DISTANCE (KM)	FREQUENCY (PER DAY)	VIA
Ankara	60	8	550	hourly	Afyon
Antalya	55	6½	450	hourly	Aydın
Bergama	13	2	110	frequent	Menemen
Bodrum	27	3	286	half-hourly in high season	Milas
Bursa	35	5	300	hourly	Balıkesir
Çanakkale	40	4½	340	hourly	Ayvalık
Çeşme	15	1½	116	frequent	Alaçatı
Denizli	25	4	250	hourly	Aydın
Foça	8	2	86	frequent	Menemen
İstanbul	60	8½	575	hourly	Bursa
Konya	43	8	575	every 2 hours	Afyon
Kuşadası	15	1¼	95	frequent	Selçuk
Manisa	10	¾	45	frequent	Sarnıç
Marmaris	30	4	320	hourly	Aydın
Salihli	17	1½	90	frequent	Sardis
Selçuk	9	1	80	frequent	Belevi

Manisa

There are six daily trains to/from Manisa (₺4.50 to ₺7, 1¾ hours).

Selçuk

Seven daily trains travel to Selçuk from Basmane station (₺6, 1½ hours) between 7.45am and 6.15pm.

❶ Getting Around

TO/FROM THE AIRPORT

İzmir's Adnan Menderes Airport is 18km south of the city on the way to Ephesus and Kuşadası.

Bus

Local buses 200 and 202 run hourly between both arrivals terminals and the Swissôtel Büyük Efes hotel via Üçkuyular bus station; 204 runs between both arrivals terminals and the otogar via Bornova metro. Both cost two credits.

Shuttle

Havaş buses (₺15, 30 minutes) leave hourly from Gazi Osmanpaşa Bulvarı near the Swissôtel Büyük Efes between 3.30am and 11.30pm; and to the same hotel from domestic arrivals, leaving 25 minutes after flights arrive.

Taxi

A taxi to/from the airport costs about ₺50.

TO/FROM THE BUS STATIONS

If you arrived at the main otogar on an intercity bus operated by one of the larger bus companies, a free *servis* (shuttle bus) is provided to the centre, normally Dokuz Eylül Meydanı. If you arrive on a local bus, you can catch a dolmuş (₺2, 25 minutes) that runs every 15 minutes between the otogar and both Konak and Basmane Garı, or you can take buses 54 and 64 (every 20 minutes) to Konak or 505 to Bornova metro (every 30 minutes). Passes can be bought at the bus stop.

To get to the otogar, the easiest way is to buy a ticket on an intercity bus at Dokuz Eylül Meydanı and take the bus company's *servis*. However, if you're catching a local bus from the otogar (eg to Salihli), take the metro to Bornova then pick up bus 505.

To get to Üçkuyular bus station, catch bus 169 from the Konak bus terminal.

BICYCLE

İzmir has a cycle-share hiring scheme called **Bisim** (☎ 433 5155; www.bisim.com.tr; 1st hour ₺2, then per hour ₺1; ☺ 6am-11pm), with a couple of dozen docking stations, most along the seafront *kordon*.

---

❶ TRAVEL CARDS

İzmir has two travel cards, covering bus, metro and ferry, which are available at stations, piers and shops with the Kent Kart sign.

Kent Kart (City Card) You pay a ₺6 deposit when you buy the card and then top it up with credit. When you use the card, ₺2 is debited from it, then every journey you make for the next 90 minutes is free.

Üç-Beş (3-5) This card with two/three/five credits, each valid for a single journey, costs ₺6.50/9.40/15.20.

BOAT

The most pleasant way to cross İzmir is by **İzdeniz Ferry** (www.izdeniz.com.tr; ☺ 7am-11pm). Roughly half-hourly timetabled services, with more at the beginning and end of the working day, link the piers at Karşiyaka, Bayraklı, Alsancak, Pasaport, Konak and Göztepe. The fare is ₺3.

BUS

Buses 86 and 169 lumber down Şair Eşref Bulvarı then pass Montrö Meydanı, the bazaar and Agora (and serve the same route in reverse after terminating in Balçova, past Üçkuyular in southwest İzmir); 169 runs down Talatpaşa Bulvarı and Cumhuriyet Caddesi to Konak Meydanı.

CAR

Large international car-hire franchises, including Budget, Europcar, Hertz, National Alamo and Avis, and smaller companies have 24-hour desks at the airport, and some have an office in town. **Green Car** (☎ 0232-446 9060; www.greenautorent.com; Mithatpaşa Caddesi 57) is one of the largest car-hire companies in the Aegean region.

You'll pay to park. The car park in Kültürpark, for example, charges ₺5.50/11 per half/full day.

METRO

İzmir Metro (www.izmirmetro.com.tr; fares ₺2; ☺ 6.30am-11.30pm) is clean, quick and cheap. There are currently 17 stations running from Fahrettin Altay to Ege Üniversitesi (Aegean University) via Konak, Çankaya, Basmane and to Bornova. There are plans to expand the network.

TAXI

You can hail a taxi on the street or pick up one from a taxi stand or outside one of the big hotels. Fares start at ₺3 then cost ₺0.25 per 100m. Make sure the meter is switched on.

Manisa

☑ 0236 / POP 315,500

Backed by mountains, the modern town of Manisa was once the ancient town of Magnesia ad Sipylum. The early Ottoman sultans left Manisa many fine mosques, now lovingly restored. The main reasons to visit are to inspect the mosque and the city's two fine museums or to take in the Mesir Macunu Festivalı.

⊙ Sights & Activities

Of Manisa's many old mosques, the Muradiye Camii (1586), the last work of the celebrated architect Mimar Sinan, has the most impressive tile work especially in its *mihrab* (niche in a minaret indicating the direction of Mecca). The adjoining building, originally constructed as an *imaret* (soup kitchen), is now the Manisa Museum (Manisa Müzesi; ☑ 231 1071; Murat Caddesi 107; admission ₺5;

⊙ 8am-5pm Tue-Sun), which houses some fine mosaics and other important finds from Sardis as well as ethnographic collections. The exhibits on traditional Turkish *eski yazı* (old writing) calligraphy is especially good.

Opposite the Muradiye in the Valide complex, the Sultan Camii (1523) is not as impressive but has a magnificently carved *mimber* (pulpit). Ayşe Hafsa Sultan Hamamı (☑ 231 2051; www.sultanhamammanisa.com; admission ₺20-25; ⊙ men 7am-11.30pm, women 10am-8pm) next door, named after the mother of Süleyman the Magnificent, has separate entrances for men and women. In the old hospital in the same complex is the new Medical History Museum (Tıp Tarihi Müzesi; ⊙ 10am-10pm) FREE, which painlessly traces the history of medicine under the Ottomans in seven rooms. Don't miss the mock-ups of operations, the pharmacy and the exhibit on the history and making of Manisa's most famous product, the addictive Mesir paste.

WORTH A TRIP

SARDIS

Sardis was once the capital of the powerful Lydian kingdom that dominated much of the Aegean before the Persians arrived. It is also one of the Seven Churches of the Revelation (or Apocalypse) mentioned in the New Testament. Its ruins, scattered around the village of Sartmustafa (or Sart), some 90km east of İzmir, make a particularly worthwhile excursion.

The ruins of Sardis (admission ₺8; ⊙ 8am-5pm, to 7pm Apr-Sep) lie at the eastern end of the village, immediately north of the road. Information panels dot the site.

You enter the site along an 18m-long paved Roman road, past a well-preserved Byzantine latrine and a row of almost 30 Byzantine shops, which belonged to Jewish merchants and artisans in the 4th century AD. Jews settled here as early as 547 BC.

Turn left at the end of the Roman road to enter the synagogue *(havra)*, impressive because of its size and beautiful decoration: fine geometric mosaic paving and coloured stone on the walls. The southern shrine housed the Torah.

Next to the synagogue is the *palestra*, an open expanse where athletes trained and where the gymnasium and baths once stood. This complex was probably built in the early 3rd century AD and abandoned after a Sassanian invasion in 616.

Right at the end is a striking two-storey building called the Marble Court of the Hall of the Imperial Cult, which, though heavily restored, gives an idea of the former grandeur of the building.

Excavations on the way to the village to the south have uncovered a stretch of the Lydian city wall and a Roman villa with painted walls on top of an earlier Lydian residence.

A sign points south to the Temple of Artemis, just over 1km away. Today only a few columns of the once magnificent but never completed building still stand. Nevertheless, the temple's plan is clearly visible and very impressive. Perhaps more interesting is the early Christian church dating from the 4th century AD.

Half-hourly buses to Salihli (₺17, 1½ hours, 90km) leave from İzmir's otogar, and pass Sartmustafa. You can also catch dolmuşes to Sartmustafa (₺1.5, 15 minutes, 9km) from behind the Salihli otogar.

Buses can be hailed along the highway from Salihli to Manisa (₺5, one hour), making it possible – just – to visit both Manisa and Sardis in the same day.

⭐ Festivals & Events

Mesir Macunu Festivalı   CULTURAL
(Mesir Festival; www.unesco.org/culture/ich/
RL/00642) If you're able to visit Manisa
around the spring equinox (21 March), you
can catch the Mesir Macunu Festivalı, a
week-long festival in celebration of *Mesir
macunu* (Mesir paste), a scrumptious treat
made from dozens of spices that must be
tasted to be believed. You will never eat *lokum* (Turkish delight) again.

According to legend, in the early 16th
century a local pharmacist named Müslihid-
din Çelebi Merkez Efendi – there's a statue
of him in a roundabout near the Muradiye
Camii – concocted a potion to cure Ayse Hafsa Sultan, the mother of Sultan Süleyman
the Magnificent, of a mysterious ailment.
Delighted with her swift recovery, the queen
mother paid for the amazing elixir to be distributed to the local people.

These days townsfolk in period costumes
re-enact the mixing of the potion from sugar
and 41 spices and other ingredients, then toss
it from the dome of the Sultan Mosque. Locals credit the paste with calming the nerves,
stimulating the hormones and immunising
against poisonous stings. We just think it
tastes out of this world. Buy it from Hafsa
Sultan Aktar (www.hafsasultanaktar.com; Murat
Caddesi 79; ⊙ 8.30am-9.30pm), a shop near the
entrance to the Manisa Museum.

❶ Getting There & Around

It's easiest to get to Manisa by half-hourly bus
from İzmir (₺10, 40 minutes, 30km), although
trains also run. From Manisa, buses to Salihli
pass Sardis (₺7, one hour). To get to Manisa's
historic mosques, take a dolmuş from in front of
the otogar (₺2).

Çeşme

📶 0232 / POP 22,950

With its long seafront, hilltop castle overlooking a windswept bay and winding, busy market streets, Çeşme makes a pleasant base for
exploring the surrounding peninsula and is
the springboard for the Greek island of Chios,
8km across the water. It's popular with week-
ending İzmiris and can get busy during the
school holidays, when prices rise accordingly.
All in all, though, it's hard to imagine tarrying
too long in raffish Çeşme when beauty contest
winner Alaçatı is so close.

◉ Sights & Activities

Çeşme Fortress   FORTRESS
(Çeşme Kalesi; 1001 Sokak 1; ⊙ 9am-7pm Apr-Sep,
to 5pm Oct-Mar) **FREE** This Genoese fortress,
whose dramatic walls dominate the town
centre, was built in 1508 and repaired by
Sultan Beyazıt II, son of Sultan Mehmet
the Conqueror (Mehmet Fatih), to defend
the coast from attack by pirates. Later, the
Rhodes-based Knights of St John of Jerusalem also made use of it. The battlements offer excellent views of Çeşme, and it's good to
walk around inside – under arches, up and
down steps, and through towers.

Çeşme Museum   MUSEUM
(Çeşme Müzesi; 📞 712 6609; 1001 Sokak 1; admission ₺8; ⊙ 9am-7pm Tue-Sun Apr-Sep, to 5pm Oct-
Mar) Housed in the castle's Umur Bey tower,
this museum displays archaeological finds
(mostly coins) from nearby Erythrae (now
Ildırı), the Bağlararası Bronze Age harbour
settlement (tools, a curious stone phallus)
and the Roman era (superb gold diadems).
Much is made of the attack by Russian empress Catherine the Great's navy on 5 July
1770 that wiped out the Ottoman fleet.

**Statue of Cezayirli Gazi
Hasan Paşa**   MONUMENT
With its back to the fortress and facing the
sea is this statue of the great Ottoman admiral (1714–90), who was sold into slavery
but became a grand vizier and was fleet
commander during the Battle of Çeşme
against the Russians. He is shown accompanied by a lion, which he supposedly
brought back from Africa.

Ayios Haralambos Church   CHURCH
(Ayios Haralambos Kilisesi; İnkılap Caddesi) North
of Çeşme Fortress, this imposing but redun-
dant 19th-century Greek Orthodox church,
fully restored in 2012, is used for temporary
exhibitions.

Boat Trips   BOAT TOUR
From late May to September, *gülets* (traditional wooden yachts) offer one-day boat
trips to nearby Black Island, Donkey Island
and Wind Bay, where you can swim and
snorkel. Browse the waterfront to compare
prices and negotiate; they should cost between ₺50 and ₺80, including a cooked
lunch. Boats leave around 10am and return
around 5pm.

Çeşme

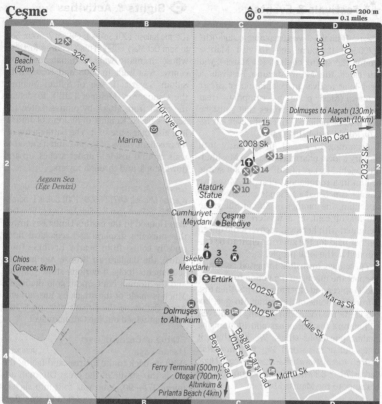

Beach (50m)

3264 Sk

Hürriyet Cad

Marina

Aegean Sea (Ege Denizi)

Chios (Greece; 8km)

3010 Sk

3001 Sk

Dolmuşes to Alaçatı (130m); Alaçatı (10km)

İnkılap Cad

2032 Sk

2008 Sk

Atatürk Statue

Cumhuriyet Meydanı

Çeşme Belediye

İskele Meydanı

Ertürk

Dolmuşes to Altınkum

1002 Sk

1010 Sk

Maraş Sk

Kale Sk

Bağlar Çarşı Cad

Beyazit Cad

1015 Sk

Müftü Sk

Ferry Terminal (500m); Otogar (700m); Altınkum & Pırlanta Beach (4km)

0   200 m
0   0.1 miles

İZMİR & THE NORTH AEGEAN ÇEŞME

Çeşme

◎ Sights

1 Ayios Haralambos Church.....................C2
2 Çeşme Fortress......................................C3
3 Çeşme Museum......................................C3
4 Statue of Cezayirli Gazi Hasan
    Paşa..C3

✚ Activities, Courses & Tours

5 Boat Trips...B3

🛏 Sleeping

6 Antik Rıdvan Otel..................................C4
7 Işık Pansiyon...C4

8 Kanuni Kervansaray Historical
    Hotel...C4
9 Yalçın Otel...C3

🍴 Eating

10 İmren Lokantası....................................C2
11 Kumrucu Tani..C2
12 Pasifik Otel Restaurant.......................A1
13 Rumeli Pastanesi..................................C2
14 Tiko's Cafe...C2

🍷 Drinking & Nightlife

15 Friendly Corner.....................................C2

🛏 Sleeping

★ **Yalçın Otel**   HOTEL €

(☎712 6981; www.yalcinotel.com; 1002 Sokak 14; s/d ₺60/80; ☺Apr-Oct; ❉@🛱) Perched on the hillside overlooking the harbour, this hotel has 18 spotless, well-maintained rooms. The biggest drawcards are the two large terraces with sunbeds and fabulous views, and its midrange quality for a budget price. Bülent is the consummate host; call in advance out of season. The excellent family-style set-menu dinner costs ₺25.

Antik Rıdvan Otel
HOTEL €€

(☑ 712 9772; www.antikridvanotel.com; 1015 Sokak 10; s/d ₺50/75; ❄ 🛜) This odd 'antique hotel', contained in a hulking old mansion painted red, feels somehow half-finished, but the open-air courtyard is welcomed in summer, the 15 rooms are clean and comfortable enough (some with sea views), and the price is certainly right.

Işık Pansiyon
PENSION €€

(Light Pension; ☑ 712 6305; www.facebook.com/Pansiyonlsik; 1021 Sokak 8; s ₺40-60, d ₺70-100; ❄ 🛜) The sunny courtyard and friendly owners make this basic little pension worth considering, though the 14 rooms are pokey and dark. Still, they all have small TVs and huge fridges. It's just 150m south of the marina.

Kanuni Kervansaray Historical Hotel
HISTORIC HOTEL €€€

(☑ 712 0630; www.cesmekervansaray.com.tr; 1015 Sokak, Çarşı Mevki, Kale yanı; r ₺160-350; ❄ 🛜 ☀) Contained in a caravanserai built under Sultan Süleyman the Magnificent in 1528, this 'historic' hotel is novel and perfectly located. The Ottoman facade impresses from afar; inside the 29 rooms are large, with showy, over-the-top baroque furnishings. You might stick to the **Kubbe Restaurant**, which is good, though service is slow. Wi-fi is dodgy due to the thick stone walls.

✗ Eating

The mostly touristy restaurants are along the waterfront. For cheaper, more locally oriented places, head up İnkılap Caddesi. Specialities include *kumru* (a bread roll sprinkled with sesame seeds) and *sakızlı reçel* (jam made from mastic, the resin of a local gum tree).

Rumeli Pastanesi
BAKERY €

(☑ 712 6759; www.rumelidondurma.com.tr; İnkılap Caddesi 44a; ice cream per scoop ₺2; ⏰ 8am-2am) Occupying an Ottoman stone house since 1945, this *pastane* (patisserie) sells great ice cream – try the mastic flavour – from its side window, and stocks all manner of local jams and preserves.

Tiko's Cafe
TURKISH €

(2008 Sokak 8a; mains ₺15; ⏰ 6am-3am) This Ottoman-feeling establishment near the Greek Orthodox church throngs with locals at lunchtime and with yachties and party-goers till the wee hours throughout summer. The regular menu includes seafood and grilled meat, and there is a revolving display of fresh meze. Friendly place.

Kumrucu Tani
KEBAP €

(☑ 712 1149; 2008 Sokak 4; kebap ₺10; ⏰ 9am-1am) Run by a local sporting identity, this is a friendly, straight-up kebap joint with delicious, healthy side dishes.

İmren Lokantası
TURKISH €€

(☑ 712 7620; İnkılap Caddesi 6; mains ₺12; ⏰ noon-1am) Çeşme's first restaurant, which opened back in 1953, is set in a bamboo-roofed atrium with a fountain and plants. It's famous locally for its traditional, high-quality Turkish food, including stews.

Pasifik Otel Restaurant
SEAFOOD €€€

(☑ 712 1767; www.pasifikotel.com; Tekke Plajı Mevkii 16; mains ₺18-25; ⏰ 8am-midnight) If you fancy a walk and some fish, head to this hotel restaurant at the far northern end of the seafront, where you can enjoy a great fish casserole behind a ceiling-high glass window overlooking a small beach. It's one of the better 'local' restaurants in Çeşme.

🍺 Drinking & Entertainment

Some of the restaurants along the marina turn into live-music venues during summer.

Friendly Corner
PUB, CAFE

(☑ 712 1751; 3025 Sokak 2; ⏰ 9am-2am) This self-proclaimed amicable hang-out must be just that as it attracts both locals and members of the wafer-thin community of expats. Münür, owner-chef-bartender, is a joy.

ℹ Information

The helpful **tourist office** (☑ 712 6653; İskele Meydanı 4; ⏰ 8.30am-noon & 1-5.30pm Mon-Fri, 9am-5pm Sat & Sun Jun-Sep), ferry and bus ticket offices and banks with ATMs are all within two blocks of Cumhuriyet Meydanı, the main square near the waterfront with the inevitable Atatürk statue. You can access the internet at the very central **Sahil Net** (Hürriyet Caddesi; per hour ₺2; ⏰ 9am-1am).

ℹ Getting There & Around

BUS

You have to change in İzmir to travel between Çeşme and most places (and transit in Çeşme to get to other parts of the peninsula). Çeşme's otogar is a kilometre south of Cumhuriyet Meydanı, though you can pick up dolmuşes in the centre.

Ankara

Metro and Ulusoy offer services to Ankara (₺73, nine hours)

İstanbul

There are morning and evening services to İstanbul (₺78, 10 hours) with Metro and Ulusoy; in summer other companies offer additional buses.

İzmir

Buses run every 15 minutes to İzmir's main otogar (₺13, 1¾ hours) and the city's smaller, western Üçkuyular bus station (₺12, 1½ hours).

DOLMUŞ

Alaçatı

Dolmuşes for Alaçatı (₺4) leave every five minutes in summer and half-hourly in winter, from the corner of İnkılap Caddesi and 2052 Sokak.

Altınkum

Dolmuşes to Altınkum (₺4) leave half-hourly from Çeşme's otogar, and pick up on the main street 20m south of the tourist office.

FERRY

As times (and destinations) change every year, always check the relevant website.

Chios (Sakız)

Both normal ferries (one-way/return passenger ₺60/100, car ₺215/360, 1½ hours) as well as new high-speed ones (one-way ₺85, 20 minutes) link Çeşme and the nearby Greek island of Chios (Sakız in Turkish). They sail at least twice a day between mid-May and mid-September. Outside that period, they go and return on Wednesday, Saturday and Sunday. Tickets can be bought direct from **Ertürk** ([icon] 712 6768; www.erturk.com.tr; Beyazıt Caddesi 6 & 7; [icon] 9am-8pm); you don't need to purchase your ticket in advance unless you have a car.

TAXI

A taxi to Alaçatı costs ₺45.

Pırlanta Beach & Altınkum

Southwest of Çeşme, **Diamond Beach** (Pırlantı Plajı) is good for kitesurfing and windsurfing. Two companies rent equipment here; **Adrenaline Sports** ([icon] 0541 803 9733, 722 2377; www.adrenalinesports.com.tr; [icon] May-Sep) offers tuition as well.

Back on the main road from Çeşme, turn right to reach the increasingly built-up resort of **Altınkum**, which boasts a series of delightful sandy coves. There's a cafe with sunloungers on a clean beach with turquoise water right where the dolmuşes stop.

Half-hourly dolmuşes run from Çeşme to Altınkum (₺4) via Pırlanta Beach (₺3.50).

Alaçatı

[icon] 0232 / POP 9550

A mere two decades ago this rather unassuming erstwhile Greek village, some 10km southeast of Çeşme, was known mostly for its excellent olive oil and world-class windsurfing. But thanks to some forward-thinking hoteliers, who turned the dilapidated *taş evleri* (stone houses) into high-end boutique accommodation, Alaçatı has become one of Turkey's hottest destinations for the free-spending middle class.

At the same time, development has spawned an impressive culinary and social scene and two food-related festivals are very much now on Alaçatı's calendar. The **Alaçatı Herb Festival** (Alaçatı Ot Festivalı; www.alacatiotfestivali.com) takes place in April and the new **Festival of Vanishing Tastes** (Kaybolan Lezzetler Festivali; www.kaybolanlezzetler.com), which examines the region's rich culinary heritage influences by Levantines, Greeks and Jews, is held in June.

Aside from a shoulder-to-shoulder high season stroll along Kemalpaşa Caddesi, there are not a lot of activities on offer or sights to tick off. But that's all the more reason to don your designer sunglasses and join the flashy Turkish city slickers for a glass of wine, some top-class nosh and a comprehensive lesson in Turkish chic.

[icon] Sleeping

Prices drop sharply in the low season, though most hotels and restaurants only open from mid-May to mid-October and for Christmas and the New Year. Reservations are essential in the high season.

Çiprika Pansiyon PENSION €€
([icon] 716 7303; www.ciprika.com; 3045 Sokak 1; s ₺75-100, d ₺125-180; [icon][icon]) An old Alaçatı family presides over this humble pension that contends with the more glamorous competition. Çiprika is one of a few real pensions in the town, offering seven decently sized but frayed stone rooms, with TVs and small writing tables. The big plus is the huge corner garden for watching the crowds stroll by.

★ **Alaçatı Taş Otel** BOUTIQUE HOTEL €€€
(Alaçatı Stone Hotel; [icon] 716 7772; www.tasotel.com; Kemalpaşa Caddesi 132; s €100-135, d €125-165; [icon][icon][icon]) This is Alaçatı's first, and some would say the still best, boutique hotel. Owner Zeynep, assisted by manager-with-the-mostest Salih, has a

knack for determining guests' needs and designed all seven recently renovated, understated rooms overlooking a walled garden. We especially like large room 6 in the main building and the two guesthouses in their own independent buildings.

The poolside afternoon teas included in the price are lavish, featuring freshly baked cakes. It's open year-round.

İncirliev
BOUTIQUE HOTEL €€€

(Fig Tree House; ☑716 0353; www.incirliev.com; Mahmut Hoca Sokak 3; r €100-185; ❄❆) The eight rooms at this century-old property showcase Aegean interior design; our favourites are the Blue Room in a former stable, the stone Terrace Room with floor-length windows and a fireplace, and the White Room with a 50-sq-metre bathroom. Guests will relish breakfast (including 36 different jams!) and afternoon tea beneath the leafy namesake with charming owners Sabahat and Osman.

Tash Mahal Otel
BOUTIQUE HOTEL €€€

(☑716 0122; www.tashmahalotel.com; 1005 Sokak 68; r ₺260-450; ❄❆) The belaboured pun of its names notwithstanding, this former wine house built in 1864 is one of Alaçatı's most enchanting small hotels. Hidden down a backstreet, the Tash avoids the heavy foot traffic of some of its rivals.

It's hard to pick a favourite from the eight rooms. 'Romance' has travertine-stone walls and storybook windows, while 'Provence', a former warehouse with a loft, has a fireplace and opens onto the hotel gardens and the signature eagle-headed stone mosaic on the floor.

Sailors Otel Meydan
BOUTIQUE HOTEL €€€

(☑716 8765; www.sailorsotel.com; Kemalpaşa Caddesi 66; r ₺190-300; ❄❆) One of two Sailors properties in Alaçatı, this hotel occupies a 150-year-old Greek house on the main square. Rustic but refined, the five blue-and-white rooms have enclosed balconies. The cafe-restaurant downstairs is a local meeting place.

WINDSURFING IN ALAÇATI

Alaçatı was 'discovered' as a windsurfer's paradise in the 1970s by a handful of intrepid German campers. Its strong, consistent northerly winds – blowing at up to 25 knots – make it a big hit with the surfing community. The main windsurfing beach, Alaçatı Surf Paradise (Alaçatı Sörf Cenneti), is now generally recognised as the prime location outside Europe.

The windsurfing beach has suffered here in recent years, however. The construction of a marina cannibalised 1km of the beach, reducing it to 2km and leading to fears for the surfers' safety with boats motoring past. The road there is now lined with large houses, which are part of the ongoing Port Alaçatı residential development.

For now, windsurfing continues largely unhindered, with the main season running from mid-May to the beginning of November (outside which many operators close). The Windsurf World Cup takes place here in August. With seven schools at Alaçatı Surf Paradise (and one across the bay), more than 5000 people start windsurfing here every year.

ASPC and Myga Surf Company are the largest operators. English-speaking instructors are normally available at the following centres, as are kitesurf boards. Hiring boards for longer periods lowers daily rates.

ASPC (Alaçatı Surf Paradise Club; ☑716 6611; www.alacati.info; 8012 Sokak 3) This Turkish-German operation offers good courses and high-quality equipment, charging ₺125 to ₺225 for a package (board, wetsuit, harness and shoes) for one day. Book ahead for the lower rate. JP/Neil Pryde and, for beginners, Gaastra Freetime boards are available. A starter course consisting of five hours (10 hours for three students or more) across three days costs ₺520.

Myga Surf Company (☑716 6468; www.myga.com.tr) This outfit has a range of equipment, and charges ₺150 to ₺220 for a one-day package. It also hires out paddle boards. A five-hour starter course (7½ hours for two students, 10 hours for three or more), which can be spread across a few days, costs ₺500.

Active Alaçatı Windsurf Centre (☑716 6383; www.active-surf.com) Recommended by readers, the smaller Active charges ₺120 to ₺200 for a one-day package. A starter course costs ₺560.

✖ Eating

There are few better places to eat in the whole Aegean than Alaçatı. Most restaurants target the smart set, with mains typically starting at ₺20. Many restaurants close for lunch, when everyone heads to the beach, and open only at weekends in low season.

The rather soulless Alaçatı marina, several kilometres south, has a few restaurants, including the excellent fish restaurant **Ferdi Baba** (☑568 6034; Liman Caddesi, Yat Limanı; mains ₺20-35; ⊙10am-midnight), which most agree is the best on the waterfront.

Eftalya
CAFE ₺

(☑716 9337; Cami Arkası Sakarya 3; gözleme ₺10; ⊙9am-1am, to 7pm in winter) In the line of cafes next to the mosque, Eftalya's *gözleme*, packed with cheese and greens, is a hearty breakfast choice. Homemade lemonade, meat-filled *çiğ börek* and *mantı* are also available.

★ Asma Yaprağı
AEGEAN ₺₺

(☑716 0178; www.asmayapragi.com.tr; 1005 Sokak 50; meze ₺7.50-15; ⊙10am-midnight) Communal meals in the one-room 'Vine Leaf' are an Alaçatı experience for gastronomes and lucky stragglers. Tin-plated Aegean meze alternate weekly, but expect plenty of fresh herbs, lashings of olive oil, vegetables and eponymous vine leaves. Dessert is a mastic appreciation ceremony. Located at the mosque-end of the antique district. There's outside seating, too.

Şerefe Meyhane
MEZE ₺₺

(☑716 0508; 1001 Sokak 19; mains ₺20, meze ₺9-11; ⊙8am-1am) There are some who say the 'Cheers Tavern' serves the best meze in town. We can only vouch for the salt fish (₺20), which goes down a treat with a cold Efes.

Kaptan'nın Yeri
SEAFOOD ₺₺

(☑716 8030; Uğur Mumcu Caddesi; fish ₺15-20; ⊙11am-midnight) The dining scene in Alaçatı can get a little precious, but 'Captain's Place' is one of the cheapest down-to-earth spots to eat fish in town. The squid and mussels are exemplary, and the service is warm and friendly. Just south of the car park.

Yusuf Usta Ev Yemekleri
TURKISH ₺₺

(Master Joseph's Home Cooking; ☑716 8823; Zeytinci İş Merkezi 1; mains ₺18; ⊙noon-8pm) At this restaurant on the south side of the ring road, near the turn-off into Alaçatı, the ₺5 salad bar and steam trays with meat and vegetable are popular at lunchtime. This is cheap traditional food done well – getting both is a rarity.

Agrilia
FUSION ₺₺₺

(☑716 8594; 1005 Sokak 68; mains ₺25-70; ⊙1.30pm-midnight daily, Fri-Sun only in winter) This long-running alternative to traditional Turkish fare specialises in creative pasta fusion dishes and Argentine grilled meats. It occupies an old Greek town house next to the Tash Mahal boutique hotel, with which it shares the garden.

Barbun
MODERN TURKISH ₺₺₺

(☑716 8308; 1001 Sokak 5; dishes ₺20-40; ⊙6pm-2am Jun-Sep, 2.30pm-midnight Oct-May) This stylish new kid on the block would probably sit more comfortably in İstanbul's Beyoğlu than Alaçatı. It serves (very) Modern Turkish dishes – try the Karaburnu sardines or the octopus with orange and capers – and is committed to using only locally sourced as well as foraged produce. A guilt-free meal then!

Rasim Usta'nin Yeri
TURKISH ₺₺₺

(☑716 8420; Kemalpaşa Caddesi 54/A; mains ₺15-30; ⊙9am-midnight) 'Master Rasim's Place' is one of the oldest and still most dependable restaurants in town. Choose from delicious soups and salads, and a few meat and pasta dishes rotating daily. Ask the grill chef to turn the fish and chicken to order. It's just west of the main square.

🍷 Drinking & Nightlife

Pole
BAR

(Cumhuriyet Meydanı; beer ₺8; ⊙10am-midnight; 🛜) Although its prices follow the Alaçatı trend and shoot up at the height of summer, this very central bar-cafe is one of the best-value places for a drink.

Makah
BAR

(☑716 6611; Cark Mevkii 1; ⊙10am-late) Outside high season, this club on Makah Beach, in the heart of the windsurfing scene, is a great place for a beer and burger. In high season, it's party time.

ℹ️ Getting There & Around

BICYCLE

ASPC (p215) rents out mountain bikes (per day/week from ₺30/170).

BUS

Metro has an office by the car park, selling tickets to nationwide destinations (normally via İzmir).

CAR

You can rent cars from **Işıltı** (☑716 8514; www.isiltirentacar.com; Uğur Mumcu Caddesi 16; per day from ₺80).

DOLMUŞ

Frequent dolmuşes run to/from Çeşme (₺4, 10 minutes, 10km) and İzmir (₺12, one hour, 75km). Between mid-May and September, dolmuşes run to/from Alaçatı Surf Paradise (₺3), which is 4km south of town on the western side of the *liman* (harbour).

Sığacık

☑ 0232 / POP 5000

Sığacık is an isolated port village clustered around a crumbling 16th-century Genoese castle. With no beach, there's not much to do here except stroll the picturesque waterfront, take a boat trip and watch the fishermen returning with their famous catch of *kalamar* (squid) and *barbunya* (red mullet).

🛏 Sleeping & Eating

Dağ Motel MOTEL €

(☑ 745 7060; www.dagmotel.net; r ₺70-100) The 'Mountain Motel', with 20 renovated rooms, has an excellent and relatively isolated location on the north side of Sığacık Bay. Its fine restaurant (mains ₺20) is part of the regional Slow Food movement. Service is prompt.

Teos Pansiyon PENSION €€

(☑ 745 7463; www.teospension.com.tr; 126 Sokak 26; d ₺140-150; ❄ 🎧) With a nice family feel to it and seven spacious, very attractive rooms, the Teos is good value. Sofas, sea views (suites 4 and 7 are the best) and big white beds all feature. You can buy fresh fish from the market and ask the obliging family to cook it for you.

Beyaz Ev PENSION €€

(☑ 0532 598 1760; www.sigacikpansiyon.net; Sığacık Caddesi; s/d ₺50/100; ❄ 🎧) The three-room 'White House' is a lovely pension, slightly inland but with a huge terrace overlooking the seafront . Rooms are spacious and bright, with thin wooden floorboards and curious furniture. There's also a lovely garden.

Liman SEAFOOD €€

(☑ 745 7011; Liman Meydanı 19; mains ₺20; ⊙ noon-midnight) The 'Harbour', which is right on, well, just that, doesn't disappoint with its fresh fish, great meze and seafront views through huge plate-glass windows.

ℹ Getting There & Away

ÇEŞME

You must travel via İzmir.

İZMİR

Take a bus or dolmuş to Seferihisar from İzmir's Üçkuyular otogar (₺5, 50 minutes, half-hourly). From Seferihisar, half-hourly dolmuşes run to Sığacık (₺2, 10 minutes, 5km).

Akkum & Teos

☑ 0232

Two kilometres over the hill from Sığacık is the waterfront settlement of Akkum. In summer its protected cove used to attract windsurfers in their thousands, but it has been eclipsed by Alaçatı. Today it's quieter and cheaper than Alaçatı and has larger waves.

Of its two smooth, sandy beaches, Büyük Akkum has the better facilities – windsurfing, sea kayaking and diving equipment and instruction are available – but Küçük Akkum is likely to be quieter.

Before Akkum, turn left to reach the scattered ruins at Teos, 5km from Sığacık: primarily picturesque fluted columns from a famous temple dedicated to Dionysus and re-erected here. Teos was once a vast Ionian city, and you can roam the fields in search of other remnants, including a theatre used for Dionysian festivals south of the acropolis. Following the footpath to the southwest for a short distance leads to the ancient harbour with mooring stones. Note the excavated Hellenistic wall from the 3rd century BC along the way.

🍴 Eating

On the road to the ruins, 1km from the turnoff, is Teos Park, a forestry department picnic grove. There's a shady restaurant here and a shop where you can buy snacks and cold drinks to enjoy beneath the pine trees overlooking the sea.

Above Küçük Akkum, Yakamoz (☑ 0536 256 1415, 745 7599; 3216 Sokak 8; mains ₺18) has a great terrace, serving seafood and Turkish classics as well as English breakfast.

ℹ Getting There & Away

DOLMUŞ

In summer frequent dolmuşes run to Teos from Seferihisar (₺2.50, 20 minutes) via Sığacık and Akkum.

TAXI

A taxi from Sığacık to Akkum costs about ₺10; a return trip to Teos (including waiting time) costs ₺30.

Ephesus, Bodrum & the South Aegean

Best Places to Eat

➡ Limon Aile Lokantası (p264)

➡ Ney (p270)

➡ Bozburun Restaurant (p277)

➡ Nazik Ana (p258)

Best Places to Stay

➡ Mehmet Ali Ağa Konağı (p274)

➡ Casa Dell'Arte (p267)

➡ Su Otel (p258)

➡ Villa Konak (p241)

➡ Hotel Bella (p233)

Why Go?

Turkey's sparkling Aegean coast boasts 4000 years of civilisation – and it's got the ruins to prove it, the most famous being the capital of Roman Asia Minor itself: Ephesus. Nearby, the ancient ports of Priene and Miletus, and the temple at Didyma, give the complete picture of the Aegean in centuries past.

In summer, the coast's population swells as millions of tourists descend on Marmaris, Kuşadası and, especially, Bodrum, Turkey's most glamorous seaside getaway. This whitewashed town beneath a 15th-century castle somehow maintains an air of refinement through the non-stop partying, while boutique hotels and elegant eateries keep springing up, both here and in the sophisticated coastal villages of the Bodrum Peninsula. On the remote Datça and Bozburun Peninsulas, more elemental pleasures await in the rugged terrain and fishing villages with spectacular Aegean views.

The coast is most peaceful in spring or fall (when prices drop, too).

When to Go
Selçuk

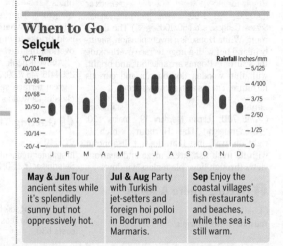

May & Jun Tour ancient sites while it's splendidly sunny but not oppressively hot.

Jul & Aug Party with Turkish jet-setters and foreign hoi polloi in Bodrum and Marmaris.

Sep Enjoy the coastal villages' fish restaurants and beaches, while the sea is still warm.

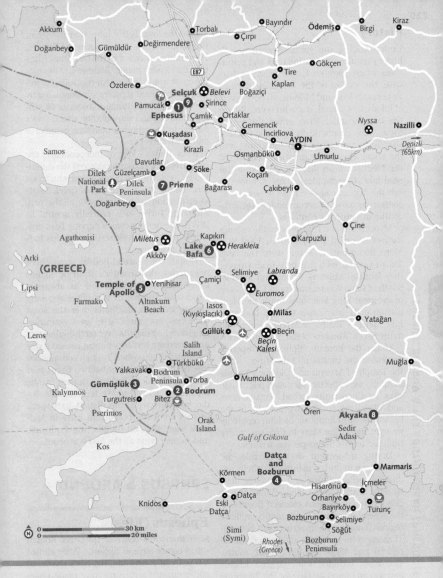

Ephesus, Bodrum & the South Aegean Highlights

1 Walk the marble streets of **Ephesus** (p220), Europe's best-preserved ancient city.

2 Indulge in the sophisticated dining and nightlife of **Bodrum** (p253).

3 Enjoy sea views over fresh fish in Bodrum Peninsula villages such as **Gümüşlük** (p262).

4 Feel miles from anywhere on the rugged **Datça and Bozburun** Peninsulas (p272).

5 Gape in wonder at the soaring columns of Didyma's **Temple of Apollo** (p248).

6 Toast sunset in a village among Byzantine ruins on **Lake Bafa** (p249).

7 Survey rolling fields where the sea once lay from the ancient port of **Priene** (p245).

8 Escape the Aegean crowds in **Akyaka** (p277), a river-mouth beach town among pine-clad mountains.

9 Try seasonal produce at the region's weekly markets in **Selçuk** (p230).

History

Understanding the south Aegean coast's history requires visualising bays and peninsulas where they no longer exist – otherwise, the stories of the key ancient cities Ephesus, Priene and Miletus, all now several kilometres inland, make no sense. Before the lazy Meander River silted things up, these were economically and strategically significant port cities, fully integrated into the wider Greco-Roman world back when the Mediterranean Sea was dubbed a 'Roman lake'. Geographical changes, however, saw the Aegean coast's centres of power and commerce move to accommodate the subcontinent's evolving contours.

Mycenaeans and Hittites were the region's earliest recorded peoples (from 1200 BC). More important, however, were the later Ionian Greeks, who fled here from Greece; they founded Ephesus, Priene and Miletus. South of Ionia was mountainous Caria – site of the great King Mausolus' tomb, the Mausoleum of Halicarnassus (today's Bodrum). Like Ephesus' Temple of Artemis, it was one of the Seven Wonders of the Ancient World.

Under the Romans, Ephesus prospered, becoming the capital of Asia Minor, while the Temple of Artemis and Didyma's Temple of Apollo were spectacular pagan pilgrimage sites. As Christianity spread, pagans, Jews and Christians coexisted peacefully in the big towns. Most famously, St John reputedly brought the Virgin Mary to Ephesus, where tradition attests his gospel was written.

During subsequent Byzantine rule, the coastal communities maintained their traditional social, cultural and economic links with the nearby Greek islands. While the precise territorial divisions changed frequently, the general division of the Byzantine military regions (known as themes) here was between Thracesion (in the north and central coastal region) and Kibyrrhaeoton (in the south). The latter included some Aegean islands and was an important base for the Byzantine navy, especially when Arab fleets menaced.

In the late 11th and 12th centuries, overland Seljuk expansion coincided with Crusaders on the move to the Holy Land – along with the decline of the Byzantine navy, which allowed Italian fleets to eventually rule the Mediterranean. In 1402 the Knights Hospitaller (who then owned much of the Greek Dodecanese islands) built a grand castle in Halicarnassus – scandalously, using stone from the ancient mausoleum – and they re-

named the town Petronium. After Süleyman the Magnificent's 1522 conquest of Rhodes, Petronium was ceded to the Ottomans (thus the Turkicised name 'Bodrum'). Although the coast would be Turkish-controlled thereafter, it remained significantly populated by Greeks; their traditional knowledge of sailing, shipping and shipbuilding would prove crucial to the empire's maritime commerce and naval success.

After Turkey's War of Independence, the 1923 Treaty of Lausanne decreed the tumultuous Greek-Turkish population exchanges – terminating three millennia of Greek coastal civilisation with one stroke of the pen. Although Turkey was officially neutral in WWII, the Aegean coast's curving bays provided cover for Greek resistance ships harassing the Germans.

Despite the peaceful holiday atmosphere here today, this frontier's strategic significance remains as vital now as always – Greek and Turkish fighter pilots regularly engage in mock dogfights over the coast (fatalities are rare). The two countries' long-standing dispute over territorial waters and sovereign territory almost caused a war in January 1996, when Turkish commandos briefly stormed the uninhabited Greek islet of Imia (Kardak in Turkish), causing frantic diplomatic activity in Western capitals. Today, you can gaze at this distant, hazy speck of rock from the beachfront cafes in laid-back Gümüşlük, on the Bodrum Peninsula, and wonder what all the fuss was about.

EPHESUS & AROUND

Ephesus (Efes)

More than anywhere else, the Greco-Roman world comes alive at Ephesus. After almost 150 years of excavation, the city's recovered and renovated structures have made Ephesus Europe's most complete classical metropolis – and that's with 82% of the city still to be unearthed.

As capital of Roman Asia Minor, Ephesus was a vibrant city of over 250,000 inhabitants. Counting traders, sailors and pilgrims to the Temple of Artemis, these numbers were even higher, meaning that in Ephesus one could encounter the full diversity of the Mediterranean world and its peoples. So important and wealthy was Ephesus that its

Temple of Artemis (en route to present-day Selçuk) was the biggest on earth, and one of the Seven Wonders of the Ancient World.

Excavations are ongoing, with new surprises popping up as archaeologists continue to dig. In 2007 a gladiator's cemetery was discovered near the Stadium, and Roman-era synagogue remains reportedly lie behind the library; these are among several areas where new discoveries may be made.

In the future, Turkish authorities are planning to wage war against the silt accumulation that defeated all previous Ephesian civilisations. If accomplished, their marvellous idea of dredging a canal to the Aegean would allow visitors to come to Ephesus by boat, or to gaze out from it onto the sea, thus restoring the city's original identity as a romantic port.

History

Early Legend

According to legend, 10th-century-BC Dorian incursions forced Androclus, Ionian prince of Athens, to seek a safer settlement. First, however, he consulted the famed Delphic oracle, which foresaw 'the fish, the fire and the boar' as markers of the new Ionian city.

After crossing the Aegean, Androclus and his crew rested on the Anatolian shore and cooked a freshly caught fish – so fresh, in fact, that it jumped out of the pan. The toppled coals set the nearby forest ablaze, smoking out a wild boar that Androclus chased down and killed; on that very spot, he resolved to build Ephesus (near today's ruins of the Temple of Artemis).

Allegiance to Artemis

Androclus and his Ionian followers had been preceded on the coast by the Lelegians, who worshipped the Anatolian maternal fertility goddess Cybele. The Ionians fused Lelegian ritual with their own, making the Artemis worshipped in Ephesus a unique fertility goddess. Despite the 7th-century-BC flood that damaged the temple, and the Cimmerian invaders who razed the entire city around 650 BC, the Artemis cult continued, and the determined population rebuilt their temple after each setback.

Croesus & the Persians

Ephesus' massive wealth, accumulated from maritime trade and pilgrims to the Temple of Artemis, aroused the envy of Lydia's King Croesus, who attacked in around 560 BC. Autocratic Croesus relocated the populace

inland, where the new Ephesus was built (near the temple's southern edge). However, the Lydian king also respected the cult, funding the temple's reconstruction over the next 10 years.

Everyday life continued as the Ephesians paid tribute to Lydia and, later, to Persian invaders. Ephesus revolted in 498 BC, sparking the Greco-Persian War, which briefly drove out the eastern invaders, and Ephesus joined Athens and Sparta in the Delian League. However, in the later Ionian War, Ephesus picked the losing side and was again ruled by Persia.

In 356 BC, a young notoriety seeker, Herostratus, burned down the Temple of Artemis, to ensure his name would resound forever. The disgusted Ephesian elders executed Herostratus and declared that anyone who mentioned his name would also be killed. A new temple, bigger and better than anything before, was immediately envisioned. In 334 BC, an admiring Alexander the Great offered to pay for construction – if the temple would be dedicated to him. But the Ephesians, who were fiercely protective of their goddess, declined, cunningly pointing out that it was unfitting for one god to make a dedication to another. When completed, the temple was recognised as one of the Seven Wonders of the Ancient World.

From Lysimachus to the Romans

Upon Alexander's death, Lysimachus (one of his generals) took Ionia. However, by then silt from the River Cayster (Küçük Menderes in Turkish; 'Little Meander') had already started to block Ephesus' harbour, and Lysimachus moved the population to today's Ephesus site, strategically set between two hills. When the Ephesians revolted again, Lysimachus' Seleucid rivals invaded, leading to a messy period of conquest and reconquest that only ended when Ephesus became Roman in 133 BC.

Augustus' decision to make Ephesus capital of Asia Minor in 27 BC proved a windfall for the city; its population grew to around 250,000, drawing immigrants, merchants and imperial patronage. The annual festival of Artemis (Diana to the Romans) became a month-long spring party drawing thousands from across the empire. Yet Ephesus also attracted Christian settlers, including St John, who supposedly settled here with the Virgin Mary and wrote his gospel here. St Paul also lived in Ephesus for three years (probably in the AD 60s).

Ephesus (Efes)

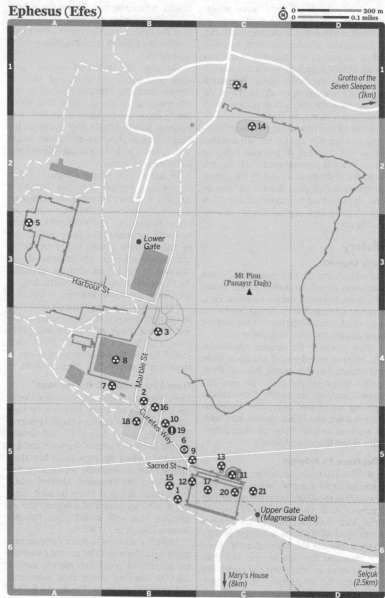

N
0 ——————— 200 m
0 ——————— 0.1 miles

Grotto of the
Seven Sleepers
(1km)

Lower
Gate

Mt Pion
(Panayır Dağı)

Harbour St

Marble St

Curetes Way

Sacred St

Upper Gate
(Magnesia Gate)

Mary's House
(8km)

Selçuk
(2.5km)

End of Ancient Ephesus & Its Byzantine Epilogue

Despite Attalus II of Pergamum rebuilding the harbour, and Nero's proconsul dredging it in AD 54, the harbour continued to silt up. A century later, Emperor Hadrian tried diverting the Cayster, but silt eventually pushed the sea back to today's Pamucak. Malarial swamps developed, the port was lost, and Ephesus' increasingly Christian composition meant diminished funds for the Artemis/Diana cult. In 263, Germanic

Ephesus (Efes)

◉ Sights

Goths sacked Ephesus, burning the temple yet again.

Nevertheless, Ephesus' association with two disciples of Christ (not to mention his mother), and its status as one of the Seven Churches of Asia (mentioned in the Book of Revelation), inspired pious Byzantine emperors to salvage what they could. Fourth-century emperor Constantine the Great rebuilt many public buildings, with additional works overseen by Arcadius (r 395–408). And 6th-century emperor Justinian I built a basilica dedicated to St John on Ayasuluk Hill (in today's Selçuk).

The fortress settlement there later became known as Agios Theologos (the 'Holy Theologian' in Greek) – hence the later Turkicised name, Ayasuluk. Amusingly, medieval Crusaders versed in the classics were surprised to find a forlorn village here, rather than the epic ancient city they had expected.

◉ Sights

Ephesus (adult/student/parking ₺30/20/7.50; ⊙ 8am-7.30pm May-Oct, 8am-5pm Nov-Apr, last admission one hour before closing) takes at least two hours to explore (add 30 minutes if visiting the Terraced Houses). Visit in the early morning or late afternoon to avoid crowds and the bright midday sun (between 9.30am and 1.30pm is busiest). The softer morning light is best for photographing the ruins, but the site is generally quietest after 3pm, when the cruise-liner groups return to their departing boats. Take a hat, sunglasses, sunscreen and water, or you will have to pick them up in the overpriced shops and cafes at the entrances.

Ephesus' two gates are 3km apart. The most popular entrance is the Upper Gate (also known as the Magnesia Gate), which allows you to walk down the Curetes Way with the Library of Celsus below you and exit through the Lower Gate. If you end up entering and exiting through the same gate, retracing your steps is not a huge hardship as you will see the site twice.

◉ Upper Ephesus

Varius Baths RUIN
Baths were situated at the main entrances to ancient cities so that visitors could wash before entering, and these stand at the entrance to Upper Ephesus. Greco-Roman baths also served a social function as a meeting and massage destination.

Upper Agora RUIN
This large square once used for legislation and local political talk was flanked by grand columns and filled with polished marble. In the middle was a small **Temple of Isis** – testament to the cultural and trade connections between Ephesus and Alexandria in Egypt. The agora's columns would later be reused for a Christian basilica, which was a typically Byzantine three-nave structure with a wooden roof. From here, there are several archways in the distance, once food-storage houses.

Odeon RUIN
Primarily used for municipal meetings, this once-lavish 5000-seat theatre boasts marble seats and carved ornamentation. Ephesus had one of the ancient world's most advanced aqueduct systems, and there are signs of this in terracotta piping for water along the way to the building.

Prytaneum RUIN
Two of six original Doric columns mark the entrance to the ruined Prytaneum (town hall) and city treasury. Here and elsewhere in Ephesus, note the differences between the Ionian Greeks' heavily ornamented,

Ephesus

A DAY IN THE LIFE OF THE ANCIENT CITY

Visiting Ephesus might seem disorienting, but meandering through the city that was once second only to Rome is a highlight of any trip to Turkey. The illustration shows Ephesus in its heyday – but since barely 18% of Ephesus has been excavated, there's much more lurking underfoot than is possible to depict here. Keep an eye out for archaeologists digging away – exciting new discoveries continue to be made every year.

A typical Ephesian day might begin with a municipal debate at the Odeon **1** . These deliberations could then be pondered further while strolling the Curetes Way **2** to the Latrines **3** , perhaps marvelling on the way at imperial greatness in the sculpted form of Emperor Trajan standing atop a globe, by the Trajan fountain. The Ephesian might then have a look at the merchandise on offer down at the Lower Agora, before heading back to the Terraced Houses **4** for a leisurely lunch at home. Afterwards, they might read the classics at the Library of Celsus **5** , or engage in other sorts of activities at the Brothel **6** . The good citizen might then supplicate the gods at the Temple of Hadrian **7** , before settling in for a dramatic performance at Ephesus' magnificent Great Theatre **8** .

FACT FILE

» Ephesus was famous for its female artists, such as Timarata, who painted images of the city's patron goddess, Artemis.

» The Great Theatre could hold up to 25,000 spectators.

» According to ancient Greek legend, Ephesus was founded by Amazons, the mythical female warriors.

» Among Ephesus' 'native sons' was the great pre-Socratic philosopher, Heraclitus.

Brothel
As in other places in the ancient Mediterranean, a visit to the brothel was considered rather normal for men. Visitors would undertake progressive stages of cleansing after entering, and finally arrive in the marble interior, which was decorated with statues of Venus, the goddess of love. A foot imprint on the pavement outside the rubble indicates the way in.

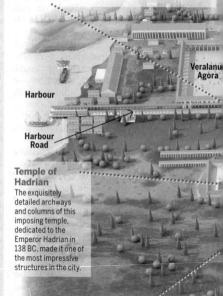

Veralanu Agora

Harbour

Harbour Road

Temple of Hadrian
The exquisitely detailed archways and columns of this imposing temple, dedicated to the Emperor Hadrian in 138 BC, made it one of the most impressive structures in the city.

Library of Celsus
Generations of great thinkers studied at this architecturally advanced library, built in the 2nd century AD. The third-largest library in the ancient world (after Alexandria and Pergamum), it was designed to guard its 12,000 scrolls from extremes of temperature and moisture.

Great Theatre

Built into what is today known as Mt Panayır, the Great Theatre was where Ephesians went to enjoy works of classical drama and comedy. Its three storeys of seating, decorated with ornate sculpture, were often packed with crowds.

Latrines

A fixture of any ancient Greco-Roman city, the latrines employed a complex drainage system. Some wealthier Ephesians possessed a 'membership', which allowed them to reserve their own seat.

Odeon

The 5000-seat Odeon, with its great acoustics, was used for municipal meetings. Here, debates and deliberations were carried out by masters of oratory – a skill much prized by ancient Greeks and Romans.

Lower Agora

Trajan Fountain

Hercules Gate

Upper Agora

Terraced Houses

These homes of wealthy locals provide the most intimate glimpse into the lives of ancient Ephesians. Hewn of marble and adorned with mosaics and frescoes, they were places of luxury and comfort.

Curetes Way

Ephesus' grandest street, the long marble length of the Curetes Way, was once lined with buzzing shops and statues of local luminaries, emperors and deities.

spiralling columns, and their smooth, unadorned Roman counterparts. Both coexist randomly across the site, due to ancient retrofitting and modern relocations. A similar difference is notable in arches: the genius of single-material, harmoniously balanced Ionian Greek arches, and the pragmatic use of mortar cement by the Romans.

Temple of Hestia Boulaea   RUIN
The Prytaneum hosted this shrine, where the city's eternal flame was tended to by vestal virgins, and was fronted by a giant Artemis statue. The fertility goddess was carved with huge breasts and welcoming arms extending from her body, though her hands (probably crafted from gold) are long gone. Many of the statues of deities, emperors and other luminaries here originally had precious gemstones for eyes – another indicator of Ephesian wealth.

Asclepion   RUIN
A side street called the 'Sacred St' led to Ephesus' Asclepion (hospital). Protected by the god Asclepius and his daughter Hygieia, doctors used the Asclepian snake symbol, often etched into the stone; its symbolic meaning was the snake's ability to shed its skin and renew itself, while the ancients also knew that snake venom had curative powers. Ephesus was famous for its medical school.

Temple of Domitian   RUIN
This ruined temple recalls Domitian (r AD 81–96), the tyrant who banished St John to Patmos (where he wrote the Book of Revelation) and executed his own nephew for showing interest in Christianity. The temple, which the unpopular ruler demanded be made in his honour, was promptly demolished when he died.

Pollio Fountain   RUIN
Like the nearby Memius Monument, the Pollio Fountain hints at the lavish nature of ancient Ephesus' fountains, which filled the city with the relaxing sound of rushing water, again indicating its wealth.

◉ Curetes Way

Curetes Way   RUIN
Named for the demigods who helped Lena give birth to Artemis and Apollo, the Curetes Way was Ephesus' main thoroughfare, lined with statuary, great buildings and rows of shops selling incense, silk and other goods. Walking this street is the best way to understand Ephesian daily life.

Circular depressions and linear grooves are sporadically gouged into the marble, to keep pedestrians from slipping on the slick surface. This was important not only during winter rains, but also during the searing summer heat; shopkeepers would regularly douse the slippery marble street with water from the fountains to cool the air.

Flowering trees that once shaded the street and shops also lowered the temperature. Right under where they stood, there are occasional stone abutments adorned with 12 circular depressions – boards for games of chance that ancient Ephesians would play for fun, and even bet on: the contest was known in Latin as *ludus duodecim scriptorum,* the 'game of twelve markings'.

There's a rather patchwork look to the Way's marble blocks – many are not in their

---

LOCAL KNOWLEDGE

VISITING EPHESUS & SELÇUK

Tips for getting the most out of your visit by Mehmet Esenkaya, owner of No Frills Ephesus Tours (p228).

➡ Enter Ephesus from the Lower Gate. This way you avoid a lot of the crowds from the cruise ships and tour buses that start from the Upper Gate.

➡ In the hot summer months take an umbrella with you, as there is no shade at all.

➡ Toilets are located at the entry gates – there are no toilets once you are inside the site.

➡ Terraced Houses are a must-see!

➡ The House of Virgin Mary is best seen in the afternoon, when it's quieter and the weather is cooler up there.

➡ Stay in Selçuk at least two nights as there is much to see in the area besides Ephesus. If you can incorporate it, Saturday is Selçuk's market day where you can taste fresh seasonal fruits and vegetables and pick up souvenirs.

original places, due to ancient and modern retrofitting. An intriguing element in some blocks are the tiny, carved Greek-language initials; they denoted the name of the specific builder responsible for the relevant section. This helped labourers collect their pay, as it proved they had actually worked.

Several structures along the Way have occasional oval depressions in the walls – these held the oil lamps that lent a magical glow to the city's main thoroughfare by night.

Hercules Gate   GATE
With reliefs of Hercules on both main pillars, this two-storey gate was constructed in the 4th century AD. One of its functions was to prevent wagons from entering the Curetes Way.

Trajan Fountain   MONUMENT
This honorary fountain was once dominated by a huge statue of the great emperor, grasping a pennant and standing on a globe; the inscription reads, 'I have conquered it all, and it's now under my foot.' Today, only the globe and a single foot survive. The fountain's water flowed under the statue, spilling onto and cleaning the Way.

Men's Latrines   RUIN
This square structure has toilet 'seats' along the back walls. Although wealthy men had private home bathrooms, they also used the public toilets; some even paid a membership fee to claim a specific seat. Turning into the structure's entrance, you'll note a small aperture; here stood the clerk, who collected fees from visitors. While the whole experience was indeed a public one, the flowing Roman toga would have provided a modicum of privacy.

Temple of Hadrian   RUIN
One of Ephesus' star attractions, this ornate Corinthian-style temple honours Trajan's successor, and originally had a wooden roof and doors. Note its main arch: supported by a central keystone, this architectural marvel remains perfectly balanced, with no need for cement or mortar. The temple's designers also covered it with intricate decorative details and patterns – Tyche, goddess of chance, adorns the first arch, while Medusa wards off evil spirits on the second.

Sailors and traders in particular invoked Tyche, to protect them on their long journeys. After the first arch, in the upper-left corner is a relief of a man on a horse chasing a boar – a representation of Ephesus' foundation myth. At shoulder height are backwards swastikas representing the nearby Meander River.

Terraced Houses   RUIN
(admission ₺15) The roofed complex here contains (at present) seven well-preserved Roman homes, which are well worth the extra ₺15. As you ascend the snaking stairs through the enclosure, detailed signs explain each structure's evolving use during different periods. Even if you aren't a history buff, the colourful mosaics, painted frescoes and marbles provide breathtaking insight into the lost world of Ephesus and its aristocracy.

In dwelling 2, keep an eye out for wall graffiti: these hand-scrawled images include everything from pictures of gladiators and animals to names and love poems. Dwelling 6 once contained a huge marble hall, which has been partly restored, as well as remarkable hot and cold baths, dating from the 3rd century AD.

The whole residential area was originally a graveyard – the Romans built the terraces for their homes over this and other Hellenistic structures.

Brothel   RUIN
Unsurprisingly, this site is eagerly anticipated by tourists, but its rather dishevelled state makes envisioning licentious goings-on a challenge. Indeed, some experts believe that visiting sailors and merchants simply used it as a guesthouse and bath, which of course would not necessarily exclude prostitution services on demand.

Whatever the brothel's fundamental purpose was, its administrators reputedly required visitors to this windowless structure to undergo various degrees of cleansing before entering the inner areas, which were adorned with little statues of Venus. Rumours also abound about the possible existence of a secret underground tunnel connecting the brothel to the Library of Celsus opposite; you may encounter locals who swear to have walked through it as recently as 15 to 20 years ago.

☉ Lower Ephesus

Library of Celsus   RUIN
The early 2nd-century-AD governor of Asia Minor, Celsus Polemaeanus, was commemorated in this magnificent library. Originally built as part of a complex, the library looks bigger than it actually is: the convex facade

base heightens the central elements, while the central columns and capitals are larger than those at the ends. Facade niches hold replica statues of the Greek Virtues: Arete (Goodness), Ennoia (Thought), Episteme (Knowledge) and Sophia (Wisdom).

The originals are in Vienna's Ephesus Museum (the Austrian Archaeological Institute restored the library).

As a Greek and Latin inscription on the front staircase attests, Celsus' son, Consul Tiberius Julius Aquila, built the library in 114 to honour his deceased father, who was buried under the building's western side. Capable of holding 12,000 scrolls in its wall niches, the Celsus was the third-largest ancient library (after Alexandria and Pergamum). The valuable texts were protected from temperature and humidity extremes by a 1m gap between the inner and outer walls.

Lower Agora   RUIN
This 110-sq-metre former textile and food market once had a massive colonnade.

Marble Street   RUIN
Ephesus' third-largest street was a thoroughfare between the Library of Celsus and the Great Theatre.

Great Theatre   RUIN
Originally built under Hellenistic king Lysimachus, the Great Theatre was reconstructed by the Romans between AD 41 and AD 117. However, they incorporated original design elements, including the ingenious shape of the *cavea* (seating area). Seating rows are pitched slightly steeper as they ascend, meaning that upper-row spectators still enjoyed good views and acoustics – useful, considering that the theatre could hold 25,000 people.

Indeed, Ephesus' estimated peak population (250,000) is supported by the archaeologists' method of estimation: simply multiply theatre capacity by 10.

Harbour Street   RUIN
Formally the Arcadian Way, Harbour St was built by Byzantine emperor Arcadius (r 395–408) in a late attempt to revive the fading city. At the time, it was Ephesus' most lavish thoroughfare, illuminated at night by 50 streetlights on its colonnades, while water and sewage channels ran beneath its marble flagstones. It greeted visitors after they patronised the Harbour Baths.

Look for the high column at the arcade's end to see how far inland the sea reached in those days.

Stadium   RUIN
Outside the Lower Gate, the Stadium dates from the 2nd century AD. The Byzantines removed most of its finely cut stones to build the castle on Ayasuluk Hill. This 'quarrying' of pre-cut building stone from older, often earthquake-ruined structures was a constant feature of Ephesian history.

Gymnasium of Vedius   RUIN
On the side road between the lower car park and the Selçuk–Kuşadası road, this ruined 2nd-century-AD structure has exercise fields, baths, toilets, covered exercise rooms, a swimming pool and a ceremonial hall.

☞ Tours

If signing up to a tour in a distant town or cruise port, try to ascertain that your guide is licensed and well informed, and understand exactly how much time you'll get onsite, compared to how much time will be spent on detours to carpet shops.

Random guides lurk at the entrances, asking about ₺150 for two hours. The garbled and uninformative multilingual audioguides (₺20) available at the gates are not recommended. Many of the ruins have English-language signage.

★ No Frills Ephesus Tours   TOUR
(☏ 0232-892 8828; www.nofrillsephesustours. com; St Jean Caddesi 3/A, Selçuk; half-/full-day tours from €40/50; ☺ tours 9am daily Apr-Oct) Noticing how carpet-selling tactics and underhand practices were irritating time-poor independent travellers, Mehmet Esenkaya and his Australian wife Christine launched these small-group tours. Other tours may be cheaper, but this is often because their prices are being subsidised by expected commission on carpet-shop sales after the tour, which can translate into pressure on tourists to buy, as well as wasted time.

Tours include transport, entrance and parking fees, and are led by entertaining and well-informed guides – without any side trips to tacky souvenir shops. Both tours visit the Temple of Artemis, Ephesus and the Basilica of St John, with Mary's House also included in the full-day tour. The Terraced Houses and Şirince village can be added on (€10 each).

Selcukephesus.com SCENIC FLIGHTS, SKYDIVING
(☑0530 884 0854; www.selcukephesus.com; 20-/30-/60-min flight ₺150/200/400) For a totally different take on Ephesus, see it from above in a two-seater microlight out of Selçuk Airport, just east of Ephesus. Your journey will take you over the main sights of Selçuk and Ephesus, before looping over the Kuşadası coast for sea views. Book online.

ℹ Getting There & Away

Hotels are not allowed to take guests to Ephesus, so take a taxi, car or tour. Selçuk is roughly a 3.5km walk from both entrances, with the Temple of Artemis and shade provided by mulberry trees en route to the Lower Gate.

Dolmuşes (minibuses) serve the Lower Gate (₺3, half-hourly in summer, hourly in winter). Alternatively, dolmuşes between Selçuk and Kuşadası drop off and pick up at the turn-off for the Lower Gate, about a 20-minute walk from the site.

A taxi to/from either gate costs ₺15 to ₺20.

Around Ephesus

Most Ephesus tours also visit the following nearby sites, though ask in advance.

◉ Sights

Mary's House HISTORIC BUILDING, RELIGIOUS
(Meryemana; ☑894 1012; admission ₺15, parking ₺8; ☉8am-6pm, mass 10.30am Sun, 6pm Sun-Fri Apr-Oct, 5pm Sun-Fri Nov-Mar, Assumption service 15 Aug) Atop the foundations of a ruined house on the wooded slope of Bülbül Dağı (Mt Coressos), thought to be where the Virgin Mary lived, the enterprising Turks let a chapel be built, which receives streams of bussed-in pilgrims and curious tourists. 'Appropriate dress' is required. You may not have space to see much inside the tiny chapel through all the visitors, but note the pale red line on its side after exiting – everything beneath it is from the original foundation.

A 'wishing wall' below the chapel is covered in bits of rag, indicative of Turkic folk custom that visitors have imitated by tying their own bits of cloth, paper, plastic (or anything at hand) to a frame and making a wish. Taps here produce water from a spring.

The house foundations, discovered in 1881 by French priest Julien Gouyet, are from the 6th century AD (though certain elements are older). Although legend had long attested that St John brought the Virgin Mary to Ephesus near the end of her life

(AD 37–45), it took until the 19th century for conditions to be right for commercialisation. Gouyet claimed to have found Mary's house based on the visions of a 'mystic', bedridden German nun, Catherina Emmerich, and four popes have visited since then (most recently, Benedict XVI in 2006). Although the Vatican has not taken an official position on the case, the late John Paul II did declare Emmerich a saint in 2004, during the frenzy of last-minute sanctifications before his death.

Multilingual information panels exist, and brochures and booklets are available. *Mary's House* by Donald Carroll is a recommended book. At the entrance are cafes, shops and toilets, and the leafy site is good for a picnic.

The site is 7km from Ephesus' Upper Gate and 8.5km from the Lower Gate. It's not serviced by dolmuşes, and taxis from Selçuk otogar (bus station) are ₺40/70 single/return (including a 30-minute wait).

Grotto of the Seven Sleepers RUIN
FREE The road between Ephesus' two gates passes this cave tomb, where seven legendary Christians, persecuted by Emperor Decius in AD 250, are buried. Walk 200m from the grotto car park to see the ruins, following the hill path to the right. The grotto is clearly visible through a wire fence, and a warden may open the gate in exchange for a small tip.

The story goes that, having refused to recant their beliefs, the Sleepers gave their possessions to the poor and went to pray in this cave on Mt Pion. They soon fell asleep, and Decius had the cave sealed. When the men were awoken centuries later by a landowner seeking to use the cave, they felt they had slept but a day, and warily sent someone into pagan Ephesus. The dazed young emissary was just as surprised to find Christian churches there as the Ephesians were to find someone presenting 200-year-old coins. The local bishop, Stephen, met the Sleepers, who later died and were buried in their cave.

The bishop quickly proclaimed the miracle (in around 450), immediately creating a Byzantine pilgrimage cult that would last for over 1000 years. The legend became famous as far away as France and England, and there's even a Koranic variant.

Excavation, begun in 1927, has unearthed hundreds of 4th- and 5th-century terracotta oil lamps, decorated with Christian and in some cases pagan symbols. Regardless of the legend's verisimilitude, it's clear from these finds and the scores of rock-carved graves in this necropolis that the area was important to many people for many years.

Nearby vendors sell drinks and snacks.

Selçuk

☑ 0232 / POP 28,213

Were it not for nearby Ephesus, Selçuk might be just another Turkish farming town, with its lively markets and ploughs rusting away on side streets. That said, the gateway to Ephesus does have plenty of its own attractions – many topped with a picture-perfect stork's nest: Roman/Byzantine aqueduct arches, a lone pillar remaining from one of the Seven Wonders of the Ancient World, and the hilltop Byzantine ruins of the Basilica of St John and Ayasuluk Fortress.

Like all small places catering to short-term visitors, there is plenty of competition in the local tourism trade, which can result in both good deals for visitors and less-welcome pressure. Yet all in all, Selçuk remains a likeable, down-to-earth town, mixing a traditional country feel with a tourist buzz and family-run pensions offering a taste of Turkish hospitality and home cooking.

◉ Sights

Ephesus Museum   MUSEUM

(Uğur Mumcu Sevgi Yolu Caddesi; admission ₺10; ⊙8.30am-6.30pm Apr-Oct, to 4.30pm Nov-Mar) This museum holds artefacts from Ephesus' Terraced Houses, including scales, jewellery and cosmetic boxes, plus coins, funerary goods and ancient statuary. The famous effigy of Phallic god Priapus, visible by pressing a button, draws giggles, and a whole room is dedicated to Eros in sculpted form. The punters also get a rise out of the multi-breasted marble Artemis statue, a very fine work indeed.

Finds from a gladiators' cemetery excavation are displayed, with commentary on their weaponry, training regimes and occupational hazards. Also worth seeing is the frieze from the Temple of Hadrian that shows four heroic Amazons with their breasts cut off – early Greek writers attributed Ephesus' founding to them.

The museum is ideally visited after touring Ephesus and seeing where the finds come from. After midday, however, it fills with cruise crowds being rushed through.

Byzantine Aqueduct   RUIN

Running intermittently east from Ayasuluk Hill, the long and tall Roman/Byzantine aqueducts are festively adorned with the huge nests of migrating storks, who stand guard from March through September.

Basilica of St John   RUIN, HISTORIC SITE

(St Jean Caddesi; admission incl Ayasuluk Fortress ₺10; ⊙8am-6.30pm Apr-Oct, to 4.30pm Nov-Mar) Despite a century of restoration, the once-great basilica built by Byzantine emperor Justinian (r 527–65) is still but a skeleton of its former self. Nonetheless, it is an atmospheric site with excellent hilltop views, and the best place in the area for a sunset photo. The information panels and scale model highlight the building's original grandeur, as do the marble steps and monumental gate.

Over time, earthquakes and attackers ruined Justinian's church, which was inspired by the local connection with St John, who reportedly visited Ephesus twice. His first visit (AD 37 to 48) was with the Virgin Mary; the second (AD 95) was when he wrote his gospel, on this very hill. These legends, and the existence of a 4th-century tomb supposedly housing John's relics, inspired Justinian to build the basilica here, drawing thousands of pilgrims in Byzantine times. John's tomb can be seen, surrounded by the cruciform outlines of Justinian's basilica and a 4th-century predecessor.

Ayasuluk Fortress   CASTLE

(2013 Sokak; admission incl Basilica of St John ₺10; ⊙8am-6.30pm Apr-Oct, to 4.30pm Nov-Mar) Selçuk's crowning achievement is accessed on the same ticket as the neighbouring Basilica of St John. Excavation is ongoing and, at the time of writing, entry was by intermittent guided tours; hopefully regular access will soon be established. The digs here, begun in 1990, have proven that there were castles on Ayasuluk Hill going back beyond the original Ephesian settlement to the Neolithic age. The partially restored fortress' remains today date from Byzantine, Seljuk and Ottoman times.

Guides will likely point out ruins including a hamam, basements and a mescit (small mosque) with a discernible *mihrab* (niche indicating the direction of Mecca).

One section of the castle, the mostly ruined Fortress Mansion, made waves when excavated in 2009, because it had last been mentioned by British traveller John Covell in 1670. Built for a ruling Ottoman family, the structure was probably created by the same architects as nearby İsa Bey Camii.

Excavations of the Inner Fortress here have also uncovered the remains of three houses in the Kale Mosque, an area comprised of 15 bedrooms now dubbed the Southern Terrace. Since 2010, more than 100m of the western walls and towers have been restored using original materials.

İsa Bey Camii
MOSQUE

(St Jean Caddesi) At the base of Ayasuluk Hill, this mosque (1375) was built in a post-Seljuk/pre-Ottoman transitional style, when Selçuk was capital of the Aydın Emirate. It contains a bust of its patron, the Emir of Aydın, and is open to visitors (except at prayer times).

Temple of Artemis
RUIN

(Artemis Tapınağı; off Dr Sabrı Yayla Bulvarı; ⊘8am-7pm Apr-Oct, 8.30am-6pm Nov-Mar) FREE In an empty field on Selçuk's western extremities, this solitary reconstructed pillar is all that remains of the massive Temple of Artemis, one of the Seven Wonders of the Ancient World. At its zenith, the structure had 127 columns; today, the only way to get any sense of this grandeur is to see Didyma's better-preserved Temple of Apollo (p248), which had 122 columns.

The temple was damaged by flooding and various invaders during its 1000-year lifespan, but it was always rebuilt – a sign of the great love and attachment Ephesians felt for their fertility avatar, the cult of which brought tremendous wealth to the city from pilgrims and benefactors who included the greatest kings and emperors of their day.

From the south, there is a good view of the stork's-nest-topped pillar with İsa Bey Camii and Ayasuluk Hill beyond.

Saturday Market
MARKET

(Şahabettin Dede Caddesi; ⊘9am-5pm winter, 8am-7pm summer) Self-caterers and sightseers alike will enjoy this market. Like the Wednesday market (⊘9am-5pm winter, 8am-7pm summer), it offer fruits, veg and cheeses from village farms.

🛏 Sleeping

Selçuk specialises in good-value, family-run pensions, with more upscale hotels also available. Unfortunately, with all of the attentive service, free extras, bus station pick-ups, airport transfers and eager assistance, there can be pressure to buy (carpets, tours etc). You should be OK at the places listed here.

★ Atilla's Getaway
HOSTEL, RESORT €

(☑892 3847; www.atillasgetaway.com; Acarlar Köyü; dm/s/d/tw/tr €16/26/42/42/63, camping €8; ❋@🛜🏊) This 'backpacker resort', named after its friendly Turkish-Australian owner, is all about relaxation, with a classically themed chill-out area gazing at the hills and a bar with pool table and nightly fires. Twice-weekly barbecues and six kinds of breakfast are offered and the volleyball court and table tennis add to the fun.

The roadside complex is about 3km south of Selçuk, linked by free shuttles, and a 50-minute walk through the hills from Ephesus' Upper Gate. The bungalows with shared facilities are fairly basic, but comfortable modern en-suite rooms are available, as are half board and accommodation-only packages.

Barım Pension
PENSION €

(☑892 6923; info@barimpension.com; 1045 Sokak 34; s ₺45-50, d ₺80-90; ❋🛜) This long-running pension stands out for its unusual and winding wire art, crafted by two friendly metalworking brothers who run Barım with their wives. The pension occupies a characterful 140-year-old stone house, with a leafy back garden to breakfast in. The 10 rooms are reasonably modern; 2 and 5 are good doubles, the latter up its own private staircase. Adnan, a keen cyclist, can suggest local rides and organise bike rental.

Nur Pension
PENSION €

(☑892 6595; www.nurpension.com; 3004 Sokak 20; dm/s/d/tw/tr €10/20/30/30/40; ❋🛜) In a quiet residential area with farm machinery in the streets, the Turkish-Japanese 'Divine Light' has basic but clean and bright rooms on two floors, including options with shared bathroom. There is a kitchen and covered courtyard for drinking çay and lounging.

Alihan Guesthouse
PENSION €

(☑892 9496; www.alihanguesthouse.com; 1045 Sokak 34; s/d ₺50/70; ❋🛜) The friendly Alihan has basic but clean rooms, a kitchen for self-caterers and an enclosed breakfast terrace.

Tuncay Pension
PENSION €

(☑892 6260; www.tuncaypension.com; 2015 Sokak 1; s/d ₺50/70; ❋🛜) Tuncay's rooms are sparse and modern with threadbare carpets, but some doubles are spacious and the pension has a terrace with castle views and a courtyard decorated with knick-knacks.

Selçuk

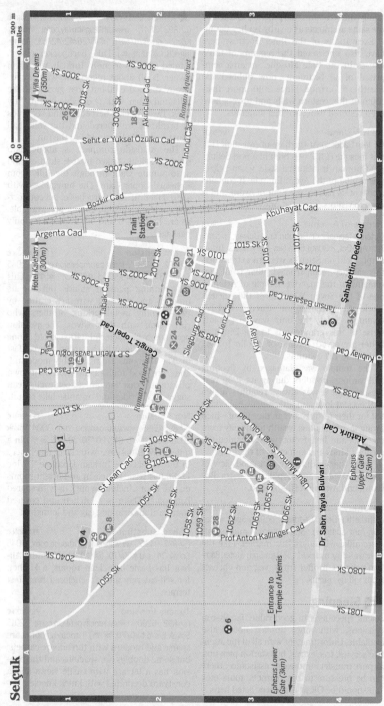

200 m
0.1 miles

Villa Dreams (350m)

3005 Sk
3018 Sk
3004 Sk
26
3008 Sk
3006 Sk
Akıncılar Cad
18
Roman Aqueduct
İnönü Cad
Sehit er Yuksel Özülkü Cad
3007 Sk
3002 Sk
Bozkir Cad
Abuhayat Cad
Argenta Cad
Hotel Kalehan (300m)
Train Station
2006 Sk
Tabak Cad
2002 Sk
2001 Sk
20
21
1010 Sk
1007 Sk
1006 Sk
1015 Sk
1016 Sk
1017 Sk
1014 Sk
Sahabettin Dede Cad
Cengiz Topel Cad
Roman Aqueduct
Fevzi Pasa Cad
S.P. Metin Tavsitioğlu Cad
16
2003 Sk
27
25
24
2
Siegburg Cad
1003 Sk
Lienz Cad
14
Tahsin Başaran Cad
5
23
Kızılay Cad
1013 Sk
Kubilay Cad
15
13
St Jean Cad
2013 Sk
1046 Sk
1038 Sk
Atatürk Cad
7
1
12
17
11
22
1045 Sk
Uğur Mumcu Sevgi Yolu Cad
3
Ephesus Upper Gate (3.5km)
1050 Sk
1051 Sk
9
10
1065 Sk
1066 Sk
Dr Sabri Yayla Bulvari
1054 Sk
1056 Sk
1058 Sk
1059 Sk
1062 Sk
1063 Sk
28
Prof Anton Kallinger Cad
8
4
29
2040 Sk
1055 Sk
1080 Sk
1081 Sk
Entrance to Temple of Artemis
6
Ephesus Lower Gate (3km)

Selçuk

★ **Hotel Bella**　　　　　　　　　　HOTEL €€
(☑ 892 3944; www.hotelbella.com; St Jean Caddesi 7; s ₺110-155, d & tw ₺120-165, tr/f ₺185/210; ❄@⊛) This posh little hotel comes complete with a carpet and jewellery shop, and well-designed rooms with Ottoman flourishes in the decor. Even the economy rooms have a certain grandeur in their carpets and pictures of the harem, while antiques and artefacts decorate the rooftop lounge and restaurant.

Uniquely, Bella provides transport for guests to Ephesus, having opened a travel agency in order to get the licence to do so.

★ **Boomerang**　　　　GUESTHOUSE, HOSTEL €€
(☑ 892 4879; www.boomerangguesthouse. com; 1047 Sokak 10; dm/s/d/tw/tr/f from €10/30/40/40/60/70; ❄⊛) People do indeed keep coming back to this Turkish-Chinese operation, to spend chilled-out evenings among the trees in the stone courtyard, where the recommended bar-restaurant (mains ₺12 to ₺20) serves dishes including kebaps, Chinese food and cheesy *köfte*. Some rooms have balconies, while budget options are also available (single/double/twin/triple €20/30/30/45) along with extras such as a travel desk and bike hire.

Nazar Hotel　　　　　　　　　　HOTEL €€
(☑ 892 2222; www.nazarhotel.com; S.P. Metin Tavaslıoğlu Caddesi 34; s/d/tr/f from €35/40/60/80; ❄@⊛✸) In a rustic residential area beneath Ayasuluk Fortress, the Turkish-French Nazar stands out for its excellent service. Nothing is too much trouble for owner İlk-

er and the breakfasts and dinners (€10) on the roof terrace are home-cooked feasts with views of the Basilica of St John. Rooms are plain with small bathrooms, and some have a balcony.

Homeros Pension　　　　　　　PENSION €€
(☑ 892 3995; www.homerospension.com; 1048 Sokak 3; s/d ₺50/100; ❄⊛) Recommended by readers, this long-time favourite offers a dozen rooms in two buildings, unique for their colourful hanging textiles and handcrafted furniture made by owner Derviş, a carpenter and antiques collector. Enjoy good views and dinners on the roof terraces. There are also budget rooms with shared bathroom.

Jimmy's Place　　　　　　　　　HOTEL €€
(☑ 892 1982; www.artemisguesthouse.com; 1016 Sokak 19; s €25-60, d €30-70; ❄@⊛✸) In a modern yellow building, multilingual Cumhur 'Jimmy' has created a comfortable hotel with 27 tastefully decorated rooms featuring wood-panelled floors and spacious bathrooms. The travel library and information service, covered terrace and buffet breakfast with filter coffee all combine to make a top-notch operation.

Akay Hotel　　　　　　　　　　　HOTEL €€
(☑ 892 3172; www.hotelakay.com; 1054 Sokak 7; s/d from ₺100/150; ❄@⊛✸) This smart, Swiss-owned hotel near İsa Bey Camii has well-appointed rooms overlooking an inviting turquoise pool and bar. Dinners (€10) are on the relaxing roof terrace. The poolside rooms are not worth the extra expenditure.

Villa Dreams
PENSION €€

(☑892 3514; www.ephesusvilladreams.com; 3046 Sokak 15; s/d ₺70/100; ✲ 🕯 ≋) Recommended by readers, Villa Dreams offers great views, an outdoor swimming pool and a communal kitchen. It has modern standard rooms and two big family rooms with shiny wood floors and balconies. The rooftop terrace affords fantastic castle views, and a free shuttle is provided to and from the centre.

Wallabies Aquaduct Hotel
HOTEL €€

(☑892 3204; www.wallabiesaquaducthotel.com; Cengiz Topel Caddesi 2; s/d ₺75/120; ✲ 🕯) Beside the Byzantine Aqueduct, Wallabies has smart rooms in black and white, with views from the upper floors into the stork's nest atop the ruins or across town. It lacks atmosphere, but is pleasant enough with a small lift, buffet breakfast and double-glazed windows to keep noise at bay.

Nilya Hotel
BOUTIQUE HOTEL €€€

(☑892 9081; www.nilya.com; 1051 Sokak 7; s/d/tr/ste ₺180/200/240/260; ✲ 🕯) Under the same ownership as nearby Hotel Bella, Nilya shows similar artistic flourishes in the hand-carved walnut headboards and ceiling roses, Kütahya tiles, Ottoman miniatures and travertine bathrooms adorning the 12 rooms. The renovated stone house has a balcony gazing across the flats at the Aegean and a pleasant courtyard.

Naz Han
BOUTIQUE HOTEL €€€

(☑892 8731; www.nazhan.net; 1044 Sokak 2; s/d €60/70; ✲ 🕯) Naz Han occupies a century-old Greek house, its courtyard and lounge tastefully decorated with artefacts and antiques, and its rooms juxtaposing white-washed walls and carpets. Some rooms and bathrooms are more modern than others, so ask to see a few.

There's also a small roof terrace with views, and home-cooked dinners and breakfasts featuring local products including olives from Naz Han's orchard.

Hotel Kalehan
HOTEL €€€

(☑892 6154; www.kalehan.com; Atatürk Caddesi 57; s/d €55/75; ✲ 🕯 ≋) On Selçuk's northern outskirts, the 'Castle Caravanserai' has flowery gardens leading to rooms mixing mod cons with a vintage feel created by scattered antiques and black-and-white photos. The bar-restaurant is a pleasant spot to relax after a day of ruins.

✖ Eating

Selçuk's restaurants offer dependable and reasonably priced Turkish fare, although many pensions and hotels serve more exciting home cooking. The outdoor restaurants and tea gardens beside the illuminated Byzantine Aqueduct arches make for atmospheric and romantic summer dining.

Sişçi Yaşar'ın Yeri
KÖFTE, KEBAP €

(Atatürk Caddesi; mains from ₺8; ☺lunch & dinner) Under overhanging leaves next to a 14th-century mosque, Yaşar's place is good for a simple lunch of *köfte* (meatballs), *çöp şiş* (*şiş* kebap served rolled in a thin pide with onions and parsley) and *ayran* (yoghurt drink).

Ejder Restaurant
TURKISH, KEBAP €€

(Cengiz Topel Caddesi 9/E; mezes ₺6-8, mains ₺9-25; ☺lunch & dinner) Next to the Byzantine Aqueduct, this outdoor restaurant on a pedestrianised walkway is good for lunch on a sunny day, with lots of choices including the generous *tavuk şiş* (roast chicken kebap). The kind owners, Mehmet, Rahime and son Arkan, are proud to show off their guestbooks and memorabilia, which include photos from the Clinton family's visit in 1999.

Selçuk Köftecisi
KÖFTE €€

(Şahabettin Dede Caddesi; mezes ₺8, köfte ₺12; ☺lunch & dinner) In a modern building by the fish market, this long-running local favourite serves excellent *köfte*, cooked to perfection and accompanied by salad, rice and fried onions. The good selection of side salads includes a spicy walnut option.

Mehmet & Alibaba Kebab House
TURKISH €€

(1047 Sokak 4; mezes ₺5-8, kebaps ₺9-20; ☺lunch & dinner; 🕯) As the testimonials in many tongues attest, this restaurant is geared towards tourists, but you are at least assured of good service and well-prepared food from a clean kitchen. Dishes include meze platters (₺8 to ₺20), *köfte*, and kebaps including *dürüm* options (wrapped in flatbread).

Tat Restaurant
TURKISH €€

(Cengiz Topel Caddesi 19; mains ₺12; ☺lunch & dinner) Touristy Tat's food won't set the world on fire – although the *güveç* (stew) and other fiercely sizzling dishes could start a blaze – but it is a pleasant spot with seating among lanterns on a pedestrianised walkway. Multilingual waiters chat to diners and humour their children, between delivering kebaps, seafood and mezes such as fried zucchini and hummus.

TIRE MARKET

The farming town of Tire, 38km northeast of Selçuk, lies amid the fields beneath the Bozdağlar Mountains. Its popular Tuesday market provides a slice-of-life view of rural Turkey, sprawling across the town centre and filling whole streets with the aroma of freshly picked herbs. The 8.30am Islamic market prayer over the loudspeaker adds a certain exotic touch and the foodstuffs on sale at the day-long event are delicious. A smaller market takes place on Friday.

Tire clings to its traditional felt-making industry, with a few *keçe* (felt) makers, still working on blends of teased cotton and wool, on the cobbled lane running uphill from the small Leyse Camii (1543). Just off this street, Tire Keçecilik (Belediyehan Caddesi 46; ⏰8am-8pm) sells quirky and beautiful clothing, mobiles and souvenirs – affordable ways to own a piece of Turkish patterning without forking out for a carpet. The design-making process involves creating patterns, dousing with water, adding cotton and finally pressing the material for a full hour.

Up a steep and winding 5km road from Tire, the mountain village of Kaplan offers the excellent Kaplan Dağ Restorant (☎0232-512 6652; www.kaplandag.com; mezes ₺5, mains ₺13-18; ⏰1-9pm Tue-Sun; 🖉), renowned for its local dishes with lashings of olive oil and wild herbs. Seasonal mezes like stuffed zucchini flowers are offered, and mains include Tire *köfte* and *şiş* kebaps. Book ahead on Tuesdays and weekends. A taxi from Tire costs ₺20.

Dolmuşes serve Tire from Selçuk (₺7, one hour) every 40 minutes.

🍷 Drinking & Nightlife

While seaside Kuşadası has wild nightlife, Selçuk's desultory bar/cafe scene exists mainly to help local males watch televised football matches out of their homes. Drinking with your hosts and fellow guests at your accommodation is generally more worthwhile.

Selçuk's liveliest bars are found on the cobbled pedetrian streets south of the Byzantine Aqueduct, with a few mellow spots along Prof Anton Kallinger Caddesi.

Odeon Bistro Cafe   PUB

(1054 Sokak 1) Under a tent roof, this friendly watering hole decorated with hanging lanterns has a fridge full of mezes and local wines including Harman, a palatable dry red from Pamukkale.

Destina   BAR

(Prof Anton Kallinger Caddesi 24) Destina's little front garden is perfect for a late-afternoon *çay* or sunset beer, overlooking the greenery around the Temple of Artemis.

Denis   BAR

(Cengiz Topel Caddesi 20) Soundtracked by rock videos, Denis has beer bongs and outside tables on two streets.

ℹ️ Information

Tourist Office (www.selcuk.gov.tr; Agora Caddesi 35; ⏰8am-noon & 1-5.30pm daily May-Sep, Mon-Fri Oct-Apr)

DANGERS & ANNOYANCES

Look out for conniving 'coin-men': although savvy travellers won't fall for it, there are apparently still enough naive tourists willing to part with a couple hundred euros or dollars to make it worthwhile for locals to tinker with coin moulds, base metals and household chemicals to create pieces of supposedly ancient numismatic treasure. Besides the illegality of purchasing antiquities in Turkey, it's a total waste of your money. The fraudsters are most often found around St John's Hill or the gates of Ephesus.

ℹ️ Getting There & Around

TO/FROM İZMIR ADNAN MENDERES AIRPORT

Bus Take an İzmir-bound bus and get off at the highway turn-off, from where the airport is a 2km walk or a ₺15 taxi ride (you must cross the motorway to reach the taxis).

Shuttle Atlasjet and Onur Air shuttle their passengers to Selçuk for free. Going back, they depart from outside the hospital. Selçuk's local shuttle companies are generally inefficient and unreliable.

Taxi Budget on €40 to €50.

Train The simplest and cheapest public transport option, the one-hour journey to/from the airport costs ₺4.50. Services are not punctual, so you should aim to catch a train leaving Selçuk at least two hours before you are due to check in. Passengers are not assigned a seat and you may have to stand. Also note that the train's airport stop is a 15- to 20-minute walk from the departures terminal.

CHRIS CHEADLE / GETTY IMAGES ©

1. Temple of Apollo, Didyma (p248) 2. Knidos, Datça
Peninsula (p275) 3. Temple of Athena, Priene (p245)
4. Great Thatre, Miletus (p247)

DENIZ UNLUSUS / GETTY IMAGES ©

Ruins of the South Aegean

The Romans, Carians, Ionian Greeks and Byzantines were a few of the ancient civilisations that left their mark on this ruin-strewn stretch of coastline, where the very contours of the land have changed but weathered theatres and temples still stand.

Ephesus

On the flagstones of this great Roman provincial capital, you can tread in the footsteps of historical notables such as Antony and Cleopatra.

Priene

Refreshingly quiet after a visit to Ephesus, Priene was, like its busier neighbour to the north, a port city. Silted up by the Meander River, the Aegean coast receded west to its current location, stranding these ports inland and spelling their decline.

Miletus

Miletus suffered the same fate as nearby Ephesus and Pirene. Its most impressive ruin is the 15,000-seat Great Theatre, while the Temple of Apollo marked the start of a sacred road to Didyma.

Didyma

With its towering columns, Didyma's Temple of Apollo is one of Turkey's most evocative classical ruins. It also helps to visualise the lost grandeur of Ephesus' Temple of Artemis, one of the Seven Wonders of the Ancient World.

Mausoleum of Halicarnassus

The tomb of the Carian King Mausolus was also one of the Seven Wonders of the Ancient World. Displays at the site in Bodrum recreate the white-marble mausoleum topped by stepped pyramids.

Knidos

This Dorian port city, straddling two bays on the Datça Peninsula, is a stunning example of how at sites throughout Aegean and Mediterranean Turkey, ruins are given extra poetry by their lyrical settings.

BUS & DOLMUŞ

Bodrum (₺30, three hours) Pamukkale has a morning and afternoon departure in summer. In winter, you must change in Kuşadası and Söke.

Denizli (₺30, three hours) For Pamukkale and coastal destinations such as Fethiye and Antalya. Metro has a morning and afternoon departure year-round, with additional Pamukkale services in summer.

İstanbul (₺80, 10 hours) Metro has two daily departures year-round, with additional Pamukkale services in summer.

İzmir (₺9, one hour) Every 40 minutes from 6.30am to 8.30pm (winter 6pm).

Kuşadası (₺5, 25 minutes) Every 20 to 30 minutes from 6.30am to midnight (winter 7pm). Via Pamucak (₺3, 10 minutes).

Pamukkale (₺34, 3¼ hours) Direct Pamukkale bus at 4.30pm in summer. Otherwise, change in Denizli.

TAXI

A taxi across town costs about ₺10. For longer journeys, negotiating a price in advance with the driver is normally cheaper than using the meter.

TRAIN

There are roughly eight trains a day to İzmir (₺5.75, 1½ hours) via the airport (see above) and to Denizli (₺14.50, three hours).

Şirince

📞0232 / POP 960

The clustered stone-and-stucco homes, bucolic wooded setting and long winemaking tradition of Şirince, once a Greek-populated mountain village, have made it popular with Turkish and foreign tourists. It is busiest at weekends, when coaches charge up the mountain road from Selçuk. While this deluge has affected the village's original charms, it remains a beautiful place and a relaxing day trip. It's much more tranquil by night, and a handful of boutique hotels, many rather precious and overpriced, cater to well-heeled tourists.

While Şirince was probably settled when Ephesus was abandoned, today's remains date to the 19th century. Legend has it that freed Greek slaves resettled here in the 15th century, calling the village Çirkince (Ugliness) to keep others away. This altered to Kirkinje by the 19th century, and, following the exodus of the Greeks in the population exchange of the 1920s, the name Şirince (Pleasantness) was applied.

Şirince was repopulated by Turks also from northern Greece; they built a mosque, but retained the local alcohol trade, and today you can sample their unique wines (made from raspberry, peach, black mulberry and pomegranate) in local restaurants and cafes.

⊙ Sights

Crowds dissipate by evening; late morning to mid-afternoon is busiest. There's a long gauntlet of souvenir stands and tourist restaurants, which eventually disperses near the church, allowing you to enjoy the cool, crisp air and lovely old houses from the cobbled lanes on high.

Church of St John the Baptist CHURCH
(⊙8am-8pm summer, 8.30am-6.30pm winter) **FREE** This church (1805) has been sadly neglected by modern Turkey; an American charitable society is largely responsible for its upkeep. Preservation is non-existent, with graffiti scrawled where the altar once was, but there are faded Byzantine frescoes on some walls and atmosphere added by choral music and birds flitting through the windows.

If you have a spare kuruş, there's a shallow wishing well before the church entrance.

🛏 Sleeping

Doğa Pension PENSION €€
(📞0555 358 2121; s/d ₺80/150) 'Nature' Pension offers basic rooms at the far end of the village, some more modern than others, featuring stone fireplaces and rugs.

Terrace Houses BOUTIQUE HOTEL €€€
(📞0532 263 7942; www.ephesushousessirince.com; ste €125, house €150-200; ❋ 🛜) These lovingly adorned traditional 19th-century houses are in the quieter streets above the mosque, away from the tourist bustle. Some include four-poster beds and bath-tubs, and all enjoy relaxing views over the village.

Choose between the Grapevine, Olive and Fig Houses and the new addition, Clockmaker's Cottage, the latter standing just below the terrace cafe where breakfasts of local produce are served.

Güllü Konak BOUTIQUE HOTEL €€€
(📞898 3131; www.gullukonak.com; r €125-245; ❋ 🛜) Reader-recommended, this refined collection of individually decorated 35-sq-metre rooms, all named after a different type of *gül* (rose), occupies two sturdy white-and-brown mansions in a tranquil private garden.

✖ Eating & Drinking

Most restaurants here are outdoor affairs, and do a good line in all-day *köy kahvaltı* (village breakfast), which typically costs ₺15 and features numerous honeys, cheeses, rounds of çay and so on. *Kuru fasulye* (white-bean stew) is another popular local dish. Tourist restaurants, mostly licensed, are found around the mosque.

If you are ordering expensive local wine, ask for it to be poured in front of you. Mischievous waiters have been known to give refills of cheap house wine, presuming (correctly) that tourists will never know the difference.

★ **Pervin Teyze**   AEGEAN, ORGANIC €€
(gözleme ₺5-7, mezes & mains ₺8-15; 🖉) Signposted above the church, this ramshackle terrace restaurant serves simple dishes made by village ladies, with choices changing according to the season and the matriarchs' whim. Enjoy sweeping views and choral music drifting up from the church, while tucking into *gözleme* (stuffed savoury crepes), *dolmas* (vegetables or flowers stuffed with rice or meat), *mantı* (Turkish ravioli) and of course *kahvaltı*.

Şirincem Restaurant & Cafe   ANATOLIAN €€
(mains ₺9-22) This rustic restaurant under shady foliage, owned by a fruit-farming family, offers a good range of mezes, meat dishes and Anatolian wines as well as *kahvaltı*.

**Artemis Restaurant &
Şarapevi**   WINE BAR, RESTAURANT
(www.artemisrestaurant.com) At the village entrance, you can taste Şirince wines in the former Greek schoolhouse, with great views from the outside terrace and garden.

❶ Getting There & Away

Dolmuşes (₺3) leave Selçuk for Şirince half-hourly in summer, hourly in winter. Parking at the village entrance costs ₺5.

Pamucak

🖉 0232

Popular Pamucak, 7km west of Selçuk, is your nearest beach day trip, though better beaches exist to the north and south (ask locally). On weekends, Turkish families flock here, often leaving their trash behind, so it's not always the cleanest stretch of sand, but still fine for a swim. From February to March, flamingos visit the estuary wetlands (a 15-minute walk from the beach).

Dereli (🖉 893 1205; www.dereli-ephesus.com; s €38-45, d €45-65, campsite per person ₺25; 🕿) offers palm-fronted, beach-facing bungalows and a eucalyptus-shaded campsite. Grander clifftop hotels are found on the coast road south to Kuşadası.

Half-hourly dolmuşes run to/from Selçuk (₺3, 10 minutes) via the Ephesus Lower Gate turn-off, and to/from Kuşadası (₺4, 20 minutes).

Kuşadası

🖉 0256 / POP 70,143

Kuşadası is a popular package-tour destination and, as the coastal gateway to Ephesus, Turkey's busiest cruise port (roughly 30th worldwide). Lacking the sights and ambience of Bodrum and the size of Marmaris, it remains a runner-up on the Aegean party scene, but the Irish pubs, discos and multilingual touts certainly create a memorably ribald atmosphere. If you prefer to mix your Ephesus visit with nightlife and sea views than Selçuk's rural ambience, Kuşadası is ideal (albeit more

---

GETTING WET IN KUŞADASI

Aqua Fantasy (🖉 0232-850 8500; www.aquafantasy.com; Ephesus Beach; adult/child €24/17; ⊙ 10am-6.30pm) claims to be Turkey's top water park, while **Adaland** (🖉 0256-618 1252; www.adaland.com; Çamlimanı Mevkii; adult/child €15/12; ⊙ 11.30am-5pm Apr-Oct) claims to be Europe's best. Both are just north of Kuşadası near Pamucak, and have myriad pools, slides and so on. Kids under three get free at both. Aqua Fantasy offers a 10% discount if booking online, and has an adjoining hotel with restaurants, hamam and spa.

Aquaventure Diving Center (🖉 0256-612 7845; www.aquaventure.com.tr; Miracle Beach Club; ⊙ 8am-6pm) offers reef dives (from €30) and PADI open water courses (€250), although other places such as Kaş are better dive spots. It is located by Ladies Beach and provides free transfers from most hotels.

Kuşadası

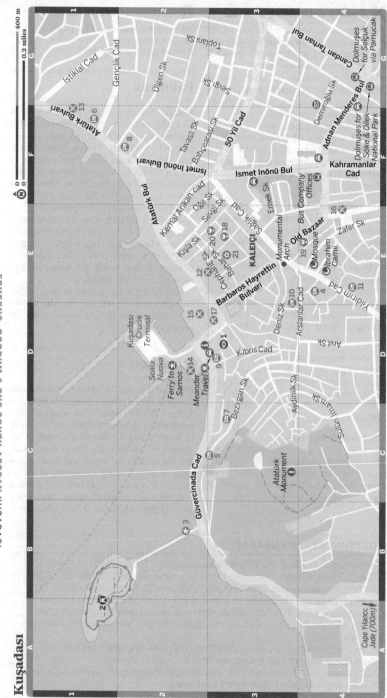

Kuşadası

expensive), with some good hotels and restaurants, a happily untraditional bazaar and two quieter old quarters.

◎ Sights & Activities

Local travel agencies offer trips to Ephesus (half/full-day €35/55), Priene, Miletus and Didyma (€45) and further-flung places such as Pamukkale (€50), all including lunch.

Bazaar   MARKET
Immediately in the line of sight of disembarking cruisers, the main bazaar area hawks 'genuine fake watches', leathery apparel, cheap jewellery and the like.

Kuşadası Castle   FORTRESS
A veritable boutique castle, Kuşadası's small stone fortress, standing on the causeway-connected Güvercin Adası (Pigeon Island), is attractively spotlit at night. A path leads around the island's eastern side with views of Kuşadası – popular with strolling couples, fishermen and cats. The castle is normally locked but a museum is set to open inside.

Boat Trips   BOAT TOUR
Boats moored at the causeway leading to Kuşadası Castle offer one-hour sunset cruises for about ₺5 and, between April and November, day trips around local bays. Operators including Ali Kaptan 2 (☑0535 515 6821; www.kusadasitekneturu.com) and Matador (☑0532 461 3889) depart daily between mid-May and mid-September (weather allowing), and charge from ₺35 including food and soft drinks.

Call in advance for a pick-up from your accommodation.

Ottoman Turkish Bath   HAMAM
(Osmanlı Türk Hamamı; ☑622 1050; hamamosmanli.com; Kadınlar Denizi; admission incl body wash & bubble massage €15; ⊙8am-11pm) Kuşadası has four hamams, but this new bath at Ladies Beach is already rumoured to be the best on the Aegean coast. It offers male, female and mixed sections, plus female attendants and free transport to/from the centre.

Beaches   BEACH
Kuşadası town's small artificial beach is eclipsed by Kadınlar Denizi (Ladies Beach), 2.5km south and served by regular dolmuşes down Güvercinada Caddesi. It's nice, but gets very crowded in summer with package tourists from the big nearby hotels. Further south are several small beaches, again backed by big hotels.

⌂ Sleeping

Kuşadası centre has pensions and business hotels, while package-tour resorts and luxury hotels cover the outlying coasts.

Sezgin Hotel Guest House   HOSTEL €
(☑614 4225; www.sezginhotel.com; Arslanlar Caddesi 68; dm/s/d/tr €15/25/35/50; ❄@ ఉ ≋) Uphill from the bar action, Sezgin has bright and spacious rooms with modern bathroom, satellite TV, fridge and hairdryer. The reception and corridors are less appealing, but the rear courtyard has a chill-out area and pool overlooked by orange trees. Friendly owner Deniz offers local information in English, German and Japanese.

★ Villa Konak   BOUTIQUE HOTEL €€
(☑614 6318; www.villakonakhotel.com; Yıldırım Caddesi 55; r €55-70; ❄ ఉ ≋) Far above the

coast in the quieter old quarter, Villa Konak occupies a restored 140-year-old stone house, with pictures of old Kuşadası and Ottoman knick-knacks scattered around the rooms. The alcove seats in the poolside garden and bookcases of paperbacks alike create the feel of a relaxing haven, completed by the homemade cookies in the complimentary afternoon tea.

Some bathrooms are newer than others, so if possible look at a few rooms.

★ Liman Hotel
HOTEL €€

(Mr Happy's; ☏ 614 7770; www.limanhotel.com; cnr Kıbrıs & Güvercinada Caddesi; s/d/tr €30/50/60; ❄@🛜) Run by seasoned traveller Hasan (aka 'Mr Happy') and an equally upbeat team, 'Harbour' Hotel's name references not just its location but Hasan's aim to provide a safe harbour and 'a solution place for travellers'. Rooms are comfortable, straightforward affairs with balconies and recently renovated bathrooms.

The real pleasure of staying here is the general vibe of holiday camaraderie, beginning at breakfast on the roof terrace, when Hasan's brother Omar sings Turkish pop songs as the cruise liners glint in the docks below. The terrace is also the venue for drinks and nightly summer barbecues, while downstairs is a lounge and help with everything from hamam visits to bus tickets and local excursions.

Anzac Golden Bed Pension
PENSION €€

(☏ 614 8708; Uğurlu Sokak 1, Cıkmazı 4; r from ₺95, tr & f ₺130; ❄@🛜) Perched in the hilltop old quarter, this Australian-owned pension has nine rooms decorated with antique furnishings and a superb rooftop garden terrace, where the view can be enjoyed over breakfast, afternoon tea, sundowners or a barbecue.

Hotel Stella
HOTEL €€

(☏ 614 1632; www.hotelstellakusadasi.com; Bezirgan Sokak 44; s €35-40, d €50-60; ❄🛜❄) Entered from the seafront in an eccentric elevator up the cliff, Stella spills down the hillside with good views of the castle and bay from its western end. Rooms are a little bland and the corridors gloomy, but pluses include balconies, a comfortable breakfast room and help booking transport and tours.

Ilayda Avant Garde
HOTEL €€€

(☏ 614 7608; www.ilaydaavantgarde.com; Atatürk Bulvarı 42; r/ste from €63/164; ❄🛜❄) Jet-setting beach bums will feel at home in this design-savvy hotel with its minimalist-on-holiday aesthetic. A blocky Tetris theme pervades the cool, neat rooms, which are slightly small but restful behind double glazing. Amenities include a lobby bar and rooftop pool and bar-restaurant.

Efe Boutique Hotel
HOTEL €€€

(☏ 614 3660; www.efeboutiquehotel.com; Güvercinada Caddesi 37; s/d/tr ₺200/300/400; ❄🛜) Sleek lights and mirrors abound in the 40 airy rooms and suites, which are coloured black, white and turquoise with furniture including writing desk, transparent chairs and mirror-mounted plasma-screen TV. All rooms have sea-facing balconies, but because of the hotel's pyramid shape, the upper rooms get more view and less space.

We recommend losing a little cat-swinging potential in exchange for more blue vista.

Hotel Ilayda
BUSINESS HOTEL €€€

(☏ 614 3807; www.hotelilayda.com; Atatürk Bulvarı 46; s/d from €50/80; ❄🛜) The older sibling of nearby Ilayda Avant Garde, Ilayda has nice design touches and a good restaurant. It has all mod cons, and great views from some rooms and the rooftop cafe.

✖ Eating

Waterfront dining is atmospheric but can be expensive – verify seafood prices before ordering. Look out for waiters sneaking a couple of lira onto the bill, used to cruise-liner passengers who don't notice. If ambience isn't important, head inland for cheaper kebap shops. Kaleiçi, Kuşadası's old quarter, offers characterful backstreet eats and some fun, more Turkish cafes. A popular street food is *midye dolma* (mussels stuffed with rice).

★ Avlu
TURKISH €

(Cephane Sokak 15, Kaleiçi; mezes from ₺5, mains from ₺8; ⏱ lunch & dinner) The great and the good have made their way to the glass-fronted 'Courtyard' restaurant to try the traditional Turkish cuisine produced by its open kitchen. Choose a kebap from the menu or point and pick daily specials and mezes.

Fish Market
SEAFOOD €

(off Atatürk Bulvarı; balık ekmek ₺5-10; ⏱ lunch & dinner) Eateries around the fountain in the modern square at the fish market do *balık ekmek* (fish kebap), consisting of fish or calamari in bread with salad. You can also buy fish here and ask nearby restaurants to cook it; restaurants should charge under ₺10 for the service, but ask your hotel to organise or you could end up paying more.

Cimino ITALIAN, PIZZERIA, CAFE €€
(Atatürk Bulvarı 56/B; mains ₺13-40; ⊙lunch & dinner) With jazz on the sound system and trumpet players on the walls, Cimino is a cool spot for Italian dishes, Lavazza coffee and cocktails.

Holiday Inn PIDE, KEBAP €€
(40 Kahramanlar Caddesi 57/5; pide ₺12, kebaps ₺15; ⊙lunch & dinner) Locals rate the pide (Turkish-style pizza), *lahmacun* (Arabic-style pizza, ₺3.50) and kebaps at this eatery, where the house special, Vali kebap (₺30), is a mix of chicken, lamb, beef and tomato. Sit on the pedestrianised street near the top of Barlar Sokak and, if you're not full, finish with some dessert from the adjoining *baklavacı* (baklava shop).

★**Ferah** SEAFOOD, AEGEAN €€€
(☑614 1281; İskele Yanı Güvercin Parkı İçi; mezes ₺6, seafood portions ₺20-22; ⊙lunch & dinner) Next to the play park, 'Pleasure' restaurant is one of Kuşadası's classier waterfront fish eateries, with great sunset sea views and good-quality seafood and mezes.

Kazım Usta SEAFOOD €€€
(☑614 1226; Balıkçı Limanı; mezes ₺8-25, mains ₺16-35; ⊙lunch & dinner) Going for over 40

WORTH A TRIP

DILEK PENINSULA

About 26km south of Kuşadası, the Dilek Peninsula juts westwards into the Aegean, almost touching Samos. West of Güzelçamlı village, **Dilek National Park** (Dilek Yarımadası Büyük Menderes Deltası Milli Parkı; www.dilekyarimadasi.com; admission per person/car ₺3/12; ⊙7am-7.30pm Jun-Sep, 8am-5pm Oct-May) is a mountainous reserve with walking trails, stunning vistas, azure coves for swimming, and deep green forests inhabited by wild boars and horses.

A brown sign just before the park gate points to **Zeus Mağarası** (Cave of Zeus), where the water's refreshingly cold in summer and warm in winter.

After the gate, four rounded bays with pebble beaches lie below the road, which has great views from designated pullover points. The road tapers off at a high-security military compound covering the peninsula's end, from where men in uniform can train their binoculars on the tourists frolicking on opposing Samos.

The first cove, **İçmeler Köyü** (1km from the entrance), has a sandy beach, but it's the busiest and somewhat dirty with views of Kuşadası's urban sprawl. About 4km further on, **Aydınlık Köyü** is a quieter, 800m-long pebble strand backed by pines, and is busy enough to warrant a lifeguard station, though it is not always manned.

About 1km further along, after the *jandarma* (provincial police) station turn-off, the signposted **kanyon** appears on the left. Boards here give information and maps of the park. A 15km walk down a forest path, **Doğanbey** village has beautiful seaside stone houses, restored by affluent incomers. A few kilometres west of Doğanbey, the fishing village and ancient Hellenistic port of **Karine** has a waterfront fish restaurant. The path's first 6km are open to all, but after that you need a permit or to be with a guide. There is also a 25km cycle track to Doğanbey from Güzelçamlı.

Dilek's third bay, **Kavaklı Burun Köyü** (1km past the canyon entrance), has a halfmoon pebble beach. The final visitable beach, pebbly **Karasu Köyü** (11km from the entrance), is the most placid, and enjoys revelatory views of mountainous Samos rising from the sea. If you're lucky, you might even see a dolphin.

Camping is forbidden – the party's over at closing time. All four beaches have free wood-slatted chairs, which are quickly taken, and umbrellas and fold-out chairs to rent. There are restaurants at the entrance and restaurant shacks on each bay.

In summer, dolmuşes run from Kuşadası every 20 minutes to Dilek (₺5, 40 minutes), but only as far as the third bay (Kavaklı Burun). Off season, if your dolmuş is empty, the driver may stop at the park gate. The park entrance fee is paid on the bus. Regular dolmuşes also run from Söke to Doğanbey (via Priene) in summer. With your own wheels, you can drive to Doğanbey, 30km southwest of Söke; look for the turn-off on the road from Priene to Miletus. In the future, if the new mayor of Kuşadası sticks to his election promises, there will be a ferry from Kuşadası to Dilek.

EPHESUS, BODRUM & THE SOUTH AEGEAN KUŞADASI

years, Kazım Usta is one of Kuşadası's top fish restaurants, serving dishes ranging from swordfish kebap to farmed bream and meat options. Order fish by the kilo (1kg is ₺80 to ₺120) and book ahead to bag a waterfront table in summer.

🍷 Drinking & Entertainment

Head up Atatürk Bulvarı for seafront tea gardens and cafes.

Orient Bar
BAR, LIVE MUSIC

(www.orientbar.com; Kışla Sokak, Kaleiçi) On a side street, this perennial favourite in an atmospheric old stone house is the perfect escape from nearby Bar St, whether you listen to the nightly acoustic guitarist or settle in for a cosy chat beneath the vine trellis.

Another Bar
BAR

(Tuna Sokak 10, Kaleiçi) On the site of an old citrus orchard, this popular local bar has tables and stools dotted among the remaining trees, but less harmoniously, a huge screen and dance floor, too.

Bar St
PUB

(Barlar Sokak) On this cacophonous strip, tattoo and piercing parlours line up alongside shamrocks, sex shops and gaudy bars, soundtracked by karaoke, televised football and loquacious touts. At the northern end, the long-standing Jimmy's Irish Bar and, opposite, Kitty O'Shea fulfill the leprechaun quota; halfway down, Kuşadası Club & Bar is a popular hang-out for young locals.

Kaleiçi
LIVE MUSIC, MEYHANE

On the atmospheric warren of streets in Kuşadası's old town, look out for Türkü Bars, where locals knock back rakı (aniseed brandy) and dance to Turkish folk music. Also known as *meyhanes* (taverns), the characterful stone-walled bars are found on streets including Cephane, Bahar, Tuna and Kışla Sokaks.

Cape Yılancı
CLUB

(Yılancı Burnu; Kutucuoğlu Ahmet Sokak) Giant bar/club/concert complexes line this waterfront strip, along the coast from Kuşadası Castle. Basically private beaches by day, they transform by night into slick bars, dance clubs, and live music stages on the water.

Jade (www.jadebeachclub.com; admission ₺30) is all palm trees, wraparound couches, mood lighting and mojitos, with a pool, sand

volleyball, beachside loungers and relaxed drinks by day, and dance floors, bars and concerts after dark.

ⓘ Information

Banks and ATMs are found all over the centre, including on Barbaros Hayrettin Bulvarı.

Özel Kuşadası Hastanesi (☑ 613 1616; Ant Sokak) Excellent, English-speaking private hospital 3km north of the centre (Selçuk road).

Tourist Office (☑ 614 1103; Liman Caddesi; ⊙ 8am-noon & 1-5pm Mon-Fri) Near the cruise-ship dock; staff speak a little English and give out maps and brochures.

ⓘ Getting There & Around

TO/FROM İZMIR ADNAN MENDERES AIRPORT

Bus Take a dolmuş to Selçuk (the best option) or a bus to İzmir and change.

Shuttle From Kuşadası's otogar, Last Minute Travel (☑ 614 6332; Otogar) runs a shuttle (₺20), departing roughly every two hours. Atlasjet and Onur Air shuttle their passengers for free to/from Jappa garage, opposite the otogar, departing Kuşadası 2¾ hours before every flight. If there is space, they will take other travellers for ₺20.

Taxi About ₺120.

BOAT

Meander Travel (☑ 612 8888; www.meander-travel.com; Güvercinada Caddesi; ⊙ 7am-11pm summer, 9am-6pm Mon-Sat winter) operates the ferry to Samos (Greece) and sells tickets. The daily service operates from April through October, with boats departing Kuşadası at 8.30am and Samos at 5pm.

There may be additional departures in high summer; check the website. Tickets for the 1¼-hour crossing cost €35 for a single, €40 for a same-day return and €55 for an open return (this includes port tax). Arrive one hour before departure for immigration formalities. If you are returning to Kuşadası, check your Turkish visa is multiple-entry.

BUS & DOLMUŞ

Kuşadası's otogar is at Kahramanlar Caddesi's southern end, on the bypass highway, with *servises* (free shuttles) running to and from the bus companies' offices on İsmet İnönü Bulvarı. Dolmuşes leave from centrally located Candan Tarhan Bulvarı, and from the otogar.

Şehiriçi minibuses (₺52) run every few minutes in summer (every 15 to 20 in winter) from the otogar to the centre, and along the coast.

Bodrum (₺33, 3½ hours) Pamukkale has morning, afternoon and evening departures in summer; in winter, take a dolmuş to Söke.

İzmir (₺17, two hours) Half-hourly buses in summer, hourly in winter.

Selçuk (₺5, 25 minutes) Dolmuşes every 20 to 30 minutes via Pamucak and the turn-off for Ephesus Lower Gate.

Söke (₺5, 30 minutes) Dolmuşes every 20 to 30 minutes.

CAR

Budget, Europcar, Avis and others rent out cars, and you can get good deals through Economy Car Rentals (p674).

TAXI

There are taxi ranks all over town, generally with their prices for longer journeys on display. Fares include €50 return to Ephesus, €60 including Mary's House. For shorter journeys, meters open on ₺4 and charge ₺4 per kilometre.

PRIENE, MILETUS, DIDYMA & AROUND

Priene

☎ 0256

Like Ephesus, Priene was once a sophisticated port city. Although its relative lack of spectacular ruins leaves more to the imagination, Priene enjoys a commanding position high on Mt Mykale, giving it a certain natural grandeur missing at Ephesus. The site also offers plenty of shady trees, less crowds and views across the patchwork fields, making a trip here cooler and more relaxing.

While up on these craggy peaks, try to imagine the sea below you, instead of today's fields. Before the Meander River silted over, Priene had two harbours, and was

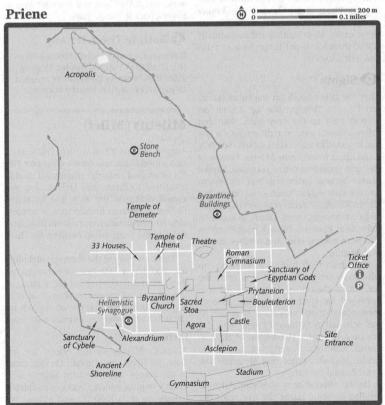

Priene

N · 0 ——————— 200 m
0 ——————— 0.1 miles

Acropolis

Stone Bench

Temple of Demeter

Byzantine Buildings

Temple of Athena

Theatre

33 Houses

Roman Gymnasium

Sanctuary of Egyptian Gods

Ticket Office

Prytaneion

Hellenistic Synagogue

Byzantine Church

Sacred Stoa

Bouleuterion

Castle

Alexandrium

Agora

Sanctuary of Cybele

Asclepion

Site Entrance

Ancient Shoreline

Stadium

Gymnasium

EPHESUS, BODRUM & THE SOUTH AEGEAN PRIENE

famed for its shipbuilding industry and sailing tradition.

There are toilets in the car park and cafes in the village below, abutting a ruined Byzantine aqueduct.

History

Priene was important by 300 BC (when the League of Ionian Cities held congresses and festivals here), peaking between then and 45 BC. Still, it was smaller than nearby Miletus, and the Romans made fewer modifications of its Hellenistic buildings, which has preserved its uniquely 'Greek' look. By the 2nd century AD, however, the silt had won, and most of the population relocated to Miletus. Amid the rubble, a tiny Greek village, Samson (later populated by Turks also) existed until 1923, when the Greeks were expelled and the remaining Turks moved to the neighbouring village of Güllübahçe.

Digging only started here in the late 19th century, led by British and German archaeologists. Plenty of marble statues and other antiquities ended up in their museums – in some cases, short-sighted sultans actually traded them for 'useful' things such as trains and technology.

◉ Sights

After the ticket booth for the ruins (admission ₺5; ☉ 8.30am-7pm May-Sep, 8.30am-5pm Oct-Apr), walk up the steep path. Note that Priene's streets meet at right angles – a system invented by Hippodamus (498–408 BC), an architect from nearby Miletus. Creator of the 'grid system' of urban planning, Hippodamus became influential, and his system was used not only in Miletus and Priene, but also in Rhodes, Piraeus (the port of Athens) and even ancient Greek Thurii, in southern Italy. As at Ephesus, Priene's marble streets also have gouged lines and notches to prevent slipping.

On a high bluff backed by stark mountain and overlooking what was once the sea, stands the ruined Temple of Athena, destroyed by earthquakes. Once Priene's biggest and most important structure, it was designed by Pythius of Priene, who also designed Bodrum's Mausoleum of Halicarnassus. An original inscription, now in the British Museum, states that Alexander the Great funded the temple.

Unlike Hippodamus – whom Aristotle recalled as being rather the free spirit (he never cut his hair and wore the same clothes year-round) – Pythius was a stickler for detail. He saw his classical Ionian temple design as solving the imperfections he perceived in preceding Doric design. Today's five re-erected columns give some sense of the temple's original look, though many others lie in unruly heaps around it.

Priene's theatre (capacity 6500) is among the best-preserved Hellenistic theatres anywhere. Whistle to test the acoustics, and slip your fingers between the lion's-paw indentations on the finely carved VIP seats in the front row.

Nearby lie Byzantine church ruins. Also see the nearby bouleuterion (council chamber), built to hold 250 interlocutors; from here a narrow path leads down to the ruined medical centre, the Asclepion (once thought to be a Temple of Zeus). Remains of a gymnasium, stadium and recently excavated Hellenistic Synagogue are also around.

You can follow the remains of the city wall, once 2.5km long and 6m high with 16 towers, back to the car park.

❶ Getting There & Away

Dolmuşes run from Söke to Güllübahçe village (₺3, 20 minutes) every 20 minutes, stopping 250m from Priene, by the Byzantine aqueduct cafes. Services are less frequent in winter.

Miletus (Milet)

☑ 0256

Ancient Miletus, 22km south of Priene amid rich cotton fields, was once a great port city. It's often (but unfairly) disparaged as dull compared to Priene and Didyma, but you should definitely not skip it – its mixed Hellenistic-Roman architecture is impressive, and the fascinating museum illustrates the original relationship between the three sites.

There are cafes at the entrance, including one flanking a 14th-century caravanserai; they are not recommended for a meal, as they are rather expensive. Stop at Miletus Museum before touring the site to pick up the informative and free 'circular tour' map.

History

Although Miletus' distant origins are unclear, it's likely that Minoan Cretans came in the Bronze Age (the word Miletus is of Cretan origin). Ionian Greeks consolidated themselves from 1000 BC, and Miletus became a leading centre of Greek thought and culture over the following centuries; most significantly, the Milesian School of philosophy (from the 6th century BC) featured great thinkers such as Thales, Anaximander and Anaximenes. Their observations of nature emphasised rational answers rather than recourse to mythical explanations, making the Milesians essentially the world's first scientists.

Like the other coastal cities, Miletus was fought over by Athens and Persia, and finally taken in 334 BC by Alexander the Great, who ushered in the city's golden age. Rome later took over, and a small Christian congregation developed following St Paul's visits (around AD 57). In Byzantine times, Miletus was an archbishopric. Unlike other coastal cities, enough of its port was free from silt build-ups for the Seljuks to use it for maritime trade through the 14th century. The Ottomans abandoned the city when its harbour finally silted up, and the Meander has since pushed Miletus 10km inland.

◎ Sights

As at Priene, you'll notice the streets of Miletus (parking ₺3, audioguide ₺10; ⊙ 24hr) FREE have a right-angle grid plan – the brainchild of local architect Hippodamus. Approaching from the car park, the Great Theatre dominates. Miletus' commercial and administrative centre from 700 BC to AD 700, the 15,000-seat Hellenistic theatre had majestic sea views. The Romans reconstructed it in the 1st century AD.

Exit the theatre through the tunnel on the right to reach the rest of the site. Above the theatre, ruined Byzantine castle ramparts provide views of the former harbour (called Lion Bay, after the lion statues that guarded it) to the left. Look right for the stadium, the northern, western and southern agoras, and between them, bouleuterion ruins.

East of the theatre, beyond a vanished ancient commercial centre, the ruined Temple of Apollo had great significance, marking the start of a 15km-long sacred road to

EPHESUS, BODRUM & THE SOUTH AEGEAN MILETUS (MILET)

Miletus (Milet)

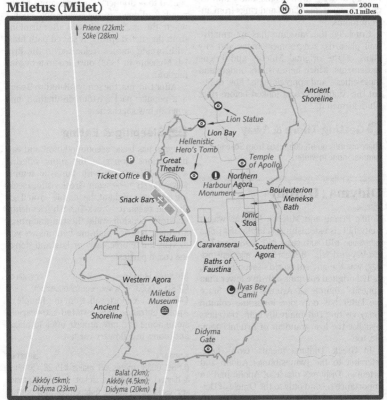

0 — 200 m
0 — 0.1 miles

Priene (22km);
Söke (28km)

Ancient Shoreline

Lion Statue

Lion Bay

Hellenistic Hero's Tomb

Temple of Apollo

Great Theatre

Ticket Office

Northern Agora

Harbour Monument

Bouleuterion

Menekse Bath

Snack Bars

Ionic Stoa

Baths   Stadium

Caravanserai

Southern Agora

Baths of Faustina

Western Agora

İlyas Bey Camii

Miletus Museum

Ancient Shoreline

Didyma Gate

Akköy (5km);
Didyma (23km)

Balat (2km);
Akköy (4.5km);
Didyma (20km)

Didyma's temple and oracle. As if by magic, the laurel trees that Greeks considered sacred to Apollo still cast their shade near the Milesian temple ruins.

The vast **Baths of Faustina**, constructed for Marcus Aurelius' wife, are worth entering; the massive walls and inner floors of the two spacious structures still survive. The designers' ingenious plan used an underground system of hot-water pipes (known as 'hypocausts') and *tubuli* (terracotta wall flues), which kept the bath interior hot. Next to it was a refreshing cold bath.

South of the ancient ruins is the post-Seljuk İlyas Bey Camii (1404), with an intricate doorway.

Miletus Museum   MUSEUM
(admission ₺5; ⊙ 8.30am-6.30pm summer, 8.30am-4pm winter) Miletus Museum exhibits finds from the site – ancient glass, pottery and votive stelae, statues (including river god Meander in repose, taken from the Baths of Faustina), numerous classical, Roman and Byzantine coins, and exquisite gold pendants, necklaces and rings from ancient tombs.

Crucially, the museum has informative wall placards, geographical maps and city plans of the original Miletus and Priene settlements, which help visitors understand these cities – and appreciate just how different the Anatolian coast looked before river silt deformed it.

ⓘ Getting There & Away

There are infrequent dolmuşes from Söke in summer; none in winter.

Didyma (Didim)

📞 0256

Unlike Priene and Miletus, Didyma wasn't a city, but its astonishing **Temple of Apollo** (admission ₺10, audioguide ₺10; ⊙ 8.30am-7pm mid-May–mid-Sep, 8.30am-5pm mid-Sep–mid-May) was the ancient world's second-largest, its 122 original columns only five fewer than Ephesus' Temple of Artemis (p231). Since the latter has only one lonesome column today, visiting Didyma really helps travellers visualise the lost grandeur of Artemis' temple, too.

In Greek, Didyma means 'twin' (here, referring to the twin siblings Apollo and Artemis). Didyma's oracle of Apollo had an importance second only to the Oracle of Del-

phi. Although destroyed by Persians in the early 5th-century BC, Alexander the Great revitalised it in 334 BC and, about 30 years later, Seleucid rulers planned to make it the world's largest temple. However, it was never completely finished and Ephesus' Temple of Artemis took the record instead.

In AD 303, the oracle allegedly supported Emperor Diocletian's harsh persecution of Christians – the last such crackdown, since Constantine the Great soon thereafter made the empire a Christian polity. The now unpopular oracle was silenced by Emperor Theodosius I (r 379–395), who closed other pagan temples such as the Delphic Oracle.

The impressive temple site is surrounded by souvenir shops, tourist restaurants and a few small pensions (being an archaeological site, building modifications aren't allowed). Entering from the ticket booth, clamber up the wide steps to marvel at the massively thick and towering columns.

Behind the temple porch, oracular poems were inscribed on a great doorway and presented to petitioners. Covered ramps by the porch lead down to the *cella* (inner room), where the oracle prophesied after drinking from the sacred spring. A sacred path lined with ornate statues (relocated to the British Museum in 1858) once led to a bygone harbour.

After Didyma, the sandy **Altınkum Beach** is a popular package-tour destination, and you can buy snacks here.

🛏 Sleeping & Eating

Didyma has basic accommodation and eating options alongside the ruins, offering a tranquil evening with fantastic temple views. It gets 'neo-pagan' Greek visitors seeking a moonlit night at the temple – you'll see the odd paean to 'Greek-Turkish friendship' on stone pension walls. Restaurant prices are high, but overnighting here allows you to visit the temple early or late and dodge the coach parties.

Medusa House   PENSION €€
(📞 811 0063; www.medusahouse.com; s/d €40/60; 🖥) A short walk from the Temple of Apollo entrance, this restored 150-year-old stone home and new annexe offer 10 pleasant rooms in a flowery garden.

Kamacı   BUFFET €€
(📞 811 0033; mezes ₺5, mains ₺15-28; ⊙ lunch & dinner) Facing the ticket booth, Kamacı serves kebaps, *köfte*, fish, *güveç* and better-

ℹ VISITING PRIENE, MILETUS & DIDYMA

Visiting the ancient settlements of Priene, Miletus and Didyma, which run in a line south of Kuşadası, is easily done in a day by car or guided tour. A tour is worth considering – the sites are less well excavated and signposted than Ephesus, so having a professional guide will help bring them to life. Travel agencies in Selçuk and Kuşadası offer the 'PMD' (Priene, Miletus and Didyma) tour for about €35 to €45, including transport, lunch, an hour at each site and possibly one or two add-ons such as Söke market and Altınkum Beach. Tours usually require at least four participants. Ascertain in advance where you'll go and for how long; make sure the tour includes the Miletus Museum (p248), which is sometimes forgotten but definitely worthwhile.

Visiting all three in a day by public transport is tricky. Regular dolmuşes connect Söke with Priene and Didyma, but you will likely have to return to Söke between the two, and there are no regular services to Miletus. Nonetheless, with luck and a few changes in Söke, it may be possible to visit all three in summer.

value mezes to locals and tourists alike, with views of the temple's two sturdiest pillars. Not to be confused with the tour-group buffet hall of the same name by the car park.

Harabe Cafe BAR, RESTAURANT
(snacks ₺7, mains ₺18) A great place to watch the sun set behind the temple pillars, with a first-floor terrace, live music and an open fire in winter. Burgers, salads, *tost* (toasted sandwich) and *kahvaltı* are on the menu.

ℹ Getting There & Away

Frequent dolmuşes run from Söke to Didyma (₺7, one hour) and Altınkum (₺8, 1¼ hours). Services are less frequent in winter.

Lake Bafa (Bafa Gölü)

☏ 0252

Landlocked (but 50% saltwater) Lake Bafa constitutes the last trace of the Aegean's former inland reach. It's a peaceful place, ringed by traditional villages such as Kapıkırı on the lake's far eastern shore. Bygone Byzantine hermitages and churches abound in the Bafa hills, and the region is a rich natural habitat boasting sights from orchids to owls, butterflies and chameleons. In particular, over 200 avian species are represented, including eagles, flamingos, pelicans and cormorants.

Above Kapıkırı rises Beşparmak Dağı (Five-Fingered Mountain; 1500m), known as Mt Latmos in the ancient Greek myth of Endymion. Although the ancient sources tell different versions, the most salacious is that this handsome shepherd boy was put into an eternal sleep by his father, Zeus, at the request of the rather smitten moon goddess,

Selene. Every night, she would visit the perfectly preserved Endymion, whose nocturnal emissions were apparently sufficiently abundant to father Selene's 50 daughters.

The ruins of the ancient port city Herakleia sprawl throughout Kapıkırı, which is populated by roving chickens, donkeys and old women hawking trinkets and crafts. Since the ruins are less exciting than elsewhere, this rustic scene and the lakeside setting comprise most of the experience.

◉ Sights & Activities

Pension owners organise boat trips (from ₺20 per person) and half-day hikes to Neolithic caves and ruins (from €20 per person), with the possibility of spending a night camping in the hills. Many can also help with birdwatching, botany and photography tours.

Herakleia RUIN
(Kapıkırı) FREE For sublime lake views, follow the road past the rock-hewn Temple of Endymion, and past the ruined Byzantine castle, which overlooks its necropolis' rock tombs.

From the beach and a ruined Byzantine church, note the island just opposite – its base conceals ancient building foundations. It's sometimes possible to walk there, when waters recede.

The large Temple of Athena, accessed on a westward path behind the agora car park, occupies a promontory overlooking the lake. Only three walls remain, but the perfectly cut blocks (no mortar) are impressive. Other signposted paths lead east to the agora, the bouleuterion and (several hundred metres across the pastures) the unrestored theatre, with barely a few seating rows remaining. Also nearby are stretches of city walls (c 300 BC).

🛏 Sleeping & Eating

Bafa is popular with German tourists and pension owners speak mostly German. Staying in idyllic Kapıkırı commands high prices, but you can get discounts for larger groups and longer stays. Most pension restaurants are open to non-guests; Bafa's unusual saltwater/freshwater composition means they serve sea and lake fish caught in the same waters.

★ Kaya Pansiyon   PENSION €€
(☎543 5579; info@kayapansiyon.com; Kapıkırı; half board per person ₺70; ❉ 🛜) 'Rock' Pension offers accommodation in wooden cabins and pastel bungalows, perched on boulders in a secluded valley. Rooms are rustic with intermittent hot water, but breakfast and dinner on the terrace are farm-fresh feasts accompanied by the lake breeze.

Karia Pansiyon   PENSION €€
(☎543 5490; www.kariapension.com; Kapıkırı; s/d incl half board €50/75, campsites per person €4; ❉ 🛜) Friendly Karia offers some of the best lake views in town from its terrace restaurant and homely rooms climbing the rocky hillside.

Agora Pansiyon   PENSION €€€
(☎543 5445; www.agorapansiyon.com; Kapıkırı; s/d incl half board from €65/100; ❉ 🛜) Nestled between gardens and a shaded terrace with hammocks, Agora has good rooms and

CARIAN TRAIL

The longest of Turkey's 20 long-distance hiking trails, the Carian Trail (www.cariantrail.com) meanders 820km from the Milas area down to the Datça and Bozburun Peninsulas, through the ancient kingdom of Caria. It passes many of the ruins covered here and offers the opportunity to see the emerald hills and azure coves of the Aegean at a slow pace, hiking beyond the tourist trail to secret corners such as Lake Bafa's Neolithic cave paintings. You can walk short sections of the route; find a guidebook, map and more information on the trail's website and at Culture Routes in Turkey (www.cultureroutesinturkey.com).

wooden cabins decorated with drawings and prints of the lake, plus a hamam.

Selene's Pension   PENSION €€€
(☎543 5221; www.bafalake.com; Kapıkırı; d incl half board €80-110; ❉ 🛜) Kapıkırı's original pension, popular Selene's is a mini-village of 15 rooms and wooden cabins, with sweeping lake views from its terrace restaurant.

❶ Getting There & Away

Buses and dolmuşes will drop you on the highway in Çamıçı village (also known as Bafa), at the turn-off for Kapıkırı. It's 10km from there to Kapıkırı; dolmuşes (₺5) are rare and a taxi costs ₺20. If you stay for a few days, your pension may provide a free pick-up.

Milas & Around
📞 0252 / POP 55,348

Mylasa (Milas) was ancient Caria's royal capital, except for during Mausolus' reign from Halicarnassus (present-day Bodrum). While this agricultural town is most interesting for its Tuesday farmers market, the surrounding area conceals unique historic sites.

◉ Sights

Milas' best sights are within a 25km radius. Ruins in town include Baltalı Kapı (Gate with an Axe), a well-preserved Roman gate. Up a steep path from Gümüşkesen Caddesi is the 2nd-century-AD Roman tomb, Gümüşkesen Mausoleum. Its name means 'That Which Cuts Silver' or 'Silver Purse', and the tomb is possibly modelled on Bodrum's Mausoleum of Halicarnassus.

Euromos   RUIN
(admission ₺5; ◷8.30am-7pm May-Sep, to 5pm Oct-Apr) Founded in the 6th century BC, Euromos peaked between 200 BC and AD 200, under Hellenistic and then Roman rule. Its indigenous deity cult had earlier been subsumed by that of Zeus, and indeed the partially restored Temple of Zeus is all that survives.

The temple is between Çamıçı and Milas, signposted from the highway near Selimiye village. To get here, take a bus or dolmuş between Milas and Çamıçı/Söke and ask to get off at the ruins, 200m north of the highway.

Iasos (Kıyıkışlacık)   RUIN
FREE Seaside Kıyıkışlacık village contains ancient Iasos, a Carian city that was once an island and prospered from fishing and the

unique red-and-white marble in the nearby hills. A member of the ancient Delian League, Iasos participated in the Peloponnesian Wars, but later weakened. Nevertheless, it was definitely a Byzantine bishopric from the 5th to the 9th centuries, before being finally abandoned in the 15th century.

Today, the hillside walled acropolis-fortress stands opposite the fishing harbour. Excavations have revealed ruins of a bouleuterion, and agora and a Roman temple of Artemis Astias (AD 190), among other structures.

Enjoy fresh fish and good views of the wave-soaked ruins at Iasos Ceyar Deniz Restaurant (⊘537 7066; mezes ₺5, seafood from ₺17; ⊘lunch & dinner). If you can't drag yourself away from this blissful fishing village, Ersan Pansiyon (⊘537 7006; r excl breakfast ₺50) has clean, modern rooms, some with balcony surveying the castle. Village breakfast is ₺10.

In summer, an hourly Kıyıkışlacık–Milas dolmuş (₺5) runs from 8.30am to 6pm, less frequently in winter. The village turn-off is marked on the highway between Çamıçı and Milas, 2km southeast of Euromos. Kıyıkışlacık is 20km south of the turn-off.

Labranda
RUIN

(admission ₺5; ⊘8am-7pm summer, to 5pm winter) The hillside site of ancient Labranda, surrounded by pines, occupies the area that supplied Mylasa's drinking water. Labranda's local deity was worshipped since at least the 6th century BC, subsequently becoming a sanctuary of Zeus, under Mylasa's control. The great Temple of Zeus honours the god's warlike aspect (Stratius, or Labrayndus means 'Axe-Bearing'). Festivals and Olympic games occurred at Labranda, which possibly possessed an oracle.

The Labranda turn-off is marked on the highway on the northern side of Milas (en route to Lake Bafa). It's 14km from there; unless you're driving, take a Milas taxi (₺40 including an hour of waiting).

Beçin Kalesi
RUIN

(Beçin Castle; admission ₺5; ⊘8am-7pm summer, to 5pm winter) At the beginning of Beçin village, 1km south of the Bodrum–Muğla highway on the road to Ören, a signposted road climbs to Beçin Kalesi, on a rocky outcropping. Originally a Byzantine fortress, it was remodelled by the short-lived 14th-century Menteşe Empirate.

The high castle walls, topped by a giant Turkish flag, offer great views of Milas below. More Menteşe-era structures can be seen across the valley, including the Kızıl-han (Red Caravanserai), the Ahmet Gazi tomb and the restored medrese (seminary) You can borrow a guidebook from the castle ticket booth.

Half-hourly dolmuşes run between Milas and Beçin village (₺2.25).

❶ Getting There & Around

Milas' otogar is 1km north of the centre, on the highway near the Labranda turn-off, and well connected to the central köy garaj (village otogar), from where dolmuşes serve local destinations.

BODRUM PENINSULA

The Bodrum Peninsula, named after the summer hot spot of Bodrum town, offers a mix of exclusive resorts and laid-back coastal villages where you can enjoy good swimming and stylish eats. Despite the glaringly visible inroads of modern tourism, tradition and tranquillity are partially preserved by local open-air vegetable markets and the rugged coastline, overlooked by scarcely populated hills in the peninsula's centre. The area has an efficient and inexpensive dolmuş network, making it easy to hop between Bodrum and the outlying coves, where you can find quality beach accommodation at reasonable rates with just a little advance planning.

❶ Getting There & Around

AIR

Milas-Bodrum Airport (BJV; www.bodrumairport.com), 36km from Bodrum town, receives flights from all over Europe, mostly with charters and budget airlines such as EasyJet and Sun Express in summer. Anadolu Jet, Atlasjet, Onur Air, Pegasus Airlines and Turkish Airlines all serve İstanbul (both airports) and/or Ankara, while Bora Jet flies to Adana and Mykonos (Greece).

Havaş (www.havas.net/en) shuttles between the airport and Bodrum otogar (₺15, 45 minutes), leaving the latter two hours before every Anadolu Jet, Onur Air, Pegasus Airlines, Sun Express and Turkish Airlines domestic departure. Atlasjet provides a free shuttle, leaving Turgutreis three hours before departures and stopping in Bitez, Gümbet, Bodrum otogar and Konacık en route to the airport. Both services

EPHESUS, BODRUM & THE SOUTH AEGEAN BODRUM PENINSULA

Bodrum Peninsula

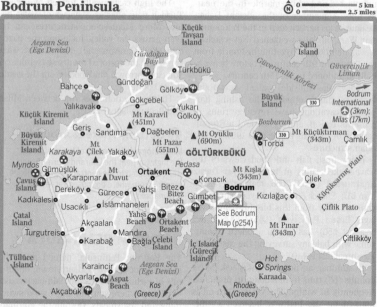

also meet arrivals. Otherwise, an expensive taxi (₺90 from the city centre; ₺100 from the airport) is your only option.

BOAT

Visit operators' offices or phone to check their website departure info, which isn't always reliable. Check, too, if your ferry is departing from Bodrum's old port near the castle or the newer cruise port south of town. Drivers in particular should book in advance; this can often be done online. **Bodrum Ferryboat Association** (Bodrum Feribot İşletmeciliği; ☎ 0252-316 0882; www.bodrumferryboat.com; Kale Caddesi 22; ⊗ 8am-9pm May-Sep, reduced hours winter) and **Bodrum Express Lines** (☎ 0252-316 1087; www.bodrumexpresslines.com; Kale Caddesi 18) serve Datça and the following Greek islands:

Datça (single/return/car ₺30/50/100; 1½ hours) Daily mid-June to late October. The ferry docks at Körmen on the peninsula's northern coast, and the fare includes the 15-minute shuttle to Datça. There will be more services in the coming years, including twice weekly in winter.

Kalymnos (one-way €30, same-day return €35, open return €50; 1¼ hours) Wednesdays early June to late October. Also Turgutreis–Kalymnos Saturdays mid-May to late October.

Kos (one-way €17, same-day return €19, open return €30; one hour) Daily mid-April to October, four times weekly November to mid-April

(weather permitting). Also Turgutreis–Kos daily late April to late October. From mid-June to October, **Yeşil Marmaris** (☎ 0252-313 5045; www.kosferry.com; İskele) offers fast daily Bodrum–Kos catamarans (20 minutes), which cost a few euros more.

Rhodes (one-way €50, same-day return €60, open return €75; 2½ hours) Saturdays and Sundays early July to late September. Yeşil Marmaris also operates services.

Symi Services suspended at the time of research, although some Rhodes boats stop here. Also served by Yeşil Marmaris.

BUS

All the major bus companies serve Bodrum otogar. Some also serve Turgutreis and Yalıkavak. Metro links Bodrum with most destinations; heading east along the coast, Pamukkale is a better option, with at least one morning and one night bus to Antalya (₺70, eight hours) via Milas, Muğla, Dalaman and Fethiye. Marmaris Koop has several daily buses to Marmaris (₺25, three hours) and beyond.

CAR & MOTORCYCLE

Numerous companies in Bodrum and at the airport rent out cars, motorbikes and scooters, including Avis (also in Turgutreis), Economy Car Rentals (p674) and **Neyzen Travel** (☎ 0252-316 7204; www.neyzen.com.tr; Kibris Sehitleri Caddesi 34, Bodrum).

DOLMUŞ

Bodrum's dolmuşes whizz around the peninsula every 10 minutes (half-hourly in winter) and display their destinations in their windows. You can get to most villages for ₺5 or less, with services running from 7am to 10pm (5am June to September). From Bodrum to Yalıkavak on the far side of the peninsula takes about 30 minutes.

There are also services between Turgutreis and Akyarlar, Gümüşlük, Yalıkavak, Gündoğan and Türkbükü, and between Yalıkavak and Gümüşlük. Otherwise, to travel between the villages, you will have to transit in Bodrum otogar or try your luck flagging down a passing dolmuş on the road.

Bodrum

🎵 0252 / POP 36,401

Although more than a million tourists flock to its beaches, boutique hotels and clubs each summer, Bodrum (Halicarnassus in ancient times) never loses its cool. More than any other Turkish seaside getaway, it has an enigmatic elegance that pervades it, from the town's grand crowning castle and glittering marina to its flower-filled cafes and white-plastered backstreets. Even in the most hectic days of high summer, you can still find little corners of serenity, in the town and especially in its outlying coastal villages.

Only in the past few decades has Bodrum come to be associated with pleasure, paradisical beaches and glittering summertime opulence. Previously, it was a simple fishing village, and old-timers can still remember when everything was in a different place or didn't exist at all. Long before the palmed promenades and epicurean seafood restaurants, Bodrum wasn't even desirable: it was the place where dissidents against the new Turkish republic were sent into exile.

All that started to change after one of the inmates took over the prison. Writer Cevat Şakir Kabaağaçlı (aka the 'Fisherman of Halicarnassus') was exiled to sleepy Bodrum in 1925, and quickly fell in love with the place. After serving his time, he proceeded to turn on a whole generation of Turkish intellectuals, writers and artists to Bodrum's charms in the mid-1940s.

From then on, there was no going back: by the 1980s, well-heeled foreigners were starting to come, and today Bodrum is a favourite getaway for everyone from European package tourists to Turkey's prime movers and shakers. But it was Kabaağaçlı's

early influence, giving the town its arty identity, which saved it from the ignominious fate of other Turkish fishing villages turned resorts.

Urban planners have also sought to preserve Bodrum's essential Aegean character, which was influenced by the Cretans who moved here during the population exchange of the 1920s. Today, laws restrict the height of buildings, and the whitewashed houses with bright-blue trim evoke a lost era. The evocative castle and the ancient ruins and Ottoman mosques around town also help keep Bodrum a discerning step above the rest.

👁 Sights

Castle of St Peter   CASTLE, MUSEUM

(🎵 316 2516; www.bodrum-museum.com; İskele Meydanı; admission ₺25, audioguide ₺10; ⊗ 8.30am-6.30pm, to 4.30pm winter, exhibition halls closed noon-1pm) There are splendid views from the battlements of Bodrum's magnificent castle, built by the Knights Hospitaller in the early 15th century. The castle houses the **Museum of Underwater Archaeology**, displaying the underwater archaeology treasures amassed during the building's renovation.

The Knights, based on Rhodes, built the castle during Tamerlane's Mongol invasion of Anatolia (1402), which weakened the Ottomans and gave the order an opportunity to establish this foothold in Anatolia. They used marble and stones from Mausolus' famed mausoleum and changed the city's name from Halicarnassus to Petronium (hence the Turkicised 'Bodrum').

By 1437 they had finished building, although they added new defensive features (moats, walls, cisterns etc) right up until 1522, when Süleyman the Magnificent captured Rhodes. The Knights were forced to cede the castle, and the victorious Muslim sultan promptly built a mosque in it. For centuries, the castle was never tested, but French shelling in WWI toppled the minaret (the Turkish government re-erected it in 1997).

Spread around the castle, the attractively lit and informative museum has reconstructions and multimedia displays to complement the antiquities, and takes about two hours to see. It gets very busy and claustrophobic in the museum's small rooms, so get here early.

➡ **Main Court**

Heading into the castle, you'll pass carved marble **Crusader coats of arms**. Next is the

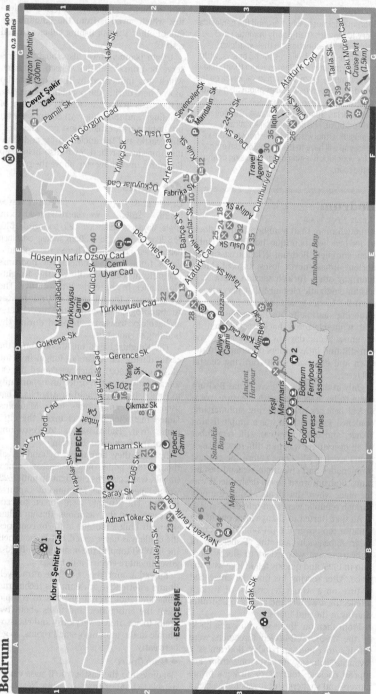

Bodrum

castle's main court, centred on an ancient mulberry tree. Here is a massive amphorae collection, with pieces from the 14th century BC to modern times, all recovered from southern-coast waters, and a courtyard cafe adorned with ancient statuary.

A tiny model and a full-sized reconstruction of a late Roman ship's stern discovered off Yassıada are displayed in the chapel. Walk the decks, take the helm and inspect the galley and wine casks below.

➜ **Glass Wreck Hall & Glass Hall**

Climbing towards the towers, you next come to the Glass Wreck Hall on the left. It houses a 16m-long, 5m-wide ship that sank in AD 1025 while carrying three tonnes of glass between Fatimid Syria and a Byzantine glass factory in the Danube or Black Sea. Archaeologists and historians were excited not only by what the find revealed about 11th-century ship construction, but also for what it indicated about Fatimid glass production and design.

Next, the small Glass Hall exhibits finds from the 15th century BC to the 14th century AD, and includes Mycenaean beads, Roman glass bottles and Islamic weights.

➜ **French Tower & Carian Princess Hall**

Beyond, the French Tower has finds from the Tektaş Burnu, the world's only fully excavated classical Greek shipwreck (dating from 480 BC to 400 BC). Amphorae, talismanic marble discs and kitchen utensils from the vessel are displayed, plus 2001 excavation photos taken at the Çeşme Peninsula site. Ancient coins (including from Croesus' Caria) are also on display.

The neighbouring Carian Princess Hall is a must-see, exhibiting a gold crown, necklace, bracelets, rings and an exquisite wreath of gold myrtle leaves. Popularly associated with the last Carian queen, Ada (reinstated by Alexander the Great after annexing Halicarnassus in 334 BC), they belonged to an unknown woman of status.

➜ **English Tower**

Guarding the castle's southeast corner, the English Tower, also known as the Lion Tower, was built during the reign of King Henry IV of England (1399–1413). In 1401 Henry became the first (and only) English monarch to host a Byzantine emperor, Manuel II Palaeologos, and he took seriously Manuel's warning about the Muslim threat to Christian Europe posed by the Turks. The tower

EPHESUS, BODRUM & THE SOUTH AEGEAN BODRUM

was thus a symbol of support for their common cause.

Today, the interior is fitted out as a medieval refectory, with a long dining table surrounded by suits of armour, stag horns, lions' heads and the standards of the Knights Hospitaller and their Turkish adversaries. Piped-in medieval music completes the farcical picture of a knightly theme restaurant. There is some interest, however, in the model of the *Sovereign of the Seven Seas,* a ship built on Charles I's orders in 1637, and the Latin graffiti, carved 500 years ago by the Knights Hospitaller.

➡ Uluburun Wreck Hall

Turn left out of the tower to follow the battlements around the castle to the Glass Hall; carry straight on for the Uluburun Wreck Hall, which contains finds from Bronze Age shipwrecks, including the world's oldest excavated wreck, the 14th-century-BC *Uluburun.* Full-size replicas of the interior and the wreck site exist. The adjoining Treasure Room displays Canaanite gold jewellery, bronze daggers, ivory cosmetic boxes, wooden writing boards and Egyptian Queen Nefertiti's golden scarab.

➡ Gatineau Tower & Snake Tower

Further north, enter the dungeons at Gatineau Tower, where the Knights imprisoned, and sometimes tortured, their enemies from 1513 to 1523. The inner gate's chilling inscription sums up the dungeon as being *Inde Deus abest* ('Where God does not exist'). Hold children's hands and mind your head – the steps down are steep and narrow.

On the way back to the exit, the Snake Tower displays more artefacts and statuary. Named after a snake carved in the stone, it was used as a hospital in the Ottoman era.

Mausoleum RUIN

(Turgutreis Caddesi; admission ₺10; ⊗8am-7pm Tue-Sun, to 5pm winter) One of the Seven Wonders of the Ancient World, the Mausoleum was the greatest achievement of Carian King Mausolus (r 376–353 BC), who also moved the Carian capital from Mylasa (Milas) to Halicarnassus. Today, the only ancient elements to survive are the pre-Mausolean stairways and tomb chambers, the Mausolean drainage system, the entry to Mausolus' tomb chamber, precinct wall bits and some large fluted marble column drums.

Before his death, the king planned his own tomb, to be designed by Pythius (architect of Priene's Temple of Athena). When he died, his wife (and sister), Artemisia, oversaw the completion of the enormous, white-marble tomb topped by stepped pyramids. Incredibly, the Mausoleum stood relatively intact until the Knights Hospitaller needed building material for the Castle of St Peter; between 1406 and 1522, almost all of it was reused or ground into powder for walls. Luckily, the more impressive ancient friezes were incorporated into the castle walls, while original statues of Mausolus and Artemisia were sent to the British Museum.

The site has relaxing gardens, with excavations to the right and a covered arcade to the left – the latter contains a copy of the famous frieze in the British Museum. Four original fragments displayed were discovered more recently. Models, drawings and documents indicate the grand dimensions of the original Mausoleum. A scale model of Mausolus' Halicarnassus and the Mausoleum also stand.

Ancient Theatre RUIN

(Kıbrıs Şehitler Caddesi) On the Gümbet road, ancient Halicarnassus' restored 4th-century-BC theatre (capacity 13,000) lies in the hillside rock, and still functions for summer concerts.

Myndos Kapısı RUIN

(Myndos Gate; off Turgutreis Caddesi) These are the restored remains of the only surviving gate from King Mausolus' 4th-century-BC 7km-long walls. Before them are the remains of a moat that took the lives of many of Alexander the Great's soldiers in 334 BC, and nearby are tombs, mosaics and other ruins.

Shipyard RUIN

(Şafak Sokak; ⊗9am-6pm Tue-Sun) **FREE** The restored Ottoman shipyard stands just beyond the marina. In 1770, Russia destroyed the entire Ottoman fleet at Çeşme; rebuilding it occurred in boatyards like this. It was fortified against pirate attacks in the 18th and 19th centuries. Although the shipyard's tower occasionally hosts art exhibitions, it's essentially a children's playground. Old tombstones, dating from the period when the Latin alphabet was replacing Arabic, are kept above. There are good views from here, too.

🏃 Activities

Travel agents all over town offer tours and activities, including a few on Dere Sokak heading inland from Cumhuriyet Caddesi.

Tours will take you to Ephesus, three hours' drive away, for about €30 (€45 including one or two stops en route such as Euromos and Miletus); taxis charge about €150 for up to five people.

Boat Trips
BOAT TOUR

(☉ daily Apr-Oct) Excursion boats moored in both bays offer day trips around the peninsula's beaches and bays, typically charging about ₺35 including five or so stops and lunch. Karaada (Black Island), with hot-spring waters gushing from a cave, is a popular destination where you can swim and loll in supposedly healthful orange mud.

Book through your hotel or direct with operators – Ezgi Boats (☎ 0542 345 4392; Cumhuriyet Caddesi) or Yağmur (☎ 0533 341 1450; Cumhuriyet Caddesi) – ideally a day ahead.

Tarihi Bardakçı Hamamı
HAMAM

(☎ 0536 687 3743; Dere Sokak 32; hamam ₺30, massage ₺30; ☉ 8am-11pm) Going since 1749, Bodrum's oldest hamam offers mixed bathing.

Neyzen Yachting
BOAT TOUR

(☎ 316 7204; www.neyzen.com.tr; Kıbrıs Şehitleri Caddesi 34) *Gület* (traditional wooden yacht) trips including a nice circular tour of the Gulf of Gökova, hugging the coast of the Datça Peninsula to Knidos.

🛏 Sleeping

In high summer, accommodation fills up fast, so be prepared to pound the pavement if you haven't booked ahead. Hotels near the marina and Bar St get the most noise from the clubs and bars. If arriving by bus, you may be harassed by touts offering 'budget accommodation' – it's best to ignore them.

Albatros Otel
PENSION €

(☎ 316 7117; www.albatrosotelbodrum.com; cnr Neyzen Tevfik Caddesi & Menekşe Çıkmazı; s/d ₺150/220; ❋ 🛜) Recommended by readers, this low-key pension offers friendly service and a location on the western bay, making it a good pick for independent travellers and small families.

Kaya Pension
PENSION €

(☎ 316 5745; www.kayapansiyon.com.tr; Eski Hükümet Sokak; s/d ₺130/160; ☉ Apr-Oct; ❋ 🛜) One of Bodrum's better pensions, Kaya has 13 clean, simple rooms with hairdryer, safe and TV, including seven with balcony. There is a roof terrace for breakfast and a flowering courtyard and comfy reception

for lounging. Helpful owner Mustafa can arrange activities.

Hotel Güleç
PENSION €

(☎ 316 5222; www.hotelgulec.com; Üçkuyular Caddesi 22; r €40-45; ❋ 🛜) This good-value little pension has a central location and simple but bright and clean rooms. The tiny bathrooms leave a little to be desired, but there is a sunny garden for breakfast and assorted brothers and cousins to help find parking and so on.

Artunç Hotel
PENSION €

(☎ 316 1550; www.artuncotel.com; Fabrika Sokak 32; s/d €57/60; ❋ 🛜 🏊) This former family home's carpets and furniture are dated, but white walls freshen up its 14 rooms. There is a flowery courtyard for breakfast. Facilities include in-room minibars and safes in reception.

Otel Atrium
HOTEL €

(☎ 316 2181; www.atriumbodrum.com; Fabrika Sokak 21; s/d incl half board from ₺100/120; ❋ 🛜 🏊) One of Bodrum's oldest hotels, the Atrium's 60 plain but spacious rooms are good value for families and independent travellers. There's a pool (with separate kid's section), a poolside bar, two restaurants and table tennis.

Turunç Pansiyon
PENSION €

(☎ 316 5333; www.turuncpansiyon.com; 1023 Sokak 4/A; s/d ₺100/160; ❋ 🛜) 'Seville Orange' Pension offers a pleasant alleyway location

EPHESUS, BODRUM & THE SOUTH AEGEAN BODRUM

> ### ℹ BODRUM BEDS
>
> It's more expensive than other coastal resorts, but if you're keen on a Bodrum-area base, try to plan in advance: many hotels offer discounted rates for advance bookings. Those that stay open in winter also drop their rates considerably compared with the silly summer season. Indeed, prices are so high across the whole Bodrum Peninsula in summer (especially August and, to a lesser extent, July) that sleeping and eating listings in this section use our İstanbul price ranges (p654). After a few months of hard work, many hoteliers close their doors and disappear from October to May; even in mid-May, resort towns such as Türkbükü sometimes resemble building sites, as decks are built and preparations made for the approaching season.

near the western bay and neat rooms with mod cons including LCD TV.

★ Su Otel
BOUTIQUE HOTEL €€

(✆316 6906; www.bodrumsuhotel.com; off Turgutreis Caddesi; s/d/ste from €65/95/135; ✢@☎☲) Epitomising Bodrum's white-and-sky-blue aesthetic, the relaxing 'Water Hotel' has 25 rooms and suites around a pool glinting with silver tiles, an Ottoman restaurant and a bar scattered with red sofas. Owner Zafer's zingy artwork decorates the premises along with hand-painted İznik tiles, Ottoman candlesticks and antiques.

A fount of local knowledge, Zafer organises on-site Turkish cookery and art classes and day trips to Ephesus.

Marina Vista
RESORT €€

(✆313 0356; www.hotelmarinavista.com; Neyzen Tevfik Caddesi 168; s/d ₺330/440; ✢☎☲) From the impressive mural in reception and pool with seating alcoves to the terrace restaurant overlooking the marina, this chain hotel is a relaxing waterfront option. A spa and children's activities are offered and the Argentine restaurant makes a change from local fare.

Antique Theatre Hotel
BOUTIQUE HOTEL €€

(✆316 6053; www.antiquetheatrehotel.com; Kıbrıs Şehitler Caddesi 169; r €120-140, ste €160-180; ✢☎☲) Taking its name from the ancient theatre across the road, this opulent place enjoys great castle and sea views, and has a big outdoor pool and one of Bodrum's best hotel restaurants. Original artwork and antiques adorn the rooms, which each have an individual character and offer better value than the suites.

Aegean Gate
BOUTIQUE HOTEL €€

(✆316 7853; www.aegeangatehotel.com; Guvercin Sokak; s/d/tr €90/120/150; ✢☎☲) About 2.5km southeast of the castle on a quiet hill, Aegean Gate has sparkling rooms and a relaxing pool with bar. The catch? A minimum two-night stay is required, and credit cards aren't accepted. It's 50m from a 24-hour taxi rank, five minutes' walk from a dolmuş connection to the centre, and a 20-minute walk from Bodrum's main party strip.

Marmara Bodrum
LUXURY HOTEL €€€

(✆999 1010; http://bodrum.themarmarahotels.com; Suluhasan Caddesi 18; s/d from €270/290; ✢@☎☲) The upmarket Marmara, high on a bluff, has great views and elegant rooms (try for one with sea views). It's part of a five-star chain, and facilities include tennis, spa, gym and two pools.

A free shuttle accesses a private beach on the peninsula. The rooftop 'party animal suite' has a big Jacuzzi, two balconies and a private roof terrace for throwing your own all-nighter.

El Vino Hotel
BOUTIQUE HOTEL €€€

(✆313 8770; www.elvinobodrum.com; Pamili Sokak; r €170-220, ste €230; ✢☎☲) This rustic place behind a stone wall in the backstreets has large and well-appointed rooms with wooden floors. Try for a room with views of the pool and garden area (where breakfast is served). The rooftop restaurant also affords nice views.

✗ Eating

Like all harbourside resorts, Bodrum's waterfront has pricey, big-menu restaurants (not all bad), but also discreet backstreet contenders, fast-food stalls, some excellent fish restaurants and various markets. Generally, western bay eateries are more upscale, while the eastern bay has more informal fare marketed to the patrons of the adjacent bars and nightclubs. Kebap stands are also found in the market hall, where the Friday fruit and veg market (p261) takes place.

★ Nazik Ana
TURKISH €

(Eski Hükümet Sokak 5; dishes from ₺6, kebaps ₺8-15; ⊙breakfast, lunch & dinner, closed Sun winter) This simple back-alley place offers prepared dishes hot and cold (viewable at the front counter), letting you sample different traditional Turkish dishes at shared tables. You can also order kebaps and *köfte*. It gets busy with workers at lunchtime, offering one of Bodrum's most authentic eating experiences.

Bodrum Denizciler Derneği
CAFE, FAST FOOD €

(İskele Meydanı 44; snacks & mains ₺5-11) Bodrum's Mariners Association cafe attracts locals from çay-drinking seadogs to young landlubbers nursing bottles of Efes Malt. Burgers, sausage and chips, *tost* and *kahvaltı* are served with a front-row view of the yachts and tour boats.

Döner Tepecik
KEBAP €

(Neyzen Tevfik Caddesi; kebaps ₺5-12; ⊙lunch & dinner) Across from the eponymous mosque, this local favourite does tasty kebaps, including the İskender (döner lamb on a bed of crumbled pide, topped with yoghurt, hot tomato sauce and browned butter), on homemade bread.

Gayıkcı
KEBAP €

(Cevat Şakir Caddesi 15/D; kebaps ₺8-21; ⊘lunch & dinner) Clean and relatively cheap, this open-fronted *kebapçı* (kebap eatery) at the entrance to the fish market serves meat feats including İskender kebaps.

Musto
INTERNATIONAL €€

(☑313 3394; Neyzen Tevfik Caddesi 130; mains ₺15-40) This bar-restaurant does draught Guinness and pub food in arty surrounds, with its packed tables creating a busy bistro atmosphere. Dishes include pasta, burgers, *kahvaltı* and cheese plates.

Avlu
MODERN TURKISH, INTERNATIONAL €€

(☑316 3694; Sanat Okulu Sokak 14; mains ₺18-38) This bistro in an old stone house decorated with black-and-white photos offers seating in its courtyard or on the cobbled lane. It has a good wine selection and serves mostly Turkish food with a few burgers thrown in.

Berk Balık Restaurant
SEAFOOD €€

(☑313 6878; Cumhuriyet Caddesi 171; meze ₺8, seafood from ₺22; ⊘lunch & dinner) In a good area for waterfront seafood restaurants, this calm spot has outside seating at white tables with blue and orange chairs. Well-heeled locals dig into meze such as stuffed calamari.

Le Man Kültür
INTERNATIONAL, CAFE €€

(Cumhuriyet Caddesi 161; mains ₺25) Decorated with comic-book art, this cool Turkish chain is popular with students for its smoothies, coffees and cocktails. It does snacks and meals including sandwiches, burgers and *kahvaltı*.

Kalamare
SEAFOOD €€

(☑316 7076; Sanat Okulu Caddesi 9; mezes ₺6, mains ₺15-30) Serving meat dishes as well as octopus, calamari, sea bass et al, Kalamare attracts a cool young crowd, who sit on the lane beneath the extravagant Gaudí-style chimney.

Fish Market
SEAFOOD €€

(off Cevat Şakir Caddesi; ⊘dinner Mon-Sat) Bodrum's fish market (sometimes called '*manavlar*' for the fruit stands at the entrance to this small network of back alleys) offers a unique sort of direct dining: you choose between myriad fresh fish and seafood on ice at fishmongers' tables and, having paid there, have them cooked at any adjoining restaurant for about ₺10.

If in doubt, waiters can help you decide – options run from top-end catches to cheaper farm fish. It should cost about ₺10

for enough farmed sea bass or bream for one, but few fishmongers will go that low and many will try to sell you a whole kilo (₺25). Sea fish costs from about ₺70 per kilo, so here and in all seafood restaurants, if you pay less than about ₺25 for a portion then you may be eating something that is not fresh or is from a farm.

The plain restaurants spill across the small streets, which get incredibly crowded and have zero atmosphere, save maybe for the people-watching. If indecisive, pick the busiest-looking place – locals are fiercely loyal to their favourites.

La Pasión
SPANISH €€€

(Restaurante Español; ☑313 4594; Uslu Sokak 8; tapas ₺10-20, mains ₺30-60; ⊘lunch & dinner) To see how far Bodrum has come in its quest to join the ranks of international seaside sophistication, head to this refined Spanish restaurant down a side street for tapas, paella or pasta. The restaurant occupies an old stone house with tables among fig trees in the flowering courtyard, and Spanish music wafting through the breeze.

Set lunch menus, which change weekly and feature intricate starters and desserts, are available in the off season.

Orfoz
SEAFOOD €€€

(☑316 4285; Cumhuriyet Caddesi 177/B; meals from ₺120, incl wine from ₺150; ⊘dinner daily Jun-Sep, dinner Tue-Sun Oct-May) Often listed as one of Turkey's best fish restaurants, Orfoz serves delectable seafood such as oysters with parmesan, baby calamari with onions and garlic, scallops, sea urchins and blue crab. Reservations essential.

Gemibaşi
SEAFOOD €€€

(☑316 1220; Neyzen Tevfik Caddesi 132; meze from ₺7.50, mains ₺25-35; ⊘lunch & dinner) A popular fish restaurant, 'Ship's Captain' has open-air seating backed by an atmospheric old stone wall.

🍷 Drinking & Entertainment

Bodrum's varied nightlife scene caters to its diverse clientele. The Turkish jet-set fills the western-bay clubs, while the foreign masses frequent the loud waterfront bars and clubs of Bar St (Dr Alim Bey Caddesi and Cumhuriyet Caddesi). In high summer, Bodrum becomes a 24/7 town, with many nightspots partying until dawn, and more bars and clubs pop up on the peninsula's beaches and coves.

The castle and ancient theatre host opera, ballet and rock performances; for upcoming event schedules, visit www.biletix.com.

Moonlight   BAR
(Cumhuriyet Caddesi 60/B) Opening onto the beach, chilled-out Moonlight is a friendly hang-out off Bar St – great to meet people or just enjoy the castle views.

Marina Yacht Club   BAR
(http://english.marinayachtclub.com; Neyzen Tevfik Caddesi 5) This big, breezy waterfront nightspot has a few bars and offers live music most nights year-round. Merrymakers congregrate at the tables dotting the water-facing deck; in winter, the inside section by the port gates is more popular.

Dr. No   NARGILE CAFE
(Cumhuriyet Caddesi 145; nargile ₺25; ⊙10am-late) With white sofas on the water's edge, Dr. No offers several flavours of Arabic tobacco and coffee, cocktails, wine and draught Efes.

Hasan Fidan Kahve   CAFE
(Külcü Sokak; ⊙Mon-Sat) Named after owner Murat's grandfather, this cafe and coffee merchant in the market hall serves cappuccinos, espressos and Turkish coffees.

Körfez   BAR
(Uslu Sokak 2) This unpretentious old favourite does rock, with a dark-wood atmosphere to match and alleyway seating. Happy-hour deals are offered, and Sunday is 'oldies but goldies' night.

Küba   CLUB
(☑313 4450; www.kubabar.com; Neyzen Tevfik Caddesi 62; ⊙7pm-4am) Bodrum's poshest and most popular address for Turkish clubbers, Küba has all the plasma screens, disaffected DJs, shiny poles and laser beams one would expect. Its outdoor bar-restaurant is a cool spot for a waterfront drink.

White House   CLUB
(Cumhuriyet Caddesi 147) This 20-year-old doyenne of Bodrum's party scene has beachfront chill-out sofas, a dance floor pumping with house music and blissed-out tourists.

Helva   CLUB
(www.helvabodrum.com; Neyzen Tevfik Caddesi 54) Just a bit less snobby than nearby Küba, Helva is also less frenetic but attracts a similarly slick Turkish crowd – more lounging and less dancing.

Halikarnas   CLUB
(☑0530 372 2985; www.halikarnas.com.tr; Cumhuriyet Caddesi 132) Touching the laser since 1979, this bacchanalian party temple, complete with faux classical columns and balconies, hosts DJs and carnivalesque shows in its various lounges and outdoor stage. Jade Jagger designed its Secret Garden restaurant. Entry is typically ₺50 including a drink.

Mavi Bar   LIVE MUSIC
(☑316 3932; Cumhuriyet Caddesi 175) This tiny white-and-blue venue stages live music most nights. It's busiest after 1am.

Marine Club Catamaran   CLUB
(☑313 3600; www.clubcatamaran.com; Dr Alim Bey Caddesi; admission ₺60-80; ⊙10pm-4.30am Jun-Sep) Europe's biggest floating disco, this party boat sails at 1.30am, keeping the licentiousness offshore for a good three hours. Its transparent dance floor can pack in 2000 clubbers plus attendant DJs. A free shuttle operates every 10 minutes to the eastern bay.

METRO SERVICES FROM BODRUM OTOGAR

DESTINATION	FARE (₺)	DURATION (HR)	DISTANCE (KM)	FREQUENCY (PER DAY)
Ankara	85	12	689	3
Antalya	70	8	496	1 morning, 1 night (Pamukkale)
Denizli (for Pamukkale)	36	5	250	8
İstanbul	90	13	851	8
İzmir	40	3½	286	hourly
Konya	70	12	626	1 morning, 1 afternoon
Kuşadası	25	3	151	1 evening

🛍 Shopping

MARKET

(Külcü Sokak) This white building hosts Bodrum's Tuesday clothes market, a treasure trove of fake T-shirts, textiles, watches and Atatürk paraphenalia, and the Friday fruit and veg market (8am to 2pm).

ℹ Information

ATMs line Cevat Şakir Caddesi and harbour-front streets.

Post Office (Cevat Şakir Caddesi; ⏱9am-12.30pm & 1.30-7.30pm Mon-Fri & 10am-4pm Sat Mar-Nov, to 5.30pm Mon-Fri Nov-Mar)

Tourist Office (☑316 1091; Kale Meydanı; ⏱8am-6pm Mon-Fri, daily Jun-Oct)

Tourist Office (Hüseyin Nafiz Özsoy Caddesi; ⏱8am-noon & 1-5pm Mon-Fri, 8am-1pm Sat) At the otogar.

ℹ Getting Around

Almost everything is in walking distance downtown. There's an intra-city dolmuş service (₺1.75), which is frequently stuck in traffic. Central Bodrum's roads are busy, slow and mostly follow a clockwise one-way system – missing your turn necessitates an irritating repetition of the process.

Taxis start with ₺4 on the meter and charge ₺4 per kilometre, with no night rate. It costs about ₺12 to cross town.

Otoparks (car parks) around town cost ₺5 for one hour, ₺20 for a day. Your hotel may be able to organise a free space nearby.

Bitez

☑0252

Less hectic than Gümbet just east, Bitez is still a major centre of coastal nightlife in summer, and draws more foreigners than Turks. However, it's an actual village, framed by lovely orchards, so it doesn't go into total hibernation in winter. The fine sandy beach, 2km below the village centre, is good for swimming and packed with umbrellas and loungers, satellites of the restaurants and cafes behind them.

In summer, Bitez Boat Cruise (☑0507 445 3940; trips incl lunch & tea ₺30) offers day trips from the beach.

For some cultural edification, visit the ruins of Pedasa, signposted above the village on the main Bodrum–Turgutreis road. A relic of the lost Lelegian civilisation that predated the Carians, this small site features defensive wall foundations and ruins, probably of a temple.

🛏 Sleeping

⭐Yalı Han HOTEL €€

(☑363 7772; www.yalihanotel.com; Bitez Yalısı; s/d/tr from €70/95/160; ❋🤶❄) The Turkish-Swedish 'Beach Caravanserai' is one of the more tasteful hotels on Bitez sands, with a gourd-shaped pool and a cafe overlooked by 16 rooms with nautical touches and myriad amenities. The seven superior rooms are a great choice for small families, offering an admirable amount of space for this sardine-aping tourist area.

Garden Life RESORT €€

(☑363 9870; www.bitezgardenlife.com; Bergamut Caddesi 52; s/d incl full-board & drinks €100/135; ❋🤶❄) In the orchards surrounding Bitez on the coast road from Gümbet, various pools, bars, a private beach and pleasant rooms in cool blues are all set in Garden Life's eponymous greenery.

3S Beach Club RESORT €€

(☑363 8001; www.3sbeachclub.com; Yalı Caddesi 112; s/d incl half board ₺300/400; ❋🤶❄) Overlooking Bitez from the western end of the beach, 3S has a poolside bar, private beach, hamam, sauna and fitness centre. Rooms are not particularly attractive but reasonably spacious with TV, minibar and balcony.

🍴 Eating

Bitez has a few good eateries working year-round. On weekends, brunch buffets at seafront restaurants have become rather the local tradition.

Bitez Mantıcı TURKISH €

(Atatürk Bulvarı 60; mains ₺10-15; ⏱lunch & dinner) On a roadside terrace in the village, this unassuming place does excellent versions of Turkey's extended carbohydrates family, from *mantı* to *börek* (filled pastry) and buttery-rich *gözleme*.

Lemon Tree INTERNATIONAL €€

(☑363 9543; Sahil Yolu 28; mains ₺18-30; ⏱8am-late) Right at the beach, near the small Yalı Mosque, this hugely popular place marked by breezy white-and-green decor lets you eat, drink and enjoy at shaded tables or on its loungers on the sand. There's an appetising blend of Turkish and international fare (try the house 'Lemon Tree chicken' – a light take on sweet-and-sour chicken).

Even locals come for the ridiculously massive and varied buffet brunch (₺25, from 10am to 2pm on weekends), while set three-course meals are a good deal at ₺38. It's a lively watering hole by night, too.

Black Cat
MODERN TURKISH €€

(Mart Kedileri; ☑363 7969; Şah Caddesi 8/7; mezes ₺8, snacks ₺8-12, mains ₺20-30; ☺lunch & dinner) The amiable Ferhan's whimsical restaurant, decorated with holidaying children's pictures of black cats, serves light meals by day and heartier fare at night. House specials are Özel ('special') kebap, featuring aubergine piled with meat and yoghurt, and *kadayıf* (dough soaked in syrup and topped with a layer of clotted cream) for dessert. Find it one block from the beach.

Ortakent

☑0252

Ortakent is becoming more popular as the relentless wave of summer-home building continues to gouge out the peninsula hillside with alarmingly uniform giant white cubes. For now, the view at sea level of the broad blue bay remains largely unblighted by development. Ortakent's 3km sand beach is mostly the domain of packed lounge chairs by summer, but the water here is nevertheless among the peninsula's cleanest (and coldest), due to wave action. The eastern Scala Beach (www.scalabeach.net) is quieter.

In early June, Sunsplash (www.sunsplash -festival.com) festival brings an eclectic mix of electronic, world and jazz DJs and musicians to Aspat Beach, a few kilometres along the coast from Ortakent in the southwest.

⌂ Sleeping

Yilmaz Hotel
HOTEL, APARTMENT €

(☑358 5508; www.yilmazhotel.com; Zümrüt Sokak; d €75, incl half board €90; ☺Jun-Oct; ❊❧❧) Oceanfront Yilmaz offers 30 rooms with sea or garden view and aims to appeal to families, independent travellers and active holidaymakers, with surfing and sailing schools and boat tours nearby. Meals feature organic vegetables from the hotel garden and afternoon tea is served. A two-bedroom apartment is also available for longer stays.

Satsuma Suites
APARTMENT €€

(☑348 4249; www.satsumasuites.com; Eren Sokak 17; r €70-130; ❊❧❧) For those looking to escape the noise of Bodrum, these luxe suites with elegantly appointed bathrooms, set around flowering trees and a welcoming pool near Scala Beach, are ideal. The breakfast is solid as well.

✗ Eating

Kefi
TURKISH, INTERNATIONAL €€

(☑348 3145; www.kefibeach.com; Asma Sokak 23/1; snacks ₺12-19, mains ₺20-40) This fledgling resort's beachfront bar-restaurant serves a range of dishes, including *köfte*, *güveç*, burgers, seafood and local speciality *çökertme* (meat fried with potato chips and slathered with yoghurt). A *fasıl* (gypsy music) band plays two nights a week.

Suites accommodating up to four go for ₺500 a night (minimum one week stay).

Gebora
SEAFOOD €€

(☑348 3340; Yahşi Yalısı; mezes ₺6, fish ₺20; ☺lunch & dinner) On the main beachfront boardwalk near the Yalı Mosque, Gebora is a straightforward, much-loved old standby for fresh fish, mezes and home-grown salads.

Turgutreis

☑0252

Once a sponge-diving centre, Turgutreis has turned its sights on tourism, particularly longer-term villa and apartment rentals, and it offers 5km of sandy beaches, a dozen tiny islets and some logistical advantages. As the peninsula's largest town after Bodrum, Turgutreis has more services, shops and ferry and dolmuş links than its neighbours – and more concrete; the Saturday market resembles dusty middle Anatolia more than an Aegean retreat. Indeed, the waterfront statue of a pregnant woman holding an olive branch is meant to represent the health, peacefulness and diversity of Anatolia. It is one of the peninsula's more workaday places, and for short stays the prettier neighbouring villages are a better option.

In 1972 the village, then called Karatoprak, was renamed after Ottoman admiral Turgut Reis, who was born here in 1485 and led many maritime battles before dying in the 1565 siege of Malta.

Gümüşlük

☑0252

Unlike the many fishing villages hijacked by modern tourism, Gümüşlük has thankfully been spared uglification because it lies around the ruins of ancient Carian Myndos. As a protected archaeological zone, the village legally cannot be overdeveloped – at least not on the waterfront where the ruins disappear into the sea, continuing out to the facing Rabbit Island, which can be reached on foot at low tide.

Accessed from the main Bodrum–Turgutreis road via a lovely side road through the hills, Gümüşlük has an escapist feel. It's good for a swim and a drink or fresh fish meal at simple yet stylish eateries on the beach. Its authenticity has, however, made it more than a little precious, with local accommodation and restaurant prices rising to match the village's increasingly upscale visitors.

It's said that famed Carian king Mausolus built Myndos (which largely awaits excavation) due to its strategic position and harbour – indeed, the sea just north of Rabbit Island is very deep. Look straight across these waters to see a hazy speck of rock, Kardak (Imia in Greek), the ownership of which almost sparked a war between Greece and Turkey in January 1996, following gratuitous flag-planting exchanges and a more serious but brief Turkish commando occupation. Today, the area is strictly off-limits.

Victoria's farmstay offers horse rides (₺40 per hour) and pony rides (₺20 per 15 minutes) and lessons from an English-speaking coach.

A car park (₺5 per day) and ATMs are close to the main beach.

🛏 Sleeping

Gümüşlük is getting expensive, but family-run pensions still exist, as do vacation rentals. In all cases, book ahead.

Victoria's   FARMSTAY ₺
(☑ 394 3264; www.victoriasclub.net; 1396 Sokak 4, Çukurbük; ✿🖘🛋) Making a refreshingly rustic change from Bodrum bling, this pastoral hideaway nestles between a farmyard and a private beach. Accommodation is in five well-equipped stilted cabins overlooking the stables, and packages including horse riding are available. The speciality of the restaurant (mains ₺15 to ₺50) is *levrek buğlama* (sea bass stew).

Club Hotel Zemda   RESORT ₺₺
(☑ 394 3151; www.clubhotelzemda.com; s/d from €75/100; ✿@🛋) At the bay's southern end, this French-run getaway in a Mediterranean mix of sunny colours and breezy white is good for activities, with sailing and windsurfing on offer. The bar-restaurant is sandwiched between the pool and beach.

Otel Gümüşlük   HOTEL, VACATION RENTAL ₺₺
(☑ 394 4828; www.otelgumusluk.com; Yalı Mevkii 28; s/d ₺255/300; ✿🖘🛋) Away from the water, this two-storey, ranch-style hotel has 36 airy, minimalist rooms around a pool. It's a three-minute walk to the dolmuş stop and the hotel offers two- to four-bedroom villa and apartment rental in Gümüşlük, Yalıkavak and Turgutreis.

🍴 Eating & Drinking

Gümüşlük's atmospheric little beach restaurants and cafes are excellent for eating, drinking or just whiling away the time. At the beach's northern end, a line of waterfront fish restaurants has fantastic views of the glittering waves and Rabbit Island.

Cash-carrying self-caterers can greet the incoming fisherfolk on the docks (8am to 10am) to relieve them of some of their burden, which otherwise will be destined for local restaurants.

Limon   SEAFOOD, AEGEAN ₺
(☑ 394 4010; Gümüşlük Köyü; mains ₺15-20; ⊙ 8.30am-8.30pm) 'Lemon' brings a little of its hilltop associate Limon Aile Lokantası's magic to town, offering a changing menu of meat and seafood dishes in casual, family-friendly surrounds.

Espavo   CAFE ₺
(Bölme Plajı; mains ₺13-20; ⊙ lunch & dinner) With outside tables surveying the sea, this circular glass building on sand-and-pebble Bölme beach does homemade burgers and other light fare. Meal deals include calamari and a glass of wine for ₺22.

ℹ HOLIDAY RENTALS

Villa rentals can be great value, particularly for longer stays, with fully furnished apartments available by the day, week and month. If self-catering at least some of the time, such offers constitute seriously good deals for those seeking extended sojourns on the secluded Bodrum coast, giving the option of shopping at local farmers markets. Rentals are available in villages including Gümüşlük, Turgutreis and Gündoğan. In addition to the listings in this book, check out websites such as www.bodrum-exclusiveholidayrentals. com, www.bodrumservice.com and www.bodrumvillarentals.com.

Mandarina
BAKERY €

(Gümüşlük Köyü; poğaça ₺1.50; ⊙breakfast)
South of the road for the car park, Mandarina's good for a light breakfast of *poğaça*
(puff pastry) or the full Turkish (₺35).

★ Limon Aile Lokantası
SEAFOOD, AEGEAN €€€

(☑394 4010; Cumhuriyet Caddesi; mezes ₺10,
mains ₺30-50; ⊙from 9.30am late Apr–mid-Oct;
☑) In the hills above Gümüşlük, Limon
sprawls across a series of garden terraces
around a whitewashed farmhouse, overlooking a Roman bath and Byzantine chapel ruins. Dishes include seafood and carpaccios,
while vegetarians will love the unique, olive
oil-soaked mezes such as stuffed zucchini
flowers and the house take on *sigara böreği*
(deep-fried cigar-shaped pastries).

Homemade goodies include the famous
cakes; five marmalades in the *kahvaltı;*
lemonade and hand-picked, vodka-soaked
petals in the *gelincik* (poppy) cocktail. Find
it on the old Myndos Rd to Yalıkavak. Open
for breakfast, lunch and dinner.

Ali Ruza'nin Yeri
SEAFOOD €€€

(☑394 3047; Gümüşlük Yalı; meze ₺8-30, mains
₺20-40; ⊙lunch & dinner) Serving expertly prepared fresh fish since 1972, this waterfront
classic is run by a local fishing clan whose
boats floats nearby. With eight different
types of rakı to choose from, the business of
feasting on fish is taken extremely seriously
here.

Mimoza
SEAFOOD €€€

(☑394 3139; www.mimoza-bodrum.com;
Gümüşlük Yalı; mezes from ₺15, mains ₺30-50;
⊙lunch & dinner May-Sep) Popular Mimoza,
on the beach's north end, has cheery white
tables perched above the sea, boats bobbing
in the secluded bay opposite. It does a good
variety of seafood mains and mezes, including house specials calamari *köfte* and green
mussels with cheese.

Unfortunately, its many charms
have made it a favourite of the Turkish
upper-crust, and prices are high. Book
ahead for evening dining.

Jazz Cafe
BAR

(☑394 3479; Çayıraltı Halk Plajı) This come-as-you-are beach bar, with a tree growing
through its corrugated-iron roof and a wood-burner for winter, hosts live jazz, blues and
flamenco on Friday and Saturday nights.

Yalıkavak
☑0252

A former fishing and sponge-diving village,
Yalıkavak has played up its relative remoteness from Bodrum to attract a more exclusive and Turkish clientele. However, it hasn't
escaped the holiday-home-construction
craze, and is known too for its upmarket private beaches – **Xuma Beach Club** and **Dodo
Beach Club** are popular. Its marina keeps
the village relatively lively out of season and
day trippers will always find a few restaurants open.

Nearby abandoned Yakaköy (between
Yalıkavak and Ortakent), the **Dibek Sofrası**
(www.dibeklihan.com; Yakaköy Çilek Caddesi 46/2;
⊙May-Oct) complex contains a museum, art
gallery, restaurant and vineyard. It exhibits
Ottoman antiques such as jewelled daggers,
antique fountain pens and ornate coffee
cups collected by the owners.

🛏 Sleeping

4 Reasons Hotel
BOUTIQUE HOTEL €€

(☑385 3212; www.4reasonshotel.com; Bakan Caddesi 2; s/d/tr/q from €171/190/255/290; 🌬❄✿)
This friendly and intimate hillside retreat
features 20 self-described 'nu-bohemian'
rooms with lots of little designer touches
and fine locally sourced marble fixtures. The
garden is a venue for bocce, massage, yoga
and pilates, and the poolside bistro serves
Aegean flavours with views of Yalıkavak Bay.

Sandima 37
BOUTIQUE HOTEL €€€

(☑385 5337; www.sandima37suites.com; Atatürk
Caddesi 37; ste €200-280; 🌬❄✿) On the hillside road into town, Sandima's seven stylish
suites are set around a lush garden with
sweeping views of the marina and surrounding headlands. The restored stone cottage by
the pool has the most ambience. Manager
Kenan is full of restaurant recommendations and advice.

🍴 Eating

Geriş Altı (Yalıkavak's western district, towards Gümüşlük) is the place for the day's
fishing catch. Thursday is market day at
Çınaraltı, 10 minutes' walk inland from the
seafront.

Özmasa
ANATOLIAN €€

(☑385 3107; İskele Meydanı; mains ₺20) Run by
a family from Gaziantep, Özmasa specialises
in Anatolian kebaps such as Testi ('pottery'),
cooked in a terracotta pot, and Halep Işi

(spicy minced beef with yoghurt and hot to-mato sauce). Homemade pide, *tuzda balık* (fish baked in salt), lamb shank and organic *köy kahvaltı* are also offered.

Le Café
INDIAN, INTERNATIONAL €€

(☑ 385 5305; İskele Caddesi 33; mains ₺16-30) This Turkish-Indian restaurant with water-front seating serves a good selection of curries and starters including samosas and pakoras. Dishes ranging from steaks to chicken parmigiana, a house speciality, are also offered.

Pamukkale Restaurant
PIZZA €€

(Atatürk Caddesi 143; mains ₺14-35) Locals head to this long-running eatery near the seafront to satisfy their pide cravings. Unusual pides such as *spesiyal karışık* (special mixed, with cheese, mince, pepper-oni, tomato and green pepper) cater to the demands of international tourists.

Gündoğan

☑ 0252

Placid Gündoğan Bay, surrounded on both sides by hills glistening with wealthy villas, offers a sandy beach with good swimming right in the centre, and stays relatively se-date at night. Most of its part- or full-time occupants are retirees of status from İstan-bul or Ankara, who, despite their secularist proclivities, have just not been able to get the local imam to turn down the volume at the mosque – about the only noise that could jolt you out of bed here.

Settlement here probably began around AD 1100, though an earlier Roman town, Vara, had existed nearby. In 1961 the village's original Greek name (Farilya) was changed to Gündoğan.

Although Gündoğan gets little atten-tion on the historical-tour circuit, its back-hills contain Lelegian rock tombs and, a 15-minute boat trip from town, Apostol Island, crowned by a fairly well-preserved Byzantine church with frescoes – ask locally to arrange trips.

🛏 Sleeping

Chichi new hotels are springing up on the western side of the bay, offering private beaches and decks.

Villa Joya
APARTMENT €

(☑ 387 8841; www.villajoyabodrum.com; Kızılbu-run Caddesi 34/A; 4-person villa €90; ❋ 🗢) One of several family-run businesses renting to self-caterers, Joya offers three apartments with kitchens and lovely gardens. While each apartment sleeps four, there's only one master bedroom (the other two beds are pull-out sleepers in the living room). Still, the price is hard to beat.

Costa Farilya
RESORT €€

(☑ 387 8487; www.costafarilya.com; Yalı Mevkii 62; r ₺350-600; ❋ 🗢 ≋) Making a change from the peninsula's ubiquitous white cubes, uber-modern Costa Farilya's 70 rooms occupy grey blocks, the newest of which is formed of crushed stone behind met-al gridding. Rooms are muted and calm-ing with low-slung beds, a grey-and-white theme and views across the bay from those with balcony.

Facilities include a spa, pool bar, fitness centre, various restaurants and biweekly yoga.

🍴 Eating

Terzi Mustafa'nin Yeri
SEAFOOD, TURKISH €€

(Plaj Cafe Restauran; ☑ 387 7089; Atatürk Cadde-si 10; mezes from ₺7, mains from ₺15) Right on the sand at the central waterfront, this local favourite run by a fishing family serves a good range of mezes and mains, marine and otherwise. There's no noise save for the wind and waves, no lights save for the moon and stars – ideal for those seeking great food and quiet conversation.

Fish prices start around ₺18 for marinat-ed sea bass, a cold meze, but big fish are the house speciality.

Türkbükü

☑ 0252

Türkbükü's reputation as Turkey's poshest beach getaway is kept alive by the Turkish celebrities, politicians and business moguls who flock here each summer. Thus consid-ering that better beaches exist elsewhere on the peninsula, visiting this privileged cove might be best understood as a sociocultural experience – not to mention an opportunity for an excellent meal and a cocktail in style.

Even in a place where women go to the beach in high-heels, sporting diamond-encrusted sunglasses, tongue-in-cheek re-minders of social divisions remain; the tiny wooden bridge between the two halves of Türkbükü's beach is jokingly said to di-vide the 'European side' from the 'Asian side' – a reference to İstanbul, and an insinuation of the wealth gap between the ultra-posh homes and hotels on the western shores, and the ever-so-slightly less-expensive ones to the east. These days, in the words of one local hotelier, with the chichi resort town's increasing beautification, it's more a case of 'Europe' and 'Eastern Europe'.

🛏 Sleeping

Türkbükü accommodation is unsurprisingly pricey, but you'll certainly have some interesting neighbours. Note that the summer clubs keep things loud until late.

★ Kaktüs Çiçeği   BOUTIQUE HOTEL €€
(☎ 377 5254; www.kaktuscicegi.com.tr; İnönü Caddesi 119; d/tr from ₺350/400; ❄ 🙝 🌊) 🏊 An echo of the old Türkbükü, before the glitterati superseded the artists and intellectuals, 'Cactus Flower' has a vintage feel in its artfully designed rooms with small balconies gazing at the hills. Bougainvillea, eucalyptus and vines fill the beachfront garden and spill onto the landings.

Owner Murak, a French- and English-speaking writer, runs the 18-room property in green style and organic produce abounds in the Mediterranean cuisine. Discounts of over 50% are offered off season.

YU   BOUTIQUE HOTEL €€
(☎ 377 5275; www.yu-otel.com; Bağarası Caddesi 26; r €180-200; ❄ 🙝 🌊) Aiming to give Türkbükü's suave clientele some city style by the sea, YU shoots for a chic look mixing minimalism with Mediterranean pizazz. The poolside bungalows are compact, cubic and sometimes clinical, but there's a snack bar and some rooms have a Jacuzzi built into the bed's headboard.

LifeCo   RESORT €€
(☎ 377 6310; www.thelifeco.com; Bağarası Mahallesi; s/d incl detox from €195/350; ❄ @ 🌊) The Türkbükü branch of LifeCo Wellbeing Centres offers a cleansing environment for detox programs, with orange and mandarin trees lining its cool walkways. One- to 21-day packages are available, as is a one-day program without accommodation (€120).

Kuum   LUXURY HOTEL €€€
(☎ 311 0060; www.kuumhotel.com; Atatürk Caddesi 150; r incl half board from €610; ❄ 🙝 🌊) A hit with the Turkish elite, this €600-a-night haven offers accommodation in brown cubes on grassy terraces, creating the dreamy feel of a 1960s science-fiction film. This impres-

sion continues in the 40- to 80-sq-metre suites, where vaguely psychedelic touches such as bubble chairs mix with the luxury of glass-walled bathroom, coffee machine and sea views.

Facilities include a private beach, spa, hamam and waterside restaurant.

Maçakızı   LUXURY HOTEL €€€
(☎ 311 2400; www.macakizi.com; Narçiçeği Sokak; r incl half board from €589; ❄ 🙝 🌊) Ground zero for Türkbükü's chic summer crowd, this luxurious place combines a resort feel with boutique trimmings and minimalist decor. There's a sociable restaurant, a lively bar and a spa, but the real eye-catcher is the long wood-slatted boardwalk extending into the languid sea, replete with cosy pillow-beds.

Maki Hotel   HOTEL €€€
(☎ 377 6105; www.makihotel.com.tr; Keleşharımı Mevkii; r from €270; ⊙ mid-May–Oct; ❄ 🙝 🌊) Popular with İstanbul's movers and shakers, the Maki is an ongoing party during summer, with a big wooden deck for lounging on throw pillows, a pool and beach bars, and a club extending over the water. The 52 smallish rooms and suites have arty elements such as headboards made of interlocking purple bars – clearly not designed with sleeping in mind.

5 Oda   BOUTIQUE HOTEL €€€
(Beş Oda; ☎ 377 6219; www.otel5oda.com; İnönü Caddesi 161; r €450; ⊙ May-Oct; ❄ 🙝) 'Five Rooms' offers exactly that, and its small size ensures good service. The eclectic boutique spot has fresh, sea-facing rooms and a striking natural stone-and-wood design.

🍴 Eating & Drinking

Deluxe hotels have excellent (and exorbitantly priced) restaurants, while others are clustered by the waterfront; some turn into standing-room-only open bars for the beautiful and the tanned. Book ahead.

Casita   TURKISH €€
(Türkbükü Yalı; mains from ₺15; ⊙ lunch & dinner) İstanbul's famous *mantı* chain graces the shores of Türkbükü, giving its summer guests a taste of home. By day it offers comfortable chaise longues for unwinding.

Miam   INTERNATIONAL €€€
(☎ 377 5612; Yalı Mevkii 51; mezes ₺7-20, mains ₺24-48) Recommended locally, this small restaurant with a few in-demand waterfront tables is a good place to take a break from

seafood. Options include deli and cheese plates, lamb chops and filet mignon with gorgonzola, cream or pepper sauce.

Garo's
SEAFOOD €€€

(☑377 6171; Türkbükü Yalı; mezes ₺15, mains ₺25-50) Local tip Garo's is pricey but popular for its mezes in particular. The owner-chef serves seafood and meat dishes such as *bonfile* (sirloin steak) at white-and-blue tablecloths under dangling lights and open Aegean skies.

Gölköy

☑0252

Gölköy Bay exists in Türkbükü's shadow, and is thus often overlooked. However, it has great nightlife, beaches and (slightly) cheaper digs, although in summer it now sees its fair share of $300 bottles of Absolut Vodka going down. Well-known Turkish bands and DJs play Bianca Beach (www.bodrumfun.com/bianca-beach-club; Akdeniz Caddesi 35; ☺10am-5am May-Oct), an open-air club on the beach frequented by models and hedonists.

Only 50m from the centre and 1km from Türkbükü, Villa Kılıc Hotel (☑357 8118; www.villakilic.com; Sahil Sokak; s/d from €160/180; ❇☎☷) offers 33 lavishly designed rooms with hardwood floors and marble accents. There's a big pool and good restaurant, or you can recline on Gölköy's largest bathing platform (300 sq metres), where DJs play and beach parties take place on Tuesdays in summer.

Torba

☑0252

Despite being a short ride from Bodrum, Torba has stayed quieter and more family-oriented. It has a nice beach, but lacks the seclusion of places on the peninsula's more distant corners and has a more workaday feel.

Non-guests can use the facilities at Voyage (☑367 1820; www.voyagehotel.com; Kızılağaç Mevkii; ❇☎☷), the village-centre resort, for the day (₺120 including food and drinks, 9am to 9pm).

⌂ Sleeping

Izer Hotel & Beach Club
RESORT €€

(☑367 1910; www.izerhotel.com; per person incl full-board, drinks & activities from €72; ☺May-Oct;

❇☎☷) Popular with British package tourists, this well-run resort has a seafront pool with attendant restaurant and bar longer than the Bodrum Peninsula. Choose between smaller rooms in the club area, where numerous activities are offered and children are well taken care of, and larger, quieter rooms in the hotel's garden villas.

A cheery, colourful place to bring the family, far from the other coves' designer dens of iniquity.

★ Casa Dell'Arte
LUXURY HOTEL, VILLA €€€

(☑367 1848; www.casadellartebodrum.com; İsmet İnönü Caddesi 64; ste €584-1026; ❇☎☷) Staying at this exquisite 'house of art and leisure', owned by an art-collecting Turkish family, is like visiting the well-appointed home of an eminent curator. Modern Turkish art and antiques decorate the flowing interior and sculptures stand around the pool – the artistic environment even includes the odd installation, a library of art books and tours of the collection.

Luxuries such as an outdoor Jacuzzi have not been overlooked and you can upgrade to a three-bedroom villa (€1728) or yacht (from €2000).

Casa Dell'Arte Family Resort
RESORT €€€

(☑367 1848; www.casadellartebodrum.com; İsmet İnönü Caddesi 66; ste €324-540; ❇☎☷) As children under 12 are not allowed in Casa Dell'Arte's neighbouring art hotel, families are catered to here with features such as a children's pool and an atelier to get kids' creative juices flowing. Children under six stay free and those under 12 for €35.

✕ Eating

Menthol
KEBAP, GRILL €€

(Atatürk Caddesi; snacks ₺7.50-10, mains ₺15-45; ☺lunch & dinner) Affordable restaurants are found in the village centre and along the road to the marina, including this *ocakbaşı* (grill house) overlooking the central roundabout. It serves a mix of international and Turkish dishes, including *dürüm* kebaps, pide and burgers.

Gonca Balık
SEAFOOD €€€

(☑367 1796; Mutlu Sokak 15; mezes ₺9, fish from ₺30; ☺lunch & dinner) With cheery orange tables strung along the ebbing waves, this is Torba's premium (and priciest) spot for a fish-and-meze meal.

Eastern Peninsula

☑ 0252

Bodrum's eastern bays are less well known, in some cases because hotels have swallowed them whole. Inland, the villages and lanes are quiet and rustic, but the area lacks the overall atmosphere and appeal of the peninsula proper.

🛏 Sleeping

Hapimag Sea Garden   RESORT €€
(☑ 311 1280; www.hapimag-seagarden.com; Yalı-çiftlik; per person incl full board & drinks €126; ❄@☲) The sprawling Sea Garden offers everything you could desire between three turquoise bays – restaurants serving food from Italian to Indonesian, a nightclub complete with a huge golden Buddha, and lots of watery fun for children.

Kempinski Barbaros Bay   LUXURY HOTEL €€€
(☑ 311 0303; www.kempinski-bodrum.com; Kızı-lağaç; s/d from €320/356; ❄☎☲) Bodrum's branch of the famed international chain is cradled within a sea-facing cliff, isolated from any outside disturbances, with its own private beach and docks. The modern rooms have all of the expected amenities, and there are five restaurants in season, a bar, spa centre and hamam.

However, the real marvel is the massive, elliptical outdoor pool, possibly Turkey's biggest, with an adjacent chill-out area featuring hanging greenery and beds. The hotel is popular with families, offering daily children's activities in summer.

MARMARIS & AROUND

Marmaris

☑ 0252 / POP 34,047

Marmaris owes its debatable desirability to the industrial-tourism concept, which sees the port town create a non-stop party atmosphere for its British, Scandinavian and Russian summer tourists, most of them packaged. Still, it does have a pretty harbour in a mountainous bay, crowned by a castle and lined with wood-hulled yachts and the vessels of visiting sailors.

Lacking Bodrum's refinement, Marmaris itself is one of the gaudier resort towns on the Turkish Med – a sort of Kuşadası on

steroids. Not many Turks you will encounter here actually come from the area, and few cultural attractions remain. The immediate surroundings, however, are spectacular, including the rugged and relatively unvisited peninsulas of Bozburun and Datça. The town also makes a good base for *gület* cruises, diving in pristine waters and visiting the Greek isle of Rhodes – and hey, there's always the nightlife.

◉ Sights & Activities

Marmaris Castle & Museum   MUSEUM
(Marmaris Kalesi ve Müzesi; admission ₺8; ⊙8am-7pm Tue-Sun) Marmaris' hilltop castle (1522) was Süleyman the Magnificent's assembly point for 200,000 troops, used to capture Hospitaller-held Rhodes. The castle hosts the small Marmaris Museum, which exhibits amphorae, tombstones, figurines, oil lamps and other finds, including from Knidos and Datça. Saunter the castle's walls and gaze down on the bustling marina.

Old Town   HISTORIC AREA
The hilly streets around Marmaris Castle, atmospheric lanes that feel far removed from the shiny new marina, contain Marmaris' few remaining traditional buildings.

Bazaar   MARKET
The mostly covered çarşı (bazaar) sells everything from haircuts to hats for concealing them.

Jinan Garden   GARDENS
(Atatürk Caddesi) This Zen-style garden, complete with a pagoda and soothing water, also has a teahouse for some suitably pensive refreshment.

Beaches   BEACH
Marmaris' narrow, pebbly town beaches allow decent swimming, but much better are İçmeler and Turunç (10km and 20km southwest, respectively). From late April to October, water taxis serve İçmeler (₺10, 30 minutes, half-hourly) and Turunç (₺12.50, hourly, 50 minutes).

Dolmuşes by 19 Mayıs Gençlik Meydanı also access İçmeler (₺3.25), Turunç (₺7) and the beach at Günlücek Park, a forest reserve 3.5km southeast of Marmaris.

Armutalan Hamamı   HAMAM
(☑ 417 5374; off Datça Caddesi, Camiavlu Ma-hallesi; bath & scrub ₺40, with oil massage ₺70; ⊙9am-midnight Apr-Oct) The enormous, full-serve 'Pear Field' Hamamı is behind the

Marmaris

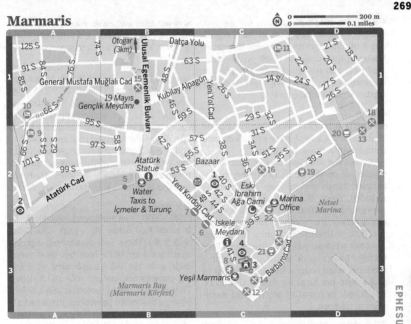

Marmaris

◉ Sights
1	Bazaar	C2
2	Jinan Garden	A2
3	Marmaris Castle & Museum	C3
4	Old Town	C3

◉ Activities, Courses & Tours
5	Boat Trips	B2
6	Calypso	C3
7	Professional Diving Centre	B2
8	Yeşil Marmaris	C3

◉ Sleeping
9	Barış Motel & Pansiyon	A2
10	Maltepe Pansiyon	A1
11	Marina Apart	C1

◉ Eating
12	Aquarium	C3
13	Chef Marine Brasserie	D2
14	Fellini	C3
15	Köfteci Ramiz	B1
16	Meryemana	C2
17	Ney	C3
18	Rota	D1

◉ Drinking & Nightlife
19	Bar St	D2
20	Kahve Dünyası	D2
21	Panorama Restaurant & Bar	C3
22	Türkü Bars	C2

government hospital and Kipa supermarket (2km west of the centre). The watery complex boasts four hamams and a swimming pool. After 6pm it's quietest, as the tour groups are gone.

Call for a free pick-up (until 8.15pm); blue No 4 dolmuşes also go there up 19 Mayıs Gençlik Meydanı (₺2).

Boat Trips

(Atatürk & Yeni Kordon Caddesis; ☺May-Oct) Marmaris Bay **day trips** (₺35 to ₺50 including lunch, soft drinks, pick-up and drop-off)

offer eye-opening views and inviting swimming holes. So many old salts advertise tours that their boats are practically bumping and grinding into one another on the docks. Before signing up, confirm all details (exact boat, itinerary, lunch etc).

Hiring a yacht, together with a group of friends or with random new ones, offers the pleasure of a **blue cruise** down the coast. Cruises offered by **Yeşil Marmaris** (☎412 6486; www.bluevoyageyachts.com; Barbaros Caddesi 13; 8-/12-/16-berth per day €1900/1800/2200, half-/full-board per person

€30/45) are recommended; as for the rest, compare prices, ask around and negotiate. Yeşil offers seven- to 10-day itineraries taking in the Turquoise Coast or the Datça Peninsula and Rhodes. Dalyan is a popular destination for shorter trips. See p366 for further advice on blue cruises.

Diving

Several dive boats opposite Ziraat Bank on Yeni Kordon Caddesi offer excursions and courses (April through October).

As with the numerous cruises, many boats operate, so choose carefully; equipment, insurance, lunch and pick-up are normally included. Since diving is potentially more life-endangering than lounging on a yacht, ask whether the company is licensed by the Turkish Underwater Sports Federation. Also, ask whether your dive leader will be a certified instructor or 'assistant instructor' – the latter often being a simple deckhand in scuba gear, not ideal for safety. And do be responsible by reporting any medical conditions in advance.

Professional Diving Centre   DIVING
(☑ 0533 456 5888; www.prodivingcentre.com; Yeni Kordon Caddesi) Offers excursions (₺80 including two dives and lunch) and a four-day PADI open-water course (€250).

Calypso   DIVING
(☑ 0537 282 7690; Yeni Kordon Caddesi) Offers daily excursions and a three-day open-water course.

🛏 Sleeping

The prevalence of package tourists (typically, sequestered in big outlying beach hotels) means that good central options are limited. Dimly lit, seedier pensions lurk around darker corners, propping up the bottom end of Marmaris' sex-tourism industry.

Maltepe Pansiyon   PENSION €
(☑ 412 1629; www.maltepepansiyon.com; 66 Sokak 9; s/d/tr/q ₺35/75/90/120; ❋ ❑) This slightly ramshackle family-run pension has a shady courtyard where guests can drink *elma* çay (apple tea) under vine trellises. A self-catering kitchen is available, as are cheaper rooms with shared bathroom.

Barış Motel & Pansiyon   PENSION €
(☑ 413 0652; www.barismotel.com; 66 Sokak 16; s/d without breakfast €20/25, breakfast €3; ❋ ❑) The popular 'Peace' has spartan but clean rooms and a front patio. If you're planning to stay out after midnight, ask for a key to get back in. Not to be confused with Barış Hotel & Apart, located in a different part of town.

Otel Dost   HOTEL, APARTMENT €€
(www.oteldost.com; General Mustafa Muğlalı Caddesi 74; s/d/tr/apt ₺100/130/180/290; ❋ ❑ ❑) Turkish-Liverpudlian couple İbrahim and Natalie offer 18 well-equipped modern rooms and a vine-covered terrace for breakfast. Across the road is a pool and snack bar, and the self-catering penthouse apartment has two bedrooms with views of the surrounding hills. Help with tours, transfers, rental cars, ferry tickets and so on is offered.

Marina Apart   APARTMENT, HOTEL €€
(☑ 412 2030; www.marinaapartotel.com; Mustafa Kemal Paşa Sokak 24; s/d/apt €30/40/50; ❋ ❑ ❑ ❑) These four-person self-catering apartments are quite bare but good value, each with the full complement of cooking implements, cutlery, sofa and balcony. There's a cafe-bar in reception and a neighbouring bakery for provisions. Rates include breakfast, and hotel services such as Dalaman Airport transfers (€50) are offered.

🍴 Eating

Beware harbourside restaurants that offer a free bottle of wine with meals, and then recoup their outlay by charging for bread, service and so on.

Meryemana   TURKISH €
(35 Sokak 5/B; mains ₺5-9) In addition to *mantı* and *gözleme*, this friendly local eatery serves delicious pre-prepared *etli yemek* (meat dishes) and *sebze yemek* (vegetable dishes). A good place to try some Turkish classics.

Köfteci Ramiz   KÖFTE, GRILL €€
(General Mustafa Muğlalı Caddesi 5/A; mains ₺8-33.50) At lunchtime, local suits queue for this 90-year-old *köfte* chain's salad bar (₺7.50). Meal deals abound and hygiene is certainly no concern – the chefs even wear hair nets.

Rota   KEBAP, GRILL €€
(Netsel Marina; mains ₺10-28.50) Safely removed from Bar St, at the far end of the shopping centre across the bridge, 'Ship's Course' serves meat dishes, pides and salads in a covered outdoor setting.

★ Ney   TURKISH €€€
(☑ 412 0217; 26 Sokak 24; mezes ₺8, mains ₺20-27; ⊙ lunch Mon-Sat, dinner daily Mar-Nov) Perched

on a winding lane above the waterfront, with views of yacht masts between the stone houses, little Ney occupies a whitewashed 250-year-old Greek house. The home-cooked dishes include some wonderful mezes and house specials *mantı* and *köfte* with yoghurt and garlic.

Aquarium   INTERNATIONAL €€€
(☑413 1522; Barbaros Caddesi; mains ₺15-40) One of the cooler and more creative waterfront eateries, Aquarium is scattered with books, magazines and a chess set (its pieces made of piping). Large grills and steaks are offered, while the lunch menu features lighter meals including fish and chips, wraps and pizzas.

Fellini   ITALIAN, INTERNATIONAL €€€
(☑413 0826; Barbaros Caddesi 71; mains ₺22-39) With cheery yellow chairs and flower arrangements, this decades-old waterfront restaurant serves great thin-crust pizzas, pasta, seafood, steaks and kebaps.

Chef Marine Brasserie   STEAK €€€
(☑413 1748; Netsel Marina; mains ₺16-45) Meat dishes including dry-aged steaks come with a view in this restaurant's glassed-in upstairs dining room. There's also an open-air terrace alongside the yachts, and pizzas, pastas, burgers and kebaps on the menu.

Drinking & Entertainment

Marmaris by night offers more neon than Vegas, and almost as many drunks certain they're just one shot away from the big score. Away from the infamous debauchery of Bar St, there are quieter spots for drinks and harbour views, including the waterfront bar-restaurants lining Barbaros Caddesi and the marina.

Bar St   STREET
(39 Sokak) This raucous stretch of licentiousness is dominated by big, bold and brassy bar-club complexes that spill out onto the street. If you like laser beams, dance music, liquored-up louts, tequilas by the half-dozen and the odd foam party, this is pretty much it. The major action takes place between Eski İbrahim Ağa Cami and the Netsel Marina footbridge. Most bars open from 7pm to 4am daily.

As the night wears on, the street becomes a veritable cacophony, as each place tries to drown out its neighbours by cranking up the volume. Beers and spirits cost ₺13 to ₺30,

shooters ₺5 to ₺10 and fishbowl cocktails around ₺70. Happy hours, free shots and buy-one-get-one-free incentives are offered, but there's no guarantee that 'name-brand' spirits will be authentic.

Heading east from the Eski İbrahim Ağa Cami, you first come to a strip of **Türkü Bars** and *meyhanes,* playing live Turkish folk and *fasıl;* worth a stop to see how Turks unwind over a few milky glasses of rakı. These peter out around the marina office and the Ibiza beats and fluorescent shooters begin.

Since the bars are so close and so interchangeable, they're best understood as a single amorphous mass. Castellated **Joy Club** is shiny and sinful with three large bars, while **Crazy Daisy** offers raised terraces and nightly laser, foam, water and dance shows. Opposite the latter are standing-room-only outdoor bars **Shame, Apollon** and, recommended locally, **B52**. The strip's only rock bar, **Davy Jones's Locker,** has live bands in summer, while **Back Street** opposite (and with another branch near Joy Club) offers multiple bars and VIP terraces. Further towards the water, **Club Areena** claims to be the world's biggest open-air nightclub (Bodrum's Halikarnas (p260) notwithstanding), with bars, terraces and nightly foam parties.

Panorama Restaurant & Bar   BAR, RESTAURANT
(☑412 8961; Hacı İmam Sokağı 40) The marina-view terrace is more famous than the food (mains ₺18 to ₺30), but it's still a nice place for sunset drinks and nibbles.

Kahve Dünyası   CAFE
(Netsel Marina) This chain cafe, resembling the left bank of the Seine in comparison with tacky Bar St across the bridge, is a relaxed spot for coffee and cake.

ℹ Information

Tourist Office (☑412 1035; İskele Meydanı 2; ⊙8am-noon & 1-5pm Mon-Fri mid-Sep–May, daily Jun–mid-Sep) Has maps, but not very helpful.

ℹ Getting There & Around

AIR

The closest aiports are Dalaman (98km southeast) and Milas-Bodrum (135km northwest). **Havaş** (www.havas.net/en) runs a shuttle bus to/from Dalaman International Airport (₺15, 1½ hours). Otherwise, Marmaris Koop has eight daily buses to Dalaman (₺15, 1½ hours), from where you can catch an (expensive) taxi to the airport.

BOAT

From June to October, daily catamarans serve Rhodes (one-way/same-day return/open return including port tax €40/42/60, one hour) from the pier 1km southeast of Marmaris, departing in both directions at 9am and 5pm. There are also sporadic departures between March and May. Greek catamaran companies also serve this route, but are generally 10% more expensive.

A ferry (car one-way/same-day return/open return €110/135/190, 2½ hours) sails on Tuesdays and Fridays from November to February and on summer Thursdays, leaving Marmaris at 9am and returning at 2pm. Foot-passenger tickets are more than double the price of the catamaran fare.

Travel agencies including **Yeşil Marmaris** (☑ 412 1033; www.rhodesferry.com; Barbaros Caddesi 13; ⊘ 9am-9pm, to 6pm Nov-Feb) and **Marmarisferry.com** (☑ 413 0230; www.marmarisferry.com; İskele Caddesi) sell tickets. Book ahead at least one day (if driving, more) and bring your passport. Be at the ferry dock one hour before departure for immigration formalities. Some agencies provide free hotel pick-up for same-day return passengers.

BUS

Marmaris' small otogar is 3km north of the centre. Dolmuşes serve it along Ulusal Egemenlik Bulvarı frequently in summer. Bus company offices line General Mustafa Muğlalı Caddesi (between 19 Mayıs Gençlik Meydanı and 84 Sokak) in the city centre; some companies provide a *servis* between here and the otogar. Destinations include:

Antalya (₺55, six hours) Daily with Kamil Koç and Pamukkale.

Bodrum (₺25, three hours) Nine daily Marmaris Koop buses.

Fethiye (₺23, three hours) Eight daily Marmaris Koop buses via Dalaman and Göcek.

İstanbul (13 hours) A few daily year-round with Metro (₺70) and Pamukkale (₺80) among others.

İzmir (4¼ hours) Hourly with Metro (₺25) and Pamukkale (₺35) among others.

DOLMUŞ

Regular dolmuşes canvas the bay from near the northern end of 19 Mayıs Gençlik Meydanı.

Datça & Bozburun Peninsulas

Far from the madding crowds of Marmaris, a more elemental and tranquil experience awaits on its outlying peninsulas, Datça (occasionally called Reşadiye) and Bozburun (or Hisarönü). The adjoining peninsulas unwind wonderfully into the blue waters at the meeting of the Aegean and Mediterranean, with stunning azure coves, hidden archipelagos and craggy, thickly forested peaks overlooking it all.

Despite a developing tourist industry, these rugged shores are far less built-up than the Bodrum Peninsula and as such reserved for escapists and anyone seeking simple village life or a sail in secluded waters. As the ancient Greek historian and geographer Strabo said of the Datça Peninsula, 'God sent his privileged believers here to have a long and healthy life'.

Datça

☑ 0252 / POP 11,261

Some 70km from Marmaris, down a winding road dotted with traditional windmills, Datça is the peninsula's major harbour town. Datça is surprisingly workaday given its seaside location, but this lends it a certain laid-back authenticity, and it has three lovely beaches: **Kumluk Plajı** (Sandy Beach), tucked behind the main street, Atatürk Caddesi; **Hastanealtı** (literally 'Below the Hospital'), the bigger, eastern-shore beach; and **Taşlık Plajı** (Stony Beach) at harbour's end, with a pool to swim in the steamy water from the **hot springs**.

Despite its nondescript downtown, Datça makes a pleasant base for seeing the area, with a string of waterside restaurants that spill onto Kumluk Plajı in summer. If you've made the long trek all the way out here, chances are high that you'll prefer nearby Eski Datça, which has preserved the traditional feel that Datça has lost. Off season, however, Datça is a safer choice, as many businesses in the neighbouring village shut their doors.

Excursion boats and travel agencies including Karnea Turizm (p274) and **Bora Es Tour** (☑ 712 2040; www.boraestour.com; Yat Limanı) offer day trips from Datça harbour (from ₺40 including lunch and soft drinks), some including the ruins of Knidos. Longer *gület* cruises are also on offer.

🛏 Sleeping

Budget pensions are available around Atatürk Caddesi and above the harbour near the square. Renting villas and apartments in Datça or nearby villages can be good value; check locally or via websites such as **Hidden Datça** (www.hiddendatca.com).

Tunç Pansiyon PENSION, APARTMENT €
(☑712 3036; www.tuncpansiyon.com; İskele Mahallesi; s/d/apt ₺60/100/160; ✳@🖥) Recommended by readers, this roundabout-area pension (look for the Ögür taxi stand and Vestel shop) has basic but sunny and spotless rooms with balcony, as well as an apartment sleeping up to five. Helpful owner Metin offers a free laundry service and car excursions for up to three to Knidos – you're charged just for the petrol (₺50).

Ilıca Camping CAMPING GROUND €
(☑712 3400; www.datcailicacamping.com; Taşlık Plajı; campsites per person ₺20, bungalows per person ₺50, d ₺200; ✳🖥) This seaside campsite shaded by eucalyptus trees has a great open grassy pitch and a restaurant.

Villa Tokur BOUTIQUE HOTEL €€€
(☑712 8728; www.hoteltokur.com; Koru Mevkii; d/ste €83/115; ✳🖥🏊) This German-owned hilltop hotel with a garden and well-groomed grounds overlooking the sea offers 15 nicely furnished rooms. It's a 10-minute walk uphill from Taşlık Plajı.

Konak Tuncel Efe HOTEL €€€
(☑712 4488; www.konaktuncelefe.com; Atatürk Caddesi 55; s/d/f from ₺190/250/250; ✳🖥) İznik tiles and exposed walls abound in this purpose-built building, with a feeling of age created in the 20 rooms by a mix of modern and vintage furniture. The cool and shadowy lobby has a bar, scattered sofas and tables piled with books, while the penthouse family rooms have skylights in their sloping ceilings.

Kumluk Otel HOTEL €€€
(☑712 2880; www.kumlukotel.com; Atatürk Caddesi 39/1; s/d from ₺160/200; ✳🖥) Behind the harbourside cafe-bar of the same name, Kumluk has 26 modern rooms with long mirrors, glass-fronted fridge and flat-screen TV. The decor mixes white with flashes of primary colours and there's a glassed-in terrace for breakfast.

✗ Eating

Datça's *keşkek* (lamb mince and coarse, pounded wheat) is its speciality.

★Zekeriya Sofrası ANATOLIAN, GRILL €
(Atatürk Caddesi 70; dishes from ₺5; 🍴) The pre-prepared and made-to-order dishes in this bright eatery, opposite Billabong on the main street, give a great-value taste of Turkish home cooking. The bains-marie contain all sorts of meat and vegetable creations

from as far afield as Şanlıurfa, where the owner's family hails from, including house speciality Borani (lamb stew). Come at lunch for the widest selection of fresh dishes.

Café Inn CAFE €€
(Kumluk Plajı 32/B; mains ₺15-20) Mixing beach-house furniture with the odd heavier animal-footed table, this breezy hang-out serves a decent cappuccino and light meals from *dolmades* (stuffed grape leaves) to pizzas. The *kahvaltı* features four preserves and a plate of fruit.

★Culinarium MODERN TURKISH €€€
(☑712 9770; Yat Limanı; mains ₺30-50; ⊘lunch & dinner) The three-course set menu (₺60) is a gourmet experience at this Turkish-German restaurant, its wraparound bar gazing at Bozburun and Symi. Fish is served in boneless fillets with light dressings; meat mains include fillet steak in mustard and tarragon sauce; and desserts are mostly based on Datça's famous almonds.

Emek Restaurant SEAFOOD €€€
(☑712 3375; Yat Limanı; mezes ₺6, mains ₺15-30; ⊘lunch & dinner) Datça's oldest and most reliable seafood joint on the marina, Emek serves good grilled catches and *köfte* with Symi views.

Mayistra ITALIAN €€€
(☑712 2822; Kumluk Plajı 14; mains ₺18-30; ⊘lunch & dinner; 🍴) This seafront pizzeria serves a wide range of pasta, pizza, antipasti and salads. It also offers a good wine selection and bottles of Efes Malt.

🍷 Drinking & Nightlife

Datça's nightlife centres on the harbour.

Sunrise BAR
(Yat Limanı 2/A) Under bougainvillea, Yaşar's bar is popular with expats for its draught beer and televised soccer and rugby.

Eclipse BAR, CLUB
(İskele Caddesi) Offering happy-hour discounts from 5pm to 10pm, Eclipse's outside deck is a great spot for a sunset beer. Inside, beneath exposed beams, pop-art superheroes overlook the dance floor.

🛍 Shopping

Shops on Atatürk Caddesi sell local products as well as figs, *lokum* (Turkish delight), honeycomb, *helva* (sweet made from sesame seeds) and herbs.

Özlü Datça FOOD & DRINK
(Atatürk Caddesi 72/H; ⊙9am-11pm summer, to 5pm winter) Datça's three main products (honey, almonds and olive oil) are sold here.

ⓘ Information

Karnea Turizm (📋712 8842; www.karneaturizm.com; Atatürk Caddesi 54/B) Run by the helpful Beycan Uğur, Karnea provides local info, books Turkish Airlines flights, organises transfers, rents out cars and scooters, and runs local trips.

ⓘ Getting There & Around

BOAT

Bodrum Buy tickets and confirm details (the website is sometimes out of date) at the **Bodrum Ferryboat Association** (📋712 2323; www.bodrumferryboat.com; Turgut Özal Meydanı; ⊙8am-8pm) in central Datça. Arrive at the office 30 minutes before departure for the *servis* to Körmen harbour at Karaköy (5km northwest of Datça). If staying in Eski Datça, with prior notice the *servis* can pick you up on the main road.

Rhodes & Symi At the time of writing, regular ferries were not running from Datça. Greek ferries made day trips from the islands to Datça on summer Saturdays. Check **Ferrylines** (www.ferrylines.com) for more information. In summer, operators including **Knidos Yachting** (📋712 9464; Yat Limanı 4/A) and **Seher Tour** (📋712 2473; www.sehertour.com; Atatürk Caddesi 88/E) offer day trips to Symi, charging about €600 for the boat (so eight passengers would each pay €75).

BUS & DOLMUŞ

Hourly summer dolmuşes serve Marmaris (₺15, 1¾ hours, every two hours in low season) from the Pamukkale office. The bus from Marmaris drops you on the main street, 500m before the square and harbourside pensions. Turkey's major bus companies all have offices on Atatürk Caddesi, and offer daily departures to cities throughout western Turkey, but Marmaris otogar offers more.

CAR & MOTORCYCLE

Akdeniz Rent a Car (📋712 2636; Ambarcı Caddesi 8/B) Rents out cars (one day ₺70 to ₺90) and scooters (one day ₺40).

Eski Datça

📋0252 / POP 8000

'Old Datça', capital of an Ottoman district stretching into today's Greece, is much more atmospheric than its 'new' counterpart. Its cobbled lanes wind beckoningly between whitewashed stone houses draped with bougainvillea, providing a blissful escape into the untroubled coast of yesteryear.

Surya Yoga Centre (📋712 2287; www.suryaturkey.com; one-week retreats €580) offers yoga retreats here.

🛏 Sleeping & Eating

★**Mehmet Ali Ağa Konağı** HISTORIC HOTEL €€€
(📋712 9257; www.kocaev.com; s/d from €180/220; ⊙May-Oct; 🅿🅰🛜🏊) In the sleepy village of Reşadiye, 1.5km north of Eski Datça, this opulent boutique hotel centres on an early 19th-century Mediterranean mansion. Its 18 historically furnished rooms sprawl across the Ottoman pile, which was renovated a decade ago and has its orginal carved wooden doors and ceilings, and a new building in similar style.

Among them, the Mansion Suite is one of Turkey's most impressive rooms, consisting of the *selamlik* (public quarters), where local notables met, and *haremlik* (family quarters) with traditional cupboard bathroom. Walkways wind through the lush gardens to the restored hamam, outdoor bar and restaurant.

Olive Farm GUESTHOUSE €€€
(📋712 4151; http://guesthouse.olivefarm.com.tr; s/d from €60/80; 🅿🛜🏊) This stylish country retreat has 13 pastel rooms with bright bedding, rustic furnishings and its own olive-based toiletries. The mix of children's playroom, garden hammocks and artisitic decoration creates the feel of a farm designed by Gaudí. Find it 2km north of Eski Datça.

Eski Datça Evleri PENSION, APARTMENT €€€
(Old Datça Houses; 📋712 2129; www.eskidatca evleri.com; s/d/tr/f from €65/85/130/165; 🛜) These new houses, Fig, Almond and Olive, are built in traditional fashion, with thick stone walls keeping the Mediterranean heat from their white interiors. Inside are hamam-style bathrooms and small kitchens, while the courtyard cafe, Ede, is a rustic hang-out decorated with numberplates and olive-oil bottles. Rates include breakfast.

Datça Sofrası TURKISH, GRILL €€
(📋712 4188; mezes ₺7, mains ₺12-15; ⊙lunch & dinner) This terrace restaurant beneath a vine-clad pergola serves good mezes and grilled meat dishes, including house speciality *bademli köfte* (with Datça almonds).

Shopping

Olive Farm FOOD & DRINK
(Güller Dağı Çiftliği; ⏰8.30am-5.30pm) Among olive groves, the farm shop offers tastings of its olives and oil, black-fig vinegar, jams and other products. It's 2km north of Eski Datça.

Getting There & Away

In summer, dolmuşes run hourly to/from Datça (₺3), 2.5km south. In low season, it's every two hours. Eski Datça is just 100m from the main road, so you can get off the dolmuş from Marmaris at the turn-off and walk (or call your accommodation for a pick-up).

Knidos

A once-prosperous Dorian port city dating to 400 BC, Knidos (admission ₺10; ⏰8am-7pm Apr-Oct, to 5pm Nov-Mar) – pronounced *kuh-nee-dos* – lies in scattered ruins across 3km of the Datça Peninsula's tip. Steep hillsides, terraced and planted with groves of olive, almond and fruit trees, rise above two idyllic bays where yachts drop anchor and a lighthouse perches dramatically on a headland.

The peninsula edge's unpredictable winds meant that ancient ships often had to wait for favourable winds at Knidos (also known by the Latinised name, Cnidus); this boosted the ship-repairs business, hospitality and general trade. St Paul, en route to Rome for trial in AD 50 or 60, was one of many maritime passengers forced to wait out the storm here.

Although little remains, the city paths are well preserved. The round temple of Aphrodite, which once contained the world's first freestanding female statue, is one of a few ruined temples. The 5000-seat Hellenistic lower theatre and 4th-century-BC sundial comprise other ancient attractions, as do the remnants of a stoa with a cross-stone balancing precariously on top.

The on-site restaurant, open in summer, offers great views, although prices are high.

Getting There & Away

Knidos is a one-hour drive from Datça, along a winding and scenic road. Hiring a car or scooter allows you to detour onto the back roads on the peninsula's southern coast.

From June to August, **Pamukkale** (Atatürk Caddesi) dolmuşes leave Datça for Knidos at 10.30am and noon, returning at 2.30pm and 4.30pm (₺20 return).

Datça harbour excursion boats also visit Knidos in summer, leaving around 9am and returning by 7pm (from ₺45 including lunch). Datça's Karnea Turizm offers this tour for ₺55 and a day trip by land for ₺80.

Selimiye

📞0252 / POP 4900
Popular with yachtspeople, this former traditional boat-builders' village on the Bozburun Peninsula is – for now – little more than a promenade, lined with restaurants, pensions and bars on a calm bay, beneath a few toppled ruins. The price of land here is rising though, along with accommodation and restaurant charges, and the village is slowly starting to resemble the chichi Bodrum Peninsula. Visit soon, while it retains its air of blissful detachment from the outside world.

Between June and September, boats offer day cruises around the bay, stopping at beaches for swimming, for about ₺50 including lunch and drinks.

The mountainous, deeply indented Bozburun Peninsula is the perfect place to escape the madness of Marmaris. For a real off-the-beaten-track adventure, kick-start a motorbike or scooter and roll down the winding country roads, into a natural paradise and villages that modernity forgot. From Marmaris, take the coast road to İçmeler and then wind through the hills to Turunç, Bayırköy, Söğüt and Bozburun, returning via Selimiye and the main Datça–Marmaris road – a circuit of about 120km.

Sleeping

Ekin Pansiyon PENSION ₺₺
(📞446 4017; Hanımpınar Mahallesi 1; s/d ₺80/160; ⏰Jun-Oct; 🛜) Reached on a wooden walkway that follows a stream from the seafront, the Yıldırım family's pension has small, basic rooms with tiled floor and fridge. A little car noise comes from the lane at the rear.

Jenny's House PENSION, VACATION RENTAL ₺₺₺
(📞446 4289; www.jennyshouse.co.uk; s/d ₺120/200; ❄🛜♨) Turkish-British couple Metin and Jenny offer lovely garden bungalows around a pool in the village. They can also help with holiday rentals.

Losta Sahil Ev BOUTIQUE HOTEL ₺₺₺
(📞446 4395; www.lunabegonvil.com.tr; Gemecit Mahallesi 9; s/d ₺180/200; ⏰Apr-Oct; ❄🛜) This little stone house decorated with sea shells and arty anchors has well-furnished rooms with small water-facing balcony.

Sardunya Bungalows HOTEL €€€

(📞 446 4003; www.sardunya.info; Silimiye Köyü; s/d ₺120/220; 🏧🛜) Fifteen family-friendly rooms in stone 'bungalows' behind the beach, with a nice garden and restaurant.

✖ Eating & Drinking

Selimiye Döner Kebap KEBAP €€

(Buruncuk Sokak; mains ₺10) In addition to the advertised kebaps, this family-run eatery in the village does home-cooked Turkish dishes.

Ceren Restaurant TURKISH, GRILL €€

(Hanımpınar Mahallesi; mains ₺15) Ceren serves *ızgara* (grilled) dishes such as *köfte* and chicken *şiş*, accompanied by warm home-baked bread, on its vine-covered terrace.

Bulent's Kitchen AEGEAN €€€

(📞 0533 326 7575; Buruncuk Sokak 54/A; mezes ₺7-8, mains ₺18-22; ⏱ lunch & dinner; 🖊) On checked tablecloths, Bulent serves cuisine combining the joys of Aegean home cooking with *meyhane*-style meze. Try the fish cooked in milk, an İzmir speciality, or go for olive-oil-drenched goodies including quince, celery, okra, broad bean, eggplant and zucchini.

Aurora SEAFOOD €€€

(📞 446 4097; mezes ₺5-15, mains ₺20-35; ⏱ lunch & dinner May-Oct) Set in an antique stone house on the seafront, Aurora is serious about mezes and seafood. Some 50 mezes are produced every night, along with mains such as fish in an oyster, tomato, wine and ginger sauce, and charcoal-cooked steak stuffed with mozarella.

❶ Getting There & Away

Dolmuşes between Marmaris (₺10, 1¼ hours) and Bozburun stop in Selimiye every few hours, on the main road at the village's northern end.

Bozburun

📞 0252 / POP 2400

Bozburun, a 30km drive down the peninsula from the Marmaris–Datça road, retains its rustic farming, fishing and *gület*-building roots, though tourism has arrived too. It's an agreeable spot far from the masses with some excellent accommodation, and you can swim in brilliantly blue waters just around the harbour to the left from the rocks (just watch out for sea urchins). Local charter boats venture into the idyllic surrounding bays. Market day is Tuesday.

🛏 Sleeping

Pensions are found on the waterfront east of the marina. Accommodation fills with Turkish tourists in July and August, so book ahead.

Pembe Yunus PENSION €€

(📞 456 2154; www.bozburunpembeyunus.com; Cumhuriyet Caddesi 131; s/d incl half board from ₺90/180; 🏧🛜) Located 700m from the marina, the 'Pink Dolphin' is a friendly, peaceful place, with white interiors and shared terraces enjoying vast sea views. Dinner is eaten on blue chairs at the water's edge and the hotel has a boat for Symi trips.

Yilmaz Pansiyon & Apart PENSION, APARTMENT €€

(📞 456 2167; www.yilmazpansion.com; İskele Mahallesi 391; s ₺120-150, d ₺140-180, apt ₺230-250; 🏧🛜) Around 100m east of the marina, this friendly pension offers simple but cheerful rooms and two-bedroom self-catering apartments (rates include breakfast), plus a modern shared kitchen, a satisfying breakfast spread and a vine-covered terrace just metres from the sea. It also arranges local boat cruises.

★ Sabrinas Haus LUXURY HOTEL €€€

(📞 456 2045; www.sabrinashaus.com; d incl half board €350-850; ⏱ Apr-Aug; 🏧🛜🏊) Reachable by boat (a liveried skipper picks up guests in a speedboat, *Hawaii Five-O* style) or a half-hour walk along the bay's eastern shore, Sabrinas Haus is the ultimate pamper ific, get-away-from-it-all place. There are 17 tastefully designed rooms and suites (think lots of natural woods and shades of white) hidden in a beautiful mature garden.

The infinity pool and seafront deck and bar are super; the spa offers myriad massages and treatments; and activities include cruises to Symi and candle-lit picnic barbecues on a neighbouring island. Note that a 50% credit card deposit is required, as is a minimum two-night stay (three nights June to mid-October), and kids under 14 aren't allowed.

✖ Eating & Drinking

Thanks to the steady stream of yachts, Bozburun's marina-facing restaurants offer extras such as laundry service and inflated prices.

Papatya Lokantası TURKISH €

(Cumhuriyet Caddesi; mains ₺6; ⏱ lunch) Locals pile into this friendly little *lokanta* (eatery serving ready-made food) by the mosque for *çorba* (soup), kebaps and homemade dishes.

★ **Bozburun Restaurant** SEAFOOD €€€
(☑ 0532 684 0920; Kordon Caddesi; mezes ₺6-12, mains from ₺25; ⊙ lunch & dinner May-Oct) A favourite of Bill Gates, this 40-year-old restaurant has a great harbourside location near the customs office and lighthouse, with outside seating to enjoy it. Dozens of different mezes are prepared every day and the house specials include grilled and fried calamari, grilled octopus and *saç kavurma* (stir-fried cubed meat dish).

Osman's Place STEAK €€€
(☑ 456 2144; mains ₺18.50-35) One of the more reasonably priced waterfront options, this Turkish-Scottish restaurant offers draught Efes, Lavazza coffee, homemade cake and a range of mains. Steaks, the owner-chef's speciality, include T-bone, Mexican and pepper.

Marin Cafe Bar BAR
(Atatürk Caddesi 115A) This chilled-out bar near Pembe Yunus pension has a resident surfing dog.

❶ Getting There & Away

Four daily dolmuşes serve Marmaris (₺12, 1½ hours) via Selimiye, with a couple of extra services in summer.
Bozburun Transfer (☑ 456 2603; www.marmaristransfer.biz; Atatürk Caddesi 10; 1-3 people €70) Transfers to/from Dalaman International Airport.

Akyaka (Gökova)
☑ 0252 / POP 2500
Tucked between pine-clad mountains and a grey sand beach on the Gulf of Gökova, Akyaka is a relaxing alternative to hectic Bodrum and Marmaris. At the mouth of the Kadın Azmağı river, it was the second town in Turkey to join the Cittaslow (Slow City) movement and has resisted unsightly development, with half-timbered houses built and restored in Ottoman style by architect Nail Çakırhan. It's sometimes called Gökova (also the name of a different town, several kilometres inland).

The road from Muğla crosses the Sakar Pass (Sakar Geçidi; 670m), offering breathtaking views of the water.

The town's Blue Flag beach is good for swimming and Çınar Beach, 2km away, has deep water for snorkelling. In summer, the fishing cooperative offers boat tours (₺30 including lunch) to local beaches, bays and Cleopatra Island, which has bright golden sand and Hellenistic and Roman ruins. Year-round boat trips glide up the lovely Kadın Azmağı (₺5, one hour) over slowly waving strands of green waterweed.

Akyaka gets steady summertime winds, making it ideal for windsurfing and kite-boarding. Half a dozen operators offer equipment rental and tuition, including Yücelen Activities (☑ 243 5108; www.gokovaruzgar.com; Akyaka Plajı; kiteboard hire per day ₺180, 8-/12-hour course €350/550; ⊙ Apr-Oct) on the beach by the hotel of the same name. Yücelen also offers sea kayaking, canoeing and stand-up paddle boarding.

Free Wheelies (☑ 0544 800 4011; Lütfiye Sakıcı Caddesi; per hour/day from ₺5/20) hires out mountain and road bikes and recommends trails up the beach or into the hills.

Wednesday is market day in Akyaka, while on Saturday it's near Gökova Bay, 4km away.

🛏 Sleeping

Numerous holiday apartments are available; contact Captain's Travel Agency (☑ 243 5398; info@captains-travel.com; Negriz Sokak), Tomsan Okaliptus (☑ 243 4370; www.tomsanokaliptus.com; Türkoğlu Sokak 8; ❋ 🛜 ☷) or Susam Hotel.

Gökova Park Camping CAMPING GROUND €
(☑ 243 5156; campsites per tent/caravan ₺30/34, d/tr/q bungalows excl breakfast ₺130/175/200, cottages excl breakfast ₺250) Beside the Yücelen Hotel on the beach, with a cafe-bar, tent pitches, bungalows, and cottages accommodating up to five.

Susam Hotel HOTEL €€
(☑ 243 5863; www.susamhotel.com; Lütfiye Sakıcı Caddesi 21; s/d/tr/q from ₺130/150/170/200; ❋ 🛜 ☷) Susam has 10 immaculate rooms (most with balconies) and a small garden, the perfect place to linger over the table-covering breakfast spread.

Big Blue HOTEL €€
(☑ 243 4544; www.bigblueakyaka.com; Sanat Sokak 6; d/ste from ₺150/350; ❋ 🛜) Six rooms with private balcony or terrace and a jaunty nautical feel courtesy of white walls and stripy cushions. Go for a cheaper and more spacious ground-floor room, although the penthouse suite is certainly pleasant with sea and forest views.

Turkuaz HOTEL, APARTMENT €€
(☑ 243 4389; Kermetur Karşısı; d/apt excl breakfast ₺125/150; ❋ 🛜) Occupying a renovated

Ottoman house with wooden balconies, Turkuaz offers comfortable and spacious rooms and self-catering apartments accommodating up to four. Ask for a room away from the Atatürk Caddesi end, where there's an outdoor bar.

Yücelen Hotel   RESORT €€€

(☑243 5108; www.yucelen.com.tr; Hamdi Yücel Gürsoy Sokak 2; s/d ₺210/300; ❄🖥🐾) This big (125-room) classic on the beach is a popular family resort and has indoor and outdoor pools, a fitness centre and a sauna. Accommodation is in Ottoman-style blocks, reached across bridges over a network of soothing streams.

✗ Eating & Drinking

Fish kebaps are sold all over town for about ₺5, including on boats moored at the river mouth; check the cleanliness of kitchens before ordering.

The beachfront cafe at Big Blue (p277) is a smart spot for a sundowner, serving cocktails and frozen milkshakes. One block inland, three popular bars on Nergiz Sokak and Lütfiye Sakıcı Caddesi draw a mixed crowd of tourists and local kitesurfers with ponytails.

Golden Roof Restaurant   INTERNATIONAL €€€

(☑243 5302; Karanfil Sokak 33; mezes ₺8, mains ₺15-40) This casual family-run eatery does dishes from fish and chips to pide and pizza, but mamma's specials are the best options, including Ottoman steak (rolled and stuffed with chestnuts, pastrami and other goodies). Affable brothers Erdal and Doğan are a good source of local information.

Tıkın House   KEBAP €€

(☑243 5444; Lütfiye Sakıcı Caddesi; mains ₺10; ⊙lunch & dinner; 🖥) Opposite the Susam Hotel, this popular kebap joint also has a changing daily menu featuring çorba, mantı and pizza.

❶ Getting There & Away

Dolmuşes serve Muğla (₺5, 30 minutes) half-hourly (hourly in winter) and Marmaris (₺7, 30 minutes) twice daily (summer only). Otherwise, walk to the highway junction (2km uphill from the beach), where transport passes in both directions every 30 minutes.

Muğla

🗐0252 / POP 62,635

While Muğla (moo-lah) is often overlooked by tourists eager to break for the coast, it's well worth a visit. With its whitewashed Ottoman quarter, traditional shops, historic buildings and museums, Muğla has plenty of cultured charm and, as a small university city, offers relaxing cafes to while away the hours amid the click of backgammon and rustling of Mediterranean foliage.

◎ Sights & Activities

Old Town   HISTORIC AREA

From Cumhuriyet Meydanı, the main square and roundabout with Atatürk's statue, walk north along Kurşunlu Caddesi to Kurşunlu Cami ('Lead-Covered Mosque'; 1493) to reach Muğla's old quarter. The white mosque's minaret and courtyard were added in 1900. Beyond here, the bazaar's narrow lanes are jammed with artisans' shops, confectioners and restaurants.

Muğla's 18th- and 19th-century Ottoman houses and the Ulu Cami (1344) are up the hill; the mosque was built by Menteşe emirs (though 19th-century repairs altered its look). Nearby, the clock tower (saatli kule), Greek-built in 1905, sounds a church bell on the hour. Further up, the renovated Ottoman Sekibaşı Hamamı hosts occasional art exhibits; its intricate architecture alone, with branching side rooms and central marble bath-table, make it worth a peek.

Zahire Pazarı   HISTORIC BUILDING

(Zahire Pazarı; ⊙8am-11pm; 🖥) This carefully restored bazaar, overlooked by an old-town mosque, features lazy cafes spilling across a leafy cloistered courtyard dotted with traditional craft shops; the city subsidises their rent to maintain traditions such as marbled paper and art, hand-woven items and intricate painted boxes. Even if you're not shopping, come for an atmospheric drink.

Muğla Museum   MUSEUM

(Postane Sokak; ⊙9am-noon & 1-5pm Tue-Sun) FREE Muğla's museum is divided into an ethnographic section with Greek and Roman pottery and an Ottoman diorama; a gladiator room with stone carvings and information about the lives of these professional combatants; and a room with fossil

EPHESUS, BODRUM & THE SOUTH AEGEAN MUĞLA

beds and other prehistoric finds from local excavation sites.

The museum is in eastern Muğla on the same square as the beautiful Konakaltı Kültür Merkezi, a traditional complex turned cultural centre.

Vakıflar Hamamı   HAMAM
(Mustafa Muğlalı Caddesi 1; hamam ₺50, scrub & massage ₺15, oil massage ₺30; ⊙7am-11pm) This mid-14th-century hamam offers mixed bathing for men and women.

🛏 Sleeping

Karya Apart & Otel   PENSION €
(☑214 4841; Saatlikule Caddesi 70; s/d excl breakfast ₺35/70; 🅿🛜) One of the old-town pensions catering primarily to student lodgers, Karya has clean rooms with functional bathrooms.

İzethan Hotel   BUSINESS HOTEL €€
(☑212 2700; www.izethanhotel.net; Abdi İpekçi Bulvarı 75-77; s/d ₺60/100; 🅿🛜🛁) Although it's a 15-minute walk northwest of Cumhuriyet Meydanı, near Nazim Hikmet Parki, the İzethan is good value with a restaurant, bar, hamam, sauna and almost 100 rooms with all mod cons.

🍴 Eating & Drinking

Market day in Muğla is Thursday.

Meşhur Bozdoğan Pidesi   KÖFTE €
(Kurşunlu Çıkmazı; meals ₺5-9.50) Down a small alleyway opposite Kurşunlu Cami, this local eatery does meal deals featuring kebap, *lahmacun,* pide, *köfte* or chicken *şiş* and *ayran.*

Arabacı   TURKISH €€
(Turgutreis Caddesi 14; mezes ₺5, mains from ₺10) 'Coachman' is Muğla's smartest restaurant, occupying an old house with a rear terrace and walled garden near Kurşunlu Cami. The menu includes *köfte,* seafood, *tandır* (slow-cooked) dishes and good meze and wine selections.

Bıcılar Han   ANATOLIAN, CAFE, BAR €€
(Saatlikule Caddesi) This restored caravanserai beneath the clock tower is fronted by a **restaurant** (mezes ₺4-5, mains ₺12-15; ⊙dinner) serving kebaps and local dishes, with live *fasıl* at night. The neighbouring cafe (snacks from ₺5; ⊙lunch) serves *gözleme, börek* and fruit juice, and in the courtyard is Efes Han bar, decked out with metalwork sculptures.

Çakarkeyf   COFFEEHOUSE, NARGILE CAFE
(Zahire Pazarı; ⊙9am-midnight) This laid-back cafe in a restored bazaar offers coffees in flavours such as white or bitter chocolate, raspberry and walnut.

Pub Uç   PUB
(Avlu; Hekimbaşı Sokak) Just north of Kurşunlu Cami, this internationally flavoured student haunt serves Tuborg and Carlsberg draught in its covered garden and bar, decorated with portraits of blues legends and Hollywood greats. Find it down a beckoning cobbled lane off an old-town alley.

Konak Kuzine   CAFE
(Kurşunlu Caddesi 13) Students play backgammon over fruit juice, homemade lemonade and çay on the front deck and upstairs balcony of this 19th-century Greek mansion, opposite Kurşunlu Cami.

ℹ Information

Tourist Office (☑214 1261; Cumhuriyet Caddesi; ⊙8am-noon & 1-5pm Mon-Fri) About 600m southeast of Cumhuriyet Meydanı. English is spoken and free maps are available.

ℹ Getting There & Away

Muğla's otogar is about 750m southwest of the main square via Zübeyde Hanım Bulvarı; bus offices are just south of the square. Buses and dolmuşes serve Antalya (₺50, 5¾ hours, daily), Bodrum (₺20, two hours, hourly), Denizli (₺26, 3¼ hours, hourly) and Marmaris (₺12, one hour, half-hourly), with more eastbound services available in the latter.

Western Anatolia

Why Go?

Durable, diverse and down to earth, Western Anatolia combines everything from ancient sites and mountain terrain to some of Turkey's heartiest food and friendliest people.

The region's diversity of ancient civilisations can be experienced directly: hike the rock-carved Phrygian Valley, pound marble pavements in the ancient cities of Sagalassos and Afrodisias, or take a woodland pilgrimage on the St Paul Trail. Original Ottoman capital Bursa, meanwhile, is a cornerstone of Turkish identity, with mosques, imperial mausoleums and the İskender kebap. The shimmering travertines of Pamukkale, on the other hand, are just great for splashing in.

The region's lesser-known attractions constitute its secret weapon, however: escapist Eğirdir, set on a tranquil lake, is perfect for hiking, a jaunt in a local fisherman's boat or doing nothing at all; while vibrant Eskişehir, a student city with an atmospheric old town, offers river gondola rides and happening bars and restaurants.

Best Places to Eat

➡ Kebapçı İskender (p292)
➡ Köfteci Yusuf (p284)
➡ Memphis (p298)

Best Places to Stay

➡ Kitap Evi (p291)
➡ Charly's Pension (p317)
➡ Melrose House (p309)

When to Go

Bursa

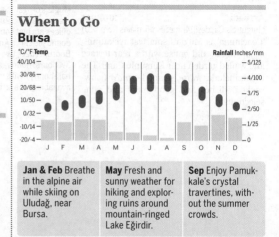

| | Jan & Feb Breathe in the alpine air while skiing on Uludağ, near Bursa. | May Fresh and sunny weather for hiking and exploring ruins around mountain-ringed Lake Eğirdir. | Sep Enjoy Pamukkale's crystal travertines, without the summer crowds. |

Western Anatolia Highlights

1 Laze in calcite travertine pools on the snow-white ridges of **Pamukkale** (p304), beneath the ruins of ancient Hierapolis.

2 Find B&B bliss by the idyllic lake in **Eğirdir** (p314), and tackle the St Paul Trail through the Taurus Mountains.

3 Channel the exhilaration of a Roman gladiator, gazing from the tunnel onto **Afrodisias's** (p312) vast stadium.

4 Ascend the lonely heights of **Sagalassos** (p320), a ruined mountain city with a magnificent rebuilt fountain.

5 Hike deep into a civilisation lost in the desolate, rock-hewn **Phrygian Valley** (p299).

6 Wind through the bazaars and unwind in a thermal hamam in the first Ottoman capital, **Bursa** (p285).

7 Indulge in the nightlife, Ottoman quarter and all-round good vibes of **Eskişehir** (p296), inner Anatolia's most European city.

İZNİK

☑ 0224 / POP 22,661

Turks are proud of İznik's Ottoman tile-making tradition, though its Byzantine incarnation as Nicaea was more significant – church councils in this fortress town shaped the future of Christianity. Today, İznik is a somewhat dusty and rundown collection of tile shops, teahouses and handicraft stalls, though the ruined fortifications and lakeside setting make visiting worthwhile. Easily accessed from İstanbul via a ferry across the Sea of Marmara to Yalova, İznik is a good candidate for a rural break from the big city.

History

Founded around 1000 BC, İznik got its classical Greek name (Nikaea; Westernised to Nicaea) when one of Alexander the Great's generals, Lysimachus, captured it in 301 BC and named it after his wife, Nikaea.

In AD 325, Emperor Constantine the Great chose Nicaea for the first Ecumenical Council, which united ecclesiastical leaders from across Christendom and set a precedent for future councils. Huge differences then existed between different Christian sects, and the council (which considered Christ's divinity, the calculation of Easter and other issues) resulted in the Nicene Creed, enabling bishops and priests to speak in an authoritative and unified way – and thus, for the religion to expand. Four centuries later, the seventh Ecumenical Council was held in Nicaea's Aya Sofya (Hagia Sofia) church.

Under Justinian I (AD 527–65), Nicaea's buildings and defensive walls were renovated. In 1204, when Constantinople fell during the Fourth Crusade, Nicaea became a Byzantine empire in exile, one of three successor states (along with Trebizond/Trabzon on the Black Sea and Epiros in Greece).

In 1331 Sultan Orhan conquered the city, establishing İznik's first Ottoman *medrese* (seminary).

◉ Sights

Most attractions are within the fortifications.

Aya Sofya HISTORIC BUILDING
(Orhanlı Camii; cnr Kılıçaslan & Atatürk Caddesi) Originally a great Justinianic church, Aya Sofya (Church of the Divine Wisdom) is now a mosque, surrounded by a rose garden. The building encompasses ruins of three differ-

ent structures. A mosaic floor and mural of Jesus, Mary and John the Baptist survive from the original church.

Destroyed by a 1065 earthquake, it was later rebuilt with the mosaics set into the walls. The Ottomans made it a mosque, but a 16th-century fire again destroyed it. Reconstruction supervised by the great architect Mimar Sinan added İznik tiles to the decoration.

Yeşil Cami MOSQUE
(off Kılıçaslan Caddesi) Built between 1378 and 1387 under Sultan Murat I, Yeşil Cami (Green Mosque) has Seljuk Turkish proportions, influenced by Seljuk homeland Iran. The minaret's green-and-blue-glazed zigzag tiles foreshadowed the famous local industry.

İznik Museum MUSEUM
(İznik Müzesi; ☑ 757 1027; Müze Sokak; admission ₺3; ⊙ 9am-1pm & 2-6pm Tue-Sun) The city museum is housed in a soup kitchen that Sultan Murat I built for his mother, Nilüfer Hatun, in 1388. Born a Byzantine princess, Nilüfer was given to Sultan Orhan to cement a diplomatic alliance.

The museum's grounds contain marble statuary, while its lofty halls display original İznik tiles, with their milky bluish-white and rich 'İznik red' hues. Other exhibits include 8000-year-old finds from a nearby *tumulus* (burial mound) at Ilıpınar, indicating links with Neolithic Balkan culture.

Opposite, see the restored 1492 **Şeyh Kutbettin Camii** (Müze Sokak).

City Walls & Gates RUIN
İznik's once-imposing Roman walls, renovated by the Byzantines, no longer dominate, but parts of their 5km circumference remain impressive. Four main gates still transect the walls, while remains of 12 minor gates and 114 towers also stand.

The most impressive walls, reaching 10m to 13m in height, stand between **Lefke Gate** and the southern **Yenişehir Gate** (Atatürk Caddesi). Lefke comprises three Byzantine gateways, and offers good views of the walls to the south.

The imposing northern **İstanbul Gate** (off Atatürk Caddesi) features huge stone carvings of heads facing outwards.

Göl (Lake) Gate has scant remains, as does the minor **Saray (Palace) Gate**, named this because Sultan Orhan (r 1326–61) had a palace nearby. Just inside Saray is a ruined 15,000-seat **Roman theatre**.

İznik

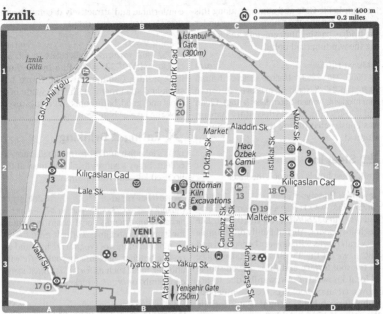

0 — 400 m
0 — 0.2 miles

İznik Gölü

İstanbul Gate (300m)

Yenişehir Gate (250m)

İznik

Church of the Koimesis   RUIN
(Dormition of the Mother of God; Çelebi Sokak)
Only some foundations remain, but the church was once famous as the burial place of the Byzantine emperor Theodore I (Lascaris). Built around AD 800 and reconstructed after a mid-11th-century earthquake, it's İznik's only church that was never converted into a mosque; unsurprisingly, it was dynamited by victorious Turks after the War of Independence.

Lascaris, who established the Empire of Nicaea after the Crusaders' 1204 conquest, built Nicaea's outer walls, which were then supported by over 100 towers and protected by a wide moat.

🏃 Activities

Viewpoint Walk   WALKING
Marked by a towering Turkish flag, İznik's hilltop viewpoint makes a good sunset walk (2km), with views of the lake stretching away beyond town. To reach it, head out

through Lefke Gate and continue along this back road for about an hour, walking under the bridge, passing the cemetery and following the winding road uphill.

Il Murat Hamamı   HAMAM
(☑ 0505 744 3259; Maltepe Sokak; adult/child ₺12/8, scrub ₺7, massage ₺9; ☺ men 6am-midnight, women 1-5pm Mon & Thu) Clean and kid-friendly, this 15th-century hamam was constructed during the reign of Sultan Murat II.

🛏 Sleeping

İznik's best hotels overlook the lake.

Kaynarca Pansiyon   HOSTEL ₺
(☑ 757 1753; www.kaynarca.net; Gündem Sokak 1; dm/s/d/tr ₺32.50/47.50/85/112.50; ☎) The English-speaking Ali and family offer simple but clean rooms with flowery bedspread and BBC news on the TV. Breakfast takes place on the roof terrace and Ali is a good source of local knowledge. Awkwardly, due to no-shows, advance bookings require a deposit to his Turkish bank account. Rates include the optional ₺7.50 breakfast.

Cem Otel   HOTEL ₺₺
(☑ 757 1687; www.cemotel.com; Göl Sahil Yolu 34; s/d ₺70/140; ✳ ☎) Well situated near the lake and walls, the Cem offers good value and friendly service. Rooms (with minibar) are comfortable and attractively decorated, and there is a terrace restaurant.

Çamlık Motel   HOTEL ₺₺
(☑ 757 1362; www.iznik-camlikmotel.com; Göl Sahil Yolu; s/d ₺70/130; ✳ ☎) Run by the English-speaking Cumhur, the 'Pine Grove' has spick-and-span rooms with crisp white bedding and good bathrooms. Balconies overlook the lake or hotel garden.

🍴 Eating & Drinking

İznik's lake fish and *köfte* (meatballs) are excellent. Enjoy a sunset drink and meal at the licensed lakeside restaurants.

★ Köfteci Yusuf   KÖFTE, GRILL ₺
(Atatürk Caddesi 73; köfte portion ₺7; ☺ lunch & dinner) This friendly local chain is famous for its plump and juicy *köfte;* it even has its own brand of *ayran* (yoghurt drink) and an on-site butcher. Accompany your *köfte* with another meat such as *kuzu şiş* (roast skewered lamb) or *tavuk* (chicken).

Karadeniz   PIDE ₺
(Kılıçaslan Caddesi 149; mains ₺8-12; ☺ lunch & dinner) 'Black Sea' specialises in pide with toppings such as *sucuk* (spicy sausage) and *lahmacun* (Arabic-style pizza; ₺2.50).

Çamlık Restaurant   SEAFOOD, TURKISH ₺₺
(Göl Sahil Yolu; mezes ₺6, mains ₺9-18) The Çamlık Motel's licensed restaurant is a local

---

İZNIK TILES

In 1514 Sultan Selim I captured Persian Tabriz, bringing its artisans to İznik. The Persian craftsmen were skilled tile-makers, and soon İznik's kilns were producing faience (tin-glazed earthenware) unequalled even today. Peaking in the 16th and 17th centuries, İznik's tile-making was a unique Ottoman artistic tradition.

However, the decreased demand for significant public works in post-Ottoman Turkey caused a rapid decline. To revive this craft, the İznik Foundation (İznik Vakıf Çinileri; www.iznik.com; Vakıf Sokak; ☺ 8am-6pm Mon-Fri) has worked with historians, university laboratories and trained craftspeople from across Turkey.

All of the İznik Foundation's designers are women, who you can watch at work. The results of their labours dot the garden and you can buy pieces in the showroom, starting at around ₺50 for an ashtray or small tile. The craftswomen meticulously design the pristine white tiles – following tradition, only floral cross-sections are painted. It takes up to 70 days to complete larger works, such as İstanbul's metro system and the World Bank in Ankara.

Made of 85% quartz from local quarries, İznik tiles' unique thermal properties keep buildings warm in winter and cool in summer. Reflected sound waves create perfect acoustic qualities – all reasons why Ottoman mosques used them. When shopping, check if you are looking at quartz or regular ceramic tiles, and if they are machine- or hand-painted.

Shops all over town sell multicoloured tiles, as well as other ceramics and handicrafts. Good shopping complexes include Nilüfer Haltun (Kılıçaslan Caddesi; ☺ 9am-7.30pm), Suleyman Paşa Medresesi (Maltepe Sokak; ☺ 9am-7.30pm) and Sultan Hamamı (Çini Çarşısı; Atatürk Caddesi; ☺ 9am-7.30pm) – there is room for bargaining at all.

favourite for grilled lake fish with views of the water. When the weather's good, enjoy a meze and drink in the lakeside garden, or angle for a table by the window in the yawning interior.

Seyir Cafe CAFE, KEBAP **€€**
(Kılıçaslan Caddesi 5; mains ₺10-13) In a garden next to Göl Gate, with olive trees, roses and kitschy classical statuettes creating pastoral vibes, Seyir offers kebaps, pizzas, burgers and an all-day breakfast buffet (₺15).

ⓘ Getting There & Away

Ankara (₺30, six hours) Daily bus via Eskişehir.
Bursa (₺10, 1½ hours, 6am to 9pm) Half-hourly midibuses.
İstanbul Regular **İDO** (www.ido.com.tr) ferries link Yalova, 62km northwest of İznik, with İstanbul Yenikapı (₺16, 1¼ hours), Pendik, Kartal and Bostancı.
Yalova (₺10, one hour) Hourly midibuses.

Bursa

📳 0224 / POP 1.7 MILLION

Modern, industrial Bursa is built around the mosques, mausoleums and other sites from its incarnation as first Ottoman capital. Despite being built-up and somewhat chaotic, its durable Ottoman core and abundant parks keep it remarkably placid in places. For some fresh air after pounding the markets, the soaring peaks of Mt Uludağ (Turkey's premier ski resort) are nearby, with Çekirge's thermal hamams en route.

As with Konya, Bursa's historic contributions to Islamic development has given it an austere reputation; you'll see a majority of head-scarved women and devout prayer in overflowing mosques. Yet locals are kind and welcoming, and you can take the occasional photo inside historic religious structures (just be respectful). In 2014, Bursa was awarded Unesco World Heritage status for being the birthplace of the Ottoman Empire.

History

Bursa was mentioned by both Aristotle and ancient geographer Strabo as a Greek city, Kios. In 202 BC, Macedonian king Philip V bequeathed it to his Bithynian counterpart, Prusias, who named it Prousa after himself (the origin of the modern name).

Under Byzantine rule, and especially under Justinian I, Prousa grew in stature,

while Çekirge's thermal baths were developed. However, tumultuous events such as the 1075 Seljuk occupation (which lasted 22 years until Crusaders rolled through) initiated a cycle of conquest and reconquest. Prousa's proximity to Nicaea (today's İznik) cemented their ties, and the cities revolted during a lurid 12th-century dynastic struggle. In one of Byzantine history's more gruesome scenes, the sadistic Emperor Andronikos I Komnenos (r 1183–85) attacked Prousa, hanging rebellious Greeks from its lovely chestnut trees, in a frenzy of mutilations, eye-gouging and impalement.

This instability made Prousa easy pickings for Seljuk conquerors. Small principalities arose around warlords such as Ertuğrul Gazi and, in 1317, Prousa was besieged by his son Osman – founder of the Ottoman line. The siege lasted years, but in 1326 Prousa was finally starved into submission, becoming Osman's capital. His successor, Orhan Gazi (r 1326–59), gradually expanded the empire toward Constantinople.

Sultan Orhan opened the first Ottoman mint, and eventually could dictate to Byzantine leaders. Although Edirne (then Hadrianople) became the capital in 1365, Bursa remained important. Both Osman and Orhan are buried here, and Muslim tourists flock to their tombs to pray and exalt their legacy. Throughout Ottoman times, Bursa's silk production was legendary and much sought-after by Turkish nobles.

Population changes began in the late 19th century, when Balkan Muslims arrived with the Ottoman Empire's decline there. In a poignant twist, the city's Greek residents chose Kios as the name of their new village in Greece, following the 1923 population exchanges. After the War of Independence, Bursa developed industrially and has been a major automotive producer since the 1960s.

◎ Sights & Activities

◎ Central Bursa

Central Cumhuriyet Alanı (Republic Sq) is also called Heykel (statue), after its large **Atatürk monument** (Map p286). Atatürk Caddesi runs west from Heykel through the commercial centre to Ulu Camii (Great Mosque). Further west, **Zafer Plaza** (Map p286; Cemal Nadir Cad) shopping centre's blue-glass pyramid is a landmark.

Central Bursa & Yeşil

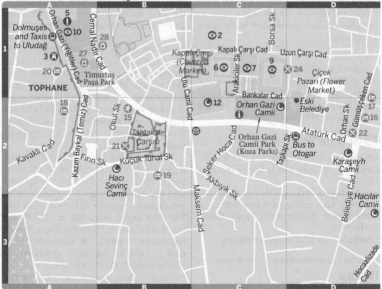

Central Bursa & Yeşil

Bursa City Museum　　　　MUSEUM
(Bursa Kent Müzesi; Map p286; ☎ 220 2626; www.
bursakentmuzesi.com; Heykel; admission ₺1.50;
⊙ 9.30am-5.30pm Tue-Sun) Chronicling Bursa's history from the earliest sultans, their
military campaigns and ornate firearms
to more recent characters such as Tarzan
impersonator Ali Atay, this lively museum
mixes cultural and ethnographic collections
with multimedia wizardry. Displays including a mock-up handicrafts bazaar give a
good understanding of local life and culture.

Ulu Camii　　　　MOSQUE
(Map p286; Atatürk Caddesi) This enormous
Seljuk-style shrine (1399) is Bursa's most dom-

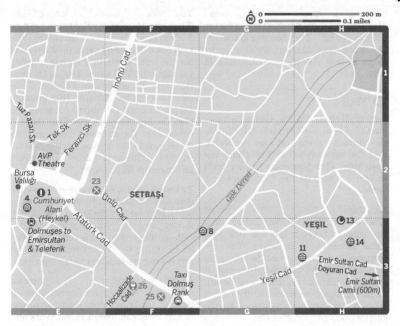

inant and durable mosque. Sultan Beyazıt I built it in a monumental compromise – having pledged to build 20 mosques after defeating the Crusaders in the Battle of Nicopolis, he settled for one mosque, with 20 small domes. Two massive minarets augment the domes, while the giant square pillars and portals within are similarly impressive. The *mimber* (pulpit) boasts fine wood carvings, and the walls feature intricate calligraphy.

Bursa's Karagöz shadow puppet theatre reportedly began with Ulu Camii's construction.

Central Markets
MARKET

(☉8.30am-8pm Mon-Sat, 10.30am-6pm Sun) Behind Ulu Camii, Bursa's sprawling Kapalı Çarşı (Covered Market) contains two historic markets: the 14th-century Bedesten (Vaulted Market; Map p286), built by Sultan Beyazıt I and reconstructed after the 1855 earthquake; and the Eski Aynalı Çarşı (Old Mirrored Market; Map p286), originally the Orhanbey Hamamı (bathhouse of the Orhan Camii Külliyesi). Built in 1335, it features a domed ceiling with skylights. Karagöz shadow puppets and other traditional items are sold here.

Just east of Eski Aynalı Çarşı is Koza Han (Cocoon Caravanserai; Map p286; Uzun Çarşı Cad), built in 1490. Expensive silk shops over-look the courtyard with its cafes and small mosque (1491) honouring Beyazıt.

Bursa was on the Silk Road, and camel caravans lodged at Emir Han (Map p286; Kapalı Çarşı Cad), entered at the rear of Ulu Camii. Drovers and merchants slept and did business upstairs, their precious cargo stored in the ground-floor rooms. The courtyard tea garden has a fine old fountain.

Bursa Citadel
CASTLE, HISTORIC AREA

(Hisar; Map p286) Some ramparts and walls still survive on the steep cliff, the site of Bursa's citadel and oldest neighbourhood, Tophane. From Ulu Camii, walk west and up Orhan Gazi (Yiğitler) Caddesi, to reach the Hisar (Fortress). On the summit, a park contains the Tombs of Sultans Osman and Orhan (Osman Gazi ve Orhan Gazi Türbeleri; Map p286; Timurtaş Paşa Park; admission by donation), the Ottoman Empire's founders.

Although the mausoleum was ruined in the 1855 earthquake, Sultan Abdülaziz rebuilt it in baroque style in 1863. Osman Gazi's tomb is the more richly decorated.

The six-storey clock tower (Map p286; Timurtaş Paşa Park), the last of four that also served as fire alarms, stands in a square with a cafe where families and couples gaze out over the valley and snap photos.

WESTERN ANATOLIA BURSA

Çakır Ağa Hamamı HAMAM

(Map p286; ☎ 221 2580; Atatürk Caddesi; hamam ₺25, massage ₺15; ☺men 6am-midnight, women 10am-10pm) Çakır Ağa, a police chief under Murat II, built this oft-restored hamam in 1484.

☉ Yeşil

East of Heykel, Atatürk Caddesi crosses the Gök Deresi (Gök Stream), which tumbles through a gorge. Just after the bridge, Yeşil Caddesi veers left to Yeşil Camii and Yeşil Türbe, while Namazgah Caddesi leads straight on towards the Uludağ *teleferik* (cable car).

Yeşil Camii MOSQUE

(Green Mosque; Map p286; Yeşil Caddesi) Built for Mehmet I between 1412 and 1419, Yeşil Camii represents a departure from the previous, Persian-influenced Seljuk architecture. Exemplifying Ottoman stylings, it contains a harmonious facade and beautiful carved marble work around the central doorway. The mosque was named for the interior wall's greenish-blue tiles.

Diverse calligraphy exists on the main door's niches. Entering the ornate interior, you'll pass beneath the *hünkar mahfili* (sultan's private box) and into a domed central hall with 15m-high *mihrab* (niche indicating the direction of Mecca). A narrow staircase leads to the sumptuously tiled *hünkar mahfili*, where the sultan stayed when in town; the harem and household staff enjoyed less plush digs on either side.

Yeşil Türbe HISTORIC BUILDING

(Green Tomb; Map p286; Yeşil Caddesi; ☺8am-noon & 1-5pm) **FREE** The mausoleum of fifth Ottoman sultan Mehmed I Çelebi (and several of his children) stands in a cypress-trimmed park opposite Yeşil Camii. During his short rule (1413–21), he reunited a fractured empire following the Mongols' 1402 invasion. Despite its name, the *türbe* is not green; the blue Kütahya tiles outside postdate the 1855 earthquake. The structure has a sublime, simple beauty, the original interior tiles exemplifying 15th-century decor. There is also an impressive tiled *mihrab*.

Turkish & Islamic Arts Museum MUSEUM

(Map p286; Yeşil Caddesi; admission ₺5; ☺8.30am-noon & 1-7pm Tue-Sun) Housed in Yeşil Camii's former *medrese,* this museum contains 14th- to 16th-century İznik ceramics, *mihrab* curtains, jewellery, embroidery, calligraphy, dervish artefacts and Karagöz puppets.

Emir Sultan Camii MOSQUE

(Emir Sultan Caddesi) An early Ottoman mosque, the 14th-century Emir Sultan was named for Sultan Bayezit I's son-in-law and adviser, a Persian scholar-dervish. Today's structure reflects renovations made after a 1766 earthquake, in the then fashionable Ottoman baroque style, echoing the romantic decadence of baroque and rococo – rich in wood, curves and outer painted arches.

Renovated by Selim III in 1805, the mosque was damaged by the 1855 earthquake and rebuilt by Sultan Abdülaziz in 1858, receiving more touch-ups in the 1990s.

SHADOW PUPPETS

Originally a Central Asian Turkic tradition, Karagöz shadow puppet theatre developed in Bursa and spread throughout the Ottoman Empire. These camel-hide puppets, made translucent after oil treatment and then painted, are manipulated by puppeteers behind a white cloth screen onto which their images are cast by backlighting.

Legend attests that Ulu Camii's foreman, Karagöz the Hunchback, distracted the workforce with the humorous antics he carried out with 'straight man' Hacivat. An infuriated sultan executed the comic slackers, whose joking became immortalised in Bursa's Karagöz shadow puppetry. In 2006, director Ezel Akay revived this legend in comic film *Killing the Shadows* (original title *Hacivat Karagöz Neden Öldürüldü?*).

Puppeteer Şinasi Çelikkol has championed Karagöz puppetry, and his shop, **Karagöz Antique Shop** (Map p286; ☎221 8727; www.karagozshop.com; Eski Aynalı Çarşı 12; ☺9.30am-7.30pm), is a lively place to see the puppets and watch an impromptu performance. Ask about his ethnographic museum in the nearby village of Misi. Çelikkol also founded the **Karagöz Museum** (Karagöz Müzesi; ☎232 3360; Çekirge Caddesi 59; admission free, Karagöz performance ₺5; ☺9.30am-5.30pm Tue-Sun, performances 10am & 2pm Tue-Fri, noon Sat), opposite the Karagöz monument. The collection includes magnificent Turkish, Uzbek, Russian and Romanian puppets and puppet-making tools.

The interior is surprisingly plain, but the mosque enjoys a nice setting beside a tree-filled cemetery overlooking the valley. Emir Sultan's tomb is here, and the oldest of several historic fountains dates to 1743.

Dolmuşes and buses marked 'Emirsultan' travel here. Walking along Emir Sultan Caddesi, another cemetery en route contains the graves of the İskender kebap dynasty, including the creator of the famous kebap, İskender Usta.

Yıldırım Beyazıt Camii   MOSQUE

(Mosque of Sultan Bayezit I) North of Emir Sultan Camii, this twin-domed mosque (1395), also referred to as just Beyazıt Camii, was built by Mehmed I Çelebi's father, Sultan Bayezit I. It houses the tombs of Yıldırım Beyazıt (Thunderbolt Bayezit), as the sultan was known, and his other son, İsa. Its adjoining *medrese* is now a medical centre.

Irgandı Köprüsü   HISTORIC BUILDING

(Irgandı Bridge; Map p286; Gök Deresi) Spanning the gorge, north of the Setbaşı road bridge, this restored Ottoman structure is home to shops, cafes and touristy artisans' workshops.

Tofaş Museum of Anatolian Carriages   MUSEUM

(☑329 3941; Kapıcı Caddesi; ☺10am-5pm Tue-Sun) Old cars and horse-drawn carts are housed in this former silk factory with gardens. It's a 550m walk uphill, signposted right after the Setbaşı road bridge.

◉ Muradiye

Muradiye Complex   HISTORIC AREA

(Map p290; off Kaplıca Caddesi) This relaxing complex contains a shady park, a cemetery with historic tombs, and the 1426 Sultan Murat II (Muradiye) Camii (Map p290). Imitating Yeşil Camii's painted decorations, the mosque features an intricate *mihrab*.

The cemetery has 12 tombs (Map p290) from the 15th to 16th century, including that of Sultan Murat II (r 1421–51). Although his son, Mehmet II, would capture Constantinople, Murat did all the hard work, annexing territory from enemy states during his reign.

Like other Islamic dynasties, the Ottoman's did not practice primogeniture – any royal son could claim power upon his father's death, which unsurprisingly resulted in numerous bloodbaths. The tombs preserve this macabre legacy: all the *şehzades* (imperial sons) interred here were killed by close relatives. While many tombs are ornate and trimmed with beautiful İznik tiles, others are simple and stark, like that of the ascetic and part-time dervish Murat II.

The 15th-century Muradiye Medresesi (Map p290) was a tuberculosis clinic in the 1950s and still houses a medical centre. The Sultan Murat II Hamamı (Map p290), which catered to the *medrese* students, is now a government building.

Ulumay Museum of Ottoman Folk Costumes & Jewellery   MUSEUM

(Osmanlı Halk Kıyafetleri ve Takıları Müzesi; Map p290; ☑222 7575; off Kaplıca Caddesi; admission ₺5; ☺8.30am-6.30pm Tue-Sun) Originally the Sair Ahmet Paşa *medrese* (1475), the museum exhibits around 70 costumes and over 350 different pieces of jewellery.

Ottoman House Museum   MUSEUM

(Osmanlı Evi Müzesi; Map p290; off Kaplıca Caddesi; ☺8am-noon & 1-5pm Tue-Sun) FREE This restored 17th-century house has a beautiful exterior and a few Ottoman dioramas inside.

Hüsnü Züber Evi   MUSEUM, HISTORIC BUILDING

(Map p290; Uzunyol Sokak 3; admission by donation; ☺10am-noon & 1-5pm Tue-Sun) Uphill behind the Sultan Murat II Hamamı, knock to gain entry to this restored 19th-century Ottoman house. The collection inside includes ornate musical instruments and intricately carved and painted Anatolian wooden spoons. Beyond here lie winding alleys, shops and crumbling Ottoman houses.

◉ Kültür Parkı & Around

North of Muradiye and down the hill, Bursa's leafy Culture Park (Kültür Parkı; Map p290) boasts fine lawns and flowers. Families enjoy its tea gardens, restaurants and playgrounds, and taking bisikleti gezisi (pedal boats; Map p290; ☺per 20 min ₺10) out on the lake.

Archaeology Museum   MUSEUM

(Arkeoloji Müzesi; Map p290; admission ₺5; ☺8am-noon & 1-5pm Tue-Sun) The museum's collection ranges from beautiful Roman pottery and figurines to stone tools and artefacts dating back to the Paleolithic era.

Atatürk House   NOTABLE BUILDING

(Atatürk Evi; Map p290; ☑234 7716; Çekirge Caddesi; ☺8am-noon & 1-7pm Tue-Sun) FREE Across the road from Kültür Parkı, Atatürk House (1895) commemorates the great leader in a pine-scented garden setting. The restored

Muradiye, Kültür Parkı & Around

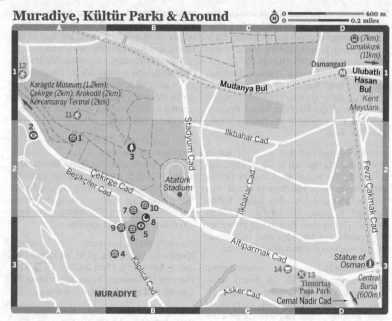

Muradiye, Kültür Parkı & Around

structure contains mostly original furnishings from when Atatürk stayed here in the 1920s and 1930s.

Yeni Kaplıca   HAMAM
(Map p290; ☏ 236 6955; Mudanya Caddesi 10; hamam men/women ₺17/15, massage ₺22; ⊙ 5am–11pm) The 'new thermal bath' is actually the city's oldest, founded by 6th-century emperor Justinian I, and renovated in 1522 by Süleyman the Magnificent's grand vizier, Rüstem Paşa. Here too are the women-only *kaynarca* (boiling) baths, and the family-oriented baths at the neighbouring Karamustafa Hotel. Yeni Kaplıca is west of Kültür Parkı, signposted downhill from Çekirge Caddesi near Atatürk House.

◉ Çekirge

Çekirge, Bursa's spa suburb, is 2km northwest of Kültür Parkı. The warm mineral-rich waters of Uludağ bubble up here and have been valued since ancient times for their curative powers. Hotels here usually have private mineral baths, and independent *kaplıcalar* (thermal baths) exist too.

Murat I (Hüdavendigâr) Camii   MOSQUE
(I Murat Caddesi) The unusual mosque (1366) features a barrel-vaulted Ottoman T-square

design, and includes ground-floor *zaviye* (dervish hostel) rooms. The only visible part of the 2nd-floor facade gallery, originally a *medrese,* is the sultan's *loge* (box), above the mosque's rear.

Sarcophagus of Murat I
TOMB

(İ Murat Caddesi; ⊘ 8am-10pm) Sultan Murat I (r 1359–89), most famous for the Battle of Kosovo that claimed his life, is interred in this huge sarcophagus opposite the mosque. Murat's remains were brought from Kosovo by his son, Bayezit I.

Eski Kaplıca
HAMAM

(☑ 233 9309; Eski Kaplıca Sokak; hamam men/women/children under 12yr ₺35/30/free, scrub ₺20, massage ₺20; ⊘ 7am-10.30pm) The bath is hewn of marble and the hot rooms have plunge pools at this restored 14th-century hamam, run by the adjacent Kervansaray Termal hotel on the eastern side of Çekirge. It also has a private section (two people ₺80).

☞ Tours

Karagöz Travel Agency
TOUR

(Map p286; ☑ 221 8727; www.karagoztravel.com; Eski Aynalı Çarşı; 1-/2-day tours ₺110/290) The English-speaking Uğur runs group tours every weekend, popular with Bursa's Turkish and expat residents. Destinations range from Eskişehir to Turkey's Aegean islands; the program is on the website. Shorter local tours can also be arranged.

✫ Festivals & Events

Uluslararası Bursa Festivali
MUSIC FESTIVAL

(International Bursa Festival; www.bursafestivali.org) Bursa's June/July music and dance festival lasts three weeks, and features diverse regional and world music, plus an international 'star' headliner or two. Free performances are offered and tickets for top acts are around ₺40.

International Golden Karagöz
Folk Dance Competition
DANCE FESTIVAL

In July this dance event sees international groups perform at the open-air theatre in Kültür Parkı.

Karagöz Festival
PUPPETRY FESTIVAL

In November of odd years, this week-long festival hosts performances by Karagöz shadow puppeteers, Western puppeteers and marionette performers.

⌕ Sleeping

⌕ Central Bursa

Despite Bursa's historical sights, the city's hotels cater mainly to business travellers, leading to to high prices. If sensitive to smoke, check the room first. For budget hotels, head to the streets east of Tahtakale Çarşısı.

Otel Çamlıbel
HOTEL €

(Map p286; ☑ 221 2565; İnebey Caddesi 71; s ₺30-40, d & tw ₺60-80; ☎) This central cheapie has seen better days but its en-suite rooms with TV are clean and comfortable. The rooms with shared bathroom are basic, but the taps normally produce hot water and renovations were underway when we visited. The blue-fronted building also contains triples and quadruples.

Safran Otel
BOUTIQUE HOTEL €€

(Map p286; ☑ 224 7216; www.safranotel.com; Kale Sokak 4; s/d/tr ₺100/150/180; ☀☎) The Safran occupies an elegant restored Ottoman house in the historic Tophane district, near the tombs of Osman and Orhan. Although the building includes a Byzantine wall, the 10 rooms are thoroughly modern affairs. Room 5 is spacious with a good street view and room 9 has a large bathroom.

Hotel Çeşmeli
HOTEL €€

(Map p286; ☑ 224 1511; Gümüşçeken Caddesi 6; s/d ₺70/130; ☀☎) Run by women, the 'Fountain' is a good spot for female travellers near the market. Although the rooms are slightly dated, they are spacious and spotlessly clean, the lobby is a pleasant environment for watching Bursa bustle past and the Çeşmeli remains a friendly central option.

Hotel Efehan
BUSINESS HOTEL €€

(Map p286; ☑ 225 2260; www.efehan.com.tr; Gümüşçeken Caddesi 34; s/d ₺60-75, d/tr ₺110/140; ☀@☎) The central Efehan offers good value, good service and fresh standard rooms, including a dozen family-sized options. The top-floor breakfast hall and bar offer good views, but avoid the room up top, which is oddly shaped and poky.

★ Kitap Evi
BOUTIQUE HOTEL €€€

(Map p286; ☑ 225 4160; www.kitapevi.com.tr; Burç Üstü 21; s ₺180-200, d ₺200-225; ☀@) The 'Book House', a former Ottoman residence and book bazaar, is a peaceful haven, tucked inside the citadel battlements far above

WESTERN ANATOLIA BURSA

Bursa's minarets and domes. The 12 eclectic rooms each have their own style (one boasts a marble-lined hamam) and the city seems far away in the courtyard, with its fountain and resident tortoise.

Well-polished wood fixtures and little touches like artwork and stained glass complement the rows of bookshelves and vintage knick-knacks. Minibars and the à la carte restaurant make it a tempting place to while away an evening.

Çekirge

For R&R, try a *kaplıca* hotel in Çekirge (4.5km northwest of Ulu Camii).

★ Marigold Hotel
LUXURY HOTEL, SPA €€€

(☑234 6020; www.marigold.com.tr; I Murat Caddesi 47; s/d incl hamam from €100/130; ❈ 🛜 ≋) Beginning in the lobby, where cleansed-looking couples pad around in towelling robes, Marigold is all about relaxation. A traditional Ottoman hamam set is among the items for sale in the rooms, and the spa features an 85-sq-metre thermal pool. The hotel is a comfortable and restful environment, with a restaurant, bar, patisserie and four-storey atrium climbing to the rooms.

Gönlüferah 1890
LUXURY HOTEL, SPA €€€

(☑232 1890; www.gonluferah.com; I Murat Caddesi; s/d incl 30min hamam from ₺200/270; ❈ 🛜 ≋) Dating from 1890 and a hotel since the early 20th century, the hilltop Gönlüferah has hosted many a famous guest and looks the part, with thick carpets and portraits of Bursa's Ottoman forefathers. Rooms range from standard with city or mountain view to 'Prince' and 'Sultan'.

The standard options are small, particularly their bathrooms, but continue the opulent tone through plush headboard, dangling lights and minibar featuring wine and spirits.

Kervansaray Termal
HOTEL €€€

(☑233 9300; www.kervansarayhotels.com.tr; off Eski Kaplıca Sokak; r without breakfast ₺200; ❈ 🛜 ≋) This chain hotel may have an ugly shell, but it rubs shoulders with the 14th-century Eski Kaplıca (p291), which guests get free entry to. The hotel has multiple restaurants, bars and pools, and comfortable rooms where decorative flourishes and well-stocked minibars raise the game above business-hotel territory.

✗ Eating & Drinking

Bursa is famous for its rich İskender kebap (döner lamb on a bed of crumbled pide, topped with yoghurt, hot tomato sauce and browned butter); also known as the Bursa kebap; and its *kestane şekeri* dessert, fashioned from candied chestnuts and also called *maron glacé*.

Hacıbey Lokantası
ESNAF LOKANTA €

(Map p286; Çelebiler Caddesi 3; mains ₺6-9) Readers recommend this *lokanta* (eatery serving ready-made food) opposite the entrance to Tahtakale Çarşısı. It serves *köfte* and dishes from the bain-marie.

Mahfel
CAFE, ICE CREAM €

(Map p286; Namazgah Caddesi 2; dondurma ₺7; ☺8am-11pm) With a nice shady ravine setting, Bursa's oldest cafe is known for its *dondurma* (ice cream). Order *bir porsiyon* (one portion) to dig into a veritable sundae.

Karadeniz Pide & Kebap Salonu
PIDE, KEBAP €€

(Selvi Sokak 2, Çekirge; lahmacun ₺3.50, mains ₺7-22.50) With photos of bygone Bursa and salmon-pink chairs, this Çekirge favourite serves an impressive selection of pide plus İskender and other kebaps, many available in *dürüm* form (wrapped in flatbread).

★ Kebapçı İskender
KEBAP €€€

(Map p286; Ünlü Caddesi 7; İskender portion ₺22; ☺11am-9pm) This refuge for serious carnivores is famous nationwide – it is where the legendary İskender kebap was created in 1867. The wood-panelled interior with tiled pillars and stained-glass windows is a refined environment for tasting the renowned dish. There is no menu: simply order *bir* (one) or *bir buçuk* (1½) portions.

This is the main branch of a dozen eponymous eateries around Bursa; the branch (Map p286; İc koza Han; İskender kebap portion ₺22; ☺11am-9pm) next to Koza Han has an atmospheric vaulted setting.

Sakarya Caddesi Fish Restaurants
SEAFOOD €€€

(Map p290; off Altıparmak Caddesi; mezes from ₺5, seafood ₺16-35; ☺lunch & dinner) In the former Jewish quarter, about a 10-minute walk from Ulu Camii, cobbled Sakarya Caddesi is a busy lane of fish restaurants. Crowds wander between the alfresco tables, joined by waiters carrying trays of rakı (aniseed brandy) and the occasional accordion-wielding *fasıl* (gypsy music) band.

Of the two-dozen eateries, the best is Arap Şükrü, named after its founder, an Independence War hero whose descendents still run it. If it is full, dining next door will likely be equally enjoyable, but be warned that your bill may be higher than you anticipate; many establishments add a cover charge.

İskender
KEBAP €€€

(Map p286; Atatürk Caddesi 60; İskender portion/child portion ₺21.50/14.75; ☺lunch) This central spot, which claims to have created the İskender kebap, does hearty versions of the local favorite at slightly cheaper prices than rival claimant Kebapçı İskender.

Gren
CAFE

(Map p290; www.grencafe.com; Sakarya Caddesi 46; ☺mains ₺12) Bursa's hip 'photography cafe' hosts exhibitions, workshops and other events matching its antique-camera decor and arty young clientele.

La Bella
BAR

(Map p286; Hocaalizade Caddesi) This relaxed bar has a terrace overlooking the leafy Gök Deresi gorge. It is entered next to Simit Sarayı cafe; look for the sign to Yener Ocakbaşı.

☆ Entertainment

Karabaş-i Veli Kültür Merkezi
CULTURAL

(Mevlâna Cultural Centre; ☎ 222 0385; www.mevlana .org.tr; Çardak Sokak 2; ☺winter 8.30pm, summer 9.30pm) FREE For about an hour every night, sit in the tea garden and watch the şeyh (master dervish) lead his students through a sema (ceremony)in this 600-year-old tekke (dervish lodge). Saturday night is a major event.

🛍 Shopping

Bursa's massive market system runs underground, overground and all around, hawking everything from fish and veg to sharp suits, home appliances and veritable mountains of silver and gold. Look out for the popular local sweet candied chestnuts, kestane şekeri.

Bali Bey Han
HANDICRAFTS

(Map p286; Cemal Nadir Caddesi) This 15th-century Ottoman caravanserai houses handicraft shops.

ℹ Information

Post office, phones and ATMs are on Atatürk Caddesi; for exchange offices visit the Kapalı Çarşı.
Tourist Office (Map p286; ☎ 220 1848; Atatürk Caddesi; ☺8am-noon & 1-5pm Mon-

BURSA SILK

Bursa's ancient *ipek* (silk) tradition is owed to both local production and the city's position on the Silk Road, which brought Chinese and Persian silk to Europe via Anatolia. Today, silk is Bursa's prime local handicraft, produced by 23 local villages. Some villagers still cultivate silkworms, buying them each April from cooperatives and letting them gorge themselves on mulberry leaves back home. The precious white cocoons spun by the worms used to be sold at Koza Han, and silkworm breeders could be seen haggling over huge sacks of cocoons, but this practice has died out.

Koza Han (p287) is still a good place to pick up silk scarves and other garments, as are boutiques around the Kapalı Çarşı. Ensure that you're buying real silk (which doesn't come cheap), not an inferior synthetic product.

Fri, 8am-12.30pm & 1.30-6pm Sat & Sun) Not particularly helpful and little English is spoken.

Bursa is heavily built-up and crowded. With its constant traffic, *tek yön* (one-way) roads and lack of street lights, it can seem bewildering. Cross Atatürk Caddesi by the *alt geçidi* (pedestrian underpasses). People with disabilities can use the lift at Atatürk Alt Geçidi (the underpass nearest to Heykel) – the nearby florist has the key.

ℹ Getting There & Away

Travelling to/from İstanbul, the metro-bus-ferry combo via Mudanya is fastest. Ferries also link İstanbul to Yalova. Otherwise, the *karayolu ile* (by road) buses turn and wind around the Bay of İzmit (four to five hours). Better are those designated *feribot ile* ('by ferry'), which take the ferry from Topçular, east of Yalova, to Eskihisar.

AIR

There are flights between Bursa's **Yenişehir Airport** (www.yenisehir.dhmi.gov.tr) and Adana, Ankara, Düsseldorf (Germany) and Northern Cyprus. See the website for further details.

BUS

Bursa's *terminal* (otogar; bus station) is 10km north of the centre on the Yalova road. The table on p294 has bus route and fare information. Bus-company offices are found throughout the centre, including next to Çakır Ağa Hamamı.

ℹ Getting Around

Visit www.burulas.com.tr for more on transport in and around Bursa.

TO/FROM THE BUS STATION

Centre Bus 38 (₺2.50, one hour). To the otogar, wait at the stop on Atatürk Caddesi opposite the *eski belediye* (old town hall). Taxi ₺30.
Çekirge Bus 96 (₺2.50, one hour). Taxi ₺35.

BUS

City buses have their destinations and stops visible. A short journey costs ₺2, a long journey ₺2.50. The buses are prepay – buy single or multi-use tickets from kiosks or shops near most bus stops (look for the BuKART sign). Stops line Atatürk Caddesi opposite Koza Parkı and the *eski belediye*. Bus 1C is useful, following a similar circuit to the dolmuş route described below.

DOLMUŞ

Taxi dolmuşes, their destinations indicated by an illuminated rooftop sign, are cheaper than buses (short journey ₺1.75, long ₺2), and faster and more frequent, especially to Çekirge. The most useful route around the city centre runs anticlockwise from Heykel up İnönü Caddesi to Kent Meydanı, Atatürk Stadium and along Çekirge Caddesi to Çekirge, returning by the same road and Altıparmak, Cemal Nadir and Atatürk Caddesis to Heykel. Drivers pick up and drop off all along the route. There is also a rank on the eastern side of the Setbaşı road bridge, from where taxi dolmuşes follow a similar route to Çekirge.

METRO

The metro (₺2.50) runs every eight to 12 minutes between 6am and midnight. The closest station to the city centre is Şehreküstü, near the Kapalı Çarşı.

TAXI

Taxis start with ₺2.50 on the meter and charge about ₺2 per kilometre. Heykel to Muradiye is about ₺12; to Çekirge ₺15.

TRAM

Red trams follow a similar route to taxi dolmuşes, from Heykel to Kent Meydanı, Atatürk Stadium and back. They are cheap (short journey ₺0.75, long ₺1.50) but slow. Buy tickets before boarding from BuKART kiosks near stations.

Around Bursa

Mudanya

☏ 0224 / POP 56,153

Mudanya is a lively seaside town most known for its İstanbul ferry. Strategically set on the Sea of Marmara, it is where the Armistice of Moudania was signed by Italy, France, Britain and Turkey on 11 October 1922 (Greece reluctantly signed three days later). Under it, all lands from Edirne eastward, including İstanbul and the Dardanelles, became Turkish. The whitewashed 19th-century house where the treaty was signed houses a **museum** (Mudanya Armistice House Museum; Mütareke Meydanı; ⏰ 8am-5pm Tue-Sun) of historic Armistice-related photos.

🛏 Sleeping & Eating

West of the museum, fish restaurants line the waterfront in the attractive Ottoman quarter.

La Fontaine BOUTIQUE HOTEL ₤₤
(☏ 543 1041; www.lafontaineotel.com.tr; Fevzipaşa Caddesi 36; s/d ₺80/140; ✳🌐) Its hotchpotch of vintage decor borders on kitsch, but the 'Fountain' is right in the old town, offering plain but spacious rooms in two renovated

SERVICES FROM BURSA'S OTOGAR

DESTINATION	FARE (₺)	DURATION (HR)	DISTANCE (KM)	FREQUENCY
Afyon	35	5	290	several daily
Ankara	45	6½	400	hourly
Bandırma	15	2	115	hourly
Çanakkale	40	5	310	hourly
Denizli	60	9	532	daily
Eskişehir	24	2½	155	hourly
İstanbul	29	3	230	hourly
İzmir	40	5½	375	hourly
Kütahya	24	3	190	several daily
Yalova	12	1¼	76	several daily

Ottoman buildings. The friendly proprietors have another property in the neighbouring fishing village of Güzelyalı.

(☑554 6464; www.esmanbutikotel.com; Mustafa Kemalpaşa Caddesi 24; s/d ₺75/150; 🕲🛜) Behind its turquoise facade with gold trim, the colour schemes in the Esman's 25 modern rooms will not be to everyone's taste, for example a pink headboard against a maroon wall. Nonetheless, it is a restful place with exposed wooden floors, a whitewashed reception and a courtyard cafe.

★ Montania   LUXURY HOTEL **€€€**
(☑544 6000; www.montaniahotel.com; İstasyon Caddesi; s/d ₺125/200; 🕲🛜🏊) Mudanya's most famous hotel occupies a French-built railway building dating to 1849, with views of the boats sailing in and out of the neighbouring ferry terminal. Rooms are split between this gorgeously renovated building and a new block, where you lose the historical character.

The restaurant, offering live Turkish music on Wednesdays and Saturdays, and the bar with train-carriage seating make good use of the older structure. Daily tours are offered to Bursa and beyond.

Coffee Shot   CAFE **€€**
(Mütareke Meydanı; mains ₺10-14) To a soundtrack of sunshine soul, the cool Başa and team serve *tost* (toasted sandwich), *mantı* (Turkish ravioli), burgers and myriad coffees and sweat treats.

ⓘ Getting There & Away

Regular **BUDO** (http://budo.burulas.com.tr) ferries link İstanbul Kabataş with Mudanya (₺22, two hours). Yellow bus 1M runs from Mudanya ferry terminal to Bursa's Emek metro station (₺3, half-hourly) and bus F1 to Bursa's *terminal* (otogar; ₺3, hourly). From Bursa to Mudanya ferry terminal, take the metro to Organize Sanayi and catch the dolmuş (₺2.75, frequent). BUDO also operates a summer Mudanya–Tekirdağ service.

Daily **İDO** (www.ido.com) ferries (more at weekends) link İstanbul Yenikapı and Kadıköy with Güzelyalı (₺28, 2¼ hours), 4km east of Mudanya ferry terminal. Regular buses connect Güzelyalı with Bursa metro.

Uludağ

☑0224
Close to Bursa and İstanbul, Uludağ (Great Mountain; 2543m) is Turkey's favourite ski resort. The resort is 33km from Bursa, but the *teleferik* (cable car) offers a short and scenic ascent to Sarıalan village (1635m), 6km by road from the resort (1865m) and its chain hotels. In summer, come for the views and clean, cool air; the resort is dead outside the December–March ski season, but chairlifts operate and paths climb the wooded slopes. Hiking routes lead to volcanic lakes on the upper slopes, but the paths are not well marked or maintained so you will need a guide or a good map and orienteering experience. Sarıalan is good for a picnic and a stroll, with quiet paths and roads winding through the trees around the village. Picnic sites and teahouses line the road up from Bursa.

Skiing and snowboarding here cost a little over ₺100 a day (lift pass about ₺70 and equipment hire about ₺40). Ski-season accommodation options are listed at www.skiingturkey.com; chains such as Kervansaray cater to an increasingly international crowd.

If simply seeking a city break in cooler climes, head 7km from Bursa toward the mountain, to İnkaya village and its celebrated 600-year-old *çınar* (plane tree) – its wildly curving, thick branches are supported partly by sturdy metal braces. Enjoy çay, snacks and views at the İnkaya Tarihi Çınaraltı Çay Bahçesi (gözleme ₺4) under the abundant foliage. Bursa bus 1C runs to the village hourly from Atatürk Caddesi via Heykel and Çekirge Caddesi (₺2.50); a taxi costs ₺20 (₺30 return).

ⓘ Getting There & Away

Teleferik Dolmuşes run from Heykel to the lower *teleferik* station (₺2, 15 minutes). Cable cars (₺20 return, 10 minutes) depart every 40 minutes between 8am and 10pm in summer and between 10am and 5pm in winter, wind and weather permitting. In season, they go whenever they fill up (30 people). The *teleferik* stops at Kadıyayla, then continues to Sarıalan, from where dolmuşes run to the ski resort (₺5).

There are plans to extend the *teleferik* to the resort in the coming years, and to move the lower station to Bursa's Setbaşı neighbourhood.

Road Dolmuşes (₺12, one hour) run several times daily in summer (more frequently in winter) from Tophane to the ski resort via Kadıyayla and Sarıalan. Taxis from Tophane cost about ₺100; in winter you will likely find someone to share the ride with or be able to haggle the price down. At the Uludağ National Park gate, 11km from the resort, motorists must pay ₺10 to enter the park.

Eskişehir

📞 0222 / POP 648,396

Eskişehir may well be Turkey's happiest city – and with a massive university population, it is certainly among its liveliest. An oasis of liberalism in austere middle Anatolia, Eskişehir is increasingly popular with Turkish weekenders, and even boasts a small community of dedicated foreigners.

Eskişehir's progressive spirit is associated with mayor Yılmaz Büyükerşen, who realised the potential of the city's Porsuk River, adding walking bridges and a sand beach, while building pedestrian thoroughfares and a smoothly efficient tram system. (In summer, you can even explore the Porsuk by gondola or boat.)

The cumulative result is Turkey's most liveable city, and a place where you can engage with the friendly and open-minded locals. With an atmospheric old quarter, roaring nightlife, cultivated cuisine, two parks and a brand-new science centre for kids, Eskişehir truly has much on offer.

History

Although regional relics date to Palaeolithic times, traces of Eskişehir's first settlements date to the Bronze Age (3000–2000 BC). Hittites came, and later Phrygians, making it an important base until the 7th-century-BC Cimmerian conquest. Alexander the Great later captured the town; subsequently a Hellenistic, Roman and Byzantine city, it was known by the Greek name Dorylaion. The 6th-century emperor Justinian had a summer palace here, and Dorylaion flourished as a bishopric.

Dorylaion's strategic location along military routes was tested by marauding Arabs in the 8th century and later by Seljuk expansion across Anatolia. In the Battle of Dorylaion (1097), Crusaders defeated Seljuk forces, but revenge was exacted in 1147. Dorylaion's continued importance as a garrison continued under the Ottomans, its fortress being referenced in records of sultans like Mehmet II and Süleyman the Magnificent. The modern name Eskişehir ('old city') – also found in historical texts as Eskihisar ('old castle') – refers to the ruined Dorylaion castle (in today's Şarhöyük suburb).

Modern Eskişehir's formative developments began with the arrival of Crimean Tatars and Caucasus natives, diversifying the population in the late 19th century. The Istanbul railroad's completion in 1892, and the later development of factories and trade, invigorated the economy. Locals are proud of their ancestors' role in the War of Independence, with important battles fought nearby. Their resolute stance toward wartime occcupiers (mostly the Greeks and Brits) was often praised by Atatürk when he visited.

⊙ Sights & Activities

New attractions have increased Eskişehir's appeal to everyone from kids to history buffs. Statues around town celebrate the city's stint as 'cultural capital of the Turkic world' for 2013; the turban-wrapped chap they show is Nasreddin Hodja, the 13th-century philosopher and humanist who lived here.

Odunpazarı　　　　　　　　　HISTORIC AREA
(Ottoman Quarter) Eskişehir's protected heritage district is a real aesthetic treat. Elegant, pastel-shaded traditional homes with distinctive overhanging stories and wood-framed shutters stand on narrow stone lanes, along with mosques and other historic structures. Many of the houses contain museums and cafes, while craftwork and vintage stalls dot the lanes. This was Eskişehir's first Turkish district, and it features Ottoman and even Seljuk structures. *Odun* means 'firewood' (the area was once a firewood bazaar).

Kurşunlu Külliyesi Complex　　HISTORIC AREA
(Mücellit Sok, Odunpazarı; ⊙8am-10pm) This sublime old-town complex was built between 1517 and 1525 by a leading master of classical Ottoman architecture, Acem Ali, though internal structures were built and rebuilt in following centuries.

Behind the 1492 **Kurşunlu Mosque** with its *kurşunlu* (leaden) dome, the **medrese** houses the **Museum of Meerschaum** (⊙8am-5pm) **FREE**, which pays homage to the region's weird and wonderful white rock, in its artistically crafted form. There are some particularly elaborate pipes on display and a handicrafts bazaar.

Next to the *medrese,* the four-domed **tabhane** (guesthouse) may also have been a harem. The vaulted **imaret** (almshouse) and adjacent, domed **aşevi** (kitchen), which respectively house glassblowing and jewellery studios, were the culinary quarters. The dining hall, kitchen and alcoved oven partly remain. The Ottoman **caravanserai,** built after 1529, is a cultural centre used for weddings.

Atlıhan Complex   MARKET, HISTORIC BUILDING
(Pazaroğlu Sokak 8, Odunpazarı; ⏰9am-8pm) Eskişehir is famous for its 'white gold', or *meerschaum* (*luletaşı* in Turkish), a light, porous white stone, mined locally and shaped into pipes and other objects. The Atlıhan Complex hosts two floors of local artisans' shops and a cafe. On the 1st floor, Mavi Sanat Merkezi (Atlıhan Complex 10) has some unusual and beautiful ceramics and jewellery.

City Museum   MUSEUM
(Kent Müzesi; Türkmen Hoca Sokak 45, Odunpazarı; ⏰10am-7pm Tue-Sun) FREE Included in this collection is Eskişehir's Museum of Contemporary Glass Art, a unique display donated by about 70 Turkish and foreign artists. The tradition of melting and fusing glass dates to the Pharaohs, and a local Egyptologist (and university professor) revived the art and opened a studio in Eskişehir. The 1st floor details local history through informative panels and interactive screens.

Osmanlı Evi   NOTABLE BUILDING, MUSEUM
(Ottoman House; Yeşil Efendi Sokak 22, Odunpazarı; admission ₺1; ⏰8.30am-7.30pm Tue-Sun) This renovated former inn opened in 1890 and Atatürk stayed here in 1920, during his military campaigning. The cafe serves traditional Turkish food.

Museum of the Republican History   MUSEUM
(Cumhuriyet Müzesi; Atatürk Bulvarı 11, Odunpazarı; ⏰8.30am-4pm Mon-Fri, 9am-5pm Sat) FREE This museum celebrates Atatürk and the Turkish Republic through hundreds of photos, paintings and collages covering seminal events like the battles of Gallipoli, Sakarya and Dumlupınar. Models of Turkish WWI warships are displayed, as are over 50 portraits of Atatürk, and visitors can watch an Atatürk documentary. The imposing building itself (built 1915) reflects the mores of contemporaneous Western European structures, and remains a striking example of Turkey's First National Period of architecture.

Archaeological Museum   MUSEUM
(Atatürk Bulvarı; admission ₺10; ⏰8am-6.30pm Tue-Sun) This modern museum showcases prehistoric artefacts, items from Hittite, Phyrygian and Classical Antiquity, including goddess figurines, floor mosaics and sarcophagi, plus many Greek, Byzantine and Ottoman coins. It has a good cafe (off Atatürk Bulvarı; mains ₺13-23) overlooking the statuary dotting the garden.

Sazova Park   PARK
(Küthaya Yolu) West of the centre on the Küthaya road, this area of cleared *sazova* (cane field) has been turned into a family-friendly paradise of fresh air and rolling lawns. The themepark-worthy attractions include a fairy-tale castle complete with staff in medieval garb, a pirate ship, a dinky open train, and playgrounds with bouncy castles, mushroom playhouses and huge dinosaur slides.

A planetarium, aquarium and zoo are also found here, as are plentiful picnic sites, tea gardens and ice-cream stands. A taxi from the centre costs ₺10 or so.

Eskişehir Science and
Experiment Centre   SCIENCE CENTRE
(Eskişehir Bilim Deney Merkezi; ☑444 8236; www. eskisehirbilimdeneymerkezi.com; Sazova Park, Küthaya Yolu; adult/student ₺2/1; ⏰10am-5pm Tue-Sun) Like a cross between a science centre and a fairground, this colourful and hugely entertaining complex illustrates the many forces of nature through hands-on experiments. Interactive classics such as the oh-so-scary infinity bridge, the fountain-triggering xylophone and the counterweighted car get visitors pulling, pushing and pedalling. Free guided tours are available.

Kent Park   PARK
(Borsa Caddesi) On the tram line near the otogar, beautiful 'City Park' is a civic masterpiece full of enticing sights and activities. The artificial sandy beach is packed in summer; there is a horse-riding enclosure (₺10 per ride) and gondola rides on the river (₺10 per boat); and paths perfect for a romantic stroll exemplify Eskişehir's chosen path as Turkey's 'Aşk-şehir' (City of Love).

⚡ Festivals & Events

Each October/November, the International Eskişehir Festival brings numerous Turkish and foreign artists, musicians and performers for nine days of concerts, exhibitions and plays.

🛏 Sleeping

Most of the following sleeping, eating, drinking and entertainment recommendations are found between the river and Anadolu University's Yunus Emre campus, walking distance from İsmet İnönü and Bağlar tram stops.

Book ahead if possible, especially at weekends, when Anatolian short-breakers hit town and some hotels hike prices.

Hosteleski
HOSTEL €

(☑220 7063; www.hosteleski.com; Yıldırımer Sokak 27/1; dm/s/d & tw without breakfast €10/15/24; ☎) Hosteleski offers all the backpacker essentials on three floors of a tall, thin building: kitchen, terrace, lounge, laundry service, bike garage and movie nights. The friendly English-speaking owners Çağrı (aka Charlie) and Deniz are happy to help and give recommendations. The two dorms, one female-only, and two private rooms share two bathrooms.

For breakfast, there is a bakery nearby on Cengiz Topel Caddesi.

★Abacı Konak Otel
HISTORIC HOTEL €€€

(☑333 0333; www.abaciotel.com; Türkmen Hoca Sokak 29; s/d ₺180/260; ❀☎) With pastel heritage homes clustered around a flowering, fountained courtyard, staying at Abacı Konak is like having your own personal Ottoman quarter. Being in Odunpazarı, it is legally a heritage site, so nothing can be changed – the vintage furnishings, wood floors and ceilings are all original, and the tasteful, subdued decor matches.

Book ahead – the hotel is popular with Turkish groups (especially on weekends). The closest tram stop is Atatürk Lisesi.

Grand Namlı Otel
HOTEL €€€

(☑322 1515; www.namliotel.com.tr; Üniversite Caddesi 14; s/d ₺149/189; ❀☎) Rising seven storeys from its ground-floor deli restaurant, the plush and friendly Grand Namlı has spacious modern rooms with expansive wardrobes and dry minibars.

Ibis Hotel
BUSINESS HOTEL €€€

(☑211 7700; www.ibishotel.com; Siloönü Sokak 5; r week/weekend ₺159/209; ❀☎) Resembling a salmon-coloured Flatiron Building, the Ibis has six floors of rooms featuring glass-fronted minibars, safes and light wooden furniture. Bathrooms are older and plainer, but overall the feel is smoother than the saxaphone-shaped beer tap in the muzak-infused bar.

✖ Eating & Drinking

Eskişehir's vast and varied restaurant and bar scene caters to its diverse community of locals, university students and expats. Cheap eats abound, with numerous snack bars tempting the students with kebaps and meal deals.

Önür Işkembe
SOUP €

(Cengis Topel Caddesi; soup ₺4-10) Eskişehir's students stagger here from nearby Barlar Sokak to chase the Efes with a bowl of *ışkembe çorba* (tripe soup). *Mercimek* (lentil) and *Kelle Paça* (sheep's head and trotters) soups are also offered, overlooked by photos of offal-loving Turkish celebrities' visits.

★Memphis
INTERNATIONAL, PUB €€

(☑320 3005; www.varunamemphis.com; İsmet İnönü Caddesi 102/C; mains ₺11-24) Exposed brick, wine racks, wall-to-floor windows and cool artwork give Memphis the feel of a craft brewery, and its draught beer selection indeed extends beyond regular Efes to Efes Malt and uber-cold Efes Şok Soğuk. The food is good too, mixing Turkish flavours with international dishes from pizza and pasta to quesadillas and fajitas; the steak burger is recommended.

On Friday nights, tables are hotter property than a Cappadocian fairy chimney with a sea view.

Dünya Köfte
KÖFTE, GRILL €€

(Üniversite Caddesi; mains ₺8-11) Just past Bağlar tram stop, this butcher's doubles as a smart restaurant selling delicious *köfte* at palatable prices. To sample different types of *köfte,* order a *karışık* (mixed) plate.

★Cafe Del Mundo
INTERNATIONAL, PUB €€€

(www.delmundocafe.com; Siloönü Sokak 3; mains ₺14-30; ⊙11am-1am Mon-Fri, 8am-1am Sat & Sun) This cosy and colourful bar – created by travellers, for travellers – is the friendliest spot in town. The cheery yellow building near Barlar Sokak is splendidly decorated with assorted international memorabilia (licence plates, tickets, travel books, many billowing flags) and, continuing the global theme, dishes from Pad Thai to pesto fusilli are available.

The three levels of bars fill by night with merry students and foreigners. Happy hour is noon to 5pm daily, quiz night is on Sunday and your second cocktail is free from 5pm to 9pm on weekdays.

Passage
INTERNATIONAL, PATISSERIE €€€

(www.eskisehirpassage.com; Kızılcıklı Mahmut Pehlivan Caddesi 15/B; mains ₺10-27) Popular for a weekend brunch, this spacious place offers everything from coffees and rich cakes to wraps, big salads, pastas and contemporary Turkish flavours. There's an open kitchen where the chefs are on display – join them for special chocolate-making courses.

This end of Kızılcıklı Mahmut Pehlivan Caddesi, near the İsmet İnönü tram stop, is good for bistros and upmarket eateries.

Barlar Sokak BAR
(Bar St; Vural Sokak) Cocktail bars, shot bars, theme bars, DJ bars, *meyhanes* (Turkish taverns), clubs and venues all jostle for attention on this well-oiled lane, along with the odd *kebapçı* (kebap eatery) to soak up the Efes. It has a more Turkish flavour than its equivalents in Bodrum and Marmaris, with more rakı, melon slices, *fasıl* bands and good-looking students in evidence than lobster-coloured louts.

Haller Gençlik Merkezi'nde CAFE, NARGILE CAFE
(Youth Centre; Üniversite Caddesi) In this restored 1930s building, cafes serve *mantı* (Turkish ravioli), *kumpir* (baked potatoes) and caffeinated sustenance, facing shops selling everything from souvenirs to body-building supplements. With exposed brick walls and an inviting smell of coffee, Kahve Evi is a mellow spot where Illy cappuccinos come with a fairy chimney of foam.

☆ Entertainment

Peyote LIVE MUSIC, DJ
(www.peyote.com.tr; Vural Sokak) This venue on Barlar Sokak hosts local acts from across the musical spectrum, including rock, metal, jazz, hip-hop and acoustic. Shows start around 11pm on Friday and Saturday and cost about ₺10; grab a drink beforehand in the adjoining courtayard.

222 Park CLUB
(www.222park.com; İsmet İnönü Caddesi 103) Housed in an enormous former wood factory, 222 (as pronounced in English) is Eskişehir's party colosseum, with a nightclub, live stage, and sundry cafes, restaurants and summer wine terrace. The owners run a tight ship, so under-18s can't enter the nightclub section, where entry is ₺30 (₺20 with a student card). It's across from the Espark shopping mall.

Eskişehir Municipal Symphony Orchestra MUSIC
(☎ 211 5500; www.eskisehir-bld.gov.tr/eng/eskisehir _kultur.php; Büyükşehir Belediye Sanat ve Kültür Sarayı/Opera Binası, İsmail Gaspıralı Caddesi 1) Since picking up its baton in 2002, Eskişehir's symphony orchestra has become one of Turkey's best, and now offers weekly concerts for an enthusiastic local audience. It also provides backup for operas and ballets. Works performed here run the gamut from classical masters to modern musicals, plus kids' shows. The orchestra tours widely abroad and cooperates with visiting musicians too.

ℹ Information

Helpful city maps are freely available at the bus and train stations and in many hotels.
Tourist Office (☎ 230 1368; İki Eylül Caddesi) Little English spoken, but helpful and maps and brochures are available. In the Valilik (regional government) building.

ℹ Getting There & Away

The train station is northwest of the centre near İsmet İnönü tram stop; the otogar is 3km east.

Regular buses serve Afyon (₺20, three hours), Ankara (₺40, 3¼ hours), Bursa (₺20, 2½ hours), İstanbul (₺30, six hours) and Kütahya (₺10, 1½ hours). *Servises* (free shuttles) and trams link the centre and otogar. A taxi from the centre costs ₺10 or so.

Trains run to/from Ankara (₺27.50, 1½ hours, several daily), Konya (₺36.25, two hours, two daily), İzmir (₺34, 11 hours, nightly) and İstanbul Pendik (₺45, 2½ hours, six daily) among other destinations.

ℹ Getting Around

Prepaid tickets (₺2) are used for most public transport; buy from a booth or kiosk with the green-and-yellow circular Es Karti sign. Dolmuş journeys cost ₺1.75 and you pay the driver.

Trams on the ESTram network run between 6am and midnight; the normal waiting time is about seven minutes. Trams display their final destination at the front, but it can still be confusing to identify which tram is which at certain crossover stops, so ask if unsure.

Taxis are plentiful, and there are electronic signal buttons on some street corner posts that you can press to hail one.

Phrygian Valley

Anatolia's mysterious Phrygians once inhabited this rock-hewn valley (Frig Vadisi), which runs haphazardly past Eskişehir, Kütahya and Afyon. It's an increasingly popular hiking destination, but is still relatively untouched and offers spectacular Phrygian relics. The rugged terrain is exhilarating and highly photogenic. The Afyon-area ruins are the best preserved, and the Eskişehir-area ruins also impress, but Kütahya's are less abundant.

For all things Phrygian, check out Phrygian Way Project (www.frigyolu.com) and Culture Routes in Turkey (cultureroutesinturkey.com), which have information on Phrygian history and hiking options. Various free brochures and maps are also available in local tourist offices. Hüseyin Sarı's Phrygian Way guidebook, available on Amazon, details the 506km hiking trail his team waymarked – making Western Anatolia's answer to Cappadocia accessible at last.

◉ Sights

◉ Eskişehir Ruins

Through Yazılıkaya Vadisi (Inscribed Rock Valley), heading from Seyitgazi to Afyon, turn south after 3km down the road marked with a brown sign pointing to Midas Şehri. Further along this rough road a sign leads right 2km to the Doğankale (Falcon Castle) and Deveboyukale (Camel-Height Castle), both riddled with formerly inhabited caves.

Further south, another rough track leads 1km to the Mezar Anıtı (Monumental Tomb), and a restored, rock-carved tomb. Continuing south, you will find another temple-like tomb, Küçük Yazılıkaya (Little Inscribed Rock).

Midas Şehri (Midas City) is at Yazılıkaya village, several kilometres from Küçük Yazılıkaya and 32km south of Seyitgazi. The Midas Türbe (Midas Tomb) is a 17m-high relief carved into volcanic tufa, and covered in geometric patterns resembling a temple facade. During festivals, an effigy of Cybele was displayed in the bottom niche. Phrygian-alphabet inscriptions – one bearing Midas' name – circle the tomb.

A path behind the tomb leading to a tunnel passes a smaller tomb, unfinished and high in the rock. Continue upwards to the high mound, where an acropolis stood. The stepped altar stone, possibly used for sacrifices, remains along with traces of walls and roads. Interestingly, the first evidence of water collection comes from here – carved holes with slatted steps that trapped rainwater for the dry season.

◉ Afyon Ruins

The Afyon-area ruins include examples from Phrygian up to Turkish times. Doğer village's han (caravanserai) dates from 1434 (if it is locked, ask for the key at the municipal building opposite). From here, dirt tracks lead to lily-covered Emre Gölü (Lake Emre), overlooked by a small building once used by dervishes, and a rock formation with a rough staircase, the Kirkmerdiven Kayalıkları (Rocky Place with 40 Stairs). The track continues 4km to Bayramaliler and Üçlerkayası, with rock formations called peribacalar (fairy chimneys), resembling Cappadocia's.

After Bayramaliler, Göynüş Vadisi (Göynüş Valley) is a 2km walk from the Eskişehir–Afyon road, with fine Phrygian rock tombs decorated with lions.

At Ayazini village there once stood a rock settlement, Metropolis, also reminiscent of Cappadocia. The apse and dome of its Byzantine church are hewn from the rock face, and several rock-cut tombs have carvings of lions, suns and moons.

Around Alanyurt, east of Ayazini, more caves exist at Selimiye; and there are more fairy chimneys at Kurtyurdu, Karakaya, Seydiler and İscehisar, including the bunker-like rock Seydiler Kalesi (Seydiler Castle).

PHRYGIANS

A mysterious Thracian tribe arriving in Anatolia around 2000 BC, the Phrygians spoke an Indo-European language, used a Greek alphabet, and ruled from Gordion, 100km southwest of Ankara and a starting point of the Phrygian Way. The Phrygians dominated during the 8th and 7th centuries BC, under the royal lineages of Midas and Gordias, and their culture continued under Cimmerian and Lydian overlords.

When hearing the word 'Phrygian', music lovers today might think of modal jazz, and indeed this mysterious ancient tribe reportedly invented numerous instruments, like the double clarinet, flute, lyre, syrinx (Pan pipes), triangle and cymbals. No doubt the caves in which these Greek- and Hittite-influenced people lived had great acoustics to test them in.

Phrygian civilisation peaked around 585 to 550 BC, when the rock-cut monuments at Midas Şehri – the most impressive surviving Phrygian stonework – were carved. Phrygian relics in museums provide fascinating insights into a lost culture that transformed Anatolia and the Aegean.

☞ Tours

In Afyon and Eskişehir respectively, travel agents Ceba Tour (☑ 0272-213 2715, 0506 437 6969; cebaturizm@gmail.com; Alparslan Türkeş Bulvarı C/2 Erçelik Sitesi, Afyon; half-day tours 1/2/3 people €60/100/150) and Ufuk Özkarabey (☑ 0222-220 0808, 0532 765 2540; Cengiz Topel Caddesi 42/E, Eskişehir) offer day trips. Agencies in towns such as Pamukkale and Selçuk also offer excursions.

ℹ Getting There & Around

The easiest way to explore the ruins is by rental car; try Europcar (☑ 0222-231 0182; www.europcar.com.tr; Kızılcıklı Mahmut Pehlivan Caddesi 22/B; 1/3 days from ₺111/315) in Eskişehir and Lider (☑ 0272-215 7122, 0532 633 5649; Süleyman Gonçer Caddesi 2; 1/2 days from ₺120/220) in Afyon. Between October and April, heavy rain sometimes renders the area's back roads impassable.

Visiting the ruins by public transport is difficult, but there are dolmuşes to the villages from Afyon otogar. Regular buses and dolmuşes on the main roads between Eskişehir, Kütahya and Afyon will also pick up from the roadside, so if you start early, it may be possible to visit a few sites in a day.

From Afyon, dolmuşes serve Ayazini (on the Afyon–Eskişehir road). From the church drop-off, walk 500m for Metropolis. To continue to Doğer, take the dolmuş back towards Afyon, but disembark at Gazlıgöl and pick up a dolmuş heading northwest.

Kütahya

☑ 0274 / POP 224,898

The industrialised city of Kütahya has Phrygian roots, though it is most unique historically as the bygone capital of the Germiyan Emirate (1302–1428), before it was swallowed up by the Ottoman Empire. There are historical attractions on its central pedestrianised boulevards, but little else, making Kütahya better for a day trip than an overnight stay.

Kütahya's association with industrial porcelain and tile production dates to the capture of Tabriz in 1514, when Selim I relocated its tile-making artisans to Kütahya and İznik. Shops around town sell tiles and ceramics, and the August Dumlupınar handicrafts fair is worth seeing.

◉ Sights & Activities

Zafer (Belediye) Meydanı, Kütahya's main square, is marked by a huge, vase-shaped fountain and overlooked by the *vilayet* (provincial government building) and *belediye* (town hall). Running southwest is pedestrianised thoroughfare Cumhuriyet Caddesi, which continues past Dönenler Cami to Ulu Cami (1410).

Tile Museum
MUSEUM

(Çini Müzesi; ☑ 223 6990; admission ₺5; ⊙ 8.45am-12.30pm & 1.30-7pm Tue-Sun) Behind Ulu Cami, the (non-working) İmaret Cami showcases Kütahya's kiln-fired past, with pottery including large jugs and plates by masters like Hacı Hafiz Mehmet Emin Efendi (who worked on İstanbul's Haydarpaşa station), plus İznik tiles and local embroidery. The 14th-century, blue-tiled tomb of Yakup Bey (r 139–1409), one of the Germanid Sultanate's last leaders, is also here.

Archaeology Museum
MUSEUM

(Arkeoloji Müzesi; admission ₺5; ⊙ 8.45am-12.30pm & 1.30-7pm Tue-Sun) Beside Ulu Cami in the Vacidiye Medresesi (1314), this museum exhibits Phrygian Valley finds including Roman votive stelae, plus a masterpiece Roman sarcophagus from Aizanoi's Temple of Zeus, carved with scenes of battling Amazons. The structure was built by Umur bin Savcı of the Germiyan clan.

Dönenler Cami
MOSQUE

Behind the mechanical rotating dervish statue, the Dönenler Cami was built in the 14th century and later used as a *mevlevihane* (home to a Mevlevi dervish group). It evokes the Seljuk past with its galleried *semahane* (hall where Sufi ceremonies are held) with paintings of tall Mevlevi hats on the columns.

Kossuth House
HISTORIC BUILDING

(Macar Evi; ⊙ 8.45am-12.30pm & 1.30-7pm Tue-Sun) FREE From the Tile Museum, follow the signs through the backstreets, past Ottoman houses in various states of decay, and turn right after the geology museum to reach this unlikely and incongruous sight. The stately whitewashed Ottoman building once housed dissident Hungarian parliamentarian Lajos Kossuth (1802–94), and the house exemplifies upper-class Kütahyan life in the mid-19th century. Along with period furnishings, costumes and weaponry, there are two floors of verandahs overlooking a rose garden and statue of Kossuth.

After demanding independence from the Austrian-dominated Hapsburg Empire, Kossuth and others were expelled; he spent a year here (1850–51) before continuing his exile in the UK, USA and Italy.

WESTERN ANATOLIA KÜTAHYA

Kütahya Fortress
CASTLE

FREE Looming over Kütahya, this originally 8th-century Byzantine fortress was restored by the Seljuks, the Germiyan emirs and the Ottomans between the 13th and 15th centuries. Dozens of round tower ruins indicate its former strength. It is a long uphill walk, or a taxi costs ₺15; afterwards take the steep path down to Ulu Cami.

🛏 Sleeping

Qtahya Otel
BUSINESS HOTEL ₺₺

(📞 226 2010; www.q-tahya.com; Atatürk Bulvarı 56; s/d ₺65/130; ✳🕙) The Qtahya is a modern block with in-room fridges, flat-screen TVs and thick red carpets; the only disappointment is the bathrooms with their rickety showers. It is arguably overpriced, but so are most options in this business town.

Hilton Garden Inn
BUSINESS HOTEL ₺₺₺

(📞 229 5555; www.kutahya.hgi.com; Atatürk Bulvarı 21; s/d ₺166/236; ✳@🕙) Yes, it's a chain, with all the patented mattresses and standard furnishings that come with it, but the Kütahya Hilton offers the best accommodation in town. Service is sharp and facilities include a lobby bar, snack bar, restaurant and business centre. Book online for major discounts.

🍴 Eating & Drinking

Konya Sofrası
PIDE, TURKISH ₺

(Atatürk Bulvarı; mains ₺5-15) This friendly family-run restaurant next to Qtahya Otel serves *tandır* (slow-cooked) dishes, *güveç* (stew) and recommended pide.

Deftardar Konağı
ANATOLIAN ₺

(Yakın Macar Evi; mains ₺5-10; 🕙9am-8pm) Occupying an Ottoman building near Kossuth House museum, with a pleasant garden and upstairs rooms featuring carved wooden ceilings, this family-run restaurant serves *mantı*, *börek* (filled pastry), *çorba* and Ottoman dishes.

Hammam-I Ziyafe
RESTAURANT ₺₺

(Cumhuriyet Caddesi; mains ₺6-15; 🖋) This restaurant in a restored hamam (1402) offers a good choice of *çorba*, mezes and salads, plus set lunch menus. House specials are *güveç*, *gözleme* (stuffed savoury crepes) and *köfte*, and you can sit beneath the brick dome or outside on the pedestrianised boulevard.

The adjoining snack bar, **Karavan Gözleme** (Cumhuriyet Caddesi; snacks from ₺3.50), serves *gözleme* and *börek*.

ℹ Information

Tourist Information Kiosk (📞 223 6213; Zafer Meydanı; 🕙9am-5.30pm Mon-Fri) Some English is spoken, and good maps are available. In front of Şekerbank.

ℹ Getting There & Away

Bus-company offices are around the Hilton Garden Inn hotel. *Servises* run to/from the otogar. Pamukkale offers at least two daily services to/from Afyon (₺15, 1½ hours), Antalya (₺40, 6½ hours), Bodrum (₺63, 9½ hours), Bursa (₺22, three hours) and Marmaris (₺55, 9½ hours), and several to/from Denizli (₺50, five hours). Anadolu has several daily buses to/from Eskişehir (₺12, 1½ hours), İstanbul (₺43, six hours) and İzmir (₺45, six hours).

Afyon (Afyonkarahisar)

📞 0272 / POP 186,991

Like nearby Kütahya, Afyon is a provincial city lying under an ancient castle – a particularly dramatic one atop a vertiginous rock, which had myriad occupants between Hittite and Ottoman times. And like its dusty counterpart, despite having a university, Afyon remains a workaday, conservative place, where the only noise at night comes from minarets and teahouses tuned into televised football matches.

Despite its prosaic qualities, Afyon (officially now 'Afyonkarahisar') has an attractive Ottoman quarter and some magnificent mosques befitting its long history. But it is Afyon's role in the War of Independence, when Atatürk briefly made it his headquarters before routing the Greeks in the 1922 Battle of Dumlupınar, that makes locals most proud. Lest there be any doubt, note the giant statue of a muscular man beating another into the ground, at the main square (Hükümet Meydanı).

◉ Sights & Activities

Mevlevihane Cami
MOSQUE

(Old Town) This 13th-century Seljuk creation was a dervish lodge when Sultan Veled (son of dervish founder Celaleddin Rumi) made Afyon the empire's most important Mevlevi centre after Konya. Today's mosque (1908), rebuilt for the ill-fated Sultan Abdülhamid II, has twin domes and twin pyramidal roofs above its courtyard. The **museum** (🕙9am-5.30pm Tue-Sun) **FREE** brings the mystical dervish ways to life.

Ulu Cami
MOSQUE

(Old Town; ⊘10am-6pm) Although among the most important surviving Seljuk mosques, the opulent Ulu Cami (1273) is often closed outside prayer times. It is supported by 40 soaring wooden columns with stalactite capitals and features a flat-beamed roof. Local green tiles decorate the minaret.

Old Town
HISTORIC AREA

Around Ulu Cami are hilly cobbled streets of pastel Ottoman wooden houses, some serving as teahouses and restaurants.

Afyon Kale
CASTLE

FREE The *kale* (castle) or *hisar* (fortress) overlooks Afyon from a craggy rock and the steep path up is signposted opposite Ulu and Yukarı Pazar Camis. The strenuous approach passes Ottoman guard towers on what was quite the formidable defensive structure. A taxi up costs about ₺15.

Hittite king Mursilis II built the first castle here, c 1350 BC. Since then, various rulers have restored the original *kara hisar* (black fortress) – most recently the Turkish government, with unorthodox white masonry. In 2004 the state also renamed Afyon, named after the *afyon* (opium) that was cultivated here, as Afyonkarahisar ('Black Castle of Opium'), thus shifting the limelight to the castle from the less savoury history of opium production.

Although the castle is empty, the views from the 226m-high summit are spectacular. However, by night it is unlit, so do not leave it too late if walking down.

İmaret Cami
MOSQUE

Afyon's major mosque complex (five minutes' walk from Hükümet Meydanı) was built for Gedik Ahmet Paşa in 1472. The blue-tiled, spiral-fluted minaret decorations indicate Seljuk preferences, though Ottoman stylings are apparent. The eastern entrance, like an *eyvan* (vaulted hall), accesses a double-domed sanctuary (as in mosques at early Ottoman capitals Bursa and Edirne). The adjoining İmaret hamam retains its original stone basins and is still used.

🛏 Sleeping

Many hotels supplement the usual Turkish breakfast with a dollop of Afyon's famous cream. The cream is made partly from the opium plant, but will not leave you in a narcotic stupor for the rest of the day.

Hotel Soydan
HOTEL €€

(✒215 2323; www.soydanhotel.com; Karagözoğlu Sokak 2; s/d ₺60/100) Apart from the tank of carnivorous fish in reception, the Soydan is an unremarkable but friendly provincial hotel. The 36 rooms are comfortable if a bit faded; some have balconies with castle view. Centrally located near Hükümet Meydanı.

Şehitoğlu Konaği
HISTORIC HOTEL €€€

(✒214 1313; www.sehitoglukonagi.com; Kuyulu Sokak 2-6; s/d ₺110/190; 🖙) This renovated Ottoman house has 20 rooms sharing balconies with good castle views. The cupboard bathrooms are cramped and the decor is rather kitsch, but it remains an atmospheric old-town option. Its restaurant (mains ₺12 to ₺18) specialises in kebaps, *ızgara* (grilled) meat and local fare such as *sucuk* (spicy sausage).

🍴 Eating & Drinking

Afyon is famous for its *sucuk* and local cheeses, both of which make regular appearances in shop windows and restaurant menus. Look out, too, for Afyon's *kaymaklı lokum* (Turkish delight including local cream).

Mihrioğlu Konağı
ANATOLIAN €€

(Türbe Caddesi 6/A; mezes ₺5-7, mains ₺10-18; ⊘8.30am-midnight) Set in an Ottoman house in the old town, Mihrioğlu offers a menu of Anatolian classics: *zeytinyağlı*-based (olive oil) dishes, *börek, saç kavurma* (stir-fried cubed meat dish), *çöp şiş* (şiş kebap served rolled in a thin pide with onions and parsley), *ızgara sucuk* and *mantı*. A rustic garden with water features and shaded alcoves provides summer seating.

Gamze Döner
KEBAP €€

(Bankalar Caddesi; kebaps ₺15) This smart *kebapçı* just off Hükümet Meydanı serves kebaps, including one featuring *sucuk*.

Sarıdere Cafe
CAFE

(Bankalar Caddesi 17) Take the lift up from AVM Alışveriş Merkezleri department store to this rooftop student cafe with great castle views from its outdoor terrace. Musicians often play in the evenings and get the students dancing and singing along.

ℹ Information

Tourist Office (✒213 5447; Hükümet Meydanı; ⊘8am-noon & 1.30-5.30pm Mon-Sat) Has useful maps, but little English spoken.

❶ Getting There & Around

Metro and Kamil Koç have offices just off Hükümet Meydanı. Metro serves Ankara (₺34, four hours, 10 daily), Antalya (₺34, five hours, 10 daily), Denizli (₺30, four hours, three daily), Eskişehir (₺25, three hours, two daily), Isparta (₺20, three hours, daily), İstanbul (₺53, eight hours, three daily), İzmir (₺35, 5½ hours, regular), Konya (₺30, 3¾ hours, frequent) and Kütahya (₺20, 1½ hours, seven daily).

Servises connect the centre and otogar, and dolmuşes run from Hükümet Meydanı (₺1.50, every 20 minutes). Taxis cost about ₺15.

PAMUKKALE REGION

The glittering white of Pamukkale's calcite cliffs jumps straight out of many Turkey tourism brochures, and day-waders come from far and wide to indulge in the warm waters of these dazzling travertines. Above them stand the ruins of ancient Hierapolis, whose inhabitants did much the same thing 2000 years ago. Other, more impressive, ruins sprawl across a green plain at lesser-visited Afrodisias, where the 270m-long stadium gives a visceral thrill. The ancient ruins of Laodicea provide another culturally edifying day-trip opportunity, while big-city Denizli serves as a transport hub for most travellers – the place where you take the bus or dolmuş to Pamukkale or other more interesting towns.

Pamukkale

☏ 0258 / POP 2630

Pamukkale has been made eternally famous by the gleaming white calcite shelves overrunning with warm, mineral-rich waters on the mountain above the village – the so-called 'Cotton Castle' (*pamuk* means 'cotton' in Turkish).

While it is tempting to wallow in the travertines, just above them lies Hierapolis, once a Roman and Byzantine spa city which has considerable ruins and a museum. Unesco World Heritage status has brought more extensive measures to protect the glistening bluffs, and put paid to the days of freely traipsing around everywhere, but the travertines remain one of Turkey's singular experiences, even with restricted bathing.

While the photogenic travertines get busloads of day-trippers passing through for a quick soak and photo op, staying

overnight allows you to visit the site at sunset and dodge some of the crowds. This also gives time for a day trip to the beautiful and little-visited ancient ruins of Afrodisias and Laodicea, and to appreciate the village of Pamukkale itself. It is a dedicated tourist town around Cumhuriyet Meydanı, but in quieter parts of the village life is still soundtracked by bleating goats and birdsong.

◉ Sights & Activities

Pamukkale's double attractions – the shimmering white travertines/terraces and the adjacent ruins of ancient Hierapolis – are a package deal. Both are accessed on the same ticket (₺25) and comprise their own national park, located on a whitewashed hill right above Pamukkale village.

Of the site's three entrances, the south gate (☉6am-9pm) is most practical. It is about 2.5km from Pamukkale, on the hill near Hierapolis' main sights, meaning you see both attractions while walking downwards, exiting through the middle gate and finishing in the village. The north gate (☉8am-8pm Apr-Oct, to 5pm Oct-Apr) is about 3km away, allowing you to enter Hierapolis via the necropolis and Frontinus St and, likewise, walk downhill to the village. Both gates are uphill from Pamukkale, better accessed by dolmuş, taxi or (in most cases) a free lift provided by your accommodation than walking; Hierapolis and the travertines comprise a large site, so save your energy.

The middle gate (☉8am-8pm Apr-Oct, to 5pm Oct-Apr), on the edge of Pamukkale itself, is at the base of the terraced mountain, meaning you walk uphill over the travertines to Hierapolis and take the same route back to the village – not a logical route, but it does offer two looks at the travertines. If you are just after a little R&R in the pools, this is the quickest and easiest entrance.

Note the entrance gates' different opening times; you can exit them when you like. Tickets are only good for one entry, so you must see the site in one go. Nevertheless, you can stay inside as long as you like, and for most people a single visit is enough; pensions are generally happy to make a picnic lunch so you can take your time and enjoy an all-day visit. Additional fees apply for the Hierapolis Archaeology Museum and Antique Pool (though you can arguably get enough out of the experience without shelling out more lira for these).

Travertines
NATURE RESERVE

The saucer-shaped travertines (or terraces, as they are also called) wind sideways down the powder-white mountain, providing stunning contrast to the clear blue sky and green plains below. To protect the unique calcite surface, guards oblige you to go barefoot, so if planning to walk down to the village via the travertines, be prepared to carry your shoes with you.

Socks and shower shoes are also allowed. Although the ridges look rough, in reality the constant water flow keeps the ground mostly smooth, even gooey in places, and the risk of slipping is greater than that of cutting your feet. To walk straight down without stops takes about 30 minutes. The constant downward motion can be hard on the knees.

Although the terrace pools are not particularly deep, you can get fully submerged in the thermal water. There is a gushing channel of warm water at the top of the path down through the travertines, where representatives of many nations sit and give their legs a good soak. If you do not have a bathing suit or shorts, or otherwise do not wish to get too wet, there are plenty of dry sections leading down. Also note that going at midday means crowds and sharp sunlight reflecting off the dazzling white surface; later afternoon is a better time to go.

Hierapolis
RUIN

The ruins of this Roman and Byzantine spa city evoke life in a bygone era, in which Greeks, Romans and Jews, pagans and Christians, and spa tourists peacefully co-existed. It became a curative centre when founded around 190 BC by Eumenes II of Pergamum, before prospering under the Romans and, even more so, the Byzantines, when large Jewish and Orthodox Christian communities comprised most of the population. Recurrent earthquakes brought disaster, and Hierapolis was finally abandoned after a 1334 tremor.

Hierapolis' location atop the tourist magnet that is the 'Cotton Castle' seems to have blessed it with a budget rather more ample than most Turkish archaeological sites. The orderly paved pathways, well-trimmed hedges, flower-filled expanses, slatted walkways and shady park benches make Hierapolis far more genteel than even Ephesus. Wild and raw it is not, but for those wishing, or needing, to see an ancient site on well-maintained terrain, Hierapolis' curvaceous mountaintop home is ideal.

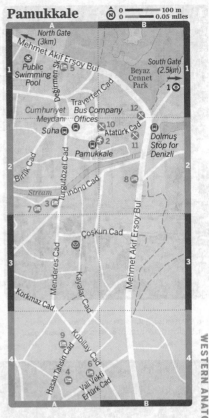

Pamukkale

1. Afrodisias (p312) 2. Roman theatre (p308), Hierapolis
3. Laodicea (Laodikya; p311) 4. Antonine Nymphaeum (p321),
Sagalassos

TIM GERARD BAKER / GETTY IMAGES ©

2 Western Anatolia Highlights

Ancient ruins scatter this region where civilisations once prospered. On street corners and windblown plateaus, weathered inscriptions and chipped statues tell the stories of the Phrygians, Greeks, Romans, Ottomans and others. Wonderfully, because most of Western Anatolia's ruins are off the tourist circuit, at some sites it might be just you, the Anatolian wind and a ticket salesman who is keen to chat. Arrive early or late to have vast theatres and civic squares to yourself.

Hierapolis

The ruins of Hierapolis, a multicultural spa city in Roman and Byzantine times, stand in decaying splendour atop Pamukkale's famous snow-white mountain of travertine rock formations.

Afrodisias

Splendiferous Afrodisias boasts two of western Turkey's most photogenic relics. The tetrapylon (monumental gateway) welcomed travellers when Afrodisias was the provincial capital of Roman Caria, and the 30,000-seat stadium still echoes with the roars of gladiators and spectators.

Sagalassos

The Roman ruins of Sagalassos, which was also a major Pisidian city, are scattered in an unbeatably poetic location at an altitude of 1500m in the Taurus Mountains.

Laodicea

Entered along a colonnaded street, Laodicea was a prosperous city on two trade routes and home to one of the Seven Churches of Asia (mentioned in the Book of Revelation).

İznik

İznik's Roman walls and Byzantine churches recall its heyday when the first Ecumenical Council, which shaped Christianity, met here.

Hierapolis

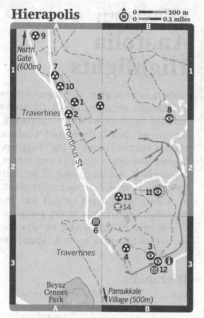

N 0 ——— 200 m
0 ——— 0.1 miles

Hierapolis

◉ Sights

◐ Activities, Courses & Tours

➡ **Byzantine Gate to the Roman Theatre**

Entering at the south gate, walk through the 5th-century Byzantine gate, built of travertine blocks and marble among other materials, and pass the Doric columns of the 1st-century gymnasium. An important building in health-orientated Hierapolis, it collapsed in a 7th-century earthquake. Continue straight on for the foundations of the Temple of Apollo. As at Didyma and

Delphi, eunuch priests tended the temple's oracle. Its alleged power derived from an adjoining spring, the Plutonium (named after the underworld god Pluto). Apparently only the priests understood the secret of holding one's breath around the toxic fumes that billowed up from Hades, immediately killing the small animals and birds they sacrificed.

The spectacular Roman theatre, built in stages by emperors Hadrian and Septimius Severus, could seat over 12,000 spectators. The stage mostly survives, along with some decorative panels and the front-row, VIP 'box' seats.

➡ **Martyrium of St Philip the Apostle**

From the theatre, tracks lead uphill and left to the less-visited but fascinating Martyrium of St Philip the Apostle, an intricate octagonal structure on terrain where St Philip was supposedly martyred. The arches of the eight individual chapels, marked with crosses, originally had heptagonal interiors.

Differing accounts from ancient sources have created confusion over precisely which Philip was commemorated here – if it really was Jesus's apostle, he was allegedly hung upside down from a tree after challenging the pagan snake-worshippers at their nearby temple. An apocryphal ancient source claims that at Philip's death, a yawning abyss opened in the earth, swallowing up the Roman proconsul, the snake-worshippers, their temple and about 7000 hapless bystanders. Righteous!

Whichever Philip was martyred here, his body has reportedly been found about 40m away, in a Byzantine structure excavated by Italian archaeologists. The sensational news of August 2011 revived interest in St Philip and Hierapolis. Considering that his martyrium clearly suffered fire damage in the 5th century, it is possible that the unearthed body was indeed relocated from the martyrium then.

➡ **Hellenistic Theatre to Frontinus Street**

From the Martyrium, a rough path with fantastic views of the site and the plains beyond leads west across the hillside to the completely ruined Hellenistic theatre, above the 2nd-century agora. One of the largest ever discovered, it was surrounded by marble porticoes with Ionic columns on three sides, and closed by a basilica on the fourth.

From the theatre, follow the steep overgrown diagonal path towards the poplars to reach the agora (alternatively, backtrack to the Martyrium of St Philip the Apostle for an easier path down). Walking downhill through the agora, you will re-emerge on the ridgeline main path. Turn right on the colonnaded Frontinus Street, where some original paving and columns remain. Monumental archways once bounded both ends of this, the city's main commercial thoroughfare. The ruined Arch of Domitian, with its twin towers, is at the northern end; just before them, the large latrine building has two floor channels, for sewage and for fresh water.

➔ Necropolis

Beyond the Arch of Domitian are the ruined Roman baths, and further past these, an Appian Way–style paved road leads to the north gate. An extraordinary necropolis (cemetery) extends several kilometres northwards. The clustered circular tombs here probably belonged to the many ancient spa tourists whom Hierapolitan healers failed to cure.

Hierapolis Archaeology Museum MUSEUM
(admission ₺5; ☉8.30am-7pm Tue-Sun summer, to 5.30pm winter) Housed in former Roman baths, this excellent museum exhibits spectacular sarcophagi from Laodicea and elsewhere; small finds including jewellery, oil lamps and stamp seals from Hierapolis and around; and in the third room, its entrance watched by a sphinx, friezes and Roman-era statuary from the nearby theatre. Left of the entrance are impressive capitals from the agora and other parts of the site.

Antique Pool SWIMMING
(admission ₺32, child 0-6/7-12yr free/₺13; ☉8am-7.30pm summer, to 5.30pm winter) The sacred pool in this spa's courtyard has submerged sections of original fluted marble columns to lounge against. The water, which is abundant in minerals and a more than balmy 36°C, was thought to have restorative powers in antiquity, and may well still do. In summer, it is busiest from 11am to 4pm.

Ballooning & Paragliding BALLOONING, GLIDING
🖋 A nascent industry is taking to the skies over Pamukkale, offering a bird's-eye view of Hierapolis and the travertines. Shop around, ask to see operators' credentials and check they are fully insured, for your personal safety as much as the good of your wallet. Try Anka Tandem Paragliding (☎272 2011; meteorgold@hotmail.com; Cumhuriyet Meydanı; 15min

flights ₺150), run by experienced paraglider Levent Ekmekçi.

🛏 Sleeping

Pamukkale's numerous pensions and small hotels are split between the bustling centre, where travertine views and touristic businesses abound and Hierapolis' middle gate is a short walk away, and rustic lanes on the south side of the village. The stiff competition translates into good service, tips and assistance. Most places offer free pick-ups from Pamukkale otogar and lifts to the Hierapolis gates; a pool (often with thermal water from the travertines or other springs) and laundry service; and help with booking bus tickets and tours to Afrodisias and elsewhere.

Try to book ahead in high summer, especially if you have a preference. Campers are usually welcome to pitch their tent on the premises for a small fee.

Beyaz Kale Pension PENSION €
(☎272 2064; www.beyazkalepension.com; Oguzkaan Caddesi 4; s/d/q/f ₺60/80/130/150; ❄🛜🏊) On a quiet street just outside the village centre, the cheery yellow 'White Castle' has 14 spotless rooms on two floors, some more modern than others. The friendly lady of the house, Hacer, serves some of the best local pension fare (dinner menu ₺20) on the relaxing rooftop terrace with travertine views. A cot is available for junior travellers.

Hotel Dört Mevsim PENSION €
(☎272 2009; www.hoteldortmevsim.com; Hasan Tahsin Caddesi 27; s ₺35-50, d ₺50-70; ❄🛜🏊) Recommended by readers, the 'Four Seasons' is run by a welcoming farming family on a quiet lane in the village. The cheaper rooms are basic, but the setting is a winner with a shaded poolside terrace for digging into the home-cooked food.

Mustafa Hotel PENSION €
(☎272 2240; mustafamotel@hotmail.com; Atatürk Caddesi 22; s/d ₺40/70; ❄🛜) The 10 rooms are basic but affordable options close to all the action in the village centre, and the excellent terrace has travertine views.

★ Melrose House HOTEL €€
(☎272 2250; www.melrosehousehotel.com; Vali Vekfi Ertürk Caddesi 8; s €35-55, d €40-55; ❄🛜🏊) The closest thing to a boutique hotel in Pamukkale, Melrose House has 17 spacious modern rooms, including a family room and suites with circular beds worthy

of a Blaxploitation movie. Decor throughout mixes handmade Kütahya tiles and pillars, wallpaper and exposed stonework, and the poolside restaurant is an agreeable place to linger.

Rooms on the upper two floors have balconies and the owners, Mehmet and Ummu, are a helpful and refreshingly impartial source of local info.

Venüs Hotel
HOTEL €€

(☑272 2152; www.venushotel.net; Hasan Tahnsin Caddesi; s/d €35/45; ❈@🖉🌐♨) Recommended by readers, the Venüs is a comfortable hideaway with a traditional Turkish poolside restaurant and quiet corners for reading or chatting with fellow travellers. Reached along corridors decorated with Ottoman tiles, the modern rooms at the rear are pleasant, with white and turquoise bedding. The owners also organise day trips to local sights.

Melrose Viewpoint
HOTEL €€

(☑272 3120; www.melroseviewpoint.com; Çay Sokak 7; s/d/tr/f from €35/41/47/55; ❈🌐♨) Resembling a turquoise cruise ship complete with porthole windows, this new hotel from the couple behind Melrose House has 17 rooms with king-size beds, full-length mirrors, small balconies and a tasteful smattering of curves and flourishes. Those on the 1st floor have travertine views and the terrace restaurant (mains ₺15 to ₺26) enjoys sweeping vistas.

Özbay Hotel
HOSTEL €€

(☑0538 981 9677; face-4-face@hotmail.com; Mehmet Akif Ersoy Bulvarı 37; dm/s/d/tr/f from €10/34/42/52/64; ❈@) Renovated in 2014, Özbay's rooms are simple but pleasantly furnished; all have a balcony and the deluxe options have amenities including fridge, hair dryer and bathrobes. In the garden and terrace restaurant, you can enjoy pide, pizza, draught beer and local wine with travertine views. The dorm is female-only.

Hotel Hal-Tur
HOTEL €€€

(☑272 2723; www.haltur.net; Mehmet Akif Ersoy Bulvarı 71; s/d €50/70; ❈🌐♨) The Hal-Tur has attractive modern rooms and fantastic travertine views. The excellent pools (with separate kid's section) and garden make it great for families.

✖ Eating & Drinking

Pamukkale's restaurants are mostly unremarkable and overpriced – your accommodation will likely offer better fare.

Ottoman House
TURKISH €

(Atatürk Caddesi 29; gözleme ₺5) For a snack and a beer after visiting the travertines, this place opposite Hierapolis' middle gate does *gözleme*, made by a lady at the entrance. Head through the Ottoman-style salon for a terrace overlooking the nearby water park and travertines. Prices for mains are less reasonable.

★ Kayaş
RESTAURANT, BAR €€

(Atatürk Caddesi 3; mezes ₺8, mains ₺16-25; ☺lunch & dinner) This central place with a long bar and big TV (for football matches, generally) is the best spot for a beer, but it also serves Turkish food at better prices than other eateries. *Sigara böreği* (deep-fried, cigar-shaped pastries filled with cheese) are among the tasty mezes, and mains include *güveç* and *şiş* kebaps.

Mustafa Hotel
PIDE, INTERNATIONAL €€

(Atatürk Caddesi 22; mains ₺10-24, menu ₺20; 🖉) Wood-fired pide and pizza are the speciality, but kebaps, crepes, felafel, hummus and other mezes are also available.

ℹ Information

Pensions offer advice, maps and assistance. As in any tourist town, most have their own favourite travel providers and disparage everyone else, so compare offers.

Tourist Office (☑272 2077; ☺8am-5.30pm summer, to 5pm winter) Has Hierapolis maps.

DANGERS & ANNOYANCES

Pamukkale's travel agencies have a bad reputation; stories of poor service and fly-by-night operations abound. They are best avoided apart from booking a day trip to Afrodisias. Definitely do not book tours and activities in other parts of Turkey, such as Cappadocia. Many agencies share offices with the bus companies, so when buying bus tickets make sure you are dealing directly with the bus operator or their appointed agent.

Travellers are sometimes taken off the *servis* from Denizli and taken to a pension to receive the hard sell. Asian travellers in particular have been targeted with this and other scams. If this happens, leave and go to your first choice of accommodation.

ℹ Getting There & Around

AIR

Turkish Airlines flies between **Denizli Çardak Airport** (www.cardak.dhmi.gov.tr) and İstanbul Atatürk, and Pegasus Airlines serves İstanbul Sabiha Gökçen. A shuttle to/from Pamukkale costs from ₺20. Make sure you will not have to change at Denizli otogar.

BUS

Most services to/from Pamukkale involve changing in Denizli, which is en route to most places anyway. Bus companies including Metro, Kamil Koç and Pamukkale have offices on and around Cumhuriyet Meydanı, and most buses drop passengers here or on Mehmet Akif Ersoy Bulvarı, the main road into town. Eager touts hawking accommodation sometimes lie in wait, but you can make up your own mind. Most accommodation will pick you up for free.

Buses and dolmuşes (₺5, 40 minutes) run frequently between Pamukkale and Denizli otogar. If you buy a ticket beginning or ending in Pamukkale, the bus company should provide a *servis* to/from the otogar.

Süha (📞 272 2248; www.suhaturizm.com. tr; Cumhuriyet Meydanı) has wo direct daily Denizli–Selçuk buses in summer (₺25).

CAR

Operators including **Europcar** (www.europcar. com.tr) offer rental cars in Denizli and at the airport.

TAXI

Taxis to Hierapolis' south gate from Pamukkale/ Denizli cost ₺20/40.

TRAIN

Daily trains run between Denizli and Selçuk. **Süha** (📞 272 2248; www.suhaturizm.com.tr; Cumhuriyet Meydanı) sells tickets including a shuttle to Denizli train station for ₺20.

Around Pamukkale

Laodicea (Laodikya)

Only 8km from Pamukkale, Laodicea was a prosperous city straddling two major trade routes, famed for its wool, banking and medicines. Cicero lived here for a time before Mark Antony had him killed, and large Orthodox Christian and Jewish populations co-existed. Today, the columns standing in the long grass have good views of the travertines.

The spread-out **ruins** (admission ₺10; ⏰8.30am-7pm mid-Apr–Sep, 8am-5pm Oct–mid-Apr) indicate Laodicea was once big. Entering up **Syria Street**, the colonnaded main drag, look out for the 2nd-century **temple**, its columns built with travertine blocks and a glass floor showing toppled pillars beneath. See also the **stadium** outlines and remains of two **theatres**; upper-tier seats remain in the second. By the **agora** and **baths** are ruins of the **basilica church** mentioned in the Book of Revelation, where Laodicea is listed as among the Seven Churches of Asia.

ℹ Getting There & Away

Pamukkale–Denizli dolmuşes pass the turn-off for Laodicea (₺3 from Pamukkale). From the

METRO SERVICES FROM DENIZLI OTOGAR

DESTINATION	FARE (₺)	DURATION (HR)	DISTANCE (KM)	FREQUENCY (PER DAY)
Afyon	32	4	240	11
Ankara	60	7	480	14
Antalya	40	4	300	6
Aydın (for Selçuk)	15	2¼	135	22
Bodrum	36	5	290	5
Bursa	50	10	532	5
Eğirdir	35	4	180	2
Isparta	25	3	175	2
İstanbul	75	12	665	11
İzmir	27	4	250	16
Konya	45	6½	440	6
Kuşadası	30	3½	190	2
Marmaris	30	4	185	6
Nevşehir (Cappadocia)	55	9	674	4

signpost on the Pamukkale–Denizli road, it is a 1km walk to the ruins past the ticket office, cafe and toilet. Alternatively, pensions can arrange transport, and it may be possible to tag Laodicea onto a visit to Afrodisias.

Kaklık Mağarası & Ak Han

A sort of underground Pamukkale, Kaklık Mağarası (Kaklık Cave; admission ₺2; ☉ 8am-10pm) gushes with calcium- and sulphur-rich water. The flow, into a large sinkhole, creates a bright, white pyramid with warm travertine pools below. Bathing is allowed in the non-aesthetic outside pool.

En route to the cave from Pamukkale, Ak Han (c 1251) is a well-preserved Seljuk caravanserai with a beautifully carved gateway.

❶ Getting There & Away

Kaklık Mağarasi is 35km from Pamukkale. Visiting on a tour from Pamukkale is easier than public transport, but the frequent dolmuşes and buses heading east from Denizli on the highway can drop you in Kaklık village (₺5), 4km south of the cave. A sign points the way from there – walk the shadeless road or flag down a farm vehicle.

Ak Han is just off the Denizli–Kaklık highway, about 1km east of the Pamukkale turn-off.

Afrodisias

The remoteness of Afrodisias, out in the Anatolian hinterland among Roman poplars, green fields and warbling birds, safeguards its serenity from the masses. While compact Ephesus boasts finer individual ruins, Afrodisias outdoes it for sheer scale, while its on-site museum is more impressive too (erstwhile European excavators relocated much Ephesian treasure to their own museums). The site is relatively untended, with some side paths disappearing into thickets and bramble, and with luck you could have it almost to yourself, creating the exotic feel of discovering lost ruins.

History

Afrodisias's acropolis began around 5000 BC as a prehistoric mound. Its later temple was a pilgrimage site from the 6th century BC and, by the 1st century BC, the city had become large and prosperous, due to its rich marble quarry and imperial favour. In the 3rd century AD, the 150,000-strong city became provincial capital of Roman Caria.

Early Byzantine Afrodisias developed into an Orthodox city, with the Temple of Aphrodite being transformed into a church, while the stone from other buildings was reused for defensive walls (c AD 350). By the 7th century, Afrodisias had been renamed Stavroupolis (City of the Cross), and historical sources attest to the prescence of Byzantine bishops here until the 10th century. Despite being abandoned in the 12th century, it remained a Byzantine titular bishopric until the 15th century.

Sometime after the city's abandonment, a Turkish village, Geyre, developed here. The village was ruined by a 1956 earthquake and relocated, allowing archaeologists to work on the site.

◉ Sights

From the car park, a tractor will tow you 500m to the entrance in a connected carriage. Take the circular site tour first, then dry your sweat over a drink, saving the cooler indoor museum for last. You have two route choices; the anticlockwise route elaborated here is less affected by the occasional mid-morning package-tour groups.

Turn right beside the museum for the grand house with Ionic and Corinthian pillars on the left. Further on the left, the elaborate tetrapylon (monumental gateway) once greeted pilgrims coming to the Temple of Aphrodite. The impressive monument has been reconstructed using 85% of its original blocks.

The tomb of Professor Kenan T Erim is on the lawn here. A Turkish professor from New York University, the trailblazing archaeologist oversaw excavations here from 1961 to 1990.

Continue down the steps on the straight footpath, and turn right across the grassy field for the 270m-long stadium. One of the biggest and best preserved classical stadiums, this massively long structure has 30,000 overgrown seats. Some were reserved for individuals or guilds, and the eastern end was a gladiatorial arena. Standing in the dark and sloping tunnel and looking out onto the huge field, you can imagine the fear, exhilaration and sheer adrenaline these ancient warriors would have felt, striding towards imminent death amidst a raucous crowd demanding blood.

The erstwhile Temple of Aphrodite, once dedicated to the goddess of love, was converted to a basilica around AD 500. Its cella was removed, its columns shifted to form a nave, and an apse was added, making it hard to visualise the original structure. Nearby, the

Afrodisias

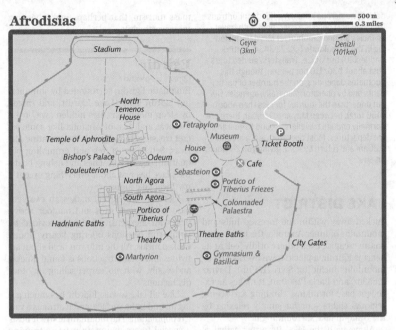

Stadium

Geyre (3km)

Denizli (101km)

North Temenos House

Tetrapylon

Temple of Aphrodite

Museum

House

Ticket Booth

Bishop's Palace

Odeum

Cafe

Bouleuterion

Sebasteion

North Agora

Portico of Tiberius Friezes

South Agora

Colonnaded Palaestra

Portico of Tiberius

Hadrianic Baths

Theatre Baths

Theatre

City Gates

Martyrion

Gymnasium & Basilica

Bishop's Palace is a grand house that previously accommodated Roman governors. Just beyond, the left fork in the path leads to the beautiful marble **bouleuterion**, preserved almost undamaged for 1000 years by mud.

Return to the fork and follow the sign to the *tiyatro* (theatre). The path leads past the **north agora** and through the early 2nd-century-AD **Hadrianic Baths** to the **south agora**, with a long, partially excavated pool, and the grand **Portico of Tiberius**.

Stone stairs up the earthen, prehistoric mound access the white marble **theatre**, a 7000-capacity auditorium complete with stage and individually seated seats. Southeast was the large **theatre baths** complex.

The path now leads downhill to the **Sebasteion**: originally a temple to the deified Roman emperors, it was visually spectacular, with a three-storey-high double colonnade decorated with friezes of Greek myths and imperial exploits. In the same area, the impressive, many-faced **friezes** come from the Portico of Tiberius.

To understand the magnitude here, see the approximately 70 (of the once-existing) 190 reliefs in the elegant **museum**. They occupy opposing sides of the main interior hall. The unique combination of friezes acknowledge a Greek culture and mythology

underpinning the worldly achievements of the pragmatic Romans. So, along with the statues illustrating mythical heroes are representations of robust emperors. Note how subjugated nations are always portrayed in female form: Trajan rips open the shirt of chaste Dacia; Nero has his way with a trembling Armenia; and Claudius delivers a death blow to the slumped figure of Britannia, her tunic revealing a bare breast.

Other marbles here include Aphrodite's 2nd-century cult statue, and busts of great writers and thinkers. One, labelled simply, 'a philosopher,' may be the great 3rd-century-AD Peripatetic philosopher, Alexander of Afrodisias. See too sculptures of Caius Julius Zoilos, Octavian's freed slave who became a wealthy local benefactor, and the interactive screen, which shows how Afrodisias would have looked in its heyday.

ℹ Information

There is an ATM, cafe and toilets in the car park, and a shop, toilets and exorbitant cafe inside the site entrance. Audioguides are available (₺10).

ℹ Getting There & Away

Visiting Afrodisias (55km southeast of Nazilli and 101km from Denizli) by public transport from Pamukkale is tricky, as you have to change dolmuş numerous times. A guided tour or transfer (transport only) is easier; book with travel agencies around Cumhuriyet Meydanı, including in the **Pamukkale** (🎵 272 3434; Atatürk Caddesi 10) bus office. Transfers/guided tours cost about ₺30/110 per person, though this fluctuates depending on the number of participants and by operator. Generally, agencies will not undertake the journey for less than about ₺150 total; between May and October, there are normally enough travellers around to guarantee departures. Most operators leave around 9.30am and return by 4pm, giving you 2½ hours on-site.

LAKE DISTRICT

Tucked away within the forested hills and mountains of inner Anatolia, the lake region has an escapist, even otherworldly feel. At its heart is Eğirdir, a placid town overlooked by mountains including Sivri (1749m), Davraz (2653m) and Barla (2800m). It makes an excellent base for hiking, climbing and seeing regional sights – or for simply relaxing by the tranquil lake surrounding it.

Along with the lake, its water activities and tasty fish, the Eğirdir area offers year-round action, including the rose harvest in May and June, the autumn apple harvest and winter skiing. History-loving hikers can explore the St Paul Trail and ascend to the lofty ruins of Sagalassos, perched among the rocky peaks of the Taurus range. But it is the kind hospitality of the locals, unaffected by

mass tourism, that perhaps makes visiting most worthwhile.

Eğirdir

🎵 0246 / POP 19,417

Enigmatic Eğirdir, surrounded by shimmering Eğirdir Gölü (Lake Eğirdir) and ringed by steep mountains, lies hidden away from the heat and dust of Anatolia like some secret treasure. Indeed, with its Byzantine fortress, Seljuk structures and crumbling old quarter ringed by beaches and fishing boats, the place has just about everything except a mythical lake monster.

Eğirdir (*ey*-eer-deer) makes an excellent base for regional sites and outdoor activities, with inexpensive lodging provided by family-run pensions offering hearty, home-cooked meals. All the info you need about activities and local attractions is found quickly and easily, with no carpet-selling or other distractions.

Like all lake towns, Eğirdir has much going on under the surface, and it attracts a varied population. The mountain above it hosts a special forces mountain warfare training base, while a distant western shore conceals its underwater equivalent. In summer, Muslim devotees of the quasi-mystical Nur movement gather in nearby Barla village. At summer's end, Yörük mountain nomads descend to do business, while autumn's influx of apple wholesalers stimulates certain dens of iniquity on Yeşilada ('Green Island'),

---

WORTH A TRIP

ISPARTA'S ROSE TOURS

While apparently just an unassuming transport hub, Isparta is famous for its attar of roses, a valuable oil for perfumes. Between mid-May and mid-June, when the flowers cover the fields between Isparta and Lake Burdrur, the production process starts anew.

At daybreak, rose petals are plucked and placed in copper vats. The steam then passed over them is drawn off and condensed, leaving the water's surface covered with a thin layer of oil that's skimmed off and bottled. The 'extra' rosewater is also sold, and there's plenty (it takes 100kg of petals to produce just 25g of attar of roses).

In season, Eğirdir pension owners can organise tours to attar-producing villages, and can incorporate a visit to Isparta Hamam (hamam incl massage ₺35; ⏰ 7am-11pm). Dutch-Turkish producer Alia (www.ecotourismbyalia.com) offers a day tour (€50) to help the villagers pick roses, see the production process, learn about rosewater and oil and try their cosmetics; book direct or through Eğirdir Outdoor Centre. Alia is also opening a spa hotel near Lake Burdur. Other local brands to look out for are the organic Senir and Gülbirlik, the world's biggest rose oil producer, with four processing plants handling 320 tonnes of petals daily.

If you haven't time for touring, numerous shops (and the bus stations) in Isparta sell rose-related creams and perfumes.

which was joined to the mainland and the rest of Eğirdir 55 years ago. Through it all, the town's dependable news source – a public loudspeaker – crackles on, reporting who has died and what utility bills are overdue.

History

Originally Hittite (c 1200 BC), the town was successively held by Phrygians and Lydians, captured by Persians and then Alexander the Great, before finally becoming Roman Prostanna. The modern mountain warfare base occupies the ancient settlement; the archaeological identity of this formerly large and prosperous town thus remains unexplored.

The Byzantines renamed it Akrotiri (Steep Mountain), making it a bishopric. Seljuks captured it in 1204, and later the Turkish Hamidoğulları tribe came; by the mid-14th century, the name had been debased to Akritur. In 1417, the Ottomans conquered, though the population (especially on Yeşilada) remained mostly Greek until the population exchange of the early 1920s.

The name Akrotiri/Akritur eventually became Eğirdir, meaning 'crooked' or 'bent'. In the 1980s, to end the jokes, it was officially renamed Eğirdir, meaning 'she is spinning'. It partly refers to a folk tale about a queen who sat at her loom, unaware that her son was dead.

◉ Sights

Hızır Bey Camii   MOSQUE
Originally a Seljuk warehouse (built in 1237), this simple stone structure became a mosque in 1308 under Hamidoğulları emir Hızır Bey. It features a clerestory (an upper row of windows) above the central hall and new tiles around the *mihrab*. Note the finely carved wooden doors and stone portal, and the minaret's faded blue tile trim.

Dündar Bey Medresesi   HISTORIC BUILDING
In 1281, Hamidoğulları emir Felekeddin Dündar Bey turned this grand stone structure – then a 67-year-old Seljuk caravanserai – into a *medrese*. The small on-site bazaar sells Galatasaray and Fenerbahçe strips, floppy hats and holiday gear.

Castle   RUINS
A few hundred metres down the peninsula stand the massive walls of Akrotiri's ruined castle, which allegedly dates back to 5th-century-BC Lydian king Croesus.

Ayastafanos Church   CHURCH
Eğirdir's last remaining Orthodox church; 13 others were torn down after the Greek community departed in the population exchange. The 12th-century Byzantine stone building originally had a roof made of a ship's hull.

Pınar Pazarı   MARKET
If around on any Sunday between July and October, buy apples, cheese, yoghurt or even a goat at this village market from the Yörük Turks, who descend from their mountain redoubts to hawk their wares and stock up for winter. In the old days, wily Yörük mothers would use these public events to negotiate marriages for their children.

Pınar is 7km southeast of Eğirdir, served by dolmuş (₺1.50).

🏃 Activities

Eğirdir Outdoor Centre   ADVENTURE SPORTS
(📱311 6688; www.egirdiroutdoorcenter.com; ⊙8am-7pm) Run by outdoor enthusiast İbrahim Ağartan and family (of Charly's Pension fame), this information and activities centre is the go-to place for everything from hiring a mountain bike (per hour/half-day/day ₺4/25/35) to laundry (₺15) and a book exchange.

The centre offers free information, and organises boat trips and group-rate transport for independent travellers to remote local sights and stops on the St Paul Trail; add your name to the list to share a ride with others heading in the same direction. A drop-off and pick-up, enabling a one-way walk along the St Paul Trail, is about ₺150 for a small group. The centre also hires out camping equipment (tent, sleeping bag, mat, rucksack and stove ₺50) and offers tours and packages covering activities from fishing to snowshoeing.

If you are a keen kayaker or windsurfer, ask here to borrow equipment from the local training centres for a nominal fee.

Eğirdir Hamam   HAMAM
(hamam ₺12, massage ₺23; ⊙7am-11pm, men Sat-Wed, women Thu & Fri) Renovated 13th-century hamam behind the post office.

Sivri Dağı   HIKING
(Mt Sivri; Akpınar) This mountain (1749m) on the St Paul Trail makes a good day walk. The walk to the peak of Sivri Dağı from the hill village of Akpınar (6km return) takes about 3½ hours. Organise transport to/from Akpınar,

Eğirdir

WESTERN ANATOLIA EĞİRDİR

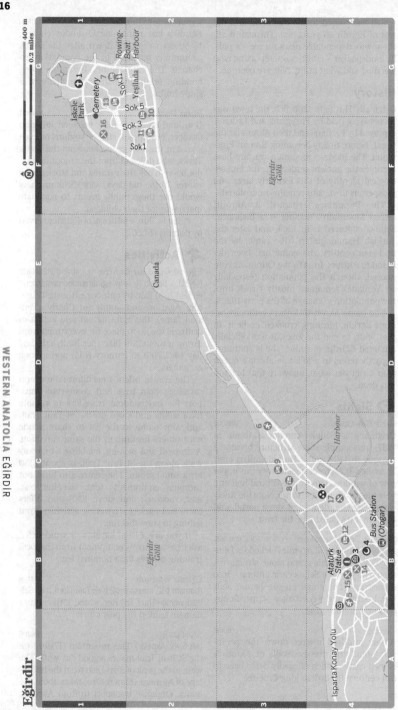

400 m
0.2 miles

Eğirdir Gölü

Eğirdir Gölü

Eğirdir Gölü

Iskele Park

Cemetery

Rowing-
Boat
Harbour

Sok 11

Yeşilada

Sok 5

Sok 3

Sok1

Canada

Harbour

Atatürk
Statue

Bus Station
(Otogar)

Isparta Konay Yolu

Eğirdir

7km from Eğirdir, through your accommodation or Eğirdir Outdoor Centre. If you have a car, Akpınar is worth a drive for its viewpoint overlooking the lake and peninsula.

Beaches & Boat Trips
From the peninsula's northern shore by the castle to its tip at Yeşilada, several relaxing small beaches exist, many with attendant food stalls and çay *ocakları* (stoves). Out of town, at Yazla (less than 1km down the Isparta road) is sandy Belediye Beach. Several kilometres further north is pebbly Altınkum Beach. In summer, dolmuşes run every 15 minutes (₺1.50) from the otogar. Taxis cost ₺12. Further north again, 11km towards Barla, is the long, sandy Bedre Beach. Cycle or catch a taxi (₺25).

Some of Eğirdir's best swimming spots are accessible only by boat trips (around €17 per person), which let you relax, try some fishing, and generally bliss out on the lake's breezy blue waters and in its verdant lagoons. Boat trips, which run from mid-June to mid-September, have traditionally provided a second income for fishermen and pension owners. However, the ever-declining number of fishermen means that prices have soared – if you solicit a boat-owner at random, expect to pay ₺35 to ₺40 per person, for only one hour on the lake.

It is wiser to arrange a trip through your pension or Eğirdir Outdoor Centre, which charges ₺50 per person for a six-hour excursion. The trip involves visiting hidden coves, swimming, sunbathing, a barbecue lunch of freshly caught fish, and gaining an insight into a local fisherman's life.

⭐ Festivals & Events

Dedegöl Dağcılık Şenliği HIKING
(Dedegöl Mountaineering Festival) Over a Friday and Saturday on or after 19 May, Eğirdir's mountaineering club organises this communal scramble up Mt Dedegöl (2998m). A night is spent at the Karagöl base camp (1600m), before a 4am start for a long day's trek to the peak and back down.

Participation is free, with transportation and meals arranged for 1000 hikers, but you must register (through Eğirdir Outdoor Centre) and organise your own equipment.

🛏 Sleeping

Eğirdir's family-run pensions cluster around the castle ruins (a close walk from the centre) and at the peninsula's far end, on the road-attached island of Yeşilada (1.5km from the centre). Make sure that your bedroom windows have screens – Eğirdir's harmless but irritating little lake bugs will fly towards any lit area, but they can't get through a screen (they are less of a nuisance when the wind is up).

Şehsuvar Peace Pension PENSION €
(☑311 2433; www.peacepension.com; Yeşilada; s/d/tr ₺40/80/100; ☺) Tucked away in the middle of the island, near Yeşilada's tranquil *meydan* (square), friendly Şehsuvar has a shaded terrace with grapevines and four bright, spotless rooms. Owner Hüseyin does not speak English, but nonethless tries to help with information about local activities.

Çetin Pansiyon PENSION €
(☑311 2154; 3 Sokak 12; s/d/tw/tr without breakfast ₺30/70/70/105) Near the castle, Çetin has six basic rooms up a narrow staircase, four with views across the lake. The room at the top has a rudimentary kitchenette. Breakfast is an additional ₺15.

⭐ Charly's Pension PENSION, HOSTEL €€
(☑311 4611; www.charlyspension.com; 5 Sokak 2; s €30-35, d €35-40, dm/tr/f €12/45/55; ❄☺) In the heart of the old Greek quarter behind the castle, İbrahim Ağartan and family offer characterful accommodation ranging from budget to top end. The three neighbouring

buildings are technically separate pensions, Charly's, Fulya and Lale, but all share a terrace restaurant in Ottoman-era Charly's with sweeping lake views.

This is the place to linger over the generous buffet breakfast or a beer, chatting to other guests while the multilingual İbrahim dispenses information and organises activities. Staying in these comfortable and relaxing digs is a memorable experience for the insights into life on the lake and the camaraderie shared by travellers of all stripes.

★ Ali's Pension
PENSION €€

(☑ 311 2547; www.alispension.com; Yeşilada; s/d/tr/f from €25/35/50/65; ❀ @ 🛜) At the far end of the island, Eğirdir's oldest pension is a great choice, with eight handsomely furnished and spotless rooms. The English- and German-speaking Birsan and her fishing family offer excellent hospitality, and the home-cooked breakfasts and dishes such as crayfish are delicious and abundant.

Göl Pension
PENSION €€

(☑ 311 2370; www.golpension.com; Yeşilada; r ₺120; ❀ @ 🛜) On the island, the family-run 'Lake' Pension has a pleasant breakfast room and great views from the roof terrace, where two rooms open onto a private section. At the top of the stairs is a cute attic-style room with sloped ceiling.

Choo Choo Pension
PENSION €€

(☑ 311 4926; www.choochoopension.com; Yeşilada; s/d/tw/f €45/50/50/65; ❀ 🛜) This island pension is run by an old fishing clan, who also run the Halikarnas restaurant on the lakefront. The nine rooms are costly, but they are spacious and modern, having been renovated in 2014 with new beds and mattresses. There is a roof terrace, and homemade *börek* features in the lakeside breakfast.

Golden Apple
BUSINESS HOTEL €€

(Altın Elma; ☑ 333 2333; www.goldenapple.com; Kale Sokak 9; s/d ₺50/100; ❀ 🛜) The Apple has smart rooms, though some are poky, and a 4th-floor breakfast terrace.

✕ Eating

Pension dinners are tasty, convenient and great for meeting fellow travellers. Local specialities include *istakoz* (crayfish) and the lake carp, bass and other fish. Between mid-March and mid-June, the fish are given a chance to breed and it is illegal to fish the lake, so any catches served then likely come from the freezer. Head to Yeşilada

for fish restaurants with a view, and to the Hızır Bey Camii area for more economic pide and kebap sandwiches. The Thursday market (☉8am-noon) is held by the castle. Eğirdir is famous for *elma* (apples), as a statue by the otogar celebrates.

Coşkun Döner
KEBAP €

(kebaps from ₺2; ☉lunch) With plastic tables on the pavement, 'Lively' Döner does kebaps in *dürüm* or sandwich form or on a plate. For a postprandial cuppa, the neighbouring çay *ocağı* serves Eğirdir's best brew according to locals.

Eğirdir Outdoor Centre
CAFE €

(mains ₺10; ☑) The activity centre does home-cooked food and olive-oil-soaked dishes including green beans and aubergine. *Gözleme* (₺5), cappuccino and espresso are also on the menu.

Poyraz
SEAFOOD €€

(Yeşilada; mezes ₺7, mains ₺10-20; ☉lunch & dinner) Poyraz offers seating on the waterfront, where fishermen pull in their nets, and in its less atmospheric interior. Being unlicensed, its prices are more assuredly reasonable than at other fish restaurants on the island. Dishes include *köfte* and grilled chops as well as seafood.

Günaylar
PIDE, KEBAP €€

(mains ₺6-17; ☉lunch & dinner) One of two pide and kebap restaurants on this small square overlooking the Atatürk statue, Günaylar also serves *güveç* and *ızgara* dishes.

ⓘ Information

The best sources of information are the Eğirdir Outdoor Centre (p315) and, if arriving by bus, the Kamil Koç office at the otogar. ATMs and banks are near the otogar.

ⓘ Getting There & Around

From Eğirdir otogar, pensions by the castle are within walking distance, whereas Yeşilada is 1.5km away (₺10 by taxi, ₺1 by dolmuş).

AIR

Turkish Airlines connects İstanbul Atatürk with Isparta Süleyman Demirel Airport. Accommodation can organise airport transfers to Eğirdir (from ₺200). A free shuttle links the airport with Isparta centre and *köy garaj* (village otogar), from where services depart to Eğirdir. Travelling to the airport, take the shuttle from outside Isparta *belediye*, or catch a dolmus from Eğirdir to Isparta, get off at Migros supermarket and take a taxi from across the road (₺15).

BUS

A few daily buses (more in summer) run to Bursa (₺48, eight hours), İstanbul (₺60, 10 hours), Denizli (for Pamukkale; ₺30, 3½ hours), Aydın (for Selçuk; ₺40, six hours), İzmir (₺45, eight hours) and Antalya (₺22, three hours). Especially over summer weekends, buy tickets at least a day in advance. The Kamil Koç and Isparta Petrol offices at Eğirdir otogar also sell tickets for other bus companies.

There are direct services to Göreme (₺60, eight hours), but you will have access to more buses if you go to Konya (₺35, four hours); if you leave Eğirdir early, you can spend a few hours sightseeing in Konya before continuing to Cappadocia.

The frequency of long-haul buses is greater from nearby Isparta, accessible by frequent buses and dolmuşes (₺4.50, 30 minutes) or taxi (₺100). In Isparta, intercity buses terminate at the main otogar and services from local destinations such as Eğirdir at the *köy garaj*, 5km away on the other side of the city centre. *Servises* connect the two.

Around Eğirdir

Within an 80km radius of Eğirdir exist numerous interesting destinations, most along the St Paul Trail – and listed here in south–north fashion.

Trips can be arranged by the Eğirdir Outdoor Centre (p315) or your pension. Otherwise, drive or take a taxi (Kovada Gölü Milli Parkı, for example, costs about ₺80). Sütçüler and Yalvaç are served by regular dolmuş (₺15).

Yazılı Canyon Nature Park & Around

The Yazılı Canyon Nature Park (Yazılı Kanyon Tabiat Parkı; admission ₺3), roughly a 65km drive south of Eğirdir, protects a forested gorge deep in the Taurus Mountains, which separate the Lake District (ancient Pisidia) and the Antalya region (Pamphylia), and their unique climatic zones. From the parking area, follow a path 3km upstream through the glorious Çandır Kanyon to alpine waterfalls. There are shady bathing spots, filled with cathartically cold water. It is busy in summer, but otherwise tranquil.

In the same area, traipse the Roman road of Adada, where a ruined agora and Trajan's temple are visible. The ruins are up a winding mountain road around the village of Sütçüler.

ST PAUL TRAIL

Almost two millennia ago, the Apostle Paul trekked northwards from Perge (near the coast and Antalya) through the Anatolian wilds to today's Yalvaç, near Eğirdir. The winding route – from sea level to a 2200m peak – passes crumbling ancient ruins. Although some hikers start from the south, you will have more options and help in Eğirdir, a good base for both the northern and southern sections of the 500km trail.

Check out Culture Routes in Turkey (www.cultureroutesinturkey.com), Trekking in Turkey (www.trekkingin turkey.com) and Kate Clow's St Paul Trail guidebook, available at the Eğirdir Outdoor Centre (p315).

Kovada Gölü Milli Parkı

Surrounding a small lake connected to Lake Eğirdir by a channel, Kovada Gölü Milli Parkı (Lake Kovada National Park) is good for hiking, picnicking and flora, especially at the nearby Kasnak Forest, which is full of butterflies and rare mountain flowers. The park is about 30km south of Eğirdir en route to Yazılı Canyon Nature Park, and the two can be visited in one day.

Zından Cave

Roughly 30km southeast of Eğirdir, and about 1km north of Aksu by a Roman bridge, is the entrance to the kilometre-long Zından Cave (Zından Mağarası), which features Byzantine ruins, stalactites and stalagmites, and the so-called 'hamam' room. The cave makes a good cycling day trip.

Mt Davraz

Rising between three lakes, Mt Davraz (Davraz Dağı; 2653m) has great skiing from mid-December to March. A day-long section of the St Paul Trail leads between here and Kasnak Forest. Davraz offers nordic and downhill skiing, plus snowboarding, and the 1.2km-long chairlift is fast and modern. A day on the slopes here (including equipment hire and lift pass) costs around €50. The ski centre has accommodation ranging from penions to five-star chains such as Sirene, but staying in Eğirdir, 25km northeast, is cheaper and not difficult.

Antiocheia-in-Pisidia

About 2km from Yalvaç is Antiocheia-in-Pisidia (⊙9am-6pm) FREE, a largely unexcavated ancient Pisidian city. St Paul of Tarsus visited several times (as recorded in the Bible's Acts of the Apostles). On the strategic borderland of ancient Phrygia and Pisidia, it became an important Byzantine city, but was abandoned in the 8th century after Arab attacks.

Beyond the gate, a Roman road leads up past triumphal arch foundations, then turns right to the theatre. Further uphill, on a flat area surrounded by a semicircular rock wall, is the main shrine. Originally dedicated to the Anatolian mother goddess Cybele, and later to the moon god Men, it became an imperial Roman cult temple of Augustus. On the left is the nymphaeum, once a spring.

Several Antiocheian aqueduct arches are visible across the fields. Downhill from the nymphaeum, the ruined Roman baths feature several excavated large chambers, and a largely intact original ceiling. The foundations of St Paul's Basilica also remain.

Yalvaç Museum (Yalvaç Müzesi; ⊙8.30am-5.30pm Tue-Sun) FREE has a modest artefact collection, and a market takes place in Yalvaç on Monday.

Sagalassos

To visit the sprawling ruins of Sagalassos, high amidst the jagged peaks of Ak Dağ (White Mountain), is to approach myth: the ruined city set in stark mountains seems to illuminate the Sagalassian perception of a sacred harmony between nature, architecture and the great gods of antiquity.

The very antithesis of the 'Ephesus experience', Sagalassos is rarely troubled by tour buses or crowds; sometimes the visiting archaeologists and sheep wandering the slopes outnumber tourists. This is a place for getting perspective, for feeling the raw Anatolian wind on your face, and of course, for seeing some very impressive ancient ruins. While you can rush through in about 90 minutes, take the time to linger and properly appreciate this mountaintop site.

Sagalassos is one of the Mediterranean's largest archaeological projects. Although repeatedly devastated by earthquakes, it was never pillaged, and reconstruction is slowly moving ahead.

History

Sagalassos was founded about 1200 BC by a warlike tribe of 'Peoples from the Sea' seeking defensive positioning. A large swamp (perhaps even a lake) probably covered part of the lowland where today's village stands. Ancient Sagalassos would thus have been protected on three sides by mountains, and on the other by water.

Sagalassos later became second only to Antiocheia-in-Pisidia in Pisidian society. The locals adopted Greek cultural, linguistic and religious mores. Alexander the Great claimed it in 333 BC, and its oldest ruins date from the Hellenistic period he opened. Although most surviving structures are Roman, inscriptions are in Greek (the ancient world's lingua franca).

Sagalassos prospered under the Romans, its grain export, mountain springs and iron ore making it economically important and self-sufficient. Despite the high elevation, Sagalassos was well integrated into Rome's Anatolian road system. In the 4th century, the city became a Christian, Byzantine outpost. However, plague and disasters like the 590 earthquake damaged the city's sophisticated structures and dispersed its surviving population. After a massive 7th-century quake, Sagalassos was abandoned; survivors moved to villages or occupied fortified hamlets among the rubble.

Seljuk warriors defeated the last Byzantine defenders in the mid-13th century, but the remote and largely ruined city had little strategic value for the Ottomans. And so it slumbered for centuries, guarded by sheep and birds, until 1706, when a French traveller commissioned by King Louis XIV 'discovered' it. Yet it was not until 1824 that the ancient city's actual name was finally deciphered, by a British reverend and antiquarian, FVJ Arundell.

◎ Sights

At the ticket booth (admission ₺10; ⊙9am-7pm summer, 8.30am-5pm winter), request the *anahtar* (key) to the oft-closed Neon Library. From the entrance you can turn up to the right, starting from the top and working your way downhill (a somewhat steeper approach), or proceed from the bottom and work your way up and around.

Following the latter, clockwise route, see the marble colonnaded street that marked the city's southern entrance from the lowland valleys. The lack of wheel indentations suggests that mainly pedestrians used this street, which is the spine and central axis of Sagalassos, stretching upwards through it.

From below, it would have appeared that the city's terraced fountains were one triple-tiered tower of water – an impressive optical illusion. Passing through the Tiberian gate, see the lower agora and the massive reconstructed Roman baths complex to the right. At the agora's rear (back up the metal staircase), the Hadrianic nymphaeum stands flanked by the mountainside. The well-preserved former fountain here contains elaborate sculptures of mythic (and mostly headless) Nereids and Muses. A ruined Odeon sits just beyond.

The main path now winds up to the upper agora, once the main civic area and political centre. Thanks to restoration, it boasts Sagalassos' most impressive attraction: the Antonine Nymphaeum, a huge fountain complex some 9m high and 28m across. Originally wrought from seven different kinds of stone, the fountain was ornately decorated with Medusa heads and fish motifs. Although it collapsed in the 590 earthquake, the rubble lay clustered, aiding modern restorers. The impressive result is a massive structure supported by rows of thick columns (including bright blue marble ones in the centre), through which huge sheets of water gush into a lengthy receptacle. The fountain is bedecked by statues, including a large marble Dionysus replica (the original is in Burdur Museum).

The agora's western edge is flanked by the bouleuterion; some of its seating remains intact. Rising over the fountain in the northwest corner is a 14m-high heroon (hero's monument). In 333 BC, Alexander the Great had a statue of himself erected here (now in Burdur Museum too). Peer over the agora's southern edge to spot the macellon (food market), dedicated to Emperor Marcus Aurelius, with its trademark Corinthian columns. Note the tholos in the middle; the deep fountain was used to sell live fish.

From here, turn right and up into the hills for the late Hellenistic Doric fountainhouse, its piping now reattached to its original Roman-era source. Behind it is the Neon Library, with its fine mosaic floor. In the darkness at the rear, an original Greek inscription commemorates Flavius Severianus Neon, a noble who funded the library in AD 120. The back podium contained curving and rectangular niches for storing reading material. The library was modified over the following centuries, with the striking mosaic of Achilles' departure for Troy commissioned during the brief reign of Emperor Julian (361–363), whose unsuccessful attempt to restore paganism to the Orthodox empire augured his demise.

Finally, atop the hill is Sagalassos' 9000-seat Roman theatre – one of Turkey's most complete, despite earthquake damage to the seating rows. Just above its top steps, walk parallel with the theatre through its eerie tunnel, where performers and contestants once entered (note that it is dark, strewn with debris and has a very low exit point). The bluff east of here offers stunning panoramic views over the city, mountains and plains.

ⓘ Information

Since Sagalassos sprawls upwards across steep terrain, wear sturdy shoes. Even on hot and sunny days, the treeless and exposed site is often windy, and clouds can suddenly arrive (bring an extra shirt or sweater). In summer, go early or late to avoid the midday sun.

It takes roughly 1½ to four hours to do Sagalassos. Signage is excellent, with detailed and colourful representations of the various structures. A map at the entrance details various routes around the site (you may wish to photograph it as it does not appear again); the itinerary we have outlined above corresponds to the two-hour route. During the summer, archaeologists sometimes give free guided tours and answer questions. Out of season, it is basically all yours.

At the ticket office is a cafe, a bookshop and toilets; **Ağlasun** (7km below) has shops, services and small restaurants.

ⓘ Getting There & Away

A transfer/taxi from Eğirdir costs about ₺60 (minimum three passengers); vehicles typically leave at 9am and return by 4pm. Organise it through your pension or Eğirdir Outdoor Centre (p315), which links up independent travellers.

Otherwise, hourly dolmuşes run from Isparta's *köy garaj* to Ağlasun (₺5, one hour, 6am onwards). Coming back, the last Ağlasun–Isparta dolmuş leaves at 9.30pm in summer, 6pm in winter; the last Isparta–Eğirdir service leaves at 9.45pm in summer, 7pm in winter. A few daily **Ağlasun Minibüs Kooperatifi** (www.aglasunkoop.com) minibuses link Ağlasun with Antalya (₺13, 2½ hours).

From Ağlasun, a steep and winding road climbs 7km to the ticket office. There is also a 3km path up. A return taxi costs ₺35 (including waiting time at Sagalassos of an hour or so); your dolmuş driver from Isparta may be persuaded to do the same for a similar fee.

Antalya & the Turquoise Coast

Why Go?

The ancient Lycians were on to something when they based their empire here. This is Turkey at its most staggeringly beautiful. Sandy sweeps of shore hug a coastline lapped by jade waters and backed by jagged, forest-blanketed slopes. The Turquoise Coast is prime sun-and-sea territory but step off the beach and you'll find the ancient cities of Xanthos, Letoön and Arykanda perched precariously on hilltops and ornate tombs carved into cliffs at Tlos and Myra. While hike any section of the 500km-long Lycian Way trail and you are rewarded with scenery well worth the sweat.

If you just want the beach though, you're in the right place. Patara's knock-'em-dead stretch of sand and Çıralı's cosseted cove are two of the best for beach-sloth inaction. Of course there are ancient sites just around the corner from both. Maybe the Lycians were partial to a bit of sandcastle action as well.

Best Places to Eat

➡ İkbal (p357)
➡ Levissi Garden (p343)
➡ Vanilla (p374)
➡ Korsan Fish Terrace (p351)
➡ Meğri Lokantasi (p336)

Best Places to Stay

➡ Hoyran Wedre Country House (p361)
➡ Hotel Villa Mahal (p350)
➡ Hideaway Hotel (p356)
➡ Mehtap Pansiyon (p360)
➡ Myland Nature (p364)

When to Go
Antalya

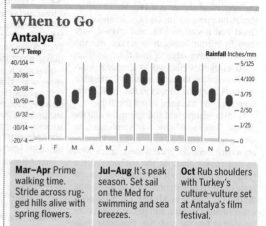

Mar–Apr Prime walking time. Stride across rugged hills alive with spring flowers.

Jul–Aug It's peak season. Set sail on the Med for swimming and sea breezes.

Oct Rub shoulders with Turkey's culture-vulture set at Antalya's film festival.

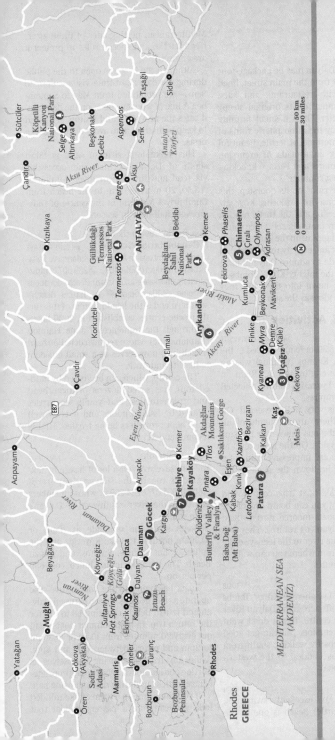

Antalya & the Turquoise Coast Highlights

1 Traversing the scenic section of the Lycian Way that begins from the haunting Greek ruins of **Kayaköy** (p342).

2 Brushing up on classical world history amid the ruins of **Patara** (p346) before an afternoon of lazing on its 20km-long beach.

3 Kayaking over Kekova Island's sunken city near the village of **Üçağız** (p358).

4 Wandering back in time within the labyrinthine alleys of **Antalya's** (p365) historic Kaleiçi district.

5 Lounging on Çıralı beach by day, then after dark hiking up to the eternal **Chimaera** (p363) flame.

6 Dusting off your explorer hat to scramble amid the lonely ruins of **Arykanda** (p361).

7 Experiencing this jaw-droppingly lush slice of the Med from the sea – setting sail from **Fethiye** or **Göcek.**

Dalyan

0252 / POP 5094

Laid-back little Dalyan may be package-tour fodder but away from the main street, lined cheek-to-jowl with restaurants and bars, it still retains much of its original sleepy riverside character. Once a small farming community, today the atmospheric ruins of Kaunos and hinterland of fertile, beautiful waterways bring an armada of excursion boats from Marmaris and Fethiye knocking on its door during summer.

As well as the ruins on its doorstep, this is an excellent base for exploring Köyceğiz Gölü (Lake Köyceğiz) and the turtle nesting grounds at nearby İztuzu Beach. Once you're done for the day lapping up the sun on a boat trip or traversing ancient city remnants, pull up a pew riverside to admire Dalyan's most famous feature: the mighty Kings' Tombs of ancient Kaunos; hewn into the cliffs, they take on a golden glow as the sun sets.

Sights & Activities

Kaunos   ARCHAEOLOGICAL SITE
(admission ₺10; 8.30am-7pm) Founded in the 9th century BC, Kaunos (Caunus) was an important Carian city by 400 BC. Right on the border with Lycia, its culture reflected aspects of both empires.

The theatre is very well preserved. On the hill above there are remnants of an acropolis and fabulous views over the surrounding countryside. On the same level as the theatre there are impressive ruins of a Roman bath while down the slope is the port agora.

Two-hour guided boat trips cost around ₺20. Alternatively, you can board one of the private rowing boats moored next to Saki restaurant in Dalyan (₺4 return). They will take you across the river to the teensy settlement of Çandır, from where you can walk to Kaunos in 20 minutes.

Kings' Tombs   TOMB
Dalyan's famous Lycian-style Kings' Tombs are set into the cliffs across the Dalyan River southwest of the centre. If you don't want to take a boat excursion, you can get good views of the tombs by walking south from town along Maraş Caddesi to the western end of Kaunos Sokak.

İztuzu Beach   BEACH
(İztuzu Kumsalı) An excellent swimming beach, İztuzu (Turtle) Beach is one of the Mediterranean nesting sites of the loggerhead turtle, and special rules to protect it are enforced.

Although the beach is open to the public during the day, night-time visits – 8pm to 8am – are prohibited from May to September. A line of wooden stakes on the beach indicates the nest sites, and visitors are asked to keep behind them to avoid disturbing the nests.

This 4.5km-long strip of sand is 13km south of Dalyan's centre and accessible via road and the Dalyan River. Minibuses (₺3.50, 20 minutes) run to the beach from Cumhuriyet Meydanı in the centre of Dalyan every half-hour in season.

Sea Turtle Research, Rescue
& Rehabilitation Centre   WILDLIFE RESERVE
(Deniz Kaplumbağaları Araştırma, Kurtarma ve Rehabilitasyon Merkezi (DEKAMER); 289 0077; http://caretta.pamukkale.edu.tr; İztuzu Beach; donations welcome; 10am-6pm) At İztuzu Beach's southern end is the headquarters of this turtle rescue centre, established in 2009 largely through the influence of June Haimoff (Kaptan June) whose reconstructed baraka (beach hut) now serves as a small museum to her life and work.

The centre, which can be visited by guided tour, has saved dozens of loggerhead and green turtles, and you'll see turtles injured by fishing hooks and nets as well as by boat propellers being treated. Highly recommended.

Boat Excursions   BOAT TOUR
You can save yourself a lot of hassle by taking boats run by the Dalyan Kooperatifi (0541 505 0777, 284 2094), whose members moor on the river southwest of Dalyan's main square.

Boats leave the quayside at 10am or 10.30am heading to Lake Köyceğiz and the Sultaniye hot springs, Kaunos, and İztuzu Beach. The tours, including lunch, cost ₺30 per person.

Boats belonging to the cooperative also operate a river dolmuş service between Dalyan and İztuzu Beach, charging ₺8 to ₺10 for the return trip. In high summer boats head out every 20 minutes from 10am or 10.30am to 2pm and return between 1pm and 6pm. Avoid any trips advertising themselves as 'turtle-spotting' tours, which inappropriately lure turtles out during daylight using bait.

If you can drum up a team of like-minded folk, you can hire a passenger boat that holds from eight to 12 people. A two-hour tour just to Kaunos costs ₺80 for the boat; if you want to visit the Sultaniye hot springs as well, count on three hours and ₺130.

Kaunos Tours   ADVENTURE SPORTS
(☑ 284 2816; www.kaunostours.com; Sarısu Sokak 1/A) On the main square opposite the landmark sea turtles statue, Kaunos Tours offers any number of organised activities both on and off the water, including canyoning (€30), sea kayaking (€30), jeep safaris (€28) and trekking (€28). Prices include lunch.

Ethos Dalyan Dive Centre   DIVING
(☑ 284 2332, 0555 412 5438; www.dalyandive.com; Yalı Sokak 5) This professional outfit offers snorkelling and diving trips. A day-long excursion including two dives and lunch is around ₺125.

🛏 Sleeping

Happy hunting grounds for hotels and pensions is Maraş Caddesi, a 1km-long road running north–south that ends at a sharp bend in the river and carries on as Kaunos Sokak. The majority of Dalyan's hotels and pensions are only open between April and late-October.

Bahaus Resort Dalyan   HOSTEL €
(☑ 284 5050, 0533 688 2988; www.bahausresort.com; İztuzu Yolu 25; dm €20-24, s/d/f €55/65/90; ❇ @ 🛜 ≋) A 'hostel resort' may sound like the ultimate oxymoron, but this is the real McCoy. The Bahaus Resort is spread over an enormous farm-like property and has both dormitories (with four to eight beds) and private rooms. Food at breakfast is locally sourced, and we love the telescope in the common room just begging for a little moon-gazing.

It's about 1km from central Dalyan, along the road to İztuzu Beach.

Dalyan Camping   CAMPING GROUND €
(☑ 284 5316, 0506 882 9173; www.dalyancamping.net; Maraş Caddesi 144; campsite per person ₺15, caravan ₺40, bungalow ₺80, without bathroom ₺50; ❇ 🛜) This well-shaded site offers

---

LOCAL KNOWLEDGE

KAPTAN JUNE: MARINE ENVIRONMENTALIST

Sea turtles were the last thing on Briton June Haimoff's mind when she sailed into Dalyan on her boat *Bouboulina* in 1975. But after 'Kaptan June' – as the locals had affectionately dubbed her – set up house in a *baraka* (hut) on İztuzu Beach, got to observe the *caretta caretta* (loggerhead turtles) at ground level and fended off, with the help of a number of Turkish and foreign environmentalists, plans to develop the beach into a 1800-bed Marmaris-style hotel resort, they became her life's work. Kaptan June set up the Sea Turtles Conservation Foundation (www.dalyanturtles.com) and was awarded an MBE in 2011 at age 89.

What is the greatest threat to the sea turtles?
Humans. The proliferation of dams and roads has devastated lots of the Mediterranean coast. The turtles' habitats are being destroyed for the sake of tourist development. As for injuries to the turtles, more than 90% are human-inflicted and come from fishing hooks and nets and, most commonly, boat propellers.

What steps has the foundation taken to reduce these?
Our first project was to give away 90 locally manufactured propeller guards to excursion boats on the Dalyan River and there are plans to hand out another 100. We are now looking into sourcing and distributing biodegradable fishing line which won't harm the turtles if they happen to ingest it.

How can visitors to İztuzu Beach reduce their impact?
The urge to see a turtle in nature is not easily satisfied; they only come out at night during mating season and the beach is closed then. Some boat companies offer 'turtle-spotting' tours by day and attract the turtles by feeding them their favourite crab or chicken, which is not suitable for them. I recommend travellers join tours run by boats with propeller guards; these can be identified by a flag bearing the foundation's logo. The boat cooperative, especially the younger captains, has been very supportive. Once visitors use the services of these captains exclusively, others will follow suit.

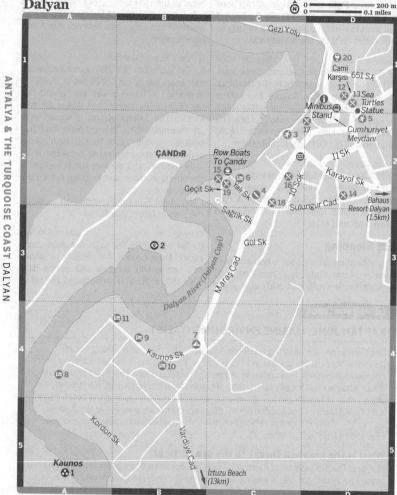

Dalyan

rustic bungalows in three sizes, with stone floors and basic furniture, as well as space to park the caravan or set up your tent. Smaller bungalows don't have en suites or air-conditioning. There's a kitchen and washing machines for guest-use and the jetty-terrace attached to the restaurant looks right over to the King's Tombs.

★ **Kilim Hotel** HOTEL €€
(☑ 284 2253, 0532 645 8400; www.kilimhotel.com; Kaunos Sokak 7; s/d/f €45/57/69; ❊ @ ☎ ❊) Whether you choose a huge, airy room in the main house, or hop over the road to the

riverside annexe cottages, you can't go wrong at this peaceful home-from-home. Owners Becky and Emrah have created a relaxing retreat where guests really do feel like friends. We especially like the cushion-strewn riverside deck – perfect for lazy lounging.

For the more active, there's also Pilates workouts three times a week. Book direct with the hotel to bag the best room deals.

Happy Caretta HOTEL €€
(☑ 284 2109, 0532 645 8400; www.happycaretta. com; Kaunos Sokak 26; s/d €50/70; ❊ @ ☎) Amid the magical garden of cypress trees

Dalyan

ANTALYA & THE TURQUOISE COAST DALYAN

and palms, the 14 rooms here are simple and rather small, but comfortable and stylishly decorated with natural materials. The lovely terrace-dock waiting for you to take the plunge is a plus, and the view of the illuminated Kings' Tombs by night is priceless.

Affable owners İlknur and Münir make their own plum and fig jams from their fruit trees and lay on a superb four-course home-cooked meal (₺45) when pre-ordered.

Midas Pension   PENSION €€
(☑ 284 2195; www.midasdalyan.com; Kaunos Sokak 32; s/d ₺90/120; ❄ 🖳) Selçuk and Saadet Nur are the welcoming hosts of this family-friendly riverside pension complete with waterside deck-cum-dock covered in shady vine trellises. The 10 simple rooms are cosy and clean with cute towel-art swans laid out to welcome you.

Çınar Sahil Otel   HOTEL €€
(☑ 284 2402, 0555 507 3035; www.cinarsahilhotel. com; Yalı Sokak 14; s/d ₺80/100; ❄ 🖳) Fronting the river and surrounded by plane trees, this simple but very central hotel has 10 impeccably clean rooms and a terrace with great views across to the Kings' Tombs. Ask for one of the four rooms with balcony and river view. Barbecues are organised in season, and there's a boat accommodating up to four people for rent.

Kamarca House Hotel   BOUTIQUE HOTEL €€€
(☑ 284 4517, 0532 283 9001; www.kamarcahotel. com; Tepearası Köyü; r €160, ste €470; ❄ 🖳 🖳) If you're seeking luxury amidst absolute tranquillity head for this boutique hotel in Tepearası village, 8km northeast of Dalyan. The five rooms and suites are wonderfully

decorated in a tactile mix of natural wood and stone, antique furnishings and original artwork. Hostess Kamer's cooking is legendary; she ran her own restaurant in the USA. For full board add €75.

Dalyan Resort   RESORT €€€
(☑ 284 5499, 0530 665 990; www.dalyanresort. com; 114 Sokak 12; s/d/ste €100/110/130; ❄ 🖳 🖳) This snazzy 58-room hotel is on its own little peninsula that juts into the river about 1.2km from the town centre. The service is discreet and there are full views of the Kings' Tombs from the classy pool. The health centre and spa are excellent; try the elegant Turkish hamam (full treatment €20).

Eating & Drinking

Dalyan's restaurant scene swings rather wildly between high quality and tourist-oriented places making generally poor versions of international staples. Saturday is market day in Dalyan – great for stocking up on fresh local produce. There are a host of bars and other drinking spots along Maraş Caddesi.

Demet Pastanesi   CAFE €
(Maraş Caddesi 39; pastries & desserts ₺4-6; ⊙ 7.30am-midnight) Excellent pastries, tantalising Turkish desserts, and decent coffee. If you're hankering for a sugar-hit, this is Dalyan's top spot. The hazelnut and walnut tart is to die for. It's also a great place to pick up breakfast and picnic supplies.

Dalyan İz   CAFE €
(☑ 0542 451 5451; www.dalyaniz.com; Sulungur Caddesi; cake ₺5-8; ⊙ 9.30am-7pm) This sweet garden cafe is hugely popular with Dalyan

expats due to the ever-changing array of homemade baking and good filter coffee. It's also home to a shop selling interesting hand-painted ceramics and tiles and the friendly owners are a great source of local information.

Çağrı PIDE €

(Gülpınar Caddesi; pide ₺7-12) This cheap and cheerful pide (Turkish-style pizza) place is nearly always packed with happy customers.

Atay Dostlar Sofrası TURKISH €€

(☑284 2156; Camı Karşısı 10; mains ₺12-20) You'll find competent staff and good prices at this local workers' restaurant where visitors are greeted warmly and fed well. There's a point-and-pick counter and dishes are freshly made.

★ Dalyan La Vie MODERN TURKISH €€€

(☑284 4142; www.dalyanlavie.com; Sağlik Sokak 5; mains ₺18-32) What was the tired Riverside Restaurant has metamorphosed into one of the most exciting new restaurants on the Turquoise Coast. The seafood dishes, especially the casseroles, are highly recommended, desserts are Turkish traditional with a twist, and the location on the river is enviable.

Saki TURKISH €€€

(☑284 5212; Geçit Sokak; mains ₺15-28; ☑) With a brilliant (and breezy) location right on the riverfront, this very authentic eatery serves some of the most wholesome Turkish food in Dalyan. There's no menu; choose from the glass cabinet of homemade meze (₺7 to ₺12) as well as meat, vegetarian and fish dishes.

Kordon SEAFOOD €€€

(☑284 2261; Çarşı İçi 2; mains ₺20-25; ☑) Dalyan's long-established (since 1987) fish restaurant, the Kordon has a commanding position on the river just up from where the excursion boats moor. Ichthyophobes can choose from a large selection of steaks and grills, and there are a half-dozen vegetarian choices on offer.

Mai Steakhouse INTERNATIONAL €€€

(☑284 2642; Sulungur Caddesi 1; mains ₺20-30) This relaxed restaurant, with a nifty blue-and-white decoration theme going on, whips up a decent steak, some Mediterranean flavours and a few other international dishes.

Jazz Bar Dalyan BAR

(www.jazzbardalyan.com; Gülpinar Caddesi; ☺9pm-late) We're not sure where the jazz is, but this lively place has regular decent live music and a fine array of cocktails on offer.

ⓘ Information

Tourist Office (☑284 4235; Cumhuriyet Medanı; ☺8am-noon & 1-5.30pm Mon-Fri) Keeps banker's hours in a modern glass-walled kiosk in Dalyan's main square.

ⓘ Getting There & Away

Dolmuşes (minibuses) stop in Cumhuriyet Meydanı, near the main mosque. There are no direct minibuses from here to Dalaman. First take a minibus to Ortaca (₺4, every 25 minutes in high season, every hour in low season, 14km) and change there. From Ortaca otogar (bus station), regular buses go to Köyceğiz (₺6, 25 minutes, 22km), Dalaman (₺4, 15 minutes, 9km) and Fethiye (₺10, 1¼ hours, 75km). A taxi to Dalaman airport from Dalyan costs ₺85.

From May to September there are daily dolmuşes from Dalyan to Köyceğiz, Marmaris, and Fethiye at 10am.

Köyceğiz

☑0252 / POP 9333

A short distance off the D400, the main coastal highway, Köyceğiz (keuy-jay-iz) lies on the northern side of Köyceğiz Gölü, a large and serene lake linked to the Mediterranean by the Dalyan River. As beautiful (and ecologically significant) as it is, a brackish lake is not major competition for the Med, and this farming community attracts only modest tourism, depending still on citrus fruits, pomegranates, honey and a bit of cotton for its livelihood. The region is also famous for its Oriental sweetgum trees (*Liquidambar orientalis*), the sap of which is used to produce frankincense. If you're looking for a place to take long walks, do a bit of boating and get away from the coastal scrum, you've come to the right place.

⊙ Sights & Activities

Köyceğiz is a town for strolling. Hit the lakeshore promenade called Kordon Boyu and walk past the pleasant town park, shady tea gardens and waterfront restaurants. Most pensions have bicycles available for free to guests, so take a ride out to the surrounding orchards and farmland. The road along the western shore of the lake to the Sultaniye mud pools offers superb views. It's 26km by road to the springs or you can take a boat excursion from the promenade.

Köyceğiz Waterfall
WATERFALL

This small waterfall, 7km northwest of Köyceğiz, is the local's favourite spot for a refreshing dip during summer. Take any dolmuş heading west towards Marmaris and Muğla and tell the driver you want to get off at the şelale (shay-*lah*-lay) or 'waterfall'. It's about a 15-minute walk from the highway.

Köyceğiz-Dalyan Nature Reserve
PARK

The Köyceğiz-Dalyan Nature Reserve has a growing reputation among outdoor types for its excellent hiking and cycling. The park is home to large swaths of Liquidambar *(Liquidambar orientalis)* trees and to wetland areas rich in birdlife.

Sultaniye Hot Springs
SPRING

(Sultaniye Kaplıcaları; admission ₺8) For some good (and dirty) fun, head for the Sultaniye Hot Springs, on the southeast shore of Lake Köyceğiz, which are accessible from both Köyceğiz and Dalyan. These bubbling hot mud pools (temperatures can reach 39°C) contain mildly radioactive mineral waters that are rich in chloride, sodium, hydrogen sulphide and bromide.

At the smaller baths just before the Dalyan River joins the lake, you can pamper yourself with a restorative body-pack of mud in a steaming sulphur pool.

To get here from Köyceğiz, take the bus headed for Ekincik (₺6) at 9.30am, which will drop you off at the springs. From Dalyan, take a dolmuş boat (₺10, 30 minutes), which leaves when full (every half-hour or so in summer, every hour otherwise) from the riverfront.

Boat Excursions
BOAT TOUR

You can take boat trips across the lake south to Dalyan and the Kaunos ruins for ₺15 to ₺30 per person including lunch.

🛏 Sleeping

Most of the town's pensions and hotels are either on or just off Kordon Boyu along the lake.

★ Flora Hotel
HOTEL €

(☎262 4976, 0535 320 8567; www.florahotel.com.tr; Kordon Boyu 96; s/d/tr €20/30/50; 🅟 @ 🛜) 🌿 This backpacker favourite gets our vote as the best place in Köyceğiz, mostly because of its enthusiastic and very 'green' owner Alp. Some of the 16 rooms have balconies with views to the lake and there are also four apartments with a kitchenette, excellent for

self-caterers. Guests can use the hotel's kayaks and bicycles for free.

Alp can arrange walks into the nearby Gölgeli Mountains for birdwatching (almost 150 species have been spotted) as well as fishing trips in the lake (catch and release) and on the sea.

Hotel Alila
HOTEL €

(☎262 1150; www.hotelalila.com; Emeksiz Caddesi 13; s/d ₺50/80; 🅟 🛜) Full of character, the bougainvillea-bedecked Alila has 20 simple rooms, 16 of which have direct views of the lake from small balconies. The friendly owner Ömer runs the place professionally and attends to every detail (right down to the swan-folded towels).

Fulya Pension
PENSION €

(☎262 2301; fulyapension@mynet.com; Ali İhsan Kalmaz Caddesi 88; s/d ₺20/40; 🅟 @ 🛜) This brilliant budget option, set back from the lake, has 16 spick-and-span rooms with balconies, and there's a large roof terrace with a bar and occasional live music. Bikes are available free of charge, and boat trips (₺20, including lunch) to the local attractions are a bargain. Guests love the breakfasts here.

Tango Hostel & Pension
HOSTEL €

(☎262 2501, 0533 811 2478; Ali İhsan Kalmaz Caddesi 112; dm/s/d ₺25/30/60; 🅟 @ 🛜) Managed by Şahin, the local school sports teacher, this place is big on activities including boat trips (₺20), trekking (₺25) and rafting (₺60). The 26 rooms (including six dorms) are bright, cheerful and well maintained, and there's a pleasant garden. It's away from the water and very much a party place. Bikes are free.

Kaunos Hotel
HOTEL €€

(☎262 3730; www.kaunoshotel.com; Ali İhsan Kalmaz Caddesi 29; s/d €45/65; 🅟 @ 🛜 🏊) This salmon-coloured colossus commands a prominent position on the waterfront, with full views of the lake from 50 of the 73 rooms. The rooms, all of which have balconies, are comfortable and pin-neat rather than remarkable. Spend most of your time at the huge terrace pool.

🍴 Eating

There are several predominantly fish restaurants bunched up along the lake and lots of cheap and cheerful eateries off the main square. You'll find several places selling *köyceğiz lokması*, a local speciality of fried dough drenched in syrup. Don't blame us for your dentist bills later.

The local market is held every Monday near the police station opposite the tourist office at the southern end of Atatürk Bulvarı.

★ **Mutlu Kardeşler** PIDE **€**

(☑262 2482; Fevzipaşa Caddesi; köfte & kebap ₺10-15, pide ₺6-12; ☉7am-11pm) Much loved by locals, this simple and exceptionally friendly place, off the main square, dishes up tasty Turkish favourites with plenty of smiles. The outdoor tables on a little shaded terrace are prime put-your-feet-up and relax territory.

Colıba MODERN TURKISH **€€**

(☑262 2987; Cengiz Topel Caddesi 64; mains ₺15-25; ☉10am-midnight) This whitewashed and wooden restaurant lakeside, serves delicious mixed meze platters, *alabalık* (trout) and grills. The shaded terrace has lovely views of the lake.

Thera Fish Restaurant SEAFOOD **€€€**

(☑0541 833 6154; Cengiz Topel Caddesi; mains ₺20-30; ☉9am-midnight) On Köyceğiz's main waterfront road, you can pick your fish fresh from the large tank on the terrace. The red mullet fillets are excellent, as is the sea bream. For a special occasion the grilled prawns are perfect for sharing.

ℹ Information

Tourist Office (☑262 4703; ☉8.30am-5pm Mon-Fri) South of the main square and almost on the lake; stocks brochures and photocopies of a simple hand-drawn map.

ℹ Getting There & Away

The otogar serving Köyceğiz is just off the main highway, about 2km from the lake; dolmuşes (₺2) run every 15 minutes or so into town. Buses go to Dalaman (₺6, 30 minutes, 26km), Marmaris (₺12, one hour, 63km), Ortaca (₺5, 25 minutes, 22km) and Fethiye (₺15, two hours, 65km) hourly.

Dalaman

☑0252 / POP 25,313

Little has changed for this agricultural town since the ever-expanding **Dalaman International Airport** (☑0252 792 5555; www.at mairport.aero/Dalaman_en/index.php) was built on the neighbouring river delta, with most arrivals moving on immediately.

It's just over 5km from the airport to the town of Dalaman and another 5km from there to the D400 coastal highway. Besides seasonal flights to many European cities, **Turkish Airlines** (www.thy.com) and **Pegasus Airlines** (www.flypgs.com/en/) operate between them four to six daily flights to İstanbul year-round, costing around ₺85 one-way.

From the airport, **Havaş Airport Buses** (☑0555 985 1165; www.havas.net/en/) have a bus schedule that meets most incoming flights. The fare to Fethiye (via Göcek) is ₺10, and to Marmaris (via Ortaca and Köyceğiz) is ₺15. A taxi into Dalaman town is ₺30 to ₺35.

From Dalaman's otogar, near the junction of Kenan Evren Bulvarı and Atatürk Caddesi, you can catch buses to Antalya (₺35, four hours, 335km), Köyceğiz (₺8, 30 minutes, 26km) and Marmaris (₺15, 1½ hours, 90km). All routes north and east pass through either Muğla (₺20, two hours, 87km) or Fethiye (₺15, one hour, 46km).

Göcek

☑0252 / POP 4285

Göcek (*geuh-*jek) is the western Mediterranean's high-end yacht spot and the attractive bay makes a relaxing alternative to Fethiye despite all the building going on in the hills surrounding the town. There's a small but clean swimming beach at the western end of the quay, and boat-charter companies scattered throughout the town.

🛏 Sleeping

Tufan Pansiyon PENSION **€**

(☑645 1334, 0546 921 7460; Belediye Marina; s/d ₺50/60; ✱) In Göcek's centre and just 25m from the sea, the family-run Tufan has eight small but spotless and rather sweet rooms, half of which have sea views from a shared balcony.

Göcek Dim Hotel HOTEL **€€**

(☑645 1294, 0532 796 2798; www.gocekdimhotel. com/eng/; Günlük Sokak 13; s/d/tr €40/50/60; ✱🛜🏊) With 15 plain but well-furnished rooms and a pleasant terrace, medium-sized pool and a location just opposite the beach, this hotel to the west of the centre offers good value. All rooms have a fridge and TV.

Villa Danlin HOTEL **€€€**

(☑645 1521; www.villadanlin.com; Çarşı İçi; s/d €65/75; ✱🛜🏊) We really like the homely, light-filled rooms and the friendly service at this lovely hotel on Göcek's main street. The charming little building at the front contains the lobby and three rooms while the other 10 are in a modern extension at the back overlooking a generously sized pool.

A&B Home Hotel
HOTEL €€€

(☑ 645 1820, 0532 255 2025; www.abhomehotel. com; Turgut Özal Caddesi; s/d €60/80; ❈ 🛜 ≋) The 11 smallish rooms here are decked out in shades of soothing lemon and the wrought iron bedsteads give them a cosy appeal. The beckoning pool on the attractive front terrace is a real winner. As is the excellent buffet breakfast.

Efe Hotel
LUXURY HOTEL €€€

(☑ 645 2646; www.efehotelgocek.com; Likya Caddesi 1; s/d €80/90, ste €100-130; ❈ 🛜 ≋) Hidden in a lush garden about 200m north of the Skopea Marina, Göcek's most ambitious hotel to date has 19 large and bright rooms, a half-Olympic-sized pool and restful mountain views. The garden bar is a delight.

✗ Eating & Drinking

West Cafe & Bistro
INTERNATIONAL €€

(☑ 645 2794; www.westcafegocek.com; Turgut Özal Caddesi; mains ₺10-25; 🛜) The views are fantastic and service is super-friendly at this relaxed restaurant with a menu that romps from burgers and wraps to seafood and more traditional Turkish fare. The coffee is possibly the best in Göcek, and the beer is welcomingly chilled, so it's a fine place to pop in just for a drink too.

Kebab Hospital Antep Sofrası
KEBAP €€

(☑ 645 1873; Turgut Özal Caddesi; mains ₺14-22; ⊙ 8am-midnight) It may have a joke name and not look like much but this is Göcek's top spot for chargrilled meat feasting. Grab a table on the marina side for kebap dining with a view. They also do pide and *lahmacun* (Arabic-style pizza) if you're not feeling in a grilled-meat mood.

Can Restaurant
SEAFOOD €€€

(☑ 645 1507; Skopea Marina; mains ₺15-30; ⊙ 7am-midnight) With a lovely terrace shaded by an old yucca tree and beachside seating, this local favourite serves a great selection of meze with some rather unusual options, including delicious seafood meze. For a special occasion, the house speciality is *tuzda balık* (fish baked in salt); expect to pay from ₺75 per kilo.

Blue Lounge Bar
BAR, RESTAURANT

(Çarşı Yolu Caddesi 36; ⊙ 8am-2am) On the marina, this relaxed and friendly bar is great for a sundowner after a day on the sea. Happy hour hails good deals on cocktails, there's a fine assortment of spirits, and the beer is always cold. The menu of steaks, seafood and some decent Asian flavours is a winner too.

🛍 Shopping

Muse Jewellery
JEWELLERY

(☑ 0533 361 6054; Turgut Özal Caddesi) Amidst all the chandlers and shops selling boat supplies is this uber-posh bling shop selling antique Ottoman jewellery. And with most of the baubles priced in euros with at least five digits, you'll almost have to be a sultan to afford them.

ℹ Getting There & Away

Buses drop you at the petrol station on the main road, from where it's a 1km walk to the centre. Dolmuşes drive into the main square, with its requisite bust of Atatürk, a PTT and ATMs. Dolmuşes depart every half-hour for Fethiye (₺7, 45 minutes, 30km). For Dalyan, change at Ortaca (₺5, 25 minutes, 19km, hourly).

Fethiye

☑ 0252 / POP 82,000

In 1958 an earthquake levelled the seaside city of Fethiye (feh-*tee*-yeh), sparing only the remains of the ancient city of Telmessos. More than half a century on and it is once again a prosperous hub of the western Mediterranean. Despite its booming growth, Fethiye is incredibly low-key for its size, due mostly to the restrictions on high-rise buildings and the transitory nature of the *gület* (Turkish yacht) business, which brings travellers flocking here April through to October.

Fethiye's natural harbour is perhaps the region's finest, tucked away in the southern reaches of a broad bay scattered with pretty islands, in particular Şövalye Adası, glimpsed briefly in the James Bond film *Skyfall*. About 15km south is Ölüdeniz, one of Turkey's seaside hot spots, and the surrounding countryside has many interesting sites to explore, including the ghost town of Kayaköy (Karmylassos), waiting patiently and in silence just over the hill.

⊙ Sights

There isn't much left to see of ancient Telmessos. Dotted around town you'll come across Lycian stone sarcophagi dating from around 450 BC and broken into by tomb robbers centuries ago. One excellent Lycian

Fethiye

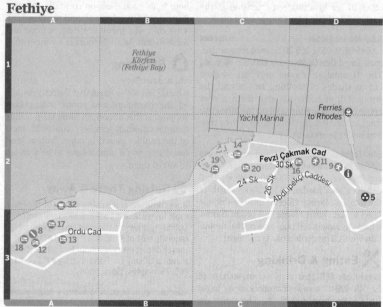

Fethiye

⊙ Sights
1 Crusader Fortress	F3
2 Fethiye Museum	G2
3 Lycian Sarcophagi	G3
4 Lycian Stone Sarcophagi	F2
5 Roman Theatre	D2
6 Tomb of Amyntas	H3

⊕ Activities, Courses & Tours
7 12-Island Tour Excursion Boats	E2
8 European Diving Centre	A3
9 Ocean Yachting Travel Agency	D2
10 Old Turkish Bath	E2
11 Yeşil Dalyan	D2

⊜ Sleeping
12 Duygu Pension	A3
13 Ferah Pension	A3
14 Hotel Doruk	C2
15 Orka Boutique Hotel	F2
16 Tan Pansiyon	D2
17 V-Go's Hotel & Guesthouse	A3
18 Villa Daffodil	A3

19 Yacht Classic Hotel	C2
20 Yildirim Guest House	C2

⊗ Eating
21 Cem & Can	F2
22 Ceyazir Usta	F2
23 Deniz Restaurant	F1
24 İskele Ocakbaşı	E2
25 Meğri Lokantasi	E2
26 Meğri Restaurant	E2
27 Nefis Pide	E2
28 Paşa Kebab	E2
29 Weekly Market	H1

⊜ Drinking & Nightlife
30 Cafe Cafe	E2
31 Car Cemetery	E2
32 Deniz Kafe	A2
33 Kismet	F1
34 Kum Saati Bar	E2

⊝ Shopping
Old Orient Carpet & Kilim Bazaar	(see 25)
35 Sister's Place	F2

sarcophagus is just east of the *belediye* (city hall). Another, good example is the **sarcophagus** serving as a traffic roundabout on Kaya Caddesi.

Fethiye Museum   MUSEUM
(www.lycianturkey.com/fethiye-museum.htm; 505 Sokak; admission ₺5; ⊗8am-5pm Tue-Sun) Focusing on Lycian finds from Telmessos as well as the ancient settlements of Tlos

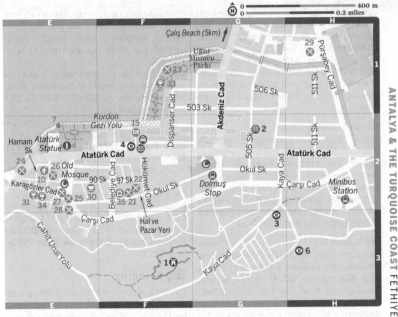

and Kaunos, this museum exhibits pottery, jewellery, small statuary and votive stones (including the important Grave Stelae and the Stelae of Promise). Its most prized significant possession, however, is the so-called Trilingual Stele from Letoön, dating from 358 BC, which was used partly to decipher the Lycian language with the help of ancient Greek and Aramaic.

The garden surrounding the museum contains an excellent lapidary of mostly Lycian sarcophagi and Roman tombstones, some of them portraying early Christian symbols and angels.

Tomb of Amyntas   TOMB
(⊘8am-7pm) FREE Fethiye's most recognisable sight is the mammoth Tomb of Amyntas, an Ionic temple facade carved into the sheer rock face in 350 BC, in honour of 'Amyntas son of Hermapias'. Located south of the centre, it is best visited at sunset. Smaller rock tombs lie about 500m to the east.

Roman Theatre   RUIN
FREE In the centre of Fethiye, just behind the harbour, is Telmessos' 6000-seat Roman theatre dating from the 2nd century BC. Neglected for years, it was undergoing serious restoration when we passed through.

Crusader Fortress   FORTRESS
On the hillside above (and south of) Fethiye and along the road to Kayaköy, you can't miss the ruined tower of a Crusader fortress, built by the Knights of St John at the start of the 15th century on earlier (perhaps Lycian, Greek and Roman) foundations.

Çalış Beach   BEACH
About 5km northeast of Fethiye's centre is Çalış, a narrow stretch of gravel beach lined with mass-produced hotels as well as pubs and chip shops patronised by resident British expats. Dolmuşes depart for Çalış (₺2, 10 minutes) from the minibus station beside the mosque every five to 10 minutes throughout the day.

🏃 Activities

Seven Capes   OUTDOORS
(☑0537 403 3779; www.sevencapes.com; Kayaköy) One of the best ways to see the Med up close is in a sea kayak. This experienced outfit offers daily kayaking tours including an excellent one between Ölüdeniz and Kabak via Butterfly Valley (€50), and a 'night paddling' tour (€45) under the stars.

They also offer daily Turkish cooking courses (€35) from their base in Kayaköy, and organise walking tours.

Ocean Yachting Travel Agency   OUTDOORS
(☑612 4807; www.oceantravelagency.com; Fevzi
Çakmak Caddesi; ◷9am-9pm Apr-Oct) Ocean
Yachting sells boat voyage trips and organises paragliding (₺150), day-long rafting
trips (₺105), jeep safaris (₺55) and plenty
of tours and boat trips in the surrounding
area including the daily 12 island boat trip
(₺30 to ₺50).

European Diving Centre   DIVING
(☑614 9771; www.europeandivingcentre.com;
Fevzi Çakmak Caddesi 133; ◷9am-7pm) British-
owned and operated European Diving
Centre, west of the main harbour in
Karagözler, offers recreational diving trips
and the full gamut of PADI dive courses
ranging from Discover Scuba dives (€47) up
to Divemaster and Instructor level.

Old Turkish Bath   HAMAM
(Tarihi Fethiye Hamamı; ☑614 9318; www.oldturkish
bath.com; Hamam Sokak 2-4, Paspatur; bath &
scrub ₺35, massage ₺25-60; ◷7am-midnight)
Low-key and small, the Old Turkish Bath
in Paspatur, the oldest section of Fethiye,
dates to the 16th century. There are separate
sections for men and women (and a mixed
section for couples). Extra services include
aromatherapy massages and facemasks.

☞ Tours

Fethiye is a major base for travellers wanting to explore the surrounding countryside
and coastline.

Many visitors not joining the longer blue
cruises opt for the 12-Island Tour (per person
incl lunch ₺30-35, on sailboat ₺50; ◷10.30am-
6pm, mid-Apr–Oct), a day-long boat trip
around Fethiye Körfezi (Fethiye Bay). The
boats usually stop at five or six islands and
cruise by the rest, but either way it's a great
way to experience the coastline. Hotels and
travel agencies sell tickets or you can deal
directly with the boat companies along the
waterfront parade at the marina.

The normal tour visits Yassıcalar (Flat
Island) for a stop and a swim, then Tersane Adası (Shipyard Island) for a dip and
a visit to the ruins, followed by Akvaryum
(Aquarium) for lunch, a swim and a snorkel. Cennet Koyu (Paradise Bay) is next for
a plunge, followed by Kleopatra Hamamı
(Cleopatra's Bath) and finally Kızılada (Red
Island) with its beach and mud baths.

Some of these boat tours are little more
than booze cruises that cram passengers
onto the boat and blast out loud music for

the entire time on the water. If this isn't your
scene make sure you check beforehand. In
general party-style tours usually charge
around ₺30 while the less-crowded boats
cost ₺50.

One reliable company based along the
waterfront promenade is Kardeşler Daily
Boat Company (☑612 4241, 0542 326 2314;
www.kardeslerboat.com).

If you have another day or so, excellent
boat tours of the same length go to or include Butterfly Valley via Ölüdeniz and allow you to walk, swim and visit ruins.

Fethiye tour agencies also organise the
popular Saklıkent Gorge Tour (per person
₺50), which includes the ruins at Tlos and a
trout lunch; and the Dalyan Tour (per person
₺50), which includes a shuttle to Dalyan, a
tour of Köyceğiz Gölü (Lake Köyceğiz), the
Sultaniye mud baths, Kaunos ruins and İz-
tuzu Beach.

🛏 Sleeping

The bulk of accommodation options are up
the hill behind the marina in Karagözler or
further west. Many pensions will organise
transport from the otogar, but there are also
frequent dolmuşes between the otogar and
Karagözler.

If you're a family looking for self-catering
accommodation, most holiday villas and
apartments are based at Çalış Beach, in the
nearby resorts of Hisarönü and Ovacık, and
in the village of Kayaköy.

★Yildirim Guest House   PENSION €
(☑614 4627, 0543 779 4732; www.yildirimguest
house.com; Fevzi Çakmak Caddesi 21; dm ₺25,
s/d/tr ₺50/80/120; ❄️🛜) This shipshape
hostel-pension just opposite the marina is
Fethiye's top pit-stop for budget travellers,
with a selection of dorms (with four to six
beds) and simple, spotless rooms. Well-
travelled host Omer Yapıs is a mine of local
information. There are free bikes for guests,
free tea and coffee, and pick-ups and excursions are all easily arranged.

Ferah Pension   PENSION €
(☑614 2816, 0532 265 0772; www.ferahpen-
sion.com; Ordu Caddesi 23; dm/s/d €15/25/38;
❄️🛜🏊) If you're looking for character you
can't bypass the Ferah. The inner-terrace,
dripping in vines and bedecked by flower
pots, has a teensy pool. The 10 simple rooms
are kept spick-and-span; grab one at the
very top of the house for harbour views to

ON THE DEEP BLUE SEA

For many travellers a four-day, three-night cruise on a *gület* (Turkish yacht) alo
Turquoise Coast – known locally as a 'blue voyage' *(mavi yolculuk)* – is the high
their trip to Turkey. Although advertised as a voyage between Fethiye and Olyn
boats usually start (or stop) at Demre and the trip to/from Olympos (1¼ hours,
bus. From Fethiye, boats usually call in at Ölüdeniz and Butterfly Valley and stop at Kaş,
Kalkan and/or Kekova, with the final night at Gökkaya Bay opposite the eastern end of
Kekova. A less common (but some say prettier) route is between Marmaris on the Aegean Sea and Fethiye.

Food is usually included in the price, but you sometimes have to pay for water and soft
drinks and always for alcohol. All boats are equipped with showers, toilets and smallish
but comfortable double and triple cabins (usually between six and eight of them). Most
people sleep on mattresses on deck as the boats are not air-conditioned.

A blue voyage is not cheap – depending on the season, the price is usually between
€165 and €250 – though some reach as high as €275 in mid-summer – so it makes
sense to shop around. Here are some suggestions to avoid getting fleeced:

➡ Ask for recommendations from other travellers.

➡ Avoid touts at the bus stations and go straight to agencies (especially those listed
below).

➡ Bargain but don't necessarily go for the cheapest option because the crew will skimp
on food and services.

➡ Check out your boat if you are on site and ask to see the guest list.

➡ Ask whether your captain and crew speak English.

➡ Don't go for gimmicks such as free water sports; they often prove to be empty
promises and boats rarely have insurance for them in case of accidents.

➡ Confirm whether the boat ever actually uses the sails (though most don't in any case)
rather than relying on a diesel engine.

➡ Avoid buying your ticket in İstanbul, as pensions and commission agents there take a
healthy cut.

➡ Book well ahead – both in high season (July and August) when spaces are in great
demand and low season when far fewer boats take to the water.

We recommend the following owner-operated outfits for running a tight ship. Boats depart at least daily between late April and October.

Before Lunch Cruises (☎ 0535 636 0076; www.beforelunch.com; Fethiye; 3-night cruise per
person €250-325) Run out of Fethiye by an experienced Turkish and Australian duo who
set their own itinerary and are more expensive than most but garner high praise from
guests.

Ocean Yachting (☎ 612 7798; www.bluecruise.com; Fethiye Marina; 3-night cruise per person
from €225) Highly professional outfit with a swag of cruise choices.

Olympos Yachting (☎ 0242-892 1145; www.olymposyachting.com; Olympos; 3-night cruise
from €185) Popular and recommended company based in Olympos.

V-Go Yachting & Travel Agency (☎ 614 4004; www.bluecruisesturkey.com; Fethiye &
Olympos; 3-night cruise €189-228) Blue cruises that target the backpacker market. Based
in Fethiye with a branch at Olympos.

---

die for. Don't leave without sampling owner
Monica's superb home cooking (dinner ₺20).

Tan Pansiyon   PENSION €
(☎ 614 1584, 0546 711 4559; www.tanpansiyon.
com; 30 Sokak 41; s/d ₺45/65; ❊⬚) If the

backpacker grind wears a bit thin, try
this pension run by the charming Öztürk
family in Karagözler. The nine rooms are
small (the bathrooms even smaller). But it's
sparkling clean and quiet. It's also good for

...terers; there's a kitchen for guests' ... on the stunning roof terrace.

Duygu Pension
PENSION €

(☑ 614 3563, 0535 736 6701; www.duygupension. com; Ordu Caddesi 54; s/d ₺50/80; ❋ ⊛ 🛜 🛎) Cute as a button, this warm and welcoming family-run pension in Karagözler, west of the harbour, has 10 homely rooms brightened by colourful wall stencils and frilly touches while the rooftop terrace has blinding sea views. Birol is your man and a great source of information.

Villa Daffodil
HOTEL €€

(☑ 614 9595; www.villadaffodil.com; Fevzi Çakmak Caddesi 139; s €37-49, d €50-75, ste €100; ❋ 🛜 🛎) This Ottoman-styled guesthouse has rooms bedecked with dark wood furnishings, old carpets and quirky details (though we're not too sure about the Ottoman-meets-Serengeti touches in some of the suites). Grab one with a sea view for the best experience. The classy pool area, at the back, is perfect for glamour-puss lounging after a long day's sightseeing.

V-Go's Hotel & Guesthouse
HOSTEL €€

(☑ 614 4004, 612 5409; www.v-gohotel.com; Fevzi Çakmak Caddesi 109; dm/s/d/f €12/30/44/60; ❋ @ 🛜 🛎) This hostel at the western end of Karagözler is a firm favourite with budget travellers looking to party. The 28 decent-sized rooms and spacious dorms are spread over two buildings between a large terrace with bar, chill-out chairs and pool. If you are looking for action, this is your place. Those after something more sedate, look elsewhere.

Yacht Classic Hotel
BOUTIQUE HOTEL €€€

(☑ 612 5067; www.yachtclassichotel.com; Fevzi Çakmak Caddesi 1; s ₺250, d ₺300-400; ❋ 🛜 🛎) This boutique hotel is a symphony in soothing pastels and cream with luxurious bathrooms and a tasteful contemporary ambience. Guests get to enjoy the large pool terrace overlooking the harbour and what could be the most stylish hotel hamam on the Med.

Orka Boutique Hotel
HOTEL €€€

(☑ 614 5010; www.orkaboutique.com; Kordon Boyu Başlangıç Mevkii 1; d from €100; ❋ 🛜) This new addition to Fethiye's hotel scene is all floor-to-ceiling glass windows and swish contemporary styling in cool pastels and lashings of white. The seafront rooms are the ones

to bag (or else your mammoth windows are wasted on a panorama of a taxi stand).

Hotel Doruk
HOTEL €€€

(☑ 614 9860; www.hoteldoruk.com; Yat Limanı; s ₺180-230, d ₺220-280; ❋ 🛜 🛎) This stalwart of the Fethiye scene is still a good choice; especially since its recent room fit-out. At least half of the 28 rooms have balconies overlooking the bay with room 103 especially well-placed. Avoid the mansard rooms on the top floor, which can feel claustrophobic.

🍴 Eating

Fethiye's enormous market takes place on Tuesday along the canal between Atatürk Caddesi and Pürşabey Caddesi next to the stadium.

Nefis Pide
PIDE €

(☑ 614 5504; Eski Cami Sokak 9; pide ₺5-12; ⊙ 9am-midnight) Tucked away in an alleyway next to the Old Mosque, Nefis serves up Fethiye's best pide, along with good value kebap and *dürüm* (kebab sandwich) plates. It's friendly, sparkling clean and has lovely outdoor seating. Order the *karaşık* (mixed) pide for a satisfying feast.

Ceyazir Usta
KEBAP

(Hal ve Pazar Yeri; ₺7.50-15; ⊙ 8am-9pm Mon-Sat) Inside the fish market, 'Master Ceyazir' will fix you up with some of the best kebaps and *dürüm* (kebab sandwich) in Fethiye, served from his tiny hole in the wall.

★ Meğri Lokantası
TURKISH €€

(☑ 614 4047; Çarşı Caddesi 26; plates ₺6-14; 🖉) Looking for us at lunchtime in Fethiye? We're usually here. Packed with locals who spill onto the streets, the Meğri offers excellent and hearty home-style cooking at very palatable prices. Mix and match your meal by choosing from the huge glass display window of vegetarian and meat dishes. It's pretty much all delicious.

İskele Ocakbaşı
KEBAP €€

(☑ 614 9423; Şehit Feti Bey Parkı; mains ₺14-26; ⊙ 9am-1am) When we're looking for a kebap-fix in Fethiye, İskele is where we head. The grill dishes from its central *ocak-başı* (barbecue) are excellent but it's the super-friendly service that really makes this place shine. The shady outdoor patio overlooking bobbing boats on the harbour is a bonus too.

Paşa Kebab
TURKISH €€

(☑ 614 9807; Çarşı Caddesi 42; pide ₺6-10, ke-baps ₺14-22; ⊙ 9am-1am) Nearly always bus-tling, and with a menu that's something of a novella, Paşa does a fine line in Turkish staples. If you're hungry, try the Paşa Special, a gigantic and delicious kebap concoction of beef, tomato bulgar and cheese.

Cem & Can
SEAFOOD €€€

(Hal ve Pazar Yeri 67) One way to taste Fethiye's fish is to buy your own (per kilo ₺18 to ₺30) from the circle of fishmongers in the fish market, then take it to one of the restaurants opposite to have them cook it. Our favourite is Cem & Can, which charges ₺8 per head for cooking the fish, plus salad and bread.

Meğri Restaurant
INTERNATIONAL €€€

(☑ 614 4046; 40 Sokak 10; meze & salads ₺7-15, mains ₺20-35; ☑) If you want a change from the tomato-cucumber-parsley Turk-ish salad combo, Meğri Restaurant (not to be confused with nearby Meğri Lokantasi) is a great choice. We really like their broc-coli and chicken salad and we love their huge meze selection. Mains range from pasta to steaks, kebap and a whole section for vegetarians.

Deniz Restaurant
SEAFOOD €€€

(☑ 612 0212; Uğur Mumcu Parkı; mains ₺15-30) Probably the best seafood restaurant in Fethiye outside of the fish market, the 'sea' restaurant exhibits everything alive and swimming in tanks (the grouper is best) and excels in making unusual meze. Try the ex-cellent *semizotu* (purslane) in yoghurt and the *ceviche* (fish preserved in lemon juice).

🍷 Drinking & Nightlife

The lion's share of Fethiye's bars and night-clubs stand cheek-by-jowl along Hamam Sokak, which runs north–south between Karagözler Caddesi and Atatürk Caddesi in the old town. Another happy hunting ground for bars is along Dispanser Caddesi, south of the Martyrs' Monument.

Cafe Cafe
CAFE

(90 Sokak; ⊙ 10am-11pm; 🛜) Fethiye's best coffee is served up here (as well as some good cakes and light snacks). Service is swift and the tables out front are prime people-watching territory.

Deniz Kafe
CAFE

(2 Karagözler Kürek Yarışları; ⊙ 9am-11pm) This little makeshift cafe-bar has tables right up to the edge of the water and even one or two on a small pier west of the marina. It's a great place to while away a lazy afternoon.

Car Cemetery
BAR

(☑ 612 7872; Haman Sokak 25; ⊙ 10am-4am) British boozer-cum-club, this place with the whacko deco and live rock music at the weekend is particularly popular with locals, when it will be standing (or falling down) room only.

Kismet
BAR

(☑ 0545 922 2301; Uğur Mumcu Parkı) This wel-coming bar (with cabaret shows most Friday nights in season – phone for an update) off Dispanser Caddesi is open all day and until the wee hours. Good crowd, and a nice place for a sundowner or something cold much later.

Kum Saati Bar
BAR

(Haman Sokak 31) What looks like just another joint along what is Fethiye's most raucous street after dark, the 'Hour Glass' keeps good time throughout the day as a bar and turns into a club with music and dancing at the bewitching hour.

🛍 Shopping

Sister's Place
SPICES

(☑ 0536 614 3877; Hal ve Pazar Yeri; ⊙ 7.30am-9.30pm Mon-Sat) This tiny Aladdin's Cave of herbs, essential oils and – for real – magic potions is where everyone comes for a cure and a spell. You're in good hands with Nes-rin and her brother Tarık – trust us.

Old Orient Carpet & Kilim Bazaar
CARPETS

(☑ 0532 510 6108; c.c_since.1993@hotmail.com; Çarşı Caddesi 5) As solid as Gibraltar and reli-able as rain, this shop is where the discern-ing buy their carpets and kilims, following the sage advice of carpet seller Celal Coşkun.

ℹ Information

Tourist Office (☑ 614 1527; İskele Meydanı; ⊙ 8am-7pm Mon-Fri, 10am-5pm Sat & Sun) Stocks a couple of glossy brochures and free town map.

ℹ Getting There & Away

Fethiye's busy otogar is 2.5km east of the town centre, with a separate station for minibuses 1km east of the centre near the petrol station.

Buses from the otogar to Antalya (₺30, six hours, 285km) head east along the coast at least every hour in high season, stopping at Kalkan (₺13, 1½ hours, 83km), Kaş (₺16, two hours,

CELAL COŞKUN: CARPET SELLER

Celal Coşkun learned to make carpets and weave kilims at his grandmother's knee in Malatya in southeastern Anatolia before apprenticing himself as a carpet repairer in İstanbul and opening his shop, Old Orient Carpet & Kilim Bazaar (p337), in Fethiye. We asked this 30-year veteran of the trade for his top tips on buying and caring for carpets and kilims.

➧ Know the basics: a carpet is wool or silk pile with single (Persian) or double (Turkish) knots; a kilim is a flat weave and reversible; a *cicim* is a kilim with one side embroidered.

➧ Establish in advance your price range and what you want in terms of size, pattern and colour.

➧ Deal only with a seller who you feel you can trust, be it through reputation, recommendation or instinct.

➧ Counting knots is only important on silk-on-silk carpets, though a double-knotted wool carpet will wear better than a single-knotted one.

➧ Most reputable carpet shops can negotiate discounts of between 5% and 10%, depending on how you may pay; anything higher than that and the price has been inflated in the first place.

➧ To extend the life of a carpet, always remove your shoes when walking on it and never beat a carpet as this breaks the knots and warp (vertical) and weft (horizontal) threads.

➧ If professional cleaning is too expensive and the traditional method – washing it with mild soap and water and drying it on wood blocks to allow air to circulate beneath it – is too much like hard work, lay the carpet face (pattern) side down for a few minutes in fresh snow (if available!).

➧ Anything made by hand – including a carpet – can be repaired by hand.

107km) and Olympos (₺30, 4¾ hours, 228km). The inland road to Antalya (₺25, 3½ hours, 200km) is much quicker.

Minibuses heading for destinations in the local vicinity depart from the handy **dolmuş stop** near the mosque downtown. Destinations include Faralya and Kabak (₺6.50), Göcek (₺5), Hisarönü (₺3.50), Kayaköy (₺4.50), Ovacık (₺3.50), Ölüdeniz (₺5), and Saklıkent (₺8.50).

Catamarans sail daily to Rhodes in Greece (one-way/same-day return/open-return €51.50/62/77, 1½ hours) from Fethiye pier opposite the tourist office. They run from late April to October, departing from Fethiye at 9am Monday, Wednesday, Thursday and Friday, and returning from Rhodes at 4.30pm. Tickets are available near the pier from Ocean Yachting Travel Agency (p334) and **Yeşil Dalyan** (☎612 4015; www.yesildalyantravel.com; Fevzi Çakmak Caddesi 35b).

ⓘ Getting Around

Minibuses (₺2) ply the one-way system along Atatürk Caddesi and up Çarşı Caddesi to the otogar, as well as along Fevzi Çakmak Caddesi to the Karagözler pensions and hotels. There are also minibuses to Çalış Beach. A taxi from the otogar to the pensions west of the centre costs

about ₺8, and to Dalaman airport between ₺80 and ₺100.

A couple of agencies in town, including **Levent Rent a Car** (☎614 8096; www.leventrentacar. net; Fevzi Çakmak Caddesi 37b), hire out scooters for ₺30 per day.

Ölüdeniz

☎0252 / POP 4708

With its sheltered (and protected) lagoon beside a lush national park, a long spit of sandy beach and Baba Dağ (Mt Baba) casting its shadow across the sea, Ölüdeniz (*eu-leu-den-eez*), some 15km south of Fethiye, is a tourist association's dream come true. Problem is, like most beautiful destinations, everyone wants to spend time here and a lot of people think package tourism has turned the motionless charms of the 'Dead Sea' into a Paradise Lost. If you're looking for an easygoing day on the beach though, you can't really go wrong here. Similarly, if you've always wanted to throw yourself off a mountain, Ölüdeniz is one of Turkey's top destinations for tandem paragliding. Nearby is the starting point for the wonderful

Lycian Way walking trail, which runs high above the fun and frolic.

◎ Sights & Activities

Ölüdeniz Beach & Lagoon   BEACH
(Ölüdeniz Caddesi; lagoon admission adult/child ₺4.50/2) The beach is why most people visit Ölüdeniz. While the decent strip of shore edging the village is free, the famed lagoon beach is a protected national park (Ölüdeniz Tabiat Parkı) that you pay to enter. Both the public beach and lagoon get heavily crowded in summer but with the mountains soaring above you, it's still a lovely place to while away a few hours. There are showers, toilets cafes and sunshades and loungers can be rented.

Paragliding   PARAGLIDING
(tandem flight ₺150-175, plus ₺25 entrance fee to Baba Dağ) Daniel Craig jumps off 1960m-high Baba Dağ in the James Bond film *Skyfall* and so can you. The descent from the mountain can take up to 40 minutes, with amazing views over the Blue Lagoon, Butterfly Valley and, on a clear day, as far as Rhodes.

Easy Riders (🖉617 0148; www.easyriders travel.8m.com; Han Camp Ölüdeniz) and **Pegas Paragliding** (🖉617 0051; www.pegasparagliding.blogspot.com.tr; Çetin Motel) are both reliable Ölüdeniz-based companies.

Whichever company you choose, ensure the company has insurance and the pilot has the appropriate qualifications. Parasailing (₺100) on the beach is also possible.

Boat Excursions   BOAT TOUR
(tour per person incl lunch ₺15-25) Throughout summer, boats set out from Ölüdeniz beach to explore the surrounding coast. A typical day-long boat tour might take in Gemile Bay (Kabak), the Blue Cave, Butterfly Valley and St Nicholas Island, with some time for swimming included. Ask the tourist office for more information.

🛏 Sleeping

Ölüdeniz definitely caters more towards the resort crowd but there is also a boutique hotel and a couple of camping grounds offering comfortable and stylish bungalows as well as tent pitches.

Sugar Beach Club   CAMPING GROUND €
(🖉617 0048; www.thesugarbeachclub.com; Ölüdeniz Caddesi 20; campsite per person ₺15, caravan incl electricity ₺25, bungalow s/d from ₺100/110; ❄@⊛) This ultra-chilled spot, run by affable Erkin, is the pick of the crop in Ölüdeniz for backpackers. The design is first class – a strip of beach shaded by palms and lounging areas, with a waterfront bar and restaurant and backed by two-dozen colourful bungalows with bathrooms and air-conditioning. It's 500m north of the lagoon entrance.

The club has its own beach, canoes and paddleboats can be hired, and special events like barbecues are a regular occurrence. If you're not staying here but want to hang out, it costs ₺7 to use the sun loungers, parasols and showers.

Sultan Motel   HOTEL €
(🖉616 6139; www.sultanmotel.com; Ölüdeniz Yolu; s/d ₺60/80; ❄⊛⊜) Just off the main road on the left as you descend from Hisarönü into Ölüdeniz, the Sultan is at a trailhead of the Lycian Way and is a favourite of walkers and trekkers. Its 16 rooms and five apartments, which also have kitchens for self-catering, are in stone chalets. Some have excellent views down to Ölüdeniz.

Seahorse Beach Club   RESORT €€
(🖉617 0123, 0532 691 4375; www.seahorsebeach club.com; Ölüdeniz Caddesi; campsite per person €7, caravan d/f €65/95; ❄) Gazing out onto Ölüdeniz Bay, Seahorse has 24 blue-and-white caravans with all the mod-cons for those who prefer a more luxurious version of camping. There is a restaurant and bar in a lofted wooden cabin and the club's very own beach is a short stroll away.

Blue Star Hotel   HOTEL €€
(🖉617 0069; www.hotelbluestaroludeniz.com; Mimar Sinan Caddesi 8; s/d €50/60; ❄⊜⊛) This well-maintained, family-run hotel was one of the first on the block when it opened just 60m from the beach in 1985. Though they're not large, the 42 rooms are light, bright and airy and most have balconies.

★Oyster Residences   BOUTIQUE HOTEL €€€
(🖉617 0765; www.oysterresidences.com; Belcekız 1 Sokak; d from €150; ⊙May-Oct; ❄⊛⊜) This delightful boutique hotel, inspired by old Fethiye-style houses, was built in 2004 but looks at least a century older. It has 26 bright and airy rooms done up in a kind of neo-troppo style that will have most mortals swooning. Rooms open up onto lush gardens that creep all the way to the beach. Stunning stuff.

✖ Eating & Drinking

Oba Motel Restaurant   INTERNATIONAL **€€**

(📞617 0158; www.obamotel.com.tr/Erestaurant.asp; Mimar Sinan Caddesi; mains ₺15-25; ☺8am-midnight; 🅿) Partly housed in a wooden cabin, the restaurant of the leafy Oba Motel has a great reputation for home-style food at palatable prices. It also does great Turkish/European breakfasts including homemade muesli with mountain yoghurt and local pine honey. The menu offers everything from snacks to full-on mains, including a half-dozen veggie options.

Buzz Beach Bar   RESTAURANT, BAR **€€€**

(📞617 0526; www.buzzbeachbar.com; Belcekız 1 Sokak; mains ₺18.50-35.50; ☺8am-2am; 🛜) With a commanding position on the waterfront, this two-level place offers a wide menu from burgers and pasta (₺14 to ₺20) to fillet steak and seafood. The roof terrace is the beachfront's top spot for a sunset cocktail or beer.

Cloud 9   RESTAURANT, BAR **€€€**

(📞617 0391; Belcekız 1 Sokak; mains ₺15-35; 🛜) Fun and friendly, Cloud 9 has a menu that meanders from pizza and pasta to steaks, seafood and Turkish grills. Sipping a mojito at one of the shaded outdoor tables here is a great end to a beach day.

Help Lounge Bar   BAR, RESTAURANT

(📞617 0650; Belcekız 1 Sokak; ☺9am-4am; 🛜) The most happening place in town, this funky joint has a large terrace with a bar right on the seafront with comfy cushioned benches, colourful murals on the walls and the front end of a Chevy coming through the wall. Happy hour is from 6pm to 8pm and again from 10.30pm till midnight.

ℹ Information

Tourist Office (📞617 0438; www.oludeniz.com.tr; Ölüdeniz Caddesi 32; ☺8.30am-11pm) Helpful information booth and booking service in the centre.

ℹ Getting There & Away

In high season, dolmuşes leave Fethiye (₺5, 25 minutes, 15km) for Ölüdeniz roughly every five to 10 minutes, passing through Ovacık and Hisarönü. In low season they go every 20 minutes by day and hourly at night. You can reach Faralya and Kabak on six minibuses a day in summer. A taxi to Kayaköy costs ₺30 to ₺35. To Fethiye, it's ₺45 to ₺55.

Butterfly Valley & Faralya

Tucked away on the Yedi Burun (Seven Capes) coast a dozen kilometres from Ölüdeniz is the village of Faralya (population 150), also called Uzunyurt. Below it is the paradise-found of Butterfly Valley, with a fine beach and some lovely walks through a lush gorge. It is home to the unique Jersey tiger butterfly, from where it takes its name.

There are two ways to reach Butterfly Valley: via boat from Ölüdeniz or on foot via a very steep path that wends its way down a cliff from Faralya. If you choose the latter, be sure to wear proper shoes and keep to the marked trail (indicated with painted red dots). It usually takes 30 to 45 minutes to descend and closer to an hour to come back up. There are fixed ropes along the path in the steepest or most dangerous parts.

Faralya is on a stage of the Lycian Way and is prime hiking territory. There is an excellent trail-blazed walk across the hill to Kabak from here.

🛌 Sleeping & Eating

★ **George House**   PENSION **€**

(📞642 1102, 0535 793 2112; www.georgehouse-faralya.com; Faralya; incl half board campsite/platform per person ₺40/45, bungalow s/d/tr ₺90/140/195, s/d without bathroom ₺110/60; ❄@🛜💦) Run by the eponymous George's enthusiastic son Hasan, this Faralya institution offers simple, spick-and-span bungalows (some with air-conditioning and bathroom), tent sites, and open-air wooden platforms with mattresses. There's also a roomy apartment with kitchenette for families who want to self-cater (₺100). Surrounded by gardens, right by the path leading down to Butterfly Valley, this is a great choice.

The views down to the valley are splendid, there's a spring-water pool perfect for a dip after a hot day's walking, and we love the homely food cooked up in the restaurant. Even if you're not staying here, this is a good place for lunch or dinner in Faralya.

Butterfly Valley   CAMPING GROUND **€**

(Kelebekler Vadisi; 📞0555 632 0237; http://thebutterflyvalley.blogspot.com.tr; Butterfly Valley; incl half board per person tent or dm ₺35, bungalow ₺42; ☺Mar-Oct) Accommodation in Butterfly Valley itself is simple: tents for rent (or bring your own), and bungalows on stilts with mattresses on the floor. Be warned that these rooms bake during the summer. For those who prefer their creature comforts, there are lots more places to stay above the valley in Faralya.

Melisa Pansiyon
PENSION €€

(☑ 642 1012, 0535 881 9051; www.melisapension. com; s/d ₺70/100; ❋ 🔊) Offering as warm a welcome as you'll find anywhere along the Yedi Burun, the Melisa has four well-maintained and cheerful rooms, a pretty garden, a fully-stocked kitchen for guests who want to self-cater, and a vine-bedecked terrace overlooking the valley. Owner Mehmet speaks English and is a good source of local information.

Onur Motel
HOTEL €€

(☑ 642 1162, 0538 260 8734; www.onurmotel-faralya.com; bungalow incl half board s/d ₺100/150, ste ₺250; ☀ Apr-Oct; ❋ 🔊) On the main road through Faralya, this place offers accommodation in 10 modern, wooden bungalows with incredible views, although they can be something of a heat trap. There are also three brand new and rather stylish suite rooms. The garden with pool is a lovely place to cool off and the restaurant dishes up excellent meals.

Die Wassermühle
LUXURY HOTEL €€€

(The Watermill; ☑ 642 1245; www.natur-reisen. de; half board per person r/ste €55/71; ☀ Apr-Oct; ❋ 🔊) This incredibly tasteful resort, owned by a long-time German resident Brigitte, is hidden within a wooded slope to the left as you enter Faralya and is the coolest – in both senses – place around. Both the suites (with kitchenettes) and standard rooms are spacious and use all-natural materials. Views from the restaurant and spring-water pool terraces are commanding.

🛈 Getting There & Away

You can take a tour of Butterfly Valley from Fethiye or Ölüdeniz, or board the shuttle boat (₺20 return), which departs from Ölüdeniz daily between April and October at 11am, 2pm and 6pm (with additional sailings at noon, 4pm and 6.30pm mid-June to mid-September). From Butterfly Valley back to Ölüdeniz, it leaves at 9.30am, 1pm and 5pm (and, in season, at 10.30am, 3pm and 6pm as well).

Six daily minibuses (₺6.50, 35 minutes, 26km) from June to September (four in spring and two in winter) link Fethiye and Faralya via Ölüdeniz. The road up here from Ölüdeniz is as memorable for its views as for its knuckle-whitening corners. A taxi from Fethiye costs about ₺100.

Kabak

☑ 0252

Six kilometres south of Faralya – and worlds away from everywhere else – Kabak is for the camping and trekking enthusiast, yoga devotee or any fan of untapped beauty. Once this region's best-kept secret – and a haven for Turkish alternative life-stylers – the cat is now definitely out of the bag, with the pine-tree-flanked valley that runs above the beach counting around 14 camps. This is still one of the Fethiye area's most tranquil spots though and anyone craving a slice of back-to-nature bliss will adore a stay here. Regardless of how you get down the steep track to Kabak Valley – by high-suspension vehicle (15 minutes) or on foot (half-hour) – you'll be rewarded with a spectacular beach flanked by two long cliffs.

🛏 Sleeping & Eating

Accommodation down in Kabak Valley (Gemile Beach) consists of camping and tented platforms and bungalows. Nearly all include half board in the price – there are no restaurants as such on Gemile Beach, only up in Kabak village, on the road to/from Faralya. Most camps open from April to October, and most can organise transport down; phone, email or text ahead.

Turan Hill Lounge
BUNGALOW €€

(☑ 642 1227, 0532 710 1077; www.turancamping. com; incl half board campsite per person ₺55, semi-open bungalow without bathroom s/d ₺110/160, deluxe tent d ₺180, bungalow d ₺280-400; ❋ 🔊) The epitome of Turkish 'glamping', Turan Hill was the first accommodation to open in Kabak and is still the trendsetter. It's long grown out of its hippyish roots to become a stylish luxe-camping getaway. There's a choice of rustic semi-open platforms and some incredibly cute boutique bungalows brimming with colourful character.

It also has lovely views and lots of mellow lounging areas. Yoga courses are held regularly on the enormous platform in the valley below.

Reflections Camping
BUNGALOW €€

(☑ 642 1020, 0538 649 9935; www.reflections camp.com; incl half board per person own tent/camp tent ₺50/55, bungalow ₺100, without bathroom ₺70; 🔊) 🖉 Original owner Chris, who built this place from scratch, has now moved on but the new owners seem to be sticking to this camp's ethos of simple, sustainable living. Reflections is a comfortable place with some of the best sea views in Kabak. Four of the bungalows are made of compacted-earth bags while others are built of bamboo.

The view from the communal toilets, with a 'living' roof planted with ferns and ginger plants, is nothing short of awesome.

Gemile Bay   BUNGALOW €€

(☑ 642 1016, 0533 511 0487; www.gemilecamping. com; per person campsite ₺50, bungalow ₺165; ✳ 🛜) Meral began Gemile Camp here in Kabak Valley 10 years ago but she's now moving the site of rustic-chic bungalows and campsites closer down to the beach. Expect a super-relaxed and friendly atmosphere and a restaurant offering well-known chef Gabriel Sponza's Mediterranean-fusion dishes.

Olive Garden   BUNGALOW €€€

(☑ 642 1083, 0536 439 8648; www.olivegarden kabak.com; incl half board s/d ₺110/220; 🛜) Oozing with charm, the Olive Garden is not at the bottom of Kabak Valley, but down a side track 100m from the village. Accommodation is in wooden bungalows surrounded by gorgeous views. Owner Fatih is a former chef and the food here is superb. Many of the ingredients come from his family's fruit trees, olive groves and vegetable gardens.

Mamma's Restaurant   TURKISH €€

(☑ 642 1071; mains ₺10-15) Quite the character, Mama dishes up simple, hearty dishes including *gözleme* (stuffed savoury crepe; ₺5) and her own homemade *ayran* (yoghurt drink; ₺3) from her front patio near the dolmuş stop in Kabak village. She also has a couple of simple and tidy rooms to rent that are popular with walkers.

🛈 Getting There & Away

The road from Faralya carries on for another 6km until it reaches tiny Kabak village. Between June and September six daily minibuses (₺6.50, 45 minutes, 32km) trundle between Fethiye and Kabak via Ölüdeniz and Faralya. They leave Kabak at 8.30am, 10.30am, 12.30pm, 2.30pm, 5.30pm and 7.30pm. There are four services in spring and two in winter.

From the dolmuş stop in the village a 4WD vehicle is usually on hand to transfer people down to the camps (₺40) or you can take the 20-minute walking path leading down into the valley.

Kayaköy

🎵 0252 / POP 2200

About nine kilometres south of Fethiye is Kayaköy (ancient Karmylassos), an eerie ghost town of 4000-odd abandoned stone houses and other structures that once made up the Greek town of Levissi. Today they form a memorial to Turkish-Greek peace and cooperation.

Levissi was deserted by its mostly Greek inhabitants in the general exchange of populations supervised by the League of Nations in 1923 after the Turkish War of Independence. Most Greek Muslims came to Turkey and most Ottoman Christians moved from coastal Turkey to Greece. The abandoned town was the inspiration for Eskibahçe, the setting of Louis de Bernières' 2004 novel, *Birds Without Wings*.

As there were far more Ottoman Greeks than Greek Muslims, many Turkish towns were left unoccupied after the population exchange. Also, Kayaköy, or Kaya as it is known locally, was badly damaged by earthquake in 1957.

With the tourism boom of the 1980s, a development company wanted to restore Kayaköy's stone houses and turn the town into a holiday village. Scenting money, the local inhabitants were delighted, but Turkish artists and architects were alarmed and saw to it that the Ministry of Culture declared Kayaköy a historic monument, safe from unregulated development. What remains is a timeless village set in a lush valley with some fine vineyards nearby. In the evening, when the stone houses are spotlit, Kayaköy is truly surreal.

⦿ Sights

Kayaköy (Levissi) Abandoned Village   RUIN

(admission ₺5, free after closing; ⊗8.30am-6.30pm) The tumbledown ruins of Levissi are highly atmospheric. The roof-less, dilapidated stone houses sit upon the slopes like sentinels over the modern village below.

Not much is intact except the two churches. The Kataponagia Church, with an ossuary containing the mouldering remains of the long-dead in its churchyard, is on the lower part of the slope while the Taxiarkis Church is near the top of the hill. Both retain some of their painted decoration and black-and-white pebble mosaic floors.

🛏 Sleeping & Eating

Selçuk Pension   PENSION €
(📞 618 0075, 0535 275 6706; istanbulrestaurant@
hotmail.com; s/d ₺50/80; ❋) Set amid flower
and vegetable gardens, the Selçuk has a doz-
en rooms that are a bit worn but spotless,
quite spacious and homely; four have lovely
views of the abandoned village.

Villa Rhapsody   GUESTHOUSE €€
(📞 618 0042, 0532 337 8285; www.villarhapsody.
com; s/d/tr €34/47/62; 🛜🌊) This welcoming
place has 16 comfortable rooms with balconies overlooking a delightful walled garden
and a swimming pool. Atilla and Jeanne, the
Turkish and Dutch owners, can offer local
advice and sketch maps for walking in the
area as well as organise bike hire. Set meals
are available on request (₺25 to ₺40).

Doğa Apartments   APARTMENT €€
(📞 618 0373, 0532 684 2514; www.dogaapart-
ments.com; apt per week from €400; ❋🛜🌊)
Just 200m from the main entrance to the
abandoned village, the six self-contained
apartments here are housed in two old farm
buildings, one of which dates back more
than 200 years. They're full of quaint decorative touches and are well equipped with
all a self-caterer could need. The poolside
bar is a delight.

⭐ Günay's Garden   VACATION RENTAL €€€
(📞 618 0033, 0537 231 7648; www.gunaysgarden.
com; Gümrük Sokak; 2-bed villa per week from
€660, 3-bed villa per week from €720; ❋@🛜🌊)
A top choice for families or groups of friends
who want to use Kayaköy as their base,
this positively scrumptious boutique resort
consists of a half-dozen self-catering villas
hidden within lush gardens and set around
a shimmering pool. Some of the villas have
both front and back balconies, and the views
of the abandoned village are evocative.

Host Rebecca organises art and yoga
courses and literary events – Louis de
Bernières, author of *Birds Without Wings*
has stayed and read here – while husband
Tolga is in command of the kitchen at the
excellent Izela restaurant, located in the
grounds.

İstanbul Restaurant   TURKISH €€
(📞 618 0148; mains ₺15-25; ⊙8am-midnight;
🖉) Friendly and fun, this place serves up
excellent homestyle grills and meze made
from the produce of the surrounding vegetable gardens and orchards. It's a delightful

HIKING FROM KAYAKÖY

The Kayaköy to Ölüdeniz section of the
Lycian Way trek takes in serene forest
scenery and jaw-droppingly beautiful
coastal panoramas. For keen walkers
who don't have time to add in a longer
trek, it's a fantastic half-day hike. The
signposted trailhead starts within Kayaköy's abandoned village ruins and is
waymarked the entire length. The walk
takes two to 2½ hours (8km).

spot for dinner, and the traditional Turkish
dishes are delicious. They offer free pick-up/
drop-off if you're not staying in Kayaköy.

Cin Bal   BARBECUE €€
(📞 618 0066; www.cinbal.com; mains ₺15-25) Arguably the most celebrated grill restaurant
in the region, Cin Bal specialises in lamb
tandir (clay oven) dishes and kebaps, and
seats 300 people inside and in its garden
courtyard under the grapevines. It's just
down a narrow lane from the abandoned village and is always heaving (and smoking!).

⭐ Levissi Garden   MEDITERRANEAN €€€
(📞 618 0108, 0533 247 5934; www.levissigarden.
com; Eski Köy Sokak; mains ₺25-44; 🖉) This
400-year-old stone building houses a stunning wine house and restaurant, with a
cellar that stocks 12,000 bottles of Turkey's
finest tipple. From its original stone oven,
the Levissi produces Mediterranean specialties such as slow-cooked lamb steaks
and mouth-watering *klevtiko* (leg of lamb
cooked in red wine, garlic and herbs) with
a wonderful meze selection. Book to avoid
disappointment.

Izela Restaurant   MEDITERRANEAN €€€
(📞 618 0033, 0537 231 7648; www.gunaysgarden.
com; mains ₺18-35) This lovely restaurant is
located in the lush grounds of Günay's Garden. It specialises in Mediterranean dishes, with more than a tip of the hat toward
modern Turkish cuisine. Almost everything
is sourced locally (as in the farm next door) –
from olive oil and vegetables to chickens,
ducks and turkeys.

❶ Getting There & Away

Dolmuşes run to Fethiye (₺4.50, 20 minutes,
8km) every half-hour or so from May to October
and every couple of hours in low season. A taxi
from Fethiye costs ₺50. All dolmuşes pass

through Hisarönü on their way to/from Kayaköy, from where dolmuşes leave every 10 minutes for Ölüdeniz. It's about a one-hour walk downhill through pine forest from Hisarönü to Kayaköy.

Tlos

On a rocky outcrop high above a pastoral plain, **Tlos** (admission ₺5; ⊙8.30am-7pm) was one of the most important cities of ancient Lycia. So effective was its elevated position that the well-guarded city remained inhabited until the early 19th century. As you climb the winding road to the ruins, look for the **acropolis** topped with an Ottoman **fortress** on the right.

Beneath the fortress, reached by a narrow path, are Lycian-era **rock tombs**, including that of the warrior Bellerophon of Chimaera fame. It has a temple-like facade carved into the rock face and to the left a fine bas-relief of our hero riding Pegasus, the winged horse.

Tlos' **theatre** is 100m further up the road from the ticket kiosk. It's in excellent condition, with most of its marble seating intact, and the stage wall is being rebuilt. Look among the rubble of the stage building for blocks carved with an eagle, a player's mask and garlands. Just across the road are ruins of the ancient **baths** (note the apothecary symbol – snake and staff – carved on an outer wall on the south side).

🛏 Sleeping

Mountain Lodge   LODGE **€€€**
(☏0252 638 2515; www.tlosmountainlodge.com; s €60, d €80-120; ❄@🛜♨) Set in a pretty garden full of birdsong, with lots of shady seating areas and a lovely spring-fed pool, Mountain Lodge is a peaceful gem of a place. The homely cabin-style rooms look like old stone houses and each has a verandah. The lodge is halfway between Güneşli and Tlos; walk the 2km from Güneşli or call beforehand for a pick-up.

For walkers and nature-lovers, it's a wonderful place to stay.

❶ Getting There & Away

From Fethiye, minibuses go to Saklıkent (₺8.50, 45 minutes) every 20 minutes via Güneşli, the jumping-off point for Tlos, which is a 4.5km hike (uphill all the way) from the junction.

Saklıkent Gorge

☏ 0252

Some 12km after the turn-off to Tlos heading south, this spectacular **gorge** (adult/student ₺4.50/2; ⊙8am-6pm) is really just a fissure in the Akdağlar, the mountains towering to the northeast. Some 18km long, the gorge is too narrow in places for even sunlight to squeeze through. Luckily *you* can, but prepare yourself for some very cold water year-round – even in summer.

You approach the gorge along a wooden boardwalk towering above the river. On wooden platforms suspended above the water, you can relax, drink tea and eat fresh trout while watching other tourists slip and slide their way across the river, hanging onto a rope, and then dropping into the gorge proper. Good footwear is essential, though plastic shoes and helmets can be rented (₺5).

Across the river from the car park is **Saklıkent Gorge Club** (☏659 0074, 0533 438 4101; www.gorgeclub.com; campsite €10, dm on platform €10, tree house without bathroom s/d €24/40, bungalow s/d €32/48; @♨), a rustic backpacker-oriented camp with basic tree houses (all have little fridges), campsites and snazzier rooms for those who don't want to rough it. It's well set up with a pool, bar and restaurant.

The club can organise various activities such as rafting (₺30/60 for 45 minutes/three hours) and canyoning (₺20/100/200 for trips of three hours/one day/two days and one night; minimum four people), as well as fishing, trekking, jeep safaris, and tours of Tlos and Patara.

❶ Getting There & Away

Minibuses run every 15 minutes between Fethiye and Saklıkent (₺8.50, one hour). The last one back is at 8.30pm.

Pınara

The spectacularly sited ruins of **Pınara** (admission ₺8; ⊙8.30am-8.30pm May-Oct, to 5pm Nov-Apr) were once one of the six highest-ranking cities in ancient Lycia. The site is vast and although the actual remnants are not the region's most impressive, the sheer splendour and isolation of the setting makes it worth visiting.

Rising high above the site is a sheer column of cliff honeycombed with **rock** tombs; archaeologists are still debating as to how and why they were cut here.

Pınara's theatre is in good condition, but its odeon and temple to Aphrodite (with heart-shaped columns) are badly ruined. Note the enormous (and anatomically correct) phallus, a kind of early graffiti carved on the steps of the latter by builders.

Just to the southeast is the Royal Tomb with particularly fine reliefs, including several showing walled Lycian cities.

ⓘ Getting There & Away

The Pınara turn-off is 46km southeast of Fethiye. The road winds through citrus orchards for 3.5km to just before Minare village, then takes a sharp left turn to climb a slope for another 2km. Infrequent minibuses from Fethiye (₺8, one hour) in season drop you at the start of the Pınara road, from where you can walk to the site.

Eşen, a village 3km southeast of the Pınara turn-off from the highway, has a few shops and basic restaurants.

Letoön

Sharing a place with the Lycian capital Xanthos on Unesco's World Heritage list since 1988, Letoön (admission ₺8; ⊘8.30am-7pm) is home to some of the finest ruins on the Lycian Way.

Letoön is a religious sanctuary dedicated to Leto who, according to legend, was Zeus' lover and bore him Apollo and Artemis. Unimpressed, Zeus' wife Hera commanded that Leto spend eternity wandering from country to country. According to local folklore she passed much time in Lycia and became the national deity.

The core of Letoön's ruins consists of three temples standing side by side and dedicated to Apollo (the Doric one on the left), Artemis (the Ionian in the middle) and Leto (the Ionian on the right and now partially reconstructed). The Apollo temple has a fine mosaic showing a lyre, a bow and arrow and floral centre.

The permanently flooded and highly atmospheric nymphaeum (ornamental fountain with statues) is inhabited by frogs which, in folklore, are said to be the shepherds who refused Leto a drink from the fountain and were punished for their lack of hospitality.

Just to the north of Letoön's main temple complex is a large Hellenistic theatre dating from the 2nd century BC.

WALKING BETWEEN LETOÖN & XANTHOS

The road between Letoön and Xanthos is an easy 5km section of the Lycian Way walking trail. Head out of Letoön and turn right at the turn-off to Kumluova village. Head straight up this road for about 1km until you get to Lycian Way signposted crossroads. Take the road signed for Xanthos and follow it until you reach Kınık village and the entrance road for the ruins.

Located about 17km south of the Pınara turn-off, this former religious centre is often considered a double-site with Xanthos but Letoön has its own romantic charm.

ⓘ Getting There & Away

Minibuses run from Fethiye via Eşen to Kumluova (₺8, 60km, one hour) every half-hour or so. They can drop you off at the (signposted) Letoön turn-off, from where it's an easy 1km walk to the site.

If driving from Pınara, turn right off the highway, go 4km and bear right at the signpost 'Letoön/Karadere'. After another 3.5km, turn left at the T-junction, then right after 100m and proceed a kilometre – all signposted – to the site through fertile fields and orchards and hectares of polytunnels full of tomato plants.

Xanthos

Once the capital of Lycia, Xanthos (admission ₺10; ⊘9am-7pm) sits on a rock outcrop above Kınık.

It's a short uphill walk to the site past the city gates and the plinth where the fabulous Nereid Monument (now in the British Museum) once stood.

Further up, opposite the car park, is the Roman theatre, agora, and the ticket office. Follow the colonnaded street to find some well-preserved mosaics, the Dancers' Sarcophagus and Lion Sarcophagus and some rock tombs.

For all its grandeur, Xanthos had a chequered history of wars and destruction. At least twice, when besieged by clearly superior enemy forces, the city's population committed mass suicide.

As many of the finest sculptures (eg the Harpies Monument) and inscriptions were carted off to London by Charles Fellows in

1842, most of the inscriptions and decorations you see today are just copies of the originals.

ℹ️ Getting There & Away

Any of the minibuses running from Fethiye's otogar south to Kalkan and Kaş can drop you off at Kınık (₺8, one hour, 63km, about every hour), from where it's a 1.5km walk to the site.

Patara

📞 0242 / POP 950

Patara, on the coast 8km south of Xanthos, can claim Turkey's longest uninterrupted beach as well as a swag of atmospheric Lycian ruins. Just inland, 1.5km from the beach and ruins, is the laid-back little village of Gelemiş. This is the perfect spot to mix ruin-rambling with some dedicated sun worship. Once very much on the hippy trail, Gelemiş is almost never filled with travellers these days – a miracle given its obvious charms – and traditional village life still goes on.

👁️ Sights & Activities

Ancient Patara　　　　　ARCHAEOLOGICAL SITE
(admission incl Patara Beach ₺5, long-stay ticket allowing 10 entries over 10 days ₺7.50; ⊘9am-7pm) Patara's grand monuments lay scattered along the road to Patara Beach. The main section of ruins is dominated by the dilapidated 5000-seat theatre. Next door is the bouleuterion, ancient Patara's 'parliament' where it is believed members of the Lycian League met. It has been thoroughly restored, following a two-year ₺8.5 million reconstruction. The colonnaded street, with re-erected columns, runs north from here. This would have been Patara's grandest boulevard, lined by shops and with the agora at its southern end.

Away from the main ruins there are plenty more remnants of Patara's long history to fossick through. From the ticket booth, along the Gelemiş–Patara Beach road, you first pass by the 2nd-century triple-arched triumphal Arch of Modestus with a necropolis containing a number of Lycian tombs nearby. As you head along the road, next is a Harbour Baths complex and the remains of a Byzantine basilica before you arrive at the central section of ruins.

From the colonnaded street a dirt track leads to a lighthouse built by Emperor Nero that lays claim to being one of the three oldest lighthouses in the world. This is the area of the ancient harbour (now a reedy wetland) and is home to the enormous Granary of Hadrian, used to store cereals and olive oil, and a Corinthian-style temple-tomb.

Patara's place in history is well documented. It was the birthplace of St Nicholas, the 4th-century Byzantine bishop of Myra who later passed into legend as Santa Claus. Before that, Patara was celebrated for its temple and oracle of Apollo, of which little remains. It was Lycia's major port – which explains the large storage granary still standing. And according to Acts 21:1–2, Saints Paul and Luke changed boats here while on their third mission from Rhodes to Phoenicia.

Patara Beach　　　　　　　　　BEACH
(admission incl Patara ruins ₺5, long-stay ticket allowing 10 entries over 10 days ₺7.50) Backed by large sand dunes, this splendid, 18km-long sandy beach is one of Turkey's best. Due to its length, even in the height of summer you can find a quiet spot. Sunshades (₺4) and loungers (₺3) can be rented and there's a cafe for when you get peckish. Depending on the season, parts of the beach are off limits as it is an important nesting ground for sea turtles. It always closes at dusk and camping is prohibited.

You can get here either by following the road for 1km past the Patara ruins, or by turning right at the Golden Pension in Gelemiş and following the track waymarked with blue arrows, which heads for the sand dunes area along the western side of the archaeological section. Between late May and October, tractor-wagons (₺2) trundle down to the beach from the village three times daily.

Kirca Travel　　　　CANOEING, HORSE RIDING
(📞843 5298; www.kircatravel.com) Kirca specialises in six-hour canoeing trips (€24) on the Xanthos River but also offers three-hour horse-riding trips through the Patara dunes and day-hikes.

🛏️ Sleeping

As you come into Gelemiş, the main road and the hillside on your left contains various hotels and pensions. A turn to the right at the Golden Pension takes you to the village centre, across the valley and up the other side to more pensions. Note that outside of summer, most of the hotels offer decent discounts on their rooms. Many of the pensions also offer self-catering apartments so this is a great base for families and long-stayers.

★ Akay Pension
PENSION €

(☑ 843 5055, 0532 410 2195; www.patara akaypension.com; s/d/tr/apt ₺60/90/120/160; ❄ @ 🛜 ➿) Run by keen-to-please Kazım and his wife, Ayşe, the Akay has a comfy Ottoman-style lounge to hang out and meet other travellers and 13 very well maintained, sweetly decorated rooms all with gleaming-new bathrooms and balconies overlooking citrus groves. There's an apartment for self-catering families too. Ayşe's cooking is legendary; sample at least one set meal (from ₺20) while here.

★ Flower Pension
PENSION €

(☑ 843 5164, 0530 511 0206; www.pataraflower pension.com; d/tr/studio/apt ₺90/120/120/150; ❄ @ 🛜 ➿) The Flower has nine bright and airy rooms with balconies overlooking the garden as well as five kitchen-equipped studios and three apartments well set up for families. Manager Bekir is a fount of local information. His mum presides over the kitchen, so guests who choose to dine in are guaranteed Turkish soul food at its best.

Zeybek 2 Pension
PENSION €

(☑ 843 5086, 0532 683 5845; www.zeybek2pension .com; s/d/apt €20/24/45; ❄ @ 🛜) This family-run pension with a slightly rural feel has nine clean and sunny, basic rooms and kitchen-equipped apartments with balconies, bedecked with traditional rugs. For the best view in town, climb up to the roof terrace that boasts 360-degree vistas of the hills and the ancient harbour.

Golden Pension
PENSION €

(☑ 843 5162; www.pataragoldenpension.com; s/d/ tr €30/35/40; ❄ 🛜) Patara's original pension, run by Arif, the village's ex-mayor, is peaceful despite its central location on the main crossroads. There are 16 homely rooms (all with balconies) and a popular restaurant that has a pretty shaded terrace. Choose a room with a garden view.

ANCIENT LYCIA 101

The Lycian civilisation was based in the Teke Peninsula, the bump of land jutting out into the sea and stretching from Dalyan in the west to Antalya in the east.

The Lycian people date back to at least the 12th century BC, but they first appear in writing in the *Iliad* when Homer records their presence during an attack on Troy. It is thought they may have been descended from the Lukkans, a tribe allied with the ancient Hittites. A matrilineal people, they spoke their own unique language – which has still not been fully decoded.

By the 6th century BC the Lycians had come under the control of the Persian Empire. Thus began a changing of the guard that occurred as regularly as today's guard at Buckingham Palace. The Persians gave in to the Athenians, who were defeated in turn by Alexander the Great, the Ptolemaic Kingdom in Egypt and then Rhodes.

Lycia was granted independence by Rome in 168 BC, and it immediately established the Lycian League, a loose confederation of 23 fiercely independent city-states. Six of the largest ones – Xanthos, Patara, Pınara, Tlos, Myra and Olympos – held three votes each, the others just one or two. The Lycian League is often cited as the first proto-democratic union in history and the *bouleuterion* (council chamber) among the ruins of Ancient Patara has been dubbed the 'world's first parliament'.

Partly as a result of this union, peace held for over a century but in 42 BC the league made the unwise decision not to pay tribute to Brutus, the murderer of Caesar, whom Lycia had supported during the Civil War. With his forces, Brutus besieged Xanthos and the city-state's outnumbered population, determined not to surrender, committed mass suicide.

Lycia recovered under the Roman Empire but in AD 43 all of Lycia was amalgamated into the neighbouring province of Pamphylia, a union that lasted until the 4th century when Pamphylia became part of Byzantium.

Lycia left behind very little in the way of material culture or written documents. What it did bequeath to posterity, however, was some of the most stunning funerary monuments from ancient times. Cliff tombs, 'house' tombs, sepulchres and sarcophagi – the Teke Peninsula's mountains and valleys are littered with them, and most are easily accessible on foot and/or by car.

Hotel Sema
HOTEL €

(☑ 843 5114, 0537 428 9661; www.semahotel.com; r/apt €29/48; ✳ ☎ ☞ ☎) Friendly Ali and Hanife run this simple but spotless hotel that sits in a garden just above the main road. There are a dozen rooms plus small apartments with kitchens. The view over the village from the pool is awesome.

Patara View Point Hotel
HOTEL €€

(☑ 843 5184, 0533 350 0347; www.pataraview-point.com; s/d €40/55, apt per week €500; ✳ @ ☞ ☎) Up the hill from the main road, Patara's most stylish hotel has a nice pool, and 27 rooms with a chic-country feel. As the name suggests, there are killer views over the valley. Owner Muzaffer has a huge interest in history and you'll find old farm implements scattered throughout, including a 2000-year-old olive press and an ancient beehive.

There is also four absolutely gorgeous, modern and spacious apartments you can rent by the week in a secluded spot right at the end of the village.

🍴 Eating & Drinking

Tlos Restaurant
TURKISH €€

(☑ 843 5135; meze ₺3-8, pide ₺6-15, mains ₺12-20; ⊙ 8am-midnight; 🖉) Run by the moustached and smiling chef-owner Osman, the Tlos has an outdoor terrace shaded by a large plane tree. The *guveç* (casserole, ₺15) is recommended and the garlicky oven-baked mushrooms meze dish is delicious.

Lazy Frog
INTERNATIONAL €€

(☑ 843 5160; mains ₺15-25; ⊙ 8am-1am) With its very own kitchen garden, this central, popular place offers steaks as well as various vegetarian options and *gözleme* (stuffed savoury crepe) on its relaxing terrace.

Medusa Bar
BAR

(☑ 843 5193; ⊙ 9am-3am; 🖉) Laid-back with cushioned benches and walls hung with old photos and posters, the Medusa plays music until the wee hours.

Gypsy Bar
BAR

(⊙ 9am-3am) Tiny but traditional and much loved locally, the Gypsy has live Turkish music from 10pm a couple of nights each week.

ℹ Getting There & Away

Any bus heading south to Kaş from Fethiye can drop you on the highway 3.5km from the village. Local dolmuşes run to the village every 30 to 40 minutes from the highway drop-off point

between mid-April to October. If you're arriving early or late in the year, ring your pension in Gelemiş to check. There are also hourly dolmuşes to Gelemiş from Kaş.

From about June to September, minibuses depart from Patara beach via Gelemiş to Fethiye (₺12, 1½ hours, 73km), Kalkan (₺7.50, 20 minutes, 15km) and Kaş (₺10, 45 minutes, 40km). There's also a daily departure to Saklıkent Gorge (₺10, one hour, 52km) at 11am.

Kalkan
☑ 0242 / POP 3349

Kalkan is a well-to-do harbourside town built largely on hills that look down on an almost perfect bay. It's as justly famous for its excellent restaurants as its small but central beach. Just be aware that Kalkan is far more touristed, expat and expensive than most other places on the coast, including neighbouring Kaş.

A thriving Greek fishing village called Kalamaki until the 1920s, Kalkan is now largely devoted to high-end tourism. Development continues up the hills, with scores of new villas appearing each season. But look for Kalkan's charms in the compact old town.

🏃 Activities

Most people use Kalkan as a base to visit the Lycian ruins or engage in the many activities in the surrounding area. Apart from the beach near the marina and Kaputaş, a perfect little sandy cove with a beach about 7km east of Kalkan on the road to Kaş, options for getting wet include swimming platforms at various hotels such as the Caretta Boutique Hotel and Hotel Villa Mahal, open to the public for a nominal fee.

Dolphin Scuba Team
DIVING

(☑ 627 9757; www.dolphinscubateam.com; 2 dives €48, PADI discover scuba €58) Kaş may have a better reputation for diving but there are a couple of wrecks and a fair amount of sealife to the west of Kalkan harbour. Dolphin Scuba offer recreational diving and the full gamut of PADI courses. Any non-diving friends and family who want some snorkelling action are welcome to come along while you dive (£15).

Anıl Boat
BOAT TOUR

(☑ 844 3030, 0533 351 7520; jacksonvictoria@ hotmail.com; Kalkan harbour) Kalkan is an excellent place for a day-long boat trip. One recommended vessel is Ali Eğriboyun's Anıl

Kalkan

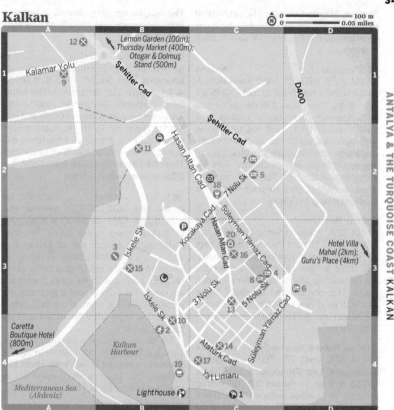

Lemon Garden (100m);
Thursday Market (400m);
Otogar & Dolmuş
Stand (500m)

Kalamar Yolu

Şehitler Cad

Şehitler Cad

D400

Hasan Altan Cad

7 Nolu Sk

Kocakaya Cad

Süleyman Yılmaz Cad

Hasan Altan Cad

İskele Sk

İskele Sk

3 Nolu Sk

5 Nolu Sk

Süleyman Yılmaz Cad

Hotel Villa
Mahal (2km);
Guru's Place (4km)

Caretta
Boutique Hotel
(800m)

Kalkan
Harbour

Atatürk Cad

Yat Limanı

Mediterranean Sea
(Akdeniz)

Lighthouse

Kalkan

◎ Sights
| 1 Public Beach | C4 |

☘ Activities, Courses & Tours
| 2 Anıl Boat | B4 |
| 3 Dolphin Scuba Team | B3 |

🛏 Sleeping
4 Courtyard Hotel	C3
5 Gül Pansiyon	C2
6 Holiday Pansiyon	D3
7 Türk Evi	C2
8 White House Pension	C3

✖ Eating
| 9 Ada Patisserie | A1 |
| 10 Aubergine | B4 |

11 Foto's Pizza	B2
12 Hünkar Ocakbaşı	A1
13 Kalamaki	C3
14 Korsan Fish Terrace	C4
15 Marina Restaurant	B3
16 Merkez Cafe	C3
17 Mussakka	C4
Zeytinlik	(see 16)

☕ Drinking & Nightlife
| 18 Moonlight Bar | C2 |
| 19 The Lighthouse | B4 |

🛍 Shopping
| 20 Just Silver | C3 |

Boat, which costs €24 per person (or about €220 for the whole boat accommodating up to eight people), including an excellent lunch. They also do evening dinner sailings.

🛏 Sleeping

Most of Kalkan's accommodation is made up of private villas and apartment rentals.

Between May and October the majority of rooms in town are block-booked by travel agencies and wholesalers, so it pays to book in advance.

Gül Pansiyon
PENSION €

(☑ 844 3099, 0533 216 8487; www.kalkangulpansiyon.com; 7 Nolu Sokak 10; s/d €30/35, apt €45; ❈ ☜) This super-friendly place run by welcoming Ömer has a rooftop with million-dollar views, small but tidy rooms with balconies, and three apartments with kitchenettes and washing machines. Try to bag one of the rooms on the 3rd floor for the views and the light. There are great discounts outside of peak summer when it's a popular pit-stop for hikers.

Holiday Pansiyon
PENSION €

(☑ 844 3154; Süleyman Yılmaz Caddesi 2; s/d ₺70/90; ❈ ☜) Though the seven rooms here are simple, they're spotless and charming. The three in the older Ottoman section are particularly atmospheric, with wooden beams, lacy curtains and delightful balconies with good views. It's run by the charming Ahmet and Şefıka, who make delicious breakfast jams.

Kelebek Hotel & Apartments
APARTMENT €

(☑ 844 3770, 0543 375 7932; www.butterfly holidays.co.uk; Karayolları Sokak 4; s/d €25/35, apt €30-60; ❈ ☜ ☷) To the north of the centre, a couple of hundred metres off the D400, this family-run hotel offers remarkably good value for self-caterers. The rooms, fronted by a large swimming pool, are clean, if slightly frayed around the edges, but the eight apartments, with kitchens, in a nearby separate block are an excellent deal.

★ Türk Evi
PENSION €€

(☑ 844 3129, 0533 335 3569; www.kalkanturkevi. com; Şehitler Caddesi 19; s €40, d €50-60; ❈ ☜) Full of character and old world Ottoman style, this old stone house (dating from the 1950s) is one of Kalkan's most charming hotels. It houses nine larger-than-average rooms individually decorated with period furniture and colourful kilims. Some of the rooms upstairs have wonderful sea views.

White House Pension
PENSION €€

(☑ 844 3738, 0532 443 0012; www.kalkanwhitehouse.co.uk; 5 Nolu Sokak 19; s/d from €40/65; ❈ ☜) Situated on a quiet corner at the top of the old town hill, this attentively run pension has 10 compact, breezy rooms – four with balconies – in a spotless family home.

The real winner here, though, is the view from the terrace and friendly owners Halıl and Marion.

Caretta Boutique Hotel
HOTEL €€

(☑ 844 3435, 0505 269 0753; www.carettahotel kalkan.com; İskele Sokak 6; s €45-58, d €69-85; ❈ ☜) A perennial favourite for its swimming platforms, home-style cooking and warm welcome from owners Gönül and son, Murat. There are 13 bright, sunny rooms; for a total away-from-it-all experience, nab one of the two terrace rooms along the cliff. There's a free boat service from below the lighthouse in Kalkan marina.

★ Hotel Villa Mahal
LUXURY HOTEL €€€

(☑ 844 3268, 0530 386 4713; www.villamahal. com; d from €220, ste €440; ❈ ☜ ☷) One of Turkey's most stylish hotels lies atop a cliff on the eastern side of Kalkan Bay. The 13 rooms, individually designed in whiter-than-white minimalism with azure splashes here and there, have panoramic sea views. The infinity pool is spectacularly suspended on the edge of the void, while a mere 180 steps takes you to the seafront bathing platform.

It's about 2km by road from Kalkan. There's a free water taxi into the centre. A normal taxi to/from Kalkan costs about ₺15. Sailboats (two Lasers and a Topper) can be hired for ₺50 per hour.

Courtyard Hotel
BOUTIQUE HOTEL €€€

(☑ 844 3738, 0532 443 0012; www.courtyard kalkan.com; Süleyman Yılmaz Caddesi 24-26; r from €120) Cobbled out of a couple of 19th-century village houses, with rooms retaining their original fireplaces, wooden ceilings and floors, the Courtyard has lashings of Ottoman old-world character. Check out room number one with its 'cave bathroom' converted from a 400-year-old water cistern. Halıl and Marion are delightful hosts.

✖ Eating

Kalkan's main market day is Thursday, though there is a much smaller one in the Akbel district to the northwest on Sunday.

In season, it's wise to book ahead no matter where you plan to eat in Kalkan.

Ada Patisserie
CAFE €

(☑ 844 2536; Kalamar Yolu; cakes & pastries ₺5-10; ☜) This charming little cafe/patisserie dishes up Turkish-style sweet and savoury delectables.

Guru's Place ANATOLIAN €€

(☑844 3848, 0536 331 1016; www.kalkanguru. com; Kaş Yolu; meze plate ₺20, mains ₺9-28; ☺8am-11pm; ☑) Affable Hüseyin and his family, who have been in the area for four centuries, have been running this seaside restaurant for 20 years. Food is authentic and fresh, coming from their own garden. The small menu is mostly focused on daily specials.

It's on the road to Kaş, so a free transfer service is provided; it's worth the short journey.

Foto's Pizza PIDE €€

(☑844 3464; www.fotospizza.com; İskele Sokak; pizza ₺13-24; ☑) Listing a pizza joint in a town of such culinary repute seems sacrilegious, but (a) Foto's has always been more pide than pizza for us and (b) the views from the terrace make it hard to overlook. There's pasta (₺11 to ₺17), omelettes and casseroles too.

Hünkar Ocakbaşı KEBAP €€

(☑844 2077; Şehitler Caddesi 38e; mains ₺9-24) This authentic *ocakbaşı* (grill restaurant) serves all the traditional kebap favourites. They also do pide and pizzas, as well as five kinds of *güveç* (casserole), including a vegetarian one.

Merkez Cafe INTERNATIONAL €€

(☑844 2823; Hasan Altan Caddesi 17; pizza & pasta ₺9-17, cakes & pastries ₺4-7; ☺8am-1am; ☑) The always buzzing Merkez makes superb pastries and cakes, including a gorgeous chocolate baklava and coconut-and-almond macaroons. More substantial fare includes pizzas and pasta.

★Korsan Fish Terrace SEAFOOD €€€

(☑844 3076; www.korsankalkan.com; Atatürk Caddesi; mains ₺26-40; ☺10am-midnight) On the roof of the 19th-century Patara Stone House, this restaurant is among the finest seafood experiences in Kalkan. Its homemade lemonade is legendary and there's live jazz on Tuesday and Saturday from 8.30pm. Ichthyophobes need not be concerned; hosts Uluç and Claire have come up with an alternative menu of modern Turkish and international dishes that are fishless.

Aubergine MODERN TURKISH €€€

(Patlıcan; ☑844 3332; www.kalkanaubergine.com; İskele Sokak; mains ₺19-36; ☺8am-3am; ☑) With a shaded terrace bang on the marina, as well as cosy seats inside, this restaurant is a magnet for its location alone. But add to that specialities such as its slow-roasted wild boar, and swordfish fillet served in a creamy vegetable sauce, and you have a winner. Caffeine fiends should note that they also make a damn fine cappuccino.

Zeytinlik MODERN TURKISH €€€

(Olive Garden; ☑844 3408; Hasan Altan Caddesi; mains ₺23-36; ☑) This British-Turkish joint venture under the guidance of Fathi and Rebecca, serves some of the most adventurous Turkish food around – try the fish *dolmas*, the samosa-like minced lamb in filo pastry triangles or any of the several vegetarian options.

Mussakka TURKISH €€€

(☑844 1576, 0537 493 2290; İskele Sokak 41; mains ₺24-40; ☺9.30am-1am; ☑) Trendy harbourfront Mussakka is lunchtime lounging central in Kalkan. Try the signature moussaka, which they insist is Turkish (it's all Greek to us). A boon for vegetarians, it offers five meatless mains (₺16 to ₺21). We love the great views and the big comfortable bar in front.

Marina Restaurant TURKISH €€€

(☑844 3384, 0535 380 0970; İskele Sokak; mains ₺23-35; ☺8am-1am) Just below the landmark Pirat Hotel, our favourite grill restaurant by the water is dearer than it used to be – what isn't? – but still does excellent grills and seafood. It also serves up excellent pide (₺10 to ₺15). Ask Hikmet to recommend from the more than a dozen meze made daily.

Kalamaki MODERN TURKISH €€€

(☑844 1555; Hasan Altan Caddesi 43; mains ₺27-39) A modern venue with a very stylish minimalist pub on the ground floor, and restaurant above, offers superb Turkish dishes with a European twist. Try the scrumptious lamb with plums or the generous vegetarian casserole. Host Tayfur takes it all in his stride – even when celebs such as Gordon Ramsay come a-calling (for real).

🍷 Drinking & Nightlife

The Lighthouse CAFE

(☑844 3752; Yat Limanı; ☺8.30am-2.30am) The closest thing Kalkan has to a tea garden, the erstwhile Fener ('lighthouse' in Turkish) – and no prizes for guessing its location – is as popular with locals as it is with expats and visitors. Looking for someone in Kalkan? Try here first.

Lemon Garden
BAR, RESTAURANT

(☑844 1634; Şehitler Caddesi 36) This garden bar and restaurant (which used to be known as the Parc Kalkan) is the expat watering hole of choice. Quiz nights are a regular feature.

Moonlight Bar
BAR

(☑844 3043; Hasan Altan Caddesi; ⊙9am-4am) Just down from the post office, Kalkan's oldest boozer is still its most 'happening'.

🔒 Shopping

Just Silver
JEWELLERY

(☑844 3136; Hasan Altan Caddesi 28) Just about the most famous shop in Kalkan has gals and dolls lining up for ear, nose, neck, finger and toe baubles.

ℹ Information

Kalkan Turkish Local News (KTLN; http://kalkan.turkishlocalnews.com) Independent, comprehensive and reliable website on all things Kalkan run by a well-informed British expat.

ℹ Getting There & Away

Dolmuşes and small buses connect Kalkan with Fethiye (₺13, 1½ hours, 83km) and Kaş (₺5, 35 minutes, 29km) via the beach at Kaputaş (₺3, 15 minutes, 7km). Minibuses also run hourly to Patara (₺5, 25 minutes, 15km).

İslamlar

This former Greek alpine village is a favourite escape from Kalkan, 8km south. The attractions here are a temperature that is 5°C cooler than the coast in summer, and the dozen or so trout restaurants that make use of icy mountain streams to fill their tanks. In the village square, have a look at one of two working mills that still use waterpower and a great millstone to turn local residents' grain into flour.

🛏 Sleeping & Eating

Grapevine Cottage
VACATION RENTAL €€

(☑838 6078, 0534 744 9255; www.grapevinecottage.host-ed.me/index.htm; cottage €70) Set among citrus groves and vineyards, this charming two bedroom, self-catering cottage is an arty, rustic retreat run by Briton Deborah. The views down to the sea from the breakfast terrace are priceless and the garden full of wandering ducks and chickens adds bags of appeal for those seeking an escape-to-the-country setting.

Transport to/from Akbel, a suburb to the northwest of the centre of Kalkan, can be arranged but getting here by public transport is not possible. It's right on the Lycian Way, so ideal for walkers.

Çiftlik
TURKISH €€

(☑838 6055, 0537 421 6129; İslamlar; trout ₺8) Our favourite İslamlar restaurant dishes up meals of fresh trout with a variety of meze, salads and chips that won't cost much more than ₺15 per person. It's due south from the village square.

Değirmen
TURKISH €€

(☑838 6295, 0532 586 2734; İslamlar; mains ₺10-20) This slightly upmarket but still authentic İslamlar restaurant serves up the local trout and makes its own tahini from sesame picked from the fields and then ground in the basement.

ℹ Getting There & Away

İslamlar village is five kilometres inland from Kalkan. There is no regular dolmuş service. A taxi from Kalkan costs about ₺20.

Bezirgan

In an elevated valley some 17km northeast of Kalkan sits the beautiful village of Bezirgan, a timeless example of Turkish rural life. Towering some 725m above the fruit orchards and fields of sticky sesame are the ruins of the Lycian hilltop citadel of Pirha.

Accommodation is available at Owlsland (☑0242-837 5214; www.owlsland.com; Bezirgan; r per person €43, self-catering cottage 3 days/week €460/790; ☎), a 150-year-old farmhouse idyllically surrounded by fruit trees and run by a charming Turkish-Scottish couple. Erol, a trained chef, turns out traditional Turkish dishes made with locally grown produce and Pauline makes her own jams and ginger cake. The three rooms are simple but cosy, contain most of their original features and are decorated with old farm implements. The upstairs room with balcony and traditional decor is especially nice. They also have a cottage for self-caterers. The signposted turning for Owlsland is past Bezirgan on the road to Elmalı, just before the road begins climbing to Sütleğen.

❶ Getting There & Away

Regular minibus services from Kalkan to Elmalî will drop you off in Bezirgan. There's also a direct bus to/from Antalya.

If you're under your own steam head north from Kalkan, cross over the D400 linking Fethiye and Kaş and follow the signs for Sütleğen and Elmalî. The road climbs steadily, with stunning views across the sea, and heads further up the mountain. Once the road crests the pass, you can see Bezirgan below. Ignore the first exit for Bezirgan and take the second.

Kaş

☑ 0242 / POP 7558

No, it may not sport the finest beaches in the region but its central location, mellow atmosphere and huge range of adventure activities on offer has made Kaş – pronounced (roughly) 'cash' – an ideal base from which to launch yourself on forays into the surrounding area. For divers this is Turkey's hub for underwater exploits with some excellent wreck diving just off shore. While a plethora of boat trips, kayaking tours and hikes are all easily arranged from here.

Extending to the west of the old town is the 6km-long Çukurbağ Peninsula. At the start of it you'll find a well-preserved ancient theatre, about all that's left of ancient Antiphellos, the name of the original Lycian town. Above Kaş several Lycian rock tombs in the mountain wall can be seen even at night when they are illuminated.

Lying just offshore, dominating the harbour view, is the geopolitical oddity of the Greek island of Meis (Kastellorizo), which can be visited on a day trip.

◉ Sights

★ Antiphellos Theatre   RUIN
(Hastane Caddesi) FREE Antiphellos was a small settlement and the port for Phellos, the much larger Lycian town further north in the hills. The small Hellenistic theatre, 500m west of Kaş' main square, could seat some 4000 spectators and is in very good condition.

King's Tomb   TOMB
(Uzun Çarşı Sokak) FREE Walk up hilly Uzun Çarşı Sokak, the Roman-era road that locals call Slippery Street, to reach the King's Tomb, a superb example of a 4th-century BC Lycian sarcophagus, which is mounted on a high base and has two lions' heads on the lid.

If you're seriously into tomb-viewing, you can also make the strenuous walk to view the rock tombs (Likya Caddesi) cut into the sheer cliffs above town.

Büyük Çakıl Beach   BEACH
(Big Pebble Beach) For swimming, head for Büyük Çakıl, a relatively clean beach 1.3km from Kaş' town centre. Although it's largely pebble-based, there's a few metres of sand at one end. There are shaded cafes for refreshments, which also rent out sun loungers and sunshades.

Liman Ağzı   BEACH
If you're after a full day on the beach, the best idea is to hop on one of the water taxis (₺12 return fare; ⊙ Jun-Aug services every 20 minutes, fewer services in spring and autumn) in Kaş harbour and head for one of three beaches on the peninsula opposite at Liman Ağzı. All three have cafes and you can rent sun loungers and sunshades. You can also hike here along a nice trail that begins at Büyük Çakıl Beach.

Akçagerme Beach   BEACH
(Akçagerme Plajı) Akçagerme Beach is a public beach opposite the exit to Gökseki, along the main road west to Kalkan from Kaş.

☞ Tours

Kaş is the regional centre for diving in the Mediterranean and there are wrecks and a lot more underwater life than you'd expect below the surface.

It's also an excellent base for exploring the region further and travel agencies here offer a huge range of day tours and adventure activities. Most companies offer more or less the same tours, but you can always tailor your own for a negotiated price.

Among the stalwarts, the various boat trips to Kekova (€25 to €30) are a fine day out and include swimming stops as well as time to see several interesting ruins. There are also very popular kayaking tours to the Kekova area.

A great idea is to charter a boat from the marina. A whole day spent around the islands of Kaş should cost from ₺200 to ₺250 for the entire boat, accommodating up to eight people.

Bougainville Travel   OUTDOOR ACTIVITIES
(☑ 836 3737; www.bougainville-turkey.com; İbrahim Serin Caddesi 10) This long-established English-Turkish tour operator has a solid reputation and much experience in organising

Kaş

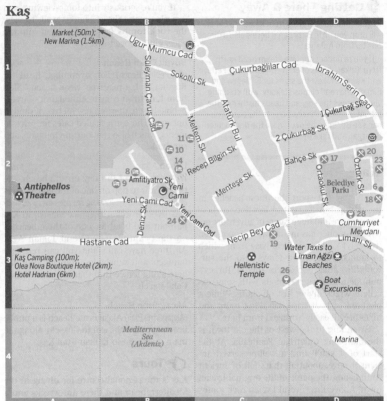

ANTALYA & THE TURQUOISE COAST KAŞ

Kaş

(€26 for one dive, including equipment). It also organises the full gamut of outdoor activities with some interesting options other tour companies don't offer. There's sea kayaking (€25 to €50), a range of day-hike options (€26 to €40) and, for the more adventurous, coasteering (from €45).

Festivals & Events

Kaş Lycia Festival — CULTURAL
The annual Kaş Lycia Festival runs for three days at the end of June. It features prominent folk-dancing troupes and musicians – and an international swimming race – and works to foster an improved relationship between Greece and Turkey.

Sleeping

Most budget and midrange accommodation in Kaş is west and northwest of the centre along the waterfront and up the hill around the Yeni Camii (New Mosque). Outside of the peak summer months of June to September, you can get excellent discounts on room rates at nearly all of the hotels in town.

Anı Pension — PENSION €
(☑ 836 1791, 0533 326 4201; www.motelani.com; Süleyman Çavuş Caddesi 12; dm/s/d ₺25/40/90; ❄@☎) The Anı leads the way for budget digs in Kaş, mostly thanks to on-the-ball host Ömer who continues to improve his pension. The decent-sized rooms all have balconies and the roof terrace is a hub where you can kick back, cool off with a beer, and swap travel stories with fellow guests.

There's a book exchange, guests can also use the kitchen, and they hold occasional barbecues (₺15).

Hilal Pansiyon — PENSION €
(☑ 836 1207, 0532 615 1061; www.hilalpension.com; Süleyman Çavuş Caddesi 8; s/d/tr/apt ₺40/70/80/50; ❄@☎) Run by friendly Süleyman, the Hilal offers 17 simple but spotless rooms and a leafy roof terrace with great views of town. There are occasional barbecues (₺15), bikes are free for guests and you also get a 10% discount on activities and tours. If you're travelling with the family in tow, Süleyman also has good-value self-catering apartments.

Kaş Camping — CAMPING GROUND €
(☑ 836 1050; www.kaskamping.com; Hastane Caddesi 3; campsite ₺25-45, standard/deluxe bungalow ₺105/225; ❄☎) Located on an attractive rocky outcropping at the start of the peninsula 800m west of Kaş, this popular site is

any number of activities and tours, including Kekova island boat tours (€30); canyoning (€50); mountain biking (€40); tandem paragliding (€90 for flights lasting 20 to 30 minutes); scuba diving (€25 per dive including all equipment, €35 for a first dive); and sea kayaking (€30).

Xanthos Travel — OUTDOOR ACTIVITIES
(☑ 836 3292; www.xanthostravel.com; İbrahim Serin Caddesi 5/A) Xanthos run extremely popular and recommendable boat day tours in the Kekova area (€25 to €35), as well as a variety of different sea-kayaking tours that get you up close with the sunken city ruins (€30 to €45). For land-lubbers there are jeep safaris (€30 to €35) and a variety of different mountain biking and trekking options.

Dragoman — OUTDOOR ACTIVITIES
(☑ 836 3614; www.dragoman-turkey.com; Uzun Çarşı Sokak) Dragoman is Kaş' diving specialist, with a variety of dive packages offered

100m from the sea and features a lively terrace bar. There's space to pitch your tent or pull up in your motor-home, as well as cute bungalows for hire.

★ Hideaway Hotel
HOTEL €€

(☑ 836 1887, 0532 261 0170; www.hotelhideaway. com; Anfitiyatro Sokak; s €40, d €50-70, ste €80; ✱◙⑤➢) The Hideaway just keeps getting better. Run by the unstoppable Ahmet, a fount of local information, this lovely hotel has large, airy rooms (six have sea views) with a fresh white-on-white minimalist feel and gleaming modern bathrooms. There's a pool for cooling off and a chilled out roof terrace with an honour-system bar and superb views.

We give this place the serious thumbs-up for attention to detail with a proper coffee machine serving up cappuccino, free water refills, and excellent dinners available (from ₺18).

Ateş Pension
PENSION €€

(☑ 836 1393, 0532 492 0680; www.atespension. com; Anfitiyatro Sokak 3; dm/s/d/tr/f ₺70/110/150/160/40; ✱◙⑤) A cut above the other pensions in Kaş, the Ateş has rooms with snuggley duvets on the beds and modern bathrooms, while black-and-white photographs grace the walls. Owners Recep and Ayşe are super-friendly hosts and also arrange barbecue feasts on the pleasant roof terrace (₺25). Guests get to use the pool at the nearby Hideaway Hotel.

Santosa Pension
PENSION €€

(☑ 836 1714, 0535 846 3584; www.santosapansiyon. com; Recep Bilgin Sokak 4; s/d/tr ₺80/100/120;

✱◙⑤) This is a quiet and homely choice with tidy, small rooms that have balconies and cheerful floral stencilling on the walls. The couple who run the show are cooks – try one of their barbecues (₺25) or vegetarian set meals (₺15).

Meltem Pension
PENSION €€

(☑ 836 1855; www.meltempansiyon.com; Meltem Sokak; s/d ₺90/110; ✱) The very simple rooms at this friendly, family-run place are bright, airy and most have balconies. The shady roof terrace is a fine spot for hanging out in the evening and during summer regular barbecues are organised there.

Nur Hotel
HOTEL €€€

(☑ 836 1203; www.nurotel.com; Hükümet Caddesi; d/f/ste €80/100/170; ✱⑤➢) There's a contemporary beachy feel to the light-filled rooms here, which feature painted wood features and lashings of white. The suites ooze luxuriant modern decadence with mammoth spa baths and oversized beds. One room has been fully fitted out for wheelchair access.

Olea Nova Boutique Hotel
BOUTIQUE HOTEL €€€

(☑ 836 2660; www.oleanova.com.tr; Demokrasi Caddesi 43; r from €100; ✱◙⑤➢) Set amid olive groves, 2km from Kaş' centre, with panoramic views across the peninsula to the Greek island of Meis, this swish boutique hotel is just the ticket for those seeking a peaceful break. The 19 rooms are all pristine white minimalism while the kidney-shaped pool and terrace bar are slothing central after a day in the sun.

MEIS EXPRESS

Visiting the teensy Greek island of Meis (Kastellorizo) is a popular day-trip from Kaş. The **Meis Express Ferry** (same-day return €25) sails throughout the year at 10am (10.30am in winter) and returns at 4pm (3pm in winter). The voyage takes 20 minutes. Meis is a simple fishing village of cute pastel-coloured houses with a sprinkling of restaurants, a superb bakery, a duty-free shop selling Greek wine and pork, some excellent hikes over the hill and a decent museum. From Meis' harbour it's also easy to arrange boat trips to swim inside the fabulously surreal blue cave along the island's coast.

It's possible to spend the night in Meis, or continue onwards into Greece proper. There are ferries to Rhodes (€21.50, five hours) three times a week and a high-speed catamaran (€35, 2½ hours, every Wednesday) in summer. Meis even has a tiny landing strip from where you can fly to Rhodes (€40, 40 minutes) at 5.30pm Friday to Wednesday. On Meis, your best source of information is **Papoutsis Travel** (☑ +30 22460 49 286).

Tickets for Meis can be bought from **Meis Express** (☑ 836 1725; www.meisexpress. com) in the harbour or any travel agency. If you haven't booked your ticket the day before, make sure you arrive a half-hour before sailing.

Hotel Hadrian HOTEL €€€
(⌂836 2856; www.hotel-hadrian.de; Doğan Kaşaroğlu Sokak 10; r from €140; ❄ 🌐 ⊠) About halfway out on the Kaş peninsula, the German-owned Hadrian is a tropical oasis with 14 rooms and suites (though the faux classical statues add a touch of Teutonic kitsch). The large seawater pool and private swimming platform are excellent, and the terrace bar has wow-factor views.

Narr Hotel HOTEL €€€
(⌂836 2024; www.narrhotel.com; Hükümet Caddesi; s/d/tr €90/100/120; ❄ 🌐 ⊠) This narrow white-and-cream hotel has 15 rooms, just opposite Küçük Çakıl Beach and its bathing platforms. All rooms are classically styled and seven of them (including 201 and 202) look directly at the sea and the Greek island of Meis.

✖ Eating

Kaş has a burgeoning dining scene with the old town packed full of eating options. You'll find some excellent restaurants to the southeast of the main square, especially around Sandıkçı Sokak.

The weekly market takes place every Friday on Ugar Mumcu Caddesi.

Havana Balık Evi SEAFOOD €
(⌂836 4111; Öztürk Sokak 7; mains ₺6-15; ⊘9am-midnight; ✎) Head here for cheap and cheerful *balık ekmek* (₺6) – the simple fish sandwich that is a staple in coastal Turkey. Keeping up the fishy theme, there are also hearty bowls of *balık guveç* (fish casserole, ₺15) and *hamsı tava* (pan-fried Turkish anchovies; ₺10). You can bring your own alcohol.

Enişte'nin Yeri TURKISH €
(⌂836 4404; Necip Bey Caddesi; dishes ₺5-15) An excellent choice for no-nonsense Turkish dishes of pide, grills, soups and salads. Head out back to eat in the pretty courtyard during the summer months.

Cafe Mola CAFE €
(⌂8361994; Bahçe Sokak; dishes ₺5-12; ⊘8.30am-11pm) This convivial cawfe is great for Turkish breakfast (₺13) and quick bites such as sandwiches (₺5) and *mantı* (₺12). Don't leave without trying their award-winning fresh lemonade with mint (₺6).

★ Şaraphane ANATOLIAN €€
(⌂836 2715, 0532 520 3262; Yeni Cami Caddesi 3; mains ₺12-25) A definite must-do for wine connoisseurs (Şaraphane is Turkish for 'wine house'), this is an intimate, cosy choice with a great atmosphere, open kitchen, and a roaring fire in the cooler months. The small menu features fresh, bold flavours and lesser-seen Turkish dishes such as *erişte* (Turkish noodles). The wine list of local and organic tipples is extensive.

Köşk ANATOLIAN €€
(⌂836 3857; Gürsoy Sokak 13; mains ₺14-25) In a lovely little square off a cobbled street just up from the water, Köşk occupies a rustic, 150-year-old house with two terraces and seating in the open courtyard. Forgo the mains and feast instead on their gorgeous meze dishes, which draw from both Mediterranean and Anatolian influence. Delicious.

Bi Lokma ANATOLIAN €€
(⌂836 3942; Hükümet Caddesi 2; mains ₺13-21; ⊘9am-midnight; ✎) Also known as 'Mama's Kitchen', this place has tables meandering around a terraced garden overlooking the harbour. Sabo – the 'mama' in question – turns out great traditional Turkish soul-food including excellent meze, and her famous *mantı* (Turkish ravioli; ₺13) and *börek* (filled pastry; ₺13).

Çınarlar Pide & Pizza House PIDE €€
(⌂836 2860; İbrahim Serin Cad 4; pide ₺8.50-14, pizza ₺12-20; ⊘8am-1am) Perennially popular with Kaş' young bloods, who come for the well-priced pide, pizza and pop music, Çınarlar has a pleasant courtyard tucked away off the street.

★ İkbal MODERN TURKISH €€€
(⌂836 3193; Sandıkçı Sokak 6; mains ₺20-34; ⊘9am-midnight) Arguably Kaş' best restaurant, run by Vecdi and his German wife, Barbara, İkbal serves excellent seafood and the house speciality, slow-cooked leg of lamb, from a small but well-chosen menu. The wine list has a good selection of Turkish wines from Mediterranean vineyards.

Retro Bistro INTERNATIONAL €€€
(⌂836 4282; İbrahim Serin Caddesi; mains ₺20-30; ⊘11am-late) New kid on the block Retro Bistro specialises in homemade pasta and sous-vide cooking, and also does a great burger but it gets our vote for its gorgeously unique and luscious desserts. Aubergine crème brûlée and beetroot pannacotta may sound a tad odd but trust us – they're scrumptious.

Blue House
TURKISH €€€

(☑836 1320; Sandıkçı Sokak 8; mains ₺20-34) Home cooking with extra finesse; the entire family pitch in to help at this sweet restaurant set in the family home. The small terrace has superb views across the bay while the cooks rustle up tasty meze and lots of seafood mains from the kitchen.

🍸 Drinking & Nightlife

Hideaway Bar & Cafe
BAR

(☑836 3369; Cumhuriyet Meydanı 16/A; ⊙4pm-3am) We adore this enchanting garden cafe and bar, accessed by a non-descript doorway on the main square. This is our favourite spot for a restorative mid-afternoon coffee and for relaxed evening drinks, only a stone's throw from the hustle and yet a world away. Sunday brunch is great here too.

Echo Cafe & Bar
BAR

(☑836 2047; www.echocafebar.com; Limanı Sokak; ⊙8am-4am) Hip and stylish, this lounge near an ancient (5 BC, anyone?) cistern on the harbour has Kaş high society sipping fruit daiquiris to both live and canned jazz. The airy gallery upstairs has nice little balconies overlooking the water.

Cafe Corner
CAFE

(☑836 3661; İbrahim Serin Caddesi 20; ⊙8am-1am) This well-positioned cafe-bar has a nice relaxed atmosphere and well-priced drinks. Sit back and watch the world go by with a decent snacks and light-meals menu for when you get peckish.

Giorgio's Bar
BAR

(☑0544 608 8687; Cumhuriyet Meydanı) Facing the harbour, Georgio's has great music (played live several times a week) and service. Drinks prices are not bad (cocktails from ₺18) when you consider the key location.

🛍 Shopping

Turqueria
HANDICRAFTS

(☑836 1631; Uzun Çarşı Sokak 21) Run by Orhan and Martina, a charming Turkish-German couple long-time resident in Kaş, Turqueria is an Aladdin's cave, with everything from old prints and advertisements to rare Turkish puppets handcut from leather.

Gallery Anatolia
CERAMICS

(☑836 1954; www.gallery-anatolia.com; Hükümet Caddesi 2; ⊙9am-11pm) This very upmarket gallery along the marina has locally designed ceramic pieces.

ℹ Information

Tourist Office (☑836 1238; Cumhuriyet Meydanı; ⊙8am-5pm) Marginally helpful office on the main square with town maps and a few brochures.

ℹ Getting There & Away

The **otogar** is along Atatürk Bulvarı 350m north of the centre. From here there are daily buses to İstanbul (₺90, 15 hours, 985km) at 6.30pm and direct buses to İzmir (₺55, 8½ hours, 440km). To reach Ankara, you must change at Fethiye.

Closer to home there are dolmuşes every half-hour to Kalkan (₺5, 35 minutes, 29km); and to Antalya (₺24, 3½ hours, 188km) via Demre (₺8, one hour, 45km) and Olympos (₺18, 2½ hours, 109km). Buses to Fethiye (₺16, 2½ hours, 107km) leave hourly. Services to Patara (₺7.50, 45 minutes, 40km) run every hour. You can also reach Saklıkent Gorge (₺12.50, one hour, 52km) from here.

Üçağız & Kekova
☑0242 / POP 400

Declared off-limits to development, Üçağız (ooch-*eye*-iz) is a quaint fishing and farming village in an absolutely idyllic setting on a bay amid islands and peninsulas. Little has changed here over the years and the teensy squiggle of lanes behind the harbour is a watercolour-worthy scene of rustic cottages and rural life. Üçağız is a regular stop on the *gület* circuit and the jumping-off point for visiting the sunken city at Kekova and the secluded settlement of Kaleköy. During summer an armada of tour buses pull into the car park, rush groups onto the waiting boats, and then shuffle their sunburnt charges back onto the buses at the end of the day, while Üçağız snaps back into snooze mode for the evening. Staying overnight, with little to do except appreciate the glorious silence, is a delight.

A few words about where you are and what's what: the village you enter from the coastal highway is Üçağız, ancient Teimiussa, with its own Lycian necropolis. Across the water on the peninsula to the southeast is Kaleköy (called Kale locally), a protected village on the site of the ancient city of Simena.

South of the villages and past the channel entrance is the long island of Kekova with its famous underwater ruins; local people generally use this name to refer to the whole area. To the west on the Sıçak Peninsula is Aperlae, an isolated and very evocative ancient Lycian city on the Lycian Way.

🛏 Sleeping & Eating

Üçağız's pensions all offer boat services to the beaches on Kekova Island. They are also excellent bases for hiking sections of the Lycian Way.

Likya Pension
PENSION €

(☑ 874 2251, 0531 596 8408; gokkaya07@mynet. com; s/d/tr ₺60/90/110; 🕸🛜) Owner Halil runs this peaceful oasis snuggled within a lush garden of fruit trees. There are eight cosy rooms here brimming with rustic charm. Guests are welcome to use the kitchen and laundry and Halil has a dingy for beach excursions nearby. The pension is in an alleyway just up from the harbour.

★ Likya Cennet Pension
PENSION €€

(☑ 874 2250, 0533 462 8554; www.likyacennet. com; s/d ₺90/120; 🕸🛜) Gregarious Mehmet (who also runs a carpet shop) and his friendly wife Zuhra have five large, bright and spotlessly clean rooms right on the waterfront, with killer views across the harbour from the terrace. We love the garden full of mulberry trees and Zuhra's homecooking (dinners ₺20 to ₺35). Mehmet can also organise boat trips and beach excursions.

Kekova Pansiyon
PENSION €€

(☑ 874 2259, 0536 550 5294; www.kekovapansi yon.com; d ₺150; 🕸🛜🌊) Set in splendid isolation on the far end of the waterfront, this pension is in a handsome old stone building with a terrace dotted with flowerpots. The eight whitewashed rooms are full of old-fashioned flair and share a lovely verandah with cushioned benches and views over the water.

Onur Pension
PENSION €€

(☑ 874 2071, 0536 675 0717; www.onurpension. com; d ₺100-120; ⊗Feb-Oct; 🕸@🛜) With a picturesque setting right on the harbour, this well-maintained pension has eight small, simple and tidy rooms (four with full sea views). It's run by locally born Onur and his Dutch wife Jacqueline. Onur can give great trekking advice and act as a guide.

Kordon Restaurant
SEAFOOD €€

(☑ 874 2067; meze ₺5-6, grills & fish per 500g ₺15-17.50; ⊗9am-midnight) With an attractive, breezy terrace overlooking the marina and fresh fish – try the excellent grilled sea bass – the Kordon is one of the better restaurants in town. Set lunch is a snip at ₺20 to ₺25.

İbrahim Restaurant
TURKISH €€

(mains ₺15-25) This popular waterfront restaurant dishes up decent kebap and seafood mains as well as a great selection of meze (₺6 per portion).

❶ Getting There & Away

There is no bus service from Kaş but nearly all of the tour companies in Kaş will let you hitch a lift on their daily boat tour transport to Üçağız if they have a spare seat (₺20 return).

EXPLORING THE KEKOVA AREA

Given the difficulty of getting to the Kekova area by public transport, most people end up taking a boat tour from Kaş or Kalkan, which starts with a bus ride to Üçağız where you'll board the boat.

Along the northern shore of Kekova island are ruins, partly submerged 6m below the sea and referred to as the **Batık Şehir** (Sunken City). These ruins are the result of a series of severe earthquakes in the 2nd century AD; most of what you can still see is a residential part of ancient Simena. Foundations of buildings, staircases and moorings are also visible. It is forbidden to anchor or swim around or near the Sunken City.

After the visit to Kekova you'll have lunch on the boat and then head on to Kaleköy, passing a couple of submerged (and very photo-worthy) Lycian tombs just offshore. There's usually about an hour to explore Kaleköy and climb up to the hilltop fortress.

Tours from Kaş, which cost €25 per person, generally leave at 10am and return around 6pm. Tours that include the nearby ruins of Aperlae usually cost €5 extra. If you're staying in Üçağız you can easily organise a tour by negotiating with any of the boat captains at the harbour directly. A three-hour boat tour costs between ₺80 to ₺120. All the pensions in Üçağız can also arrange boat tours for you.

The closest you'll get to the Kekova sunken city ruins is on a sea-kayaking tour (€25 to €30 per person, or €45 to €50 with Aperlae, including transfers and lunch) run by one of the Kaş travel agencies.

One dolmuş leaves Antalya for Üçağız daily at 2.15pm (₺20, 3½ hours). It stops in Demre enroute at 5pm (₺5, 30 minutes). From Üçağız, the dolmuş leaves at 8am.

Kaleköy (Kale)

☏ 0242 / POP 150

The watery paradise of Kaleköy is one of the western Mediterranean's truly delightful spots, home to the ruins of ancient **Simena** and an impressive Crusader **fortress** (admission ₺5) perched above the hamlet looking out to sea. Within the fortress, the ancient world's tiniest **theatre** is cut into the rock, and nearby you'll find ruins of several temples and public baths. From the top you can look down upon a field of **Lycian tombs**, and the old **city walls** are visible on the outskirts.

Kaleköy is accessible from Üçağız only by boat (10 minutes) or on foot (45 minutes) along a track that is part of the Lycian Way trail.

🛏 Sleeping & Eating

Simena Pansiyon   PENSION €€

(☏ 874 2025, 0532 779 0476; www.simenapansiyon.com; s/d €50/70; ❄ 🁢) Set slightly back from Kaleköy harbour, this gorgeous 150-year-old Greek stone house (look out for the lovely mosaic on the verandah) has four rooms brimming with colourful character and antiques. All share a wide verandah where you could happily sloth away the day staring out to sea.

★ Mehtap Pansiyon   PENSION €€€

(☏ 0535 592 1236, 874 2146; www.mehtappansiyon.com; s/d/tr €95/110/125; ❄ 🁢) The 10-room Mehtap has million-dollar views over the harbour and submerged Lycian tombs below. Four rooms are in a 200-year-old stone house so quiet and tranquil you may start snoozing as you check in; another four are in a building dating back a millennium and there's two more in a purpose-built wood cottage.

İrfan and his son, Saffet, are warm and knowledgeable hosts. Saffet's wife, Nazike, grows her own vegetables and is an excellent cook (set meal ₺40).

Kale Pansiyon   PENSION €€€

(☏ 874 2111, 0532 244 1163; www.kalepansiyon.com; s/d €50/80; ❄ 🁢) Slap on the harbour, the 10 airy rooms of the Kale Pansiyon all have balconies so close to the sea you can hear the water lapping. We like the seafront platform, complete with sun loungers, here too.

Ankh   CAFE €

(☏ 874 2171; www.ankhpansion.com; ice cream ₺8) Ankh, a cafe at a pension, makes its own peach, banana and hazelnut ice cream and boasts spectacular views from its terrace.

Hassan Deniz Restaurant   SEAFOOD €€

(☏ 874 2101; www.hassandeniz.com; mains ₺10-20) One of about five restaurants along Kaleköy seafront, Hassan Deniz is much favoured by yachties and their crews for its fresh fish and great meze. It's at the end of a long pier.

Kale (Demre)

☏ 0242 / POP 16,200

Officially 'Kale' but called by its old name 'Demre' by just about everyone, this sprawling, dusty town was once the Lycian (and later Roman) city of Myra. By the 4th century it was important enough to have its own bishop – most notably St Nicholas, who went on to catch the Western world's imagination in his starring role as Santa Claus. In AD 60, St Paul put Myra on the liturgical map by changing boats at its port, Andriake, while on his way to Rome (or so Acts 27: 4-6 tell us).

Once situated on the sea, Demre moved further inland as precious alluvium – deposits of clay, silt, sand and gravel – flowed from the Demre stream. That silting is the foundation of the town's wealth, and it remains a major centre for the growing and distribution of fruit and vegetables.

The street going west from the main square to the Church of St Nicholas is pedestrian Müze Caddesi and is lined with cafes and shops. Alakent Caddesi leads 2km north to the Lycian rock tombs of Myra (a 20-minute walk or ₺10 taxi ride), while the street going south from the square passes the otogar (100m).

◉ Sights

St Nicholas Church   CHURCH

(Müze Caddesi; admission ₺15; ⊘9am-7pm) It may not be vast like the Aya Sofya or brilliant with mosaics like İstanbul's Chora Church (Kariye Museum), but the Church of St Nicholas, where the eponymous saint was laid upon his death in AD 343, is nonetheless a star attraction for pilgrims and tourists alike. Although St Nicholas is no longer in situ (Italian merchants smashed open the sarcophagus in 1087 and supposedly carted his bones to Bari), the church features interesting Byzantine frescoes and mosaic floors.

The church was made a basilica when it was restored in 1043. Later restorations in 1862 were sponsored by Tsar Nicholas I of Russia (St Nicholas is the patron saint of Russia) and changed the church by building a vaulted ceiling and a belfry. More recent work by Turkish archaeologists is aiming to protect it from deterioration.

There are some statues of the saint – one of them the height of kitsch as Santa Claus – in the square in front of the church. St Nick's feast day (6 December) is a very big event here.

Myra   ARCHAEOLOGICAL SITE
(admission ₺15; ⊙9am-7pm) If you only have time to see one striking honeycomb of Lycian rock tombs, then choose the memorable ruins of ancient Myra. Located about 2km inland from Demre's main square, they are among the finest in Lycia. There's a well-preserved **Roman theatre** here, which includes several Roman theatrical masks carved on stones lying in the nearby area. The so-called **Painted Tomb** near the river necropolis portrays a man and his family in relief both inside and out.

Andriake   RUIN
FREE About 5km southwest of Demre's centre is the seafront settlement of Çayağzı,

called Andriake by the Romans at a time when the port was an important entrepot for grain on the sea route between the eastern Mediterranean and Rome.

The ruins of ancient Andriake are strewn over a wide area to the north and south of the access road approaching Çayağzı. The great **granary** built by Hadrian and completed in AD 139 lies in the southern section.

Much of the land is marshland so the ruins (including the granary) can be difficult to reach in wet weather. In 2009 the ruins of the first synagogue found in ancient Lycia were uncovered here.

Dolmuşes run sporadically out to Çayağzı; your best bet is probably a taxi (₺15).

🛏 Sleeping & Eating

Most visitors travel to Demre by day and sleeping options in the town centre are virtually nonexistent. If you're driving and get hungry, about 2km east of Demre, at the end of a long pebble beach, are several shacks serving freshly caught crab with chips and salad.

★**Hoyran Wedre**
Country House   BOUTIQUE HOTEL €€€
(✆875 1125, 0532 291 5762; www.hoyran.com; s/d/ ste from €90/120/140; ❉🅰❄) A destination hotel if ever there was one, this complex of stone buildings is a rural oasis up in the Taurus Mountains, with astounding views across the countryside down to the Kekova area. There are 17 rooms and suites done in

---

WORTH A TRIP

ARYKANDA

Built over five terraces, **Arykanda** (admission ₺5; ⊙9am-7pm) is one of the most dramatically situated ruins in Turkey. The city's most outstanding feature is its 10-metre tall, two-storey **baths** complex, standing next to the gymnasium on the lowest terrace.

Following a path to the next terrace you'll come to a large colonnaded **agora**. Its northern arches lead into an **odeon**. Above, is a fine 2nd-century **theatre** and **stadium**. Another agora, a bouleterion, and cistern, are found on the upper terraces.

One of the oldest sites on the peninsula, Arykanda was part of the Lycian League from its inception in the 2nd century BC but was never a member of the 'Big Six' group of cities that commanded three votes each. This may have been due to its profligate and free-wheeling ways as much as anything else. Arykanda was apparently the party town of Lycia and forever deeply in debt. Along with the rest of Lycia it was annexed by Rome in AD 43 and survived as a Byzantine settlement until the 9th century when it was abandoned.

If you're driving, head 29km northeast of Demre to the unremarkable provincial centre of Finike, where there's an exit off the D400 leading north for another 30km to Arykanda.

Dolmuşes headed for Elmalı (₺12) from Finike will drop you off at the foot of the hill leading to the site entrance from where it's a steep 3km walk to the ruins. A taxi will cost about ₺120 from Demre.

traditional fashion (wattle-and-daub plastered walls) and decorated with antiques sourced in İstanbul.

We love the nearby Lycian acropolis (which owner Süleyman can guide you through), the pool shaped like a traditional cistern, the set meals (€20) prepared entirely from locally grown produce (though some rooms have kitchens if you prefer to self-cater), and high teas at 5pm.

It's 18km west of Demre, and 3km south of Davazlar village, off the D400.

Gaziantep Restaurant　　　KEBAP €
(☑871 2812; Eynihal Caddesi; pide ₺4-8, kebap ₺9-15; ☺7am-10pm) Just opposite Demre square with the Church of St Nicholas and its accompanying faux icon shops, this simple but spotless place with outside seating is a local favourite.

Akdeniz Restaurant　　　TURKISH €
(☑871 5466; Müze Caddesi; mains ₺5-15; ☺7am-11pm) This welcoming restaurant west of St Nicholas Church has a large array of tasty precooked dishes as well as pide and *köfte* (meatballs).

Sabancı Pastaneleri　　　CAFE €
(☑871 3020; Eynihal Caddesi; pastries ₺3-8; ☺6am-11pm) This modern cafe near the otogar is great for breakfast or a snack. It also serves ice cream (₺2 per scoop).

🛈 Getting There & Away

Buses and dolmuşes travel to/from Kaş (₺8, one hour, 45km) hourly and less frequently to/from Olympos & Çıralı (₺10, 1½ hours) and Antalya (₺15, 2½ hours).

Olympos & Çıralı
☑0242
About 65km northeast of Demre, past Finike and Kumluca, a road leads southeast from the main highway (veer to the right then follow the signs for 11km) to ancient Olympos with its tumble of beachside ruins and backpacker camp community.

On the other side of the mountain and over the narrow Ulupınar Stream is Çıralı, a holiday hamlet with dozens of hotels and pensions that may look like it was born yesterday but contains that most enigmatic of classical icons: the eternal flame of the Chimaera.

Olympos
An important Lycian city in the 2nd century BC, Olympos is more famous these days for being the beach resort of choice for backpackers. Staying in an Olympos 'tree house' at one of the dozen or so camps that line the 1.5km-long track along the valley down to the ruins and beach has long been the stuff of travel legend. The former hippy-trail hot spot has gentrified considerably in past years and during summer can be pretty overcrowded and institutionalised.

Love it or hate it, Olympos still offers good value and an up-for-it party atmosphere in a lovely setting. Just remember that 'tree house' is a misnomer; huts are very firmly on the ground. If you plan on staying, don't forget to bring enough cash to last your visit; there is no ATM or bank in Olympos.

🔘 Sights & Activities

Most people come to loll about and swim at the **beach** (admission incl Olympos ruins ₺5, long-stay ticket allowing 10 entries over 10 days ₺7.50) that fronts the ruins but there are also numerous activities available from agencies and camps in Olympos including boat cruises (full-day with lunch €20 to €25); canyoning (full-day trip €30); sea kayaking (half-day trip €18); paragliding (€75); diving (try dive €25, two dives with equipment included €46); mountain-biking trips; and rock climbing. Some of the best and most difficult rock climbing is at Hörguc, a wall opposite Olympos.

All camps organise nightly transport to view the Chimaera (₺25 to ₺30).

Olympos Ruins　　　ARCHAEOLOGICAL SITE
(admission incl Olympos Beach ₺5, long-stay ticket allowing 10 entries over 10 days ₺7.50; ☺9am-7.30pm) The rambling ruins of ancient Olympos are scattered beside the trickling Ulupınar Stream inside a deep valley that runs directly to the sea. Olympos devoutly worshipped Hephaestus (Vulcan), the god of fire, which may have been inspired by the Chimaera, an eternal flame that still burns from the ground not far from the city.

Olympos went into decline in the 1st century BC. The arrival of the Romans at the end of the 1st century AD, brought about the city's rejuvenation but pirate attacks during the 3rd century caused the city's importance to wane. In the Middle Ages the Venetians and Genoese built fortresses along the coast but by the 15th century the site had been abandoned.

Olympos Adventure Center ADVENTURE SPORTS
(☑ 0532 686 1799; www.olymposadventurecenter.com; Kadır's Tree Houses; ⊙ 8.30am-10pm) Olympos' action-adventure specialists offer the full gamut of tours and activities from ATV trips (€25) to diving (one dive including equipment, €25). This is the go-to company if you're into rock climbing with a huge range of rock-climbing trips (from €10) and courses (from €129) to choose from.

🛏 Sleeping & Eating

Unless specified otherwise, the prices for accommodation at the camps listed here is per person and includes half board (ie breakfast and dinner); all drinks cost extra. Outside of peak summer months expect good discounts on accommodation. Solo travellers should note that the per person bungalow rates are based on a double so a single supplement is sometimes expected. Check when booking.

While 'tree houses' (usually small, rustic bungalows slightly raised off the ground) have shared bathrooms, most camps now boast bungalows with en suite and air-conditioning. Not all tree houses have reliable locks, so store valuables at reception.

Be extra attentive to personal hygiene while staying at Olympos. In summer, particularly, the huge numbers of visitors can stretch the camps' capacity for proper waste disposal to the limit, so be vigilant about where and what you eat. Every year some travellers wind up ill.

Şaban Pansion BUNGALOW €
(☑ 892 1265, 0507 007 6600; www.sabanpansion.com; dm ₺40, tree house ₺45, bungalow with bathroom & air-con ₺70; ❋ 🛜) Our personal favourite, this is the place to come if you want to snooze in a hammock or on cushions in the shade of orange trees. In the words of the charming manager Meral: 'It's not a party place'. Instead it sells itself on tranquillity, space and great home cooking, plus room 7 really is a tree house.

Bayrams BUNGALOW €
(☑ 892 1243, 0532 494 7454; www.bayrams.com; dm ₺40, tree house ₺50, bungalow with bathroom & air-con ₺75; ❋ 🛜) We love the lively communal feel here. Guests relax on cushioned platforms, playing backgammon or reading in the garden or puffing away on a nargile (water pipe) at the bar. Come here if you

want to socialise but not necessarily party. The camp can fit 150 guests.

Orange Pension BUNGALOW €
(☑ 892 1317, 0554 484 1265; www.olymposorange-pension.com; dm ₺30, bungalow with bathroom & air-con ₺60; ❋ 🛜) Run by well-travelled host Apo, Orange's pine-clad bungalows have a touch of Swiss Family Robinson about them and are quite spacious compared to other camps. Some even have TVs. On the downside they're more crammed together. There's a great garden out front with hammocks and shady seating.

Varuna Pansiyon TURKISH €€
(☑ 892 1347, 0532 602 7839; www.olymposvaruna.com; mains ₺10-15; ⊙ 8am-11pm; ❋ 🛜) This popular restaurant serves a fair range of snacks and mains including sandwiches (₺8), trout meals and kebaps in an attractive dining room. There's also accommodation (₺60 to ₺65) here in 11 bungalows and 13 rooms, which are bigger and have a bit more character than the typical Olympos offerings.

Çıralı

Çıralı (cher-*ah*-luh) is a relaxed, family-friendly hamlet of upscale pensions and hotels leading down to and along a beach lined with a dozen restaurants. It's a quieter alternative to the backpackers' haunt down the beach at Olympos. And it's close to the magical and mystical Chimaera.

Known in Turkish as Yanartaş or 'Burning Rock', the Chimaera (admission ₺5) is a cluster of flames that blaze spontaneously from crevices on the rocky slopes of Mt Olympos. At night it looks like hell itself has come to pay a visit, and it's not difficult to see why ancient peoples attributed these extraordinary flames to the breath of a monster – part lion, part goat and part snake – which had terrorised Lycia. The mythical hero Bellerophon supposedly killed the Chimaera by mounting the winged horse Pegasus and pouring molten lead into the monster's mouth.

Today gas still seeps from the earth and bursts into flame upon contact with the air. The exact composition of the gas is unknown, though it is thought to contain methane. Although a flame can be extinguished by covering it, it will reignite close by into a new and separate flame. At night the 20 or 30 flames in the main area are clearly visible at sea.

ANTALYA & THE TURQUOISE COAST OLYMPOS & ÇIRALI

The best time to visit is after dinner. From Çıralı, follow the road along the hillside marked for the Chimaera until you reach a valley and walk up to a car park. From there it's another 20- to 30-minute climb up a stepped path to the site; bring or rent a torch. It's a 7km walk from Olympos, but most camps also organise transport every night after dinner.

🛏 Sleeping

Çıralı may look at first like just two dirt roads lined with pensions, but it's a delightful beach community for nature lovers and post-backpackers. Driving in, you cross a small bridge where a few taxis usually wait to run people back up to the main road. Continue across the bridge and you'll come to a junction in the road with innumerable signboards – there are about 60 pensions here. Go straight on for the pensions nearest to the path up to the Chimaera. Turn right for the pensions closer to the beach and the Olympos ruins.

Outside of the June to mid-September peak season, most places here offer good discounts on rooms.

Hotel Canada HOTEL €€
(☑ 825 7233, 0532 431 3414; www.canadahotel.net; d €60, 4-person bungalow €90; ❋ 🛜 ⛲) This is a beautiful place offering the quintessential Çıralı experience: warmth, friendliness and house-made honey. The main house rooms are comfortable and the garden is filled with hammocks, citrus trees, and 11 bungalows. Canadian Carrie and foodie husband Şaban also offer excellent set meals (€10). It's 750m from the beach; grab a free bike and pedal on down.

Orange Motel PENSION €€
(☑ 825 7328, 0532 738 9570; www.orangemotel. net; d €70, 2-bedroom bungalow €100; ❋ 🛜) A smart and reasonably priced choice, the Orange is smack dab in the middle of an orange grove; come here in spring and you'll never forget the overwhelming scent. The garden is hung with hammocks and the relatively large rooms are well set up with kettles and decent-sized bathrooms. Evening meals are good value at ₺20.

Odile Hotel HOTEL €€
(☑ 825 7163; www.hotelodile.com; s/d €70/80, 2-/4-person bungalow with kitchenette €120/180) The neat bungalows here are set around a large pool, within a well-maintained garden.

Just behind the main complex surrounding another pool plus a child's pool, are larger 'luxe' bungalows made of lovely scented cedar. They are an excellent deal for families wanting to self-cater.

Sima Peace Pension BUNGALOW €€
(☑ 825 7245, 0532 238 1177; www.simapeace.com; s/d ₺80/120; ❋ 🛜) A throwback to the '60s (dig the peace sign logo), this Çıralı stalwart is about 750m up from the beach with rustic bungalows surrounded by fruit trees. Upstairs bungalows are nearing a tree-house style experience. Aynur – ably assisted by Koko the parrot – is the consummate host, and quite the character. Her cooking is legendary (dinner ₺15 to ₺20).

★ Myland Nature BUNGALOW €€€
(☑ 825 7044, 0532 488 2653; www.mylandnature. com; s/d/tr €69/93/115; ❋ 🛜) 🏄 This is an artsy, holistic and very green place that is sure to rub you up the right way (massage, free yoga and meditation workshops available). The 13 spotless and spacious wooden bungalows, with skylight features, are set around a pretty garden with hammocks strung between the orange trees. The food (vegetarian set meal ₺20) garners high praise.

Bikes are available (free for one hour, ₺7 all day) and non-guests can usually join the daily yoga sessions for ₺20.

Olympos Lodge RESORT €€€
(☑ 825 7171; www.olymposlodge.com.tr; r from €215; ❋ 🛜) The poshest place in Çıralı, Olympos Lodge is situated right on the beach within its private 1.5 hectare paradise of citrus orchards, manicured gardens and strutting peacocks. Rooms are gorgeously attired in a style that oozes bohemian glamour (rooms 1 and 2 have sea views). There's a lovely winter garden open in the cooler months.

ℹ Getting There & Away

Virtually any bus taking the coastal road between Fethiye and Antalya can drop you off or pick you up at the stops near the Olympos and Çıralı junctions. Just make sure you specify which one you want. From there, minibuses (₺5) leave for both destinations.

For Olympos (9km from the D400), minibuses depart every hour between 8am and 8pm from May to October. Returning, minibuses leave Olympos at 9am, then every hour until 7pm. From October to April they usually run hourly with the last minibus usually departing Olympos at 6pm.

To Çıralı (7km) there are minibuses every hour between 9am and 7pm between June and September but they often don't depart until they are full. They usually do a loop along the beach road, then pass the turn-off to the Chimaera and head back along the edge of the hillside. Outside of summer there is only one morning and one afternoon minibus service.

Many of the places to stay listed here will pick you up from the highway (₺20 to ₺25) if you book in advance.

Phaselis & Around

A romantically sited Lycian port, **Phaselis** (admission ₺10; ⊙9am-7pm Apr-Oct, 8.30am-5pm Nov-Mar) was founded by colonists from Rhodes as early as the 7th century BC on the border between Lycia and Pamphylia. Its wealth came from the shipment of timber, rose oil and perfume.

The extensive ruins are arranged around three bays, each with a diminutive beach. Much of what's left dates from Roman times. Look out for **Hadrian's Gate** (the emperor visited in 129 AD), the South Harbour's **agora** and the North Harbour's wonderful **colonnaded street**.

Phaselis is 6km north of the exits for Olympos and Çıralı from the D400. From the turn off it's about 1km to the site entrance and another 1km to the ruins and the sea.

Olympos Teleferik   CABLE CAR
(☑0242 242 2252; www.olymposteleferik.com; adult/child 7-16yr one-way €15/7.50, return €30/15; ⊙9.30am-6pm) If you're keen to sit on top of the world and look down on creation, this cable car climbs almost to the top of 2375m-high **Tahtalı Dağ** (Wooded Mountain), the centrepiece of **Beydağları Sahil National Park** (Beydağları Sahil Milli Parkı). The gondolas seat 80 people and depart every half-hour in summer and hourly in winter. The trip takes 10 minutes.

The turn-off from the highway is about 3km before Phaselis. A well-paved but steep road then carries on for 7km to the cable car's lower station at 725m.

ℹ Getting There & Away

Frequent buses on the highway from Antalya (₺8, 45 minutes, 58km) and Kemer (₺5, 20 minutes, 15km) pass both the exits for Phaselis and the Olympos Teleferik.

The cable-car company runs hourly shuttle buses from the highway exit to the teleferik station between 10am and 5pm. It also provides a direct bus service to/from Antalya (₺35) and Kemer (₺25), which you must book in advance.

Antalya

☑0242 / POP 1,027,551

Once seen simply as the gateway to the Turkish Riviera, Antalya today is very much a destination in its own right. Situated smack on the Gulf of Antalya (Antalya Körfezi), the largest Turkish city on the western Mediterranean coast is both classically beautiful and stylishly modern. At its core is the wonderfully preserved old city district of Kaleiçi – literally 'within the castle' – which offers atmospheric accommodation aplenty within a bundle of finely restored Ottoman houses. The old city wraps around a splendid Roman-era harbour with cliff-top views of hazy-blue mountain silhouettes that are worth raising a toast to. While just outside of the central city is one of Turkey's finest museums.

History

Antalya was named Attaleia after its 2nd-century founder Attalus II of Pergamum. His nephew Attalus III ceded the town to Rome in 133 BC. When the Roman Emperor Hadrian visited the city more than two centuries later, in 130 AD, he entered the city via a triumphal arch (now known as Hadrian's Gate), built in his honour.

There followed a succession of new 'landlords': the Byzantines took over from the Romans, followed by the Seljuk Turks in the early 13th century. The latter gave Antalya both a new name and an icon – the Yivli Minare (Fluted Minaret).

The city became part of the Ottoman Empire in 1391. After WWI, the empire collapsed and Antalya was ceded to Italy. In 1921 it was liberated by Atatürk's army and made the capital of Antalya province.

◉ Sights

★**Antalya Museum**   MUSEUM
(Map p368; ☑236 5688; www.antalyamuzesi.gov. tr/en; Konyaaltı Caddesi 1; admission ₺20; ⊙9am-6.30pm) On no account should you miss this comprehensive museum with exhibitions covering everything from the Stone and Bronze Ages to Byzantium. The Hall of Regional Excavations exhibits finds from

1. Kekova harbour (p358) 2. Fethiye (p331)
3. Ölüdeniz Beach & Lagoon (p339) 4. Kaş harbour (p353)

STUART BLACK / GETTY IMAGES ©

2

The Blue Cruise

A blue cruise is sightseeing with swags of style. Board a *gület* (Turkish yacht) to experience the Turquoise Coast's scenery in all its glory, from lazy days filled with swimming and sunbathing to sunset toasts in one of the prettiest corners of the Mediterranean.

Casting Off

Fethiye is the most popular departure point for average landlubbers who want a taste of on-the-sea life. More experienced yachties (and those chartering an entire boat rather than a cabin) often head for Göcek or Kaş.

Day One

Gülets head out from Fethiye and skim the lush green coastline to Ölüdeniz before cruising on to the cliff-hemmed beach at Butterfly Valley. The first day usually ends at St Nicholas Island, where there's plenty of time for swimming, snorkelling and – if you want your land legs back – exploring the island's ancient ruins.

4

Day Two

A full day of soaking up some sun on-board, with opportunities aplenty for swimming. On day two you usually cruise by the dinky harbour towns of Kalkan and Kaş and moor near the Liman Ağzı peninsula.

Day Three

Mixing history into the sunshine and salt spray, day three sails to Kekova Island's famous sunken-city remnants, before visiting Kaleköy to clamber up the hilltop to the fortress ruins of ancient Simena.

Day Four

On this day you head east along the coast, with plentiful swimming stops to savour the scenery. Çayağzı (the ancient harbour of Andriake), just south of Demre, is the usual disembarking point.

Antalya

Antalya

◎ **Top Sights**
1 Antalya Museum A2

✖ **Eating**
2 Can Can Pide ve Kebap Salonu D2
3 Club Arma C2
4 Güneyliler C1

🛍 **Shopping**
5 İki Kapılar Hanı D1

---

ancient cities in Lycia (such as Patara and Xanthos) and Pamphylia while the Hall of Gods displays beautiful and evocative statues of some 15 Olympian gods, many of them in near-perfect condition. Most of the statues, including the sublime Three Graces, were found at Perge.

Upstairs are coins and other gold artefacts recovered from Aspendos, Side and Byzantine sites. Taking pride of place is the so-called Elmalı Treasure of almost 2000 Lycian coins looted from Turkey in 1984 and returned from the USA some 15 years later.

The museum is about 2km west of the Kaleiçi district, accessible on the old-fashioned *tramvay* (tram) from Kale Kapısı tramstop.

★ **Hadrian's Gate**   GATE
(Hadriyanüs Kapısı; Map p370; Atatürk Caddesi) Commonly known as Üçkapılar (the 'Three Gates') in Antalya, the monumental Hadrian's Gate was erected for the Roman emperor's visit to Antalya in 130 AD.

★ **Suna & İnan Kıraç Kaleiçi Museum**   MUSEUM
(Map p370; ☎ 243 4274; www.kaleicimuzesi.org; Kocatepe Sokak 25; adult/child ₺3/2; ⊙ 9am-noon & 1-6pm Thu-Tue) This small ethnography museum is housed in a lovingly restored Antalya mansion. The 2nd floor contains a series of life-size dioramas depicting some of the most important rituals and customs of Ottoman Antalya. Much more impressive is the collection of Çanakkale and Kütahya ceramics housed in the former Greek Orthodox church of Aya Yorgi (St George), just behind the main house, which has been fully restored and is worth a look in itself.

Sultan Alaadın Camii   MOSQUE
(Map p370; Zafer Sokak) This gem of a mosque is squirreled away in the back alleys of Antalya. It began life as the Greek Orthodox Panhagia Church in 1834 and was converted to a mosque in 1958. Just inside the courtyard gate, you can climb up the spiral staircase of the church's old bell tower. Inside the prayer hall, uniquely in Antalya, the original painted ceiling, with its intricate star motifs and angels, has been preserved.

There are no official opening times but the mosque is usually open in the afternoons after midday prayer. When you see the gate open, you can visit.

Antalya Kültür Evi   HISTORIC BUILDING
(Map p370; Kadırpaşa Sokak; ⊙ 8am-5pm Tue-Sun) **FREE** This finely restored Ottoman mansion is worth a visit if you're interested in Antalya's architectural history. Down-

stairs explanation boards present the city's historical and cultural identity through its architecture. Upstairs a couple of rooms have been set up in 19th-century style replete with original furniture and dodgy mannequins.

Kesik Minare
HISTORIC SITE

(Truncated Minaret; Map p370; Hesapçı Sokak) This stump of a tower marks the ruins of a substantial building that has played a major role in Antalya's religious life over the centuries. Built originally as a 2nd-century Roman temple, converted into the Byzantine Church of the Virgin Mary in the 6th century and then a mosque three centuries later. It became a church again in 1361 but fire destroyed most of it in the 19th century.

The ruins are fenced off but you can still see bits of Roman and Byzantine marble from the outside.

Yivli Minare
HISTORIC SITE

(Fluted Minaret; Map p370; Cumhuriyet Caddesi) Antalya's symbol is the Yivli Minare, a handsome and distinctive 'fluted' minaret erected by the Seljuk Sultan Aladdin Keykubad I in the early 13th century. The adjacent mosque (1373) is still in use. Within the Yivli Minare complex is the heavily restored **Mevlevi Tekke** (Whirling Dervish Monastery; Map p370), which probably dates from the 13th century. Nearby to the west are two **türbe** (tombs; Map p370), one from the late 14th century and the other from 1502.

The broad plaza to the west with the equestrian **statue of Atatürk** (Map p370) is Cumhuriyet Meydanı.

Tekeli Mehmet Paşa Camii
MOSQUE

(Map p370; Paşa Camii Sokak) The Tekeli Mehmet Paşa Camii was built by the Beylerbey (Governor of Governors) Tekeli Mehmet Paşa. The building was repaired extensively in 1886 and 1926. Note the beautiful Arabic inscriptions in the coloured tiles above the windows.

Roman Harbour
WATERFRONT

(Map p370; İskele Caddesi) The Roman harbour at the base of Kaleiçi's slope was Antalya's lifeline from the 2nd century BC until late in the 20th century, when a new port was constructed about 12km to the west, at the far end of Konyaaltı Plajı. The harbour was restored during the 1980s and is now a marina for yachts and excursion boats.

Hıdırlık Kalesi
HISTORIC BUILDING

(Map p370; Karaalioğlu Parkı) This 14m-high tower was built in the 1st or 2nd century AD as a mausoleum and later, due to its excellent position looking over the bay, played an important role in the city's defences as a watchtower.

Karaalioğlu Parkı
PARK

(Map p370; Atatürk Caddesi) This large, attractive and flower-filled park has great panoramic views over the sea and is prime sunset promenading territory.

🏃 Activities

Sefa Hamamı
HAMAM

(Map p370; ☑241 2321, 0532 526 9407; www.sefahamam.com; Kocatepe Sokak 32; ⊙10am-9pm) The atmospheric Sefa Hamamı retains much of its 13th-century Seljuk architecture. A bath costs ₺25 and the full works with soap massage and scrub costs ₺45. Oil massages are an extra ₺30. Men and women bathe separately.

Balık Pazarı Hamamı
HAMAM

(Fish Market Bath; Map p370; ☑243 6175; Balık Pazarı Sokak; ⊙8am-11pm) The 700-year-old Balık Pazarı Hamamı offers Turkish bath packages of soak, scrub and soap for ₺40. There are separate sections for men and women.

Boat Excursions
BOAT TOUR

(Map p370; Roman Harbour) Excursion yachts tie up in the Roman harbour in Kaleiçi. Some trips go as far as Kemer, Phaselis, Olympos, Demre and even Kaş. You can take one-/two-hour trips (₺20/35) or a six-hour voyage (₺80 with lunch) which visits Kemer and Phaselis, the Gulf of Antalya islands and some beaches for a swim.

👉 Tours

Antalya is an excellent base for excursions to the ancient sites of Phaselis, Termessos, Perge, Aspendos and Selge as well as to the town of Side. There's a huge array of travel agencies in Antalya's Kaleiçi area offering tours.

Nirvana Travel Service
TOUR

(Map p370; ☑244 3893, 0532 521 6053; www.nirvanatour.com; İskele Caddesi 38/4) Offers a huge range of excursions including a full-day tour to Termessos with a stop at the Düden Şelalesi (Düden Falls) and a full-day tour to Perge and Aspendos with a side-trip to Manavgat waterfall. Both cost €45.

Kaleiçi

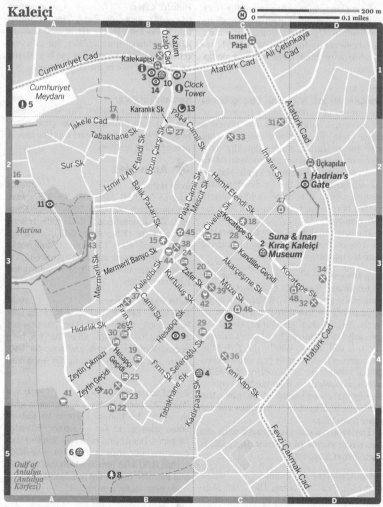

Festivals & Events

Golden Orange Film Festival FILM
(Altın Portakal Film Festivalı; www.altinportakal.org.tr; ☺ early Oct) Antalya's annual red-letter event is the Golden Orange Film Festival.

Antalya International Piano Festival MUSIC
(Antalya Uluslararası Piyano Festivali; www.antalyapiyanofestivali.com; ☺ Nov) Internationally recognised, the Antalya International Piano Festival is held at the **Antalya Cultural Centre** (Antalya Kültür Merkezi; ☎ 238 5444; 100 Yıl Bulvarı, Atatürk Kültür Parkı) west of the city centre.

Sleeping

The most atmospheric (and central) place to stay in Antalya is the old town of Kaleiçi, a virtually vehicle-free district that has everything you need. Kaleiçi's winding streets can be confusing to navigate, although signs pointing the way to most pensions are posted on street corners.

Most midrange and budget pensions offer decent discounts from October through to April.

Kaleiçi

ANTALYA & THE TURQUOISE COAST ANTALYA

★ **Sabah Pansiyon**   PENSION €
(Map p370; ☑ 247 5345, 0555 365 8376; www.
sabahpansiyon.com; Hesapçı Sokak 60; dm/s/d/tr
€13/25/30/45, 2-bedroom self-catering apt €100;
❄ ⊕ 🖥 ⊛) Our favourite budget digs in Antalya
is still going strong. The Sabah has long been
the first port of call for travellers watching
their kuruş, thanks to the Sabah brothers
who run the place with aplomb. Rooms
vary in size but all are sweet, simple and
super-clean. The shaded courtyard is prime
territory for meeting other travellers.

If you're looking for self-catering facilities,
check out their complex of five modern, spacious apartments nearby which can accommodate up to six people. Great for families.

Abad Pansiyon   PENSION €
(Map p370; ☑ 248 9723, 0537 691 4164; www.
antalyahostel.com; Hesapçı Sokak 65; dm/s/d/tr
₺25/40/60/100; ❄ 🖥) Right on the main
thoroughfare through the Kaleiçi district,
this lovely old Ottoman house has simple,
bright, if rather bland, rooms that are a solid
choice for budget travellers.

Hotel Blue Sea Garden   HOTEL €
(Map p370; ☑ 248 8213, 0537 691 4164; www.hotel-
blueseagarden.com; Hesapçı Sokak 65; s/d ₺45/75;
❄ ⊕ 🖥 ⊛) The plus here is the swimming pool
in a leafy courtyard – vital in the heat of
summer. The 16 rooms are nothing special
(with small bathrooms), but the in-house
restaurant has plenty of fans.

★ **White Garden Pansiyon**   PENSION €€
(Map p370; ☑ 241 9115; www.whitegardenpension
.com; Hesapçı Geçidi 9; s/d €32/40, self-catering
apt €110; ❄ 🖥 ⊛) A positively delightful place
to stay – full of quirky Ottoman character –
the White Garden combines tidiness and
class well beyond its price level, with impeccable service from Metin and his staff.
The building itself is a fine restoration and
the courtyard is particularly charming. The
breakfast here is one of the best you'll see
in Turkey.

There are also four self-catering apartments with good-sized rooms that would be
an excellent choice for families.

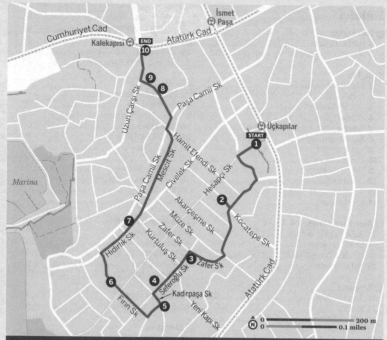

City Walk
Kaleiçi's Architecture Through the Ages

START HADRIAN'S GATE
END KALE KAPISI
LENGTH 1.5KM; TWO HOURS

Begin by strolling through the arches of ❶ **Hadrian's Gate** (p368), taking the first narrow alley to your left into the quieter residential district of Kaleiçi. You'll see some good examples of Ottoman mansions. Note the characteristic protruding shuttered oriel (*cumba* in Turkish) windows, where the women of the house would have hosted guests – being able to see out but not be seen themselves.

Turn right onto Kocatepe Sokak to visit the ❷ **Suna & İnan Kıraç Kaleiçi Museum** (p368). Then backtrack to continue along the lane until you arrive at a pretty square with trickling fountain. Turning right here onto Zafer Sokak you arrive at ❸ **Sultan Alaadın Camii** (p368). Head left by the ruins of the ❹ **Kesik Minare** (p369), then turn left again onto Kadırpaşa Sokak passing by the ❺ **Antalya Kültür Evi** (p368), noting its beautiful stone-pebble entrance.

You'll notice that nearly all of the houses are built of stone; a fire in 1895 destroyed much of the original timber housing. Turn right onto pretty ❻ **Fırın Sokak** with its mix of restored mansions now used as pensions and dilapidating houses awaiting restoration, and turn right onto Hıdırlık Sokak.

As you walk up the road you'll see the crumbling remains of the ❼ **Roman and Byzantine era walls**, which once encircled the town. Follow the road up until you come to a lonely sentinel incisor-like wall chunk marking a split in the road. Follow the left-hand road (tourist-shop-lined Paşa Camii Sokak) from where you'll notice on your right another large chunk of the ❽ **old city walls** with derelict examples of complete timber-framed Ottoman houses built into the walls.

End your walk by visiting 18th-century ❾ **Tekeli Mehmet Paşa Camii** (p369) before exiting the Old Town at ❿ **Kale Kapısı** (Fortress Gate), marked by an old stone clock tower (*saat kalesi*) and a statue of Attalus II, the city's founder.

Mavi & Anı Pansiyon
PENSION €€

(Map p370; ☑247 0056; www.maviani.com; Tabakhane Sokak 26; s/d/tr €30/45/57, self-catering apt €72-100; ※奥) This restored Ottoman house has a fabulously peaceful garden, common areas decorated with old Anatolian furniture and bric-a-brac, and rooms brimming with old-world character; some of which are Turkish style (beds on the floor). It's a wonderfully atmospheric place to stay. If you want something more contemporary they also have four newly renovated apartments, all with kitchen facilities, nearby.

Atelya Art Hotel
BOUTIQUE HOTEL €€

(Map p370; ☑241 6416; www.atelyahotel.com; Civelek Sokak 21; s/d €40/60; ※奥奥) Timelessness is hard to pin down, but the Atelya makes a bold effort in this eccentric art-inspired hotel contained in two old buildings (room 104 is great) and two newer ones. All rooms ooze an Ottoman splendour of richly coloured fabrics and beautiful furniture that capture the spirit of the past. It's an excellent midrange choice.

Agatha Lodge
BOUTIQUE HOTEL €€

(Map p370; ☑242 5082, 0542 614 9775; www.agathalodge.com; Hesapçı Sokak; s/d €40/50; ※奥) With just six rooms, Agatha Lodge is a charmingly intimate place to stay. We like the courtyard restaurant bursting with colourful pot plants and the elegantly attired rooms with gorgeously carved headboards and painted ceilings. The espresso machines in each room get a huge thumbs up too.

Secret Palace
PENSION €€

(Map p370; ☑244 1060; www.secretpalacepansion.com; Fırın Sokak 10; s/d €32/40; ※奥奥) Next door to its sister hotel, the White Garden Pansiyon, this restored traditional Turkish house has big high-ceilinged and light-filled rooms between a grand corridor with an original tiled floor. The tranquil garden outside is relaxation-central with a pool and bar surrounded by orange and tangerine trees.

Villa Verde
PENSION €€

(Map p370; ☑248 2559; www.pensionvillaverde.com; Seferoğlu Sokak 8; s/d €45/60) All the rooms at Villa Verde are named after fruit and have a fresh, minimalist appeal with liberal use of white-on-white decor with wood accents. Grab the 'Greyfurt' (Grapefruit) or 'Dut' (Mulberry) room to wake up with views over the ruins of Kesik Minare.

Villa Perla
BOUTIQUE HOTEL €€€

(Map p370; ☑248 4341; www.villaperla.com; Hesapçı Sokak 26; s/d €100/120; ※奥奥) We love this authentic Ottoman place snuggled around a courtyard complete with pool and tortoises. The seven comfortable rooms are at the top of a staircase that starts with a 12th-century stone step, the wooden ceilings are the real deal and some of the rooms have four-post beds and folk-painted cupboards. The in-house restaurant makes excellent meze.

Tuvana Hotel
BOUTIQUE HOTEL €€€

(Map p370; ☑247 6015; www.tuvanahotel.com; Karanlık Sokak 18; r €140-300; ※奥奥) This discreet compound of six Ottoman houses has been stylishly converted into a refined city hotel with 46 rooms and suites. Rooms are suitably plush, with an old-European feel, as well as mod-cons such as DVD players. The swimming pool is a bonus in the warmer months and the main restaurant Seraser (p374) is world-class.

Mediterra Art Hotel
BOUTIQUE HOTEL €€€

(Map p370; ☑244 8624; www.mediterraart.com; Zafer Sokak 5; s/d €80/90; ※奥奥) This upscale masterpiece of wood and stone once housed a Greek tavern (see the 19th-century frescoes and graffiti on the restaurant wall). The Mediterra offers sanctuary by a cutting-edge pool, a marvellous winter dining room and 28 small, though modestly luxurious, rooms spread over four buildings. On the top floor, via ancient stone steps, is a small art gallery.

✗ Eating

A nearly endless assortment of cafes and restaurants are tucked in and around the Kaleiçi area. For cheap eating, walk east to the Dönerciler Çarşısı (Market of Döner Makers; Map p370; Atatürk Caddesi) or north to the rooftop kebap places across the street from Kale Kapısı (Fortress Gate; Map p370).

Güneyliler
KEBAP €

(Map p368; ☑241 1117; 4 Sokak 12/A; meals ₺9-12) With its cafeteria-style interior, this reasonably priced locals-only joint isn't much to look at. But the wood-fired *lahmacun* (Arabic-style pizza; ₺3 to ₺6) and expertly grilled kebaps are served with so many complimentary extras, you'll want to return. If you get lost, ask for directions at the landmark Best Western Khan Hotel at Kazım Özalp Caddesi 55.

Can Can Pide ve Kebap Salonu KEBAP €

(Map p368; 243 2548; Arık Caddesi 4/A; pide & dürüm ₺8; 7am-midnight Mon-Sat) Looking for something very cheap and cheerful? Fantastically prepared *çorba* (soup), pide and Adana *dürüm* (beef kebap rolled in pitta) are here at bargain prices as are *mantı* (Turkish ravioli). It's opposite the landmark Antalya 2000 building and its Plaza Cinema.

Tarihi Balık Pazarı Unlu Mamülleri BAKERY €

(Map p370; Balık Pazarı Sokak; pastries ₺2-4) Great for lunch on the run or a mid-afternoon snack, this excellent little bakery churns out a mind-boggling array of sweet and savoury baked goods. We're particularly partial to the pastry roll crammed full of *sucuk* (spicy beef sausage) and cheese, and to the spinach *gözleme* (stuffed savoury crepe).

Paul's Place CAFE €

(Map p370; 244 3375; www.spccturkey.com; Yeni Kapı Sokak 24; latte ₺5, cakes ₺4.5, köfte ₺5-7; 9am-6pm Mon-Fri;) The good word comes in coffee cups at this informal cafe run by Christian expats in the St Paul Cultural Center. Regardless of your faith, you'll enjoy the espresso or filter coffee and scrumptious baked goods. There's a well-stocked lending library too.

Sim Restaurant TURKISH €€

(Map p370; 248 0107; Kaledibi Sokak 7; mains ₺12.50-20) Honest, home-style Turkish favourites are served up at this simple but charming restaurant run by a friendly family. When the weather's fine, dine underneath the canopy in the narrow passageway at the front, wedged against ancient Byzantine walls. The peaceful setting perfectly compliments *köfte* (meatballs), a choice of six meze and glorious *çorbalar* (soups).

Although only a few streets away from the hustle of Kaleiçi's main dining drag, you could be a world away.

Yemenli TURKISH €€

(Map p370; 247 5346; Zeytin Sokak 16; mains ₺14.50-17.50;) Tried-and-true Turkish favourites are served up at this lovely restaurant with dining either in the leafy garden courtyard or inside the charmingly renovated stone house. It's run by the same team behind the Sabah Pansiyon, so service is friendly and on-the-ball. There's a couple of excellent vegetarian options here too.

Parlak Restaurant ANATOLIAN €€

(Map p370; 241 6553; www.parlakrestaurant. com; Kazım Özalp Caddesi 7; mains ₺10-24) Opposite the jewellery bazaar and just off pedestrian Kazım Özalp Caddesi, this sprawling open-air patio restaurant in an old caravanserai is favoured by locals. It's famous for its charcoal-grilled chicken (one-half ₺10) and excellent meze.

7 Mehmet Restaurant TURKISH €€

(238 5200; www.7mehmet.com; Atatürk Kültür Parkı, Dunmlupınar 201; meze ₺6-20, mains ₺10-35) Antalya's most famous eatery is a couple of kilometres west of the centre, and its spacious indoor and outdoor dining areas occupy a hill overlooking Konyaaltı Beach and the city. The menu of grilled mains, fish and meze is unsurprising but of very high quality. Ask for a peek in the enormous kitchen.

LeMan Kültür CAFE €€

(Map p370; 243 7473; www.leman.com.tr; Atatürk Caddesi 44; mains ₺11.50-20; 9am-midnight) If you want to catch a bit of Antalya's young hipster vibe, this garden cafe south of Hadrian's Gate is the place to come. It takes as its theme cartoons and caricatures (they're all done by patrons) and is vastly popular with students. It's open for breakfast, lunch and dinner and is always packed.

Gül Restoran MEZE €€

(Map p370; 243 2284; Kocatepe Sokak 1; mains ₺9-24) On the edge of Atatürk Caddesi is this very blue intimate garden restaurant, shaded by a grove of Antalya's famous orange trees and popular with visiting German couples. The buffet of meze (₺8) – there are eight different ones each day – is well known.

★ Vanilla INTERNATIONAL €€€

(Map p370; 247 6013; www.vanillaantalya.com; Zafer Sokak 13; mains ₺22-40) One indicator of Antalya's rising stock is this outstanding, ultra-modern restaurant led by British chef Wayne and his Turkish wife, Emel. Banquettes, glass surfaces and cheery orange bucket chairs provide a streamlined and unfussy atmosphere, allowing you to concentrate on the menu: Mediterranean-inspired international dishes such as roasted courgette and leek risotto, duck confit and chicken livers with smoked pancetta.

Seraser MEDITERRANEAN €€€

(Map p370; 247 6015; www.seraserrestaurant. com; Karanlık Sokak 18, Tuvana Hotel; mains ₺25-50; 1pm-midnight) The signature restaurant at the Tuvana Hotel and among Antalya's best, Seraser offers international dishes with a Mediterranean twist – try the seabass wrapped in vine leaves or the Santorini-style octopus – in especially fine Ottoman surrounds. (We love the pasha-style chairs and the glass-bead chandelier.) The Turkish coffee *crème brûlée* is legendary.

Club Arma
SEAFOOD €€€

(Map p368; ☑ 244 9710; www.clubarma.com.tr; İskele Caddesi 75; mains ₺19-42) Housed in a former oil depot built right into the cliffside above the harbour, this upmarket *balık evi* (fish restaurant) specialises in meze (brought to you properly on a tray to choose from) and seafood in its infinite variety. On a balmy Antalya evening, the fabulous terrace with its five-star view is one of the city's most romantic dining experiences.

Hasanağa Restaurant
TURKISH €€€

(Map p370; ☑ 247 1313; Mescit Sokak 15; mains ₺20-25) Expect to find the garden dining area here chock-a-block on the nights when traditional Turkish musicians and folk dancers entertain from 8pm onwards. Dishes are predictable Turkish fare – *köfte* (meatballs), mixed grills and the like – although the cooks do produce some veggie dishes (around ₺15).

🍷 Drinking & Entertainment

Antalya has a lot to offer after dark. There are buzzy beer gardens with million-dollar views and live-music venues with everything from rock to *türkü* (Turkish folk music). Antalya also has a seedy side that we recommend steering well clear of. Many of the clubs in Kaleiçi and around the central city are little more than prostitute pick-up joints where drinks are priced exorbitantly and female illegal-immigrants are being made to work under duress.

Castle Café
CAFE

(Map p370; ☑ 248 6594; Hıdırlık Sokak 48/1; ◷ 8am-11pm) Our favourite place along the cliff's edge is this lively cafe and bar which attracts a good crowd of young Turks with its affordable drinks. Service can be slow but the jaw-dropping views from the terrace more than make up for it.

Access is either from the path just opposite the Hıdırlık Kalesi or through the back, down the stairs, off Hıdırlık Sokak.

KNOW YOUR BAZAAR

The Kaleiçi district is jam-packed full of shops and stalls that are firmly pegged for the tourist market. The northwest section of the old city is basically one big bazaar of t-shirts and souvenirs rolling down the hilly alleyways to the harbour. If you're looking for something a little less plastic-fantastic to take home, head to the **İki Kapılar Hanı** (Map p368), a sprawling covered bazaar dating to the late 15th century that is centred between Kazım Özalp Caddesi and İsmet Paşa Caddesi just north of the Kaleiçi district. There are plenty of jewellers, metalwork merchants and textiles to be found here. To buy direct from the supplier, take a wander through the copper-workshops in the alleyways west of Kazım Özalp Caddesi as well.

The Lounge
BAR

(Map p370; ☑ 247 6013; Hesapçı Sokak; ice cream ₺3.50, cakes ₺10; ◷ 9am-1am; ☜) Under the same management as (and next door to) the outstanding Vanilla restaurant, this very slick cafe-bar offers imported ice cream (it's Mövenpick) and a genuine Lavazza espresso machine for those weary of Turkish coffee. Paninis and pizza (₺10 to ₺18) are available, and there's live music on Friday and Saturday nights.

Dem-Lik
BAR

(Map p370; ☑ 247 1930; Zafer Sokak 6; beer ₺6, coffee ₺4; ◷ noon-midnight) This chilled-out garden bar-cafe, with tables scattered under shady fruit trees is where Antalya's university crowd reshapes the world between ice-cold beers while listening to (mostly) jazz, reggae and blues (live at the weekend). There's a menu of cheap pasta and other international dishes on offer as well.

Pupa Cafe
CAFE

(Map p370; Paşa Camii Sokak) We really like this casual garden-cafe with tables next to a slab of Byzantine wall. It's a relaxed and friendly place scattered with pot plants and hanging lamps. A good choice for a quiet evening of chatting and drinking. The good-value menu of seafood and Turkish staples (₺10 to ₺18) makes this place worthy of a visit too.

Kale Bar

BAR

(Map p370; ☑ 248 6591; Mermerli Sokak 2; beer
₺9, cocktails from ₺21; ⊘11am-midnight) This
patio bar attached to the CH Hotels Türkevi
may very well command the most spectacular harbour and sea view in all of Antalya.
Cocktails are priced accordingly.

Filika Cafe-Bar

LIVE MUSIC

(Map p370; ☑ 244 8266; Mescit Sokak 46;
⊘8pm-5am) This venue with live pop and
rock music, above Mescit Sokak in the
centre of Kaleiçi, attracts Antalya's hipster-
alternative crowd.

🛍 Shopping

Osmanlı Sultan Çarık

SHOES

(Map p370; ☑ 247 1540, 0532 677 0642; www.
osmanlicarik.com; Hesapcı Sokak 3) The 'Ottoman Sultan Slipper' shop will whip you up a
pair of hand-stitched pointy-toed slippers in
dyed ox and buffalo leather for ₺90 to ₺160.
Sandals (₺60 to ₺80) and boots (from ₺270)
are also available.

Owl Bookshop

BOOKS

(Map p370; ☑ 0532 632 3275; Kocatepe Sokak 9;
⊘9am-7pm Mon-Sat) Secondhand bookshop
stocked mostly with travellers' hand-me-
downs under the care of literary larrikin, Kemal Özkurt, who doles out heartfelt reading
and other advice (requested or otherwise).

Estanbul Art Gold

JEWELLERY

(Map p370; ☑ 247 2023; www.estanbulartgold.com;
Zafer Sokak 23) Saldıray Kara creates individualistic pieces of jewellery at this teensy
workshop. You can even have a go at crafting
your own piece if you want.

ℹ Information

Antalya Guide (www.antalyaguide.org) Comprehensive website with info on everything
Antalya-related from climate to cultural events.

Tourist Office (Map p370; ☑ 241 1747; Cumhuriyet Meydanı; ⊘8am-6pm) Tiny information
office just west of the Yivli Minare. Has city
maps and a few brochures.

ℹ Getting There & Away

AIR

Antalya's busy **international airport** (Antalya
Havalimanı; ☑ 444 7423; www.aytport.com) is
10km east of the city centre on the D400 highway. There's a tourist information desk and a
number of car-hire agencies have counters here
as well. **Turkish Airlines** (www.thy.com) and **Pegasus Airlines** (www.flypgs.com) both have several flights daily to/from İstanbul (₺70 to ₺120
one-way) while **SunExpress** (www.sunexpress.

BUS SERVICES FROM ANTALYA'S OTOGAR

DESTINATION	FARE (₺)	DURATION (HR)	DISTANCE (KM)	FREQUENCY (PER DAY)
Adana	55	11	565	every 2hr
Alanya	18	3	135	every 20min
Ankara	55-60	8	555	frequent
Çanakkale	70-80	12	770	9am; 2 overnight
Denizli (Pamukkale)	35-40	4	225	several
Eğirdir	20	3½	195	hourly to Isparta (transfer there)
Fethiye (coastal)	30	7½	285	hourly
Fethiye (inland)	25	4	200	several
Göreme/Ürgüp	50	9	485	2 overnight
İstanbul	70-80	11½	785	frequent
İzmir	50	8	470	several
Kaş	24	3½	188	every 30min
Kemer	12	1½	55	every 15min
Konya	45	5	305	several
Marmaris	40-50	6	365	several
Olympos/Çıralı	12	1½	80	every 30min
Side/Manavgat	12	1½	65	every 20min in season

com) operate flights to and from destinations in eastern Turkey (₺120 to ₺150 one-way).

BUS

Antalya's otogar, about 4km north of the city centre on highway D650, consists of two large terminals fronted by a park. Looking at the otogar from the main highway or its parking lot, the Şehirlerarası Terminalı (Intercity Terminal), which serves long-distance destinations, is on the right. The İlçeler Terminali (Domestic Terminal), serving nearby destinations such as Side and Alanya, is on the left.

CAR & MOTORCYCLE

There are plenty of car-rental agencies here including **Gaye Rent a Car** (☑ 247 1000; www.gaye rentacar.com; İmaret Sokak 1), hiring out cars for ₺60 to ₺90 (scooters ₺30 to ₺40) per day.

ⓘ Getting Around

TO/FROM THE AIRPORT

To reach the airport, catch bus 600 (₺2), which can be boarded from Aspendos Bulvarı. To get here you can take the AntRay south from İsmet Paşa stop to the last stop at Meydan. The bus leaves from here. A taxi will cost you about ₺35.

TO/FROM THE BUS STATION

The AntRay tram is the quickest way into town. Follow the signs from the bus station to the underpass which brings you to Otogar tramstop. You will have to buy a reloadable electronic card (₺5, valid on city buses and the *Antik tramvay* as well) at the tram-stop ticket office. It's a 20-minute journey (eight stops) to the central İsmet Paşa stop just outside Kaleiçi.

Bus 40 (₺1.75) heads for Atatürk Caddesi in the town centre every 20 minutes or so from the bus shelter near the airport taxi stand and takes about an hour. To get to the otogar from Kaleiçi, take bus 93 from the bus stop on the corner of Cumhuriyet Caddesi and Ali Fuat Cebesoy Caddesi.

A taxi between the otogar and Kaleiçi should cost ₺25.

PUBLIC TRANSPORT

Antalya's original 6km-long single-track old-style *Antik tramvay* (₺1.25) has 10 stops and provides the simplest way of crossing town. It runs every half-hour between 7.30am and 9pm. You pay as you board and exit through the rear door. The tram runs from the Antalya Museum (Müze stop) along Konyaaltı Caddesi, Cumhuriyet Caddesi, Atatürk Caddesi and Işıklar Caddesi.

A sleek, double-track tram line with 16 stations called AntRay (₺1.50 per journey), which opened in 2009, links northern areas of the city to the south and the coast, and is really only helpful for visitors getting to/from the otogar. The two tram lines are not linked at present though the İsmet

Paşa stop on the AntRay is a short walk from the central Kale Kapısı stop on the tramway.

Termessos

Hidden high in a rugged mountain valley, 34km northwest of Antalya, lies the ruined but still massive ancient city of Termessos (admission ₺5; ◷ 9am-7pm). Neither Greek nor Lycian, the inhabitants were Pisidian, fierce and prone to warring. They successfully fought off Alexander the Great in 333 BC, and the Romans (perhaps wisely) accepted Termessos' wishes to remain independent and an ally in 70 BC.

In the car park, at the end of the Termessos access road (King's Road), you come across the **lower city ruins**. The portal on the hillock to the west was once the entrance to the **Artemis-Hadrian Temple** and **Hadrian Propylaeum**. From here follow the steep path south; you'll see remains of the **lower city walls** on both sides and pass through the **city gate** before reaching, in about 20 minutes, the lower **gymnasium** and **baths** on your left.

A short distance uphill from the lower city ruins are the remnants of Termessos' **upper city walls** and a **colonnaded street**. Just above is the upper **agora** and its five

Termessos   ⬆ N   0 ▬▬▬▬ 200 m   0 ▬▬▬▬ 0.1 miles

Artemis-Hadrian Temple & Hadrian Propylaeum

Hadrian's Gate

Cistern

Lower City Walls

Rock Tomb

City Gate

Lower City Walls

Tomb of Alcetas

Colonnaded Street

Gymnasium & Baths

Upper City Walls

Termessian House

Unidentified Building

Attalos Stoa

Osbaras Stoa

Theatre

Corinthian Temple

Upper Agora

Heroon

Upper Agora

Upper Gymnasium

Southern Necropolis (2km)

Bouleuterion

Temple of Zeus

Temple of Artemis

large cisterns; an ideal spot to explore slowly and to catch a bit of shade.

On the eastern side of the upper agora is the theatre, which enjoys a positively jaw-dropping position atop a peak, surrounded by a mountain range; you can see Antalya on a clear day. Walk southwest from the theatre to view the cut-limestone bouleuterion, but use caution when scrambling across the crumbled Temple of Artemis and Temple of Zeus south of it.

Termessos' southern necropolis is at the very top of the valley, 3km (one hour's walk) up from the car park at the site entrance.

Termessos is spread out and requires much scrambling over loose rocks and up steep though well-marked paths. Allow a minimum of two hours to explore the site, and bring plenty of drinking water.

Güllükdağı Termessos National Park
PARK

(Termessos Milli Parkı) This national park, which surrounds the Termessos site, abounds in wildlife including mountain goats, speckled deer, golden eagles and 680 species of plant (80 of them endemic). At the entrance, the small Flora & Fauna Museum (admission included with the Termessos ₺5 entry fee) contains a bit of information about the ruined city, as well as about the botany and zoology of the immediate area.

❶ Getting There & Away

Taxi tours from Antalya cost around ₺170, or you could take an organised or group excursion for about ₺50 cheaper. An even cheaper option is to catch a bus from Antalya otogar bound for Korkuteli (₺12) and alight at the entrance to the national park. Taxis waiting here in the warmer months will run you up the 9km-long King's Rd to the ruins and back for about ₺25.

Perge

Some 17km east of Antalya and 2km north of Aksu on highway D400, Perge (admission ₺20; ☉9am-7pm) was one of the most important towns of ancient Pamphylia. Inside the site, walk through the massive Roman Gate with its four arches; to the left is the southern nymphaeum and well-preserved baths, and to the right the large square-shaped agora. Beyond the Hellenistic Gate, with its two huge towers, is the fine colonnaded street, where an impressive collection of columns still stands.

The water source for the narrow concave channel running down the centre of the colonnaded street was the northern nymphaeum, which dates to the 2nd century AD. From here it's possible to follow a path to the ridge of the hill with the acropolis.

Perge experienced two golden ages: during the Hellenistic period in the 2nd and 3rd centuries BC and under the Romans in the 2nd and 3rd centuries AD (from which most of the ruins here date). Turkish archaeologists first began excavations here in 1946 and a selection of the statues discovered – many in magnificent condition – can be seen at the Antalya Museum.

Excavations and restoration work continue on site. At the time of writing Perge's theatre and stadium, each of which sat 12,000 spectators, and are located along the access road before you reach the site entrance, were both closed.

❶ Getting There & Away

The easiest way to reach Perge is to take the AntRay tram to the last southern stop (Meydan) and catch bus AC03 from there to Aksu (₺3, 30 minutes, 15km). You can easily walk the remaining 2km north to the ruins. Many Antalya travel agencies run combined excursions to Perge and Aspendos. A taxi tour will be about ₺160.

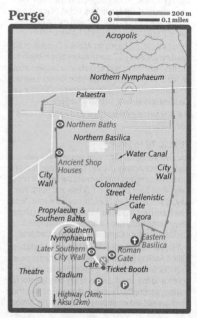

Perge · N · 0 ——— 200 m · 0 ——— 0.1 miles

- Acropolis
- Northern Nymphaeum
- Palaestra
- Northern Baths
- Northern Basilica
- Water Canal
- Ancient Shop Houses
- City Wall
- City Wall
- Colonnaded Street
- Hellenistic Gate
- Propylaeum & Southern Baths
- Agora
- Southern Nymphaeum
- Eastern Basilica
- Later Southern City Wall
- Roman Gate
- Theatre
- Cafe
- Ticket Booth
- Stadium
- Highway (2km); Aksu (2km)

Aspendos

People come in droves to ancient Aspendos (admission ₺20, parking ₺5; ☺9am-7pm) near the modern-day village of Belkıs for one reason: to view the awesome theatre, considered the best-preserved Roman theatre of the ancient world. It was built during Aspendos' golden age in the reign of Emperor Marcus Aurelius (AD 161–80), and used as a caravanserai by the Seljuks during the 13th century. The history of the city, though, goes all the way back to as far as the Hittite Empire (800 BC).

After touring the area in the early 1930s, Atatürk declared Aspendos too fine an example of classical architecture to stay unused. Following a restoration that didn't please a lot of historians, the 15,000-seat theatre again became an event venue. Operas, concerts and other events are staged here to this day. The acoustics are excellent and the atmosphere at night sublime.

Apart from the theatre, the ancient city ruins are extensive and include a stadium, agora and 3rd-century basilica, although there is little left intact. To reach them follow the trail to the right of the theatre exit. To the north are the remains of the city's aqueduct.

The theatre was closed for restoration work when we last passed through. It should be open by the time of your trip but check before making the journey out here, so you're not disappointed on arrival.

✯✯ Festivals & Events

Aspendos Opera & Ballet Festival FESTIVAL
(Aspendos Opera ve Bale Festivalı; www.aspendosfestival.gov.tr) The internationally acclaimed Aspendos Opera & Ballet Festival is held in the Roman theatre running either through June or in August and September (depending on the year). Tickets can be bought online, from the kiosk opposite the theatre and from travel agents in Antalya and Side.

ⓘ Getting There & Away

Aspendos lies 47km east of Antalya. If driving, immediately on your right as you exit the D400 for Aspendos is a restored Seljuk-era switchback bridge with seven arches spanning the Köprü River. It dates from the 13th century but was built on an earlier Roman bridge.

From Antalya, minibuses (₺12) headed for Manavgat will drop you at the Aspendos turn-off, from where you can walk (45 minutes) or hitch the remaining 4km to the site. Taxis waiting at the highway junction will take you to the theatre for an outrageous ₺20, or you can join an excursion from Antalya, stopping at Perge along the way. A taxi tour will cost about ₺160.

Selge & Köprülü Kanyon

The ruins of ancient Selge are strewn about the Taurus-top village of Altınkaya, 12km above spectacular Köprülü Kanyon and within a national park with peaks up to 2500m.

As you wander through the village and its ruins, consider that Selge once counted a population of more than 20,000. Because of the city's elevated position, its city walls and surrounding ravines, approaching undetected wasn't a simple task and the city was able to ward off most invaders. Nevertheless, the Romans eventually took hold of the territory, which survived into the Byzantine era.

About 350m of the city wall still exists, but its most striking monument is its theatre restored in the 3rd century AD. Close by is the agora.

At the foot of the ascent, you'll discover two Roman-era bridges. The first (and smaller) is the Bürüm Bridge and the second the dramatically arched Oluk Bridge spanning 14m across a deep canyon of the ancient Eurymedon (now Köprü) River. It has been in service since the Romans put it here in the 2nd century AD.

🏃 Activities

Hiking
Around the Oluk Bridge, you'll find villagers keen to guide you on hikes up from Köprülü Kanyon along the original Roman road, about two hours up (1½ hours down), for about ₺60. An excellent qualified guide who knows the area inside and out is Adem Bahar, who can be reached on ☑ 0535 762 8116 or via the Köprülü Kanyon Restaurant. He also organises rafting trips.

You can also arrange two-day mountain treks for groups to Mt Bozburun (2504m) and other points in the Kuyucak Dağları (Kuyucak Range) for about ₺120. There is a three-day walk through the Köprülü Kanyon on the St Paul's Trail.

Rafting
There are more than two-dozen companies offering rafting trips in the canyon, including larger outfits such as Gökcesu Rafting (☑ 0533 522 3205, 765 3384; www.gokcesu.net)

and smaller ones such as Antalya Rafting (☎0242-311 4845, 0532 604 0092; www.antalya-rafting.net), based at the the Köprülü Kanyon Restaurant, about 100m down from the eastern side of Oluk Bridge. An excursion on the excellent intermediate rapids is about €19, which includes hotel pick up, a lesson, a two- to three-hour trip, and lunch.

🛏 Sleeping

There are a couple of waterfront pensions with restaurants on the west side of the Köprü River, about 4km past the modern Karabük Bridge. For accommodation in Altınkaya, just minutes from the Selge ruins, contact Adem Bahar (☎0535 762 8116; per person full board ₺40).

Selge Pansiyon   PENSION €
(☎0242-765 3244, 0535 577 9475; www.selgepansiyon.com; campsite ₺20, bungalow ₺50; ❅@) Selge Pansiyon is right on the river and offers simple and homely bungalows with pine-clad interiors that are excellent value. You can pitch your tent in the garden here as well.

Perge Pansiyon   PENSION €€
(☎0242-765 3074, 0533 475 8108; www.pergepansiyon.com; campsite ₺15, bungalow s/d ₺60/120; ❅🕸) This sprawling, modern option has timber bungalows with your front door just one stride from the water's edge and surrounded by beautifully cared-for gardens.

❶ Getting There & Away

Many travel agencies in Antalya include Köprülü Kanyon Milli Parkı and Selge in their tours. Unless you have your own transport, this is your only option.

If you do have a vehicle, however, you can visit in half a day, though it deserves a lot more time. The turn-off to Selge and Köprülü Kanyon is about 5km east of the Aspendos road (51km from Antalya) along highway D400. Another 30km up into the mountains the road divides, with the left fork marked for Karabük and the right for Beşkonak. If you take the Karabük road along the river's west bank, you'll pass most of the rafting companies and the two pensions. About 11km from the turn-off is the graceful old Oluk Bridge. From here the paved road marked for Altınkaya climbs some 13km to the village and the Selge ruins through increasingly dramatic scenery.

If you follow via Beşkonak, it is 6.5km from there to the canyon and the bridge.

Side

📞 0242 / POP 11,933

Down at the harbour the re-created colonnade of the Temple of Athena marches towards the blue sea. At the top of the old town's gentle hill, Side's theatre still lords it up over the surrounding countryside. Between the two, the lanes of this once docile fishing village have long since given themselves over to souvenir peddlers and restaurant touts intent on hustling for business. Despite the constant stream of visitors hunting for bargains, the liberal scattering of glorious Roman and Hellenistic ruins sitting incongruously between shops means if you scrunch your eyes up for a minute you can just about imagine the shoppers picking over togas rather than T-shirts.

◉ Sights

★ Temples of Apollo & Athena   RUIN
This compact site is one of the most romantic on the Mediterranean coast. Dating from the 2nd century BC, a half-dozen columns from the Temple of Athena have been placed upright in their original spots, and after dark a spotlight dramatically outlines their form.

The site was cordoned off due to restoration work when we last came through town but work should hopefully be finished by the time you visit.

★ Theatre   RUIN
(Çağla Caddesi; admission ₺15; ⊙9am-7pm) Built in the 2nd century AD, Side's spectacular theatre seats up to 20,000 people and rivals the nearby theatre of Aspendos for sheer drama. Look to the wall of the *skene* (stage building) for reliefs of figures and faces, including those of Comedy and Tragedy.

Side Museum   MUSEUM
(Side Caddesi; admission ₺10; ⊙9am-6.40pm Tue-Sun) Contained within a 5th-century bathhouse, Side's museum has an impressive (if small) collection of statues and sarcophagi.

Agora   RUIN
Just east of Side Theatre and across the road from Side Museum are these agora remains, which once functioned as the ancient town's slave market.

Temple of Tyche   RUIN
The ruined circular-shaped Temple of Tyche is dedicated to the goddess of fortune. Right

Side

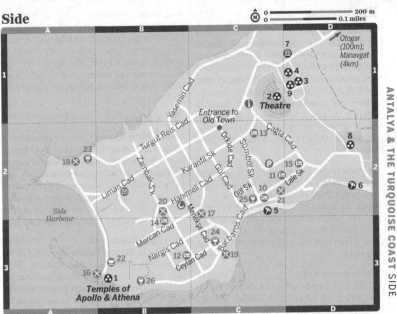

Side

◎ Top Sights

◎ Sights

◎ Sleeping

◎ Eating

◎ Drinking & Nightlife

next door is an arresting **ancient latrine** with two-dozen marble seats.

Eastern Beach　　　　　　　　　　BEACH
(Barbaros Caddesi) If you walk down Barbaros Caddesi, passing by the large **State Agora** ruin, you'll come to the lovely Eastern Beach, which is a prime spot of sand to throw down your beach towel. You can rent sun loungers and sunshades here for about ₺7 per day.

Closer is the small, narrow **beach** that runs along Barbaros Caddesi.

Sandy Beach　　　　　　　　　　BEACH
Side's main beach is Sandy Beach, north of the centre, and backed by rows of resort hotels. Follow the main road out of town (Side Caddesi) and turn left at Şarmaşık Sokak opposite the otogar (bus station). There is regular dolmuş transport to the beach from near Side Theatre.

🛏 Sleeping

⭐ Onur Pansiyon PENSION €
(📞753 2328; www.onur-pansiyon.com; Karanfil Sokak 3; s/d ₺60/90; 🏵🛜) With oodles of character at wallet-saving prices, this family-run pension oozes traditional pension style right down to the Turkish lace curtains. Rooms are charmingly cosy and there's a relaxing garden full of potted plants and climbing vines to chill-out in. The friendly manager is helpful with advice and local lore.

Sempatı Motel PENSION €
(Mercan Cad 13; s/d/tr ₺60/85/110; 🏵❄🛜) The well-maintained rooms here are kept ship-shape by manager Nihan. We particularly like the two rooms in the attic eaves with their quirky shower arrangement (due to the roof slope) and the roof terrace with great sea vistas.

Beach House Hotel HOTEL €€
(📞753 1607; www.beachhouse-hotel.com; Barbaros Caddesi; s/d/tr/f ₺60/120/150/180; 🏵🛜🏊) Once the celebrated Pamphylia Hotel, a magnet for celebrities in the 1960s, the Beach House's prime seafront location and welcoming owners lures a loyal band of regulars. Most rooms face the sea and all have balconies. We love the roof terrace (with teensy pool), the library full of beach-reads and the garden which comes complete with Byzantine ruins.

Hotel Lale Park HOTEL €€
(📞753 1131; www.hotellalepark.com; Lale Sokak 7; s/d/apt €50/55/110; 🏵❄🏊) One of Side's nicest small hotels, the 'Tulip Park' has simple, decent-sized rooms set around a manicured garden with pretty pool and alfresco bar. Management are friendly and keep everything sparkling clean. Dinner (₺25) is a good-value alternative to Side's other restaurants, and is open to outside guests. You'll need to book by noon.

Hotel Sevil HOTEL €€
(📞753 2041; www.hotelsevil.com; Zambak Sokak 32; s/d €40/50; 🏵🛜) Set around a miniforest of mulberry trees and palms, this midrange option has a smart little bar and a chilled vibe with friendly management. The rooms all have balconies (some with sea views) and feature wood panelling and classical neutral tones.

Side Doğa Pansiyon PENSION €€
(📞753 6246; www.sidedoga.com; Lale Sokak 8; s/d €20/40; 🏵🛜) Quirky, colourful wall decorations give the large rooms inside this lovely stone house a fresh, arty slant, while the flower-festooned courtyard is a chilled-out, shady spot to relax in. All up, it's a great Side choice.

🍴 Eating

Balık & Köfte Ekmek SANDWICHES €
(Harbour; sandwiches ₺7) Bobbing away gently in Side's sheltered harbour, this converted fishing boat serves up good-value fish and *köfte* (meatball) sandwiches. Meze platters are also available. In a tourist town with uniformly expensive restaurants, it's a thrifty haven for travellers watching their Lira.

Moonlight Restaurant SEAFOOD €€
(📞753 1400; Barbaros Caddesi 49; mains ₺15-30) In business since 1983, this longstayer of the Side scene offers solid Turkish cooking, an extensive local wine list and professional yet non-stuffy service. Seafood is the mainstay of the menu and is super-fresh. For romantic dining, head to the back terrace on the water.

Emir TURKISH €€
(📞753 2224; Menekşe Caddesi; meze ₺8-10, mains ₺16-25; 🍴) The Emir almost leans on the ruins of the Roman baths where Cleopatra is said to have dallied. The open kitchen produces some excellent meze, grills and a generous array of vegetarian dishes.

Soundwaves Restaurant INTERNATIONAL €€€
(📞753 1059; Barbaros Caddesi; mains ₺20-30) This long-running Side eatery has a friendly and relaxed vibe. A small, focused menu is delivered by an experienced chef, and there are regular seafood specials. Ask if the excellent swordfish kebaps are available, and kick off with a few meze and a cold beer.

Ocakbaşı TURKISH €€€
(📞753 1810; Zambak Sokak; mains ₺20-35; 🍴) With friendly service and a huge menu of tasty Turkish grills and meze, Ocakbaşı is a hugely popular Side dinner spot. Vegetarians can breathe a sigh; there's a decent choice of dishes here. It can get noisy and crowded so dine early (before 7.30pm) if you don't fancy being squeezed between tables of large tour groups.

Karma

INTERNATIONAL €€€

(Turgut Reis Caddesi; mains ₺30-45) This slick, cosmopolitan restaurant and bar has an unbeatable oceanfront garden and a menu that jumps from Turkish staples to more diverse Mediterranean and Asian-style offerings.

🍷 Drinking & Nightlife

★Apollonik

CAFE, BAR

(Liman Yolu) Right beside the Temples of Apollo and Athena, the Apollonik is a laid-back bar, perfect for a relaxed evening. It does decent food if you're peckish but most people come for the novella-length menu of cocktails (₺20), which you can sup on the terrace overlooking the harbour, or inside snuggled up on the cushion-strewn sedir seating.

Even when Side is quiet early in the season, the Apollonik will still be full of satisfied punters.

Beyaz Bar

BAR

(Turgut Reis Caddesi) Beyaz translates to 'white' in Turkish, and the interior of this restored Ottoman house near the harbour fits the bill. Inside is a romantic confection of white walls and tables, a stylish and classy backdrop to regular performances of Turkish music.

Stones Bar

BAR

(Barbaros Caddesi 119) The spectacular waterfront views here are perfect fodder for sundowner drinks. The outside terrace is, unsurprisingly, prime real estate in the early evening, so join the crowds, sit back and enjoy sunset.

Mehmet's Bar

BAR

(Barbaros Caddesi) This ever-popular spot opposite the beach might be better suited to a tropical island than a Turkish promontory. Pop in for a quiet drink and ask them to crank up the reggae.

Kiss Bar

BAR

(Barbaros Caddesi 64) This neon-lit open bar located just off the beach promenade is a great spot for people-watching.

ℹ️ Information

Aspendos Opera & Ballet Festival Ticket Office If you're in Side, the easiest way to organise your tickets to Aspendos' annual festival is through this handy office.

Tourist Office (☑753 1265; ⊗8am-5pm) German- and Turkish-speaking office about 800m north of the centre.

ℹ️ Getting There & Around

Vehicular entrance to the old town is restricted, and if you're driving you'll need a reservation at an old-town hotel or pension to gain access. If you're just visiting for the day, you'll be steered to park in the old town car park.

Side's otogar is east of the ancient city. In summer, an open-top bus (₺1) shuttles visitors from the otogar to near the entrance to the old town.

Frequent minibuses connect Side otogar with the Manavgat otogar (₺2.50), 4km to the northeast, from where buses go to Antalya (₺12, 1½ hours, 75km), Alanya (₺12, 1½ hours, 60km) and Konya (₺25, four hours, 230km). Coming into Side, most buses either drop you at the Manavgat otogar or stop by the petrol station on the highway where a free *servis* (shuttle bus) will transfer you into Side. A taxi from Side to Manavgat otogar costs about ₺15.

In summer Side has direct bus services once to three times daily to Ankara (₺45, 10 hours, 625km), İzmir (₺40, 8½ hours, 540km) and İstanbul (₺60, 13 hours, 850km).

Eastern Mediterranean

Best Places to Eat

➡ Hatay Sultan Sofrası (p413)

➡ İskele Sofrası (p387)

➡ Öz Asmaaltı (p405)

➡ Çağlayan Restaurant (p413)

Best Places to Stay

➡ Hotel Bosnalı (p405)

➡ Centauera (p387)

➡ Liwan Hotel (p412)

➡ Hotel Esya (p392)

Why Go?

This is Turkey's non-airbrushed slice of Mediterranean coastline. A handful of distinctly local-style beach resorts lie between the industrial port cities. Crumbling ruins sit among acres of intensely farmed countryside with nary a tourist in sight. In the ancient towns of Tarsus and Antakya, atmospheric old-town fragments cling on amid the modern hubbub.

The southern Hatay province's fascinating melding of religions, languages and foods is reason enough for many to linger. For others, the wealth of important early Christian sites is the eastern Med's ace up its sleeve. The area's historical riches though encompass a dizzying timeline of kings and conquerors that stretches from Karatepe's late-Hittite remnants, through Roman Anemurium, to the cliff-top castles of once-mighty Cilicia. The stretch of the Mediterranean that most people miss is full of surprises for those that make the trip.

When to Go
Antakya

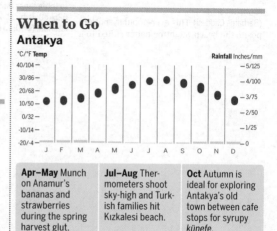

Apr–May Munch on Anamur's bananas and strawberries during the spring harvest glut.

Jul–Aug Thermometers shoot sky-high and Turkish families hit Kızkalesi beach.

Oct Autumn is ideal for exploring Antakya's old town between cafe stops for syrupy *künefe*.

Eastern Mediterranean Highlights

1 Marvel at Roman and Byzantine artistry while surrounded by some of the world's finest mosaics at the **Hatay Archaeology Museum** (p410).

2 Admire the stupendous view while sitting on the craggy, crumbling ramparts of **Yılankale** (p407).

3 Explore the beautiful remnants of **Anemurium** (p391) with grazing cows and sheep your only company.

4 Descend into the massive chasm and then test out your vertigo over Hell at the **Caves of Heaven and Hell** (p400).

5 Take a beach break in tiny **Arsuz** (p408).

6 Swot up on Hittite history amid the stone reliefs and statuary of **Karatepe** (p407).

7 Soak up the ramshackle atmosphere of bygone days in the compact old centres of **Tarsus** (p402) and **Antakya** (p411).

Alanya

📞 0242 / POP 107,486

In just a few short decades, Alanya has mushroomed from a sparsely populated town fronting a fine stretch of sandy beach to a densely populated tourist haven for predominantly Dutch and Scandinavian visitors. At night, the downtown area can resemble 'Vegas by the Sea', and aside from taking a boat cruise or a stroll along the waterfront, many visitors shuffle only between their hotel's pool and all-inclusive buffet restaurant, and then frequent the laser-shooting nightclubs after dark.

Look up from the bars and tattoo parlours for a minute, however, and you'll find Alanya does have its hidden charms. Looming high above the promontory, to the south of the modern centre, is an impressive fortress complex with the remains of a fine Seljuk castle, some atmospheric ruins, and a sprinkling of traditional red-tile roofed houses rimming the alleyways that climb up the hillside. Alanya is a tale of two cities if ever we saw it.

👁 Sights

⭐ Alanya Castle
CASTLE

(Alanya Kalesı; Kaleyolu Caddesi; admission ₺15; ☉9am-7pm) Presiding with stately grace over the clutter of bars and souvenir shops below is Alanya's awesome Seljuk-era castle with views across the city and out to the Pamphylian plain and Cilician mountains.

Right at the top of the castle area is the İç Kale (inner fortress). Within are plentiful (though poorly preserved) ruins including a half-dozen cisterns and the shell of an 11th-century Byzantine church.

The road to the fortress winds uphill for 3.5km. Catch a bus from Hürriyet Meydanı (₺1.25, hourly from 9am to 7pm) or opposite the tourist office (15 minutes past the hour and, in summer, also 15 minutes before the hour). Taxis are around ₺15.

Ehmedek
NEIGHBOURHOOD

(Kaleyolu Caddesi) As you walk up towards Alanya Castle, the road passes a turn-off for the village of Ehmedek, which was the Turkish quarter during Ottoman and Seljuk times. Today a number of old wooden houses still cluster around the fine 16th-century Süleymaniye Camii (Ehmedek Sokak), the oldest mosque in Alanya. Also here is a former Ottoman bedesten (vaulted covered market) and the Akşebe Türbesi, a distinctive 13th-century mausoleum.

Red Tower
HISTORIC BUILDING

(Kızılkule; İskele Caddesi; admission ₺4, combined ticket with Tersane & guard house ₺10; ☉9am-7pm) This five-storey octagonal defence tower, measuring nearly 30m in diameter, more than 30m in height and with a central cistern within for water storage, looms over the harbour at the lower end of İskele Caddesi. Constructed in 1226 by Seljuk Sultan Alaeddin Keykubad I (who also built Alanya Castle), it was the first structure erected after the Armenian-controlled town surrendered to the sultan.

Tersane
HISTORIC BUILDING

(admission ₺4, combined ticket with Red Tower & guard house ₺10) A wooden walkway runs south along the old harbour walls from the Red Tower to the Tersane, the only Seljuk-built shipyard remaining in Turkey. With the waves sloshing through its restored stone arches, it's highly atmospheric. From here the walkway continues further along the shoreline to a small guard house (admission ₺4, combined ticket with Red Tower & Tersane ₺10), which would have served as a coastal watchtower during the Seljuk era.

Alanya Museum
MUSEUM

(İsmet Hilmi Balcı Caddesi; admission ₺5; ☉9am-7pm) Alanya's small museum is worth a visit for its artefacts, which include tools, jugs and jewellery collected from other Pamphylian sites in the area.

Cleopatra's Beach
BEACH

(Kleopatra Plajı) Sandy and quite secluded in low season, and with fine views of the fortress, Cleopatra's Beach is the city's best. Alanya's main beaches are also decent, although east of the centre they're fronted by a busy main road.

Dripstone Cave
CAVE

(Damlataş Mağarası; adult/child ₺4.50/2.25; ☉10am-7pm) Close to Cleopatra's Beach, this stalactite-studded cave has humidity levels of 95% and is said to produce a certain kind of air that, if inhaled and exhaled long enough, has the ability to relieve asthma sufferers.

Alanya Aqua Park
AMUSEMENT PARK

(www.alanyaaquapark.net; İsmet Hilmi Balcı Caddesi 62; adult/child ₺25/15; ☉9am-6pm) Kids had enough of castles and ruins? This large water park, near Alanya centre, has plenty of wet and wild fun with pools and slides appropriate for both older children and little ones. There's a nice area with sun loungers for wiped out parents, too.

🏃 Activities & Tours

Many local operators organise tours to the ruins along the coast west of Alanya and to Anamur. A typical tour to Aspendos, Side and Manavgat will cost around €20 per person, while trips to Anamur and ancient Anemurium will cost about €35 per person. Tours to Sapadere Canyon (p390) are usually €25 per person.

Excursion Boats   BOAT TOUR
(per person incl lunch ₺35) Every day at around 10.30am, boats leave from near Rıhtım Caddesi for a six-hour voyage around the promontory, visiting several caves, as well as Cleopatra's Beach. Other cruises include sunset jaunts around the harbour (from ₺20).

🛌 Sleeping

Alanya has hundreds of hotels and pensions although almost all of them are designed for groups. İskele Caddesi is the best place to look for budget offerings while the Tophane district under the castle is now home to a scattering of boutique hotels set in beautifully restored Ottoman houses.

Temiz Otel   HOTEL €
(☏ 513 1016; http://temizotel.com.tr; İskele Caddesi 12; s/d ₺60/90; ※ 🛜) If you want to be slam in the centre of the downtown action, the Temiz has 32 decently sized, if bland, rooms. Rooms at the front have balconies, but light sleepers should steer clear and ask for a room at the back as the thumping noise from the bars goes on into the wee hours.

Tayfun Pansiyon   PENSION €
(☏ 513 2916; Tolupaşa Sokak 17a; s/d ₺20/30) Tucked away in a central residential neighbourhood, the Tayfun is one of the last cheap sleeps in Alanya. Rooms are definitely basic, but clean and spacious enough, and there's an adjacent leafy garden for end-of-day relaxing. Breakfast isn't included, but there are plenty of cafes around the corner on Damlataş Caddesi.

Lemon Villa   BOUTIQUE HOTEL €€
(☏ 513 4461; www.lemonvilla.com; Tophane Caddesi 20; r from ₺150; ※ 🛜) The stone-walled rooms at this restored Ottoman house are full of authentic details with ornate wooden ceiling panels, hanging lamps and original fire places. The two suites at the top are particularly sumptuous with suitably grand sea views to top it off.

★Centauera   BOUTIQUE HOTEL €€€
(☏ 519 0016; www.centauera.com; Andızlı Camii Sokak 4, Tophane; r €60-120; ※ 🛜) A 10-minute stroll from the harbour, the romantic Centauera is a world away from downtown Alanya, with views across the elegant sweep of bay and birdsong the only sound you hear most mornings. This restored Ottoman house is packed full of old world elegance and ably run by friendly owner Koray. With just five rooms it's an intimate choice.

We love the roll-top baths in the deluxe rooms and little luxurious touches such as coffee makers in all rooms. Dinner is also available on request if you pre-order.

Villa Turka   BOUTIQUE HOTEL €€€
(☏ 513 7999; www.hotelvillaturka.com; Kargı Sokak 7, Tophane; r €72, ste €166; ※ 🛜) This 200-year-old Ottoman mansion has been lovingly restored to showcase its original wooden ceilings and tiled floors. The 10 rooms here feature quality bed linen, honey-toned cedar decor and antiques, while views take in the Taurus mountains and the nearby Red Tower. Breakfast often incorporates organic goodies from farms surrounding Alanya.

Seaport Hotel   BUSINESS HOTEL €€€
(☏ 513 6487; www.hotelseaport.com; İskele Caddesi 82; s/d ₺130/220; ※ 🛜) This bustling business-style hotel right on Alanya harbour offers no-nonsense, classically styled rooms (half with brilliant sea views) and efficient service. Rates include a breakfast and dinner buffet, but unfortunately the food can be disappointing.

🍴 Eating

★İskele Sofrası   TURKISH €€
(Tophane Caddesi 2b; meze ₺6-8, mains ₺15-35) Eschew the glitzier harbour restaurants and head for this intimate option, run by the friendly Öz family. The menu includes more than 70 meze, including *girit ezmesi,* an unforgettable mash of feta, walnuts and olive oil. All the usual grills and loads of seafood headline the menu, but there are also pasta and veggie options.

The terrace with harbour views is a delight, perfect with a cold beer.

Sofra   ANATOLIAN €€
(İskele Caddesi 8a; mains ₺12-16) Sofra delivers a modern spin on the traditional Turkish eatery with tasty kebaps, *mantı* (Turkish

Alanya

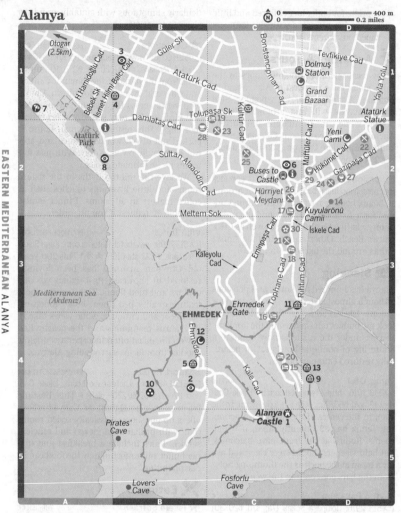

ravioli) and eastern Anatolian *içli köfte* (ground lamb and onion in a bulgur wheat shell). You can peruse the interesting black-and-white photographs of historic Alanya while waiting for your meal.

Lokanta Su
MEDITERRANEAN €€€

(☑512 1500; www.lokantasualanya.com; Damlataş Caddesi 14a; mains ₺23-45) From Italy to the Middle East, Lokanta Su's menu covers the best of the Mediterranean, but the beautiful courtyard of this Ottoman house (originally the residence of the Governor of Alanya) is also a lovely spot to come for a drink with

one of the best wine lists in town. The pizza menu (₺23 to ₺30) showcases some innovative touches.

Ottoman House
TURKISH €€€

(☑511 1421; www.ottomanhousealanya.com; Damlataş Caddesi 31; mains ₺20-45) Inside a 100-year-old stone villa surrounded by lush gardens, Ottoman House is an atmospheric dining experience. The *beğendili taş kebabı*, a traditional Ottoman combination of sautéed lamb and aubergine purée, and the grilled seafood dishes are all good. Visit on

Alanya

EASTERN MEDITERRANEAN ALANYA

Thursday or Sunday night for the all-you-can-eat barbecue (€15).

Köyüm Gaziantep Başpınar ANATOLIAN €€€
(📞513 5664; Hükümet Caddesi; meze ₺10-13, mains ₺20-30) For something more adventurous than the usual grills, this is one of central Alanya's best traditional Turkish options. Dishes from the eastern city of Gaziantep are on offer; try the *patlıcan kebabı* (aubergine kebaps) or the *beyti sarması* (spicy meatballs wrapped in flatbread).

Mahperi Restaurant INTERNATIONAL €€€
(📞512 5491; www.mahperi.com; Rıhtım Caddesi; mains ₺25-35) Quite a feat in fly-by-night Alanya, this classy waterfront fish and steak restaurant has been in operation since 1947 and offers a good selection of international-style dishes.

🍷 Drinking & Entertainment

Alanya features some of the most bawdy, bright and banging nightclubs in all of Turkey. It's all good fun if that's what you're looking for, though solo female travellers may find some of the late-night scene a little on the sleazy side. For the non-party animals there are also more restrained entertainment options.

Ehl-i-Keyf NARGILE CAFE
(Damlataş Caddesi 32) The shaded garden of this restored Ottoman residence is a trendy hang-out for Alanya's bright young things, and a great antidote to the more touristy bars and cafes around town. Enjoy a relaxing combo of tea, nargile (water pipe) and backgammon, or a freshly squeezed juice. Note that only alcohol-free beer is available.

**Red Tower Brewery
Restaurant** BAR, RESTAURANT
(www.redtowerbrewery.com; İskele Caddesi 80) It's fusion confusion at this multistorey pleasure palace with harbour views. The ground-floor brew pub serves two decent beers, there's an international restaurant on the 1st floor, Turkish dishes on the 3rd floor, and sushi and live guitar music in the 6th floor Sky Lounge. Our pick is a pint of the authentically hoppy Pilsner on Red Tower's alfresco deck.

Club İstanbul CLUB
(Rıhtım Caddesi 34) One of Alanya's most popular clubs gets packed with a fun, young and up-for-it crowd of both local and holidaying revellers. There's usually a different DJ every night during the height of summer and a decent mesh of popular music.

Havana Club CLUB
(www.clubhavanaalanya.com; Hükümet Caddesi 13) This venue is a summer holiday favourite for partying young Turks, with DJs who play a mix of club classics, modern pop and R&B dance hits.

Cello
LIVE MUSIC

(İskele Caddesi 36) Cello is a rustic wooden bar showcasing 'protest and folk music' (their words, not ours) and is a top spot for an acoustic-fuelled night combining rakı (aniseed brandy) or a few beers. Friendly locals crowd in, escaping the booming manufactured beats in the super clubs down by the harbour. Gigs kick off at 10.30pm most nights.

❶ Information

Tourist Office (☑ 513 1240; Damlataş Caddesi 1; ☉ 8am-5pm) Near the Alanya Museum.

Tourist Office (Damlataş Caddesi; ☉ 9am-6pm Mon-Fri) Small branch near Alanya's belediye (Town Hall).

❶ Getting There & Away

The otogar (bus station) is on the coastal highway (Atatürk Caddesi), 3km west of the centre. Most services are less frequent off-season, but buses generally leave hourly for Antalya (₺18, two hours, 115km) and eight times daily to Adana (₺60, 10 hours, 440km). Buses to Konya (₺35, 6½ hours, 320km) take the Akseki–Beyşehir route.

If you're travelling down the coast from Side, most buses from Manavgat otogar conveniently drop you off at the dolmuş station downtown behind the Grand Bazaar.

❶ Getting Around

Dolmuşes (minibuses) to the otogar (₺1.50) can be picked up at the **dolmuş station** near the mosque behind the Grand Bazaar, north of Atatürk Caddesi. From the otogar, walk out towards the coast road and the dolmuş stand is on the right. A taxi to the otogar from the centre costs ₺15.

Around Alanya

There are several notable attractions on or just north of the D400 as you travel east from Alanya, including the seldom-visited ancient sites of **Laertes** and **Syedra**. A turn-off near the 11km marker leads northward for 6km to **Dim Cave** (Dim Mağarası; www.dimcave.com.tr; adult/child ₺10/4; ☉ 9am-7pm), a subterranean fairyland of spectacular stalactite and stalagmite formations with a crystal clear pool at the deepest depth. A 360m-long walkway leads you through the entire length of the cave. Dolmuşes headed for Kestel from Alanya (hourly in season) will drop you off near the entrance to the cave. A return taxi will cost about ₺70. A turning at 27km and another road leading 18km northeast takes you to beautiful **Sapadere Canyon** (Sapadera Kanyonu; adult/child ₺4/2; ☉ 9am-7pm). Access for walkers through the gorge is along a 750m-long path. A return taxi from Alanya is around ₺120, and tours from Alanya are €25 per person.

Around 30km west towards Antalya and just after Incekum beach is a turning for a road leading north for 9km to **Alarahan**, a 13th-century *han* (caravanserai), which can be explored with a torch. At the head of the

---

ARMENIAN KINGDOM OF CILICIA

During the early 11th century, the Seljuk Turks swept westwards from Iran, wresting control of much of Anatolia from a weakened Byzantium and pushing into the Armenian highlands. Thousands of Armenians fled south, taking refuge in the rugged Taurus Mountains and along the Mediterranean coast, where in 1080 they founded the kingdom of Cilicia (or Lesser Armenia) under the young Prince Reuben.

While Greater Armenia struggled against foreign invaders and the subsequent loss of its statehood, the Cilician Armenians lived in wealth and prosperity. Geographically, they were in the ideal place for trade and they quickly embraced European ideas, including its feudal class structure. Cilicia became a country of barons, knights and serfs, the court at Sis (today's Kozan) even adopted Western-style clothing. Latin and French became the national languages. During the Crusades the Christian armies used the kingdom's castles as safe havens on their way to the Holy Land.

This period of Armenian history is regarded as the most exciting for science and culture, as schools and monasteries flourished, teaching theology, philosophy, medicine and mathematics. It was also the golden age of Armenian ecclesiastical manuscript painting, noted for its lavish decoration and Western influences.

The Cilician kingdom thrived for nearly 300 years before it fell to the Mamluks of Egypt. The last Armenian ruler, Leo V, spent his final years wandering Europe trying to raise support to recapture his kingdom before dying in Paris in 1393.

valley nearby are the 13th-century ruins of Alara Castle (Alara Kalesi).

Southeast from Alanya, the twisting clifftop road occasionally descends to the ocean to pass through the fertile delta of a stream, planted with bananas, or crowded with greenhouses. It's a long drive to Anamur, but it's a beautiful procession of sea views and cool pine forests. This region was ancient Cilicia Tracheia (Rugged Cilicia), a somewhat forbidding part of the world because of the mountains and fearsome pirates, who preyed on ships from the hidden coves.

Anamur

☏ 0324 / POP 35,319

Surrounded by fertile fields of banana plantations and mammoth polytunnels hiding strawberry crops, Anamur is a prosperous farming town and laid-back resort. The waterfront İskele district with its decent strip of sand springs into action on summer weekends when locals head to the coast to cool off. The beach's eastern end is capped by the storybook bulk of Mamure Castle, while just to the west of town is the massive Byzantine city of Anemurium, with tumble-down ruins galore.

Whether it's the ruins or relaxed beach life that bring you here, don't leave town without sampling the local *muzler* (bananas). Shorter and sweeter than imported varieties, piles of bananas are on sale everywhere. Do as the holidaying Turks do and buy them by the bagful to munch on the sand.

◉ Sights

Anamur lies north of highway D400. About 2.5km southeast of the main roundabout is the İskele beach front area. Anemurium is 8.5km west while Mamure Castle is 7km east.

★ Anemurium

Ancient City   ARCHAEOLOGICAL SITE

(Anemurium Antik Kenti; admission ₺5; ⊙ 9am-7pm) Anemurium's sprawling and eerily quiet ruins stretch for 500m down to the pebble beach with mammoth city walls scaling the mountainside above. From Anemurium car park beside the huge necropolis area, walk southeast past a 4th-century basilica; look behind it for a pathway of mosaic tiles leading to the sea. Above the church is one of two aqueducts. The best-preserved structure in Anemurium is the baths complex with coloured mosaic tiles that still decorate portions of the floor.

Also worth seeking out is the theatre dating from the 2nd century AD and, opposite, the more complete odeon, with 900 seats and a tile floor.

Although founded by the Phoenicians in the 4th century BC, Anemurium suffered a number of devastating setbacks, including an attack in AD 52 by a vicious Cilician tribe, and most of the ruins visible date from the late Roman and Byzantine periods onward. Archaeologists have also uncovered evidence that an earthquake destroyed the city in about 580.

Approaching Anamur from the west or down from the Cilician mountains, a sign points south towards the ruins of Anemurium Antik Kenti. The road then bumps along for 2km to the *gişe* (ticket kiosk); it's another 500m to the car park.

Mamure Castle   CASTLE

(Mamure Kalesi; admission ₺5; ⊙ 8am-7.30pm) This tremendous castle, with its crenellated walls, 39 towers and part of its moat still intact, is the biggest and best-preserved fortification on the Turkish Mediterranean coast. The rear of the castle sits on the beach, where sea turtles come in summer to lay their eggs, while its front end almost reaches the highway.

At the time of writing, the castle was undergoing an extensive (and long overdue) restoration, which should be completed by the time you get here.

Mamure Castle dates from the 13th century; it was constructed by the rulers of the Armenian kingdom of Cilicia on the site of a Roman fortress dating from the 3rd century AD. Mamure was taken by Karamanoğlu Mehmet Bey and his troops in 1308 and alterations began, including the addition of a mosque in the eastern courtyard. Here you'll also see remnants of an aqueduct that brought water from the mountains 5km away, a stable that looks like a garage, and the holes in the walls that served as the guards' barracks. To the west is the kalesi (castle interior), where the castle commander and other top brass lived.

Climbing the castle's towers, especially the one with a dungeon within, is something of an adventure, although some stairs are pretty crumbled, so use extreme caution. Your reward is an astounding view of the sea and the ruins of Softa Castle (Softa Kalesi), another fortress built by the Armenian rulers of Cilicia near Bozyazı some 18km to the east.

Anamur Museum
MUSEUM

(Anamur Müzesi; Adnan Menderes Caddesi 3; ⊙8.30am-5pm) FREE Highlights of this museum are archaeological finds from Anemurium, including frescoes from private houses, bathhouse mosaics, an unusual clay sarcophagus, plus jewellery, oil lamps and early Christian religious objects. Look for the iron scales in the shape of a woman, her bulging eyes staring emptily into space.

🛏 Sleeping

The popular İskele (harbour) district is where most visitors to Anamur end up. Pensions and hotels run along Fevzi Çakmak Caddesi (or İskele Yolu) down to the harbour and around İnönü Caddesi, the main street running along the waterfront. Town buses stop at the beachfront intersection.

★ Hotel Esya
PENSION €

(☑ 816 6595, 0539 491 0211; www.anamur.gen.tr/hotelesya; İnönü Caddesi 55; s/d ₺50/90; ❄ 🛜) Quite possibly Anamur's friendliest family runs this excellent pension just a short walk from the beach. The simple rooms are brimming with charming quaintness, and breakfast usually includes freshly cooked *sigara böreği* (fried filo and cheese pastries). Often the family's English-speaking son is on hand, but loads of smiles create a warm welcome even if he's not around.

Hotel Luna Piena
HOTEL €€

(☑ 814 9045; www.hotellunapiena.com; Süleyman Bal Sokak 14; s/d/f ₺60/120/150; ❄ 🛜) Just paces from the beach, this comfortable hotel offers 32 rooms with parquet floors, balconies with full sea views, spacious showers and a preference for sparkling white decor.

Yan Hotel
HOTEL €€

(☑ 814 2123; www.yanhotel.com; Adnan Menderes Caddesi; s/d ₺70/100; ❄ 🛜) Good sea views and a lovely leafy garden are the bonuses of staying at this hotel, just 30m from the beachfront. The downstairs bar is good for a beer, too. Rooms are basic but very light and airy.

🍴 Eating & Drinking

İskele Sofrası
TURKISH €€

(Sokak 1909; mains ₺8-18) Just one block back from the beach, this popular family eatery turns out top-notch meze and heaving grills – order the *patlıcan* (eggplant) kebap – and try not to feed the very patient Labrador usually parked outside. Good fish dishes and Anamur's best pide round out the menu, and cold beer is also available.

Mare Vista Restaurant
INTERNATIONAL €€

(☑ 814 2001; İnönü Caddesi 28; mains ₺10-25) Directly opposite the beach, the 'Sea View'

TURTLES AT RISK!

The beach at Anamur is one of a dozen nesting sites of the loggerhead turtle (*deniz kaplumbağası*) – a large, flat-headed turtle that spends most of its life in the water – along Turkey's Mediterranean coast.

Between May and September, females come ashore at night to lay their eggs in the sand. Using their back flippers they scoop out a nest about 40cm deep, lay between 70 and 120 soft-shelled white eggs the size of ping-pong balls, then cover them over. If disturbed, the turtles may abandon the nests and return to the sea.

The eggs incubate in the sand for some 60 days and the temperature at which they do determines the gender of the hatchlings: below 30°C and all the young will be male, above 30°C and they will be female. At a steady 30°C a mix is assured.

As soon as they're born (at night when it's cool and fewer predators are about), the young turtles make their way towards the sea, drawn by the reflected light. If hotels and restaurants are built too close to the beach (as is often the case in the western Mediterranean), their lights can confuse the youngsters, leading them to move up the beach towards danger – in Anamur's case, the D400 highway.

The loggerhead turtle also nests on the beaches at Demirtaş and Gazipaşa, both southeast of Alanya, and in the Göksu Delta. In the western Mediterranean, important nesting grounds are at Dalyan, Fethiye, Patara, Demre (Kale), Kumluca and Tekirova (both northeast of Demre), and Belek (east of Antalya).

For more on the conservation of these majestic creatures, see p650.

dishes up a range of international and some Italian-themed dishes (including the ubiquitous pizza), as well as salads and sandwiches. Service can be slow, so count on ordering a second beer. Keep an eye on the noticeboard out front for details of occasional live music.

Masalim TEA GARDEN

(İnönü Caddesi) We really like this sand-between-your-toes tea garden smack-dab on the seafront. Run by a couple of friendly sisters, highlights include cheap eats and a couple of kilim-bedecked day beds. Fire up a nargile session, or order a cold beer and listen to the bouncy Turkish pop music cascading over nearby waves.

ⓘ Information

Tourist Office (☑ 814 5058; ⏰ 8am-noon & 1-5pm Mon-Fri) In the otogar complex behind the police station.

ⓘ Getting There & Away

Anamur's otogar is on the intersection of the D400 highway and 19 Mayıs Caddesi. Several buses depart daily to Alanya (₺25, three hours, 130km), Taşucu/Silifke (₺25, three hours, 140km) and Adana (₺35, six hours, 305km).

ⓘ Getting Around

Town buses to İskele depart from a small stand behind the otogar (₺1.50, every 30 minutes). You have to buy a pre-paid ticket before boarding the bus. The small *bakkal* (grocery shop) across the road from the bus stand sells them. A taxi between İskele and the otogar costs ₺12.

If you're heading to Anemurium, flag down a dolmuş to Ören (₺2, half-hourly) from outside the Yağmur Market, opposite the mosque in front of the otogar. Let the driver know and he can drop you off at the Anemurium turn-off on the main highway, from where it's a 2.5km walk. Expect to pay ₺60 for a taxi to Anemurium and back, with an hour's waiting time.

Frequent dolmuşes headed for Bozyazı (₺2) will drop you off outside Mamure Castle, or it's about a 3.5km walk along the beach from İskele. Walk east to the end of İnönü Caddesi and across the bridge where the fishing boats dock in the river, then take the dirt track down to the beach and walk towards the battlements.

Taşucu

☑ 0324 / POP 8953

It may be the working port of nearby Silifke, but a lovely strip of beach and well-maintained seafront promenade make Taşucu (tah-shoo-joo) a destination in its own right. This is an extremely low-key holiday resort that's a favourite stop for birdwatchers who want to combine some swimming and sunbathing with visits to the nearby wetlands of the Göksu Delta.

Taşucu is also an important transport hub, with ferries for both walk-on passengers and cars travelling to/from Girne in Northern Cyprus. The beach is fronted by Sahil Caddesi, which stretches east from the ferry pier and has several good pensions. Around the harbour, excursion boats depart for day trips (per person ₺30) along the coastline and to nearby islands.

🛏 Sleeping

Outside of summer there are excellent discounts on room prices at all of the hotels.

Lades Motel HOTEL €€

(☑ 741 4008; www.ladesmotel.com; İsmet İnönü Caddesi 45; s/d ₺80/100; ❄ 🐕 ☀) The facade of this hotel may be rather worn, but the rooms, with balconies overlooking the pool and harbour, have been spruced up to a high standard with new beds and modern bathrooms. It's a favourite with birdwatchers and the downstairs bar is prime territory for comparing 'twitching' notes with fellow birders. It's on the road down to the harbour.

Meltem Pansiyon PENSION €€

(☑ 741 4391; 0533 360 0726; www.meltempansi yon.net; Sahil Caddesi 75; s/d/tr ₺80/100/120; ❄ @ 🐕) Super-friendly and smack on the beach, this family-run pension is a homely choice. Some eight of the 20 modest rooms face the sea. The rest of the rooms have balconies facing the street. Breakfast (₺7.50 extra) is served on the delightful seafront back patio.

Holmi Pansiyon PENSION €€

(☑ 741 5378; 0545 948 3806; www.holmipansiyon. com; Sahil Caddesi 23; d ₺100; ❄ 🐕) The rooftop terrace at this 15-room pension on the main harbourfront road is particularly nice on a hot day. Around half the rooms have sea views, and a shared guests' kitchen is also available. All the rooms have benefited from a recent renovation and now boast shiny modern bathrooms.

Taşucu Motel PENSION €€

(☑ 741 2417; www.tasucumotel.com; Sahil Caddesi 25; d/tr ₺150/200; ❄ 🐕) Going through a spangly new refit when we called in, the

Taşucu has big airy rooms with great seafront views and a chilled-out roof terrace for end-of-day relaxing. It's directly opposite the harbour promenade on the main road.

🍴 Eating

For a good-value seafood fix, head to one of the excursion boats lining the harbour. They also double as restaurants with fish sandwiches (₺5) and grilled seafood.

Alo Dürüm
TURKISH €

(📞 741 5657; İsmet İnönü Caddesi 17; dishes ₺6-12) Ebullient host Ahmet runs this cheerful open-air kebap place right in the middle of the main drag along the seafront. His hearty portions of döner (spit-roasted lamb slices) and *dürüm* (döner sandwiches) are popular with locals and travellers alike. Don't miss the *tantuni dürüm* (sandwich of beef, peppers, garlic, and onion; ₺6).

Baba Restaurant
SEAFOOD €€

(📞 741 5991; İsmet İnönü Caddesi 43; mains ₺15-25) Regarded as the area's best eatery, the Baba's terrace is a beautiful place to sip a cold beer or slurp imported Italian gelato (₺4 to ₺6). It's the excellent food that really lures diners though, especially the tempting cart of meze (₺3 to ₺5).

ℹ Getting There & Away

BOAT

Fergün Denizcilik (📞 741 2323; www.fergun. net; İsmet İnönü Caddesi) runs *feribotlar* (car ferries) between Taşucu and Girne in Northern Cyprus from Sunday to Wednesday (passenger one-way/return ₺75/130, with car one-way/return ₺175/330). Boats board at midnight and depart from the harbour at 2am, arriving in Girne at 8am. You must be at the harbour to clear immigration at 10.30pm. For the return leg, ferries leave Girne every Monday, Tuesday, Wednesday and Friday at 2pm. Not included in the fare is the harbour tax: ₺12 out of Taşucu and ₺33 from Girne.

The same company also used to run a daily hydrofoil between Taşucu and Girne during the summer months, but services were cancelled in 2013 due to lack of demand. Enquire at their Taşucu office to see if they've been reinstated.

BUS

Buses heading south to Silifke can drop you (if you let them know) on the main highway just past the turn-off for the road down to the harbour. It's an easy five-minute walk to the waterfront and the hotels.

There are dolmuşes every half hour between Taşucu and Silifke otogar (₺2) where you can make long-distance bus connections. The dolmuş route trundles the full length of the waterfront and can be flagged down anywhere along Sahil Caddesi and İsmet İnönü Caddesi.

Silifke

📞 0324 / POP 56,163

Silifke is a riverside country town with a long history. A striking castle towers above the mineral-rich blue-green Göksu River, dubbed the Calycadnus in ancient times. In the vicinity are other archaeological and natural sights that deserve a visit.

Seleucia ad Calycadnum, as Silifke was once known, was founded by Seleucus I Nicator in the 3rd century BC. He was one of Alexander the Great's most able generals and founder of the Seleucid dynasty that ruled Syria after Alexander's death.

The town's other claim to fame is that Emperor Frederick Barbarossa (r 1152–90) drowned in the river near here while leading his troops on the Third Crusade. It was apparently the weight of his armour that brought him down.

Silifke's accommodation options are mediocre at best, and the town is best visited as a day trip from nearby Taşucu.

◎ Sights

Silifke Castle
CASTLE

(Silifke Kalesi) **FREE** This Byzantine hilltop fortress, with its moat, two dozen towers and vaulted underground chambers was once Silifke's command centre. The walls are its most impressive feature as the interior is still undergoing excavation work. Keep an eye out for the friendly Ahmet Kulali. He speaks excellent English and has extensive knowledge on local history. Tip him well – he's worth it.

Tekir Ambarı
CISTERN

(Su Sarnıcı; Eğitim Sokak) **FREE** The Tekir Ambarı is an ancient cistern carved from rock that can be entered via a spiral staircase. To reach the cistern, head to the junction of İnönü Bulvarı and Menderes Caddesi, then walk up the alleyway (348 Sokak) to the left of the Küçük Hacı Kaşaplar butcher shop. Turn left onto Eğitim Sokak, just before the school. The cistern is hidden in a mound just behind a basketball court.

Silifke Museum
MUSEUM

(Taşucu Caddesi 29; admission ₺5; ⊗8am-5pm Tue-Sun) To the east of Silifke's centre, on the main road heading to Taşucu, this local museum showcases Roman figures and busts. The collection also includes ancient coins and jewellery, amphorae and pottery, and tools and weapons from the Roman and Hellenistic eras.

Necropolis
RUIN

(İnönü Bulvarı) Ancient Silifke's necropolis, alongside busy İnönü Bulvarı has been fenced off so all you can do is peek between the railings at the rather sad ruins of the Roman Temple of Jupiter with its columns used by storks as nesting posts. The temple dates from the 2nd century AD, but was turned into a Christian basilica sometime in the 5th century.

Merkez Camii
MOSQUE

(Central Mosque; Fevzi Çakmak Caddesi) Also called the Alaeddin Camii, or Aladdin's Mosque, the Seljuk-era Merkez Camii dates from 1228, although it's seen many renovations over the centuries.

Reşadiye Camii
MOSQUE

(İnönü Bulvarı 138) Built by the Ottomans, the Roman columns supporting the back and front porticoes were originally from the Temple of Jupiter.

Stone Bridge
BRIDGE

The stone bridge over the Göksu dates back to AD 78 and has been restored many times, including twice in the last century (1922 and 1972).

Church of St Thekla
CHURCH

(Aya Tekla; Aya Tekla Sokak; admission ₺5; ⊗9am-5pm) This Christian site is dedicated to Saint Thekla, one of Saint Paul's early devotees. Thekla is said to have spent her later years here, trying to convert the locals of Seleucia to Paul's teachings. Having ruffled the feathers of local healers, they decided to kill her, but on their arrival at her cave she vanished into thin air.

The very atmospheric though modest church carved out of the cave where she lived is an important pilgrimage site.

In the 5th century a large basilica was built on the grassy knoll above the cave, but only an incisor-like chunk of the apse is still standing.

The church is signposted off the D400 highway, 3km southwest of Silifke. Any dolmuş travelling between Taşucu and Silifke can drop you at the turn-off, from where it's a 1km walk to the site.

🍴 Eating & Drinking

Try the *Silifke yoğurdu* – a local yoghurt famous throughout Turkey.

Kale Restaurant
TURKISH €€

(Silifke Castle; mains ₺8-20) This restaurant, just below the walls and looming towers of Silifke Castle, has fantastic views across town and serves up simple dishes at reasonable prices. It's the best place within kilometres for a sundowner.

OFF THE BEATEN TRACK

ALAHAN MONASTERY

This remarkable monastery complex (admission ₺5; ⊗9am-5pm) perches on a terraced slope with tumbling views of the Göksu Valley below.

Above the site entrance is a cave-church chiselled into the cliff face. A grand entry adorned with richly carved reliefs of angels and demons leads into the ruins of the west basilica with its re-erected Corinthian columns. More ruins dot the path up to the mammoth, well-preserved 5th century east basilica, thought to be one of the most ambitious early examples of domed-basilica architecture.

Although today the location amid the pine-forested slopes of the Taurus Mountains has a middle-of-nowhere feel, during the Byzantine age the monastery sat near a vital trade and communications route, and archaeologists believe Alahan was probably one of Turkey's most important religious centres during the 5th and 6th centuries.

The journey here takes in some of the region's most beautiful scenery, with the Göksu River, rimmed by soaring jagged cliffs, scything through the countryside. Take the inland (D715) highway from Silifke to Mut (1½ hours, 76km) and then continue north for another 24km to the village of Geçimli, where a signposted turnoff to the monastery leads for 3km up a steep incline.

Gözde Restaurant
KEBAP €€

(Balıkçılar Sokak 7; mains ₺8-15) This kebap and *lahmacun* (Arabic-style pizza) joint also serves up delicious soups, meze and grills in a shaded outdoor dining area down a small street.

Göksu Pastanesi
TEA GARDEN

We like this large and shaded terrace off Cavit Erdem Caddesi, perched atop the rumbling Göksu River and close to the stone bridge. Snack on pastries from ₺2.

ⓘ Information

Tourist Office (☑ 714 1151; Veli Gürten Bozbey Caddesi 6; ☺ 8am-5pm Mon-Fri) Just north of Atatürk Caddesi, this office has a surprisingly good array of English-language info on the region, a decent town map and helpful staff.

ⓘ Getting There & Away

Buses from Silifke otogar depart hourly for Adana (₺20, 2½ hours, 165km). Other frequent services include Mersin (₺15, two hours, 95km), Alanya (₺35, six hours, 265km) and Antalya (₺45, nine hours, 395km).

Dolmuşes to Taşucu (₺2) depart every 20 minutes from a stand on the south bank of the Göksu, near the stone bridge; they pass by the otogar on their way out of town. A taxi to Taşucu costs ₺25.

Around Silifke

Just southeast of Silifke are the lush salt marshes, lakes and sand dunes of the Göksu Delta, an important wetland area and home to some 330 bird species. To the north and northeast, the slopes of the maquis-covered Olba Plateau stretch along the coast for about 60km before the Cilician plain opens into an ever-widening swathe of fertile land. It is one of Turkey's richest areas for archaeological sites and includes many destinations more easily accessed from Kızkalesi.

Uzuncaburç

The remnants of Roman Diocaesarea sit within the village of Uzuncaburç (admission ₺3; ☺ 8am-7pm), 30km northeast of Silifke. Originally this was the Hellenistic city of Olba, home to a zealous cult that worshipped Zeus Olbius.

The impressive Temple of Zeus Olbius, with two dozen erect columns, lies to the left of the colonnaded street. Beside the temple are various sarcophagi bearing reliefs. Important Roman structures include a nymphaeum (2nd century AD), an arched city gate, and the Temple of Tyche (1st century AD).

Just before the entrance to the main site is a small Roman theatre. To view a Hellenistic structure built before the Romans sacked Olba, head north through the village, where you'll pass a massive, five-storey watch tower with a Roman road behind it. Another 600m down into the valley leads to a long, roadside necropolis of rock-cut tombs and more sarcophagi.

On the road to Uzuncaburç some 8km out of Silifke at Demircili – ancient Imbriogon – you'll pass several superb examples of Roman monumental tombs that resemble houses.

ⓘ Getting There & Away

Minibuses to Uzuncaburç (₺6) leave from a side street near the Silifke tourist office at 11am and noon. From Uzuncaburç there is one service to Silifke at 3pm.

Hiring a taxi costs ₺120 return, usually incorporating a visit to the tombs at Demircili.

Kızkalesi

☑ 0324 / POP 1750

The coastal village of Kızkalesi boasts a lovely swath of beach capped by a castle and another island castle just offshore that seems to be floating on the sea. Unfortunately the town itself is a grid of rather grim-looking concrete slab apartment blocks that look like they were slapped up in five minutes. Kızkalesi only springs into action from June to September when locals make a beeline for the beach on steaming hot weekends. For archaeology and history buffs though, the village is a popular base as a springboard for the virtual open-air museum of ruins scattered across the Olba Plateau.

◎ Sights

Kızkalesi Castle
CASTLE

(Maiden's Castle; ☺ 9am-5pm) FREE Lying 300m from the shore, Kızkalesi Castle is like a suspended dream. Check out the mosaics in the central courtyard and the vaulted gallery, and climb one of the four towers (the one at the southeast corner has the best views). It's possible to swim to the castle, but most people catch the boat (₺5) from the beach pier near Corycus Castle. Another option is to rent a dolphin-themed pedalo (around ₺10) and pedal on over.

Corycus Castle
CASTLE

(Korykos Kalesı; admission ₺5; ⊙8am-8pm) At the northern end of Kızkalesi beach, Corycus Castle was either built or rebuilt by the Byzantines, briefly occupied by the Armenian kingdom of Cilicia and once connected to Kızkalesi by a causeway. Walk carefully up the worn stairway to the east, where a ruined tower affords a fine view of Kızkalesi Castle.

Across the highway is a **necropolis**, once the burial ground for tradespeople. Tombs and rock carvings include a 5th-century relief of a warrior with a raised sword.

Elaiussa-Sebaste
ARCHAEOLOGICAL SITE

`FREE` Some 4km northeast of Kızkalesi at Ayaş, are the extensive remains of ancient Elaiussa-Sebaste, a city dating back to the early Roman period and perhaps even to the Hittite era. Important structures on the left (west) side include a 2300-seat hilltop **theatre**, the remains of a **Byzantine basilica**, a **Roman temple** with floor mosaics of fish and dolphins, and a total-immersion cruciform **baptistery**. The ruins of a **Byzantine palace** are on the eastern side of the highway.

🛌 Sleeping

Yaka Hotel
HOTEL **€€**

(☑ 523 2444 ; 0542 432 1996 ; www.yakahotel.com. tr; s/d €30/45; 🏵@🛜) Yakup Kahveci, the Yaka's multilingual and quick-witted owner, runs the most welcoming hotel in Kızkalesi. The 17 rooms are impeccably tidy, breakfast (or specially ordered dinner) is eaten in the attractive garden, and there's nothing in the area Yakup doesn't know and/or can't organise. The Yaka is also a great place to meet other travellers, especially those interested in archaeology.

Hotel Hantur
HOTEL **€€**

(☑523 2367; www.hotelhantur.com; s/d/f €40/50/60; 🏵@🛜) The Hantur has a front-row seat on the sea and the 20 colourful rooms are cool and comfortable. Only the back rooms have balconies, but for a true seaside experience forgo the balcony and grab a room facing the sea (such as room 301). The breezy front garden is another bonus, as is the helpful and friendly family who run the hotel.

Rain Hotel
HOTEL **€€€**

(☑523 2782; www.rainhotel.com; s/d/tr/f €50/70/80/90; 🏵@) With a warm and friendly vibe, the Rain is a perennially popular choice, with 18 spotless and spacious rooms, a few with tiny balconies. The homely downstairs lounge is a good place to kick back and meet other travellers and the onsite travel agency can organise pretty much any activity or tour for guests.

🍴 Eating & Drinking

A lovely dining option is the 10-minute bus ride (₺2.50, every 30 minutes) to the seafood restaurants at Narlıkuyu.

Cafe Rain
INTERNATIONAL **€€**

(☑523 2234; mains ₺15-25; ⊙May-Oct) The rainbow decor here complements the cheery menu of tasty, good-value international favourites as well as what might be the finest *börek* (pastry filled with cheese or meat) on the eastern Mediterranean. In the evenings, travellers transform it into a companionable cocktail bar.

Paşa Restaurant
KEBAP **€€**

(☑523 2230; Plaj Yolu 5; mains ₺8-16; ⊙May-Oct) Just off central Cumhuriyet Meydanı, this large open spot has grills and meze at better prices than the beachfront restaurants. Keeping things super-competitive is the adjacent and equally good value **Tanem** ('Sweetheart') restaurant.

Turkish Turtles Club
BAR

Exposed bricks and giant beer cans make this the funkiest place in town. You may be keeping company with Turkish teenagers from Adana or Mersin, proudly showing off the newly inked tattoos they've just scored around the corner.

Albatross
BAR, RESTAURANT

(⊙May-Oct) It's a restaurant as well, but visit here for sundowners around the outdoor bar, with full views of the sea castle. They've been known to overcharge Western travellers, so check prices when you order your drinks.

ℹ️ Getting There & Away

Frequent buses link Kızkalesi with Silifke (₺5, 30 minutes, 24km) and Mersin (₺8, 1½ hours, 60km).

1. Mosaic, Anemurium Ancient City (p391) 2. Alahan Monastery (p395) 3. Karatepe-Aslantaş Open-Air Museum (p407) 4. Mosaic, Hatay Archaeology Museum (p410)

Antiquities of the Eastern Med

Want to explore rugged crumbling ruins without the crowds? The eastern Mediterranean is chock-a-block full of vast archaeological sites, important early Christian sites and craggy clifftop castles that are all the more fun to explore because of their half-forgotten ambience.

Anemurium Ancient City

This swath of rickety ruins tumbles down the cliffside to the beach. Soak up the heady atmosphere of long-lost grandeur while surveying the city from high on the citadel walls, or clambering through the once lavish Roman baths.

Caves of Heaven & Hell

The underworld has come a-calling. Stand over Hell's abyss and inside the wide, yawning mouth of Heaven and check visiting the abode of gods off your list.

Yılankale

If you only see one castle in the eastern Mediterranean, pick this wondrous pile of ramparts and towers clinging onto a hilltop south of Adana. It's a sweat-inducing scramble to get up to the highest tower, but the views are worth it.

Karatepe

Giant slabs of inscribed reliefs guarded by glaring-eye sphinxes and lions are all that are left of the 8th-century-BC Hittite town of Azatiwataya.

Hatay Archaeology Museum

Be dazzled by the intricate beauty and artistic mastery of one of the world's great mosaic collections on show at this region's top museum.

THE BEST CHRISTIAN SITES

➡ Church of St Peter (p411)
➡ Tarsus (p402)
➡ Alahan Monastery (p395)
➡ Church of St Thekla (p395)

Around Kızkalesi

There are several places to the southwest and northeast of Kızkalesi that are of genuine historical interest and importance. They include everything from an idyllic seaside village with an important mosaic to a descent into the very bowels of the earth.

Narlıkuyu

On a cove 5km southwest of Kızkalesi, Narlıkuyu has popular fish restaurants, a mosaic of singular beauty and other-worldly mountain caves nearby.

Inside the village's **Mosaic Museum** (Mozaik Müzesi) `FREE`, in a compact 4th-century Roman bath on the waterfront, is a wonderful mosaic of the Three Graces – Aglaia, Thalia and Euphrosyne – the daughters of Zeus. The museum is usually kept locked, but the guardian is always on hand to open it up for visitors.

The cove here is home to several seafood restaurants, with dining terraces right next to the sea. They all do seafood meals complete with huge piles of salads and scrumptious meze for about ₺40. Try the **Kerim** (seafood priced by weight, meals ₺40-60), near the museum, or the **Narlıkuyu** (seafood priced by weight, meals ₺35-70) on the opposite side of the cove.

Frequent dolmuşes run between Kızkalesi and Silifke via Narlıkuyu (₺2.50). Get off here to walk 1.5km up the steep hill to the Caves of Heaven and Hell.

Caves of Heaven & Hell

Near Narlıkuyu, a road winds north for 1.5km to the **Caves of Heaven and Hell** (admission ₺10; ⊙8am-7pm), sinkholes carved out by a subterranean river and places of great mythological significance. The walk from Narlıkuyu junction to the main entrance gate is quite steep. Enterprising locals usually offer taxi services up the hill for ₺5 one-way.

The mammoth underground **Chasm of Heaven** (Cennet Mağarası) – 200m long, 90m wide and 70m deep – is reached via 450-odd steps to the left of the ticket booth. Right in front of the cave mouth is the tiny but beautiful remains of the 5th-century Byzantine **Chapel of the Virgin Mary**, used for a short time in the 19th century as a mosque. Once inside the cave, the stairs

can be wet and slippery and there are no handrails, so wear decent shoes. At the furthest end inside the colossal grotto is the **Cave of Typhon** (Tayfun Mağarası), a damp, jagged-edged, devilish theatre. Locals believe this to be a gateway to the eternal furnace and Strabo mentions it in his Geography. According to legend, the cave's underground river connects with the hellish River Styx.

Follow the path from the ticket office further up the hill to the **Gorge of Hell** (Cehennem Mağarası) with its almost vertical walls that you view by stepping out onto a heart-stopping platform extending over the 120m-deep pit. This charred hole is supposedly where Zeus imprisoned the 100-headed, fire-breathing monster Typhon after defeating him in battle.

Around 600m west of the main entrance is the **Asthma Cave** (Astim Mağarası), which supposedly relieves sufferers of the affliction.

Adamkayalar

Tricky to get to but well worth the effort is Adamkayalar (Men Rock Cliff), some 17 Roman-era reliefs carved on a cliff face about 8km north of Kızkalesi. They are part of a 1st century AD necropolis and immortalise warriors wielding axes, swords and lances, and citizens, sometimes accompanied by their wives and children.

At the necropolis opposite Corycus Castle a sign points west to the site. Follow the road uphill for 5km and, at another sign, turn left; the car park is just under 3km down this road. Follow the painted blue arrows down a rather tricky incline into the glen for about 750m and don't go alone: you might fall and be stranded.

Kanlıdivane

About 8.5km northeast of Kızkalesi at Kumkuyu is the road leading 3km to the ruins of **Kanlıdivane** (admission ₺5; ⊙8am-7pm), the ancient city of Kanytelis.

Central to Kanlıdivane ('Bloody Place of Madness'), is a 60m-deep chasm where criminals were tossed to wild animals. Peering down, you'll see reliefs on the cliff walls of a six-member family (southwest) and a Roman soldier (northwest). Ruins ring the pit including four **Byzantine churches** and a **necropolis** to the northeast with a 2nd-century **temple tomb**.

Mersin (İçel)

📞 0324 / POP 898.813

Mersin was earmarked a half-century ago as the seaside outlet for Adana and its rich agricultural hinterland. Today it is the largest port on the Turkish Mediterranean and for the most part a sprawling, soulless place that most people leave quickly. But Mersin, whose official new name İçel (also the name of the province of which it is capital) is ignored by most everyone, does have its moments. If you scrunch up your eyes, some of the streets near the sea almost have a Marseilles feel to them, and there are definitely worse ways to while away an afternoon than a lazy seafood lunch on the excursion boats lining the harbour.

◉ Sights

Mersin Museum
MUSEUM

(Atatürk Caddesi Kültür Merkezi; ⊘ 8am-noon & 1-4.45pm) **FREE** Mersin's archaeology museum has finds from nearby tumuli (burial mounds) and sites (including Elaiussa-Sebaste near Kızkalesi), a great bronze of Dionysus and curious odds and ends such as a Roman-era glass theatre 'token' on the ground floor.

Greek Orthodox Church
CHURCH

(Atatürk Caddesi Kültür Merkezi; ⊘ divine liturgy 9-11.15am Sun) Next to Mersin Museum, this walled 1852 church is still in use and has a lovely iconostasis. To gain entry, go to the left side of the church facing 4302 Sokak and ring the bell.

Atatürk Evi
MUSEUM

(Atatürk House; Atatürk Caddesi 36; ⊘ 8am-5pm Tue-Sun) **FREE** Along the pedestrianised section of Atatürk Caddesi is a museum in a beautiful seven-room villa where Atatürk once stayed.

🛏 Sleeping

Budget and midrange hotels huddle around the otogar.

Tahtalı Hotel
HOTEL €

(www.hoteltahtali.com; Mersinli Ahmet Caddesi 21; s/d ₺40/80; ❀ 🤶) Despite its less than pretty bus station location – it's right across the road from Mersin's otogar – the Tahtalı is a decent budget sleep. The rooms are nothing to write home about, but it's clean, safe and friendly.

Nobel Oteli
BUSINESS HOTEL €€

(📞 237 2210; www.nobeloteli.com; İstiklal Caddesi 73; s/d ₺110/160; ❀🤶) Behind the big, brash and very yellow exterior, the Nobel is a smart choice in the heart of the city with 74 big, comfortable rooms that come with some deft design touches and satellite TV. The foyer is a hive of business activity, and the adjoining restaurant is popular at lunch.

Kardelen Hotel
HOTEL €€

(📞 337 2798; www.kardelen.com.tr; Mesudiye Fasih Kayabak Caddesi; s/d ₺60/100; ❀🤶) This newish hotel is around 300m from the city's otogar. It wouldn't win any style awards, but it's clean, safe and the staff try hard to please. Central Mersin and the city's main restaurant area is around 600m away.

🍴 Eating & Drinking

Mersin's local speciality is *tantuni* kebap – chopped beef sautéed with onions, garlic and peppers, and wrapped in pita-like *lavaş ekmek*. *Tantuni* is often accompanied by *şalgam suyu*, a crimson-coloured juice made by boiling turnips and adding vinegar. For something sweet, try *cezerye*, a semigelatinous confection made from carrots and packed with walnuts. For a cheap seafood fix, try the floating fish restaurants around the harbour. Fish sandwiches and a beer are both around ₺5.

Hacıbaba
TURKISH €€

(📞 238 0023; İstiklal Caddesi 82; mains ₺7-14) Opposite the Nobel Oteli, the delightful Hacıbaba does excellent *zeytinyağli biber dolması* (stuffed peppers), and there are good kebaps, *lahmacun* and pide, too.

Deniz Yıldızı
SEAFOOD €€

(📞 237 7124; 4701 Sokak 10b; mains ₺12-20) The 'Starfish' is the best of several fish restaurants between Silifke Caddesi and Atatürk Caddesi, in the centre of town.

Piknik
BAR

(5218 Sokak) This bar-cum-cafe-cum-teahouse is one of a collection of humming little working-class drinking venues in the Taşhan Antik Galerya on a street between İsmet İnönü Caddesi and Uray Caddesi.

ℹ Information

Tourist Office (📞 238 3271; İsmet İnönü Bulvarı; ⊘ 8am-noon & 1-5pm Mon-Fri) Near the harbour at the eastern end of town.

EASTERN MEDITERRANEAN MERSİN (İÇEL)

① Getting There & Away

BUS

Mersin's otogar is on the city's eastern outskirts. To get to the centre, leave by the main exit, turn right and walk up to the main road (Gazi Mustafa Kemal Bulvarı). Cross to the far side and catch a city bus travelling west (₺1.50). Buses from town to the otogar leave from outside the train station, as well as from a stop opposite the Mersin Oteli.

From the otogar, frequent buses run to Adana (₺12, 1½ hours, 75km), Silifke (₺15, two hours, 85km, three per hour) via Kızkalesi (₺8, one hour), and Alanya (₺45, 8½ hours, 375km, eight per day). There are also dolmuşes every 30 minutes to Tarsus (₺4).

TRAIN

There are frequent rail services to Tarsus (₺3, 20 minutes) and Adana (₺5, 45 minutes) between 6am and 10.30pm.

Tarsus

🖉 0324 / POP 249,010

Should Tarsus' most famous son return two millennia after his birth, St Paul would hardly recognise the place through the sprawl of concrete apartment blocks. For pilgrims and history buffs the scattering of early Christian sites here is reason enough to linger, but stroll through the historic city core, with its twisting narrow lanes rimmed by houses slouching in various states of dilapidation, and you'll really find this town's timeless appeal.

⊙ Sights

Old City   HISTORIC AREA
(Antik Şehir) The compact Old City lies between Adana Bulvarı and Hal Caddesi. It

---

A PLACE OF PILGRIMAGE

Jewish by birth, Paul (born Saul) was one of early Christianity's most zealous proselytisers and during his lifetime converted hundreds of pagans and Jews to the new religion throughout the ancient world. After his death in Rome about AD 67, the location of his birthplace became sacred to his followers. Today pilgrims still flock to the site of his ruined house in Tarsus to take a drink from the 30m-deep well on the grounds.

---

includes a wonderful 60m-long stretch of Roman road, and a labyrinth of alleyways hemmed by historical Tarsus houses, one now housing the Konak Efsus boutique hotel.

Just southeast are several historical mosques, including the Eski Cami (Old Mosque), a medieval structure that was originally a church dedicated to St Paul. Adjacent looms the barely recognisable brickwork of a huge old Roman bath.

Across Atatürk Caddesi is the late-19th-century Makam Camii (Official Mosque), and to the east is believed to be the tomb of the Prophet Daniel. To the west is the 16th-century Ulu Cami (Great Mosque), sporting a curious 19th-century minaret moonlighting as a clock tower. Next door is the 19th-century Kırkkaşık Bedesten (Forty Spoons Market), still used as a covered bazaar.

St Paul's Well   HISTORIC SITE
(St Paul Kuyusu; Hal Caddesi; admission ₺3; ⊙8am-7pm) Just on the edge of the Old City (signs point the way from Atatürk Bulvarı) are the ruins of St Paul's house, his supposed birthplace, which can be viewed underneath sheets of plexiglass.

Church of St Paul   CHURCH
(St Paul Kilisesi; Abdı İpekçi Caddesi; ⊙8am-8pm) FREE South of the Old City, this Orthodox church was originally built in the 1850s to commemorate St Paul. It was utilised as a storage depot (among other uses) up until the mid-1990s when the Ministry of Culture began a restoration and it was opened up for services again in 2011. There are simple frescoes on the interior ceiling.

Cleopatra's Gate   GATE
Walk 1km southwest of the Old City along İsmetpaşa Bulvarı to get to the Roman Kancık Kapısı, literally the 'Gate of the Bitch', but better known as Cleopatra's Gate. Despite the name it has nothing to do with the Egyptian queen, although she is thought to have had a rendezvous with Mark Antony here in 41 BC. Heavy-handed restoration has unfortunately robbed it of any sense of antiquity.

Tarsus Museum   MUSEUM
(Adile Hala Caddesi; ⊙8am-7.30pm) FREE About 750m southwest of the Old City, this museum showcases a small but interesting trove of ancient statuary and coins, one from the 6th century BC.

Waterfall
WATERFALL

Catch a dolmuş (₺1.5) in front of the Eski Cami to a cooling waterfall *(şelale)* on the Tarsus River (the Cydnus River in ancient times), some 3km to the north. There are tea gardens and restaurants nearby.

Sleeping & Eating

★ Konak Efsus
BOUTIQUE HOTEL €€

(☑ 614 0807; www.konakefsus.com; Tarihi Evler Sokak 31-33; s/d €40/60; ❈ 🛜) Tarsus' best accommodation is this delightful boutique hotel converted from a traditional Ottoman house. The eight rooms, with stone walls, antique furniture and 21st-century plumbing, are all unique and bear different names. The Cleopatra Suite is especially fine, as is the lovely patio. It's very popular, especially at weekends, so booking ahead is recommended.

The courtyard restaurant is also great.

Cafe Maça
CAFE €

(Tarihi Evler Sokak; mantı ₺6, cakes ₺3-6) We're big fans of this rather funky cafe snuggled inside a creaky 200-year-old house just up the road from the Konak Efsus hotel. Run by a super-friendly arty couple, this is a top spot for delicious homemade *mantı* as well as a good coffee and cake stop.

ⓘ Information

Tourist Office (☑ 613 3888; Atatürk Bulvarı; ☺ 8am-5pm Mon-Sat) In front of the Roman road. Usually locked and unmanned though.

ⓘ Getting There & Away

Tarsus' otogar is 3km east of the centre. A taxi is ₺10 and a city bus is ₺1.25. Frequent small buses and dolmuşes connect Tarsus with Mersin (₺4, 29km) and Adana (₺4, 42km). They always pick up and drop off passengers from just beside Cleopatra's Gate and also along Adana Bulvarı.

The train station, with regular services to Mersin (₺3) and Adana (₺4), is northwest of the tourist office at the end of Hilmi Seçkin Caddesi.

Adana

☑ 0322 / POP 1.61 MILLION

Turkey's fourth-largest city is a thoroughly modern affair with just a handful of sights, some pretty good cafes and bars, and excellent transportation links. Adana makes a good base for exploring the little-visited historic sites and ruins to the southwest, and if you've been travelling lazily along the Med, the urban buzz may be just the city-slicker injection you need.

Adana is more or less cut in two by the D400 highway. North of the road (called Turan Cemal Beriker Bulvarı in town and running west to east and over Kennedy Bridge) are leafy and well-heeled districts. South of the trendy high-rise apartments and sidewalk bars and cafes, the mood deepens, and housing starts to sprawl. The Seyhan River delimits the city centre to the east.

◉ Sights & Activities

★ Sabancı Merkez Camii
MOSQUE

(Sabancı Central Mosque; Turan Cemal Beriker Bulvarı) The most imposing mosque in Adana is the six-minaret Sabancı Merkez Camii, on the left bank of the Seyhan River beside the Kennedy Bridge. The largest mosque between İstanbul and Saudi Arabia, it was built by the late industrial magnate Sakıp Sabancı (1933–2004) – philanthropist and founder of the second-richest family dynasty in Turkey – and is covered top to tail in marble and gold leaf. The mosque can accommodate an estimated 28,000 worshippers.

Archaeology Museum
MUSEUM

(Fuzuli Caddesi 10; ☺ 8am-5pm Tue-Sun) Adana's Archaeology Museum is rich in Roman statuary from the Cilician Gates, north of Tarsus. These 'gates' were the main passage through the Taurus Mountains and an important transit point as far back as Roman times. Note especially the 2nd-century Achilles sarcophagus, decorated with scenes from the *Iliad*. Hittite artefacts and Hellenistic monuments are also on display.

At the time of writing the museum was closed to visitors and reports were that it was going to reopen in a new location. Ask at the Adana tourist office for an update.

Adana Ethnography Museum
MUSEUM

(Ziyapaşa Bulvarı 143; admission ₺5; ☺ 8am-5pm Tue-Sun) Just off İnönü Caddesi, this museum is housed in a former Crusader church that later served as a mosque. It has been undergoing a painfully slow restoration since 2011 and remained closed at the time of writing. If open when you pass through, its showcase of carpets and kilims (pileless woven rugs), weapons, manuscripts and funeral monuments are definitely worthy of a visit.

Adana

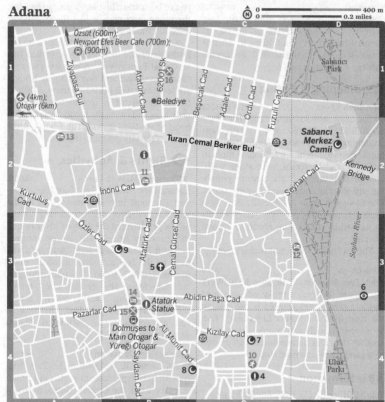

Adana

◎ Top Sights
1 Sabancı Merkez Camii	D2

◎ Sights
2 Adana Ethnography Museum	A2
3 Archaeology Museum	C2
4 Great Clock Tower	C4
5 St Paul's Catholic Church	B3
6 Stone Bridge	D3
7 Ulu Cami	C4
8 Yağ Camii	B4
9 Yeni Cami	B3

◆ Activities, Courses & Tours
10 Çarşı Hamamı	C4
Mestan Hamamı	(see 15)

◰ Sleeping
11 Akdeniz Oteli	B2
12 Hotel Bosnalı	D3
13 Ibis Hotel	A2
14 Otel Mercan	B3

◉ Eating
15 Öz Asmaaltı	B4
16 Şen	B1

Ulu Cami   MOSQUE
(Great Mosque; Kızılay Caddesi) The attractive 16th-century Ulu Cami (Great Mosque) is reminiscent of the Mamluk mosques of Cairo, with black-and-white banded marble and elaborate window surrounds. The tiles in the *mihrab* (niche indicating the direction of Mecca) came from Kütahya and İznik.

Stone Bridge   BRIDGE
(Taşköprü; Abidin Paşa Caddesi) This Roman-era stone bridge over the Seyhan at the eastern end of Abidin Paşa Caddesi was built under

Hadrian (r 117–138) and repaired in the 6th century. The bridge's 300m-long span has 21 arches, but you can only see 14 – the rest are underwater.

Yeni Cami
MOSQUE

(New Mosque; Özler Caddesi) Built in 1724, the central Yeni Cami follows the general square plan of the city's Ulu Cami, with 10 domes.

Yağ Camii
MOSQUE

(Oil Mosque; Ali Münif Caddesi) The Yağ Camii (1501), with its imposing portal, started life as the Church of St James.

St Paul's Catholic Church
CHURCH

(Bebekli Kilise; 10 Sokak) Built in 1870 by the Armenian community, this church is still in service today as a Roman Catholic place of worship.

Great Clock Tower
MONUMENT

(Büyük Saat Kulesi; Ali Münif Caddesi) Near Adana's sprawling covered market *(kapalı çarşı),* the Great Clock Tower dates back to 1881.

Mestan Hamamı
HAMAM

(Merry Hamam; Pazarlar Caddesi 3; soak & scrub ₺15; ⊙5am-11pm) The Mestan Hamamı, right in the centre of town, is a great place to experience a soak and scrub.

Çarşı Hamamı
HAMAM

(Market Hamam; Ali Münif Caddesi 145; ⊙men 5-9am & 4-10pm, women 9am-3.30pm) This very local hamam is a good opportunity to enjoy a traditional Turkish bath.

Sleeping

Otel Mercan
HOTEL €

(☑351 2603; www.otelmercan.com; Küçüksaat Meydanı 5; s/d ₺60/90; ❄ি) The Mercan wins our award for friendliest hotel in Adana. Both staff and management go out of their way to help, and the location, right in the middle of the city centre is super convenient. The freshly renovated lobby is a surprisingly chic addition, although the vibe isn't transferred to the more prosaic but still comfortable rooms.

★Hotel Bosnalı
BOUTIQUE HOTEL €€

(☑359 8000; www.hotelbosnali.com; Seyhan Caddesi 29; s/d ₺130/150, ste ₺200-250; ❄ি) This splurge-worthy treat is one of the eastern Mediterranean's best places to stay. Housed in a mansion dating back to 1889, the Bosnalı is all stone-tile floors, hand-carved wooden ceilings and antique Ottoman furnishings. The city views from the rooftop restaurant are lovely, and the staff are uniformly friendly and professional. Top stuff.

Ibis Hotel
BUSINESS HOTEL €€

(☑355 9500; www.ibishotel.com; Turhan Cemal Beriker Bulvari 49; r ₺137; ❄ি) In true Ibis style, the compact rooms here are chic and modern with all mod cons, and we also applaud their decision to incorporate non-smoking floors. On the downside, the location – a slam-dunk on the main highway through town with a huddle of grim car-repair workshops for neighbours – isn't so appealing.

Akdeniz Oteli
HOTEL €€

(☑363 1510; fax 363 1510; İnönü Caddesi 22; s/d ₺70/100; ❄ি) Centrally located near lots of restaurants, this clean two-star place is starting to look a little rough around the edges, but is still a safe bet to rest your head in Adana. Don't miss the psychedelic mirrored staircase leading from the lobby to the 2nd-floor bar.

✖ Eating & Drinking

Famous worldwide is Adana kebap: minced beef or lamb mixed with powdered red pepper grilled on a skewer. It is served with sliced onions dusted with the slightly acidic herb sumac and barbecued tomatoes.

Şen
TURKISH €

(62001 Sokak; mains ₺7-12; ☑) Heading north on Ataturk Caddesi, turn right into 62002 Sokak and then left into 62001 Sokak to find this relaxed neighbourhood *lokanta* (restaurant serving ready-made food) popular with desk jockeys from nearby offices and featuring loads of vegetarian options. The best place to sit is on the terrace shaded by a rambling arbour. There's no menu, so check out what looks good.

Özsüt
CAFE €

(Ziyapaşa Bulvarı 15c; cakes ₺4.50-8; ⊙8am-midnight) Cakes, puddings and a delightfully delicious assortment of ice creams are available at this branch of a popular chain.

★Öz Asmaaltı
KEBAP €€

(☑351 4028; Pazarlar Caddesi 9; Adana kebap meal ₺22) This local favourite is just about the best restaurant of its class in Adana. It's a spartan place, but the mains and meze are delightful. This is *the* place to try Adana kebap, and you'll get a bundle of meze, salad and the dentist-nightmare dessert of *kadayıf* (dough soaked in syrup and topped with clotted cream) with your meal.

Newport Efes Beer Cafe
PUB

(Şinasi Efendi Caddesi 23) Retro Americana decor, an outdoor terrace and a range of draught beers are the key attractions for a young and cosmopolitan crowd at this bustling pub, tucked away in a leafy, up-market neighbourhood. Look for the red British-style phone booth out front. Hearty food comes with a Turkish, Italian or Mexican accent. Alfresco bars and cafes dot the surrounding streets.

ⓘ Information

Tourist Office (☑ 363 1448; Atatürk Caddesi 7; ☉ 8am-noon & 1-5pm Mon-Sat) One block north of İnönü Caddesi, with excellent city maps and pretty good English spoken.

ⓘ Getting There & Away

Adana's airport (Şakirpaşa Havaalanı) is 4km west of the centre on the D400. The otogar is 2km further west on the north side of the D400. The train station is at the northern end of Ziyapaşa Bulvarı, 1.5km north of İnönü Caddesi.

BUS

Adana's large otogar has direct bus and/or dolmuş services to just about everywhere in Turkey. Note that dolmuşes to Kadirli (₺10, two hours, 108km) and Kozan (₺8, one hour, 72km) leave from the Yüreği otogar, on the right bank of the Seyhan River.

TRAIN

The *Çukurova Ekspresi* sleeper train links the ornate *gar* (station) at the northern end of Ziyapaşa Bulvarı with Ankara (7.30pm, ₺29, 12 hours). Both the *Toros Ekspresi* train (7am, ₺22, 6½ hours) and the *İçanadolu Mavi* train (3.45pm, ₺22, 6½ hours) head to Konya daily. There are trains almost twice an hour between 6am and 11.15pm to Mersin (₺4) via Tarsus (₺3).

ⓘ Getting Around

A taxi from the airport into town costs ₺15, and from the otogar into town it's about ₺25. A taxi from the city centre to the Yüreği otogar will cost ₺7.50.

Around Adana

Inland from the Bay of İskenderun (İskenderun Körfezi) are the little visited remains of castles and settlements connected with the Armenian kingdom of Cilicia, including its capital, Sis at Kozan. Some, such as Anazarbus, date back to Roman times or earlier.

Kozan

This large market town and district seat 72km northeast of Adana via the D815 was once Sis, the capital of the kingdom of Cilicia and the linchpin keystone of a cavalcade of castles overlooking the expansive (and hard-to-defend) Çukurova plain. Towering above the plain is stunning **Kozan Castle** (Kozan Kalesi) FREE, built by Leo II (r 1187–1219), stretching some 900m along a narrow ridge.

SERVICES FROM ADANA'S OTOGAR

DESTINATION	FARE (₺)	DURATION (HR)	DISTANCE (KM)	FREQUENCY (PER DAY)
Adıyaman (for Nemrut Dağı)	30	6	335	7 buses
Alanya	45-55	10	440	up to 8 buses
Ankara	45-55	7	475	hourly
Antakya	20	3½	190	hourly
Antalya	55	11	565	2 or 3 buses
Diyarbakır	40	8	535	several
Gaziantep	20	3	220	several
İstanbul	60	14	920	hourly
Kayseri	30	6	355	several
Konya	40	6	335	several
Şanlıurfa	30	6	360	several
Silifke	20	2½	165	14 buses
Van	60	15	910	at least 1 bus

Along the kilometre-long road to the castle are the ruins of a church, locally called the *manastır* (monastery). From 1293 until 1921 this was the seat of the Katholikos (Patriarchate) of Sis, one of the two senior patriarchs of the Armenian Church.

Inside the castle is a mess of ruined buildings, overgrown with weeds, but continue upward to the many-towered keep on the right. On the left is a massive tower, which once held the royal apartments. In all there are 44 towers and lookouts and the remains of a *bedesten* (warehouse).

Kozan has some lovely old houses and makes a good day trip by minibus from Adana (₺8, one hour). An old house dating from 1890 is now a quirky inn called **Yaver'in Konağı** (Yaver's Mansion; ☑ 515 0999; www.yaverinkonagi.com; Manastır Sokak 5; s/d ₺60/90; ❀@☎), which features 13 rustic but comfortable rooms in the traditional three-storey house, and two newer outbuildings at the bottom of the ascent to the castle. There's a good restaurant, serving superb *lahmacun* baked in an open-air stone oven.

Anazarbus (Anavarza)

When the Romans moved into this area in 19 BC, they built this fortress city on top of a hill dominating the fertile plain and called it Caesarea ad Anazarbus. Later, when Cilicia was divided in two, Tarsus remained the capital of the west and Anazarbus the main seat in the east. It changed hands at least 10 times over the centuries, falling to the Persians, Arabs, Byzantines, the Hamdanid princes of Aleppo, the Crusaders, a local Armenian king, the Byzantines again, the Turks and the Mamluks. When that last group finally swept away the Armenian kingdom of Cilicia in 1375, the city was abandoned.

Some 5km after leaving the highway, you reach a T-junction and a large **gateway** set in the city walls; beyond this was the fortress city, now just fields strewn with ancient stones. Turn right and you'll soon reach the house of the *bekçi* (watchman); look for the blue gate. His own property contains **Roman sarcophagi** (one with the face of the 3rd-century Emperor Septimius Severus) and pools with glorious **mosaics** of Titus and dolphins, fish and sea birds. A guided walk (be generous) will showcase the stadium, theatre and baths. Make sure you see the dedication stone of the ruined

---

WORTH A TRIP

YILANKALE

Built in the mid-13th century, when this area was part of the Armenian kingdom of Cilicia, **Yılankale** (Snake Castle) `FREE` took its name from a serpent once entwined in the coat of arms above the entrance. From the car park there's a well-laid path for 100m then a rough trail. Reaching the castle's highest point requires a steep climb over the rocks, past gatehouse, cisterns and vaulted chambers. Standing high above the wheat fields, though, you'll feel on top of the world.

Yılankale is 38km east of Adana and just over 3km south of the D400 highway.

6th-century **Church of the Apostles** in the field, with a carved cross and the alpha and omega symbols, the very rare Roman vaulted stables south of the castle, and the main aqueduct with several arches still standing.

The hilltop **castle** looms above the ruins and village. If you are hiking up to the castle (up 400 steps), make sure to wear good walking shoes. The furthest portion of the extensive fortress remnants that trail across the ridge are extremely precarious and shouldn't be entered; at least one traveller has died in recent years trying to climb through to the castle's outermost keep.

⊙ Getting There & Away

If driving from Yılankale, return to the D400 highway and take the exit to the D817 (Kozan/ Kadirli) north for 27km to the village of Ayşehoca, where a road on the right is marked for Anavarza/Anazarbus, 5km to the east. If you're in a dolmuş or minibus you can get out here and hitch a ride. From Kozan follow the D817 south for 28km and turn left at Ayşehoca.

Karatepe-Aslantaş Open-Air Museum

Archaeology buffs should make a beeline for the **Karatepe-Aslantaş Open-Air Museum** (Karatepe-Aslantaş Açık Hava Müzesi; admission ₺5; ⊙10am-7pm) within the national park of the same name. The ruins date from the 8th century BC, when this was an important town for the late-Hittite kings of Cilicia, the greatest of whom was named Azitawatas. Today the remains on display consist of statuary, stone reliefs and inscribed tablets – some of which have played a critical role in helping archaeologists decipher the hieroglyphic Luwian language.

Karatepe's small but excellent **museum**, beside the entrance gate, displays items unearthed by excavations here and has plenty of information panels explaining the site's significance. There is also a scale model of the site, which helps put everything into perspective.

The first group of Karatepe's statuary is displayed at the **Palace Gate** with views across the forested hilltop overlooking Lake Ceyhan (Ceyhan Gölü), an artificial lake used for hydroelectric power and recreation. From here, traces of the 1km-long walls that defended the town are still evident. Under the protective shelter are statue representations of lions and sphinxes and rows of fine stone reliefs including one showing a relaxed feast at Azitawatas' court, complete with sacrificial bull, musicians and chariots.

The northeast **Lower Gate** is home to Karatepe's best stone carvings, including reliefs of a galley with oarsmen, warriors doing battle with lions, a woman suckling a child under a tree and the Hittite sun god. The sphinx statues guarding the reliefs are extremely well-preserved.

A sign at the site entrance states that visits are only allowed in guided groups, but nobody seems to pay any attention to that. Independent travellers will simply be accompanied around the site's circular path by a guard.

❶ Getting There & Away

It's easiest to reach Karatepe with your own transport. From Adana head east to Osmaniye (95km) and then take route 80-76 for 30km to the site. If you're driving from Kozan, follow route 817 for 18km to Çukurköprü and then head east for another 18km to Kadirli, from where a secondary road leads for 22km to the site.

Without your own wheels take a dolmuş to Osmaniye from either Adana (₺8, 1½ hours, 95km) or İskenderun (₺8.50, 1½ hours, 105km) and organise a taxi from there. From Osmaniye, a return trip to Karatepe with a stop at the ruined Hellenistic city of **Hierapolis-Castabala** will cost around ₺100.

İskenderun

📞 0326 / POP 188.643

İskenderun (Alexandretta in ancient times), a modern industrial city with a working port, is the gateway to the Hatay province.

Strategically located, the town has changed hands more than once. Alexander the Great took charge in 333 BC, and it was occupied by the British in 1918. The following year the French took charge until 1938. In 1939 the Republic of Hatay voted to join the nascent Turkish Republic.

With an attractive waterfront and an excellent museum, İskenderun is a handy stopover between Adana and Antakya. It's also a springboard to the beach town of Arsuz.

The main road along the waterfront is Atatürk Bulvarı. Şehir Pamir Caddesi is İskenderun's 'high street', running north from the waterfront and the massive monument to Atatürk and friends.

WORTH A TRIP

ARSUZ

For a little R&R between exploring the dusty remains of the Armenian Kingdom of Cilicia, head for Arsuz (Uluçınar), a delightful fishing town jutting out into the sea, 33km southwest of İskenderun. Relaxing highlights include swimming, gazing at the distant mountains, or trying your luck fishing in the nearby river.

The accommodation of choice is at the **Arsuz Otel** (📞 643 2444; www.arsuzotel.com; Atatürk Bulvarı 2; s/d from ₺100/150; 🛜), a rambling 'Olde Worlde' (though really only 50 years old) hotel fronting the sea, with its own beach and 50 spacious and airy rooms. Splash out and take something over-the-top like room 28, a two-bedroom suite called Cennet (Paradise), with a huge balcony. The lobby, with its old-fashioned tiles and piano, has a vague South of France ambience to it, and the restaurant features grilled *mercan* (Red Sea bream) and local Hatay meze such as *oruk* (spicy beef croquette) and *sürk* (soft cheese flavoured with dried red pepper).

Dolmuşes link Arsuz and İskenderun (₺4, 30 minutes) throughout the day.

◉ Sights

İskenderun Museum of the Sea MUSEUM
(İskenderun Deniz Müzesi; Atatürk Bulvarı; admission ₺6; ☺9am-5pm Tue-Sun) This excellent private museum fills a restored colonial mansion with an interesting showcase of Turkish naval history along with a room dedicated to covering the fascinating role of the Hatay region in Turkish history. There's plenty of English language translations, and highlights include a mini-armada of model ships and displays of Ottoman navy campaigns up to and including the Gallipoli campaign. The museum is around 600m west on Atatürk Bulvarı, to the right if you're facing inland.

🛏 Sleeping

Altındişler Otel HOTEL ₵
(☑617 1011; www.altindislerotel.com; Şehir Pamir Caddesi 11; s/d ₺50/90; ❊ 🛜) This good-value hotel has prosaic but spotless rooms brightened by colourful prints and friendly staff. Note that the nearby mosque kicks off the day with the call to prayer around 4.30am.

Hataylı Oteli BUSINESS HOTEL ₵₵
(☑614 1590; www.hataylioteli.com; Mete Aslan Bulvarı; s/d ₺100/150; ❊ 🛜) This three-star hotel with all mod cons is ideally located near the water at the eastern end of Atatürk Bulvarı. The excellent lobby bar has a mildly equine theme, and the 62 rooms are huge and handsome. The terrace restaurant offers a glorious breakfast vista across the Med.

İmrenay Hotel HOTEL ₵₵
(☑613 2117; www.imrenayhotel.com; Şehir Pamir Caddesi 5; s/d ₺75/120; ❊ 🛜) At first this hotel is a tad gloomy, with dark-brown parquet floors at reception, but the 33 smallish rooms have recently been renovated and are light and airy. The early-morning call to prayer of the nearby mosque is a factor to consider when staying here. Reception brings an open mind to negotiation.

🍴 Eating

Petek SWEETS ₵
(Mareşal Çakmak Caddesi 16; cakes ₺4-8) Stylish Petek has been serving very fine *künefe* (layers of kadayıf cemented together with sweet cheese, doused in syrup and served hot with a sprinkling of pistachio) since 1942; pair with espresso to offset the exceptional sweetness. Find it one block inland from Atatürk Bulvarı and three blocks west from Şehir Pamir Caddesi, to the right when facing inland.

Kücük Kervan TURKISH ₵₵
(19 Sokak 7/3; meze ₺2-4, mains ₺8-12) Compile a meze platter at this excellent local eatery, serving İskenderun residents for over 40 years. Kebaps include a mini-mountain of fresh herbs and salad. It's located off a sleepy square seemingly transplanted from Naples or Marseille. Find Kücük Kervan two blocks inland from Atatürk Bulvarı and two blocks west from Şehir Pamir Caddesi, to the right when facing inland.

Sirinyer SEAFOOD ₵₵₵
(☑641 3050; www.sirinyerrestaurant.com; Akdeniz Caddesi 113; mains ₺15-25) Reputed to have some of the Turkish Mediterranean's freshest fish, this upmarket destination restaurant with a lovely seafront terrace is around 5km southwest of the centre, on the old road to Arsuz. Beer, rakı and wine mix freely with the nautical atmosphere, and it's a perfect splurge-worthy opportunity if you haven't seen the coast much during your eastern Turkey travels.

❶ Getting There & Away

The otogar is about 2km southeast of the centre, just off the main highway through town and has fairly regular bus services to Adana (₺10, two hours, 135km) and Antakya (₺6, one hour, 58km). It's quicker though to use the dolmuşes, which all leave from various bus stands just east of the pedestrian overpass along the main highway (Prof Muammer Aksoy Caddesi). There are dolmuş services at least every half hour to Adana, Antakya, Arsuz (also known as Uluçınar; ₺4, 30 minutes, 33km) and Osmaniye (₺8.50, 1½ hours, 66km) from here.

Antakya (Hatay)

☑0326 / POP 217,072

Built on the site of ancient Antiocheia ad Orontem, Antakya, officially known as Hatay, is a prosperous and modern city near the Syrian border. Under the Romans, Antioch's important Christian community developed out of the already large Jewish population that was at one time led by St Paul. Today Antakya is home to a mixture of faiths – Sunni, Alevi and Orthodox Christian – and has a cosmopolitan and civilised air. Locals call their hometown Barış Şehri (City of Peace), and that's just what it is. In the ecumenical city of Antakya you'll find at least five different religions and sects represented within a couple of blocks of one another.

Antakya (Hatay)

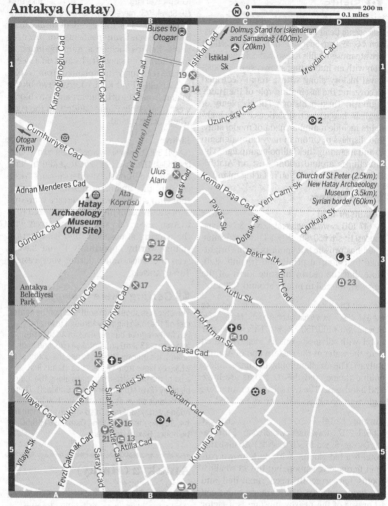

0 —————— 200 m
0 —————— 0.1 miles

Buses to Otogar

Dolmuş Stand for İskenderun and Samandağ (400m); (20km)

İstiklal Cad
İstiklal Sk
19
14

Meydan Cad

Karaoğlanoğlu Cad

Atatürk Cad

Kanatlı Cad

Asi (Orontes) River

Uzunçarşı Cad

2

Cumhuriyet Cad
Otogar (7km)

Ulus Alanı
18
İsa Sk
Kemal Paşa Cad
9

Yeni Cami Sk

Church of St Peter (2.5km); New Hatay Archaeology Museum (3.5km); Syrian border (60km)

Adnan Menderes Cad

1
Hatay Archaeology Museum (Old Site)

Ata Köprüsü

Payas Sk

Dolaşık Sk

Çankaya Sk

Gündüz Cad

12
22

Bekir Sıtkı

Kunt Cad

3
23

Antakya Belediyesi Park

İnönü Cad

Hürriyet Cad

17

Kutlu Sk

Prof Atman Sk
6
10

Gazipaşa Cad

7

15
5

11
Hükümet Cad

Şinasi Sk

Sevdam Cad

Kurtuluş Cad

8

Silahlı Kuvvetler Cad

16
4

Vilayet Cad

Vilayet Sk

Fevzi Çakmak Cad

Saray Cad

21
13
Atilla Cad

20

The Arab influence permeates local life, food and language; indeed, the city only became part of Turkey in 1939 after centuries conjoined in some form or another to Syria. Most visitors come to Antakya for its archaeology museum or as pilgrims to the Church of St Peter. Be sure to take time to stroll along the Orontes (Asi) River and through the bazaars and back lanes of a city we rate as an underrated jewel of the Turkish Mediterranean.

Sights

★ Hatay Archaeology Museum (Old Site)   MUSEUM

(Hatay Arkeoloji Müzesi; Gündüz Caddesi 1; admission ₺10; 9am-6.30pm Tue-Sun) This museum contains one of the world's finest collections of Roman and Byzantine mosaics, covering a period from the 1st century AD to the 5th century. Many were recovered almost intact from Tarsus or Harbiye (Daphne in ancient times), 9km to the south.

Antakya (Hatay)

EASTERN MEDITERRANEAN ANTAKYA (HATAY)

At the time of writing, the museum was in the final stages of its long-awaited move to purpose-built premises on the main road to Reyhanlı, about 1km past the Church of St Peter.

The new museum is set to provide a brilliant modern canvas to display the dazzling collection, much of which has never been put on show before due to a lack of room at the old museum.

Among the museum's highlight pieces are the full-body mosaic of **Oceanus & Thetis** (2nd century) and the **Buffet Mosaic** (3rd century), with its depictions of dishes of chicken, fish and eggs. **Thalassa & the Nude Fishermen** shows children riding whales and dolphins, while the fabulous 3rd-century mosaics of **Narcissus** and **Orpheus** depict stories from mythology. Other mosaics in the collection have quirkier subjects: three of the museum's most famous are the happy hunchback with an oversized phallus; the black fisherman; and the mysterious portrayal of a raven, a scorpion, a dog and a pitchfork attacking an 'evil eye'.

As well as the mosaics, the museum also showcases artefacts recovered from various mounds and tumuli (burial mounds) in the area, including a Hittite mound near Dörtyol, 16km north of İskenderun. Taking pride of place in the collection is the so-called **Antakya Sarcophagus** (Antakya Lahdı), an impossibly ornate tomb with an unfinished reclining figure on the lid.

Church of St Peter
CHURCH

(St Pierre Kilisesi; admission ₺10; ⊙9am-noon & 1-6pm) This early Christian church cut into the slopes of Mt Staurin (Mountain of the Cross) is thought to be the earliest place where the newly converted met and prayed secretly. Both Peter and Paul lived in Antioch for a few years and they almost certainly preached here. Tradition has it that this cave was the property of St Luke the Evangelist, who was born in Antioch, and that he donated it to the burgeoning Christian congregation.

When the First Crusaders took Antioch in 1098, they constructed the wall at the front and the narthex, the narrow vestibule along the west side of the church. To the right of the altar faint traces of an early fresco can be seen, and some of the simple mosaic floor survives. The water dripping in the corner is said to cure disease.

At the time of writing, the church was at the end (so we were assured) stages of a very drawn-out restoration, and should be open when you get here.

Just 2.5km northeast of town, the church is accessible on foot in about half an hour along Kurtuluş Caddesi.

Old Town
HISTORIC SITE

The squiggle of lanes between Kurtuluş Caddesi and Hurriyet Caddesi are an atmospheric huddle of Antakya's remaining old houses, with carved lintels, wooden overhangs and hidden courtyards within the compounds. Slightly north, around the 7th-century **Habibi Neccar Camii** (Kurtuluş Caddesi) you'll find more preserved examples of Antakya architecture. The priests at the Catholic church believe St Peter would have lived in this area between AD 42 and 48, as it was then the Jewish neighbourhood.

THE CHANGING FACE OF ANTAKYA

Long neglected and slipping into slouching dilapidation, Antakya's central old town district is undergoing something of a rebirth of late with the derelict old houses rimming the back lanes being slowly restored and converted into cafes, restaurants and bars. The biggest sign of Antakya's new-found confidence though is the new Hatay Archaeology Museum (p410), which is slated to be open by the time you read this. The entire mosaic collection from the old museum in the centre of Antakya is being moved to spangly new premises that will boast the world's largest mosaic display area. The new museum will be out of town on the road to Reyhanlı, about 1km past the Church of St Peter which, after a long restoration project, is also planned to reopen to visitors at around the same time.

Orthodox Church
CHURCH

(Hürriyet Caddesi 53; ☉divine liturgy 8.30am & 6pm) Most of the city's 1200-strong Christian population worships at the fine Orthodox church. Rebuilt after a devastating earthquake in 1900 with Russian assistance, the church is fronted by a lovely courtyard up some steps from the street, and contains some beautiful icons, an ancient stone lectern and valuable church plate.

Roman Catholic Church
CHURCH

(Prof Atman Sokak; ☉10am-noon & 3-5pm, mass 8.30am daily & 6pm Sun) The Italian-ministered Roman Catholic Church was built in 1852 and occupies two houses in the city's old quarter, with the chapel in the former living room of one house.

Sermaye Camii
MOSQUE

(Capital Mosque; Kurtuluş Caddesi 56) The Sermaye Camii has a wonderfully ornate şerefe (balcony) on its minaret (you'll see it on posters of Antakya). A little further south on Kurtuluş Caddesi, you'll see the facade of Antakya's old synagogue (Kurtuluş Caddesi 56).

Bazaar
BAZAAR

A sprawling market fills the backstreets north of Kemal Paşa Caddesi. The easier way to see it is to follow Uzunçarşı Caddesi, the main shopping street.

🛏 Sleeping

Antakya Catholic Church Guesthouse
GUESTHOUSE €

(☎215 6703; www.anadolukatolikkilisesi.org/antakya; Prof Atman Sokak; per person ₺30; ❄) A positively delightful place to stay (if you can get in), this guest house run by the local Catholic church has nine tidy double rooms wrapped around a leafy (and suitably reflective) courtyard. Guests are invited (though not required) to attend daily mass in the church opposite.

Hotel Saray
HOTEL €

(☎214 9001; Hürriyet Caddesi 3; s/d/tr ₺50/80/120; ☎) A bit rugged and definitely not what its name suggests, 'the Palace' has 35 good-sized, light-filled but very basic rooms, some even with tiny balconies and mountain views. Look forward to a super-central location near the bazaar and good restaurants. If you can get the staff to crack a smile you're doing better than us.

Antik Beyazıt Hotel
BOUTIQUE HOTEL €€

(☎216 2900; www.antikbeyazitoteli.com; Hükümet Caddesi 4; s/d/tr 110/150/200; ❄☎) Housed in a pretty French Levantine colonial house (1903), Antakya's first boutique hotel is looking a bit frayed, though it's as friendly as ever and the antique furnishings, oriental carpets and ornate chandelier in the lobby still evoke a more elegant past. The 27 rooms are fairly basic; the ones on the 1st floor have the most character.

Mozaik Otel
HOTEL €€

(☎215 5020; www.mozaikotel.com; İstiklal Caddesi 18; s/d ₺85/130; ❄☎) The rooms at this midrange choice are surprisingly peaceful despite its great central position near the bazaar. Service here lets the side down slightly, being rather haphazard, but the two dozen rooms are decorated with folksy bedspreads and mosaic reproductions, and the excellent Sultan Sofrası restaurant is just next door.

★ Liwan Hotel
BOUTIQUE HOTEL €€€

(☎215 7777; www.theliwanhotel.com; Silahlı Kuvvetler Caddesi 5; s/d ₺130/200; ❄☎) This 1920s eclectic-style building was once owned by the president of Syria, and contains two dozen tastefully furnished rooms across four floors. The restaurant is in an open courtyard (once an internal garden with ogee arches) that is covered in chillier months. For those who adore old-timer hotels, there is bucket loads of atmosphere to lap up here.

Due to the quirky nature of the room set-up, note that not all rooms have windows, so check when you book. The atmospheric stone bar features live music from 11pm to 2.30am most weekends, so if you're a light sleeper you may be more comfortable elsewhere.

✗ Eating & Drinking

There are many restaurants either on or just off Hürriyet Caddesi. Good places to relax over a drink and a snack are the tea gardens in the riverside Antakya Belediyesi Parkı, on the left bank of the Asi River.

★ **Çağlayan Restaurant** KEBAP €
(Hürriyet Caddesi 17; dürüm ₺8) Döner kebap places may be a dime a dozen on Hürriyet Caddesi, but Çağlayan's *dürüm* (döner meat sandwiches) are in a league of their own: spectacularly tasty and so packed full of goodies that one is a feast all by itself. Make sure to order the spicy sauce.

★ **Hatay Sultan Sofrası** ANATOLIAN €€
(www.sultansofrasi.com; İstiklal Caddesi 20a; mains ₺10-16) Antakya's premier spot for affordable tasty meals, this bustling place is just the ticket to dive into Hatay's fusion of Middle Eastern and Turkish cuisine. The articulate manager loves to guide diners through the menu, and will help you pick from the diverse array of meze and spicy local kebap options. Leave room to order *künefe* for dessert.

Antakya Evi ANATOLIAN €€
(Silahlı Kuvvetler Caddesi 3; mains ₺7-15) This restaurant is located in an old villa decorated with photos and antique furniture. There are loads of spicy Hatay specialities,

local meze (₺6 to ₺8) and robust grills. Look forward to live Turkish folk music on Friday and Saturday night.

Anadolu Restaurant TURKISH €€€
(Hürriyet Caddesi 30a; mains ₺15-35) Popular with families, the local glitterati and the expense-account brigade, Antakya's culinary hot spot serves a long list of fine meze on gold-coloured tablecloths in a splendid al-fresco garden, where the palm trees push through the roof. Meat dishes include Anad-olu kebap and the special *kağıt*, or 'paper' kebab.

Affan Kahvesi COFFEEHOUSE
(Kurtuluş Caddesi 42) This authentic coffee-house, in a building dating back to 1911, has Old-World ambience in spades. Pull up a wooden chair inside (don't forget to marvel at the gorgeous tiled floor), or head out back to the shady courtyard, to drink an Antakya coffee. They're famed for their *Haytah* des-sert: an electric-pink layered pudding of ice cream and rose water.

Nargiz Vitamin Bar JUICE BAR
(Hürriyet Caddesi 7; juice ₺3-8) Need a vitamin injection after some hard travelling on the road? This friendly place (blasting out a fine line in '80s rock classics) is where to go for freshly squeezed juices or an 'atom shake' (₺7), a regional speciality of banana, pista-chio, honey, apricot and yoghurt that will keep you full for half a day.

Barudi Bar BAR
(Silahlı Kuvvetler Caddesi) The Barudi Bar is one of Antakya's most happening hang-outs, with its hideaway inner courtyard, decent range of imported beers and impressive list of cocktails.

EASTERN MEDITERRANEAN ANTAKYA (HATAY)

GOOD EATING IN ANTAKYA

Arab – particularly Syrian – influences permeate Hatay's local cuisine. Handfuls of mint and wedges of lemon accompany kebaps, hummus is readily available, and the unique *kekik salatası* (fresh thyme salad made with spring onions and tomatoes) is a zingy treat.

Be sure to try the following: *muhammara*, a meze dip of crushed walnuts, red pepper and olive oil (also called *cevizli biber*); *oruk*, a torpedo-shaped croquette of spicy minced beef encased in bulgur wheat flour and fried – not unlike Lebanese *kibbeh*; and *sürk*, a tangy soft cheese flavoured with dried red pepper.

For dessert, you can't miss *künefe* (layers of kadayıf cemented together with sweet cheese, doused in syrup and served hot with a sprinkling of pistachio). Several places near the Ulu Cami make a mean one for around ₺5, including Hatay Künefe (Ulus Alanı, İnönü Caddesi; künefe ₺5).

🛍 Shopping

Doğal Defne Dünyası HOMEWARES
(Kurtuluş Caddesi) High-quality soaps from ancient Daphne (now Harbiye to the south), as well as gorgeous silk scarves woven and block-printed by hand are sold here.

ℹ Getting There & Around

AIR

Antakya's **Hatay Airport** (☑ 235 1300; www.hatay.dhmi.gov.tr) is 20km north of the city. Both **Pegasus Airlines** (www.flypgs.com) and **Turkish Airlines** (www.turkishairlines.com) have regular flights to/from İstanbul starting from about ₺70. A taxi from the airport is around ₺30, and **Havaş** (☑ 0555 985 1101; www.havas. net; per person ₺10) run a regular airport shuttle bus into central Antakya.

BUS

Antakya's intercity otogar is 7km to the northwest of the centre. A taxi to/from the centre will cost ₺15. Many of the big bus companies run free serviş (shuttle bus) transfers into central Antakya. Ask on arrival. Buses 5, 9, 16 and 17 (₺1.50) run from just outside the otogar to the western bank of the Asi (Orontes) River, central to hotels.

Direct buses go to Ankara, Antalya, İstanbul, İzmir, Kayseri and Konya, usually travelling via Adana (₺20, 3½ hours, 190km). There are also frequent services to Gaziantep (₺25, four hours, 262km) and Şanlıurfa (₺30, seven hours, 400km).

Minibuses and dolmuşes for İskenderun (₺6, one hour, 58km) and Samandağ (₺5, 40 minutes, 28km) leave near the Shell petrol station along Yavuz Sultan Selim Caddesi, at the top of İstiklal Caddesi.

Around Antakya

Monastery of St Simeon

The remains of the 6th-century **Monastery of St Simeon** (Aziz Simon Manastırı) **FREE** sit atop a mountain 18km southwest of Antakya on the road to Samandağ. The cross-shaped monastery contains the ruins of three churches. Fragments of mosaics can be seen in the floor of the first (north) church, but the central Church of the Holy Trinity, is the most beautiful. The south church is more austere.

The monastery is currently closed to visitors for a restoration project that is unlikely to finish until 2017.

The site's most interesting item is the octagonal base of a pillar, atop which Saint Simeon Stylite the Younger (521–597), imitating a 5th-century Syrian predecessor deemed the 'Elder', would preach against the iniquities of Antioch.

ℹ Getting There & Away

The turn-off is just past the village of Karaçay, reachable by a Samandağ dolmuş (₺3, 20 minutes) from Antakya. After travelling 5km through a wind turbine farm, the road branches, and the monastery remains are 2km up the right hand road. A taxi from Antakya and back with an hour at the site will cost about ₺100.

Çevlik

The scant ruins of **Seleuceia in Pieria** at Çevlik, Antioch's port in ancient times 5km northwest of Samandağ, are hardly impressive, but they include the **Titus & Vespasian Tunnel** (Titüs ve Vespasiyanüs Tüneli; admission ₺5; ⊙ 9am-7pm), an astonishing feat of Roman engineering. Seleucia lived under the constant threat of flooding from a stream that descended from the mountains and flowed through the town. To counter this threat, 1st-century Roman emperors Titus and Vespasian ordered that a 1.4km-long channel be cut through the solid rock to divert the stream.

From the *gişe* (ticket kiosk), follow the trail along an irrigation canal and past some shelters cut into the rock, finally arriving at a Roman arch spanning the gorge and the entrance to the tunnel. Bring a torch with you as the path can be slippery. At the far end of the channel an inscription provides a date for the work carried out by sailors and prisoners from Judea. About 100m from the tunnel are a dozen Roman **rock tombs** with reliefs, including the excellent **Beşikli Mağarası** (Cave with a Crib).

ℹ Getting There & Away

Dolmuşes run between Antakya and Samandağ (₺8, 40 minutes, 28km), where you can change for another bound for Çevlik (₺3, 15 minutes).

Ankara & Central Anatolia

Best Places to Eat

➡ Konak Konya Mutfağı (p459)
➡ Sema Hanımın Yeri (p453)
➡ Somatçi (p459)
➡ Balıkçıköy (p425)

Best Places to Stay

➡ Gordion Hotel (p423)
➡ Imren Lokum Konak (p432)
➡ Hich Hotel (p458)
➡ Deeps Hostel (p422)
➡ Derviş Otel (p458)

Why Go?

Somewhere between the cracks in the Hittite ruins, the fissures in the Phrygian burial mounds and the scratches in the Seljuk caravanserais, the mythical, mighty Turks raced across this highland desert steppe with big ideas and bigger swords. Nearby, Alexander the Great cut the Gordian knot, King Midas displayed his deft golden touch and Julius Caesar came, saw and conquered. It was also in this part of Turkey where the whirling dervishes first twizzled like human spinning tops and it was here that Atatürk forged his secular revolution along dusty Roman roads that all lead to Ankara, an underrated capital city and geopolitical centre. Further north through the nation's fruitbowl, in Safranbolu and Amasya, 'Ottomania' is still in full swing. Here wealthy weekenders sip çay with time-rich locals who preside over dark timber mansions. Central Anatolia is the meeting point between the fabled past and the prosperous present – a sojourn here will enlighten and enchant.

When to Go
Ankara

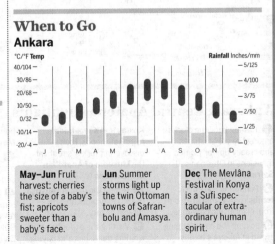

May–Jun Fruit harvest: cherries the size of a baby's fist; apricots sweeter than a baby's face.

Jun Summer storms light up the twin Ottoman towns of Safranbolu and Amasya.

Dec The Mevlâna Festival in Konya is a Sufi spectacular of extraordinary human spirit.

Ankara & Central Anatolia Highlights

1 Turning back the clocks among the cobblestones and creaky timber-framed mansions in Ottomanised **Safranbolu** (p429).

2 Pondering the **Pontic tombs** (p444) that poke out from cliffs in ancient Amasya.

3 Joining the cafe-hopping crowd in Ankara's trendy **Kızılay** and **Kavaklıdere** neighbourhoods, then discovering Turkey's roots at the **Museum of Anatolian Civilisations** (p417).

4 Hitting the hills at **Hattuşa** (p438) to explore ancient Turkish history.

5 Visiting the ex-lodge of the whirling dervishes and paying homage to Rumi at Konya's **Mevlâna Museum** (p454).

6 Marvelling at the blue-tiled magnificence of the *medreses* and mosques of **Sivas** (p451).

7 Exploring the rock-cut tombs and chapels and relishing the rural vibe of **Gökyurt** (p462): the little Cappadocia.

Ankara

📞 0312 / POP 4.7 MILLION

Turkey's 'other' city may not have any showy Ottoman palaces or regal facades, but Ankara thrums to a vivacious, youthful beat unmarred by the tug of history. Drawing comparisons with İstanbul is pointless – the flat, modest surroundings are hardly the stuff of national poetry – but the civic success of this dynamic and intellectual city is assured thanks to student panache and foreign-embassy intrigue.

The country's capital has made remarkable progress from a dusty Anatolian backwater to today's sophisticated arena for international affairs. Turkey's economic success is reflected in the booming restaurant scene around Kavaklıdere and the ripped-jean politik of Kızılay's sidewalk cafes, frequented by hip students, old-timers and businessmen alike. And while the dynamic street-life is enough of a reason to visit, Ankara also boasts two extraordinary monuments central to the Turkish story – the beautifully conceived Museum of Anatolian Civilisations and the Anıt Kabir, a colossal tribute to Atatürk, modern Turkey's founder.

History

Although Hittite remains dating back to before 1200 BC have been found in Ankara, the town really prospered as a Phrygian settlement on the north–south and east–west trade routes. Later it was taken by Alexander the Great, claimed by the Seleucids and finally occupied by the Galatians around 250 BC. Augustus Caesar annexed it to Rome as Ankyra.

The Byzantines held the town for centuries, with intermittent raids by the Persians and Arabs. When the Seljuk Turks came to Anatolia, they grabbed the city, but held it with difficulty. Later, the Ottoman sultan Yıldırım Beyazıt was captured near here by Central Asian conqueror Tamerlane and subsequently died in captivity. Spurned as a jinxed endeavour, the city slowly slumped into a backwater, prized for nothing but its goats.

That all changed when Atatürk chose Angora, as the city was known until 1930, to be his base in the struggle for independence. When he set up his provisional government here in 1920, the city was just a small, dusty settlement of some 30,000 people. After his victory in the War of Independence, Atatürk declared it the new Turkish capital, and set about developing it. From 1919 to 1927, Atatürk never set foot in İstanbul, preferring to work at making Ankara top dog.

◉ Sights

★ **Museum of Anatolian Civilisations**   MUSEUM

(Anadolu Medeniyetleri Müzesi; Map p420; 📞 0312-324 3160; Gözcü Sokak 2; admission ₺15; ⊙ 8.30am-6.15pm Apr-Oct, to 5pm Nov-Mar; Ⓜ Ulus) The superb Museum of Anatolian Civilisations is the perfect introduction to the complex weave of Turkey's ancient past, housing artefacts cherry-picked from just about every significant archaeological site in Anatolia.

The museum is housed in a 15th-century *bedesten* (covered market). The central room houses reliefs and statues, while the surrounding hall displays exhibits from Palaeolithic, Neolithic, Chalcolithic, Bronze Age, Assyrian, Hittite, Phrygian, Urartian and Lydian periods. Downstairs are classical Greek and Roman artefacts and a display on Ankara's history.

The exhibits are chronologically arranged in a spiral: start at the Palaeolithic and Neolithic displays in the room to the right of the entrance, then continue in an anticlockwise direction, visiting the central room last.

Items from one of the most important Neolithic sites in the world – Çatalhöyük, southeast of Konya – are displayed here. There's a mock-up of the inside of a dwelling typical of those uncovered at the site, one of the most famous mother goddess sculptures unearthed from the excavations and wall paintings of hunting scenes.

Also on show are many finds from the Assyrian trading colony Kültepe, one of the world's oldest and wealthiest bazaars. These include baked-clay tablets found at the site, which dates to the beginning of the 2nd millennium BC.

One of the striking Hittite figures of bulls and stags in the next room used to be the emblem of Ankara. The Hittites were known for their relief work, and some mighty slabs representing the best pieces found in the country, generally from around Hattuşa, are on display in the museum's central room.

Most of the finds from the Phrygian capital Gordion, including incredible inlaid wooden furniture, are on display in the museum's last rooms. The exhibits also include limestone blocks with

Ankara

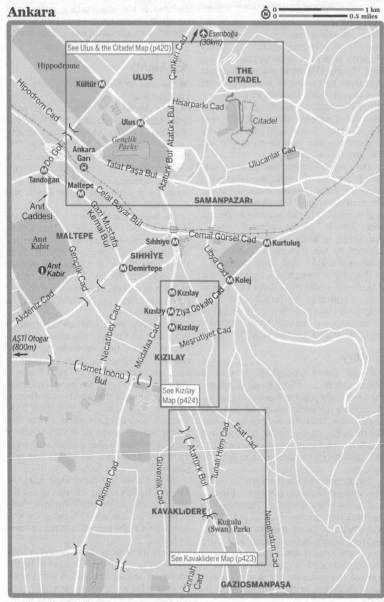

ANKARA & CENTRAL ANATOLIA ANKARA

still-indecipherable inscriptions resembling the Greek alphabet, and lion- and ram-head ritual vessels that show the high quality of Phrygian metalwork.

Urartian artefacts are also on display here. Spurred by rich metal deposits, the Urartians were Anatolia's foremost metalworkers, as the knives, horse-bits, votive plates and shields on display demonstrate.

There are also terracotta figures of gods in human form, some revealing their divine powers by growing scorpion tails, and neo-Hittite artefacts.

Downstairs, classical-period finds and regional history displays provide a local picture. Excavations have unearthed a Roman road near the Column of Julian, and Ankara has its own 'missing link', the 9.8-million-year-old Ankarapithecus (a 30kg, fruit-eating primate).

At the time of research all but one of the rooms in the museum was closed for major renovations. It will have all reopened by the time this book hits the shelves, but the order of displays may be different to that explained here. Renovations or not, get there early to avoid the flood of tour groups and school parties.

Citadel
NEIGHBOURHOOD

(Ankara Kalesi; Map p420; Ⓜ Ulus) The imposing *hisar* is the most interesting part of Ankara to poke about in. This well-preserved quarter of thick walls and intriguing winding streets took its present shape in the 9th century AD, when the Byzantine emperor Michael II constructed the outer ramparts. The inner walls date from the 7th century.

After you've entered **Parmak Kapısı** (Finger Gate; Map p420), the main gate, and passed through a gate to your left, you'll see **Alaettin Camii** (Map p420; Alitaş Sokak) on the left. The citadel mosque dates from the 12th century, but has been extensively rebuilt. To your right a steep road leads to a flight of stairs that leads to the **Şark Kulesi** (Eastern Tower; Map p420), with panoramic city views. Although it's much harder to find, a tower to the north, **Ak Kale** (White Fort), also offers fine views.

Inside the citadel local people still live as they would in a traditional Turkish village, and you'll see women beating and sorting skeins of wool. Broken column drums, bits of marble statuary and inscribed lintels are incorporated into the walls.

At the time of research a major renovation project was underway to tart the citadel up. The project will take a few years to complete, but already there were mumblings from some quarters about how the newly gentrified citadel was losing the ramshackle character that gave it its charm (a certain dirty, run-down charm, but charm all the same). Others, though, say much the opposite. You decide for yourself.

Anıt Kabir
MONUMENT

(Atatürk Mausoleum & Museum; Map p418; www.anitkabir.org; Gençlik Caddesi; audioguide ₺10; ⊙9am-5pm May-Oct, to 4pm Nov-Apr; Ⓜ Tandoğan) **FREE** The monumental mausoleum of Mustafa Kemal Atatürk (1881–1938), the founder of modern Turkey, sits high above the city with its abundance of marble and air of veneration. The tomb itself actually makes up only a small part of this fascinating complex, which consists of museums and a ceremonial courtyard. For many Turks a visit is virtually a pilgrimage, and it's not unusual to see people visibly moved. Allow at least two hours in order to visit the whole site.

The main entrance to the complex is via the **Lion Road**, a 262m walkway lined with 24 lion statues – Hittite symbols of power used to represent the strength of the Turkish nation. The path leads to a massive courtyard, framed by colonnaded walkways, with steps leading up to the huge tomb on the left.

To the right of the tomb, the extensive **museum** displays Atatürk memorabilia, personal effects, gifts from famous admirers, and recreations of his childhood home and school. Just as revealing as all the rich artefacts are his simple rowing machine and huge multilingual library, which includes tomes he wrote.

Downstairs, extensive exhibits about the War of Independence and the formation of the republic move from battlefield murals with sound effects to overdetailed explanations of post-1923 reforms. At the end, a gift shop sells Atatürk items of all shapes and sizes.

As you approach the tomb itself, look left and right at the gilded inscriptions, which are quotations from Atatürk's speech celebrating the republic's 10th anniversary in 1932. Remove your hat as you enter, and bend your neck to view the ceiling of the lofty hall, lined in marble and sparingly decorated with 15th- and 16th-century Ottoman mosaics. At the northern end stands an immense marble **cenotaph**, cut from a single piece of stone weighing 40 tonnes. The actual tomb is in a chamber beneath it.

The memorial straddles a hill in a park about 2km west of Kızılay and 1.2km south of Tandoğan, the closest Ankaray-line metro station to the entrance. A free shuttle regularly zips up and down the hill from the entrance; alternatively, it's a pleasant walk

Ulus & the Citadel

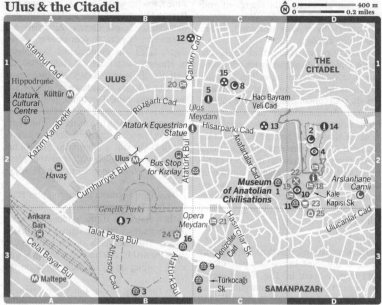

Ulus & the Citadel

◎ Top Sights
1 Museum of Anatolian Civilisations C2

◎ Sights
2 Alaettin Camii D2
3 Cer Modern... B3
4 Citadel D2
5 Column of Julian C1
6 Ethnography Museum............................ C3
7 Gençlik Parkı... B3
8 Hacı Bayram Camii C1
9 Painting and Sculpture Museum C3
10 Parmak Kapısı D2
11 Rahmi M Koç Industrial Museum D2
12 Roman Baths B1
13 Roman Theatre C2
14 Şark Kulesi D2
15 Temple of Augustus and Rome C1
16 Vakıf Eserleri Müzesi B3

◎ Sleeping
17 And Butik Hotel.. D2
18 Angora House Hotel D2
19 Divan Çukurhan D2
20 Hotel Taç B1
21 Otel Mithat... C3

◎ Eating
Çengelhan .... (see 11)
Kınacızade Konağı .... (see 18)
22 Zenger Paşa Konağı D2

◎ Drinking & Nightlife
23 Kirit Cafe D2

◎ Entertainment
24 Ankara State Opera House B3

◎ Shopping
25 Hisar Area D3

to the mausoleum (about 15 minutes). Note that security checks, including a bag scan, are carried out on entry.

Gençlik Parkı
PARK
(Youth Park; Map p420; Atatürk Bulvarı) The biggest afternoon out for Ankara families is the Gençlik Parkı, in the heart of the city. It's a classic Middle Eastern–style park with several pleasant *çay bahçesi* (tea gardens; single women should go for those with the word *aile* (family) in their name), lots of fountains lit in garish colours, and a few plastic dinosaurs (obviously). The Luna Park funfair provides amusement for children and, thanks to a few terrifying-looking rides, cheap thrills for teenagers.

Rahmi M Koç Industrial Museum   MUSEUM
(Map p420; ☑ 0312-309 6800; www.rmk-museum. org.tr; Depo Sokak 1; adult/child ₺6/3; ⊘ 10am-5pm Tue-Fri, to 6pm Sat & Sun; Ⓜ Ulus) The surprisingly absorbing Rahmi M Koç Industrial Museum, which is located inside the beautifully restored Çengelhan building (which is also home to a posh hotel and restaurant), has three floors covering subjects as diverse as transport, science, music, computing, Atatürk and carpets; some displays have interactive features.

Anyone born before about 1985 should be prepared for the somewhat depressing shock of seeing childhood memories such as ZX Spectrum computers, cassette tapes and things you could have sworn blind were only invented a year or so back being deemed old enough to be worthy of museum status.

Cer Modern   GALLERY
(Map p420; ☑ 0312-310 0000; www.cermodern. org; Altınsoy Caddesi 3; admission ₺12; ⊘ 10am-6pm Tue-Sun; Ⓜ Ulus) Located in an old train depot, this huge artists' park and gallery exhibits modern and challenging art from across Europe, plus there's an excellent cafe and shop. Cultural events are also staged here. The area around the Cer Modern is currently undergoing a significant redevelopment that will eventually give rise to the birth of a massive new cultural centre.

Vakıf Eserleri Müzesi   MUSEUM
(Ankara Museum of Religious Foundation Works; Map p420; Atatürk Bulvarı; ⊘ 9am-5pm Tue-Sun; Ⓜ Ulus) FREE The tradition of carpets being gifted to mosques has helped preserve many of Turkey's finest specimens. This extensive collection – which once graced the floors of mosques throughout the country – was put on display to the public in 2007. A must for anyone interested in Turkish textiles, the exhibits also include a fascinating Ottoman manuscript collection, tile-work, metalwork and intricately carved wood panels.

All of it is superbly displayed with detailed information panels in English (labelling for individual items though is generally only in Turkish) explaining the history of Turkish crafts.

Ethnography Museum   MUSEUM
(Etnografya Müzesi; Map p420; Türkocağı Sokak, Samanpazarı; admission ₺10; ⊘ 8.30am-7pm Tue-Sun; Ⓜ Ulus) The Ethnography Museum is housed inside a white marble post-Ottoman building (1927) that served as Atatürk's mausoleum until 1953.

Past the equestrian statue out the front, the mausoleum is preserved in the entrance hall. Around the walls are photographs of Atatürk's funeral. The collection is superb, with displays covering henna ceremonies, Anatolian jewellery, rug-making, Seljuk ceramics, early-15th-century doors, and (opposite the anxious-looking mannequins in the circumcision display) coffee.

Painting and Sculpture Museum   MUSEUM
(Resim ve Heykel Müzesi; Map p420; Türkocağı Sokak, Samanpazarı; ⊘ 9am-noon & 1-5pm; Ⓜ Ulus) FREE The Painting and Sculpture Museum showcases the cream of Turkish artists. Ranging from angular war scenes to society portraits, the pieces demonstrate that 19th- and 20th-century artistic developments in Turkey paralleled those in Europe, with increasingly abstract form.

Hacı Bayram Camii   MOSQUE
(Map p420; Hacı Bayram Veli Caddesi; Ⓜ Ulus) Ankara's most revered mosque is Hacı Bayram Camii. Hacı Bayram Veli was a Muslim 'saint' who founded the Bayramiye dervish order around 1400. Ankara was the order's centre and Hacı Bayram Veli is still revered by pious Muslims. The mosque was built in the 15th century, with tiling added in the 18th century. Surrounding shops sell religious paraphernalia (including wooden toothbrushes as used, supposedly, by the Prophet Mohammed).

Kocatepe Camii   MOSQUE
(Map p424; Bankacı Sokak; Ⓜ Kızılay) The huge outline of Kocatepe Camii is the symbol of Ankara. It is one of the world's largest mosques, but it is also very new (it was built between 1967 and 1987). In the basement of the mosque is a supermarket, which says much about the priorities of modern Turkey!

Roman Ruins
The Ulus area of the city has a handful of Roman ruins that can be easily seen in a half-day.

Roman Baths   RUIN
(Roma Hamaları; Map p420; Çankırı Caddesi; admission ₺5; ⊘ 8.30am-5pm; Ⓜ Ulus) At the sprawling 3rd-century Roman Baths ruins, the layout is still clearly visible; look for the standard Roman *apoditerium* (dressing room), *frigidarium* (cold room), *tepidarium* (warm room) and *caldarium* (hot room). A Byzantine tomb and Phrygian remains have also been found here.

Temple of Augustus and Rome RUIN

(Map p420; Hacı Bayram Veli Caddesi; admission ₺5; ⊙8.30am-5pm Tue-Sun; ⓂUlus) Except for a couple of imposing, inscribed walls, not much remains of this temple (AD 25) built to honour the Roman Emperor Augustus.

Column of Julian MONUMENT

(Jülyanus Sütunu; Map p420; Çam Sokak; ⓂUlus) Erected in honour of Roman Emperor Julian the Apostate's visit to Ankara, the Column of Julian sits proudly in a square ringed by government buildings, it is usually topped by a stork's nest.

Roman Theatre RUIN

(Map p420; Hisarparkı Caddesi; ⓂUlus) Along Hisarparkı Caddesi, you can see the remains of a Roman theatre from around 200 to 100 BC.

★☆ Festivals & Events

Ankara Music Festival MUSIC

(www.ankarafestival.com) Three weeks of classical performances in April.

Ankara Film Festival FILM

(www.filmfestankara.org.tr/en) The city's film festival normally kicks off in March, but in 2014 it was moved to mid-June. The festival hosts a selection of both local and foreign cinema.

Büyük Ankara Festivali MUSIC, FAMILY

FREE This week-long event in July exists somewhere between summer concert series and carnival.

🛏 Sleeping

🛏 Ulus & the Citadel

Otel Mithat HOTEL €€

(Map p420; ☑0312-311 5410; www.otelmithat. com.tr; Tavus Sokak 2; s/d €30/43; ❄🐾; ⓂUlus) With groovy carpeting and sleek neutral bed linen, the Mithat's rooms are fresh and modern. The teensy bathrooms do let the side down somewhat, but this is a minor complaint about what is, overall, an excellent budget choice. Non-smokers will be pleased that unlike most Ankara hotels in this price range, the Mithat takes their no-smoking policy seriously.

Angora House Hotel HISTORIC HOTEL €€€

(Map p420; ☑0312-309 8380; www.angorahouse. com.tr; Kale Kapısı Sokak 16; s/d €70/100; 🐾; ⓂUlus) Be utterly charmed by this restored

Ottoman house, which oozes subtle elegance at every turn. The six spacious rooms are infused with loads of old-world atmosphere, featuring dark wood accents, creamy 19th-century design textiles and colourful Turkish carpets, while the walled courtyard garden is the perfect retreat from the citadel streets. Delightfully helpful staff add to the appeal.

And Butik Hotel HISTORIC HOTEL €€

(Map p420; ☑310 2303, 0312-310 2304; www.and-butikhotel.com; İstek Sokak 2; s/d from ₺100/125; 🐾; ⓂUlus) Right in the heart of the Citadel, this place, which is so cheap you might wonder if you heard the price right, is housed inside a pleasingly renovated Ottoman-era building. The small rooms are crammed with character, there's a warm welcome from your hosts, and a little courtyard garden. The only small niggle is that wi-fi doesn't generally reach the rooms.

Hotel Taç HOTEL €€

(Map p420; ☑0312-324 3195; Çankırı Caddesi 35; s/d ₺70/100; ❄🐾; ⓂUlus) It may not look like much from outside, but the Taç delivers a fair deal. Cute floral rugs and nice art inject a bit of personality into the rooms, which all come with extras such as a kettle, hair dryer and flat-screen TV. Light sleepers should avoid the front rooms if possible as they can be insanely noisy.

Divan Çukurhan HISTORIC HOTEL €€€

(Map p420; ☑0312-306 6400; www.divan.com. tr; Depo Sokak 3, Ankara Kalesi; s/d €130/150, ste €180-400; ❄🐾; ⓂUlus) This fabulous up-market hotel offers guests a chance to soak up the historic ambience of staying in the 16th-century Çukurhan caravanserai. Set around a dramatic glass-ceilinged interior courtyard, each individually themed room blends ornate decadence with sassy contemporary style. Ankara's best bet for those who want to be dazzled by oodles of sumptuous luxury and sleek service.

Booking online often results in healthy discounts.

🛏 Kızılay

★Deeps Hostel HOSTEL €

(Map p424; ☑0312-213 6338; www.deepshostelankara.com; Ataç Sokak 46; dm/s/d without breakfast ₺30/50/75; 🐾; ⓂKızılay) At Ankara's best budget choice, friendly Şeyda, the owner of Deeps, has created a colourful, light-filled hostel with spacious dorms and rooms, and squeaky-clean, modern shared bathrooms. It's all topped off by masses of advice and information, a fully equipped kitchen and a cute communal area downstairs where you can swap your Turkish travel tales.

Hotel Eyüboğlu
BUSINESS HOTEL **€€€**

(Map p424; 0312-417 6400; www.eyubogluhotel. com; Karanfıl Sokak 73; r ₺580; ❄ 🛜; Ⓜ Kızılay) Although lacking in character, this very smart business-class hotel has tinkly piano music in the lobby, staff that go out of their way to help, and no-nonsense, neutral toned rooms boasting beds so comfy you'll happily ignore your alarm clock. There's a wealth of nearby places to eat.

🛏 Kavaklıdere

Hotel Aldino
HOTEL **€€**

(Map p423; 0312-468 6510; www.hotelaldino. com; Bülten Sokak 22; s/d €60/80; 🛜) Good-sized rooms and professional service make this hotel a bit of a deal. Everything is spotlessly clean, the staff speak English and you can't beat the location. Just look past their fondness for granny-ish dried flower arrangements and floral bed linen.

★ Gordion Hotel
HISTORIC HOTEL **€€€**

(Map p423; 0312-427 8080; www.gordionhotel. com; Büklüm Sokak 59; s/d ₺170/200; ❄🛜🏊) This independent hotel in the middle of the Kavaklıdere neighbourhood, is a fabulously cultured inner-city residence with grand and stately rooms, a basement swimming pool, Vakko textiles in the lobby, centuries-old art engravings, a conservatory restaurant, beautiful beds and an extensive DVD library. At current rates it's an out and out bargain.

✖ Eating

✖ Ulus & the Citadel

Most Ulus options are basic. The southern end of Anafartalar Caddesi is the perfect hunting ground for cheap and cheerful *kebapçis* (kebap eateries).

By contrast there are a number of more upmarket, tourist-oriented places in and around the Citadel where reasonably good food is almost invariably combined with a pleasant atmosphere.

Zenger Paşa Konağı
ANATOLIAN **€€**

(Map p420; 0312-311 7070; www.zengerpasa. com; Doyran Sokak 13; mains ₺15-25; Ⓜ Ulus)

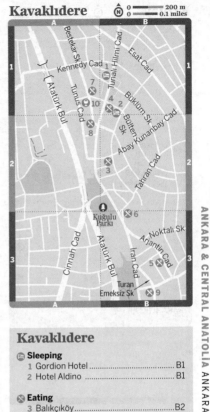

Kavaklıdere

Crammed with Ottoman ephemera, the Zenger Paşa at first looks like a deserted ethnographic museum, but climb up the rickety stairs and you'll find views of the city that are worth a visit alone. Wealthy locals love the pide (Turkish-style pizza), meze and grills, still cooked in the original Ottoman oven.

Bands playing traditional music often provide a weekend accompaniment, and it's not all that unusual for spontaneous dancing to break out.

Kızılay

Kınacızade Konağı TURKISH €€
(Map p420; ☎0312-324 5714; www.kinacizade-konagi.com; Kale Kapısı Sokak 28; mains ₺6-23; ⊙9am-9pm Mon-Sat; Ⓜ Ulus) This Ottoman house serves up a range of typical Turkish kebap dishes alongside cheaper pide and delicious *gözleme* (stuffed savoury crepes). The shady courtyard, enclosed by picturesque timber-framed facades in various states of higgledy-piggledy disrepair, is a delightful place to while away time over a lazy lunch.

Çengelhan MODERN TURKISH €€€
(Map p420; ☎0312-309 6800; Depo Sokak 1; mains ₺25-50; ⊙Tue-Sun; Ⓜ Ulus) Inside an old caravanserai, the restaurant of the Rahmi M Koç Industrial Museum offers sleek dining in novel surroundings, with tables nestled between museum displays of vintage cars, aeroplanes aiming for the heavens and Ottoman paraphernalia. A top choice to sample traditional Turkish dishes with a contemporary twist. Reservations are essential.

✗ Kızılay

It's all about street-side eating and cafe-hopping in the trendy hang-outs here. You'll find everything from stalls serving döner kebap (spit-roasted lamb slices) and corn on the cob to hip bistros blasting pop tunes, their tables graced by cooler-than-thou student types. Much of the food on offer here though is a fairly identical mix of snacky or fast-food type meals and finding a decent restaurant can be harder than it might first appear.

Çomlek Ev Yemekleri TURKISH €
(Map p424; Konur Sokak; set menu ₺7; ⊙noon-9pm Mon-Sat; Ⓜ Kızılay) This unpretentious place is crammed with students who slurp down simple but filling daily lunch specials. Choose the *güveç* (meat and vegetable stews cooked in a terracotta pot) for a tasty, wholesome meal.

Le Man Kültür INTERNATIONAL €
(Map p424; ☎0312-310 8617; www.lmk.com.tr; Konur Sokak 8; mains ₺8-20; Ⓜ Kızılay) Named after a cult Turkish comic strip – and decorated accordingly – this is still the pre-party pick for a substantial feed and for spotting beautiful young educated things. The food is generally of the meatballs, burgers and grilled meats variety. Drinks are reasonably priced and the speakers crank everything from indie-electro to Türk pop.

Masabaşı Kebapçisi KEBAP €€
(Map p424; ☎0312-417 0781; www.masabasi.com.tr; Mithat Pasa Caddesi; ₺18-25; ⊙11am-11pm;

Ⓜ Kizilay) At seemingly any time of the day there's a mass of people here tucking into an impressive selection of different kebaps and other grilled meats and many people will tell you it's the best such place in the neighbourhood to eat.

✖ Kavaklıdere

Elizinn
DESSERTS €

(Map p423; www.elizinn.com.tr; Tunali Hilmi Caddesi 81; cakes ₺7-9; ⊙ 7.30am-8pm) You like sweet and naughty things? Then you, alongside zillions of locals who pour in here every afternoon, will love Elizinn and its irresistible range of pastries, cakes and other sugar-coated treats.

Mangal
TURKISH €€

(Map p423; ☑ 0312-466 2460; www.mangalkebap.com; Bestekar Sokak; mains ₺15-25; ⊙ 9am-10pm) For over twenty years this neighbourhood star has been churning out perfectly prepared pide and every kind of kebap or grilled meat you can think of as well as many you can't. It's fairly smart, which makes the low prices an unexpected surprise.

★ Balıkçıköy
SEAFOOD €€€

(Map p423; ☑ 0312-466 0450; Abay Kunanbay Caddesi 4/1; mains ₺18-25; ⊙ noon-midnight) This is the third instalment of Ankara's favourite seafood restaurant. Take the waiter's recommendations for the cold meze, then take your pick of the fried and grilled fish – the fried whitebait (₺13) is a favourite – all perfectly cooked and quick to the table. Book ahead to avoid disappointment.

Marmaris Balıkçisi
SEAFOOD €€€

(Map p423; ☑ 0312-427 2212; Bestekar Sokak 88/14A; mains ₺17-30; ⊙ 11am-11pm) At this well-regarded, and very fairly priced, seafood restaurant, with its suitably blue and white oceanic theme, you can pluck your creature of the deep off its bed of ice and have it quickly grilled or fried up and doused in olive oil and lemon ready for your taste buds to enjoy.

Although the menu is very long, they normally only have a fraction of what is listed, thus indicating that everything is freshly caught and in season.

Mezzaluna
ITALIAN €€€

(Map p423; ☑ 0312-467 5818; Turan Emeksiz Sokak 1; mains ₺22-40; ⊙ noon-11pm) The capital's classiest Italian restaurant is busy busy busy, with chefs crafting some of Ankara's best pasta and slapping pizzas on the counter for apron-clad waiters to deliver. The choices include antipasti, risotto, wood-fired pizzas, and seafood (a better bet than the steaks).

Günaydın
STEAKHOUSE €€€

(Map p423; ☑ 0312 466 7666; www.gunaydin.com; Arjantin Caddesi 6; mains ₺20-30; ⊙ midday-3pm & 6-10pm) Ankara's favourite steakhouse seriously knows its meat. This carnivore heaven serves up T-bones, porterhouse and beef ribs with snappy, professional service. And there's kebaps – of course!

La Gioia
INTERNATIONAL €€€

(Map p423; www.lagioia.com.tr; Tahran Caddesi 2; mains ₺15-27; ⊙ 10am-midnight) This ever-so swanky cafe-bistro at the heart of the embassy district looks seriously Parisian – as do much of the clientele. If you're in need of a break from the endless kebaps of central Turkey then you'll enjoy the exciting salads here: black rice salad, grilled bream salad and goats cheese salad are just some of those on offer. The main dining room is a giant conservatory-style affair, but when it's fine you can also eat at the outdoor tables.

🍸 Drinking & Nightlife

Kızılay is Ankara's cafe central, with terraces lining virtually every inch of space south of Ziya Gökalp Caddesi. The area is also ripe for a night out with Ankara's student population – try Bayındır Sokak, between Sakarya and Tuna Caddesis. The tall, thin buildings pack in up to five floors of bars, cafes and gazinos (nightclubs). Many of the clubs offer live Turkish pop music, and women travellers should feel OK in most of them. It almost goes without saying that names change fast and the hot club of the moment changes even faster. And remember, the bars and cafes around here are filled with the young and gorgeous – so come suitably attired to mix with the crowd.

Aylak Madam
CAFE

(Map p424; ☑ 0312-419 7412; Karanfil Sokak 2; ⊙ 10am-late; Ⓜ Kızılay) A super-cool French bistro/cafe with a mean weekend brunch (from 10am to 2.30pm), plus sandwiches, head-kicking cappuccinos, and a jazz-fusion soundtrack. Postgraduates and writers alike hang out here, hunched over their laptops or with their pens tapping against half-finished manuscripts.

ANGORA WOOL

Can you tell the difference between a goat and a rabbit? It's not as easy as you think – or at least not if all you have to go on is the wool. One of the most popular misconceptions about Ankara's famous angora wool is that it comes from angora goats, a hardy breed believed to be descended from wild Himalayan goats. Not so: the soft, fluffy wool produced from these goats is correctly known as mohair. Angora wool in the strictest sense comes from angora rabbits, also local but much cuter and whose fur, weight for weight, was once worth as much as gold.

Kirit Cafe
CAFE

(Map p420; Koyunpazarı Sokak; M Ulus) With a fun felt shop on the ground floor and quirky local art gracing the walls of the cafe upstairs, this place is a lovely find. They brew a decent coffee if you just want a drink, but their burgers, pasta and cheesecake hit the spot as well.

Hayyami
WINE BAR

(Map p423; ☑ 0312-466 1052; Bestekar Sokak 82B; ☺ noon-late) Named after the renowned Sufi philosopher, this thriving wine house/restaurant attracts a hobnobbing crowd to its lowered courtyard. It boasts a long and diverse wine selection, which you can savour with a tapas-like array of dishes including *salçalı sosis* (barbecued sausage) and devilishly large cheese platters (mains ₺12 to ₺25).

Bibar
BAR

(Map p424; Inkılap Sokak 19; M Kızılay) Bibar attracts everyone from pale-faced student goths, alternative rockers and people who just want to boogie. The music can be as mixed as the crowd on the right night. There are dozens of other rowdy, beer swilling bars with big outdoor terraces on the same road.

Café des Cafés
CAFE

(Map p423; ☑ 0312-428 0176; Tunalı Hilmi Caddesi 83; ☺ 8.30am-11pm) Quirky vintage styling and comfy sofas make Café des Cafés a popular Kavaklıdere haunt. Pull up a chair on the tiny streetside terrace and sharpen up your people-watching skills. The orange and cinnamon hot chocolate is bliss in a glass.

☆ Entertainment

Ankara State Opera House
PERFORMING ARTS

(Opera Sahnesi; Map p420; ☑ 0312-324 6801; www.dobgm.gov.tr; Atatürk Bulvarı 20; M Ulus) This venue plays host to all the large productions staged by the Ankara State Opera and Ballet. The season generally runs from September to June and it's worthwhile trying to catch a performance if you're in town at that time.

🔒 Shopping

To see what fashionable Turkey spends its money on, head south along Tunalı Hilmi Caddesi in Kavaklıdere where lots of local stores stand alongside more familiar names such as Mango and British department store Marks & Spencer. There are several massive malls outside of the central city including the AnkaMall, easily accessed by alighting at Akköprü metro station.

Hisar Area
HANDICRAFTS

(Map p420; M Ulus) The alleyways southeast of the Parmak Kapısı entrance to the citadel were traditionally the centre for trading in angora wool. Walk downhill from the dried-fruit stalls in front of the gate, and you'll come across copper-beaters, as well as plenty of carpet and antique stores, small galleries and craft shops that are good for a rummage.

Dost Kitabevi
BOOKS

(Map p424; ☑ 0312-418 8327; Karanfil Sokak, Kızılay; M Kızılay) Head downstairs at this buzzing book store to browse their reasonable (and very decently priced) selection of English-language novels.

ⓘ Information

MEDICAL SERVICES

Pharmacists take it in turns to open around the clock; look out for the *nobetçi* (open 24 hours) sign.

Bayındır Hospital (☑ 0312-428 0808; www. bayindirhastanesi.com.tr; Atatürk Bulvarı 201, Çankaya) An up-to-date private hospital.

MONEY

There are lots of banks with ATMs in Ulus, Kızılay and Kavaklıdere. To change money, *döviz bürosu* (currency-exchange offices) generally offer the best rates, often without commission.

POST & TELEPHONE

The **Main Post Office** (Map p420; Atatürk Bulvarı) is in Ulus. There are also PTT branches in Kızılay. All have phone booths nearby.

TOURIST INFORMATION

Tourist Office (Map p420; ☑ 0312-310 3044; Kale Kapısı Sokak; ⊙10am-5pm; Ⓜ Ulus) Ankara's main tourist office is inside the Citadel. There are also (usually unmanned) branches at the AŞTİ otogar and at the train station.

❶ Getting There & Away

AIR

Although domestic and international budget carriers serve Ankara's **Esenboğa airport** (☑ 0312-590 4000; www.esenbogaairport.com; Özal Bulvarı, Esenboğa), İstanbul's airports offer more choice. Even flying domestically, it may save you time and money to travel via İstanbul.

Lufthansa, Pegasus Airlines and Qatar Airways offer international connections while every Turkish budget airline links Ankara with an array of different Turkish cities.

BUS

Every Turkish city or town of any size has direct buses to Ankara. The gigantic otogar (bus station), also referred to as **AŞTİ** (Ankara Şehirlerarası Terminali İşletmesi; Mevlâna Bulvarı), is at the western end of the Ankaray underground train line, 4.5km west of Kızılay.

Buses to/from İstanbul (₺19 to ₺45, six hours), Antalya (₺20 to ₺50, eight hours), İzmir (₺24 to ₺55, eight hours) and other major destinations leave numerous times daily. Buses to Cappadocia (₺35, five hours) often terminate in Nevşehir. Be sure your ticket states your *final* destination (eg Göreme, Ürgüp).

Because there are so many buses to many parts of the country, you can often turn up, buy a ticket and be on your way in less than an hour. Don't try this during public holidays, though.

The *emanet* (left-luggage room) on the lower level charges ₺4 per item stored; you'll need to show your passport.

TRAIN

A new high-speed train line linking **Ankara Train Station** (Ankara Garı; Talat Paşa Bulvarı) with İstanbul Pendik (a suburb 25km east of İstanbul) started in 2014. There are around six trains a day and the journey takes just 3½ hours. Economy class tickets cost ₺75. Get to the station at least 15 minutes before departure as there are a number of security checks to pass through.

High-speed train services run to Eskişehir (economy/business class ₺25/35, 1½ hours, 10 daily) and Konya (economy/business class ₺27.50/35, two hours, eight daily) and are comfortable, fast and efficient.

The Trans-Asia train to Iran leaves at 10.25am every Wednesday, pulling into Tehran Station on Friday at 8.20pm.

❶ Getting Around

TO/FROM THE AIRPORT

Esenboğa airport is 33km north of the city. **Havaş** (Map p420; ☑ 0312-444 0487; www. havas.net; Kazım Karabekir Caddesi, Gate B, 19 May Stadium, Ulus) airport buses link the airport with Ulus (₺10, 40 minutes) and the AŞTİ otogar (main bus station; ₺10, one hour). Departures are every half-hour between 3am and 9.30pm daily. After 9.30pm buses leave according to flight departure times.

Buses leave from in front of the passenger arrivals gate H (domestic arrivals); international arrivals should walk left on leaving the airport terminal. The Havas bus terminal in Ulus is basically a parking lot in the middle of a massive road junction system and walking from here to your hotel is not advised. A taxi from here to the hotels in the Citadel should cost around ₺20. Havaş have an information booth at the otogar, near the main exit on the ground floor.

LONG-DISTANCE SERVICES FROM ANKARA GARI

DESTINATION	VIA (MAJOR STOPS)	TRAIN NAME	TIME (HOURS)	DEPARTURE TIME
Adana	Kayseri	*Çukurova Mavi Tren*	11	8.05pm daily
Diyarbakır	Kayseri, Sivas, Malatya	*Eylül Mavi Tren*	22¼	11.15am daily
İzmir	Eskişehir	*İzmir Mavi Tren*	13¼	7.50pm daily
Kars	Kayseri, Sivas, Erzurum	*Doğu Ekspresi*	27¾	6.30pm daily
Kurtalan	Kayseri, Sivas, Malatya, Diyarbakır	*Güney/Kurtalan Ekspresi*	26¾	1.33am Mon & Wed-Sat
Tatvan (for ferry to Van)	Kayseri, Sivas, Malatya	*Vangölü Ekspresi*	36	1.33am Tue & Sun

Don't pay more than ₺70 for a taxi between the airport and the city.

TO/FROM THE BUS STATION

The easiest way to get into town is on the Ankaray metro line, which has a station at the AŞTİ otogar. Get off at Maltepe for the train station (a 10-minute walk), or go to Kızılay for midrange hotels. Change at Kızılay (to the Metro line) for Ulus and cheaper hotels.

A taxi costs about ₺30 to the city centre.

TO/FROM THE TRAIN STATION

Ankara Train Station is about 1km southwest of Ulus Meydanı and 2km northwest of Kızılay. Many dolmuşes head northeast along Cumhuriyet Bulvarı to Ulus, and east on Talat Paşa Bulvarı to Kızılay.

It's just over 1km from the station to Opera Meydanı; any bus heading east along Talat Paşa Bulvarı will drop you within a few hundred metres if you ask for Gazi Lisesi.

BUS

Ankara has a good bus, dolmuş and minibus network. Signs on the front and side of the vehicles are better guides than route numbers. Buses marked 'Ulus' and 'Çankaya' run the length of Atatürk Bulvarı. Those marked 'Gar' go to the train station, those marked 'AŞTİ' to the otogar.

Standard ₺3.50 transport cards (valid for two journeys) are available at subway stations and major bus stops or anywhere displaying an EGO Bilet sign. They work on most buses as well as the subway. These tickets are not valid on express buses, which are the longer buses with ticket counters halfway down the vehicle.

CAR

Driving within Ankara is chaotic and signs are inadequate; it's easier to ditch your car and use public transport.

If you plan to hire a car to drive out of Ankara, there are many small local companies alongside the major international firms; most have offices in Kavaklıdere along Tunus Caddesi, and/or at Esenboğa airport. For your sanity it's probably easier to get a bus out to the airport and hire a car there, thus hopefully avoiding driving in Ankara.

METRO

Ankara's underground train network is the easiest way to get between Ulus and Kızılay and the transport terminals. There are currently two lines: the Ankaray line running between AŞTİ otogar in the west through Maltepe and Kızılay to Dikimevi in the east; and the Metro line running from Kızılay northwest via Sıhhiye and Ulus to Batıkent. The two lines interconnect at Kızılay. Trains run from 6.15am to 11.45pm daily.

A one-way fare costs ₺1.75. Tickets are available at all stations for two journeys (₺3.50) and five journeys (₺8.75).

TAXI

Taxis are everywhere and they all have meters (normally built into the mirror), with a ₺2.70 base rate. It costs about ₺10 to cross the centre; charges rise at night and the same trip will cost well over ₺15.

Around Ankara

You don't have to go far from Ankara to hit some major pieces of Anatolian history, but if it's a leisurely day trip you're after rather than an overnighter, consider the Phrygian archaeological site at Gordion or the small Ottoman town of Beypazarı.

Gordion

The capital of ancient Phrygia, with some 3000 years of settlement behind it, Gordion lies 106km southwest of Ankara in the village of Yassıhöyük.

Gordion was occupied by the Phrygians as early as the 9th century BC, and soon afterwards became their capital. Although destroyed during the Cimmerian invasion, it was rebuilt before being conquered by the Lydians and then the Persians. Alexander the Great came through here and famously cut the Gordian knot in 333 BC, but by 278 BC the Galatian occupation had effectively destroyed the city.

The moonscape-like terrain around Yassıhöyük is dotted with tumuli (burial mounds) that mark the graves of the Phrygian kings. Of some 90 identified tumuli, 35 have been excavated; you can enter the largest tomb, and also view the site of the Gordion acropolis, where digs revealed five main levels of civilisation from the Bronze Age to Galatian times.

There are no real facilities in Yassıhöyük, although at weekends you might find something to eat.

◉ Sights

Midas Tumulus & Gordion Museum   RUIN
(admission incl museum ₺5; ⊙ 8.30am-7pm) In 1957 Austrian archaeologist Alfred Koerte discovered Gordion, and with it the intact tomb of a Phrygian king, probably buried sometime between 740 and 718 BC. The tomb is actually a gabled 'cottage' of cedar surrounded by juniper logs, buried inside a

tumulus 53m high and 300m in diameter. It's the oldest wooden structure ever found in Anatolia, and perhaps even in the world. The tunnel leading into the depths of the tumulus is a modern addition.

Inside the tomb archaeologists found the body of a man between 61 and 65 years of age, 1.59m tall, surrounded by burial objects, including tables, bronze situlas (containers) and bowls said to be part of the funerary burial feast. The occupant's name remains unknown (although Gordius and Midas were popular names for Phrygian kings).

In the museum opposite, Macedonian and Babylonian coins show Gordion's position at the centre of Anatolian trade, communications and military activities, as do the bronze figurines and glass-bead jewellery from the Syro-Levantine region of Mesopotamia.

Acropolis   RUIN

FREE Just beyond Yassıhöyük village is the weather-beaten 8th-century-BC acropolis. Excavations here have yielded a wealth of data on Gordion's many civilisations. The site is a mass of jumbled, half-buried walls and, thanks to the scarcity of other visitors, feels remote and forgotten.

The lofty main gate on the western side of the acropolis was approached by a 6m-wide ramp. Within the fortified enclosure were four megara (square halls) from which the king and his priests and ministers ruled the empire. The mosaics found in one of these halls, the so-called Citadel of Midas, are on display outside the Gordion Museum.

ⓘ Getting There & Away

Baysal Turizm buses connect Ankara's otogar with Polatlı every half-hour (₺8, one hour). Dolmuş also go direct to Polatlı from a small bus station (more of a parking lot really) on the edge of Ulus. Once in Polatlı, you can travel the last 18km to Yassıhöyük in a minibus (₺5), but this involves a 1.5km walk across town to the minibus stand, and services depart very sporadically. You'd be lucky to get a taxi from Polatlı for less than ₺100 return with waiting time. You could also try to hitch from Polatlı. The road to Gordion is signed just 50m from the otogar. However, even if you get a lift from here you'll probably be dropped off at the junction 7km from Yassıhöyük from where you may well have to walk (and then walk back to the junction again).

Beypazarı

☏ 0312 / POP 36.900

A considered approach from a proactive town mayor has turned this picturesque Ottoman town, set high above the İnözü Vadisi, into the weekend destination *du jour* for Ankara's escapees. More than 3000 Ottoman houses line the narrow streets in the hilltop old quarter, where 500-plus buildings and some 30 streets have been restored. Coppersmiths and carpenters beaver away, shopkeepers flog model Ottoman houses in little bags to Ankaralı day-trippers, and the 200-year-old market recalls Beypazarı's position on the Silk Road.

Occupying a sizeable Ottoman mansion **Beypazarı Museum** (Beypazarı Tarih ve Kültür Evi) was closed at the time of research. Check to see if it has reopened.

On the first weekend in June, the local food festival **Havuç Guveç** celebrates the humble carrot (the area grows more than half of the carrots consumed in Turkey). Additional attractions, if any are needed, include craftwork markets and Ottoman house tours.

While you're here try the local delicacies, which include *havuç lokum* (carrot-flavoured Turkish delight), clumpy *cevizli sucuğu* (walnuts coated in grape jelly) and Beypazarı mineral water, bottled here and swigged throughout the country.

ⓘ Getting There & Away

From Ankara, buses to Beypazarı (₺10; 1¾ hours) leave from a small, dedicated bus station a kilometre or so north of Ulus. A taxi from the Citadel to the station costs ₺12. The bus also stops close to the AnkaMall, which you can reach via the Akköprü metro station.

Safranbolu

☏ 0370 / POP 42.800

Turkey's most thoroughly preserved Ottoman town is so gloriously dinky, it's as if it slid off the lid of a chocolate box. Safranbolu's old town, known as Çarşı, is a vision of red-tiled roofs and meandering alleys chock-a-block full of candy stores and cobblers. Having first found fame with traders as an isolated source of the precious spice saffron, people flock here today to recapture the heady scent of yesteryear within the muddle of timber-framed mansions now converted into quirky boutique hotels. Spending the

Safranbolu - Çarşı

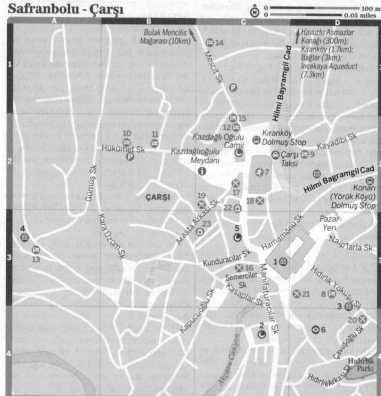

Safranbolu - Çarşı

◉ Sights
1	Cinci Hanı	C3
2	İzzet Paşa Camii	C4
3	Kaymakamlar Müze Evi	D3
4	Kent Tarihi Müzesi	A3
5	Köprülü Mehmet Paşa Camii	C3
6	Ottoman Houses	D4

◉ Activities, Courses & Tours
7	Cinci Hamam	C2

◉ Sleeping
8	Bastoncu Pansiyon	D3
9	Efe Backpackers Pension	D2
10	Gülevi	B2
11	İmren Lokum Konak	B2
12	Kahveciler Konağı	C2
13	Leyla Hanım Konağı	A3
14	Mehveş Hanım Konağı	C1
15	Selvili Köşk	C2

◉ Eating
16	Bizim Cafe	C3
17	Çizgi Cafe	C2
18	Hanım Sultan	C2
19	Kadıoğlu Şehzade Sofrası	C2
20	Taşev	D4
21	Zencefil	D3

◉ Shopping
22	Safrantat	C2
23	Yemeniciler Arastası	C3

night here is all about soaking up the enchanting Ottoman scene – all creaky wooden floors, exuberantly carved ceilings and traditional cupboard-bathrooms. A day at the old hamam or browsing the market shops and revelling in the cobblestone quaintness is about as strenuous as it gets, but if history begins to feel a bit like old news, then hiking in the wondrous Yenice Forest nearby, remapped and rediscovered, will show you exactly why Unesco stamped this region as a World Heritage Site in 1994.

History

During the 17th century, the main Ottoman trade route between Gerede and the Black Sea coast passed through Safranbolu, bringing commerce, prominence and money to the town. During the 18th and 19th centuries, Safranbolu's wealthy inhabitants built mansions of sun-dried mudbricks, wood and stucco, while the larger population of prosperous artisans built less impressive but similarly sturdy homes. Safranbolu owes its fame to the large numbers of these dwellings that have survived.

The most prosperous Safranbolulus maintained two households. In winter they occupied town houses in the Çarşı (market) district, which is situated at the meeting point of three valleys and so protected from winter winds. During the warm months they moved to summer houses in the garden suburb of Bağlar (vineyards). When the iron- and steelworks at Karabük were established in 1938, modern factory houses started to encroach on Bağlar, but Çarşı has remained virtually untouched.

During the 19th century about 20% of Safranbolu's inhabitants were Ottoman Greeks, but most of their descendants moved to Greece during the population exchange after WWI. Their principal church, dedicated to St Stephen, was converted into Kıranköy's Ulu Cami (Great Mosque).

◉ Sights & Activities

Ottoman Houses HISTORIC BUILDING
Just walking through Çarşı is a feast for the eyes. Virtually every house in the district is an original, and what little modern development there is has been held in check. Many of the finest historic houses have been restored, and as time goes on, more and more are being saved from deterioration and turned into hotels, shops or museums.

Kaymakamlar Müze Evi MUSEUM
(Hıdırlık Yokuşu Sokak; adult/student ₺4/3; ⊙ 9am-5.30pm) This typical Safranbolu home has all the classic features of Ottoman houses. It was owned by a lieutenant colonel and still feels like an address of note as you climb the stairs towards the wooden ceiling decoration. Tableaux (featuring some rather

weary mannequins) recreate scenes such as bathing in a cupboard and a wedding feast.

Cinci Hanı HISTORIC BUILDING
(Eski Çarşı Çeşme Mahallesi; admission ₺1) Çarşı's most famous and imposing structure is this brooding 17th-century caravanserai that's now a hotel. Non-guests are welcome to come and explore: climb up to the rooftop for red-tiled-roof panoramas over the town. On Saturdays a market takes place in the square behind it.

İzzet Paşa Camii MOSQUE
(Manifaturacılar Sokak) This is one of the largest mosques constructed during the Ottoman Empire. It was built by the grand vizier (prime minister) in 1796 and restored in 1903. Its design was influenced by European architecture.

Kent Tarihi Müzesi MUSEUM
(City History Museum; ☑ 0370-712 1314; Çeşme Mahallesi Hükümet Sokak; adult/child ₺4/3; ⊙ 9am-5.30pm Tue-Sun) Inside the mustard-yellow Eski Hükümet Konağı (old government building), on a hill overlooking the town, the exhibits at this museum are a decent introduction to local life.

Just behind is the **clock tower** (1797), built by grand vizier İzzet Mehmet Paşa.

Köprülü Mehmet Paşa Camii MOSQUE
(Manifaturacılar Sokak) This beefy, helmet-roofed building beside the Yemeniciler Arastası (a row of shops beside a mosque) dates to 1661. The metal sundial in the courtyard was added in the mid-19th century.

Cinci Hamam HAMAM
(☑ 0370-712 2103; Kazdağlıoğlu Meydanı; full treatment ₺35; ⊙ men 6am-11pm, women 9am-10pm) One of the most renowned bathhouses in all of Turkey, with separate baths for men and women.

🎊 Festivals & Events

Geleneksel Sezzetler Şenliği FOOD
A popular May food festival run by the Association of Anatolian Cuisine.

Safranbolu Architectural Treasures & Folklore Week CULTURAL
FREE In September, with exhibitions and performances across town.

🛏 Sleeping

Safranbolu is very popular with Turkish tourists during weekends and holidays.

Prices may rise at particularly busy times, and it can be worth booking ahead. Splashing out a bit is virtually an obligation, as you may never get another chance to sleep anywhere so authentically restored. If you'd rather stay in a family home than a hotel, the tourist office has a list of basic pensions (the *Safranbolu'daki Ev Pansiyonları Listesi*). They are cheaper than hotels, though often of lower quality.

Efe Backpackers Pension
PENSION €

(☑ 0370-725 2688; www.backpackerspension.com; Kayadibi Sokak 8; dm/s/d ₺25/70/90; ☎) This place dishes up all of Safranbolu's Ottoman charm at a smidgen of the cost of other hotels. Efe is the kind of hostel where being on a budget doesn't mean scrimping on quality, cleanliness or efficiency. There's a basic dorm for those really saving their lira and the snug private rooms are packed full of local character.

Yasemin, the polyglot matriarch, runs a tight ship with a host of extras on offer such as free otogar transfers and daily tours (these require a minimum of five people). The stunning views over town from the terrace top it all off.

Bastoncu Pansiyon
PENSION €

(☑ 0370-712 3411; www.bastoncupension.com; Hıdırlık Yokuşu Sokak; dm/s/d ₺25/60/90; ☎) In a 350-year-old building, Bastoncu is a Safranbolu institution with a superb higgledy-piggledy feel. Connected by a labyrinth of staircases, rooms and dorms have all their original wood panelling, jars of dried flowers, and some (slightly pongy) cupboard bathrooms. It's run by a friendly couple who speak English and Japanese and appreciate travellers' needs.

★ Imren Lokum Konak
HISTORIC HOTEL €€

(☑ 0370-725 2324; www.imrenkonak.com; Kayyim Ali Sokak; s/d ₺160/230; ☎) This old Ottoman building houses a fine hotel with rooms that, though keeping all their old Safranbolu flavour, have enough modern touches to make them truly user friendly. There's a large open courtyard and restaurant that attract many an overnighting tourist from Ankara at weekends and this ensures a holiday vibe.

Leyla Hanim Konaği
HISTORIC HOTEL €€

(☑ 0370-725 1272; www.leylahanimkonagi.com; Çeşme Mahallesi Hükümet Sokak 25; s/d from €50/75; ☎) This place was once a barracks for soldiers, but if those men could see it today they'd probably never guess that this now wonderful boutique hotel was once their, no-doubt, rather grimy home. Today it's all ye-olde elegance mixed with flashes of modernity such as deep purple theatre curtains draped over exposed stone walls.

Kahveciler Konağı
HISTORIC HOTEL €€

(☑ 0370-725 5453; www.kahvecilerkonagi.com; Mescit Sokak 7; s/d ₺75/120; ☎) The large rooms here have whitewashed walls, glorious wood-panel ceilings and lovely views of red-tiled roofs. Amiable host Erşan has transformed his grandfather's house into a comfortable home away from home. As a bonus for those less agile, the bathrooms are big by Safranbolu standards and require no climbing into cupboards.

Selvili Köşk
HISTORIC HOTEL €€

(☑ 0370-712 8646; www.selvilikosk.com; Mescit Sokak 23; s/d ₺100/120; ☎) From the engraved banisters to the carved ceilings, this wonderful restoration job offers a regal-feeling, romantic retreat. Dazzling carpets cover every inch of floor and are layered over the *sedirs* (bench seating that runs along the walls), and local embroidered linens grace the beds in sun-drenched rooms.

Ingeniously hidden bathrooms are found through opening cupboard doors (for those who cannot, or will not, climb into a cupboard to use the bathroom, it might pay to look elsewhere).

Mehveş Hanım Konağı
HISTORIC HOTEL €€

(☑ 0370-712 8787; www.mehveshanimkonagi.com.tr; Mescit Sokak 30; s ₺80, d ₺100-150; ☎) With every nook and cranny crammed with curios and Ottoman paraphernalia, the Mehveş is a beautiful and authentic place to stay. Run with cheerful competency, the spacious rooms have intricately carved wooden ceilings, *sedir* seating, teensy cupboard bathrooms (some rooms share much larger and more modern bathrooms) and Ottoman princess nets around the beds. There's also a lovely hidden garden.

Havuzlu Asmazlar Konağı
HISTORIC HOTEL €€

(☑ 0370-725 2883; Çelik Gülersoy Caddesi 18; s/d weekday ₺120/160, weekend from ₺160/210; ❄☎) The tiny, lobby-side pool, with tinkling fountains (the noise of which was once used to prevent women listening in on men's important conversations – about football and such) is just one of the audacious quirks in this beautifully restored hotel. The comfortable rooms are furnished with brass beds, *sedirs* and kilims.

The hotel is a couple of minutes' walk north of the main square.

Gülevi　　　　HISTORIC HOTEL €€€
(☑0370-725 4645; www.canbulat.com.tr; Hükümet Sokak 46; s €75-95, d €100-125, ste €150-175; ☞) Architect-design couple İbrahim and Gül have crafted what might be Safranbolu's most striking reinterpretation of the Ottoman aesthetic. 'Rose House' is an affordable masterpiece where urban luxury mingles seamlessly with traditional Ottoman design. Amid a shaded, grassy garden, the rooms (spread over three houses) are all soft colours, wood panelling and Turkman carpets, set off by flamboyant artistic touches.

Guests lucky enough to stay here can enjoy a drink in the tiny underground cave bar (once the treasury of the house) or dine at the private restaurant where the pick of local produce is on the menu.

✕ Eating

Bizim Cafe　　　　ANATOLIAN €
(Çeşme Mahallesi; mains ₺5-10) Deep in the old shopping district is this welcoming little family-run restaurant that serves whatever's on the stove, which luckily is always pretty good, including dolmades rolled on the street and deliciously spicy soups. Locals love it.

Zencefil　　　　TURKISH €
(☑0370-712 5120; Arkasi Sokak 24, Cinci Hani; mains ₺7-15; ☺9am-9pm) Run by a foodie couple, this place dishes up all the regional classics as well as a few less common items such as yayım (noodles with walnuts), which is a twist on the town's more normal pasta and walnuts. All the food is cooked up right in front of you and service is friendly.

Hanım Sultan　　　　ANATOLIAN €
(Akın Sokak 6, Çeşme Mahallesi; mains ₺5-10) Squirreled away down a little alleyway, this place rustles up rustic, wholesome cooking. Try the divine pot of etli dolma (vine leaves stuffed with meat) for a hearty, delicious lunch.

Çızgi Cafe　　　　ANATOLIAN €€
(☑0370-717 7840; Arasta Arkası Sokak; mains ₺7-15) Eat on the cushioned benches outside or dine inside in one of the cosily intimate cubby-hole dining areas. Çızgi is an easygoing place where local dishes such as cevizli yayım (macaroni topped with walnuts) and mantı (Turkish ravioli) are on the small menu, and it's all about wasting hours talking over coffee and nargile (water pipe) afterwards.

Kadıoğlu Şehzade Sofrası　　　　TURKISH €€
(☑0370-712 5657; Arasta Arkası Sokak 8; mains ₺11-23; ☺11.30am-10.30pm) It's all traditional Ottoman-style seating at this converted mansion restaurant. The huge, steaming hot pide, çorba, grills and zerde (saffron dessert) are all recommended.

Taşev　　　　MODERN TURKISH €€€
(☑0370-725 5300; www.tasevsanatvesarapevi.com; Hıdırlık Yokuşu Sokak 14; mains ₺17-25; ☺10am-11pm Tue-Sun) This is Safranbolu's bona fide contemporary dining option and it delivers with thick steaks and creamy pasta dishes. The Turkish cheese platter is a must for cheese lovers. Service is warm and they'll helpfully explain menu items and help you choose from the extensive wine list.

🔒 Shopping

Safranbolu is a great place to pick up handicrafts – especially textiles, metalwork, shoes and wooden artefacts – whether locally made or shipped in from elsewhere to supply coach tourists.

Yemeniciler Arastası　　　　MARKET
(Peasant Shoe-Maker's Bazaar; Arasta Arkası Sokak) The restored Yemeniciler Arastası is the best

place to start looking for crafts, although the makers of the light, flat-heeled shoes who used to work here have long since moved out. The further you go from the *arasta* the more likely you are to come across shops occupied by authentic working saddle-makers, felt-makers and other artisans.

Safrantat FOOD
(Manifaturacılar Sokak) Although Safranbolu is so packed with sweet shops that you half expect the houses to be made out of ginger-bread, Safrantat is one of the top picks for sugary delights. Don't leave without trying the regional speciality, *yaprak helvası* – delicious chewy layers of white *helva* (halva) spotted with ground walnuts.

ℹ️ Information

Çarşı has a bank with an ATM on Kazdağlıoğulu Meydanı.

Tourist Office (📍 0370-712 3863; www.safran-bolu.gov.tr; Kazdağlıoğlu Meydanı; ⊘ 9am-5.30pm) One of Turkey's most helpful tourist information offices. Informed, multilingual staff can provide loads of tips and advice, and will even help with booking bus tickets.

ℹ️ Getting There & Away

Most buses stop in Karabük first and then finish at Kıranköy otogar (upper Safranbolu), from where minibuses or a *servis* (shuttle bus) can deposit you in central Kıranköy, near the dolmuş stand for Çarşı.

There are several bus company offices along Sadrı Artunç Caddesi and just off Adnan Menderes Caddesi in Kıranköy, where you can buy tickets to destinations including Ankara (₺25, three hours), İstanbul (₺45, seven hours) and Kastamonu (₺17, two hours).

For Amasra take a bus to Bartın (₺20, 1½ hours) and change there. Buses to Bartın go every hour at quarter past.

If you're driving, exit the Ankara–İstanbul highway at Gerede and head north, following the signs for Karabük/Safranbolu.

There is a direct train from Karabük to Ankara, but the bus is a much easier option.

ℹ️ Getting Around

Dolmuşes (₺1.25) ply the route from Çarşı's main square, over the hills, and into central Kıranköy every 15 minutes. From the last stop you can catch another minibus to Karabük. You only have to pay the bus fare once if you're going all the way. A taxi from Çarşı to Kıranköy will cost you ₺10 to ₺12.

Around Safranbolu

Yörük Köyü

Along the Kastamonu road, 15km east of Safranbolu, Yörük Köyü (Nomad Village) is a beautiful settlement of crumbling old houses once inhabited by the dervish Bektaşi sect. The government forced them to settle here so it could tax them, and once they'd put down roots, these new villagers grew rich from their baking prowess.

Sipahioğlu Konağı Gezi Evi (Leyla Gencer Sokağı; admission ₺5; ⊘ 8.30am-sunset) is one of the village's enormous Ottoman houses. The builder's warring sons divided the mansion in two, and you tour the *selamlık* and *haremlik* separately.

Nearby in Cemil İpekçi Sokağı is the 300-year-old *çamaşırhane* (laundry), with arched hearths where the water was heated in cauldrons. Ask at Sipahioğlu Konağı Gezi Evi for the key.

ℹ️ Getting There & Away

There is no direct bus service from Safranbolu to Yörük Köyü, but dolmuşes to the nearby village of Konarı (five daily, ₺5) can drop you at the Yörük Köyü turn-off on the main road. From there it's a 1km walk to the village (and in fact the drivers will often deviate off their course to take you right up to the village).

Çarşı Taksi (📍 0370-725 2595; Hilmi Bay-ramgil Caddesi) charges ₺40 return, including waiting time, to Yörük Köyü, and many hotels can organise tours. For ₺100 they will whisk you around Yörük Köyü, the caves at Bulak Mencilis Mağarası and the İncekaya Aqueduct.

Bulak Mencilis Mağarası

Deep in the Gürleyik hills 10km northwest of Safranbolu, the impressive **Bulak Mencilis Mağarası** (adult/child ₺3.50/2.50; ⊘ 9am-8pm) cave network opened to the public a decade ago, although troglodytes may have lived here many millennia before. You can walk through 400m of the 6km-long network, enough to reveal a fine array of stalactites and stalagmites with inevitable anthropomorphic nicknames.

There are steps up to the cave and you should wear sturdy shoes as the metal walkway inside can be slippery and wet.

A taxi from Safranbolu costs ₺40 return.

İncekaya Aqueduct

Originally built in Byzantine times but restored in the 1790s by İzzet Mehmet Paşa, İncekaya Aqueduct (Su Kemeri) is just over 7km north of Safranbolu. Its name means 'thin rock' and the walk across it, high above the beautiful Tokatlı Gorge, would not suit sufferers of vertigo.

A taxi from Safranbolu costs ₺35 return.

Kastamonu

📱 0366 / POP 98,450

At first glance Kastamonu doesn't seem to be anything other than a busy provincial town of little obvious tourist appeal, but veer into the helter-skelter of alleyways off bustling Cumhuriyet Caddesi and you'll discover decaying remnants of former glory at every turn. A wealth of Ottoman mansions slowly slumping and sliding into picturesque abandon line Kastamonu's lanes, while market streets throng with locals on a bargain-hunt. It's a glimpse of provincial Turkey yet to be trussed up for the tourists. Just out of town, Kasaba's intricately carved and painted wooden mosque provides enough of a reason to spend the night.

History

Kastamonu's history has been as chequered as that of most central Turkish towns. Archaeological evidence suggests there was a settlement here as far back as 2000 BC, but the Hittites, Persians, Macedonians and Pontic (Black Sea) kings all left their mark. In the 11th century the Seljuks descended, then the Danişmends. The 13th-century Byzantine emperor John Comnenus tried to hold out here, but the Mongols soon swept in, followed by the Ottomans.

Kastamonu's modern history is inextricably linked to headgear: Atatürk launched his hat reforms here in 1925, banning the fez due to its religious connotations and insisting on the adoption of European-style titfers.

👁 Sights

Archaeology Museum   MUSEUM
(📱 0366-214 1070; Cumhuriyet Caddesi; ⊙ 8.30am-12.30pm & 1.30-5.30pm Tue-Sun) **FREE** South of Nasrullah Bridge, this small museum has beautifully displayed exhibits and detailed information panels in English. The

central hall is devoted to Kastamonu's role in Atatürk's sartorial revolution, while the left-hand room houses Hellenic and Roman finds. Upstairs are Hittite and Bronze Age exhibits from regional excavations.

Perhaps the highlight of the collection is the Roman period sarcophagus containing a female skeleton complete with half a mane of hair still on her head.

Nasrullah Meydanı   SQUARE
(off Cumhuriyet Caddesi) Leading off from Nasrullah Bridge, the square centres on the Ottoman Nasrullah Camii (1506). Poet Mehmet Akif Ersoy delivered speeches in this mosque during the War of Independence. The former Münire Medresesi (seminary) at the rear houses craft shops. West of the square are old market buildings, including the Aşirefendi Hanı and the 15th-century İsmail Bey Hanı.

Castle   CASTLE
(Kale; ⊙ 9am-sunset) **FREE** One block south of the town's Archaeology Museum, turn right onto Şeyh Şaban Veli Caddesi and follow the road up to the scant remains of Kastamonu's castle. Parts of the building date from Byzantine times, but most belong to Seljuk and Ottoman reconstructions.

Ethnography Museum   MUSEUM
(📱 0366-214 0149; Sakayra Caddesi 5; admission ₺5; ⊙ 8.30am-7pm Tue-Sun) South of Nasrullah Bridge on Cumhuriyet Caddesi, turn right after Gazi Paşa school to reach the restored 1870 Liva Paşa Konağı, with its upstairs salons furnished as it would have been in Ottoman times.

🛏 Sleeping

Kastamonu has a fair range of accommodation with most of the cheaper hotels clustered around Nasrullah Bridge. The bus companies' offices and internet cafes are in the same area.

Uğurlu Konakları   HISTORIC HOTEL €€
(📱 0366-212 8202; www.kastamonukonaklari.com; Şeyh Şaban Veli Caddesi 47-51; s/d ₺140/200; 🕸) A short walk from the town centre and the castle, this hotel comprises two houses faithfully restored with Indian carpets, red-brown trimmings and a private garden. Rooms in the front house are more appealing, leading off from atmospheric communal salons. It's very popular and worth booking ahead.

Osmanlı Sarayı HISTORIC HOTEL €€

(Ottoman Palace; ☑ 0366-214 8408; www.kasta
monuosmanlisarayi.com; Belediye Caddesi 81; s/d
₺70/140; 🛜) Atatürk once visited this grand
building in its former incarnation as Kastamonu's town hall. Breathe in the history in
the high-ceilinged rooms, which have authentic fittings and cupboard-bathrooms.

🍴 Eating & Drinking

The winding streets to the west of Nasrullah
Meydanı are great for a wander and a çay.

Münire Sultan Sofrası ANATOLIAN €€

(Nasrullah Meydanı; mains ₺7-14; ⊘ noon-10pm
Tue-Sun) Tucked inside the Münire Medresesi
complex, we like this place for its local specialities. If you're hungry try the *banduma*
(chicken and filo pastry drenched in butter
and chopped walnuts) and order a glass of
eğşi (sour plum drink) to wash it all down.
It's one of those rare places that has high-
chairs for babies.

ℹ Getting There & Away

Kastamonu's **otogar** (Kazım Karabekir Caddesi)
offers regular departures for Ankara (₺30, four
hours), İstanbul (₺50, eight hours), Karabük
(₺20, two hours), Samsun (₺35, 5½ hours) and
Sinop (₺25, three hours).

Minibuses for İnebolu (₺10, two hours) also
leave from the otogar.

If you're heading to Çorum first take a bus to
Tosya (₺17, 1¼ hours, hourly) from where buses
to Çorum (₺18; 2½ hours) leave at 8.30am,
12.45pm and 4.30pm. The bus station in Kastamonu can call ahead and reserve you a place on
one of these buses.

Around Kastamonu

Kasaba

Amid rolling hills and fertile fields, the tiny
hamlet of Kasaba, 17km northwest of Kastamonu, is a pretty but unlikely place to find
one of Turkey's finest surviving wooden
mosques. The restored interior of Mahmud
Bey Camii (1366) has four painted wooden
columns, a wooden gallery and finely painted ceiling rafters. You can climb some rough
ladders to the third storey of the gallery to
look at the ornate beam-ends and interlocking motifs topping the pillars.

A return taxi from Kastamonu, with waiting time, costs ₺50. A cheaper option is to
take the Pınarbaşı bus and jump off at the

Kasaba turn-off, but it is a 4km walk to the
village from there.

Boğazkale, Hattuşa & Yazılıkaya

Out in the centre of the Anatolian plains,
two Unesco World Heritage Sites evoke a vital historical moment at the height of Hittite
civilisation. Hattuşa was the Hittite capital,
while Yazılıkaya was a religious sanctuary
with fine rock carvings.

The best base for visiting the sites around
here is Boğazkale, a farming village 200km
east of Ankara. Boğazkale has simple traveller
services; if you want or need something fancier you'll need to stay in Çorum or, if you get
going early enough in the morning, Ankara.

Boğazkale

☑ 0364 / POP 1350

The village of Boğazkale has ducks, cows
and wheelbarrow-racing children wandering its cobbled streets; farmyards with
Hittite and Byzantine gates; and a constant
sense that a once-great city is just over the
brow. Most visitors come solely to visit Hattuşa and Yazılıkaya, which can be accessed
on foot if it's not too hot, but there is more to
explore. Surrounded by valleys with Hittite
caves, eagles' nests, butterflies and a Neolithic fort, the area around Hattuşa is ripe
for hiking. Head 4km east of Yazılıkaya and
climb Yazılıkaya Dağı to watch the sun set
on the sites, or head to the swimming hole
(locally known as *hoşur*) on the Budaközü
river to cool off after a long day in the ruins.

Late in the day, the silence in Boğazkale is
broken only by the occasional car kicking up
dust on the main street, and the rural solitude may tempt you to stay an extra night.
Apart from the accommodation options, the
village's only facilities are some small shops,
a post office and a bank with an ATM.

◉ Sights

Boğazkale Museum MUSEUM

(Sungurlu Asfalt Caddesi; ⊘ 8am-7pm Tue-Sun)
FREE Unsurprisingly, Hittite artefacts dominate the small Boğazkale Museum. The pride
of the collection are the two sphinx statues
that once stood guard at Hattuşa's Yer Kapı
gate. They were only returned to Boğazkale
in 2011, having previously been on display
in Berlin and İstanbul. Free audioguides are
available.

🛏 Sleeping & Eating

The following properties offer camping for about ₺25 per person, including the use of electricity and hot water.

Aşıkoğlu Hotel & Pension
HOTEL €€

(☑0364-452 2004; www.hattusas.com; Sungurlu Asfalt Caddesi; s ₺25-80, d ₺40-120; 🗪) The friendly service sets this place apart, and the simple, spick-and-span rooms in a range of styles are just the ticket for resting your head after visiting Hattuşa, although in winter the unheated rooms get very cold. There's a cosy Ottoman-style cafe-restaurant and Hittite documentaries are shown on a cinevision screen in the evening.

Dishes at the restaurant cost ₺8 to ₺20 (including a decent, wood-fired pide for ₺8 to ₺12). If you ring ahead the hotel can organise taxi transfers from Sungurlu otogar.

Kale Hotel
HOTEL €€

(☑0364-452 3126; Yazılıkaya Yolu Üzeri; s ₺55, d ₺70-100; ☺Apr-Oct; 🗪) Kale's colourful rooms have cheery floral linen and decent beds; the top rooms at the front have good views and some have balconies. It's all wonderfully quiet and peaceful. The restaurant, with its adjoining terrace, mostly caters to groups, but even so the food is delicious.

Otel Başkent
HOTEL €€

(☑0364-452 2037; www.baskenthattusa.com; s/d ₺70/120; 🗪) Easily the smartest rooms in town, the Başkent has central heating for cold winter nights and a surprising amount of comfort for so small a place. There have, however, been allegations of rooms being used by locals 'by the hour', if you get our drift.

Hittite Houses
HOTEL €€

(☑0364-452 2004; www.hattusas.com; Sungurlu Asfalt Caddesi; s/d ₺60/100) Behind a mocked-up Hittite wall-facade, this hotel has plain but light-filled rooms. It's run by the knowledgeable owners of the Aşıkoğlu Hotel opposite, so guests have access to all the facilities and services there.

ℹ Getting There & Away

To get to Boğazkale by public transport, you'll need to go via Sungurlu (₺5). From Sungurlu otogar your bus should provide a *servis* to the Boğazkale dolmuş stand, 1km from the otogar near the football stadium and park. There is no set dolmuş schedule, but there are more in the

Boğazkale & Hattuşa

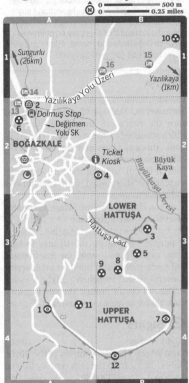

Boğazkale & Hattuşa

morning with the first leaving around 7am and they run until around 5.30pm. Taking a taxi may be your only resort at the weekend; don't pay more than ₺40. Travellers coming from Cappadocia should note that there are no dolmuşes between Boğazkale and Yozgat, 41km southeast. You're better off going via Sungurlu.

Hattuşa

The mountainous, isolated site of **Hattuşa** (admission incl Yazılıkaya ₺8; ☉8am-7pm) was once the capital of the Hittite kingdom, which stretched from Syria to Europe. At its zenith this was a busy and impressive city of 15,000 inhabitants with defensive walls over 6km in length, some of the thickest in the ancient world, studded with watchtowers and secret tunnels.

As you climb out of the village to the site, an evocative reconstruction of a section of city wall comes into view. Imagine the sense of purpose that drove the Hittites to haul stone to this remote spot, far from oceans and trade routes, and build an engineering masterpiece that launched a mighty empire.

The full circuit around the site is a long walk, taking at least three hours.

◉ Sights

Büyük Mabet
TEMPLE

(Great Temple) The vast complex of the Büyük Mabet, dating from the 14th century BC and destroyed around 1200 BC, is the closest archaeological site to the entrance gate and the best preserved of Hattuşa's Hittite temple ruins, but even so you'll still need plenty of imagination.

As you walk down the wide processional street, the administrative quarters of the temple are to your left. The well-worn cube of green nephrite rock here is thought to

have played a significant role in the Hittite religion.

The main temple, to your right, was surrounded by storerooms thought to be three storeys high. In the early 20th century, huge clay storage jars and thousands of cuneiform tablets were found in these rooms. Look for the threshold stones at the base of some of the doorways to see the hole for the hinge-post and the arc worn by the door's movement. The temple is believed to have been a ritual altar for the deities Teshub and Hepatu; the large stone base of one of their statues remains.

Sarı Kale & Yenıce Kale
RUIN

About 250m south of the Büyük Mabet, the road forks; take the right fork and follow the winding road up the hillside. On your left in the midst of the old city you can see several ruined structures. The rock-top ruins of the **Sarı Kale** (Yellow Fortress) may be a Phrygian fort on Hittite foundations. On another rock outcrop are the remains of the **Yenıce Kale**, which may have been a royal residence or small temple. You can climb to the summit from the east side.

Aslanlı Kapı
GATE

(Lion's Gate) At Aslanlı Kapı, two stone lions (one rather poorly reconstructed) protect the city from evil spirits. This is one of at least six gates in Hattuşa's 4000-year-old defensive walls, though it may never have been completed. You can see the best-preserved parts of Hattuşa's fortifications from here, stretching southeast to Yer Kapı and from there to Kral Kapı.

The walls illustrate the Hittites' engineering ingenuity, which enabled them to either build in sympathy with the terrain or transform the landscape, depending on

---

ⓘ VISITING HATTUŞA

➡ The ruins are an easy, and extremely pretty, walk from town.

➡ Arrive early in the morning to tour the ruins before the 21st century intrudes in the form of coaches and souvenir sellers.

➡ Enter the Büyük Mabet temple ruins from the trail uphill of Hattuşa's ticket kiosk, opposite the remains of a house on the slope.

➡ The circuit is a hilly 5km loop; if you want to walk, wear sturdy shoes and take enough water (there is no shop on site).

➡ There is very little shade so don't forget a hat and sunblock.

➡ Your Hattuşa ticket is also valid for Yazılıkaya, but staff at the ticket office in Hattuşa do sometimes have to be prompted to give a ticket, so make sure you do get one.

THE HITTITES OF HATTUŞA

While the name may evoke images of skin-clad barbarians, the Hittites were a sophisticated people who commanded a vast Middle Eastern empire, conquered Babylon and challenged the Egyptian pharaohs more than 3000 years ago. Apart from a few written references in the Bible and Babylonian tablets, there were few clues to their existence until 1834 when a French traveller, Charles Texier, stumbled upon the ruins of the Hittite capital of Hattuşa.

In 1905 excavations turned up notable works of art and the Hittite state archives, written in cuneiform on thousands of clay tablets. From these tablets, historians and archaeologists were able to construct a history of the Hittite empire.

The original Indo-European Hittites swept into Anatolia around 2000 BC, conquering the local Hatti, from whom they borrowed their culture and name. They established themselves at Hattuşa, the Hatti capital, and in the course of a millennium enlarged and beautified the city. From about 1375 to 1200 BC Hattuşa was the capital of a Hittite empire that, at its height, shared Syria with Egypt and extended as far as Europe.

The Hittites worshipped over a thousand different deities; the most important were Teshub, the storm or weather god, and Hepatu, the sun goddess. The cuneiform tablets revealed a well-ordered society with more than 200 laws. The death sentence was prescribed for bestiality, while thieves got off more lightly provided they paid their victims compensation.

Although it defeated Egypt in 1298 BC, the empire declined in the following centuries, undone by internal squabbles and new threats such as the Greek 'sea peoples'. Hattuşa was torched and its inhabitants dispersed. Only the city states of Syria survived until they, too, were swallowed by the Assyrians.

what was required. Natural outcrops were appropriated as part of the walls, and massive ramparts were built to create artificial fortresses.

Yer Kapı
GATE

(Earth Gate) The Yer Kapı is Hattuşa's most impressive gate, with an artificial mound pierced by a 70m-long tunnel. The Hittites built the tunnel using a corbelled arch (two flat faces of stones leaning towards one another), as the 'true' arch was not invented until later.

Primitive or not, the arch of Yer Kapı has done its job for millennia, and you can still pass down the stony tunnel as Hittite soldiers did, emerging from the postern. Afterwards, re-enter the city via one of the monumental stairways up the wide stone glacis and pass through the Sphinx Gate, once defended by four great sphinxes. One is still in situ, two are in the Boğazkale museum and the other has been lost. There are wonderful views over the upper city temple district from here.

Kral Kapı
GATE

(King's Gate) Kral Kapı is named after the regal-looking figure in the relief carving. The kingly character, a Hittite warrior god protecting

the city, is a copy; the original was removed to Ankara for safekeeping.

Nişantaş & Güney Kale
RUIN

At Nişantaş a rock with a faintly visible Hittite inscription cut into it narrates the deeds of Suppiluliuma II (1215–1200 BC), the final Hittite king. Immediately opposite, a path leads up to the excavated Güney Kale (Southern Fortress) with a fine (fenced-off) hieroglyphics chamber with human figure reliefs.

Büyük Kale
RUIN

(Great Fortress) Although most of the Büyük Kale site has been excavated, many of the older layers of development have been re-covered to protect them, so what you see today can be hard to decipher. This fortress held the royal palace and the Hittite state archives.

Tours

Hattuşaş Taxi
CULTURAL TOUR

(☑0535 389 1089; www.hattusastaxi.com) A mine of Hittite information is Murat Bektaş, who runs excellent tours in Hattuşa and around the surrounding area. For those with little time, his full-day Hittite tour of Hattuşa, Yazılıkaya and Alacahöyük (₺80 to ₺90 per person) is highly recommended.

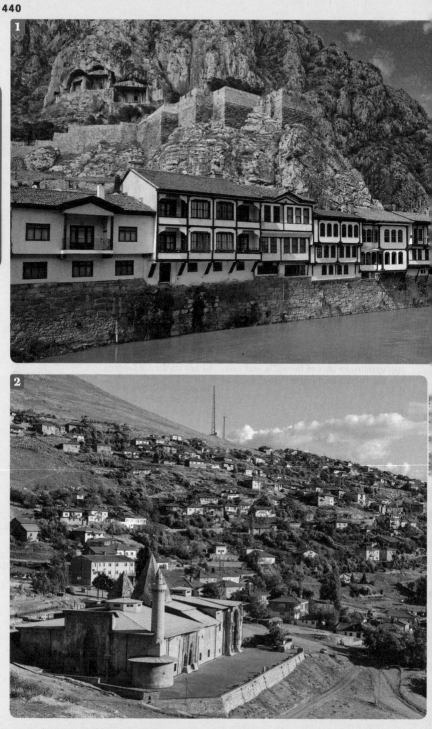

IZZET KERIBAR / GETTY IMAGES ©

1. Yeşilırmak River, Amasya (p443) 2. Divriği 's Ulu Cami & Darüşşifa (p452), near Sivas 3. Kral Kapı (p439), Hattuşa

Archives of Anatolia

Written in the rocks, buried underground and carved into the cliffs, the high plateaus of central Anatolia are heavy with history. This is where the world's oldest wooden structure was discovered and where Atatürk came up with the vision for Turkey. Visit the following sites to reveal the full extent of modern Turkey's yesteryears.

Hattuşa

The mountainous, isolated site of Hattuşa was once the capital of the Hittite kingdom. At its epoch this was one of the most powerful empires in the world. Today the tumbledown walls still recall past glories.

Museum of Anatolian Civilisations

With breathtaking artefacts cherry-picked from just about every significant archaeological site in Anatolia, Ankara's recently renovated Museum of Anatolian Civilisations provides the ultimate history lesson.

Gordion

Alexander the Great may have cut the Gordian knot here, but the real interest lies in the wooden tomb of a Phrygian king hidden for nearly 3000 years under a burial mound.

Sivas

With a colourful history and some of the finest Seljuk buildings ever erected, the main square of the often-overlooked town of Sivas showcases Islamic art and architecture at its best.

Amasya

A pretty riverside town with a history as long as time. Amasya has rock-cut tombs carved into cliffs, graceful Islamic buildings from across the ages, castles perched precariously along mountain summits, a museum of gory mummies and another filled with terrifying-looking medical instuments.

ⓘ Getting Around

To get around Hattuşa and Yazılıkaya without your own transport you'll need to walk or hire a taxi. It's 1km from the Aşıkoğlu Hotel to the Hattuşa ticket kiosk. From there the road looping around the site from the ticket kiosk (not including Yazılıkaya) is another 5km. The walk itself takes at least an hour and a half, plus time spent exploring the ruins, so figure on spending a good three hours here.

Yazılıkaya

Yazılıkaya (Yazılıkaya Yolu Üzeri; admission incl Hattuşa ₺8) means 'Inscribed Rock', and that's exactly what you'll find in these outdoor rock galleries, just under 3km from Hattuşa. There are two galleries: the larger one, to the left, was the Hittite empire's holiest religious sanctuary; the narrower one, to the right, has the best-preserved carvings. Together they form the largest known Hittite rock sanctuary, sufficiently preserved to make you wish you could have seen the carvings when they were new.

In the larger gallery, **Chamber A**, there are the faded reliefs of numerous goddesses and pointy-hatted gods marching in procession. Heads and feet are shown in profile, but the torso is shown front on, a common feature of Hittite relief art. The lines of men and women lead to some large reliefs depicting a godly meeting. Teshub stands on two deified mountains (depicted as men) alongside his wife Hepatu, who is standing on the back of a panther. Behind her, their son and (possibly) two daughters are respectively carried by a smaller panther and a double-headed eagle. The largest relief, on the opposite wall, depicts the complex's bearded founder, King Tudhaliya IV, standing on two mountains. The rock ledges were probably used for offerings or sacrifices and the basins for libations.

On the way into **Chamber B**, you should supposedly ask permission of the winged, lion-headed guard depicted by the entrance before entering. The narrow gallery is thought to be a memorial chapel for Tudhaliya IV, dedicated by his son Suppiluliuma II. The large limestone block could have been the base of a statue of the king. Buried until a century ago and better protected from the elements, the carvings include a procession of 12 scimitar-wielding underworld gods. On the opposite wall, the detailed relief of Nergal depicts the underworld deity as a sword; the four lion heads on the handle (two pointing towards the blade, one to the left and the other to the right) double as the deity's knees and shoulders.

Alacahöyük

The tiny farming hamlet of Alacahöyük is 36km north of Boğazkale and 52km south of Çorum. The site is very old, but the excavation area is small and most of the movable monuments are now in Ankara's Museum of Anatolian Civilisations (p417), so it's really only worth the effort if you've got some spare time after visiting Hattuşa.

The **museum** (incl excavation area admission ₺5; ⏰8am-7pm) is beside the ruins, displaying artists' impressions of the site at various points in its history, as well as finds dating back to the Chalcolithic and Old Bronze ages.

At the ruins, the **monumental gate** has two eyeless sphinxes guarding the door. The detailed reliefs (copies, the originals are in Ankara) show musicians, a sword swallower, animals for sacrifice and the Hittite king and queen – all part of festivities and ceremonies dedicated to Teshub, shown here as a bull. Once through the gate, the main excavations on the right-hand side are of a Hittite palace/temple complex.

To the left, protected under plastic covers, are the pre-Hittite royal **shaft graves**. Dating from 2300 to 2100 BC, each skeleton was buried individually along with a variety of personal belongings and several oxen skulls, which archaeologists presume to be the leftovers of a funereal meal.

On the far left of the back of the site is an underground **tunnel**. Walk through it and look down at the fields to see how the site was built up over the millennia.

ⓘ Getting There & Away

There's no public transport between Alacahöyük and Boğazkale, so the best way to reach the site is by taxi or with your own transport. If you're really keen, you could take a bus or dolmuş from Çorum to Alaca and another from Alaca to Alacahöyük (one or two services per day, none at weekends).

Çorum

☏0364 / POP 236,730

Set on an alluvial plain on a branch of the Çorum River, Çorum is a prosperous, but unremarkable provincial capital, resting on its modest fame as the chickpea capital of Turkey. The town is full of *leblebiciler* (chickpea roasters) and sacks upon sacks of the chalky little pulses, sorted according to fine distinctions obvious only to a chickpea dealer.

The Çorum Museum is excellent preparation for Hattuşa and the other Hittite sites to the southwest, and the busy and bustling town centre offers some glimpses of provincial Turkish life.

◎ Sights

★ **Çorum Museum** MUSEUM
(Cengiz Topel Caddesi; admission ₺5; ⊘ 8am-7pm Tue-Sun) By the time a traveller reaches Çorum, there's a good chance they'll have seen more than enough small-town museums, but don't make the assumption that Çorum's version of the same is not worth visiting – quite the opposite in fact. This excellent museum, one of the best in central Turkey, uses impressive exhibits, computer graphics and film to display Anatolian history from the Bronze Age to the Roman period, with a major focus on Hittite history.

The centrepiece is a reconstruction of the royal tomb at Alacahöyük, with bull skulls and a crumpled skeleton clad in a crown, and there are some incredible artefacts such as a Hittite ceremonial jug with water-spouting bulls around its rim, and a good collection of Hittite cuneiform tablets.

Next door, and included in the entrance fee, is the less impressive **Ethnographic Museum** containing the usual selection of mannequins making pots, drinking çay and so forth.

The museum is just over the main road from the otogar.

🍽 Sleeping & Eating

There are plenty of kebap-style places to eat throughout the town.

Grand Park Hotel HOTEL €€
(✉ 0364-225 4131; www.grandpark.com.tr; İnönü Caddesi 60; s/d ₺60/120; ❊🛜) This smart hotel has small rooms with light modern decor and shipshape bathrooms. The friendly staff and lightning-bolt fast wi-fi are a bonus. It's 250m up the road from the otogar. There are several similar places nearby.

★ **Anitta Otel** LUXURY HOTEL €€€
(✉ 0364-666 0999, 0364-213 8515; www.anitta hotel.com; İnönü Caddesi 80; s ₺95-140, d ₺145-200; ❊🛜🏊) The town's snazziest offering probably doesn't deserve the five-stars it's been awarded, but nevertheless this is a genuinely comfortable place to stay. There are numerous facilities and a roof-top restaurant that produces excellent Turkish and international dishes. There are two types of room on offer, with only size and desk space differing between them.

❶ Getting There & Away

Being on the main Ankara–Samsun highway, Çorum has good bus connections. Regular buses go to Alaca (₺5, 45 minutes), Amasya (₺15, two hours), Ankara (₺20, four hours), Kayseri (₺30, 4¾ hours), Samsun (₺20, three hours) and Sungurlu (₺6, 1¼ hours).

Amasya

☑ 0358 / POP 96,220

Amasya is a tale of two shores. On the north of the Yeşilırmak River, rows of half-timbered Ottoman houses sit squeezed together like chocolate cakes in a patisserie window. To the south, the newer, more modern Turkey tries to get on with things in an outward-looking ode to the succession of empires that reigned in this narrow, rocky valley. Towering above the minarets and the *medreses* (seminaries) are pockmarks of Pontic tombs, etched into the highrise bluff and guarded by a lofty citadel. Amasya's setting may evoke high drama, but life here unfolds as slowly as the train takes apples out of town via a mountain tunnel. In local folklore, these tunnels were dug by Ferhat, a tragic star-crossed figure who was in love with Sirin, the sister of a sultan queen.

History

Called Hakmış by the Hittites, the Amasya area has been inhabited continuously since around 5500 BC. Alexander the Great conquered Amasya in the 4th century BC, then it became the capital of a successor kingdom ruled by a family of Persian *satraps* (provincial governors). By the time of King Mithridates II (281 BC), the Kingdom of Pontus entered a golden age and dominated a large part of Anatolia from its Amasya HQ. During the latter part of Pontus' flowering, Amasya was the birthplace of Strabo (c 63 BC to AD 25), the world's first geographer.

Amasya's golden age continued under the Romans, who named it a 'first city' and used it as an administrative centre for rulers such as Pompey. It was Julius Caesar's conquest of a local town that prompted his immortal words '*Veni, vidi, vici*' – 'I came, I saw, I conquered'.

Amasya

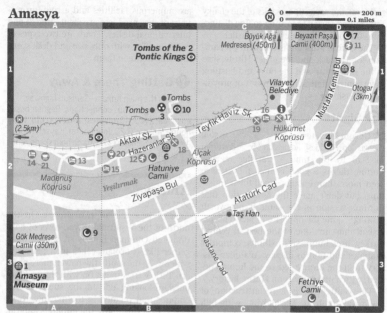

Amasya

◎ Top Sights

◎ Sights

◎ Activities, Courses & Tours

◎ Sleeping

◎ Eating

◎ Drinking & Nightlife

After the Romans came the Byzantines, the Danışmend Turks, the Seljuks, the Mongols, and the national republic of Abazhistan. In Ottoman times, Amasya was an important military base and testing ground for the sultans' heirs; it also became a centre of Islamic study, with as many as 18 *medreses* and 2000 theological students by the 19th century.

After WWI, Atatürk met his supporters here and hammered out the basic principles of the Turkish struggle for independence, which were published in the Amasya Circular.

◉ Sights

◉ North of the River

★ Tombs of the Pontic Kings   TOMB
(Kral Kaya Mezarları; admission ₺5; ⏰ 8.30am-6.30pm May-Oct, to 4.45pm Nov-Apr) Looming above the northern bank of the river is a

sheer rock face with the conspicuous cut-rock Tombs of the Pontic Kings. The tombs, cut deep into the limestone as early as the 4th century BC, were used for cult worship of the deified rulers. There are more than 20 (empty) tombs in the valley and they're at their most striking when viewed from the southern river bank. At night they are lit up in a memorably garish fashion.

Climb the steps from the souvenir stalls to the ticket office. Just past the office the path divides: turn right to view the most impressive tombs, with good panoramas of Amasya. Turn left to find the remnants of the Baths of the Maidens Palace, built in the 14th century, and, through a rock-hewn tunnel, a couple more tombs.

Hatuniye Mahallesi   NEIGHBOURHOOD

The Hatuniye Mahallesi is Amasya's wonderful neighbourhood of restored Ottoman houses, interspersed with good modern reproductions to make a harmonious whole.

The Hazeranlar Konağı (Hazeranlar Sokak; admission ₺5; ⊘8.30am-noon & 1-4.45pm Tue-Sun), constructed in 1865 and restored in 1979, was built by Hasan Talat, the accountant of governor-poet Ziya Paşa, for his sister, Hazeran Hanım. The restored rooms are beautifully furnished in period style, with a refined feel to their chandeliers and carved wood. The Directorate of Fine Arts gallery in the basement has changing exhibitions.

Harşena Castle   CASTLE

(Kale; admission ₺5; ⊘8am-7pm Apr-Oct, to 4.45pm Nov-Mar) Perched precariously atop rocky Mt Harşena, the kale offers magnificent views down the valley. The remnants of the walls date from Pontic times, perhaps around King Mithridates' reign, but a fort stood here from the early Bronze Age. Destroyed and repaired by several empires, it had eight defensive layers descending 300m to the Yeşilırmak River, and a tunnel with 150 steps cut into the mountain.

To reach the castle turn left when you get to the Büyük Ağa Medresesi and follow the road for about 1km to a street on the left marked 'Kale'. It's 1.7km up the mountainside to a car park, then another steep 15-minute climb to the summit. Although the castle is popular with families, travellers of either sex are advised not to go up unaccompanied on foot later in the day.

Büyük Ağa Medresesi   MEDRESE

The impressive Büyük Ağa Medresesi (1488) has an octagonal layout, rarely seen in Ottoman medrese architecture. It was built by Sultan Beyazıt II's chief white eunuch Hüseyin Ağa, also known as Grandagha. It still serves as a seminary for boys who are training to be hafız (theologians who have memorised the entire Koran) and is not open to the public.

Just before the medresesi is a small, and not totally natural, waterfall that's a hit with local families.

⊙ South of the River

★ Amasya Museum   MUSEUM

(☑0358-218 4513; Atatürk Caddesi; admission ₺5; ⊘8.15am-noon & 1-4.45pm) This superb museum packs in beautifully laid out treasures from the Bronze Age, Hittite, Pontic and Roman eras. Look out for the famous Statuette of Amasya, a bronze figure of the Hittite storm god Teshub. The highlight though is a collection of mummies dating from the 14th-century İlkhan period. The bodies, mummified without removing the organs, were discovered beneath the Burmalı Minare Camii. They're not very suitable for squeamish or young eyes.

There's also a wealth of manuscripts, Ottoman artefacts, an armoury of flintlock guns and the original wooden doors from Amasya's Gök Medrese Camii. All the displays have detailed information panels in English.

Sabuncuoğlu History of Medicine Museum   MUSEUM

(Darüşşifa; Mustafa Kemal Bulvarı; adult/child ₺4/2; ⊘8.30am-5pm Tue-Sun) Built as a mental hospital in 1309 by Ilduş Hatun, wife of the İlkhanid Sultan Olcaytu, the Darüşşifa (also called Bimarhane) may have been the first place to try to treat psychiatric disorders with music. It was used as a hospital until the 18th century. One of the most important physicians who worked here was Serefedin Sabuncuoğlu; today the hospital is a museum to his work and includes surgical equipment and some fascinating (and rather graphic) illustrations of treatments.

Sultan Beyazıt II Camii   MOSQUE

(Ziyapaşa Bulvarı) The graceful Sultan Beyazıt II Camii (1486) is Amasya's largest külliye (mosque complex), with a medrese, fountain, imaret (soup kitchen) and library. The main door, mihrab (niche in a minaret indicating the direction of Mecca) and pulpit are made of white marble, and its windows feature *kündekari* (interlocking wooden carvings). It's surrounded by manicured lawns and is popular with locals.

In the mosque grounds is the small and rather eccentric **Minyatür Amasya Müzesi** (Ziyapaşa Bulvarı, Sultan Beyazıt II Camii; ₺2; ⊙9am-noon & 1-7pm May-Oct, 8am-noon & 1-5pm Nov-Mar), which is a near perfect recreation of Amasya in miniature. Use it to plan your route up to the castle and stay for nightfall to listen to the call to prayer. Children will love this one.

Gök Medrese Camii
MOSQUE

(Mosque of the Sky-Blue Seminary; Atatürk Caddesi) The Gök Medrese Camii was built from 1266 to 1267 for Seyfettin Torumtay, the Seljuk governor of Amasya. The *eyvan* (vaulted recess) serving as its main portal is unique in Anatolia, while the *kümbet* (domed tomb) was once covered in *gök* (sky-blue) tiles, hence the name.

Mehmet Paşa Camii
MOSQUE

(Mustafa Kemal Bulvarı) The pretty Mehmet Paşa Camii was built in 1486 by Lala Mehmet Paşa, tutor to Şehzade Ahmet, the son of Sultan Beyazıt II. Don't miss the beautiful marble *mimber* (pulpit). The complex originally included the builder's tomb, an *imaret, tabhane* (hospital), hamam and *handan* (inn).

Beyazıt Paşa Camii
MOSQUE

(Mustafa Kemal Bulvarı) This early Ottoman mosque (1419) follows a twin-domed plan that was a forebear in style to the famous Yeşil Cami in Bursa. It's closed except at prayer times, but its most interesting features are external anyway.

Gümüşlü Cami
MOSQUE

(Silvery Mosque; Meydanı, Atatürk Caddesi) The Gümüşlü Cami (1326) is the earliest Ottoman mosque in Amasya, but has been rebuilt several times: in 1491 after an earthquake, in 1612 after a fire, and again in 1688. It was added to in 1903 and restored again in 1988.

🕴 Activities

Hamams
HAMAM

Amasya has several venerable hamams that are still in operation. The **Yıldız Hamamı** (Star Hamam; Hazeranlar Sokak; wash & massage ₺12) was built by a Seljuk commander in the 13th century and restored in the 16th century. On the southern side of the river is the Ottoman **Mustafa Bey Hamamı** (Mustafa Kemal Bulvarı; wash & massage ₺12), built in 1436. Both are open from about 6am to 10am and 4pm to 11pm for men and from 10am to 4pm for women.

🛏 Sleeping

Gönül Sefası
GUESTHOUSE ₺₺

(☑0358-212 9461; www.gonulsefasi.com; Yalıboyu Sokak 24; s/d/tr ₺60/100/120) Antique farming equipment decorates the courtyard while Ottoman curios fill every nook in the little restaurant, adding lots of local character to this family-run hotel. The large rooms are kept elegantly simple with comfy beds. Grab one of the two hosting teensy balconies over the Yeşilırmak River to make the most of this delightfully dinky place.

Emin Efendi Konağı
HISTORIC HOTEL ₺₺

(☑0358-213 0033; www.eminefendi.com; Hazeranlar Sokak 66-85; s/d ₺90/130; ❋🖭) Brought to life by one of Amasya's oldest families, Emin Efendi is a collection of five neighbouring old buildings (the names of each building varies slightly). The style of all though is of gentle old elegance and some have river views. Sound proofing though is non-existent. The courtyard restaurant (mains ₺5 to ₺25) is the place for fine dining.

Şükrübey Konağı
GUESTHOUSE ₺₺

(☑0358-212 6285; www.sukrubeykonagi.com.tr; Hazeranlar Sokak 55; s/d ₺70/140; 🖭) A sweet family choice with simple, cosy rooms set around a courtyard, Şükrübey is a winner for its genuinely warm and welcoming atmosphere. Rooms lead out to narrow balconies with views of either the courtyard or the Yeşilırmak River. Some of the rooms were being renovated at the time of research so it should soon be even better.

The hotel is quite discreet, with only a very small sign.

Uluhan Otel
HOTEL ₺₺

(☑0358-212 7575; www.oteluluhan.com; Teyfik Haviz Sokak 15; r ₺150-180; 🖭) While the cheaper rooms here are elegant and old-fashioned, it's the river-facing rooms, covered in glitter paint and coloured dots that make this place stand out from the pack. Even so, it seems a little overpriced.

🍴 Eating & Drinking

Amasya's best eating is found in its hotels, but there are a few reasonable cafes and restaurants in Hatuniye Mahallesi and a smattering of more basic options around town.

Amasya is famed for its apples, which give autumn visitors one more thing to sink their teeth into.

Elif & Be Kafeterya
ANATOLIAN €

(Hazeranlar Sokak; mains ₺6-8; ⊘9am-10pm) This cute little flower-filled cafe and restaurant serves light meals such as *gözleme* and attracts masses of people for a drink or snack. It's next to the Hazeranlar Konaği.

Strabon Restaurant
MODERN TURKISH €€

(☑0358-212 4012; Teyfik Havız Sokak; mains ₺8-16; ⊘8.30am-11pm) Our favourite riverside deck in Amasya. The hot or cold mezes (₺6 to ₺12) are tasty and fresh, the meat grills are low on oil, and the grilled *balık* (fish) is so perfectly cooked it literally falls off the bone. If you're not hungry, Strabon doubles as a fun venue for drinking booze.

Amasya Şehir Derneği
TURKISH €€

(Teyfik Havız Sokak; mains ₺10-20) Beloved by a suited-and-booted clientele, this popular restaurant has three tiers to choose from and a menu of typical Turkish grills. The balcony is the place to be, especially in the evening when the river views provide a respite from the live music entertainment inside.

Hadi Heeri
TURKISH €€

(Hazeranlar Sokak 21/A; mains ₺8-12; ⊘noon-11pm) With a raised riverfront terrace this is one of the more popular cafe-restaurants in the old town. People tend to congregate here for food at lunchtime and çay in the evening. Don't miss trying the chickpea soup.

Eylül Buğusa Avlu
BAR

(Hazeranlar Sokak) It may have no view, but this shaded courtyard is a pleasant spot for a couple of beers and some light eats (snacks ₺5 to ₺8).

Seyran Cafe
NARGILE CAFE

(Hazeranlar Sokak) The coveted seating is on the tiny balcony of this mellow cafe.

❶ Information

Tourist Office (Hükümet Köprüsü; ⊘8am-5pm) Inside a small wooden hut, the tourist office can dole out a couple of leaflets, but that's about the limit of things.

❶ Getting There & Away

The **otogar** (Atatürk Caddesi) has daily services to locations including Ankara (₺30, five hours), Çorum (₺10, two hours), İstanbul (₺60, 11 hours), Kayseri (₺40, eight hours), Nevşehir (₺50, nine hours), Samsun (₺15, 2½ hours), Si-vas (₺30, 3½ hours) and Tokat (₺15, two hours). A taxi from the otogar to the city centre costs around ₺15 depending on where you hop out.

Amasya **train station** (☑218 1239; İstasyon Caddesi; ⊘4am-10pm) is served by daily local trains to Samsun (₺6, three hours, 4.55am and 8.40am) and Sivas (₺11, 5½ hours, 2.25pm).

Tokat
☑0356 / POP 134,000

Locals claim you can hear the steps of civilisations creeping up behind you in Tokat, where history buffs gorge themselves on the mosques, mansions, hamams and *hans* (caravanserais) in this ancient town at the heart of Anatolia.

Physically on the rise due to seven centuries of sodden silt, Tokat's booming antique trade and architectural treats guarantee the town won't sink into obscurity any time soon. You can easily spend a day rummaging through the *yazma* (headscarf) and copperware stalls, or getting knuckled by Tokat's notorious masseurs.

◎ Sights

★Tokat Müzesi
MUSEUM

(Sulusokak Caddesi, Arastalı Bedesten; ⊘8am-noon & 1-5pm) FREE Housed within the impressively restored Arastalı Bedesten (covered market) the excellent collection here packs in Roman tombs, Seljuk carpets, Hellenic jewellery and local folkloric dresses, with informative signs in English. Look out for Bronze Age and Hittite artefacts, icons and relics from Tokat's churches (including a Greek Orthodox representation of John the Baptist with his head on a platter) and dervish ceremonial tools and weapons.

Gök Medrese
HISTORIC BUILDING

(Blue Seminary; GOP Bulvarı) Constructed after the fall of the Seljuks and the coming of the Mongols by Pervane Muhinedin Süleyman, a local potentate, the 13th-century Gök Medrese has also served as a hospital and a school. Very few of the building's *gök* tiles are left on the facade, but there are enough on the interior courtyard walls to give an idea of what it must have looked like in its glory days.

At the time of writing the medrese was closed for renovations.

Mevlevihane
MUSEUM

(Bey Sokağı; ⊘8am-6pm Mon-Fri, 9am-6pm Sat & Sun) FREE Turn left on GOP Bulvarı just before Latifoğlu Konağı and cross the canal to get to this restored dervish lodge with its museum to all things dervish, built in 1613 by Muslu Ağa, vizier to Sultan Ahmet I (r 1603–17). One of the most tranquil corners of Tokat, the building is set inside a small garden compound in a neighbourhood of cobbled streets and Ottoman houses buckling under the weight of years.

The exhibits inside include metalwork, illustrated Korans and prayer carpets gathered from mosques throughout the region. The *semahane* (where whirling ceremonies were held) is upstairs. The room contains an interesting collection of dervish paraphernalia, but the effect is unfortunately tarnished by the tacky mannequins illustrating the *sema*.

Follow the garden path round to the back of the building to get to Muslu Ağa Köşkü, which the vizier used as his family residence.

Just outside, back across the canal, is Tokat's Ottoman Clock Tower; the numbers on its faces are in Arabic.

Sulusokak Caddesi
NEIGHBOURHOOD

Many of Tokat's old buildings still survive, though in ruins, along Sulusokak Caddesi, which was the main thoroughfare before the perpendicular Samsun–Sivas road was improved in the 1960s. With its ancient buildings and dusty side-streets it's an interesting area to poke about.

Sulusokak Caddesi runs west from the north side of Cumhuriyet Meydanı on GOP Bulvarı, past Ali Paşa Camii (1572), which has classical Ottoman features on its grand central dome. Continue along the road and on the right you'll see the tiny Ali Tusi Türbesi (1233), a brick Seljuk work that incorporates some fine blue tiles.

Further on, on the same side of the road, the brick-and-wood Sulu Han is still in use, with its interior painted turquoise and white. This 17th-century Ottoman caravanserai provided accommodation for merchants visiting the Arastalı Bedesten (covered market) next door, which has been superbly reconstructed and now houses the Tokat Müzesi (p447). Right after the bedesten is the 16th-century Takyeciler Camii, displaying the nine-domed style of great Ottoman mosques.

Across the road from the bedesten are two spectacular buildings that are currently being restored: the Yağıbasan Medresisi (1152), one of Anatolia's first open-domed medreses, and beside it the enormous bulk of the 16th-century Ottoman Deveciler Hanı, one of Tokat's finest caravanserais.

Carry on up the road and you'll come to the tiny 14th-century Kadı Hasan Camii and the Ottoman Paşa Hamamı (1434).

Taş Han & Around
HISTORIC BUILDING

(GOP Bulvarı; ⊙8am-8pm) FREE The 17th-century Taş Han, is an Ottoman caravanserai and workshop with a cafe in the courtyard. Two floors of shops sell a mixture of local garb and copperware, and paintings of sailboats and doe-eyed puppies.

Behind the Taş Han are streets lined with old half-timbered Ottoman houses. There are more shops in this area selling crafts; some of the designs you see on *yazmas*, kilims and carpets were assimilated from Afghan refugees who settled here during the Soviet invasion of Afghanistan in the 1980s.

In the fruit and vegetable market, across GOP Bulvarı from the Taş Han, stand the Hatuniye Camii and ruined medrese, dating from 1485 and the reign of Sultan Beyazıt II.

A few hundred metres north of the Taş Han, behind some plastic sandal stands on the same side of the street, look out for Sümbül Baba Türbesi (1291), an octagonal Seljuk tomb. Beside it a road leads up for around 1km to the citadel, built in the 5th century and restored during the Seljuk

---

AUBERGINE DREAM

The town's culinary contribution to the world, the Tokat kebap is made up of skewers of lamb and sliced aubergine (eggplant) hung vertically, then baked in a wood-fired oven. Tomatoes and peppers, which take less time to cook, are baked on separate skewers. As the lamb cooks, it releases juices that baste the aubergine. All these goodies are then served together with a huge fist of roasted garlic, adding an extra punch to the mix.

It's almost worth coming to Tokat just to sample the dish, and in fact you might have to; it's inexplicably failed to catch on in places much further afield than Sivas or Amasya, and Tokat's chefs do it best anyway. Standard aubergine döners that crop up are a far cry from the glorious blow-out of the original.

and Ottoman eras. Little remains but the fine view, and women travellers should not go up alone.

Latifoğlu Konağı   MUSEUM

(GOP Bulvarı; ⊙ 8am-noon & 1-5pm) FREE Two blocks south of Cumhuriyet Meydanı, the splendid 19th-century Latifoğlu Konağı is a fine example of baroque architecture in the Ottoman style. The rooms have been restored to their former finery with elaborately carved wood ceilings and intricately embellished plasterwork detail.

🏃 Activities

Ali Paşa Hamam   HAMAM

(GOP Bulvarı; ⊙ 5am-11pm for men, 9am-5pm for women) These baths, under domes studded with glass bulbs to admit natural light, were built in 1572 for Ali Paşa, one of the sons of Süleyman the Magnificent. They have separate bathing areas for men and women, and the full works should cost around ₺15.

🛏 Sleeping

Çavuşoğlu Otel   HOTEL €

(☑ 0356-213 0908; GOP Bulvarı 168; s/d ₺50/70; ❄❡) The price is right at this central bargain. Fair-sized rooms are well cared for, and if you get a back room they are that rare thing for Turkey – quiet – well fairly! There's fast wi-fi, hairdryers in the bathrooms, and the towels are nice and new.

Çavuşoğlu Tower Hotel   BUSINESS HOTEL €€€

(☑ 0356-212 3570; www.cavusoglutowerhotel.com; GOP Blvd 172/A; s/d from ₺130/180; ❄❡❧) The smartest address in town has enormous rooms with floor to ceiling windows (that from the upper levels will make a vertigo sufferer wobble), there are big desks and the beds have glittery bedspreads, which is probably just what every businessman wants. There's an impressive breakfast spread, fast internet, a pool and a gym.

🍽 Eating

Konak Café   CAFE €

(☑ 0356-214 4146; GOP Bulvarı; mains ₺7-15; ⊙ 9am-11pm) This friendly cafe has multi-level outdoor shaded seating to lounge on after stomping all those historic streets. The menu does the usual *köftes* and kebaps, but it's a good place to just chill out with a juice and puff on a nargile as well. It's located at the rear of the Latifoğlu Konağı.

Mis Kebap   KEBAP €€

(Hükümet Caddesi; mains ₺9-25; ⊙ 10am-11pm) Ask a local where the best Tokat kebaps (and pretty much any other kind of kebap) can be found and there's a good chance they will send you to this bustling, upmarket restaurant where smartly turned out waiters explain what everything is and assure you that you are indeed hungry enough to eat a monster-sized Tokat kebap.

Plevne Restaurant   TURKISH €€

(Sulusokak Caddesi; mains ₺10-15; ⊙ 8am-10pm) The wavy, black-and-white murals lend a modern tinge to this bright canteen-like place. The food consists of well-prepared Turkish classics and the pide is particularly special: deliciously thin with just the right amount of crunch.

ℹ Getting There & Away

Tokat's small **otogar** (Gültekin Topçam Bulvarı) is about 1.7km northeast of the main square. Bus companies should provide a *servis* to ferry you to/from town; otherwise, if you don't want to wait for a dolmuş, a taxi will cost about ₺12.

Several bus companies have ticket offices around Cumhuriyet Meydanı.

Tokat doesn't have all that many bus departures, so it's worth confirming departure times and booking tickets as early as possible. There are buses to the following: Amasya (₺15, two hours), Ankara (₺45, 7½ hours), İstanbul (₺70, 12 hours), Samsun (₺30, three hours) and Sivas (₺15, 1½ hours).

Local minibuses leave from the separate İlce ve Köy terminal, one block east from the Taş Han.

Around Tokat

Ballıca Cave

The **Ballıca Cave** (Ballıca Mağarası; ☑ 0356-261 4236; adult/child ₺8/4; ⊙ 8am-sunset), 26km southwest of Tokat, is one of Turkey's most famous caves. The limestone labyrinth, 3.4 million years old and 8km long (680m is open to the public), bristles with rock formations such as onion-shaped stalactites and mushroom-like stalagmites. Smugglers used to live here and the squeaks of the current residents, dwarf bats, add to the atmosphere created by dripping water.

Unfortunately, the ambience is quickly lost if you share the metal walkways with many others, and with its copious lighting and signposts, the cave can feel like an underground theme park.

The views from the cafe, over the forested hills and oh-so-pretty mountains are enough to make you want to lace up some hiking boots, and the good news is that these caves now sit at the heart of the new Ballıca Nature Park. It's hoped that in the near future a number of signed hiking trails will lead off from the caves.

To get to Ballıca, take a minibus from Tokat's İlçe ve Köy minibus terminal to Pazar (₺4, 40 minutes), where a taxi will be waiting to run you up the winding country road to the cave (8km). Drivers prefer to do a round trip with waiting time, but they also like to keep the meter running while they wait so you may end up paying as much as ₺60 to ₺80. If you are driving from Amasya, Pazar is signposted 14km south of the main road to Tokat.

Sivas

☏ 0346 / POP 315,100

With a colourful, sometimes tragic history and some of the finest Seljuk buildings ever erected, Sivas is a good stopover en route to the wild east. The city lies at the heart of Turkey politically as well as geographically, thanks to its role in the run-up to the War of Independence. The Congress building resounded with plans, strategies and principles as Atatürk and his adherents discussed their great goal of liberation. The Turkish hero commented: 'Here is where we laid the foundations of our republic'. At night, as the red flags on the *meydan* (town square) compete for attention with the spotlit minarets nearby, İnönü Bulvarı might be central Anatolia's slickest thoroughfare outside Ankara. The occasional horse and cart gallops down the boulevard, past the neon lights, like a ghost of Anatolia's past.

History

The tumulus at nearby Maltepe shows evidence of settlement as early as 2600 BC, but Sivas itself was probably founded by the Hittite king Hattushilish I around 1500 BC. It was ruled in turn by the Assyrians, Medes and Persians, before coming under the sway of the kings of Cappadocia and Pontus. Eventually the city fell to the Romans, who called it Megalopolis; this was later changed to Sebastea, then shortened to Sivas by the Turks.

The Seljuks and the Danışmends slogged it out for supremacy here between 1152 and 1175 until the Seljuks finally prevailed, only to be dispossessed by the Mongol invasion of 1243. The İlkhanids succeeded the Mongols, and the city was then grabbed by the Ottomans (1398), Tamerlane (1400) and the Ottomans again (1408).

More recently Sivas was the location for the famous Sivas Congress in September 1919. Seeking to consolidate Turkish resistance to the Allied occupation and partition of his country, Atatürk arrived here from Samsun and Amasya, and gathered delegates to confirm decisions made at the Erzurum Congress. The two congresses heralded the War of Independence.

SIVAS MASSACRE

Sivas' Otel Madımak was the site of one of modern Turkey's worst hate crimes, on 2 July 1993, when 37 Alevi intellectuals and artists were burned alive in a mob arson attack. The victims, who had come for a cultural festival, included Aziz Nesin, the Turkish publisher of Salman Rushdie's *Satanic Verses*. A crowd of 1000 extreme Islamist demonstrators gathered outside the hotel after Friday prayers to protest about the book's publication, and in the ensuing chaos the hotel was set alight and burned to the ground.

Despite continual calls from the victim's families for the site to be turned into a memorial, the Madımak was reopened and run as a hotel and kebap shop until 2010 when the government purchased the building. In 2011 it reopened as a children's science and cultural education centre with a small memorial corner that lists the names of those who died.

The scars from the tragedy show no signs of fading, though. Every year, on the anniversary, demonstrators gather at the site in remembrance, and many of the victim's families and supporters still say that justice has yet to be served. In March 2012 five further suspects in the attack had the case against them dropped due to the statute of limitations. Of the 190 people initially charged for their role in the attack only 31 are still in prison, serving sentences of life imprisonment.

Sivas

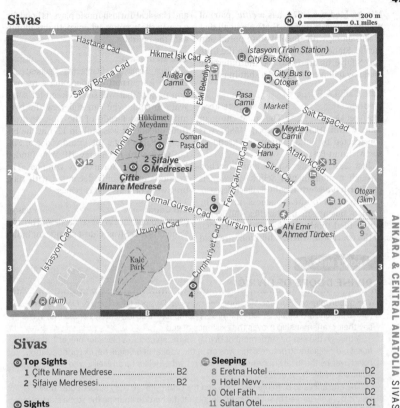

Sivas

◉ Sights & Activities

★ Şifaiye Medresesi   MEDRESE

(Hükümet Meydanı) **FREE** Dating to 1218, this was one of the most important medical schools built by the Seljuks and was once Anatolia's foremost hospital. But it wasn't just built to help the sick. It was built to look good, and 800 years later it still impresses.

The decoration features stylised sun/lion and moon/bull motifs, beautiful blue Azeri tile work and a poem in Arabic composed by the sultan.

The main courtyard has four *eyvans* (vaulted halls), with sun and moon symbols on either side of the eastern one. Look to the right as you enter the courtyard to see the porch that was walled up as a tomb for Sultan İzzettin Keykavus I, who commissioned the building before he died of tuberculosis.

Today the courtyard is filled with the tables and chairs of teahouses serving çay. Come in the early evening as the sun sets and swallows scream between the minarets of the neighbouring mosques and you could imagine yourself in Iran.

★ Çifte Minare Medrese   MEDRESE

(Seminary of the Twin Minarets; Hükümet Meydanı) **FREE** Commissioned by the Mongol-İlkhanid vizier Şemsettin Güveyni after defeating the Seljuks at the battle of Kosedağ, the Çifte

Minare Medrese (1271) has a *çifte* (pair) of mighty minarets. In fact, that's about all that is left, along with the elaborate portal and facade. Stand on the path between the Çifte and Şifaiye medreses to see the difference made by half a century and a shift in power.

Kale Camii & Bürüciye Medresesi
HISTORIC BUILDING

(Hükümet Meydanı) FREE The squat Ottoman Kale Camii (Hükümet Meydanı) (1580) was constructed by Sultan Murat III's grand vizier Mahmut Paşa.

Just east of the Kale Camii, reached through a monumental Seljuk gateway, is the Bürüciye Medresesi (Hükümet Meydanı), built to teach 'positive sciences' in 1271 by Iranian businessman Muzaffer Bürücerdi, whose tiled tomb is inside. The tea garden in the courtyard, where exhibitions are held

and classical Turkish music plays, is good for a çay in the evening, when spotlights illuminate the building.

Gök Medrese
MEDRESE

(Sky-blue Seminary; Cumhuriyet Caddesi) Although it's currently undergoing a restoration project that will see it closed for some years to come, you can still view the twin minarets and facade of the Gök Medrese from outside. It was built in 1271 at the behest of Sahib-i Ata, the grand vizier of Sultan Gıyasettin Keyhüsrev III, who funded Konya's Sahib-i Ata mosque complex. The facade is exuberantly decorated with tiles, brickwork designs and carvings.

Ulu Cami
MOSQUE

(Great Mosque; Cemal Gürsel Caddesi) The Ulu Cami (1197) is Sivas' oldest significant build-

---

DON'T MISS

DIVINE DOORS OF DİVRİĞİ

The quadruplet of 780-year-old stone doorways on Divriği's Ulu Cami & Darüşşifa (Grand Mosque & Hospital; ⊘8am-5pm) FREE complex are so intricately carved that some say their craftsmanship proves the existence of god.

Although the sleepy settlement of Divriği seems an obscure place for one of Turkey's finest old religious structures, this was once the capital of a Seljuk *beylik* (principality), ruled over by the local emir Ahmet Şah and his wife, Melike Turan Melik, who founded the adjoining institutions in 1228.

The entrances to both the Ulu Cami and the Darüşşifa are truly stupendous, their reliefs densely carved in such minute detail that it's hard to imagine the stone started out flat. It's the tasteful Seljuk equivalent of having a cinema in your house, the sort of thing only a provincial emir with more money than sense could have dreamt of building.

Entered through the 14m-high Darüşşifa Gate, the hospital (one of the oldest in Anatolia) is pervaded by an air of serenity. The vast domed inner courtyard is centred around an octagonal pool with a spiral run-off, which allowed the tinkle of running water to break the silence of the room and soothe patients' nerves. A platform raised above the main floor may have been for musicians who likewise soothed the patients. The building was used as a medrese from the 18th century.

Next door, the West Gate of the mosque is a riot of kilim motifs, rosettes and textured effects. Note the carvings of the two-headed eagles on the far sides of the gate. Inside the mosque is very simple, with an intricately carved wooden *mimber* (pulpit in a mosque) and unique *mihrab* (niche in a minaret indicating the direction of Mecca). On the northern side of the mosque is the spectacular North Gate, a dizzying cornucopia of floral designs, Arabic inscriptions and a wealth of geometric patterns and medallions. Climb the stairs to the eastern side to view the smaller Shah's Gate.

Dolmuş services from Sivas leave from the terminal beside Sivas otogar at 9am, noon, 3pm and 5pm (₺25, 2½ hours), and from Divriği back to Sivas at 5am, 8.30am, noon and 4.30pm. All stop in Kangal. It is just about possible to see Balıklı Kaplıca and Divriği on the same day using public transport as long as you take the 9am bus and visit Balıklı Kaplıca first.

A return taxi from Sivas, stopping in Balıklı Kaplıca on the way, costs about ₺200. Take ID as there is sometimes a police checkpoint after Kangal.

Drivers should note that there's no through road to Erzincan from Divriği, forcing you to head northwest to Zara and the highway before you can start driving east.

ing, and one of Anatolia's oldest mosques. Built by the Danışmends, it's a large, low room with a forest of 50 columns. The super-fat brick minaret was added in 1213 and if you look at it from the southern side of the road you'll notice it has a very distinct tilt. Inside, 11 handmade stone bands surround the main praying area and the ornate *mihrab* was discovered during renovations in 1955.

Kurşunlu Hamam
HAMAM

(☑for men 0346-222 1378, for women 0346-221 4790; Kurşunlu Caddesi; soak & scrub ₺15; ⊙7am-11pm for men, 9am-6pm for women) Built in 1576 this huge, multiple-domed structure had the indignity of being put to work as a salt warehouse for 30 years before it was restored to its former glory and put back into service as a hamam. There are separate men's and women's sections.

🛏 Sleeping

Otel Fatih
HOTEL €

(☑0346-223 4313; www.sivasfatihoteli.com; Kurşunlu Caddesi 22; s/d ₺60/90; 🖥) Amid a row of cheap hotels, the Fatih wouldn't win any style awards, but it's a certified bargain, with decent-sized rooms, good bathrooms and staff who are used to seeing the odd foreigner walk through the door.

★ Eretna Hotel
BUSINESS HOTEL €€

(☑0346-223 1717; www.eretnahotel.com; Atatürk Caddesi 36; d ₺150; 🖥) In Istanbul or at a beach resort you'd be lucky to get a basic guesthouse for these kind of prices, but in Sivas you can sleep like a lord in this glittering four-star hotel with softly toned rooms and helpful management. Front-facing rooms can be a little noisy, so opt for a rear-facing one and snooze like a baby.

Sultan Otel
HOTEL €€

(☑0346-221 2986; www.sultanotel.com.tr; Eski Belediye Sokak 18; s/d ₺120/140; ❋🖥) The rooms here are brushed up with swanky fixtures and furnishings in soft sage and neutral tones, while the bathrooms are sparkling and modern. It's all squeaky-clean and professionally run, with a rooftop bar-restaurant and extensive breakfast buffet to add to the mix.

Hotel Nevv
HOTEL €€

(☑0346-221 6363; www.hotelnevv.com.tr; Atatürk Caddesi 96; s/d ₺100/150; ❋🖥) There are lots of bright colours and green accents at the Nevv as well as decent-sized, modern bath-

rooms and rare double-glazed windows to cut down on the amount of exterior noise breaking into your sweet dreams.

🍴 Eating

★ Sema Hanımın Yeri
ANATOLIAN €

(☑0346-223 9496; İstaasyon Caddesi, Öncu Market; mains ₺6-12; ⊙8am-midnight) In this rustic, wood-panelled restaurant, the welcoming Madame Sema serves home-cooked food such as *içli köfte* (meatballs stuffed with spices and nuts) to a packed audience of young locals. If you've never eaten in a Turkish home before then this is the next best thing.

Sultan Sofrasi
KEBAP €

(Atatürk Cad 67; mains ₺8-12; ⊙11am-11pm) Attracting an eclectic mix of love-struck young couples, tired workers and domino slapping old guys in flat caps, this is an ever-bustling kebap place serving hearty, meaty meals.

❶ Getting There & Away

BUS

Bus services from Sivas aren't all that frequent. From the otogar (₺15 from the city centre by taxi) there are fairly regular services to Amasya (₺30, 3½ hours), Ankara (₺35, seven hours), İstanbul (₺70, 13 hours), Kayseri (₺20, three hours), Samsun (₺35, six hours) and Tokat (₺15, 1½ hours).

Buses should provide a *servis* into the city centre. Otherwise, catch any city bus heading to the city centre from their terminal, next to the otogar. Buses head up Atatürk Caddesi and end their run just uphill from the Paşa Camii.

TRAIN

Sivas **train station** (☑221 7000; İstasyon Caddesi) is a major rail junction for both east–west and north–south lines. The main express services are the *Doğu Ekspresi* to Kars (16 hours, daily) and the *4 Eylül Mavi Tren* to Diyarbakır (12 hours, daily). There are also local services to Kangal, Divriği and Amasya.

Around Sivas

Balıklı Kaplıca

The place where the fish-pedicure craze has it origins, bathing at Balıklı Kaplıca (Hot Springs with Fish; ☑0346-469 1151; www.balikli. org; visitor/patient ₺8/50; ⊙8am-6pm) is a satisfyingly unusual experience. The spa complex has six segregated pools set amid trees, a cafe above the mineral water, and the musty Balıklı Kaplıca Hotel (☑ 0346-469 1151; www.balikli.org; s/d ₺120/150; ❄ ❞ ☒). Hot springs rates depend on whether you define yourself as 'visitor' or 'patient'.

According to local lore a shepherd boy discovered the healing qualities of the local mineral water here, high in the dermatologically curative element selenium, and noticed that the warm water was inhabited by 'doctor fish' that sloughed dead skin off any body part you offered them. The fish supposedly favour psoriasis-inflicted skin and the spa attracts patients from all over the world, but the swarming school happily gets stuck into any patch of flesh. It is wonderfully therapeutic to dangle your feet in the water and feel nature giving you a thorough pedicure, with the nippers tickling and then soothing like tiny vacuum cleaners.

The recommended course for genuine patients is eight hours a day in the pool for three weeks.

Dolmuşes from the terminal beside Sivas' otogar run to Kangal (₺10, one hour, hourly); from there you can take a taxi to the resort (₺20). Balıklı Kaplıca offers group transfers from Sivas.

Konya

☑ 0332 / POP 1,138,170

An economic powerhouse that is religiously inspired and a busy university city that's as conservative as they come: Konya treads a delicate path between its historical significance as the home town of the whirling dervish orders and a bastion of Seljuk culture, and its modern importance as an economic boom town. The city derives considerable charm from this juxtaposition of old and new. Ancient mosques and the maze-like market district rub up against contemporary Konya around Alaaddin Tepesi, where hip-looking university students talk religion and politics in the tea gardens. If you are passing through this region, say from the coast to Cappadocia, then make time to explore one of Turkey's most compelling cities.

History

Almost 4000 years ago the Hittites called this city 'Kuwanna'. It was Kowania to the Phrygians, Iconium to the Romans and then Konya to the Turks. Iconium was an important provincial town visited several times by Sts Paul and Barnabas.

From about 1150 to 1300, Konya was the capital of the Seljuk Sultanate of Rum, which encompassed most of Anatolia. The Seljuk sultans endowed Konya with dozens of fine buildings in an architectural style that was decidedly Turkish, but had its roots in Persia and Byzantium. Traditionally Konya lay at the heart of Turkey's rich farming 'bread basket', but these days light industry and pilgrimage tourism are at least as important.

◉ Sights

★ Mevlâna Museum   MUSEUM
(☑ 0332-351 1215; admission ₺5, audioguide ₺10; ◷ 10am-5pm Mon, 9am-5pm Tue-Sun) For Muslims and non-Muslims alike, the main reason to come to Konya is to visit the Mevlâna Museum, the former lodge of the whirling dervishes. It's Celaleddin Rumi (later known as Mevlâna) that we have to thank for giving the world the whirling dervishes and, indirectly, the Mevlâna Museum. Calling it a mere museum, however, makes it sound dead and stale, but the truth couldn't be more different. As one of the biggest pilgrimage centres in Turkey, the museum constantly buzzes with energy.

For Muslims, this is a very holy place, and more than 1.5 million people visit it a year, most of them Turkish. You will see many people praying for Rumi's help. When entering, women should cover their head and shoulders, and no one should wear shorts.

The lodge is visible from some distance, its fluted dome of turquoise tiles one of Turkey's most distinctive sights. After walking through a pretty garden you pass through the Dervişan Kapısı (Gate of the Dervishes) and enter a courtyard with an ablutions fountain in the centre.

Remove your shoes and pass into the Tilavet (Koran reading) room, also known as the calligraphy room due to its calligraphic displays.

At the entrance to the mausoleum, the Ottoman silver door bears the inscription, 'Those who enter here incomplete will come out perfect'. Entering the mausoleum, look out for the big bronze Nisan tası (April bowl) on the left. April rainwater, vital to the farmers of this region, is still considered sacred and was collected in this 13th-century bowl. The tip of Mevlâna's turban was dipped in the water and offered to those in need of

DON'T MISS

WATCHING THE WHIRLING DERVISHES

The Mevlevi worship ceremony (sema), is a ritual dance representing union with God; it's what gives the dervishes their famous whirl, and appears on Unesco's third Proclamation of Masterpieces of the Oral and Intangible Heritage of Humanity. Watching a sema can be an evocative, romantic, unforgettable experience. There are many dervish orders worldwide that perform similar rituals, but the original Turkish version is the smoothest and purest, more of an elegant, trancelike dance than the raw energy seen elsewhere.

The dervishes dress in long white robes with full skirts that represent their shrouds. Their voluminous black cloaks symbolise their worldly tombs, their conical felt hats their tombstones.

The ceremony begins when the hafız, a scholar who has committed the entire Koran to memory, intones a prayer for Mevlâna and a verse from the Koran. A kettledrum booms out, followed by the plaintive sound of the ney (reed flute). Then the şeyh (master) bows and leads the dervishes in a circle around the hall. After three circuits, the dervishes drop their black cloaks to symbolise their deliverance from worldly attachments. Then one by one, arms folded on their breasts, they spin out onto the floor as they relinquish the earthly life to be reborn in mystical union with God.

By holding their right arms up, they receive the blessings of heaven, which are communicated to earth by holding their left arms turned down. As they whirl, they form a 'constellation' of revolving bodies, which itself slowly rotates. The şeyh walks among them to check that each dervish is performing the ritual properly.

The dance is repeated over and over again. Finally, the hafız again chants passages from the Koran, thus sealing the mystical union with God.

It's worthwhile planning your Konya trip to be here on a Saturday when the sema ceremony is performed at the Mevlâna Culture Centre (Whirling Dervish Performance; Aslanlı Kışla Caddesi; ☺9pm Sat) FREE. Those interested in learning more about the philosophy and beliefs of Sufis (Muslim mystics) can also attend a lecture on the teachings of Mevlâna beforehand at 8pm. There's usually no need to book, but you might want to arrive early to guarantee your seat.

ANKARA & CENTRAL ANATOLIA KONYA

healing. Also on the left are six sarcophagi belonging to Bahaeddin Veled's supporters who followed him from Afghanistan.

Continue through to the part of the room directly under the fluted dome. Here you can see Mevlâna's Tomb (the largest), flanked by that of his son Sultan Veled and those of other eminent dervishes. They are all covered in velvet shrouds heavy with gold embroidery, but those of Mevlâna and Veled bear huge turbans, symbols of spiritual authority; the number of wraps denotes the level of spiritual importance. Bahaeddin Veled's wooden tomb stands on one end, leading devotees to say Mevlâna was so holy that even his father stands to show respect. There are 66 sarcophagi on the platform, not all visible.

Mevlâna's tomb dates from Seljuk times. The mosque and semahane, where whirling ceremonies were held, were added later by Ottoman sultans (Mehmet the Conqueror was a Mevlevi adherent and Süleyman the Magnificent made charitable donations to the order). Selim I, conqueror of Egypt, donated the Mamluk crystal lamps.

The small mosque and semahane to the left of the sepulchral chamber contain exhibits such as musical instruments, the original copy of the Mathnawi, Mevlâna's prayer rug, and a 9th-century gazelle-skin Christian manuscript. There is a casket containing strands of Mohammed's beard, and a copy of the Koran so tiny that its author went blind writing it. Look to the left of the mihrab for a seccade (prayer carpet) bearing a picture of the Kaaba at Mecca. Made in Iran of silk and wool, it's extremely fine, with some three million knots (144 per square centimetre).

The matbah (kitchen) of the lodge is in the southwest corner of the courtyard. It is decorated as it would have been in Mevlâna's day, with mannequins dressed as dervishes. Look out for the wooden practise board, used by novice dervishes to learn to whirl. The dervish cells (where the dervishes lived) run along the northern and western

Konya

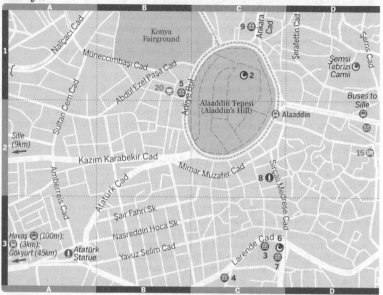

Konya

◎ Top Sights

◎ Sights

◎ Sleeping

◎ Eating

◎ Drinking & Nightlife

◎ Shopping

sides of the courtyard. Inside are a host of ethnographical displays relating to dervish life.

The complex can get oppressively busy, and seeing any of the contents of the museum display cases can be a pushing and shoving, head-ducking affair. Come early on a weekday if you want to see all the items in peace. On the other hand, the atmosphere on busy days is almost addictive and more than makes up for not being able to properly examine the museum pieces.

Beside the museum is the **Selimiye Camii**, built between 1566 and 1574 when Sultan Selim II was the governor of Konya.

Tile Museum   MUSEUM

(Karatay Medresesi Çini Müzesi; ☎0332-351 1914; Alaaddin Meydanı; admission ₺5; ◎9am-6.40pm) Gorgeously restored, the interior central dome and walls of this former Seljuk theo-

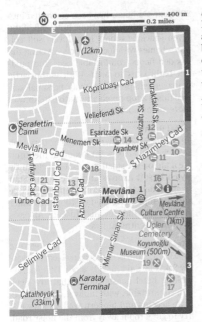

Alaaddin Camii — MOSQUE

Konya's most important religious building after the Mevlâna shrine, this Seljuk mosque bestrides Alaaddin Tepesi. Built for Alaeddin Keykubad I, Sultan of Rum from 1219 to 1231, the rambling 13th-century building was designed by a Damascene architect in Arab style. Over the centuries it was embellished, refurbished, ruined and restored. The grand original entrance on the northern side incorporates decoration from earlier Byzantine and Roman buildings.

Surrounding the mosque is the Alaaddin Tepesi, the town's favourite flower garden and park. It is at its sweetest in the spring when its summit is a glowing carpet of tulips. There are several pleasant tea shops and cafes here.

Sahib-i Ata Külliyesi — MOSQUE

(Larende Caddesi; ⊙9am-noon & 1-5pm) Behind its requisite grand entrance with built-in minaret is the Sahib-i Ata Külliyesi, originally constructed during the reign of Alaaddin Keykavus. Destroyed by fire in 1871, it was rebuilt in 13th-century style. The *mihrab* is a fine example of blue Seljuk tile work.

Around the corner, in the old dervish lodge, is the Sahib-i Ata Vakıf Müzesi (Sırçalı Medrese Caddesi; ⊙9am-5pm) **FREE** with its red-brick and blue-tiled interior now home to an interesting collection of religious artefacts.

Sırçalı Medresi — MONUMENT

(Glass Seminary; Sırçalı Medresi Caddesi; ⊙8.30am-5.30pm) **FREE** Sponsored by the Seljuk vizier Bedreddin Muhlis, the 13th-century Sırçalı Medresi was named after its tiled exterior. The *eyvan* (vaulted hall) on the western side of the courtyard was used for classes; it is decorated with blue tiles and its arch has a band of particularly fine calligraphic tile work.

Archaeological & Ethnographic Museums — MUSEUM

The rather dusty Archaeological Museum (☑0332-351 3207; Larende Caddesi; admission ₺5; ⊙9am-12.30pm & 1.30-5pm Tue-Sun) houses finds from Çatalhöyük, including the skeleton of a baby girl, clutching jewellery made of stone and bone. Other artefacts range across the millennia, from Chalcolithic terracotta jars to Hittite hieroglyphs, an Assyrian oil lamp shaped like a bunch of grapes, and bronze and stone Roman sarcophagi, one narrating the labours of Hercules in high-relief carvings. Nearby, the little-visited

logical school (1251) showcase some finely preserved blue-and-white Seljuk tilework. There is also an outstanding collection of ceramics on display including exhibits of the octagonal Seljuk tiles unearthed during excavations at Kubad Abad Palace on Lake Beyşehir. Emir Celaleddin Karatay, a Seljuk general, vizier and statesman who built the *medrese*, is buried in one of the corner rooms.

Museum of Wooden Artefacts and Stone Carving — MUSEUM

(Tas ve Ahsap Eserler Müzesi; ☑0332-351 3204; Adliye Bulvarı; admission ₺5; ⊙9am-12.30pm & 1.30-6.40pm Tue-Sun) The İnce Minare Medresesi (Seminary of the Slender Minaret), now the Museum of Wooden Artefacts and Stone Carving, was built in 1264 for Seljuk vizier Sahip Ata. Inside, many of the carvings feature motifs similar to those used in tiles and ceramics. The Seljuks didn't heed Islam's traditional prohibition of human and animal images: there are images of birds (the Seljuk double-headed eagle, for example), humans, lions and leopards.

The octagonal minaret in turquoise relief outside is over 600 years old and gave the seminary its popular name. If it looks short, this is because the top was sliced off by lightning.

Ethnographic Museum (Larende Caddesi; admission ₺5; ☺8.30am-12.30pm & 1.30-5pm Tue-Sun) has a good collection of Ottoman craftwork, including some keys the size of 21st-century doors.

Koyunoğlu Museum MUSEUM
(Kerimler Caddesi 25; ☺8am-12.30pm & 1.30-5pm Tue-Sun) FREE This curious museum contains the legacy of railway inspector Izzet Koyunoğlu who built up his esoteric collection of rare, er, collectables on his travels through Turkey. Our heart goes out to the tired-looking stuffed pelican, but there is a wonderful variety of exhibits, encompassing prehistoric bones, rhinoceros-horn rosaries, mammoth bones, boxwood spoons bearing words of wisdom about food, 19th-century carriage clocks, and old photos of Konya.

⭐ Festivals & Events

Mevlâna Festival CULTURAL
The annual Mevlâna Festival runs for a fortnight, culminating on 17 December, the anniversary of Mevlâna's 'wedding night' with Allah. Tickets (and accommodation) should be booked well in advance; contact the tourist office for assistance. If you can't get a ticket, other venues around town host dancers during the festival, although they are not of the same quality.

🛏 Sleeping

There's certainly no shortage of hotels in Konya, but the steady flow of pilgrims can lead to high prices.

Ulusan Otel HOTEL €
(☑0332-351 5004; Çarşı PTT Arkası 4; s/d without bathroom ₺35/70; ☎) This is the pick of the Konya cheapies. The rooms may be totally basic, but they're bright and spotlessly clean. Shared bathrooms are immaculately kept (some rooms have private bathrooms) and the communal area is full of homely knick-knacks.

Hotel Yasin HOTEL €
(☑0332-351 1624; Yusuf Ağa Sokak 21; s/d ₺35/70; ☎) In the heart of the souk, this place has more than just price going for it. Backpackers will find amply proportioned rooms that are well looked after, and behind the reception there's a helpful English-speaking chap.

⭐ Derviş Otel BOUTIQUE HOTEL €€
(☑0332-350 0842; www.dervishotel.com; Güngör Sokak 7; r €55-80; ❊☎) This airy, light-filled

200-year-old house has been converted into a rather wonderful boutique hotel. All of the seven spacious rooms have lovely soft colour schemes with local carpets covering the wooden floors, comfortable beds and modern bathrooms to boot. With enthusiastic management providing truly personal service this is a top-notch alternative to Konya's more anonymous hotels.

Hotel Rumi HOTEL €€
(☑0332-353 1121; www.rumihotel.com; Durakfakih Sokak 5; d ₺100-180; ❊☎) Rooms at the Rumi are a tad on the small side, but are elegantly styled in soft mauves and sage green. Staff seem to delight in offering genuine service and the top-level breakfast room has killer views over to the Mevlâna Museum. An oasis of calm in central Konya.

Otel Derya HOTEL €€
(☑0332-352 0154; www.deryaotel.com.tr; Ayanbey Sokak 18; s/d ₺75/130; ❊☎) This snazzy-looking hotel boasts rooms that are sleek and comfortable, with funky grey and chocolate accents and modern walk-in showers. Try to get a room away from the noisy road.

⭐ Hich Hotel BOUTIQUE HOTEL €€€
(☑0332-353 4424; www.hichhotel.com; Aziziye Mah Celal Sokak 6; s €69-89, d €89-109; ❊☎) A beautiful new addition to the Konya hotel scene, this design hotel mixes modern touches such as coloured stained-glass windows and contemporary furnishings with the elegant structure of the two 150-year-old buildings the hotel occupies. There's a sunny garden terrace and you can spin your way down to the Mevlâna Museum in but a moment.

🍴 Eating & Drinking

Konya's speciality is *fırın* kebap, slices of (hopefully) tender, fairly greasy roasted mutton served on puffy bread. The city bakers also make excellent fresh pide topped with minced lamb, cheese or eggs, but in Konya pide is called *etli ekmek* (bread with meat). Some restaurants around the Mevlâna Museum have great views, but their food is not recommended. The fast-food restaurants on Adilye Bulvarı, competing with the golden arches, are lively places for a snack, but check that the swift grub is thoroughly cooked.

Şifa Lokantası KEBAP €
(☑0332-352 0519; Mevlâna Caddesi 29; mains ₺6-14; ☺7am-9.30pm) Super-fast and super-

friendly service make this cheap and cheerful restaurant a sure-fire favourite. The pide is filling, fresh and tasty, and the kebaps succulent and flavourful.

★ **Konak Konya Mutfağı** ANATOLIAN €€
(☑0332-352 8547; Piriesat Caddesi 5; mains ₺15-20; ☺11am-10pm) This excellent traditional restaurant is run by well-known food writer Nevin Halıcı, who puts her personal twist on Turkish classics. Grab an outside table and dine beside vine-draped pillars and a fragrant rose garden. Aubergine aficionados shouldn't miss the *sebzeli közleme* (a grill of smoked aubergine and lamb) and sweet tooths should definitely save room to try the unusual desserts.

★ **Somatçı** ANATOLIAN €€
(☑0332-351 6696; www.somatci.com; Mengüc Sokak 36; mains ₺12-17; ☺9am-11pm) Rekindling old recipes, this exciting new restaurant uses the finest ingredients and cooks

everything with panache. Staff are happy to advise on dishes and the setting inside a carefully restored old building is spot on.

Gülbahçesı Konya Mutfağı TURKISH €€
(☑0332-351 0768; Gülbahçe Sokak 3; mains ₺9-18; ☺8am-10pm) One of Konya's best restaurants, mostly because of its upstairs terrace with views of the Mevlâna Museum. Dishes include *yaprak sarma* (stuffed vine leaves), Adana kebap and *etli ekmek*. It's a little hidden away in a mainly pedestrianised zone behind the tourist office.

★ **Osmanlı Çarşısı** CAFE
(☑0332-353 3257; İnce Minare Sokak 35A) An atmospheric early-20th-century house with terraces, pavement seating and cushions galore where students talk politics while sucking on nargile and old-timers slapping dominoes down sit in the same chairs they've occupied for years and years.

RUMI – THE MAN WHO MADE THE DERVISHES WHIRL

Celaleddin Rumi, the Seljuk Sultanate of Rum, was one of the world's great mystic philosophers. His poetry and religious writings, mostly in Persian, the literary language of the day, are among the most beloved and respected in the Islamic world. Rumi later became known as Mevlâna (Our Guide) to his followers.

Rumi was born in 1207 in Balkh (Afghanistan). His family fled the impending Mongol invasion by moving to Mecca and then to the Sultanate of Rum, reaching Konya by 1228. His father, Bahaeddin Veled, was a noted preacher, known as the Sultan of Scholars, and Rumi became a brilliant student of Islamic theology. After his father's death in 1231, he studied in Aleppo and Damascus, returning to live in Konya by 1240.

In 1244 he met Mehmet Şemseddin Tebrizi (Şemsi Tebrizi or Şems of Tabriz), one of his father's Sufi (Muslim mystic) disciples. Tebrizi had a profound influence on Rumi but, jealous of his overwhelming influence on their master, an angry crowd of Rumi's disciples put Tebrizi to death in 1247. Stunned by the loss, Rumi withdrew from the world to meditate, and wrote his greatest poetic work, the 25,000-verse Mathnawi (Mesnevi in Turkish). He also wrote many aphorisms, ruba'i and ghazal poems, collected into his 'Great Opus', the Divan-i Kebir.

Tolerance is central to Mevlâna's teachings, as in this famous verse:

Come, whoever you may be. Even if you may be an infidel, a pagan, or a fire-worshipper, come. Ours is not a brotherhood of despair. Even if you have broken your vows of repentance a hundred times, come.

Rumi died on 17 December 1273, the date now known as his 'wedding night' with Allah. His son, Sultan Veled, organised his followers into the brotherhood called the Mevlevi, or whirling dervishes.

In the centuries following Mevlâna's death, over 100 dervish lodges were founded throughout the Ottoman domains. Dervish orders exerted considerable conservative influence on the country's political, social and economic life, and numerous Ottoman sultans were Mevlevi Sufis. Atatürk saw the dervishes as an obstacle to advancement for the Turkish people and banned them in 1925, but several orders survived on a technicality as religious fraternities. The Konya lodge was revived in 1957 as a 'cultural association' intended to preserve a historical tradition.

🛍 Shopping

Bazaar
MARKET

Konya's bazaar sprawls back from the PTT building virtually all the way to the Mevlâna Museum, cramming the narrow streets with stalls, roving vendors and the occasional horse-drawn cart. There's a concentration of shops selling religious paraphernalia and tacky souvenirs at the Mevlâna Museum end.

ℹ Information

Tourist Office (☎ 0332-353 4020; Aslanı Kışla Caddesi; ⊙ 9am-5pm Mon-Sat) Gives out a city map and a leaflet covering the Mevlâna Museum; can also organise guides for the museum and has information on the weekly whirling dervish shows.

DANGERS & ANNOYANCES

Konya has a long-standing reputation for religious conservatism. Not that this should inconvenience you, but take special care not to upset the pious and make sure you're not an annoyance. If you visit during Ramadan, be aware that many restaurants will be closed during the daylight fasting hours; as a courtesy to those who are fasting, don't eat or drink in public during the day.

Non-Muslim women seem to encounter more hassle in this bastion of propriety than in many other Turkish cities, and dressing conservatively will help you avoid problems. Men can wander around in shorts without encountering any tension, but may prefer to wear something longer to fit in with local customs.

Male travellers have reported being propositioned in the Tarihi Mahkeme Hamamı.

ℹ Getting There & Away

AIR

Both **Turkish Airlines** (☎ 0332-321 2100; Ferit Paşa Caddesi; ⊙ 8.30am-5.30pm Mon-Fri, to 1.30pm Sat) and **Pegasus Airlines** operate daily flights to and from İstanbul.

The airport is about 13km northeast of the city centre; expect to pay ₺40 to ₺50 by taxi.

Depending on flight arrival/departure times, **Havaş** (☎ 0332-239 0105; www.havas.net; Ferit Paşa Caddesi, Turkish Airlines Office) airport buses run five to seven shuttle-bus services between the airport and central Konya per day (₺10, 30 minutes). Buses leave from outside the Turkish Airlines office and Alaaddin Tepesi.

BUS

Konya's **otogar** (İstanbul Caddesi) is about 7km north of Alaaddin Tepesi, accessible by tram from town. Regular buses serve all major destinations, including Ankara (₺25, 3½ hours), Antalya (₺42, five hours), İstanbul (₺68, 11½ hours), Kayseri (₺40, four hours) and Sivas (₺60, seven hours). There are lots of ticket offices on Mevlâna Caddesi and around Alaaddin Tepesi.

The **Karatay Terminal** (Eski Garaj; Pırıeasat Caddesi), 1km southwest of the Mevlâna Museum, has bus and dolmuş services to local villages.

WORTH A TRIP

SILK ROAD SPLENDOUR AT SULTANHANI

The highway between Konya and Aksaray crosses quintessential Anatolian steppe: flat grasslands as far as the eye can see, with only the occasional tumbleweed and a few mountains in the distance breaking the monotony. The Seljuks built a string of *hans* (caravanserais) along this Silk Road route and, 110km from Konya, 42km from Aksaray, the dreary village of Sultanhanı is home to one of the most stunning *hans* still standing.

The largest in Anatolia, the Sultanhanı (admission ₺5; ⊙ 7am-7pm) was constructed in 1229, during the reign of the Seljuk sultan Alaeddin Keykubad I, and restored in 1278 after a fire (when it became Turkey's largest *han*). Through the wonderful carved entrance in the 50m-long east wall, there is a raised *mescit* (prayer room) in the middle of the open courtyard, which is ringed with rooms used for sleeping, dining and cooking. A small, simple doorway leads to the atmospheric *ahır* (stable), with arches, domes and pillars in the pigeon-soundtracked gloom.

The site is a popular stop for tour groups, and you may field invitations to visit the nearby carpet-repair workshop. If you resist such offers, you could easily explore Sultanhanı in half an hour.

Regular buses run from Aksaray's otogar from Monday to Friday (₺10, 45 minutes); there are fewer services at weekends. Leaving Sultanhanı, flag down a bus or village minibus heading to Aksaray or Konya on the main highway. If you start out early you can hop off the bus, see the *han* and be on your way again an hour or so later.

BINBIRKILISE

Just before WWI, the great British traveller Gertrude Bell travelled 42km northwest of the small town of Karaman and recorded the existence of a cluster of Byzantine churches set high on a lonely hillside and rather generously known as Binbirkilise (1001 Churches). Later Irfan Orga came here in search of the last remaining nomads, a journey recorded in his book *The Caravan Moves On*. You won't see any nomads around these days, or indeed much to mark the ruins out as churches, but half a dozen families live around the ruins (and in them, in the case of some of their animals) and the site is a rural alternative to busier attractions.

It's easiest to reach the churches with your own transport. Drive out of Karaman on the Karapınar road and follow the yellow signs. The first sizeable ruin pops up in the village of Madenşehir, 36km north, after which the road becomes increasingly rough. There are fantastic views all along the road, which is just as well, as you'll have to come back the same way.

A taxi from Karaman's otogar should cost around ₺150 for the return trip; the drivers know where the churches are.

TRAIN

The **train station** (📞 332 3670; Alay Caddesi) is about 3km southwest of the centre. There are eight high-speed train links between Konya and Ankara daily (adult/child ₺27.50/13, 1¾ hours).

🛈 Getting Around

In order to use Konya's city buses, trams and minibuses you need to have a travel pass (₺1), which can be bought from booths at any of the larger transport stations.

To get to the city centre from the otogar take any tram from the east side of the station to Alaaddin Tepesi (30 minutes); tickets, which cover two journeys, cost ₺3. Trams run 24 hours a day, with one per hour after midnight. A taxi costs around ₺25.

There are half-hourly minibuses from the train station to the centre. A taxi from the station to Hükümet Meydanı costs about ₺15.

Innumerable minibuses and city buses ply Mevlâna Caddesi. Buy an electronic ticket from the booths beside the bus stands (₺3, valid for two journeys).

Around Konya

Çatalhöyük

No, this isn't a hallucination brought on by the parched Konya plain. Rising 20m above the flatlands, the East Mound at Çatalhöyük (🕗 8am-5pm) FREE is left over from one of the largest Neolithic settlements on earth. About 9000 years ago, up to 8000 people lived here, and the mound comprises 13 levels of buildings, each containing around 1000 structures. Little remains of the ancient centre other than the excavation areas, which draw archaeologists from all over the world.

If you visit between June and September, when the digs mostly take place, you might find an expert to chat to. At other times, the museum does a good job of explaining the site and the excavations, which began in 1961 under British archaeologist James Mellaart and have continued with the involvement of the local community. Mellaart's controversial theories about mother-goddess worship here caused the Turkish government to close the site for 30 years.

Near the museum entrance stands the experimental house, a reconstructed mud-brick hut used to test various theories about Neolithic culture. People at Çatalhöyük lived in tightly packed dwellings that were connected by ladders between the roofs instead of streets, and were filled in and built over when they started to wear out. Skeletons were found buried under the floors and most of the houses may have doubled as shrines. The settlement was highly organised, but there are no obvious signs of any central government system.

From the museum you can then walk across the mound to the dome-covered north shelter where excavation work has uncovered the remains of several buildings with their outlines still visible. A short trail then leads to the south area. With 21m of archaeological deposits, many of the site's most famous discoveries were made here. The lowest level of excavation, begun by Mellaart, is the deepest at Çatalhöyük and holds deposits left more than 9000 years ago. There are information panels on the viewing platforms of both excavation areas which help you decipher the site.

To get here by public transport from Konya, 33km northwest, get the Karkın minibus, which leaves the Karatay Terminal (also called Eski Garaj) at 7am, 9.30am and 4.50pm on weekdays. Get off at Kük Koy (₺7.50, 45 minutes) and walk 1km to the site, or you may be able to persuade the driver to take you the whole way. Going back, minibuses leave Kük Koy at 7.15am, 3pm and 7pm. Getting there by bus at the weekend is much harder: there are buses at 9am and midday on Saturdays and none on Sundays.

A taxi from Konya to the site and back will cost about ₺50.

Gökyurt (Kilistra, Lystra)

A little piece of Cappadocia to the southwest of Konya, the landscape at Gökyurt is reminiscent of what you'll see in Güzelyurt or the Ihlara Valley: a gorge with dwellings and medieval churches cut into the rock face, but without the crowds.

St Paul is thought to have stayed here on his three Anatolian expeditions and the area has long been a Christian pilgrimage site; especially for 12 months from June 2008, declared by Pope Benedict XVI as 'the year of St Paul' to celebrate the 2000th anniversary of the saint's birth.

There's one particularly fine church cut completely out of the rock, but no frescoes. A trip out here makes a lovely half-day excursion. The village the cave dwellings are found in is full of ever-smiling farming folk who will literally take you by the hand and lead you to the best of the caves. After you've finished exploring here set out to create your own adventures by taking a walk through the stunning surrounding landscape and looking for more cave dwellings.

❶ Getting There & Away

The easiest way to get here from Konya, 45km away, is by car or taxi; the latter will charge ₺150 to ₺200 return (including waiting time). There

are several daily buses from Konya's Karatay Terminal to Hatunsaray, 18km from Gökyurt, but taxis there are actually more expensive than from Konya as the drivers make the most of their captive audience.

Driving, you should take the Antalya road, then follow signs to Akören. After about 34km, and a few kilometres before Hatunsaray, look for a tiny brown-and-white sign on the right (marked 'Kilistra-Gökyurt, 16km'). Cyclists need to watch out for sheepdogs roaming about.

Sille

📞 0332 / POP 2000

If you're looking for an excursion from Konya, head to the pretty village of Sille, where a rock face full of cave dwellings and chapels overlooks bendy-beamed village houses in several states of decay and a few bridges across the dry river.

The domed Byzantine St Helen's Church (Ayaelena Kilisesi), near the last bus stop, was reputedly founded by Empress Helena, mother of Constantine the Great. Recently renovated, it's often kept locked – ask for the key at the security office just below the church (next to the cafeteria). There are some wonderful faded wall frescoes hidden behind an altar painted with pictures of the saints.

On the hill to the north stands a small chapel, the Küçük Kilese. It too has been recently renovated, but is normally locked Monday to Friday. Even so it's still worth the scramble up for the views over the village.

Running behind the village a whole series of cave dwellings and chapels are carved into the soft rock. None are in very good condition, but they're fun to explore.

❶ Getting There & Away

Bus 64 from Mevlâna Caddesi (near the post office) in Konya leaves every half-hour or so for Sille (₺3, 25 minutes).

Cappadocia

Best Places to Eat

➡ Cappadocia Home Cooking (p496)
➡ Ziggy's (p492)
➡ Seten Restaurant (p473)
➡ Topdeck Cave Restaurant (p473)
➡ Alamet-i Farika (p507)

Best Places to Stay

➡ Hezen Cave Hotel (p488)
➡ Koza Cave Hotel (p473)
➡ Kelebek Hotel & Cave Pension (p471)
➡ Esbelli Evi (p490)
➡ Kale Konak (p477)

Why Go?

As if plucked from a whimsical fairy tale and set down upon the stark Anatolian plains, Cappadocia is a geological oddity of honeycombed hills and towering boulders of otherworldly beauty. The fantastical topography is matched by the human history here. People have long utilised the region's soft stone, seeking shelter underground and leaving the countryside scattered with fascinating troglodyte-style architecture. The fresco-adorned rock-cut churches of Göreme Open-Air Museum and the subterranean refuges of Derinkuyu and Kaymaklı are the most famous sights, while simply bedding down in one of Cappadocia's cave hotels is an experience in 21st-century cavern dwelling.

Whether you're wooed here by the hiking potential, the history or the bragging rights of unique accommodation, it's the lunarscape panoramas that you'll remember. This region's accordion-ridged valleys, shaded in a palette of dusky orange and cream, are an epiphany of a landscape – the stuff of psychedelic daydreams.

When to Go

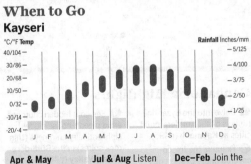

Kayseri

Apr & May Wildflowers shock the valley moonscapes into a dazzlingly photogenic riot of colour.

Jul & Aug Listen to classical-music concerts in natural outdoor rock venues.

Dec–Feb Join the snow bunnies at the Erciyes Dağı (Mt Erciyes) ski resort.

Cappadocia Highlights

1 Delve into the Byzantine tunnels of such underground cities as **Kaymaklı** (p495).

2 Examine the fresco-covered finery of churches in the **Göreme Open-Air Museum** (p466).

3 Tackle nature on the mountain trails of **Ala Dağlar National Park** (p499).

4 Seek out hidden churches amid pigeon-house-riddled cliffs and fairy chimneys (thin rock spires) in the **Güllüdere (Rose) Valley** (p469).

5 Clamber atop **Uçhisar Castle** (p476) to gaze out over a panorama of rippling rock.

6 Imagine cave-cut village life while exploring the warren of abandoned caverns in **Zelve** (p480).

7 Stroll between verdant fields and soaring cliffs to search out rock-cut churches in the **Ihlara Valley** (p500).

8 Hike through a secluded monastic settlement in **Soğanlı** (p497).

History

The Hittites settled Cappadocia (Kapadokya) from 1800 BC to 1200 BC, after which smaller kingdoms held power. Then came the Persians, followed by the Romans, who established the capital of Caesarea (today's Kayseri). During the Roman and Byzantine periods, Cappadocia became a refuge for early Christians and from the 4th to the 11th century Christianity flourished here; most churches, monasteries and underground cities date from this period. Later, under Seljuk and Ottoman rule, Christians were treated with tolerance.

Cappadocia progressively lost its importance in Anatolia. Its rich past was all but forgotten until a French priest rediscovered the rock-hewn churches in 1907. The tourist boom in the 1980s kick-started a new era, and now Cappadocia is one of Turkey's most famous and popular destinations.

Dangers & Annoyances

Most buses arriving in Cappadocia from the west terminate in Nevşehir, from where a free *servis* (shuttle bus) will ferry you to your final destination. Make sure that your ticket states that it is for Göreme, Ürgüp etc, not just 'Cappadocia'. Be aware that tour companies based at Nevşehir otogar (bus station) have a bad reputation for attempting to get tourists onto their private shuttle buses and then proceeding to hard-sell them tours and accommodation in Nevşehir. We suggest that you avoid any dealings with the tour agents here. The official bus-company *servises* usually meet your bus as it arrives and are clearly marked with the bus-company logo.

If you do find yourself without a *servis* or taxi and you have booked a hotel, it is worth phoning it for assistance; Nevşehir's otogar has long been problematic for travellers and the tourist industry in the rest of Cappadocia is well aware of it.

Walking in central Cappadocia's valleys is a wonderful experience and should not be missed, but solo travellers who do not want to hire a guide should buddy up before venturing into the more-isolated areas as there have been several attacks on female tourists in the valleys in recent years. It's also advisable to avoid the valleys and the unlit roads between villages in the evenings.

That said, compared to many other popular traveller destinations across the world, Cappadocia remains an incredibly safe place for solo female travellers and – anxious to maintain this reputation – the local tourism industry has installed patrolling watchmen in some of the valleys. As with any destination, common sense should prevail. Solo travellers should be wary of accepting invitations to go out into the valleys with new acquaintances and all hikers with mobile phones should program their hotel's number into it and take it while walking as a sensible precaution in case you get lost or have an accident.

☞ Tours

Tour companies abound in Cappadocia. Prices are usually determined by all operators at the beginning of each season. Make your decision based on the quality of the guide and the extent of the itinerary.

Most tour companies offer two standard full-day tours referred to locally as the Red Tour and the Green Tour. The itineraries do differ slightly between agencies, so it pays to look around.

The Red Tour usually includes visits to Göreme Open-Air Museum, Uçhisar rock castle, Paşabağı and Devrent Valleys, and Avanos. The Green Tour generally includes a hike in the Ihlara Valley and a trip to an underground city. Most companies charge between ₺100 and ₺110 for the Red Tour and ₺120 for the Green Tour.

Most itineraries finish at a carpet shop, onyx factory or pottery workshop, but it is still worth taking a tour. It is interesting to see traditional Cappadocian craftspeople at work, but make it clear before the trip begins if you are not interested. Most of the pensions either operate their own tours or work with one of the travel agencies.

Guided day hikes, usually in the Güllüdere (Rose), Kızılçukur (Red) or Meskendir Valleys, are also offered by most operators. Costs vary according to destination, degree of difficulty and length.

Other popular tour destinations are Soğanlı Valley (including stops at Keşlik Monastery and Sobesos) and multi-day trips to Nemrut Dağı (Mt Nemrut).

We strongly advise you to avoid booking an expensive Cappadocia tour package upon arrival in İstanbul. If your time is limited and you want to take a tour in Cappadocia, you're better off booking directly with an agent in Cappadocia itself.

ⓘ Getting There & Away

AIR

Two airports serve central Cappadocia: Kayseri Airport (p508) and Nevşehir Airport (p486). Both have several flights daily to/from İstanbul starting from about ₺85. The main operators are Turkish Airlines (www.turkishairlines.com) and Pegasus Airlines (www.flypgs.com).

BUS

Most buses from İstanbul and other western Turkey destinations travel to Cappadocia overnight and bring you to Nevşehir, where (if the bus is terminating there) a bus-company *servis* will take you on to Uçhisar, Göreme, Avanos or Ürgüp. From Ankara there are several services throughout the day.

TRAIN

The nearest train stations are at Niğde and Kayseri.

ⓘ Getting Around

TO/FROM THE AIRPORT

Very reasonably priced airport shuttle-bus services operate between both Cappadocia airports and the various villages. They must be pre-booked before arrival. If you have booked your accommodation the easiest solution is to request your hotel or pension to arrange an airport-shuttle pick-up for you. You can also book directly with the shuttle-bus service. There are a few companies, but **Helios Transfer** (☑ 0384 271 2257; www.heliostransfer.com; Adnan Menderes Caddesi 24/A, Göreme; per passenger to/from either airport €10) and **Cappadocia Express** (☑ 0384 271 3070; www.cappadociatransport.com; Iceridere Sokak 3, Göreme; per passenger to/from Nevşehir Airport ₺20, to/from Kayseri Airport ₺25) seem to be the pick of the bunch, with services operating for all flights coming into and going out of both airports. Both will pick up from and drop off to hotels in Avanos, Çavuşin, Göreme, Nevşehir, Ortahisar, Uçhisar and Ürgüp.

BUS

Dolmuşes (minibuses; ₺2.50 to ₺3.50 depending on where you get on and off) travel between Ürgüp and Avanos via Ortahisar, the Göreme Open-Air Museum, Göreme, Çavuşin, Paşabağı and Zelve. The services leave Ürgüp otogar hourly between 8am and 7pm. Going in the opposite direction, starting from Avanos, the dolmuşes operate hourly between 8am and 8pm. You can hop on and off anywhere along the route.

There are several other dolmuş services between villages. See the transport information under individual destinations for details.

The Ihlara Valley in southwest Cappadocia can be visited on a day tour from Göreme. If you want to visit it independently, plan to spend the night, as bus changes in Nevşehir and Aksaray prolong travelling time.

CAR & MOTORCYCLE

Cappadocia is great for self-drive visits. Roads are often empty and their condition is reasonable. There is ample parking space, but pulling up outside some cave hotels might be tricky.

Göreme

☑ 0384 / POP 2101

Surrounded by epic sweeps of golden, moonscape valley, this remarkable honey-coloured village hollowed out of the hills may have long since grown beyond its farming-hamlet roots, but its charm has not diminished. In the back alleys new boutique cave hotels are constantly popping up, but tourists still have to stop for tractors trundling up narrow, winding streets where elderly ladies knit on sunny stoops. Nearby, the Göreme Open-Air Museum is an all-in-one testament to Byzantine life, while if you wander out of town you'll find storybook landscapes and little-visited rock-cut churches at every turn. With its easy-going allure and stunning setting, it's no wonder Göreme continues to send travellers giddy.

⊙ Sights

★ **Göreme Open-Air Museum** MUSEUM
(Göreme Açık Hava Müzesi; ☑ 271 2167; Müze Caddesi; admission ₺20; ⊙ 8am-6.30pm) One of Turkey's Unesco World Heritage Sites, the Göreme Open-Air Museum is an essential stop on any Cappadocian itinerary and deserves a two-hour visit. First an important Byzantine monastic settlement that housed some 20 monks, then a pilgrimage site from the 17th century, this splendid cluster of monastic Byzantine artistry with its rock-cut churches, chapels and monasteries is 1km uphill from Göreme's centre.

Note that the museum's highlight – the Karanlık Kilise – has an additional ₺10 entrance fee.

From the museum ticket booth, follow the cobbled path until you reach the **Aziz Basil Şapeli** (Chapel of St Basil), dedicated to Kayseri-born St Basil, one of Cappadocia's most important saints. In the main room, St Basil is pictured on the left; a Maltese cross is on the right, along with St George and St Theodore slaying a (faded) dragon, symbolising paganism. On the right of the apse, Mary holds baby Jesus with a cross in his halo.

Just above, bow down to enter the 12th-century **Elmalı Kilise** (Apple Church), overlooking a valley of poplars. Relatively well preserved, it contains both simple, red-ochre daubs and professionally painted frescoes of biblical scenes. The Ascension is pictured above the door. The church's name is thought to derive from an apple tree that grew nearby or from a misinterpretation of the globe held by the Archangel Gabriel, in the third dome.

Byzantine soldiers carved the 11th-century **Azize Barbara Şapeli** (Chapel of St Barbara), dedicated to their patron saint, who is depicted on the left as you enter. They also painted the mysterious red ochre scenes on the roof – the middle one could represent the Ascension; above the St George representation on the far wall, the strange creature could be a dragon, and the two crosses the beast's usual slayers.

Uphill is the **Yılanlı Kilise** (Snake Church), also called the Church of St Onuphrius, where St George's ubiquitous dragon-foe is still having a bad day. To add insult to fatal injury, the church got its current moniker when locals mistook the pictured dragon for a snake. The hermetic hermaphrodite St Onuphrius is depicted on the right, holding a genitalia-covering palm leaf. Straight ahead, the small figure next to Jesus is one of the church's financiers.

The stunning, fresco-filled **Karanlık Kilise** (Dark Church; admission ₺10) is the most famous of the Open-Air Museum's churches. It takes its name from the fact that it originally had very few windows. Luckily, this lack of light preserved the vivid colour of the frescoes, which show, among other things, Christ as Pantocrator, Christ on the cross and the Betrayal by Judas. The church was restored at great expense and the entrance fee is intended to limit visitor numbers to further preserve the frescoes.

Just past the Karanlık Kilise, the small **Azize Katarina Şapeli** (Chapel of St Catherine) has frescoes of St George, St Catherine and the Deesis (a seated Christ flanked by the Virgin and John the Baptist).

The 13th-century **Çarıklı Kilise** (Sandal Church) is named for the footprints marked in the floor, representing the last imprints left by Jesus before he ascended to heaven. The four gospel writers are depicted below

---

ℹ️ VISITING THE MUSEUM

➡ Arrive early in the morning or near closing to bypass tour groups.

➡ Avoid weekends, when the museum is at its busiest.

➡ Don't skimp on Karanlık Kilise – it's worth the extra ₺10.

➡ Your ticket is valid all day, so you can leave and come back.

➡ The museum is an easy, though uphill, 1km walk from town.

➡ Beware the sun – this is an 'open-air' museum.

---

the central dome; in the arch over the door to the left is the Betrayal by Judas.

Downhill, the cordoned-off **Rahibeler Manastırı** (Nunnery) was originally several storeys high; all that remain are a large plain dining hall and, up some steps, a small chapel with unremarkable frescoes.

When you exit the Open-Air Museum, don't forget to cross the road to visit the **Tokalı Kilise** (Buckle Church), 50m down the hill towards Göreme and covered by the same ticket. This is one of Göreme's biggest and finest churches, with an underground chapel and fabulous, recently restored frescoes painted in a narrative (rather than liturgical) cycle. Entry is via the barrel-vaulted chamber of the 10th-century 'old' Tokalı Kilise, with frescoes portraying the life of Christ. Upstairs, the 'new' church, built less than a hundred years later, is also alive with frescoes on a similar theme. The holes in the floor once contained tombs, taken by departing Greek Christians during Turkey's population exchange.

El Nazar Kilise CHURCH
(Church of the Evil Eye; admission ₺5; ☉8am-5pm) Carved from a ubiquitous cone-like rock formation, the 10th-century El Nazar Kilise has been well restored with its snug interior a riot of colourful frescoes. To find it, take the signposted Zemi Valley trailhead off Müze Caddesi.

Saklı Kilise CHURCH
(Hidden Church) A yellow sign points the way off Müze Caddesi to the Saklı Kilise, only rediscovered in 1956. When you reach the top of the hill, follow the track to the left and look out for steps leading downhill to the right.

CAPPADOCIA GÖREME

Göreme

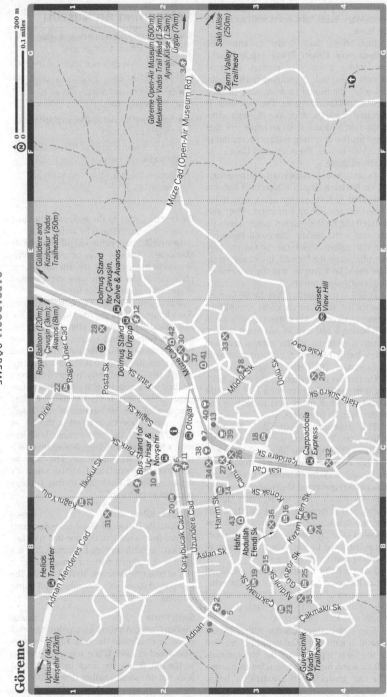

Uchisar (4km); Nevşehir (12km)

Helios Transfer

Adnan Menderes Cad

Royal Balloon (120m); Çavuşin (3km); Avanos (8km)

Ragıp Üner Cad

Güllüdere and Kızılçukur Vadisi Trailheads (50m)

Dolmuş Stand for Çavuşin, Zelve & Avanos

Göreme Open-Air Museum (500m); Meskendir Vadisi Trail Head (1.5km); Aynalı Kilise (1.5km); Ürgüp (7km)

Müze Cad (Open-Air Museum Rd)

Sakli Kilise (250m)

Zemi Valley Trailhead

Sunset View Hill

Kale Cad

Hafız Şükrü Sk

Cappadocia Express

Dolmuş Stand for Ürgüp

Posta Sk

Direk Sk

Fatih Sk

Park Sk

İlkokul Sk

Kağnı Yolu

Sağlık Sk

Müze Cad

Ünlü Sk

Müdür Sk

Otogar

Bus Stand for Uçhisar & Nevşehir

İsali Cad

İçeridere Sk

Camii Sk

Karşıbucak Cad

Uzundere Cad

Harim Sk

Aslan Sk

Konak Sk

Kazım Eren Sk

Hafız Abdullah Efendi Sk

Gül Sk

Güngör Sk

Aydınlı Sk

Çakmaklı Sk

Çakmaklı Sk

Adnan

Güvercinlik Vadisi Trailhead

200 m
0.1 miles

Göreme

Aynalı Kilise CHURCH
(Mirror Church; admission ₺5) From the Open-Air Museum entrance, a 1km walk uphill along Müze Caddesi brings you to the sign-posted trail leading down to the little-visited Aynalı Kilise. The main chapel is adorned with simple red ochre geometric decorations, but the highlight is shimmying through the network of narrow tunnels interconnecting a series of rooms within the rock face. Ahmet, the on-site guardian, provides torches.

Güllüdere Valley PARK
The trails that loop around Güllüdere (Rose) Valley are easily accessible to all levels of walkers and provide some of the finest fairy-chimney strewn vistas in Cappadocia. As well as this, though, they hide fabulous, little-visited rock-cut churches boasting vibrant fresco fragments and intricate carvings hewn into the stone. If you only have time to hike through one valley in Cappadocia, this is the one to choose.

Follow the signs from the Güllüdere Valley trailhead to the Kolonlu Kilise (Columned Church) FREE, chiselled out of a nondescript rock facade. Take the trail through the orchard and then cross the tiny bridge over the gully to enter the church's gloomy lower chamber. Climb up the staircase and you'll find a white stone nave studded with sturdy columns carved out of the rock.

From there, backtrack through the orchard and follow the main trail to the Haçlı Kilise (Church of the Cross) FREE, where the shady cave cafe at the entrance is the perfect pit stop. The church, accessed by a rickety wooden staircase, has frescoes dating to the 9th century on its apse and a spectacular large cross carved into its ceiling.

Head north from the Haçlı Kilise and, when the trail branches, take the right-hand path to reach the Üç Haçlı Kilise (Church of the Three Crosses) FREE, with its stunning ceiling relief and damaged frescoes featuring an enthroned Jesus.

🏃 Activities

Mehmet Güngör HIKING
(📱 0532 382 2069; www.walkingmehmet.net; 4hr/full day €60/80) Mehmet Güngör's nickname, 'Walking Mehmet', says it all. Göreme's most experienced local walking guide has an encyclopaedic knowledge of the surrounding valley trails and can put together itineraries to suit all interests and levels of fitness. Highly recommended.

LOCAL KNOWLEDGE

MEHMET GÜNGÖR: CAPPADOCIA'S WALKING GURU

Mehmet Güngör (aka Walking Mehmet) has been guiding visitors through the maze of valley trails surrounding Göreme for the past 14 years. We asked him for his top tips for DIY hikers.

Best morning walk? Görkündere Valley is perfect for early-morning walks as the sun's angle at this time highlights the rock formations perfectly.

Best walk if you only have one day? Güllüdere and Kızılçukur Valleys are my absolute favourite walks. Every corner reveals a different frame. For the best light, walk here in the afternoon.

Best adventurous walk? Walk from Zelve, via Paşabağı, to Çavuşin and take the trails opposite the old village ruins that lead up to the Boztepe ridge. Hike all the way along here to the Kızılçukur viewpoint, then walk down through Kızılçukur and Güllüdere Valleys.

Best walk to escape the crowds? Zemi Valley still sees very few visitors and is extremely pretty. Further away from Göreme, Gomeda Valley (between Ürgüp and Mustafapaşa) and Çat Valley (trailheads in Çat village and near Gülşehir's Open Palace ruin) are rarely visited.

Which church should walkers not miss? The Kolonlu Kilise (p469) always surprises people as it's very well hidden and in the middle of nowhere.

Fatma's Turkish Cooking Class
COOKING COURSE

(☑271 2597; www.cafesafak.weebly.com; per person ₺75) These cooking classes – operated out of the Çingitaş family's home – will have you rustling up the hearty dishes of the Anatolian plains like a pro. Classes run from 9am to 1pm and take you through the Turkish staples of lentil soup, stuffed vine leaves, stuffed aubergines (eggplants) and the Cappadocian *aside* pudding. Book through Cafe Şafak (28 Müze Caddesi).

Elis Kapadokya Hamam
HAMAM

(☑271 2974; Adnan Menderes Caddesi; soak, scrub & massage €25; ⊙10am-10pm) This hamam provides a typical soak-and-scrub experience with mixed and women-only areas. Be aware that the included 'massage' is a blink-of-the-eye effort. You need to pay extra (₺2 per minute) for a proper oil massage.

Kelebek Turkish Bath Spa
HAMAM

(☑271 2531; Kelebek Hotel, Yavuz Sokak; soak & scrub €35) Unwind after the chimney-spotting and treat yourself to Cappadocia's most luxurious hamam experience with a full range of spa-style added extras.

☞ Tours

The following tour businesses have been recommended by Lonely Planet readers or can be vouched for by us. However, the list is by no means exhaustive.

Heritage Travel
GUIDED TOUR

(☑271 2687; www.turkishheritagetravel.com; Uzundere Caddesi) This highly recommended local agency specialises in tailormade Turkey packages but also runs three popular guided day tours (€60 per person) including an excellent 'Undiscovered Cappadocia' trip to Soğanlı. A range of more off-beat activities, from photography safaris (€125 per person) to cooking classes (€50 per person) and day trips to Hacıbektaş are also offered.

Middle Earth Travel
ADVENTURE TOUR

(☑271 2559; www.middleearthtravel.com; Karsıbucak Caddesi) The adventure-travel specialist offers a range of day hikes (€50 to €90 per person depending on numbers and itinerary) as well as multi-day treks through Ala Dağlar National Park, along the Lycian Way or St Pauls' Trail, through the Kaçkar Mountains or up Mt Ararat.

Nomad Travel
GUIDED TOUR

(☑271 2767; www.nomadtravel.com.tr; Belediye Caddesi) Nomad has the typical Cappadocia guided day-trip offerings of the Green Tour (Ihlara Valley; ₺120 per person) and the Red Tour (regional highlights; ₺100 per person), along with an excellent Soğanlı tour (₺150 per person). Its three-day Nemrut Dağı (Mt Nemrut) tour, which leaves on Monday, is a worthwhile option if you're short on time to explore further east.

Metis Travel GUIDED TOUR

(📞271 2188; www.metistravel.com; Müdür Sokak 9) This boutique travel agency is run by the same folk behind Koza Cave Hotel, so attention to detail and personalised service are on top form. They run three daily tours (€50 per person) taking in different Cappadocia highlights and can also arrange itineraries covering the breadth of Turkey.

Yama Tours GUIDED TOUR

(📞271 2508; www.yamatours.com; Müze Caddesi 2) This popular backpacker-friendly travel agency runs daily Red (regional highlights; ₺110) and Green (Ihlara Valley; ₺120) tours and can book a bagful of other Cappadocia adventures and activities for you.

★ Festivals & Events

Klasik Keyifler CLASSICAL MUSIC

(📞0532 614 4955; www.klasikkeyifler.org; ☺Aug) Klasik Keyifler is an innovative organisation that holds chamber-music concerts by Turkey's brightest stars in intimate natural settings. The summer series hits Cappadocia in August, when you can hear the sounds of Schumann bouncing off the valley walls in Zelve and Mustafapaşa. Workshops run in conjunction with the performance.

🛏 Sleeping

Most Göreme hotels now open all year round and offer decent discounts between November and March. This is only a small sample of the huge amount of rock-cut retreats in this fairy-chimney-punctured village.

Köse Pension HOSTEL €

(📞271 2294; www.kosepension.com; Ragıp Üner Caddesi; dm ₺15, d/tr ₺100/120, s/tr without bathroom ₺30/90; 🛜🏊) It may have no cave character, but travellers' favourite Köse is still the pick of Göreme's budget digs. Ably managed by Sabina, this friendly place provides a range of spotless rooms featuring brilliant bathrooms, bright linens and comfortable beds, more basic rooms, and a spacious rooftop dorm. The swimming pool is a bonus after a long, hot hike.

Breakfasts here (not included; ₺5 to ₺8) include a swag of options.

Kemal's Guest House PENSION €

(📞271 2234; www.kemalsguesthouse.com; Karşıbucak Caddesi; dm/d/tr/ste €15/45/65/80; 🛜) It may not have the razzmatazz of Göreme's newer offerings, but this pension delivers old-fashioned hospitality in spades. Kemal

is a terrific cook (dinner feasts €15) and his Dutch wife, Barbara, knows her way around Cappadocia's hiking trails like no other hotelier. Pull up a comfy seat in the sun-dappled garden and thumb your nose at your 'boutique' friends.

Ali's Guest House HOSTEL €

(📞271 2434; www.alisguesthouse.com; Harım Sokak 13; dm/d €6/30; 🛜) We've whinged about Göreme's backpacker digs trussing themselves up to cater for the boutique crowd, so a big thumbs up to this newcomer aimed squarely at the budget end of the market. Ali's has two snug cave dorms sharing small but extremely clean bathrooms, and three cosy private rooms upstairs. The outdoor courtyard is a pot-plant-strewn communal haven.

Dorm Cave HOSTEL €

(📞271 2770; www.travellerscave.com; Hafız Abdullah Efendi Sokak 4; dm €10, d/tr €30/45; 🛜) Who needs to pay wads of cash to stay in a Cappadocian cave when you can get the cavern experience on the cheap? This superb hostel shuns the boutique craze, offering instead three very spacious cave dorms (mixed and female-only) that share small but modern bathrooms across a pretty courtyard. Upstairs, the three petite private rooms are also brilliant value.

Shoestring Cave Pension HOSTEL €

(📞271 2450; www.shoestringcave.com; Kazım Eren Sokak; dm €10, s/d/tr €30/40/50, ste €55-65; 🛜🏊) The double rooms at this old-school backpacker paradise have been jazzed up significantly in recent years, while the funky cave dorm means those counting their kuruş still have a dependable place to crash. The courtyard picnic tables and cool terrace swimming-pool area provide a proper communal feel, so pull up a pew and swap a couple of Turkish travel tales.

★Kelebek Hotel & Cave Pension HOTEL €€

(📞271 2531; www.kelebekhotel.com; Yavuz Sokak 31; fairy chimney s/d €44/55, deluxe s/d €56/70, ste €85-130; 🛜🏊) It's reassuring to know the oldie is still the goodie. Local guru Ali Yavuz leads a charming team at one of Göreme's original boutique hotels that has seen a travel industry virtually spring from beneath its stunning terrace. Exuding Anatolian inspiration at every turn, the rooms are spread over two gorgeous stone houses, each with a fairy chimney protruding skyward.

CAPPADOCIA GÖREME

With an in-house hamam, and a village-garden project offering guests a slice of the Cappadocia of old – valley breakfasts, cooking classes and autumn grape-harvesting trips – Kelebek continues to innovate. It's no wonder people leave smitten.

Taşkonak
HOTEL €€

(📞270 2680; www.taskonak.com; Güngör Sokak 23; s/d/ste/f €35/40/80/110; 🛖) Angela and Yılmaz provide huge helpings of hospitality at this friendly and highly relaxed hideaway. Standard rooms are snug but sweet, while the spacious cave suites are among the best-value deals in town. Killer views from the terrace and a breakfast feast of homemade spreads, freshly baked delights and proper coffee will leave you grinning at your good fortune.

Kismet Cave House
HOTEL €€

(📞271 2416; www.kismetcavehouse.com; Kağnı Yolu 9; s €52, d €65-95, f €130; 🛖) Kismet's fate is assured. Guests consistently rave about the intimate experience here, created by welcoming, well-travelled host Faruk. The rooms are full of local antiques, carved wood features, colourful rugs and quirky artwork, while communal areas are home to cosy cushion-scattered nooks. This honest-to-impending-greatness Anatolian cave house is delightfully homey in every way.

Hanzade Suites
BOUTIQUE HOTEL €€

(📞271 3536; www.hanzadesuites.com; Ali Çavuş Sokak 7; d €65, ste €70-100; 🛖) Good things definitely do come in small packages. This once-typical village dwelling has been transformed by owner Mustafa into a haven of just seven generously proportioned rooms that effortlessly blend local craftwork with modern elegance and a hat-tip to minimalism. We're particularly enamoured with the drop-dead-gorgeous onyx and travertine flooring and the glamorously high beds. Superb stuff.

ErenBey Cave Hotel
BOUTIQUE HOTEL €€

(📞271 2131; www.erenbeycavehotel.com; Kazım Eren Sokak 19; d/f/ste €70/85/120; 🛖) This rather lush new boutique-style hotel plays up its quirkily shaped cave rooms

---

DON'T MISS

WALKING IN THE VALLEYS AROUND GÖREME

Göreme village is surrounded by the magnificent Göreme National Park. The valleys are easily explored on foot; each needs about one to three hours. Most are interconnected, so you could easily combine several in a day, especially with the help of the area's many dolmuşes (minibuses). Don't forget a bottle of water and sunscreen.

Some of the most interesting and accessible valleys:

Bağlıdere Vadısı (White Valley) From Uçhisar to Göreme.

Görkündere Vadısı (Love Valley) Trailheads off Zemi Valley and from Sunset View Hill in Göreme; particularly spectacular rock formations.

Güllüdere Vadısı (Rose Valley) Trailheads just north of Göreme, at Çavuşin, and Kızılçukur viewpoint (opposite the Ortahisar turn-off); superb churches and panoramic views.

Güvercinlik Vadısı (Pigeon Valley) Connecting Göreme and Uçhisar; colourful dovecotes.

İçeridere Vadısı Running south from İçeridere Sokak in Göreme.

Kılıçlar Vadısı (Swords Valley) Running north off Müze Caddesi on the way to the Göreme Open-Air Museum.

Kızılçukur Vadısı (Red Valley) Running between the Güllüdere and Meskendir Valleys; great views and vibrant dovecotes.

Meskendir Vadısı Trailhead next to Kaya Camping, running north off Müze Caddesi past the Göreme Open-Air Museum; tunnels and dovecotes.

Zemi Vadısı Trailhead running south off Müze Caddesi.

A word of warning: Although many of the valleys now have trailhead signposts and signage has been put up at strategic points along the paths of Güllüdere and Kızılçukur Valleys, many of the trails remain only basically marked and there's no detailed map of the area available. It's quite easy to get lost if you don't stick to the trails.

with aplomb. The Eren family have converted their generations-old homestead into nine exceedingly spacious and rather swish rooms that all have bucketloads of idiosyncratic design. Room nine, with its rock-carved four-pillared bed and bathtub-with-a-view, is the stuff of romantic-getaway dreams.

★**Koza Cave Hotel** BOUTIQUE HOTEL €€€
(☑271 2466; www.kozacavehotel.com; Çakmaklı Sokak 49; d €80-90, ste €110-175; ☜) ✒ Bringing a new level of eco-inspired chic to Göreme, Koza Cave is a masterclass in stylish sustainable tourism. Passionate owner Derviş spent decades living in Holland and has incorporated Dutch eco-sensibility into every cave crevice of the 10 stunning rooms. Grey water is reused, and recycled materials and local handcrafted furniture are utilised in abundance to create sophisticated spaces. Highly recommended.

Aydınlı Cave House BOUTIQUE HOTEL €€€
(☑271 2263; www.thecavehotel.com; Aydınlı Sokak 12; r €70-85, f €110, ste €100-200; ☜) Proprietor Mustafa has masterfully converted his family home into a haven for honeymooners and those requiring swags of swanky rock-cut style. Guests rave about the warm service and immaculate, spacious cave rooms, formerly used for drying fruits and making wine. Antiques and farming utensils decorate the terraces, while swoon-worthy suites blend local character with sheer class.

✖ Eating

Pick up fresh produce, locally made cheese and all sorts of other foodie delights at the weekly Wednesday market (☺9am-4pm).

Nazar Börek TURKISH €
(☑271 2441; Müze Caddesi; gözleme & börek ₺6-9; ☜✒) Head here for supremely tasty traditional Turkish staples served up by friendly Rafik and his team. Nazar remains our longstanding favourite for its hearty plates of *gözleme* (savoury pancakes) and *sosyete böregi* (stuffed spiral pastries served with yoghurt and tomato sauce). The convivial atmosphere encourages diners to linger long after their meal has finished.

Fırın Express PIDE €
(☑271 2266; Eski Belediye Yanı Sokak; pide ₺6-10; ☜✒) Simply the best pide (Turkish-style pizza) in town is found in this local haunt. The cavernous wood oven fires up meat and vegetarian options and anything doused

with egg. We suggest adding an *ayran* (yoghurt drink) and a *çoban salatası* (shepherd's salad) for a delicious bargain feed.

Sarmaşık TURKISH €
(☑0541 490 3797; Eski Belediye Altı 1; mains ₺5-18) Cheap and cheerful Turkish staples are dished out at this itsy-bitsy cafe – great if you're looking for a lunch that won't break the bank. In a completely unexpected twist it also serves sushi. (You need to make a reservation by lunchtime for a sushi dinner.)

Köy Evi ANATOLIAN €€
(☑271 2008; Aydınkıragı Sokak 40; meze ₺7-10, mains ₺12-18, kebap plates ₺20-40; ✒) The simple, wholesome flavours of village food are the main act at this brilliant rustic-style restaurant where charming staff serve up a taste-bud tour of Göreme while the female chefs shovel out more steaming-hot bread from the *tandır* (oven). The warren of cave rooms has been kept authentically basic, which adds to the homespun appeal.

Bring your appetite and prepare to feast on the soul food that fuelled Cappadocian farmers for centuries.

Pumpkin Cafe ANATOLIAN €€
(☑0542 808 5050; İçeridere Sokak 7; set menu ₺35; ☺6-11pm) With its dinky balcony decorated with whimsically carved-out pumpkins (what else), this cute-as-a-button cafe is one of the cosiest dining picks in Göreme. The daily-changing four-course set menu is a fresh feast of simple Anatolian dishes, all presented with delightful flourishes.

★**Seten Restaurant** MODERN TURKISH €€€
(☑271 3025; www.setenrestaurant.com; Aydınlı Sokak; mains ₺16-40; ✒) Brimming with an artful Anatolian aesthetic, Seten is a feast for the eye as well as for the stomach. Named after the old millstones used to grind bulgur wheat, this restaurant is an education for newcomers to Turkish cuisine and a treat for well-travelled palates. Attentive service complements classic main dishes and myriad luscious and unusual meze. It's by far Göreme's most sophisticated dining experience.

★**Topdeck Cave Restaurant** ANATOLIAN €€€
(☑271 2474; Hafız Abdullah Efendi Sokak 15; mains ₺18-30; ☺6-10pm Wed-Mon; ✒) If it feels as though you're dining in a family home, it's because you are. Talented chef Mustafa (aka Topdeck) and his gracious clan have transformed an atmospheric cave room in their house into a cosy restaurant where the kids

EKREM ILHAN: GÖREME'S HORSE WHISPERER

When Persia ruled Turkey, Katpatuka (Cappadocia) was famous throughout the empire for its beautiful horses. In Iran's Persepolis palace, among the reliefs depicting delegates from Persia's subject states, visitors from Katpatuka are pictured with equine offerings.

It seems appropriate, then, that present-day Göreme has a horse whisperer. Ekrem Ilhan brings wild horses to Göreme from Erciyes Dağı (Mt Erciyes), where a tribe of 400 has grown as local farmers have replaced them with machinery.

'They are in shock when they arrive here, but when their eyes open they see me, talking and giving them sweet things,' he says. 'People teach animals to bite and kick, because they are angry with them. But when you're friends, and you talk to them and give them some carrot and cucumber, you don't have any problems.'

Looking like a Cappadocian Clint Eastwood in a hat brought from America by a carpet-dealing friend, Ilhan tells a story about two pregnant mares he returned to Mt Erciyes to give birth. 'One year later, I went into the mountains, among the 400 horses, and called their names and they came directly to me.'

Ilhan treats the 11 horses in his cave stable using homemade remedies, such as grape water to extract parasites, and olive oil, mint and egg for indigestion.

He has started a horse-trekking company, called **Dalton Brothers** ([☎]0532 275 6869; www.cappadociahorseriding.com; Müze Caddesi ; 2/4hr €40/75), at the suggestion of a Canadian traveller and *Lucky Luke* fan. 'People like wild horses because it's difficult riding in the mountains; it's rocky; and the horses are used to it,' he says. Many of the horses are not suitable for first-time riders. If you're not an experienced rider please make sure you specify this before signing up.

pitch in with the serving and diners dig into hearty helpings of Anatolian favourites with a spicy twist.

Choose the mixed meze plate (₺21) for a flavour-packed blowout your stomach will thank you for. Reservations are essential.

Rasoi INDIAN €€€
([☑]271 2463; Cevizler Sokak; mains ₺15-40; [✐]) Göreme was for years a culinary desert if you craved anything other than Turkish cuisine, and then in waltzed this game-changing Indian restaurant. We're not fond of the dining room, which is a bit stuffy, but full marks for the Punjabi specialities of *shahi paneer* (curd cheese in a rich tomato gravy) and *chana masala* (spicy chickpeas).

Dibek ANATOLIAN €€€
([☑]271 2209; Hakkı Paşa Meydanı 1; mains ₺13-35; [✐]) Diners sprawl on cushions and feast on traditional dishes and homemade wine at this family restaurant, set inside a 475-year-old building. Many book ahead (at least three hours) for the slow-cooked *testi kebap* ('pottery kebap'; meat, chicken or vegetables cooked in a sealed terracotta pot; ₺35).

Orient Restaurant INTERNATIONAL €€€
([☑]2712346; Adnan Menderes Caddesi; mains ₺20-40) Juicy steaks and racks of lamb head up Orient's impressively meaty menu, which romps from traditional Turkish to more continental-style options with ease. The outside seating, among blooming roses, is delightful and the service is completely charming.

🍷 Drinking & Nightlife

Fat Boys BAR, RESTAURANT
([☑]0535 386 4484; Belediye Caddesi; beer ₺10, mains ₺10-30; [🕘]noon-late; [🛜]) This bar-restaurant combo is a winner. We love the terrace, strewn with fat cushions, and curling up on the couches inside.The hungry can order from a global menu that stars good-value Turkish staples along with Aussie-style pies, pasta, and nachos. The friendly staff, well-stocked bar and relaxed atmosphere make this place Göreme's most popular evening hang-out.

Cafe Şafak CAFE
(Müze Caddesi; coffee ₺6-7; [🛜]) Fellow coffee geeks, you have found your nirvana. Şafak delivers cappuccino, espresso and flat whites (yes, really) as good as you'd get in coffee-hipster Melbourne – which, unsurprisingly, is where owner Ali trained as a barista. Hands down the best caffeine fix in Cappadocia.

Mydonos Cafe
CAFE

(Müze Caddesi 18; drinks ₺6-10) Subdued jazzy background music and wall displays of old vinyl dust jackets fill the interior with subtle bohemian flair, while the roof terrace is the perfect pit stop for sunny Cappadocian afternoons. There's good French-press coffee and delicious hot chocolate. The mellow vibe extends to the service, so don't expect it to be snappy.

Red Red Wine House
BAR

(🖉271 2183; Müze Caddesi; glass of wine ₺10) In a former stable with arched ceilings, this seductive local feels like an ancient bootlegger's secret mixing den decorated by lovers of adult contemporary. A steady chain of guests smoke fruity pipes and sip increasingly palatable Cappadocian wines.

🛍 Shopping

Tribal Collections
CARPETS

(🖉271 2760; www.tribalcollections.net; Köşe Cikmazı Sokak 1; ⊙9am-9pm) As well as being the proprietor of this mighty fine rug shop, owner Ruth is well known for her highly recommended carpet educationals (think of it as a carpets 101), which explain the history and artistry of these coveted textiles.

Sultan's Charm
BATHWARE

(Müze Caddesi 32) Loved all those hamam towels in İstanbul's twee boutiques but shuddered at the cost? Sultan's Charm has beautiful stacks of sensibly priced hand-loomed and organic-cotton Turkish hamam products as well as gorgeous soaps from Harbiye.

Argos
CERAMICS

(🖉271 2750; Cevizler Sokak 22) A classy selection of handmade ceramics, both modern and Asian-inspired, as well as unusual stone pieces.

❶ Information

There are standalone clusters of ATM booths on and around Uzundere Caddesi. Some of the town's travel agencies will exchange money, although you're probably better off going to the **post office** (PTT; Posta Sokak) or **Deniz Bank** (Müze Caddesi 3).

There's a **tourist-information booth** at the otogar that is open when most long-distance buses arrive, but it's run by the **Göreme Turizmciler Derneği** (Göreme Tourism Society; 🖉271 2558; www.goreme.org) and not an official tourist office. This coalition of hotel and restaurant owners is solely aimed at directing travellers to accommodation in the village and staff can't supply any meaningful information. They do give out free maps and sell one for ₺5.

❶ Getting There & Away

There are daily long-distance buses to all over Turkey from Göreme's **otogar**, although normally you're ferried to Nevşehir's otogar to pick up the main service (which can add nearly an hour to your travelling time). Note that the morning bus to İstanbul goes via Ankara and so takes an hour longer than the overnight bus. For Aksaray, change in Nevşehir.

❶ Getting Around

BUS

Göreme has good connections to the other Cappadocian villages. The Ürgüp–Avanos

SERVICES FROM GÖREME'S OTOGAR

DESTINATION	FARE (₺)	DURATION (HR)	FREQUENCY (PER DAY)
Adana	40	5	1 morning & 1 evening
Ankara	40	4½	2 morning & 3 afternoon
Antalya	50	9	1 morning & 3 evening
Çanakkale	80	16	3 evening
Denizli (for Pamukkale)	55	11	2 evening
Fethiye	65	14	1 evening
İstanbul	60	11-12	1 morning & 2 evening
İzmir	60	11½	2 evening
Konya	25	3	2 morning & 3 evening
Marmaris/Bodrum	60	13	1 evening
Selçuk	60	11½	2 evening
Şanlıurfa	65	11	1 evening

dolmuş picks up/drops off passengers on its way through town in both directions. To Ürgüp it usually stops in Göreme at 25 minutes past the hour between 8am and 8pm, and to Avanos at 15 minutes past the hour between 8am and 7pm.

As well as this, Göreme Belediye Bus Corp has a regular bus service from Göreme to Nevşehir via Uçhisar (₺2.50 to ₺3 depending on where you get off, every 30 minutes between 8am and 7pm) that leaves from the otogar.

CAR & MOTORCYCLE

There are several places to hire mountain bikes, scooters, cars and quads, including **Hitchhiker** (📞 271 2169; www.cappadociahitchhiker.com; Uzundere Caddesi) and **Oz Cappadocia** (📞 271 2159; www.ozcappadocia.com; Uzundere Caddesi), which are both near the otogar entrance. It pays to shop around, as prices vary dramatically.

Since there are no petrol stations in Göreme and your rental car comes with a near-empty tank, head to one of the garages on the main road near Ortahisar to fill up.

Uçhisar

📞 0384 / POP 3874

Pretty little Uçhisar has undergone rapid development since the heady Club Med days. The French love affair with the clifftop village continues each summer as busloads of Gallic tourists unpack their *joie de vivre* in trendy hotels at the foot of Uçhisar Castle. The royal rectangular crag, visible from nearby Göreme, is the dramatic centrepiece of a stylish Cappadocian aesthetic, albeit at times a touch manufactured. Unfortunately, some ill-judged hotel construction here has spoilt one of this village's most dream-like fairy-chimney vistas, which somewhat disrupts Uçhisar's famously surreal setting. Despite this, it remains a quieter alternative to Göreme as a base for exploring the region.

There are Vakif Bank and Garanti Bankası ATMs on the main square, and the **post office** (Adnan Menderes Caddesi) is nearby.

⊙ Sights & Activities

There are some excellent hiking possibilities around Uçhisar, with trailheads to both Bağlıdere Vadısı (White Valley) and Güvercinlik Vadısı (Pigeon Valley) on the outskirts of town.

Uçhisar Castle   FORTRESS
(Uçhisar Kalesi; admission ₺3; ⊙ 8am-8.15pm) This tall volcanic-rock outcrop is one of Cappadocia's most prominent landmarks and visible for miles around. Riddled with tunnels, it was used for centuries by villagers as a place of refuge when enemy armies overtook the surrounding plains. Climbing through its mazy core to the panoramic vantage point of its peak is a sublime way to watch the sun set over the rock valleys of the Cappadocian countryside.

The castle is a major tourist attraction, so try to go early or late in the day to avoid the tour-bus groups. The lack of barriers means you should be very careful – one photographer died when he fell over the edge after stepping back to get a good shot.

Kocabağ Winery   WINERY
(www.kocabag.com; Adnan Menderes Caddesi; ⊙ 10am-7pm) This rather swish outlet for Cappadocia's Kocabağ Winery is the best place in town for a spot of wine tasting. Just outside, a small selection of vines displays the different grape varieties for interested connoisseurs, while the shop displays all of Kocabağ's wines and offers tastings. It's on the main road off Uçhisar's town square.

🛏 Sleeping

Kilim Pension   PENSION €€
(📞 219 2774; www.sisik.com; Tekelli Mahallesi; s €35, d €47-70; 🛜) The pride of fun-loving, multilingual 'Şişik', Kilim Pension is an unpretentious home-away-from-home with a glorious vine-draped terrace and a cosy restaurant that dishes up first-class local fare. Spacious rooms are smartly simple, light and airy, with swish bathrooms as a bonus. The complimentary chaperoned hikes into the valleys are highly recommended.

Taka Ev   HOTEL €€
(📞 0532 740 4177; www.takaev.net; Kayabaşi Sokak 43; r from €70; 🛜) Run by friendly Murat, charmingly cute Taka Ev is an intimate place festooned with flowerpots and colourful *suzani* (Uzbek bedspread) embroideries. The seven light-filled rooms have tonnes of local character and homely touches, along with swanky bathrooms that host powerful showers.

Uçhisar Pension   PENSION €€
(📞 219 2662; www.uchisarpension.com; Göreme Caddesi; s/d ₺80/100, cave r €50-80; 🛜) Mustafa and Gül dispense lashings of old-fashioned Turkish hospitality in their cosy pension. Simple rooms are spick-and-span with white-washed walls and small but squeaky-clean bathrooms. Downstairs, the roomy cave suites are decorated traditionally. In

HOW TO MAKE A FAIRY-CHIMNEY LANDSCAPE

The *peribacalar* (fairy chimneys) that have made Cappadocia so famous began their life when a series of megalithic volcanic eruptions was unleashed over this region about 12 million years ago. A common misconception is that the culprits for this reign of fire were the now-dormant volcanic peaks of Erciyes Dağı (Mt Erciyes) and Hasan Dağı (Mt Hasan) that still lord it over Cappadocia's landscape. These volcanoes were formed much later, however. The true perpetrators have long since been leveled by erosion, leaving only slight evidence of their once mighty power.

During this active volcanic period – which lasted several million years – violent eruptions occurred across the region, spewing volcanic ash that hardened into multiple layers of rock geologically known as tuff (consolidated volcanic ash). These layers were then slowly but surely whittled away by the grinding effects of wind, water and ice.

This natural erosion is the sculptor responsible for the weird and wacky Cappadocian landscape. Where areas of a harder rock layer sit above a softer rock layer, the soft rock directly underneath is protected while the rest gets winnowed away, creating the bizarre isolated pinnacles nicknamed 'fairy chimneys'. Depending on your perspective, they look like giant phalluses or outsized mushrooms. The villagers call them simply *kalelar* (castles).

summer swing from the rooftop hammock and pinch yourself for your luck on finding million-dollar views for budget prices.

★**Kale Konak** BOUTIQUE HOTEL €€€
(☑ 219 2828; www.kalekonak.com; Kale Sokak 9; s €100, d €120, ste €135-150; 🛜) Take a handful of minimalist retreat-chic, blend it with touches of artistic flair and balance it all out with wads of Ottoman style and you get this effortlessly elegant hotel. Spacious rooms lead out through underground passageways to comfortable reading corners, communal areas strewn with fat cushions, and shady terraces in the shadow of Uçhisar's craggy *kale*.

The marble hamam tops off what has to be Uçhisar's most super-sophisticated place to stay. The epitome of casual luxury.

Şira Hotel HOTEL €€€
(☑ 219 3037; www.hotelsira.com; Göreme Caddesi 87; s/d €125/150; 🛜) Multilingual Filiz and her family have created a beautiful retreat where modern comfort and traditional architecture sit in harmony side by side. The panoramic views from the terrace may be enough to tempt you never to leave, but the real bonus is the management's appreciation for wine, food and nature – all on show in the restaurant's flavourful feasts.

Les Maisons de Cappadoce VACATION RENTAL €€€
(☑ 219 2813; www.cappadoce.com; studios €140-190, villas €240-980; 🛜) If only real-estate barons everywhere could use French architect Jacques Avizou's tasteful expansion policy, then maybe we could all live in places like Les Maisons de Cappadoce in the old quarters of ancient towns with little breakfast baskets hanging on our door every morning. These intelligently designed serviced villas range from studios to sublime family funhouses.

Argos LUXURY HOTEL €€€
(☑ 219 3130; www.argosincappadocia.com; Kayabaşi Sokak; r from €165, ste from €680; ❄️ 🛜) Designer luxury meets caveman chic head-on at this offering from the Istanbul advertising firm with its feet now in the hotel game. The hotel spills over the hillside in a cluster of 'mansions' and cave warrens connected by alleyways and manicured lawns. The original hotel area, sporting renowned architect Turgur Cansever's sympathetic restorative edge, has the most authentic atmosphere.

✖ Eating

House of Memories TURKISH €€
(Göreme Caddesi; meze ₺5, mains ₺16-20) Bags of homespun rustic appeal and kooky service are why we like this little restaurant serving up traditional Turkish favourites. It's behind Uçhisar Castle on the main hotel road.

Restaurante du Mustafa TURKISH €€
(Kale Sokak; gözleme ₺5, mains ₺15-30) It may not be as flashy as other restaurants in Uçhisar, but Mustafa's delivers on fresh, local flavour, serving up Turkish favourites with unpretentious flair.

★ **Center Café & Restaurant**   TURKISH **€€€**
(☑219 3117; Belediye Meydanı; mains ₺10-35)
A former top-notch Club Med chef now
presides over this humble town-square
cafe-restaurant with a menu of tasty meze,
kebap plates and flavourful tagines. The
verdant garden setting is a shady haven in
summer months, perfect for lazy lunches
watching the hum of village life. We almost
wish this place was still secret.

Şıra   MODERN TURKISH **€€€**
(Göreme Caddesi 87; mains ₺20-40) Bringing a
modern touch to Turkish classic dishes, with
some more international-style options thrown
in for good measure, Şıra is a lovely choice for
dinner in Uçhisar. The huge range of local
wines is a bonus, as are the gorgeous views.

🛍 Shopping

Göreme Onyx   JEWELLERY
(Güvercinlik Vadisi Karşısı) The full gamut of
precious stones is on offer in this large shop
on the outskirts of Uçhisar.

❶ Getting There & Away

The Nevşehir–Avanos bus and the Nevşehir–
Göreme dolmuş both pass through Uçhisar and
drop off/pick up passengers on the main highway at the bottom of the village.

Dolmuşes to Nevşehir (₺2.50) leave from outside the *belediye* (town hall) on the main square
every half-hour between 7am and 7.30pm.

A taxi to Göreme costs ₺15 and to Ürgüp ₺35.

Çavuşin

☑0384
Midway between Göreme and Avanos is
little Çavuşin, dominated by a cliff where
a cluster of abandoned houses spills down
the slope in a crumbling stone jumble. The
main hive of activity is the clutch of souvenir stands at the cliff base, which spring into
action when the midday tour buses roll into
town. When the last bus has left for the day,
Çavuşin hits the snooze button and resumes
its slumber. The village has no bank or ATM.

⊙ Sights & Activities

Çavuşin is the starting point for scenic
hikes through Güllüdere Vadısı (Rose Valley), Kızılçukur Vadısı (Red Valley) and
Meskendir Vadısı. You can even go as far as
the Kızılçukur viewpoint (6.5km), then walk
out to the Ürgüp–Ortahisar road and catch
a dolmuş back to your base.

Çavuşin Church   CHURCH
(Big Pigeon House Church; admission ₺8; ⊙8am-
5pm) Just off the highway on the northern
edge of Çavuşin you'll find this church, accessed via a steep and rickety iron stairway.
Cappadocia's first post-iconoclastic church,
it served as a pigeon house for many years
and is home to some fine frescoes.

Çavuşin Old Village Ruins   RUIN
FREE Walk up the hill through the new
part of Çavuşin and continue past the main
square to find the old village ruins. Carved
into the steep cliff face here is a labyrinthine complex of abandoned houses that
you can wander through by climbing up the
cliff path. The timeless ambience has been
slightly lost due to the hotel that has been
slapped right in the middle of the ruins, but
there's still plenty to explore.

Church of St John the Baptist   CHURCH
FREE Right at the top of Çavuşin's village-
ruins rock outcrop is the Church of St
John the Baptist, one of the oldest churches in Cappadocia. While the interior frescoes are severely damaged and faded, the
still-standing columns inside the cavern are
impressive and the views across the countryside from the church entry are sublime.

🍃 Tours

Mephisto Voyage   ADVENTURE TOURS
(☑532 7070; www.mephistovoyage.com) Based
at the İn Pension, this group has a good
reputation. It's been operating for over a
decade and offers trekking and camping
packages ranging from a two-day local wander to a 14-day trip around Cappadocia and
the Taurus Mountains (€500). It rents out
bicycles and offers tours by bike, horse and
cart and, for mobility-impaired people, the
Joëlette system.

🛌 Sleeping & Eating

İn Pension   PENSION **€**
(☑532 7070; www.pensionincappadocia.com; Mehmet Yılmaz Caddesi; old wing d €30, new wing d/
tr €40/50, ste €70-100; 🅰) This little pension
by the main square comes with built-in travel advice courtesy of owner Mephisto Voyage. There are a couple of simple and small
budget rooms, while the new wing has a
range of spruced-up, bright doubles with little bathrooms. Downstairs the deluxe rooms
come with loads of traditional stone features
and lovely decorative touches.

Village Cave Hotel
BOUTIQUE HOTEL €€

(☑532 7197; www.thevillagecave.com; r from €65; ☎) The most interesting lodging in Çavuşin is this restored 18th-century stone house with six bedrooms carved on two floors in view of the gorgeous tumble of the old village. Decorated with minimalist chic, the seriously quirky cave shapes here are the stand out feature. Friendly host Halim is the third generation to manage the property.

★ Azure Cave Suites
BOUTIQUE HOTEL €€€

(☑532 7111; www.azurecavesuites.com; r €75-100; ☎) This gorgeous warren of caves, right at the top of Çavuşin hill, is a romantic refuge with incredible views across the countryside and over the old village ruins opposite. A Mediterranean-inspired decorative touch gives a distinctly fresh approach to Cappadocia's cave aesthetic, while we're particularly enamoured with the colourful pansy-filled patios and vistas from the rooftop terrace.

CAPPADOCIA FROM ABOVE

If you've never taken a flight in a hot-air balloon, Cappadocia is one of the best places in the world to try it. Flight conditions are especially favourable here, with balloons operating most mornings throughout the year. Seeing this area's remarkable landscape from above is a truly magical experience and many travellers judge it to be the highlight of their trip. Transport between your hotel and the balloon launch site is included in the hefty price, as is a champagne toast.

Flights take place just after dawn. Unfortunately, due to demand, even most of the reputable companies now offer a second, later-morning flight as well. Winds can become unreliable and potentially dangerous later in the morning, so you should always book the dawn flight.

You'll quickly realise that there's a fair amount of hot air among the operators about who is and isn't inexperienced, ill-equipped and under-insured. Be aware that, despite the aura of luxury that surrounds the hot-air ballooning industry, this is an adventure activity and is not without its risks. There was a fatal ballooning accident here in 2013. It's your responsibility to check the credentials of your chosen operator carefully and make sure that your pilot is experienced and savvy – even if it means asking to see their licences and logbooks. And don't pick the cheapest operator if it means they might be taking shortcuts with safety or overfilling the balloon baskets (which, if nothing else, will mean you won't be able to see the views you've paid a princely sum for).

It's important to note that the balloons travel with the wind, and that the companies can't ensure a particular flight path on a particular day. All companies try to fly over the fairy chimneys, but sometimes – albeit rarely – the wind doesn't allow this. Occasionally, unfavourable weather means that the pilot will cancel the flight for safety reasons; if this happens you'll be offered a flight on the next day or will have your payment refunded. Although this may be an inconvenience, it is preferable to flying in dangerous conditions.

All passengers should take a warm jumper or jacket and should wear flat shoes and trousers. Children under six will not be taken up by reputable companies.

The following agencies are in Göreme and have good credentials.

Butterfly Balloons (☑271 3010; www.butterflyballoons.com; Uzundere Caddesi 29) This seamless operation has an excellent reputation, with highly skilled and professional pilots including Englishman Mike, who has vast international experience and is a fellowship member of the Royal Meteorological Society. Standard flights (one hour, up to 20 passengers) cost €175.

Royal Balloon (☑271 3300; www.royalballoon.com; Dutlu Sokak 9) Seasoned pilot Suat Ulusoy heads up this reputable balloon operation. Standard flights (one hour, up to 20 passengers) cost €175.

Voyager Balloons (☑271 3030; www.voyagerballoons.com; Müze Caddesi 36/1) Recommended for its multilingual pilots and professional service. Standard flights (one hour, up to 28 passengers) cost €160.

Panorama Restaurant
TURKISH €€

(☑532 7002; dishes ₺7-20; ☑) This cheap and cheerful garden restaurant, near the trailhead into Rose Valley, is our favourite place to rest up at lunchtime after a morning hike. It also has simple pension-style rooms in the building behind.

Ayse & Mustafa's Place
TURKISH €€

(dishes ₺5-20; ⊘9am-5pm; ☑) Sit under the plum trees and enjoy Ayse's home-cooked *gözleme* (savoury pancakes) and *menemen* (scrambled eggs with peppers, tomatoes and cheese) – a hit with the lunchtime tour-bus crowd.

ℹ Getting There & Away

Çavuşin is on the route of both the hourly Nevşehir–Avanos bus and the Ürgüp–Avanos dolmuş service.

Paşabağı

This valley, halfway along the turn-off road to Zelve near a fairy-chimney *jandarma* (police station), has a three-headed rock formation and some of Cappadocia's best examples of mushroom-shaped fairy chimneys. Monks inhabited the valley and you can climb up inside one chimney to a monk's quarters, decorated with Hellenic crosses. Wooden steps lead to a chapel where three iconoclastic paintings escaped the vandals; the central one depicts the Virgin holding baby Jesus.

Zelve

The road between Çavuşin and Avanos passes a turn-off to the Zelve Open-Air Museum (Zelve Açık Hava Müzesi; admission ₺10; ⊘8am-7pm), where three valleys of abandoned homes and churches converge. Zelve was a monastic retreat from the 9th to the 13th century and although it doesn't have as many impressive painted churches as the Göreme Open-Air Museum, its sinewy valley walls with rock antennae are a wonderfully picturesque place for poking around.

The valleys were inhabited until 1952, when they were deemed too dangerous to live in and the villagers were resettled a few kilometres away in Aktepe, also known as Yeni Zelve (New Zelve). Remnants of village life include the small, unadorned, rock-cut mosque in Valley Three and the old değirmen (mill), with a grindstone and graffitied wooden beam, in Valley One.

Beyond the mill, the Balıklı Kilise (Fish Church) has fish figuring in one of the primitive paintings. Adjoining it is the more impressive Üzümlü Kilise (Grape Church), with obvious bunches of grapes. In Valley Two what's left of the Geyikli Kilise (Church with Deer) is worth seeing.

An excellent walking trail loops around the valleys allowing access to the various caverns, although erosion continues to eat into the valley structures and certain areas are cordoned off due to rockfalls.

There are cafes in the car park outside.

PRESERVING CAPPADOCIA

Like many regions that have witnessed a tourism boom, Cappadocia walks a tightrope between hanging onto its authentic soul (which attracted travellers here in the first place) and responding to the push for progress. The showstopping landscapes and ancient rock-cut shelters have transformed this area's economy from subsistence agriculture to one of the world's most unique tourism destinations.

Its burgeoning popularity with travellers, though, has not been without problems. The hot-air-ballooning industry's rush to cater for increasing numbers has led to the bulldozing of sections of valley to make way for multiple take-off sites. The popularity of jeep and ATV tours into the valleys has caused needless erosion. Hotel construction has boomed – with a handful of entrepreneurs more interested in cashing in than in preserving Cappadocia's rich natural heritage.

Luckily, however, most Cappadocians know the inherent value of their gorgeous region. Recent laws have banned vehicles from going into the valleys and limited the number of balloon companies. Even more encouragingly, locals led the way in protesting against an inappropriate hotel development in Uçhisar and recently succeeded in getting a court order to stop construction. With the local tourism industry on board, that tightrope looks like it's being walked responsibly.

❶ Getting There & Away

The Ürgüp–Avanos dolmuş stops at both Paşabağı and Zelve. If you're heading onward to Avanos after your visit, the dolmuş swings by Zelve car park at roughly 30 minutes past the hour; going the other way, towards Göreme and Ürgüp, it passes at 15 minutes past the hour.

It's an easy 1.5km flat walk along the road from Paşabağı to Zelve.

Devrent Valley

Look: it's a camel! Stunning Devrent Valley's volcanic cones are some of the best formed and most thickly clustered in Cappadocia, and looking at their fantastic shapes is like gazing at the clouds as a child. See if you can spot the dolphin, seals, Napoleon's hat, kissing birds, Virgin Mary and various reptilian forms.

Most of the rosy rock cones are topped by flattish, darker stones of harder rock that sheltered the cones from the rain until all the surrounding rock was eaten away, a process known as differential erosion.

To get to Devrent Valley (also known as Imagination Valley) from Zelve, go about 200m back down the access road to where the road forks and take the right road, marked for Ürgüp. After about 2km you'll come to the village of Aktepe (Yeni Zelve). Bear right and follow the Ürgüp road uphill for less than 2km. The Ürgüp–Avanos dolmuş can drop you off at Aktepe.

Avanos

📞 0384 / POP 13,250 / ELEV 910M

The Kızılırmak (Red River) is the slow-paced pulse of this provincial town and the unusual source of its livelihood, the distinctive red clay that, mixed with a white, mountain mud variety, is spun to produce the region's famed pottery. Typically painted in turquoise or the earthy browns and yellows favoured by the Hittites, the beautiful pieces are traditionally thrown by men and painted by women. Aside from the regulation tour groups (who, quicker than an eye-blink, get bussed into the pottery workshops and then bussed out again), Avanos is relatively devoid of foreign visitors, leaving you alone to meander the alleys that snake up the hillside, lined with gently decaying grand Greek houses. Occasional (and slightly incongruous) Venetian-style gondolas now ply the river, but riverside is still the place to ponder the sunset as you sip your umpteenth çay.

◉ Sights

Most visitors come to Avanos to see the town's pottery artisans at work. Tour groups are shuffled into the pottery warehouses outside of town. Others should patronise one of the smaller **pottery workshops** in the centre, most of which will happily show you how to throw a pot or two.

Chez Galip Hair Museum   MUSEUM
(Firin Sokak 24; ⊙ 10am-8pm) ᴹᴿᴱᴱ Not content with being home to some fine ceramic art, this pottery workshop and gallery also hosts Cappadocia's infamous hair museum. Yes, that's right: it's a museum dedicated to locks of hair that past visitors have left here for posterity – roughly 16,000 samples of hair cover the walls and ceiling of the back cave here. You'll find it either kookily hilarious or kind of (OK, a lot) creepy. Feel free to add your own contribution. Scissors are provided.

Find it opposite the post office in the centre of town.

Güray Ceramic Museum   MUSEUM
(Dereyamanlı Caddesi; admission ₺3; ⊙ 9am-7pm) This rather snazzy museum sits in a mammoth series of newly tunnelled-out caves underneath the Güray Ceramic showroom. It displays its private collection of ceramic art amassed over the years, with the ancient ceramics hall featuring pieces from as far back as the Chalcolithic era.

To get here from Avanos centre, cross the river at Taş Köprü bridge (at Atatürk Caddesi's western end), take the first right-hand turn onto Kapadokya Caddesi and follow the signs.

☞ Tours

Kirkit Voyage   GUIDED TOURS
(📞 511 3148; www.kirkit.com; Atatürk Caddesi 50) This company has an excellent reputation and friendly multilingual staff. As well as the usual guided tours, it can arrange walking, biking, canoeing, horse-riding and snowshoeing trips and can arrange airport transfers (reservation essential). The highly recommended guided horse-riding treks range from €40 for two hours to €80 for a full day and include proper riding equipment.

🛏 Sleeping

Ada Camping   CAMPING GROUND €
(📞 511 2429; www.adacampingavanos.com; Jan Zakari Caddesi 20; campsites per person ₺15; 🐾) This large, family-run camping ground is

in a superb setting near the river. The toilet block could be cleaner, but there's lots of shade and grass, a restaurant and a cold but inviting swimming pool. It's on the southern bank of the river, west of the main bridge.

★**Kirkit Pension**　　　　PENSION **€€**
(☑511 3148; www.kirkitpension.com; Genç Ağa Sokak; s/d/tr/f €40/55/70/90; ☎) This Avanos institution, right in the centre of town, is a rambling stone house with rooms full of kilims (pileless woven rugs), old black-and-white photographs, intricately carved cupboards and *suzanis* (Uzbek bedspreads), all set around a courtyard brimming with plants and quirky antiques. Looked after by incredibly knowledgeable and helpful management, Kirkit is the perfect base for trips around Cappadocia.

Venessa Pansiyon　　　　PENSION **€€**
(☑511 3840; www.venessapension.con; 800 Sokak 20; r ₺120-150; ☎) Owned by enthusiastic local history expert Mükremin Tokmak, the Venessa is a homely Avanos option with simple and bright rooms full of local kilims and traditional *yastık* cushions, and a cosy rooftop terrace with great views and bundles of local character. The pension also has its own small Cappadocian art exhibition and museum.

Sofa Hotel　　　　BOUTIQUE HOTEL **€€**
(☑511 5186; www.sofahotel.com; Gedik Sokak 9; d €40-70; ☎) A higgledy-piggledy wonderland for adults struck by wanderlust, the Sofa is the creation of artist Hoja, who has spent a fair chunk of his life redesigning the Ottoman houses that make up the hotel. Rooms merge eclectic-chic and traditional decoration with ease. Service is more aloof than elsewhere, but it's not often you get to stay somewhere so lavishly offbeat.

✗ Eating

The grassy banks of the Kızılırmak river have recently been spruced up and are prime picnicking territory. There are also plenty of shady riverside cafes to relax in.

Avanos' huge Friday market (☺9am-5pm) is the best in the region. It's held on the south bank of the river, near Taş Köprü bridge.

Hanım Eli　　　　ANATOLIAN **€**
(Atatürk Caddesi; mains ₺7-10) This modest little diner serves up wholesome local dishes packed full of fresh, local flavour. This is home-style cooking executed brilliantly and without pretentious flourish. The *mantı*

(Turkish ravioli) we had here was the best in Cappadocia.

Avanos Kadın Girişimciler Koop Restaurant　　　　ANATOLIAN **€€**
(Avanos Women's Cooperative Restaurant; Uğur Mumcu Caddesi; mains ₺10-15) Want to sample *içli köfte* (ground lamb and onion with a bulgur coating, often served as a hot meze) the way a Turkish mamma does it? The industrious women of Avanos have got together to offer a taste of home cooking in this restaurant just off Avanos' main square. Portions are on the small side, but it's good value.

Kapadokya Urfa Sofrası　　　　KEBAP **€€**
(Atatürk Caddesi; pide & dürüm ₺6-7, mains ₺12-20) Our pick of Avanos' multitude of kebap joints is this welcoming place right near the main square with cheerful service and excellent-value meals. Looking for a cheap, tasty lunch? We recommend ordering a couple of *lahmacun* (Arabic-style pizza; ₺3). Want something more substantial? The *beyti sarma* (spicy ground meat baked in a thin layer of bread; ₺14) here is superb.

★**Dayının Yeri**　　　　KEBAP **€€€**
(☑511 6840; Atatürk Caddesi; mains ₺13-25) Locals grumble that it's not as cheap as it used to be, but this modern grill restaurant is one of Cappadocia's best. Steer clear of the meze and it's still good value, too. Don't leave without sampling the *künefe* – layers of *kadayıf* dough cemented together with sweet cheese, doused in syrup and served hot with a sprinkling of pistachio.

It's right beside Taş Köprü (the town's main bridge).

Bizim Ev　　　　INTERNATIONAL **€€€**
(☑511 5525; Baklacı Sokak 1; mains ₺15-25) The cave wine cellar could easily tempt you into a few lost hours, but if you can make it upstairs the terrace is the place for atmospheric dining. Service is sleekly unobtrusive and the menu ranges from steaks to kebaps to casseroles.

🔒 Shopping

Avanos' many small ceramic workshops are located in the alleyways around the main square and in the group of shops opposite the post office.

Le Palais du Urdu　　　　CERAMICS
(☺10am-6pm) Our favourite Avanos artisan haunt, this unique drum-making and pottery studio caused a minor stir in ceramic

circles with a recent TV appearance. It's just off the main square, to your right if you're facing the hill.

ⓘ Information

Tourist Office (☑ 511 4360; Atatürk Caddesi; ⊙ 8.30am-5pm) Based in a beautifully restored Ottoman mansion opposite Taş Köprü (Avanos' main bridge). Extremely helpful staff and good town maps.

ⓘ Getting There & Around

Buses from Avanos to Nevşehir (₺3) leave every 30 minutes between 7am and 7pm. Services departing on the hour travel via Çavuşin, Göreme and Uçhisar (₺2.50); the half-hour departures take the direct route.

Dolmuşes to Ürgüp (₺3.50) leave hourly between 7am and 8pm, travelling via Zelve, Paşabağı, Çavuşin, Göreme and Göreme Open-Air Museum.

Both these services drop off and pick up passengers along Atatürk Caddesi.

Monday to Friday there is a dolmuş service to Özkonak underground city hourly between 8.30am and 5.30pm. The dolmuşes leave from behind the post office near the main square.

Kirkit Voyage (p481) hires out mountain bikes for ₺50 per day.

Around Avanos

Sarıhan

Built in 1249, the Sarıhan (Yellow Caravanserai; admission ₺3; ⊙ 9am-midnight) has an elaborate gateway with a small mosque above it. Having been restored in the late 1980s, it's one of the best remaining Seljuk caravanserais. Gunning down the highway towards it makes you feel like a 13th-century trader, ready to rest his camels and catch up with his fellow dealers.

Inside, you also have to use your imagination in the bare stone courtyard. Visitors are allowed on the roof.

The main reason to come to the Sarıhan is the nightly 45-minute whirling dervish ceremony (Sema; ☑ 511 3795; admission €25; ⊙ 9.30pm). You must book ahead – most hotels in Cappadocia will arrange it for you. The price may vary according to how much commission your tour agent or hotel is skimming off the top. Though the setting is extremely atmospheric, the *sema* is nowhere near as impressive as those staged in İstan-

bul. If you've seen one of those you should probably give this a miss.

Getting to the Sarıhan, 6km east of Avanos, without your own transport is difficult, as there are no dolmuşes and few vehicles with which to hitch a ride. An Avanos taxi driver will probably want around ₺30 to take you there and back, including waiting time.

Özkonak Underground City

About 15km north of Avanos, the village of Özkonak hosts a smaller version of the underground cities of Kaymaklı and Derinkuyu, with the same wine reservoirs and rolling stone doors. Although Özkonak underground city (admission ₺10; ⊙ 8am-6.30pm) is neither as dramatic nor as impressive as the larger ones, it's much less crowded.

The easiest way to get there is by dolmuş from Avanos (₺2, 30 minutes, hourly between 8.30am and 5.30pm Monday to Friday). There are no services on the weekend. Ask to be let off for the *yeraltı şehri* (underground city); the bus stops at the petrol station, a 500m stroll from the entrance.

Nevşehir

☑ 0384 / POP 94,189 / ELEV 1260M

Poor old Nevşehir. Surrounded by the stunning countryside of Cappadocia, this provincial capital offers travellers little incentive to linger. According to local lore, if you set eyes on the beautiful view from Nevşehir's hilltop castle, you'll be compelled to stay here for seven years. We're pretty sure the modern panorama of bland high-rises wasn't quite what they were talking about when that legend began. Nevşehir's accommodation is also bleak. Even if you arrive at night, we recommend that you make your way to nearby Göreme, where the accommodation is infinitely superior.

⊙ Sights

Nevşehir Museum   MUSEUM
(☑ 213 1447; Türbe Sokak 1; admission ₺3; ⊙ 8am-noon & 1-5pm Tue-Sun) This tiny museum is housed in an ugly building 1km from the centre. The collection includes an archaeological room with Phrygian, Hittite and Bronze Age pots and implements, as well as Roman, Byzantine and Ottoman articles. Upstairs, the dusty ethnographic section is less interesting.

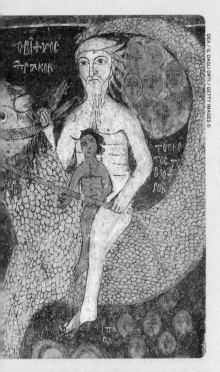

Cappadocian Frescoes 101

The frescoes of Cappadocia's rock-cut churches are, to be exact, *seccos* (whereby tempera paints are applied to dry plaster). Most of the frescoes here date from the 10th to the 12th centuries.

Christ Pantocrator

Christ 'the All-Powerful: typically painted on the church dome, depicting Jesus holding a book in one hand and giving a blessing with his other.

Nativity

Jesus' birth in Bethlehem. The Nativity in Eski Gümüşler Monastery is particularly striking.

Transfiguration

Portrayal of the miracle of Christ's metamorphosis in front of his disciples. A good depiction of this scene is in the Tokalı Kilise.

Anastasis

The 'Resurrection': Christ pictured with prophets, freeing souls from hell. The Karanlık Kilise has a superb example.

Deesis

Similar to 'Christ Pantocrator', Deesis scenes show a seated Christ flanked by the Virgin Mary and St John the Baptist.

Last Judgement

'Judgement Day': when righteous souls will ascend to heaven. The depiction in the Church of St Jean in Gülşehir is vividly well preserved.

Know Your Fresco Saints

St George Legend says this epic dragon slaughter took place upon Erciyes Dağı.

St Basil the Great Archbishop of Caesarea, credited with beginning monasticism in Cappadocia.

St Gregory the Theologian Friend of St Basil and Archbishop of Constantinople.

St Barbara Early Syrian Christian convert, martyred by being beheaded by her father.

1. Last Judgement fresco, Church of St Jean (p486), Gülşehir 2. Nativity fresco, Eski Gümüşler Monastery (p498) 3. Christ Pantocrator fresco, Karanlık Kilise (p467), Göreme

🛏 Sleeping & Eating

Hotel Safir   HOTEL €€
(☑ 214 3545; www.otelsafir.com; Paşa Bulvarı 27;
s/d ₺70/110; ❋ 🛜) Finally, a half-decent hotel
in Nevşehir, with large, tiled, spotless rooms,
a swanky lift and keen-enough staff. If, for
any obscure reason, you get stuck in town
for the night, this is a safe and solid option.

Nevşehir Konaği   ANATOLIAN €
(☑ 213 6183; Aksaray Caddesi 46; meze ₺3-5,
mains ₺7-15; ⊘ 9am-9.30pm) This municipal
restaurant, in an Ottoman-style building in
the park of the Kültür Merkezi (City Cultural
Centre), 1.5km southwest of the centre, serves
Cappadocian specialities such as *bamya çorba* (okra soup) and *dolma mantı* (ravioli).

ℹ Getting There & Away

Nevşehir is the main regional transport hub for
the nearby Cappadocian villages.

A taxi to Göreme should cost around ₺35.

AIR
Nevşehir Airport (Nevşehir Kapadokya Hav-
alimanı ; ☑ 0384 421 4451; www.kapadokya.
dhmi.gov.tr; Nevşehir Kapadokya Havaalanı
Yolu, Gülşehir) is 30km northwest of town, past
Gülşehir. Airport shuttle buses run between the
airport and the villages of central Cappadocia.
They must be pre-booked.

BUS
Nevşehir otogar is 2.5km southwest of the city.
Most bus services from İstanbul and other towns
in western Turkey terminate in Nevşehir but then
provide a free *servis* bus service to Göreme,
Ürgüp, Avanos and Uçhisar. See Dangers & An-
noyances (p465) for more information.

Nevşehir has excellent transport links to the
surrounding Cappadocian villages from its dolmuş stand on Osmanlı Caddesi in the city centre.
From here local dolmuşes run to Göreme (₺3,
every 30 minutes from 8am to 7.30pm); Uçhisar
(₺2.50, every 30 minutes from 7.30am to 6pm);
Ürgüp (₺3.50, every 15 to 20 minutes from 7am
to 10.30pm); Avanos (₺3, every 30 minutes from
7am to 7pm); Ortahisar (₺3, hourly from 8am to
5pm); and to Kaymaklı and Derinkuyu (₺3, every
30 minutes between 9am and 6.30pm). Buses
to Hacıbektaş leave from the Has Hacıbektaş
office, just around the corner.

Around Nevşehir

The sights north of Nevşehir may not be as
famous as their central Cappadocian cousins, but don't believe for a second that this
means they're second rate. Hiding just off

the road to Gülşehir is one of the region's
most fabulous fresco-filled churches, while
Hacıbektaş is the spiritual home of the fascinating Bektaşi Alevi sect.

Gülşehir
☑ 0384 / POP 12,219
This small town 19km north of Nevşehir has
two rocky attractions on its outskirts that
are definitely worth visiting if you're passing
through.

◉ Sights

Church of St Jean   CHURCH
(Karşı Kilise; admission ₺5; ⊘ 8am-5pm) On the
main highway into Gülşehir, just before the
turn-off to the centre (another 2km further)
is a signposted trail leading to the incredible 13th-century Church of St Jean. This
two-levelled, rock-cut church is home to marvellous frescoes, including scenes depicting
the Annunciation, the Descent from the Cross,
the Last Supper, the Betrayal by Judas, and
the Last Judgement (rarely depicted in Cappadocian churches), which were all painstakingly restored to their original glory in 1995.

Open Palace   MONASTERY
(Açık Saray; ⊘ 8am-5pm) **FREE** This fine rock-
cut monastery complex has a cluster of
churches, refectories, dormitories and a
kitchen, all carved out of fairy chimneys
and dating from the 6th and 7th centuries. It's signposted off the main Gülşehir–
Nevşehir road, about 4km before Gülşehir's
town centre.

ℹ Getting There & Away

Dolmuşes to Gülşehir (₺2.50, 25 minutes,
every 30 minutes) from Nevşehir depart from a
dolmuş stand on Lale Caddesi, just north of the
Alibey Camii. Ask to be let off at the Açık Saray
or Karşı Kilise to save a walk back from town.
Returning, just flag the bus down from the side
of the highway. You can also flag down dolmuşes
heading onward to Hacıbektaş from the highway.

Hacıbektaş

Hacıbektaş could be any unremarkable,
small Anatolian town if it weren't for the
beautiful dervish *dergah* (lodge) and museum set right in the main square. A visit here
is a glimpse of the history and culture of the
Bektaşi Alevi religious sect. The annual Hacı
Bektaş Veli pilgrimage and festival (August
16 to 18) is a fascinating experience if you're
here at that time.

◉ Sights

Hacıbektaş Veli Museum   MUSEUM
(Hacıbektaş Veli Müzesi; admission ₺5; ⊘8am-7pm Tue-Sun) Right in Hacıbektaş' centre is this tranquil dervish *dergah* (lodge), now a museum as well as a place of pilgrimage for those of the Bektaşı faith. Several rooms are arranged as they might have been when the Bektaşı order lived here, with dioramas of dervish life and beautiful exhibits of clothing, musical instruments and jewellery. The **Meydan Evi** (meeting house), where initiation ceremonies were performed, has an intricate wooden dove-tailed ceiling, its crossbeams symbolising the nine levels of heaven.

Amid the rose gardens of the museum's inner courtyard is the **Pir Evi** (House of the Masters), which contains the **Mausoleum of Haci Bektaş Veli**. Walk down the stairs, passing the tiny cell where dervishes would retreat to pray, to enter the Kırklar Meydanı (where dervish ceremonies took place), its walls decorated with colourful floral and geometric motifs. Haci Bektaş Veli's tomb is in a separate room to the right.

Across the rose gardens from the Pir Evi is the **Mausoleum of Balım Sultan** (another important religious leader), with a 700-year-old mulberry tree – its aged branches propped up by wooden posts – just outside.

❶ Getting There & Away

From Nevşehir, dolmuşes leave from the Has Hacıbektaş office on Lale Caddesi, near the Alibey Camii (₺5, one hour, hourly between 8.45am and 2.45pm). From Hacıbektaş, catch a returning dolmuş from the Mermerler Seyahat office, on Atatürk Bulvarı, across the road from the Hacıbektaş Veli Museum (₺5, one hour, hourly between 8am and 5pm) or five minutes later at Hacıbektaş' otogar. There are also seven daily departures for Ankara.

Ortahisar

📞 0384 / POP 3562

When Cappadocia's cartographers first got together, the farming village of Ortahisar must have been left off the tourist map. Known for the jagged castle that gives the town its name, Ortahisar is the epitome of Cappadocia's rustic agricultural soul. Wander downwards from the central square and you'll discover cobbled streets rimmed by gorgeously worn stone-house ruins leading out to a gorge of pigeon-house-speckled rock. Head upwards (towards the highway) and you'll see the cave complexes where Turkey's citrus-fruit supply is still stashed. Change, though, is in the air: a handful of offbeat and beautiful boutique hotels has popped up as visitors searching for the Cappadocia-of-old begin to discover Ortahisar's beguiling, arcadian beauty.

If you need information head to Crazy Ali's antique shop, next to the castle. Ali can help with walking directions into the surrounding valleys. There is a standalone ATM in the main square.

◉ Sights & Activities

Ortahisar Castle   CASTLE
(Cumhuriyet Meydanı; admission ₺5; ⊘9am-6pm) Slap in the middle of Ortahisar's town centre, this 18m-high rock outcrop was used as a fortress in Byzantine times. It reopened after a restoration project stabilised the

---

HACI BEKTAŞ VELI & THE BEKTAŞI SECT

Born in Nishapur in Iran in the 13th century, Hacı Bektaş Veli inspired a religious and political following that blended aspects of Islam (both Sunni and Shi'ite) with Orthodox Christianity. During his life he is known to have travelled around Anatolia and to have lived in Kayseri, Sivas and Kırşehir, but eventually he settled in the hamlet that is now the small town of Hacıbektaş.

Although not much is known about Hacı Bektaş himself, the book he wrote, the *Makalât*, describes a mystical philosophy less austere than mainstream Islam. In it he laid out a four-stage path to enlightenment (the Four Doors). Though often scorned by mainstream Islamic clerics, Bektaşı dervishes attained considerable political and religious influence in Ottoman times. Along with all the other dervishes, they were outlawed by Atatürk in 1925.

The annual pilgrimage of Bektaşı dervishes is an extremely important event for the modern Alevi community. Politicians tend to hijack the first day's proceedings, but days two and three are given over to music and dance.

crumbling edifice; you can now climb the precarious stairways to the top and admire the glorious view.

Culture Folk Museum   MUSEUM

(Kültür Müzesi; Cumhuriyet Meydanı 15; admission ₺5; ⊙9am-5pm) On the main square near Ortahisar's castle, the Culture Folk Museum gets bombarded with tour groups but is a good place to get to grips with the basics of local culture. In the dioramas, with their multilingual interpretive panels, mannequins in headscarves and old men's *şapkas* (hats) make *yufka* (thinly rolled, unleavened bread), *pekmez* (syrup made from grape juice) and kilims.

Hallacdere Monastery   MONASTERY

FREE The columned church of this rock-cut monastery complex contains unusual decorative features. Look for the animal heads on the column capitals and the human figure sculpted onto the wall. It's just off the main road into town, 1km northeast of Ortahisar centre.

Pancarlı Kilise   CHURCH

(Beetroot Church; admission ₺5; ⊙9am-4.30pm Apr-Oct) This rarely visited 11th-century church is snuggled amid a particularly photogenic vista of orange-hued rock. The small nave has a dazzling interior of well-preserved frescoes, while the surrounding cliff face is pockmarked with a warren of rooms that once served as living areas for hermit monks. To find it, head southeast from Ortahisar Castle, following Hacı Telegraf Sokak down the hill. Cross the bridge across the gully and take the eastern (signposted) farm track for 3km.

Cemal Ranch   HORSE RIDING

(☑0532 291 0211; cemalhome50@hotmail.com; İsak Kale; incl pick-up from Göreme or Ürgüp 1/2/4hr ₺50/100/200) Set amid stunning valley views, Cemel offers riding excursions in the surrounding countryside. All horseback tours include a traditional *gözleme* (savoury pancake) lunch. One-hour rides go through Ortahisar Valley and visit the Hallacdere Monastery. Four-hour treks explore the secluded Üzengi Valley. The ranch is 1km east of Ortahisar centre.

🍴 Sleeping & Eating

Castle Inn   HOTEL €€

(☑343 3022; www.castleinn.com.tr; Bahçe Sokak 5; r €50-90) With just five rooms, this old Greek house a stone's throw from the vil-

lage square is a snug choice, with friendly advice and historical titbits dished out by personable host Suat. Each of the stone-arch rooms (and one cave suite) is scattered with mementos picked up on Suat's travels, while the terrace has sweeping village views.

★ Hezen Cave Hotel   BOUTIQUE HOTEL €€€

(☑343 3005; www.hezenhotel.com; Tahir Bey Sokak 87; s/d €120/140, ste €210-270; 🐾) We think we've fallen in love. From the foyer's statement-piece ceiling of recycled *hezen* (telegraph poles) to the gourmet-feast breakfasts, every detail at this gorgeous design hotel has been thought through. A riot of quirky colours enlivens doors, windowframes and fixtures, adding a shot of contemporary chic to cave rooms that exude effortless cool.

The honesty bar, complimentary goodies and free shuttle service just top off an experience where you wonder if you've wandered into a VIP's daydream. Don't pinch us. We don't want to wake up.

Queen's Cave   BOUTIQUE HOTEL €€€

(☑343 3040; www.queenshotelcappadocia.com; Dere Sokak 24-26; r €80-140) Snuggled at the bottom of Ortahisar village is this intimate hideaway amid gardens of lavender and pansies. Cave and traditional stone-cut rooms merge modern comforts and lashings of natural wood and stone to emerge with a distinctively stylish cave-house vibe. For a touch of troglodyte whimsy, reserve the fairy-chimney room.

Ciğerci Bilalin Yeri   ANATOLIAN €€

(Huseyin Galif Efendi Caddesi; meals ₺10-18; ⊙Apr-Aug) The normally Mersin-based chef opens up his second operation in Ortahisar to feed the citrus-fruit workers when they're in town. Grab a table at the cubby-hole diner during these months and you're guaranteed plates of perfectly grilled meat skewers, served with a mountain of fresh *lavaş* bread and crunchy salad. It's on the main road uphill from the town square.

Tandır Restaurant   ANATOLIAN €€€

(☑477 8575; Manzara ve Kültür Park, Esentepe Mahallesi; mains ₺15-20; 🍴) Inside a lovely park, with gorgeous views over a tumble of village houses, hides this traditional restaurant where dishes such as *kabak çiçeği dolması* (stuffed zucchini flowers) and *tandır kuzu* (lamb tandoor) are served up with gracious aplomb.

ℹ️ Getting There & Away

Dolmuşes leave from the main square to Ürgüp (₺2, every 30 minutes from 8am to 5pm Monday to Saturday). Heading to Göreme, you have to walk 1km uphill to the Ortahisar turn-off on the main highway, where you can catch the Ürgüp–Avanos dolmuş as it goes by.

Ürgüp

📞 0384 / POP 20,061

When Ürgüp's Greek population was evicted in 1923, the town's wealth of fine stone-cut houses was left teetering into gentle dilapidation until tourism began to take off. Now, 90 years later, these remnants of another era have found a new lease of life as some of Cappadocia's most luxurious boutique hotels. Ürgüp is the rural retreat for those who don't fancy being too rural, with its bustling, modern downtown area a direct foil to the old village back lanes still clinging to the hillside rim. There's not a lot to do in town itself. Instead, Ürgüp has cleverly positioned itself as the connoisseur's base for exploring the geographical heart of Cappadocia, with boutique-hotel frippery and fine dining at your fingertips.

◉ Sights & Activities

★ Old Village   NEIGHBOURHOOD
The back alleys of Ürgüp are home to many fine examples of the traditional stone architecture of this region, and are well worth a stroll.

Temenni Wishing Hill   VIEWPOINT
(⊙ 9am-11pm) Home to a saint's tomb and a cafe, this viewpoint has 360-degree views over Ürgüp.

Museum   MUSEUM
(Kayseri Caddesi; ⊙ 8am-noon & 1-5pm Tue-Sun) FREE The museum features some 10-million-year-old teeth from a forerunner of the elephant, unearthed at Mustafapaşa, but the overall collection is uninspiring.

Turasan Winery   WINERY
(📞 341 4961; Tevfik Fikret Caddesi; vineyard tour & wine tasting €5; ⊙ 8.30am-7pm) The abundant sunshine and fertile volcanic soil of Cappadocia produce delicious sweet grapes, and several wineries carry on the Ottoman Greek winemaking tradition. You can sample some of the local produce here.

Tarihi Şehir Hamamı   HAMAM
(📞 341 2241; İstiklal Caddesi; soak, scrub & massage ₺25; ⊙ 7am-11pm) Partly housed in what was once a small church, the hamam offers mixed but respectable bathing.

☞ Tours

Several Ürgüp-based travel agents run tours around Cappadocia.

Argeus Tours   GUIDED TOUR
(📞 341 4688; www.argeus.com.tr; İstiklal Caddesi 47) Offers three- to nine-day packages, including a nine-day mountain-biking option, as well as day tours, flights and car hire. It's Ürgüp's Turkish Airlines representative.

Peerless Travel Services   GUIDED TOUR
(📞 341 6970; www.peerlessexcursions.com; İstiklal Caddesi 41) A range of one-day private tours as well as two- to six-day Cappadocia packages. Can also arrange car rental, airport transfers and tours throughout Turkey.

🛏️ Sleeping

Ürgüp has a glut of luxury boutique hotels, mostly on and around Esbelli Mahallesi (Esbelli Hill). If you're looking for a good selection of midrange and budget options, you're better off in Göreme. Some hotels close between November and March, when Ürgüp's weather keeps locals indoors and travellers elsewhere.

Hotel Elvan   PENSION €€
(📞 341 4191; www.hotelelvan.com; Barbaros Hayrettin Sokak 11; s/d/tr ₺70/120/180; 🖥️) Bah! – who needs boutique-style when you have pensions like the Elvan, where Hasan and family dish out oodles of homespun hospitality? Set around an internal courtyard brimming with colourful pot plants, the 20 neat rooms feature daisy bedspreads, pinewood floors and tiny bathrooms, all kept sparkling clean.

Cappadocia Palace   HOTEL €€
(📞 341 2510; www.hotel-cappadocia.com; Mektep Sokak 2; s/d/tr ₺80/130/170, cave s/d/tr ₺120/200/240; 🖥️) This Ürgüp old-timer has helpful management and a choice of either enormous cave rooms hosting bathrooms big enough to boogie in, or plainer (and smaller) motel-style rooms for those who aspire to the boutique scene but don't have the budget to match.

Ürgüp

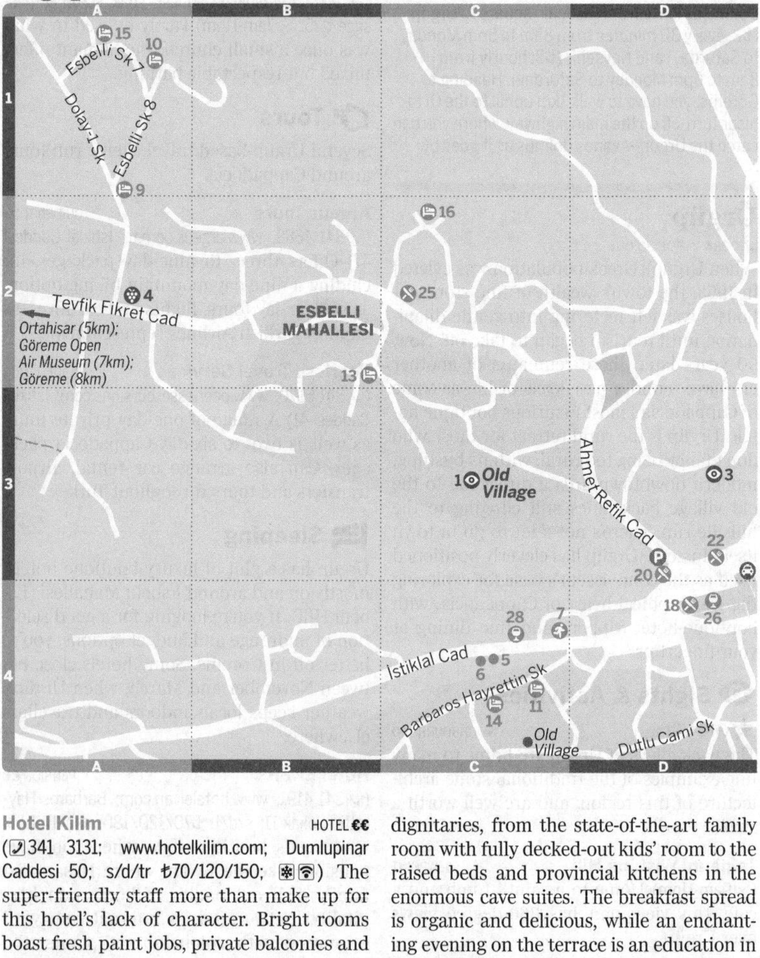

Hotel Kilim HOTEL €€
(☎341 3131; www.hotelkilim.com; Dumlupinar Caddesi 50; s/d/tr ₺70/120/150; ❄📶) The super-friendly staff more than make up for this hotel's lack of character. Bright rooms boast fresh paint jobs, private balconies and new linen.

★**Esbelli Evi** BOUTIQUE HOTEL €€€
(☎341 3395; www.esbelli.com; Esbelli Sokak 8; d €110, ste €160-220; 📶) Jazz in the bathroom, whisky by the tub, secret tunnels to secluded walled gardens draped in vines – this is one of Cappadocia's most individual boutique hotels. A lawyer who never practised, Süha Ersöz instead (thank God) purchased the 12 surrounding properties over two decades and created a highly cultured yet decidedly unpretentious hotel that stands out on exclusive Esbelli Hill.

The 14 detailed rooms feel more like first-class holiday apartments for visiting dignitaries, from the state-of-the-art family room with fully decked-out kids' room to the raised beds and provincial kitchens in the enormous cave suites. The breakfast spread is organic and delicious, while an enchanting evening on the terrace is an education in local history, humility and grace.

Serinn House BOUTIQUE HOTEL €€€
(☎341 6076; www.serinnhouse.com; Esbelli Sokak 36; d €120-145; 📶) Charming hostess Eren Serpen has truly set a new standard for hotel design in Cappadocia with this contemporary effort that seamlessly merges İstanbul's European aesthetic with Turkish provincial life. The six minimally furnished rooms employ dashes of colour and feature Archimedes lamps, signature chairs, hip floor rugs and tables too cool for coffee.

The toiletries are top shelf, breakfasts feature Eren's fabulous home-baking, and relaxing on the sun-drenched courtyard leaves guests in no doubt that humankind

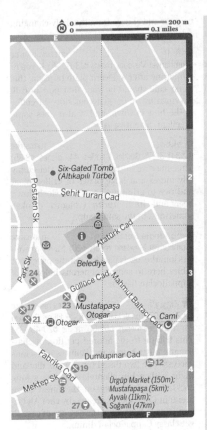

has evolved from that staid old prehistoric cave life.

Melekler Evi　　　　BOUTIQUE HOTEL €€€
(☑341 7131; www.meleklerevi.com.tr; Dere Sokak 59; d €100-160; ☎) Architectural duo Muammer and Arzu have created a sweet little hideaway that brims with inspired artistic flourishes. Each room is an individual piece of interior-design heaven, where hi-fi music and high-tech shower systems merge with smatterings of winged sculpture, grand old stone fireplaces and touches of homespun whimsy.

Delectable meals are prepared each day on request in a former stable, as enchanted residents come and go with a handmade map in one hand and a glass of local *şarap* (wine) in the other.

Yunak Evleri　　　　LUXURY HOTEL €€€
(☑341 6920; www.yunak.com; Yunak Mahallesi; s/d €130/140, ste €160-200; ☎) Warranting its own postcode, Yunak is a labyrinth of good taste cut into the cliffside. The hotel's mazy structure – in some parts dating back to the 5th century – unfurls itself in a string of Arabic lights that guide guests to its elegant carved-stone chambers. This is a hotel for connoisseurs of exceptional travel.

Sacred House　　　　LUXURY HOTEL €€€
(☑341 7102; www.sacred-house.com; Barbaros Hayrettin Sokak 25; d €200-500; ☎) This *haute couture* abode employs a maximum-design philosophy with huge helpings of Gothic-inspired baroque style. Chandeliers swing from ceilings, while ostentatious statues, pillars and objets d'art grace every corner and niche. The winter-garden bar and restaurant are a delight, though the underground

hamam and pool bedecked with Roman columns may leave you wondering where you misplaced your toga.

Hotel Assiana
HOTEL €€€

(☑ 341 4960; www.assianahouse.com; Dolay Sokak 1; d/ste €85/100; ☎) It may not be as polished as neighbouring hotels, but Assiana has an old-fashioned charm and a cosy, authentic edge. Interiors have hints of country-house grandeur with gilded mirrors, stately armchairs, stone fireplaces and *sedir* (traditional U-shaped floor-cushion seating arrangement), and we love the womb-like cave room with its separate tunnel entry.

🍴 Eating

Ürgüp's mammoth Saturday **market** (Fabrika Caddesi; ⊙9am-4pm) is a buzzing hive of activity and full of local produce. It's held in the Migros Supermarket car park.

Develili Deringöller Pide ve Kebap Salonu
PIDE €

(Dumlupınar Caddesi; pide ₺6-12; ☑) Shh... We're going to tell you a secret the locals have been trying to hide for years: this is, hands down, the best pide in Cappadocia.

Merkez Pastane ve Dondurma
ICE CREAM €

(Güllüce Caddesi; scoops ₺2) Cappadocian locals have been known to drive to Ürgüp just to buy a *dondurma* (ice cream). Check out the honey-and-almond flavour and you'll see why.

Zeytin Cafe
TURKISH €€

(☑ 341 7399; Atatürk Bulvarı; dishes ₺6-15; ☑) Our top lunchtime spot in Ürgüp is this thoroughly welcoming, modern *lokanta* (eatery serving ready-made food) dishing up wholesome homemade stews, *mantı* (ravioli) and Turkish staples. Head inside to the counter and choose from the daily-changing selection.

Cafe In
INTERNATIONAL €€

(Cumhuriyet Meydanı; mains ₺13-17; ☑) If you're hankering after a decent plate of pasta, this dinky cafe should be your first port of call. Servings are on the generous side, the coffee is the best in town, and it also does some excellent, inventive salads.

Ocakbaşı
TURKISH €€

(☑ 341 3277; Güllüce Caddesi 44; dishes ₺8-25) This massive restaurant serves delectably oily mezes and huge plates of grilled meat and rice to grinning locals who slosh down beer and fresh *ayran* (yoghurt drinks), sometimes in the same gulp.

Cappadocia Restaurant
TURKISH €€

(Cumhuriyet Meydanı; meals ₺20) Savvy travellers join the locals packing out the pavement tables here to sample generous helpings of Cappadocian flavour.

★ Ziggy's
MODERN TURKISH €€€

(☑ 341 7107; Yunak Mahallesi, Tevfik Fikret Caddesi 24; meze set menus ₺55-60, mains ₺20-45; ☑) This tribute to the adored pet dog of charismatic hosts Nuray and Selim is a luscious success. The two-tiered terrace fills day and night with a hip clientele enjoying strong cocktails and feasting on the finest meze menu in Cappadocia, created by chef Ali Ozkan. Ziggy's has nailed the essence of casual-yet-classy Cappadocian dining.

Don't miss a browse in Nuray's treasure-trove atelier downstairs, where she sells her beautiful handmade jewellery and quirky giftware.

Muti
MODERN TURKISH €€€

(☑ 341 5808; Cumhuriyet Meydanı 26; mains ₺28-46) Cherrypicking influences from Arabic,

SERVICES FROM ÜRGÜP'S OTOGAR

DESTINATION	FARE (₺)	DURATION (HR)	FREQUENCY (PER DAY)
Adana (via Nevşehir)	40	5	2 morning & 1 evening
Ankara	40	5	7
Antalya	50	10	2 evening & 1 morning
Çanakkale	80	17	1 evening
İstanbul	60	11	1 morning & 2 evening
İzmir & Selçuk	60	11½	1 evening
Kayseri	10	1¼	8
Konya	30	4	6
Marmaris/Bodrum/Pamukkale	70	11-15	1 evening

Armenian and old Ottoman cuisine, Muti offers formal Turkish dining with a fusion flourish. Meaty mains such as oven-baked veal tail and lamb shank rule the menu within the atmospheric low-lit stone restaurant. Downstairs, the charming courtyard bar is a convivial place for post-dinner drinks.

Han Çirağan Restaurant
TURKISH, BAR €€€

(☑341 2566; Cumhuriyet Meydanı; mains ₺15-35; ☑) The menu here is a meander through Turkish favourites with a modern twist, and service is super-friendly. After dinner, retire to the very cool bar downstairs, under the vine trellis, that has a city atmosphere and an excellent wine list, and serves up a mean martini.

🍸 Drinking & Nightlife

Ürgüp's main square (Cumhuriyet Meydanı) is the best place to grab a drink at an outside table and watch Cappadocia cruise by. Bookended by carpet shops, the pedestrian walkway running northeast from Ehlikeyf restaurant is full of cafes fronted by old men playing backgammon.

By far the most convivial and relaxed place for a drink in Ürgüp is at the bar in Han Çirağan restaurant, but if you want to go exploring, a few other places pass muster.

La Vita
BAR

(☑341 6927; İstiklal Caddesi) This comfy, low-key Ürgüp bar has chatty staff and a decent soundtrack, and hosts live music in the evening.

Angel Café Bistro
BAR, RESTAURANT

(☑341 6894; Cumhuriyet Meydanı) Ürgüp's bright young things lounge around on the red beanbags out the front and hip-hop blasts from the stereo. It comes into its own after dark.

Barfiks
BAR, RESTAURANT

(☑341 8442; Fabrika Caddesi) The downstairs cave bar is a wonderfully atmospheric setting for soulful, traditional tunes from local musicians. Don't expect to be able to have a conversation because it really is loud.

ℹ Information

There are several banks with ATMs on or around Cumhuriyet Meydanı.

Tourist Office (☑341 4059; Kayseri Caddesi 37; ☉8am-5.30pm Mon-Fri) The helpful tourist office gives out a town map and has a list of Ürgüp's hotels.

ℹ Getting There & Away

From the **otogar** (Güllüce Caddesi) dolmuşes travel to Nevşehir every 15 to 20 minutes from 7am to 10.30pm (₺3). The dolmuş service between Ürgüp and Avanos (₺3.50), via the Ortahisar turn-off, the Göreme Open-Air Museum, Göreme village, Çavuşin and Zelve, leaves from the otogar hourly between 8am and 7pm.

Dolmuşes to Mustafapaşa leave roughly every 30 minutes between 8am and 8.30pm (₺2) and to Ortahisar every 30 minutes between 8am and 7pm (₺2). Both these services leave from the **Mustafapaşa otogar** (Güllüce Caddesi), next to the main otogar.

ℹ Getting Around

If you don't fancy the steep walk from the centre of town up to Esbelli Mahallesi you can catch a **taxi** (fare ₺5) from the rank on the main square.

Ürgüp is a good base for hiring a car, with most agencies located on the main square or İstiklal Caddesi. Rates hover around ₺90 to ₺100 per day for a small manual sedan such as a Fiat Palio and climb to ₺120 to ₺140 for a larger automatic. Companies include **Europcar** (☑341 8855; İstiklal Caddesi 10), **National** (☑341 6541; Cumhuriyet Meydanı), **Avis** (☑341 2177; İstiklal Caddesi 19) and **Astral** (☑341 3344; www.astralrentacar.com; İstiklal Caddesi 19).

Several outlets rent mopeds and motorcycles from ₺50 a day, and bicycles from ₺25.

Mustafapaşa

☑0384 / POP 1600

This beautiful Cappadocian village is shifting slowly from yesteryear but remains well beneath the tourist radar. Still known widely by its pre-WWI Greek name of Sinasos, Mustafapaşa is home to some of the region's loveliest examples of typical Greek stone-carved-mansion architecture, serving as a reminder of its prosperous past when wealthy Greek-Ottoman merchants made up a sizeable portion of the community. When you've finished admiring the faded grandeur of the facades, the minor rock-cut churches amid the outlying valleys allow a decent dose of natural scenery.

You enter Mustafapaşa at an enlarged intersection, the Sinasos Meydanı, where a signboard indicating the whereabouts of the local rock-cut churches is located. Follow the road downhill and you'll come to Cumhuriyet Meydanı, the centre of the village, which sports the ubiquitous bust of Atatürk and several teahouses.

There is one ATM, but no bank, in town.

CAPPADOCIA MUSTAFAPAŞA

GOING UNDERGROUND

Thought to have been carved out by the Hittites, the vast network of underground cities in this region was first mentioned by the ancient Greek historian Xenophon in his *Anabasis* (written in the 4th century BC).

During the 6th and 7th centuries, Byzantine Christians extended and enlarged the cities and used them as a means by which to escape persecution. If Persian or Arab armies were approaching, a series of beacons would be lit in warning – the message could travel from Jerusalem to Constantinople in hours. When it reached Cappadocia, the Christians would gather their belongings and relocate to the underground cities, hiding in the subterranean vaults for months at a time.

One of the defense mechanisms developed by the cities' inhabitants was to disguise the air shafts as wells. Attackers might throw poison into these 'wells', thinking they were contaminating the water supply. The resulting fires were easy to quench, and the smoke was either absorbed by the soft tuff rock or dispersed in the shafts – leaving the attackers none the wiser.

The shafts, which descend almost 100m in some of the cities, also served another purpose. As new rooms were constructed, debris would be excavated into the shafts, which would then be cleared and deepened so work could begin on the next floor. Some of the cities are remarkable in scale – it is thought that Derinkuyu and Kaymaklı housed about 10,000 and 3000 people respectively.

Around 37 underground cities have already been opened. There are at least 100 more, though the full extent of these subterranean refuges may never be known.

Touring the cities is like tackling an assault course for history buffs. Narrow walkways lead you into the depths of the earth, through stables with handles used to tether animals, churches with altars and baptism pools, walls with air-circulation holes, granaries with grindstones, and blackened kitchens with ovens. While it's a fascinating experience, be prepared for unpleasantly crowded and sometimes claustrophobic passages. Avoid visiting on weekends, when busloads of domestic tourists descend. Even if you don't normally like having a guide, it's worth having one: they can conjure up the details of life below the ground better than you can on your own.

◉ Sights

There are churches in **Monastery Valley**, but they're disappointing compared with others in Cappadocia. Nonetheless, it's a lovely walk. To the west of Mustafapaşa there are 4km to 8km walks in **Gomeda Valley**. Local guide Niyazi, who charges €25 for individuals and groups, can be contacted through Old Greek House hotel.

Ayios Kostantinos-Eleni Kilise   CHURCH
(Church of SS Constantine & Helena; Cumhuriyet Meydanı; admission ₺5; ⊙8.30am-5.30pm) Right on Mustafapaşa's main square is the imposing Ayios Kostantinos-Eleni Kilise, erected in 1729 and restored in 1850. A fine stone grapevine runs around the door, while the ruined domed interior with faded 19th-century frescoes has a picturesquely shabby ambience.

Ayios Vasilios Kilise   CHURCH
(St Basil Church; admission ₺5; ⊙9am-6pm) A sign pointing off Sinasos Meydanı leads 1km to the 12th-century Ayios Vasilios Kilise, perched near the top of a ravine. Its interior features unimpressive 20th-century frescoes. There should be someone there with a key; if not, enquire at the *belediye* (town hall).

Medrese   MEDRESE
FREE Between Sinasos Meydanı and Cumhuriyet Meydanı is a 19th-century *medrese* (seminary; now utilised as a school) with a finely carved portal. The stone columns on either side of the doorway are supposed to swivel when there's movement in the foundations, thus warning of earthquake damage.

⊨ Sleeping & Eating

Both Old Greek House and Hotel Pacha double as restaurants.

Old Greek House   HISTORIC HOTEL €€
(☑353 5306; www.oldgreekhouse.com; Şahin Caddesi; r ₺150; 🕸) If this 250-year-old Greek mansion is good enough for the ex-mayor to

Below are four of the most interesting to visit. There are also underground cities in the village of Güzelyurt (p503), and at Özkonak (p483) near Avanos.

Kaymaklı Underground City (admission ₺20; ⊘ 8am-6.30pm) Kaymaklı underground city features a maze of tunnels and rooms carved eight levels deep into the earth (only four are open). As this is the most convenient and popular of the underground cities, you should aim to get here early in July and August to beat the tour groups, or from about 12.30pm to 1.30pm, when they tend to be having lunch.

Derinkuyu Underground City (admission ₺20; ⊘ 8am-6.30pm) Derinkuyu underground city, 10km south of Kaymaklı, has large, cavernous rooms arrayed on seven levels. When you get all the way to the bottom, look up the ventilation shaft to see just how far down you are – claustrophobics, beware!

Özlüce Underground City (⊘ 9am-6.30pm) To reach Özlüce underground city, turn right as you enter Kaymaklı village from the north and you'll be heading for the small village of Özlüce, 7km further away. More modest than the caves of Kaymaklı or Derinkuyu, this underground city is also much less developed and less crowded.

Gaziemir Underground City (admission ₺3; ⊘ 8am-6pm) Some 18km east of Güzelyurt, just off the road to Derinkuyu, is Gaziemir underground city, only opened in 2007. Churches, a winery with wine barrels, food depots, hamams and tandoor fireplaces can be seen. Camel bones and loopholes in the rock for tethering animals suggest that it also served as a subterranean caravanserai.

Getting There & Away

Although you can visit one of the cities as part of a day tour from Göreme, Avanos or Ürgüp, it's also easy to see them on your own. From Nevşehir, Derinkuyu Koop runs dolmuşes to Derinkuyu (₺3, 45 minutes, every 30 minutes between 9am and 6.30pm), which also stop in Kaymaklı (₺2.50, 30 minutes). Dolmuşes leave from the central bus stand on Osmanlı Caddesi.

You'll need a taxi or a hire-car to take you to Özlüce from Kaymaklı or to visit Gaziemir.

sleep in, it's good enough for us. Although it's best known for its Ottoman-flavoured set menus (₺40 to ₺50), enjoyed in the atmospheric grand halls, this place also has 14 generously sized, spotlessly clean rooms with an antique vibe.

Hotel Pacha PENSION €€
(☑ 353 5331; www.pachahotel.com; Sinasos Meydanı; s/d ₺75/100; ☏) This sprawling Ottoman-Greek house boasts neat-as-a-pin rooms and a tasty upstairs restaurant (meals €10) full of local bric-a-brac. The vine-covered courtyard provides sunseeker bliss on lazy summer afternoons.

Upper Greek House HOTEL €€
(☑ 353 5352; www.uppergreekhouse.com; Zafer Sokak; r ₺150-200; ☏) Right at the top of Mustafapaşa's hill, this quiet retreat has big and airy stone-arch rooms, decorated with simple elegance and opening onto large terraces or the shady courtyard downstairs.

Perimasali Cave Hotel HOTEL €€€
(☑ 353 5090; www.perimasalihotel.com; Sehit Aslan Yakar Sokak 6; d €120, ste €200-280; ☏) Over-the-top sculpture, gilded accents and spotlight features; this opulent Cappadocian hideaway has rooms that do nothing by half. The attention to detail befits a five-star hotel, though the decor won't be to everyone's taste. Service is charming and the terrace provides killer above-ground views.

Hanımeli Kapadokya Restaurant ANATOLIAN €€
(Yılmaz Sokak 14; set menu per person ₺40) Set on the Karagöz family's rooftop, this friendly place rustles up hearty home-cooking feasts. Local mezes are followed by your choice of wholesome mains – have the *testi kebap* (meat, chicken or vegetables cooked in a terracotta pot); it's particularly good here. If you manage to demolish that lot, you're doing better than we are and– there's still dessert to go.

ℹ Getting There & Away

Dolmuşes to Ürgüp leave from the main square (₺2, every 30 minutes between 8am and 6pm). A taxi costs ₺25.

Ayvalı

📞 0384 / POP 500

This lovely little village in a valley south of Ürgüp is a snapshot of the Cappadocia of old. It's a sleepy place surrounded by farming plots with a meander of cobbled alleyways rimmed by wonky stone houses. Tourists are virtually unsighted...for now.

If you don't have your own transport, getting to Ayvalı is a bit tricky. From Ürgüp's Mustafapaşa otogar, dolmuses depart for Ayvalı at 8.30am, 2pm and 5pm (₺2, 20 minutes). Returning from Ayvalı to Ürgüp the dolmuses leave at 8am, 9.30am and 3pm.

🛏 Sleeping & Eating

Aravan Evi
GUESTHOUSE €€

(📞 354 5838; www.aravan.com; d €80; 🖥) Looking for a slice of the simple life without sacrificing modern comforts? This charming guesthouse has just three lovely stone-arch rooms elegantly decorated in traditional fashion. A stay here is a welcoming time-out from the bustle of life. The gorgeous terrace restaurant (open to non-guests, reservations essential) is a flavourful trip through Cappadocian dishes and specialises in *tandır* (clay-oven) cooking.

Öykü Evi
HOTEL €€€

(📞 354 5852; www.oykuevi.net; Ayvalı Koyu 100; d €130; 🖥) 'Story House' is a tranquil haven snuggled into the rock and overlooking a secluded gorge where the only sound at night is the frogs. It's run by friendly owner (and author) Ayşe, who has stamped her whimsical taste throughout. Colourful pottery, pansies and wind charms abound on the terrace, while cosy rooms are a riot of colour and rustic charm.

⭐ Cappadocia Home Cooking
ANATOLIAN €€

(📞 354 5907; www.cappadociahomecooking.com; per person incl cooking class & meal €50) Tolga and his family have swung open the doors to their home – surrounded by their organic garden and overlooking Ayvalı's deep gorge – to offer a taste of true home-style Cappadocian cooking. They offer meals and highly recommended cooking classes with hands-on appeal, guided by Tolga's tiny dy-

namo of a mother, Hava. It's a foodie haven. Reservations are essential.

It's on the Ayvalı main road. Tolga can arrange transport to/from Ayvalı from your base in Cappadocia.

Soğanlı

📞 0352 / POP 500

Let's get one thing straight: despite its science-fiction setting, no scene in *Star Wars* was ever filmed near Soğanlı, or anywhere else in Turkey. But don't despair, Chewbacca fans – there's still ample reason to travel to this tiny village 36km south of Mustafapaşa; namely, a reverential series of rock-cut churches hidden amid the two dramatic, secluded valleys of Aşağı (Lower) Soğanlı and Yukarı (Upper) Soğanlı. An afternoon exploring at the foot of these sheer faces may inspire you to write your own script.

To reach Soğanlı turn off the main road from Mustafapaşa to Yeşilhisar and proceed 4km to the village. The **ticket office** (adult/child ₺5/free; ⊙8am-8.30pm) for the site is near the Kapadokya Restaurant. In the village square, local women sell the dolls for which Soğanlı is supposedly famous.

👁 Sights

Soğanlı's valleys were first used by the Romans as necropolises and later by the Byzantines for monastic purposes.

The most interesting churches are in the Yukarı Soğanlı valley (the right-hand turn on entering the village) and are easily circuited on foot in about two hours. All are signposted, but be careful as many are in a state of disrepair.

The Aşağı Soğanlı valley is accessed by taking the left-hand path from Soğanlı village.

Tokalı Kilise
CHURCH

(Buckle Church) On the main road into Soğanlı, about 800m before the ticket office, signs point to the Tokalı Kilise on the right, reached by a steep flight of worn steps.

Gök Kilise
CHURCH

(Sky Church) The Gök Kilise is just to the left of the Tokalı Kilise. It has twin naves separated by columns and ending in apses. The double frieze of saints is badly worn.

Karabaş Kilisesi
CHURCH

(Black Hat Church) The first church on the right after entering the Yukarı Valley, the

SOĞANLI ROAD TRIP

If you only rent a car once on your trip, the day you visit Soğanlı could be the time to do it. Not only are the valleys tricky to reach by public transport, but also the drive there is beautiful. The open countryside makes a change from central Cappadocia's canyons and you can stop in sleepy country villages that give an idea of what Göreme was like 30 years ago. Here our are top stops along the way.

Cemil Church Signposted from the main Soğanlı road, some 6km south of Musta-fapaşa, is the town of **Cemil**, where chickens rule the cobblestone paths, overlooked by abandoned Greek mansions on the hillside that are teetering into disrepair. Follow the signposted alleyway through the village to the picturesque blue-columned Cemil Church with its fresco fragments (all extremely defaced).

Keşlik Monastery (admission ₺5; ⊗9am-6.30pm Mar-Nov) This rock-cut Byzantine complex, 10km south of Mustafapaşa, is a labyrinth of a place with 16 houses where hundreds of monks lived. Inside the dwellings you can see fireplaces, bookshelves and grey nicks left on the rock by metal chisels. The **kitchen** features a hatch for passing meals to the **refectory**, which has seats at the far end for the teachers. The **Stephanos Church** here has a very well-preserved cross-form ceiling fresco that extends all along the vault.

Taşkınpaşa Mosque Some 7km south of Keşlik Monastery, tractors bounce along hilly, cobbled streets in Taşkınpaşa, which is named after its 600-year-old Seljuk mosque. The original, 14th-century pulpit is now in Ankara's Ethnography Museum. Outside, Taşkın Paşa himself is buried in one of the two **Seljuk tombs**; traders stayed under the arches during the caravanserai days. On the way back to the main road you will see a **medrese** (seminary) with an ornate door frame.

Sobesos (⊗8.30am-5.30pm) At the ancient city of Sobesos, signposted from Şahinefendi village, the various sections of the **Roman baths** can easily be distinguished. There are also some fine Roman mosaics, a mummy and a **Byzantine church**, built during renovations of the Roman city in the late 4th century. The main road through Şahinefendi itself is lined by cliffs pockmarked by hundreds of caves, carved out and used to store potatoes.

Karabaş Kilisesi is covered in paintings showing the life of Christ, with Gabriel and various saints. A pigeon in the fresco reflects the importance of pigeons to the monks, who wooed them with dovecotes cut into the rock.

Yılanlı Kilise   CHURCH
(Church of St George, Snake Church) The Yılanlı Kilise sits in the furthest corner of the Yukarı Valley, its frescoes deliberately painted over with black paint, probably to protect them. The hole in the roof of one chamber, surrounded by blackened rock, shows that fires were lit there.

Kubbeli Kilise   CHURCH
(Domed Church) Turn left at the Yılanlı Kilise, cross the Yukarı Valley floor and climb the far hillside to find the Kubbeli Kilise. The Kubbeli is unusual because of its Eastern-style cupola cut clean out of the rock.

Saklı Kilise   CHURCH
(Hidden Church) Nestling in the Yukarı Valley hillside, very near the Kubbeli Kilise, is the Saklı Kilise, which as its name suggests is indeed completely obscured from view until you get close.

Geyikli Kilise   CHURCH
(Deer Church) In the Aşağı Valley, the Geyikli Kilise has a monks' refectory and a still-visible fresco on the wall of St Eustace with a deer (from where the church's name is derived).

Tahtalı Kilise   CHURCH
(Church of St Barbara) The Tahtalı Kilise sits at the further end of the Aşağı Valley. It has well-preserved Byzantine and Seljuk decorative patterns.

🍴 Sleeping & Eating

Emek Pansiyon   PENSION €
(☑653 1029; soganli_emekpansion@hotmail.com; dm incl half board ₺50) We love this place for its authentic Cappadocian charm. The cave rooms (with shared bathroom) sleep up to six on traditional *sedir*-style beds, layered with carpets and cut into the rock. The

terrace cafe above, brimming with antiques and old photos, is a relaxing place to while away a few hours whether you stay the night or not.

Soğanlı Restaurant
TURKISH €€

(☑653 1016; mains ₺10-15; ☑) This popular lunch pit stop for Soğanlı day tours rustles up a mean *gözleme* (savoury pancake) and some tasty casseroles. The very basic pension rooms (₺35 per person) at the back are small but serviceable.

Kapadokya Restaurant
TURKISH €€

(☑653 1045; mains ₺10-15; ☑) Under shady trees, Kapadokya serves stodgy but acceptable omelettes, casseroles and soups. The campground (₺5 per site) is a patch of grass with a decrepit toilet block.

ⓘ Getting There & Away

It's basically impossible to get to Soğanlı by public transport. Best bet: go to Yeşilhisar from Kayseri (₺2.50, every 30 minutes from 7am to 9pm), then negotiate for a taxi to take you the last 15km. It's easier, though, to rent a car or sign up for a day tour in Ürgüp or Göreme.

Niğde

☑0388 / POP 124,774

Backed by the snowcapped Ala Dağlar range, Niğde, 85km south of Nevşehir, is a busy agricultural centre with a small clutch of historic buildings dating back to its foundation by the Seljuks. You won't want to stay but may have to if you want to visit the fabulous Eski Gümüşler Monastery, 10km northeast. You may also pass through en route to the base-camp villages for trekking in the Ala Dağlar National Park.

French is spoken in the helpful tourist office (☑232 3393; Belediye Sarayı 38/39; ⊗8am-noon & 1-5pm Mon-Fri), located on the 1st floor of the ugly Kültür Merkezi (City Cultural Centre) on Bor Caddesi. ATMs are dotted along Bankalar/İstiklal/Bor Caddesi.

◉ Sights

Niğde Museum
MUSEUM

(Niğde Müzesi; ☑232 3397; Dışarı Caddesi; admission ₺5; ⊗8am-noon & 1-5pm Tue-Sun) Niğde Museum houses a well-presented selection of finds from the Assyrian city of Acemhöyük near Aksaray, through the Hittite and Phrygian ages to sculptures from Tyana (now Kemerhisar), the former Roman centre and Hittite capital 19km southwest of Niğde. Several mummies are exhibited too, including the 11th-century mummy of a blonde nun discovered in the 1960s in the Ihlara Valley.

🛏 Sleeping & Eating

Hotel Şahiner
HOTEL €€

(☑232 2121; www.hotelsahiner.com; Giray Sokak 4; s/d ₺80/120; ❄ ☎) Sure, it doesn't have much

WORTH A TRIP

ESKI GÜMÜŞLER MONASTERY

Some of Cappadocia's best-preserved and most captivating frescoes are hidden within the rarely visited, ancient rock-hewn Eski Gümüşler Monastery (admission ₺5; ⊗8.30am-5pm), which was only rediscovered in 1963.

The lofty main church is covered with colourful Byzantine frescoes, painted between the 7th and 11th centuries. Of particular interest is the striking Virgin and Child to the left of the apse, which depicts the elongated Mary giving a Mona Lisa smile – it's said to be the only smiling Mary in existence.

Although the frescoes are the monastery's most famous feature, the warren of rooms here is fun to explore too. You enter the complex via a rock-cut passage, which opens onto a large courtyard with reservoirs for wine and oil, and rock-cut dwellings, crypts, a kitchen and a refectory. A small hole in the ground acts as a vent for a 9m-deep shaft leading to two levels of subterranean rooms. You can descend through the chambers or climb to an upstairs bedroom.

The monastery sprawls along the base of a cliff about 10km northeast of Niğde. To get there, Gümüşler Belediyesi dolmuşes (₺1.50, 15 minutes) depart every hour from Niğde's *eski* otogar (old bus station). As you enter Gümüşler, don't worry when the bus passes a couple of signs pointing to the monastery – it eventually passes right by it. To catch a bus back to Niğde, walk to the roundabout 500m from the monastery entrance and flag down a dolmuş heading to the left.

character, but decent-size, clean rooms with comfortable beds make the Şahiner a solid choice if you need to stay the night in Niğde. It's in an alleyway off Bankalar Caddesi, right in the centre of town.

Sini Lezzet Sofrası TURKISH €€
(İsmail Hakkı Altan Caddesi; mains ₺7-18) On Niğde's bustling pedestrian strip (one block down from the Atatürk statue), this *lokanta* (eatery serving ready-made food) dishes up huge plates of pide, spicy *güveç* (stew) and sizzling kebaps, all served with mountains of complimentary bread and salad.

ℹ Getting There & Away

BUS
Niğde's otogar is 4km out of town on the main highway. It has buses to Adana (₺20, 2¾ hours, five daily), Aksaray (₺15, 1½ hours, hourly between 7am and 9pm), İstanbul (₺60, 11 hours, five daily), Kayseri (₺15, 1½ hours, hourly between 7am and 9pm), Konya (₺25, 3½ hours, 10 daily), Nevşehir (₺10, one hour, hourly from 7am to 6pm) and Şanlıurfa (₺60, nine hours, two daily).

The *eski* otogar (old bus station) is right in the centre of town on Esin Erışıngı Caddesi. It has regular dolmuşes to Eski Gümüşler Monastery (₺1.50, 15 minutes, hourly) and Çamardı (₺5, 1½ hours, hourly) as well as frequent services to outlying villages.

Niğde city buses (₺1.50) scoot between the otogar and the centre of town – passing right beside the *eski* otogar – every 20 minutes during the day.

TRAIN
Niğde's train station, on the Ankara–Adana train line, is at the end of İstasyon Caddesi in the town centre. A daily service leaves for Ankara at 11.19pm (₺22.25, 9½ hours) and for Adana there are departures at 3.50am (₺9, four hours) and 8.55am (₺12.50, 3¾ hours).

Ala Dağlar National Park

The Ala Dağlar National Park (Ala Dağlar Milli Parkı) protects the rugged middle range of the Taurus Mountains between Kayseri, Niğde and Adana. It's famous throughout the country for its extraordinary trekking routes, which make their way through craggy limestone ranges dotted with waterfalls. It's best to trek between mid-June and late September; at other times weather conditions can be particularly hazardous, especially since there are few villages and little support other than some mountaineers' huts. Bring warm gear and prepare for extreme conditions.

The most popular walks start at the small villages of Çukurbağ and Demirkazık, which lie beneath Demirkazık Dağı (Mt Demirkazık, 3756m), 40km east of Niğde.

You can also reach the mountains via Yahyalı, 80km due south of Kayseri. From here it's another 60km to the impressive Kapuzbaşı Waterfalls (best seen between March and May) on the Zamantı River.

Although there are a variety of walks in the mountains, many people opt for the two-day-minimum walk to the beautiful Yedigöller (Seven Lakes, 3500m), which starts and finishes at Demirkazık. An easier three- to four-day walk begins at Çukurbağ and leads through the forested Emli Valley, before finishing at Demirkazık.

Although solo trekkers do sometimes venture into the mountains, unless you're experienced and prepared you should consider paying for a guide or joining a tour. All trekking arrangements, including guide and equipment hire, can be made through the guesthouses in Çukurbağ. A guide should cost around €100 per day; horses (to carry luggage) will also need to be added onto the price. If you prefer to trek as part of an organised tour, Middle Earth Travel (p470) is a good first port of call in Göreme. The agency offers both a three-day and a five-day program in the Ala Dağlar, with prices starting at €190 per person for a minimum of four people on the three-day option. Other agencies such as Demavend Travel (☑0388 232 7363; www.demavendtravel.com; 4th fl, Yildiz Is Merkesi 10, Sefik Soyer Meydanı) and Sobek Travel (☑0388 232 1507; www.trekkinginturkeys. com; Avanoğlu Apt 70/17, Bor Caddesi) are based in Niğde.

Çukurbağ has basic shops for supplies.

🛏 Sleeping

Ala Dağlar Camping CAMPING GROUND €
(☑0534 201 8995; www.aladaglarcamping.com; Çukurbağ Köyü Martı Mahallesi; campsites per person €7, cabin d/tr without bathroom €24/30, bungalow d/tr without bathroom €30/40, chalet s/d €40/50) Run by climbing couple Zeynep and Recep, this alpine hideaway has an ample camping area and basic mountain-log-cabin accommodation. Shared amenities (including kitchen) are good and there's a cafe if you're not in the cooking mood. Trekking and climbing guides as well as a host of

SULTAN MARSHES

An afternoon ploughing the Sultan Marshes in your gumboots might not sound like your cup of birdseed, but there's something undeniably fascinating about observing a flock of flamingos at a waterhole or an eagle swooping to snap the neck of a curious baby squirrel. The giant patch of wetland in between Soğanlı and Ala Dağlar is world famous among the twitching fraternity, which descends here year-round to spot the 300-odd species on stopover from Africa, Russia and continental Europe. Despite a local myth that bushfires have killed all the ornithology, birdlife here is thriving, and even a short detour to the flat, open fields can be richly rewarding.

If you decide to stay, the Sultan Pansiyon (☑0352 658 5549; www.sultanbirding.com; Sultansazlığı, Ovaçiftliği; s/d/tr €30/50/65; ❄@) is pretty much your only option. Luckily, it's very comfortable and backs onto the marshes themselves. The affable owners and resident birdfreaks can whip you around in their car and help you tick off your newly discovered hit list. It's free and easy to drive yourself, as long as it's not too wet.

activities can be arranged. It's a 2km walk from Çukurbağ junction and village.

Özşafak Pension PENSION €€
(☑0536 230 3120; www.ozsafak.net; Çukurbağ; r per person incl half board €30, campsites per person €10) This delightfully homey pension is run by enthusiastic local guide Beşir, who can organise all your trekking or birdwatching activities. Rooms are super-simple but clean, with beds piled high with snugly thick duvets. There are majestic mountain views from the pension's balcony and both breakfast and dinner are feasts of fresh, hearty local fare.

It's right on the main road's intersection to Çukurbağ village. All the dolmuş drivers can drop you off here if you let them know.

Şafak Pension & Camping PENSION €€
(☑0388 724 7039; www.safaktravel.com; Çurkurbağ Village; r per person incl half board €30, campsites per person €10) Run by friendly local guide Hasan, who can organise pretty much any activity, Şafak offers simple, clean rooms with hot water, heating and comfortable beds. Campsites have electricity and their own bathroom facilities, and the terrace and garden command magnificent views of Mt Demirkazık. It's on the main-road intersection with the Çurkurbağ village turn-off.

❶ Getting There & Away

From Niğde's *eski* otogar, take a Çamardı-bound dolmuş (₺5, 1½ hours, hourly between 7am and 5pm from Monday to Saturday, fewer services on Sunday) and ask to be let off at Çukurbağ junction and village (it's 5km before Çamardı). From Çamardı there are 10 services to Niğde between 6am and 5.30pm from Monday to Saturday and three services on Sunday.

Ihlara Valley
☑0382

Southeast of Aksaray, the Ihlara Valley scythes through the stubbly fields and today is home to one of the prettiest strolls in the world. Once called Peristrema, the valley was a favourite retreat of Byzantine monks, who cut churches into the base of its towering cliffs.

Following the Melendiz River, hemmed in by jagged cliffs, as it snakes between painted churches, piles of boulders and a sea of greenery ringing with birdsong and croaking frogs, is an unforgettable experience. Good times to visit are midweek in May or September, when fewer people are about.

There is an ATM in Ihlara village.

◉ Sights

Ihlara Valley HISTORIC SITE
(Ihlara Vadısı; admission incl Selime Monastery ₺10; ⊙8am-6.30pm) Hiking the full trail between Ihlara village and Selime is a wonderfully bucolic day out. Most visitors come on a tour and only walk the short stretch with most of the churches, entering via the 360 steps of the Ihlara Vadısı Turistik Tesisleri (Ihlara Valley Tourist Facility) ticket booth and exiting at Belisırma. This means the rest of the path is blissfully serene, with farmers tilling their fields and shepherds grazing their flocks the only people you're likely to meet.

Other entrances are at Ihlara village, Belisırma and Selime. It takes about an hour to walk from Ihlara village to the Ihlara Vadısı Turistik Tesisleri stairs, 1½ hours to walk from there to Belisırma, and about another two hours to walk from Belisırma to Selime.

If you're planning to walk the entire trail it's best to start early in the day, particularly in summer, when you'll need to take shelter from the fierce sun. Along the valley floor, signs mark the different churches. Some of the best to seek out on your hike are listed below

Kokar Kilise
CHURCH
(Fragrant Church) This church has some fabulous frescoes – the Nativity and the Crucifixion for starters – dating from the 9th and 11th centuries.

Pürenli Seki Kelisesi
CHURCH
This double-nave church has a wealth of 10th- and 12th-century frescoes depicting stories from the Gospels.

Ağaçaltı Kilise
CHURCH
(Daniel Pantonassa Church) This cruciform-plan church is most famous for its incredibly well-preserved fresco ceiling depicting the Ascension.

Sümbüllü Kilise
CHURCH
(Hyacinth Church) Some frescoes remain, but the church is mostly noteworthy for its simple-but-elegant facade.

Yılanlı Kilise
CHURCH
(Snake Church) Many of the frescoes are damaged, but it's possible to make out the one outlining the punishments for sinners, especially the three-headed snake with a sinner in each mouth and the nipple-clamped women (ouch) who didn't breastfeed their young.

Kırk Dam Altı Kilise
CHURCH
(St George's Church) Although badly graffitied, the frescoes are still gloriously vibrant, and above the entrance you can see St George on a white horse, slaying a three-headed snake.

Direkli Kilise
CHURCH
This cross-shaped church has four columns, with lovely partially-preserved frescoes of saints. The large adjoining chamber originally had two storeys, as you can see from what's left of the steps and the holes in the walls from the supporting beams. A sign near the Belisırma ticket booth points the way to the entry.

Bahattın'ın Samanlığı Kilise
CHURCH
(Bahattın's Granary) Some of the Ihlara Valley's best-preserved frescoes – depicting scenes from the life of Christ – are contained in this tiny church (named after a local who used to store grain here). The entry is slightly

hidden. From the Direkli Kilise, walk to the right (facing the road) along the cliff track to find it.

Selime Monastery
MONASTERY
(admission incl Ihlara Valley ₺10; ☉ dawn-dusk) The monastery at Selime is an astonishing rock-cut structure incorporating a vast kitchen with a soaring chimney, a church with a gallery around it, stables with rock-carved feed troughs and other evidence of the troglodyte lifestyle.

☞ Tours

Travel agencies in Göreme, Avanos and Ürgüp offer tours incorporating Ihlara for about ₺120 per person.

🛏 Sleeping & Eating

If you want to walk all of the gorge and don't have your own transport, you'll have to stay overnight. There are modest pensions

Ihlara Valley
Ⓝ 0 — 1 km
0 — 0.5 miles

Aksaray (45km)
Çatlak Hotel
● Selime
Selime Monastery
Güzelyurt (9km)
Ⓘ Piri Pension
Çatlak Restaurant ⊗
Ticket Office
Yaprakhisar
Anatolia Valley Restaurant & Camping;
Tandırcı Restaurant & Camping;
Belisırma Restaurant
Melendiz River
● Belisırma
Ticket Office
Bahattın'ın Samanlığı Kilise Ⓘ Ⓘ Direkli Kilise
Kırk Dam Altı Kilise Ⓘ Ⓘ Yılanlı Kilise
Sümbüllü Kilise Ⓘ Ağaçaltı
Ihlara Vadısı Turistik Tesisleri Ⓘ Kilise
Pürenli Seki Ⓘ Kokar
Kelisesi Ⓘ Kilise
Ticket Office ●
Star Restaurant & Pension ⊗
Ihlara Village ⊗
Akar Pansion 🛏 Ilısu (2km);
& Restaurant Güzelyurt (13km)

BIG HASAN

If a stroll through the Ihlara Valley gets you salivating for more walking, the stark beauty of the trail up to the peak of Hasan Dağı (Mt Hasan), Cappadocia's second-highest mountain, provides a challenging trek. The closest village to the 3268m inactive volcano is **Helvadere**, about 10km southwest of Ihlara village and 20km east of Taşpınar. Helvadere is the site of the ancient city of Nora, the architecturally unique remains of which can be seen 1km east of the village. From the mountain hut, 8km southwest of Helvadere, it takes eight hours to hike to and from the summit, where the basement of what was once Turkey's highest church remains. There are views of the Ala Dağlar and Bolkar ranges and Tuz Gölü, the country's second-largest salt lake. You can get more information in Göreme at Middle Earth Travel (p470), which offers a two-day trip incorporating Kaymaklı and the Ihlara Valley from €190 per person.

handily placed at both ends of the gorge (in Ihlara village and Selime). Note that most accommodation is closed from December to March.

Ihlara Village

Akar Pansion & Restaurant PENSION €€
(☑ 453 7018; www.ihlara-akarmotel.com; Ihlara Village; s/d/tr ₺50/100/120; ☏) One of the best options in the valley, Akar's large rooms have cheerfully bright linen and are kept spotlessly clean. Grab one of the rooms in the new building with private balconies. Helpful English-speaking staff can fill you in on any Ihlara queries, the restaurant serves tasty local dishes (₺10 to ₺20) and the attached shop sells picnic ingredients.

Star Restaurant & Pension TURKISH €€
(☑ 453 7020; www.ihlarapansion.com; Ihlara Village; mains ₺18-20; ☏ ☑) Right beside the river, the wonderful shady terrace at this friendly, family-run place is just the spot for dinner and chilling out with a beer after a day's hike. Local trout is the speciality, but there are also meaty casseroles and vegetarian options. It also has 10 simple rooms upstairs (singles/doubles ₺40/80) and a small, grassy camping area (sites ₺30).

Belisırma

Midway along the gorge, below Belisırma village, a cluster of low-key restaurants feed hungry hikers, with dining on platforms upon the river. All serve basic meals of grilled trout, kebaps, salads and soups, and have campsites.

Tandırcı Restaurant & Camping TURKISH €€
(☑ 457 3110; lunch ₺15) Tour groups often bypass this restaurant, leaving a mellow, shady

spot and a chance of scoring a river platform for lunch. Campsites are free.

Belisırma Restaurant TURKISH €€
(☑ 457 3057; lunch ₺15-20) Popular with tour groups, this place serves up the standard trout and *güveç* (stew) mains with friendly service. Free campsites.

Anatolia Valley Restaurant & Camping TURKISH €€
(☑ 457 3040; lunch ₺15-20) Efficient service and plenty of river-platform seating mean Anatolia is packed most summer lunchtimes. Campsites are ₺15.

Selime

Piri Pension PENSION €
(☑ 454 5114; Selime; s/d ₺45/90, campsites ₺20) This ramshackle yellow house, right beside Selime Monastery and a cluster of fairy chimneys, has six very basic rooms. You can also camp in the garden out front.

Çatlak Hotel HOTEL €€
(☑ 454 5006; www.catlakturizm.com.tr; Selime; s/d ₺80/100; ☏) Despite the gaudy 1970s-style decor, Çatlak has good-size rooms and smiley staff. Its riverside restaurant (a few steps from the Selime entry to Ihlara Valley) is a great place to have dinner.

❶ Getting There & Away

On weekdays six dolmuşes per day make the run between Aksaray and Ihlara village, travelling down the valley via Selime and Belisırma. Dolmuşes leave Aksaray at 7.30am, 10am, noon, 2pm, 4pm and 6pm. They leave Ihlara village for the return run at 6.45am, 8am, 9am, 11am, 1pm and 4pm (₺5, 45 minutes). On weekends there are fewer services. To get to Güzelyurt ask the driver to drop you at the Selime T-junction, where you can wait for a Güzelyurt dolmuş.

Güzelyurt

📞 0382 / POP 2647 / ELEV 1485M

This hillside tumble of crumbling stone houses, with back alleys presided over by strutting cockerels and the odd stray cow, leads down to a valley studded with the remnants of rock-cut churches. Surrounded by rolling hills, a lakeside monastery, and with the silhouette of Hasan Dağı (Mt Hasan) glowering over the horizon, the gentle-paced rhythm of life here is a refreshing glimpse of rural Cappadocia.

The town was known as Karballa (Gelveri) in Ottoman times, up till the population exchanges of 1924 it was inhabited by 1000 Ottoman Greek families and 50 Turkish Muslim families. Afterwards the Greeks of Gelveri went to Nea Karvali in Greece, while Turkish families from Kozan and Kastoria in Greece moved here. The relationship between the two countries is now celebrated in an annual Turks & Greeks Friendship Festival in July.

Güzelyurt main street has several shops, a bank (but no ATM) and a helpful tourist office (🕑 8.30am-7pm), though it is unfortunately often shut.

◎ Sights

Monastery Valley   RUINS
(admission ₺5; 🕑 8am-6.30pm) The 4.5km Monastery Valley is full of rock-cut churches and dwellings cut into the cliff walls. It's a lovely place for a stroll and panoramic viewpoints abound. From Güzelyurt's main square, take the signposted right-hand turn and follow the street down about 400m to the ticket booth.

Right beside the ticket office is Güzelyurt Underground City. The restored complex ranges across several levels and includes one hair-raising section where you descend through a hole in the floor.

The impressive facade of the Büyük Kilise Camii (Mosque of the Great Church) is the first major building after the ticket office. Built as the Church of St Gregory of Nazianzus in 385, it was restored in 1835 and turned into a mosque following the population exchange in 1924. St Gregory (330–90) grew up locally and became a theologian, patriarch and one of the four Fathers of the Greek Church. Check out the wooden sermon desk that was reputedly a gift from a Russian tsar. The church is quite plain inside but there are plans to uncover the whitewashed frescoes.

Opposite the Büyük Kilise Camii, a set of stairs leads up to the tranquil Sivişli Kilisesi (Church of the Panagia), with damaged but still colourful frescoes decorating the apse and domed ceiling. There are fantastic views over Güzelyurt if you climb up to the ridge from here.

Some 2km after the ticket office, you enter a gorge hemmed by high cliffs. The Kalburlu Kilisesi (Church with a Screen) with its superb chiselled entrance is the first rock-outcrop building in the group. Almost adjoining it is the Kömürlü Kilisesi (Coal Church), which has carvings including an elaborate lintel above the entrance and some Maltese crosses.

Yüksek Kilise & Manastır   MONASTERY
(High Church & Monastery) This religious complex is perched high on a rock overlooking Güzelyurt lake, some 2km south of a signposted turn-off on the Ihlara road 1km west of Güzelyurt. The walled compound containing the plain church and monastery is graffitied inside and looks more impressive from afar but has sweeping views of the lake and mountains.

Kızıl Kilise   CHURCH
(Red Church) Against a backdrop of stark, sweeping fields, the red masonry of the Kızıl Kilise stands out for miles. One of Cappadocia's oldest churches, it is currently undergoing a drawn-out restoration but can still be visited. It's 8km out of Güzelyurt on the Niğde road, just past the village of Sivrihisar.

🍴 Sleeping & Eating

There are three *lokantas* on and around the main square, serving cheap beer and rakı (aniseed brandy) and dishes such as kebaps and pide.

★ Hotel Karballa   HISTORIC HOTEL €€
(📞 451 2103; www.karballahotel.com; s/d/tr/f €40/50/75/90, ste s/d/tr €50/60/85; ❄️ 🛜 🏊) Occupying a 19th-century Greek monastery, the Karballa is named after its former inhabitants, and we bet the monks enjoyed living here. All rooms have colourful *suzani* bedspreads and carpets, but it's worth splashing out for a room in the main building. The cross-shaped windows and stone-vaulted ceilings are seriously atmospheric.

The hotel is to the left of the tea garden in Güzelyurt centre.

Halil Pension
PENSION €€

(☑451 2707; Yukarı Mahallesi Amaç Sokak; s/d ₺60/120; ☞) This family home has rooms in a modern extension to the original 140-year-old Greek house. Rooms are simple and small but have loads of natural light. There's a roof terrace with magnificent views over Güzelyurt lake. As you enter town from the west, it's signposted off to the right, a short walk downhill from the centre.

❶ Getting There & Away

From Aksaray, dolmuşes leave for Güzelyurt at 7.30am, 9.45am, 11.30am, 1.30pm, 3.30pm, 5.30pm and 6.30pm. Returning dolmuşes travel from Güzelyurt to Aksaray (₺5, one hour) at 6.30am, 7.30am and then every two hours, with the last at 5.30pm. On weekends there are fewer services. Going either way, dolmuşes can drop you at the T-junction near Selime, from where you can wait for an Ihlara Valley–bound dolmuş.

Aksaray
☑0382 / POP 189,977

Sitting in the shadow of Hasan Dağı, Aksaray is symptomatic of Turkey's economic rise: quietly prospering, with high consumer confidence. With an ugly modern town centre, the city doesn't have much to hold your interest, but as it's a jumping-off point for the Ihlara Valley you may find yourself snared here for a couple of hours. If so, an afternoon among the throng in the attractive town square surrounded by gaudy government buildings is an unequivocally Anatolian experience.

◎ Sights

Aksaray Museum
MUSEUM

(Aksaray Müzesi; Konya Caddesi; ⊙8.30am-5.30pm Tue-Sun) **FREE** Well, you certainly won't have problems finding this massive museum en route from the otogar along the main road to Aksaray centre. The recently revamped displays covering early Cappadocian human history have excellent English information boards, but the prize exhibit is the small collection of mummies unearthed in the Ihlara Valley.

Ulu Cami
MOSQUE

(Bankalar Caddesi) The Ulu Cami has decoration characteristic of the post–Seljuk Beylik period. A little of the original yellow stone remains in the grand doorway.

Eğri Minare
MONUMENT

(Crooked Minaret; Nevşehir Caddesi) Built in 1236 and leaning at an angle of 27 degrees, the curious Eğri Minare in the older part of Aksaray is, inevitably, known to locals as the 'Turkish Tower of Pisa'.

🛏 Sleeping & Eating

The following are within walking distance of the main square.

Otel Vadim
HOTEL €

(Otel Vadi; ☑212 8200; 818 Vadi Sokak 13; s/d/tr ₺55/75/90; ☞) Located in a quiet side street off Büyük Kergi Caddesi (the southern extension of Bankalar Caddesi), the Vadim is nothing special, but rooms are spacious and clean and the staff try hard to please.

Harman
TURKISH €

(☑212 3311; Bankalar Caddesi 16a; mains ₺7-12) Aksaray's best restaurant is adorned with photos of visiting celebrities posing with the star-struck waiters. It offers a great selection of *ızgara* (grills), döner kebaps (spit-roasted lamb slices), pide and soups.

❶ Getting There & Away

From Aksaray's **otogar** (Konya Caddesi), buses go to Ankara (₺30, 3½ hours); Göreme (₺10, 1½ hours) via Nevşehir (₺10, one hour); Konya (₺20, two hours) via Sultanhanı (₺5, 45 minutes); and Niğde (₺10, 1½ hours). Minibuses make the regular trundle from the otogar into the centre of town. A taxi to the centre will cost around ₺13.

Dolmuşes run between the **Eski Garaj** (Old Otogar; Atatürk Bulvarı), little more than a group of bus stands next to Migros supermarket in the centre, to Güzelyurt (₺5, one hour) and the Ihlara Valley (₺5, 45 minutes). There is a plan to begin the Ihlara and Güzelyurt dolmuş services from the otogar, so if you've just pulled in and are heading that way, check if you need to go into the centre or not.

Around Aksaray

The road between Aksaray and Nevşehir follows one of the oldest trade routes in the world, the Uzun Yol (Long Road). The route linked Konya, the Seljuk capital, with its other great cities (Kayseri, Sivas and Erzurum) and ultimately with Persia (Iran).

The Long Road was formerly dotted with *hans* (caravanserais) where the traders would stop for accommodation and business. The remains of three of these can be visited from Aksaray, the best preserved

SKI ERCİYES DAĞI

Erciyes Dağı Ski Resort (www.kayserierciyes.com.tr; Erciyes Dağı; 1-day ski pass ₺25), on the northeastern side of ruggedly beautiful Erciyes Dağı, is undergoing a multimillion-lira revamp intended to establish the mountain as a rival to European ski destinations. The ski runs themselves, and the modern gondola ski-lift system connecting them, are fantastic, with pistes to suit both beginners and hardcore snow-bunnies looking for empty slopes.

Accommodation remains thin on the ground for now, but it's within easy driving distance of Cappadocia's villages.

The resort plans to have 21 hotels right on the slope – with a focus on high-end accommodation. It looked a long way from completion when we visited (five hotels were open), although we were given an optimistic-sounding finishing date of 2015. At the time of writing lift passes and equipment hire remained exceedingly cheap by international standards – all the more reason to go now before the jet-setter ski crowd descends.

being the impressive **Ağzıkara Hanı** (admission ₺3; ⊙8am-6pm), 16km northeast of Aksaray, which was built between 1231 and 1239. From Aksaray a taxi will charge about ₺50 for the run there and back. You can also catch any bus heading to Nevşehir and jump off at the Ağzıkara Hanı.

Further towards Nevşehir you'll pass the scant remains of the 13th-century **Tepesidelik Hanı**, 23km northeast of Aksaray, and the 12th-century **Alay Hanı**, another 10km on.

Kayseri

🖉 0352 / POP 1 MILLION / ELEV 1067M

Mixing Seljuk tombs, mosques and modern developments, Kayseri is both Turkey's most Islamic city after Konya, and one of the economic powerhouses nicknamed the 'Anatolian tigers'. Most travellers whizz through town on their way from the airport to Cappadocia's villages, only seeing the shabby high-rises and ugly industrial factories on Kayseri's outskirts. The city centre of this Turkish boom town, though, is full of surprises. An afternoon pottering within the huge bazaar and poking about the Seljuk and Ottoman monuments – all loomed over by mighty Erciyes Dağı – is an interesting contrast to exploring the more famous fairy-chimney vistas to the city's west.

◉ Sights

★ **Museum of Seljuk Civilisation**   MUSEUM
(Selçuklu Uygarlığı Müzesi; Mimar Sinan Parkı; admission ₺2; ⊙9am-7pm) This excellent museum is set in the restored Çifte Medrese, a 13th-century twin hospital and seminary built at the bequest of Seljuk sultan Key-

hüsrev I and his sister Gevher Nesibe Sultan and thought to be one of the world's first medical training schools. The strikingly serene architecture is offset by beautiful exhibits of Seljuk artistry, culture and history, complemented by up-to-the-minute multimedia displays. Our one grumble is that not enough of the information panels have English translations.

★ **Güpgüpoğlu Konağı**   MUSEUM
(Ethnography Museum; Tennuri Sokak; ⊙8am-5pm Tue-Sun) FREE Ignore the scruffy mannequin-inhabited dioramas acting out Ottoman daily life and instead feast your eyes on the glorious interior of this grand mansion's painted wooden wall panels and ceilings. The building dates from the 15th century and Mamluk architectural influence is obvious in its regal black-and-white stone facade. During the 19th century the house's multicoloured beams and intricately carved woodwork were home to composer and lyricist Ahmet Mithat Güpgüpoğlu.

Mahperi Hunat Hatun Complex   HISTORIC BUILDING
(Seyyid Burhaneddin (Talas) Caddesi) FREE The austere and stately Mahperi Hunat Hatun complex is one of Kayseri's finest Seljuk monuments, built in the 13th century during the reign of Sultan Alaattin Keykubat. It comprises the **Hunat Hatun Medresesi**, with its shady courtyard now used as a cafe, the **Mahperi Hunat Hatun Camii** (mosque) and a still-functioning **hamam**.

Kayseri Castle   CASTLE
(Kayseri Kalesi; Cumhuriyet Meydanı) The monumental black-basalt walls of Kayseri castle were first constructed under the Roman

CAPPADOCIA KAYSERI

Kayseri

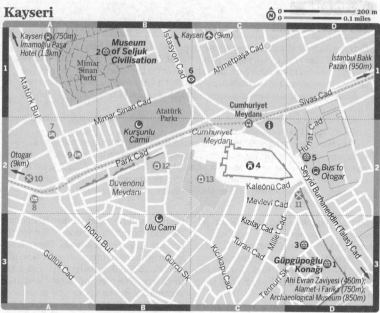

Kayseri

◎ **Top Sights**

◎ **Sights**

▣ **Sleeping**

✕ **Eating**

🛍 **Shopping**

emperor Gordian III and were rebuilt by the Byzantine emperor Justinian 300 years later. The imposing edifice you see today, though, is mostly the work of 13th-century Seljuk sultan Alaattin Keykubat. The castle is undergoing a mammoth restoration project, which will transform its internal area into a museum, art centre and park.

Atatürk Evi   HISTORIC BUILDING
(Tennuri Sokak; ☺8am-5pm Mon-Fri) FREE This creaky 19th-century Ottoman house, with its doll-house-proportioned mezzanine and 1st floor furnished in late Ottoman style, was where Turkey's founder, Kemal Atatürk, stayed when he visited Kayseri in August 1919.

Sahabiye Medresesi   MEDRESE
(Ahmetpaşa Caddesi) This Seljuk theological school dates from 1268 and its interior now functions as a book bazaar. Its richly decorated doorway with stalactite detailing is particularly notable.

Archaeological Museum   MUSEUM
(Hoca Ahmet Yesevi Bulvarı; admission ₺5; ☺8am-5.30pm Tue-Sun) Kayseri's small archaeological museum is a minor magpie's nest, featuring finds from nearby Kültepe (ancient Kanesh, chief city of the Hatti people and the first Hittite capital). Other exhibits include a stunning sarcophagus illustrating Hercules' labours, and a fascinatingly creepy exhibit of child mummies. It's a 1.5km stroll from Cumhuriyet Meydani. To find it walk down Talas Caddesi

until you get to the cemetery. Turn left, walk behind the cemetery and you'll see the museum on the far right-hand corner.

Ahi Evran Zaviyesi MUSEUM
(Esnaf ve Sanatkarlar Müzesi; Seyyid Burhaneddin (Talas) Caddesi; ⊙ 9am-5pm) FREE The gloomy interior of this 13th-century technical school for artisans and craftspeople is great to poke about in. It's crammed with a jumble-sale-style delight of dusty exhibits from calligraphy to metalwork, and agricultural implements to carpet looms. It's 1km down Talas Caddesi, opposite the cemetery.

Surup Krikor Lusavoriç Kilise CHURCH
(Church of St Gregory the Illuminator; Necip Fazıl Bulvarı) The 19th-century Surup Krikor Lusavoriç Kilise is one of Anatolia's few remaining Armenian churches. Its domed interior, complete with dilapidated frescoes and three gilded altars, was undergoing a long-overdue restoration when we last passed through Kayseri that will, hopefully, see the church returned to its original splendour. If finished by the time you arrive, the painting on the left, with four fiery columns topped by flaming crosses, depicts the vision of St Gregory, who grew up in Kayseri.

The church is located 1.6km southwest of Cumhuriyet Meydanı. The most direct way to get here from İnönü Bulvarı is to turn right onto Nazım Bey Bulvarı and then left onto Necip Fazıl Bulvarı. The church is three blocks down the road.

🛏 Sleeping

İmamoğlu Paşa Hotel HOTEL €€
(☑ 336 9090; www.imamoglupasaotel.com.tr; Kocasinan Bulvarı 24; s/d ₺90/140; ❇ 🖥) Near the train station, only a short jaunt from Kayseri centre, is this jazzy place with modern rooms decked out in neutral beige and grey tones and probably the most comfortable beds in town. Unlike most Kayseri hotels, it has some designated non-smoking rooms, so you don't have to wake up to the lingering smell of stale tobacco.

Hotel Almer HOTEL €€
(☑ 320 7970; www.almer.com.tr; Osman Kavuncu Caddesi 1; s/d ₺70/140; ❇ 🖥) A tribute to the 1980s-style architectural obsession with reflective glass, the Almer is a safe and solid choice in central Kayseri. Rooms are business-bland but comfortable and the glitzy lobby has a decent bar.

Bent Hotel HOTEL €€
(☑ 221 2400; www.benthotel.com; Atatürk Bulvarı 40; s/d ₺110/180; ❇🖥) The name – and the unfortunate use of red neon lighting across the exterior – may not inspire confidence, but the Bent has friendly staff and small (unfortunately smoky) rooms that are kept neat and clean.

Hotel Çapari HOTEL €€
(☑ 222 5278; Donanma Caddesi 12; s/d ₺70/110; ❇🖥) Enthusiastic staff, a great, central but quiet location and tidy rooms make the Çapari a decent place to rest your head for the night in Kayseri.

🍴 Eating

Kayseri boasts a few special dishes, among them *pastırma* (salted, sundried veal coated with *çemen,* a spicy concoction of garlic, red peppers, parsley and water) – the original pastrami.

Anadolu Lokantası TURKISH €
(☑ 320 5209; Osman Kavuncu Caddesi 10; dishes ₺5-14) No fuss. No frills. Just hearty portions of Turkish staples, served to an endless stream of lunchtime customers.

★ Alamet-i Farika ANATOLIAN €€
(☑ 232 1080; Deliklitaş Caddesi 8; mains ₺10-24) The interior is all European-style elegance, but the food is top-notch Anatolian. Tuck into the *mantı* (ravioli), devour the meaty speciality *çentik kebap* (grilled meat served atop potatoes with a yoghurt and tomato sauce) and save room for the naughtily sweet desserts. Finish up with Turkish coffee, served in dainty teacups with a shot glass of lemonade on the side.

To find it head straight down Talas Caddesi for 1.5km (past the cemetery) until you get to Hüma Hastanesi (a hospital) and the

---

OFF THE BEATEN TRACK

SULTAN HAN

Now finely restored, the Seljuk royal caravan lodging **Sultan Han** (admission ₺3; ⊙ dawn-dusk) was built in the 1230s, and is one of the largest in Anatolia. It's 45km northeast of Kayseri, near Tuzhisar, on the old Kayseri–Sivas highway.

To get here from Kayseri, take a Sivas-bound bus (₺5), or a dolmuş (₺2.50) heading to Sarıoğlan or Akkışla from the doğu (east) garage.

CAPPADOCIA KAYSERI

mosque. Take the right-hand turn into Deliklitaş Caddesi straight after the mosque and the restaurant is on the first block.

Elmacioğlu İskander Merkez — KEBAP €€
(222 6965; 1st & 2nd fl, Millet Caddesi 5; mains ₺10-22) Bring on the calories. Skip the diet for the day and ascend the lift to the top-floor dining hall, with views over the citadel, to order the house speciality, İskender kebap (döner kebap on fresh pide and topped with savoury tomato sauce and browned butter). Your waistline won't thank us, but your tastebuds will.

İstanbul Balık Pazarı — FISH €€
(231 8973; Sivas Caddesi; mains ₺15-20) Choose your fish from the glistening catches in the fishmongers by the door, then head to the dining room out back, with its jaunty mishmash of nautical and historical paintings, to dig into seafood flavours.

Shopping

Kapalı Çarşı — MARKET
(Vaulted Bazaar; Cumhuriyet Meydanı) Set at the intersection of age-old trade routes, Kayseri has long been an important commercial centre. Its Kapalı Çarşı was one of the largest bazaars built by the Ottomans. Restored in the 1870s and again in the 1980s, it remains the heart of the city and is well worth a wander.

Bedesten — MARKET
Adjoining the vast Kapalı Çarşı is the *bedesten* (warehouse), built in 1497. It was first dedicated to the sale of textiles and is still a good place to peruse great fat rolls of Turkish carpets and kilims.

Information

You'll find banks with ATMs in the centre.
Tourist Office (222 3903; Cumhuriyet Meydanı; 8am-5pm Mon-Fri) The helpful tourist office gives out maps and various brochures.

Getting There & Away

AIR
Kayseri Airport (Kayseri Erkilet Havalimanı; 337 5494; www.kayseri.dhmi.gov.tr; Kayseri Caddesi) is 9km north of the centre. A taxi from the central city to the airport costs around ₺15, or hop on a city bus for ₺1.25. If you're heading straight to one of the Cappadocian villages, airport shuttle buses pick up/drop off passengers at the airport. They must be pre-booked.

BUS
Kayseri's massive **otogar** (336 4373; Osman Kavuncu Bulvarı) is 9km west of the centre. Nearly all bus companies provide a free *servis* into the central city. If there's no *servis*, grab a taxi (₺15), catch a local bus (₺1.25) from the main road or take the tram (₺1.70).

Dolmuşes to Ürgüp (₺5, one hour, nine services between 8am and 7.30pm) leave from the smaller building across the car park from the main otogar. There is no direct dolmuş service to Göreme, but you can take the Ürgüp service and change there or hop on any of the big bus-company services travelling to Nevşehir. Most will drop you in Nevşehir, where you can get a *servis*. Some, though, will drop off passengers in Göreme along the way on request. Your best bets for a direct drop-off are Süha and Metro bus companies.

TRAIN
Kayseri Train Station (Kayseri Garı; Kocasinan Bulvarı) is served by the daily *4 Eylül Mavi* train (between Ankara and Malatya), the *Doğu Ekspresi* (between Ankara and Kars) and the *Çukurova Mavi* (between Ankara and Adana). There is also the daily *Erciyes Ekspresi*, which runs between Kayseri and Adana. The weekly Trans-Asia service to Tehran (Iran) also pulls in here.

To reach the centre from the train station, walk out of the station, cross the big avenue and board any bus heading down Atatürk Bulvarı towards Cumhuriyet Meydanı. Alternatively, you could walk along Altan Caddesi, which isn't as busy as Atatürk Bulvarı.

Getting Around

A state-of-the-art **tram** system called the KayseRay runs through central Kayseri from 6am to 2am daily. It's a very efficient way of getting around and single tickets cost ₺1.70. The nearest tram station to the otogar is Selimiye, a 10-minute walk away. From Selimiye it's 14 tram stops (25 minutes) to the central Cumhuriyet Meydanı tram station.

Black Sea Coast

Best Places to Eat

➜ Okyanus Balık Evi (p517)
➜ Mustafa Amca'nin Yeri (p512)
➜ Pamuk Kardeşler Balık Restaurant (p519)
➜ Kalender (p529)
➜ Orta Kahve (p524)

Best Places to Stay

➜ Sebile Hanım Konaği (p521)
➜ Denizci Otel (p516)
➜ Taşbaşı Butik Otel (p522)
➜ Hotel Nur (p528)

Why Go?

While many visitors flock south to the Mediterranean or west to the Aegean, the Black Sea (Karadeniz) is equally deserving, particularly because it is so different from the other coasts. After Amasra's seaside-holiday vibe and Trabzon's big-city buzz, you can relax in pint-size fishing villages or head inland and up to alpine *yaylalar* (mountain pastures). And the spectacular coastline makes for a scenic route across Turkey to other parts of Anatolia.

This is a historic region, scattered with the legacies of civilisations and empires that have ebbed and flowed like Black Sea waves. Castles, churches, monasteries and architecturally important mosques recall the days of the kings of Pontus, the Genoese and the Ottomans. Queen Hippolyte and her tribe of female Amazon warriors supposedly lived here, and the seafront chapel at Yason Burnu (Cape Jason) marks the spot where Jason and his Argonauts passed by.

When to Go
Trabzon

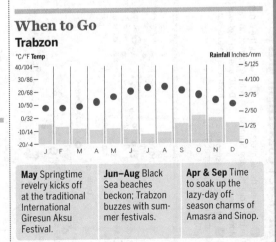

May Springtime revelry kicks off at the traditional International Giresun Aksu Festival.

Jun–Aug Black Sea beaches beckon; Trabzon buzzes with summer festivals.

Apr & Sep Time to soak up the lazy-day off-season charms of Amasra and Sinop.

Black Coast Highlights

1 Climbing through forests up to the cliff-hugging **Sumela Monastery** (p531).

2 Enjoying the easygoing ambience of the port at **Sinop** (p514).

3 Counting the vertigo-inducing curves on the scenic **D010 coastal highway** (p513) from Amasra to Sinop.

4 Exploring the winding labyrinth of alleys in **Amasra Castle** (p511).

5 Cruising big-city streets and enjoying a massage at a hamam in **Trabzon** (p525).

6 Discovering mountain plateaus and alpine hamlets on a day trip to villages such as **Uzungöl** (p534).

7 Stepping back in time along **Ünye's** rat-a-tat-tat

8 Hopping on the **cable car** (p522) and enjoying a picnic high above **Ordu** (p522).

Bakırcılar Sokak (Street of Coppersmiths) (p521).

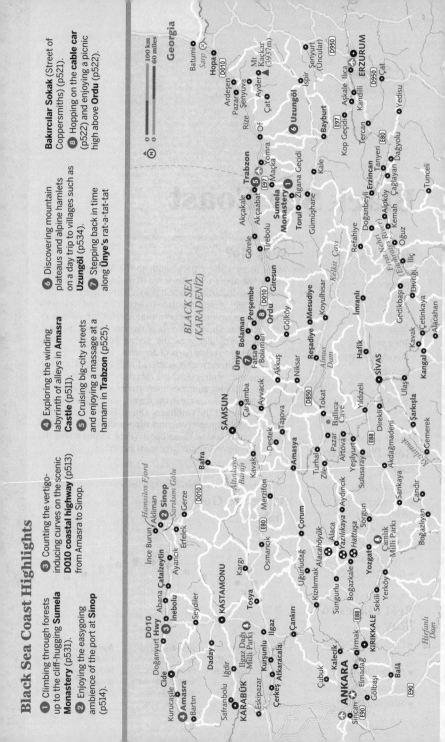

Amasra

☑ 0378 / POP 6650

It's a six-hour, 450km-long journey from İstanbul to Amasra, but your first glimpse of the city from the hills above will tell you that the trip was worthwhile. Straddling a peninsula with two bays and a rocky island reached by a Roman bridge, the town is the Black Sea's prettiest port. It's a popular tourist centre, but low-key in comparison with many Aegean and Mediterranean resorts.

A Greek colony called Sesamos Amastris and mentioned by Homer was established here in the 6th century BC. The Byzantines held Amasra as part of the Pontic kingdom but rented the port to the Genoese as a trading station from 1270 until 1460, when Mehmet the Conqueror took it without a fight. Under Ottoman rule, Amasra lost its commercial importance to other Black Sea ports, and today it's a laid-back spot to relax.

Restaurants and bars can be found on both Büyük Liman (Big Harbour) to the east and prettier Küçük Liman (Little Harbour) to the west. Most accommodation is closer to the former. The statue in the square overlooking Küçük Liman is of Turkish rock star Barış Akarsu, a much-loved local boy who died in a car accident at age 28 in 2007.

◎ Sights & Activities

Amasra Castle   CASTLE
(Amasra Kalesi) FREE Reached through three massive gateways from Küçük Liman or via steps from Büyük Liman, Amasra's citadel occupies the promontory fortified by the Byzantines. The Dereağzı Tunnel under the castle leads to a fresh-water pool.

The citadel precincts are now mostly residential, but the impressive original walls and some relics survive, including the restored 9th-century Byzantine Church Mosque (Kilese Camii), which functioned as the former and then the latter until 1930.

Amasra Museum   MUSEUM
(Amasra Müzesi; www.amasramuzesi.com; Çamlık Sokak 4; admission ₺5; ☺ 8.30am-5pm Tue-Sun, to 7pm Apr-Oct) This excellent museum occupies a 19th-century naval school at the southern end of Küçük Liman. Exhibits, from coins to carpets and including Roman, Byzantine, Hellenistic and Ottoman finds, showcase Amasra's multi-layered history.

Boat Trips   BOAT TOUR
(Büyük Liman) Amasra and its castle are best viewed from the sea. Operators in Büyük Liman offer boat trips around the harbours and nearby island (from ₺10 for a 45-minute tour, and ₺40 for six hours, including swimming stops and lunch on the island). Boats mostly run on summer weekends but you'll find a few year-round.

🛏 Sleeping

Rates on busy summer weekends from mid-June to mid-September are up to 50% higher than during other periods, and many places will charge solo travellers the cost of a double room. Most hotels open only at the weekend from November to April.

Balkaya Pansiyon   PENSION €
(☑ 315 1434; www.balkayapansiyon.com; General Mithat Ceylan Caddesi 35; s/d without breakfast ₺40/70; ☏) This is one of Amasra's cheapest pensions, offering 15 small, basic, but renovated, rooms on a side street behind the tourist office on Büyük Liman. Choose 104 for a room with a view.

Kuşna Pansiyon   PENSION €€
(☑ 315 1033; www.kusnapansiyon.com; Kurşuna Sokak 36/A; s/d ₺50/100; ❋ @ ☏) The friendly Doğu family has really thought of travellers' requirements at this pension in the castle precincts. Nine bright, modern rooms, including a cute attic room in the main house, overlook a verdant garden and rocky cove. Breakfast features homemade jam and unlimited tea and coffee. It's near the Church Mosque; access via the steps near the Büyük Liman tour boats.

Timur Otel   HOTEL €€
(☑ 315 2589; www.timurotel.com; Çekiciler Caddesi 53; s/d ₺50/100; ❋ ☏) This very friendly hostelry has 25 spotless (though somewhat dark) rooms overlooking a square with a fountain, just off Büyük Liman. Double-glazing ensures a good night's sleep despite the nearby mosque. Some rooms have views.

Çarşı Butik Otel   BOUTIQUE HOTEL €€
(☑ 315 1146; www.carsibutikotel.com; Çekiciler Caddesi 23; s/d ₺60/120; ❋ ☏) Overlooked by the castle walls near the souvenir market, the Çarşı's dozen or so wood-trimmed rooms have private verandahs decorated with comfy cushions. The term 'boutique' is used generously, and some bad decorating decisions have been made (eg some awful leopard-skin

bedspreads), but it's a friendly and conveniently positioned place to stay.

Sahil Otel
HOTEL €€

(☑315 2211; www.amasra.net/sahil-otel-amasra. html; Turgut Işık Caddesi 82; s/d ₺60/120; ❄@🕸) Opposite the Amasra Yelken Kulübü (Amasra Sailing Club) at the far end of Büyük Liman, the compact but modern Coast Hotel has 13 rooms with small balconies. Waterfront eating and drinking is just a stroll away.

✗ Eating

Amasra's mostly licensed (ie selling booze) seafront restaurants serve fresh fish by the *porsiyon* (portion). Alternatively, get a takeaway and take your pick of the two harbours.

Hamam Cafe
CAFE €

(☑315 3878; www.hamamcafe.com; Büyük Liman; gözleme ₺6; ⊙8.30am-11.30pm; 🕸) In an Ottoman-era hamam by the tourist office booth, this easygoing cafe is perfect for sipping tea and playing backgammon among colourful lights on the disused *göbek taşı* (heated central 'navel stone'). The *peynirli gözleme* (stuffed savoury crepes with cheese) are moreish and the *Amasra mantısı* (Turkish ravioli; ₺12) a speciality.

Mavi Yeşil
SEAFOOD €€

(☑315 2727; www.amasramaviyesil.com/; Büyük Liman Caddesi; fish portion ₺12.50-35; ⊙10am-midnight) Smart black tables with red overlays populate the first-floor dining room of the 'Blue Green', which rises from Upper Beach (Plaj Üstü) opposite Ziraat Bank. It serves calamari and *köfte* (meatballs) as well as the day's catch; the balcony with views along the coast doubles as the smoking area.

Amasra Sofrası
TURKISH €€

(☑315 2483; Iskele Sokak 25; mains ₺8-15; ⊙7am-midnight; 🕸) On a quiet square just west of Büyük Liman, this friendly grill house and *lokanta* (eatery serving ready-made food) has alfresco tables. Choose among the many vegetable dishes, pide, kebaps and fish.

Balıkçının Yeri
SEAFOOD €€

(☑315 2109; www.balikcininyeri.com; Büyük Liman Caddesi 57/A; fish portion ₺12-20; ⊙8am-midnight) 'Fisherman's Place' is the standout in a row of cheaper seafood restaurants lining the northern edge of Büyük Liman. Sea views are limited, but you can buy a takeaway *balık ekmek* (fish sandwich, ₺6).

★ Mustafa Amca'nin Yeri
SEAFOOD €€€

(☑315 2606; www.amasracanlibalik.com; Küçük Liman Caddesi 8; fish portion ₺10-45, meze ₺6; ⊙8am-midnight) Locals recommend this restaurant for its excellent *canlı balık* (fresh fish), unsurpassed service and big windows offering sweeping sea views. In situ since 1945, 'Uncle Mustafa's Place' is unmissable – a chalet-like frontage outside hiding a nautical theme within.

🍷 Drinking & Nightlife

★ Lutfiye
CAFE

(☑315 3222; www.lutfiye.com; Küçük Liman Caddesi 20/A; ⊙9am-midnight) This super classy cafe serves cappuccinos, snacks and breakfast to a chilled-out soundtrack. It's also a lovely alternative to Amasra's kitsch souvenir market, selling marmalade, nut-studded *lokum* (Turkish delight) and *helva* (sesame-seed sweet).

Çınar
BAR

(☑315 1018; www.amasracinarbalik.com; Küçük Liman Caddesi 1; ⊙9am-midnight) The west-facing 'Plane Tree' is a winner for Amasra sunsets and sweeping harbour views. It serves crisply chilled draught beer, a wide range of cocktail-ready spirits and meze.

Ağlayan Ağaç Çay Bahçesi
TEA GARDEN

(Weeping Tree Tea Garden; ☑315 2930; Nöbethane Sokak) Head up through the castle precincts to this cliff-top tea garden with views of squawking seagulls circling the island; signs point the way.

Cafe 'N Bistro
PUB

(☑315 3535; Küçük Liman Caddesi 1; ⊙11am-late) This wood-fronted corner bar is male-dominated inside, but its outside tables are hot property for watching the evening roll in. It's at the end of the souvenir market, with snacks such as *börek* (filled pastry) and chips available.

Arma Cafe & Patisserie
CAFE

(Cumhuriyet Caddesi 1; ⊙8am-11pm) Just back from Küçük Liman, the 'Rigging' is nautical in name only, with landlubbers enjoying coffees, teas and hot chocolates in its windows. Pastries (including cupcakes) and Turkish breakfast also on offer.

Han Cafe & Bar
BAR

(☑315 2775; www.amasra.gen.tr/han-bar; Küçük Liman Caddesi 17; ⊙10am-late) This is the most popular of Amasra's small cluster of pubs away from the water and is sandwiched between houses next to the main castle gate. There's often live music at night in season.

Sesamos Cafe BAR

(Turgut Isık Caddesi; ⊙7am-1am) Facing the Büyük Liman, Sesamos has ramshackle appeal, with nautical clobber balancing on wooden beams and seating among fishing boats on the beach.

Çekek Cafe BAR

(Turgut Isık Caddesi 1; ⊙8.30am-midnight) Opposite Ziraat Bank and away from the Küçük Liman clamour, Çekek is a mellow place to start the evening with a cocktail. There's seating on the beach and a little jetty, plus eats such as breakfast, burgers and fish.

ℹ Information

There are a few internet cafes on Özdemirhan Sokak just east of Küçük Liman.

Tourist Office (Büyük Liman; ⊙Jun-Sep) In a small kiosk beside Hamam Cafe. Opening hours are often restricted to weekends.

ℹ Getting There & Away

Heading east along the coast, get an early start. Dolmuşes (minibuses) become increasingly scarce later in the day.

Intercity bus companies don't travel to Amasra. Instead, minibuses to Bartın (₺4, 30 minutes) leave every 30 minutes from near the PTT (post office). From Bartın there are buses to Safranbolu (₺18, two hours), Ankara (₺30, five hours) and İstanbul (₺45, seven hours). For Sinop, you will need to change in Karabük (₺18, two hours) and/or Kastamonu (₺25, four hours).

Metro and Kamil Koç have offices in the main square next to the Atatürk statue in Amasra.

Amasra to Sinop

Winding sinuously around rugged hills hugging the sea, the D010 from Amasra to Sinop (320km) is breathtakingly scenic. Expect minimal traffic and stunning views at every turn, with glistening turquoise waters, lush forested headlands and rugged cliffs of *marla,* a distinctive slate-like volcanic rock used for roofing. Though the condition of these paved roads is good, the average driving speed is about 45km/h, which means that it takes over seven hours to reach Sinop. By public transport, you'll need to use local services between the small towns and villages along the way. Get going at daybreak and don't expect to complete the journey in a day.

A few villages have camping grounds, including Çakraz, just west of Bozköy Beach. Kurucaşile, 45km east of Amasra, has some pensions and modest hotels, and you can see boats being built in the village. Other spots within day-trip distance of Amasra are the picturesque two-beach village of Kapısuyu and, 10km further east, the tiny harbour at Gideros, the idyllic cove of your dreams. There are a couple of restaurants here where you can feast on local seafood and watch the sunset, including Günbatımı (☑0366-871 8140; Gideros Koyu; mains ₺12). From here the road descends to Kalafat and Kumluca, a sand-and-pebble beach stretching 8km. Many dolmuşes terminate in Cide, 3km east of Kumluca. Seafront pensions, mostly only open from June to September, and fish restaurants huddle at the western end of town, around 2km from the central otogar (bus station).

The road beyond Cide is particularly bendy and hilly. Around 12km east, a signpost points to Kuscu Köyü, a small village with access to the Aydos Canyon, a steep river ravine. Doğanyurt, 31km before İnebolu and about 4½ hours from Amasra, is yet another pleasant harbour town, with a Friday market, a big pier and a few little cafes and *lokantalar* (eateries serving ready-made food).

About 150km (three hours) west of Sinop, İnebolu is a possible stopping point; onward transport may be hard to find by late afternoon. The Yakamoz Tatıl Köyü (Phosphorescence Holiday Village; ☑0366-811 3100; www.yakamoztatilkoyu.com.tr; İsmetpaşa Caddesi; bungalow s/d ₺55/85, room s/d ₺70/105, mains ₺20; ❄❂❄) is a beachside resort 800m west of the centre, with a cafe and licensed restaurant; book ahead in summer. In the town centre are old Ottoman houses painted a distinctive oxblood red and a relatively lively seafront promenade; eat at the İne Balık & Et (☑366-811 4123; Hacı Mehmet Aydın Caddesi 9; mains ₺10-35).

Abana, 24km east of İnebolu, has a decent beach, and about 23km further on, near Çatalzeytin, is a long pebble beach surrounded by beautiful scenery. Not far east, about 4km before reaching Türkeli, is the delightful Güllüsu Aile Balık Lokantası (Güllüsu Family Fish Restaurant; ☑0368-684 8046; Güllüsu Mevkii, Türkeli; mains ₺10-25) for another fish feast. At Ayancık the road divides, with the northern route offering the more scenic journey to Sinop (58km). To get onto this route, cross the bridge and continue through Ayancık.

BLACK SEA COAST AMASRA TO SINOP

Sinop

☎ 0368 / POP 38,600

Wrapped around a rocky promontory, delightful Sinop is a town of superlatives. It is the most northerly point in Anatolia and the only southern-facing spot on the coast. According to an old salty saying, 'the Black Sea has three harbours – July, August and Sinop'. The naturally sheltered harbour here is safe even in the roughest winter weather, when it can be dangerous for ships to enter other ports.

Colonised from Miletus on Anatolia's Aegean coast in the 8th century BC, Sinop's trade grew, and successive rulers – including the Pontic kings (who made it their capital), Romans and Byzantines – turned it into a busy trading centre. The Seljuks took Sinop in 1214 and used it as a port, but the Ottomans preferred to develop nearby Samsun, which had better land communications. On 30 November 1853, a Russian armada attacked Sinop without warning, overwhelming the local garrison and killing or wounding about 3000 people. The battle brought on the Crimean War, in which the Ottomans allied themselves with the British and French to fight Russian ambitions to expand westward and southward.

Sinop is today a holiday town with a cosmopolitan air; its heritage as a trading port for nigh on three millennia is reflected in model shops on sale in shops all over town. Book accommodation ahead in peak season (mid-June to mid-September).

◉ Sights

Sinop Fortress FORTRESS

(Sinop Kalesi) **FREE** Open to attack from the sea, Sinop was first fortified by the Hittites around 2000 BC. The existing walls are additions made by the Romans, Byzantines, Seljuks and Ottomans of those erected in 72 BC by Pontic King Mithridates VI. At one time the walls, some 3m thick, were more than 2km long, with 25m-high towers and seven gates, including still extant Kumkapı (Sand Gate; Batur Sokak) and Lonca Kapı (Guild Gate) to the northwest.

Between the two gates and next to the village otogar is a statue of Diogenes the Cynic (Sakarya Caddesi), the Greek philosopher born in Sinop in about 413 BC.

Tarihi Sinop Cezaevi HISTORIC BUILDING

(Historical Sinop Prison; http://sinopale.org/historical -sinop-prison; Sakarya Caddesi; admission ₺5; ⊙ 9am-5pm, to 7pm Apr-Sep) The cells, empty corridors, exercise yards and children's reform school of this hulking former prison within the fortress are haunting, particularly if you've seen *Midnight Express*, Alan Parker's frightening 1978 film about an American drug dealer trapped in the Turkish penal system. Founded in 1887, it 'did time' as a prison until 1997 when inmates were moved to a more modern facility nearby. Many notable Turkish writers were imprisoned here; it remains very much alive in Turkish collective memory.

Sinop Archaeological Museum MUSEUM

(Sinop Arkeoloji Müzesi; www.sinopmuzesi.gov. tr; Okullar Caddesi 2; admission ₺3; ⊙ 8am-5pm Tue-Sun) Highlights of this excellent museum include the fabulous Meydankapı mosaic from the 4th century AD depicting the four seasons and seven muses; a marble statue of lions savaging a deer from the 4th century BC; various coin hoards, including the celebrated one from Gelincik; and an excellent collection of Byzantine religious objects, including icons from local churches. The garden contains pillars, more mosaics, turban-topped gravestones and a pleasant fish pond.

Alaaddin Camii MOSQUE

(Aladdin Mosque; Sakarya Caddesi) Set in an expansive walled courtyard, this mosque was constructed for Süleyman Pervane in 1267. It has been repaired many times; the local Candaroğlu emir added the marble *mihrab* (niche indicating the direction of Mecca) and wooden *mimber* (pulpit), sadly damaged when one of the three domes collapsed. The austere interior and spacious courtyard are oases from Sinop's buzz.

Pervane Medresesi HISTORIC BUILDING

(Batur Sokak; ⊙ 8am-10pm) The powerful Seljuk grand vizier Süleyman Pervane built this seminary in 1262 to commemorate the conquest of Sinop a half-century earlier. It now houses a cafe and shops selling local crafts, including lovely embroidered linen, a Sinop speciality.

Şehitler Çeşmesi MEMORIAL

(Martyrs' Fountain; Kurtuluş Caddesi) Secreted away near the harbour, next to the Hacı Ömer Camii (1903), the poignant Martyrs'

Sinop

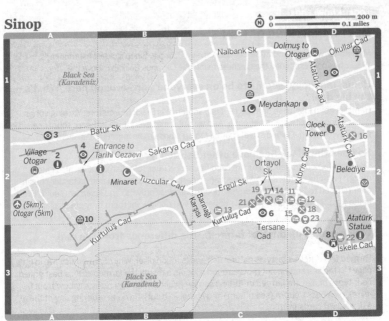

Sinop

⊙ Sights

⊜ Sleeping

⊗ Eating

⊜ Drinking & Nightlife

⊜ Shopping

Fountain commemorates the Turkish soldiers who died in the surprise Russian attack of 1853. It was built using money recovered from the soldiers' pockets.

Sinop Martyrs' Monument MEMORIAL
(Atatürk Caddesi) This monument near the museum contains the remains of soldiers killed in the Crimean War.

⊨ Sleeping

Yılmaz Aile Pansiyonu PENSION €
(☎261 5752; www.facebook.com/pages/Sinop-yıl maz-aile-pansiyon/378816672219753; Tersane Çarşısı, Tersane Caddesi; per person without breakfast ₺35, without bathroom ₺25; @🖤) Tucked away down a narrow lane, this friendly, family-run pension a few steps from the waterfront has 12 simple but renovated rooms. Room 47 has its own bathroom and a sea view.

MERT KANAL: KING OF FISH

Mert Kanal, whose grandfather opened Mevsim Balıkçılk, Sinop's oldest fishmonger's, in the 1930s, has now expanded the business to include Okyanus Balık Evi above the shop.

Hamsi (anchovy) seems to be on everyone's lips around here. What's the big deal?

Hamsi is not a just a fish or a food – it is tradition, it is Black Sea culture. We sing songs, dance dances, write poems about it. And we put it into everything – bread, soup, rice pilaf. There's even a jellied sweet *(hamsi tatlısı)* whose main ingredient is anchovy.

So does the Black Sea have other fish to fry?

The most famous is *kalkan* (turbot) and the best is *lüfer* (bluefish). But we also catch *mezgit* (whiting), *istavrit* (horse mackerel), *barbunya* (red mullet) and its tastier cousin *tekir* (striped red mullet). Be careful, though: *karides* (prawns) and *kalamar* (squid) live in the Mediterranean and Aegean, not here. If you really want them they are available, but frozen.

Which makes us think of farmed... Big difference from the real McCoy?

Farmed fish is not as tasty as natural fish and is much oilier. Why? Farmed fish live in little cages in the sea and do not move around a lot. As a result, the farmed stuff is best grilled. Four types of fish are farmed in Turkey: *somon* ('salmon', though really rainbow trout), *levrek* (sea bass), *çupra* (sea bream) and *alabalık* (trout). If you're ordering any of these, ask where it came from.

Any secrets for testing for freshness?

Use your senses. Smell is obvious but look at the fish carefully. The eyes should be bright and clear, the gills red (not purple), the skin shiny. In Turkey, fishmongers use very strong lights so they reflect on the fish, making it look fresh. Take it out of the light. Feel it. The skin should be almost slimy, the meat firm. If soft, it is not fresh.

★ **Denizci Otel**
HOTEL €€

(☑260 5934; www.denizciotel.com.tr; Kurtuluş Caddesi 13; s/d ₺70/120; ❉ 🛜) It's all change at the waterfront 'Sailor', which has been given a complete makeover and now bears a homey Ottoman retro feel. It's a superb option, with reproductions of slightly erotic Lawrence Alma-Tadema paintings decorating the corridors and 27 large rooms with big plasma-screen TVs and window alcoves. Room 503 should be your first choice.

Otel 57
HOTEL €€

(Elli Yedi; ☑261 5462; www.otel57.com; Kurtuluş Caddesi 29; s/d ₺80/100; ❉ 🛜) At this friendly place, spick-and-span leatherette chairs in reception give way to 20 comfortable (though smallish) rooms. There's a plentiful breakfast buffet and the clientele is a mix of Turkish businessmen and tourists. If you must know (and we did) '57' is the number of Sinop province and appears on local licence plates.

Otel Mola
HOTEL €€

(☑261 1814; www.sinopmolaotel.com.tr; Barınağı Karşısı 34; s/d ₺80/140; ❉ 🛜) Overlooking the harbour, 'Hotel Rest' has two-dozen rooms, many of them (including rooms 201 and 202) facing the sea. Real wooden parquet floors with carpets, balconies and a back garden with ancient walls complete the picture. High marks also go to the friendly staff.

Sinopark Otel
BUSINESS HOTEL €€

(☑261 3257; www.sinoparkotel.com; Kurtuluş Caddesi 9; s/d ₺90/140; ❉ 🛜) The Sinopark is the closest Sinop gets to having a designer hotel. Its 23 rooms spread over five floors, half of which face the harbour, come with LCD TV, well-stocked minibar and tiled bathrooms.

🍴 Eating

Sinop's waterfront is lined with licensed open-air restaurants. Try Sinop-style *mantı* (Turkish ravioli) with lashings of yoghurt. To sweeten a stroll along the nearby harbour, head to **Dolunay Pastaneleri** (⌨261 8688; Kurtuluş Caddesi 14; desserts from ₺2; ☺4am-midnight) for ice cream and baklava.

Mangal   TURKISH €
(Kurtuluş Caddesi 15; mains ₺9-15; ☺8am-9pm) With walls decorated with fishing photos and guns, this homely grill house serves *mantı* and grilled fish, chicken and *köfte*.

Antep Sofrası   KEBAP, PIDE €
(⌨260 3434; Atatürk Caddesi 3/A; mains ₺7-15; ☺8am-10pm) Locals head to Antep's upstairs salon for kebaps, from *patlıcan* (aubergine) to İskender (döner kebap on fresh pide topped with savoury tomato sauce and browned butter). A welcoming place that's good for female travellers, it's not far from the museum.

Sahil Ocakbaşi   KÖFTE, FISH €
(⌨260 3645; Ortayol Sokak 12; mains ₺8-15; ☺8am-10pm) In this hole-in-the-wall side-street grill house, watch *köfte* being rolled in the kitchen and cooked on the grill, which diners sit around. Served with onion, tomato and pepper, the result is lip-smacking. Blokey but friendly ambience.

Öz Diyarbakır Mangal Sofrası   TURKISH €
(⌨261 1909; Kurtuluş Caddesi 18; mains ₺9; ☺10am-midnight) 🍴 Close to the seafront bars and hotels, this large but simple place serves good *lahmacun* (Arabic-style pizza), soup, pide and a range of kebaps. *Paket servis* (takeaway) is available.

★**Okyanus Balık Evi**   SEAFOOD €€
(Ocean Fish House; ⌨0532 361 27 33; www. mevsimbalikcilik.com; Kurtuluş Caddesi; mains ₺15-53; ☺11am-11am) Probably the best seafood restaurant on the Black Sea coast, the 'Ocean Fish House' is run by Mert Kanal, whose grandfather founded the fishmonger's on the ground floor. Expect fresher than fresh and only in season. Excellent and unusual meze too.

Zeyden Mutfak   CAFE, BREAKFAST €€
(⌨261 9923; Yalı Kahvesi Karşısı; breakfast ₺12.50; ☺7am-4pm) This coolly minimalist cafe serves village breakfasts composed of 17 different things, including olives, jams and *sahanda yumurtalar* (fried eggs).

Saray Restaurant   SEAFOOD €€
(⌨261 1729; www.sarayrestaurant.com.tr; Rıhtım Sokak 5/A; fish mains ₺15-20, meze ₺8-9; ☺8am-11pm) Grab a table on the pier and begin your meal with the 'Palace's' excellent mezes. Fish (mostly farmed) dishes take no risks but salads are good.

🍷 Drinking & Nightlife

Tea gardens line the seafront, offering backgammon and other board games. Stroll along and decide which has the best vantage point.

Burç Café   CAFE, BAR
(Sinop Kalesi, Tersane Caddesi; ☺8am-6pm, to midnight Apr-Sep) In a tower of the fortress, this atmospheric spot attracts a young crowd for live music (in season) and ocean views. Bring something warm to wear as it can get chilly even in the summer.

Nihavent   PUB
(⌨261 6633; Balıkçı Yolu Aralığı 3; beer ₺8; ☺11am-2am) As much a restaurant but more fun as a pub, this friendly place down a narrow alley towards the harbour has several beers on tap and live music in summer.

🛍 Shopping

Yöresel El Sanatları Satış Mağazası   HANDICRAFTS
(Regional Handicrafts Shop; Batur Sokak, Pervane Medresesi; ☺9am-5pm Mon-Sat) This lovely shop in the restored Pervane Medresesi sells both new and antique embroidered linen tablecloths, scarves and decorative items. The charming and helpful English-speaking staff can provide tourist information.

BUS SERVICES FROM SİNOP'S OTOGAR

DESTINATION	FARE (₺)	DURATION (HR)	DISTANCE (KM)	FREQUENCY (PER DAY)
Ankara	50	7	443	13
İstanbul	60	11	700	11
Karabük (for Safranbolu & Amasra)	40	6	340	1
Kastamonu	25	4½	170	2
Samsun (for Trabzon)	25	3	168	hourly

ℹ Information

There are internet cafes on Kaledibi Aralığı Sokak near the town hall.

The most helpful source of information in English is the Yöresel El Sanatları Satış Mağazası (p517) at Pervane Medresesi. The **tourist office** (İskele Caddesi; ⊙ 8am-7pm mid-Jun–mid-Sep, 9am-5pm May–mid-Jun & mid-Sep–Oct) and **booth** (Sakarya Caddesi, Tarihi Cezaevi; ⊙ 8am-5pm, to 7pm Apr-Sep) are less so (when open).

ℹ Getting There & Around

Turkish Airlines (www.thy.com) flies to/from İstanbul only. A taxi to the airport, 5km west of the centre, costs ₺25.

Sinop's otogar is 5km southwest of town on the main road to Kastamonu. **Dolmuşes** run there from Okullar Caddesi next to the museum (₺2).

Dolmuşes run to villages such as Akliman and Gerze from the **village otogar** (Sakarya Caddesi).

Samsun

☑ 0362 / POP 577,000

Few travellers stop in the sprawling port city of Samsun for more than a change of bus. Indeed, even the enterprising Genoese only paused long enough to burn the city to the ground in the 15th century. But with accommodation and eateries handily located around Cumhuriyet Meydanı (Republic Sq) and a couple of decent museums, Samsun makes a convenient stop on your journey east or west. From Cumhuriyet Meydanı, Cumhuriyet Caddesi runs eastwards, along the south side of Atatürk Park, which is bordered to the north by Atatürk Bulvarı (the coastal highway). The main thoroughfare heading west from the square is Gazi Caddesi.

⊙ Sights

Archaeology & Ethnography Museum
MUSEUM

(Arkeoloji ve Etnoğrafya Müzesi; www.samsunkent muzesi.com; Samsun Fuar Alanı; admission ₺3; ⊙ 8am-5pm Tue-Sun, to 7pm Apr-Sep) The most striking item in this museum is the huge Romano-Byzantine mosaic found at nearby Kara Samsun (Amisos). It depicts Thetis and Achilles from the Trojan War and the four seasons alongside sea monsters and nymphs. Other highlights include elegant gold jewellery dating from the 1st century BC – the time of the legendary Pontic King Mithridates VI. The museum is at the entrance to the Samsun Fairgrounds and just

west of the landmark pink *valilik* (provincial government headquarters) building.

Gazi Museum
MUSEUM

(Gazi Müzesi; www.samsunkulturturizm.gov.tr/TR; Gazi Caddesi; ⊙ 8am-5pm Tue-Sun, to 7pm Apr-Sep) **FREE** One block south of Cumhuriyet Meydanı, this museum commemorates the start of the War of Independence in Samsun on 19 May 1919, and the Turkish Republic's subsequent foundation. Several of Atatürk's hats feature.

Amisos Antik Kenti
ARCHAEOLOGICAL SITE

(Amisos Ancient City; Amisos Tepesi) **FREE** If you'd like to see where the Amisos treasure in the Archaeology & Ethnography Museum came from in 1995, head west for 3km to Batıpark (West Park) on the coast and board the **Samsun Amisos Hill Cable Car** (Samsun Amisos Tepesi Teleferik Hattı; Batıpark & Amisos Tepesi; admission ₺2.5; ⊙ 9am-10pm), which will take you in just four minutes to the site of two mounds laid over burial chambers. Reach the cable car's lower station via the SHRS (p520) tram (stop: Baruthane).

On the hill, the south tumulus has a rock-hewn tomb with two chambers; the north one contains a tomb with three linked chambers. There's a boardwalk running round them with some explanatory signs.

🛏 Sleeping

Explore the Tarihi Bedesten Çarşısı (Old Bazaar Market) area west of the main square Cumhuriyet Meydanı for more budget accommodation options.

Otel Necmi
HOTEL €

(☑ 432 7164; www.otelnecmi.com.tr; Tarihi Bedestan Sokak 6; s/d/tr without bathroom ₺45/75/105; ❄ 🖲) This homely budget choice at the beginning of the old bazaar west of the main square Cumhuriyet Meydanı feels like your eccentric uncle's house, with pot plants, mirrors and big old chairs in reception. The 20 rooms are poky and none too salubrious, but the staff are helpful, offering maps and advice.

Otel Vidinli
HOTEL €€

(☑ 431 6050; www.otelvidinli.com.tr; Kazımpaşa Caddesi 4; s/d without breakfast ₺80/130, breakfast ₺10; ❄ 🖲) Going strong since 1957, the 35-room Vidinli has traditionally been Samsun's best hotel, with expansive views across the main square. There's now a lot more competition but it remains popular for its swift but old fashioned lift, spacious rooms, stunning 6th-floor breakfast room and excellent licensed restaurant. Ask for room 401; it's huge and overlooks Cumhuriyet Meydanı.

Yıldızoğlu Hotel   BUSINESS HOTEL €€
(☑333 3400; www.yildizogluhotel.com; Talimhane Caddesi 13; s/d ₺90/130; ❄🕭) This stylish option, due east of the central square Cumhuriyet Meydanı and opposite the police station, offers 46 rooms with turquoise trimmings, little black lampshades, minibars and walk-in showers. Facilities include a fitness centre, sauna (₺20) and bar in the blue-lit reception area. The generous breakfast stretches to soup, *börek* (filled pastry) and *dolmas* (vegetables stuffed with rice or meat).

Samsun Park Otel   BUSINESS HOTEL €€
(☑435 0095; www.samsunparkotel.com; Cumhuriyet Caddesi 38; s/d/tr ₺70/100/130; ❄@🕭) Book ahead to bag a compact but comfortable room at the all-white Samsun Park. It's 200m east of the main square Cumhuriyet Meydanı and has 37 rooms; our favourite is 601.

🍴 Eating & Drinking

Gaziantep Kebap Salonu   KEBAP, TURKISH €
(Osmaniye Caddesi 7; mains ₺4-8; ☺8am-11pm) This slice of southeast Turkey is a relaxed neighbourhood *kebapçı* (kebab eatery), where couples and male groups snack on *lahmacun* and local *ayran* (yoghurt drink) from nearby Tokat. Heading east on Cumhuriyet Caddesi, turn right after the Hotel Amisos.

Divan Pastanesi   CAFE
(☑432 3434; Cumhuriyet Caddesi 6; ☺6am-11pm) A block east of the central square, Cumhuriyet Meydanı, among the bus-company offices, this lovely patisserie is good for a morning caffeine fix and there's

an outdoor patio. Frothy cappuccinos, baklava and *börek* (filled pastries) are served among baskets of oranges and boxes of chocolates. Always a warm welcome.

Sıla Restaurant   KÖFTE, KEBAP €€
(Cumhuriyet Caddesi 36; mains ₺8-20; ☺8am-8pm) Sıla, 100m east of the main square Cumhuriyet Meydanı, is popular for a meaty lunch; try the chicken *şiş* kebap served with fiery peppers. Split your gaze between the strange, egg-like sculptures outside the Culture & Art Gallery (Kültür ve Sanat Galerisi) at the southeast corner of Atatürk Park, and the darting waiters – artistes of hustle-bustle even by Turkish standards.

★ Pamuk Kardeşler Balık
Restaurant   SEAFOOD €€€
(☑445 0433; www.pamukkardesler.com; Batıpark; mains ₺15-45; ☺11.30am-midnight) A trinity of seafood restaurants line the marina near the cable car in Batıpark and this licensed one is far and away the best. Reach it on foot via the Sahil Yürüyüş Yolu (Coastal Walking Path) or the Samulaş tram (stop: Fener).

ℹ Information

There are internet cafes on Hürriyet Sokak, which runs south from Cumhuriyet Caddesi.

Tourist Office (☑431 1228; Atatürk Kültür Merkezi, Atatürk Bulvarı; ☺9am-5pm Mon-Fri, to 6pm Sat & Sun Jun-Sep) Helpful office with limited handouts between the Büyük Samsun Otel and the Atatürk Kültür Merkezi (Atatürk Cultural Centre).

ℹ Getting There & Away

AIR

Regular **Havaş** (☑444 0487; www.havas.net) shuttle buses link the city and Samsun Çarşamba Airport (₺9, half-hour); they depart from the

BUS SERVICES FROM SAMSUN'S OTOGAR

DESTINATION	FARE (₺)	DURATION (HR)	DISTANCE (KM)	FREQUENCY (PER DAY)
Amasya	15	2½	130	frequent
Ankara	50	7	420	frequent
Giresun	25	3½	220	15
Hopa	40	9½	520	three
İstanbul	60	11	750	11
Kayseri	50	7	530	10
Sinop	25	3½	168	hourly
Trabzon	30	6	355	10
Ünye	12	1½	95	half-hourly

Atatürk Kültür Merkezi car park next to the tourist office. Havaş also connects the airport and Ordu (₺20, two hours) via Ünye and Fatsa (₺15).

Anadolu Jet (www.anadolujet.com) Flies to/from Ankara and İstanbul.

Onur Air (www.onurair.com) Flies to İstanbul.

Pegasus Airlines (www.flypgs.com) Flies to İstanbul and İzmir.

Sun Express (www.sunexpress.com) Flies to Antalya, İstanbul, İzmir and a dozen European cities.

Turkish Airlines (www.thy.com) Flies to Ankara and İstanbul and several cities in Germany.

BUS

Bus companies have offices at the Cumhuriyet Meydanı end of Cumhuriyet Caddesi. *Servises* (shuttle buses) run between there and the otogar, 3km inland. There are also frequent dolmuşes (₺2) from the otogar to Cumhuriyet Meydanı, and left-luggage facilities at the otogar.

CAR & MOTORCYCLE

You can hire a car in the city or at Samsun Çarşamba Airport through a number of agencies, including Economy Car Rentals (p674).

ⓘ Getting Around

You probably won't be using it extensively but Samsun's tram line, **SHRS** (Samsun Hafif Raylı Sistem; www.samulas.com.tr), is simple to use and runs for 15km along the coast, serving 21 stations. It's most useful for points west (eg Batıpark and the cable car).

Trams run every five to 15 minutes from 6.15am to just before midnight. Buy tickets (₺2.75) and board it near the entrance to the Samsun Fairgrounds (stop: Cumhuriyet Meydanı).

Ünye

☑ 0452 / POP 79,000

This seaside town 90km east of Samsun has one of Anatolia's longest settlement histories. There is evidence of civilisation during the Stone Age, and Ünye was an important port at the junction of the Silk Road and the coastal highway during the Ottoman period. Smaller and more conservative than Samsun and Ordu but prettier than either, with some lovely Ottoman and Greek architecture, Ünye is worth a stop for its coastal promenade and labyrinth of well-kept winding streets and lanes. These fan out from the main square (Cumhuriyet Meydanı) across the coastal road from the seafront.

⊙ Sights & Activities

Ünye Castle CASTLE, RUIN

(Ünye Kalesi) FREE About 7km inland from the town stands Ünye Castle, a ruined fortress founded by the Pontics and rebuilt by the Byzantines, with an ancient tomb cut into the rock face below. Catch a minibus (₺2) heading to Kaleköy or Akkuş on the D850 road to Niksar and Tokat, and ask to be dropped off at the road to the castle. It's a further 2km trek to the top. A taxi will cost ₺30 (or ₺40 for waiting and return).

Tozkoparan Rock Tomb TOMB

(Tozkoparan Mağara Mezarı) FREE This millennia-old cave tomb, one of a few in the area, is off the D010 coastal road 5km east of the centre. Carved bull figures flank the entrance to the tomb, which is thought to date to between 7000 BC and 5000 BC. Eastbound minibus-

---

THE LEGEND OF THE AMAZONS

The Samsun-Ünye region, especially around the town of Terme (Themiskyra) is often associated with the Amazons, one of the most enduring Greek myths. This race of warrior women, famed for cutting off one breast to allow them to use their bows more effectively, were said to have ruled the coast in pre-Pontic times. Homer, Herodotus and Amasya's own Strabo all relate tales of strapping female soldiers. Reputedly their reproductive habits involved annual intercourse with a neighbouring tribe, or 'breeding colonies' of captive male sex slaves, who would then be killed. Some early biographers even claim Alexander the Great fathered a child with the Amazonian queen Thalestris.

Sadly there is little evidence to support any Amazonian presence in the Black Sea region. The myth may have evolved from the role of high priestesses in mother-goddess cults. Other historians believe that it arose from travellers encountering Anatolian tribes with strange matriarchal systems.

This enduring classical myth continued to capture public imagination across following centuries, and eventually provided the name for the world's largest river (though the more credible etymology is *amassona* from the local Indian language for 'boat destroyer').

---

es can drop you by the cement factory at the turn for the tomb (₺2). A taxi will cost ₺30 (or ₺40 waiting and return).

Ünye Müze Evi — MUSEUM
(Ünye Museum House; www.facebook.com/muze evi; cnr Hacı Emin Caddesi & Alicer Sokak; ⊙9am-6pm Tue-Sun) FREE This tiny but ambitious museum up the hill west of the main square Cumhuriyet Meydanı looks at the history, lifestyles and folklore of the nine different ethnic groups who have made Ünye their home over the centuries.

Bakırcılar Sokak — STREET
(Street of Coppersmiths) Just near Orta Camii (Middle Mosque), this street of bygone times is home to a handful of coppersmiths, including Bizim Bakırcı (Our Coppersmith; Bakırcılar Sokak 13) who still hammer and shape items for the home, as their forebears have done for centuries.

Eski Hamam — HAMAM
(Old Hamam; Cumhuriyet Meydanı; admission ₺14; ⊙men 5am-midnight Mon, Wed, Thu & Sun, women 11am-5pm Tue, Fri & Sat) The Old Hamam occupies a former church on the southeast corner of the main square.

🛏 Sleeping

Otel Güney — HOTEL €
(☑323 8406; www.otelguney.com; Belediye Caddesi 14; s/d ₺40/80; ❄ 🏧) An excellent choice south of the main square, this hotel is spotless, has 17 rooms with modern bathrooms and a fabulous rooftop cafe on the 4th floor.

Gülen Plaj Camping — CAMPING GROUND €
(☑324 6686; Devlet Sahil Yolu, Uzunkum; campsites ₺40, bungalow ₺160) Overlooking an idyllic sweep of beach 2.5km west of the centre, Gülen's wooden bungalows with balconies and kitchenettes sleep up to four among the trees.

Hotel Kılıç — HOTEL €
(☑323 1224; Haciemin Caddesi; s/d without breakfast ₺35/70) Ünye's first hotel, the 'Sword' is pretty far down in the pecking order but offers an excellent location right behind the mosque on the main square. The 18 rooms are nondescript but clean and there's a dingy lounge.

★ Sebile Hanım Konağı — BOUTIQUE HOTEL €€
(☑323 7474; www.sebilehanimkonagi.com; Çubukçu Arif Sokak 10; s ₺75-120, d ₺120-180, ste ₺150-230; ❄ @ 🛜) In the former Armenian district, this gloriously restored and romantic hilltop property dating to 1870 has 14 cosy wood-lined rooms with private hamam, fridge and lovely fabrics on the walls. The cheapest rooms are mansard ones on the top floor. Go instead for the deluxe room 104 with two windows or one of the two huge suites (105 or 205).

There's also an excellent licensed restaurant (mains ₺8 to ₺25) open 10am to 11pm daily with courtyard seating in the warmer months. From the central square Cumhuriyet Meydanı follow the signs uphill from the western edge of the old city walls.

🍴 Eating & Drinking

Kaptan Balıkçılık — SEAFOOD €
(Captain Fishery; ☑323 2333; Kasaplar Sokak 11; mains ₺10; ⊙10am-11pm) Hidden in the market next to a fishmonger's, Kaptan Balıkçılık is Ünye's newest and best budget fish eatery. Try the *karides güveç* (prawn stew; ₺10). A fish sandwich and drink will set you back just ₺5.

Cafe Vanilya — CAFE
(Cumhuriyet Meydanı 3; snacks ₺5; ⊙10am-11pm; 🛜) Set in a restored villa-style town house on the southwest edge of the main square, the 'Vanilla' is a popular but down-to-earth terrace cafe serving Ünye's bright young things. Expect offerings such as *tost* (toasted sandwiches) and burgers.

İskele — SEAFOOD, TURKISH €€
(☑323 3053; www.iskelerestoran.com; Devlet Sahil Yolu 32; mains ₺12-20; ⊙8am-11pm) The 'Pier' has a waterside location and a reputation for seafood and grilled meats. Ignore the diversions into Italian – mostly pizzas – and stick with fish and Turkish classics. No alcohol.

Sofra — TURKISH €€
(☑323 4083; Belediye Caddesi 25/A; mains ₺11-13; ⊙7am-10pm) Sofra is in a lovely stone house and serves pide, kebaps and *Osmanlı mutfağı* (Ottoman cuisine). It's wildly popular at lunch and just a couple of blocks east of the main square.

ℹ Information

Tourist Office (☑323 4952; Hukumet Binası, Cumhuriyet Meydanı; ⊙8.30am-5.30pm Mon-Fri) In a kiosk next to Ziraat Bank on the southeast side of the main square.

BLACK SEA COAST ÜNYE

OLD COAST ROAD

At Bolaman, 30km east of Ünye, the D010 runs inland and doesn't touch the coast again until 7km short of Ordu. It's a spectacular stretch, traversing one of Turkey's longest road tunnels (3.82km), and the diversion inland has created a lovely alternative route on the old coast road.

A winding few kilometres northeast from Bolaman, a small brown sign points 500m left to rugged Yason Burnu (Cape Jason), where a tiny chapel (1868) has replaced an ancient temple erected by sailors marking the spot where Jason and his Argonauts braved the waters around the cape en route to Colchis (now in Georgia) in search of the golden fleece. A nearby cafe serves fish and *köfte* (meatballs). To the east is lovely Çaka, a 400m strip of white sand regarded as the Black Sea's best beach. There's a leafy picnic area here too.

Some 15km west of Ordu, the fishing port of Perşembe is an attractive, slow-paced Black Sea village. Later at night locals fish from the slender pier and fish restaurants prepare the day's 'catch', presumably collected from the dozens of fish farms visible from shore. Across the main road from the seafront fish restaurants, peaceful Otel Dede Evi (☑ 0452-517 3802; Atatürk Bulvarı 266; s/d ₺60/120; ❈ ⬧) has shipshape rooms with TV and fridge.

This meandering detour is best attempted with your own transport, but there are dolmuşes (₺2.75) to Perşembe from Fatsa to the west and Ordu to the east.

ⓘ Getting There & Away

Bus companies have offices on the coast road. Minibuses and vans travel to Samsun (₺12, 1½ hours) and Ordu (₺10, 1¼ hours). Go to Fatsa (₺5) to catch a bus along the old coast road to Perşembe (₺10).

Ordu

☑ 0452 / POP 148,000

Ordu, with a well-kept centre around a palm-tree-lined seafront boulevard, is 63km east of Ünye. The city sprawls in both directions, but winding narrow lanes give central Ordu a village-like feel. It can be very confusing making your way around in town; ask the tourist office (if open) or any of the hotels for a map.

⊙ Sights

Paşaoğlu Mansion & Ethnography Museum MUSEUM
(Paşaoğlu Konağı ve Etnoğrafya Müzesi; www.ordu kulturturizm.gov.tr; Taşocak Caddesi; admission ₺3; ⊙ 9am-noon & 1.30-5pm Tue-Sun) This interesting museum occupies an ornate mansion (1896) 500m northwest (and uphill) from the main square Cumhuriyet Meydanı past a bazaar; look for signs reading 'Müze – Museum'. The recreated 1st-floor rooms – large bedrooms, lounges – are reminders that upper-class Ottomans enjoyed a sophisticated and cosmopolitan life

before it all came to an end in the early 20th century.

The ethnographic exhibits include the usual dusty weapons and folk costumes though the sand mosaic of Atatürk (who tarried here in 1924) is unusual.

Ordu Boztepe Cable Car CABLE CAR
(Ordu Boztepe Teleferik Hattı; admission Mon-Fri ₺5, Sat & Sun ₺6 ; ⊙ 10am-9.30pm) Take a seven-minute *teleferik* (cable car) ride from the seafront a short distance from the Mıdı restaurant up Boztepe (498m) for breathtaking views and fresh air. If the restaurant and cafe don't tempt you, there's a park with a picnic area here as well.

Taşbaşı Cultural Centre HISTORIC BUILDING
(Taşbaşı Kültür Merkezi; Menekşe Sokak) FREE
Now a cultural centre, this erstwhile Armenian church (1853) overlooks the seafront from a hillside location about 500m west of the tourist office. The surrounding old Greek quarter is an attractive neighbourhood of tumbledown houses and a couple of lovely boutique hotels.

⌂ Sleeping

★ **Taşbaşı Butik Otel** BOUTIQUE HOTEL ₺₺
(☑ 223 3530; www.tasbasibutikotel.com; Kesim Evi Sokak 1; s/d ₺70/120; ❈ ⬧) The decor occasionally strays into chintz territory, but the Black Sea views are terrific from this restored hilltop mansion, behind and up

the steps from the Taşbaşı Cultural Centre (p522) in Ordu's old Greek neighbourhood. Each of the six rooms is named after an Ordu district; our absolute favourite is Zaferi Milli.

Atlıhan Hotel HOTEL €€
(✏️212 0565; www.atlihanhotel.com.tr; Kazım Karabekir Caddesi 9; s/d ₺70/120; ✸ 🛜) This sprawling establishment, one block back from the seafront behind the town hall, has sea views from the top-floor restaurant/jazz club. The 39 rooms are a very good size and the bathrooms up to date. Choose room 304 for a double-window sea view. The same group runs two other boutique hotels, including the hilltop Hotel İkizevler.

Hotel İkizevler BOUTIQUE HOTEL €€
(Twins Hotel; ✏️225 0081; www.ikizevlerhotel.com.tr; Sıtkıcan Caddesi 54; s/d ₺90/150; ✸ 🛜) The name may mean 'Twins', but this hilltop boutique hotel is unified in delivering 12 rooms of gracious Ottoman style. The property was originally two stately homes, and it now dominates a hilltop a short distance northwest of the Taşbaşı Cultural Centre. Wooden floors, antique rugs and huge bathrooms all support the relaxed heritage ambience.

Hotel Kervansaray HOTEL €€
(✏️214 1330; Kazım Karabekir Caddesi 1; s/d ₺60/110; ✸ 🛜) The Kervansaray is friendly and good value, with 30 spacious and comfortable rooms (glow-in-the-dark green bedspreads notwithstanding). Breakfast is pleasant in the 1st floor **Kervansaray Cafe** among bright pink and purple chairs; it's open to the public too from 7am to 10pm daily. Ask for a room away from the noisy main street.

✕ Eating & Drinking

Ordu Kervansaray Lokantası TURKISH €
(✏️212 2815; www.kervansaray.com.tr; Kazım Karabekir Caddesi 1; mains ₺10; ⏰6am-9pm) Below the hotel of the same name but unrelated, this attractive, modern lunchtime eatery serves a good range of kebaps and even a few desserts on place mats bearing pictures of old Ordu. Mouth-watering *hazır yemek* (ready-to-eat food) awaits in the steam tables.

Jazz Café CAFE €
(Kazım Karabekir Caddesi 7; snacks ₺8-12; ⏰9am-8.30pm Mon-Sat, 11am-8.30pm Sun; 🛜) A sleek and cosmopolitan spot next to the Atlıhan Hotel, serving cappuccino and sweet treats

including hot chocolate and waffles. Savoury palates shouldn't miss the excellent *sigara böreği* (feta cheese and pastry snacks). Sit outside on the tiny terrace or among photos of Frank Sinatra and Dizzy Gillespie.

Mıdı Restaurant SEAFOOD €€
(✏️214 0340; Sahil Caddesi 55; mains ₺10-20, meze ₺5; ⏰10am-midnight) This rather chaotic restaurant on the pier has great views but no booze. Watch the cable car climb from the seafront and enjoy a good range of local seafood and fresh meze, including Ordu specialities and aubergine served in a number of ways.

Jazz Pub LIVE MUSIC
(✏️0532 450 5069; Kazım Karabekir Caddesi 9; ⏰4pm-2am) On the 5th floor of the Atlıhan Hotel, this cool jazz bar has live music at 9.30pm on Wednesday, Saturday and Sunday nights. With low lighting and English-speaking staff manning the long bar, it's a mellow spot for a relaxed evening out.

ℹ️ Information

Tourist Office (✏️223 1444; www.ordu.gov.tr; Atatürk Bulvarı; ⏰10am-6pm Mon-Thu, to 8pm Fri & Sat, to 2pm Sun) Fairly helpful tourist office is housed in a kiosk next to the Halk Bankası on the inland side of the coast road about 250m west of the town hall.

ℹ️ Getting There & Around

Ordu's otogar is 5km east on the coast road. Buses depart regularly to Giresun (₺7, one hour), Ünye (₺10, 1¼ hours) and Perşembe (₺2.75, 20 minutes). You can also usually flag down buses along the coast road.

From Ziraat Bank in the centre, local dolmuşes run uphill to Taşbaşı Cultural Centre in one direction, and near the otogar in the other (₺1.75).

Giresun

📞0454 / POP 102,300

The historic town of Giresun, 45km east of Ordu, was founded more than 2000 years ago as the Greek colony of Cerasus (Kerasos). Because its ancient name means 'cherry' in Greek, the town is credited with introducing cherries to Europe. Today, however, the ubiquitous hazelnut (*fındık*) drives Giresun's economy. The climate in these parts is perfect for the humble little nut and the area has Turkey's finest orchards. Note the bronze statue of hazelnut pickers in the town centre.

Giresun's centre is Taşbaşı Parkı on the coast road. Don't confuse it with the square with a clocktower a few hundred metres to the west. The town hall is on the inland side of the park; the cobbled pedestrian main drag, Gazi Caddesi, climbs uphill from here.

In May Giresun holds the International Giresun Aksu Festival (Uluslararası Giresun Aksu Festivalı), which ends with a trip round tiny Giresun Island, just 1.5km off the eastern end of Giresun Bay.

◎ Sights

Giresun Museum MUSEUM
(Giresun Müzesi; Sokakbaşı Caddesi 57-62; admission ₺3; ⊙8.30am-5pm) With an impressive archaeological and ethnographic collection, Giresun's museum occupies the well-preserved 18th-century Gogora church with a painted dome. Check out the minaret-shaped stove and ancient cellar filled with amphora. The museum is 1.5km around the promontory east of the centre on the coast road; catch any dolmuş marked 'Hastanes' (Hospital) heading east (₺1.25).

Kalepark PARK
Perched on the steep hillside above Giresun, this shady park with the remains of a castle has panoramic views, beer gardens and barbecues. No public transport serves Kalepark, so you'll need to walk about 2km on Gazi Caddesi and turn left onto Bekirpaşa Caddesi. Alternatively, a taxi from town costs ₺10.

⌑ Sleeping

Kit-Tur Otel HOTEL €€
(☑212 0245; www.otelkittur.com; Arifbey Caddesi 27; s/d ₺60/100; ✴🕸) Overlooking Gazi Caddesi, the very friendly Kit-Tur is perfect for relaxing after a long drive, with comfy chairs in the big, marble reception and low beds in the 50 rooms. The views from the huge rooftop (5th floor) restaurant are breathtaking.

Otel Çarıkçı HOTEL €€
(☑216 1026; Osmanağa Caddesi 6; s/d ₺75/120; ✴🕸) At the very start of Gazi Caddesi near the pedestrian bridge over the coastal road, the two-star 'Sandal Maker' has a traditional Turkish curly-toed slipper as its logo. Staff speak English and the brown, compact rooms with pine floors have tiled, modern bathrooms. Room 502 is a good choice for sea views.

Hotel Başar HOTEL €€€
(☑212 9920; www.hotelbasar.com.tr; Atatürk Bulvarı; s/d ₺100/180; ✴🕸) Across the footbridge from the centre, this eight-storey, blue-and-yellow limestone palace has a licensed penthouse restaurant, surveying the port and sea. Staff speak good English and the 54 spacious rooms, reached from the atrium by glass-bubble lift, feature beer-stocked minibars and slightly aged bathrooms with hair-dryer and phone.

✕ Eating

Deniz Lokantası TURKISH €
(☑216 1158; Alpaslan Caddesi 3; mains ₺5-10; ⊙24hr) Next to the town hall, this modernised cafeteria that never sleeps has been churning out good-value meals since 1953. Expect a short wait at lunchtime, but it's worth it.

Ellez PIDE, KEBAP €
(Fatih Caddesi 7; pide ₺8-10; ⊙7am-9pm) One block inland from the centre, this friendly, compact *pideci* (pizza place) with a tiny balcony and log-cabin feel attracts a younger crowd. Pide, kebaps (₺8) and *lahmacun* (₺2) are available.

★Orta Kahve CAFE €€
(☑216 5100; www.ortakahve.com.tr; Topal Sokak 1; mains ₺10-17.50; ⊙8.30am-10.30pm) In this cosy hang-out for Giresun's more cosmopolitan crowd, old typewriters provide a backdrop for newspapers, magazines, and different teas and coffees. It's good for breakfast (₺12), and healthy eats include salads, crepes and wraps. Turn left about 75m uphill on Gazi Caddesi, after the small green mosque (Şeyh Kerameddin Camii) on the right.

🛍 Shopping

Fındıkevi FOOD
(Hazelnut House; ☑216 6128; www.findikcim.com. tr; Gazi Caddesi 15; ⊙9am-6pm) This shop at the bottom of the main pedestrian street is devoted to the hazelnut in all its guises: salted, chillied, ground and/or covered in chocolate. Don't go home without some.

ⓘ Information

Internet cafes are on and around Gazi Caddesi near the post office, a few hundred metres uphill from the town hall.

ℹ️ Getting There & Away

The bus station is 4km west of the centre, but buses usually drop people in the centre, too. For Trabzon (₺15, two hours) and Ordu (₺7, one hour), it's easiest to pick up minibuses from the coastal road, either below the mosque overlooking the park or by the clock tower opposite the port entrance. Bus company offices are next to the town hall and offer services to Samsun (₺25, 3½ hours).

Trabzon

🎵 0462 / POP 244,000

The Black Sea's busiest port, Trabzon mixes cosmopolitan buzz with a somewhat louche, seaside-town feel. Not the Black Sea coast's largest city but certainly its most sophisticated, Trabzon is too caught up in its own whirl of activity to worry about what's happening in far-off İstanbul or Ankara.

Contrasting with the gracious, medieval church (now mosque) of Aya Sofya, and the one-time Byzantine monastery at nearby Sumela, the modern world shines through on Atatürk Alanı, Trabzon's busy main square in the eastern section of the city centre. Indeed, the exotic city Rose Macaulay described in *The Towers of Trebizond* (1956) is very much a distant memory now.

East of Atatürk Alanı (also known as Meydan Parkı) and down a steep hill is the port. There are cafes and restaurants around Atatürk Alanı and west along Uzun Sokak and Kahramanmaraş Caddesi. West of the centre, past the bazaar, is Ortahisar, a picturesque old neighbourhood straddling a ravine.

History

Trabzon's recorded history begins in the middle of the 8th century BC, when Miletus colonists came from Sinop and founded a settlement, Trapezus, with an acropolis on the *trapezi* (Greek for 'table') of land above the harbour.

The port town did well for 2000 years, until the Christian soldiers of the Fourth Crusade seized and sacked Constantinople in 1204, forcing its noble families to seek refuge in Anatolia. The Comnenus imperial family subsequently established an empire along the Black Sea coast in 1204, with Alexius Comnenus I reigning as the emperor of Trebizond.

Over the next two centuries the Trapezuntine emperors and empresses skilfully balanced alliances with the Seljuks, Mongols and Genoese. Prospering through trade with eastern Anatolia and Persia, the empire peaked under Alexius II (1297–1330), before declining in factional disputes. The empire of Trebizond survived until the Ottoman conquest in 1461, eight years longer than Constantinople.

◉ Sights & Activities

Trabzon Museum MUSEUM
(Trabzon Müzesi; www.trabzon.bel.tr/english/trb museum.html; Zeytinlik Caddesi 10; admission ₺3; ⏰9.15am-5.45pm Tue-Sun) The Italian-designed Kostaki Mansion (1913), built for a Russian merchant and mixing elements of rococo, art nouveau and neoclassical architecture, briefly hosted Atatürk in 1924 and again in 1937. One of the most beautiful museums in provincial Turkey, the ornate rooms, with painted ceilings, carved wooden doors and original furnishings, display reasonably interesting ethnographic and Ottoman artefacts, mostly labelled in English.

The basement archaeological section has more significant pieces, including a flattened bronze statue of Hermes unearthed at Tabakhane in 1997 as well as beautiful wooden Byzantine icons dating from the 5th to 15th centuries.

Bazaar District MARKET
(Çarşı (Market) Quarter) Pedestrianised Kunduracılar Caddesi leads from Atatürk Alanı to Trabzon's bazaar, located in the Çarşı (Market) quarter. Near the restored Çarşı Camii (Market Mosque; Çarşı Quarter) (1842), central Trabzon's largest mosque, is the Taş Han (Vakıf Han; Çarşı Quarter), a caravanserai with an open courtyard constructed around 1533 and the Bedesten (covered bazaar), Trabzon's oldest marketplace, now full of workshops, stores and cafes.

Gülbahar Hatun Camii MOSQUE
Sultan Selim I the Grim, the great Ottoman conqueror of Syria and Egypt, built this mosque southwest of the bazaar in 1514 in honour of his mother, Gülbahar Hatun. Next to it are a tea garden and reconstructed wooden *serender* (granary). It's a pleasant walk west from the centre over Tabakhane Bridge, with plant nursery below it. Soon after crossing the next bridge (Zağnos Köprüsü), turn left.

Trabzon

Trabzon

◉ Sights

◉ Activities, Courses & Tours

◉ Sleeping

◉ Eating

◉ Drinking & Nightlife

N 0 ——————— 200 m
0 ——————— 0.1 miles

Liman Mukli İdare

Kale Park

Devlet Sahil Yolu Cad

KEMERKAYA

2 Nolu Gazipaşa Sk

Passenger Terminal for
Ferries to Sochi (250m)

Balıkpazarı Sk

Sh Ercan Aygun Sk

Topal Hakim Sk

Gazipaşa Cad

Dolmuş to
Havaalani
(Airport)

Kunduracılar Cad

Halkevi Sk

Ziyad Nemli
Sanat Sk

KTÜ

Dolmuş to
Otogar

Deniz Sk

S Yazıcıoğlu Sk

İskele Cad

12   10

15

17

Sıra Mağazalar Cad

14

11

Sh Karaoğlan oğlu İbrahim Cad

Kahramanmaraş Cad

23

31   20

30

Atatürk Alanı

26

18

Dolmuşes to
Coşandere &
Maçka

22

28

19

25

Dervişoğlu Sk

8   7

İskender
Paşa Camii

Kasımoğlu Sk

Uzun Sk

16

Cami Sk

27

13

Cudibey Mektep Sk

Ulusoy   Metro

Dolmuşes to
Aya Sofya, Otogar,
Sumela Monastery

6

Taksim
İshani Sk

İran Cad

Otogar (3km);
(5km)

BLACK SEA COAST TRABZON

Atatürk Mansion   HISTORIC BUILDING

(Atatürk Köşkü; ☎231 0028; Köşk Caddesi; admission ₺2; ⊙8am-5pm, to 7pm Apr-Sep) Nestled in the leafy, hilltop neighbourhood of Soğuksu 5km southwest of Atatürk Alanı, this three-storey, blindingly white mansion (1903) has fine views and lovely gardens. Built for a wealthy Trabzon banking family in the Black Sea style popular in the Crimea, it was bequeathed to Atatürk when he visited in 1924. Don't miss the simple table in the study with a map of the WWI Dardanelles campaign scratched into the wood.

City buses labelled 'Köşk' leave from opposite the post office on Kahramanmaraş Caddesi and drop you outside the mansion (₺2). A taxi will cost about ₺15.

Meydan Hamamı   HAMAM

(www.meydanhamami.com; Kahramanmaraş Caddesi 3; hamam ₺20, scrub ₺6, massage ₺7; ⊙men 6am-11pm, women 8am-8pm) The 'Hamam on the Square' is clean and efficiently run.

There are separate areas for men and women; the **women's entrance** is around the corner.

Sekiz Direkli Hamamı   HAMAM

(Eight Pillar Hamam; 8 Direkli Hamamı Sokak 1; sauna & massage ₺25; ⊙men 8am-11pm Fri-Wed, women 8am-5pm Thu) Sekiz Direkli means 'With Eight Pillars' and the rough-hewn columns inside date from Seljuk times (although the rest of the building has been modernised). A few of the old-timers working here appear to be only slightly younger than the hamam. Expect a robust massage nonetheless.

☞ Tours

Local operators run organised day trips to places of interest around Trabzon including Sumela (₺30, 10am to 3pm); Uzungöl (₺40, 10am to 6pm) daily; Ayder (₺50, minimum five people) three days a week; and Batumi, Georgia (₺75, 7am to 9.30pm).

Eyce Tours TOUR
(☑326 7174; www.eycetours.com; Taksim İşhanı Sokak 11, 1st fl)

Vazelontours TOUR
(☑321 0080; www.vazelontur.com.tr; Atatürk Alanı 23/a, Taksim İs Merkezi; ⊙9am-7pm) Accommodating tour operator.

🛌 Sleeping

Many of the hotels along Güzelhisar Caddesi are popular with business travellers, so book ahead during the week and ask for a discount at weekends.

Hotel Can HOTEL €
(☑326 8281; Güzelhisar Caddesi 2; s/d ₺30/50; ❋ 🛜) There isn't much difference between the tall, thin 18-room 'Hotel Soul' and some of its neighbours – except for the price and the friendly staff. This is probably Trabzon's top budget choice and the best place to meet fellow travellers.

Elif Otel HOTEL €
(☑326 6616; Güzelhisar Caddesi 8; s/d ₺50/80; 🛜) The renovated reception and warm welcome make the Elif a good choice along Güzelhisar Caddesi hotels. The dozen rooms

have smart bathrooms and lumpy white duvets on the beds; room 203 is bright and looks down on to the street.

★ Hotel Nur HOTEL €€
(☑323 0445; www.nurotel.net; Cami Sokak 15; s/d ₺70/140, without bathroom ₺45/90; ❋ 🛜) A long-standing travellers' favourite, with a fabulous lounge/bar on the rooftop and very helpful staff, the Nur has 10 rooms with bathrooms and five with shared facilities. Some rooms are indeed pint-size but the views across Atatürk Alanı make up for the squeeze. The nearby mosque doesn't skimp on the 5am call to prayer.

Otel Ural BUSINESS HOTEL €€
(☑321 1414; www.otelural.com; Güzelhisar Caddesi 1; s/d ₺60/120; ❋ @ 🛜) With warm, chocolate-brown decor, flat-screen TVs and flash bathrooms, the Ural's 26 spacious and spotless rooms raise the bar along Trabzon's hotel alley.

Hotel Nazar HOTEL €€
(☑323 0081; www.nazarotel.com.tr; Güzelhisar Caddesi 5; s/d ₺80/140; ❋ 🛜) The 'Evil Eye' looks better than ever since its renovation, with new carpets and spot-on showers

---

DON'T MISS

AYA SOFYA MOSQUE & MUSEUM

Aya Sofya Mosque & Museum (Aya Sofya Müzesi ve Camii; ☑223 3043; www.trabzon-muzesi.gov.tr; Aya Sofya Sokak; ⊙9am-7pm Jun-Aug, 9am-6pm Apr-May & Sep-Oct, 8am-5pm Nov-Mar) Originally called Hagia Sophia (Church of Divine Wisdom), Aya Sofya sits 4km west of Trabzon's centre on a terrace close to the sea. Built between 1238 and 1263, it was influenced by Georgian and Seljuk design, although the wall paintings and mosaic floors follow the prevailing Constantinople style of the time. It was converted to a mosque after Ottoman conquest in 1461, and later used as an ammunition-storage depot and hospital by the Russians, before restoration in the 1960s.

In 2013 local religious authorities gained control of the building and converted it into a mosque again. A local judge has ruled the transformation of the former church to be illegal and ordered it to be maintained as a museum. For the moment it is both, though some of the ceiling frescoes and floor mosaics have been covered. You may be charged ₺10 admission if it reverts to being just a museum.

The church has a cross-in-square plan, topped by a single dome, showing Georgian influence. A stone frieze on the south porch depicts the expulsion of Adam and Eve from the Garden of Eden. On the western side of the building, the vaulted narthex has the best-preserved frescoes of various biblical themes, and the facade has a relief of an eagle, symbol of the church's founders, the Comnenus family. Unfortunately, most of the frescoes within arm's reach have been heavily defaced. The best frescoes (Annunciation, Visitation, Doubting Thomas etc) are in the main apse. The astonishing Christ Pantocartor on the ceiling dome is now covered with a tarpaulin.

The museum stands in gardens with a square bell tower erected in 1427. The site is signposted uphill from the coastal highway; it can be reached by dolmuş (₺1.75) from near the southeastern end of Atatürk Alanı. A taxi costs about ₺15.

upgrading the 41 rooms. Some rooms have balconies and sea views (try room 404).

Otel Horon
HOTEL €€

(📞 326 6455; www.hotelhoron.com; Sıra Mağazalar Caddesi 4; s/d ₺130/170; ❄🛜) In business since 1967, the aubergine-coloured Horon has a good central position and 44 attractively decorated, though somewhat faded, rooms with good showers. Efes is among the cold drinks in the well-stocked minibars and the 5th-floor restaurant has city views. Somewhat pricey for what it is though.

🍴 Eating

A few good eateries line Atatürk Alanı and the two streets running west. Got a sweet tooth? Head to Uzun Sokak for ice cream and pastries at **Kılıcoğlu** (Uzun Sokak 36; desserts from ₺7; ⊙7am-midnight); *kuruyemiş* (dried fruits and nuts), *lokum* (Turkish delight), *pestil* (dried fruit 'leather'), *bal* (honey) and cheeses at **Yeşil Mandıra** (Green Dairy; Sıra Mağazalar Caddesi 13/A; ⊙8am-10pm); *helva* (sweet made from sesame seeds) at **Beton Helva** (Uzun Sokak 15; ⊙10am-10pm); and hazelnuts and confectionary at **Cirav Fındık** (Ticaret Mektep Sokak 8; ⊙8am-10pm).

Üstad
TURKISH €

(Atatürk Alanı 18/B; mains ₺8; ⊙24hr) Locals squeeze into this compact *lokanta* (eatery serving ready-made food), located right on the main square. The lunchtime staples include *biber dolması* (stuffed peppers).

⭐Kalender
TURKISH €€

(📞 323 1011; Zeytinlik Caddesi 16/B; mains ₺13, salads ₺4-9; ⊙8.30am-9pm) This welcoming cafe-restaurant just south of the museum has a cosmopolitan vibe. It's perfect for a post-museum coffee and brunch of *menemen* (scrambled eggs with peppers and tomatoes) or *gözleme* (stuffed savoury crepe). The front tables overlook a side street and, on weekdays, you can choose a mixed plate of three/four of the seven or eight hot (₺13/15) and cold (₺7/9.50) daily dishes.

Bordo Mavi
INTERNATIONAL €€

(📞 323 3325; www.bordomavirestaurant.com; Halkevi Sokak 12; mains ₺14-27; ⊙8am-11pm) This cosmopolitan garden-cafe adjoins the clubhouse of Trabzonspor, the idolised local football team, and the waiters wear the team strip. Pizzas, pastas and sandwiches are on the menu alongside breakfast and Turkish meals.

Reis'in Yeri
TURKISH, TEAHOUSE €€

(Reis' Place; Liman Mukli İdare; mains ₺15-22; ⊙8am-11pm) Head down Gazipaşa Caddesi from Atatürk Alanı and across the footbridge to this sprawling fish/chicken/*köfte* grill house, which doubles as a tea garden. It's guaranteed dolmuş-free, and you can even hire rowing boats to steer around the tiny cove.

Cemilusta
FISH, KÖFTE €€

(📞 321 6161; www.cemilusta.com.tr; Atatürk Alanı 6; mains ₺11, salads ₺4; ⊙9am-9pm) Trabzon families flock to this spot for the fish and köfte house specialties, and views of the square from the outside tables and 1st-floor dining room. Various types of *köfte* are available, including the local one from Akçaabat, eaten with peppers, rice and salad. This place serves among the best baklava we have ever eaten.

Fevzi Hoca Balık-Köfte
SEAFOOD, KÖFTE €€

(www.fevzihoca.com.tr; İpekyolu İş Merkezi, 2nd fl, Kahramanmaraş Caddesi 8; mains ₺15; ⊙noon-10pm) There are no menus in this stylish fish restaurant. Just choose a *büyük* (big) or *küçük* (small) beastie and it comes in a meal deal with salad, pickles and dessert. *Köfte* set meals are also available.

Lezzet Lokantası
TURKISH €€

(Gazipaşa Caddesi 1; mains ₺8-12; ⊙6am-8pm) In business since 1935, this *lokanta* serves lunchtime staples, chunky chips, kebaps and commendable *lahmacun*. It all comes with outside seats overlooking the square and a soundtrack of waiters calling to passers-by.

🍷 Drinking & Nightlife

Koza Caffe
CAFE

(1st fl, Ziyad Nemli Sanat Sokağı 1; ⊙11am-11pm; 🛜) Diagonally opposite Şekerbank, 'Cocoon Cafe' has a refreshingly funky interior with a mishmash of fish tanks and faux medieval decor. Grab a seat on one of the tiny outdoor balconies and settle in for coffee and snacks.

Ehl-i Keyf
CAFE

(📞 321 3044; Cemal Sokak 2; 🛜) One of Trabzon's best live music and nargile spots, the former Stress Cafe has now become the 'Tame Fun' and it's so laid-back it's almost horizontal. The Ottomans-R-Us decor is slightly naff, but this is a relaxing haven. Live music kicks off on the top floor at 7.30pm most nights.

Edward's Coffee
CAFE

(☑326 8026; www.edwardscoffee.com; Cudibey Mektep Sokak 42/B; ☺7am-11pm) This small Anatolian chain serves cappuccino and other non-Turkish coffees. It has outside seating and a menu featuring sandwiches and salads.

Paticafe
CAFE, BAR

(6th fl, Kahramanmaraş Caddesi 10/A; ☺9am-10pm) On the rooftop of a shopping arcade, Paticafe serves Efes at outside tables with views uphill of Trabzon's Hollywood-style sign put up in 2011.

Efes Pub
PUB

(Kahramanmaraş Caddesi 5; ☺11am-11pm) Two floors of smoky, blokey ambience with draught Efes in 0.5L glasses and 2L 'beer towers'. Climb to the roof terrace for views down Kahramanmaraş Caddesi.

ℹ️ Information

There are numerous internet cafes and travel agencies around the main square and on and just off Kahramanmaraş Caddesi.

Tourist Office (☑326 4760; Atatürk Alanı; ☺8am-5.30pm Jun-Sep, 8am-5pm Mon-Fri Oct-May) This place next to the small police station on the south side of Atatürk Alanı is helpful and English-speaking.

ℹ️ Getting There & Away

AIR

Anadolu Jet (www.anadolujet.com) Flies to/from Ankara and İstanbul.

Onur Air (www.onurair.com.tr) Flies to İstanbul and Nicosia (Lefkoşa) in Northern Cyprus.

Pegasus Airlines (www.flypgs.com) Flies to Ankara and İstanbul.

SunExpress (www.sunexpress.com.tr) Flies to Antalya, İzmir and 16 European cities.

Turkish Airlines (www.thy.com) Flies to Ankara and İstanbul.

BOAT

Timetables for ferries to Sochi, Russia, change regularly. Check the latest situation at the shipping offices by the port entrance or online at **Sarı Denizcilik** (www.saridenizcilik.com), **Port of Trabzon** (www.al-port.com) and **Ferrylines.com** (www.ferrylines.com).

Depending on demand, be prepared to wait a few days or longer for a departure. Tickets cost from about US$150 with sleepers from US$50 extra.

You usually need to report to the port police several hours before departure time. The journey takes four hours (fast afternoon ferry) to 12 hours (slow overnight ferry).

BUS

Bus company offices, such as **Metro** (www.metroturizm.com.tr) and **Ulusoy** (www.ulusoy.com.tr), are scattered around Atatürk Alanı and serve destinations including Batumi and Tblisi in Georgia.

For Ayder and the Kaçkar Mountains, catch a Hopa-bound bus and change at Ardeşen or, better, Pazar. If you miss the daily Kars bus, head to Hopa or Erzurum for more services. For Yerevan in Armenia, you must change at Tbilisi in Georgia.

CAR

You can hire a car to pick up, or drop off, in Trabzon or at the airport through Economy Car Rentals (p674). The following rental agencies also have offices in town or at the airport: **Avis**

BUS SERVICES FROM TRABZON'S OTOGAR

DESTINATION	FARE (₺)	DURATION (HR)	DISTANCE (KM)	FREQUENCY (PER DAY)
Ankara	50	12	780	5
Artvin	30	4½	255	7
Erzurum	30	5	325	4
Hopa	20	3½	165	hourly
İstanbul	70	17	1110	3
Kars	40	10	525	1
Kayseri	60	12	686	1
Rize	8	1½	75	hourly
Samsun	30	6	355	10
Sinop	50	10	533	1 (at 9.30pm)
Tbilisi, Georgia (via Batumi)	50	11	430	1 (at 8pm)

BLACK SEA FLAVOURS

The local Black Sea cuisine provides a few taste sensations that you won't find anywhere else.

Not surprisingly fish reigns supreme in these parts and the *hamsi* (anchovy) is lord of them all. The damp coastal climate is perfect for things such as tea and hazelnuts but bad for wheat, which is replaced by more accommodating corn (maize). Popular here is *muhlama* (or *mıhlama*), a polenta-like dish of cornmeal cooked with butter and cheese and *kuymak*, where an egg is added for a lighter effect. Both types are eaten as a staple and if consumed at breakfast will set you up for a long day's trekking.

Despite what you may have read elsewhere, Tembel and Fadime – slang for a man and a woman from the Black Sea region – do not have a preference for cabbage surpassed only by certain Eastern European countries. Cabbage is *lahana* in Turkish and is almost always pickled. What people eat in abundance here – in soups, stews, salads and dolmas – is *karalahana*, literally 'black cabbage' but actually, a weedy-looking variety of collard. *Lahana sarması* (stuffed collard rolls) often contain corn or fish. *Karalahana çorbası* (collard soup, with various other vegetables, including sweet green peppers, and cornmeal) is a speciality of Rize.

If your taste buds aren't reacting to these savoury treats, there's also *Laz böreği*, a delicious flaky pastry layered with custard and hazelnuts. Like most Turkish desserts, a few bites can easily turn into a daily addiction. And when you consider that many Turkish pastry chefs hail from the Black Sea, you know it's going to be good.

The best place to try Black Sea cuisine is Kayadibi Saklıbahçe (p532) in Maçka or, in a pinch, Rize's Evvel Zaman (p535).

(☑ 325 5582; www.avis.com.tr), **Dollar Rent A Car** (☑ 444 1170; www.dollar.com.tr; Taksim Caddesi), **Europcar** (☑ 444 1399; www.europcar.com.tr; Cikmaz Sokak 38/1A, off Kunduracılar Caddesi) and **National** (☑ 325 3252; www.nationalcar.com.tr).

❶ Getting Around

TO/FROM THE AIRPORT
Dolmuşes to the *havaalanı* (airport, ₺1.75), 5.5km east of the centre, leave from a side street on the northern side of Atatürk Alanı. They drop you on the opposite side of the coast road from the airport, 500m from the terminal entrance across a pedestrian bridge.

A taxi costs ₺25. Buses bearing 'Park' or 'Meydan' go to Atatürk Alanı from the airport.

Havaş (☑ 325 9575; www.havas.net) operates shuttle buses to/from the airport (₺5), but they are inconvenient as they run along Yavuz Selim Bulvarı south of the centre. More useful are Havaş shuttles to/from Ardeşen (₺17) via Of and Rize (₺13). There's also a Havaş bus to/from Giresun (₺20).

BUS & DOLMUŞ
Trabzon's otogar is 3km east of the port, on the interior side of the coastal road. To reach Atatürk Alanı from the otogar, cross the shore road in front of the terminal, turn left, walk to the bus stop and catch any bus with 'Park' or 'Meydan' in its name. The dolmuş for Atatürk Alanı

is marked 'Garajlar-Meydan'. A taxi between the otogar and Atatürk Alanı costs ₺10.

To get to the otogar, catch a dolmuş marked 'Garajlar' from near the southeastern end of Atatürk Alanı, or one marked '**KTÜ**' from next to Otel Horon.

Dolmuşes (₺1.75) mainly leave from under the flyover near the southeastern end of Atatürk Alanı, although you can flag them down along their routes.

Sumela Monastery

The Greek Orthodox Monastery of the Virgin Mary, better known as **Sumela Monastery** (Sümela Manastırı; www.sumela.com; admission ₺15; ☾ 9am-7pm Jun-Sep, to 5pm Apr, to 6pm May, to 4pm Oct-Mar), 46km south of Trabzon, is one of the historical highlights of the Black Sea coast. The monastery was founded in the 4th century AD and abandoned in 1923 after the creation of the Turkish Republic and the so-called exchange of populations. The highlight of the complex is the main church, with damaged but stunningly coloured frescoes both inside and out.

Sumela, whose name is derived from nearby Mt Melat, clings improbably to a sheer rock wall, high above evergreen forests and a rushing mountain stream. It's a mysterious place, especially when mists swirl in the tree-lined valley below (most of the time) and the call of a hidden mosque drifts ethereally through the forest.

Visit early or late to avoid the hordes of Turkish tourists. At the entrance to the Altındere Vadisi Milli Parkı (Altındere Valley National Park) there's a ₺10/5 charge for cars/motorbikes. About 2km further on are a shady riverside park with picnic tables and a restaurant.

The main trail to the monastery begins over the footbridge past the restaurant, and is steep but easy to follow. You'll ascend 300m in about a half-hour, the air growing noticeably cooler as you climb through forests and alpine meadows. A second trail begins further up the valley. Follow the concreted road 1km uphill and across two bridges until you come to a wooden footbridge over the stream on the right. This trail cuts straight up through the trees, past the shell of the Ayavarvara Chapel. It's usually much quieter than the main route and takes the same amount of time.

You can drive almost to the monastery ticket office; the 3km drive is challenging at busy times, with cars coming the other way on the narrow mountain road. En route are waterfalls and a lookout point, from where you can see the monastery suspended on a cliff face high above the forest.

From the car park it's a 300m walk along a very rough and steep trail to the ticket office and monastery complex, sheltered underneath a hefty outcrop. On the way to the main church you'll pass the remains of a 19th-century aqueduct, a guards room, a library with a fireplace, a kitchen, a bakery and a vaulted refectory. The two-part church, formed from a natural cave and also built in the shape of an extended apse, is covered both inside and out with colourful frescoes depicting everything from the life of the Virgin Mary to the Last Judgement. The earliest examples date from the 9th century, but most of them are from the 19th century. Sadly, many have been defaced, some of them deliberately – recently.

The monastery has been substantially restored to showcase the various chapels and rooms used by pious types in earlier centuries. Continuing restoration in no way detracts from the experience, although on busy days, the views of the building will likely be more memorable than touring its cramped interiors.

Sleeping & Eating

From Maçka, some 29km south of Trabzon, the road winds for 17km through dense evergreen forests, following a rushing mountain stream past commercial trout pools, fish restaurants, pensions and campsites. There's a cafe with snacks in a renovated building just to the left after entering the monastery complex.

Coşandere Tourist Resort
PENSION, MOTEL €€

(Coşandere Turistik Tesisleri; ☑0462-531 1190; www.cosandere.com; Sumela Yolu, Coşandere; r ₺70-100, 4-person bungalow ₺140-170; 🛜) Located in Coşandere, a stream-fed village 5km southeast of Maçka, this pension has converted, pine-clad *serenderler* (granaries) sleeping up to six, and a huge wooden motel-like building favoured by groups. It's a handy way to get out and about in the mountains without your own transport, as various tours, treks and day trips are offered, including *yayla* (mountain) safaris.

The restaurant, with outside tables, makes a cool and pleasant lunch stop for Akçaabat *köfte* or *saç kavurma* (cubed lamb or beef cooked in a heavy metal skillet).

Kayadibi Saklıbahçe
BLACK SEA CUISINE €

(☑0462-512 2318; www.kayadibisaklibahce.com; Tünel Çıkışı, Maçka; mains ₺10; ⊙8am-11pm) This 'Hidden Garden' restaurant with great views in Maçka wins hands down for offering the best Black Sea dishes in the region, including polenta-like cheesy *kuymak*, *etli karalahana sarması* (mince-stuffed collard leaves) and *mısır ekmeği* (corn bread). It's worth the trip in itself.

Getting There & Away

Ulusoy and Metro run buses from Trabzon (₺25 return, one hour), leaving at 10am and departing from Sumela at 1pm/2pm in winter/summer. Both Eyce Tours (p528) and Vazelontours (p528) in Trabzon run organised tours.

Dolmuşes to Maçka (₺3, every 20 minutes) depart from the minibus ranks downhill from Atatürk Alanı, across the coast road from the port. Some carry on to Coşandere or even Sumela. A taxi to Maçka/Sumela costs ₺90/130; from Maçka to Sumela it's ₺40.

Driving from Trabzon, take E97 Hwy south and turn left at Maçka, 29km south of Trabzon. The monastery is also signposted as Meryemana (Virgin Mary), as it is known in the area.

BATUMI, GEORGIA

A rewarding excursion from the eastern Black Sea coast is Batumi in Georgia, just 37km north of Hopa. Citizens of most countries do not require visas, and transport links to/ from Turkey are frequent and inexpensive. At the time of writing, €1/US$1 was worth about 2.4/1.7 GEL.

Georgia is an ancient nation with a proud, hospitable people whose distinctive language has its own unique alphabet. It was the second nation (after Armenia) to embrace Christianity, and it is believed to be the birthplace of wine (*ghvino* in Georgian). It's *very* different from Turkey.

With a backdrop of mist-wrapped hills, Georgia's traditional summer holiday capital has sprouted new hotels and attractions like mushrooms in recent years, largely due to Turkish investment. But Batumi (Batum in Turkish; population 125,800) still owes much of its charm to the fin-de-siècle elegance of its original boom years a century ago.

Stroll or cycle (2 GEL per hour) along the seafront Batumi Boulevard (www.boulevard.ge), laid out in 1881 and lined with curious sculptures and structures, including the zany Alphabet Tower, a monument to Georgian script, and Ali & Nino, recalling the ill-fated lovers in Kurban Said's eponymous novel. Must-see sights are few but don't miss Europe Sq, with its striking monument to Medea holding her husband Jason's golden fleece and the Georgian Orthodox St Nicholas Church (1865). If time is on your side visit Batumi Botanical Gardens (www.bbg.ge; admission 6 GEL; ⊘8am-9pm), 9km to the north and one of the best in Europe. Gonio Apsaros Fortress (adult/student 3/1 GEL, audioguide 5 GEL; ⊘9am-6pm), 11km south of Batumi near the Turkish border, dates to Roman times and may be where Jason spent the night and the Apostle Matthias is buried.

The choice of places to stay in Batumi is legion. At the budget end the friendly 60-bed Globus (☏422-276721; www.hostelbatumi-globus.com; Mazniashvili 54; d 20-25 GEL, d 65 GEL; ❄☎), with open courtyard, a great kitchen and free laundry service, is everything you want a hostel to be. For midrange accommodation opt for the spic-and-span Hotel Brighton (☏422-274135; http://brighton.ge; Nodar Dumbadze 10; s & d 150-180 GEL; ❄☎) with 15 rooms just off Europe Sq. For a real treat book into the Piazza Boutique Hotel (☏322-601537; www.piazza.ge; Parnavaz Mepe 25; s 180-300 GEL, d 200-320 GEL; ❄☎), with 16 themed rooms (from Japanese and Art Deco to English) with balconies in a curious 13-storey bell tower.

Georgian cuisine is unique, with a particular taste for walnuts, aubergine and grilled meats. The great staple is *khachapuri,* essentially a cheese pie, and *khinkali,* spicy dumplings filled with mince, potato or mushrooms. Sample these dishes at Cafe Retro (☏422-276116; E Takaishvili 10; khachapuri 6.50-15 GEL; ⊘9am-10.30pm) or the more central (but less atmospheric) Shemoikhede (☏422-217110; www.gmcgroup.ge; Zhordania 8; mains 7-15 GEL; ⊘10am-midnight). For a more refined evening out, choose the wonderful Old Boulevard (☏592-222241; Ninoshvili 23a; mains 10-20 GEL).

Batumi is very much a café society. Cool your heels while enjoying something warm and sweet at the Kafe Literaturuli (☏422-272013; K Gamsakhurdia 18; cakes 2.30-6.80 GEL; ⊘10am-11pm; ☎), famous for its cookies, or at Privet iz Batuma (☏422-277766; Memed Abashidze 39; mains 2-8 GEL; ⊘10am-12.30am), with a pre-1917 nautical theme. Sample and buy Georgia's unique wines at Winery Khareba (☏422-270027; www.winery-khareba.com; K Gamsakhurdia 28-30; tasting 3-7 GEL; ⊘10.30am-8pm, to 10pm summer).

The helpful tourist information centre (☏577-909091; www.visitbatumi.travel; Ninoshvili qucha) is in a kiosk diagonally opposite the landmark Intourist Palace Hotel (1939).

A *marshrutka* (dolmuş) to/from the Turkish border at Sarpi, 17km south, is 1 GEL; in Batumi they leave from Tbilisi Sq. Bus 16 (0.80 GEL) runs from there from the train station via Tbilisi Sq and vice versa. Taxis to/from the border cost 30 GEL. From Sarpi a dolmuş will take you to Hopa. The border is open 24 hours daily and crossing it is normally straightforward, though there can be queues at weekends.

AMONG THE LAZ

Rize is the last major centre of the Laz people, a loose community numbering around 250,000, two-thirds of whom still speak the Caucasian-based Lazuri language related to Georgian. Known for their colourful traditional costumes and distinctive folk music and dances including the *horon*, Laz cultural performances take place at major local festivals in the Rize region. The sound of the piercing *tulum* (bagpipe) will stay with you forever.

The name Laz is not so easily defined, however. The Turkish Laz dispute any categorisation that would lump them in with their Georgian counterparts. Non-Laz locals distinguish themselves as 'Karadenizli' (from the Black Sea), but many Turks use Laz as a catch-all term for anyone living east of Samsun.

The majority population in towns such as Pazar and Ardeşen, the Laz are just as keen to distance themselves from other coastal citizens, and dismiss the demeaning stereotype of the simple, *hamsi*-swallowing Laz fisherfolk. The Laz, however, remain anchored to the sea; many Turkish shipping lines are owned by wealthy Laz families.

Uzungöl

📞 0462 / POP 1560

With its lakeside mosque and forested mountains that recall Switzerland, Uzungöl (Long Lake) remains idyllic, but be prepared for more than a few tacky hotels (there are currently 1500 rooms here) and a growing number of visitors from the Gulf States, where they never see rain or green grass. Uzungöl feels artificial compared with much of the Kaçkars further east, but it makes a good base for hikes in the Soğanlı Mountains and to the tiny lakes around Demirkapı in the Haldizen Mountains. Summer weekends get very busy, so try to visit during the week.

At the southern end of the lake is a clutch of wood-trimmed resorts, motels and pensions, many with freestanding bungalows. One of the best-value options is İnan Kardeşler (📞 656 6222; www.inankardesler.com.tr; s ₺70-100, d ₺120-140; 🛜), the charmingly named 'Trust Brothers', with 42 hotel rooms and 25 one- and two-bedroom bungalows sleeping up to five. There are cheaper and scruffier pensions on the main road into Uzungöl.

Minibuses travel to/from Of (₺8), 43km north, and Trabzon (₺15). You can rent mountain bikes (₺5 per hour) at the far end of the lake.

Rize

📞 0464 / POP 104,900

In the heart of Turkey's picturesque tea-growing area, Rize is a modern city centred on an attractive square. The hillsides above town are planted with *çay*, which is dried, blended, and shipped throughout Turkey. The hilltop tea garden is a good spot for a refreshing cuppa courtesy of the local tea giant Çaykur. Rizeans are equally proud of local boy turned prime minister Recep Tayyip Erdoğan, who grew up here and now has a university named after him.

The main square, with the inevitable Atatürk monument, beautifully reconstructed PTT and the Şeyh Camii (Sheik Mosque), is 200m inland from the coastal road. Principal thoroughfares Cumhuriyet Caddesi and Atatürk Caddesi run east from the square and parallel with the coast.

👁 Sights

Tea Garden   GARDENS
(tea ₺0.75) Rize's fragrant and floral tea garden is next to the Çaykur tea factory; 20 minutes' walk above town via the steep main road (Zihni Derin Caddesi) leading uphill behind the Şeyh Camii. Enjoy the superb views with a fresh brew of local leaves – a typical Rize experience. Taxis charge ₺8 from the main square up to the tea garden. If you don't make it here, sip tea in town at the competing Doğus (Cumhuriyet Caddesi 141; ⊙ 8am-6pm) shop.

Rize Castle   CASTLE
(Rize Kalesi; tea ₺1.50; ⊙ 8am-11pm) Built by the Genoese on the steep hill at the back of town, Rize's ancient *kale* has both a Lower Castle and the so-called Inner Castle above it. The latter contains a cafe with sweeping coastal views. To reach the castle head west of the main square along Atatürk Caddesi. Some 50m past the Petrol Ofisi gas station and opposite the Türkcell shop, turn left up Kale Sokak. A taxi here is ₺8.

Rize Museum
MUSEUM

(Rize Müzesi; ☑ 214 0235; Antika Sokak 4; ⏰ 9am-noon & 1-4pm Tue-Sun) **FREE** Just behind the tourist office kiosk, this fine reconstructed Ottoman house is decorated in traditional style, with recreated bridal room, weaving room, kitchen and so on filled with antique furniture, cooking implements and musical instruments. An old record player reminds us that the 20th-century Ottomans were very much part of the modern age. Mannequins model traditional Laz costumes from central Rize and Hemşin costumes from the Ayder region.

In the basement you'll find fine carved baroque and rococo furniture from Italy and near the entrance a *serender,* a traditional wooden granary on stilts.

🛏 Sleeping & Eating

Hotel Milano
HOTEL €€

(☑ 213 0028; www.hotelmilanorize.com; Cumhuriyet Caddesi 115/A; s/d/tr ₺80/120/160; ✱ 🛜) An unattractive seven-storey block in the centre of town houses this rather charming hotel. The 35 bright and airy rooms are well-sized and offer Rize's strongest shower pressure. Ask for one at the rear of the building for less noise from the main drag. Staff in the first-floor reception are welcoming and quite helpful.

Otel Kaçkar
HOTEL €€

(☑ 213 1490; www.otelkackar.com; Cumhuriyet Caddesi 101; s/d/tr ₺70/100/130; ✱ 🛜) On the north side of the main square, the lower-midrange Kaçkar's mosaic facade conceals 29 neat and simple rooms, with once-smart black furniture, basic bathrooms and new parquet floors.

Huzur
KEBAP, PIDE €

(☑ 217 1511; Cumhuriyet Caddesi 111/D; mains ₺8-12; ⏰ 8am-11pm) A cut above most *lokantalar,* 'Repose' is chilled, with a modern interior and seating on pedestrianised Deniz Caddesi. Dishes on the pictorial menu, delivered by waiters in bow ties and aprons, include top-notch pide.

Dergah Pastaneleri
SWEETS €

(Deniz Caddesi 19/A; mains ₺5-12; ⏰ 8am-midnight; 🛜) Stop for baklava or cake and *dondurma* (ice cream) at this gleaming modern *pastane* (patisserie). You can survey Rize from the roof terrace. There's also a branch (Atatürk Caddesi 35) near the main square.

Evvel Zaman
BLACK SEA CUISINE €

(www.evvelzaman.com.tr; Harem Sokak 2; mains ₺9-10; ⏰ 9am-11pm) This lovingly restored Ottoman house – the interior is like a joyously jumbled museum, stretching to a display case of swords and daggers – is a good place to try traditional Black Sea dishes, though the food can be hit-or-miss. The pictorial menu also features breakfasts with produce from local villages and there are shaded tables in the garden.

It's at the southeast (uphill) edge of the main square.

ℹ Information

Tourist Office (☑ 213 0408; Atatürk Caddesi 35/G; ⏰ 8.30am-5pm Mon-Fri) In a seldom-open kiosk down from the Rize Museum.

ℹ Getting There & Away

Bus-company offices and travel agents front the main square.

Frequent minibuses run to Hopa (₺14, 1½ hours) and Trabzon (₺8, 1¼ hours). For the northern Kaçkars, take an east-bound minibus to Ardeşen (₺4) or, better, Pazar (₺5) and change.

The otogar is along the old coast road, 2km northwest of the main square. For Trabzon, Pazar, Ardeşen and Hopa, it's easier to pick up a local minibus from the small otogar next to Halkbank, a few blocks northeast of the main square.

Hopa

☑ 0466 / POP 18,500

Just 37km southwest of the Georgian border, Hopa is the archetypal border town, with cheap hotels, traders markets and takeaway-food shops. On the leafy streets inland from the seafront highway are shoe shiners, barbers and a town going about its everyday business, seamlessly mixing old and new, headscarves and mobile-phone shops, in classic Turkish fashion. It's not worth overnighting here unless you arrive late en route to/from Georgia. There's a PTT, internet cafes and, near the pedestrian bridge, money changers and banks with ATMs.

🛏 Sleeping

Otel Huzur
HOTEL €

(☑ 351 4095; Cumhuriyet Caddesi 25; s ₺30-35, d ₺50-60; ✱ 🛜) Friendly Huzur's wood-panelled reception area and lounge is good for observing border-bound characters. The

20 rooms are reasonably comfortable; the cheaper have a shower but share a toilet.

Otel Heyamo BUSINESS HOTEL €€
(☑ 351 2315; www.otelheyamo.com; Cumhuriyet Caddesi 44; s ₺60-90, d ₺80-120; ❀ ☎) The welcoming, recently renovated lobby leads to 40 attractively decorated bedrooms, with flat-screen TVs, small desks and carved-wood panelling and French-pattern wallpaper. Eight rooms (eg 806) have balconies facing the sea and there's a huge bright breakfast room on the roof.

🍴 Eating & Drinking

Eateries cluster around the hotels. There's a *tekel bayii* (off-licence kiosk) at the pedestrian bridge 100m west of the Green Garden Kebap.

Green Garden Kebap PIDE, KEBAP €
(☑ 351 4277; Cumhuriyet Caddesi, Belediye Parkı; mains ₺8-12) A few hundred metres east of the main hotel strip, two terraces and a brick dining room dish up pide and kebaps in a shady park, with a pictorial menu and helpful staff.

ℹ Getting There & Away

Hopa's otogar is on the old coastal road 1.5km west of town (₺1 by dolmuş). **Ulusoy** (www.ulusoy.com.tr) and **Artvin Ekspres** (www.yesilartvinekspres.com.tr) buses to Erzurum (₺40, eight hours) leave at 6.30am, 9am and 4pm. Artvin Ekspres regularly serves Artvin (₺14, 1½ hours), and Kars (₺40) at 10.30am. Ulusoy has hourly minibuses to Rize (₺14, 1½ hours) and Trabzon (₺20, three hours).

For Georgia, **Metro** (www.metroturizm.com.tr) serves Tbilisi (₺40, eight hours) at 7am and 1am via Batumi (₺10, one hour, hourly). From Batumi take bus 16 to the border, then a waiting minibus to Hopa.

A taxi to the Georgian border from Hopa costs ₺35.

Northeastern Anatolia

Best Places to Eat

➡ Ocakbaşı Restoran (p559)

➡ Erzurum Evleri (p541)

➡ Çagin Cağ Kebapcısı (p541)

➡ Publik Bistro (p545)

➡ Hanimeli Kars Mutfagi (p558)

Best Places to Stay

➡ Ekodanitap (p545)

➡ Otel Doğa (p548)

➡ Karahan Pension (p551)

➡ Laşet Tesisleri (p555)

➡ Hotel Cheltikov (p557)

Why Go?

If you've a soft spot for far-flung outposts, it's time to discover Turkey's greatest secret. Despite its wealth of attractions, northeastern Anatolia remains largely untouched by even the domestic tourist circuit, and its glorious landscapes are refreshingly coach-party free. Particularly outside the Turkish summer holidays, you may have precipitous gorges and expansive steppe, muscular mountains and highland pastures to yourself. No wonder the region is prime territory for trekking (make a beeline for the Kaçkar Mountains and Mt Ararat), white-water rafting and skiing.

Culturally, the ruins of Ani and Işhak Paşa Palace are famously romantic, and numerous secluded treasures recall once-flourishing ancient civilisations. Palaces, castles, Georgian churches, Armenian monuments and Ottoman humpback bridges all stand in splendid isolation. For urban vibes, Kars is a laid-back city with a Russian aesthetic – a staging post in this region of open spaces, mountain solitude and moody skies above the steppe.

When to Go
Erzurum

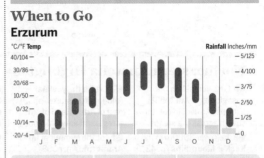

May Vivid hues and scents as the steppe blossoms, and spring warmth awakens mountain pastures.

Jun–Sep Hike and raft around the Kaçkar Mountains, scale Mt Ararat, catch festivals.

Dec–Apr Ski at Palandöken and Sarıkamış resorts, cross-country ski in the Kaçkars.

ERZURUM & AROUND

Erzurum

📞 0442 / POP 395,000 / ELEV 1853M

Lovers of architecture will be in paradise in Erzurum, where fantastic Seljuk, Saltuk and Mongol mosques and *medreses* (seminaries) line the main drag. Take it all in from atop the citadel, with mountains and steppe forming a heavenly backdrop to the jumble of billboards and minarets.

Erzurum is not a city resting on its considerable laurels of historical signifi-

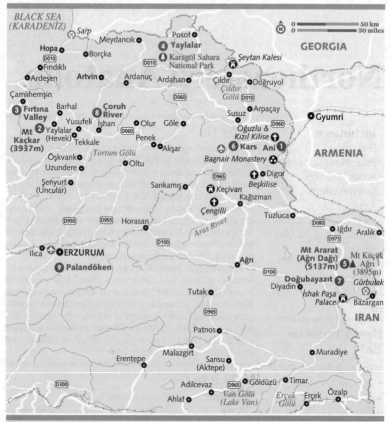

Northeastern Anatolia Highlights

❶ Lose yourself in the past glories of **Ani** (p561), a former Armenian capital strewn across the steppe.

❷ Trek over 3000m in the **Kaçkar Mountains** (p542), or tackle day walks from nearby serene villages like Barhal and Yaylalar.

❸ Experience Hemşin culture and cuisine in the **Fırtına Valley's** (p548).

❹ Cruise the **yaylalar** (mountain pastures; p552) east of Artvin, land of pine forests and emerald slopes.

❺ Hit the summit of **Mt Ararat** (5137m; p568), Turkey's highest mountain.

❻ Hang out in distinctive **Kars** (p556) and discover Georgian and Armenian ruins nearby.

❼ Meet the Kurds in **Doğubayazıt** (p565) and explore sights like İshak Paşa Palace.

❽ Test your mettle on a white-water run down the **Çoruh River** (p544).

❾ Rip up some powder at **Palandöken** (p542) ski resort.

cance; the vibrant life coursing along its shopping-centre-lined streets has earned it a reputation as a modern metropolis and eastern Turkish hub. Although it's one of Turkey's most pious, conservative cities, the hip-looking university students add a relaxed buzz to the pavements and cafes. And come winter, the nearby high-octane Palandöken ski resort has a thriving nightlife.

History

Being in a strategic position at the confluence of roads to Constantinople, Russia and Persia, Erzurum was conquered and lost by armies of Armenians, Persians, Romans, Byzantines, Arabs, Saltuk Turks, Seljuk Turks and Mongols. As for the Ottomans, it was Selim the Grim who conquered the city in 1515. It was captured by Russian troops in 1882 and again in 1916.

In July 1919 Atatürk came to Erzurum to attend the congress that provided the rallying cry for the Turkish independence struggle. The Erzurum Congress is most famous for determining the boundaries of what became known as the territories of the National Pact, the lands that became part of the Turkish Republic.

◎ Sights

Between Yakutiye Medrese and Çifte Minareli Medrese on Cumhuriyet Caddesi are the classical Lala Mustafa Paşa Camii (1562), small Ottoman Caferiye Camii (nd restrained but elegant Ulu Cami (1179), built by the Saltuk Turkish emir of Erzurum.

★Yakutiye Medrese   MUSEUM, MEDRESE
(Yakutiye Seminary; Cumhuriyet Caddesi) Rising above a central square, this imposing Mongol theological seminary dates from 1310. The Mongols borrowed the basics of Seljuk architecture and developed their own variations, as seen in the entrance with its geometric, plant and animal motifs. Of the two original minarets, only the base of one and the lower part of the other have survived. The one sporting superb mosaic tilework wouldn't look out of place in Central Asia.

Turkish-Islamic Arts & Ethnography Museum   MUSEUM
(Türk-İslam Eserleri ve Etnoğrafya Müzesi; admission ₺3; ⊙8am-5pm Tue-Sun) Housed in the Yakutiye Medrese, this museum's striking central dome is lined with faceted stalactite work that catches light from the central

opening to make a delightful pattern. Surrounded by leafy gardens, it's perfect for a tea break.

Kale   FORTRESS
(admission ₺5; ⊙8am-5pm) For Erzurum's best views, head up to the citadel, erected by the emperor Theodosius around the 5th century and subsequently damaged and repaired numerous times. Inside, spiral stairs and a step ladder climb to the top of the 12th-century clock tower.

★Çifte Minareli Medrese   MEDRESE
(Twin Minaret Seminary; Cumhuriyet Caddesi) East of the city centre, this building dates from the 1200s when Erzurum was a wealthy Seljuk city, before suffering attack and devastation by the Mongols in 1242. The twin brick minarets are decorated with eye-catching small blue tiles. Walk to the back of the building to see the grand, 12-sided domed hall at the far end of the main courtyard from the entrance. It served as the Hatuniye Türbesi, tomb of Huand Hatun, the *medrese's* founder.

Its facade exemplifies how the Seljuks liked to try out variation even while aiming for symmetry: the panels on either side of the entrance are identical in size and position but different in motif. The building is under restoration until 2015.

★Üç Kümbetler   TOMBS
(Three Tombs) Walk south between the Çifte Minareli and Ulu Cami until you come to a T-junction. Turn left then immediately right and walk a short block uphill to these three 13th-century mausoleums in a fenced enclosure. Note the near-conical roofs and the elaborately decorated side panels.

🛏 Sleeping

Erzurum has dependable budget and mid-range options, but for top-end accommodation stay at the Palandöken ski resort, 5km south of Erzurum.

Hekimoğlu Hotel   HOTEL €
(☑234 3049; Kazım Karabekir Caddesi 66; s/d/tr ₺60/90/120; ☎) With halls bedecked with colourful carpets and a jovial team at reception, the Hekimoğlu is a good-value option in Erzurum's main hotel area. Rooms are on the small side, but simple and clean. There's a busy *lokanta* (eatery serving ready-made food) downstairs, so that's everything sorted after a long Anatolian bus ride.

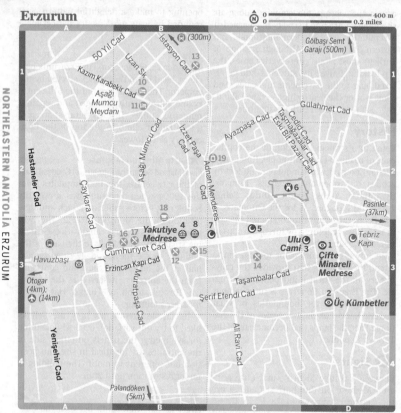

Erzurum

Top Sights

1	Çifte Minareli Medrese	D3
2	Üç Kümbetler	D3
3	Ulu Cami	D3
4	Yakutiye Medrese	B3

Sights

5	Caferiye Camii	C3
6	Kale	C2
7	Lala Mustafa Paşa Camii	C3
8	Turkish-Islamic Arts & Ethnography Museum	B3

Sleeping

9	Esadaş Otel	A3
10	Grand Hotel Hitit	B1
11	Hekimoğlu Hotel	B1

Eating

12	Arzen	B3
13	Çagin Cağ Kebapcısı	B1
14	Erzurum Evleri	C3
15	Güzelyurt Restorant	B3
16	Kılıçoğlu	B3
17	Salon Asya	B3

Drinking & Nightlife

	Daşhane	(see 14)
	Şahane	(see 14)
18	Yakutiye Park Alışveriş Merkezi	B2

Shopping

19	Rüstem Paşa Çarşısı	C2

Grand Hotel Hitit HOTEL €€
(☎ 233 5001; grandhitit@gmail.com; Kazım Karabekir Caddesi 26; s/d/tr ₺90/150/180; ☎) On a street with budget and lower midrange hotels, the Hitit has pleasant rooms with TV, dark wood decor, well-sprung mattresses,

big showers, minibars and safes. It's professionally managed and a good choice for solo women travellers.

Esadaş Otel
HOTEL €€

(📋 233 5425; www.esadas.com; Cumhuriyet Caddesi 7; s/d ₺100/160; 🛜) Pros: right on the main thoroughfare and close to everything. Cons: right on the main thoroughfare so a bit noisy (traffic ceases around 11pm). That said, it's well maintained and efficiently run and has excellent breakfast too. Bargain down the prices a bit if it's slack.

🍴 Eating & Drinking

Eateries on Cumhuriyet Caddesi around Yakutiye Medrese serve everything from *çiğ köfte* (raw ground lamb mixed with pounded bulgur, onion, clove, cinnamon, salt and hot black pepper) to *lokum* (Turkish delight). Head to **Arzen** (Cumhuriyet Caddesi; snacks from ₺3) and **Kılıçoğlu** (Cumhuriyet Caddesi; snacks from ₺3) for baklava, ice cream and espresso coffee.

Salon Asya
KEBAP €

(Cumhuriyet Caddesi 27; mains ₺8-12) Asya does a lively lunchtime trade, keeping a clientele ranging from students to policemen happy with Turkish classics.

⭐Erzurum Evleri
CAFE €€

(Yüzbaşı Sokak 5; entry ₺2, mains ₺10-20; ⊙10am-11pm) This old wooden house, signposted from Cumhuriyet Caddesi, is filled with Ottoman paraphernalia. Dishes include soup, *börek* (filled pastry) and *tandır kebap* (stew), served in private alcoves with cushions and low tables. Overlooking the courtyard, **Şahane** offers *çay*, Turkish coffee and, from 6pm, traditional live music. Round the back, **Daşhane** has nargiles (water pipes) and bean-bags. There is a small entry fee for all this heritage ambience.

Çagin Cağ Kebapcısı
KEBAP €€

(www.meshurcagkebapcisi.com; Gürcükapı Caddesi; mains ₺6-18; ⊙11am-10pm) Our choice of Erzurum's restaurants, specialising in *cağ kebap* (mutton with onions grilled on horizontal skewers). Either eat the wood-fired morsels with a fork, or do as the locals do and chomp away straight from the skewer. Each skewer is ₺5 and comes with flatbread and tasty salads and dips. The waiter will keep offering you more until you're full.

Güzelyurt Restorant
MEZE, INTERNATIONAL €€

(📋 234 5001; www.guzelyurtrestaurant.com.tr; Cumhuriyet Caddesi 42; mains ₺11-23; ⊙11am-10pm; 🍴) Erzurum's smartest restaurant, in business since 1928, is quaintly anachronistic, with shrouded windows, thick carpets and bow-tied waiters creating an old-fashioned charm. It's licensed, and a good place to splurge on a great meal. The meze (₺4 to ₺8) are the headliner, with about 20 different specialities, including lots of vegetarian options.

Yakutiye Park Alışveriş Merkezi
CAFE, LIVE MUSIC

(Yakutiye Meydanı; ⊙10am-late) Step inside this building, its tower aping the Yakutiye Medrese in glass and red lights, and enter Erzurum's student world. Lifts climb between five floors of unlicensed cafes offering *canlı* (live) music and other entertainment including snooker, table tennis and foosball. Combine nargiles and a bowling alley, and you're guaranteed a good night.

🛍 Shopping

Shops near Çifte Minareli Medrese sell carpets, antiques and souvenirs. There are jewellery shops on the northern side of Cumhuriyet Caddesi, east of Ulu Cami.

Rüstem Paşa Çarşısı
JEWELLERY

(Adnan Menderes Caddesi; ⊙11am-10pm) Erzurum is known for the manufacture of jewellery and other items from *oltutaşı*, the local black amber. Buy it in this atmospheric *çarşı* (market; 1550), built by Süleyman the Magnificent's grand vizier.

ℹ Information

MONEY
Banks and ATMs are on Cumhuriyet Caddesi.

ℹ Getting There & Away

Anadolu Jet (www.anadolujet.com) flies to/from İstanbul and Ankara, **Pegasus Airlines** (www.flypgs.com) to/from İstanbul, **Onur Air** (www.onurair.com.tr) to/from İstanbul, **Sun Express** (www.sunexpress.com.tr) to/from İzmir, and **Turkish Airlines** (📋 0850-333 0849; www.thy.com) to/from İstanbul and Ankara.

BUS
The otogar (bus station) is 4km from the centre along the airport road. Bus companies have offices around Esadaş Otel on Cumhuriyet Caddesi.

SERVICES FROM ERZURUM'S OTOGAR

DESTINATION	FARE (₺)	DURATION (HR)	DISTANCE (KM)	FREQUENCY (PER DAY)
Ankara	60	13	925	about 10 buses
Diyarbakır	35	8	485	5 buses
Doğubayazıt	25	4½	285	5 buses
İstanbul	70	19	1275	7 buses
Kars	20	3	205	frequent
Kayseri	50	10	628	several
Trabzon	30	6	325	several
Van	40	6½	410	about 3 buses

Metro serves most destinations, while Hasbingöl travels to Diyarbakır and Doğubayazıt.

For Iran, take a bus to Doğubayazıt.

The **Gölbaşı Semt Garajı**, about 1km northeast of Adnan Menderes Caddesi (take a taxi there), has local minibuses to the north and east. Daily departures include Artvin (₺30), Hopa (₺35), Rize (₺35) and Yusufeli (₺20).

TRAIN

The daily *Doğu Ekspresi* runs to Kars at 12.30pm, and to Ankara via Sivas at 2.30pm.

ℹ Getting Around

A taxi to/from the airport, about 14km northwest of town, costs around ₺50. Buses meet planes and run into central Erzurum for ₺3, with a bus stop on Hastaneler Caddesi, north of the roundabout at Cumhuriyet Caddesi's western end.

Minibuses and city buses pass the otogar and continue to town for ₺1. Some bus companies run servis minibuses into the city. A taxi costs about ₺15.

Car-rental operators, including National, Europcar and Avis, have branches in Erzurum.

Palandöken

☑ 0442

Just 5km south of Erzurum, Palandöken is Turkey's best ski resort. Runs for all levels descend from 3100m, and infrastructure includes ski lifts, cable cars and snowboard parks. Palandöken hosted the Winter Universiade (World University Games) in 2011.

The season runs from late November to early April. Weekends are busy, and there's also an après-ski scene with bars and discos.

Unlike Sarıkamış, there are no opportunities for summer hiking on the largely austere slopes, but some of Palandöken's hotels are comfortable accommodation options outside of winter.

🛏 Sleeping & Eating

Hotels have restaurants, bars, discos, hire outfits, hamams, saunas and fitness centres. Prices quoted are high-season winter weekend rates (expect discounts of around 30% to 50% in low season). They're usually negotiable, and in winter 'full board plus' packages, including all meals and lift pass, are offered.

Xanadu Snow White   HOTEL €€€

(☑ 230 3030; www.xanaduhotels.com.tr; s/d incl full board ₺500/650; ❄ 🛜 ⛷) Stylish, with great views of Erzurum, and open year-round. Check online for good deals.

Ski Lodge Dedeman   HOTEL €€€

(☑ 317 0500; www.dedeman.com; s/d from €60/75; ⊙ Dec-Apr; ❄ 🛜) This place is stylish and intimate.

ℹ Getting There & Away

From central Erzurum, a taxi costs ₺30 to ₺35.

KAÇKAR MOUNTAINS

The Kaçkar Mountains (Kaçkar Dağları) form a rugged range between the Black Sea and the Çoruh River, stretching roughly 30km northeast. Dense forest covers the lower valleys, but above about 2000m grasslands carpet the passes and plateaus, and the jagged ranges are studded with lakes and alpine summer *yaylalar* (mountina pastures).

The Kaçkars are renowned for their trekking opportunities. Popular locations include the highest point, **Mt Kaçkar** (Kaçkar Dağı; 3937m), with a glacier on its northern face, and the northeastern ranges around the peak of **Altıparmak** (3310m). Spend a few days here to explore this stunning region.

Kaçkar Mountains

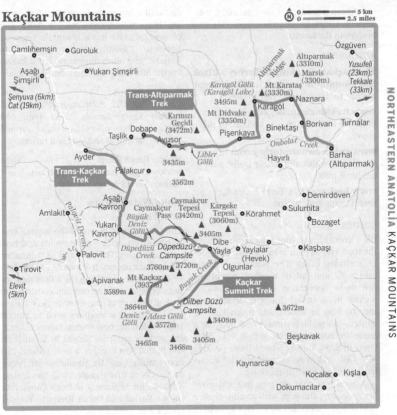

🏃 Activities

Hiking

The Kaçkars hiking season is short; you can only hike the higher mountain routes between mid-July and mid-August, when the snowline is highest. From May to mid-September there are plenty of walks on the lower slopes. If you are content not to cross the mountains, conditions are more dependably dry and clear in June and September, and the autumn colours in September and October are beautiful.

Very popular is the Trans-Kaçkar Trek: two to three days from Olgunlar to Ayder via the Çaymakçur Pass (approximately 3100m). The hike to the Kaçkar Summit by its southern face takes two to three days from Olgunlar, and may require specialist snow equipment. Without a guide, you can tackle the ascent to Dilber Düzü camp site beneath Mt Kaçkar (the path is well defined); allow seven to eight hours for this out-and-back

walk from Olgunlar. The three- to four-day Trans-Altıparmak route is similar to the Trans-Kaçkar, except that it crosses the Altıparmak range and doesn't climb the summit. From Barhal, trek for four to five hours up to Karagöl Lake, camp overnight, and return the next day.

Çamlıhemşin and Yusufeli are easily accessible, and public transport of varying frequency serves Ayder, Şenyuva, Çat, Barhal, Yaylalar and Olgunlar. High in the northwestern Kaçkars around 2000m, there are basic pensions in Yukarı Kavron, Amlakit, Palovit and Elevit. These spots and Avusor, all served by dolmuş in summer, are good spots for day walks around the slopes and lakes. As a general rule, you have to climb above about 1900m to leave the forests and get panoramic views. Culture Routes in Turkey (www.cultureroutesinturkey.com) has marked day walks around Barhal, Yaylalar and Olgunlar. Walks at lower altitudes, with or without a guide, are also stunning, with ancient Georgian churches and Ottoman bridges in the forests.

RESOURCES

The Kaçkar: Trekking in Turkey's Black Sea Mountains The book details different Kaçkar routes over the high passes.

www.trekkinginturkey.com Useful practical information and updates to the above.

www.culturalroutesturkey.com Recommends day walks and longer trails; with practical info.

www.kackar.org In Turkish, but has useful maps and photos.

GUIDES

It's a good idea to hire a local who knows the tracks if you plan to tackle high altitudes or multiday hikes. The walks are mostly unsigned, and misty weather conditions can make orientation difficult. Arranging a guide upon arrival can be difficult – they may be busy in season, and unavailable in winter – so making contact and booking a guide in advance is recommended. Zafer Onay of **East Turkey Expeditions** (✆ 0543 480 4764; zaferonay@hotmail.com) is knowledgeable and English-speaking.

A good tent, mat, sleeping bag and stove are necessary, although with an all-inclusive operator you could get away with a sleeping bag, walking boots and warm clothes. For fully guided tours for two people, including tents, mat, transport and food, expect to pay around US$300 per day from Ayder.

If you don't want to arrange a guide beforehand, many of the pensions we've included can provide guiding services and give pointers. Especially recommended are Barhal Pansiyon (p551) and Karahan Pension (p551) in Barhal, and Çamyuva Pension (p552) in Yaylalar. Guides can also be arranged through pensions in mountain villages such as Yukarı Kavron, but beware of false guides. Professional operations typically charge about ₺200 to ₺250 per day for a mule and a guide. A mule can carry three people's bags. Minimise costs by providing your own food and camping equipment.

Turku Tour
HIKING
(✆ 0464-651 7230; www.turkutour.com; İnönü Caddesi 35, Çamlıhemşin) Mehmet Demirci, a friendly local entrepreneur and owner of pensions in Ayder and Çamlıhemşin, offers day walks, longer treks, 4WD safaris, rafting, horse riding, cross-country skiing and photography. He has a mountain house at Kotençur (2300m), one hour's walk from Amlakit, and offers alternative treks following the Silk Road and Xenophon's *Anabasis*.

Cumhur Bayrak
HIKING
(✆ 0537 562 4713; cumhurbayrak@hotmail.com; Yusufeli) Knowledgeable about flora and fauna, Cumhur offers day walks around Yusufeli, as well as trekking and rafting.

Middle Earth Travel
HIKING
(www.middleearthtravel.com) Cappadocia-based nationwide hiking specialists.

White-Water Rafting

YUSUFELİ

The Çoruh River is one of the world's best rafting rivers, with superb rapids and brilliant play holes. The river and its tributaries offer rafting options from grade 2 to grade 5.

At the time of writing the following trips were popular, but the ongoing construction and utilisation of the dam project means local operators sometimes need to amend trips or develop new routes. More challenging options are from Sarıgöl to Yusufeli on the Barhal River (grade 3 to 4, around two hours rafting), and the Yusufeli to Artvin run on the Çoruh River (grade 3 to 5, two hours). Suitable for beginners is from Çamkertan on the Barhal and Çoruh Rivers to Yusufeli (grade 2 to 3, three hours).

Local operators run day trips for about ₺110 per person (three or four people ₺80 per person) for around three hours of rafting.

Necmettin Coşkun
RAFTING
(✆ 0505 541 2522; www.coruhriver.com) In Yusufeli in June/July; speaks good English (see the boxed text).

Oktay Alkan
RAFTING
(✆ 0466-811 3620; www.birolrafting.com; Greenpiece Camping & Pansiyon) Former kayak champion; in Yusufeli over the summer.

ÇAMLIHEMŞİN

White-water rafting is possible in July and August on the rapids around Çamlıhemşin. The rapids are smaller than the more exciting waters near Yusufeli, but the Black Sea region has arguably the more impressive scenery. There are operators on the Ardeşen–Çamlıhemşin road, including **Dağraft** (✆ 0464-752 4070; www.dagraft.com.tr; per person ₺50-70), which has tours geared to-

NECMETTİN COŞKUN: RAFTING GUIDE

Best season The main rafting season begins in June. For beginners, it's best to come in July or August, because the level of water is lower and the rapids less challenging.

Why it's special here The Çoruh and its tributaries are long rivers; you can paddle for hours, even several days if you want. And for serious action, the Çoruh is simply world-class, with thrilling sections complete with rapids, pools and big rocks – they're not called 'King Kong' and 'High Tension' for nothing. The scenery adds to the appeal, with deep gorges, castles and picturesque villages.

Beginners' corner We begin with a practice session and a briefing on a calm section of the river before tackling more thrilling sections, though there's no obligation to overdo it. There's always a guide on the boat, who gives the instructions to the team, and a mini-bus follows along the road and picks us up at the end of the ride.

What if the Yusufeli dam project... I think we still have a few more years before the dam becomes reality. Anyway, once it's completed, we'll find alternative sections on the Çoruh, Ispir or Barhal Rivers.

wards rafters from amateurs to professionals (grades 1 to 2 and 3 to 4; 3km to 9km). It also offers zip-lining.

Northern Kaçkars

Çamlıhemşin & Around

☏ 0464 / POP 3000

At an altitude of 300m, 20km off the coast road, Çamlıhemşin is a climatic transition point. Mist and drizzle indicate that you've left the coastal zone, and once you continue up the valleys past Çamlıhemşin, expect a stronger alpine influence in the climate, terrain and vegetation. The village is a functional, workaday spot, but has an appealing authenticity in comparison with Ayder. The locals are mostly Hemşin.

Just beyond Çamlıhemşin the road forks. The right fork leads up the Fırtına Valley; the left over the bridge and uphill to Ayder (17km). On the Ayder road, you'll pass several ancient humpback bridges across the Fırtına Çayı (Storm Stream), which were restored for the Turkish Republic's 75th anniversary (1998).

Çamlıhemşin has a post office, supermarket, garage, and an ATM. Stock up on provisions. Turku Tour (p544) organises excursions in the Kaçkars.

There are a couple of camping spots en route from the coast. For more comfortable accommodation, the highly original Ekodanitap (☏ 651 7787; www.ekodanitap.com; per person Hemşin house/treehouse ₺90/75, dinner

₺30; ☏) 🏔 is hidden up a winding road (just before Çamlıhemşin on the right) and along a forest footpath. Traditional Hemşin houses and treehouses overlook a terrace perched above a river valley with a mountain at the far end. With an organic garden and solar power, sustainability is a priority, but there are modern features such as showers. Eating with gregarious owner Mehmet Demirci and his family is a pleasure. Ekodanitap is open year-round.

A recent addition to Çamlıhemşin's accommodation scene is the excellent Taşmektep Otel (☏ 651 7010; www.camlihemsintasmektep.com; Halil Şişman Caddesi; r ₺200; ☏). Around 1km from the village en route to the Fırtına Valley, a historic stone schoolhouse has been transformed into a boutique hotel. Rooms are spacious and airy, and trimmed with colourful artwork and carpets. Nearby are a couple of surprisingly sophisticated and arty cafes.

Çamlıhemşin has basic cafes and the licensed Publik Bistro (☏ 651 7270; İnönü Caddesi 35; meals ₺12; ◷8am-5pm winter, to 10pm summer; ☏), with a riverside terrace and black-and-white Kaçkar scenes overlooking its wooden benches, a small library and backgammon sets. The breakfast is kingly, particularly if you incorporate *soğanlı yumurta* (eggs with onion), and dishes include kebaps, pasta and *muhlama* (fondue-like Hemşin dish).

Frequent dolmuş traffic runs to/from Pazar (₺8), with connections to/from Rize (₺12) and Ardeşen (₺8).

1. Nemrut Dağı (p587) 2. Ruins of Ani (p561) 3. Göbekli Tepe (p579)
4. Sumela Monastery (p531)

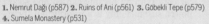

IZZET KERIBAR / GETTY IMAGES ©

Historical Highlights

Across the rugged swath of northern and eastern Anatolia the historical ebb and flow of conquering, trading and colonising civilisations is revealed in a compelling roll-call of ancient cities, grandiose monuments and hushed religious structures. Amid this sprawling region of deserts, mountains and steppe, look forward to being immersed in wildly scenic landscapes as you discover testaments to 12 millennia of history.

Sumela Monastery

From the silvery coastline of the Black Sea, ascend through misty forests to this Byzantine monastery. Founded in the 4th century it now seemingly defies gravity as it clings to sheer rocks.

Ani

On the desolate steppe bordering Turkey and Armenia, consider the power, glory and eventual downfall of this once world-leading city that was a vital stop on the ancient Silk Road trade route.

Göbekli Tepe

Secure a front-row view of the unfolding of human history as this ancient site is carefully excavated. Echoes of the ages reverberate around this compact mound estimated to be 12,000 years old.

Gaziantep Zeugma Mosaic Museum

Journey to bustling Gaziantep to experience this world-leading showcase of astounding Roman mosaics. Witness centuries-old lifestyles in carefully preserved villa interiors and the kohl-enhanced eyes of the poignant *Gypsy Girl* mosaic.

Nemrut Dağı

Be astounded by one man's megalomania amid the giant stone heads on this peak rising from ancient lands. Spending sunrise or sunset atop the summit reinforces a sense of the march of time and the transience of all great empires.

Fırtına Valley

☑ 0464

This beautiful river valley, used as a location in the Turkish film *Bal* (Honey), is a great place to experience traditional Hemşin life. Even the 6km stretch from Çamlıhemşin to Şenyuva is special; winch wires, used to hoist goods up to remote mountain houses, criss-cross the verdant slopes above the road. Look for the hilltop mansions built in the early 20th century, when locals returned flush with cash after working as chefs and bakers in pre-Revolutionary Russia.

In **Şenyuva** is the graceful arch of the 1696 **Şenyuva Köprüsü** (Şenyuva Bridge). The **teahouse** 200m further on has a supreme view of the bridge from its riverside terrace. Don't cross the nearby bridge, but continue along the river and into the hills for 6km to reach the restored **Zil Castle** (Zil Kale). It's a tough but scenic walk. En route, after 2.5km, a sign points to **Pavolit Şelâlesi** – the waterfall is a one-hour walk from here. Lush rhododendron forests surround the spectacularly situated castle, a round stone tower on a stark rock base.

Another 15km on a good road takes you to **Çat** (1250m), a riverside hamlet used as a trekking base, and the start of rougher roads into the mountains. A further 3.5km uphill is **Çat summer village** (1800m), where locals move in the warmer months when the road is passable. It's well worth the walk for the *yaylalar*, overlooked by snowy peaks and swathed in buttercups in spring. Turn left after the humpback stone Ottoman **Çılanç Köprüsü**.

🛏 Sleeping

Booking ahead is recommended in summer. The pensions mostly close from October to April. There's a food shop in Çat.

★ **Otel Doğa** GUESTHOUSE €

(☑ 651 7455; Şenyuva Yolu; half board per person ₺70; 🛜) About 4.5km from Çamlıhemşin, this friendly old guesthouse has a spacious sitting room and riverside dining room, where home-cooked food is served. The French- and English-speaking owner, İdris Duman, is a passionate champion of the Kaçkars; he will help you get your bearings at the wall map in the kitchen. Most bedrooms have private bathrooms and balconies; go for a corner room.

Toşi Pansiyon PENSION €

(☑ 654 4002; www.tosipansiyon.com; half board per person ₺85; 🛜) The first pension you come to on the outskirts of Çat, Toşi is clean and friendly with a riverside terrace and accommodation in wooden cabins. Rafting can be arranged and trekking advice is available.

Cancik PENSION €

(☑ 654 4120; www.cancikpansiyon.com; Çat village; per person ₺60) Just across the bridge in Çat village, this atmospheric pension features rustic but comfortable wooden rooms and cabins. The attached teahouse, restaurant and shop doubles as a social hub for the tiny hamlet, so get ready to meet the locals. Dinner of grilled trout is just the thing after a day's trekking.

ℹ Getting There & Away

On summer mornings, a dolmuş heads up the valley from Çamlıhemşin to Çat (₺15) and onto *yaylalar* villages. Turku Tour (p544) runs a minibus on Saturday and Thursday, leaving Çamlıhemşin at 8am and heading up the valley to Amlakit (2000m) via Elevit, Tirovit and Palovit, arriving at 11am and returning at 3pm. At other times, you will likely have to walk or take a taxi from Çamlıhemşin (Şenyuva ₺20, Çat ₺80).

The road currently ends in Amlakit, but improvements to the route between there and Sal will eventually make it possible to drive a one-way loop from Şenyuva, returning to the village along a ridge at 2000m. This will be feasible in summer, by both dolmuş and hire car.

Ayder

☑ 0464

The tourism hub of the Kaçkars, this high-pasture village revels amidst a valley perched at 1300m. Snowy slopes slide towards Ayder's rooftops between woodland in various shades of green, and waterfalls cascade to the river below. Charming alpine-chalet structures dot the steep hillside; new buildings must be in traditional style (ie sheathed in wood). Sadly, aesthetics aren't everything and Ayder's proliferation of pensions has made it more like a ski resort than a village. Çamlıhemşin and the Fırtına Valley have more authenticity and character, but Ayder is worth visiting for an accessible taste of glorious Kaçkars scenery.

Ayder is also firmly on the domestic holiday circuit, and becoming increasingly popular with Georgian tourists and Arab visitors from the Gulf states. Consequently, its budget-travel ethos is creeping upmarket, resulting in a better standard of accommodation but also higher prices.

The village is still really only busy during summer weekends and the trekking season (mid-May to mid-September); at other times there may only be a few local families living here. During the Çamlıhemşin Ayder Festival (second week of June) accommodation can be almost impossible to secure, and over weekends from June to August, Turkish tourists fill most pensions by mid-afternoon.

Lower Ayder has an ATM, restaurants, food shops, internet cafe, dolmuş and taxi stand, and accommodation and more eateries are scattered for about 1km uphill from this base.

About 4.5km below Ayder is the entrance gate to the Kaçkar Dağları Milli Parkı (Kaçkar Mountains National Park; ₺10 per vehicle).

🏃 Activities

Kaplıca SPA
(Hot Springs; ☑657 2102; www.ayderkaplicalari.com; Ayder; admission ₺10, private bath ₺40; ⊙8am-7pm) Post-trek muscle relief is offered in marble environs at Ayder's spotless *kaplıca* (spa), where water temperatures reach 56°C.

🛏 Sleeping

Many pensions perch halfway up the hill above the road. Getting up to them can be tricky when the mist rolls in. Often your bags will be dragged up the hill on nifty winch arrangements. Many businesses close from roughly October to April.

Fora Pansiyon PENSION €
(☑657 2153; www.forapansiyon.com; half board per person ₺90) This hillside pension provides a cosy sitting room and rustic pine-clad bedrooms, some with shared bathrooms. Dinner on the view-laden terrace shouldn't be missed, and new rooms with private bathrooms are especially comfortable. The laundry is a welcome feature if you've been on the road for a while.

Zirve Ahşap Pansiyon PENSION €
(☑657 2177; mirayzirve@hotmail.com; per person ₺50; ☎) In lower Ayder, this solid budget option has two floors of spick-and-span rooms, some with bathroom and some without. Views are lacking but the old chairs in reception are great for chatting to the friendly owner.

Kardelen BUNGALOWS €€
(☑657 2107; www.ayderkardelen.com; s/d ₺100/140; ☎) These reader-recommended spacious and private bungalows are around 1km uphill from lower Ayder. Despite the uphill trek, the quieter location, waterfall and meadow views, and good food and drinks – including cold beer – are definitely worth it. Owner Nadir speaks good English and can advise on local activities and walks.

Kalegon Butik Otel HOTEL €€
(☑657 2135; www.ayderkalegon.com; s/d ₺75/150; ☎) Centrally located in the main area of Ayder, the Kalegon has clean and cosy wood-lined rooms, and regular live music on summer weekends.

🍴 Eating & Drinking

Most people opt for half board accommodation at their pensions.

Yılmaz Cafeterya ANATOLIAN €
(snacks & meals ₺5-15) Run by the welcoming Yılmaz family – Kamil shouts choices at you like *çorba* and *pilau*, before whisking you towards a hearty meal, whipped up by his wife and daughters – this cafe offers chicken and fish dishes, plus local specialities like *muhlama*.

Zümrut Café CAFE €€
(mains ₺10-20) Sip a çay or Turkish coffee, and in season, fish dishes, kebaps, *muhlama* and sweet nibbles including *laz böreği* (a creamy custard and pastry treat) are all on offer. More expensive than other nearby places, but worth it for the brilliant waterfall views from the back terrace.

> ### HEMŞİN CULTURE
>
> If you visit the Ayder area over a summer weekend you may see some of the last surviving Hemşin culture. In village meadows, groups of Hemşin holidaymakers often gather to dance the *horon*, a cross between the conga and the hokey-cokey set to the distinctive whining skirl of the *tulum*, a type of goatskin bagpipe. You'll also see women all around the mountains wearing splendid headdresses, often incongruously matched with cardigans, long skirts and running shoes or woollen boots. Many Hemşin émigrés return from overseas for the Çamlıhemşin Ayder Festival.

❶ Getting There & Away

In summer, there are frequent dolmuşes to/from Pazar and Ardeşen (₺12) via Çamlıhemşin (₺6). Services are scarcer in winter, when passengers are mostly shoppers from the mountain villages, so dolmuşes descend from Ayder in the morning and return in the afternoon. A taxi from Çamlıhemşin to Ayder costs about ₺35.

On summer mornings, dolmuşes run into the mountains. Check with locals for exact schedules, but services generally run to Yukarı Kavron (₺12, one hour) every two hours, returning hourly between 2pm and 5pm; and to Avusor at 9am, returning at 3pm.

Southern Kaçkars

Yusufeli

📞 0466 / POP 6400 / ELEV 560M

This likeable river valley town is sadly slated to vanish underwater. Despite local and international resistance, the Yusufeli dam project – part of Turkey's national plan to harness hydroelectricty and achieve greater energy independence – is scheduled to be completed around 2018. Planning is underway to relocate Yeni ('New') Yusufeli higher in the mountains. Turkish officials have guaranteed that no churches in the nearby Georgian valleys will be submerged.

For now, Yusufeli is the gateway to the southern Kaçkars and a good base for the Georgian Valleys. The Çoruh River and its tributaries offer magical white-water experiences for both first-time runners and seasoned enthusiasts.

⌷ Sleeping

The following are all by the Barhal River. To reach Barcelona and Greenpiece, cross either of the bridges, turn right and follow the river for about 700m.

Greenpiece Camping & Pansiyon　PENSION €
(📞 811 3620; www.birolrafting.com; Arıklı Mahallesi; s/d ₺45/90, camping/caravans ₺5/15; @ 🛜) Birol Alkan and his twin daughters run this laid-back pension in a peaceful spot. There's a camping area with bathroom facilities, and accommodation includes a traditional wooden, chalet-style unit, and a new upstairs addition with spacious rooms and a pleasant restaurant. Rafting trips can be organised here.

Hotel Baraka　HOTEL €
(📞 0538 604 1775; s/d/tr without breakfast ₺30/40/50; 🛜) Centrally located next to the suspension footbridge, some rooms in this good budget option have river views. Rooms are clean, and bathrooms are small but functional.

Otel Almatur　HOTEL €€
(📞 811 4056; www.almatur.com.tr; s/d ₺75/125; 🛜) Look forward to flat-screen TVs, fridges, big beds with crisp linen, and windows with sweeping views, particularly from the 4th-floor corner suite. The bathrooms, however, are small. The 5th-floor restaurant's tinted windows have more stunning views and dishes include İskender kebap, *köfte* and meze. Next to the road bridge, the hotel also has a sauna. Breakfast is an excellent spread.

Otel Barcelona　HOTEL €€
(📞 811 2627; info@hotelbarcelona.com.tr; Arıklı Mahallesi; s/d €55/75; 🛁🛜❄) Popular with tour groups, Otel Barcelona has a bar-restaurant, hamam and fitness centre. Smart rooms have black-and-white tiled floors, stylish furniture and flat-screen TVs.

İhtiyaroğlu　GUESTHOUSE €€
(📞 824 4086; www.apartagara.com; Sarıgöl Yolu; campsites per person ₺20, s/d ₺60/100; 🛜) En route to Sarıgöl and the mountains, a steep winding dirt road descends 500m to this place of easy bliss. Chalet-like buildings have 20 impeccable, pine-clad rooms and you can camp on the grass. Enjoy barbecued trout (₺15) in riverside gazebos. Located riverside on the road to Barhal, and easily accessible by minibus from Yusufeli (₺8).

✘ Eating

Köşk Cafe & Restaurant　TURKISH €
(mains ₺7-12) This jolly venture above the tourist office has a good view of Yusufeli boulevardiers sauntering down the main drag. It's good for a simple breakfast or fish and chicken dishes.

Çardak Döner Restaurant　ANATOLIAN €
(mains ₺7-10; ⊙6am-2pm) Choose between goodies such as *kahvaltı* (breakfast), *hazır yemek* (ready-made food) and homemade baklava before retiring to the beautful *çardak* (balcony). It's next to the suspension footbridge.

ℹ Information

Yusufeli has internet cafes, banks with ATMs, a post office, a petrol station and a **tourist office** (☺ 8am-9.30pm daily May-Oct, 8am-5.30pm Mon-Fri Nov-Apr).

ℹ Getting There & Away

Yusufeli's central otogar is near the tourist office. There are morning buses to Artvin (₺17), Erzurum (₺20, three hours) and the Black Sea coast. You can also take a dolmuş (₺5) or taxi (₺30) to the intersection of the Artvin and Erzurum roads and catch passing buses, including the Kars bus, which passes around 1pm (₺35).

To/from Barhal (₺12.50), Yaylalar (₺30) and Olgunlar (₺30), a few dolmuşes descend to Yusufeli between about 5.30am and 7am, returning between 2pm and 5pm. Yaylalar is officially the end of the line, but it should be possible to persuade the driver to continue to Olgunlar. Outside those times, you will likely have to hire a taxi, around ₺130 between Yusufeli and Barhal, and ₺220 from Yusufeli to Yaylalar.

Driving into the Kaçkars, the road is surfaced from Yusufeli via Sarıgöl (about 18km), and on to Barhal (a further 10km). Thereafter the road is unsurfaced. If it's dry, the winding, narrow road can be braved by confident drivers in an ordinary car with good clearance all the way to Olgunlar. Allow plenty of time, seek local advice before setting off, and beware rockfalls and landslides in wet weather and when the snow is melting; springtime is risky. The road is particularly rocky above Yaylalar.

Tekkale & Dörtkilise

📞 0466 / POP 2500

Peaceful Tekkale lies 7km southwest of Yusufeli. On the way there a ruined 10th-century Georgian castle towers above the road. From Tekkale follow a road uphill 7km northwest to Dörtkilise (Four Churches), a ruined 9th-century Georgian monastery. The building is domeless, with a gabled roof and very few frescoes. Similar to the smaller Barhal church, it's a picturesque ruin with weeds and vines springing from mossy stones. With a guide, walk around 3km (one hour) to a chapel where monks from the complex kept guard.

Dolmuşes run from Yusufeli to Tekkale (₺2) at 11am, 3pm and 5pm. Services depart from across the road bridge opposite the Otel Almatur. A taxi to Tekkale costs about ₺35; ₺80 return to Dörtkilise (including waiting time). Work traffic heads towards

dams being built beyond Tekkale, so hitching is possible. From Tekkale, you can hike to Dörtkilise; look out for the church high up amid the vegetation on the left of the road. Driving, the road is mostly surfaced but narrow and slightly rough from Tekkale; take care in wet weather.

Barhal (Altıparmak)

📞 0466 / POP 1500 / ELEV 1300M

About 27km northwest of Yusufeli, Barhal is an alluring base for forays into the Kaçkars. The *köy* (village) nestles in a verdant valley, with a rippling stream running through its heart, a beautiful mountainscape, and inviting pensions which offer trekking guides and advice on day walks and longer expeditions. Another pull is the well-preserved 10th-century Georgian church next to Karahan Pension. For views over the village and the jagged peaks beyond, walk up to two small ruined chapels across the valley from the church, from where the upper chapel is visible on a ridge. The walk (unsigned, around 5km, 90 minutes return) starts over a plank footbridge near the bottom of Karahan Pension's driveway.

🍽 Sleeping & Eating

There are food shops for provisions to assemble a picnic.

⭐ **Karahan Pension** GUESTHOUSE €
(📞 0538 351 5023, 826 2071; www.karahanpension.com; Altıparmak Köyü; B&B/half board/full board per person €15/25/28) Run by Mehmet and son Bekir (who speaks some English), cosy Karahan has an adorable hillside setting 1km above the village, and a terrace with sofas perfect for unwinding. Rooms are appealing despite bare floorboards, and there are excellent views down the valley. Enjoy homemade honey and homestyle cuisine on the covered terrace.

Barhal Pansiyon GUESTHOUSE €
(📞 0535 264 6765; www.barhalpansiyon.com; half board per person ₺65, half board dm ₺45; 🖻) Over the road from the river, Barhal Pansiyon has 22 modern rooms, including wooden bungalows and simpler budget accommodation with shared facilities. It's good for hikers, with a Kaçkars map for sale, local expertise on hand, and a pleasant dining room and garden for planning. No views to speak of, but dinners feature multiple dishes.

Yaylalar (Hevek)

☑ 0466 / POP 700

It's a winding and narrow ride up to Yaylalar, 22km from Barhal, but you'll be rewarded with an uberbucolic setting – expect plenty of traditional farmhouses and scenic *yaylalar* (mountain pastures) all around. Particularly off season, the village is livelier than Olgunlar; you may well agree with the sign proclaiming Yaylalar 'heaven on earth'.

The best place to stay in both Yaylalar and Olgunlar, and the most reliably open year-round, Çamyuva Pension (☑ 0534 361 6959, 832 2001; www.kackar3937.com; half board per person ₺80; 🕾) resembles a big Swiss chalet, with comfortable rooms and balconies for watching the village go by. Alongside the well-stocked food shop and bakery (owned by Çamyuva proprietors İsmail and Naim, who also drive the dolmuşes to/from Yusufeli) are wooden cabins with porches and the stream gurgling underneath – soothing in summer, chilly in winter. Dinner and breakfast are hearty affairs, satisfying appetites built up in the mountain air.

Olgunlar

☑ 0466 / POP 50

About 3km further up from Yaylalar on a scenic white-knuckle road, the quiet hamlet of Olgunlar really feels like the end of the line. Standing in splendid isolation, it's a bucolic spot with soaring peaks, soul-stirring vistas, babbling brooks and some of Turkey's purest air.

🛏 Sleeping & Eating

A top choice for walkers, Kaçkar Pansiyon (☑ 832 2047, 0538 306 4564; www.kackar.net; half board per person ₺70; 🕾) is a haven of peace complete with pine cladding. It features super-clean rooms, a kitchen for guests' use, a comfy sitting area and delectable meals. Bag a room overlooking the stream. Friendly owner İsmail speaks some English.

Olgunlar Pansiyon (☑ 832 2159; half board per person ₺55) offers more basic accommodation, geared towards hardy trekkers.

There's a small cafe at the end of the hamlet where the walking trail starts, open from roughly June until September/October. It serves dishes like *menemen* (scrambled eggs with tomatoes and peppers) and *muhlama,* and sells basic foodstuffs.

FAR NORTHEAST

Georgian Valleys

The spectacular, mountainous country southeast of Yusufeli is a culturally peculiar area. It was once part of the medieval kingdom of Georgia, with numerous churches and castles to show for it – seldom-visited buildings mixing characteristics of Armenian, Seljuk and Persian styles. The villages in the mountains and valleys are a delight to explore, and their cherry and apricot orchards bear fruit around mid-June.

Tony Anderson's *Bread and Ashes: A Walk Through the Mountains of Georgia* has a chapter on this corner of Turkey.

History

The Persians and Byzantines squabbled over this region from the 4th century AD. It was conquered by the Arabs in the 7th century, recovered by the Byzantines, lost again and so on. The region was part of the medieval Georgian kingdom in the 10th century, governed by the Bagratids, from the same lineage as the Armenian Bagratids ruling over the Kars region. The isolation brought about by the rugged terrain, piety and support of Byzantium fostered a flourishing culture that produced the churches.

In 1008, ambitious King Bagrat III looked outside the sheltered valleys and unified Georgia's warring kingdoms. Bagrat shifted the focus of the newly formed kingdom by moving the capital from Tbilisi, nominally under Arab control, to Kutaisi; and by gradually disengaging from the southwest valleys that had been under the sway of the Byzantines since 1001.

The Byzantines and Georgians coexisted relatively harmoniously, but the Seljuk Turks' arrival in 1064 destabilised the area until 1122, when King David IV ('The Builder'; 1089–1125) defeated the Seljuks. David took up where Bagrat had left off, by reunifying Georgia with Tbilisi and the southwest provinces. So began the 'golden age' for Georgian culture, which peaked during Queen Tamar's reign (1184–1213).

Following the Mongol conqueror Tamerlane's arrival in 1386, the Ottoman capture of Constantinople (1453) ended the protection the Georgians had enjoyed under quasi-Byzantine rule. The kingdom went into decline, the Ottomans annexed the Georgian

Georgian Valleys & Around

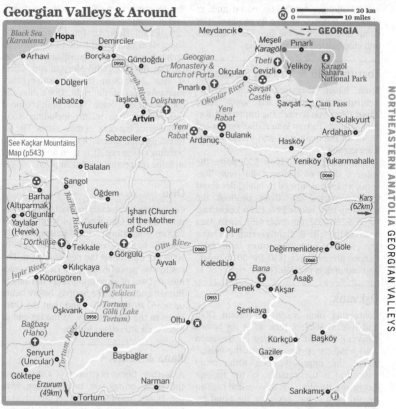

Valleys and, later, imperial Russia took care of the rest. Today, many locals have Georgian heritage.

❶ Getting There & Away

Hiring a car in Erzurum is the easiest way to see the valleys. Public transport mostly consists of minibuses that head from the villages to Yusufeli in the morning, returning in the afternoon. It's possible to catch an afternoon minibus from Yusufeli to a village such as İşhan, then walk back down to the main road and pick up a passing bus to Yusufeli. If you're catching an Erzurum-bound bus from Yusufeli, you will have to walk/hitch to sights off the main road. Hiring a taxi in Yusufeli costs about ₺100 to İşhan return (including waiting time) or ₺300 for a day.

The following itinerary starts from Yusufeli.

İşhan

From Yusufeli, drive to the intersection on the Artvin–Erzurum road (9km), turn right

and follow the brown 'İşhan Kilisesi' signposts for 21km. İşhan upper village is spectacularly situated, 7km up a steep, narrow road carved out of the mountainside. Drive slowly in wet weather, when the road gets slippery.

Located below İşhan's modern white mosque, the wonderful 7th-century **Church of the Mother of God** was enlarged in the 12th century. There are traces of blue frescoes (25 years ago whole walls were covered in them) in the near-conical dome, and a superb arcade of horseshoe-shaped arches in the apse, all with different capitals. The four pillars are impressive, as in Öşkvank, and recent careful restoration has faithfully resurrected the church's roof.

The most detailed of the many fine external reliefs – above the portal of the small neighbouring chapel – ascribes the founding of the church to King Bagrat III. Also worth admiring are the inscriptions above the main building's bricked-up portal and an elaborate fretwork around its windows. The drum also sports some fine blind arcades and elegantly carved colonnades.

Tortum Gölü & Tortum Şelalesi

From İşhan, backtrack to the Artvin–Erzurum road and turn left (south). After about 15km, you'll reach the impressive Tortum Şelalesi (Tortum Waterfalls), signposted 700m off the main road and overlooked by a tea garden.

Continuing south, Hwy 950 skirts the western shore of Tortum Gölü (Lake Tortum), which was formed by landslides about three centuries ago. Cafes overlook the 8km-long lake. İskele Et & Balık Lokantası (☏ 0535 366 9052; fish dishes ₺15), about 4km south of the falls, is slightly scruffy but has a great location on a promontory in the lake. Canoes are available (₺10 for 30 minutes) and camping is possible (₺10).

Öşkvank

Continuing 8km south of Tortum Gölü and Tortum Şelalesi, turn off at the brown 'Öşkvank Kilesesi' sign. Keep on the main road winding up the valley to the village, where the impressive late 10th-century cathedral is the grandest of the region's Georgian cathedrals, its three-aisled basilica topped by a dome. Look for the blind arcades and the reliefs of archangels.

The interior is jaw-dropping. The central nave has two walled-off aisles on either side. The southwest aisle, like the triple-arched narthex, is still in relatively good shape; note the intricate carvings on the capitals, with elaborate geometric designs, typical of Georgian church decoration. There are other fine relief carvings, both on the massive capitals that supported the equally majestic dome and on the exterior walls. Look for the fine relief of the Three Wise Men, to the right (northeast) of the main entrance.

Much of the roof has fallen in, but there are still well-preserved fragments of frescoes; look in the half dome on the inside of the main porched portal.

Bağbaşı

Continue south along Hwy 950 past Uzundere, where a castle perches dramatically on a rocky outcrop. About 15km south of

the Öşkvank turn-off is another turn-off, over a humpbacked bridge, to Bağbaşı village (called Haho by the Georgians). Go about 4km up the asphalted road through orchards and fields to the village, then bear right at the 'Taş Camii Meryem Ani Kilisesi' sign. After 3km, the late 10th-century monastery is on the right. Don't miss the conical-topped dome with multicoloured tiles, or the fine reliefs, including stone eagles grasping does in their claws. The alternating light and dark stones adds to the building's elegance. It is used as a mosque, so some restoration has taken place.

Oltu

Continuing south from Bağbaşı on Hwy 950, turn onto the Oltu road, which climbs over 2300m. A startling restored kalesi (citadel), thought to have been built by Urartus in 1000 BC, dominates the peaceful town. The castle was probably used by Genoese colonies and was of some importance during the Roman and Byzantine periods, before being occupied by the Seljuks and then the Ottomans in the 16th century. At the far end of town is an attractive church.

Bana & Penek

A further 18km northeast of Oltu, along the D955, brings you to a junction with the D060. Turning left, after about 4km you'll see a castle on the right at the end of a ridge. It's an eerie sight, in keeping with the surreal landscape, where craggy gorges alternate with reddish bluffs. About 400m further on you'll see a second crumbling clifftop castle on the right, overlooking a poplar-lined river from a rocky outcrop.

Backtrack to the junction with Hwy 955 and turn left onto the D060. A further 14.2km leads you over a bridge crossing the Penek Çayı (signposted). About 100m past the bridge, take the side track on the left. It goes uphill for 2km to Penek. Continue through the village and the awesome Armenian church of Bana soon comes into view, perching on a hill with the mountains forming a fantastic backdrop. Its most distinctive architectural feature is its rotunda shape.

Approach the church by following a dirt road that branches off to the left about 600m after leaving the village (*don't* brave it in wet weather with an ordinary car).

Artvin

📱0466 / POP 25,234 / ELEV 600M

Artvin's main claim to fame is its spectacular mountain setting – its vertiginous streets zigzag crazily up a steep hill. Sadly, kilometres of dam and road works have scarred the valley below. The main reasons to pass through are the region's beauteous *yaylalar* (mountain pastures) and the Kafkasör Kültür ve Sanat Festivalı (Caucasus Culture & Arts Festival). Held in the Kafkasör Yaylası pasture, 7km southwest of town, in late June or early July, the festival features *boğa güreşleri* (bloodless bull-wrestling matches). The bulls, classified by the thick-ness of their necks and matched accordingly, lock horns in Turkey's only bullfighting ring. Weakened bulls are regarded as defeated, and withdrawn from combat.

Tourist information is available at the tourist office (Ministry of Culture & Tourism; 📱212 3071; www.artvinkulturturizm.gov.tr; ⊙8am-5pm Mon-Fri), where English is spoken. It's in a 19th-century Russian military building, up the steep steps next to Vakıf Bank.

🛏 Sleeping & Eating

Most hotels are near the *valiliği* (provincial government building). Along İnönü Caddesi are good eateries and pastry shops.

A MAGICAL TRIP IN THE BACKCOUNTRY

In spring and summer, the area northeast of Artvin is simply stunning: a tapestry of lakes, rivers, canyons, mountains, forests, *yaylalar* (mountain passes) and traditional wooden houses, with the added appeal of a Caucasian flavour, courtesy of its proximity to Georgia. Among the off-the-beaten-track villages and towns, several churches and castles stand in delightful settings.

A DIY approach with your own wheels is preferable, as public transport is infrequent. The Artvin tourist office has maps of the area. Seek local advice before attempting secondary roads, which may be in bad shape.

About 11km east of Artvin on the D010, a signposted turn-off ('Dolişhane Kilisesi 3km') climbs to the beautiful 10th-century Dolişhane church, with a few reliefs. Back on the D010, signs 3km further on point right along the scenic Ardanuç road to Ferhatlı castle (look up on your right after 3km; it's perched on a rocky outcrop) and, a few kilometres further southeast, Gevernik castle ('Adakale') and Ardanuç, set in a dramatic canyon guarded by an impregnable fortress. About 17km past Ardanuç, near Bulanık village, is the harder-to-reach church of Yeni Rabat. Seek advice at Ardanuç before driving any further, as some sections of the road may have deteriorated.

Back on the D010, 12.5km northeast of the Ardanuç turning, a brown sign on the left points 2km up to the 10th-century Georgian Monastery and Church of Porta. About 17km further northeast on the D010, a tarred road leads north to Meydancık, a quintessential *yaylalar* settlement near the Georgian border.

In the lower section of Şavşat, an old Georgian town, a fairy-tale castle stands sentinel. Just past the castle, a brown sign points left 27km to Karagöl Sahara National Park. Cross the bridge, turn right at the T-junction and follow the winding sealed road. After 7km, a brown 'Cevisli Kilesesi' sign on the left points 4km to the ruined 10th-century Tbeti church, standing in an idyllic *yaylalar* village. Look for the elaborately carved windows. Karagöl Sahara National Park (📱0466-517 1156; www.savsat karagol.com; cars ₺7) encompasses spectacular mountain scenery and the pine-fringed Meşeli Karagöl, where you can hire a rowboat (30 minutes, ₺10). Overlooking the lake, the Karagöl Pansiyon (📱0466-531 2137; half board per person ₺120) has rustic rooms.

Back in Şavşat, the D010 leaves the lush, wooded valleys behind and snakes steeply around numerous twists and turns over the Çam Pass (2640m) to Ardahan, a typical steppe town. Licensed Laşet Tesisleri (📱0466-571 2136; www.laset.com.tr; Şavşat-Ardahan Karayolu; mains ₺10-28, s/d ₺80/120), 10km from Şavşat, serves fish and kebaps in a beautiful forested setting. Wood-lined rooms upstairs are cosy and comfortable, and there are also wooden chalets 2km away. Owner Mete speaks good English.

Mersivan Otel HOTEL €€

(☑212 3333; www.hotelmersivan.com; İnönü Caddesi; s/d ₺70/100; ☜) Located on Artvin's hilly main drag, the Mersivan is a dependable choice in close proximity to bus company offices and decent restaurants and cafes. Rooms are a tad dated, but still clean and relatively spacious.

ℹ Getting There & Around

Artvin's new otogar lies around 5km downhill from the town centre near the intersection to Ardahan. Minibuses (₺1.50) run from İnönü Caddesi in the centre of town to the otogar.

There are hourly minibuses to local towns including Hopa (₺15, 1½ hours), Yusufeli (₺17, 2¼ hours) and Şavşat (₺15, 1½ hours).

Artvin Express serves Erzurum (₺30, five hours, 6am, 9.30am, 11am and 5.30pm) and Trabzon (₺30, five hours, frequent from 7.30am to 5pm).

There are also departures to Ardahan (₺30, 11am and 1.30pm) and a daily bus to Kars (₺35, noon).

The Metro company serves various long-haul destinations.

Kars

☎0474 / POP 76,700 / ELEV 1768M

With its stately, pastel-coloured stone buildings dating from the Russian occupation, and its well-organised grid plan, Kars looks like a slice of Russia teleported to northeastern Anatolia. And the city's mix of influences – Azeri, Turkmen, Kurdish, Turkish and Russian – adds to its distinct feel. No wonder it provided the setting for Orhan Pamuk's acclaimed novel *Kar* (Snow).

Kars is usually regarded as a base for Ani, but it's worth spending a day exploring its sights, soaking up the eclectic vibe, and sampling the delicious local *bal* (honey) and *peynir* (cheese). It also makes a convenient base for exploring remote villages and sights in the surrounding steppe.

History

Dominated by a stark medieval fortress, Kars was once an Armenian stronghold, capital of the Armenian Bagratid kingdom (before Ani) and later a pawn in the imperial land-grabbing tussle played out by Turkey and Russia during the 19th century. The Russians captured Kars in 1878, installed a garrison and held it until 1920 and the Turk-ish War of Independence, when the republican forces retook it. Many of the sturdier stone buildings along the main streets date back to the Russian occupation.

The locals are said to be descended from the Karsaks, a Turkic tribe that came from the Caucasus in the 2nd century BC and gave their name to the town.

◉ Sights & Activities

Russian Monuments HISTORIC BUILDINGS

Around town are Russian belle époque mansions and other examples of Baltic architecture. On Ordu Caddesi are the Health Directorate Building (1907), with columns and floral motifs; the yellow-and-white Old Governor's Mansion (1883), where the Treaty of Kars was signed in 1921; and the Gazi Kars Anatolian High School, occupying a late-19th-century winter mansion. The Fethiye Camii, a converted 19th-century Russian Orthodox church, stands majestically south of the centre.

Kars Museum MUSEUM

(Kars Müzesi; Cumhuriyet Caddesi; ☺8am-5pm) FREE Northeast of the centre en route to Ani, the city museum has exhibits from the Old Bronze Age, the Urartian, Roman and Greek periods, and the Seljuk and Ottoman eras. Photographs show excavations at Ani and Kars province's ruined Armenian churches, as well as the Neolithic cave paintings at Camuslu, south of Kars between Keçivan and Çengilli.

Kars Culture & Art Association MUSEUM

(Kars Kültür Sanat Derneği; Bakırcılar Cad 39; ☺8am-5pm Mon-Sat) FREE Local historian Vedat's paint shop doubles as a small library and a museum about the Molokans ('milk-drinkers' in Russian) order, to which his grandmother belonged. The peaceful Christian group disagreed with the Russian Orthodox Church and came to Kars during the Russian occupation. Last century, rather than fight for the Ottomans, they scattered to the former USSR, USA and Canada.

Balyolu HIKING

(www.balyolu.com) For a sweet, lingering look at the surrounding steppe, hit the 'honey road' with the Kars- and USA-based Balyolu. The operator's one-week honey-tasting walking tours include mountain hikes and visits to remote rural communities.

DON'T MISS

KARS CASTLE WALK

North of the river in the older part of the city, **Kars Castle** (Kars Kalesi) `FREE` is well worth the knee-jarring climb, with excellent views over the town and the steppe in fine weather.

On the way to the castle along the riverbanks huddle assorted reminders of Kars' history, notably the imposing, basalt **Kümbet Camii**. Built between 932 and 937 for the Bagratid King Abas, it was called the Apostles' Church; reliefs representing the 12 apostles and Maltese Crosses remain on the exterior. It was converted to a mosque in 1064, when the Seljuks conquered Kars, then used as a church again in the late 19th century by the Russians, who added the porches.

Beyond the Kümbet Camii is the 17th-century **Ulu Cami**, Kars' largest Ottoman mosque, and, behind the school, the **Beylerbeyi Sarayı** (Beylerbeyi Palace) nestling beneath the castle.

Records show that Saltuk Turks built a fortress here in 1153. It was demolished by the Mongol conqueror Tamerlane in 1386 and rebuilt several times over the following centuries. The fortress was the scene of bitter fighting during and after WWI. When the Russian armies withdrew in 1920, control of Kars was left in the hands of the Armenian forces, until the republican armies took the castle. Inside are a Janissary barracks, arsenal, *mescit* (small mosque) and tomb.

One of the more attractive – and intact – structures in the older part of the city is the 16th-century basalt bridge, **Taş Köprü**. Destroyed by a flood and rebuilt by the Ottomans in 1719, the bridge is flanked by the ruined Ottoman **Muradiye Hamam** and **Cuma Hamam**. The basalt, rectangular 18th-century **Mazlum Ağa Hamam** is just before the bridge back to central Kars and the leafy riverside tea garden **İstihkam Çay Bahçesi** (Atatürk Caddesi).

🛏 Sleeping

Hotel Temel
HOTEL €

(📞 223 1376; www.hoteltemel.com; Yenipazar Caddesi 9; s/d ₺60/80; 🛜) Hotel Base offers neat rooms with immaculate sheets and a soothing blue-and-yellow colour scheme, but its wood-panelled interiors are dated and gloomy. Thankfully it's near the minibus terminal and has a lift and satellite TV. Nearby, **Hotel Temel 2** (📞 223 1376; Yenipazar Caddesi; s/d/tr ₺25/40/60; 🛜) has rooms that are small and old but clean.

Güngören Otel
HOTEL €€

(📞 212 6767; www.gungorenhotel.com; Millet Sokak; s/d/tr ₺90/160/210; 🛜) The Güngören is a stalwart on the travelling circuit with smart rooms with flat-screen TVs and tiled bathroom. The staff speak some English, and the location on a quiet street is convenient. Some upper-floor rooms have not been renovated, so check when you book.

★ Hotel Cheltikov
BOUTIQUE HOTEL €€€

(📞 212 0035; www.hotelcheltikov.com; Şehit Hulusi Aytekin Caddesi 63; s/d ₺180/250; 🛜) In a sleepy residential neighbourhood 10 minutes' walk from central Kars, this boutique hotel fills a stately 19th-century building that was formerly a maternity hospital. Rooms are spacious and elegant, many with carved wooden ceilings and chandeliers. Accommodation in the 'Store Room' section at the building's front incorporate dramatic stone walls, and the bathrooms are most likely eastern Turkey's best.

Kar's Otel
BOUTIQUE HOTEL €€€

(📞 212 1616; www.karsotel.com; Halit Paşa Caddesi; s/d €99/129; ❄🛜) This eight-room boutique hotel in a 19th-century Russian mansion feels like a luxurious cocoon. The rooms are very comfortable, though some might find the pastel decor too clinical. With its contemporary furnishings and mood lighting, the licensed Italian restaurant is ideal for romantic meals, and offers some diversity to kebap-jaded palates.

🍴 Eating

Kars is noted for its excellent honey, sold in several shops along Kazım Paşa Caddesi and Halit Paşa Caddesi towards the minibus terminal. They also sell the local *kaşar peyniri* (a mild yellow cheese), *kuruyemiş* (dried fruits) and other ingredients for a picnic on the steppe.

Kars

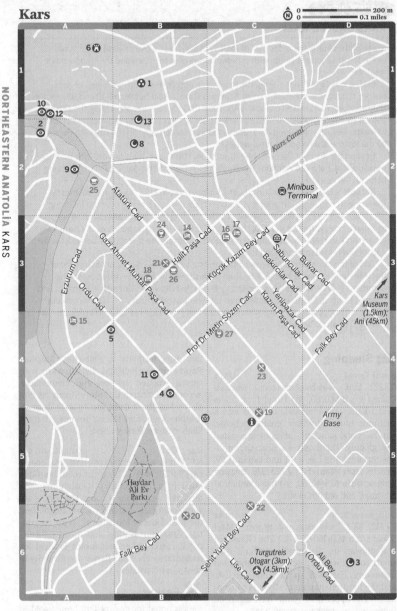

Local dishes to look out for are *piti*, a rich Caucasian-influenced lamb and chickpea stew served over shredded *lavaş* (pita bread), and *tandirda kaz* (roast duck). You'll need to order duck ahead of time. Count on around ₺45 per person.

★ **Hanimeli Kars Mutfagi**   ANATOLIAN **€€**
(www.karshanimeli.com; Faik Bey Caddesi 156; mains ₺10-15; ⊙11am-9pm) With a rustic, country-kitchen vibe, Hanimeli specialises in homestyle cooking influenced by the broader Caucasian region. Dishes include

Kars

Armemian-style *Erivan köfte* (meatballs), a silkily smooth pasta soup called *eriste aşi,* and the ravioli-like *hangel.* Roast duck is on offer, delicious Kars honey for sale, and a refreshing local drink is *reyhane* made from purple-coloured red basil.

Ocakbaşı Restoran   TURKISH €€
(📞212 0056; www.kaygisizocakbasi.com; Atatürk Caddesi 276; mains ₺10-15; 🍴) This 40-year-old favourite serves unusual Turkish dishes, such as its house specialities *ali nazık* (aubergine purée with yoghurt and beef tenderloin; ask for *et siz* for the vegetarian version) and *ejder kebap* (sesame bread stuffed with meat, cheese, parsley, nuts and eggs).

Kars Evleri   TURKISH €€
(www.karsevleri.com; Şehit Yusuf Bey Caddesi 41; mains ₺7-15) Nooks, crannies, and Turkish carpets and kilims punctuate this rambling Baltic house that's renowned for rustic homestyle cooking. A friendly family team turns out hearty renditions of local pastas, pastries and grilled fish dishes. Roast duck is ₺40 per person, and the *kahvalti* combo of cheese, honey and *kaymak* (clotted cream) for ₺9 is worth skipping your hotel breakfast for.

Kamer Mutfak
Ve Cafe   ANATOLIAN, INTERNATIONAL €€
(Halit Paşşa Caddesi 41; mains ₺10-15; 🍴✏️) Kamer offers Turkish favourites like *manti* (ravioli-like dumplings), roast duck with *pilav,* and table-covering breakfasts with local cheese and honey. International flavours include crepes, steaks and pasta, and the leafy outdoor seating is perfect for çay or coffee.

Waitstaff are friendly young women, and proceeds go to a organisation to empower women's participation in society. Good vegetarian options too.

Antik Cafe & Pastane   CAFE €€
(Gazi Ahmet Muhtar Paşa Caddesi; mains ₺8-12; 🍴) This modern, roomy cafe is a good place to recharge after walking round the centre. Cakes, baklava, *sütlaç* (rice pudding), biscuits, pizza, snacks and a breakfast buffet are offered.

🍷 Drinking & Nightlife

KarStore   CAFE
(www.karstore.com.tr; Halit Paşşa Caddesi) Breakfast and light meals are served, but the best reason to come to the KarStore is to pair Georgian wines with local cheeses, and experience regular live music during evenings. The restored Russian building is full of interesting antiques and also houses a decent gift shop with local arts and crafts.

Barış Türkü Cafe Pub   PUB, CAFE
(Atatürk Caddesi; ⏰8am-late) Housed in a historic mansion, this cafe-bar-disco attracts students of both sexes, with an energetic buzz and live music most nights. Meze, backgammon and nargiles are also available. The basement disco is the most happening place in town.

Soframız   JUICE BAR
(Prof Dr Metin Sözen Caddesi; 🍴) This fruit juice bar also does espresso coffee. Get a vitamin boost from freshly squeezed juices or an Atom smoothie.

ℹ Information

MONEY

Banks with ATMs are plentiful.

TOURIST INFORMATION

The **tourist office** (☑ 212 1705; cnr Faik Bey & Gazi Ahmet Muhtar Paşa Caddesi; ⊘ 8am-5pm Mon-Fri) has Kars and Ani maps and brochures.

ℹ Getting There & Around

Without your own transport, the best way to see Ani and the countryside around Kars is with **Celil Ersoğlu** (☑ 0532 226 3966; celilani@hotmail.com), who acts as a private driver (guiding is extra) and speaks good English. Hiring a taxi and a cooperative driver is another option.

AIR

A *servis* (₺5) runs from travel agencies to the airport, leaving 1½ hours before departures. In the opposite direction, you'll have to take a taxi (₺20 to ₺25).

Anadolu Jet (www.anadolujet.com) To/from İstanbul and Ankara.

Sun Express (www.sunexpress.com.tr) To/from İstanbul and İzmir.

Turkish Airlines (www.thy.com) To/from Ankara and İstanbul.

Kayadır Turizm (☑ 223 7035; Atatürk Caddesi 122) Sells tickets for Turkish airlines.

BUS

Kars' **otogar**, for long-distance services, is 2km southeast of the centre. *Servises* ferry passengers to/from the bus companies' city-centre offices, which are mostly on and around Faik Bey Caddesi. Major local companies include **Doğu Kars**, **İğdırlı Turizm** (☑ 0476 227 2877; www.igdirliturizm.com.tr) and **Turgutreis** (cnr Faik Bey & Atatürk Caddesis), which takes passengers to its own otogar. **Metro** (www.metroturizm.com.tr) has a daily service to Adana (₺80), Amasya (₺60), Erzurum (₺20), İstanbul (₺80), Kayseri (₺60) and Mersin (₺80).

Minibuses to local towns leave from the **minibus terminal** (Küçük Kazım Bey Caddesi). Destinations include Ardahan (₺15), Erzurum (₺20), Iğdır (₺20, for Doğubayazıt and Azerbaijan), Posof (₺30, for Georgia) and Sarıkamış (₺7), most served hourly.

Artvin and the Black Sea coast Yeşil Artvin Ekspres runs to the Black Sea with a 9.30am departure to Artvin (₺40), Hopa (₺45) for Georgia, Rize (₺50) and Trabzon (₺50).

Doğubayazıt Take a minibus to Iğdır and change.

Van Turgutreis has a daily service at 8.30am (₺50).

Yusufeli Take a bus or minibus bound for Artvin or the Black Sea coast and ask to be dropped at the junction, about 10km from Yusufeli on the Artvin–Erzurum road. Dolmuşes run from there to Yusufeli.

ℹ GETTING TO GEORGIA

At the time of writing, travellers to Georgia from Kars had the following three options, but services change regularly, and we recommend contacting Kars/Ani tour guide Celil Ersoğlu (above) for the latest.

The most straightforward option is the direct Golden Turizm bus from Kars to Tbilisi departing Kars daily at 10am. Including the border crossing, this bus takes around eight hours and costs ₺70.

A second option is to catch a minibus to Ardahan (₺15) and link up with the bus from the Özlem Ardahan company travelling from İstanbul to Tbilisi. Buses depart Ardahan travelling to Tbilisi daily at 7.30am and at 10.30am on Monday, Wednesday and Saturday. From Ardahan to Tbilisi is around seven hours and costs ₺60. In Ardahan, sleeping options include the **Hotel Huzur** (☑ 0478-211 2838; Kongre Caddesi 119; s/d ₺50/80), with poky but clean rooms across the main road from the bus station.

A third option is to catch a minibus from Kars to Posof (₺30), 17km southwest of the border at Türkgözü. You will then have to ask the driver to continue to the border (₺10) or take a taxi (₺45). After crossing the border, take a taxi to Vale (7km) and a *marshrutka* (minibus) to Akhaltsikhe, the nearest substantial town. Continue by bus to Borjomi, where you can find accommodation and onward transport to Tbilisi.

Note that minibuses from Kars to Posof run via Ardahan.

At the time of writing a new border crossing from near Çıldır Gölü in Turkey to Ahalkalaki in Georgia was scheduled to open late 2014. Contact Celil Ersoğlu in Kars for the latest information and transport details from Kars. Once this border is open it will be a quicker route from Turkey via Georgia to Armenia.

A good route to western Georgia is via Hopa on the Black Sea coast. Metro runs from here to Tbilisi, via Batumi, early in the morning.

Steer clear of the car companies in central Kars, as they don't provide proper insurance. It's possible to hire in Erzurum.

The daily Doğu Ekspresi to Ankara via Erzurum, Sivas and Kayseri departs at 9.45am.

North of Kars

Very few tourists even suspect the existence of Çıldır Gölü, but this loch-like expanse of water about 60km north of Kars offers complete peace and quiet. It's also an important breeding ground for endangered birds, best observed at Akçekale Island. Turn right at the petrol station in Doğruyol, the only significant town on the eastern shore, to see the mosque incorporating an ancient Georgian church.

A few kilometres past the town of Çıldır, on the northern shore east of Ardahan, a signpost on the right points 1km to Yıldırımtepe village. At the beginning of the village, take the left fork and follow the road around the top of Yıldırımtepe. When it ends, take the right-hand dirt track, park and walk along the hillside for about 700m for spectacular views of Şeytan Kalesi (Devil's Castle), standing sentinel on a rocky bluff in the gorge. Walk to the 6th-century Georgian castle in 45 minutes.

Driving, follow signs for Arpaçay from Kars.

South of Kars

At Ortaköy village, 45km south of Kars, a secondary road climbs 8km through an emerald-green valley, its sides flowing with mountain run-off in spring, to the clifftop village of Keçivan. The impressive remains of Keçivan's double-walled 9th-century castle straddle a ridge between two canyons.

About 25km further south of Ortaköy, 1km before the road crosses the Aras River and meets the Iğdır–Erzurum road, a brown sign opposite the petrol station points 24km to Çengilli köyü kilisesi (village church). Looming over the Kurdish mountain village is a dramatic medieval Georgian monastery with superb carving recalling the area's Armenian chucrhes. A few kilometres beyond the village is a gölü (lake) with unforgettable views over the Aras mountains.

The roads climbing to Çengilli and Keçivan are navigable in a normal car, but care should be taken and local advice sought. They may deteriorate in rainfall and are so steep (both villages are located at about 2000m) that car engines can burn out in summer. Hire-car insurance policies are unlikely to cover these minor roads.

Ani

The ruins of Ani (admission ₺8; ☺ 8.30am-6pm May-Sep, to 3pm Oct-Apr), 45km east of Kars, are an absolute must-see, even if you're not an architecture buff. Your first view is stunning: wrecks of great stone buildings adrift on a sea of undulating grass, landmarks in a ghost city that was once the stately Armenian capital and home to nearly 100,000 people, rivalling Constantinople in power and glory. The poignant ruins, the windswept plateau overlooking the Turkish–Armenian border, and the total lack of crowds make for an eerie ambience that is unforgettable. In the silence broken only by the river gurgling along the border, ponder what went before: the thriving kingdom; the solemn ceremony of the Armenian liturgy; and the travellers, merchants and nobles bustling about their business in this Silk Road entrepôt.

History

On an important east–west trade route and well served by its natural defences, Ani was selected by the Bagratid king Ashot III (r 952-77) as the site of his new capital in 961, when he moved here from Kars. Ashot's successors Smbat II (r 977-89) and Gagik I (r 990-1020) presided over Ani's continued prosperity, but internecine feuds and Byzantine encroachment later weakened the Armenian state.

The Byzantines took over in 1045, then in 1064 came the Great Seljuks from Persia, followed by the Kingdom of Georgia and, for a time, local Kurdish emirs. The struggle for the city went on until the Mongols arrived in 1239 and decisively cleared everybody else out. The nomadic Mongols had no use for city life, so cared little when the great earthquake of 1319 toppled much of Ani. The depredations of Tamerlane later that century hastened the decline; trade routes shifted, Ani lost what revenues it had managed to retain, and the city died. The earthquake-damaged hulks of its great buildings have been slowly crumbling away ever since.

⊙ Sights

Ani is entered through Arslan Kapısı. Allow at least 2½ hours to explore the area. There's a simple teahouse, but it's a good idea to bring food and water. Note some parts are off limits.

★ **Arslan Kapısı** GATE
Sturdy Arslan Kapısı (or Aslan Kapısı – Lion Gate) was supposedly named after Alp Arslan, the Seljuk sultan who conquered Ani in 1064, but probably also after the *aslan* (lion) relief on the inner wall.

★ **Church of the Redeemer** CHURCH
Near the remains of an oil press is the Church of the Redeemer (Church of St Prkitch; 1034–36). Half the structure was destroyed by lightning in 1957. The church was supposedly built to house a portion of the True Cross, brought here from Constantinople; the facade's Armenian inscriptions relay the history. The facade also sports a superb *khatchkar* (cross stone) designed on an elaborate rectangular background, about 3m above ground around the building from the path.

★ **Church of St Gregory (Tigran Honentz)** CHURCH
Below the 11th-century hamam, down by the walls separating Ani from the gorge of the Arpa Çayı, is the Church of St Gregory the Illuminator (in Turkish, Resimli Kilise – Church with Pictures). Built by a pious nobleman in 1215, it's in better condition than most buildings here. Look for the long Armenian inscription carved on the exterior walls, as well as the colourful and lively frescoes depicting scenes from the Bible and Armenian church history.

It also features well-preserved relief work, including animal motifs.

Convent of the Virgins CHURCH
(Kusanatz) Dramatically perched on the edge of the Arpa Çayı gorge, the Convent of the Virgins is unfortunately off limits. Also built by Tigran Honentz, its distinctive, serrated-domed chapel is enclosed by a defensive wall. It's clearly visible from the Menüçer Camii, but for a closer look, descend the rocky steps leading down the Silk Road into the gorge. Scant ruins of a bridge, also off limits, stand further on, right below the Menüçer Camii and visible from there.

★ **Cathedral** CHURCH
Ani's cathedral, renamed the Fethiye Camii (Victory Mosque) by the Seljuk conquerors, is the largest and most impressive building. Ani was once the seat of the Armenian Orthodox Patriarchate; the three doorways served as separate entrances for the patriarch, the king and the people. The building was transformed into a mosque whenever Muslims held Ani, but reverted to a church when the Christians took it back again. The spacious dome, once supported by four massive columns, fell down centuries ago.

Seen from a distance, the building looks quite featureless, but a closer inspection reveals eye-catching decorative elements, including several porthole windows, slender windows surrounded by elegant fretwork, several triangular niches, inscriptions in Armenian near the main entrance, and a blind arcade with slim columns running around the structure.

Continuing towards the Menüçer Camii, you'll pass an excavated area, supposed to be a former street lined with shops. Further north are the ruins of a toppled minaret, thought to have belonged to the Ebul Muhammeran Camii.

Menüçer Camii MOSQUE
With a tall octagonal, truncated minaret and six vaults, the Menüçer Camii was built by the Seljuk Turks in 1072. The blend of Armenian and Seljuk design resulted from the Seljuks employing Armenian architects and artisans. Distinctive features are the red-and-black stonework, and also the polychrome stone inlays adorning the ceilings. The minaret sports an Arabic inscription: *bismillah* ('in the name of Allah'). Climb the dingy spiral staircase inside for excellent views. There's no parapet so take care.

Nearby is an excavated area, containing remains of houses, with ovens, a granary and bathrooms. The structure next to the mosque may have been a Seljuk medrese or palace.

İç Kale FORTRESS
Across the rolling grass, southwest of the mosque, rises the monumental İç Kale (the Keep), which holds within its extensive ruins half a ruined church. Beyond İç Kale, on a pinnacle of rock above the Arpa Çayı, is the small church called the Kız Kalesi (Maiden's Castle). You'll have to look from a distance; both sites are out of bounds.

Ani

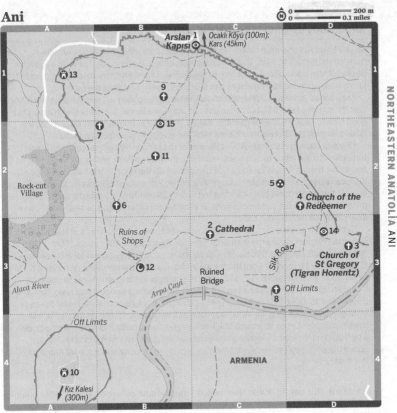

Ani

⊚ Top Sights

1 Arslan Kapısı	C1
2 Cathedral	C3
3 Church of St Gregory (Tigran Honentz)	D3
4 Church of the Redeemer	D2

⊚ Sights

5 Bezirhane (Oil Press)	C2
6 Church of St Gregory (Abughamrentz)	B2
7 Church of St Gregory (Gagik I)	B2
8 Convent of the Virgins	C3
9 Georgian Church (Gürcü Kilisesi)	B1
10 İç Kale	A4
11 Kervansaray (Church of the Holy Apostles)	B2
12 Menüçer Camii	B3
13 Seljuk Palace	A1
14 Small Hamam	D3
15 Zoroastrian Temple (Fire Temple)	B2

Church of St Gregory (Abughamrentz)
CHURCH

This rotunda-shaped church topped by a conical roof dates from about 994. It was built for the wealthy Pahlavuni family by the same architect as the Church of the Redeemer. On the 12-sided exterior, a series of deep niches are topped by scallop-shell carvings; above them, the windows of the drum are framed by a double set of blind arcades. From here you can savour the view of a rock-cut village beyond the river escarpment.

Kervansaray (Church of the Holy Apostles)
CHURCH

The Church of the Holy Apostles (Arak Elots Kilisesi) dates from 1031, but after the

DON'T MISS

ARMENIAN CHURCHES AROUND ANI

So you loved Ani and want more? No problem, there are other impressive Armenian ruins en route back to Kars. The sites have awesome settings in the middle of the steppe. Seeking them out is also a great way to see a slice of rural Anatolia: most are in muddy farmyards, surrounded by tractors and sheds and even used as cattle pens.

Kars-based guides and drivers such as Celil Ersoğlu (p560) will add the sites to an Ani visit for an extra fee. The sites can usually be accessed by car, but visiting with a local is a good idea to facilitate meetings with villagers, and handle potential pitfalls, such as ferocious farm dogs. There are no tourist facilities, so stock up on food and water.

Heading back to Kars from Ani, at the end of the second village you come to, Essen, turn left onto the reddy brown track. Head into the hills for 8km, with good views of Ani, and follow the *büyük kilisesi* (big church) signpost on the right. In the Kurdish village of Kozluca is Bagnair Monastery, consisting of two Armenian monuments. The larger church, thought to have been constructed in the 10th century, is badly damaged; the minor one, 200m across a small ravine, is in better condition, with a nice 12-sided domedrum adorned with blind arcades.

Back on the asphalt road, continue 10km towards Kars and turn right at the far end of Subatan village, opposite the memorial, towards Başgedikler. After about 15km, a signpost on the left points to Oğuzlu, 3km along a dirt track. The monumental 10th-century Oğuzlu Church rises up from the steppe and dominates the surrounding houses. It's in a bad state: an earthquake in 1936 caused the dome and other structures to collapse.

Backtrack 3km to the asphalt road, turn left at the brown signpost and head 7km past Başgedikler to Yağkesen *köyü kilise* (village church). You'll be overwhelmed by the eerie sight of Kızıl Kilise (Karmir Vank) standing on a small mound. The church is the sole towering element in an otherwise flat, treeless grassland. Outstanding features include a conical roof, V-shaped exterior niches, slender windows, an inscription in Armenian above the portal and some handsome carvings. If you're lucky, you'll see Mt Ararat in the distance.

Seljuks took the city in 1064, they added a gateway with a fine dome and used the building as a caravanserai – hence its name.

It's fairly well preserved, with decorative carvings, porthole windows, diagonally intersecting arches in the nave, and ceilings sporting geometric patterns made of polychromatic stone inlays. Look also for the various Armenian inscriptions and *khatchkar* carved on a rectangular background.

Zoroastrian Temple (Fire Temple) TEMPLE

This ruined temple is thought to have been built between the early 1st century and the first half of the 4th century AD. It might have been converted into a Christian chapel afterwards. The only remains consist of four circular columns, not exceeding 1.5m in height. They lie between the Kervansaray and the Georgian Church, about 100m north of the former.

Church of St Gregory (Gagik I) CHURCH

Northwest of the Kervansaray, this gigantic church was begun in 998 to plans by the same architect as Ani's cathedral. Its ambi-

tious dome collapsed shortly after completion, and the rest of the building is now also ruined. You can still see the outer walls and a jumble of columns.

Seljuk Palace PALACE

Beyond the Church of St Gregory (Gagik I) is a Seljuk palace built into the city's defensive walls – and so painstakingly over-restored that it looks quite out of place.

Georgian Church (Gürcü Kilisesi) CHURCH

You can't miss the only surviving wall of this Georgian Church, probably erected in the 13th century. It used to be a large building, but most of the south wall collapsed around 1840. Of the three remaining arcades, two sport bas-reliefs, one representing the Annunciation, the other the Visitation.

ⓘ Getting There & Away

The easiest option for Ani is a taxi minibus to the site (50 minutes), organised by Celil Ersoğlu (p560) or the Kars tourist office. One person will pay roughly ₺140, two pay ₺70 each, three pay ₺50 each and four to six pay ₺35 each. If there are other travellers around, you'll share the ride and the expense. This includes 2½ hours' waiting time. If you hire a taxi, make sure your driver understands that you want at least 2½ hours (preferably three) at Ani.

Sarıkamış

The town and ski resort of Sarıkamış, 55km southwest of Kars, has deep, dry powder and terrain for skiers and snowboarders. There are also cross-country options. It's more low-key and family-oriented than Palandöken, and also less windy. The slopes are also more scenic, with vast expanses of Scotch pines. The ski season runs from November to early April, and unlike Palandöken, Sarıkamış can also be enjoyed in summer with a good network of hiking trails.

Infrastructure comprises three chairlifts climbing to 2650m, and nine ski runs (three beginner, three intermediate and three advanced), between 1750m and 3500m long. Rental equipment is available at the hotels (about ₺50 per day) and lift passes are usually included in winter rates.

At the resort, 3km from Sarıkamış centre, the best option is the **Çamkar Hotel** (⌕0474-413 5259; www.camkarotel.com; summer per person ₺70, winter full board per person ₺110-190; @⌗) with restaurants, hamam and bar.

In town, **Güleryurt Lokantası** (mains ₺8-12; ⊙8am-9pm) is the best spot for soups, salads, çiğ köfte and kebaps.

Regular minibuses run to/from Kars (₺7, 45 minutes). From Sarıkamış, take a taxi to the resort (₺15). In winter, shuttles link the resort and Kars airport.

Leaving town on the old Erzurum road, Czar Nicholas II's hunting lodge is visible on the hillside on the left as you cross the railway lines. Built during the Russian occupation of Kars, the derelict stone-and-wood building was later used as an Ottoman barracks.

Kars to Doğubayazıt

The quickest route from Kars to Doğubayazıt (about 240km) takes you along the Armenian frontier and past Mt Ararat – via Digor, Tuzluca and Iğdır.

You may have to change bus or minibus in Iğdır. In central Iğdır, the friendly **Gökçe Restaurant** (Evrenpaşa Caddesi Dörtyol Mevkii; mains ₺10-12; ⊙7am-9pm) serves kebaps, pide and hazır yemek in modern surrounds.

If you get stuck in Iğdır, accommodation is available near Gökçe at the two-star **Otel Olimpia** (⌕0476 227 1866; Evrenpaşa Caddesi Dörtyol Mevkii 13; s/d/tr ₺70/120/160). It's clean, pleasantly decorated and slightly less decrepit than Iğdır's other hotels.

Bus companies serving numerous destinations have offices on the main drag around Otel Olimpia. The otogar is 1km north of the centre, off the Kars road; from the south, turn left at the roundabout with the bird statues. Pick up regular minibuses to Kars (₺25, three hours) and Doğubayazıt (₺7, 45 minutes) from here or along the main drag in the centre.

Doğubayazıt

⌕0472 / POP 73,505 / ELEV 1950M

Doğubayazıt's setting is superb. On one side, the talismanic Mt Ararat (Ağrı Dağı, 5137m), Turkey's highest mountain, hovers majestically over the horizon. On the other side, İshak Paşa Palace, a breathtakingly beautiful fortress-palace-mosque complex, surveys town from its rocky perch. The town itself doesn't have many obvious attractions, but it's an obvious base for climbing Mt Ararat and exploring a few nearby sights. Nicknamed 'doggy biscuit' by travellers on the hippie trail, it's a friendly place with an appealing sense of border-town wildness. Coming from Erzurum or Kars, you'll quickly notice the distinct atmosphere here. Predominantly Kurdish, Doğubayazıt prides itself on its strong Kurdish heritage, which is celebrated at the **Kültür Sanat ve Turizm Festivalı** (Culture and Arts Festival). Held in June or July, the summer festival allows you to immerse yourself in Kurdish heritage through music, dance and theatre performances. Locals gather to watch outdoor concerts and Doğubayazıt's çay evis (teahouses) fill.

◉ Sights & Activities

İshak Paşa Palace   PALACE
(İshak Paşa Sarayı; admission ₺5; ⊙8am-7pm) Located 6km southeast of town, İshak Paşa Palace is perched on a small plateau abutting stark cliffs. Combining Seljuk, Ottoman, Georgian, Persian and Armenian architecture, the palace was begun in 1685 and completed in 1784. Minibuses (₺1.50) rattle between the centre and the palace. Taxis charge about ₺15 to ₺20 one way; ₺25 to ₺30 return, including

Doğubayazıt

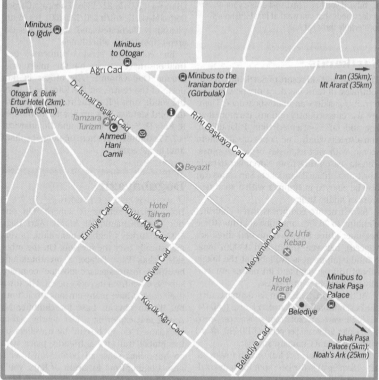

Minibus to Iğdır

Minibus to Otogar

Ağrı Cad

Minibus to the Iranian border (Gürbulak)

Iran (35km); Mt Ararat (35km)

Otogar & Butik Ertur Hotel (2km); Diyadin (50km)

Dr İsmail Beşikçi Cad

Tamzara Turizm

Ahmedi Hani Camii

Rıfkı Başkaya Cad

Beyazit

Hotel Tahran

Emniyet Cad

Büyük Ağrı Cad

Güven Cad

Küçük Ağrı Cad

Meryemana Cad

Öz Urfa Kebap

Hotel Ararat

Belediye Cad

Belediye

Minibus to İshak Paşa Palace

İshak Paşa Palace (5km); Noah's Ark (25km)

---

a one-hour wait. The protective glass roofing means you can visit on a rainy day.

The palace's elaborate main entrance leads into the first courtyard, which would have been open to merchants and guests.

Only family and special guests would have been allowed into the second courtyard, where you can see the entrance to the *haremlik* (family/women's quarters), *selamlık* (public/men's quarters), guards' lodgings and granaries. An elaborate tomb is richly decorated with a mix of Seljuk carvings and Persian relief styles. Steps lead down to the sarcophagi.

From the second courtyard, pass through the marvellously decorated portal of the *haremlik* into the palace living quarters. The highlight here is undoubtedly the beautiful dining room, a melange of styles with walls topped by Seljuk triangular stonework, Armenian floral-relief decoration, ornate column capitals showing Georgian

influence, and both black and white stone incorporated. There's a hamam and rooms with stone-carved fireplaces and windows surveying Doğubayazıt.

Returning to the second courtyard, climb a staircase to the *selamlık*. Entry is via the stately hall where guests would have been greeted before being entertained in the ceremonial hall-courtyard to the right. The *selamlık* also has a library, terrace and lovely mosque, which has kept much of its original relief decoration (note the life tree) and ceiling frescoes.

Across the valley from the palace are the ruined foundations of Eski Beyazıt (Old Beyazıt), probably founded in Urartian times c 800 BC. You can also spot a mosque, tomb and ruined fortress, which may date from Urartian times (13th to 7th centuries BC). The peaks above the car park here have excellent views of the palace with Doğubayazıt and Mt Ararat beyond.

📖 Sleeping

Good, reliable accommodation options are scarce. Women travellers are advised to stick to the following.

Hotel Tahran
HOTEL €

(☑312 0195; www.hoteltahran.com; Büyük Ağrı Caddesi 124; s/d/tr ₺35/60/80; ☎) The well-managed Tahran exudes mellow vibes. Although small and old, rooms have crisp white sheets, and the top-floor kitchen and dining room have glimpses of Mt Ararat and İshak Paşa Palace. There's a laundry service, book exchange, and reception with inviting chairs and offers of çay. Affable, English-speaking manager Bilal is clued up on subjects such as getting to Iran.

Hotel Ararat
HOTEL €

(☑312 4988; www.hotelararatturkey.com; Belediye Caddesi 16; s/d ₺40/70; ☎) Beyond Ararat's grand marbled reception, the comfortable lilac rooms have features including fridge, satellite TV and phone. Some have balconies with views of the hotel's namesake, and there's an outdoor terrace for breakfast in summer.

Murat Camping
CAMPING GROUND €

(☑0542 437 3699; www.muratcamping.com; İshakpaşa Yolu; campsite/campervan ₺10/15, dm ₺30, s & d ₺80; ☎) Located right beneath İshak Paşa Palace, Murat offers camping, campervan parking, and simple rooms and dorms. Trekking and mountaineering advice and expeditions are available, and there's a decent restaurant with Ararat views. Future plans include some private bungalows.

Butik Ertur Hotel
HOTEL €€

(☑312 7866; www.butikerturhotel.com; Güburlak Çevreyolu Üzeri; s/d ₺100/160) 'Butik (boutique)' is stretching it, but this recently refurbished hotel near the otogar is the most comfortable place in town. Bathrooms are spacious and spotless, and the licensed restaurant downstairs is a good spot for a beer and decent food. Kurdish weddings are sometimes held in an adjacent reception hall, and curious hotel guests are usually welcome to join the fun.

🍴 Eating & Drinking

Öz Urfa Kebap
KEBAP €€

(Dr İsmail Beşikçi Caddesi; mains ₺0-12) With its attractive, wood-panelled dining room reached up steep stairs, Öz Urfa is popular locally. The lamb kebap and frothy *ayran* are recommended.

Beyazit
ANATOLIAN €€

(Dr İsmail Beşikçi Caddesi; mains ₺8-13) Look for the big colourful photos of Doğubayazıt's two most famous attractions – Ararat and İshak Paşa Palace – and ascend to the second floor for good main drag views. Beyazit's combo of pide, kebaps and local dishes is popular with families.

ℹ️ Information

Banks in the centre have ATMs and there are also moneychangers if you're Iran-bound. Travel agencies can organise day trips.

English is spoken at the **Tourist Information Office** (Rıfkı Başkaya Caddesi; ⊙7.30am-12.30pm & 1.30-4.30pm Mon-Fri) where there's a good selection of maps and brochures.

ℹ️ Getting There & Around

The otogar is 2km west of town on the D100 to Ağrı. Minibuses to/from the hospital link with the centre (₺1). For long-distance destinations, travel via Erzurum (₺25, four hours, 285km).

Kars Take a minibus to Iğdır and change.

Van Minibuses leave the otogar at approximately 6.30am, 9am, noon and 2pm daily, with an extra summer service at 4pm (₺18, three hours, 185km).

Minibuses to Iğdır and Gürbulak (for Iran) leave from separate stops in central Doğubayazıt.

Iğdır Minibuses leave every 30 minutes (₺7, 45 minutes).

Iran Minibuses run to the Iranian border (Gürbulak, ₺7, 30 minutes). Get going before 10am, when many people travel to the border; after that you will have to wait longer for vehicles to fill up.

If you're flying into Iğdır or Ağrı, Turkish Airlines run minibuses (₺15) to Doğubayazıt.

> **ℹ️ GETTING TO AZERBAIJAN**
>
> From Iğdır, **Iğdırlı Turizm** (www.igdirliturizm.com.tr) has direct daily services east to the Azerbaijani enclave of Nakhichevan (₺15, 3½ hours). The company has a few offices in Iğdır town centre on the main drag. Note that you need a visa (there's an Azerbaijani consulate in Kars). To get to Baku from Nakhichevan, which is cut off from the rest of Azerbaijan by Armenia, you'll have to fly.

NORTHEASTERN ANATOLIA DOĞUBAYAZIT

Around Doğubayazıt

Travel agencies and hotels in Doğubayazıt can help organise an excursion to nearby sights. Half-day tours cost about ₺80 per person; if there are a few of you, a taxi is a cheaper option (about ₺150).

Ask your driver to take the scenic back road (less advisable after heavy rains) through the hills from İshak Paşa Palace to Noah's Ark (Nu'hun Gemisi). The elongated oval mound on a hillside is one of half a dozen possible ark sites around Mt Ararat. It's also signposted to the south of the D100, 20km from Doğubayazıt en route to the Iranian border.

Turn left (northeast) at the border and follow the signpost to reach the meteor crater *(meteor çukuru)*, supposedly dating to 1892. The site is right on the border (the village you can see from here is in Iran), so someone in your vehicle will need to leave their passport or ID at the military check point en route.

Further afield are villages at the base of Mt Ararat and Diyadin Hot Springs, west of Doğubayazıt. There are day walks around Mt Ararat and in the hills above Doğubayazıt.

Mt Ararat (Ağrı Dağı)

A highlight of any trip to eastern Turkey, the twin peaks of Mt Ararat have figured in legends since time began, most notably as the supposed resting place of Noah's Ark. The left-hand peak, called Büyük Ağrı (Great Ararat), is 5137m high, while Küçük Ağrı (Little Ararat) rises to about 3895m.

Climbing Mt Ararat

For many years permission to climb Ararat was routinely refused because of security concerns, but this fantastic summit is now accessible, albeit with restrictions.

A permit and guide are mandatory. Permits (US$50) are issued in Ağrı or Iğdır and the process takes up to two weeks. Apply in advance through reputable travel agencies listed here. The paperwork may be included in the overall price. Tamzara Turizm shows the information required for applications on its website (click on Climbing Permit). You need a permit to get past military posts on the approaches to the mountain and for your own safety – to ensure help will be on

YENI HAMAM

To rejuvenate tired and sore muscles after conquering Mt Ararat, Doğubayazıt's Yeni Hamam (Şehit Mehmet Özer Caddesi; admission ₺8; ☉men 6am-midnight, women 7am-6pm), southwest of the centre, comes recommended by trekking guides and locals alike. It's well run and as clean as a whistle. Go for a private massage (₺20); women enjoy the Turkish coffee massage.

hand if something goes wrong on the climb. People have died on the mountain; in 2010, Scotsman Donald Mackenzie went missing while searching for Noah's Ark.

If unofficial guides, hotel staff and touts in Doğubayazıt tell you they can get the permit quickly and cut costs: *don't* believe them. There's probably some bribery involved or, even worse, they will let you think they've obtained the permit but in reality will be taking you up Ararat unofficially. This scam has landed hikers in prison. Follow the official procedure, even if you have to endure the slow-turning wheels of bureaucracy, and ask for evidence that the permit has been granted.

Prices vary between agency and package, and drop for larger groups. Shop around, check what's included and consider joining a group if there are just one or two people in your party. Typically, agencies charge about €500 per person to lead a four-person group on a four- to five-day trek from Doğubayazıt, including guides, camping and food. Most reputable agencies recommend five-day treks in order to facilitate acclimatisation before tackling the summit.

Despite the costs involved, climbing Ararat is a fantastic experience. Expect stupendous views and stunning landscapes. The best weather for walking is between mid-June and mid-September; views are best in July and August. You'll need to be comfortable with snow-climbing techniques using crampons past 4800m, even in the height of summer.

A possible route is the southern one, starting from Eliköyü, an abandoned village in the foothills, at about 2200m. There's another route starting from the village of Çevirme (2250m). The first camp site is at 3200m, and the second one at 4200m.

You can also do one- and two-day treks around the mountain, including the Fish Lake walk. Provided you stay under 2500m you won't have to go through as much official hoo-ha, but it's still best to go with a local guide; risks include ferocious shepherd dogs. Expect to pay around €150 per person.

Another option is to hike through the hills around Doğubayazıt, on sections of the Silk Road between İshak Paşa Palace and Iran.

Guides

Cappadocia-based nationwide trekking specialist Middle Earth Travel (p544) is also worth considering.

East Turkey Expeditions   HIKING
(☑ 055 1111 8998; zaferonay@hotmail.com) Zafer Onay (who also covers the Kaçkars) is knowledgeable and English-speaking.

Tamzara Turizm   HIKING
(☑ 0544 555 3582; www.mtararattour.com; off Dr İsmail Beşikçi Caddesi) Based in Doğubayazıt, Tamzara is run by English-speaking Mustafa Arsin. The website is a useful source of information. Also offers walk-and-ski tours.

Mount Ararat Trek   HIKING
(☑ 0537 502 6683; www.mountararattrek.com) Run by American Amy Beam and a local team. The website is a useful source of information. Also offers walk-and-ski tours.

Southeastern Anatolia

Best Places to Eat

➡ Orkide (p576)

➡ Şirvan (p576)

➡ Diyarbakır Kahvaltı Evi
(p599)

➡ Seyr-İ-Mardin (p604)

➡ Sütçü Fevzi & Sütçü Kenan
(p614)

Best Places to Stay

➡ Asude Konak (p575)

➡ Nomad Tours Village
Homestays (p582)

➡ Dara Konağı (p603)

➡ Kasr-ı Nehroz (p606)

➡ Hacı Abdullah Bey Konağı
(p606)

Why Go?

Southeastern Anatolia is a unique part of Turkey, and apart from small Arabic and Christian pockets, this expansive region is predominantly Kurdish and extremely welcoming to visitors. Choose from a menu of historical cities, including Mardin, on a hill dominating Mesopotamia; Şanlıurfa, swathed in historical mystique and featuring the incredible temple of Göbekli Tepe; the old city of Diyarbakır, ensnared in mighty basalt walls; and the endangered honey-coloured riverside town of Hasankeyf. Move on to Nemrut Dağı (Mt Nemrut), topped with colossal ancient statues, or shimmering Lake Van, edged with snowcapped mountains. Wonderfully isolated spots include Darende and the perfect hilltop village of Savur, while Gaziantep is a must-visit destination for its astounding mosaics and superb local food. A few places could be off limits to foreigners when you visit – mainly near the borders with Iraq and Syria – but most of southeastern Anatolia is safe and accessible to independent travellers.

When to Go

Gaziantep

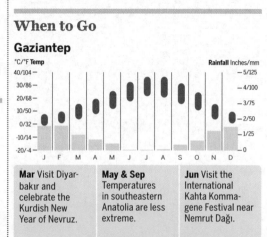

Mar Visit Diyarbakır and celebrate the Kurdish New Year of Nevruz.

May & Sep Temperatures in southeastern Anatolia are less extreme.

Jun Visit the International Kahta Kommagene Festival near Nemrut Dağı.

Gaziantep (Antep)

📞 0342 / POP 1.54 MILLION

There's one Turkish word you should learn before visiting Gaziantep: *fıstık* (pistachio). This fast-paced and epicurean city has around 180 pastry shops producing the world's best pistachio baklava. Other culinary treats are also on offer for adventurous foodie travellers.

With the biggest city park this side of the Euphrates and a buzzing cafe culture, Gaziantep oozes panache and self-confidence. It also has one astounding attraction definitely worth travelling across Turkey for: the superb Gaziantep Zeugma Mosaic Museum.

The older parts of the city are being reinvigorated, and the fortress, bazaars, caravanserai and old stone houses have been lovingly restored.

History

By the time the Arabs conquered the town in 638, the Persians, Alexander the Great, the Romans and the Byzantines had all left their imprints on Aintab (as Gaziantep was formerly known). The region remained politically unstable until the Seljuk Turks arrived from the east around 1070.

Aintab remained a city of Seljuk culture, ruled by petty Turkish lords, until the coming of the Ottomans under Selim the Grim in 1516.

During the Ottoman period, Aintab had a sizeable Christian population, including a large proportion of Armenians. Armenian churches and mansions punctuate the city's historical core.

In 1920, as the victorious Allies sought to carve up the Ottoman territories, Aintab was besieged by French forces intent on adding Turkish lands to their holdings in Syria and Lebanon. Aintab's fierce nationalist defenders finally surrendered on 8 February 1921. The epithet 'Gazi' (War Hero) was added to Antep in 1973, commemorating their tenacious defence.

With its proximity to Syria, Gaziantep has recently become a haven for refugees fleeing the conflict across the border, and the area around İnönü Caddesi's western end has developed as a 'Little Aleppo'. In August 2014, it was estimated that around 10% of Gaziantep's total population were Syrian refugees, and this influx has had a major impact on housing and employment in the city.

◉ Sights & Activities

The tourist office (p577) has the *Gaziantep Tarih ve Kültür Yolu* (Gaziantep History & Culture Road) brochure detailing 40 sights. Gaziantep is also promoting itself as a 'museum city'; recent openings include a war museum and an Atatürk museum. Ask at the tourist office.

★ Gaziantep Zeugma Mosaic Museum   MUSEUM

(www.gaziantepmuzesi.gov.tr; Sehitkamil Caddesi; admission ₺10; ⊙ 8.30am-5.30pm Tue-Sun) This modern museum showcases superb mosaics unearthed at the Roman site of Belkıs-Zeugma before the Birecik Dam flooded most of the site forever. The 2nd floor has excellent views of virtually complete floor mosaics retrieved from Roman villas, providing a detailed insight into past centuries. Other incredibly well-preserved highlights include the poignant *Gypsy Girl* and the *Birth of Venus* mosaics, and modern interactive technology also brings history to life in a compelling way.

To find the museum, follow the underpass on the left of the train station, continue under the busy main highway, turn right, and then continue on for another 400m. A taxi from central Gaziantep should be around ₺10.

★ Kale   FORTRESS

(Citadel; ⊙ 8.30am-5.30pm) **FREE** Thought to have been constructed by the Romans, the citadel was restored by Emperor Justinian in the 6th century AD, and rebuilt extensively by the Seljuks in the 12th and 13th centuries. The interior of the castle contains the Gaziantep Defence and Heroism Panoramic Museum (admission ₺1; ⊙ 8.30am-5.30pm), a tribute to the fighters who bravely defended the city against the French in 1920.

Gaziantep Museum   MUSEUM

(İstasyon Caddesi; admission ₺3; ⊙ 8.30am-noon & 1-5pm Tue-Sun) This museum previously housed the city's astounding collection of mosaics. Following their relocation to the Gaziantep Zeugma Mosaic Museum, this location now focuses on ancient seals, and Hittite carvings and sculpture.

★ Bakircilar Çarşisi   MARKET

Gaziantep's labyrinthine bazaar includes the Zincirli Bedesten (Coppersmiths' Market), now restored and full of metalworkers and shoemakers. Excellent food markets include

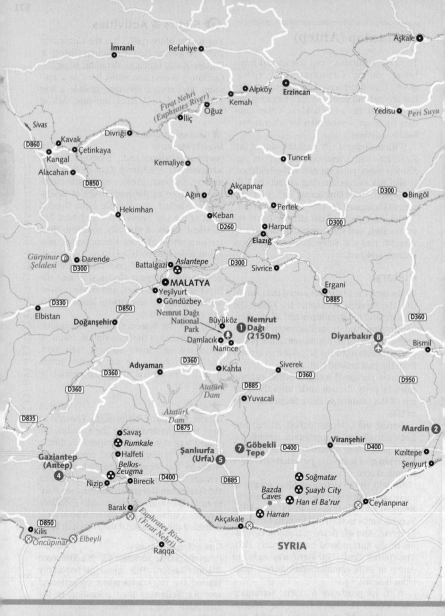

Southeastern Anatolia Highlights

1 Feel elation while watching the sun set (or rise) from **Nemrut Dağı** (p587), the 'thrones of gods'.

2 Go heritage-hunting among the historic buildings and honey-coloured stone houses of pretty **Mardin** (p601).

3 Bliss out by a gushing river in the perfect valley-village seclusion of **Savur** (p605).

4 Fall in love with the *Gypsy Girl* and feast on culinary delights in **Gaziantep** (p571).

5 Nourish your soul in the great pilgrimage city of **Şanlıurfa** (p578).

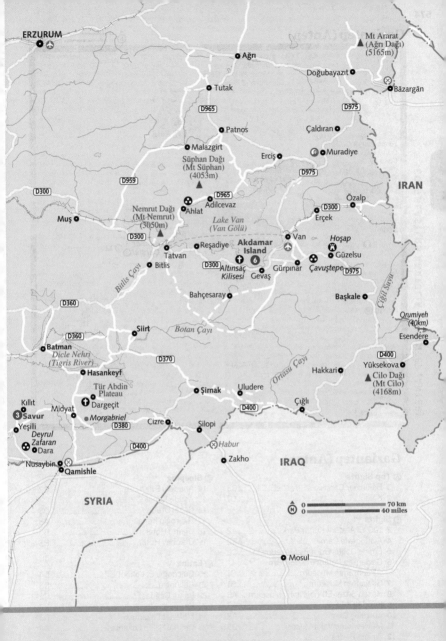

ERZURUM

Mt Ararat
(Ağrı Dağı)
(5165m)

Ağrı

Doğubayazıt

Bāzargān

Tutak

D965

D975

Patnos

Çaldıran

Malazgirt

Erciş

Muradiye

Süphan Dağı
(Mt Süphan)
(4053m)

D959

IRAN

D975

Özalp

Nemrut Dağı
(Mt Nemrut)
(3050m)

D965

Adilcevaz

D300

Erçek

Ahlat

Lake Van
(Van Gölü)

D300

Muş

Van

Hoşap

Reşadiye

Akdamar
Island

Güzelsu

Tatvan

Altınsaç
Kilisesi

Güvpınar

Çavuştepe

Bitlis

Gevaş

D975

D300

Bahçesaray

Başkale

Çiğli Suyu

D360

Siirt

Botan Çayı

Orumiyeh
(40km)

D360

Esendere

Batman

Dicle Nehri
(Tigris River)

D370

Ortasu Çayı

Hakkari

D400

Yüksekova

Hasankeyf

Cilo Dağı
(Mt Cilo)
(4168m)

Tür Abdin
Plateau

Şırnak

Uludere

Kıllıt

Midyat

Dargeçit

Çığlı

Savur

Morgabriel

Cizre

Silopi

D400

Yeşilli

Deyrul
Zafaran

Dara

D380

Habur

Nusaybin

Qamishle

Zakho

IRAQ

SYRIA

Mosul

0   70 km
0   40 miles

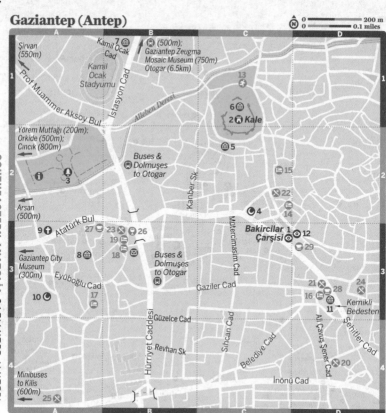

Gaziantep (Antep)

Gaziantep (Antep)

mini-mountains of spices and graceful garlands of dried chillies. South of the Zincirli Bedesten, in the **Elmacı Pazarı** area, is the original Güllüoğlu (p576) baklava shop.

The nearby **Tahmis Kahvesi** (Buğdaypazarı Sokak; ◷10am-10pm) is Gaziantep's most atmospheric *kahvehane* (coffeehouse).

Gaziantep City Museum
MUSEUM

(Gaziantep Kent Müzesi; Atatürk Bulvarı; admission ₺1; ◷8am-5pm) Interactive displays and foreign-language audioguides showcase the story of baklava and Gaziantep's history of shoemaking. Relax with a tea, coffee or cold beer in the Bayazhan's courtyard cafes. There's also occasional live music, and stalls selling local crafts.

Emine Göğüş Culinary Museum
MUSEUM

(Köprübaşı Sokak; admission ₺1; ◷8am-5pm) This interesting museum provides both information and inspiration for exploring Gaziantep's terrific eateries. English-language translations are key ingredients in the museum's successful recipe of explaining what dishes to try in local restaurants.

Hasan Süzer Ethnography Museum
MUSEUM

(Hanefioğlu Sokak; admission ₺3; ◷8am-5pm) This restored 200-year-old stone house features a central *hayat* (courtyard) patterned with light and dark stones. Rooms on the ground floor were for service; those on the 1st floor made up the *selamlık* (quarters for male family members and their visitors); and those on the 2nd floor were the *haremlik* (for female family members and their visitors).

Kurtuluş Camii
MOSQUE

Initially constructed as a cathedral in 1892, this impressive building features alternating black-and-white stone banding. Restoration work was scheduled to finish in late 2015.

Also worth seeking out is **Alaüddevle Camii** near the Zincirli Bedesten. For other recently restored mosques, see the tourist office's *Gaziantep History & Culture Road* brochure.

Kendirli Kilisesi
CHURCH

(Atatürk Bulvarı) Wedged between modern buildings, this church was constructed by French priests with the help of Napoleon III in 1860. A closer inspection of the building reveals eye-catching black-and-white medallions.

Mevlevihane Vakıf Müzesi
MUSEUM

(Tekke Camii Yanı; ◷9am-5pm Tue-Sun) FREE This museum focuses on the Mevlevi Sufis (a dervish order) and features artworks, kilims (woven rugs), manuscripts, and clothing worn by the Mevlevi.

100 Yıl Atatürk Kültür Parkı
PARK

This central park is a green haven for nature lovers, families and courting 20-somethings. There are also a couple of good places for a relaxed sunset beer.

Naib Hamami
HAMAM

(Kale Arası; spa & massage ₺30; ◷women 9.30am-5pm, men 6pm-midnight) An elegant restored hamam north of the citadel.

🛏 Sleeping

Hotel prices can be high compared with other eastern Turkish cities, but Gaziantep has good boutique hotels.

Güzel Otel
HOTEL €

(☑221 3216; Gaziler Caddesi 7; s/d ₺35/60; ❄🛜) A convenient location near the market, and clean rooms make this one of Gaziantep's best-value budget hotels.

Utkubey Hotel
HOTEL €€

(☑222 0349; www.velichotelleri.com; Teyfik Uygunlar Sokak; s/d ₺80/120; ❄🛜) This friendly spot has recently refurbished rooms and a quiet location in a sleepy lane near the city's main drag. Rooms are relatively compact, but some have castle views, and some floors are non-smoking – a rarity in eastern Turkey.

Uğurlu Hotel
HOTEL €€

(☑220 9690; Teyfik Uygunlar Sokak; s/d ₺60/100; ❄🛜) Simple but clean rooms in a quiet, but central, backstreet filled with other good-value accommodation.

Hıdıroğlu Konak
BOUTIQUE HOTEL €€

(☑230 4555; www.hidiroglukonak.com; Hıdır Sokak 19; r ₺130-200; ❄🛜) Six rooms fill a restored century-old mansion in Gaziantep's former Armenian neighbourhood. Vaulted wooden ceilings and antique furniture instil a heritage ambience, and the stone construction and spacious courtyard is a cooling haven during a Gaziantep summer.

★ Asude Konak
BOUTIQUE HOTEL €€€

(☑0532 577 8792, 230 4104; www.asudekonak.com; Arkası Millet Sokak 20; s €35-45, d €70-85; ❄@🛜) You'll feel like you're staying with friends or family at this lovingly restored courtyard house. Meals are prepared by host

GAZİANTEP FOR THE SWEET TOOTH

For baklava devotees, Gaziantep is Shangri-la. The city is reckoned to produce the best *fıstıklı* (pistachio) baklava in Turkey, if not in the world. Served ultrafresh, they're impossible to beat, and some baklava shops have reached cult status, such as Güllüoğlu (Elmacı Pazarı; snacks from ₺3; ☉8am-6pm), and the talismanic İmam Çağdaş, established in 1887.

Jale Özaslan, and can include gossamer-light *katmer* (flatbread layered with nuts and clotted cream) for breakfast, and the local speciality of *yuvarlama* (soup made with rice, meat, chickpeas and yoghurt) for dinner. Evening meals are often lingering alfresco affairs.

Anadolu Evleri
BOUTIQUE HOTEL €€€
(☎220 9525; www.anadoluevleri.com; Köroğlu Sokak; s/d €60/100, 1-/2-person ste €95/130; ❀@☎) In this restored stone mansion, local tradition is celebrated with a beguiling courtyard, beamed or painted ceilings, mosaic floors, secret passageways, and antique furniture and artefacts. It's near the bustling bazaar and good restaurants, yet still feels quiet and restful behind its historic, storied walls.

✖ Eating

Available at the tourist office, the *Gaziantep Mutfağı* (Gaziantep Cuisine) booklet describes the city's iconic dishes.

Katmerci Murat
BAKERY €
(Atatürk Bulvarı 11; katmer ₺10; ☉7am-3pm) The best entertainment of your day could be watching the graceful actions of Murat's head pastry chef as he transforms a compact ball of dough into a plate of feather-light *katmer*, a delicious baked confection combining clotted cream, chopped nuts, and delicate green pistachios.

Orijinal Halep Lokantası
MIDDLE EASTERN €
(Kozalnı Cami Sokak; snacks & mains ₺6-10) In Gaziantep's emerging 'Little Aleppo' neighbourhood, this simple restaurant serves *fatteh* (flatbread), felafel and hummus, and is also a bustling hub for journalists, NGOs and Syrian opposition activists.

★ Orkide
BAKERY €
(www.orkidepastanesi.com; Gazimuhtarpaşa Bulvarı 17; cakes ₺4-6) Renowned as the city's finest *pastane* (patisserie), Orkide also serves the best brunch (₺30) in town. Look forward to *katmer*, local cheeses, jams, honey and salads, all partnered with warm and fluffy flatbread. Turn north along Gazimuhtarpaşa Bulvarı 400m west of the tourist office.

İmam Çağdaş
TURKISH €€
(Kale Civarı Uzun Çarşı; mains ₺10-20; ☉10am-10pm) The Çağdaş family's pistachio baklava is delivered daily to customers throughout Turkey. The secret of their success is fresh, carefully chosen ingredients; also good are the creamy, chargrilled aubergine (eggplant) flavours of the *ali nazik* kebap. The restaurant is popular with Turkish tourists.

Yörem Mutfağı
ANATOLIAN €€
(Sokak 15; mains ₺10-15; ☉11am-9pm) The good-value homestyle lunches here are a pick-and-point affair – the dishes change daily – while dinner is more formal with a wider range. Look for the AK Parti sign on the street skirting the northern edge of the Atatürk Kültür Parkı, and turn right down the street before the sign.

Çulcuoğlu Et Lokantası
TURKISH €€
(Kalender Sokak; mains ₺8-18; ☉11am-2pm & 5-9pm) Çulcuoğlu's lamb kebaps and grilled chicken are both great. Don't be fooled by the unremarkable entrance, as there's a dining area at the back. It's tucked away down a narrow side street about 20m from a little mosque called Nur Ali.

Metanet Lokantası
TURKISH €€
(Kozluca Camii Yanı; mains ₺11-18; ☉8am-8pm) Tucked away near Kozluca Camii, Metanet is a top place to try *beyran*, a popular breakfast and lunch dish combining soup, rice and slowly-cooked *tandir* (clay-oven) meat. Arrive early to avoid missing out.

★ Şirvan
KEBAP €€€
(Ali Fuat Cebesoy Bulvarı; mains ₺16-22; ☉11am-10pm) Lauded as home of the city's finest kebaps, Şirvan is definitely worth the short taxi ride from central Gaziantep for seasonal specialities such as kebaps with *keme mantari* (local truffles), or *Malta eriği* (loquats). Zingy salads, house-made *ayran* (salted yoghurt drink), and superlative baklava are other reasons to seek out Şirvan.

Drinking & Nightlife

★Papirüs Cafeteria CAFE
(Noter Sokak; ⊙10am-10pm) A student crowd gathers in this historic Armenian mansion off Atatürk Bulvarı; you'll find them swapping phone numbers in the leafy courtyard. Don't miss the historic, delicately faded frescoes upstairs.

Adana Şalgamacısı – Gürbüz Usta JUICE BAR
(Hürriyet Caddesi; juices from ₺2; ⊙8:30am-11pm) Fuel on freshly squeezed juices, or try the delicious 'atom shake' combining milk, honey, banana, hazelnuts and pistachios.

Cıncık BAR, RESTAURANT
(Atatürk Kültür Parkı; ⊙noon-11pm) Cıncık's grills, meze and salads are good, and there's also a relaxed garden with Antep folk kicking back with draught Efes beer and the occasional nargile (water pipe). It's a shortish stroll through Atatürk Kültür Parkı from the city centre.

Tütün Hanı TEA GARDEN
(Eski Saray Caddesi Yanı; ⊙8.30am-11pm) In the restored Tütün Hanı, this teahouse is a great place for tea and nargile. Turkish tourists love the rugs, low wooden tables and cushions, and there's live music from 7.30pm to 11pm on Friday and Saturday nights. Good luck choosing between more than 40 nargile flavours.

ℹ Information

The post office and ATMs are around the main square.

Arsan (☏220 6464; www.arsan.com.tr; Nolu Sokak; ⊙8am-7pm) Various tours (from €45 per person), including the 'Magical Triangle'

(Birecik, Halfeti/Rumkale, Belkıs-Zeugma). Car rental is available for more flexible exploration.

Tourist Office (☏230 5969; www.gaziantep city.info; 100 Yıl Atatürk Kültür Parkı İçi; ⊙8am-noon & 1-5pm Mon-Fri) In a black and grey building in the city park. English and German spoken; and city maps and brochures provided.

ℹ Getting There & Away

AIR

Gaziantep's Oğuzeli airport is 20km from the centre. The Havas (www.havas.net) bus (₺10) meets all flights. A taxi is around ₺50.

Onur Air (www.onurair.com.tr) To/from İstanbul.

Pegasus (www.flypgs.com) To/from İstanbul.

Turkish Airlines (www.turkishairlines.com) To/from İstanbul and Ankara.

BUS

The otogar (bus station) is 6.5km from the town centre. Catch a bus (₺2.50) or minibus in Hürriyet Caddesi, north of Gaziler Caddesi, or in İstasyon Caddesi, about 400m further north. A taxi costs about ₺25.

Minibuses to Kilis (₺7, 65km) leave every 20 minutes from a separate garaj (minibus terminal) on İnönü Caddesi. It's located just past the Petrol Ofisi petrol station.

CAR

To see surrounding sights, Arsan can arrange car rental. Plan on around ₺130 a day.

TRAIN

At the time of writing, trains to/from Gaziantep were suspended for long-term line maintenance.

The train station is around 1km north of the city centre.

SERVICES FROM GAZIANTEP'S OTOGAR

DESTINATION	FARE (₺)	DURATION (HR)	DISTANCE (KM)	FREQUENCY (PER DAY)
Adana	25	4	220	frequent
Adıyaman	20	3	162	frequent
Ankara	50	10	705	frequent
Antakya	25	4	200	frequent
Diyarbakır	30	5	330	frequent
İstanbul	70	15	1136	several
Kahramanmaraş	12	1½	80	frequent
Mardin	40	6	330	several
Şanlıurfa	20	2½	145	frequent
Van	60	12	740	several

Around Gaziantep

Kilis

✆ 0348 / POP 91,000

Kilis bristles with lovely ancient buildings including mausoleums, caravanserais, hamams, mosques, fountains and *konaks* (mansions). Many have been recently restored. On or around the main square, look for the superb Adliye, the Mevlevi Hane, the Tekye Camii, the Paşa Hamamı and the Kadı Camii. The Cuneyne Camii and Çalik Camii are a bit more difficult to find (ask around).

There are frequent minibus services from Gaziantep (₺7, 65km, one hour).

Belkıs-Zeugma

Belkıs-Zeugma was founded by one of Alexander the Great's generals around 300 BC. It had its golden age with the Romans, and later became a major trading station along the Silk Road.

In modern times, much of the remains of the city disappeared under the waters of the Birecik Dam, and the most interesting mosaics are now on display in Gaziantep. At the original site, a modern pavilion on the shores of the Euphrates shelters the remains of the Roman villas of Dionysos and Danae. Kitchens, latrines and spacious rooms are all evident – along with more mosaics in situ.

The site is about 50km from Gaziantep and 8km east of Nizip, off the main road to Şanlıurfa. (It's signposted from the village of Dutlu). There is no public transport, so you'll need to rent a car or consider a tour with Arsan (p577) in Gaziantep.

Halfeti & Rumkale

With attractive houses trickling down a hillside above the Euphrates river, the peaceful town of Halfeti lies about 40km north of Birecik. Sadly, construction of the Birecik Dam meant that half of the town, including several archaeological sites, was inundated and part of the population had to be resettled.

Licensed restaurants now dot the riverside, and accommodation is available in the Socrates Boutique Hotel (✆ 0542-895 5606, 0414 751 5022; www.halfetevleri.com; Orta Caddesi 13/1; r ₺100-140; ❉ ☎). Visit on a weekday for a quieter stay. On summer weekends, the peace can be ambushed by jet-skiiers, water-skiiers and wakeboarders. Kayaking is also available.

From Halfeti, boats to Rumkale can be organised (about ₺100 for the whole boat). Individual travellers can join a group for about ₺30. Boats travel 20 minutes to the base of the rocky bluff on top of which sits a ruined fortress. The fortress features a mosque, church and monastery, all relatively well preserved, but closed for restoration at the time of writing. Boats continue for 10 minutes until Savaş, another partly inundated village.

Regular dolmuş departures leave from Gaziantep's otogar to Birecik (₺12), and there are also minibuses to Birecik from Urfa (₺14). Minibuses ply the route between Birecik and Halfeti (₺6), leaving from the Birecik market, around 300m past Hotel Acar. Make sure you stress you want to go *Eski Halfeti* though, as many of the minibuses stop at Yeni Halfeti, the newer village around 9km from Eski Halfeti.

Halfeti is relatively accessible by public transport on weekdays, but we definitely recommend an early start from Gaziantep or Urfa. Dolmuş traffic from Birecik to Eski Halfeti slows to a trickle on weekends, but the site's popularity as a destination for Turkish tourists means that hitching is a viable option.

Şanlıurfa (Urfa)

✆ 0414 / POP 585,000 / ELEV 518M

Şanlıurfa (the Prophets' City; also known as Urfa) is a pilgrimage town and spiritual centre. This is where the prophets Job and Abraham left their marks, and the Dergah complex of mosques and the holy Gölbaşı area is imbued with a compelling atmosphere redolent of the Middle East.

Women cloaked in black chadors elbow their way through the odorous crush of the bazaar, and moustachioed gents in *şalvar* (traditional baggy Arabic pants) swill tea and click-clack backgammon pieces in shady courtyards.

Fuelled by investment in the nearby Southeastern Anatolia Project (known as GAP), combining irrigation projects and community development, a cosmopolitan sheen now complements Urfa's centuries-old heritage. The city's streets hum with an energetic buzz, and the nearby temple of Göbekli Tepe is one of eastern Turkey's unmissable destinations.

History

The Hittites imposed their rule over the area around 1370 BC. After a period of Assyrian rule, Alexander the Great conquered Urfa and named the town Edessa, after a former capital of Macedonia. It remained the capital of a Seleucid province until 132 BC, when the local Aramaean population set up an independent kingdom and renamed the town Orhai. This was only temporary, as Orhai finally succumbed to the Romans.

Astride the fault line between the Persian and Roman empires, control of Edessa was batted back and forth from one to the other. In 533, the two empires signed a Treaty of Endless Peace – lasting just seven years. The Arabs swept in and cleared them all out in 637, and Edessa enjoyed three centuries of peace.

Turks, Arabs, Armenians and Byzantines then battled for the city from 944 until 1098, when the First Crusade established the Latin County of Edessa. This lasted until 1144, when it was conquered by the Seljuk Turkish *emir* Zengi, who was succeeded by Saladin, and then by the Mamluks. Edessa became Urfa in 1637, when the Ottomans finally took over.

Urfa became Şanlıurfa (Glorious Urfa) in 1984. Since 1973, when Gaziantep (War Hero Antep) was given its special epithet, the citizens of Urfa had been chafing under a relative loss of dignity. Now that their city is 'Glorious', the inhabitants can look the citizens of War Hero Antep straight in the eye.

◉ Sights

Göbekli Tepe   RUIN
(www.gobeklitepe.info; admission ₺5; ◌ daylight hours) Around 11km northeast of Urfa, 'Pot Belly Hill' was first unearthed in 1995, and its circle of Neolithic megaliths is estimated to date from 9500 BC, around 6500 years before Stonehenge. A wooden walkway circles the site, making it easy to study the centuries-old stone pillars with exquisitely stylised carvings of lions, foxes and vultures. Previously the site was thought to be a medieval cemetery, but is now thought to be the world's first place of worship

The symbols on the Göbekli Tepe megaliths also predate Sumerian hieroglyphics (traditionally thought to be the basis of written languages) by about 8000 years. Geomagnetic surveys and ground-penetrating radar systems have identified another 16 ancient megalithic rings buried nearby, and

at present only 5% of the entire site has been excavated.

A return taxi to Göbekli Tepe from Şanlıurfa is around ₺40. The site can also be visited with Harran-Nemrut Tours (p584), Mustafa Çaycı (p584) and Nomad Tours Turkey (p582).

★ Gölbaşı   HISTORIC AREA
Legend claims that Abraham (İbrahim), the Islamic prophet, was in old Urfa destroying pagan gods when Nimrod, the local Assyrian king, took offence. Nimrod had Abraham immolated on a funeral pyre, but God turned the fire into water and the burning coals into fish. Abraham was hurled into the air from where the fortress stands, landing safely in a bed of roses. Urfa's picturesque Gölbaşı area of fish-filled pools and rose gardens is a symbolic re-creation of this story.

Two rectangular **pools of water** (Balıklı Göl and Ayn-i Zeliha) are filled with supposedly sacred carp, while the area west of the Hasan Padişah Camii is a gorgeous **rose garden**. Local legend has it that anyone catching the carp will go blind.

On the northern side of Balıklı Göl is the elegant **Rızvaniye Vakfı Camii & Medresesi**, with a much-photographed arcaded wall, while at the western end is the **Halilur Rahman Camii**. This 13th-century building, replacing an earlier Byzantine church, marks the site where Abraham fell to the ground. The two pools are fed by a spring at the base of Damlacık hill, on which the castle is built.

Edessa Mosaic Museum   MUSEUM
(Haleplibaçhe Caddesi; admission incl Şanlıurfa Archaeology Museum ₺8; ◌ 8am-5pm Tue-Sat) This modern domed structure protects the excellent Haleplibaçhe (Aleppo Gardens) mosaics, part of a Roman villa complex only discovered in 2006 when construction started on a planned theme park. Highlights include wonderfully detailed mosaics showing Amazon warrior queens and the life of Achilles. The theme park has been usurped by Şanlıurfa's sprawling Archeopark, also taking in the city's massive new archaeology museum.

Şanlıurfa Archeology Museum   MUSEUM
(Haleplibaçhe Caddesi; admission incl Edessa Mosaic Museum ₺8; ◌ 8am-5pm Tue-Sat) Opened in late 2014, Şanlıurfa's spectacular new Archeology Museum forms the city's Archeopark with the new Edessa Mosaic Museum.

Şanlıurfa (Urfa)

Across three massive floors, the region's archaeological heritage includes sculpture and art from Göbekli Tepe, and a stunning cavalcade of history from Paleolithic times. To get the best from a visit to Göbekli Tepe, we recommend visiting this museum first.

★ Bazaar
MARKET

(⊙ Mon-Sat) Urfa's bazaar features everything from sheepskins and pigeons to jeans and handmade shoes. It was largely built by Süleyman the Magnificent in the mid-16th century. One of the most interesting areas is the

Şanlıurfa (Urfa)

bedesten, an ancient caravanserai where silk goods including colourful local scarves are sold. Around the bazaar are several ancient and cheap hamams, including Arasa Hamamı.

★ **Kale** FORTRESS
(Citadel; admission ₺5; ⊘ 8am-8pm) Urfa's fortress on Damlacık hill, from which Abraham was supposedly tossed, has good city views, but there's not much to see at the actual site. On the top, most interesting are the two columns dubbed the Throne of Nemrut after the supposed founder of Urfa, the biblical King Nimrod. We've received reports of women travellers being hassled on the slopes behind the castle, so we recommend visiting during daylight hours and sticking to busy areas.

Multiple conflicting histories claim the fortress was either (a) built in Hellenistic times, (b) built by the Byzantines, (c) built during the Crusades or (d) built by the Turks.

Dergah PARK
Southeast of Gölbaşı is the Dergah complex of mosques and parks surrounding the colonnaded courtyard of the Hazreti İbrahim Halilullah (Prophet Abraham's Birth Cave; admission ₺1), built and rebuilt over the centuries as a place of pilgrimage. Its western side is marked by the Mevlid-i Halil Camii, a large Ottoman-style mosque. At its southern side is the en-trance to the cave where Abraham was reputedly born. He lived here in hiding for his first seven years – King Nimrod, responding to a prophecy he'd received in a dream, feared that a newborn would eventually steal his crown, so he had all babies killed.

To visit these important places of worship you should be modestly dressed.

Ulu Cami MOSQUE
(Divan Yolu Caddesi) Urfa's Syrian-style Ulu Cami dates from the period 1170–75. Its 13 *eyvans* (vaulted halls) open onto a spacious forecourt with a tall tower topped by a clock with Ottoman numerals.

Hüseyin Paşa Camii MOSQUE
(Kara Meydanı) At Kara Meydanı, the square midway between the *belediye* (town hall) and Dergah, is the Hüseyin Paşa Camii, a late-Ottoman construction built in 1849.

Selahattin Eyubi Camii MOSQUE
(Vali Fuat Caddesi) On Vali Fuat Caddesi, which leads up from behind Gölbaşı, is this enormous, beautifully restored mosque. It was once St John's Church, as evidenced by the altar.

Yeni Fırfırlı Camii MOSQUE
(Yeni Fırfırlı Camii) North of Selahattin Eyubi Camii is Yeni Fırfırlı Camii, a finely restored building, once the Armenian Church of the Twelve Apostles.

Güzel Sanatlar Galerisi   GALLERY
(⊙8am-5.30pm Mon-Fri, noon-4pm Sat) Urfa's backstreets have many distinctive limestone houses with protruding bays supported on stone corbels. A few have been restored, most notably the house of Hacı Hafızlar. It's near the PTT, and is now an art gallery.

İl Özel İdaresi Kültür ve
Sanat Merkezi   HISTORIC BUILDING
North of the bazaar, in the neighbourhood called Beykapı Mahallesi (take 1001 Sokak), this splendid house, restored in 2002, was once a church.

🛏 Sleeping

Hotel Uğur   HOTEL €
(☏313 1340, 0532 685 2942; musma63@yahoo. com; Köprübaşı Caddesi 3; per person without bathroom ₺30; ❋🛜) Rooms are sparsely decorated and relatively compact, but clean and spotless. There's a great travellers' vibe, enhanced by a few cold beers on the hotel's terrace as you watch Urfa's cinematic buzz unfold before you. Rates exclude breakfast, but there's a good *kahvaltı salonu* (breakfast restaurant) downstairs.

Hotel Bakay   HOTEL €
(☏215 8975; Asfalt Caddesi; s/d ₺45/75; ❋@🛜) A safe bet that won't hurt the hip pocket, but be prepared to trip over your backpack

in the tiny rooms. Some are brighter than others, so check out a few before settling in.

Aslan Konuk Evi   PENSION €€
(☏215 1575, 0542 761 3065; www.aslankonukevi. com; Demokrasi Caddesi 10; dm/r incl breakfast ₺30/100; ❋@🛜) Simple but spacious high-ceilinged rooms are arranged around a shared central courtyard in a heritage Urfa building. Accommodation options range from shared dorm rooms to double rooms with private bathrooms. Good food and cold beer is available in the rooftop terrace restaurant. Nonguests are welcome for dinner, but you'll need to make a booking in the morning.

Otel Urhay   HISTORIC HOTEL €€
(☏216 2222, 0544 215 7201; www.otelurhay. com; Sarayönü Caddesi, Beyaz Sokak; s/d/tr ₺70/100/120; ❋🛜) A cool kilim-decorated lounge-restaurant combines with simple whitewashed rooms that feature both air-con – essential during an Urfa summer – and private bathrooms. The quiet inner courtyard is perfect for drinking tea. Note that weddings and parties are sometimes hosted on weekends.

Hotel Güven   HOTEL €€
(☏215 1700; www.hotelguven.com; Sarayönü Caddesi; s/d ₺85/140; ❋🛜) The Güven features

---

WORTH A TRIP

VILLAGE HOMESTAYS & ABRAHAM'S PATH

Around Şanlıurfa, a scattering of Kurdish and Alevi villages host an excellent **homestay program** (☏Turkey 0542 517 1808, UK 0044 776 777 4194; www.nomadtoursturkey.com; per person half-/full board €30/35). Accommodation is in simple but spotless village houses with shared facilities. During summer the best sleeping option is often on the roof, under the stars, waking up to the early-morning sounds of the host families' fat-tailed sheep. The same sheep provide milk for homemade cheese and yoghurt, perfect with freshly made flatbread for breakfast. Dinner is a shared affair, and in the Alevi village of Kisas, traditional music is performed.

The homestay program supports local kindergartens and schools, and is a friendly option to break up the southeastern Anatolian routine of cheap pensions and hotels.

Nomad Tours Turkey, which runs the program, also runs full-day tours to Harran (€80), Şanlıurfa (€80), Nemrut Dağı (€110) and Diyarbakır (€100). Longer multiday tours can incorporate Gaziantep, Halfeti, Mardin, Midyat and Hasankeyf. Tours to Şanlıurfa and Harran also include a visit to the temple of Göbekli Tepe.

Nomad Tours has been influential in establishing the Turkish component of **Abraham's Path** (www.abrahampath.org), a walking trail in the footsteps of the prophet Abraham traversing Israel, Palestine and the West Bank, Jordan, Syria and Turkey. Because of ongoing conflicts, not all parts of the path were open at the time of writing, but the southeast Anatolian part of the route is safe and accessible, and incorporates Kurdish and Alevi village homestays and visits to Şanlıurfa, Harran and Göbekli Tepe. Options include day walks from €55 per person and a six-day trek including accommodation in Urfa (€480 per person).

URFA'S SPECIAL PLACES

Urfa is famed for its *konuk evi* – 19th-century stone mansions now converted into restaurants and hotels. They usually feature a courtyard around which are arranged several comfy *şark odası* (Ottoman-style lounges). They are smart places to get a typical Urfa experience but can be noisy at weekends when they host *sıra geceleri* (live-music evenings) or weddings. Not all rooms have private facilities, and you're usually paying a premium for the heritage ambience.

Cevahir Konuk Evi (☑215 4678; www.cevahirkonukevi.com; Yeni Mahalle Sokak; s/d ₺180/250, mains ₺10-20; 🕸🛜) Excellent *tebbule* (tabouleh) and faultlessly cooked *tavuk şiş* (roast chicken kebap) is served on the expansive terrace. Accommodation-wise, the rooms are slightly disappointing, with kitsch paintings of Ye Olde Ottoman times and mismatched antique furniture.

smartly renovated rooms decked out in chocolate-brown and wooden tones. Flash bathrooms and flat-screen TVs transform the Güven into one of central Urfa's best places to stay.

Hilton Garden Inn　　　　　HOTEL €€€
(☑318 5000; www.hilton.com; Nisan Fuar Caddesi 11; s/d ₺150/220; 🕸🛜🏊) Rooms are very spacious, and one of Turkey's best breakfast buffets awaits dowstairs. Hotel facilities include an atrium tea garden and an indoor pool and sauna complex, and you're just a short stroll from Urfa's newest museums.

Manici Hotel　　　　HISTORIC HOTEL €€€
(☑215 9911; www.manici.com.tr; Balıklı Göl Mevkii; r ₺160-200; 🕸🛜) The opulent Manici has restored and romantic rooms. The luxe furnishings stop just short of being over the top, and there's more of a contemporary vibe than at other heritage accommodation around town. The attached restaurant serves beer and wine.

🍴 Eating

Local specialities include Urfa kebap (skewered lamb with tomatoes, sliced onions and hot peppers); *çiğ köfte* (raw ground lamb with bulgar and spices), and *şıllık* (crepes filled with walnuts and syrup). Urfa folk like their food spicy, and many dishes come with *ızot* (dried flaked peppers). Pomegranate dressing adds a sweet but zingy touch to salads.

Be careful what you eat in Urfa, especially in summer, because the heat makes food poisoning more likely.

İkiler Ciğer Salonu　　　　　KEBAP €
(Faaliyet Alanı; kebaps ₺7-10; ⊙10am-11pm) Informal streetside *ciğer salonu* (simple eateries serving grilled meats) are easy to find throughout the city. Grab a cornerside table

at İkiler, and tuck into a mini-feast of grilled lamb, chicken or liver, served on tea-towel-sized flatbreads with spice-laden onions and grilled peppers.

Beyaz Köşk　　　　　KEBAP €
(Akarbaşı Göl Cadessi 20; mains ₺7-10; ⊙10am-10pm) Turkey's best *lahmacun* (Arabic-style pizza) restaurants reputedly huddle in Gölbaşı's labyrinth of lanes, and the 'White House' is a great place to try plate-covering pizza sprinkled with spicy *ızot*. Head upstairs to the breezy terrace and observe Urfa's gentle mayhem down below.

Zahter Kahvaltı &
Kebap Salonu　　　　　BREAKFAST €
(Köprübaşı Caddesi; mains ₺5-10) Skip your hotel's breakfast and instead wolf down gooey honey, *pekmez* (grape syrup), jam and *kaymak* (clotted cream) on flatbread. Wash it all down with a large glass of çay or *ayran* – all for around ₺10.

Baklavacı Badıllı Dedeoğlu　　　SWEETS €
(Sarayönü Caddesi; pastries ₺3) Death by pistachio baklava and pistachio *sarması* ('vine leaves').

Çift Mağara　　　　　TURKISH €€
(Çift Kubbe Altı Balıklıgöl; mains ₺10-20; ⊙10am-11pm) The dining room is carved into a rocky bluff overlooking Gölbaşı, but the lovely terrace for dining alfresco beats the cavernous interior. Try the *içli köfte* (ground lamb and onion with a bulgur coating).

Gülhan Restaurant　　　　TURKISH €€
(Atatürk Caddesi; mains ₺10-15; ⊙11am-10pm) Razor-sharp waiters and salubrious surroundings combine with a pictorial menu of grills and local dishes with English translations. For dessert, try the *şıllık*.

Çardaklı Köşk
TURKISH €€

(Vali Fuat Caddesi, Tünel Çıkışı; mains ₺12-18; ⊙11am-11pm) Food is only so-so – the real draw is live music and the view over Gölbaşı from the upstairs terrace.

Manici Hotel
TURKISH €€€

(☑215 9911; Balıklı Göl Mevkii; meze ₺6-8, mains ₺15-20; ⊙noon-2pm & 6-11pm) With excellent meze and traditional Turkish mains, the licensed restaurant at the Manici Hotel is an elegant affair framed by paintings of Ottoman Sultans.

🍷 Drinking & Nightlife

Head for the leafy çay bahçesi (tea gardens) around Gölbaşı. For a cold beer, try the Altin Kupa pub, or dine at the Aslan Konuk Evi or Manici Hotel.

Gümrük Hanı
COFFEEHOUSE

(Customs Depot; Urfa bazaar; coffee ₺4) This delightful courtyard is full of tea- or coffee-swilling moustached gents playing backgammon and is the ideal spot for the first coffee of the day. Ask for *kahve mirra,* the super-strong and bitter local variation. It is a wonderfully restored caravanserai crowded with locals. We've had reader feedback that the ambience can sometimes be slightly intimidating for solo women travellers.

Şampiyon Vitamin
JUICE BAR

(Akarbaşı Göl Cadessi; juices from ₺2) Recharge at this juice bar on the edge on the bazaar. We found the zingy *greyfurt suyu* (grapefruit juice) especially refreshing.

Altin Kupa
PUB

(Köprübaşı Kışla Caddesi 4; beers ₺7; ⊙11am-11pm) This pub and beer garden is a haven from the Anatolian heat. It's too blokey for single female travellers, but we've seen local couples together here.

☆ Entertainment

Urfa is an city of contrast: pious during the day, wild in the evening. What makes the city tick are the *sıra geceleri* (live-music evenings) that are held in the *konuk evi* (p583), usually at weekends. Guests sit, eat, sing and dance in *şark odası* (Ottoman-style lounges) and, after the meal, a live band plays old favourites that keep revellers rocking and dancing. Foreigners are welcome to join the party. BYO earplugs if you're sleeping upstairs.

ℹ️ Information

The post office and ATMs are on Urfa's main drag.

Harran-Nemrut Tours (☑215 1575, 0542 761 3065; www.aslankonukevi.com; Demokrasi Caddesi 12) Run by Özcan Aslan, a local teacher who speaks good English, and has maps and brochures. Tours to nearby sites (including Göbekli Tepe, Harran, Şuayb City, Soğmatar, Mardin and Nemrut Dağı) range from €10 to €40 per person. Find Özcan at the Aslan Konuk Evi (p582), or see the website.

Mustafa Çaycı (☑0532 685 2942, 313 1340; musma63@yahoo.com; Hotel Uğur, Köprübaşı Caddesi 3) Mustafa Çaycı from Hotel Uğur (p582) runs short and long tours to Harran (per person ₺40/90), excursions to Göbekli Tepe (per person ₺35), and longer trips to Nemrut Dağı (per person ₺140).

Tourist Information Kiosk (⊙8am-5pm) Handily located near Balıklı Göl with English spoken and good local maps. Opening hours can be erratic.

SERVICES FROM ŞANLIURFA'S OTOGAR

DESTINATION	FARE (₺)	DURATION (HR)	DISTANCE (KM)	FREQUENCY (PER DAY)
Adana	35	5	365	several
Ankara	70	12	850	several
Diyarbakır	16	3	190	several
Erzurum	60	9	665	2.30pm & 7pm
Gaziantep	20	2	145	several
İstanbul	90	16	1290	3pm & 4.30pm
Kayseri	40	8	515	several
Malatya	40	4	270	2.30pm
Mardin	30	3	188	9am & 11am
Van	60	9	585	2.30pm, 8.30pm & 11pm

ℹ️ Getting There & Away

AIR

The airport is 45km from Urfa on the road to Diyarbakır. Ask about the Havas airport bus (www.havas.net, ☏10) at **Kalıru Turizm** (☏ 215 3344; www.kaliruturizm.com.tr; Sarayönü Caddesi; ⏱ 8.30am-6.30pm).

Onur Air (www.onurair.com.tr) To/from İstanbul.

Pegasus Airlines (www.flypgs.com) To/from İstanbul and Izmir.

Turkish Airlines (www.turkishairlines.com) To/from Ankara and İstanbul.

BUS

Urfa's otogar is 5km north of town off the road to Diyarbakır. Some buses will drop passengers at a roundabout around 300m from the otogar. Buses to the otogar can be caught on Atatürk Caddesi (☏1.50). Note that you'll need to buy an UrfaKart (☏3), but this allows you two rides. Taxis usually ask ☏25. Minibuses to Harran (☏5) and Kahta (☏15) leave from the regional minibus terminal beneath the otogar.

CAR

For car hire (around ☏100 per day) try Mustafa Çaycı or Harran-Nemrut Tours.

Harran

☏ 0414 / POP 6900

Harran is reputedly one of the oldest continuously inhabited spots on earth. The Book of Genesis mentions Harran and its most famous resident, Abraham, who stayed for a few years in 1900 BC. Its ruined walls, crumbling fortress and beehive houses give the town a feeling of deep antiquity. Traditionally locals lived by farming and smuggling, but the irrigation projects of the Atatürk Dam have seen cotton fields sprouting over what was once arid desert.

On arrival buy a ticket (☏5) from the booth near the car park. If anyone else in the castle tries to charge you, insist on being given the official ticket. Cheeky local kids can be slightly annoying, so an English-speaking guide (around ☏15) is a worthwhile investment.

Harran gets very busy with domestic Turkish tourists at weekends, so try to visit on a more quiet weekday.

History

Besides being the place of Abraham's sojourn, Harran is famous as a centre of worship of Sin, god of the moon. Worship of the sun, moon and planets was popular in Harran, and at neighbouring Soğmatar, from about 800 BC until AD 830, although Harran's temple to the moon god was destroyed by the Byzantine emperor Theodosius in AD 382. Battles between Arabs and Byzantines occupied the townsfolk until the Crusaders came. The fortress, which some say was built on the ruins of the moon god's temple, was restored by the Crusaders.

👁️ Sights

Beehive Houses   HISTORIC AREA

Harran is famous for its beehive houses, a design dating back to the 3rd century BC, although the present examples were mostly constructed within the last 200 years. The design evolved partly in response to a lack of wood for roofing and partly because the ruins provided a source of reusable bricks. The Harran houses are unique in Turkey, but similar buildings are in northern Syria.

The **Harran Kültür Evi**, within walking distance of the castle, allows visitors to see inside one of the houses, and then sip cold drinks in the walled courtyard afterwards.

Kale   FORTRESS

On the far (east) side of the hill, the crumbling *kale* stands right by some beehive houses. A castle probably already existed here during Hittite times, but the current construction dates mainly from after 1059, when the Fatimids took over and restored it. Originally, there were four multi-angular corner towers, but only two remain. At the time of writing it was closed for restoration, and scheduled to reopen in mid- to late-2015.

City Walls   RUINS

The crumbling stone city walls were once 4km long and studded with 187 towers and four gates. Of these, only the overly restored **Aleppo Gate**, near the new part of town, remains.

Ulu Camii   MOSQUE

Of the ruins inside the village, other than the *kale,* the Ulu Camii is most prominent. It was built in the 8th century by Marwan II, last of the Umayyad caliphs. You'll recognise it by its tall, square and very un-Turkish minaret. It's said to be the oldest mosque in Anatolia. Near here stood the first Islamic university, and on the hillside above it you'll see the low-level ruins of ancient Harran, dating back some 5000 years.

ℹ Getting There & Away

Minibuses (₺5, one hour) leave from Urfa's otogar approximately every hour and stop at modern Harran near the *belediye* (town hall) and PTT – it's then a 10-minute walk to the castle. Minibus traffic back to Urfa diminishes from mid-afternoon so check timings at the Urfa otogar before you leave.

Around Harran

Although the sites beyond Harran are missable if you're pushed for time, it would be a shame not to see the astonishing transformation wrought on the local scenery by the GAP irrigation project (p608): field upon field of cotton and barley where once there was just desert.

To get around the sites without your own transport is virtually impossible unless you have limitless time, so consider a tour by Nomad Tours (p582), Harran-Nemrut Tours (p584) or Mustafa Çaycı (p584) in Şanlıurfa. You may need to take a picnic lunch, or you might have a village lunch stop. It's useful to have a pocketful of change for tips along the way. The Harran 'long tour' usually incorporates most of the nearby sights listed below, but is slow going on a rough road in need of repair.

◉ Sights

Bazda Caves   RUINS
About 20km east of Harran, the impressive Bazda Caves (signed 'Bazda Mağaları') are supposed to have been used to build the walls of Harran.

Han el Ba'rur   RUINS
About 6km east from the Bazda Caves are the remains of the Seljuk Han el Ba'rur, a caravanserai built in 1128 to service the local trade caravans.

Şuayb City   RUINS
Around 12km northeast of Han el Ba'rur are the extensive remains of Şuayb City, where hefty stone walls and lintels survive above a network of subterranean rooms. One of these contains a mosque on the site of the supposed home of the prophet Jethro. Bring a torch and wear sturdy shoes.

Soğmatar   RUINS
About 18km north of Şuayb, the isolated village of Soğmatar is very atmospheric. Sacrifices were made to the sun and moon gods, whose effigies are carved into the side of the ledge. Like Harran, Soğmatar was a centre for the cult worship of Sin, the moon god, from about AD 150 to 200. This open-air altar was the main temple.

In a cave are 12 carved statues as well as Assyrian inscriptions. From the ruin's summit, remains of seven other temples on surrounding hills are evident.

Kahta

☎ 0416 / POP 64,500
Dusty Kahta doesn't exactly scream 'holiday', but it's well set up for visits to Nemrut Dağı. Accommodation actually on the mountain, around the village of Karadut, is more inspiring and scenic.

Around 25 June, the three-day **International Kahta Kommagene Festival** has music and folk dancing. Book accommodation ahead at this time.

🛏 Sleeping

Kommagene Hotel   HOTEL €
(☎725 9726, 0532 200 3856; www.kommagene hotel.com; Mustafa Kemal Caddesi 1; s/d ₺50/90; ❄@✿) Cosy woodlined rooms all have private bathrooms, there's a guest kitchen and laundry, and free pickups are available from the Kahta otogar or Adiyaman airport. During summer, the hotel will shuttle guests out to a nearby lake for swimming. Packages incorporating accommodation and a tour to Nemrut Daği are ₺155 per person. Daily departures are guaranteed from April to November.

Other longer trips taking in Şanlıurfa, Harran, Mardin or Diyarbakır are available, and camping is also available in the hotel grounds.

Zeus Hotel   HOTEL €€
(☎725 5694; www.zeushotel.com.tr; Mustafa Kemal Caddesi; campsites per person ₺20, s/d/ste €60/80/110; ❄✿🏊) This solid three-star option gets an A+ for its swimming pool and manicured garden – blissful after a long day travelling by bus. Campers can pitch tents in the parking lot, and have access to their own ablutions block.

🍴 Eating

For something different, take a taxi (₺20) to the lake formed by the Atatürk Dam, about 4km east of Kahta. Licensed restaurants with lovely views over the lake serve grilled fish.

Kahta Sofrası
TURKISH €

(Mustafa Kemal Caddesi; mains ₺6-11) Right on Kahta's Dort Yol ('Four Roads') intersection, Kahta Sofrası's huge kitchen and woodfired oven turn out excellent kebaps, pide, and a few eastern Anatolian dishes if you've just arrived from Cappadocia.

Neşetin Yeri
RESTAURANT, BAR €€

(Baraj Yolu; mains ₺10-15; ⊙ 11.30am-10pm) The leafy garden of this whitewashed restaurant is soothingly positioned right by the lake. Tuck into a faultless grilled *alabalık* (trout), served in a *kiremit* (clay pot), and team a cold beer or robust rakı (aniseed brandy) with lakeside views.

❶ Getting There & Away

Kahta's otogar is in the town centre, with taxi stands right beside it. There are regular buses to Adıyaman (₺4, 30 minutes, 32km), Ankara (₺60, 12 hours, 807km), İstanbul (₺90, 20 hours, 1352km), Kayseri (₺48 seven hours, 487km), Malatya (₺28, 3½ hours, 225km), Şanlıurfa (₺20, 2½ hours, 106km), and Diyarbakır (₺30, four hours, 174km). For accurate information about buses, visit the otogar and check for yourself, rather than rely on what some locals may tell you.

Also, despite what some may say, there are definitely minibuses every couple of hours from 8am to 6pm to Karadut (₺6). We recommend getting a morning start from Kahta. The buses return from Karadut between 7.30am and 8.30am the next day. Departures are less frequent on Saturday and Sunday.

Nemrut Dağı National Park

The spellbinding peak of Nemrut Dağı (admission ₺8; ⊙ dawn-dusk) rises to a height of 2150m in the Anti-Taurus Range between the provincial capital of Malatya to the north and Kahta in Adıyaman province to the south (it's not to be confused with the less-visited Nemrut Dağı near Lake Van).

Nobody knew anything about Nemrut Dağı (*nehm*-root dah-uh) until 1881, when a German engineer, employed by the Ottomans to assess transport routes, was astounded to come across the statues covering this remote mountaintop. Archaeological work began in 1953 by the American School of Oriental Research.

The summit was created when a megalomaniac pre-Roman local king cut two ledges in the rock, filled them with colossal statues

of himself and the gods (his relatives – or so he thought), then ordered an artificial mountain peak of crushed rock 50m high to be piled between them. The king's tomb and those of three female relatives are reputed to lie beneath those tonnes of rock.

Earthquakes have toppled the heads from most of the statues, and now many of the colossal bodies sit silently in rows, with the 2m-high heads watching from the ground.

Although it's relatively easy to get to the summit with your own vehicle, most people take tours, organised in either Kahta or Malatya, or as a longer day trip from Şanlıurfa or Cappadocia.

Plan to visit Nemrut between late May and mid-October, and preferably in July or August; the road to the summit becomes impassable with snow at other times. Even in high summer it will be chilly and windy on top of the mountain. This is especially true at sunrise, the coldest time of the day. Take warm clothing no matter when you go.

There are three ways of approaching the summit. From the southern side, you pass through Karadut, a village 12km from the top, before embarking upon the last few kilometres to the car park. From the southwestern side, a secondary road goes past Eski Kale (Arsameia) and climbs steeply for about 10km until it merges with the Karadut road, some 6km before the car park at the summit. This secondary road is quite rough in parts, and should only be attempted by confident drivers. Travellers staying in Karadut can walk the 12km to the summit. It's a clearly marked road with a steady gradient. At the time of writing a more scenic off-road walking track was being established. Ask at Karadut accommodation options for the latest information about this.

From the northern side, travel from Malatya is via a good 96km road until the Güneş Hotel, near the summit. It is not possible to cross the summit by car from the northern side to the southern side.

Coming from the southwest, the entrance gate (₺11) is at the turn-off to Eski Kale; from the south, the gate is just past Çeşme Pansion; from the north, the gate is at the Güneş Hotel.

History

From 250 BC onwards, this region straddled the border between the Seleucid Empire and the Parthian Empire.

Under the Seleucid Empire, the governor of Commagene declared his kingdom's

Nemrut Dağı Area

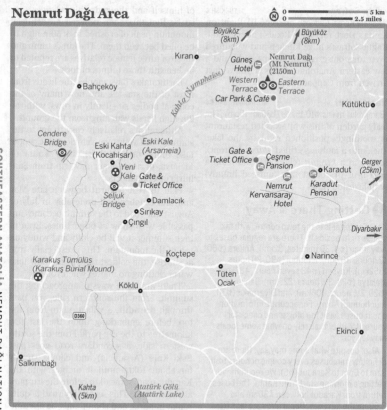

independence. In 80 BC, with the Seleucids in disarray and Roman power spreading into Anatolia, a Roman ally named Mithridates I Callinicus proclaimed himself king and set up his capital at Arsameia, near the modern village of Eski Kahta.

Mithridates died in 64 BC and was succeeded by his son Antiochus I Epiphanes (r 64–38 BC), who consolidated his kingdom's security by immediately signing a nonaggression treaty with Rome, turning his kingdom into a Roman buffer against attack from the Parthians. His good relations with both sides allowed him to revel in delusions of grandeur, and it was Antiochus who ordered the building of Nemrut's fabulous temples and funerary mound.

In the third decade of his reign, Antiochus sided with the Parthians in a squabble with Rome, and in 38 BC the Romans deposed him. The great days of Commagene were thus limited to the 26-year reign of Antiochus.

Sights & Activities

Karakuş Tümülüs
RUIN

Highway D360, marked for Nemrut Dağı Milli Parkı, starts in Kahta next to the Kommagene Hotel. After a few kilometres, the road forks left 1.5km to Karakuş Tümülüs, built in 36 BC. A handful of columns ring the mound – there were more, but the limestone blocks were used by the Romans to build the Cendere Bridge.

An eagle tops a column at the car park, a lion tops another around the mound, and a third has an inscribed slab explaining that the burial mound holds female relatives of King Mithridates II.

Cendere Bridge
BRIDGE

Some 10km from the Karakuş Tümülüs is a modern bridge over the Cendere River. To the left you'll see a magnificent humpback Roman bridge built in the 2nd century AD. The surviving Latin stelae state that the bridge was built in honour of Emperor Septimius Severus. Of the four original Corinthian columns (two at either end), three are still standing.

Eski Kahta (Kocahisar) & Yeni Kale   RUINS
About 5km from the Cendere bridge is a 1km detour to Eski Kahta. There was once a palace here, but what's now evident are the ruins of a 13th-century Mamluk castle, Yeni Kale (New Fortress). The castle was being renovated at the time of writing and due to reopen in 2015.

After Yeni Kale, cross the Kahta (Nymphaios) River to see the old road and the graceful Seljuk Bridge.

Eski Kale (Arsameia)   RUINS
About 1.5km further, the main road forks left 2km to Eski Kale, the ancient Commagene capital of Arsameia. Nearby is the park entrance for Arsameia and summit access. At Eski Kale there is a large stele depicting Mithras (or Apollo), the sun god. Further along are the bases of two stelae depicting Mithridates I Callinicus, with Antiochus I, the taller stele, holding a sceptre. Behind here, a cave entrance leads to an underground chamber built for Mithras-worshipping rites.

Further uphill is a stone relief portraying Mithridates I shaking hands with the ancient hero Heracles. Adjacent, another cave temple descends 158m through the rock; the steps into the temple are dangerous. The long Greek inscription above the cave describes the founding of Arsameia; the water trough beside it may have been used for religious ablutions.

On the hilltop are the ruined foundations of Mithridates' capital.

Summit   RUINS
(admission ₺11; ☉dawn-dusk) The park entrance is 200m from Çeşme Pension and 2.5km before the junction to to Eski Kale. From that car park, hike 600m uphill (about 20 minutes) to the western terrace. Antiochus I Epiphanes ordered the construction of a combined tomb and temple here. Antiochus and his fellow gods sit in state, although their bodies and heads have partly tumbled down. From the western terrace it's five minutes' walk around to the eastern terrace. Here the bodies are largely intact, except for the fallen heads, which seem more badly weathered than the western heads.

On the backs of the eastern statues are inscriptions in Greek. Both terraces have similar plans, with the syncretistic gods,

the 'ancestors' of Antiochus, seated. From left to right they are Apollo, the sun god (Mithra to the Persians; Helios or Hermes to the Greeks); Fortuna, or Tyche; Zeus-Ahura Mazda in the centre; then King Antiochus; and on the far right Heracles, also known as Ares or Artagnes.

Low walls at the sides of each temple once held carved reliefs showing processions of ancient Persian and Greek royalty, Antiochus' 'predecessors'. Statues of eagles represent Zeus.

The site was to be approached by a ceremonial road and was to incorporate what Antiochus termed 'the thrones of the gods', which would be based 'on a foundation that will never be demolished'.

🛏 Sleeping & Eating
There are several places to stay on the road from Karadut to the summit.

Karadut Pension   PENSION €
(☑0416-737 2169, 0533 616 4564; www.karadut pansiyon.net; Karadut; per person ₺40, campsite ₺10; ❄@) This pension in Karadut has 14 neat, compact rooms (some with air-con), cleanish bathrooms and a shared kitchen. Meals are available along with wine, beer or rakı in the alfresco terrace bar. Campers can pitch their tent in a partially shaded plot at the back. They'll pick you up from Kahta for ₺30.

Nemrut Kervansaray Hotel   HOTEL €€
(☑0416 737 2190; www.nemrutkervansaray.com; Karadut; s/d from €35/45; ❄🛜🏊) One of Karadut's established hotels has new rooms with mountain views and private balconies. Good English is spoken, there is a decent on-site restaurant with wine and cold beer, and the whole operation is friendly and very well run. The swimming pool is a welcome addition on summer days, and minibus transport to the summit is ₺100.

Güneş Hotel   HOTEL €
(☑0536 873 0534; ramo4483@hotmail.com; half-board incl transport from Malatya per person ₺120) Standing in Gothic isolation about 2.5km from the eastern terrace, this hotel is used by travellers coming from Malatya. The setting amid rocky boulders is dramatic (bordering on spooky on a cloudy day), the hush is enjoyable and the rooms are ordinary yet clean. Contact Ramazan Karataş (p593) about staying here on an overnight trip from Malatya.

ORGANISED TOURS TO NEMRUT DAĞI (MT NEMRUT)

The main tour centres are Kahta and Malatya, but there are also tours from Karadut, Şanlıurfa and Cappadocia.

From Karadut

Pensions and hotels in Karadut offer return trips to the summit – with one hour at the top – from about ₺60 per vehicle.

From Kahta

Historically Kahta has had a reputation as a rip-off town. Always check exactly what you'll be seeing during the tour (in addition to the summit) and how long you'll be away for.

From Kahta, visitors to the mountain have the option of a 'long tour' or a 'short tour'. The majority of 'long' tours are timed to capture a dramatic sunrise or sunset. If you opt for the sunrise tours, you'll leave Kahta at about 2am via Narince and Karadut, arriving at Nemrut Daği for sunrise. After an hour or so, you'll go down again following the upgraded direct road to Arsameia. Then you'll stop at Eski Kahta, Yeni Kale, Cendere Bridge and Karakuş Tümülüs. Expect to be back in Kahta at about 10am.

If you sign up for the sunset tour, you'll do the same loop but in the reverse direction. You'll leave around 1.30pm and start with the sights around Arsameia, then go up to the summit, before descending via Karadut and Narince. You'll be back in Kahta by 9.30pm. Mt Nemrut Tours (www.nemrutguide.com) at the Kommagene Hotel (p586) offers a 'long tour' package including accommodation for ₺155 per person. Tours are also available at the Zeus Hotel (p586).

A 'short tour' lasts about three hours, and zips you from Kahta to the summit and back again, allowing about an hour for sightseeing. It's less expensive, but skips the other interesting sights in the region.

If you're in a group, another option is to hire a taxi at the Kahta otogar. Prices are around ₺120 for the 'short tour' and ₺150 for the 'long tour'. Don't expect any informed commentary for these options.

Çeşme Pansion   PENSION €
(☏ 0416-737 2032; www.cesmepansion.com; per person half board ₺60, campsite ₺10) The closest shut-eye option to the summit (only 6km; the owners will drive you there for around ₺50). The rooms (all with private bathrooms) are basic but clean, and campers will enjoy the shaded garden setting.

ⓘ Getting There & Away

CAR

To ascend the southern slopes of Nemrut from Kahta, drive along the D360 via Narince and Karadut, or take a longer but more scenic route that includes Karakuş, Cendere, Eski Kahta and Eski Kale, then the 15km shortcut to the summit.

Make sure you have fuel for at least 250km of normal driving. Though the trip to the summit and back is at most 160km, you have to drive some of that in low gear, which uses more fuel. On the more scenic route, be prepared for some driving on rough and winding roads. Confident drivers only please.

You can also approach the summit from Malatya (98km, 90 minutes one way) and drive right up to the Güneş Hotel on a good road. From there, a rough road leads to the eastern terrace, a further 2.5km. It's OK with a normal car in dry weather, but is quite narrow and winding.

Note there is no road at the summit linking the southern and the northern sides, but a (very!) rough road does skirt the base of the mountain linking the Kahta (southern) side to the Malatya (northern) side. From Kocahisar, a road goes 21km to the village of Büyüköz. The first 7km, up to the village of Kıran, are surfaced. The next 6km, to the hamlet of Taşkale, deteriorates markedly and gradually becomes gravel; the last 8km, up to Büyüköz, is unsurfaced, narrow and very steep (expect nerve-racking twists and turns). Don't brave it in wet weather and seek local advice at Kocahisar (if you're coming from Kahta and going to Malatya) or at Büyüköz (if you're doing Malatya–Kahta) before setting off.

TAXI & MINIBUS

During the summer season there are minibuses (₺10) around every two hours from 8am to 6pm between Kahta and the Çeşme Pansion, about 6km from the summit. They stop at Karadut village (₺6) on the way. Pension owners can also pick you up at Kahta's otogar (agree the price

From Malatya

Malatya offers an alternative way to approach Nemrut Dağı. However, visiting Nemrut from this northern side means you miss out on the other fascinating sights on the southern flanks (reached from Kahta). Get the best of both worlds by traversing the top by foot and hitching a ride to Kahta. If you're travelling by car from Malatya, you'll have to take the long route via Adıyaman.

Hassle-free minibus tours to Nemrut Dağı are available from early May to the end of September, or to mid-October if the weather is still warm. Contact Ramazan Karataş (p593) in Malatya for bookings.

The three-hour drive to the summit traverses a sealed road, and after enjoying the sunset for two hours, you overnight at the Güneş Hotel (p589) before heading back up to the summit for sunrise. After breakfast at the Güneş, you return to Malatya at around 9.30am.

The per-person cost of ₺120 (minimum two people) includes transport, dinner, bed and breakfast, but excludes admission to the national park and the site. In theory, the tours run daily, but solo travellers may have to pay more if no one else is around to join you.

From Şanlıurfa

Tours (€40 per person, minimum two) to Nemrut are available from Harran-Nemrut Tours (p584)in Şanlıurfa. Mustafa Çaycı (p584) at the Hotel Uğur (₺140 per person, minimum two) also offers trips. Nomad Tours Turkey (p582) also runs full-day tours (€110 per person).

From Cappadocia

Many companies in Cappadocia offer minibus tours to Nemrut from mid-April to mid-November, despite the distance of over 500km each way. Two-day tours cost about ₺400 and involve many hours of breakneck driving. If you have enough time, opt for a more leisurely three-day tour. Three-day tours usually also include Harran and Şanlıurfa. Ask for details on night stops and driving times before committing.

beforehand). Don't believe anyone in Kahta who tells you there are no minibuses to the Çeşme Pansion and Karadut village from Kahta.

All pensions and hotels can run you up to the summit and back, but don't expect anything in the way of information. The closer to the summit, the cheaper it will be.

Malatya

☎ 0422 / POP 494,000 / ELEV 964M

Malatya's architecture wins no prizes and sights are sparse, but the city soon grows on you. The city's rewards include verdant parks, tree-lined boulevards, chaotic bazaars and the smug feeling that you're the only tourist for miles around. For cultural sustenance, there's the nearby historic sites of Battalgazi and Aslantepe, and operators also offer tours to Nemrut Dağı.

Malatya is Turkey's *kayısı* (apricot) capital, and after the late-June harvest, thousands of tonnes of the luscious fruit are shipped internationally.

History

The Assyrians and Persians alternately conquered the city, and later the kings of Cappadocia and Pontus did the same. In 66 BC Pompey defeated Mithridates and took the town, then known as Melita. The Byzantines, Sassanids, Arabs and Danışmend *emirs* held it until the Seljuks arrived in 1105. Then came the Ottomans (1399), the armies of Tamerlane (1401), the Mamluks, Dülkadır *emirs* and the Ottomans again (1515).

When the Egyptian forces of Mohammed Ali invaded Anatolia in 1839, the Ottomans garrisoned Malatya, leaving much of it in ruins on their departure. Later the residents returned and established a new city on the present site. You can visit the remains of old Malatya (Eski Malatya), now called Battalgazi, nearby.

◎ Sights

★ Bazaar   MARKET

(⊙daily) Malatya's vibrant market sprawls north from PTT Caddesi. Especially

Malatya

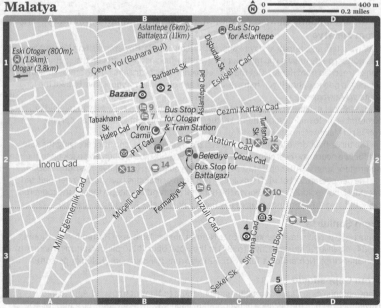

Malatya

◉ Top Sights

◉ Sights

◎ Sleeping

⊗ Eating

◉ Drinking & Nightlife

fascinating is the lively metalworking area. Brush up your Turkish and wind your way to the **Apricot Market** (*kayisi pazarı or şire pazarı*). Don't leave town without trying the chocolate-covered apricots.

Malatya Ethnographic Museum MUSEUM
(Sinema Caddesi; ◎8am-5pm) FREE English-language information brings alive this showcase of jewellery, weaving and a fearsome collection of old weapons. It's all housed near five restored old **Malatyan houses** along Sinema Caddesi.

Museum MUSEUM
(Fuzuli Caddesi; admission ₺3; ◎8am-5pm Tue-Sun) About 750m from the town centre, Malatya's museum has interesting finds from the excavations at Aslantepe.

🛏 Sleeping

Park Otel HOTEL €
(☑321 1691; parkotelmalatya@mynet.com; Atatürk Caddesi 7; s/d from ₺40/70; ❀⟩) The best budget accommodation in town with a central location and 19 rooms decked out in colourful tones. Around half the rooms have private bathrooms, but the shared facilities are clean and well kept.

Malatya Büyük Otel
HOTEL €€

(☑325 2828; www.malatyabuyukotel.com; Halep Caddesi, Yeni Cami Karşısı; s/d ₺80/120; ❉) Behind the Yeni Cami, this older hotel has recently renovated rooms with modern wooden decor, sparkling bathrooms, and lots of English-language local knowledge at reception. The location near the bazaar is very handy.

Yeni Hotel
HOTEL €€

(☑323 1423; www.malatyayenihotel.com; Yeni Cami Karşısı Zafer İşhanı; s/d ₺70/100; ❉) This well-run establishment enlivens its rooms with pastel hues, electric-blue bedspreads and spotless laminated floors. Keen shoppers should relish the location, right on the edge of the market area.

Hanem Hotel
HOTEL €€€

(☑324 1818; www.hanemhotel.com.tr; Fuzuli Caddesi 13; s/d ₺100/180; ❉ 🌐) The flashest rooms in central Malatya, with a solid four-star rating validated by modern decor, a bar, and perfect English spoken at reception. It has a central location on a shopping street that is quiet after dark.

✖ Eating

Atatürk Caddesi is awash with inexpensive eateries, and Kanal Boyu's tree-lined boulevard features cafes and ice-cream shops.

Osmanlı Kahvesi
CAFE €

(Atatürk Caddesi 67D; snacks ₺2.50) Organic coffee, freshly squeezed juices and delicious *gözleme* (savoury crepes) are available at this friendly slice of Anatolian village life in downtown Malatya. Try the *gözleme* with cheese, spinach and potato.

Beşkonaklar Malatya Mutfaği
ANATOLIAN €€

(Sinema Caddesi; mains ₺10-15; ⊙11am-9pm) Beşkonaklar Malatya Mutfaği showcases traditional local food in a restored Ottoman house. The interior is crammed with antiques, and you can adjourn to the spacious garden to enjoy interesting dishes like *anali kizli* (soup with marble-sized meatballs and chickpeas).

Mangal Vadisi
TURKISH €€

(Kışla Caddesi; mains ₺10-15; ⊙noon-10pm) Vegetarians, don't even bother reading this review: the huge *mangals* (barbecues) that take centre stage on the ground floor set the tone. This well-regarded restaurant has

grilled meat aplenty, and is in a little lane off Atatürk Caddesi.

Sarı Kurdela
TURKISH €€

(İnönü Caddesi; mains ₺6-16) Look forward to contemporary decor, efficient waitstaff and an extensive menu including pide, ready-made meals, and vegetarian dishes. Prices are cheaper in the downstairs cafeteria, and the food is just as good.

▼ Drinking & Nightlife

★Nostalji
CAFE

(Müçelli Caddesi; snacks ₺5-8; ⊙10am-11pm; 🌐) This squeaky-boarded, old Malatya mansion is packed with memorabilia. Soak up the cool karma in the light-filled main lounge while listening to mellow music and sipping Turkish coffee. Simple dishes are also available, and it's a good place to meet local students.

Taşkent
CAFE

(Kanal Boyu; ⊙7am-11pm; 🌐) One of the busier spots along Kanal Boyu, Taşkent cafe offers a laid-back atmosphere with excellent *manti* (Turkish ravioli), a menu full of nargile flavours, and the after-dark attention of Malatya's younger populace.

❶ Information

Tourist Office (☑323 2942; Sinema Caddesi; ⊙9am-5pm Mon-Fri) Adjacent to the Ethnographic Museum; little English is spoken, but has a few local brochures.

Ramazan Karataş (☑0536 873 0534; ramo4483@hotmail.com) Organises overnight trips from Malatya to Nemrut Dağı. Pick-ups from your hotel, or meet the minibus at the Malatya tourist office.

❶ Getting There & Away

AIR

The airport is 35km northwest of the centre. Ask the travel agencies on Atatürk Caddesi about the Havas bus (www.havas.net; ₺10).

Onur Air (www.onurair.com.tr) To/from İstanbul.

Pegasus Airlines (www.flypgs.com) To/from İstanbul and Ankara.

Turkish Airlines (www.thy.com) To/from İstanbul and Ankara.

BUS

Malatya's enormous **otogar**, MAŞTİ, is around 4km west of town. Most bus companies operate *servises* (shuttle minibuses) to the town centre. Minibuses from the otogar travel along Turgut

SOUTHEASTERN ANATOLIA MALATYA

Özal Bulvarı/Buhara Bulvarı but aren't allowed into the centre. Ask to be let off at the corner of Turan Temelli and Buhara Caddesis, and walk from there. City buses to the otogar (₺1.75) leave from near the *vilayet* (government building). You'll need to buy a ₺3 *kart* from the nearby booth. A taxi to the otogar costs about ₺35.

CAR

Meydan Rent a Car (☑ 325 3434; www.meydan oto.com.tr; İnönü Caddesi, Sıtmapınarı Ziraat Bankası Bitişiği; ☺ 8am-7pm) is a reliable outlet.

TRAIN

The *Vangölü Ekspresi* leaves for Ankara via Sivas and Kayseri on Tuesday and Thursday at 6.49pm. For Elazığ it leaves on Wednesday and Monday at 2.30am. Passengers are then transferred to another train for Tatvan at Elazığ.

The *Güney Ekspresi* departs for Sivas, Kayseri and Ankara on Monday, Wednesday, Friday and Sunday at 6.49pm; and for Diyarbakır at 2.30am on Tuesday, Thursday, Saturday and Sunday.

The *4 Eylül Ekspresi* departs daily for Ankara via Sivas and Kayseri at 6.30pm.

Malatya's train station can be reached by 'İstasyon' buses (₺1.50). Buses marked 'Vilayet' run from the station to the centre.

Around Malatya

Aslantepe

If you have an interest in Anatolian archaeology you'll enjoy the pretty village of Aslantepe, around 6km from Malatya. A modern pavilion has transformed the archaeological site (admission ₺3; ☺ 8am-5pm Tue-Sun) into an open-air museum, and excellent information in English and Italian brings alive the impact of the site on modern culture and society.

When the Phrygians invaded the Hittite kingdom at Boğazkale, around 1200 BC, many Hittites fled southeast over the Taurus Mountains to resettle and build walled cities. The city of Milidia, now known as Aslantepe, was one of these neo-Hittite city-states. Sporadic excavations since the 1930s have so far uncovered seven layers of remains.

To get to Aslantepe from Malatya, catch a number 59 or 401 bus marked 'Orduzu' (₺1.75, 15 minutes) from the southern side of Buhara Bulvarı near the junction with Akpınar Caddesi. These buses pass the entrance gates.

Battalgazi (Old Malatya)

You don't need to be an archaeology buff to be captivated by the remains of Old Malatya, the walled city settled alongside Aslantepe, about 11km north of Malatya at Battalgazi.

As you come into the village you'll see the ruins of the old city walls with their 95 towers, built during Roman times and completed in the 6th century.

The bus from Malatya terminates in the main square. Just off here, beside the mosque with the smooth-topped minaret, is the Silahtar Mustafa Paşa Hanı, a restored Ottoman caravanserai dating from the 17th century. Also near the main square, explore Sanat Sokağı, a street of restored heritage houses now trimmed with interesting contemporary ceramic art.

From the caravanserai, turn right and follow Osman Ateş Caddesi for about 600m until you see the broken brick minaret of the finely restored 13th-century Ulu Cami on the left. This stunning, if fast-fading, Seljuk building dates from the reign of Alaettin Keykubad I. Also worthy of interest is the Ak Minare Camii (White Minaret Mosque),

SERVICES FROM MALATYA'S OTOGAR

DESTINATION	FARE (₺)	DURATION (HR)	DISTANCE (KM)	FREQUENCY (PER DAY)
Adana	30	8	425	3-4
Adıyaman	15	2½	144	frequent
Ankara	40	11	685	frequent
Diyarbakır	30	4	260	3-4
Elazığ	10	1¾	101	hourly
Gaziantep	25	4	250	3-4
İstanbul	60	18	1130	3-4
Kayseri	30	4	354	several
Sivas	30	5	235	several

DARENDE – THE FORGOTTEN OASIS

About 110km west of Malatya, Darende is a terrific place to kick off your shoes for a day or two in a fabulous setting. There's a splendid canyon right on its doorstep, as well as well-preserved architectural treasures, including the **Somuncu Baba Camii ve Külliyesi**; the **Kudret Havuzu**, a rock pool set in the **Tohma Canyon**; and the stark **Zengibar Kalesi**, perched high on a rocky outcrop.

Along the riverbank of the canyon are restaurants specialising in fresh trout. **Hasbahçe** (☑ 0422-615 2215; Somuncu Baba Camii Civari; mains ₺8-12) is a firm favourite. In summer, men only (sorry) can swim in the Kudret Havuzu, and **rafting** (☑ 0422-615 3513, 0555 565 4935; per person from ₺40) (for everyone) is also possible in the Tohma Canyon; see the Tiryandafil Otel for more information and bookings. Don't expect massive thrills, but look forward to transiting through stunning canyons against the background of a stark cobalt sky.

The **Tiryandafil Otel** (☑ 0422-615 3095; s/d ₺120/175; 图 @) is conveniently located about 1km before the canyon and monuments. It has impeccable, spacious rooms, and the on-site restaurant (meals ₺15 to ₺20) has local specialities – try the *şelale sızdırma* (meat with melted cheese, mushrooms and butter). Ask for Talha, who speaks excellent English and can help with any queries.

With your own wheels, visit the **Gürpinar Şelalesi** (waterfalls), about 7km from Darende (from the hotel, follow the road to Ankara for 6km; then it's signposted). Don't expect Niagara-like falls, but it's an excellent picnic spot.

Regular minibuses (₺10) link Malatya and Darende. In Malatya, they depart from the shabby minibus terminal known as Eski Otogar or Köy Garagj on Çevre Yol. Buses from Kayseri also run to Darende (₺30), making it a good stop if you're travelling east from Cappadocia.

about 50m from the Ulu Cami. This also dates from the 13th century.

Close by is the 13th-century **Halfetih Minaret**, made completely of bricks, and the **Nezir Gazi Tomb**.

Buses to Battalgazi (₺1.75, 15 minutes) leave regularly from central Malatya.

Diyarbakır

☑ 0412 / POP 963,000 / ELEV 60M

Full of heart, soul and character, Diyar is finally tapping into its fantastic potential as a destination for travellers. While it's proud of being symbolic of Kurdish identity and tenacity, increasing promotion and restoration programs have seen Turkish and foreign tourists streaming back. Behind the grim basalt walls, the old city's twisting alleyways are crammed full of historical buildings and Arab-style mosques.

In past decades, Diyarbakır has witnessed pro-Kurdish demonstrations and riots, but with the recent and current rapprochement between the PKK (Kurdistan Workers Party) and the Turkish government, pride in being Kurdish is now more openly expressed.

Banned until a few years ago, the Nevruz festival takes place on 21 March and is a great occasion to immerse yourself in Kurdish culture. Another big Kurdish celebration takes place on 1 May for May Day, and apart from a few street kids on the walls, Diyarbakır is as safe as any other city in the region.

History

Mesopotamia, the land between the Tigris and Euphrates Valleys, saw the dawn of the world's first great empires. Diyarbakır's history began with the Hurrian kingdom of Mitanni around 1500 BC and proceeded through domination by the civilisations of Urartu (900 BC), Assyria (1356–612 BC), Persia (600–330 BC) and Alexander the Great and his successors, the Seleucids.

The Romans took over in AD 115, but because of its strategic position the city changed hands numerous times until it was conquered by the Arabs in 639. The Arab tribe of Beni Bakr that settled here named their new home Diyar Bakr, which means the Realm of Bakr.

For the next few centuries the city was occupied by various tribes, until 1497 when the Safavid dynasty founded by Shah İsmail took over Iran, putting an end to more than a century of Turkoman rule in this area. The Ottomans came and conquered in 1515, but even then, Diyarbakır was not to know lasting peace. In subsequent centuries, invading armies from Anatolia, Persia and Syria all overcame the city's walls.

In more modern times (since the 1980s), the city has been the centre of the Kurdish resistance movement. Throughout the 1990s many refugees from the conflict between the PKK and the Turkish government moved to the city, and Diyarbakır continues to be one of the east's fastest-growing urban centres.

On the road to Şanlıurfa in particular, phalanxes of new apartment blocks are forever multiplying, and the attraction for rural Kurds to the city is now based in economic and employment reasons.

◉ Sights

When visiting Diyarbakır's mosques, time your visit for 20 to 25 minutes after the call to prayer (when the prayers should be finished), as some are locked outside prayer times.

★ City Walls & Gates   FORTRESS

Diyarbakır's single most conspicuous feature is its great circuit of basalt walls, probably dating from Roman times – although the present walls, around 6km in total length, date from early Byzantine times (AD 330–500). Be prudent when walking on and along the walls as there have been reports of attempted robberies. Try to go in a group and keep personal items and cameras safe.

There were originally four main gates: Harput Kapısı (north), Mardin Kapısı (south), Yenikapı (east) and Urfa Kapısı (west). Fortunately, the most accessible stretch of walls is also the most interesting in terms of inscriptions and decoration. Start near the Mardin Kapısı close to the Deliller Han, a stone caravanserai now home to the Otel Büyük Kervansaray. Don't miss Nur Burcu, the Yedi Kardeş Burcu, with two Seljuk lion bas-reliefs – only visible from outside the walls – and the bas-reliefs of the Malikşah Burcu.

Ascend the walls of the İç Kale (keep) for fine views of the Tigris. The İç Kale has been undergoing restoration for several years, and includes the beautifully resurrected 3rd-century-AD St George Church. Other ongoing restoration projects include using an historic prison as a new location for the city's Archaeology Museum.

At various spots inside the walls are brightly painted, open-air Sufi sarcophagi, notable for their turbans; their size is a symbol of spiritual authority. There's a cluster a few hundred metres northeast of the Urfa Kapısı.

★ Dengbêj Evi   CULTURAL CENTRE

(http://turizm.diyarbakir.bel.tr/en/s/Dengbej_House; Kılıççı Sokak, near Behram Paşa Camii; ◷ 9am-6pm Tue-Sun) The Dengbêj Evi (House of Dengbêj) showcases the Kurdish tradition of *dengbêj*, storytelling by song. Kurdish elders gather together in informal groups and take turns to sing and chant in an ethereal and mesmerising style. Their associates add bold affirmations to underpin the melancholy and yearning melodies, and it's a compelling way to spend an hour or so in Turkey's most important Kurdish city. The complex also houses a tea garden.

★ Ulu Cami   MOSQUE

Diyarbakır's most impressive mosque is the Ulu Cami, built in 1091 by a Seljuk sultan. Incorporating elements from an earlier Byzantine church on the site, it was restored in 1155 after a fire.

The rectangular layout is Arabic, rather than Ottoman. The entrance portal, adorned with two medallions figuring a lion and a bull, leads to a huge courtyard with two-storey arcades, two cone-shaped *şadırvans* (ritual ablutions fountains), elaborate pillars, and friezes featuring fruits and vegetables.

Nebi Camii   MOSQUE

At the main intersection of Gazi and İzzet Paşa/İnönü Caddesi, is Nebi Camii, featuring a detached minaret sporting a stunning combination of black-and-white stone. This alternating black-and-white banding is characteristic of Diyarbakır's mosques, many dating from the Akkoyunlu dynasty.

Behram Paşa Camii   MOSQUE

The Behram Paşa Camii, in a residential area deep in the maze of narrow streets, is Diyarbakır's largest mosque.

Safa Camii   MOSQUE

Persian in style, the Safa Camii has a highly decorated minaret with blue tiles incorporated in its design.

Şeyh Mutahhar Camii   MOSQUE

The Şeyh Mutahhar Camii is famous for its minaret, but its engineering is even more interesting – the tower stands on four slender pillars about 2m high, earning it the name Dört Ayaklı Minare (Four-Legged Minaret).

Hazreti Süleyman Camii   MOSQUE

This 12th-century mosque, beside the İç Kale, is particularly revered because it houses the tombs of heroes of past Islamic wars.

Diyarbakır Houses   NOTABLE BUILDINGS

Predominantly owned by Armenian families, Diyarbakır houses were made of black basalt and decorated with stone stencilling. They were divided into summer and winter quarters. In the summer part the *eyvan* was a vaulted room opening onto the courtyard with a fountain. During warmer weather, the family moved high wooden platforms called *tahts* into the courtyard for sleeping, making it possible to catch any breeze. Good examples are the Esma Ocak Evi and the Cahit Sıtkı Tarancı Museum.

Esma Ocak Evi   HISTORIC BUILDING

`FREE` The beautiful grey-and-white-striped Esma Ocak Evi was built in 1899 by the Armenian Şakarer family and restored in 1996 by the female writer Esma Ocak. Now it houses a very pleasant and relaxing tea garden.

Cahit Sıtkı Tarancı Museum   MUSEUM

(Ziya Gökalp Sokak; ⊙8am-5pm Tue-Sun) `FREE` The poet Cahit Sıtkı Tarancı (1910–56) was born in this two-storey black basalt house built in 1820 in a side street about 50m north of the Ulu Cami. It now houses the Cahit Sıtkı Tarancı Museum exhibiting the poet's personal effects and furnishings.

Keldani Kilisesi   CHURCH

(Chaldean Church; ⊙9am-5pm) The population of Diyarbakır used to include many Christians, mainly Armenians and Chaldeans, but most were pushed out or perished during the troubles in the early 20th century – or, more recently, with the Hezbollah.

Off Yenikapı Caddesi, this plain, brightly lit church is still used by a few Christian families of the Syrian rite (in communion with the Roman Catholic church). It is signposted from near the Şeyh Mutahhar Camii.

Surp Giragos Kilisesi   CHURCH

This Armenian church has been reopened after a wonderful restoration. Highlights include a superb wooden ceiling, and the church's cloisters showcase interesting historic photographs of Diyarbakır's Armenian heritage. Press the doorbell and someone will usually appear from within or from the surrounding neighbourhood to provide access.

Meryem Ana Kilisesi   CHURCH

(Church of the Virgin Mary; admission ₺2; ⊙services 8-11am Sun) Still used by Syrian Orthodox Christians, this church is beautifully maintained, although only about three families still attend services. Local kids will show you the way.

Gazi Köşkü   HISTORIC BUILDING

(admission ₺1) About 1km south of the Mardin Kapısı, the fine Gazi Köşkü is the sort of Diyarbakır house to which wealthier citizens would retire during summer. The house dates from the time of the 15th-century Akkoyunlu Turkoman dynasty and stands in a well-tended park. The caretaker will expect a tip for showing you around. To get there, it's a pleasant, if rather isolated, downhill walk. Taxis charge around ₺20. About 1km further south is the 11th-century **On Gözlu Köprüsü** (Ten-Eyed Bridge).

Archaeology Museum   MUSEUM

(Arkeoloji Müzesi; İç Kale; admission ₺3) Diyarbakır's Archaeology Museum was closed at the time of writing, and scheduled to reopen in 2015 inside an old prison in İç Kale. Ask at the tourist office for an update. Before the move, the well-presented collection included finds from the Neolithic site of Çayönü (7500–6500 BC), 65km north of Diyarbakır. Also showcased was a decent Urartian collection and relics from the Karakoyunlu and Akkoyunlu, powerful tribal dynasties that ruled much of eastern Anatolia and Iran between 1378 and 1502.

🛏 Sleeping

Most accommodation is on Kıbrıs Caddesi and nearby İnönü Caddesi. Kıbrıs Caddesi does suffer from traffic noise, so try to secure a room at the back.

Hotel Surkent   HOTEL €

(☏228 1014; www.hotelsurkent.com; İzzet Paşa Caddesi; s/d ₺35/70; ❄ 🛜) In a quiet, centrally located street, the colourful Surkent is a popular choice for overland travellers. Top-floor rooms boast good views – for singles, rooms 501, 502 and 503 are the best. Avoid the downstairs rooms near reception as they can be noisy. Breakfast is an additional ₺5 and there's no lift (elevator).

Diyarbakır

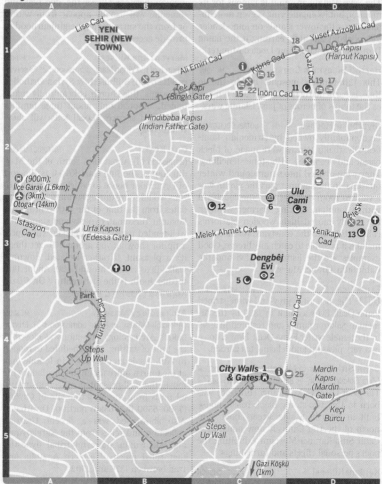

New Tigris Hotel　　　　HOTEL €€
(☎ 224 9696; www.newtigrishotel.com; Kıbrıs Caddesi 3; s/d ₺90/130; ❄️🛜) In close proximity to good restaurants, the New Tigris has lifted the game for competing hotels along bustling Kıbrıs Caddesi. Wooden floors, neutral decor, and sparkling and spacious bathrooms make the New Tigris one of the best midrange deals in town.

Otel Ertem　　　　HOTEL €€
(☎ 223 4047; İzzet Paşa Caddesi; s/d ₺70/120) Compact rooms, modern decor and gleaming bathrooms all combine at one of Diyarbakır's newest hotels. Reception is particularly snazzy and the rooms upstairs are just as trendy.

Hotel Ekin　　　　HOTEL €€
(☎ 224 90 01; http://hotelekin.com; Kıbrıs Caddesi 38; s/d ₺70/100; ❄️🛜) Opened in 2009, the Ekin is a good addition to the Kıbrıs Caddesi hotel scene. Rooms are relatively spacious and sunny, and the views from the rooftop breakfast salon will have you lingering for another glass of tea.

Hotel Kaplan　　　　HOTEL €€
(☎ 229 3300; www.kaplanhotel.com; Kıbrıs Caddesi 25; s/d ₺80/120; ❄️🛜) One of Diyarbakır's

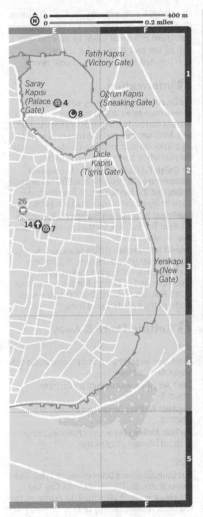

Diyarbakır

superb crisp wood-fired pide and is open around the clock if you arrive on a late bus.

★**Diyarbakır Kahvaltı Evi** CAFE €€
(www.diyarbakirevi.com; Dicle Sokak 20; breakfast ₺15, snacks & mains ₺7-15; 🛜) Kick off another fascinating Diyarbakır day with a leisurely breakfast in the leafy courtyard of this heritage mansion. A posse of cats occasionally mooches in from nearby laneways, and there's live music with jazz, rock and Kurdish tunes most Saturday nights from 8pm. Drop by and see what's scheduled. From the Şeyh Mutahhar Camii, turn left.

Meşhur Kahvaltıcı CAFE €€
(Hasan Paşa Hanı; breakfast ₺25) More expensive than the *kahvaltı* (breakfast) spots along Kıbrıs Caddesi, but worth it for the glorious ambience of the restored Hasan Paşa Hanı. Enjoy a leisurely breakfast of multiple small

older hotels has been freshened up with a recent renovation. Rooms are spacious and, despite the location on bustling Kıbrıs Caddesi, usually very quiet.

✕ Eating

Kıbrıs Caddesi has plenty of good-value, informal eateries.

Şafak Kahvaltı & Yemek Salonu TURKISH €
(Kıbrıs Caddesi; mains ₺8-12; ⊙24hr) Nosh on freshly prepared meat dishes, hearty casseroles and stuffed vegetables in this brisk Diyarbakır institution. It also does

plates on the balcony, and feel very pleased with yourself for adding Diyarbakır to your Turkish itinerary.

Çarşı Konağı TURKISH €€

(Gazi Caddesi; mains ₺10-18) This restored 450-year-old house conceals a leafy courtyard and poignant reminders of its former Jewish owners. (Look for the carved Star of David in the wooden ceiling.) Kebaps, grilled fish and salads are on offer, and you'll probably be invited for an extended çay session with friendly Diyar locals. It's popular with local women, so good for female travellers.

Selim Amca'nın Sofra Salonu TURKISH €€

(Ali Emiri Caddesi; set menu for two people ₺65) This bright eatery outside the city walls is famous for its *kaburga dolması* (lamb stuffed with rice and almonds). Round it off with a devilish *İrmik helvası* (a gooey dessert).

Drinking & Entertainment

★Hasan Paşa Hanı COFFEEHOUSE

(Gazi Caddesi; ⊙8am-10pm) Opposite the Ulu Cami, this restored 16th-century caravanserai is occupied by jewellers and carpet shops, and is perfect for a leisurely breakfast. Live music is also regularly advertised, and the friendly Kamer Avlu cafe downstairs is run by an organisation supporting women's rights in eastern Turkey.

Samo CAFE

(Surp Gragos Kilisesi Arkası) Let the hard-to-miss signage guide you through Diyarbakır's compelling labyrinth to this bohemian courtyard house with well-priced snacks and meze, Assyrian wine, and live music from 6pm to 9pm from Friday to Sunday.

Otel Büyük Kervansaray TEA GARDEN

(Gazi Caddesi; ⊙11am-10pm) The expansive courtyard is a great place to unwind over a cup of tea and take in the atmosphere. It's also licensed if you feel like a cold beer.

ⓘ Information

Old Diyarbakır is encircled by walls, pierced by several main gates. Within the walls the city is a maze of narrow, twisting, mostly unmarked alleys. Most services useful to travellers are in Old Diyarbakır, on or around Gazi Caddesi, including the post office, travel agencies and ATMs.

Ali Çalişir (✆0532 283 2367; bbcnews44@ hotmail.com) After working as a BBC cameraman throughout the Middle East, he has returned home to Diyarbakır to work as a local guide.

Municipal Information Bureau (⊙9am-noon & 1-6pm Tue-Sat) Ask for the English-language map. Irregular hours.

Tourist Information Office (www.turizm. diyarbakir.bel.tr; Gazi Caddesi; ⊙8am-5pm Tue-Sun) Excellent English spoken, good brochures, and an English-Kurdish phrasebook called *Welcome to Amed*. Don't miss the scale model of the walled city out front.

ⓘ Getting There & Away

AIR

There is no airport bus. A taxi will cost about ₺15 from Kıbrıs Caddesi.

Onur Air (www.onurair.com.tr) To/from İstanbul.

Pegasus Airlines (www.flypgs.com) To/from İstanbul.

Turkish Airlines (www.turkishairlines.com) To/from İstanbul and Ankara.

BUS

Bus companies have ticket offices on İnönü Caddesi or along Gazi Caddesi near the Dağ Kapısı. The otogar is about 14km from the centre, on the road to Urfa (about ₺25 by taxi).

SERVICES FROM DİYARBAKIR'S OTOGAR

DESTINATION	FARE (₺)	DURATION (HR)	DISTANCE (KM)	FREQUENCY (PER DAY)
Adana	40	8	550	several
Ankara	70	13	945	several
Erzurum	45	8	485	several
Malatya	30	5	260	frequent
Mardin	15	1½	95	hourly
Şanlıurfa	20	3	190	frequent
Sivas	50	10	500	several
Tatvan	30	4	264	several
Van	45	7	410	several

ⓘ GETTING TO KURDISH IRAQ

Direct buses – departing at 11am, 5.30pm and 8pm – travel from Diyarbakır to Dohuk (₺50, six hours) or Erbil (₺60, nine hours). See the bus companies along Kıbrıs Caddesi. You may need to supply your passport details the day before you travel. Note that the bus can be slower to cross the border than a shared taxi, so if time is a consideration, catch a bus from Diyarbakır to Silopi (₺30, 4½ hours), and pick up a more expensive taxi through to the Iraqi border town of Zakho.

Buses to Kurdish Iraq also travel from the Turkish city of Cizre (₺35), around four hours south of Diyarbakır. From Diyarbakır to the border at Habur, it's around four hours, and then it's another 1½ hours to Dohuk, and three hours to Erbil.

For more about travelling in Kurdish Iraq, check out the 'Travel to Kurdistan' fact sheet at www.krg.org, the website of the Kurdistan Regional Government.

At the time of writing, the security situation in northern Iraq was increasingly dangerous and unstable, so assess the current situation and check government travel advisories very carefully before planning visits to this area.

There's a separate minibus terminal (İlçe Garajı), about 1.5km southwest of the city walls, with services to Batman (₺10, 1½ hours), Mardin (₺8, 1¼ hours), Malatya (₺30, five hours) and Siverek (to get to Kahta without going right round the lake via Adıyaman). For Hasankeyf, change in Batman (₺10). To get to the minibus terminal, catch a bus (₺1.50) on Kıbrıs Caddesi, or take a taxi (₺15).

CAR

Avis (☑ 229 0275, 236 1324; www.avis.com.tr; Elazığ Caddesi; ⊙ 8am-7pm) Opposite the *belediye* (town hall) and at the airport.

TRAIN

The train station is about 1.5km from the centre, at the western end of İstasyon Caddesi. The *Güney Ekspresi* leaves for Ankara via Malatya and Sivas at 1.14pm on Monday, Wednesday, Friday and Sunday.

Mardin

☑ 0482 / POP 88,000 / ELEV 1325M

Mardin is a highly addictive and unmissable spot. Minarets emerge from a baked brown labyrinth of meandering lanes, a castle dominates the old city, and stone houses cascade down the hillside above the Mesopotamian plains. As a melting pot of Kurdish, Yezidi, Christian and Syrian cultures, it also has a fascinating cultural mix.

Just don't expect to have the whole place to yourself. With regular flights from İstanbul, İzmir and Ankara, you'll see lots of local visitors in summer. The Turkish government also has plans to promote Mardin internationally as an iconic Turkish destination like Ephesus and Pamukkale, and have (optimistically) projected up to five million domestic and overseas visitors annually by 2025.

Mardin's honey-coloured collage of old buildings and markets is still definitely worth a look though, and for somewhere extra special, detour to Dara or Savur.

History

As with Diyarbakır, Mardin's history is one of disputes between rival armies over millennia, though in recent years the only dispute that anyone has really cared about is the one between the PKK (Kurdistan Workers Party) and the government.

A castle has stood on this hill from time immemorial. The Turkish army has traditionally occupied the castle to assert authority, but now that relations between the PKK and the government are progressing positively, castle access for visitors is planned for the future. Check at the tourist office.

Assyrian Christians settled here during the 5th century, and the Arabs occupied Mardin between 640 and 1104. After that, it had a succession of Seljuk Turkish, Kurdish, Mongol and Persian overlords, until the Ottomans under Sultan Selim the Grim took it in 1517. In the early 20th century many of the Assyrian Christians were pushed out or perished during the troubles, and in the last few decades many have emigrated. A few hundred Christians remain, with several churches still in use on a rotational basis.

⊙ Sights & Activities

⭐ **Sakıp Sabancı Mardin City Museum**　　　　　MUSEUM
(Sakıp Sabancı Mardin Kent Müzesi; www.sabancimuzesimardin.gov.tr; Eski Hükümet Caddesi;

Mardin

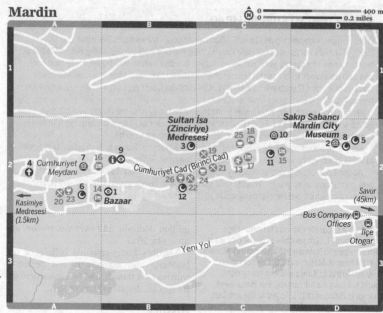

SOUTHEASTERN ANATOLIA MARDIN

Mardin

admission ₺2; ⊙8am-5pm Tue-Sun) Housed in former army barracks, this superb museum showcases the fascinating history and culture of Mardin. Excellent English-language translations and effective use of audio and video reinforce how cosmopolitan and multicultural the city's past was. Downstairs is used as an art gallery for a rotating series of exhibitions, often including images by iconic Turkish photographers.

★**Sultan İsa (Zinciriye)
Medresesi** MOSQUE

(Cumhuriyet Caddesi) Dating from 1385, the complex's highlight is the imposing recessed doorway, but make sure you wander through the pretty courtyards, lovingly tended by the caretaker, and onto the roof to enjoy the cityscape. The tea garden is a top spot to sit and survey Mardin's beauty.

★**Bazaar** MARKET

Mardin's rambling commercial hub parallels Cumhuriyet Caddesi one block down the hill. Donkeys are still a main form of transport; look out for saddle repairers resurrecting even the shabbiest examples.

Make time for the secluded **Ulu Cami**, a 12th-century Iraqi Seljuk structure that suffered badly during the Kurdish rebellion of 1832. Inside it's fairly plain, but the delicate reliefs adorning the minaret make a visit worthwhile.

Forty Martyrs Church CHURCH

(Kırklar Kilisesi; Sağlık Sokak) This church dates back to the 4th century, and was renamed in the 15th century to commemorate Cappadocian martyrs, now remembered in the fine carvings above the entrance. Services are held here each Sunday, and there's a wonderful inner courtyard. A caretaker is usually on hand to provide access to the church's compact but beautiful interior.

Mardin Museum MUSEUM

(Mardin Müzesi; Cumhuriyet Caddesi; admission ₺5; ⊙8am-5pm Tue-Sun) This superbly restored late-19th-century mansion sports carved pillars and elegant arcades on the upper floor. Inside, it has a small but well-displayed collection including a finely detailed 7th-century-BC Assyrian vase and finds from Girnavaz, a Bronze Age site 4km north of Nusaybin.

East along Cumhuriyet Caddesi is the beautiful three-arched facade of an ornately carved **old Mardin house**.

Post Office HISTORIC BUILDING

(Cumhuriyet Caddesi) Turkey's most impressive former post office is housed in a 17th-century caravanserai covered with carvings, including teardrops in stone dripping down the walls. Restoration is ongoing.

Şehidiye Camii MOSQUE

(Cumhuriyet Caddesi) Look for the elegant, slender minaret of this 14th-century mosque. Also worth visiting is the 14th-century **Latifiye Camii**, behind the Akbank, where a shady courtyard has a şadırvan (ablutions fountain) in the middle. Nearby, the eye-catching **Hatuniye** and **Melik Mahmut Camii** have been fully restored.

Kasımiye Medresesi MOSQUE

Built in 1469, two domes stand over the tombs of Kasım Paşa and his sister, but the highlights are the courtyard with arched colonnades and a magnificent carved doorway. Upstairs, see the students' quarters, before ascending for another great Mardin rooftop panorama. It's signposted 800m south of Yeni Yol.

Emir Hamamı HAMAM

(Cumhuriyet Caddesi; treatments from ₺25; ⊙men 6.30am-noon & 6-10pm, women noon-5.30pm) This hamam's history goes back to Roman times. Unfortunately the heritage interior is muddied by fluorescent lighting, but there are great post-hamam views from the terrace.

🛏 Sleeping

Mardin's popularity means that accommodation is expensive. The city's boutique hotels are undeniably atmospheric, but rooms can be small and lack natural light. Ask the right questions when you book. Summer weekends are very busy with Turkish tourists, so consider Mardin as a day trip from Midyat or Diyarbakır. Mardin accommodation is generally cheaper from Sunday to Thursday.

Şahmeran Otanik Pansiyon PENSION €

(🖉213 2300; www.sahmeranpansiyon.com; Cumhuriyet Caddesi, 246 Sokak 10; dm ₺30, r per person ₺70, without bathroom ₺50; 🕸) This rustic pension is arrayed around a honey-coloured stone courtyard just a short uphill meander from Mardin's main thoroughfare. Kilims and heritage features decorate the simply furnished rooms and shared dorms. Breakfast is an additional ₺5.

★**Dara Konaği** BOUTIQUE HOTEL €€

(🖉212 3272; www.darakonagi.com; Şehidiye Mahallesi 39; s/d €35/55; ❋🕸) In an 800-year-old mansion with views of the Plains of Mesopotamia, Dara Konaği is one of Mardin's best boutique hotels. Most rooms are relatively spacious although some have limited natural light, but the shared courtyard and verandah are tranquil and welcoming. Heritage furniture completes the deal, and the friendly English-speaking owner offers good local information.

İpek Yolu Guesthouse GUESTHOUSE €€

(🖉212 1477; www.ipekyolukadinkoop.com; Cumhuriyet Caddesi, Sokak 7; s/d ₺80/160; ❋🕸) Antique radios add a quirky touch to this restored heritage guesthouse a short stroll from Mardin's main street, and flowers brighten up the (mainly) spacious rooms.

Head to the top floor for excellent views of Mardin's honey-coloured architectural jumble, or get your travel diary up-to-date in the lovely shared courtyard.

Antik Tatlıede Butik Hotel   BOUTIQUE HOTEL €€
(🖉 213 2720; www.tatlidede.com.tr; Medrese Mahallesi; s/d/tr ₺100/150/200; 🕸🛜) In a quiet location near Mardin's bazaar, a labyrinthine heritage mansion is filled with rooms of varying sizes. Most are fairly spacious, and all are filled with a rustic mix of old kilims and antique furniture.

Reyhani Kasrı   BOUTIQUE HOTEL €€€
(🖉 212 1333; www.reyhanikasri.com.tr; Cumhuriyet Caddesi; s/d from ₺120/190; 🕸🛜) Sleek and modern rooms are concealed within a lovingly restored historic mansion, providing a more contemporary spin on the usual Mardin boutique hotel experience. Multiple floors cascade down the hillside, making it one of Mardin's more spectacular buildings. Pop in for a drink at the hotel's remarkable 'Sky Terrace' bar.

✗ Eating & Drinking

★ Seyr-İ-Mardin   ANATOLIAN €€
(Cumhuriyet Caddesi 249; meze & mains ₺6-25; ⊘9am-10pm) Translating to 'Mardin's Eye', this multilevel cafe, teahouse and restaurant has superb views. Settle in to one of the colourful couches and feast on excellent grills or the *meze tabagi* (mixed meze). Look forward to good service courtesy of the owner, who speaks very good English.

Rido'nun Yeri   KEBAP €€
(Cumhuriyet Caddesi 219; mains ₺12; ⊘11am-10pm) Keeping it simple for several generations of the same family with perfectly grilled lamb, fluffy flatbreads, and rustic bowls of *ayran*.

Antik Sur   TURKISH €€
(Cumhuriyet Caddesi; mains ₺10-20; ⊘10am-midnight) Ease into the shaded surrounds of this restored caravanserai. Turkish tourists love the local flavours and the opportunity to try Assyrian wine. Live music kicks off around 8pm most weekends, often incurring an additional fee of ₺30. This is not always made clear by the waiters, so check before sitting down. Bring along your backgammon 'A game' for the teahouse upstairs.

Cercis Murat Konağı   ANATOLIAN €€€
(🖉 213 6841; Cumhuriyet Caddesi; mains ₺25; ⊘noon-11pm) The Cercis occupies a traditional Syrian Christian home with two finely decorated rooms and a terrace with stunning views. *Mekbuss* (aubergine pickles with walnut), *kitel raha* (Syrian-style meatballs) and *dobo* (lamb with garlic, spices and black pepper) rank among the highlights. Dive into the meze platters (₺30 to ₺50) for a taste of everything that's good.

Try to book a couple of days ahead, or drop by at lunchtime and book for dinner. Wine and beer (₺10) are also served.

Çamli Kösk   TEAHOUSE
(Cumhuriyet Caddesi; ⊘5am-10pm) Join the moustachioed throngs in Mardin's most authentic tea- and coffeehouse. In between blokey rounds of backgammon, cards and *okey* (a tile-based game), the faded patina of the interior also showcases the elaborate ritual of *mirra* coffee, a stronger and more bitter variant popular in southeast Turkey.

Leylan Cafe & Kitap   CAFE
(Cumhuriyet Caddesi; ⊘11am-late) Part cafe, part bookshop, and part performance space with occasional live Kurdish music. There's also beer, wine and a balcony looking out over Mardin's bustling main drag.

Abbabar Bar   BAR
(www.abbabarbar.com; Cumhuriyet Caddesi; ⊘11am-midnight) Either retire to the expansive terrace for views, or grab an indoor table and a cold beer and wait for the live music to kick off. From Wednesday to Saturday, that's usually from 8pm to 1am.

Vitamin   JUICE BAR
(Cumhuriyet Caddesi; juices from ₺3; ⊘9am-6pm) With bright orange walls adorned with musical instruments, this pea-sized joint is Mardin's kookiest spot. The owner is a local muso of note.

Atilla Çay Bahçesi   TEA GARDEN
(Cumhuriyet Caddesi; ⊘7am-11pm) Tea garden with phenomenal views over old Mardin and the Plains of Mesopotamia.

ⓘ Information

Banks and ATMs are on Cumhuriyet Caddesi, old Mardin's one-way main street.

Tourist Information Office (Cumhuriyet Caddesi; ⊘9am-5.30pm) English spoken and good maps and brochures.

ℹ️ Getting There & Away

AIR

Mardin airport is around 20km south of Mardin. There's no airport shuttle, but any minibus to Kızıltepe can drop you (₺2.50). A taxi from the airport to old Mardin is around ₺30.

Pegasus Airlines (www.flypgs.com) To/from İstanbul and Izmir.

Turkish Airlines (www.turkishairlines.com) To/from İstanbul and Ankara.

BUS

Most buses leave from the **İlçe Otogar** east of the centre. At the time of writing a new regional bus station was planned, so this may change. Check at the tourist information office.

For long-distance destinations, buses stop in front of the **bus company offices** in the old town and in new Mardin. From around 4pm services dwindle, so make an early start.

Minibuses depart around every hour for Diyarbakır (₺12, 1¼ hours), and Midyat (₺10, 1¼ hours). There are also relatively frequent minibuses to Savur (₺8, one hour). Other destinations include Şanlıurfa (₺30, three hours), and Cizre (₺25, 2½ hours) for onward travel to Kurdish Iraq.

Around Mardin

Deyrul Zafaran

The magnificent Deyrul Zafaran (Monastery of Mar Hanania; adult/concession ₺6/3; ⊘9am-noon & 1-6pm) stands about 6km along a good road in the rocky hills east of Mardin. The monastery was once the seat of the Syrian Orthodox patriarchate but this has now moved to Damascus.

In 495 the first monastery was built on a site previously dedicated to the worship of the sun. Destroyed by the Persians in 607, it was rebuilt, only to be looted by Tamerlane six centuries later.

Shortly after entering the walled enclosure via a portal bearing a Syriac (a dialect of Aramaic) inscription, you'll see the original sanctuary, an eerie underground chamber with a ceiling of huge, closely fitted stones. This room was allegedly used by sun-worshippers, who viewed their god rising through a window at the eastern end. A niche on the southern wall is said to have been for sacrifices. Nearby is a pair of 300-year-old doors leading to the tombs of the patriarchs and metropolitans who have served here.

In the chapel, the patriarch's throne to the left of the altar bears the names of all the patriarchs who have served the monastery since 792. Past patriarchs are buried seated and facing east, wearing full robes so they're ready and dressed for God.

To the right of the altar is the throne of the metropolitan. The present stone altar replaces a wooden one that burnt down about half a century ago. The walls are adorned with wonderful paintings and wall hangings. Services in Aramaic are held here.

In the next rooms you'll see litters used to transport the church dignitaries, and a baptismal font. In a small side room is a 300-year-old wooden throne. The floor mosaic is about 1500 years old.

A flight of stairs leads to very simple guest rooms for those coming for worship. The patriarch's small, simple bedroom and parlour are also up here.

There's no public transport here so you must take a taxi or walk around 90 minutes from Mardin. Hopeful drivers wait outside the bus company offices in Mardin and will ask around ₺50 to run you there and back.

Try to visit on a weekday or the monastic hush could be disturbed by busloads of Turkish tourists. You must visit the monastery in the company of a guide.

Dara

About 30km southeast of Mardin is a magnificent ancient Roman city forgotten in time. Dating back to the 6th century, Dara (admission free) is where Mesopotamia's first dam and irrigation canals were built. Ongoing excavation promises to reveal one of southeastern Anatolia's forgotten gems. The highlight is walking down ancient stairways into the towers of Dara's underground aqueducts and cisterns. Natural light ebbs and flows into the expanse to create a remarkable cathedral-like ambience.

Except for a couple of teahouses, there are no facilities in Dara. From Mardin, there are three daily buses (₺5).

Savur

Savur is like a miniature Mardin, without the crowds. The setting is enchanting, with a weighty citadel surrounded by honey-coloured old houses, lots of greenery and a gushing river running in the valley.

With your own car, drive to **Kıllıt** (Dereiçi) about 7km east of Savur. This Syrian Orthodox village has two restored churches.

Sleeping & Eating

Hacı Abdullah Bey Konaği PENSION €
(☏0535 275 2569; savurkonagi@hotmail.com; r per person half board ₺100) Perched on the hilltop, this gorgeous *konak* has seven rooms cosily outfitted with kilims, brass beds and antiques. Another pull is the friendly welcome of the Öztürk family. They don't speak much English, but offer a convivial atmosphere and serve traditional meals prepared from fresh ingredients. Bathrooms are shared.

**Uğur Alabalık Tesisleri
Perili Bahçe** TURKISH €€
(☏0482-571 2832; mains ₺8-14; ⊙8am-9pm) For a leisurely alfresco meal, head to this shady garden by the gushing river. Relish fresh trout, salads from local organic veggies, and *içli köfte,* and sluice it all down with a glass of local wine or rakı.

❶ Getting There & Away

From Mardin, around 10 daily minibus services cover the 45km to Savur (₺8, one hour). In winter services are more restricted.

Midyat

☏0482 / POP 105,000
About 65km east of Mardin lies sprawling Midyat, with a drab new section Estel, around 3km from the inviting old town (Eski Midyat).

The centrepiece of Eksi Midyat is a traffic roundabout, but nearby, honey-coloured houses are tucked away behind silver shops. Alleyways are lined with houses with demure doorways opening onto huge courtyards surrounded by intricately carved walls, windows and recesses.

Like Mardin, Midyat's Christian population suffered in the early 20th century and during the last few decades, and much of the community has emigrated. There are nine Syrian Orthodox churches in the town, though not all regularly hold services. Although you can see the steeples, it's hard to find the churches in the maze of streets, so accept the assistance of one of the local pint-sized guides. They'll expect a small tip.

Sleeping & Eating

Hotel Demirdağ HOTEL €€
(☏462 2000; www.hoteldemirdag.com; Mardin Caddesi 103; s/d ₺60/90; ❋@☎) Across in Estel (new Midyat), the Demirdağ has well-equipped rooms, colourful as a box of Smarties. Just avoid windowless rooms 107 and 109. Its location is handy – the otogar is just one block behind.

Kasr-ı Nehroz BOUTIQUE HOTEL €€€
(☏464 2525; www.hotelnehroz.com; Işıklar Mahallesi Caddesi, Sokak 219; r from ₺210; ❋@☎) Luxury bathrooms combine with pristine stone walls and colourful kilims, while the spacious inner courtyard demands exploration with staircases and turrets leading to views of Midyat's centuries-old rooftops. Standard rooms are a tad compact, but the glorious shared spaces – including a library and reading room – are where you'll feel right at home.

Shmayaa BOUTIQUE HOTEL €€€
(☏464 0696; www.shmayaa.com; Akçakaya Mahallesi Kışla Cadessi 126, Sokak 12; r ₺220-600; ❋☎) Parts of Shmayaa's magnificent mansion date back 1600 years, and from 1915 to 1930 the building was used as military

WORTH A TRIP

HIDDEN GEMS AROUND THE TÜR ABDIN PLATEAU

In your own car or by arranging a taxi for the day in Midyat, it's easy to explore the plateau of Tür Abdin, a traditional homeland of the Syrian Orthodox Church. Dotted around the plateau to the east of Midyat (towards Dargeçit) are historic village churches and monasteries, some recently restored. Not-to-be-missed places include **Mor Yakup**, near Barıştepe; **Mor Izozoal**, perched on a knoll in Altıntaş; **Mor Kyriakos** in Bağlarbaşı; **Mor Dimet** in İzbarak; **Meryemana** in Anıtlı; and **Mor Eliyo** in Alagöz (about 3km from Anıtlı).

Roads are asphalted, villages are signposted and villagers will point you in the right direction. From Midyat, take the road to Hasankeyf (due north). After about 7km the turn-off to Mor Yakup is on the right.

garrison. Now the emphasis is on romance, with 15 beautiful rooms dotted throughout the honey-coloured labyrinth. Three honeymoon suites come complete with delicately arched stone ceilings.

Cihan Lokantası TURKISH €
(Cizre Yolu; mains ₺7-10) Near Eski Midyat's main roundabout, Cihan is the locals' favourite with local dishes like *perde pilavı* (rice and shredded chicken).

Tarihi Midyat Gelüşke Han TURKISH €€
(Eski Midyat Kuyumcular Çarşişi; snacks & mains ₺7-20) Located in an old caravanserai, this sprawling eatery is a favourite for domestic tour groups, but there's a good mix of local dishes, and the heritage ambience is quite lovely. It's located in Eski Midyat, just past the old town's silver shops.

🛈 Getting There & Away

Minibuses regularly run the 3km from Estel to old Midyat. Midyat has two otogars, one in new Midyat (one block behind Hotel Demirdağ) and one in old Midyat, some 200m south of the roundabout along the road to Cizre. There are frequent services for Hasankeyf (₺9, 45 minutes), Batman (₺10, 1½ hours) and Mardin (₺9, 1¼ hours) from the new Midyat otogar. Minibuses for Cizre (₺14, 1½ hours) and Silopi (₺20, two hours), for Iraq, leave from the otogar in old Midyat.

Minibuses from Mardin will pass through the new town, then drop you off at the roundabout in the old town. You can easily base yourself in Midyat and make a day trip to Mardin or Hasankeyf.

Around Midyat

Morgabriel

About 18km east of Midyat, **Morgabriel (Deyrul Umur) Monastery** (⊘ 8.30-11am & 12.30-3pm) FREE is surrounded by gently rollling hills dotted with olive groves. Though much restored, the monastery dates back to 397. St Gabriel, the namesake of the monastery, is buried here, and the sand beside his tomb is said to cure illness. You'll see various frescoes as well as the immense ancient dome built by Theodora, wife of Byzantine emperor Justinian.

Morgabriel is home to the archbishop of Tür Abdin (Mountain of the Servants of God), the surrounding plateau. These days he presides over a much-diminished flock of around 70 people, the majority students from nearby villages.

The monastery's land continues to be threatened by ongoing legal claims from nearby villages – despite the monastery having been established for more than 1600 years. See the website of the World Council of Arameans (www.wca-ngo.org) for more information. (Search for 'Mor Gabriel'.)

From Midyat, take a Cizre minibus (₺8) to the signposted road junction and walk 2.5km uphill to the gate. Start early in the morning as minibuses become less frequent later in the day. A taxi is about ₺80 return, including waiting time.

Hasankeyf
☏ 0488 / POP 5500

Hasankeyf is a heartbreaker. This gorgeous honey-coloured village clinging to a rocky gorge above the Tigris River is a definite must-see, but it's slated to vanish underwater. This is rumoured for 2016 or 2017, but at the time of writing there was no definitive timing. Meanwhile the foundations of Yeni (New) Hasankeyf are taking shape across the river on higher gound.

⊙ Sights

On the main road towards Batman is the restored **Zeynel Bey Türbesi**, isolated in a riverside field. The conical turquoise-tiled tomb was built in the mid-15th century for Zeynel, son of the Akkoyunlu governor, and is a rare survivor from this period. At the time of writing, plans were announced to move the tomb to protect it from the impending waters of the İlisu Dam, but no definitive timing was finalised.

A modern bridge now spans the Tigris, but to the right are the broken arches of the **Eski Köprü** (Old Bridge). Their size reinforces the importance of Hasankeyf in the period immediately before the arrival of the Ottomans.

Across the bridge is the **kale** (castle) and **mağaras** (caves). Due to safety reasons, access to the castle was not possible at the time of writing. The nearby **El-Rizk Camii** (1409) sports a beautiful, slender minaret topped with a stork's nest.

This strategic site has been occupied since Byzantine times, but most relics visible today were built during the reign of the 14th-century Ayyubids. At the top of the rock are the ruins of the 14th-century **Küçük Saray** (Small Palace), with pots

HASANKEYF UNDER THREAT

The cloud of a giant engineering project hangs menacingly above Hasakeyf. Despite its beauty and history, the town is destined to vanish beneath the waters of the Ilisu Dam, part of the GAP irrigation and hydroelectricity project. The proposed dam will flood a region from Batman to Midyat, drowning this historic site and several other archaeological treasures, and displacing more than 37 villages. Read more about this project on p651.

A good source of information is the excellent Hasankeyf Matters blog (www.hasankeyf matters.com), which includes discussion on all relevant issues, and a guide to exploring the site.

built into the ceiling and walls for sound insulation.

Nearby is a small mosque (once a Byzantine church) and the Büyük Saray (Big Palace), with a creepy jail underneath. Adjacent is a former watchtower teetering on the edge of the cliff. The 14th-century Ulu Cami was built on the site of a church.

🛏 Sleeping & Eating

Another option is to visit from Midyat or Diyarbakır (via Batman) as a day trip.

Hasankeyf Motel   GUESTHOUSE €
(☑381 2005, 0507 506 49 40; www.hasankeyf motel.com; Dicle Sokak; s/d ₺30/60) This modest 'motel' has a good location, right by the Tigris bridge, but rooms are definitely no-frills, carpets are faded, and the simple bathrooms have shared (Turkish) toilets. Rooms at the back have balconies.

Based at the motel, Ercan Altue offers walking tours (one/two persons ₺100/150) around the ancient caves dotting the hills above the town.

Hasankeyf Hasbahçe   GUESTHOUSE €
(☑381 2624, 0530 929 1527; www.hasankeyfhas bahce.com; s/d ₺60/120, camping ₺35 per couple; 🛜) This quirky place combines simple but colourful guesthouse rooms, fish ponds, organic gardens and fruit trees. Rabbits and the occasional lamb linger across the sprawling complex, and Fırat Argun, the friendly owner, is a wealth of information in rudimentary English. Cross the bridge past the motel and walk left for around 300m. Excellent trout is often served for dinner.

Hasankeyf Elit   TURKISH €
(kebap with rice & salad ₺15) This simple *lokanta* with excellent river views stretches the meaning of *elit* (elite) somewhat, but it's still one of the best-value options along Hasankeyf's path to the castle.

🅘 Getting There & Away

Frequent minibuses run from Batman to Midyat, transiting at Hasankeyf (₺10, 40 minutes). Another option is to visit from Diyarbakır (₺15, two hours), changing buses in Batman.

Bitlis

☑0434 / POP 46,300

Bitlis has one of the highest concentrations of restored historic buildings in eastern Anatolia, many of them EU-sponsored projects. The town is squeezed into a narrow river canyon.

A castle dominates the town, and two ancient bridges span the stream. Make a beeline for the Ulu Cami (1126); the newer Şerefiye Camii dates from the 16th century. Other must-sees include the splendid İhlasiye Medrese (Koranic school), the most significant building in Bitlis, and the Gökmeydan Camii.

The İl Kültür Merkez (Cumhuriyet Caddesi; ☺8am-5pm Mon-Fri) FREE has good maps of the city and brochures covering the area. It's housed inside the İhlasiye Medrese.

The Dideban Hotel (☑226 2821; dideban otel@hotmail.com; Nur Caddesi; s/d ₺70/100) is conveniently located about 100m from the minibus stand for Tatvan.

Try the excellent local *bal* (honey). Bitlis is also renowned for its *büryan kebap* (lamb baked in a pit and served with flatbread), usually served for breakfast and lunch.

Regular minibuses travel from Tatvan to Bitlis (₺5, 30 minutes).

Tatvan

☑0434 / POP 67,000

Tatvan is ideally positioned to visit spectacular Nemrut Dağı (not to be confused with the higher-profile Nemrut Dağı south of Malatya), Ahlat and Bitlis. Several kilometres long and just a few blocks wide, Tatvan is prosaic, but its setting on the shores of Lake Van is magnificent. It is also the western port for Lake Van ferries.

Sleeping & Eating

Hotel Dilek   HOTEL **€**
(📞827 1516; Yeni Çarşı; s/d ₺50/80) The Dilek gets good marks for colourful rooms with tiled bathrooms. Singles are tiny, so angle for rooms 201, 202, 301 or 302, which are more spacious and get more natural light.

Otel Dinç   HOTEL **€€**
(📞827 5960; www.oteldinc.com; Sahil Mahallesi İşletme Caaddesi 9; s/d ₺90/140; ✳ 🛜) Owned by a friendly family, the Dinç features brightly coloured and modern rooms. It's down a quiet side street on the southern side of town, and there are excellent lake and mountain views from the top-floor breakfast room.

Eyvan Pide Salonu   PIDE **€**
(1 Sokak; mains ₺6-10) This compact joint is the best place in town for thin-crust pide or *lahmacun* (Arabic-style pizza). Eyvan is tucked away to the right of the Star taxi stand on Tatvan's main street.

Gökte Ada   PIDE, KEBAP **€**
(Cumhuriyet Caddesi; mains ₺7-14) This snazzy spot atop Tatvan's modern shopping complex combines tasty pide and kebaps with expansive views of Lake Van.

🛈 Getting There & Away

Buses to Van run around the southern shore of the lake (₺20, three hours). The otogar is at the northern edge of town. A ferry crosses the lake twice a day (₺10, about four hours), but its schedule is inconsistent.

Minibuses to Ahlat (₺5, 30 minutes) leave about hourly from PTT Caddesi, beside Türk Telekom. The minibus stand for Bitlis (₺5, 30 minutes) is just up the street. Direct minibuses to Adilcevaz are infrequent; change in Ahlat.

Around Tatvan

Nemrut Dağı (Mt Nemrut)

Nemrut Dağı (3050m), rising to the north of Tatvan, is an inactive volcano with several crater lakes.

On the crater rim (13km from the main road) are sensational views over Lake Van, Tatvan, and nearby water-filled craters.

From the rim you can hike to the summit (about 45 minutes) – just follow the lip of the crater (the last stretch is a bit of a scramble). Midweek, the only company will be shepherds with their flocks and sturdy sheepdogs. Follow the dirt road leading down to the lake from the crater rim and find your own picnic area.

Visits are only possible from around mid-May to the end of October; at other times the summit is under snow.

🛈 Getting There & Away

A taxi from Tatvan is around ₺150 return. On summer weekends hitching is an option.

With your own transport, leave Tatvan heading to Bitlis, and turn right at a sign saying 'Nemrut 13km'. At the time of writing, this previously rough road was being resealed for improved access. You'll then reach the crater rim, from where a dirt road winds down into the crater and connects with other dirt roads snaking around the crater.

Guided trips can be undertaken with Alkans Tours (p613) in Van.

Lake Van (South Shore)
📞0432

After the rigours of central Anatolia, this vast expanse of water surrounded by snowcapped mountains sounds deceptively promising for beaches and water sports. Lake Van (Van Gölü) has great potential for such activities, but nothing has been really developed yet. On the positive side, it's very scenic and virtually untouched.

The most conspicuous feature on the map of southeastern Turkey, this 3750-sq-km lake was formed when a volcano (Nemrut Dağı) blocked its natural outflow.

Travelling south around the lake between Van and Tatvan offers beautiful scenery, but there's little reason to stop. The exception is 5km west of Gevaş, where the 10th-century Akdamar Kilisesi on Akdamar Island is a glorious must-see.

🛈 Sights

Gevaş Cemetery   CEMETERY
Like Ahlat on the north shore, Gevaş has a cemetery full of tombstones dating from the 14th to 17th centuries. Notable is the polygonal Halime Hatun Türbesi, built in 1358 for a female member of the Karakoyunlu dynasty.

★ **Akdamar Kilisesi** CHURCH
(Church of the Holy Cross; admission ₺5; ⏱8am-6pm) One of the marvels of Armenian architecture is the carefully restored Akdamar Kilisesi, perched on an island 3km out in Lake Van. In 921 Gagik Artzruni, King of Vaspurkan, built a palace, church and monastery on the island. Little remains of the palace and monastery, but the church walls are in superb condition and the wonderful relief carvings are among the masterworks of Armenian art.

If you're familiar with biblical stories, you'll immediately recognise Adam and Eve, Jonah and the whale (with the head of a dog), David and Goliath, Abraham about to sacrifice Isaac, Daniel in the lions' den, Samson etc. There are also some faded frescoes inside the church.

Altınsaç Kilisesi CHURCH
Another relatively well-preserved Armenian church, Altınsaç Kilisesi, is perched on a mound overlooking the lake. From Akdamar, drive 12km towards Tatvan until you reach a junction. Turn right onto the road marked for Altınsaç. After 3km the asphalt road ends and becomes a gravel road. The road skirts the shore of the lake for another 14km, until you reach the village of Altınsaç. From the village it's another 2km to the church.

🛏 Sleeping & Eating

Akdamar Restaurant & Camping CAMPING GROUND
(📞214 3479, 0542 743 1361; www.akdamarrestaurant.net; ⏱Apr-Sep; @🛜) This basic camping ground is opposite the ferry departure point for Akdamar Island. The **restaurant** (mains ₺20) has a terrace with lake views. A speciality is *kürt tavası* (meat, tomato and peppers cooked in a clay pot). It's licensed so grab a beer (₺10) while you're waiting for a boat to Akdamar to fill up. If you're camping (for free), you'll be expected to eat in the restaurant.

ℹ Getting There & Away

Minibuses run the 44km from Van to Akdamar harbour for ₺6 during high season. At other times, there's an hourly minibus to Gevaş (₺6). Most drivers will arrange for you to be transferred to another minibus from Gevaş to Akdamar harbour for an additional ₺2. Alternatively, catch a minibus heading to Tatvan and ask to be let off at Akdamar harbour. Make sure you're out on the highway flagging a bus back to Van by 4pm, as soon afterwards the traffic dries up and buses may be full.

Boats to Akdamar Island (per person ₺15) run as and when visitor numbers warrant it (minimum 15 people). From May to September, boats fill up on a regular basis so waiting time is usually minimal. Outside of the summer season, you may need to charter your own boat (around ₺150).

Lake Van (North Shore)
📞 0432
The journey around the north shore of Lake Van from Tatvan to Van is even more beautiful than the south shore.

The major bus companies take the shortest route around the south of the lake from Tatvan to Van. To travel around the north shore take a minibus to Ahlat from Tatvan, then hop on another minibus to Adilcevaz, where you can overnight. The next morning catch another bus to Van.

Ahlat

A further 42km along the lakeshore from Tatvan is the underrated town of Ahlat, famous for its splendid Seljuk Turkish tombs and graveyard.

Founded during the reign of Caliph Omar (AD 581–644), Ahlat became a Seljuk stronghold in the 1060s. When the Seljuk sultan Alp Arslan rode out to meet the Byzantine emperor Romanus Diogenes in battle on the field of Manzikert, Ahlat was his base.

Just west of Ahlat is an overgrown polygonal 13th-century tomb, **Usta Şağırt Kümbeti** (Ulu Kümbeti), 300m off the highway. It's the largest Seljuk tomb in the area.

Further along the highway on the left is a museum, and behind it a vast **Selçuk Mezarlığı** (Seljuk cemetery), with stele-like headstones of lichen-covered grey or red volcanic tuff with intricate web patterns and bands of Kufic lettering.

Over the centuries earthquakes, wind and water have set the stones at all angles, a striking sight with spectacular Nemrut Dağı as a backdrop. Most stones have a crow as sentinel, and tortoises patrol the ruins.

The small **museum** (⏱8am-noon & 1-5pm Tue-Sun) FREE has a reasonable collection including Urartian bronze belts and needles. At the time of writing a new museum around 300m back towards Tatvan was being completed.

On the northeastern side of the graveyard is the unusual Bayındır Kümbeti ve Camii (Bayındır Tomb and Mosque; 1477), with a colonnaded porch and its own *mihrab* (niche indicating the direction of Mecca).

Other sites include the Çifte Kümbet (Twin Tombs), about 2km from the old museum towards the town centre, and the Ahlat Sahil Kalesi (Ahlat Lakeside Fortress), south of the Çifte Kümbet, which was built during the reign of Süleyman the Magnificent.

❶ Getting There & Away

From Tatvan, minibuses leave for Ahlat (₺6, 30 minutes) from beside Türk Telekom and the PTT. Get off at the museum on the western outskirts of Ahlat, or you'll have to walk 2km back from the town centre. From Ahlat, there are regular minibuses to Adilcevaz (₺5, 20 minutes).

Adilcevaz

About 25km east of Ahlat is the town of Adilcevaz, once a Urartian town but now dominated by a great Seljuk Turkish fortress (1571).

Snowmelt from the year-round snowfields on Süphan Dağı flows down to Adilcevaz, making its surroundings lush and fertile. On the western edge of town is the Ulu Camii, built in the 13th century and still used for daily prayer.

From the centre of town, take a taxi to the Kef Kalesi, another Urartian citadel perched higher up in the valley (about ₺40 return).

The best accommodation in town is the Cevizlibağ Otel (☎ 0434-311 3152; www.cevizli bagotel.com; Recep Tayyip Erdoğan Bulvarı 31/1; s/d ₺50/90; ❀ ⬤), handily located midway between the otogar and the town centre. The spacious rooms are trimmed in shiny marble with wooden floors and spotless bathrooms. There's a good restaurant, and it's a short stroll to lakefront tea gardens.

❶ Getting There & Away

From Adilcevaz, there are five direct buses to Van (₺20, 2½ hours), but the last one departs around 2pm – make sure you start out early in the day.

Van

☎ 0432 / POP 353,500 / ELEV 1727M

More urban, more casual and less rigorous, Van is very different in spirit from the rest of southeastern Anatolia. Young couples walk hand in hand on the main drag, live bands knock out Kurdish tunes in pubs, and a resilient population coping with the impact of recent earthquakes inspires a satisfying urban buzz.

While Van boasts a brilliant location near the eponymous lake, forget about water sports and beaches. Instead, focus on the striking monuments, including Van Kalesi (Van Castle or the Rock of Van), spend a few days journeying around the lake, and explore the nearby historic sites of Çavuştepe and Hoşap.

Hotels, restaurants, ATMs, the post office and bus company offices all lie on or around Cumhuriyet Caddesi.

History

The kingdom of Urartu, the biblical Ararat, flourished from the 13th to the 7th centuries BC. Its capital was on the outskirts of present-day Van. The Urartians borrowed much of their culture (including cuneiform writing) from the neighbouring Assyrians, with whom they were more or less permanently at war. The powerful Assyrians never subdued the Urartians, but when several waves of Cimmerians, Scythians and Medes swept into Urartu and joined in the battle, the kingdom met its downfall.

Later the region was resettled by a people whom the Persians called Armenians. By the 6th century BC the area was governed by Persian and Median *satraps* (provincial governors).

In the 8th century AD, Arab armies flooded through from the south, forcing the Armenian prince to take refuge on Akdamar Island. Unable to fend off the Arabs, he agreed to pay tribute to the caliph. When the Arabs retreated, the Byzantines and Persians took their place, and overlordship of Armenia seesawed between them as one or the other gained military advantage.

After defeating the Byzantines in 1071 at Manzikert, north of Lake Van, the Seljuk Turks marched on, with a flood of Turkoman nomads in tow, to found the sultanate of Rum, based in Konya. The domination of eastern Anatolia by Turkish *emirs* followed

Van

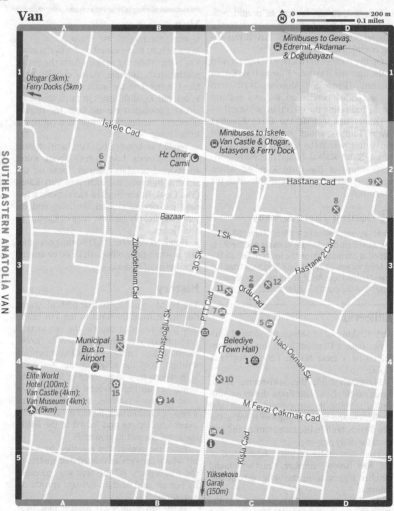

SOUTHEASTERN ANATOLIA VAN

Otogar (3km);
Ferry Docks (5km)

İskele Cad

Minibuses to Gevaş,
Edremit, Akdamar
& Doğubayazıt

Minibuses to İskele,
Van Castle & Otogar,
İstasyon & Ferry Dock

Hz Ömer
Camii

Hastane Cad

Bazaar

1 Sk

Hastane 2 Cad

Zübeydehanım Cad

30 Sk

PTT Cad

Ordu Cad

Yüzbaşıoğlu Sk

Municipal
Bus to
Airport

Belediye
(Town Hall)

Hacı Osman Sk

Elite World
Hotel (100m);
Van Castle (4km);
Van Museum (4km);
(5km)

M Fevzi Çakmak Cad

Kışla Cad

Yüksekova
Garaji
(150m)

and continued until the coming of the Ottomans in 1468.

During WWI, Armenian guerrilla bands intent on founding an independent Armenian state collaborated with the Russians to defeat the Ottoman armies in Turkey's east. From then on the Armenians, formerly loyal subjects of the sultan, were viewed by the Turks as traitors. Bitter fighting between Turkish and Kurdish forces on the one side and Armenian and Russian forces on the other brought devastation to the entire region and to Van.

The Ottomans destroyed the old city of Van (near Van Castle) before the Russians occupied it in 1915. Ottoman forces counterattacked but were unable to drive the invaders out, and Van remained under Russian occupation until the armistice of 1917. After the founding of the Turkish Republic, a new planned city of Van was built 4km east of the old site.

On 23 October 2011, Van was shaken by a 7.1 magnitude earthquake, causing around 100 deaths in the city and destroying more than 1000 buildings. A significant aftershock of magnitude 5.7 struck central Van on 9 No-

Van

vember 2011, causing more fatalities and the destruction of several inner-city hotels.

At the time of writing, three years after the earthquakes, most residents had returned to Van, and the city was again bustling. The Turkish government had also completed new housing developments on the hills above the city.

⊙ Sights

Van Castle (Van Kalesi) & Eski Van　RUIN
About 4km west of the centre, **Van Castle** (Rock of Van; admission ₺5; ⊙9am-dusk) dominates the view of the city. Visit at sunset for great views across the lake. Catch a 'Kale' minibus (₺2) from İskele Caddesi to the castle's northwestern corner for the ticket office. From the summit the foundations of **Eski Van** – the old city destroyed in WWI – reveal themselves on the southern side of the rock.

A few surviving buildings include the restored Hüsrev Paşa Külliyesi (1567); the nearby Kaya Çelebi Camii (1662), with a striped minaret; the brick minaret of the Seljuk Ulu Camii; and the Kızıl Camii (Red Mosque).

Just past the ticket office is an old stone bridge. To the left, a stairway leads up the rock past a ruined mosque and an arched-roof building which used to be a Koranic school.

At the ticket office ask the custodian (he'll expect a tip) to show you the huge cuneiform inscriptions (ask for the tabela), as well as the numerous *khachkars* (Armenian crosses) that are carved into the southern side of the rock. Look out also for the water reservoir, an ancient hamam and a ruined palace (not visible from the top of the rock). The Kızıl Camii and Ulu Camii can also easily be approached further south.

On the way back to the ticket office, in a willow forest is Sardur Burcu (Sardur Tower; 840–830 BC). This large black stone rectangle sports cuneiform inscriptions in Assyrian praising the Urartian King Sardur I.

Van Museum　MUSEUM
(Van Müzesi; Kale Yolu, below Van Castle; admission ₺5; ⊙8am-noon & 1-5pm Tue-Sun) Van's original museum was damaged in the 2011 earthquakes, and this gleaming new glass structure at the foot of Van Castle was opened in late 2014. The museum boasts the world's pre-eminent collection of Urartian exhibits, including exquisite gold jewellery, and an array of bronze belts, helmets, horse armour and terracotta figures. Ethnographic exhibits include local Kurdish and Turkoman kilims.

Just past a nearby roundabout back towards Van is the **Van Kedi Evi** (Van Cat House), ostensibly a touristy silver studio and shop, but a good opportunity to see some Van cats – pure white and often with eyes of two different colours.

⊂Ⅎ Tours

Alkans Tours　TRAVEL AGENCY
(☑215 2092, 0530 349 2793; www.easternturkey tour.org; Ordu Caddesi) The friendly Alkan family can advise on train travel to Iran, and also runs day trips (per person €25, minimum four people) taking in Hoşap, Çavuştepe and Akdamar Island. Longer tours throughout eastern Turkey, Georgia and Armenia are available, and excursions to Kars, Doğubayazıt, and Nemrut Dağı near Tatvan can be arranged. Ordu Caddesi runs east of Cumhuriyet Caddesi opposite

BREAKFASTS OF CHAMPIONS

Van is famed for its tasty *kahvaltı* (breakfast). Skip your hotel breakfast and head to Eski Sümerbank Sokak, also called 'Kahvaltı Sokak' (Breakfast Street), a pedestrianised side street running parallel to Cumhuriyet Caddesi. Here you'll find eateries specialising in complete Turkish breakfasts, including **Sütçü Fevzi** (☑216 6618; Eski Sümerbank Sokak; ◷7am-3pm) and **Sütçü Kenan** (☑216 8499; Eski Sümerbank Sokak; ◷7am-3pm).

On summer mornings the street literally heaves with punters sampling *otlu peynir* (cheese mixed with a tangy herb), *beyaz peynir* (a mild yellow cheese), honey from the highlands, olives, *kaymak* (clotted cream), butter, tomatoes, cucumbers and *sucuklu yumurta* (omelette with sausage). A full breakfast will set you back around ₺20 to ₺25.

In June 2014, almost 52,000 hungry locals had breakfast at Van Castle, gaining the city the Guinness World Record for the planet's biggest breakfast.

the Yapı Kredi bank. Call or email ahead as they may change address during the life of this book.

🛏 Sleeping

Otel Side
HOTEL €

(☑216 6265; www.otelside.com; Sıhke Caddesi Trafik Sokak 2; s/d ₺60/90) This newish hotel (built post-earthquakes in 2012) has spacious rooms decked out in chocolate brown and cream, and is in a quiet location a 10-minute walk to the restaurants, cafes and shopping of Van's bustling main street.

Otel Bahar
HOTEL €

(☑215 5748, 0539 729 6838; Ordu Caddesi 20; s/d from ₺25/35) One of the acceptable cheapies in town, the Bahar features simple rooms and compact balconies. When the nearby mosque wakes you early in the morning, take in laneway views with teashops and barbers. The cheapest rooms share bathrooms.

Royal Berk Hotel
HOTEL €€

(☑215 0050; www.royalberkhotel.com; Bankası Bitişiği Sokak 5; s/d from ₺90/130) Built after the 2011 earthquakes, the Royal Berk combines spacious and very comfortable rooms with a brilliant location in a quiet laneway just metres from Van's main street. Decor stays just the right side of over the top, the crew at reception are easygoing and friendly, and the huge breakfast spread closely replicates what's on offer in the city's famed *kahvaltı* restaurants.

Büyük Asur Oteli
HOTEL €€

(☑216 8792; www.buyukasur.com; Cumhuriyet Caddesi, Turizm Sokak; s/d ₺80/120; ❄🛜) Even if you're on a tight budget, consider spending a little more to enjoy the comforts of this reliable midrange venture. The rooms

are colourful and come complete with fresh linen, TV and well-scrubbed bathrooms. English is spoken and the hotel can organise tours to Akdamar Island, Hoşap Castle and other local attractions.

Ada Palas
HOTEL €€

(☑216 2716; vanadapalas@gmail.com; Cumhuriyet Caddesi; s/d ₺80/140; ❄) The 2nd floor is *yeşil* (green), the 3rd floor canary yellow and the 4th floor electric *mavi* (blue). The friendly owners of the centrally located and well-organised Ada Palas certainly like to add colour to life.

Elite World Hotel
HOTEL €€€

(☑0212-444 0883; www.eliteworldhotels.com.tr; Kazım Karabekir Caddesi 54; s/d €65/85; ❄@🛜🏊) Van's most comfortable hotel overflows with business-traveller-friendly features including a bar, non-smoking rooms, and a spa, sauna and swimming pool. Combined with luxury decor, it's easily Van's top place to stay.

🍴 Eating

Firavîn
KURDISH €

(Hastane Caddesi; mains ₺8-10; ◷10am-3pm; ☑) Translating to 'Lunch' in Kurdish, Firavîn offers an ever-changing daily menu of homestyle Kurdish cooking. It's very popular, so get there before 1pm for local dishes like *keledos* (chickpea, wheat, leeks and beans topped with chilli and fresh herbs). There's always a good vegetarian selection too.

Aişe
ANATOLIAN €

(Özok is Merkezi Karşi 5; mains ₺7-10; ◷10am-4pm; ☑) Run by an enterprising group of local women, Aişe presents around six different Turkish and Kurdish dishes each day. Count on around ₺10 to ₺12 for a full meal including bread and soup, all best enjoyed in the restaurant's colourful outdoor patio.

Kervansaray
ANATOLIAN €€

(Cumhuriyet Caddesi; mains ₺12-16) Upstairs from the bustle of Cumhuriyet Caddesi, Kervansaray is Van's go-to spot for a more elegant and refined dining experience. Dive into a few shared plates of excellent meze as you peruse a menu containing a few local specialities. Fans of lamb should try the tender *kağıt kebap* (paper kebap), wrapped and cooked in paper.

Tamara Ocakbaşı
STEAK €€

(Yüzbaşıoğlu Sokak; mains ₺15-25; ⊙5pm-late) In the Tamara Hotel, this eatery features 40 *ocak* (grills) – each table has its own. High-quality meat and fish dishes feature prominently, but the list of meze is equally impressive, and beer and wine is available.

Halil İbrahim Sofrası
TURKISH €€

(Cumhuriyet Caddesi; mains ₺8-15) Food is well presented and of high quality, with service to match, and served in sleek surrounds. Highlights include excellent pide and grills.

🍷 Drinking & Entertainment

Niçhe
BAR

(Maraş Caddesi; ⊙noon-late) Get to know Van's student population over frosty glasses of Efes beer at this friendly cafe-bar.

Halay Türkü Bar
LIVE MUSIC

(Kazım Karabekir Caddesi; ⊙noon-late) Multiple floors add up to multiple ways to enjoy Van's nightlife scene. Kick off with tasty meze and grilled meat before graduating to draught beer, generously poured local spirits, and regular live music.

ℹ️ Information

ATMs and banks line Cumhuriyet Caddesi.

Tourist Office (📠216 2530; Cumhuriyet Caddesi; ⊙8.30am-noon & 1-5.30pm Mon-Fri) English is spoken; good maps and brochures.

ℹ️ Getting There & Away

AIR

A taxi to the airport costs about ₺35. A municipal airport bus (₺1.50) leaves frequently from near the Akdamar Hotel.

Pegasus Airlines (www.flypgs.com) To/from İstanbul and Ankara.

Turkish Airlines (www.turkishairlines.com) To/from İstanbul and Ankara.

BOAT

A ferry crosses Lake Van between Tatvan and Van most days. There's no fixed schedule. The trip costs ₺10 per passenger and takes about four hours. 'İskele' dolmuşes ply the route from İskele Caddesi to the harbour (₺2).

BUS

Many bus companies have ticket offices at the intersection of Cumhuriyet and Kazım Karabekir Caddesis. They provide *servises* to shuttle passengers to and from the otogar on the northwestern outskirts.

For Hoşap and Çavuştepe (₺8, 45 minutes), take a minibus from the Yüksekova Garajı or the Başkale Garajı, both on Cumhuriyet Caddesi, a few hundred metres south of the Büyük Asur Oteli. Buses to Hakkari also travel past Hoşap and Çavuştepe.

Minibuses to Gevaş and Akdamar (₺6, about 45 minutes) depart from a dusty car park down a side street on the right of the northern extension of Cumhuriyet Caddesi. Transport to Doğubayazıt (₺20) also leaves from here, an 185km run that's worth taking for the scenery

SERVICES FROM VAN'S OTOGAR

DESTINATION	FARE (₺)	DURATION (HR)	DISTANCE (KM)	FREQUENCY (PER DAY)
Ağrı	30	4	213	frequent
Ankara	90	17	1250	frequent
Diyarbakır	40	7	410	frequent
Erciş	10	1¼	95	several
Erzurum	40	7	410	several
Hakkari	20	4	205	3-4
Malatya	60	12	500	frequent
Şanlıurfa	60	11	585	3-4
Tatvan	15	2	156	frequent
Trabzon	75	15	733	3-4 direct, most via Erzurum

en route, especially if you can pause at the Muradiye Waterfalls.

There are direct buses to Orumiyeh (in Iran). Ask at Van's bus company offices.

CAR

Consider renting a car (around ₺120 per day) to journey around Lake Van. Rental agencies line Cumhuriyet Caddesi.

TRAIN

The twice-weekly *Vangölü Ekspresi* from Ankara terminates at Tatvan; from Tatvan, the ferry will bring you to the dock at Van. The weekly *Trans Asya Ekspresi* runs from Ankara to Tehran and Tabriz, departing Van for Iran at 10.25am on Wednesday. Confirm exact times at the train station or with Alkans Tours (p613). Note it's not possible to book trains running from Van to Ankara once in Turkey. This leg needs to be booked in Iran.

The main train station is northwest of the centre near the otogar, with another station, İskele İstasyonu, several kilometres to the northwest on the lakeshore. Catch 'İstasyon' minibuses from İskele Caddesi.

❶ Getting Around

For Van Kalesi and the *iskele* (ferry dock), catch a minibus from İskele Caddesi.

Hoşap & Çavuştepe

A day excursion southeast of Van along the road to Başkale and Hakkari takes you to the Urartian site at Çavuştepe (25km from Van), and the spectacular Kurdish castle at Hoşap, 33km further along.

Hoşap Castle (admission ₺5) perches atop a rocky outcrop alongside sleepy Güzelsu. Cross one of two bridges to the far side of the hill to reach the castle entrance, above

which are superb lion reliefs. Looking east is a row of mud defensive walls that once encircled the village. Built in 1643 by a local Kurdish chieftain, Mahmudi Süleyman, the castle has an impressive gateway in a round tower.

The narrow hill on the left side of the highway at Çavuştepe was once crowned by the fortress-palace Sarduri-Hinili, home of the kings of Urartu and built between 764 and 735 BC by King Sardur II. These are the best-preserved foundations of any Urartian palace.

From the car park, the yukarı kale (upper fortress) is to the left, and the vast aşağı kale (lower fortress) to the right.

Climb the rocky hill to the lower fortress temple ruins, marked by a gate of black basalt blocks polished to a gloss; a few blocks on the left-hand side are inscribed in cuneiform. Mehmet Kuşman, one of the only people who can understand Urartian, is often on hand to translate.

Note other illustrations of Urartian engineering ingenuity, including the cisterns under the pathways, the storage vessels, the kitchen and palace. Down on the plains to the south are canals also created by the Urartians.

❶ Getting There & Away

To get to the Hoşap and Çavuştepe sites by public transport, catch a minibus from Van heading to Başkale or Yüksekova and get out at Hoşap (₺6). After seeing the castle, flag down a bus back to Çavuştepe, 500m off the highway, and then catch a third bus back to Van. Getting to Hoşap and Çavuştepe from Van is relatively easy, but return transport can be difficult to secure. Consider the Alkans Tours (p613) day trip, which also takes in Akdamar Island.

Understand Turkey

Turkey Today

A loyal Western ally in a troubled neighbourhood, Turkey remains pivotal on the world stage. After more than a decade of strong economic growth, Turks have seen their standard of living rise significantly, but long-standing political tensions remain as the processes of modernisation and democratisation continue.

Best in Print

Birds Without Wings
(Louis de Bernières)
Turkish Awakening (Alev Scott)
The Assassin from Apricot City
(Witold Szablowski)
Portrait of a Turkish Family
(Irfan Orga)
The Museum of Innocence
(Orhan Pamuk)
Meander: East to West along a Turkish River (Jeremy Seal)
Turkish Coast: Through Writers' Eyes (Rupert Scott)
The Winter Thief (Jenny White)

Best on Film

Vizontele Quirky comedy about the first family to get a TV in a small town.
Winter Sleep Poignant character study in snowy Anatolia.
Çoğunluk (Majority) Travails of love between a rebellious youth and a Kurdish girl.
Once Upon a Time in Anatolia Nighttime rambles on the steppe in search of a corpse.
Babam ve Oğlum Portrays the generation gap in an Aegean village.
Hamam Turkish expat inherits a hamam; addresses gay issues.
Cosmos A mysterious stranger appears in a remote border town.

Political Progress?

The Turks may be a laid-back people but their political scene is certainly feisty, particularly so in recent years. The Justice and Development Party (AKP) headed by Recep Tayyip Erdoğan has been in power since 2002 and has overseen an extended period of economic growth. The standard of living and infrastructure across the country have improved markedly, but critics allege the government is increasingly authoritarian. Some allege it has a secret Islamist agenda, citing recent restrictions on alcohol sales and advertising as evidence.

Criticism of the AKP came to a head during the Gezi Park protests of 2013, when plans for a shopping-mall project in an İstanbul park catalysed various groups that disapproved of Erdoğan's governing style. He promptly dismissed protesters as *çapulcular* (looters), but they appropriated his insult, claiming that 'chapulling' meant 'fighting for your rights'. Protests spread and continued for several weeks, with up to eight civilians, and two policemen, killed.

In December 2013 allegations of extensive corruption were levelled at senior members of the AKP. Several ministers were dismissed and Erdoğan's own son was accused. This triggered the government's fierce denunciation of the Gulen educational movement, which it accused of concocting the allegations. Many predicted that the AKP would suffer a loss in popularity, but in the municipal elections of early 2014, after fierce campaigning, the AKP emerged as victors. This clearly demonstrated that despite having many vocal detractors its message still resonates with many Turks. Tensions increased again in early 2014 after the Soma mining disaster, where 301 miners died, with many criticising Erdoğan's response. Erdoğan then campaigned frantically for the first direct presidential elections in Turkey's history. He won in the first round, ensuring a five-year stay in the presidential palace.

A Tough Neighbourhood

While Turkey may have been enjoying an economic boom, its neighbours have been doing it tough of late. Turkey's stated goal to become a regional leader remains unfulfilled at best. Unrest in Syria has been ongoing since 2011 and and continues to escalate. The Turkish government is stridently opposed to Assad, the Syrian president, and on occasions the two countries have come close to an outbreak of hostilities. According to some reports Turkey is hosting up to one million Syrian refugees within its borders, and some cities, including Gaziantep, now have noticeable Syrian precincts.

In Iraq the situation isn't much better. The rise of the so-called Islamic State and its declaration of a 'caliphate' have set off alarm bells in Turkey, and elsewhere, particularly after Turkish diplomatic staff were kidnapped in Mosul. The Kurdish regime in Iraq has forged strong business links with Turkey, however, and remains a staunch ally. Meanwhile, relations with neighbouring Iran remain cordial under new president Rouhani, and relations with Armenia inch forward in fits and starts towards normalisation.

The Many Facets of the Nation

One area where the AKP has made clear gains in recent years is in attempts to solve the Kurdish question. This has been a pressing political issue for Turkey since the 1980s, when the Kurdistan Workers Party (PKK) began a military campaign to establish an independent Kurdish state. The government recently pushed forward with discussions with Abdullah Öcalan, the PKK's imprisoned leader, resulting in a ceasefire in early 2013 and the evacuation of PKK military units from Turkish soil. The stage is now set for a comprehensive peace.

These days Turkey holds much less tenaciously to the nationalist idea that ethnic diversity is a threat to the nation-state. There is much more acknowledgment of the contributions of Armenians, Greeks, Syrians and others, and as a consequence Turkey's diverse ethnic communities are more visible and confident in day-to-day life.

POPULATION: **81,619,392**

AREA: **783,562 SQ KM**

GDP: **$821.8 BILLION (2013 EST.)**

INFLATION: **7.6% (2013 EST.)**

UNEMPLOYMENT: **9.3% (2013 EST.)**

if Turkey were 100 people

80 would be Muslims
19 would be Alevi Muslims
1 other religions

ethnic groups
(% of population)

70 Turkish
20 Kurdish
10 Other

population per sq km

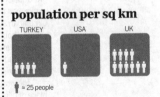

TURKEY   USA   UK

≈ 25 people

History

Fate has put Turkey at the junction of two continents. A land bridge, meeting point and battleground, it has seen peoples – mystics, merchants, nomads and conquerors – moving between Europe and Asia since time immemorial. Many have left their mark, so that the Turkish landscape is littered with Byzantine castles, Greek and Roman ruins, Seljuk caravanserais and Ottoman palaces, and the great book of Turkish history is full of remarkable and intriguing events, cultures and individuals.

Early Cultures, Cities & Clashes

Archaeologist Ian Hodder's *Çatalhöyük: The Leopard's Tale* is an account of the excavation of the site and vividly portrays life as it was during the city's heyday.

Archaeological finds indicate that Anatolia (the Turkish landmass in Asia) was inhabited by hunter-gatherers during the Palaeolithic era. Neolithic man carved the stone pillars at Göbekli Tepe around 9500 BC. By the 7th millennium BC some folk formed settlements; Çatalhöyük arose around 6500 BC. Perhaps the first-ever city, it was a centre of innovation, with locals creating distinctive pottery. Relics can be seen at Ankara's Museum of Anatolian Civilisations (p417).

During the Chalcolithic age, communities in southeast Anatolia absorbed Mesopotamian influences, including the use of metal tools. Across Anatolia more and larger communities sprung up and interacted. By 3000 BC advances in metallurgy lead to the creation of various Anatolian kingdoms. One such was at Alacahöyük, in the heart of Anatolia, yet even this place showed Caucasian influence, evidence of trade beyond the Anatolian plateau.

Trade was increasing on the western coast too, with Troy trading with the Aegean islands and mainland Greece. Around 2000 BC, the Hatti established a capital at Kanesh near Kayseri, ruling over a web of trading communities. Here for the first time Anatolian history materialises and becomes 'real', with clay tablets providing written records of dates, events and names.

No singular Anatolian civilisation had yet emerged, but the tone was set for millennia to come: cultural interaction, trade and war would be recurring themes in Anatolian history.

TIMELINE	c 9500 BC	c 6500 BC	c 4000–3000 BC
	At Göbekli Tepe, Neolithic man creates the circular array of megaliths, thought to be a medieval cemetery. Current study suggests that the site may be the world's oldest place of pilgrimage yet discovered.	Founding of Çatalhöyük, the world's first city. Over time 13 layers of houses were built, beehive style, interconnected and linked with ladders. At its peak the city housed around 8000.	Hattian culture develops at Alacahöyük during the early Bronze Age, though settlement has been continuous since the Chalcolithic age. The Hatti develop distinctive jewellery, metalwork and weapons.

Ages of Bronze: the Hittites

The Hatti soon declined and the Hittites swallowed their territory. From Alacahöyük, the Hittites shifted their capital to Hattuşa (near present-day Boğazkale) around 1800 BC. The Hittites' legacy consisted of their capital, as well as their state archives and distinctive artistic styles. By 1450 BC the kingdom, having endured internal ructions, re-emerged as an empire. In creating the first Anatolian empire, the Hittites were warlike but displayed other imperial trappings, ruling over vassal states while also displaying a sense of ethics and a penchant for diplomacy. This didn't prevent them overrunning Ramses II of Egypt in 1298 BC, but did allow them to patch things up by marrying the crestfallen Ramses to a Hittite princess.

The Hittite empire was harassed in later years by subject principalities, including Troy. The final straw was the invasion of the iron-smelting Greeks, generally known as the 'sea peoples'. The landlocked Hittites were disadvantaged during an era of burgeoning sea trade and lacked the latest technology: iron.

Meanwhile a new dynasty at Troy became a regional power. The Trojans, in turn, were harried by the Greeks, which led to the Trojan War in 1250 BC. This allowed the Hittites breathing space but later arrivals hastened their demise. Some pockets of Hittite culture persisted. Later city-states created a neo-Hittite culture, which became the conduit for Mesopotamian religion and arts to reach Greece.

> Until the rediscovery of the ruins at Boğazkale in the 19th century, the Hittites were known only through several obscure references in the Old Testament.

Classical Empires: Greece & Persia

Post-Hittite Anatolia was a patchwork of peoples, indigenous Anatolians and recent interlopers. In the east, the Urartians forged a kingdom near Lake Van. By the 8th century BC the Phrygians arrived in western Anatolia. Under King Gordius, of Gordian knot fame, the Phrygians created a capital at Gordion, their power peaking later under King Midas. In 725 BC Gordion was put to the sword by horse-borne Cimmerians, a fate that even Midas' golden touch couldn't avert.

On the southwest coast, the Lycians established a confederation of city-states extending from modern-day Fethiye to Antalya. Inland, the Lydians dominated western Anatolia from their capital at Sardis and created the first-ever coinage.

Meanwhile, Greek colonies spread along the Mediterranean coast and Greek influence infiltrated Anatolia. Most of the Anatolian peoples were influenced by the Greeks: Phrygia's King Midas had a Greek wife; the Lycians borrowed the legend of the Chimera; and Lydian art was an amalgam of Greek and Persian art forms. It seems that the admiration was mutual: the Lycians were the only Anatolian people the Greeks

> Homer, the Greek author of the *Iliad*, which told the story of the Trojan War, is believed to have been born in Smyrna (present-day İzmir) before 700 BC.

c 2000 BC	c 1200 BC	547 BC	333 BC
The Hittites, an Indo-European people, arrive in Anatolia and conquer the Hatti, claiming their capital at Hattuşa. The Hittites go on to create a kingdom extending to Babylon and Egypt.	The destruction of Troy, later immortalised in Homer's *Iliad*. For 10 years the Mycenaeans had besieged the city strategically placed above the Dardanelles and the key to Black Sea trade.	Cyrus of Persia overruns Anatolia, setting the scene for a long Greco-Persian rivalry. Later Darius I and Xerxes further Persian influence in Anatolia and forestall the expansion of Greek colonies.	Alexander the Great rolls the Persians and conquers most of Anatolia. Persian emperor Darius abandons his wife, children and mother, who is so appalled she disowns him and 'adopts' Alexander.

didn't deride as 'barbarians', and the Greeks were so impressed by the wealth of the Lydian king Croesus that they coined the expression 'as rich as Croesus'.

Introducing the Ancient Greeks: From Bronze Age Seafarers to Navigators of the Western Mind by Edith Hall highlights how Greek communities scattered across Turkey and elsewhere carried the baton of human progress for many centuries.

Heightened Hellenic influence didn't go unnoticed. Cyrus, the Persian emperor, would not countenance this in his backyard. He invaded in 547 BC, initially defeating the Lydians, then extending control to the Aegean. Under emperors Darius I and Xerxes, the Persians checked the expansion of coastal Greek colonies. They also subdued the interior, ending the era of home-grown Anatolian kingdoms.

Ruling Anatolia through local proxies, the Persians didn't have it all their own way. There was periodic resistance from feisty Anatolians, such as the revolt of the Ionian city of Miletus in 494 BC. Allegedly fomented from Athens, the revolt was abruptly put down. The Persians used the connivance of Athens as a pretext to invade mainland Greece, but were routed at Marathon.

Alexander & After

Persian control continued until 334 BC, when Alexander and his adventurers crossed the Dardanelles, intent on relieving Anatolia of the Persian yoke. Sweeping down the coast, they rolled the Persians near Troy then pushed down to Sardis, which willingly surrendered. After later besieging Halicarnassus (modern-day Bodrum), Alexander ricocheted ever-eastwards, disposing of another Persian force on the Cilician plain.

Alexander was more a conqueror than a nation-builder. When he died leaving no successor, his empire was divided in a flurry of civil wars. However, if Alexander's intention was to remove Persian influence and bring Anatolia within the Hellenic sphere, he was entirely successful. In the wake of Alexander's armies, steady Hellenisation occurred, a culmination of a process begun centuries earlier. A formidable network of municipal trading communities spread across Anatolia. The most notable of these was Pergamum (now Bergama). The Pergamene kings were great warriors and patrons of the arts. Greatest of the Pergamene kings was

ALEXANDER & THE GORDIAN KNOT

In 333 BC in the former Phrygian capital of Gordion, Alexander encountered the Gordian knot. Tradition stated that whoever untied it would come to rule Asia. Frustrated in his attempts to untie it, Alexander dispatched it with a blow of his sword. He resumed his eastward advance, Asia laying before him. He thundered across Persia to the Indus until all the known world was his dominion. However, the enormous empire Alexander created was to prove short-lived – perhaps he should have been more patient unravelling that pesky twine.

205 BC	133 BC	AD 330	395
The Lycian League is formed by a group of city-states along the Mediterranean coast including Xanthos, Patara and Olympos. Later Phaselis joined. The leagues persisted after the imposition of Roman rule.	On his deathbed, Pergamene king Attalus III leaves his state to Rome. The Romans swiftly establish a capital at Ephesus, an already buzzing port, and capitalise on vigorous sea trade.	Constantine declares his 'New Rome', later Constantinople, as the capital of the eastern Roman Empire (Byzantium). He had earlier converted to Christianity and in 325 hosted the Council of Nicaea.	Under Theodosius the Roman Empire becomes Christian, with paganism forbidden and Greek influence pervasive. Upon his death, the empire is split along the line Diocletian had set a century earlier.

Eumenes II, who built much of what remains of Pergamum's acropolis. As notable as the building of Hellenic temples and aqueducts in Anatolia, was the gradual spread of the Greek language, which eventually extinguished native Anatolian languages.

The cauldron of Anatolian cultures continued to produce various flavour-of-the-month kingdoms. In 279 BC the Celts romped in, establishing the kingdom of Galatia, centred on Ancyra (Ankara). To the northeast Mithridates carved out the kingdom of Pontus, centred on Amasya, and the Armenians (from the Lake Van region) reasserted themselves, having been granted autonomy under Alexander.

Meanwhile, the increasingly powerful Romans, based on the other side of the Aegean, eyed off Anatolia's rich trade networks.

Roman Rule

Roman legions defeated the Seleucid king at Magnesia (Manisa) in 190 BC. Later Pergamum, the greatest post-Alexandrian city, became the beachhead for the Roman embrace of Anatolia when King Attalus III died, bequeathing the city to Rome. By 129 BC, Ephesus was capital of the Roman province of Asia and within 60 years the Romans had extended their rule to the Persian border.

Over time, Roman might dissipated. In the late 3rd century AD Diocletian tried to steady the empire by splitting it into eastern and western administrative units, simultaneously attempting to wipe out Christianity. Both endeavours failed. The fledgling religion of Christianity spread, albeit clandestinely and subject to intermittent persecution. Tradition states that St John retired to Ephesus to write the fourth Gospel, bringing Mary with him. The indefatigable St Paul capitalised on the Roman road system, roaming across Anatolia to spread the word. Meanwhile, Diocletian's reforms resulted in a civil war, which Constantine won. An earlier convert to Christianity, Constantine was said to have been guided by angels to build a 'New Rome' on the ancient Greek town of Byzantium. The city came to be known as Constantinople (now İstanbul). On his deathbed, Constantine was baptised and by the end of the 4th century Christianity was the official religion of the empire.

> Julius Caesar made his famous 'Veni, vidi, vici' ('I came, I saw, I conquered') speech about a military victory at Zile, near Tokat, in 47 BC.

Rome Falls, Byzantium Arises

Even with a new capital at Constantinople, the Roman Empire proved unwieldy. Once the steadying hand of Theodosius (379–95) was gone, the empire split. The western (Roman) half of the empire succumbed to decadence and 'barbarians'; the eastern half (Byzantium) prospered, adopting Christianity and the Greek language.

Under Justinian (527–65), Byzantium took up the mantle of imperialism that was previously Rome's. Justinian built the Hagia Sophia (Aya

412	527–65	654–76	867
Theodosius II builds the land walls of Constantinople to protect the riches of his capital. They prove effective, withstanding multiple sieges, and are only to be breached once: by Mehmet II in 1453.	During the reign of Justinian, Byzantium enjoys a golden age. His military conquests include much of North Africa and Spain. He also pursues reform within the empire and embarks on building programs.	Muslim Arab armies capture Ankara and besiege Constantinople. Arab incursions in the west are temporary but the eastern and southern fringes (Syria and Egypt) of the Byzantine domain are lost forever.	Basil I helps to restore Byzantium's fortunes, catalysing a resurgence in military power and a flourishing of the arts. He was known as the 'Macedonian' but was actually an Armenian from Thrace.

BYZANTIUM: THE UNDERRATED EUROPEAN EMPIRE

Byzantium is often relegated to an afterthought in European history. As the Byzantines never accepted the authority of the popes in Rome they were regarded as being outside Latin Christendom, hence barely a part of Europe. Nonetheless, Byzantium acted as a bulwark for Europe, protecting it for centuries against the expanding armies of Islam. On the periphery of Europe, with its combination of Greek learning and language and Orthodox Christianity, Byzantium forged a magnificent cultural and artistic legacy for 11 centuries, yet it is generally – and somewhat dismissively – remembered merely for the complexity of its politics.

After the fall of Constantinople in 1453, Europe largely forgot the Greeks. Only in the 19th century did Greece again became flavour of the month when the Romantics, such as Lord Byron and other Hellenophiles, rallied to the cause of Greek liberation. But it was the glories of classical Greece that they aspired to, the Greece of Plato, Aristotle and Sappho, rather than Byzantium.

Sofya), codified Roman law, and extended the empire's boundaries to envelop southern Spain, North Africa and Italy. It was then that Byzantium came to be an entity distinct from Rome, although sentimental attachment to the idea of Rome remained: the Greek-speaking Byzantines still called themselves Romans, and later the Turks would refer to them as 'Rum'. However, Justinian's ambition overstretched the empire. Plague and encroaching Slavic tribes curtailed further expansion.

Later a drawn-out struggle with age-old rivals, the Persians, further weakened the Byzantines, leaving eastern Anatolia easy prey for the Arab armies exploding out of Arabia. The Arabs took Ankara in 654 and by 669 had besieged Constantinople. Here was a new people, bringing a new language, civilisation and religion: Islam.

Byzantium: The Surprising Life of a Medieval Empire by Judith Herrin takes a thematic approach to life in the Byzantine realm and in doing so reveals the secrets of the little-understood empire.

On the western front, Goths and Lombards advanced; by the 8th century Byzantium was pushed back into the Balkans and Anatolia. The empire hunkered down until Basil assumed the throne in 867 and boosted the empire's fortunes, chalking up victories against Islamic Egypt, the Bulgars and Russia. Basil II (976–1025) earned the moniker the 'Bulgar Slayer' after allegedly putting out the eyes of 14,000 Bulgarian prisoners of war. When Basil died, the empire lacked anyone of his calibre – or ferocity, perhaps – and the era of Byzantine expansion comprehensively ended.

First Turkic Empire: the Seljuks

From about the 8th century, nomadic Turks had moved westward from Central Asia, encountering the Persians and converting to Islam. Vigor-

976–1025	1071	1080	1204
Under Basil II (the Bulgar Slayer), Byzantium reaches its high-tide mark. He overcomes internal crises, pushes the frontiers to Armenia in the east, retakes Italy and defeats the Bulgarians.	New arrivals, the Seljuk Turks, take on and defeat a large Byzantine force at Manzikert. The Seljuks don't immediately follow on their success but it is a body blow for the Byzantines.	The Armenians, fleeing the Seljuks in Anatolia, establish the kingdom of Cilicia on the Mediterranean coast. The kingdom raises Armenian culture to new heights and lasts almost 300 years.	The rabble of the Fourth Crusade sack Constantinople, an indication of the contempt with which the Western Christians regard the Eastern Orthodox church.

ous and martial, the Turks swallowed up parts of the Abbasid empire, and built an empire of their own centred on Persia. Tuğrul, of the Turkish Seljuk clan, took the title of sultan in Baghdad, and from there the Seljuks began raiding Byzantine territory. In 1071 Tuğrul's son Alp Arslan faced down a Byzantine army at Manzikert. The nimble Turkish cavalry prevailed, laying Anatolia open to wandering Turkic bands and beginning the demise of the Byzantine Empire.

Not everything went the Seljuks' way, however. The 12th and 13th centuries saw incursions by Crusaders, who established short-lived statelets at Antioch (modern-day Antakya) and Edessa (now Şanlıurfa). In a sideshow to the Seljuks, an unruly army of Crusaders sacked Constantinople, the capital of the Byzantines, ostensibly the allies of the Crusaders. Meanwhile the Seljuks succumbed to power struggles and their empire fragmented.

The Seljuk legacy persisted in Anatolia in the Sultanate of Rum, centred on Konya. Celaleddin Rumi, the Sufi mystic who founded the Mevlevi, or whirling dervish, order, was an exemplar of the cultural and artistic heights reached in Konya. Although ethnically Turkish, the Seljuks were purveyors of Persian culture and art. They introduced woollen rugs to Anatolia, as well as remarkable architecture – still visible at Erzurum, Divriği, Amasya and Sivas. These buildings were the first truly Islamic art forms in Anatolia, and were to become the prototypes for Ottoman art.

In the meantime, the Mongol descendants of Genghis Khan rumbled through Anatolia, defeating a Seljuk army at Köse Dağ in 1243. Anatolia fractured into a mosaic of Turkish *beyliks* (principalities), but by 1300 a single Turkish *bey* (tribal leader), Osman, established a dynasty that would eventually end the Byzantine line.

> In 1054, the line along which the Roman Empire had split in 395 became the dividing line between Catholicism and Orthodox Christianity; a line that persists to this day.

Fledgling Ottoman State

Osman's bands flitted around the borderlands between Byzantine and Seljuk territory. In an era marked by destruction and dissolution, they provided an ideal that attracted legions of followers and quickly established an administrative and military model that allowed them to expand. From the outset they embraced all the cultures of Anatolia – as many Anatolian civilisations before them had done – and their traditions became an amalgam of Greek and Turkish, Islamic and Christian elements.

Seemingly invincible, the Ottomans forged westward, establishing a first capital at Bursa, then crossing into Europe and taking Adrianople (now Edirne) in 1362. By 1371 they had reached the Adriatic and in 1389 they met and vanquished the Serbs at Kosovo Polje, effectively taking control of the Balkans.

> Defending Constatinople, Emperor Constantine placed a chain across the Golden Horn to prevent Ottoman ships entering. Mehmet II ordered his ships over land – rolled over oiled logs – to breach the blockade and demoralise the Byzantine defenders.

1207–70	1243	1300	1324
The lifetime of Celaleddin Rumi, known as Mevlâna, founder of the Mevlevi Sufi order of whirling dervishes. A great mystic poet and philosopher, Rumi lived in Konya after fleeing the Mongols.	The Mongols rumble out of Central Asia, taking Erzurum and defeating the Seljuks at Köse Dağ. The Seljuk empire limps on and the Mongols depart, leaving only some minor states.	Near Eskişehir on the marches between the moribund Byzantines and the shell-shocked Seljuks, Osman comes to prominence. He takes on the Byzantine army, slowly attracting followers and gaining momentum.	Osman dies while campaigning against the Byzantines at Bursa; he installs his son, Orhan, as his successor. Bursa becomes the first Ottoman capital, ruling over a rapidly expanding realm.

In the Balkans, the Ottomans encountered resolute Christian communities and absorbed them neatly into the state with the creation of the *millet* system, by which minority communities were officially recognised and allowed to govern their own affairs. However, neither Christian insolence nor military bravado were countenanced: Sultan Beyazıt trounced the armies of the last Crusade at Nicopolis in Bulgaria in 1396. Beyazıt perhaps took military victories for granted thereafter, taunting the Tatar warlord Tamerlane. Beyazıt was captured, his army defeated and the burgeoning Ottoman Empire abruptly halted as Tamerlane lurched through Anatolia.

Painting portraits of the great port cities of Smyrna (modern İzmir), Beirut and Alexandria, *Levant: Splendour and Catastrophe on the Mediterranean* by Philip Mansel tells of the rise and fall of these centres of Ottoman wealth and culture.

Ottomans Ascendant: Constantinople & Beyond

The dust settled slowly after Tamerlane dragged a no-doubt chastened Beyazıt away. Beyazıt's sons wrestled for control until Mehmet I emerged in control and the Ottomans got back to the job at hand: expansion. With renewed momentum they scooped up the rest of Anatolia, rolled through Greece, made a first attempt at Constantinople and beat the Serbs for a second time.

The Ottomans had regained their mojo when Mehmet II became sultan in 1451. Constantinople, the last redoubt of the Byzantines, was encircled by Ottoman territory. Mehmet, as an untested sultan, had no choice but to claim it. He built a fortress on the Bosphorus, imposed a naval blockade and amassed his army. The Byzantines appealed forlornly to Europe for help. After seven weeks of siege the city fell on 29 May 1453. Christendom shuddered at the seemingly unstoppable Ottomans, and fawning diplomats declared Mehmet – now known as Mehmet the Conqueror – a worthy successor to earlier Roman and Byzantine emperors.

Byzantium experienced centuries of jockeying for power through palace intrigues, shifting alliances and skulduggery. Its legacy lives on: in modern times describing something as 'Byzantine' means it is complex and fraught.

The Ottoman machine rolled on, alternating campaigns between eastern and western fronts. The janissary system, where Christian youths were converted and trained for the military, meant that the Ottomans had the only standing army in Europe. They were agile and highly organised. Successive sultans expanded the realm, with Selim the Grim capturing the Hejaz in 1517, and with it Mecca and Medina, thus claiming for the Ottomans the status as the guardians of Islam's holiest places. It wasn't all mindless militarism, however: Sultan Beyazıt II demonstrated the multicultural nature of the empire when he invited the Jews expelled by the Spanish Inquisition to İstanbul in 1492.

The Ottoman golden age came during the reign of Sultan Süleyman (1520–66). A remarkable figure, Süleyman the Magnificent was lauded for codifying Ottoman law as well as for military prowess. Under Süleyman, the Ottomans enjoyed victories over the Hungarians and absorbed

1349	1396	1402	1453
As allies of the Byzantines, the Ottomans, under Orhan, make their first military foray into Europe. Orhan had earlier consolidated Islam as the religion of the Ottomans.	The Crusade of Nicopolis, a group of Eastern and Western European forces, aims to forestall the Turks marching into Europe with impunity. Ottoman forces abruptly defeat them; Europe is left unguarded.	Beyazıt, victor over the Crusade of Nicopolis, turns his focus to the ultimate prize, Constantinople. Ever cocky, he takes on the forces of Tatar warlord Tamerlane. His army is crushed and he is enslaved.	Mehmet II lays siege to Constantinople, coinciding with a lunar eclipse. The defending Byzantines interpret this as a fatal omen, presaging the doom of Christendom. Sure enough, the Turks are soon victorious.

the Mediterranean coast of Algeria and Tunisia; Süleyman's legal code was a visionary amalgam of secular and Islamic law, and his patronage saw the Ottomans reach their artistic zenith.

Süleyman was also notable as the first Ottoman sultan to marry. Where previously sultans had enjoyed the comforts of concubines, Süleyman fell in love and married Roxelana. Sadly, monogamy did not make for domestic bliss: palace intrigues brought about the death of his first two sons and the period after Roxelana's ascension became known as the 'Sultanate of Women'. A wearied Süleyman died campaigning on the Danube in 1566.

Sick Man of Europe

Determining exactly when or why the Ottoman rot set in is tricky, but some historians pinpoint the death of Süleyman. The sultans following Süleyman were not up to the task. His son by Roxelana, Selim, known disparagingly as 'the Sot', lasted only briefly as sultan, overseeing the naval catastrophe at Lepanto, which spelled the end of Ottoman naval supremacy. Süleyman was the last sultan to lead his army into the field. Those who came after him were sequestered in the fineries of the palace, having minimal experience of everyday life and little inclination to administer the empire. This, coupled with the inertia that was inevitable after 250 years of expansion, meant that Ottoman military might, once famously referred to by Martin Luther as irresistible, was declining.

The siege of Vienna in 1683 was the Ottomans' last tilt at expansion. It failed. Thereafter it was a downward spiral. The empire was vast and powerful, but was falling behind the West militarily and scientifically. Napoleon's 1799 Egypt campaign indicated that Europe was willing to take the battle up to the Ottomans. Meanwhile, the Habsburgs in central Europe and the Russians were increasingly assertive. The Ottomans, for their part, remained inward-looking and unaware of the advances happening elsewhere.

It was nationalism, an idea imported from the West, that sped the Ottoman demise. For centuries, manifold ethnic groups had coexisted relatively harmoniously in the empire, but the creation of nation-states in Europe sparked a desire among subject peoples to throw off the Ottoman 'yoke' and determine their own destinies. Soon, pieces of the Ottoman jigsaw splintered: Greece attained its freedom in 1830. In 1878 Romania, Montenegro, Serbia and Bosnia followed suit.

As the Ottoman Empire shrunk there were attempts at reform, but too little, too late. In 1876, Abdülhamid allowed the creation of an Ottoman constitution and the first-ever Ottoman parliament, but he used the events of 1878 as an excuse for overturning the constitution. His reign henceforth grew increasingly authoritarian.

Roxelana, the wife of Süleyman, has inspired many artistic works, including paintings, Joseph Haydn's Symphony No 63, and novels in Ukrainian, English and French.

Subjects of the Sultan: Culture and Daily Life in the Ottoman Empire, by Suraiya Faroqhi, portrays what life was like for everyday Ottoman folk, looking at townships, ceremonies, festivals, food and drink, and storytelling in the empire.

1480–1	1512–17	1520–66	1571
Mehmet II endeavours to establish himself as a true heir to Roman glory by invading Italy. He succeeds in capturing Otranto in Puglia, but he dies before he can march on Rome.	Selim the Grim defeats the Persians at Çaldiran. He proceeds to take Syria and Egypt, assuming the mantle of Caliph, then captures the holy cities of Mecca and Medina.	The reign of Süleyman the Magnificent, the zenith of the Ottoman Empire. Süleyman leads his forces to take Budapest, Belgrade and Rhodes, doubling the size of the empire.	The Ottoman navy is destroyed at Lepanto by resurgent European powers who are in control of Atlantic and Indian Ocean trades, and who are experiencing the advances of the Renaissance.

It wasn't just subject peoples who were restless: educated Turks, too, looked for ways to improve their lot. In Macedonia the Committee for Union and Progress (CUP) was created. Reform-minded and influenced by the West, in 1908 the CUP, who came to be known as the 'Young Turks', forced Abdülhamid to abdicate and reinstate the constitution. Any rejoicing proved short-lived. The First Balkan War saw Bulgaria and Macedonia removed from the Ottoman map, with Bulgarian, Greek and Serbian troops advancing rapidly on İstanbul.

The Ottoman regime, once feared and respected, was now deemed the 'sick man of Europe'. European diplomats plotted how to cherry-pick the empire's choicest parts.

WWI & Its Aftermath

The military crisis saw three nationalistic CUP *paşas* (generals) take control of the ever-shrinking empire. They managed to push back the Balkan alliance and save İstanbul, then they allied with the Central Powers in the looming world war. Consequently the Ottomans had to fend off the Western powers on multiple fronts: Greece in Thrace, Russia in northeast Anatolia, Britain in Arabia and a multinational force at Gallipoli. It was during this turmoil that the Armenian tragedy unfolded.

In *Gallipoli*, historian Peter Hart takes a detailed look at the tragic WWI campaign, from its planning stages to the bloody disembarkations at Anzac Cove and the eventual retreat.

By the end of WWI the Turks were in disarray. The French, Italians, Greeks and Armenians, with Russian support, controlled parts of Anatolia. The Treaty of Sèvres in 1920 demanded the dismembering of the empire, with only a sliver of steppe left to the Turks. European triumphalism did not count on a Turkish backlash, but a Turkish nationalist movement developed, motivated by the humiliation of Sèvres. Leading was Mustafa Kemal, the victorious commander at Gallipoli. He began organising resistance and established a national assembly in Ankara, far from opposing armies and meddling diplomats.

Meanwhile, a Greek force pushed out from İzmir. The Greeks saw an opportunity to realise their *megali idea* (great idea) of re-establishing the Byzantine Empire. They took Bursa and Edirne. This was just the provocation that Mustafa Kemal needed to galvanise Turkish support. After initial skirmishes, the Greeks pressed on for Ankara, seeking to crush the Turks. But stubborn Turkish resistance stalled them at the Battle of Sakarya. The two armies faced off again at Dumlupınar. Here the Turks savaged the Greeks, sending them in retreat towards İzmir, where they were expelled from Anatolia amid pillage and looting.

Mustafa Kemal emerged as the hero of the Turkish people; he realised the earlier dream of the 'Young Turks': to create a Turkish nation-state. The Treaty of Lausanne in 1923 undid the humiliations of Sèvres and saw foreign powers leave Turkey. The borders of the modern Turkish state were set.

1595–1603	1639	1683	1760–90s
Stay-at-home sultan, Mehmet, has his 19 brothers strangled to protect his throne. His successor institutes 'the Cage' to keep potential claimants to the throne distracted with concubines and confections.	The Ottomans sign the Treaty of Zohrab with Persia, finally bringing peace between the two Islamic states after nearly 150 years of intermittent war on the eastern fringe of Anatolia.	Sultan Mehmet IV besieges Vienna, ending in the rout of his army. By century's end, the Ottomans have sued for peace for the first time and have lost the Peloponnese, Hungary and Transylvania.	Despite attempts to modernise, and military training from France, the Ottomans lose ground to the Russians under Catherine the Great, who anoints herself protector of the Ottomans' Orthodox subjects.

GALLIPOLI CAMPAIGN

Engaged on multiple fronts during WWI, the Ottomans held fast only at Gallipoli. This was due partially to inept British command but also to the brilliance of Turkish commander Mustafa Kemal. Iron-willed, he inspired his men to hold their lines, while also inflicting shocking casualties on the invading British and Anzac forces, who had landed on 25 April 1915.

Difficult territory, exposure to the elements and the nature of hand-to-hand trench warfare meant that the campaign was a stalemate; however, there are reports of remarkable civility between invading and defensive forces. The Allies withdrew after eight months.

Unbeknown to anyone at the time, two enduring legends of nationhood were born on the blood-spattered sands of Gallipoli: Australians see the campaign as the birth of their national consciousness, while Turks regard the successful campaign to defend Gallipoli as the genesis of their independence.

Atatürk & the Republic

The Turks consolidated Ankara as their capital and abolished the sultanate. Mustafa Kemal assumed the newly created presidency of the secular republic, later taking the name Atatürk – literally, 'Father Turk'). Thereupon the Turks set to work. Mustafa Kemal's energy was apparently limitless; his vision was to see Turkey take its place among the modern, developed countries of Europe.

At the time, the country was devastated after years of war, so a firm hand was needed. The Atatürk era was one of enlightened despotism. Atatürk established the institutions of democracy while never allowing any opposition to impede him. Yet his ultimate motivation was the betterment of his people. One aspect of the Kemalist vision, however, was to have ongoing consequences: the insistence that the nation be solely Turkish. Encouraging national unity made sense, considering the nationalist separatist movements that had bedevilled the Ottoman Empire, but in doing so a cultural existence was denied the Kurds. Sure enough, within a few years a Kurdish revolt erupted, the first of several to recur throughout the 20th century.

The desire to create homogenous nation-states on the Aegean also prompted population exchanges: Greek-speaking communities from Anatolia were shipped to Greece, while Muslim residents of Greece were transferred to Turkey. These exchanges brought great disruption and the creation of ghost villages, such as Kayaköy (Karmylassos). It was aimed at forestalling ethnic violence, but it was a melancholy episode and it hobbled the development of the new state. Turkey found itself without

1826	1839	1876	1908
Major attempts at reform under Mahmut II. He centralises the administration and modernises the army, resulting in the 'Auspicious Event' where the unruly janissaries are put to the sword.	Reform continues with the Tanzimat, a charter of legal and political rights, the underlying principle of which is the equality of the empire's Muslim and non-Muslim subjects.	Abdülhamid II takes the throne. The National Assembly meets for the first time and a constitution is created, but Serbia and Montenegro, emboldened by the pan-Slavic movement, fight for independence.	The Young Turks of the Committee for Union and Progress (CUP), based in Salonika, demand the reintroduction of the constitution. In the ensuing elections the CUP wins a convincing majority.

the majority of the educated elites of Ottoman society, many of whom had not been Turkish speakers.

Atatürk's vision gave the Turkish state a comprehensive makeover. Everything from headgear to language was scrutinised and where necessary reformed. Turkey adopted the Gregorian calendar (as used in the West), reformed its alphabet (adopting the Roman script), standardised the language, outlawed the fez, instituted universal suffrage and decreed that Turks should take surnames, something they had previously not had. By the time of his death in November 1938, Atatürk had, to a large degree, lived up to his name, spearheading the creation of the nation-state and dragging it into the modern era.

Bruce Clark's *Twice a Stranger* is an investigation of the Greek–Turkish population exchanges of the 1920s. Analysing background events and interviewing those who were transported, Clark shines new light on the two countries' fraught relationship.

Working Towards Democratisation

Though reform proceeded apace, Turkey remained economically and militarily weak, and Atatürk's successor, İsmet İnönü, avoided involvement in WWII. The war over, Turkey found itself allied to the USA. A bulwark against the Soviets, Turkey was of strategic importance and received significant US aid. The new friendship was cemented when Turkish troops fought in Korea, and Turkey became a member of NATO.

Meanwhile, democratic reform gained momentum. In 1950 the Democratic Party swept to power. Ruling for a decade, the Democrats failed to live up to their name and became increasingly autocratic; the army intervened in 1960 and removed them. Army rule lasted briefly, and resulted in the liberalisation of the constitution, but it set the tone for future decades. The military considered themselves the guardians of Atatürk's vision and felt obliged to step in when necessary to ensure the republic maintained the right trajectory.

The 1960s and '70s saw the creation of political parties of all stripes, but profusion did not make for robust democracy. The late 1960s were characterised by left-wing activism and political violence, which prompted a move to the right by centrist parties. The army stepped in again in 1971, before handing power back in 1973.

Political chaos reigned through the '70s, so the military seized power again to re-establish order in 1980. This they did through the creation of the highly feared National Security Council, but they allowed elections in 1983. Here, for the first time in decades, was a happy result. Turgut Özal, leader of the Motherland Party (ANAP), won a majority and was able to set Turkey back on course. An astute economist and pro-Islamic, Özal made vital economic and legal reforms that brought Turkey in line with the international community and sowed the seeds of its current vitality.

1912–13	1915–18	1919–20	1922
The First and Second Balkan Wars. An alliance of Serbian, Greek and Bulgarian forces take Salonika, previously the second city of the Ottoman Empire, and Edirne. The alliance later turns on itself.	Turks fight in WWI on the side of the Central Powers. Encroached upon on four fronts, the Turks repel invaders only at Gallipoli. At war's ends, a British fleet is positioned off the coast of İstanbul.	The Turkish War of Independence begins. The Treaty of Sèvres (1920) reduces Turkey to a strip of Anatolian territory but the Turks, led by Mustafa Kemal, rise to defend their homeland.	The Turks push back the Greek expeditionary force, which had advanced into Anatolia, and eject them from Smyrna (İzmir). Turkey reasserts its independence and the European powers accede.

Turn of the Millennium

In 1991, Turkey supported the allied invasion of Iraq, with Özal allowing air strikes from bases in southern Anatolia. Thus, Turkey, after decades in the wilderness, affirmed its place in the international community and as an important US ally. At the end of the Gulf War millions of Iraqi Kurds fled into Anatolia. The exodus caught the attention of the international media, bringing the Kurdish issue into the spotlight, and resulting in the establishment of a Kurdish safe haven in northern Iraq. This, in

ARMENIANS OF ANATOLIA

The twilight of the Ottoman Empire saw human misery on an epic scale, but nothing has proved as enduringly melancholic and controversial as the fate of Anatolia's Armenians. The tale begins with eyewitness accounts, in April 1915, of Ottoman army units marching Armenian populations towards the Syrian desert. It ends with an Anatolian hinterland virtually devoid of Armenians. What happened in between remains mired in conjecture, obfuscation and propaganda.

Armenians maintain that they were subject to the 20th century's first orchestrated 'genocide', that 1.5 million Armenians were summarily executed or killed on death marches and that Ottoman authorities intended to remove the Armenian presence from Anatolia. To this day, Armenians demand an acknowledgment of this 'genocide'.

Turkey, though, refutes that any 'genocide' occurred. It admits that thousands of Armenians died but claim the order had been to 'relocate' Armenians without intending to eradicate them. The deaths, according to Turkish officials, were due to disease and starvation, consequences of the chaos of war. Some even claim that Turks were subjected to 'genocide' by Armenian militias.

A century later the issue is unresolved. The murder of outspoken Turkish-Armenian journalist Hrant Dink in 2007 by Turkish ultranationalists appeared to confirm that antagonism is insurmountable, but apparently reconciliatory progress is being made: thousands of Turks, bearing placards saying 'We are all Armenians', marched in solidarity with the slain journalist.

Diplomatic contact has been re-established between Turkish and Armenian governments, but progress on resolving differences is patchy. There is also increasing contact between Turkish and Armenian artists, students, academics and civil-society groups. Political obstacles remain, however, with both sides finding it difficult to compromise, particularly as nationalistic voices tend to be loudest. Turkey is concerned that America might officially recognise the 'genocide'. This issue frequently reignites, causing diplomatic arguments and accusations, but as long as the question remains officially unresolved between Turkish and Armenian governments, it will continue to resurface.

Meanwhile, brisk Turkish–Armenian trade continues, despite their border being closed. Turkish manufacturers send goods to Armenia via neighbouring Georgia, proof that Turks and Armenians have much to gain if they bury their mutual distrust.

1923	1938	1945–50	1971
The Treaty of Lausanne, signed by the steadfast İsmet İnönü, undoes the wrongs of Sèvres. The Republic of Turkey is unanimously supported by the members of the National Assembly.	Atatürk dies, at the age of 57, in the Dolmabahçe Palace in İstanbul on 10 November – all the clocks in the palace are stopped at the time that he died: 9.05am.	After WWII, which the Turks avoided, the Truman Doctrine brings aid to Turkey on the condition of democratisation. Democratic elections are held (1950) and the Democratic Party emerges victorious.	Increasing political strife prompts the military to step in again to restore order. The military chief handed the prime minister a written ultimatum, thus this was known as a 'coup by memorandum'.

turn, emboldened the Kurdistan Workers Party (PKK), which stepped up its terror campaign aimed at creating a Kurdish state. The Turkish military responded with an iron fist, such that the southeast effectively endured a civil war.

Meanwhile, Turgut Özal died suddenly in 1993, creating a power vacuum. Weak coalition governments followed throughout the 1990s, with a cast of figures flitting across the political stage. Tansu Çiller served briefly as Turkey's first female prime minister, but despite high expectations she did not solve the Kurdish issue or cure the ailing economy.

In December 1995 the religious Refah (Welfare) Party formed a government led by veteran politician Necmettin Erbakan. Heady with power, Refah politicians made Islamist statements that raised the ire of the military. In 1997 the military declared that Refah had flouted the constitutional ban on religion in politics. Faced with a so-called 'postmodern coup', the government resigned and Refah was disbanded.

The capture of PKK leader Abdullah Öcalan in early 1999 seemed like a good omen after the torrid '90s. His capture offered an opportunity – still being pursued – to settle the Kurdish question. Later that year disastrous

FATHER OF THE MOTHERLAND

Many Western travellers remark on the Turks' devotion to Atatürk. In response, the Turks reply that the Turkish state is a result of his energy and vision: without him there would be no Turkey. From the era of Stalin, Hitler and Mussolini, Atatürk stands as a beacon of statesmanship and proves that radical reform, deftly handled, can be hugely successful.

The Turks' gratitude to Atatürk manifests itself throughout the country. He appears on stamps, banknotes and statues across the country. His name is affixed to innumerable bridges, airports and highways. And seemingly every house in which he spent a night, from the southern Aegean to the Black Sea, is now a museum; İzmir's (p203) is worth a visit.

Turkish schoolchildren learn by rote and can dutifully recite Atatürk's life story. But it may be that the history-book image of Atatürk is more simplistic than the reality. An avowed champion of Turkish culture, he preferred opera to Turkish music. Though calling himself 'Father Turk', he had no offspring.

Atatürk died relatively young (aged 57) in 1938. No doubt years as a military man, reformer and public figure took their toll. His friend and successor as president, İsmet İnönü, ensured that he was to be lauded by his countrymen. The praise continues. Indeed, any perceived insult to Atatürk is considered highly offensive and is illegal.

There are several outstanding Atatürk biographies: Patrick Kinross' *Ataturk: Rebirth of a Nation* sticks closely to the official Turkish view; Andrew Mango's *Atatürk* is detached and detailed; while *Atatürk: An Intellectual Biography* by Şükrü Hanioğlu examines the intellectual currents that inspired him.

1980	1983	1985–99	1997
The third of Turkey's military coups, this time as the military moves to stop widespread street violence between left- and right-wing groups. The National Security Council is formed.	In elections after the 1980 coup, the Özal era begins. A populist and pragmatic leader, Özal embarks on economic reform, encouraging foreign investment. Turkey opens to the West and the tourism industry takes off.	Abdullah Öcalan establishes the Kurdistan Workers Party (PKK), a terror group calling for a Kurdish state. There is a long, low-intensity war in southeast Anatolia until Öcalan's capture in 1999.	The coalition government headed by Necmettin Erbakan's Islamically inspired Refah (Welfare) Party is disbanded, apparently under military pressure, in what has been called a 'post modern coup'.

earthquakes struck İzmit, ending any premillennial optimism. The government's handling of the crisis was inadequate; however, the global outpouring of aid and sympathy did much to reassure Turks they were valued members of the world community.

A new political force arose in the new millennium: Recep Tayyip Erdoğan's Justice and Development Party (AKP) won government in 2002, heralding an era of societal reforms, capitalising on improved economic conditions. With Islamist roots, the AKP sought to pursue Turkey's entry to the EU and to end military intervention in the political scene.

Much of the support for the AKP arose in the burgeoning cities of Anatolia. The cities of the interior were experiencing an economic boom, proof that the modernising and economic development projects begun earlier were finally bearing fruit. In fact, the Turkish economy continues to grow strongly, with consistently high annual GDP growth, even during the global financial crisis of 2008, so many Turks are relieved not be in the EU, thus avoiding the economic perils that have beset Greece.

The AKP pursued a new direction in foreign policy, attempting to restore relations with Turkey's near neighbours, a modestly successful policy until the Syrian civil war in 2012. Domestically, the AKP worked to curtail military intervention in Turkey's political sphere, while also initiating 'openings' to address long-term dilemmas such as minority rights, the Kurdish issue, acrimonious relations with Armenia and recognising the rights of the Alevis, an Anatolian Muslim minority. However, thus far these 'openings' have not produced long-term solutions. The AKP has also attracted criticism at home and abroad, particularly for curtailing press freedoms, including social media. Others contend that its Islamic political philosophy is consciously restricting long-held social freedoms such as drinking alcohol. Grandiose schemes put forward by Prime Minister Erdoğan – include digging a canal between the Black and Marmara Seas, and building the world's biggest mosque at Çamlıca in İstanbul – raise many eyebrows, too.

Such controversies create very strong views: Turks are either entirely in support of, or entirely against the AKP and its agenda, making for a polarised society. Whatever your position, however, it is clear that Turkey is on the move.

European observers referred to Anatolia as 'Turchia' as early as the 12th century. The Turks themselves didn't do this until the 1920s.

An appetiser for those wanting to know more, *Turkey: A Short History* by Norman Stone is a succinct and pacey wrap-up of the crucial events and personalities of Turkey's long history.

2002	2005	2007–11	May–July 2013
Recep Tayyip Erdoğan's Justice and Development Party (AKP) wins a landslide election victory, a reflection of the Turkish public's disgruntlement with the established parties. The economy recovers.	EU-accession talks begin, and economic and legal reforms begin to be implemented. Resistance to Turkish membership by some EU states leads to a decrease in approval by some Turks.	Further resounding election victories for the AKP, which increases its share of the vote, as well as winning two referenda in favour of rewriting the constitution.	Following a heavy-handed police response, an environmental sit-in in Istanbul's Gezi Park escalates, sparking a wave of protests against the government, continuing for weeks.

Architecture

Settled over millennia by countless civilisations, Turkey boasts a dizzying array of architectural styles and remnants that reveal diverse cultural influences, technical prowess and engineering techniques.

The visually stunning *Constantinople: Istanbul's Historical Heritage*, by Stéphane Yerasimos, provides history and context to many of the city's magnificent buildings.

Ancient (950–550 BC)

The earliest Anatolian architectural remnants, the carved megaliths of Göbekli Tepe (p579), date back to 9500 BC. The mud-brick constructions of Çatalhöyük (p461), that were accessed through their roofs, are almost 8500 years old. Alacahöyük (p442), dating from 4000 BC, was characterised by more complex buildings. By the time Troy was established, classical temple design was beginning to develop. Elsewhere, the Hittite remains at Hattuşa (p438), including hefty gates, walls and ramparts, reveal increasing sophistication in working with the landscape.

In the treeless southeast, distinctive 'beehive' construction techniques developed; these can still be seen at Harran (p585).

Greek & Roman (550 BC–AD 330)

The architects of ancient Greece displayed a heightened sense of planning and sophistication in design and construction, incorporating vaults and arches into their buildings. Later the Romans built upon the developments of the Greeks. The Romans were also accomplished road builders, establishing a comprehensive network linking trading communities.

Elements of classical design such as the amphitheatre, agora and forum can be seen at Side (p380), while Letoön (p345) features fine examples of temple-building that characterise Greco-Roman architecture. Other superb sites include Afrodisias (p312), Termessos (p377), Bergama and Patara (p346).

Byzantine (AD 330–1071)

Ecclesiastical construction distinguishes Byzantine architecture from that of the pagan Greeks. The Byzantines developed church design while working in new media, such as brick and plaster, and displaying a genius for dome construction, as seen in Aya Sofya (p65).

CAPITAL OF ROMAN ASIA

Ephesus (Efes; p223) is the pre-eminent example of Roman city construction in Turkey; its flagstoned streets, gymnasium, sewerage system, mosaics and theatre form a neat set-piece of Roman design and architecture.

A prosperous trading city, Ephesus was endowed with significant buildings. The Temple of Artemis, boasting a forest of mighty columns, was one of the Wonders of the Ancient World, but was later destroyed under orders of a Byzantine archbishop. The Great Theatre, one of the biggest in the Roman world, is evidence of Roman expertise in theatre design and acoustics, while the Library of Celsus is ingeniously designed to appear larger than it actually is.

Kariye Museum (Chora Church; p93), İstanbul

Mosaics were a principal Byzantine design feature; fine examples can be seen in the Hatay Archaeology Museum (p410) or in situ at the nearby Church of St Peter (p411). The Chora Church (p93; now called the Kariye Museum) in İstanbul features a sumptuous array of mosaics. An example of the burgeoning skill of Byzantine civil engineers is the Basilica Cistern (p75), also in İstanbul.

In the east, Armenian stonemasons developed their own distinctive architectural style. The 10th-century church at Akdamar (p610) is a stunning example, while the site of Ani (p561) includes fascinating ruins and remnants.

Seljuk (1071–1300)

The architecture of the Seljuks reveals significant Persian influences in design and decorative flourishes, including Kufic lettering and intricate stonework. The Seljuks created cosmopolitan styles incorporating elements of nomadic Turkic design traditions with Persian know-how and the Mediterranean-influenced architecture of the Anatolian Greeks. The Seljuks left a legacy of magnificent mosques and *medreses* (seminaries), distinguished by their elaborate entrances; you can see the best of them in Konya, Sivas and Divriği. As patrons of the Silk Road, the Seljuks also built a string of caravanserais through Anatolia, such as at Sultanhanı and in Cappadocia. The Anatolian countryside is also stippled with the grand conical *türbe* (tombs) of the Seljuks, such as those at Hasankeyf, Konya, Battalgazi and on both shores of Lake Van.

In the southeast, competitors to the Seljuks, the Artuklu Turks created the cityscapes of Mardin and Hasankeyf, featuring distinctive honey-toned stonework and brick tombs, while also embellishing and adding to the imposing black basalt walls of Diyarbakır.

For a scholarly investigation of the challenges faced by Byzantine architects, see *The Master Builders of Byzantium* by Robert Ousterhout.

Dolmabahçe Palace (p98), İstanbul

Ottoman (1300–1750)

From the 14th century, as the Ottomans expanded across Anatolia, they became increasingly influenced by Byzantine styles, especially ecclesiastical architecture. Ottoman architects absorbed Byzantine influences, particularly the use of domes, and incorporated them into their existing Persian architectural repertoire to develop a completely new style: the T-shape plan. The Üç Şerefeli Mosque (p145) in Edirne became the model for other mosques. One of the first forays into the T-plan, it was the first Ottoman mosque to have a wide dome and a forecourt with an ablutions fountain.

Aside from mosques, the Ottomans also developed a distinctive style of domestic architecture, consisting of multistorey houses with a stone ground floor topped by protruding upper floors balanced on carved

IMPERIAL MOSQUES

The rippling domes and piercing minarets of mosques are the quintessential image of Turkey for many travellers. The most impressive mosques, in size and grandness, are the imperial mosques commissioned by members of the royal households.

Each imperial mosque had a *külliye,* or collection of charitable institutions, clustered around it. These might include a hospital, asylum, orphanage, *imaret* (soup kitchen), hospice for travellers, *medrese* (seminary), library, baths and a cemetery in which the mosque's imperial patron and other notables could be buried. Over time, many of these buildings were demolished or altered, but İstanbul's Süleymaniye Mosque (p88) complex still has much of its *külliye* intact.

The design, perfected by the revered Ottoman architect Mimar Sinan during the reign of Süleyman the Magnificent, proved so durable that it is still being used, with variations, for mosque construction all over Turkey.

brackets. These houses featured separate women's and men's areas (*haremlik* and *selamlık* respectively), and often included woodwork detailing on ceilings and joinery, ornate fireplaces and expansive rooms lined with *sedirs* (low benches) ideal for the communal interaction that was a feature of Ottoman life. Cities including Amasya, Safranbolu, Muğla and Beypazarı still feature houses of this design.

In later centuries in İstanbul, architects developed the *yalı* (grand seaside mansions constructed solely of wood) to which notable families would escape at the height of summer. Prime examples are still visible on the Bosphorus.

Turkish Baroque & Neoclassical (1750–1920)

From the mid-18th century, rococo and baroque influences hit Turkey, resulting in a pastiche of curves, frills, scrolls and murals, sometimes described as 'Turkish baroque'. The period's archetype is the extravagant Dolmabahçe Palace (p98). Although building mosques was passé, the later Ottomans still adored pavilions where they could enjoy the outdoors; the Küçüksu Kasrı (p103) in İstanbul is a good example.

In the 19th and early 20th centuries, foreign or foreign-trained architects began to concoct a neoclassical blend: European architecture mixed in with Turkish baroque and some concessions to classic Ottoman style. Vedat Tek, a Turkish architect educated in Paris, built the capital's central post office, a melange of Ottoman elements and European symmetry. His style is sometimes seen as part of the first nationalist architecture movement, part of the modernisation project of the early Turkish Republic. This movement sought to create a 'national' style specific to Turkey by drawing on Ottoman design elements and melding them with modern European styles. Notable buildings in this style include the Ethnography Museum in Ankara (p421) and Bebek Mosque in İstanbul. Sirkeci Train Station, by the German architect Jachmund, is another example of this eclectic neoclassicism.

Modern (1920–present)

The rapid growth that Turkey has experienced since the 1940s has seen a profusion of bland, grey apartment blocks and office buildings pop up in Anatolian cities and towns. Yet even these, taken in context of the Turkish landscape, climate and bustle of convivial neighbourhood interaction, have a distinctive quality all their own.

During the 1940s and '50s a new nationalist architecture movement developed as Turkish-trained architects working on government buildings sought to create a homegrown style reflecting Turkish tradition and aspirations of the new republic. This architecture tended to be sturdy and monumental; examples include the Anıt Kabir (p419) in Ankara and the Çanakkale Şehitleri Anıtı (p158) at Gallipoli.

Since the 1990s there has been more private-sector investment in architecture, leading to a diversification of building styles. The Levent business district in İstanbul has seen the mushrooming of shimmering office towers, and other futuristic buildings have arisen, such as the Esenboğa Airport in Ankara.

The most interesting development in recent decades is that Turks have begun to take more notice of their history, particularly the Ottoman era. This has meant reclaiming their architectural heritage, especially those parts of it that can be turned into dollars via the tourism industry. These days, restorations and new buildings built in Sultanahmet and other parts of İstanbul – and even Göreme, in Cappadocia – are most likely to be in classic Ottoman style.

Ottoman architectural styles spread beyond the boundaries of modern Turkey. There are still Ottoman constructions (mosques, fortresses, mansions and bridges) throughout the Balkans.

Turkey: Modern Architectures in History, by Sibel Bozdoğan and Esra Akcan, examines the philosophy and impact of architecture in the new Turkey.

ARCHITECTURE TURKISH BAROQUE & NEOCLASSICAL (1750–1920)

The Turkish Table

In Turkey, meals are events to be celebrated. The national cuisine is made memorable by the use of fresh seasonal ingredients, and a local expertise in grilling meat and fish that has been perfected over centuries. Here, kebaps are succulent, meze dips are made daily with the best seasonal ingredients, and freshly caught fish is expertly cooked over coals and served unadorned, accompanied by Turkey's famous aniseed-flavoured drink, rakı. When you eat out here, you're sure to finish your meal replete and supremely satisfied.

The Ottomans were masters of the evocative culinary description, inventing such delights as 'Ladies' Thighs', 'The Sultan's Delight', 'Harem Navel' and 'Nightingale Nests'.

What to Eat

Turkey is one of the few countries that can feed itself from its own produce and have leftovers. This means that produce makes its way from ground to table quickly, ensuring freshness and flavour.

Mezes

Mezes (small, tapas-like dishes) aren't just a type of dish, they're a whole eating experience. If you eat in a local household, your host may put out a few lovingly prepared mezes for guests to nibble on before the main course is served. In *meyhanes* (Turkish taverns), waiters heave around enormous trays full of cold mezes that customers can choose from – hot mezes are ordered from the menu. Mezes are usually vegetable-based, though seafood dishes can also feature.

Meat

Overall, the Turks are huge meat-eaters, which can be a problem if you're a vegetarian. Beef, lamb, mutton, liver and chicken are prepared in a number of ways. The most famous of these is the kebap – *şiş* and *döner* – but *köfte* (meatballs), *saç kavurma* (stir-fried cubed meat dishes) and *güveç* (meat and vegetable stews cooked in a terracotta pot) are just as common.

The most popular sausage in Turkey is the spicy beef *sucuk*. Garlicky *pastırma* (pressed beef preserved in spices) is regularly used as an accompaniment to egg dishes; it's occasionally served with warm hummus (chickpea, tahini and lemon dip) as a meze.

Fish

Fish is wonderful here, but can be pricey. In a *balık restoran* (fish restaurant) you should always try to do as the locals do and choose your own fish from the display. After doing this, the fish will be weighed, and the price computed at the day's per-kilogram rate.

Popular species include *hamsi* (anchovy), *lüfer* (bluefish), *kalkan* (turbot), *levrek* (sea bass), *lahos* (white grouper), *mezgit* (whiting), *çupra* (gilthead bream) and *palamut* (bonito).

Vegetables & Salads

Turks love vegetables, eating them fresh in summer and pickling them for winter (*türşu* means pickled vegetables). There are two particularly Turkish ways of preparing vegetables: the first is known as *zeytinyağlı* (sautéed in olive oil) and the second *dolma* (stuffed with rice or meat).

Simplicity is the key to Turkish *salata* (salads), with crunchy fresh ingredients being adorned with a shake of oil and vinegar at the table and eaten with gusto as a meze or as an accompaniment to a meat or fish main course.

Sweets

Turks don't usually finish their meal with a dessert, preferring to serve fruit as a finale. Most of them love a mid-afternoon sugar hit, though, and will often pop into a *muhallebici* (milk pudding shop), *pastane* (cake shop) or *baklavacı* (baklava shop) for a piece of syrup-drenched baklava, a plate of chocolate-crowned profiteroles or a *fırın sütlaç* (rice pudding) tasting of milk, sugar and just a hint of exotic spices. Other Turkish sweet specialities worth sampling are *kadayıf*, dough soaked in syrup and topped with a layer of *kaymak* (clotted cream); *künefe*, layers of *kadayıf* cemented together with sweet cheese, doused in syrup and served hot with a sprinkling of pistachio; and *katmer*, thin layers of pastry filled with *kaymak* and pistachio and served hot.

What to Drink

Alcoholic Drinks

Turkey's most beloved tipple is rakı, a grape spirit infused with aniseed. Similar to Greek ouzo, it's served in long thin glasses and is drunk neat or with water, which turns the clear liquid chalky white; if you want to add ice *(buz)*, do so after adding water, as dropping ice straight into rakı kills its flavour.

Bira (beer) is also popular. The local drop, Efes, is a perky pilsner that comes in bottles, cans and on tap.

Turkey grows and bottles its own *şarap* (wine), which has greatly improved in quality over the past decade but is quite expensive due to high government taxes. If you want red wine ask for *kırmızı şarap;* for white ask for *beyaz şarap*. Popular local varietals include *boğazkere,* a strong-bodied red; *kalecik karası,* an elegant red with an aroma of vanilla and cocoa; *emir,* a light and floral white; and *narince,* a fruity yet dry white.

Nonalcoholic Drinks

Drinking çay is the national pastime, and the country's cup of choice is made with leaves from the Black Sea region. Sugar cubes are the only accompaniment and you'll find these are needed to counter the effects of long brewing, although you can always try asking for it *açık* (weaker).

The wholly chemical *elma çay* (apple tea) is caffeine-free and only for tourists – locals wouldn't be seen dead drinking the stuff.

Türk kahve (Turkish coffee) is a thick and powerful brew drunk in a couple of short sips. If you order a cup, you will be asked how sweet you like it – *çok şekerli* means 'very sweet', *orta şekerli* 'middling', *az şekerli* 'slightly sweet' and *şekersiz or sade* 'not at all'.

Ayran is a refreshing drink made by whipping yoghurt with water and salt; it's the traditional accompaniment to kebaps.

Sahlep is a hot milky drink that takes off the winter chill. Made from wild orchid bulbs, it's reputed to be an aphrodisiac.

THE TURKISH TABLE WHAT TO DRINK

The Turks say 'Afiyet olsun' ('May it be good for your health') before starting to eat. After the meal, they say 'Elinize sağlık' ('Health to your hands') to compliment the host or hostess on their cooking.

Menu Decoder

acılı ezme	spicy tomato and onion paste
Adana kebap	spicy *köfte* wrapped around a flat skewer and grilled
alinazik	eggplant (aubergine) puree with yoghurt and ground *köfte*
balık ekmek	fish sandwich
beyti sarma	spicy ground meat baked in bread and served with yoghurt
börek	sweet or savoury filled pastry
büryan	lamb slow-cooked in a pit
çacık	yoghurt dip with garlic and mint
çiğ köfte	raw ground lamb mixed with pounded bulgur and spices
çoban salatası	salad of tomato, cucumber, onion and sweet pepper
döner kebap	lamb cooked on a revolving upright skewer, then thinly sliced
fava salatası	mashed broad-bean salad
fıstıklı kebap	minced lamb studded with pistachios
gözleme	filled savoury pancake
haydari	yoghurt dip with roasted eggplant and garlic
hünkâr beğendi	lamb or beef stew served on a mound of rich eggplant puree
içli köfte	ground lamb and onion with a bulgur coating
imam bayıldı	eggplant, onion, tomato and peppers slow-cooked in olive oil
işkembe çorbası	tripe soup
İskender (Bursa) kebap	*döner* served on a bed of pide and yoghurt topped with tomato and burnt-butter sauces
karıışık ızgara	mixed grilled lamb
kısır	bulgur salad
kokoreç	seasoned, grilled lamb/mutton intestines
köfte	meatballs; *izgara köfte* means grilled meatballs
kuru fasulye	haricot beans cooked in a spicy tomato sauce
lahmacun	thin and crispy Arabic-style pizza topped with minced lamb
mantı	ravioli stuffed with meat, topped with yoghurt, tomato and butter
mercimek çorbası	lentil soup
muhammara	dip of walnuts, bread, tahini, olive oil and lemon juice
pastırma	pressed beef preserved in spices
patlıcan kebap	cubed or minced lamb grilled with eggplant
patlıcan kızartması	fried eggplant with tomato
perde pilavı	chicken and rice cooked in pastry
pide	Turkish pizza
piyaz	white-bean salad
sigara böreği	deep-fried cigar-shaped pastries filled with white cheese
şiş kebap	small pieces of lamb grilled on a skewer
su böreği	lasagne-like layered pastry laced with white cheese and parsley
tavuk şiş	small boneless chicken pieces grilled on a skewer
testi kebap	lamb or chicken slow-cooked in a sealed terracotta pot
Tokat kebap	lamb cubes grilled with potato, tomato, eggplant and garlic
Urfa kebap	a mild version of the Adana kebap
yaprak sarma/dolması	vine leaves stuffed with rice and herbs

Arts

Turkey's artistic traditions are rich and diverse, displaying influences of the many cultures and civilisations that have waxed and waned in Anatolia over the centuries.

Carpets

The art form that travellers are most likely to associate with Turkey is the carpet – there are few visitors who do not end up in a carpet shop at some time.

The carpets that travellers know and love are the culmination of an ages-old textile-making tradition. Long ago Turkic nomads weaved tents and saddle bags and established carpet-making techniques on the Central Asian steppes.

As in many aspects of their culture, the Turks adopted and adapted from other traditions. Moving ever-westward, the Turks eventually brought hand-woven carpets, into which they incorporated Persian designs and Chinese cloud patterns, to Anatolia in the 12th century.

Within Anatolia, distinctive regional designs evolved. Uşak carpets, with star and medallion motifs, were the first to attract attention in Europe: Renaissance artist Holbein included copies of them in his paintings. Thereafter, carpet-making gradually shifted from cottage industry to big business. Village women still weave carpets but usually work to fixed contracts, using a pattern and being paid for their final effort rather than for each hour of work.

Fearing the loss of old carpet-making methods, the Ministry of Culture has sponsored projects to revive weaving and dyeing methods. One scheme is the Natural Dye Research and Development Project (Doğal Boya Arıştırma ve Geliştirme Projesi). Some shops keep stocks of these 'project carpets', which are usually high quality.

A magnificent collection of images gathered over decades, *No-mads in Anatolia* by Harald Böhmer and Josephine Powell looks at the lost nomadic traditions of textile- and carpet-making in Anatolia. Difficult to find but hugely rewarding.

Literature

Only in the last century has Turkey developed a tradition of novel-writing, but there is a wealth of writing by Turks and about Turkey that offers insight into the country and its people.

The Turkish literary canon is made up of warrior epics, mystical verses, including those of Rumi (founder of the Mevlevi order of whirling dervishes), and the elegies of wandering *aşık* (minstrels). Travellers may encounter tales of Nasreddin Hoca, a semi-legendary quasi-holy man noted for his quirky humour and left-of-centre 'wisdom'.

Yaşar Kemal was the first Turkish novelist to win international attention, writing gritty novels of rural life. His *Memed, My Hawk*, a tale of impoverished Anatolian villagers, won him nomination for the Nobel Prize for Literature.

Recently, the prolific Turkish-American writer and academic Elif Şafak has attracted an international following. Her first novel to be translated into English, *The Flea Palace*, tells of an elegant-but-fading İstanbul apartment building. Her novels, the most recent of which is *The*

One of the giants of Turkish literature was Evliya Çelebi, who travelled the Ottoman realm for 40 years and produced a 10-volume travel-ogue from 1630. A recent edition, *An Ottoman Traveller*, presents a selection of his quirky observations.

ORHAN PAMUK: NOBEL LAUREATE

The biggest name in Turkish literature is Orhan Pamuk. Long feted in Turkey, Pamuk has built a worldwide audience since first being translated in the 1990s. He is an inventive prose stylist, creating elaborate plots and finely sketched characters while dealing with the issues confronting contemporary Turkey.

His *Black Book* is an existential whodunnit told through a series of newspaper columns, while *My Name is Red* is a 16th-century murder mystery that also philosophises on conceptions of art. In his nonfiction *İstanbul: Memories and the City,* Pamuk ruminates on his complex relationship with the beguiling city. *Cevdet Bey and His Sons,* one of his earliest works, has recently been translated into English for the first time.

The Museum of Innocence, his latest novel, details an affair between wealthy Kemal and shop girl Füsun and illustrates Pamuk's uncanny ability to evoke the ambience of modern Turkey. In 2012 Pamuk opened a museum (p95) in İstanbul based on that in the novel and displaying the ephemera of everyday life.

Pamuk was awarded the Nobel Prize for Literature in 2006. He is the only Turk to have won a Nobel Prize.

Architect's Apprentice, deal with issues confronting modern Turkey as well as its historical richness.

Ayşe Kulin has a huge following and her novels have been translated widely. *Last Train to İstanbul* is her novel of Turkish diplomats' attempts to save Jewish families from the Nazis, while *Farewell* is set during the era of Allied occupation after WWI.

Irfan Orga's autobiographical *Portrait of a Turkish Family,* set during the late Ottoman/early Republican era, describes the collapse of his well-to-do İstanbullu family. In *The Caravan Moves On* Orga offers a glimpse of rural life in the 1950s as he travels with nomads in the Taurus Mountains.

Jewish-Turkish writer Moris Farhi's pacy and episodic *Young Turk* draws on events from his own life, and is a compelling account of adolescence in old İstanbul.

Music

Even in the era of YouTube and pervasive Western cultural influences, Turkish musical traditions and styles have remained strong, and homegrown stars continue to emerge.

Pop, Rock, Experimental

You'll hear Turkish pop everywhere: in taxis, bars and long-distance buses. With its skittish rhythms and strident vocals, it's undeniably energetic and distinctive.

Sezen Aksu is lauded as the queen of Turkish pop music, releasing a string of albums in diverse styles since the 1970s. However, it is Tarkan, the pretty-boy pop star, who has achieved most international recognition. His 1994 album, *A-acayıpsin,* sold mightily in Turkey and Europe, establishing him as Turkey's biggest-selling pop sensation. 'Şımarık', released in 1999, became his first European number one. He continues to release albums and his metrosexual hip-swivelling ensures he remains a household name in Turkey.

Burhan Öçal is one of the country's finest percussionists. His seminal *New Dream* is a funky take on classical Turkish music, and his Trakya All-Stars albums are investigations of the music of his native Thrace.

Mercan Dede has released a string of albums incorporating traditional instruments and electronic beats. In a similar vein, BaBa ZuLa create a

One of Turkey's biggest cultural exports in recent years has been *Muhteşem Yüzyıl* (literally 'Magnificent Century'), a sumptuous TV series detailing the life and loves of Sultan Süleyman the Magnificent, which has attracted an enormous audience in Turkey and elsewhere.

fusion of dub, *saz* (Turkish lute) and pop – accompanied by live belly dancing!

Notable rock bands include Duman and Mor ve Ötesi. maNga create an intriguing mix of metal, rock and Anatolian folk. Their 2012 album *e-akustik* is worth seeking out.

Folk

Turkish folk music includes various subgenres that may be indistinguishable to Western ears. Ensembles consist of *saz* accompanied by various drums and flutes. Arrangements include plaintive vocals and swelling choruses. Names to look out for include female Kurdish singers Aynur Doğan and the ululating Rojin, whose hit 'Hejaye' has an addictive, sing-along chorus.

Fasıl is a lightweight version of Ottoman classical. This is the music you hear at *meyhanes* (taverns), usually played by gypsies. This skittish music is played with clarinet, *kanun* (zither), *darbuka* (a drum shaped like an hourglass), *ud* (Arabic lute) and violin.

Arabesk

A favourite of taxi drivers across Turkey is arabesk, an Arabic-influenced blend of crooning backed by string choruses and rippling percussion.

The two biggest names in arabesk are the hugely successful Kurdish singer İbrahim Tatlıses, a burly, moustachioed, former construction worker who survived an assassination attempt in 2011; and Orhan Gencebay, a prolific artist and actor.

Cinema

Turkey has long been a favoured location for foreign filmmakers; the James Bond pic, *Skyfall* (2012) and the Liam Neeson thriller *Taken 2* (2012) include scenes shot in İstanbul. The Turkish film industry itself came of age in the 1960s and '70s, when films with a political edge were being made alongside innumerable lightweight Bollywood-style movies, labelled *Yeşilçam* movies. During the 1980s, the film industry went into decline as TV siphoned off audiences, but during the 1990s Turkish cinema re-emerged.

Yılmaz Güney was the first Turkish filmmaker to attract international attention. Joint winner of the best film award at Cannes in 1982, his film *Yol* explored the dilemmas of men on weekend-release from prison, a tragic tale that Turks were forbidden to watch until 2000. Güney's

The biggest cinema event in the Turkish calendar, the Antalya Golden Orange Film Festival (www.altinportakal.org.tr/en) brings together film-industry figures, glitterati and a range of Turkish and international films every October.

A BEGINNERS' GUIDE TO TURKISH MUSIC

These are our picks to start your collection.

➡ *Turkish Groove* (compilation) Must-have introduction to Turkish music, with all the big names.

➡ *Crossing the Bridge: the Sound of İstanbul* (compilation) Soundtrack to a documentary about İstanbul's music scene.

➡ *Işık Doğdan Yükselir* – Sezen Aksu (contemporary folk) Stunning collection drawing on regional folk styles.

➡ *Nefes* – Mercan Dede (Sufi-electronic-techno fusion) Highly danceable synthesis of beats and Sufi mysticism.

➡ *Duble Oryantal* – BaBa ZuLa (fusion) BaBa ZuLa's classic, 'Belly Double', mixed by British dub master Mad Professor.

➡ *Gipsy Rum* – Burhan Öçal and İstanbul Oriental Ensemble (gypsy) A thigh-slapping introduction to Turkey's gypsy music.

uncompromising stance lead to confrontations with authorities and several stints in prison. He died in exile in France in 1984.

Turkish directors have comedic flair, too. Yılmaz Erdoğan's *Vizontele* is a wry look at the arrival of the first TV in Hakkari, a remote town in the southeast. *Düğün Dernek* is similarly quirky and entertaining. Ferzan Özpetek received international acclaim for *Hamam* (Turkish Bath), which follows a Turk living in Italy who reluctantly travels to İstanbul after he inherits a hamam.

Fatih Akin captured the spotlight after winning the Golden Bear award at the 2004 Berlin Film Festival with *Duvara Karşı* (Head On), a gripping telling of Turkish immigrant life in Germany. He followed this with *Edge of Heaven,* again pondering the Turkish experience in Germany. In 2010 Semih Kaplanoğlu won the Golden Bear award with *Bal* (Honey), a coming-of-age tale in the Black Sea region; while Reha Erdem's *Jîn* is an intriguing allegory.

Visual Arts

Turkey does not have a long tradition of painting or portraiture. Turks channelled their artistic talents into textile- and carpet-making, as well as *ebru* (paper marbling), calligraphy and ceramics. İznik became a centre for tile production from the 16th century. The exuberant tiles that adorn İstanbul's Blue Mosque and other Ottoman-era mosques hail from İznik. You'll find examples of *ebru,* calligraphy and ceramics in bazaars across Turkey.

İstanbul is the place to see what modern Turkish artists are up to. İstanbul Modern (p94) is one of the country's best modern-art galleries, but the small private art galleries along İstiklal Caddesi are worth seeing, too.

Ara Güler is one of Turkey's most respected photographers. For almost 60 years he has documented Turkish life; his *Ara Güler's İstanbul* is a poignant photographic record of the great city.

Dance

Turkey boasts a range of folk dances ranging from the frenetic to the hypnotic, and Turks tend to be enthusiastic and unselfconscious dancers, swivelling hips and shaking shoulders in ways entirely different from Western dance styles.

Folk dance can be divided into several broad categories. Originally a dance of central Anatolia, the *halay is* led by a dancer waving a handkerchief, and can be seen especially at weddings and in *meyhanes,* when everyone has downed plenty of rakı. The *horon,* from the Black Sea region, is most eye-catching – it involves plenty of Cossack-style kicking.

The *sema* (dervish ceremony) of the whirling dervishes is not unique to Turkey, but it's here that you are most likely to see it performed.

Panoramic Photographs of Turkey, by noted film director Nuri Bilge Ceylan, is a cloth-bound, limited-edition album of stunningly beautiful images of Turkish landscapes and cityscapes.

Belly dancing may not have originated in Turkey, but Turkish women have mastered the art, reputedly dancing with the least inhibition and the most revealing costumes.

A CINEMA AUTEUR IN ANATOLIA

Internationally, Nuri Bilge Ceylan has become the most widely recognised Turkish director. Since emerging in 2002 with *Uzak* (Distant), a meditation on the lives of migrants in Turkey, he has been a consistent favourite at international film festivals. *Uzak* won the Grand Prix at Cannes in 2003; Ceylan also won best director at Cannes in 2008 for *Üç Maymun* (Three Monkeys).

His 2011 release, *Once Upon a Time in Anatolia,* with brooding landscape shots and quirky dialogue, is an intriguing all-night search for a corpse in the Turkish backwoods. In 2014 he won the Palme d'Or at the Cannes Film Festival with *Winter Sleep*. He is the first Turkish director to win since Yılmaz Güney.

People

Turkey has a population of almost 80 million, the great majority of whom are Muslim and Turkish. Kurds form the largest minority, but there is an assortment of other groups – both Muslim and non-Muslim – leading some to say Turkey is comprised of 40 nations.

Since the 1950s there has been a steady movement of people into urban areas, so today 70% of the population lives in cities. Cities such as İstanbul have turned into pervasive sprawls, their historic hearts encircled by rings of largely unplanned new neighbourhoods.

Nonetheless, whether urban or rural, Muslim or Christian, Turkish, Kurdish or otherwise, the peoples of Turkey tend to be family-focused, easy-going, hospitable, gregarious and welcoming.

Turks

The first mentions of the Turks were in medieval Chinese sources, which record them as the Tujue in 6th-century Mongolia. The modern Turks descended from Central Asian tribes that moved westward through Eurasia over 1000 years ago. As such the Turks retain cultural links with various peoples through southern Russia, Azerbaijan, Iran, the nations of Central Asia, and western China.

As they moved westward Turkic groups encountered the Persians and converted to Islam. The Seljuks established the Middle East's first Turkic empire. The Seljuks' defeat of the Byzantines in 1071 opened up Anatolia to wandering Turkish groups, accelerating the westward drift of the Turks. Over succeeding centuries, Anatolia became the core of the Ottoman Empire and of the modern Turkish Republic. During the Ottoman centuries, Turkish rule extended into southeast Europe so today there are people of Turkish descent in Cyprus, Iraq, Macedonia, Greece, Bulgaria and Ukraine.

Shared ancestry with peoples in Central Asia and the Balkans means that Turks can merrily chat to locals all the way from Novi Pazar in Serbia

> Various (not exactly academically rigorous) theories state that the Turks are descendants of Japheth, the grandson of Noah. The Ottomans themselves claimed that Osman could trace his genealogy back through 52 generations to Noah.

IN THE FAMILY WAY

Turks retain a strong sense of family and community. One endearing habit is to use familial titles to embrace friends, acquaintances and even strangers. A teacher may address his student as '*çocuğum*' (my child); passers-by call old men in the street '*dede*' (literally, 'grandfather'); and old women are comfortable being called '*teyze*' (auntie) by strangers.

It is also common for children to call family friends '*amca*' (uncle) and for males of all ages to address older men as '*ağabey*' (roughly equivalent to the English 'guv'nor'). You will also hear small children referring to older girls as '*abla*', equivalent to 'big sister', which is charming in its simplicity.

These terms are a sign of respect but also of inclusiveness. Perhaps this intimacy explains how the sense of community persists amid the tower blocks of sprawling cities, where most Turks now live.

to Kashgar in China. Turkish is one of the Turkic languages, a family of languages spoken by more than 150 million people across Eurasia.

Kurds

Kurds have lived for millennia in the mountains where the modern borders of Turkey, Iran, Iraq and Syria meet. Turkey's Kurdish minority is estimated at more than 15 million people. Sparsely populated southeastern Anatolia is home to perhaps eight million Kurds, while seven million more live elsewhere in the country, largely integrated into mainstream Turkish society. The majority of Turkish Kurds are Sunni Muslims.

Despite having lived side by side with Turks for centuries, the Kurds retain a distinct culture and folklore and speak a language related to Persian. Some Kurds claim descent from the Medes of ancient Persia. The Kurds have their own foundation myth which is associated with Nevruz, the Persian New Year (21 March).

The struggle between Kurds and Turks has been very well documented. Kurds fought alongside the Turks during the battle for independence in the 1920s, but they were not guaranteed rights as a minority under the 1923 Treaty of Lausanne. The Turkish state was decreed to be homogenous – inhabited solely by Turks – hence the Kurds were denied a cultural existence. After the fragmentation, along ethnic lines, of the Ottoman Empire, such an approach may have seemed prudent, but as the Kurds were so numerous problems swiftly arose.

Until relatively recently the Turkish government refused to recognise the existence of the Kurds, insisting they were 'Mountain Turks'. Even today the census form and identity cards do not allow anyone to identify as Kurdish. However, this lack of recognition is being overcome. There are now Kurdish newspapers, books and media outlets and the Kurdish language is taught in some schools. Indicative of greater acceptance of Kurdish voices, Selahattin Demirtaş, a Kurdish politician, campaigned for president in 2014, winning 10% of the vote and praise for his engaging political style.

A Modern History of the Kurds by David McDowall investigates the plight of Kurds in Turkey, Iraq and Iran, examining how they have fared over the last two centuries as modern states have arisen in the Middle East.

Muslim Minorities

Turkey is home to several other Muslim minorities, both indigenous and recent arrivals, most of whom are regarded as Turks, but who nonetheless retain aspects of their culture and native tongue.

Laz & Hemşin

The Black Sea region is home to the Laz and the Hemşin peoples, two of the largest Muslim minorities after the Kurds.

The Laz mainly inhabit the valleys between Trabzon and Rize. East of Trabzon you can't miss the women in their maroon-striped shawls. Laz men were once among the most feared of Turkish warriors. Once Christian but now Muslim, the Laz are a Caucasian people speaking a language related to Georgian. They are renowned for their sense of humour and business acumen.

Like the Laz, the Hemşin were originally Christian. They mainly come from the far-eastern end of the Black Sea coast, although perhaps no more than 15,000 still live there; most have migrated to the cities where they earn a living as bread and pastry cooks. In and around Ayder, Hemşin women are easily identified by their leopard-print scarves coiled into elaborate headdresses.

Others

The last link to the wandering Turkic groups who arrived in Anatolia in the 11th century, the Yörük maintain a nomadic lifestyle around the Taurus Mountains. Named from the verb *yürük* (to walk), the Yörük move herds of sheep between summer and winter pastures.

In Turkey's far southeast, along the Syrian border, there are communities of Arabic speakers. Throughout Turkey there are also various Muslim groups that arrived from the Caucasus and the Balkans during the later years of the Ottoman Empire. These include Circassians, Abkhazians, Crimean Tatars, Bosnians, and Uighurs from China.

Non-Muslim Groups

The Ottoman Empire was notable for its large Christian and Jewish populations. These have diminished considerably in the last century.

> Small numbers of Turkish Kurds profess the Yazidi faith, a complex mix of indigenous beliefs and Sufi tradition, in which *Tavus Melek* (a peacock angel) is seen as an earthly guardian appointed by God.

ISLAM IN TURKEY

For many travellers, Turkey is their first experience of Islam. While it may seem 'foreign', Islam actually shares much with Christianity and Judaism. Like Christians, Muslims believe that Allah (God) created the world, pretty much according to the biblical account. They also revere Adam, Noah, Abraham, Moses and Jesus as prophets, although they don't believe Jesus was divine. Muslims call Jews and Christians 'People of the Book', meaning those with a revealed religion (in the Torah and Bible) that preceded Islam.

Where Islam differs from Christianity and Judaism is in the belief that Islam is the 'perfection' of these earlier traditions. Although Moses and Jesus were prophets, Mohammed was the greatest and last, to whom Allah communicated his final revelation.

Islam has diversified into many 'versions' over the centuries; however, the five 'pillars' of Islam – the profession of faith, daily prayers, alms giving, the fasting month of Ramazan, pilgrimage to Mecca – are shared by the entire Muslim community.

Islam is the most widely held belief in Turkey, however many Turks take a relaxed approach to religious duties and practices. Fasting during Ramazan is widespread and Islam's holy days and festivals are observed, but for many Turks Islamic holidays are the only times they'll visit a mosque. Turkish Muslims have also absorbed and adapted other traditions over the years, so it's not uncommon to see Muslims praying at Greek Orthodox shrines, while the Alevis, a heterodox Muslim minority, have developed a tradition combining elements of Anatolian folklore, Sufism and Shia Islam.

There has been a Jewish presence in Anatolia for over 2000 years. A large influx of Jews arrived in the 16th century, fleeing the Spanish Inquisition. Today most of Turkey's Jews live in İstanbul, and some still speak Ladino, a Judaeo-Spanish language.

Armenians have lived in Anatolia for a very long time; a distinct Armenian people existed by the 4th century, when they became the first nation to collectively convert to Christianity. The Armenians created their own alphabet and established various kingdoms in the borderlands between Byzantine, Persian and Ottoman empires. Until 1915 there were significant communities throughout Anatolia. The controversy surrounding the Armenians in the final years of the Ottoman Empire means that relations between Turks and Armenians remain predominantly sour. About 70,000 Armenians still live in Turkey, mainly in İstanbul and in pockets in Anatolia, particularly Diyarbakır.

The Turkic Speaking Peoples, edited by Ergün Çağatay and Doğan Kuban, is a monumental doorstop of a volume investigating, in full colour, the traditions and cultures of Turkic groups across Eurasia.

Turkish-Armenian relations are tense, but there are signs of rapprochement. In the last decade Armenian churches on Akdamar Island and in Diyarbakır have been refurbished. There have been services held in the refurbished churches (annually on Akdamar) attracting Armenian worshippers from across the border.

The Greeks are Turkey's other significant Christian minority. Greek populations once lived throughout the Ottoman realm, but after the population exchanges of the early Republican era and acrimonious events in the 1950s, the Greeks were reduced to a small community in İstanbul. Recent years, however, have seen a warming of relations and the return of some young Greek professionals and students to İstanbul.

Rugged southeastern Anatolia is also home to ancient Christian communities. These include adherents of the Syriac Orthodox Church, centred on Midyat, who speak Aramaic and maintain the monastery of Deyrul Zafaran. There are also some Chaldean Catholics remaining in Diyarbakır.

Environment

Turkey has one foot in Europe and another in Asia, its two parts separated by İstanbul's famous Bosphorus, the Sea of Marmara and the Dardanelles. Given this position at the meeting of continents, Turkey has a rich environment with flora and fauna ranging from Kangal dogs to purple bougainvillea. Unfortunately, the country faces the unenviable challenge of balancing environmental management with rapid economic growth and urbanisation, and to date it's done a sloppy job.

The Land

Boasting 7200km of coastline, snowcapped mountains, rolling steppe, vast lakes and broad rivers, Turkey is stupendously diverse. Eastern Thrace (European Turkey) makes up a mere 3% of its 769,632-sq-km land area; the remaining 97% is Anatolia (Asian Turkey).

The country's western edge is the Aegean coast, lined with coves and beaches and the Aegean islands, most belonging to Greece and within a few kilometres of mainland Turkey. Inland, western Anatolia has the vast Lake District and Uludağ (Great Mountain, 2543m), one of more than 50 Turkish peaks above 2000m.

The Mediterranean coast is backed by the jagged Taurus Mountains. East of Antalya, it opens up into a fertile plain, before the mountains close in again after Alanya.

Central Anatolia consists of a vast high plateau of rolling steppe, broken by mountain ranges and Cappadocia's fantastical valleys of fairy chimneys (rock formations).

Like the Mediterranean, the Black Sea is often hemmed in by mountains, and the coastline is frequently rugged and vertiginous. At the eastern end, Mt Kaçkar (Kaçkar Dağı; 3937m) is the highest point in the Kaçkar range, where peaks and glaciers ring mountain lakes and *yaylalar* (highland pastures).

Mountainous and somewhat forbidding, the rest of northeastern Anatolia is also wildly beautiful, from Yusufeli's valleys and raging Çoruh River via the steppe around Kars to snowcapped Mt Ararat (Ağrı Dağı; 5137m), dominating the area bordering Iran, Armenia and Azerbaijan. Southeastern Anatolia offers windswept rolling steppe, jagged outcrops of rock, and the extraordinary alkaline, mountain-ringed Lake Van (Van Gölü).

Wildlife

Animals

In theory, you could see bears, deer, jackals, caracal, wild boars and wolves, although you're unlikely to spot any wild animals unless you're trekking.

Birds

Some 400 species of bird are found in Turkey, with about 250 of these passing through on migration from Africa to Europe. Spring and autumn are particularly good times to see the feathered commuters. It's particularly easy to spot eagles, storks, (beige) hoopoes, (blue) rollers and (green) bee-eaters. There are several *kuş cennetleri* (bird sanctuaries)

Top Bird-watching Spots

Çıldır Gölü
(Çıldır Lake)

Göksu Delta,
near Silifke

Pamucak,
near Selçuk

dotted about the country, but they are often popular with noisy, picnicking locals who frighten the birds away.

Endangered Species

Anatolia's lions, beavers and Caspian tigers are extinct, and its lynx, striped hyena and Anatolian leopard have all but disappeared. A leopard was shot in Diyarbakır province in 2013, following a dramatic clifftop battle with a shepherd; the only previous sightings were in Siirt province in 2010 and outside Beypazarı in 1974. Another feline, the beautiful, pure-white Van cat, often with one blue and one amber eye, has also become endangered in its native Turkey.

Rare loggerhead turtles nest on various Mediterranean beaches, including Anamur, Patara, İztuzu Beach at Dalyan, and the Göksu Delta. A few rare Mediterranean monk seals live around Foça, but you would be lucky to see them. Greenpeace has criticised Turkey for not following international fishing quotas relating to Mediterranean bluefin tuna, which is facing extinction.

Plants

Turkey is one of the world's most biodiverse temperate-zone countries. Not only does its fertile soil produce an incredible range of fruit and vegetables, it is blessed with an exceptionally rich flora: more than 9000 species, over a third endemic and many found nowhere else on earth.

Common trees and plants are pine, cypress, myrtle, laurel, rosemary, lavender, thyme, and on the coast, purple bougainvillea, introduced from South America. Isparta is one of the world's leading producers of attar of roses, a valuable oil extracted from rose petals and used in perfumes and cosmetics.

Kangal dogs were originally bred to protect sheep from wolves and bears on mountain pastures. People wandering off the beaten track, especially in eastern Turkey, are sometimes startled by these huge, yellow-coated, black-headed animals, with optional spiked collar to protect against wolves. Their mongrel descendants live on Turkey's streets.

National Parks & Reserves

In the last few years, thanks to EU aspirations, Turkey has stepped up its environmental protection practices. It has 14 Ramsar sites (wetlands of international importance) and is a member of Cites, which covers international trade of endangered species. There are now almost 100 areas designated as *milli parkıs* (national parks), nature reserves and nature parks, where the environment is supposedly protected, and hunting controlled. Sometimes the regulations are carefully enforced, but in other cases problems such as litter-dropping picnickers persist.

Tourism is not well developed in the national parks, which are rarely well set up with facilities. It is not the norm for footpaths to be clearly marked, and camping spots are often unavailable. Most of the well-frequented national parks are as popular for their historic monuments as they are for the surrounding natural environment.

Environmental Issues

Inadequate enforcement of environmental laws, lack of finances and poor education have placed the environment a long way down Turkey's list of priorities. But there are glimmers of improvement, largely due to the country's desire to join the EU.

Nuclear Energy

One of the biggest challenges facing Turkey's environmentalists is the government's plan to build two nuclear power plants by 2023. Construction is set to begin at Akkuyu, on the eastern Mediterranean coast, in 2016. Previous plans to build a plant at this controversial site, located 25km from a seismic fault line, were scrapped in 2000. The second location is the Black Sea town of Sinop, with a vocal opponent in the community-run **Sinop is Ours** (www.sinopbizim.org). The country's seismic vulnerabilities increase the risk posed by nuclear reactors, but more plants are set to follow.

The government says the plants will aid economic growth and reduce dependency on natural gas supplies from Russia and Iran. Electricity consumption is increasing by about 6% a year in Turkey, which only has significant domestic supplies of coal.

Experts also claim that sharing a border with Iran (which has a nuclear-power program) has pushed Turkey to develop some nuclear capacity. In 2010 Turkey and Brazil tried to help Iran avoid further international sanctions by negotiating a deal in which Iran would outsource its uranium enrichment to Turkey.

The Bosphorus

One of the biggest environmental challenges facing Turkey is the threat from maritime traffic along the Bosphorus. The 1936 Montreux Convention decreed that, although Turkey has sovereignty over the strait, it must permit the free passage of shipping through it. At that time, perhaps a few thousand ships a year passed through, but this has risen to over 45,000 vessels annually; around 10% are tankers, which carry over 100 million tonness of hazardous substances through the strait every year.

There have already been serious accidents, such as the 1979 *Independenta* collision with another vessel, which killed 43 people and spilt and burnt some 95,000 tonnes of oil (around 2½ times the amount spilt by the famous *Exxon Valdez* in Alaska). Following the Gulf of Mexico disaster in 2010, the Turkish government renewed its efforts to find alternative routes for oil transportation. Its ambitious plans include a US$12 billion canal to divert tankers, which would see the creation of two new cities by the Bosphorus and the world's largest airport. There is already an 1800km-long pipeline between Baku, Azerbaijan and the Turkish eastern Mediterranean port of Ceyhan, and another pipeline is planned between Samsun on the Black Sea and Ceyhan.

Construction & Dams

Building development is taking a terrible toll on the environment, especially along the Aegean and Mediterranean coasts. Spots such as Kuşadası and Marmaris, once pleasant fishing villages, have been overwhelmed by urban sprawl and are in danger of losing all appeal. Worse still, much of the development is only used during the warmer months, placing intensive strain on the infrastructure. The number of secluded bays glimpsed on 'blue cruises' has plummeted, and the development continues to spread; examples in the Bodrum area alone include the new Port Iasos Marina and expansion of Yalıkavak marina.

Short of water and electricity, Turkey is one of the world's major builders of dams. There are already more than 600 dams and many more on the way, with controversy surrounding proposed developments. The gigantic Southeastern Anatolia Project, known as GAP, is one of Turkey's

Southwest Turkey, especially around Köyceğiz, is one of the last remaining sources of *Liquidambar orientalis* (frankincense trees). Their resin, once used by the Egyptians in embalming, is exported for use in perfume and incense. The world's last remaining populations of *Phoenix theophrastii* (Datça palm) grow in southwest Turkey and Crete.

ENVIRONMENT ENVIRONMENTAL ISSUES

EARTHQUAKE DANGER

More than 25 major earthquakes, measuring up to 7.8 on the Richter scale, have been recorded since 1939. A 7.6-magnitude quake in 1999 hit İzmit (Kocaeli) and Adapazarı (Sakarya) in northwestern Anatolia, killing more than 18,000. A 7.1-magnitude earthquake shook Van in 2011, killing more than 600, injuring over 4000 and damaging over 11,000 buildings, with thousands left homeless.

If a major quake struck İstanbul, much of the city would be devastated, due to unlicensed, jerry-built construction. When a 4.4-magnitude earthquake hit in 2010, no deaths or damage were caused, but it highlighted how ill-prepared the city was, with many locals hitting the phone and social networking sites rather than evacuating their houses.

major construction efforts. Harnessing the headwaters of the Tigris and Euphrates Rivers, it's creating a potential political time bomb, causing friction with the arid countries downstream that also depend on this water. Iraq, Syria and Georgia have all protested, and a UN report said the project is in danger of violating human rights.

In 2008, Hasankeyf featured on the World Monuments Watch list of the planet's 100 most endangered sites (not the first or last time Turkey has appeared on the list) – thanks to the İlisu Dam Project's plans to drown the historic southeastern town. This is now slated for 2016 or 2017, and work has begun on a replacement for the town, which was a Silk Road commercial centre on the border of Anatolia and Mesopotamia. Organised opposition is ongoing, but the ruins look set to vanish, along with their atmospheric setting on the Tigris River and dozens of villages. Up to 70,000 people will be displaced, many of them Kurds and minority groups.

The ruins of the world's oldest-known spa settlement, Allianoi, disappeared beneath the waters of the Yortanlı Dam in 2011. A last-ditch appeal from the tenor Plácido Domingo, president of the European cultural heritage federation Europa Nostra, failed to save the 2nd-century Roman spa near Bergama.

Other Issues

Blue recycling bins are an increasingly common sight on the streets of İstanbul, but the government still has a long way to go in terms of educating its citizens and businesses. Issues for Turkey to address as part of its bid to join the EU include water treatment, waste-water disposal, food safety, soil erosion, deforestation, degradation of biodiversity, air quality, industrial pollution control and risk management, climate change and nature protection.

Many feel the government often shuts the gate after the horse has bolted. In early 2006, fines for dumping toxic waste increased from a maximum of €4500 to €1.5 million – legislative changes that were announced only after barrels of toxic waste were discovered in empty lots around İstanbul. One of the worst-hit places was Dilovası, with deaths from cancer nearly three times the world average, and a report saying it should be evacuated and labelled a medical disaster area. Neither happened, and the over-industrialised area on the Sea of Marmara remains a reminder of the country's environmental shortcomings.

Documentary *Polluting Paradise* is a poignant comment on Turkey's environmental issues, telling the heartbreaking story of the village of director Fatih Akın, which was wrecked by a waste landfill site.

Despite its environmental shortcomings, Turkey is doing well at beach cleanliness, with 379 beaches and 22 marinas qualifying for Blue Flag status; see www.blueflag.org. Dolphins survive in İstanbul's Bosphorus and the Anatolian wild sheep, unique to the Konya region, has protected status. Turkey also ratified the Kyoto Protocol in 2009.

POPULAR PARKS

The following are among the most popular with foreign visitors to Turkey. Visit the Turkish Ministry of Culture and Tourism (www.turizm.gov.tr) for more information.

Gallipoli Historical National Park (p151) Historic battlefield sites on a gloriously unspoilt peninsula surrounded by coves.

Göreme National Park (p472) Extraordinary gorges and fairy chimneys.

Kaçkar Dağları National Park (Kaçkar Mountains National Park; p542) Stunning high mountain ranges popular with trekkers.

Köprülü Kanyon National Park (Bridge Canyon National Park; p379) Dramatic canyon with spectacular scenery and white-water rafting facilities.

Nemrut Dağı National Park (Mt Nemrut National Park; p587) Pre-Roman stone heads surmounting a man-made mound with wonderful views.

Saklıkent National Park (p344) Famous for its 18km-long gorge.

Survival Guide

Directory A–Z

Accommodation

Turkey has accommodation options to suit all budgets, with concentrations of good, value-for-money hotels, pensions and hostels in places most visited by independent travellers, such as İstanbul and Cappadocia.

Rooms are discounted by about 20% during the low season (October to April; late November to mid-March in İstanbul), but not during the Christmas and Easter periods and major Islamic holidays. Places within easy reach of İstanbul and Ankara may hike their prices during summer weekends.

If you plan to stay a week or more in a coastal resort, check package-holiday deals. British, German and French tour companies in particular often offer money-saving flight-and-accommodation packages to the south Aegean and Mediterranean.

Accommodation options in more Westernised spots such as İstanbul often quote tariffs in euros as well as (or instead of) lira; establishments in less-touristy locations generally quote in lira. Many places will accept euro (or even US dollars in İstanbul). We've used the currency quoted by the business being reviewed.

Sleeping options generally have a website where reservations can be made.

Many pensions operate in informal chains, referring travellers from one to another. If you've enjoyed staying in a place, you may enjoy its owner's recommendations, but stay firm and try not to sign up to anything sight unseen.

Price Ranges

Ranges are based on the cost of a double room. The rates quoted in this book are for high season (June to August; apart from İstanbul, where high season is April, May, September, October, Christmas and Easter). Unless otherwise mentioned, rates include tax (KDV), an en suite bathroom and breakfast. Listings are ordered by price range, starting with budget, and within those groups by preference.

When this book was researched, the Turkish lira had weakened to an exchange rate of 3-1 against the euro. In tourist areas, hoteliers peg their room prices to the euro to insulate their businesses against fluctuations in the lira; their rates in lira thus rise and fall according to the currency's value against the euro. Contrastingly, hoteliers in less-touristy areas are more likely to simply set their rates in lira – a difference that compounds the already huge regional variations across Turkey. We have thus allowed some leeway in our price ranges; in some cases, for example, a budget pension that is edged into the midrange bracket by the euro-lira exchange rate will still be marked as budget.

İstanbul & Bodrum Peninsula
€ less than €90
€€ €90 to €200
€€€ more than €200

Rest of Turkey
₺ less than ₺90
₺₺ ₺90 to ₺180
₺₺₺ more than ₺180

Apartments

➡ Good value for money, especially for families and small groups.

➡ Outside a few Aegean and Mediterranean locations, apartments for holiday rental are often thin on the ground.

➡ In coastal spots such as Kaş, Antalya and the Bodrum Peninsula, *emlakçı* (real-estate agents) hold lists of available holiday rentals.

→ *Emlakçı* are used to dealing with foreigners.

→ Also look out for *apart otels:* hotels containing self-catering units.

WEBSITES

www.exclusiveescapes.co.uk
www.holidaylettings.co.uk
www.ownersdirect.co.uk
www.perfectplaces.com
www.simpsontravel.com
www.turkeyrenting.com
www.villarenters.com
www.vrbo.com

Camping

→ Most camping facilities are along the coasts and are usually privately run.

→ Camping facilities are fairly rare inland, with the exception of Cappadocia and Nemrut Dağı National Park.

→ Best facilities inland are often on Orman Dinlenme Yeri (Forestry Department land); you usually need your own transport to reach these.

→ Pensions and hostels often let you camp on their grounds and use their facilities for a fee.

→ Female travellers should stick to official sites and camp where there are plenty of people, especially out east.

Camping outside official sites is often more hassle than it's worth:

→ The police may drop by to check you out and possibly move you on.

→ Out east, there are wolves in the wild; be wary, and don't leave food and rubbish outside your tent.

→ Also look out for Kangal dogs.

Hostels

→ There are plenty of hostels with dormitories in popular destinations.

→ Dorm beds are usually ₺30 to ₺45 per night.

NO VACANCY

Along the Aegean, Mediterranean and Black Sea coasts, the majority of hotels, pensions and camping grounds close roughly from mid-October to late April. Before visiting those regions in the low season, check accommodation is available.

→ Hostelling International has accommodation in İstanbul, Cappadocia and the Aegean and Turquoise Coast areas.

Hotels
BUDGET

→ Good, inexpensive beds are readily available in most cities and resort towns.

→ Difficult places to find good cheap rooms include İstanbul, Ankara, İzmir and package-holiday resort towns such as Alanya and Çeşme.

→ The cheapest hotels typically charge from around ₺35/40 for a single room without/with private bathroom, including breakfast.

→ Outside tourist areas, solo travellers of both sexes should be cautious about staying in budget options and carefully suss out the staff and atmosphere in reception; thefts and even sexual assaults have occurred in budget establishments (albeit very rarely).

MIDRANGE

→ One- and two-star hotels are less oppressively masculine in atmosphere, even when clientele is mainly male.

→ Such hotels charge around ₺90 to ₺130 for an en suite double, including breakfast.

→ Hotels in more traditional towns normally offer only Turkish TV, Turkish breakfast and none of the 'extras' commonplace in pensions.

→ In many midrange hotels, a maid will not make your bed and tidy your room unless you ask on reception or hang the sign on the handle.

→ Prices should be displayed in reception.

→ You should never pay more than the prices on display, and will often be charged less.

→ Often you will be able to haggle.

→ Unmarried foreign couples don't usually have problems sharing rooms.

→ Out east, couples are often given a twin room, even if they ask for a double.

→ Many establishments refuse to accept an unmarried couple when one of the parties is Turkish.

→ The cheaper the hotel, and the more remote the location, the more conservative its management tends to be.

Boutique Hotels

→ Old Ottoman mansions, caravanserais and other historic buildings have been refurbished, or completely rebuilt, as hotels.

→ Equipped with all mod-cons and bags of character.

→ Most in the midrange and top-end price brackets.

→ Many reviewed at **Small Hotels** (www.boutiquesmallhotels.com).

Pensions

In destinations popular with travellers you'll find *pansiyons* (pensions): simple, family-run guesthouses, where you can get a good, clean single/double from around ₺50/80. Many also have triple and quadruple rooms. Be sure to remove your shoes when you enter.

In touristy areas in particular, the advantages of

staying in a pension, as opposed to a cheap hotel, include:

➜ A choice of simple meals

➜ Book exchange

➜ Laundry service

➜ International TV channels

➜ Staff who speak at least one foreign language

Ev Pansiyonu

In a few places, old-fashioned *ev pansiyonu* (pension in a private home) survive. These are simply rooms in a family house that are let to visitors at busy times of year. They do not normally advertise their existence in a formal way: ask locals where to find them and look out for *kiralık oda* (room for rent) signs. English is rarely spoken by the proprietors, so some knowledge of Turkish would be helpful.

Tree Houses

Olympos is famous for its 'tree houses': rough-and-ready shelters in forested settings near the beach. The success of these backpacker hang-outs has spawned imitators elsewhere in the western Mediterranean, for example in nearby Çıralı and Saklıkent Gorge.

Touts

In smaller tourist towns such as Selçuk, touts may approach you as you step from the bus and offer you accommodation. Some may string you a line about the pension you're looking for, in the hope of reeling you in and getting a commission from another pension. Taxi drivers also play this game.

It's generally best to politely decline these offers, but if you're on a budget, touts sometimes work for newly opened establishments offering cheap rates. Before they take you to the pension, establish that you're only looking and are under no obligation to stay.

Customs Regulations

Imports

Jewellery and items valued over US$15,000 should be declared, to ensure you can take it out when you leave. Goods including the following can be imported duty-free:

➜ 200 cigarettes

➜ 200g of tobacco

➜ 1kg each of coffee, instant coffee, chocolate and sugar products

➜ 500g of tea

➜ 1L bottle or two 750mL bottles of wine or spirits

➜ Five bottles of perfume (max 120mL each)

➜ One camera with five films

➜ One video camera with 10 tapes

➜ One laptop

➜ Unlimited currency

➜ Souvenirs/gifts worth up to €300 (€145 if aged under 15)

Exports

➜ Buying and exporting genuine antiquities is illegal.

➜ Carpet shops should be able to provide a form certifying that your purchase is not an antiquity.

➜ Ask for advice from vendors you buy from.

➜ Keep receipts and paperwork.

Discount Cards

The Museum Pass İstanbul offers a possible ₺40 saving on entry to the city's major sights, and allows holders to skip admission queues. Rechargeable travel card the İstanbulkart offers savings on the city's public transport (see p136).

The following offer discounts on accommodation, eating, entertainment, transport and tours. They are available in Turkey but easier to get in your home country.

International Student Identity Card (ISIC; www.isic.org)

International Youth Travel Card (IYTC; www.isic.org)

International Teacher Identity Card (ITIC; www.isic.org)

Electricity

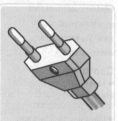

230V/50Hz

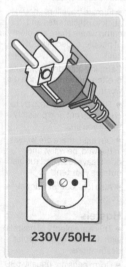

230V/50Hz

Embassies & Consulates

➡ Most embassies and consulates in Turkey open from 8am or 9am to noon Monday to Friday, then after lunch until 5pm or 6pm for people to pick up visas.

➡ Embassies of some Muslim countries may open Sunday to Thursday.

➡ To ask the way to an embassy, say: '[Country] başkonsolosluğu nerede?'

➡ Embassies are generally in Ankara.

➡ There are consulates in other Turkish cities (check the websites listed in the table for their locations).

Food

This book uses the following price ranges, based on the cost of a main course.

İstanbul & Bodrum Peninsula
€ less than ₺20
€€ ₺20 to ₺30
€€€ more than ₺30

Rest of Turkey
€ less than ₺9
€€ ₺9 to ₺17.50
€€€ more than ₺17.50

For more information on food in Turkey, see p44 and p638.

Gay & Lesbian Travellers

Homosexuality is not a criminal offence in Turkey, but prejudice remains strong and there are sporadic reports of violence towards gay people – the message is discretion.

İstanbul has a flourishing gay scene, as does Ankara. In other cities there may be a gay bar. For more on the challenges facing LGBT people in Turkey, visit http://iglhrc.org/region/turkey and www.ilga-europe.org.

Kaos GL (www.kaosgl.com) Based in Ankara, the LGBT rights organisation publishes a gay-and-lesbian magazine and its website has news and information in English.

Lambda (www.lambdaistanbul.org) Lambda is the Turkish branch of the International Lesbian, Gay, Bisexual, Trans and Intersexual Association.

LGBTI News Turkey (http://lgbtinewsturkey.com) News and links.

Pride Travel Agency (www.turkey-gay-travel.com) Gay-friendly Turkish travel agent, with useful links on its website.

EMBASSIES IN ANKARA

EMBASSY	CONTACT DETAILS	ADDRESS
Armenian	Contact Russian embassy; www.mfa.am/en	
Australian	0312-459 9500; www.turkey.embassy.gov.au	7th fl, MNG Building, Uğur Mumcu Caddesi 88, Gaziosmanpaşa
Azerbaijani	0312-491 1681; www.azembassy.org.tr	Diplomatik Site, Bakü Sokak 1, Oran
Bulgarian	0312-467 2071; www.mfa.bg/embassies/turkey	Atatürk Bulvarı 124, Kavaklıdere
Canadian	0312-409 2700; www.canadainternational.gc.ca	Cinnah Caddesi 58, Çankaya
Dutch	0312-409 1800; turkije.nlambassade.org	Hollanda Caddesi 5, Hilal Mahallesi
French	0312-455 4545; www.ambafrance-tr.org	Paris Caddesi 70, Kavaklıdere
Georgian	0312-491 8030; www.turkey.mfa.gov.ge	Diplomatik Site, Kılıç Ali Sokak 12, Oran
German	0312-455 5100; www.ankara.diplo.de	Atatürk Bulvarı 114, Kavaklıdere
Greek	0312-448 0647; www.mfa.gr/ankara	Zia Ür Rahman Caddesi 9-11, Gaziosmanpaşa
Iranian	0312-468 2821; en.mfa.ir	Tehran Caddesi 10, Kavaklıdere
Iraqi	0312-468 7421; www.mofamission.gov.iq	Turan Emeksiz Sokak 11, Gaziosmanpaşa
Irish	0312-459 1000; www.embassyofireland.org.tr	3rd fl, MNG Building, Uğur Mumcu Caddesi 88, Gaziosmanpaşa
New Zealand	0312-446 3333; www.nzembassy.com/turkey	Kizkulesi Sokak 11, Gaziosmanpaşa
Russian	0312-439 2122; www.turkey.mid.ru	Karyağdı Sokak 5, Çankaya
UK	0312-455 3344; ukinturkey.fco.gov.uk	Şehit Ersan Caddesi 46a, Çankaya
USA	0312-455 5555; turkey.usembassy.gov	Atatürk Bulvarı 110, Kavaklıdere

Insurance

→ A travel insurance policy covering theft, loss and medical expenses is recommended.

→ Huge variety of policies available; check small print.

→ Some policies exclude 'dangerous activities', which can include scuba diving, motorcycling and even trekking.

→ Some policies may not cover you if you travel to regions of the country where your government warns against travel.

→ If you cancel your trip on the advice of an official warning against travel, your insurer may not cover you.

→ Look into whether your regular health insurance and motor insurance will cover you in Turkey.

→ Worldwide travel insurance is available at www.lonelyplanet.com/travel-insurance. You can buy, extend and claim online anytime – even if you're already on the road.

Internet Access

→ Throughout Turkey, the majority of accommodation options of all standards offer wi-fi.

→ Wi-fi networks are also found at locations from cafes and carpet shops to otogars (bus stations) and ferry terminals.

→ In this book, the wi-fi access icon (🛜) indicates that a business offers a network.

→ Internet access icon (@) indicates that an establishment provides a computer with internet access for guest use.

Internet Cafes

→ Internet cafes are common, although declining with the proliferation of wi-fi and handheld devices.

→ They are typically open from 9am until midnight, and charge around ₺2 an hour (İstanbul ₺3).

→ Connection speeds vary, but are generally fast.

→ Viruses are rife.

→ The best cafes have English keyboards.

→ Some cafes have Turkish keyboards, on which 'ı' occupies the position occupied by 'i' on English keyboards.

→ On Turkish keyboards, create the '@' symbol by holding down the 'q' and ALT keys at the same time.

Language Courses

İstanbul is the most popular place to learn Turkish, though there are also courses in Ankara, İzmir and a few other spots across the country. Try to sit in on a class before you commit, as the quality of your experience definitely depends on the teacher and your classmates.

Private tuition is more expensive, but tutors often advertise at http://istanbul.en.craigslist.com.tr and in the classifieds section of the expat website www.mymerhaba.com. Many books and online resources are available; the books and CDs by David and Asuman Pollard in the 'Teach Yourself' series are recommended.

Dilmer (www.dilmer.com) A popular school, located near İstanbul's Taksim Sq. Its courses last from one to 12 weeks, catering to seven levels of proficiency (€50 to €384).

EFINST Turkish Centre (www.turkishlesson.com) The school in Levent, İstanbul, offers options including intensive two-week courses (€500), part-time 7½- to 16-week courses (€600) and private lessons (from €50). Can arrange accommodation.

Spoken Turkish (www.spokenenglishtr.com) Conveniently located on İstanbul's İstiklal Caddesi, but relatively untested, it offers part-time courses lasting four hours a week.

Tömer (tomer.ankara.edu.tr) Affiliated with Ankara University, Tömer offers four- and eight-week courses.

Turkish Language Center (www.turkishlanguagecenter. com) School in İzmir offering full-time one- to 12-week courses (€240 to €1740) and private tuition. Can also arrange accommodation.

Legal Matters

Technically, you should carry your passport at all times. In practice, you may prefer to carry a photocopy.

There are laws against lese-majesty, buying and smuggling antiquities, and illegal drugs. Turkish jails are not places where you want to spend any time.

Maps

Maps are widely available at tourist offices and bookshops, although quality maps are hard to find. In İstanbul, try on İstiklal Caddesi; online, check Tulumba.com and Amazon.

Mep Medya's city and regional maps are recommended, as are its touring maps including:

→ Türkiye Karayolları Haritası (1:1,200,000) A sheet map of the whole country

→ Adım Adım Türkiye Yol Atlası (Step by Step Turkey Road Atlas; 1:400,000)

Money

Turkey's currency is the Türk Lirası (Turkish lira; ₺). The lira comes in notes of five, 10, 20, 50, 100 and 200, and coins of one, five, 10, 25 and 50 kuruş and one lira.

The Yeni Türk Lirası (new Turkish lira; YTL) was used between 2005 and 2008 as an anti-inflationary measure. Yeni Türk Lirası is no longer valid, but if you have some notes and coins left over from a previous visit to Turkey, branches of Ziraat bank will exchange your 'new' lira for the same value of today's lira.

Lack of change is a constant problem; try to keep a supply of coins and small notes for minor payments. Post offices have Western Union counters.

ATMs

ATMs dispense Turkish lira, and occasionally euros and US dollars, to Visa, Master-Card, Cirrus and Maestro card holders. Look for these logos on machines, which are found in most towns. Machines generally offer instructions in foreign languages including English.

It's possible to get around Turkey using only ATMs if you draw out money in the towns to tide you through the villages that don't have them. Also keep some cash in reserve for the inevitable day when the machine throws a wobbly. If your card is swallowed by a stand-alone ATM booth, it may be tricky to get it back. The booths are often run by franchisees rather than by the banks themselves.

Credit Cards

Visa and MasterCard are widely accepted by hotels, shops and restaurants, although often not by pensions and local restaurants outside the main tourist areas. You can also get cash advances on these cards. Amex is less commonly accepted outside top-end establishments. Inform your credit-card provider of your travel plans; otherwise, transactions may be stopped, as credit-card fraud does happen in Turkey.

Foreign Currencies

Euros and US dollars are the most readily accepted foreign currencies. Shops, hotels and restaurants in many tourist areas accept foreign currencies, and taxi drivers will take them for big journeys.

Moneychangers

The Turkish lira is weak against Western currencies, and you will probably get a better exchange rate in Turkey than elsewhere. The lira is virtually worthless outside Turkey, so make sure you spend it all before leaving.

US dollars and euros are the easiest currencies to exchange, although many exchange offices and banks will also change other major currencies such as UK pounds and Japanese yen.

You'll get better rates at exchange offices, which often

THE ART OF BARGAINING

Traditionally, when customers enter a Turkish shop to make a significant purchase, they're offered a comfortable seat and a drink (çay, coffee or a soft drink). There is some general chitchat, then discussion of the shop's goods in general, then of the customer's tastes, preferences and requirements. Finally, a number of items are displayed for the customer's inspection.

The customer asks the price; the shop owner gives it; the customer looks doubtful and makes a counter-offer 25% to 50% lower. This procedure goes back and forth several times before a price acceptable to both parties is arrived at. It's considered bad form to haggle over a price, come to an agreement, and then change your mind.

If you can't agree on a price, it's perfectly acceptable to say goodbye and walk out of the shop. In fact, walking out is one of the best ways to test the authenticity of the last offer. If shopkeepers know you can find the item elsewhere for less, they'll probably call after you and drop their price. Even if they don't stop you, there's nothing to prevent you from returning later and buying the item for what they quoted.

To bargain effectively you must be prepared to take your time, and you must know something about the items in question, not to mention their market price. The best way to do this is to look at similar goods in several shops, asking prices but not making counter-offers. Always stay good-humoured and polite when you are bargaining – if you do this the shopkeeper will too. When bargaining, you can often get a discount by offering to buy several items at once, by paying in a strong major currency, or by paying in cash.

If you don't have sufficient time to shop around, follow the age-old rule: find something you like at a price you're willing to pay, buy it, enjoy it, and don't worry about whether or not you received the world's lowest price.

In general, you shouldn't bargain in food shops or over transport costs. Outside tourist areas, hotels may expect to 'negotiate' the room price with you. In tourist areas pension owners are usually fairly clear about their prices, although if you're travelling in winter or staying a long time, it's worth asking about *indirim* (discounts).

PRACTICALITIES

➡ Turkey uses the metric system for weights and measures.

➡ Electrical current is 230V AC, 50Hz.

➡ You can buy electrical plug adaptors at most electrical shops. A universal AC adaptor is also a good investment.

➡ **Today's Zaman** (www.todayszaman.com), **Hürriyet Daily News** (www.hurriyetdailynews.com) and **Daily Sabah** (www.sabahenglish.com) are English-language newspapers.

➡ **Journal of Turkish Weekly** (www.turkishweekly.net), published by an Ankara-based think tank, carries news and commentary in English.

➡ **Turkishpress.com** (turkishpress.com) is an American site covering Turkish news.

➡ **Cornucopia** (www.cornucopia.net) is a glossy magazine in English about Turkey.

➡ Turkish Airlines' in-flight monthly, **Skylife** (www.skylife.com/en), is worth a read.

➡ TRT broadcasts news daily, in languages including English, on radio and at www.trt-world.com.

➡ Digiturk offers numerous Turkish and international TV channels.

don't charge commission, than at banks. Exchange offices operate in tourist and market areas, with better rates often found in the latter, and some post offices (PTTs), shops and hotels. They generally keep longer hours than banks.

Banks are more likely to change minor currencies, although they tend to make heavy weather of it. Turkey has no black market.

Tipping

Turkey is fairly European in its approach to tipping and you won't be pestered with demands for baksheesh as elsewhere in the Middle East.

Some more expensive restaurants automatically add the *servis ücreti* (service charge) to your bill, although there's no guarantee this goes to the staff.

Travellers Cheques

Banks, shops and hotels usually see it as a burden to change travellers cheques, and will either try to persuade you to go elsewhere or charge you a premium for the service. If you do have to change them, try one of the major banks.

Opening Hours

Most museums close on Monday; from April to October, they shut 1½ to two hours later than usual. Other businesses with seasonal variations include bars, which are likely to stay open later in summer than in winter, and tourist offices in popular locations, which open for longer hours and at weekends during summer.

The working day shortens during the holy month of Ramazan, which currently falls during summer. More devout Islamic cities such as Konya and Kayseri virtually shut down during noon prayers on Friday (the Muslim sabbath); apart from that, Friday is a normal working day.

Listings in this book include opening hours only when they differ significantly from these standard hours.

Information 8.30am-noon & 1.30-5pm Mon-Fri

Eating breakfast 7.30-10am, lunch noon-2.30pm, dinner 6.30-10pm

Drinking 4pm-late

Nightclubs 11pm-late

Shopping 9am-6pm Mon-Fri (longer in tourist areas and big cities – including weekend opening)

Government departments, offices and banks 8.30am-noon & 1.30-5pm Mon-Fri

Photography

People in Turkey are generally receptive to having their photo taken. The major exception is when they are praying or performing other religious activities. As in most countries, do not photograph military sites, airfields, police stations and so on, as it could arouse the authorities' suspicions.

Post

Turkish *postanes* (post offices) are indicated by black-on-yellow 'PTT' signs. Most post offices follow the office hours we've listed above, but a few offices in major cities have extended opening hours.

Letters take between one and several weeks to get to/from Turkey. Postcards sent abroad cost about ₺2.50.

When posting letters, the *yurtdışı* slot is for mail to foreign countries, *yurtiçi* for mail to other Turkish cities, and şehiriçi for local mail. Visit www.ptt.gov.tr for more information.

Parcels

If you are shipping something from Turkey, don't close your parcel before it has been inspected by a customs official. Take packing and wrapping materials with you to the post office.

Airmail tariffs are typically about ₺40 for the first kilogram, with an additional charge for every extra kilogram (typically ₺5 to Europe).

Parcels take months to arrive.

International couriers including DHL also operate in Turkey.

Public Holidays

New Year's Day (Yılbaşı; 1 January)

National Sovereignty & Children's Day (Ulusal Egemenlik ve Çocuk Günü; 23 April) Commemorates the first meeting of the Turkish Grand National Assembly in 1920.

International Workers' Day (May Day; 1 May) Reinstated in 2010, the holiday features marches through İstanbul. Thousands gather around Taksim Sq, where the Taksim Square Massacre happened on 1 May 1977 during a period of political violence.

Youth & Sports Day (Gençlik ve Spor Günü; 19 May) Dedicated to Atatürk and the youth of the republic.

Şeker Bayramı (Sweets Holiday; see table) Also known as Ramazan Bayramı, it celebrates the end of Ramazan.

Victory Day (Zafer Bayramı; 30 August) Commemorates the republican army's victory over the invading Greek army at Dumlupınar during the War of Independence.

Kurban Bayramı (Festival of the Sacrifice; see table) The most important holiday of the year, it marks İbrahim's near-sacrifice of İsmael on Mt Moriah (Koran, Sura 37; Genesis 22). Transport and accommodation fill up fast.

Republic Day (Cumhuriyet Bayramı; 28 to 29 October) Commemorates the proclamation of the republic by Atatürk in 1923.

Safe Travel

Although Turkey is by no means a dangerous country to visit, it's always wise to be a little cautious, especially if you're travelling alone.

Turkey is not a safety-conscious country: holes in pavements go unmended; precipitous drops go unguarded; safety belts are not always worn; lifeguards on beaches are rare; dolmuş (minibus) drivers negotiate bends while counting out change.

The two areas to be most cautious are İstanbul, where various scams operate, and southeastern Anatolia, where the 30-year conflict between the Turkish state and the PKK (Kurdistan Workers' Party) ended in 2013. Peace talks subsequently stalled, and

the civil war in neighbouring Syria has complicated the situation, but both sides are committed to finding a solution. If fighting resumes, PKK attacks generally happen far from travellers' routes in remote parts of mountainous southeastern Anatolia, but check the latest situation if visiting the area.

Assaults

Sexual assaults have occurred against travellers of both sexes in hotels in central and eastern Anatolia. Make enquiries, check forums and do a little research in advance if you are travelling alone or heading off the beaten track.

Demonstrations

Marches and demonstrations are a regular sight in Turkish cities, especially İstanbul. These are best avoided as they can lead to clashes with the police, as happened on Taksim Sq in 2013.

Flies & Mosquitoes

In high summer, mosquitoes are troublesome even in İstanbul; they can make a stay along the coast a nightmare. Some hotel rooms come equipped with nets and/or plug-in bugbusters, but it's a good idea to bring some insect repellent and mosquito coils.

Lese-Majesty

The laws against insulting, defaming or making light of Atatürk, the Turkish flag, the Turkish people, the Turkish Republic and so on are

---

MAJOR ISLAMIC HOLIDAYS

The rhythms of Islamic practice are tied to the lunar calendar, which is slightly shorter than its Gregorian equivalent, so the Muslim calendar begins around 11 days earlier each year. The following dates are approximate.

ISLAMIC YEAR	NEW YEAR	PROPHET'S BIRTHDAY	RAMAZAN	ŞEKER BAYRAMI	KURBAN BAYRAMI
1436	25 Oct 2014	3 Jan 2015	18 Jun 2015	17 Jul 2015	23 Sep 2015
1437	14 Oct 2015	23 Dec 2015	7 Jun 2016	6 Jul 2016	12 Sep 2016
1438	3 Oct 2016	12 Dec 2016	27 May 2017	25 Jun 2017	3 Sep 2017

taken very seriously. Making derogatory remarks, even in the heat of a quarrel, can be enough to get a foreigner carted off to jail.

Scams & Druggings

In a notorious İstanbul scam, normally targeted at single men, a pleasant local guy befriends you in the street and takes you to a bar. After a few drinks, and possibly the attention of some women (to whom you offer drinks) the bill arrives. The prices are astronomical and the proprietors can produce a menu showing the same prices. If you don't have enough cash, you'll be frogmarched to the nearest ATM. If this happens to you, report it to the tourist police; some travellers have taken the police back to the bar and received a refund.

A less common variation on this trick involves the traveller having their drink spiked and waking up in an unexpected place with their belongings, right down to their shoes, missing – or worse.

Single men should not accept invitations from unknown folk in large cities without sizing the situation up carefully. You could invite your newfound friends to a bar of *your* choice; if they're not keen to go, chances are they are shady characters.

The spiking scam has also been reported on overnight trains, with passengers getting robbed. Turks are often genuinely sociable and generous travelling companions, but be cautious about accepting food and drinks from people you are not 100% sure about.

ANTIQUITIES

Do not buy coins or other artefacts offered to you by touts at ancient sites such as Ephesus and Perge. It is a serious crime here, punishable by long prison terms, and the touts are likely in cahoots with the local policemen.

SHOE CLEANERS

In Sultanahmet, İstanbul, if a shoe cleaner walking in front of you drops his brush, don't pick it up. He will insist on giving you a 'free' clean in return, before demanding an extortionate fee.

Smoking

Turks love smoking and there's even a joke about the country's propensity for puffing: Who smokes more than a Turk? Two Turks.

Note that smoking in enclosed public spaces is banned, and punishable by a fine. Hotels, restaurants and bars are generally smoke-free, although bars sometimes relax the rules as the evening wears on. Off the tourist trail in budget and midrange hotels, the ban is enforced in public areas but more leniently in rooms, which often have ashtrays.

Public transport is meant to be smoke-free, although taxi and bus drivers sometimes smoke at the wheel.

Traffic

As a pedestrian, note that some Turks are aggressive, dangerous drivers; 'right of way' doesn't compute with many motorists, despite the little green man on traffic lights. Give way to vehicles in all situations, even if you have to jump out of the way.

Telephone

Türk Telekom (www.turk telekom.com.tr) has a monopoly on phone services, and service is efficient if costly. Within Turkey, numbers starting with 444 don't require area codes and, wherever you call from, are charged at the local rate.

Kontörlü Telefon

If you only want to make one quick call, it's easiest to look for a booth with a sign saying *kontörlü telefon* (metered telephone). You make your call and the owner reads the meter and charges you accordingly. In touristy areas you can get rates as low as ₺0.50 per minute to Europe, the UK, the US and Australia.

Mobile Phones

➡ Turks adore mobile (*cep*, pocket) phones.

• Reception is excellent across most of Turkey.

• Mobile phone numbers start with a four-figure number beginning with 05.

• Major networks are **Turkcell** (www.turkcell. tr), the most comprehensive, **Vodafone** (www.vodafone. com.tr) and **Avea** (www.avea. com.tr).

• Service is often better in the smaller networks' stores, but Turkcell coverage is considerably better out east.

• A pay-as-you-go Turkcell SIM costs ₺50 (including ₺5 credit) or ₺60 (with ₺20 credit).

• You need to show your passport, and ensure the seller phones through or inputs your details to activate your account.

• SIM cards and *kontör* (credit) are widely available – at streetside booths and shops as well as mobile-phone outlets.

• You can buy a local SIM and use it in your mobile from home, but the network detects and bars foreign phones within about two weeks (sometimes after a day or two).

• To avoid barring, register your phone when you buy your Turkish SIM (or soon afterwards). At a certified mobile-phone shop, show your passport and fill in a short form declaring your phone is in Turkey. The process costs about ₺100. You can only declare one phone. The registered phone cannot be used with another Turkish SIM card for two years.

• You can pick up a second-hand mobile phone for about ₺50 to ₺70.

• Turkcell credit comes in cards with units of ₺5, ₺10, ₺15, ₺20, ₺30, ₺50, ₺95 and ₺180.

• Most shops charge a small commission on credit (eg ₺20 credit costs ₺22).

• The bigger the card, the better the rates you receive.

• The networks offer SMS bundles (for Turkey or abroad).

• Dial *123# to check credit.

• For assistance and information in English, call 8088/500 on Turkcell/Avea.

• On Turkcell, reverse charges by dialling *135*53, followed by the number, followed by #.

Payphones & Phonecards

• Türk Telekom payphones can be found in most major public buildings, facilities and squares, and transport terminals.

• International calls can be made from payphones.

• All payphones require cards that can be bought at telephone centres or, for a small mark-up, at some shops. Some payphones accept credit cards.

• Two types of card are in use: floppy cards with a magnetic strip, and Smart cards, embedded with a chip.

• The cards come in units of 50 (₺3.75), 100 (₺7.50), 200 (₺15) and 350 (₺19).

• Fifty units are sufficient for local calls and short intercity calls; 100 units are suitable for intercity or short international conversations.

INTERNATIONAL PHONECARDS

• Phonecards are the cheapest way to make international calls.

• Cards can be used on landlines, payphones and mobiles.

• As in other countries, you call the access number, key in the PIN on the card and dial away.

• Stick to reputable phonecards such as **IPC** (www.ipccard.com).

• With a ₺20 IPC card you can speak for over 200 minutes to landlines in the USA, UK, continental Europe, Australia and beyond.

• Cards are widely available in the tourist areas of major cities, but can be difficult to find elsewhere.

Time

• Standard Turkish time is two hours ahead of GMT/UTC.

• During daylight saving (summer time), the clocks go forward one hour, and Turkey is three hours ahead of GMT/UTC.

• Daylight saving runs from the last Sunday in March until the last Sunday in October.

• Turkish bus timetables and so on use the 24-hour clock,

TIME DIFFERENCES IN SUMMER

COUNTRY	CAPITAL CITY	DIFFERENCE FROM TURKEY (HRS)
Australia	Canberra	+7
Canada	Ottawa	-7
France	Paris	-1
Germany	Berlin	-1
Japan	Tokyo	+6
Netherlands	Amsterdam	-1
New Zealand	Wellington	+9
UK	London	-2
USA	Washington DC	-7

but Turks rarely use it when speaking.

➡ Visit www.timeanddate.com for more on time differences.

Toilets

Most hotels have sit-down toilets, but hole-in-the-ground models – with a conventional flush, or a tap and jug – are common. Toilet paper is often unavailable, so keep some with you. Many taps are unmarked and reversed (cold on the left, hot on the right).

In most bathrooms you can flush paper down the toilet, but in some places this may flood the premises. This is the case in much of İstanbul's old city. If you're not sure, play it safe and dispose of the paper in the bin provided. Signs often advise patrons to use the bin. This may seem slightly gross to the uninitiated, but many Turks (as well as people from other Middle Eastern and Asian countries) use a jet spray of water to clean themselves after defecating, applying paper to pat dry. The used paper is thus just damp, rather than soiled.

Public toilets can usually be found at major attractions and transport hubs; most require a payment of around 50 kuruş. In an emergency it's worth remembering that mosques have basic toilets (for both men and women).

Tourist Information

Every Turkish town of any size has an official tourist office run by the **Ministry of Culture and Tourism** (www.turizm.gov.tr). Staff are often enthusiastic and helpful, particularly when it comes to supplying brochures, but may have sketchy knowledge of the area, and English speakers are rare. Tour operators, pension owners and so

on are often better sources of information.

Visit the Ministry of Culture and Tourism website for details of Turkish tourist offices overseas.

Travellers with Disabilities

Improvements are being made, but Turkey is a challenging destination for disabled (*özürlü*) travellers. Ramps, wide doorways and properly equipped toilets are rare, as are Braille and audio information at sights. Crossing most streets is particularly challenging, as everyone does so at their peril.

Airlines and the top hotels and resorts have some provision for wheelchair (*tekerlekli sandalye*) access, and ramps are beginning to appear elsewhere. Dropped kerb edges are being introduced to cities, especially in western Turkey – in places such as Edirne, Bursa and İzmir they seem to have been sensibly designed. Selçuk, Bodrum and Fethiye have been identified as relatively user-friendly towns for people with mobility problems because their pavements and roads are fairly level. In İstanbul, the tram, metro, funicular railways and catamaran ferries are the most wheelchair-accessible forms of public transport. İstanbul Deniz Otobüsleri's (İDO) Sea Bus catamaran ferries, which cross the Sea of Marmara and head up the Bosphorus from İstanbul, are generally accessible. Urban and inter-city buses often accommodate wheelchairs, but fully accessible vehicles are uncommon. Ankara and İzmir's metros are also accessible. A breakdown of how the major cities are making their transport networks more accessible can be found at www.raillynews.com/2014/accessibility-disabled-2015-target-turkey.

Turkish Airlines offers 20% discounts on most

international and domestic flights to travellers with minimum 40% disability, and their companions. Some Turkish trains have disabled-accessible lifts, toilets and other facilities, although many are still boarded by steps. The bigger bus and ferry companies also often offer discounts.

Organisations

Businesses and resources serving travellers with disabilities include:

Access-Able (www.access-able.com) Has a small list of accommodation and tour and transport operators in Turkey.

Apparelyzed (www.apparelyzed.com) Features a report on facilities in İstanbul under 'Accessible Holidays'.

Hotel Rolli (www.hotel-rolli.de; Anamur) Specially designed for wheelchair users.

Mephisto Voyages (www.mephistovoyage.com; Cappadocia) Special tours for mobility-impaired people, utilising the Joëlette wheelchair system.

Physically Disabled Support Association (www.bedd.org.tr) Based in İstanbul.

SATH (www.sath.org) Society for Accessible Travel and Hospitality.

Visas

➡ Nationals of countries including Denmark, Finland, France, Germany, Israel, Italy, Japan, New Zealand, Sweden and Switzerland don't need a visa to visit Turkey for up to 90 days.

➡ Nationals of countries including Australia, Austria, Belgium, Canada, Ireland, the Netherlands, Norway, Portugal, Spain, the UK and USA need a visa, which must be purchased online at www.evisa.gov.tr before travelling.

➡ Most nationalities, including the above, are given a 90-day multiple-entry visa.

➡ You must enter details of your passport and date of

arrival in Turkey, click on the link in the confirmation email and pay with a MasterCard or Visa credit or debit card.

➡ Having completed this process, the e-visa can be downloaded in Adobe PDF format; a link is also emailed so it can be printed out later.

➡ The e-visa must be printed out to show on arrival in Turkey, and kept while in the country.

➡ It is recommended that applications are made at least 48 hours before departure.

➡ Your passport should be valid for at least six months from the date you enter Turkey.

➡ At the time of writing, the e-visa charge was US$20 for most nationalities, with a few exceptions including Australians and Canadians, who paid US$60, and South Africans, who received it free.

➡ In most cases, the 90-day visa stipulates 'per period 180 days'. This means you can spend three months in Turkey within a six-month period; when you leave after three months, you can't re-enter for three months.

➡ Check the **Ministry of Foreign Affairs** (www.mfa. gov.tr) for more information.

➡ No photos required.

Residency Permits

➡ There are various types of *ikamet tezkeresi* (residence permit).

➡ Apply at a *yabalcılar şube* (foreigners police/aliens department) soon after arrival.

➡ Plug http://yabancilar. iem.gov.tr (the foreign department of İstanbul's *emniyet müdürlüğü* – security police) into a website translator for more information.

➡ If you don't have a Turkish employer or spouse to support your application, you

can get a permit for touristic purposes.

➡ Touristic permits are typically valid for one year; the price varies according to the applicant's nationality, with charges starting at a few hundred lira including administrative charges.

➡ To apply for a residence permit in İstanbul, make an appointment with the *emniyet müdürlüğü* in Fatih; visit e-randevu. iem.gov.tr. The process can be demoralising and assistance hard to come by; those working behind the desks in cities such as İzmir (www.izmirpolis.gov.tr) are reputedly more helpful.

➡ Little English is spoken, so take a Turkish-speaking friend with you if possible.

➡ If your application is successful, you will be given a touristic residency card.

➡ More details in Pat Yale's *A Handbook for Living in Turkey,* which was being updated at the time of writing.

➡ Websites mentioned under Work are also sources of (anecdotal) information and advice.

Working Visas

➡ Visit www.konsolosluk. gov.tr for information on obtaining a *çalışma izni* (work permit).

➡ Your Turkish employer should help you get the visa.

➡ If it's an employer such as a school or international company, they should be well versed in the process and can handle the majority of the paperwork.

➡ The visa can be obtained in Turkey or from a Turkish embassy or consulate.

Volunteering

Opportunities include everything from teaching to working on an organic farm.

Alternative Camp (www. ayder.org.tr) A volunteer-based organisation running camps for disabled people.

Culture Routes in Turkey (cultureroutesinturkey.com/c/ about-the-trails/volunteering) Opportunities to help waymark and repair its hiking trails such as the Lycian Way. A project to renovate old buildings for use as trekking accommodation is coming up.

European Youth Portal (europa.eu/youth/evs_data-base) Database of European Union–accredited opportunities.

Gençlik Servisleri Merkezi (Youth Services Centre; www. gsm.org.tr/en) GSM runs voluntary work camps for young people in Turkey.

Gençtur (genctur.com.tr) Organises voluntourism including farmstays, with offices in İstanbul and Berlin.

GoAbroad.com (www.volun teerabroad.com) A US-based company listing a range of opportunities in Turkey, mostly through international organisations.

Ta Tu Ta (www.tatuta.org) Turkey's branch of WWOOF (Worldwide Opportunities on Organic Farms) organises work on dozens of organic farms around the country, where you receive accommodation and board in exchange for labour.

Women Travellers

Travelling in Turkey is straightforward for women, provided you follow some simple guidelines.

Accommodation

Outside tourist areas, the cheapest hotels, as well as often being fleapits, are generally not suitable for lone women. Stick with family-oriented midrange hotels.

If conversation in the lobby grinds to a halt as you enter, the hotel is not likely to be a great place for a woman.

If there is a knock on your hotel door late at night, don't open it; in the morning, complain to the manager.

We recommend female travellers stick to official camping grounds and camp where there are plenty of people around – especially out east. If you do otherwise, you will be taking a risk.

Clothing

Tailor your behaviour and your clothing to your surrounds. Look at what local women are wearing. On the streets of Beyoğlu in İstanbul you'll see skimpy tops and tight jeans, but cleavage and short skirts without leggings are a no-no everywhere except nightclubs in İstanbul and heavily touristed destinations along the coast.

Bring a shawl to cover your head when visiting mosques.

On the street, you don't need to don a headscarf, but in eastern Anatolia long sleeves and baggy long pants should attract the least attention.

Eating & Drinking

Restaurants and tea gardens aiming to attract women and children usually set aside a special family *(aile)* room or area. Look for the term *aile salonu* (family dining room).

Holiday Romances

It is not unheard of, particularly in romantic spots such as Cappadocia, for women to have holiday romances with local men. As well as fuelling the common Middle Eastern misconception that Western women are more 'available', this has led to occasional cases of men exploiting such relationships. Some men, for example, develop close friendships with visiting women, then invent sob stories and ask them to help out financially.

Regional Differences

Having a banter with men in restaurants and shops in western Turkey can be fun, and many men won't necessarily think much of it.

Particularly out east, however, passing through some

towns, you can count the number of women you see on one hand, and those you do see will be headscarved and wearing long coats. Life here for women is largely restricted to the home. Eastern Anatolia is not the place to practise your Turkish (or Kurdish) and expect men not to get the wrong idea; even just smiling at a man or catching his eye is considered an invitation. Keep your dealings with men formal and polite, not friendly.

Transport

When travelling by taxi and dolmuş, avoid getting into the seat beside the driver, as this can be misinterpeted as a come-on.

On the bus, lone women are often assigned seats at the front near the driver. There have been cases of male passengers or conductors on night buses harassing female travellers. If this happens to you, complain loudly, making sure that others on the bus hear, and repeat your complaint on arrival at your destination; you have a right to be treated with respect.

Work

Outside professional fields such as academia and the corporate sector, bagging a job in Turkey is tough. Most people teach English or nanny.

Check whether potential employers will help you get a work permit. Many employers, notably language schools, are happy to employ foreigners on an informal basis, but unwilling to organise work permits due to the time and money involved in the bureaucratic process. This necessitates working illegally on a tourist visa/residence permit. The '90 days within 180 days' regulation stipulated by tourist visas rules out the option of cross-border 'visa runs' to pick up a new visa on re-entry to Turkey.

Locals also occasionally report illegal workers, and there have even been cases of English teachers being deported.

Job hunters may pick up leads on the following expat and advertising websites:

➡ http://istanbul.craigslist.org
➡ www.mymerhaba.com
➡ www.sahibinden.com
➡ www.sublimeportal.org
➡ www.turkeycentral.com

Nannying

One of the most lucrative non-specialist jobs open to foreigners is nannying for the wealthy urban elite, or looking after their teenage children and helping them develop their language skills.

There are opportunities for English, French and German speakers, and openings for young men as well as women, all mostly in İstanbul.

You must be prepared for long hours, demanding employers and spoilt children.

Accommodation is normally included, and the digs will likely be luxurious. However, living with the family means you are always on call, and you may be based in the suburbs.

Teaching English

You can earn a decent living, mostly in İstanbul and the other major cities, as an English teacher at a university or a school. Good jobs require a university degree and TEFL (Teaching English as a Foreign Language) certificate or similar.

As well as the job-hunting resources listed in the introduction to this section, log onto www.eslcafe.com, which has a Turkey forum, and www.tefl.com.

If you want to proactively contact potential employers, Wikipedia has a list of universities in Turkey.

DERSHANE

There are lots of jobs at *dershane* (private schools), which pay good wages and offer attractions such as accommodation (although it may be on or near the school campus in the suburbs) and work permits. Some even pay for your flight to Turkey and/or flights home.

Jobs are available at all levels, from kindergarten to high school. Teachers who can't speak Turkish often find very young children challenging; many are spoilt and misbehave around foreign teachers. The best preschools pair a foreign teacher with a Turkish colleague.

You will often be required to commit to an unpaid trial period, lasting a week or two.

Unless a teacher has dropped out before the end of their contract, these jobs are mostly advertised around May and June, when employers are recruiting in preparation for the beginning of the academic year in September. Teachers are contracted until the end of the academic year in June.

LANGUAGE SCHOOLS

Teaching at a language school is not recommended. The majority are exploitative institutions untroubled by professional ethics; for example, making false promises in

job interviews. A few Turkish schools are 'blacklisted' at teflblacklist.blogspot.com.

At some you teach in a central classroom, but at business English schools you often have to schlep around the city between the clients' workplaces.

Schools often promise you a certain number of hours a week, but classes are then cancelled, normally at the last minute, making this a frustrating and difficult way to make a living in Turkey.

PRIVATE TUITION

The advantage of this is you don't need a TEFL certificate or even a university degree. You can advertise your services on http://istanbul.craigslist.org and www.sahibinden.com.

The disadvantage is that, unless you are willing to travel to clients' offices and homes (which is time-consuming, and potentially risky for women), they tend to cancel when they get busy and learning English suddenly becomes a low priority. As with business English schools, most teaching takes place on weekends and evenings, when the students have spare time.

UNIVERSITIES

University jobs command the best wages, with work permits and, often, flights thrown in. Universities also generally operate more professionally than many establishments in the above sectors.

The teacher's job is often to prepare freshman students for courses that will largely be taught in English.

As with *dershane,* jobs are advertised around May and June, and run roughly from September until June.

TOURISM

Travellers sometimes work illegally for room and board in pensions, bars and other businesses in tourist areas. These jobs are generally badly paid and only last a few weeks, but they are a fun way to stay in a place and get to know the locals.

Given that you will be in direct competition with unskilled locals for such employment, and working in the public eye, there is a danger of being reported to authorities and deported.

Transport

GETTING THERE & AWAY

Flights, cars and tours can be booked online at lonely planet.com/bookings.

Entering the Country

Most visitors need an e-visa, purchased online before travelling. See p664.

Passport

Make sure your passport will still have at least six months' validity after you enter Turkey.

Air

It's a good idea to book flights months in advance if you plan to arrive in Turkey any time from April until late August. If you plan to visit a resort, check with travel agents for flight and accommodation deals. Sometimes you can find cheap flights with Turkish carriers and less-usual airlines.

Airports

The main international airports are in western Turkey.

İstanbul Atatürk (www. ataturkairport.com) Turkey's principal international airport.

İstanbul Sabiha Gökçen (www.sgairport.com) Served by many European budget carriers.

Antalya International Airport (www.aytport.com)

İzmir International Airport (www.adnanmenderes airport.com)

Bodrum International Airport (www.bodrum-airport. com)

Dalaman International Airport (www.atmairport. aero)

Ankara International Airport (www.esenboga airport.com)

Airlines

Turkish Airlines (☎0850-333 0849; www.thy.com), the national carrier, has extensive international and domestic networks, including budget subsidiaries **Sun Express** (☎444 0797; www. sunexpress.com) and **Anadolu Jet** (☎444 2538; www. anadolujet.com). It is generally considered a safe airline, and its operational safety is certified by the International Air Transport Association (IATA). Like many airlines, it has had accidents and incidents over the years – nine crashes since 1974, most recently at Amsterdam's Schiphol airport in 2009.

Other airlines serving Turkey are listed in this section by region.

AUSTRALIA & NEW ZEALAND

You can fly from the main cities in Australia and New Zealand to İstanbul, normally

---

CLIMATE CHANGE & TRAVEL

Every form of transport that relies on carbon-based fuel generates CO_2, the main cause of human-induced climate change. Modern travel is dependent on aeroplanes, which might use less fuel per kilometre per person than most cars but travel much greater distances. The altitude at which aircraft emit gases (including CO_2) and particles also contributes to their climate change impact. Many websites offer 'carbon calculators' that allow people to estimate the carbon emissions generated by their journey and, for those who wish to do so, to offset the impact of the greenhouse gases emitted with contributions to portfolios of climate-friendly initiatives throughout the world. Lonely Planet offsets the carbon footprint of all staff and author travel.

via Dubai, Kuala Lumpur or Singapore.

You can often get cheaper flights with European airlines, if you're prepared to change flights again in Europe.

CONTINENTAL EUROPE

There's not much variation in fares from one European airport to another; with the exception of Germany, which has the biggest Turkish community outside Turkey, enabling some great deals.

Most European national carriers fly direct to İstanbul. Cheaper indirect flights can be found, for example changing in Frankfurt en route from Amsterdam to İstanbul.

Charter airlines fly between several German cities and the major western Turkish airports.

Condor (www.condor.com)

Corendon Airlines (www.corendon-airlines.com)

Germanwings (www.german wings.com)

Pegasus Airlines (www.pegasusairlines.com)

Sun Express (www.sunexpress.com)

MIDDLE EAST & ASIA

From Central Asia and the Middle East, you can usually pick up flights with Turkish Airlines or the country's national carrier.

Affordable flights from further afield normally travel to İstanbul via Dubai, Kuala Lumpur or Singapore.

Atlasjet (www.atlasjet.com)

Azerbaijan Airlines (www.azal.az)

Corendon Airlines (www.corendonairlines.com)

Onur Air (www.onurair.com.tr)

Pegasus Airlines (www.pegasusairlines.com)

UK & IRELAND

In addition to the airlines listed, flights are available with European carriers via continental Europe. With major airlines such as British Airways and Turkish Airlines,

the cheapest flights are normally in and out of London airports.

Charter flights are a good option, particularly at the beginning and end of the peak summer holiday season. Try the online charter and discounted flight agents

Atlasjet (www.atlasjet.com)

EasyJet (www.easyjet.com)

Just the Flight (www.justtheflight.co.uk).

Pegasus Airlines (www.pegasusairlines.com)

Thomson (www.thomsonfly.com)

USA & CANADA

Most flights connect with İstanbul-bound flights in the UK or continental Europe, so it's worth looking at European and British airlines in addition to North American airlines.

Another option is to cross the Atlantic to, say, London or Paris, and continue on a separate ticket with a budget carrier.

Land

If you're travelling by train or bus, expect to be held up at the border for two to three hours – or even longer if your fellow passengers don't have their paperwork in order. You'll usually have to disembark and endure paperwork and baggage checks – on both sides of the border. Security at the crossings to/from countries to the east and southeast (Georgia, Azerbaijan, Iran, Iraq and Syria) is tightest. The process is lengthened by a trainload of passengers or the long lines of trucks and cars that build up at some crossings.

Turkey's relationships with most of its neighbours tend to be tense, which can affect when and where you can cross. Check for the most up-to-date information – Lonely Planet's Thorn Tree forum and the Turkish embassy in

your country are two sources of information.

Crossing the border into Turkey with your own vehicle should be fairly straightforward, providing your paperwork is in order.

Armenia

At the time of writing, the Turkey–Armenia border was closed.

BUS

Buses run to Tbilisi (Georgia), with connections to Armenia.

Azerbaijan

The remote Borualan–Sadarak crossing, east of Iğdır (Turkey), leads to the Azerbaijani enclave of Nakhichevan, from where you need to fly across Armenian-occupied Nagorno-Karabakh to reach capital Baku and the rest of Azerbaijan.

BUS

Buses run from İstanbul and Trabzon to Baku, and to Tbilisi (Georgia) with onward connections to Baku. There are also daily buses from Iğdır to Nakhichevan. The following serve the İstanbul–Baku route:

Alpar (www.alparturizm.com.tr; Emniyet Garajı)

Mahmut (www.mahmutturizm.com.tr; Emniyet Garajı)

Metro Turizm (☑444 3455; www.metroturizm.com.tr)

Öznuhoğlu (www.oznuhogluseyahat.com)

TRAIN

The Kars–Tbilisi–Baku line is set to open in 2015.

Bulgaria & Eastern Europe

Bulgarian border guards only occasionally allow pedestrians to cross the frontier; take a bus or hitch a lift with a cooperative motorist. There are three border crossings:

Kapitan Andreevo–Kapıkule This 24-hour post is the main crossing, and the world's second-busiest land-border crossing.

Located 18km northwest of Edirne (Turkey) on the E80 and 9km from Svilengrad (Bulgaria).

Lesovo–Hamzabeyli Some 25km northeast of Edirne, this is favoured by big trucks and should be avoided.

Malko Tărnovo–Aziziye Some 70km northeast of Edirne via Kırklareli and 92km south of Burgas (Bulgaria), this is only useful for those heading to Bulgaria's Black Sea resorts.

BUS

Half a dozen companies have daily departures between İstanbul and Eastern European destinations including Albania, Bulgaria, Kosovo, Macedonia and Romania. Many use İstanbul's Emniyet Garajı, rather than the main bus station.

Alpar (www.alparturizm.com. tr; Emniyet Garajı)

Huntur (www.hunturturizm. com)

Metro Turizm (444 3455; www.metroturizm.com.tr)

Nişikli (www.nisikli.com.tr)

Ulusoy (444 1888; www. ulusoy.com.tr)

Varan (444 8999; www. varan.com.tr)

Vardar (www.vardarturizm. com.tr)

TRAIN

The daily **Bosfor/Balkan Ekspresi** runs from İstanbul to Bucharest (Romania) and Sofia (Bulgaria), with onward connections.

Note that the Turkey–Bulgaria border crossing is in the early hours of the morning and you need to leave the train to get your passport stamped. We've heard stories of harassment, especially of women, at the border, so lone women may be best taking an alternative route. For more information, see p134, **The Man in Seat Sixty-One** (www.seat61.com/ turkey2) and **Turkish State Railways** (444 8233; www. tcdd.gov.tr).

Georgia

Sarp The main, 24-hour crossing, on the Black Sea coast between Hopa (Turkey) and Batumi (Georgia).

Türkgözü Near Posof (Turkey), north of Kars and southwest of Akhaltsikhe (Georgia). The border should open from 8am to 8pm, but in winter you might want to double-check it's open at all.

Çıldır South of Türkgözü, a new crossing is set to open between here and Ahalkalaki (Georgia), reducing the travel time to Armenia.

BUS

Several bus companies depart from İstanbul, Ankara, Trabzon and other cities to Batumi, Kutaisi and Tbilisi.

Mahmut (www.mahmut turizm.com.tr; Emniyet Garajı) İstanbul–Tbilisi daily.

TRAIN

The Kars–Tbilisi–Baku line is set to open in 2015.

Greece & Western Europe

Greek and Turkish border guards allow you to cross the frontier on foot. The following are open 24 hours.

Kastanies–Pazarkule About 9km southwest of Edirne.

Kipi–İpsala Located 29km northeast of Alexandroupolis (Greece) and 35km west of Keşan (Turkey).

BUS

Germany, Austria and Greece have most direct buses to İstanbul, so if you're travelling from other European countries you'll likely have to catch a connecting bus. Several companies have daily departures for Greece and beyond.

Derya Tur (www.deryatur. com.tr) Serves Athens (Greece).

Metro Turizm (444 3455; www.metroturizm.com.tr) Destinations including Athens.

Ulusoy (444 1888; www. ulusoy.com.tr) To/from Austria, Germany, Greece and Hungary.

Varan (444 8999; www. varan.com.tr) Austria, Germany, Greece and Hungary.

CAR & MOTORCYCLE

The E80 highway makes its way through the Balkans to Edirne and İstanbul, then on to Ankara. Using the car ferries from Italy and Greece can shorten driving times from Western Europe, but at a price.

From Alexandroupolis, the main road leads to Kipi-İpsala, then to Keşan and east to İstanbul or south to Gallipoli, Çanakkale and the Aegean.

TRAIN

From Western Europe, you will come via Eastern Europe. A suggested route from London to İstanbul is the three-night journey via Paris, Munich, Zagreb, Belgrade and Sofia (or Paris, Munich, Budapest and Bucharest); see www.seat61.com/turkey for more information.

Iran

Gürbulak–Bazargan This busy post, 35km southeast of Doğubayazıt, is open 24 hours.

Esendere–Sero Southeast of Van, this crossing takes you through the breathtaking scenery of far southeastern Anatolia. It should be open from 8am until midnight, but double-check in winter.

BUS

There are regular buses from İstanbul and Ankara. **Thor Tourism** (www.thortourism. com) offers three buses a week from Ankara to Tabriz and Tehran.

From Doğubayazıt Catch a dolmuş to Gürbulak, then walk or catch a shared taxi across the border. It's Iran's busiest border crossing, and Turkey's second busiest. The crossing might take up to an hour, although tourists are normally waved through without much fuss. Change any unused Turkish lira in Bazargan, as it's harder to do so in Tabriz and Tehran. There are onward buses from Bazargan.

From Van There are direct buses to Orumiyeh (Iran).

TRAIN

For more information visit www.tcdd.gov.tr and www. seat61.com/iran.

Trans-Asya Ekspresi Leaves Ankara every Wednesday morning and arrives in Tehran on Friday evening, travelling via Van and Tabriz, with a ferry crossing of Lake Van.

Van–Tabriz (nine hours) Leaves Wednesday evening.

Iraq

Between Silopi (Turkey) and Zahko (Kurdish Iraq), there's no town or village at the Habur–Ibrahim al-Khalil crossing and you can't walk across it.

BUS

There are direct daily buses from Diyarbakır to Dohuk (₺50, six hours) or Erbil (₺60, nine hours) in Kurdish Iraq, and from Cizre.

TAXI

More hassle than the bus, a taxi from Silopi to Zakho costs between US$50 and US$70. Your driver will manoeuvre through a maze of checkpoints and handle the paperwork. On the return journey, watch out for taxi drivers slipping contraband into your bag.

Syria

At the time of writing, advisories warned against all travel to Syria due to the civil war there. Check government travel advice and www.lonely planet.com/thorntree for updates.

Sea

Departure times change between seasons, with fewer ferries generally running in the winter. The routes available also change from year to year. A good starting point

for information is **Ferrylines** (www.ferrylines.com).

Day trips on ferries to Greece are popular. Ensure that you take your passport, and that you have a multiple-entry Turkish visa so you can get back into the country at the end of the day. (Tourist visas issued on arrival in Turkey normally allow multiple entries.)

Routes

Ayvalık–Lesvos (Midilli), Greece See www.jaletour.com

Bodrum–Kalymnos, Kos, Rhodes and Symi, Greece www. bodrumexpresslines.com, www. bodrumferryboat.com, www. meisexpress.com, www.rhodes ferry.com

Çeşme–Chios, Greece www. erturk.com.tr

İstanbul–Illyichevsk (Odessa), Ukraine www.sea-lines.net

Kaş–Meis (Kastellorizo), Greece www.meisexpress.com

Kuşadası–Samos, Greece www. meandertravel.com

Marmaris–Rhodes www.marma risferry.com, www.meisexpress. com, www.rhodesferry.com

Mersin–Damietta, Egypt www. mega-mar.com.tr

Taşucu–Girne, Northern Cyprus www.akgunlerdenizcilik. com, www.fergun.net

Trabzon–Sochi, Russia www. al-port.com, www.saridenizcilik. com/en

Turgutreis–Kalymnos www. bodrumexpresslines.com, www. bodrumferryboat.com

Turgutreis–Kos www.bodrume xpresslines.com, www.bodrum ferryboat.com

Tours

Many international tour companies offer trips to Turkey.

Backroads (www.backroads. com; USA) Offers a combined bike and sailing tour on the Mediterranean and Aegean.

Cultural Folk Tours (www. culturalfolktours.com; USA)

Group and private cultural and history tours.

Dragoman (www.dragoman. com; UK) Overland itineraries starting in İstanbul and heading through Turkey and the Middle East to various far-flung destinations.

EWP (www.ewpnet.com; UK) Mountaineering and trekking specialist covering the Kaçkars, Ararat, Lycian Way, Cappadocia and elsewhere.

Exodus (www.exodus.co.uk; UK) Adventure company offering a range of tours covering walking, biking, kayaking and history.

Green Island Holidays (www.greenislandholidays.com; UK) Packages covering Turkey and Northern Cyprus, including boutique hotels in İstanbul and Alaçatı, north Aegean.

Imaginative Traveller (www.imaginative-traveller.com; UK) Various trips with themes such as food.

Intrepid Travel (www. intrepidtravel.com; Australia) Offers a variety of small-group tours, covering Turkey, the Middle East and Eastern Europe, for travellers who like the philosophy of independent travel but prefer to travel with others.

Pacha Tours (www.pacha tours.com; USA, Turkey, France & Brazil) Long-running Turkey specialist offering general tours plus special-interest packages and itineraries incorporating Greece.

GETTING AROUND

Air

Airlines

Turkey is well connected by air throughout the country, although many flights go via the hubs of İstanbul or Ankara. Internal flights are a good option in such a large country, and competition between the following airlines keeps tickets affordable.

AnadoluJet (✆444 2538; www.anadolujet.com) The Turkish Airlines subsidiary serves a large network of some 40 airports.

Atlasjet (✆0850-222 0000; www.atlasjet.com) A limited network including Adana, Antalya, Bodrum, Dalaman, İstanbul, İzmir, and Lefkoşa (Nicosia) in Northern Cyprus.

Onur Air (✆0850-210 6687; www.onurair.com.tr) Flies between İstanbul and a dozen locations from Adana to Trabzon.

Pegasus Airlines (✆0850-250 0737; www.pegasusairlines.com) A useful network of some 30 airports, including far-flung eastern spots such as Batman and Erzurum.

Sun Express (✆444 0797; www.sunexpress.com.tr) The Turkish Airlines subsidiary has a useful network of about 20 airports, with most flights from Antalya and İzmir.

Turkish Airlines (✆0850-333 0849; www.thy.com) State-owned Turkish Airlines provides the main domestic network, covering airports from Çanakkale to Kars.

Bicycle

Turkish cycling highlights include spectacular scenery, easy access to archaeological sites, which you may have all to yourself in some obscure corners, and the curiosity and hospitality of locals, especially out east.

Bicycles & Parts

Good-quality spare parts are generally only available in İstanbul and Ankara. Bisan (www.bisan.com.tr) is the main bike manufacturer in Turkey, but you can buy international brands in shops such as Delta Bisiklet (www.deltabisiklet.com), which has branches in İstanbul, Ankara, İzmir, Antalya, Adana, Konya and Kayseri. Delta services bicycles and can send parts throughout the country.

Hazards

These include Turkey's notorious road-hog drivers, rotten road edges and, out east, stone-throwing children, wolves and ferocious Kangal dogs. Avoid main roads between cities; secondary roads are safer and more scenic.

Hire

You can hire bikes for short periods in tourist towns along the coast and in Cappadocia.

Maps

The best map for touring by bike is the Köy Köy Türkiye Yol Atlası, available in bookshops in İstanbul.

Transport

You can sometimes transport your bike by bus, train or ferry free of charge, although some will charge for the space it takes up.

Boat

İstanbul Deniz Otobüsleri (İDO; ✆ 444 4436; www.ido.com.tr) and **BUDO** (budo.burulas.com.tr) operate passenger and car ferries across the Sea of Marmara. Routes to/from İstanbul:

➜ Kabataş–Princes' Islands

➜ Kabataş–Bursa

➜ Kadıköy–Bursa

➜ Yenikapı–Bandırma, Bursa and Yalova

Gestaş (www.gestasdeniz ulasim.com.tr) operates passenger and car ferries across the Dardanelles and to/from the Turkish Aegean islands of Bozcaada and Gökçeada.

Bus

Turkey's intercity bus system is as good as any you'll find, with modern, comfortable coaches crossing the country at all hours and for very reasonable prices. On the journey, you'll be treated to hot drinks and snacks, plus liberal sprinklings of the Turks' beloved kolonya (lemon cologne).

Companies

These are some of the best companies, with extensive route networks:

Kamil Koç (✆444 0562; www.kamilkoc.com.tr) Serves most major cities and towns throughout western and central Turkey and along the Black Sea coast.

Metro Turizm (✆444 3455; www.metroturizm.com.tr) Serves most cities and towns throughout Turkey.

Ulusoy (✆444 1888; www.ulusoy.com.tr) Serves most major cities and towns throughout western and central Turkey and along the Black Sea coast.

Varan (✆444 8999; www.varan.com.tr) Mostly western Turkey, plus Ankara and the Black Sea coast.

Costs

Bus fares are subject to fierce competition between companies, and bargains such as student discounts may be offered. Prices reflect what the market will bear, so the fare from a big city to a village is likely to be different to the fare in the opposite direction.

Tickets

Although you can usually walk into an otogar (bus station) and buy a ticket for the next bus, it's wise to plan ahead on public holidays, at weekends and during the school holidays from mid-June to mid-September. You can buy or reserve seats online with some of the companies listed.

At the otogar When you enter bigger otogars prepare for a few touts offering buses to the destination of your choice. It's usually a good idea to stick to the reputable big-name companies. You may pay a bit more, but you can be more confident the bus is well maintained, will run on time, and will have a relief driver on really long hauls. For shorter trips, some companies have big regional networks.

Men and women Unmarried men and women are not supposed to sit together, but the bus companies rarely enforce this in the case of foreigners. You may be asked if you are married, without having to produce any proof of your wedlock, or both travellers may find their tickets marked with *bay* (man).

Refunds Getting a refund can be difficult; exchanging it for another ticket with the same company is easier.

SEATS

All seats can be reserved, and your ticket will bear a specific seat number. The ticket agent will have a chart of the seats with those already sold crossed off. They will often assign you a seat, but if you ask to look at the chart and choose a place, you can avoid sitting in the following blackspots:

At the front On night buses you may want to avoid the front row of seats behind the driver, which have little legroom, plus you may have to inhale his cigarette smoke and listen to him chatting to his conductor into the early hours.

Above the wheels Can get bumpy.

In front of the middle door Seats don't recline.

Behind the middle door Little legroom.

At the back Can get stuffy, and may have 'back of the cinema' connotations if you are a lone woman.

Otogar

Most Turkish cities and towns have a bus station, called the otogar, *garaj* or *terminal*, generally located on the outskirts. Besides intercity buses, otogars often handle dolmuşes (minibuses that follow prescribed routes) to outlying districts or villages. Most have an *emanetçi* (left-luggage) room, which you can use for a nominal fee.

Don't believe taxi drivers at otogars who tell you there is no bus or dolmuş to your destination; they may be trying to trick you into taking their taxi. Check with the bus and dolmuş operators.

Servis

Because most bus stations are some distance from the town or city centre, the bus companies provide free *servis* shuttle minibuses. These take you to the bus company's office or another central location, possibly with stops en route to drop off other passengers. Ask ' *Servis var mı?*'('Is there a *servis*?'). Rare cities without such a service include Ankara and Konya.

LEAVING TOWN

Ask about the *servis* when you buy your ticket at the bus company's central office; they will likely instruct you to arrive at the office an hour before the official departure time.

DRAWBACKS

The *servis* saves you a taxi or local bus fare to the otogar, but involves a lot of hanging around. If you only have limited time in a location, a taxi fare may be a good investment.

SCAMS

Pension owners may try to convince you the private minibus to their pension is a *servis*. Taxi drivers may say the *servis* has left or isn't operating in the hope of convincing you that their cab is the only option. If you do miss a *servis*, inquire at the bus company office – they normally run regularly.

Car & Motorcycle

Driving around Turkey gives you unparalleled freedom to explore the marvellous countryside and coastline, and to follow back roads to hidden villages and obscure ruins.

Bear in mind that Turkey is a huge country and covering

long distances by car will eat up your time and money. Consider planes, trains and buses for long journeys, and cars for localised travel.

Public transport is a much easier and less stressful way of getting around the traffic-clogged cities.

Automobile Associations

Turkey's main motoring organisation is the **Türkiye Turing ve Otomobil Kurumu** (TTOK; Turkish Touring & Automobile Club; www.turing. org.tr).

Motorcyclist website **Horizons Unlimited** (www. horizonsunlimited.com/ country/turkey) also has Turkey-related information and contacts.

Motorcyclists may want to check out **One More Mile Riders Turkey** (www.omm riders.com), a community resource for riding in Turkey.

Bring Your Own Vehicle

You can bring your vehicle into Turkey for six months without charge. Ensure you have your car's registration papers, tax number and insurance policy with you. The fact that you brought a vehicle to Turkey will be marked in your passport to ensure you take it back out again.

Checkpoints

Roadblocks are common in eastern Turkey, with police checking vehicles and paperwork are in order. In southeastern Anatolia, you may encounter military roadblocks and roads are sometimes closed completely if there is trouble ahead.

Driving Licences

Drivers must have a valid driving licence. Your own national licence should be sufficient, but an international driving permit (IDP) may be useful if your licence is from a country likely to seem obscure to a Turkish police officer.

Fines

You may be stopped by blue-uniformed *trafik polis*, who can fine you on the spot for speeding. If you know you have done nothing wrong and the police appear to be asking for money, play dumb. You'll probably have to pay up if they persist, but insisting on proof of payment may dissuade them from extracting a fine destined only for their pocket. If they don't ask for on-the-spot payment, contact your car-rental company (or mention the incident when you return the vehicle), as it can pay the fine and take the money from your card. Do the same in the case of fines for other offences, such as not paying a motorway toll.

Fuel & Spare Parts

Turkey has the world's second-highest petrol prices. Petrol/diesel cost about ₺5 per litre. Petrol stations are widespread in western Turkey, and many are mega enterprises. In the vast empty spaces of central and eastern Anatolia, it's a good idea to have a full tank when you start out in the morning.

Yedek parçaları (spare parts) are readily available in the major cities, especially for European models. Elsewhere, you may have to wait a day or two for parts to be ordered and delivered. Ingenious Turkish mechanics can contrive to keep some US models in service. The *sanayi bölgesi* (industrial zone) on the outskirts of every town generally has a repair shop; for tyre repairs find an *oto lastikçi* (tyre repairer).

Spare motorcycle parts may be hard to come by everywhere except major cities.

Hire

You need to be at least 21 years old, with a year's driving experience, to hire a car in Turkey. Most car-hire companies require a credit card. Most hire cars have standard (manual) transmission; you'll pay more for automatic. The majority of the big-name companies charge hefty one-way fees, starting at around ₺150 and climbing to hundreds of euros for longer distances.

The big international companies – including Avis, Budget, Europcar, Hertz, National and Sixt – operate in the main cities, towns and most airports. Particularly in eastern Anatolia, stick to the major companies, as the local agencies often do not have insurance. Even some of the major operations are actually franchises in the east, so check the contract carefully, particularly the section relating to insurance. Ask for a copy in English.

If your car incurs any accident damage, or if you cause any, do not move the car before finding a police officer and obtaining a *kaza raporu* (accident report). Contact your car-rental company as soon as possible. In the case of an accident, your hire-car insurance may be void if it can be shown you were operating under the influence of alcohol or drugs, were speeding, or if you did not submit the required accident report within 48 hours to the rental company.

Agencies generally deliver cars with virtually no fuel, unless you specifically request otherwise.

CarHireExpress.co.uk (www.carhireexpress.co.uk/turkey/) A booking engine.

Economy Car Hire (www.economycarhire.com) Gets good rates with other companies, including Avis and Thrifty.

Economy Car Rentals (www.economycarrentals.com) Gets good rates with other companies, including Budget and National.

Rentalcars.com (www.rentalcars.com) Good rates with other companies, including Alamo.

Insurance

You must have international insurance, covering third-party damage, if you are bringing your own car into the country (further information is available at www.turing.org.tr/eng/green_card.asp). Buying it at the border is a straightforward process (one month costs €80).

When hiring a car, 100%, no-excess insurance is increasingly the only option on offer. If this is not the only option, the basic, mandatory insurance package should cover damage to the vehicle and theft protection – with an excess, which you can reduce or waive for an extra payment.

As in other countries, insurance generally does not cover windows and tyres. You will likely be offered cover for an extra few euros a day.

Road Conditions

Road surfaces and signage are generally good – on the main roads, at least. There are good *otoyols* (motorways) from the Bulgarian border near Edirne to İstanbul and Ankara, and from İzmir around the coast to Antalya.

Elsewhere, roads are being steadily upgraded, although they still tend to be worst in the east, where severe winters play havoc with the surfaces. In northeastern Anatolia, road conditions change from year to year; seek local advice before setting off on secondary roads. There are frequent roadworks in the northeast; even on main roads traffic can crawl along at 30km/hour. The new dams near Artvin and Yusufeli will flood some roads, and the construction causes waits of up to half an hour. Ask locally about the timing of your journey; on some roads, traffic flows according to a regular timetable, posted at the roadside.

In winter, be careful of icy roads. In bad winters, you will need chains on your wheels almost everywhere except along the Aegean and Mediterranean coasts. The police may stop you in more-remote areas to check you're properly prepared for emergencies. In mountainous areas such as northeastern Anatolia, landslides and rockfalls are a danger, caused by wet weather and snowmelt in spring. Between İstanbul and Ankara, be aware of the fog belt around Bolu that can seriously reduce visibility, even in summer.

Road Rules

In theory, Turks drive on the right and yield to traffic approaching from the right. In practice, they often drive in the middle and yield to no one. Maximum speed limits, unless otherwise posted, are 50km/h in towns, 90km/h on highways and 120km/h on *otoyols*.

Safety

Turkey's roads are not particularly safe, and claim about 10,000 lives a year. Turkish drivers are impatient and incautious; rarely use their indicators and pay little attention to anyone else's; drive too fast both on the open road and through towns; and have an irrepressible urge to overtake – including on blind corners. To survive on Turkey's roads:

➡ Drive cautiously and defensively.

➡ Do not expect your fellow motorists to obey road signs or behave in a manner you would generally expect at home.

➡ As there are only a few divided highways and many two-lane roads are serpentine, reconcile yourself to spending hours crawling along behind slow, overladen trucks.

➡ Avoid driving at night, when you won't be able to see potholes, animals, or even vehicles driving without lights, with lights missing, or stopped in the

middle of the road. Drivers sometimes flash their lights to announce their approach.

➡ Rather than trying to tackle secondary, gravel roads when visiting remote sights, hire a taxi for the day. It's an extra expense, but the driver should know the terrain and the peace of mind is invaluable.

➡ The US embassy in Ankara has a page of safety tips for drivers at http://turkey.usembassy.gov/driver_safety_briefing.html.

Tolls

Turkey has a motorway toll system, known as HGS (Hızlı Geçiş Sistemi - 'fast transit system'). Paying tolls should be automatic if you hire a car in Turkey; the vehicle should be equipped with an electronic-chip sticker or a small plastic toll transponder. You simply pay the rental company a flat fee of about €10 for unlimited use of the *otoyols*. Confirm that the car is equipped with a device, which should be located in the top centre of the windscreen. If it is not, you will likely end up with a fine.

If you are driving your own car, you must register the vehicle and buy credit at the earliest opportunity in a branch of the PTT (post office).

Dolmuşes & Midibuses

As well as providing transport within cities and towns, dolmuşes (minibuses) run between places; you'll usually use them to travel between small towns and villages. Ask, '[Your destination] *dolmuş var mı?'* (Is there a dolmuş to [your destination]?). Some dolmuşes depart at set times, but they often wait until every seat is taken before leaving. To let the driver know that you want to hop out, say '*inecek var'* (someone wants to get out).

Midibuses generally operate on routes that are too long for dolmuşes, but not popular enough for full-size buses. They usually have narrow seats with rigid upright backs, which can be uncomfortable on long stretches.

Local Transport

Bus

For most city buses you must buy your *bilet* (ticket) in advance at a special ticket kiosk. Kiosks are found at major bus terminals and transfer points, and sometimes attached to shops near bus stops. The fare is normally around ₺2.

Private buses sometimes operate on the same routes as municipal buses; they are usually older, and accept either cash or tickets.

Local Dolmuş

Dolmuşes are minibuses or, occasionally, *taksi dolmuşes* (shared taxis) that operate on set routes within a city. They're usually faster, more comfortable and only slightly more expensive than the bus. In larger cities, dolmuş stops are marked by signs; look for a 'D' and text reading '*Dolmuş İndirme Bindirme Yeri*' (Dolmuş Boarding and Alighting Place). Stops are usually conveniently located near major squares, terminals and intersections.

Metro

Several cities have underground metros, including İstanbul, İzmir, Bursa and Ankara. These are usually quick and simple to use, although you may have to go through the ticket barriers to find a route map. Most metros require you to buy a *jeton* (transport token; around ₺2) and insert it into the ticket barrier.

Taxi

Turkish taxis are fitted with digital meters. If your driver doesn't start his, mention it right away by saying 'saati-niz' (your meter). Check your driver is running the right rate, which varies from city to city. The gece (night) rate is 50% more than the gündüz (daytime) rate, but some places, including İstanbul, do not have a night rate.

Some taxi drivers – particularly in İstanbul – try to demand a flat payment from foreigners. In this situation, drivers sometimes offer a decent fare; for example to take you to an airport, where they can pick up a good fare on the return journey. It is more often the case that they demand an exorbitant amount, give you grief, and refuse to run the meter. If this happens find another cab and, if convenient, complain to the police. Generally, only when you are using a taxi for a private tour involving waiting time (eg to an archaeological site) should you agree on a set fare, which should work out cheaper than using the meter. Taxi companies normally have set fees for longer journeys written in a ledger at the rank – they can be haggled down a little. Always confirm such fares in advance to avoid argument later.

Tram

Several cities have tramvays (trams), which are a quick and efficient way of getting around, and normally cost around ₺2 to use.

Tours

Every year we receive complaints from travellers who feel they have been fleeced by local travel agents, especially some of those operating in Sultanahmet, İstanbul. However, there are plenty of good agents alongside the sharks. Figure out a ballpark figure for doing the same trip yourself, and shop around before committing.

Operators

Amber Travel (www. ambertravel.com) British-run adventure travel company specialising in hiking, biking and sea kayaking.

Bougainville Travel (☎ 836 3737; www.bougainville-turkey. com; İbrahim Serin Caddesi 10, Kaş) Long-established English-Turkish tour operator based in Kaş offering a range of Mediterranean activities and tours.

Crowded House Tours (☎814 1565; www.crowded housegallipoli.com; Huseyin Avni Sokak 4, Eceabat) Tours of the Gallipoli Peninsula and other areas including Cappadocia and Ephesus. Based in Eceabat.

Eastern Turkey Tours (☎215 2092, 0530 349 2793; www.easternturkeytour. org; Ordu Caddesi, Van) Recommended Van-based outfit specialising in eastern Anatolia, Georgia and Armenia.

Fez Travel (www.feztravel. com) Tours around Turkey, including the Gallipoli Peninsula and 'Fez Bus' backpacker tours.

Hassle Free Travel Agency (☎213 5969; www. anzachouse.com; Cumhuriyet Meydanı 59, Çanakkale) Tours of the Gallipoli Peninsula and other parts of western Turkey and gület cruises. Based in Çanakkale.

Kirkit Voyage (www.kirkit. com) Cappadocia specialists offering customised tours around Turkey, including İstanbul and Ephesus. French spoken too.

Train

Train travel through Turkey is becoming increasingly popular as improvements are made, with high-speed lines such as İstanbul–Ankara appearing.

If you're on a budget, an overnight train journey is a great way to save accommodation costs. Many fans also appreciate no-rush travel experiences such as the stunning scenery rolling by and meeting fellow passengers.

Occasional unannounced hold-ups and toilets gone feral by the end of the long journey are all part of the adventure.

Classes

Following a modernisation effort, Turkish trains are mostly as good as regular trains in Western Europe. Most have carpeted air-conditioned carriages with reclining Pullman seats; some have six-seat compartments. Riding the 250km/hour Yüksek Hızlı Treni (high-speed trains, known as YHT) is a treat, with two classes to choose between and a cafeteria car.

Many regular trains have restaurant cars and küşet (couchette) wagons with shared four-person compartments with seats that fold down into shelf-like beds. Bedding is not provided unless it's an örtülü küşetli ('covered' couchette). A yataklı vagon (sleeping car) has one- and two-bed compartments, with a washbasin, bedding, fridge and even a shared shower; the best option for women travelling alone on overnight trips.

Costs

Train tickets are usually about half the price of bus tickets, with the exception of high-speed services. A return ticket is 20% cheaper than two singles. Students (though you may need a Turkish student card), ISIC cardholders and seniors (60 years plus) get a 20% discount. Children under eight travel free.

InterRail Global and One Country passes and Balkan Flexipass cover the Turkish railway network, as do the Eurail Global and Select passes. Train Tour Cards, available at major stations, allow unlimited travel on Turkish inter-city trains for a month. There are also Tour Cards covering just high-speed trains, inter-city trains (apart from sleeping and couchette wagons) or couchettes and sleeping cars.

Long-Distance Trips

The following trains depart from Ankara:

➡ Adana via Kayseri

➡ Diyarbakır via Kayseri, Sivas and Malatya

➡ İzmir via Eskişehir

➡ Kars via Kayseri, Sivas and Erzurum

➡ Kurtalan (near Hasankeyf) via Kayseri, Sivas, Malatya and Diyarbakır

➡ Tatvan (Lake Van) via Kayseri, Sivas and Malatya

Network

The **Turkish State Railways** (✆444 8233; www.tcdd.gov.tr) network covers the country fairly well, with the notable exception of the coastlines. For the Aegean and Mediterranean coasts you can travel by train to either İzmir or Konya, and take the bus from there.

At the time of writing, to access Turkish State Railways' Anatolian network from İstanbul, you had to cross the city to Pendik (25km southeast of the centre near Sabiha Gökçen International Airport, reached via metro to Kartal and bus or taxi from there). From Pendik, high-speed trains run to Ankara via Eskişehir. Alternatively, catch a ferry across the Sea of Marmara to Bandırma, from where trains depart to İzmir. Trains to eastern Anatolia depart from Ankara. For updates visit www.seat61.com/Turkey2.

High-speed routes:

➡ Ankara–Konya

➡ Eskişehir–Konya

➡ İstanbul Pendik–Eskişehir–Ankara

Other useful routes:

➡ İstanbul–İzmir (including ferry to/from Bandırma)

➡ İzmir–Selçuk–Denizli

Reservations

It is wise to reserve your seat at least a few days before travelling, although they can be paid for shortly before departure. For the *yataklı* wagons, reserve as far in advance as possible, especially if a religious or public holiday is looming. Weekend trains tend to be busiest.

You can buy tickets at stations (only major stations for sleeping-car tickets), through travel agencies and, with more difficulty, at www.tcdd.gov.tr; www.seat61.com/Turkey2.htm gives step-by-step instructions for navigating the transaction.

Timetables

You can double-check train departure times, which do change, at www.tcdd.gov.tr.

Timetables sometimes indicate stations rather than cities, eg Basmane rather than İzmir.

Health

BEFORE YOU GO

Recommended Vaccinations

The following are recommended as routine for travellers, regardless of the region they are visiting:

➡ diphtheria-tetanus-pertussis (whooping cough)

➡ influenza

➡ measles-mumps-rubella (MMR)

➡ polio

➡ varicella (chickenpox)

The following are also recommended for travellers to Turkey:

➡ hepatitis A and B

➡ tetanus

➡ typhoid

Rabies is endemic in Turkey, so if you will be travelling off the beaten track, consider an antirabies vaccination.

Malaria is found from May to October in the provinces of Diyarbakır, Mardin and Şanlıurfa.

Get vaccinations four to eight weeks before departure, and ask for an International Certificate of Vaccination or Prophylaxis (ICVP or 'yellow card'), listing all the vaccinations you've received.

Medical Checklist

Consider packing the following in your medical kit:

➡ acetaminophen/paracetamol (Tylenol) or aspirin

➡ adhesive or paper tape

➡ antibacterial cream or ointment

➡ antibiotics (if travelling off the beaten track)

➡ antidiarrhoeal drugs (eg loperamide)

➡ antihistamines (for hay fever and allergic reactions)

➡ anti-inflammatory drugs (eg ibuprofen)

➡ bandages, gauze and gauze rolls

➡ DEET-based insect repellent for the skin

➡ insect spray for clothing, tents and bed nets

➡ water purification tablets

➡ oral rehydration salts (eg Dioralyte)

➡ pocket knife, scissors, safety pins and tweezers

➡ steroid cream or cortisone

➡ sunblock (it's expensive in Turkey)

➡ syringes and sterile needles (if travelling to remote areas)

➡ thermometer

Websites

Consult your government's travel health website before departure, if one is available. The Health & Safety section at www.lonelyplanet.com/turkey has links to travel health websites and recommendations for further reading.

IN TURKEY

Prevention is the key to staying healthy while travelling in Turkey. Infectious diseases here are usually associated

INSURANCE

Turkish doctors generally expect payment in cash. Find out in advance if your travel insurance will reimburse you for overseas health expenditures or, less likely, pay providers directly. If you are required to pay upfront, keep all documentation. Some policies ask you to call a centre in your home country (reverse charges) for an immediate assessment of your problem. It's also worth ensuring your insurance covers ambulances and transport. Not all policies cover emergency medical evacuation home or to a hospital in a major city, which may be necessary in a serious emergency.

> ## TRAVELLER'S DIARRHOEA
>
> To prevent diarrhoea, avoid tap water unless it has been boiled, filtered or chemically disinfected (with iodine or purification tablets). Eat fresh fruit or vegetables only if they're cooked or you have peeled them yourself, and avoid dairy products that might contain unpasteurised milk. Buffet meals are risky since food may not be kept hot enough; meals freshly cooked in front of you in a busy restaurant are safer.
>
> If you develop diarrhoea, drink plenty of fluids, and preferably an oral rehydration solution containing salt and sugar. A few loose stools don't require treatment, but if you start having more than four or five motions a day, you should take an antidiarrhoeal agent (such as loperamide) or, if that's unavailable, an antibiotic (usually a quinolone drug). If diarrhoea is bloody, persists for more than 72 hours or is accompanied by fever, shaking chills or severe abdominal pain, you should seek medical attention.

with poor living conditions and poverty, and can be avoided with a few precautions.

Availability & Cost of Health Care

Getting Treated

If you need basic care for problems such as cuts, bruises and jabs, you could ask for the local *sağlık ocağı* (health centre), but don't expect anyone to speak anything but Turkish.

If your hotel can't recommend the nearest source of medical help, try the travel assistance provided by your insurance or, in an emergency, your embassy or consulate.

Standards

The best private hospitals in İstanbul and Ankara offer world-class service, but they are expensive. Elsewhere, even private hospitals don't always have high standards of care and their state-run equivalents even less so.

Hospitals & clinics Medicine, and even sterile dressings or intravenous fluids, may need to be bought from a local pharmacy. Nursing care is often limited or rudimentary, as family and friends often look after Turkish patients.

Dentists Standards vary and there is a risk of hepatitis B and HIV transmission via poorly sterilised equipment, so watch the tools in use carefully. Travel insurance will usually only cover emergency dental treatment.

Pharmacists For minor illnesses, pharmacists can often provide advice and sell over-the-counter medication, including drugs that would require a prescription in your home country. They can also advise when more specialised help is needed.

Infectious Diseases

Diphtheria

Spread through Close respiratory contact.

Symptoms & effects A high temperature and severe sore throat. Sometimes a membrane forms across the throat, requiring a tracheotomy to prevent suffocation.

Prevention The vaccine is given as an injection, normally with tetanus and in many countries as a routine childhood jab. Recommended for those likely to be in close contact with the local population in infected areas.

Hepatitis A

Spread through Contaminated food (particularly shellfish) and water.

Symptoms & effects Jaundice, dark urine, a yellow colour to the whites of the eyes, fever and abdominal pain. Although rarely fatal, it can cause prolonged lethargy and delayed recovery.

Prevention Vaccine given as an injection, with a booster extending the protection offered. Available in some countries as a combined single-dose vaccine with hepatitis B or typhoid.

Hepatitis B

Spread through Infected blood, contaminated needles and sexual intercourse.

Symptoms & effects Jaundice and liver problems (occasionally failure).

Prevention The vaccine is worth considering for Turkey, where the disease is endemic. Many countries give it as part of routine childhood vaccinations.

Leishmaniasis

Spread through The bite of an infected sandfly or dog. More prevalent in areas bordering Syria.

Symptoms & effects A slowly growing skin lump or ulcer. It may develop into a serious, life-threatening fever, usually accompanied by anaemia and weight loss.

Leptospirosis

Spread through The excreta of infected rodents, especially rats. It is unusual for travellers to be affected unless living in poor sanitary conditions.

Symptoms & effects Fever, jaundice, and hepatitis and renal failure that may be fatal.

Malaria

Spread through Mosquito bites. Check with your doctor if you are considering travelling to south-eastern Turkey. Elsewhere, the risk is minimal to zero.

Symptoms & effects Malaria almost always starts with marked shivering, fever and sweating. Muscle pain, headache and vomiting are common. Symptoms may occur anywhere from a few days to three weeks after a bite by an infected mosquito. The illness can start while you are taking preventative tablets, if they are not fully effective, or after you have finished taking your tablets. Malaria symptoms can be mistaken for flu by travellers who return home during winter.

Prevention Taking antimalarial tablets is inconvenient, but malaria can kill. You must take them if the risk is significant.

Rabies
Spread through Bites or licks on broken skin from an infected animal.

Symptoms & effects Initially, pain or tingling at the site of the bite, with fever, loss of appetite and headache. With 'furious' rabies, there is a growing sense of anxiety, jumpiness, disorientation, neck stiffness, sometimes seizures or convulsions, and hydrophobia (fear of water). 'Dumb' rabies (less common) affects the spinal cord, causing muscle paralysis then heart and lung failure. If untreated, both forms are fatal.

Prevention People travelling to remote areas, where a reliable source of post-bite vaccine is not available within 24 hours, should be vaccinated. Any bite, scratch or lick from a warm-blooded, furry animal should immediately be thoroughly cleaned. If you have not been vaccinated and you get bitten, you will need a course of injections starting as soon as possible after the injury. Vaccination does not provide immunity, it merely buys you more time to seek medical help.

Tuberculosis
Spread through Close respiratory contact and, occasionally, infected milk or milk products.

Symptoms & effects Can be asymptomatic, although symptoms can include a cough, weight loss or fever months or even years after exposure. An X-ray is the best way to confirm if you have tuberculosis.

Prevention BCG vaccine is recommended for those likely to be mixing closely with the local population – visiting family,

planning a long stay, or working as a teacher or healthcare worker. As it's a live vaccine, it should not be given to pregnant women or immunocompromised individuals.

Typhoid
Spread through Food or water contaminated by infected human faeces.

Symptoms & effects Initially, usually fever or a pink rash on the abdomen. Septicaemia (blood poisoning) may also occur.

Prevention Vaccination given by injection. In some countries, an oral vaccine is available.

Environmental Hazards
Heat Illness
Causes Sweating heavily, fluid loss and inadequate replacement of fluids and salt. Particularly common when you exercise outside in a hot climate.

Symptoms & effects Headache, dizziness and tiredness.

Prevention Drink sufficient water (you should produce pale, diluted urine). By the time you are thirsty, you are already dehydrated.

Treatment Replace fluids by drinking water, fruit juice or both, and cool down with cold water and fans. Treat salt loss by consuming salty fluids, such as soup or broth, and adding a little more table salt to foods.

Heatstroke
Causes Extreme heat; high humidity; dehydration; drug or alcohol use or physical exertion in the sun. Occurs when the body's heat-regulating mechanism breaks down.

Symptoms & effects An excessive rise in body temperature, sweating stops, irrational and hyperactive behaviour, and

eventually loss of consciousness and death.

Treatment Rapidly cool down by spraying the body with water and using a fan. Emergency fluids and replacing electrolytes by intravenous drip is usually also required.

Insect Bites & Stings
Causes Mosquitoes, sandflies (located around the Mediterranean beaches), scorpions (found in arid or dry climates), bees and wasps (in the Aegean and Mediterranean coastal areas, particularly around Marmaris), centipedes.

Symptoms & effects Even if mosquitoes do not carry malaria, they can cause irritation and infected bites. Sandflies have a nasty, itchy bite, and occasionally carry leishmaniasis or Pappataci fever. Turkey's small white scorpions can give a painful sting that will bother you for up to 24 hours.

Prevention DEET-based insect repellent. Citronella candles. Cover up with light-coloured clothing. Avoid riversides and marshy areas from late afternoon onwards. Take a mosquito head net and bed net.

Treatment Antihistamine cream to sooth and reduce inflammation.

Snake Bites
Prevention Do not walk barefoot or stick your hands into holes or cracks when exploring nature or touring overgrown ruins and little-visited historic sites.

Treatment Do not panic: half of those bitten by venomous snakes are not actually injected with poison (envenomed). Immobilise the bitten limb with a splint (eg a stick) and bandage the site with firm pressure. Do not apply a tourniquet, or cut or suck the bite. Note the snake's appearance for identification purposes, and get medical help as soon as possible so that antivenene can be given.

TAP WATER
It's not wise to drink tap water if you're only in Turkey on a short visit. Stick to bottled water, boil tap water for 10 minutes, or use purification tablets or a filter. Do not drink river or lake water, which may lead to diarrhoea or vomiting.

Language

Turkish belongs to the Ural-Altaic language family. It's the official language of Turkey and Northern Cyprus, and has approximately 70 million speakers worldwide.

Pronouncing Turkish is pretty simple for English speakers as most Turkish sounds are also found in English. If you read our coloured pronunciation guides as if they were English, you should be understood just fine. Note that the symbol ew represents the sound 'ee' pronounced with rounded lips (as in 'few'), and that the symbol uh is pronounced like the 'a' in 'ago'. The Turkish r is always rolled and v is pronounced a little softer than in English.

Word stress is quite light in Turkish – in our pronunciation guides the stressed syllables are in italics.

BASICS

Hello.
Merhaba.   mer·ha·ba

Goodbye.
Hoşçakal.   hosh·cha·kal
(said by person leaving)

Güle güle.   gew·le gew·le
(said by person staying)

Yes.
Evet.   e·vet

No.
Hayır.   ha·yuhr

WANT MORE?

For in-depth language information and handy phrases, check out Lonely Planet's *Turkish Phrasebook*. You'll find it at **shop.lonelyplanet.com**.

Excuse me.
Bakar mısınız.   ba·kar muh·suh·nuhz

Sorry.
Özür dilerim.   er·zewr dee·le·reem

Please.
Lütfen.   lewt·fen

Thank you.
Teşekkür ederim.   te·shek·kewr e·de·reem

You're welcome.
Birşey değil.   beer·shay de·eel

How are you?
Nasılsınız?   na·suhl·suh·nuhz

Fine, and you?
İyiyim, ya siz?   ee·yee·yeem ya seez

What's your name?
Adınız nedir?   a·duh·nuhz ne·deer

My name is ...
Benim adım ...   be·neem a·duhm ...

Do you speak English?
İngilizce   een·gee·leez·je
konuşuyor   ko·noo·shoo·yor
musunuz?   moo·soo·nooz

I understand.
Anlıyorum.   an·luh·yo·room

I don't understand.
Anlamıyorum.   an·la·muh·yo·room

ACCOMMODATION

Where can I   Nerede ...   ne·re·de ...
find a ...?   bulabilirim?   boo·la·bee·
                                        lee·reem

campsite   kamp yeri   kamp ye·ree
guesthouse   misafirhane   mee·sa·feer·
                                        ha·ne
hotel   otel   o·tel
pension   pansiyon   pan·see·yon
youth hostel   gençlik   gench·leek
                     hosteli   hos·te·lee

How much is it per night/person?
Geceliği/Kişi
başına ne kadar? · ge·je·lee·ee/kee·shee ba·shuh·na ne ka·dar

Is breakfast included?
Kahvaltı dahil mi? · kah·val·tuh da·heel mee

Do you have a ...?	... odanız var mı?	... o·da·nuz var muh
single room	Tek kişilik	tek kee·shee·leek
double room	İki kişilik	ee·kee kee·shee·leek

air conditioning	klima	klee·ma
bathroom	banyo	ban·yo
window	pencere	pen·je·re

DIRECTIONS

Where is ...?
... nerede? · ... ne·re·de

What's the address?
Adresi nedir? · ad·re·see ne·deer

Could you write it down, please?
Lütfen yazar
mısınız? · lewt·fen ya·zar muh·suh·nuhz

Can you show me (on the map)?
Bana (haritada)
gösterebilir
misiniz? · ba·na (ha·ree·ta·da) gers·te·re·bee·leer mee·seen·neez

It's straight ahead.
Tam karşıda. · tam kar·shuh·da

at the traffic lights
trafik
ışıklarından · tra·feek uh·shuhk·la·ruhn·dan

at the corner	köşeden	ker·she·den
behind	arkasında	ar·ka·suhn·da
far (from)	uzak	oo·zak
in front of	önünde	er·newn·de
near (to)	yakınında	ya·kuh·nuhn·da
opposite	karşısında	kar·shuh·suhn·da
Turn left.	Sola dön.	so·la dern
Turn right.	Sağa dön.	sa·a dern

EATING & DRINKING

What would you recommend?
Ne tavsiye
edersiniz? · ne tav·see·ye e·der·see·neez

What's in that dish?
Bu yemekte neler var? · boo ye·mek·te ne·ler var

I don't eat ...
... yemiyorum. · ... ye·mee·yo·room

Cheers!
Şerefe! · she·re·fe

KEY PATTERNS

To get by in Turkish, mix and match these simple patterns with words of your choice:

When's (the next bus)?
(Sonraki otobüs)
ne zaman? · (son·ra·kee o·to·bews) ne za·man

Where's (the market)?
(Pazar yeri) nerede? · (pa·zar ye·ree) ne·re·de

Where can I (buy a ticket)?
Nereden (bilet
alabilirim)? · ne·re·den (bee·let a·la·bee·lee·reem)

I have (a reservation).
(Rezervasyonum)
var. · (re·zer·vas·yo·noom) var

Do you have (a map)?
(Haritanız)
var mı? · (ha·ree·ta·nuhz) var muh

Is there (a toilet)?
(Tuvalet) var mı? · (too·va·let) var muh

I'd like (the menu).
(Menüyü)
istiyorum. · (me·new·yew) ees·tee·yo·room

I want to (make a call).
(Bir görüşme
yapmak)
istiyorum. · (beer ger·rewsh·me yap·mak) ees·tee·yo·room

Do I have to (declare this)?
(Bunu beyan
etmem) gerekli mi? · (boo·noo be·yan et·mem) ge·rek·lee mee

I need (assistance).
(Yardıma)
ihtiyacım var. · (yar·duh·ma) eeh·tee·ya·juhm var

That was delicious!
Nefisti! · ne·fees·tee

The bill/check, please.
Hesap lütfen. · he·sap lewt·fen

I'd like a table for ...	... bir masa ayırtmak istiyorum.	... beer ma·sa a·yuhrt·mak ees·tee·yo·room
(eight) o'clock	Saat (sekiz) için	sa·at (se·keez) ee·cheen
(two) people	(İki) kişilik	(ee·kee) kee·shee·leek

Key Words

appetisers	mezeler	me·ze·ler
bottle	şişe	shee·she
bowl	kase	ka·se
breakfast	kahvaltı	kah·val·tuh
(too) cold	(çok) soğuk	(chok) so·ook

cup	fincan	feen·jan
delicatessen	şarküteri	shar·kew·te·ree
dinner	akşam yemeği	ak·sham ye·me·ee
dish	yemek	ye·mek
food	yiyecek	yee·ye·jek
fork	çatal	cha·tal
glass	bardak	bar·dak
grocery	bakkal	bak·kal
halal	helal	he·lal
highchair	mama sandalyesi	ma·ma san·dal·ye·see
hot (warm)	sıcak	suh·jak
knife	bıçak	buh·chak
kosher	koşer	ko·sher
lunch	öğle yemeği	er·le ye·me·ee
main courses	ana yemekler	a·na ye·mek·ler
market	pazar	pa·zar
menu	yemek listesi	ye·mek lees·te·see
plate	tabak	ta·bak
restaurant	restoran	res·to·ran
spicy	acı	a·juh
spoon	kaşık	ka·shuhk
vegetarian	vejeteryan	ve·zhe·ter·yan

Meat & Fish

anchovy	hamsi	ham·see
beef	sığır eti	suh·uhr e·tee
calamari	kalamares	ka·la·ma·res
chicken	piliç/ tavuk	pee·leech/ ta·vook
fish	balık	ba·luhk
lamb	kuzu	koo·zoo
liver	ciğer	jee·er
mussels	midye	meed·ye
pork	domuz eti	do·mooz e·tee
veal	dana eti	da·na e·tee

Fruit & Vegetables

apple	elma	el·ma
apricot	kayısı	ka·yuh·suh
banana	muz	mooz
capsicum	biber	bee·ber
carrot	havuç	ha·vooch
cucumber	salatalık	sa·la·ta·luhk
fruit	meyve	may·ve
grape	üzüm	ew·zewm
melon	kavun	ka·voon

olive	zeytin	zay·teen
onion	soğan	so·an
orange	portakal	por·ta·kal
peach	şeftali	shef·ta·lee
potato	patates	pa·ta·tes
spinach	ıspanak	uhs·pa·nak
tomato	domates	do·ma·tes
watermelon	karpuz	kar·pooz

Other

bread	ekmek	ek·mek
cheese	peynir	pay·neer
egg	yumurta	yoo·moor·ta
honey	bal	bal
ice	buz	booz
pepper	kara biber	ka·ra bee·ber
rice	pirinç/ pilav	pee·reench/ pee·lav
salt	tuz	tooz
soup	çorba	chor·ba
sugar	şeker	she·ker
Turkish delight	lokum	lo·koom

Drinks

beer	bira	bee·ra
coffee	kahve	kah·ve
(orange) juice	(portakal) suyu	(por·ta·kal soo·yoo)
milk	süt	sewt
mineral water	maden suyu	ma·den soo·yoo
soft drink	alkolsüz içecek	al·kol·sewz ee·che·jek
tea	çay	chai
water	su	soo
wine	şarap	sha·rap
yoghurt	yoğurt	yo·oort

Signs	
Açık	Open
Bay	Male
Bayan	Female
Çıkışı	Exit
Giriş	Entrance
Kapalı	Closed
Sigara İçilmez	No Smoking
Tuvaletler	Toilets
Yasak	Prohibited

EMERGENCIES

Help!
İmdat! eem·dat

I'm lost.
Kayboldum. kai·bol·doom

Leave me alone!
Git başımdan! geet ba·shuhm·dan

There's been an accident.
Bir kaza oldu. beer ka·za ol·doo

Can I use your phone?
Telefonunuzu te·le·fo·noo·noo·zoo
kullanabilir miyim? kool·la·na·bee·leer mee·yeem

Call a doctor!
Doktor çağırın! dok·tor cha·uh·ruhn

Call the police!
Polis çağırın! po·lees cha·uh·ruhn

I'm ill.
Hastayım. has·ta·yuhm

It hurts here.
Burası ağrıyor. boo·ra·suh a·ruh·yor

I'm allergic to (nuts).
(Çerezlere) (che·rez·le·re)
alerjim var. a·ler·zheem var

SHOPPING & SERVICES

I'd like to buy ...
... almak istiyorum. ... al·mak ees·tee·yo·room

I'm just looking.
Sadece bakıyorum. sa·de·je ba·kuh·yo·room

May I look at it?
Bakabilir miyim? ba·ka·bee·leer mee·yeem

The quality isn't good.
Kalitesi iyi değil. ka·lee·te·see ee·yee de·eel

How much is it?
Ne kadar? ne ka·dar

It's too expensive.
Bu çok pahalı. boo chok pa·ha·luh

Do you have something cheaper?
Daha ucuz birşey da·ha oo·jooz beer·shay
var mı? var muh

There's a mistake in the bill.
Hesapta bir he·sap·ta beer
yanlışlık var. yan·luhsh·luhk var

Question Words

How?	*Nasıl?*	na·seel
What?	*Ne?*	ne
When?	*Ne zaman?*	ne za·man
Where?	*Nerede?*	ne·re·de
Which?	*Hangi?*	han·gee
Who?	*Kim?*	keem
Why?	*Neden?*	ne·den

ATM	*bankamatik*	ban·ka·ma·teek
credit card	*kredi kartı*	kre·dee kar·tuh
post office	*postane*	pos·ta·ne
signature	*imza*	eem·za
tourist office	*turizm*	too·reezm
	bürosu	bew·ro·soo

TIME & DATES

What time is it? *Saat kaç?* sa·at kach
It's (10) o'clock. *Saat (on).* sa·at (on)
Half past (10). *(On) buçuk.* (on) boo·chook

in the morning	*öğleden evvel*	er·le·den ev·vel
in the afternoon	*öğleden sonra*	er·le·den son·ra
in the evening	*akşam*	ak·sham
yesterday	*dün*	dewn
today	*bugün*	boo·gewn
tomorrow	*yarın*	ya·ruhn

Monday	*Pazartesi*	pa·zar·te·see
Tuesday	*Salı*	sa·luh
Wednesday	*Çarşamba*	char·sham·ba
Thursday	*Perşembe*	per·shem·be
Friday	*Cuma*	joo·ma
Saturday	*Cumartesi*	joo·mar·te·see
Sunday	*Pazar*	pa·zar

January	*Ocak*	o·jak
February	*Şubat*	shoo·bat
March	*Mart*	mart
April	*Nisan*	nee·san
May	*Mayıs*	ma·yuhs
June	*Haziran*	ha·zee·ran
July	*Temmuz*	tem·mooz
August	*Ağustos*	a·oos·tos
September	*Eylül*	ay·lewl
October	*Ekim*	e·keem
November	*Kasım*	ka·suhm
December	*Aralık*	a·ra·luhk

TRANSPORT

Public Transport

At what time	*... ne zaman*	*... ne za·man*
does the ...	*kalkacak/*	kal·ka·jak/
leave/arrive?	*varır?*	va·ruhr
boat	*Vapur*	va·poor
bus	*Otobüs*	o·to·bews
plane	*Uçak*	oo·chak
train	*Tren*	tren

LANGUAGE DRIVING & CYCLING

Numbers

1	bir	beer
2	iki	ee·kee
3	üç	ewch
4	dört	dert
5	beş	besh
6	altı	al·tuh
7	yedi	ye·dee
8	sekiz	se·keez
9	dokuz	do·kooz
10	on	on
20	yirmi	yeer·mee
30	otuz	o·tooz
40	kırk	kuhrk
50	elli	el·lee
60	altmış	alt·muhsh
70	yetmiş	yet·meesh
80	seksen	sek·sen
90	doksan	dok·san
100	yüz	yewz
1000	bin	been

Does it stop at (Maltepe)?
(Maltepe'de) *(mal·te·pe·de)*
durur mu? *doo·roor moo*

What's the next stop?
Sonraki durak *son·ra·kee doo·rak*
hangisi? *han·gee·see*

Please tell me when we get to (Beşiktaş).
(Beşiktaş'a) *(be·sheek·ta·sha)*
vardığımızda *var·duh·uh·muhz·da*
lütfen bana *lewt·fen ba·na*
söyleyin. *say·le·yeen*

I'd like to get off at (Kadıköy).
(Kadıköy'de) inmek *(ka·duh·kay·de) een·mek*
istiyorum. *ees·tee·yo·room*

I'd like a ... (Bostancı'ya) *(bos·tan·juh·ya)*
ticket to ... bir bilet *... beer bee·let*
(Bostancı). lütfen. *lewt·fen*

1st-class	Birinci mevki	bee·reen·jee mev·kee
2nd-class	İkinci mevki	ee·keen·jee mev·kee
one-way	Gidiş	gee·deesh
return	Gidiş-dönüş	gee·deesh·der·newsh

first	ilk	eelk
last	son	son
next	geleçek	ge·le·jek

I'd like ... bir yer ... beer yer
a/an ... seat. istiyorum. ees·tee·yo·room

| aisle | Koridor tarafında | ko·ree·dor ta·ra·fuhn·da |
| window | Cam kenarı | jam ke·na·ruh |

cancelled	iptal edildi	eep·tal e·deel·dee
delayed	ertelendi	er·te·len·dee
platform	peron	pe·ron
ticket office	bilet gişesi	bee·let gee·she·see
timetable	tarife	ta·ree·fe
train station	istasyon	ees·tas·yon

Driving & Cycling

I'd like to Bir ... beer ...
hire a ... kiralamak kee·ra·la·mak
istiyorum. ees·tee·yo·room

4WD	dört çeker	dert che·ker
bicycle	bisiklet	bee·seek·let
car	araba	a·ra·ba
motorcycle	motosiklet	mo·to·seek·let

bike shop	bisikletçi	bee·seek·let·chee
child seat	çocuk koltuğu	cho·jook kol·too·oo
diesel	dizel	dee·zel
helmet	kask	kask
mechanic	araba tamircisi	a·ra·ba ta·meer·jee·see
petrol/gas	benzin	ben·zeen
service station	benzin istasyonu	ben·zeen ees·tas·yo·noo

Is this the road to (Taksim)?
(Taksim'e) giden *(tak·see·me) gee·den*
yol bu mu? *yol boo moo*

(How long) Can I park here?
Buraya (ne kadar *boo·ra·ya (ne ka·dar*
süre) park *sew·re) park*
edebilirim? *e·de·bee·lee·reem*

The car/motorbike has broken down (at Osmanbey).
Arabam/ *a·ra·bam/*
Motosikletim *mo·to·seek·le·teem*
(Osmanbey'de) *(os·man·bay·de)*
bozuldu. *bo·zool·doo*

I have a flat tyre.
Lastiğim patladı. *las·tee·eem pat·la·duh*

I've run out of petrol.
Benzinim bitti. *ben·zee·neem beet·tee*

GLOSSARY

acropolis – hilltop citadel and temples of a classical Hellenic city

ada(sı) – island

agora – open space for commerce and politics in a Greco-Roman city

Anatolia – the Asian part of Turkey; also called *Asia Minor*

arabesk – Arabic-style Turkish music

arasta – row of shops near a mosque, the rent from which supports the mosque

Asia Minor – see *Anatolia*

bahçe(si) – garden

bedesten – vaulted, fireproof market enclosure where valuable goods are kept

belediye (sarayı) – municipal council, town hall

bey – polite form of address for a man; follows the name

bilet – ticket

bouleuterion – place of assembly, council meeting place in a classical Hellenic city

bulvar(ı) – boulevard or avenue; often abbreviated to 'bul'

cadde(si) – street; often abbreviated to 'cad'

cami(i) – mosque

caravanserai – large fortified way-station for (trade) caravans

çarşı(sı) – market, bazaar; sometimes town centre

çay bahçesi – tea garden

çayı – stream

çeşme – spring, fountain

Cilician Gates – a pass in the Taurus Mountains in southern Turkey

dağ(ı) – mountain

deniz – sea

dervish – member of Mevlevi Muslim brotherhood

dolmuş – shared taxi; can be a minibus or sedan

döviz (bürosu) – currency exchange (office)

emir – Turkish tribal chieftain

eski – old (thing, not person)

ev pansiyonu – pension in a private home

eyvan – vaulted hall opening into a central court in a *medrese* or mosque; balcony

fasıl – Ottoman classical music, usually played by gypsies

GAP – Southeastern Anatolia Project, a mammoth hydroelectric and irrigation project

geçit, geçidi – (mountain) pass

gişe – ticket kiosk

göl(ü) – lake

gület – traditional Turkish wooden yacht

hamam(ı) – Turkish bathhouse

han(ı) – see *caravanserai*

hanım – polite form of address for a woman

haremlik – family/women's quarters of a residence; see also *selamlık*

heykel – statue

hisar(ı) – fortress or citadel

Hittites – nation of people inhabiting Anatolia during 2nd millennium BC

hükümet konağı – government house, provincial government headquarters

imam – prayer leader, Muslim cleric

imaret(i) – soup kitchen for the poor, usually attached to a *medrese*

indirim – discount

iskele(si) – jetty, quay

jeton – transport token

kale(si) – fortress, citadel

kapı(sı) – door, gate

kaplıca – thermal spring or baths

Karagöz – shadow-puppet theatre

kaya – cave

KDV – katma değer vergisi, Turkey's value-added tax

kebapçı – place selling kebaps

kervansaray(ı) – Turkish for *caravanserai*

kilim – flat-weave rug

kilise(si) – church

köfte – meatballs

köfteci – *köfte* maker or seller

konak, konağı – mansion, government headquarters

köprü(sü) – bridge

köşk(ü) – pavilion, villa

köy(ü) – village

kule(si) – tower

külliye(si) – mosque complex including seminary, hospital and soup kitchen

kümbet – vault, cupola, dome; tomb topped by this

liman(ı) – harbour

lokanta – eatery serving ready-made food

mağara(sı) – cave

mahalle(si) – neighbourhood, district of a city

medrese(si) – Islamic theological seminary or school attached to a mosque

mescit, mescidi – prayer room, small mosque

Mevlâna – also known as Celaleddin Rumi, a great mystic and poet (1207–73), founder of the Mevlevi whirling *dervish* order

meydan(ı) – public square, open place

meyhane – tavern, wine shop

mihrab – niche in a mosque indicating the direction of Mecca

milli parkı – national park

mimber – pulpit in a mosque

müze(si) – museum

nargile – traditional water pipe (for smoking); hookah

necropolis – city of the dead, cemetery

oda(sı) – room

otobüs – bus

otogar – bus station

Ottoman – of or pertaining to the Ottoman Empire, which lasted from the end of the 13th century to the end of WWI

pansiyon – pension, B&B, guesthouse

paşa – general, governor

pastane – pastry shop (patisserie); also *pastahane*

pazar(ı) – weekly market, bazaar

peribacalar – fairy chimneys (rock formation)

pideci – pide maker or seller

plaj – beach

PTT – Posta, Telefon, Telegraf; post, telephone and telegraph office

Ramazan – Islamic holy month of fasting

saat kulesi – clock tower

şadırvan – fountain where Muslims perform ritual ablutions

saray(ı) – palace

sedir – bench seating that doubled as a bed in Ottoman houses

şehir – city; municipality

selamlık – public/men's quarters of a residence; see also *haremlik*

Seljuk – of or pertaining to the Seljuk Turks, the first Turkish state to rule Anatolia from the 11th to 13th centuries

sema – *dervish* ceremony

semahane – hall where whirling *dervish* ceremonies are held

servis – shuttle minibus service to and from the *otogar*

sinema – cinema

sokak, sokağı – street or lane; often abbreviated to 'sk'

Sufi – Muslim mystic, member of a mystic (*dervish*) brotherhood

TCDD – Turkish State Railways

tekke(si) – *dervish* lodge

tersane – shipyard

Thrace – the European part of Turkey

tramvay – tram

TRT – Türkiye Radyo ve Televizyon, Turkish broadcasting corporation

tuff, tufa – soft stone laid down as volcanic ash

türbe(si) – tomb, grave, mausoleum

valide sultan – mother of the reigning sultan

vilayet, valilik, valiliği – provincial government headquarters

yalı – grand waterside residence

yayla – highland pastures

yeni – new

yol(u) – road, way

Behind the Scenes

SEND US YOUR FEEDBACK

We love to hear from travellers – your comments keep us on our toes and help make our books better. Our well-travelled team reads every word on what you loved or loathed about this book. Although we cannot reply individually to your submissions, we always guarantee that your feedback goes straight to the appropriate authors, in time for the next edition. Each person who sends us information is thanked in the next edition – the most useful submissions are rewarded with a selection of digital PDF chapters.

Visit **lonelyplanet.com/contact** to submit your updates and suggestions or to ask for help. Our award-winning website also features inspirational travel stories, news and discussions.

Note: We may edit, reproduce and incorporate your comments in Lonely Planet products such as guidebooks, websites and digital products, so let us know if you don't want your comments reproduced or your name acknowledged. For a copy of our privacy policy visit lonelyplanet.com/privacy.

OUR READERS

Many thanks to the travellers who used the last edition and wrote to us with helpful hints, useful advice and interesting anecdotes:

Adele Kilpatrick, Alan Garner, Alen Lai, Andrea Lai, Alex Thomas, Alexis krikorian, Anna Miriam Benini, Anthony Sheppard, Arlene Renney, Bec Goodwin, Cate Concannon, Christian Runkel, Cihan Yörükoğlu, Claudia Tonini, Daniel Britten, Daniel Munday, David Neely, Dianne Hoff & Jim Stiles, Dr Ahsen Hussain, Earl Luetzelschwab, Edwina Mullany, Elske van Lonkhuyzen, Eric Labonne, Erica Bettiol, Erika Chagnon-Monarque, Geoff Davies, Graham Churchman, Hasan Kemal, Isabella Cunha Soares Coelho, Janet Bond, Jennifer Campbell, Joseph Stanik, Julia Ward, Karen Smith, Kenn Clacher, Kerem İpek, Koenraad Janssens, Kyle Uhlmann, Lucie Verreault, Lynda Ozgur, Manuel Porras, Martin Zuther, Maureen Van Duijn, Michael Jobst, Michael Moses, Morgan McDaniel, Necdet Celtek, Pau Ruiz-Sanchis, Peter Larsson, Philip Host, Prachi Jain, Rachel Zhou, René Rood, Ricardo Jorge Lopes, Roscoe Ward, Rovena Aga, Sain Alizada, Sarah Österreicher, Serkan Konuralp, Shan Chong, Simon Walo, Susan Sklar, Teri Bergstrom, Xiaochuan Zheng, Yanqin Lin

AUTHOR THANKS
James Bainbridge

A heartfelt *çok teşekkürler* to everyone who helped me on my journey around the Aegean coves and Anatolian backwoods: in Selçuk, Mehmet, Christine, İlker from Nazar, and Jimmy from Jimmy's; Mr Happy in Kuşadası; Zafer in Bodrum and everyone on the peninsula; the guys at Ney in Marmaris; Metin in Datça; John from Ludlow in Selimiye; Ali in İznik; Şinasi and Uğur in Bursa; Çağrı and Deniz in Eskişehir; Mehmet and Ummu in Pamukkale; İbrahim, Müslüm, Munny and Birsan in Eğirdir.

Brett Atkinson

A huge thanks to Sahabattin and family in Van, and in Gaziantep thanks to Jale and Filiz for the trip's definite culinary highlights. In the Kaçkars it's always a pleasure to see Mehmet and İdris amid glorious mountain scenery, and around Urfa and Gollu I really enjoyed the company of Mary (and her Mum). At LP, cheers to my fellow scribes and the hardworking editors and cartos, and final thanks to Carol for holding the fort back home in Yeni Zelanda.

Stuart Butler

Thank you to everyone who helped out with my chapter of this book. In particular I would like to thank Deniz Aşık in Hattuşa. Closer to home a big thanks to my wife, Heather, and children, Jake and Grace, for putting up with my absence again.

Steve Fallon

Didi madlobat/çok teşekkürler to those who provided assistance, ideas and/or hospitality along the way: Salih Mutlu in Alaçatı; Mamuka Berdzenishvili & Maya Gavrilyuk in Batumi; Ece Alton in Behramkale; staff at Les Les Pergamon, Bergama; Volkan Pehlivan in Bozcaada; Bayram at Sakız Alsancak, İzmir; Mehmet & Ummu Gulec in Pamukkale; Akil Vidinli in Samsun; Mert Kanal in Sinop; and Hasan Şimşek in Ünye. My partner, Michael Rothschild, was a helpful travelling companion for a spell.

Will Gourlay

Thanks to Jo Cooke for asking me to join the Turkey team again. Thanks also to the authors and in-house team at Lonely Planet. In Turkey, thanks to Pat Yale for gossip, insight and info, to the Veni Vidi boys in İstanbul and the Surkent crew in Diyarbakır. Finally, thanks to Claire, Bridget and Tommy, my all-time favourite Turkey travel companions. Let's do it again, soon. *Hayde gidelim!*

Jessica Lee

A huge *çok teşekkürler* to Ömer Yapıs; Kazım and Ayşe Akay and Bekir Kırca (for cake and great local gossip); Ömer and Ahmet in Kaş; Meral in Olympos; Yakup Kahveci; Beşir Şafak; Nil Tuncer (for Kayseri-fun); Angela Şisman (for getting food-poisoned instead of me, thanks Ange!); Pat Yale; Ruth Lockwood; and Jodie Redding. A special acknowledgment to Mustafa Turgut, whose Cappadocian fresco knowledge contributed hugely to that chapter, and who sadly died while I was writing it.

Virginia Maxwell

Many thanks to Pat Yale, Mehmet Umur, Emel Güntaş, Faruk Boyacı, Atilla Tuna, Tahir Karabaş, Jen Hartin, Eveline Zoutendijk, George Grundy, Barbara Nadel, Ercan Tanrıvermiş, Ann Nevans, Tina Nevans, Jennifer Gaudet, Özlem Tuna, Ansel Mullins, Ken Dakan and the many others who shared their knowledge and love of the city with me.

ACKNOWLEDGMENTS

Climate map data adapted from Peel MC, Finlayson BL & McMahon TA (2007) 'Updated World Map of the Köppen-Geiger Climate Classification', Hydrology and Earth System Sciences, 11, 1633–44.

Illustrations pp66-7, pp80-1, and pp224-5 by Javier Zarracina

Cover photograph: Rock formations near Görkündere Vadısı (Love Valley), Cappodocia, Turkey, Naomi Parker

THIS BOOK

This 14th edition of Lonely Planet's *Turkey* guidebook was researched and written by James Bainbridge, Brett Atkinson, Stuart Butler, Steve Fallon, Will Gourlay, Jessica Lee and Virginia Maxwell. The previous two editions were also written by the authors listed above and Jean-Bernard Carillet, Chris Deliso, Brandon Presser and Tom Spurling. This guidebook was commissioned in Lonely Planet's London office, and produced by the following:
Commissioning Editor Clifton Wilkinson
Destination Editor Joanna Cooke
Product Editor Penny Cordner
Senior Cartographer Corey Hutchison
Book Designer Wibowo Rusli
Assisting Editors Sarah Bailey, Carolyn Bain, Katie Connolly, Peter Cruttenden, Carly Hall, Gabrielle Innes, Rosie Nicholson, Kristin Odijk, Gabrielle Stefanos, Saralinda Turner
Assisting Cartographer Mick Garrett
Cover Researcher Naomi Parker
Thanks to Bruce Evans, Ryan Evans, Larissa Frost, Jouve India, Elizabeth Jones, Wayne Murphy, Claire Naylor, Karyn Noble, Samantha Tyson, Lauren Wellicome

Index

NOTES

Map Legend

Sights
- Beach
- Bird Sanctuary
- Buddhist
- Castle/Palace
- Christian
- Confucian
- Hindu
- Islamic
- Jain
- Jewish
- Monument
- Museum/Gallery/Historic Building
- Ruin
- Shinto
- Sikh
- Taoist
- Winery/Vineyard
- Zoo/Wildlife Sanctuary
- Other Sight

Activities, Courses & Tours
- Bodysurfing
- Diving
- Canoeing/Kayaking
- Course/Tour
- Sento Hot Baths/Onsen
- Skiing
- Snorkelling
- Surfing
- Swimming/Pool
- Walking
- Windsurfing
- Other Activity

Sleeping
- Sleeping
- Camping

Eating
- Eating

Drinking & Nightlife
- Drinking & Nightlife
- Cafe

Entertainment
- Entertainment

Shopping
- Shopping

Information
- Bank
- Embassy/Consulate
- Hospital/Medical
- Internet
- Police
- Post Office
- Telephone
- Toilet
- Tourist Information
- Other Information

Geographic
- Beach
- Hut/Shelter
- Lighthouse
- Lookout
- Mountain/Volcano
- Oasis
- Park
- Pass
- Picnic Area
- Waterfall

Population
- Capital (National)
- Capital (State/Province)
- City/Large Town
- Town/Village

Transport
- Airport
- Border crossing
- Bus
- Cable car/Funicular
- Cycling
- Ferry
- Metro station
- Monorail
- Parking
- Petrol station
- S-Bahn/Subway station
- Taxi
- T-bane/Tunnelbana station
- Train station/Railway
- Tram
- Tube station
- U-Bahn/Underground station
- Other Transport

Note: Not all symbols displayed above appear on the maps in this book

Routes
- Tollway
- Freeway
- Primary
- Secondary
- Tertiary
- Lane
- Unsealed road
- Road under construction
- Plaza/Mall
- Steps
- Tunnel
- Pedestrian overpass
- Walking Tour
- Walking Tour detour
- Path/Walking Trail

Boundaries
- International
- State/Province
- Disputed
- Regional/Suburb
- Marine Park
- Cliff
- Wall

Hydrography
- River, Creek
- Intermittent River
- Canal
- Water
- Dry/Salt/Intermittent Lake
- Reef

Areas
- Airport/Runway
- Beach/Desert
- Cemetery (Christian)
- Cemetery (Other)
- Glacier
- Mudflat
- Park/Forest
- Sight (Building)
- Sportsground
- Swamp/Mangrove

Steve Fallon

İzmir & the North Aegean, Black Sea Coast With a house in Kalkan on the Turquoise Coast, Steve considers Turkey to be a second home. This assignment took him pretty far from said home, however, starting at the easternmost end of the Black Sea Coast (with a quick foray into delightful Georgia) and continuing down the North Aegean coastline to Turkey's greatest city: İzmir. OK ... Türkçe'yi hala mağara adamı gibi konuşuyor (he still speaks Turkish like a caveman), but no Turk has called him Fred – yet.

Will Gourlay

Will has been leaving his home base of Melbourne on regular Turkish forays for over 20 years. As a backpacker, English teacher and writer he has explored all corners of Anatolia – the more remote the better. His most recent trips have been with his wife and children in tow, although they usually stay on the beach while he rummages around in the backwoods or takes the train into Iran. He is currently researching a PhD on Turkish politics and society. Will wrote the following Understand chapters: Turkey Today, History, Architecture, Arts and People.

Jessica Lee

Antalya & the Turquoise Coast, Eastern Mediterranean, Cappadocia After four years leading adventure-tours around Turkey, Jessica moved here to live. Between writing, she battles Turkish verbs and tries to restore a village home. This edition of *Turkey* saw her hiking between Lycian splendour on the Turquoise coast, hunting down early Christian remnants in the eastern Mediterranean, and scrambling up cliffs to hidden rock-cut churches in Cappadocia. She also covers Egypt and Cyprus for Lonely Planet and writes about Turkey for a variety of publications.

Virginia Maxwell

İstanbul, Thrace & Marmara Although based in Australia, Virginia spends much of her year researching guidebooks in the Mediterranean region. Of these, Turkey is unquestionably her favourite. As well as working on the previous five editions of this country guide, she is also the author of Lonely Planet's *İstanbul* city and pocket guides, and she writes about the city for a host of international magazines and websites. Virginia usually travels with partner Peter and son Max, who have grown to love Turkey as much as she does. For this edition of *Turkey* Virginia also wrote the Eat & Drink Like a Local and Turkish Table chapters.

OUR STORY

A beat-up old car, a few dollars in the pocket and a sense of adventure. In 1972 that's all Tony and Maureen Wheeler needed for the trip of a lifetime – across Europe and Asia overland to Australia. It took several months, and at the end – broke but inspired – they sat at their kitchen table writing and stapling together their first travel guide, *Across Asia on the Cheap*. Within a week they'd sold 1500 copies. Lonely Planet was born. Today, Lonely Planet has offices in Franklin, London, Melbourne, Oakland, Beijing and Delhi, with more than 600 staff and writers. We share Tony's belief that 'a great guidebook should do three things: inform, educate and amuse'.

OUR WRITERS

James Bainbridge

Coordinating Author; Ephesus, Bodrum & the South Aegean; Western Anatolia Coordinating this guide four times, various media assignments and extra-curricular wanderings have taken James to most of Turkey's far-flung regions. He lived in İstanbul (Cihangir to be exact) while coordinating a previous edition of this book and learnt to love suffixes on a Turkish-language course. For this edition, discovering western Turkey's dramatic classical ruins and exploring the various peninsulas jutting into the Aegean showed him yet another side of this multifaceted and endlessly intriguing country. When he's not roaming the Anatolian steppe, James works as a travel writer and tour guide in Cape Town, South Africa. Visit James' website at www.jamesbainbridge.net. James also wrote most of the Plan Your Trip chapters, the Understand Enivronment essay and Survival Guide chapters this edition.

Read more about James at:
lonelyplanet.com/members/james_bains

Brett Atkinson

Northeastern Anatolia, Southeastern Anatolia Since first visiting Turkey in 1985, Brett has returned regularly to one of his favourite countries. For his fourth Lonely Planet trip to Turkey, he explored the Kurdish heartland of southeastern Anatolia. After 15 years Brett returned to fascinating northeastern destinations like Kars, Ani and the Kaçkar Mountains. Brett is based in Auckland, New Zealand and has covered around 50 countries as a guidebook author and travel and food writer. See www.brett-atkinson.net for his most recent work and upcoming travels.

Stuart Butler

Ankara & Central Anatolia Stuart has travelled widely across Turkey, particularly in the east and southeast of the country and the greater Middle East region. His travels for Lonely Planet, and a wide variety of magazines, have taken him beyond Turkey to the shores of the Arctic, the deserts of Asia and the forests of Africa. Stuart lives on the beaches of southwest France with his wife and two young children. His website is www.stuartbutlerjournalist.com.

Read more about Stuart at:
lonelyplanet.com/members/stuartbutler

OVER | MORE
PAGE | WRITERS

Published by Lonely Planet Publications Pty Ltd
ABN 36 005 607 983
14th edition – April 2015
ISBN 978 1 74321 577 7
© Lonely Planet 2015   Photographs © as indicated 2015
10 9 8 7 6 5 4 3 2 1
Printed in China

Although the authors and Lonely Planet have taken all reasonable care in preparing this book, we make no warranty about the accuracy or completeness of its content and, to the maximum extent permitted, disclaim all liability arising from its use.